WILLIAM OF OCKHAM

LEFF, Gordon. William of Ockham; the metamorphosis of scholastic discourse. Rowman and Littlefield, 1975. 666p bibl 74-34588. 47.50. ISBN 0-87471-679-9. C.I.P.

CHOICE   *DEC. '75*

Philosophy

A noted authority on medieval thought, Leff (York) has written the first comprehensive study in English of Ockham's system of thought. Its three parts successively examine Ockham's epistemology and logic, his theology, and his philosophy of nature; a final chapter considers his political ideas in relationship to the rest of his thinking. Although this is not a historical study, attention has been paid to the relation between Ockham's different works, virtually all of which have been used. For Leff Ockham's importance lies in his systematic rethinking of scholastic assumptions, and it is upon this foundation that Ockham's innovative conclusions rest. Scholars will differ over some of Leff's interpretations, but this book will remain the definitive study for years to come. A good deal of its value lies in its careful detailing of many of Ocham's most penetrating arguments. Thus it is of immense value to serious students of Ockham, since English translations are extremely fragmentary and the printed Latin is difficult to read. Highly recommended for graduate libraries. Bibliography and indexes.

TO THE MEMORY OF

Terence Jones

FORMERLY SECRETARY
TO THE
MANCHESTER
UNIVERSITY PRESS

CONTENTS

PREFACE

At a time when the study of Ockham's thought in its different facets is becoming more intensive, an attempt to present his outlook as a whole may not be inappropriate. Over a thinker as distinctive as Ockham there are bound to be varying, if not conflicting, judgements. But I hope I have at least presented the issues which engaged his thought and the manner in which he responded to them.

I wish to express my appreciation for the help I have received from many sources: in particular, to the British Academy for a grant towards the costs of publication; to the Vatican Library, Bodleian Library, Bibliothèques Mazarine and Nationale, Paris, Bibliothèque Royale, Brussels, and the British School at Rome; to Miss Beryl Smalley, Professor T. F. Torrance and Fr. J. A. Weisheipl for reading the typescript; and to the Manchester University Press for maintaining unimpaired their tradition of co-operativeness of which I have so frequently been the beneficiary.

October 1974   G. L.

ABBREVIATIONS

GENERAL TITLES

Archives—Archives d'histoire doctrinale et littéraire du moyen-âge
AFH—Archivum Franciscanum Historicum
FcS—Franciscan Studies
FS—Franziskanische Studien
Recherches—Recherches de théologie ancienne et médiévale
RHE—Revue d'histoire ecclésiastique

OCKHAM'S WORKS

An Princeps—An Princeps pro succursu, scilicet possit recipere bona ecclesiarum, etiam invito papa guerrae (OP, I, 223-271)
Breviloquium—Breviloquium de principatu tyrannico super divina et humana, ed. R. Scholz, in *Wilhelm von Ockham als politischer Denker und sein Breviloquium de principatu tyrannico* (Leipzig, 1944; reprinted Stuttgart, 1952) 39-220
Contra Benedictum—Tractatus contra Benedictum (OP, III, 157-322)
Contra Ioannem—Tractatus contra Ioannem (OP, III, 19-156)
De Imp—Tractatus de Imperatorum et Pontificum Potestate, ed. C. K. Brampton (Oxford, 1927)
De Sacramento—De Sacramento Altaris, MSS.: Vatican Library, Borghese Lat. 151; Ottoboni Lat. 179. Printed Strasbourg, 1491
De Successivis—The 'Tractatus de successivis' attributed to William Ockham, ed. P. Boehner (New York, 1944)
De Praedestinatione—The 'Tractatus de praedestinatione et De praescientia Dei et de futuris contingentibus of William Ockham, ed. P. Boehner (New York, 1945)
Dialogus—Dialogus de Imperio et Pontifica Potestate (Lyon, 1494; reprinted as vol. 1 of *Opera Plurima,* 1962)
EA—Expositio Aurea et admodum utilis super artem veterem edita per venerabilem G. de Ockham cum quaestionibus Alberti Parvi de Saxonia (Bologna 1496; reprinted, 1965). Contains Ockham's Commentaries on Porphyry's *Isagogue* and Aristotle's *Categories* and *Perihermenias*
Elementarium—Guillelmi Ockham, Elementarium Logicae, ed. E. M. Buytaert in *FcS* 25 (1965), 170-276; 26 (1966), 66-173
Elench.—Tractatus super libros Elenchorum, MS. Paris, Bib. Nat. 14721
Expositio—Expositionis in libros artis logicae prooemium et Expositio in librum Prophyrii De Praedicabilibus, ed. E. A. Moody (New York, 1965)
Logicae Minor—Logicae Minor Tractatus, ed. E. M. Buytaert, in *FcS* 24 (1964), 55-100
Octo Quaestiones—Octo Quaestiones de Potestate Papae, OP, I (1-222)
OND—Opus Nonaginta Dierum, chs. 1-6 (OP, I, 289-374); chs. 7-124 (OP, II, 375-858)
OP, I-III—Guillelmi de Ockham Opera Politica, vol. I, ed. J. G. Sikes *et al.* (Manchester, 1940); vol. II, ed. H. S. Offler (Manchester, 1963); vol. III, ed. H. S. Offler (Manchester, 1956)
Ordinatio—Commentary on the Sentences, book 1: (a) Prologue and distinctions 1-3 in OT 1 and II; (b) Distinctions 4-48 in *Super IV Libros Sententiarum* (Lyon, 1495; reprinted by

Gregg in *Opera Plurima*, III, 1962); (c) MSS.: Florence, Bib. Naz, conv. soppr. A.3-801; Paris, Bib. Mazarine, 894; 962

OT, I-II—*Guillelmi de Ockham, Scriptum in Librum Primum Sententiarum Ordinatio*, ed. G. Gál and S. Brown, vol. I: Prologus et Distinctio Prima (New York, 1967); vol. II: Distinctiones II-III (New York, 1970)

Questiones—*Questiones in libros Physicorum* MSS.: Paris, Bib. Nat. Lat. 17841; Vat. Lat. 956

Quodlibet—*Quodlibeta Septem* (Strasbourg, 1491; reprinted Louvain, 1962) MSS. Paris, Bib. Nat. 17841; Vatican Vat. Lat. 956, 3075. I have followed the Strasbourg order of questions

Reportatio—*Super IV Libros Sententiarum*, books II-IV (Lyons, 1495); reprinted in *Opera Plurima*, IV, edited by Gregg, 1962); MSS.: Florence, Bib. Naz. Conv. Soppr. A. 3. 801; Paris, Bib. Mazarine 893

Philosophical Writings—*Ockham, Philosophical Writings: A Selection*, ed. and trans. by P. Boehner (New York, 1957)

SL—*Summa Logicae*, pts. I, II, III (i), ed. P. Boehner: I (New York, 1957), II-III (i) (1962); *Summa Totius Logicae*, pt. III (ii)-(iii) (Oxford, 1675); MSS. Paris, Bib. Nat. Lat. 6431; Paris, Bib. Mazarine, 3521

SP—*Summulae Physicorum* (*Philosophia Naturalis Guilielmi Ockham* (Rome, 1637))

INTRODUCTION

Ockham was an innovator; and until recently he has had to suffer for being judged by his supposed influence upon others rather than for his own achievement. The judgement was almost uniformly derogatory because no distinction was made between his outlook and Ockhamism; the latter's earlier extravagances and later barrenness were transposed to this thought. He was made the destroyer of scholasticism, responsible for upsetting its fine balance between faith and reason, by a combination of ruthless logic and religious insensitivity, if indeed not scepticism. In the last thirty or so years the studies begun by Hochstetter, Vignaux, Moody, Baudry, Boehner,[1] and his pupils, have gradually disposed of the old cartoon and helped to restore the original Ockham as an authentic Christian thinker in the scholastic tradition. However he may have transformed that tradition and, whatever his place in it, the inappropriateness of the older labels of 'nominalist' and 'fideist' and the groundlessness of calling him a sceptic are now sufficiently plain.

I have not sought to replace these by other labels. In earlier books I have been guilty of just this misrepresentation through viewing Ockham from the same false perspective of Ockhamism. In the present book—which is in the nature of a retractation—I have sought to see his thought whole, in its own terms, not in pedigrees or, save in passing, by its subsequent effects. It is not principally an historical study. In part that is due to inadequate knowledge; but it is due in greater part to the belief that an outlook must first be known before it can be related to anything. That would scarcely be worth saying but for the widespread assumption prevalent among those engaged in the history of ideas that identification and assessment of an outlook begin with a thinker's antecedents, both intellectual and circumstantial. On that view, the way to any unknown system of thought is through the thought and circumstances that are deemed to have influenced it. That in effect means the search for sources in the thought of others and the life of the thinker concerned.

As with most half-truths, there is enough in this one to make it plausible. No one is likely to contest that there is some kind of interplay between different outlooks or that without some framework in which to measure a system it will remain largely unintelligible. The fallacy, however, is to confuse the dependence—if there is one—of a thinker upon his antecedents with our dependence upon the same antecedents for subsequent knowledge of his outlook. The first is a real order of succession; the second is an order of intelligibility. Not only does the first not entail the second, but the order of the second must be inverted because any empirical

[1] See bibliography.

xiii

investigation begins from what has to be explained. If we already knew the antecedent we could explain the consequence from it deductively. There would then
be no need for investigation. In any relation, however, logically we must know the
terms before we can know they are related: just as we can know that someone is a
man without knowing that he is a father or a son, so we can know—in the sense of
at least formulating its concepts—Ockham's outlook independently of knowing its
circumstances or sources. Conceptually, on the other hand, we only gain more
perfect, i.e. complete and perhaps intelligible, knowledge when we know the other
terms in a relation—where they exist. It is the failure to observe that distinction
which confuses more complete knowledge, that comes from knowing the antecedent conditions with knowing the object at all; the former may well be the condition of a proper assessment and so—conceptually—inseparable from adequate
knowledge of an outlook; but it remains distinct from and logically dependent
upon prior knowledge of what is to be assessed.

   That again would perhaps not be worth saying were it not for the impoverishing
effects of an order which puts the antecedents first. It is equivalent to reducing a
sufficient cause to its necessary conditions, a view which is both contradictory and
naive. It is contradictory because it assumes that what is to be identified can be
explained by what precedes it. But that would preclude the capacity to account for
the untypical and the new—the very problem presented by an outlook like Ockham's. There is all the difference between defining one thing in terms of others,
including negatively, and explaining something in terms of other things. The first
is involved in any act of identification and does not entail dependence or likeness;
we can as well say 'A man is not an ass' as 'A man is a rational being'. The second,
however, makes just that assumption of assimilability to what already exists or is
known. To accept it as the mode of procedure would be to deny irreducible
difference, since knowledge of anything would be contained in its antecedents.
That would exclude independent agency. For given the conditions, the consequences would be bound to follow. In fact it is just the difference of response within
a common framework—of assumptions, conventions, texts, authorities, and problems—that differentiates one thinker from another and does not permit their
identification with it or their reduction to it.

   In practice, of course, few—if any—would assert that it did. There is no dispute
over the real difference between Aquinas or Scotus or Ockham. Nevertheless the
effect of the neopositivist search for antecedents is to substitute an emphasis upon
influences for the nature of the thought itself: to assess it for its rapport with others
rather than for its own meaning; to stress circumstances rather than agents; to displace inner coherence by external dependence. It is there that the impoverishing
effects lie, in making it almost a methodological postulate—which runs directly
counter to the standing presumption in any such enquiry of individual difference—

that the new can be assimilated to the old, and the untypical explained by the typical. Of itself, of course, it is no less legitimate to study similarities rather than differences; the mistake is to subsume difference under similarities instead of recognising their reciprocity, which comes from their distinctiveness.

For that reason too, reliance upon sources to identify an outlook is also naive; for it assumes that a source is always the same source. That, to say the least, is a dubious assumption, and nowhere more than among medieval thinkers, concerned constantly to be reconciled with their authorities. There is not one Aristotle or Augustine in the middle ages but many. Whose then do we choose? Those of Grosseteste? Alexander of Hales? Albert the Great? Thomas Aquinas? Henry of Ghent? Duns Scotus? Ockham? That is a question of direct concern to the study of Ockham. As we shall see throughout this book, he justifies his ontology, epistemology, psychology, logic, and natural philosophy, all by appeal to Aristotle. Yet his is not the Aristotle of Aristotle's own writings (if he can be identified), nor the Aristotle of Aquinas or Averroes or Siger of Brabant, each in turn different. Left to themselves none of those will provide the reason; if it is to be found, that will be within the context of Ockham's own outlook.

What has been said is not intended to depreciate the study of circumstances. It is to stress that the questions they answer are by definition circumstantial—of person, place, time, influence, text; not of the nature of the thought itself. The misconception is to think that they do or that they are the prerequisites for doing so. It is then that distortion arises, either in magnifying or in misinterpreting the role of an idea, as Ockham's theory of concepts has been magnified and his theory of God's absolute power misrepresented, through being judged by extrinsic criteria; or by introducing irrelevant considerations, such as the provenance of a particular notion or doctrine which, whatever its interest taken for itself or in other contexts, is incidental to Ockham's own thought: in terms of its role in his outlook what would it matter whether Ockham had learned canon law at his mother's knee rather than, say, at Oxford? And does our present ignorance of where it was add to or detract from its role in his political theories? Only if we are concerned with the diffusion of canon law or Ockham's own biography does the question then arise. But those are different questions designed to meet different problems. Accordingly there is not only one kind of significance and one kind of question which serves it. In this book they are measured by reference to Ockham's own thought and only incidentally to the origin or subsequent import of his ideas. I have done so not in vindication of a particular thesis or approach but in answer to the questions, What did Ockham think, and what was the nature of his thought? For that I have sought to observe Ockham's own emphases. Hence the disparity in length between the different parts of this study.

In that context little need be said of the little that is known about his life and circumstances.[2] He was born probably between 1280 and 1285 at Ockham in Surrey; he entered the Franciscan order and was probably ordained subdeacon in 1306; he studied at Oxford where he commented the *Sentences* probably between 1317 and 1319 and certainly before 1323, in which year fifty-six extracts from them were taken by the recent chancellor of the University, John Lutterell, and presented to the pope at Avignon for censure. The pope set up a commission and Ockham was summoned to Avignon. He remained there for four years until 1327. During that time two versions of the commission's articles of censure, totalling fifty-one, were drawn up.[3] They included his doctrine of the eucharist where, as we shall see in chapter nine, he denied the independent existence of quantity as something distinct from substances and qualities, and upheld the annihilation of the bread rather than its inner transformation; God's power to suspend the normal operation of secondary causes and to act directly himself in such matters as rewarding acts not performed in grace, producing immediate knowledge of what was not present, enabling bodies to be simultaneously in different places; and a series of propositions radically simplifying relations both within God and among creatures, as well as limiting the area of evidential knowledge. In the context of Ockham's outlook these different propositions appear neither paradoxical nor incongruous with faith. Taken out of his context and put in the context of a rather rigid Thomism, which Lutterell seemed to have upheld, they appear to be both, as they did to the Avignon Commissioners who variously described the views contained in the censured articles as 'heretical', 'false', 'dangerous', 'erroneous', 'rash' and 'contradictory'. These responses indicate the distance between Ockham's thinking and previous conceptions. But it was not for these that he was to be excommunicated. That came from his defection to the pope's enemy, the German emperor, together with

[2] For Ockham's life see especially L. Baudry, *Guillaume d'Occam: sa vie, ses oeuvres, ses idées* (Paris, 1950); *Tractatus de Successivis*, edited by P. Boehner (New York, 1944), 1–15; C. K. Brampton, 'Chronological gleanings from Martival episcopal register', *AFH* 58 (1965), 369–93; H. Junghans, *Ockham im Lichte der neuren Forschung* (Berlin and Hamburg, 1968), 25–41; and J. Miethke, *Ockhams Weg zur Sozialphilosophie* (Berlin, 1969), 1–136. The books of Junghans and Miethke are—from different standpoints—general assessments of Ockham. That of Junghans is a survey of what he calls the new picture of Ockham by reference principally to P. Boehner's writings; it is a comprehensive, if at times apologetic, survey of the main writings upon Ockham in the light of present knowledge, to which it is a valuable introduction. Miethke's book is no less valuable as a thoroughgoing re-examination of Ockham's life and works and certain aspects of his thought; but it is less comprehensive, and unfortunately does not reveal the intellectual—as opposed to the biographical—path to Ockham's social philosophy.

[3] Lutterell's list of fifty-six articles as well as his own refutation of them in his *Libellus contra doctrinam Guillelmi Occam* has been edited by F. Hoffmann, *Die Schriften des Oxforder Kanzlers Johannes Lutterell* (Leipzig, 1959), 3–102; his list and his replies are also to be found in J. Koch, 'Neue Aktenstücke zu dem gegen Wilhelm Ockham in Avignon geführten Prozess', *Recherches* 7 (1935), 375–80. The fifty-one articles of the Commission of Avignon were in two lists, differing principally in their order, with the second also fuller in certain places. They have been edited by Koch, 'Neue Aktenstücke', *Recherches* 8 (1936), 83–93, 168–97. Previously the second list only was edited by A. Pelzer, 'Les 51 Articles de Guillaume d'Occam censurés en Avignon, en 1326', *RHE* 18 (1922), 240–70, who first discovered them.

the general of his order, Michael of Cesena, who had also been at Avignon, summoned to answer for his opposition to pope John XXII's condemnation of the Franciscan doctrine of absolute evangelical poverty: a matter which we shall touch upon in the final chapter. In 1328 Ockham and Michael of Cesena with other of their confrères fled from Avignon to Ludwig of Bavaria at Pisa, then engaged in a war of words against the pope over the latter's refusal to recognise his imperial title. Henceforth Ockham became one of a band of distinguished emigrés at the imperial court, spending the rest of his life as a political polemicist against papal pretensions, first in defence of Franciscan poverty and then of independent temporal authority, until his death at Munich in 1349.

The flight from Avignon divided Ockham's career in two. Until 1328 he remained an academic scholastic, probably writing his *Summa Logicae* and perhaps his *De Sacramento Altaris* in Avignon. After 1328 he became a polemicist, or publicist, engaged in a continual struggle to vindicate his order, or rather its erstwhile leaders and principles, and his protector the emperor, and to inculpate popes John XXII and then Benedict XII for heresy and abuse of spiritual power. This book is devoted principally to the first phase, of Ockham as theologian, philosopher and logician. But the last chapter will attempt briefly to discern its connection with the political doctrines of the second phase.

Unlike the writings of his political period, the sequence of Ockham's speculative works is far from settled. Without attempting here to give reasons, which will appear at different times in subsequent chapters, especially chapter two, I am inclined to place Ockham's Commentary on the *Sentences* as the earliest of his works. As it has survived, it is in two different forms. The first book is an *ordinatio*, that is, a completed and edited version, and in this case revised to distinction twenty-seven, by Ockham himself. It is much fuller and more considered than the reports (*reportationes*) that constitute the other three books. These were not edited by Ockham; they remain unrevised and may not even have been corrected by him. They also contain questions which probably did not belong to the original (book two, questions 8, part of 20, 25 from U, in the 1495 edition; book three, questions 5, 12 (which is also found again in *Quodlibet* four as question 6, where it also does not belong), questions 13–15; and the 'Additiones' at the end of book four in the printed edition).[4] These were probably from separate disputations, although their authenticity is not in doubt, nor their pertinence to the other topics. The first book has now been edited to the end of distinction three in the first two volumes of the new collected edition of Ockham's theological and philosophical works by the Franciscan Institute at St Bonaventure, New York. The remainder of the Commentary is in the edition of Treschel printed at Lyon in 1495 which I have used in conjunction with the manuscripts given in the list of abbreviations. In view

[4] P. Boehner, *Collected Articles on Ockham* (New York and Louvain, 1958) 24.

of the different forms of the first and the other three books of the Commentary, I have followed Boehner in calling the first book the *Ordinatio* and the remaining three books the *Reportatio*. In order to avoid confusion I have adopted what might appear to be the inconsistency of referring to the three books of the *Reportatio* as two, three and four, and reserved book one for the *Ordinatio*. They are sufficiently different to be treated separately; and as I shall discuss in chapter two, the *Ordinatio*, in having been itself revised, represents a distinct work and a more considered expression of Ockham's thinking than the three unedited and unrevised books of the *Reportatio*. Together, however, they provide the foundation of his thought in containing all its principal elements, especially his epistemology, theology and moral philosophy. To that extent his Commentary on the *Sentences* taken as a whole can be regarded as his most representative work as a conspectus of his outlook. It does not, however, have the preponderating place in his outlook that, say, Duns Scotus's Commentary—the *Opus Oxoniense*—has in his. That is in part due to the incomplete state of the last three books as *reportationes*; but it is also because the one real synthesis and the most constructive of all his writings comes towards the end of the first phase of his career in the *Summa Logicae*, written between 1323 and 1329, probably by 1327. A Commentary on the *Sentences* was, in origin at least, always a work of apprenticeship as the first important independent exercise undertaken by a bachelor of theology towards his doctorate (which, for reasons unknown, Ockham did not obtain: hence his title, 'Venerable Inceptor' as one who had incepted or qualified to become a doctor, save in the final requirement of presiding at a special ceremonial disputation and delivering a formal doctoral lecture).[5] Ockham's Commentary was no exception. His *Logic*, by contrast, was composed probably between five and ten years later. It is correspondingly more mature, and, to my mind, Ockham's master work. As we shall see, above all in chapters three and four, Ockham's conception of logic was central to his outlook, not through reducing all problems to questions of logic or in the formal sense of approaching them logically —all scholastics did that—but as the means of ordering all knowledge and of ascertaining the different degrees of certainty which men can have.

Between these two *termini*, the Commentary on the *Sentences* and the *Logic*, come the Commentaries on Aristotle's so-called old Logic, of the *Categories*, *Perihermenias* and *Sophistical Questions*, together with a Commentary on Porphyry's Introduction to the *Categories* (the *Isagoge*) which was its then almost inseparable accompaniment. Their chronological relation to the Commentary on the *Sentences* will be considered in chapter two, over Ockham's theory of concepts. Here it need only be said that unlike the Commentary on the *Sentences* the four Logical Com-

---

[5] This is the interpretation of Boehner, which I accept, together with its combination by Miethke (*op. cit.*, 32–4) with Brampton's suggestion, 'Guillaume d'Ockham, fut-il maître en théologie?', *Études Franciscaines* 13 (1963), 53–9, that Ockham had already left Oxford for another Franciscan house where he lectured on Aristotle's logic.

mentaries (of which the first two and the last have become traditionally and ground-lessly known as the *Summa Aurea*, from the title given to them by their first editor, Mark of Benevento, at the end of the fifteenth century) would almost certainly have been from lectures by Ockham after he had left Oxford to teach in a Franciscan house of studies—perhaps at Reading.[6] The same can be said of his Commentary on the *Physics*, like the Commentary on the *Sophistical Questions* still unprinted, which probably dates from the same period. Between these Aristotelian Commentaries and the *Logic* come the free, quodlibetal, Questions (*Quodlibets*) and the Questions on the *Physics*. When and where and how they originated we do not know. The *Quodlibets* could have been from free disputations either within the theological faculty at Oxford or in one of the Franciscan houses; Ockham could have either disputed under some master or perhaps himself presided at the disputations. The Questions on the *Physics*, on the other hand, probably derived from Ockham's teaching activity within his order, since they would not have formed part of the theological course. What can be said is that they come after the *Quodlibets*, to which they refer in a number of different places.[7]

Finally there are the two remaining independent works of his philosophical period. The first is the uncompleted *Summulae Physicorum* designed to comprehend nature in all its aspects according to Aristotelian principles; it forms the basis of part of chapter nine below. It again is a work of comparative maturity, and one can only surmise that it came either at the end of Ockham's time in England or at Avignon: I incline to the second alternative mainly on grounds of credibility: it is more than enough to believe that Ockham composed a Commentary on the *Sentences* in four books, four Logical Commentaries, the Commentary and Questions on the *Physics*, within at most seven years from 1317 to 1324. Similar considerations apply to his two opuscles on the eucharist; I have used only the second and longer treatise, which generally goes under the single name of *De Sacramento Altaris*.[8] As should be apparent in chapter nine, it was designed to vindicate Ockham's views on transubstantiation which Lutterell had included for censure. Whether or not one or both treatises were written at Oxford or Avignon, they must, it seems to me, have been written after 1323, in response to Lutterell's action.

These are the works upon which, except for the last chapter where Ockham's polemical works will be considered separately, I have drawn in this book; to them should be added the shorter treatises on Predestination and Successives and two later and lesser logical treatises, the *Elements of Logic* and the *Minor Treatise of Logic*,

---

[6] I agree here with Brampton, 'The probable order of Ockham's non-polemical works', *Traditio* 19 (1963), 480–1. For his suggestion of the Franciscan House at Reading see 'Chronological gleanings from Martival register', 380–93.

[7] For their relation, see Miethke, *Ockhams Weg*, 43–7.

[8] Boehner, *Collected Articles*, 10–11; L. Baudry, 'Sur trois manuscrits occomistes', *Archives* 10–11 (1935–6), 129–62.

which date from his Munich period in the 1340s. The various editions and manuscripts will be found in the list of Abbreviations. I have excluded what appear to
me to be the unauthentic or doubtful *Centiloquium*, against accepting which as
Ockham's work the arguments of Baudry and Boehner seem overwhelming,[9] and
also the *Tractatus de Principiis Theologiae*. But I have cited the *Tractatus de Successivis*
since it is a compilation from Ockham's Commentary on the *Physics*.

Despite their diversity and the still uncertain state of most of the texts, these works
have a remarkable unity. They are shaped by the same principles which recur
throughout Ockham's writings: for all the repetitions, and the contrast between
the prolixities of the earlier commentaries and the comparative economy of the
Quodlibets, the two shorter works on physics and the *Logic*, taken together they are
like variations upon a set of common themes. Whatever the modifications still to
come as his works are properly edited, it is inconceivable that they will alter the
configuration of Ockham's thought.

It is founded upon the discrepancy between the conceptual and the ontological,
expressed in the contrast between the individual nature of all being and the universal nature of our concepts and terms constituting proper knowledge of it.
Instead of assuming or attempting to establish a direct rapport between them,
Ockham was the first thinker systematically to explore their difference whilst
accepting their interdependence. If nominalism means the elimination of universals,
Ockham was the opposite of a nominalist, just as if realism means accepting the
independent reality of universals, he was the opposite of a realist. He neither
excluded concepts from a world in which only individuals were real, nor, like the
great majority of his predecessors, sought to explain them as the expression of real
natures or essences. In making that distinction Ockham, as Moody was the first
explicitly to recognise,[10] was safeguarding concepts from the status of merely
mental constructs; he was also safeguarding being from subordination to them.
Where the nominalist position denied concepts any epistemological standing, the
varying degrees of realism (to employ conventional but, it should become clear,
largely irrelevant terminology) allowed no means of distinguishing logically
between the mental and the real, if, like universal natures and essences, what was
known could only be known conceptually. The distinction between concepts and
what they represented then vanishes, and with it the power of differentiating true
from false propositions, where the things of which they are affirmed or denied are
not known independently of their propositions.

It was towards exposing what he regarded as the falsity of this position that
Ockham's thinking above all tended. His success reversed the direction of schol-

[9] Boehner, *Collected Articles*, 33–42; Baudry, *Guillaume d'Occam*, 270–1, 286; and 'Les
Rapports de la raison et de la foi', *Archives* 29 (1962), 87 f.
[10] E. A. Moody, *The Logic of William of Ockham* (London 1935; reprinted New York 1965),
37–8.

asticism. From having been predominantly metaphysical in attempting to extend the area of speculation beyond natural experience, it now came to be focused upon natural experience and the limits upon knowledge which it imposed. Where being had been subsumed under what could be conceived as metaphysically possible, the conceptual was now restricted to what could be known naturally from experience, or inferred from what was believed. Even in the increasingly critical atmosphere engendered by thinkers like Duns Scotus and Peter Aureole preceding Ockham, the emphasis had still been upon establishing the direct rapport between concepts and reality, either in an ascending order of abstraction with being as the highest and most universal term, or in the distinctions that could be discerned within actual beings, expressed in the formal distinction of Duns Scotus. Ockham was the first consistently to combine an epistemology based upon the primacy of individual cognition—which as we shall see in the first chapter he adopted from Duns Scotus —with an exclusively individual ontology which had no place for anything beyond or within the individual which was not itself individual. For him the central question was no longer to explain the individual by reference to the universal but rather to account for universals in a world of individuals.

How he did so is the subject of the first part of this book. It consisted in treating universals solely as concepts and analysing their role in knowledge logically and grammatically according to the different kinds of terms that can stand for them and the different modes in which they can be employed, significatively and non-significatively. He thereby substituted a logical for a metaphysical order. In doing so he discarded the long-standing assumption of a pre-existing harmony between concepts and reality, transforming what had been taken as a hierarchy of being into a diversity of ways of signifying individual beings. It was there in displacing the previous modes and assumptions that Ockham's impact lay.

If it was destructive of previous systems in exposing the misconceptions on which they were built, and if it in turn encouraged new—although now logical and theological as opposed to metaphysical—speculative extravagances among his successors, it is in my view—and contrary to my earlier opinion—entirely misconceived to regard Ockham as either merely destructive or extravagant. If he did not attempt to substitute a new system—in the sense of an embracing metaphysics and noetic—for those he rejected, his own outlook was itself a comprehensive rethinking of the whole field of scholastic enquiry. As this book will I hope show, Ockham was not a logician devaluing theology and metaphysics; he was no less a philosopher and theologican than his predecessors. He accepted the same framework of knowledge and belief. The difference was that he was concerned with their meaning and evidence to the exclusion of treating their concepts as metaphysical bricks from which to build systems.

Ockham was not in that sense a speculative thinker. If any two words could be said to characterise his outlook, they are 'meaning' and 'evidence', measured on the one hand by his principle of verification in individual existence and on the other by the contingency of all existence. For Ockham, the entire problem of knowledge centred upon the dualism between the actual and the possible, not in the metaphysical sense of Aristotle and Aquinas, as gradations of being—although they have a place in nature, as we shall consider in chapter nine—but logically and theologically. What has so often been misconstrued as Ockham's scepticism, in substituting what could be for what is, in fact sprang from a Christian awareness of the dependence of everything for its existence and its place in the order of existence upon God as creator and conserver. Combined with it was the recognition of the logical implications of that dependence in God's power to displace, conserve, destroy, or create separately or differently what ordinarily existed in the conjunction in which it was encountered by experience or held on faith. The difference affected the certainty of the entire created order, whether experience of existence—the foundation of all evident knowledge—natural phenomena, or supernatural habits and the economy of grace and merit. We shall encounter all of these aspects. What they show is not a distrust in the reliability of nature or God, but the inherent contingency of all creation and hence the limitations upon natural certainty, in the light of the supernatural certainty of God's ominipotence. Since God cannot act contradictorily or in contradiction of his own perfections, the question of a deceiving God does not arise. The dialectic is not therefore between fideism and sceptism, but between what holds *de facto* and *de inesse* and what can be *de possibili*. It is the main thread in Ockham's thinking, philosophical, logical, theological and political, expressing the absence of necessity in everything created. However we may regard its consequences, it was essentially the response of a Christian thinker, and at the opposite extreme of the natural determinism which had dominated the arts faculty at Paris in the 1270s.

As it concerned knowledge, the problem for Ockham was that if evidence was only of what could be known immediately to exist, and all existence was contingent, how could any evident knowledge give necessary knowledge? As we shall see, it led Ockham to a very restricted view of demonstrative knowledge as universally necessary knowledge, and the substitution over a wide range of questions of only probable arguments or persuasions for what had until then been the accepted as demonstrations. Much of Ockham's criticism of previous thinkers, especially Duns Scotus with whose conclusions he so frequently agreed, was precisely over their failure to recognise the limited efficacy of their arguments and/or the untenability of their concepts. Ockham's insistence that only propositions which were removed from the mode of existence to the mode of possibility, while bearing upon real existence, could be necessary, and his reduction of real meaning to the signification of real things, changed the whole basis of discourse. It precluded inferring the existence of what was not known, including God, from what was known: in Ockham's terminology intuitive knowledge of one thing does not give intuitive knowledge of something else; it transposed the diversity hitherto attributed to being—as universal and individual, essence and existence—to the diversity of terms—abstract, concrete, absolute, connotative—signifying the same individual being diversely; it distinguished between merely affirming one term of another and signifying real things or properties, as well as between essential definitions and necessary propositions; and it denied all virtual and formal distinctions which were not real, all evidence of cause from effect, all knowledge of the more universal from the less universal—in short the assumption of a direct order from the conceptual to the real. Instead, for Ockham, all knowledge must be ultimately—if it was not already directly—reducible to knowledge of existence. Verification was therefore founded upon experience rather than demonstration, with evidence taking priority over self-evidence. Proper knowledge lay precisely in analysing the logical and grammatical forms of terms, their significative or non-significative role in propositions, and the implicative connection between propositions in syllogisms and arguments.

Within the limits of certainty governing the natural order, it cannot be emphasised too strongly that Ockham totally accepted the regularities of nature and the constancy of moral norms. If his was a universe of individuals they were not self-contained or discrete. The natural order—as well as knowledge of it—was founded upon the uniformity of nature both ontologically, in the similarities between individuals of the same species and genera, and causally in their dependence upon one another. Nothing therefore could be more misconceived than the older widespread belief that Ockham denied causality or relation in general. What he did was to conceive them empirically, as opposed to logically, as deriving from observation and abstraction. Hence it cannot be logically inferred that one thing is the cause of something else unless the dependence of one upon the other[11] through temporal succession is already known in existence; and correspondingly with individuals of the same species. But once known, that experience can be generalised to all other cases or individuals of the same nature. Such generalisation is the basis of all proper knowledge, contained in universal propositions; without it, as Ockham reiterated, the way of knowledge would be closed. It is not too much to say that causality and similarity are the pivots upon which for Ockham all order and intelligibility turn. In the same way his conception of the moral order in his doctrine of the virtues and vices was based upon the immutability of right reason as the criterion of what should and should not be done. All good and bad acts consisted in the will freely

---

[11] E. Hochstetter, *Studien zur Metaphysik und Erkenntnislehre Wilhelms von Ockham* (Berlin and Leipzig, 1927) was the first to show that systematically. He can be rightly regarded as the pioneer of the new critical study of Ockham.

conforming to or rejecting its dictates. Ockham's confidence in the intelligibility of the world and its essential right ordering is nowhere better illustrated than in his confidence in man's power to do God's will expressed in his commandments.

It is complemented in his theology, which, as in the rest of his outlook, eschews all unnecessary distinctions and speculations either within God or in his relation to creatures. The difference is that theology is exclusively founded upon faith. Its truths are not therefore susceptible to experience or demonstration, but can only serve as assumptions from which implications can be derived explaining or elucidating their meaning. Ockham takes as given all the articles of faith, both as found in the Bible and among the saints and doctors and, until the time of his flight from Avignon, as defined by the Roman church. His theological seriousness of purpose can hardly be questioned. He employed reason to support faith not only where they were consonant, including persuasion of God's existence from the argument of a first conserving cause, but also where they were discrepant, above all in upholding a formal distinction—itself abhorrent to reason—between the divine essence and the the divine persons, together with God's necessary knowledge of what is contingent. It is that same restricted, non-speculative acceptance of what is given in revealed truth that equally accounts for Ockham's one area of speculation, namely that involving God's relation to his creatures. For it is governed by the truth of God's omnipotence which for Ockham means his power to do whatever does not involve a contradiction. Hence, just as reason must cede to theological truths which it cannot comprehend, belief must in turn accept theological implications which surpass the ordained limits of the present dispensation. They are all facets of the same body of faith to be taken, like everything known or believed, in their full implications. In their pursuit Ockham cut through the received wisdom in theology as he did in philosophy and logic.

It was there that his impact lay. If Ockham had a razor it was in dispensing with all unwarranted assumptions, above all those contained in the systems of his predecessors. They, rather than reason or faith taken by themselves, were the victims of his criticisms. In confining himself to what could be ultimately derived from evident knowledge of individual existence or implied from revealed truth, he changed the terms of scholastic discourse. However we may regard his effects, scholasticism after Ockham was never again the same.

PART ONE

The cognitive order

CHAPTER ONE

Simple cognition

OCKHAM'S EPISTEMOLOGY is founded upon the primacy of individual cognition. As coming first in the order of knowing, it is the complement to his view of the individual nature of all being. Together they inaugurated a new outlook. Others, notably Duns Scotus—from whom, as we shall see, Ockham derived his own categories of intuitive and abstractive knowledge—had upheld direct cognition of individuals; and the nominalists of the later eleventh century had denied the existence of any but individuals. No one, however, until Ockham sought to explain all knowledge as the outcome of individual cognition while at the same time insisting upon the universal character of all necessary knowledge and the indispensability of universal concepts in its attainment. If we except the limited efforts of Abelard, Ockham was the first thinker to incorporate universal knowledge into an individual ontology, systematically reducing, as we shall consider in chapters two, three, and four, concepts, terms and propositions to their individual import. He thereby reversed the direction which Christian thought had for the most part followed from the time of St Augustine. Instead of asking how the individual derives from a universal nature or essence he sought to explain how in a world of individuals we come to have knowledge which is not individual. What had been an ontological question became a psychological and logical question, to be resolved not by an appeal to metaphysical principles, but conceptually. Ockham was the first scholastic who had no need of a theory of individuation: the individual as the measure of existence was also the measure of what could be known.

As it affected cognition, Ockham followed Duns Scotus in making the individual directly accessible to the intellect. This was to repudiate the long-standing belief—fostered alike by Neoplatonism and Aristotle—that the proper objects of the intellect were intelligible ideas and concepts freed from their sensory and individual associations. It carried with it the assumption, made explicit by St Augustine and the Augustinian tradition, that intelligible knowledge of what was universal was superior to knowledge of individuals, reached through the senses. The same notion was expressed in Aristotle's dictum that the intellect apprehends universals but the senses individuals: *Intellectus est universalium, sensus autem particularium.*[1] It was

[1] *De Anima*, II, ch. 5, 417 b, 22–3. For a discussion of the implications of this doctrine and

reinforced by the Aristotelian doctrine of abstraction, widely adopted in the thirteenth century, by which the active intellect in abstracting or disengaging the essence or nature of intelligible species within individual things is able to know these as universal forms or qualities in themselves, freed from their contingent individual associations. As upheld by St Thomas Aquinas this doctrine was taken to mean that only universals can be directly known by the intellect; its knowledge of individuals was confined to their image or *similitudo* into which sensory knowledge was converted in the imagination.[2] For, as Aristotle also said, 'the soul never thinks without an image'.[3] The justification for confining the intellect to universals was that as an immaterial nature it could only know what is immaterial and hence only what is universal. This, as S. Day has said, expresses a metaphysical *a priori* view of natures or essences as in themselves defining the nature of the actions which arise from them.[4] Although enshrined in the Thomist axiom *agere sequitur esse*, it can hardly, however, as Day thinks, be identified solely with medieval Aristotelianism. Certainly so far as the soul is concerned, there was before the last two decades of the thirteenth century no more apparent readiness on the part of Augustinian thinkers than Aristotelians to mingle sensory existence with intellectual understanding.

Indeed it is a paradox that the development of the theory of intellectual cognition of individuals came from those who did not accept Aristotle's interpretation that all knowledge came through the senses. If the soul was an autonomous spiritual being it must, as St Augustine held, know everything independently of the senses; hence, by extension, if it were to know individual things outside the soul it must also know them independently and immediately in the way it seized all knowledge. This final corollary did not it seems emerge until the 1280s with thinkers like Matthew of Aquasparta, Peter John Olivi and Vital du Four, and finally, at the beginning of the fourteenth century, Duns Scotus. There seems reason to suppose that it came about partly at least in reaction against the impasse to which the soul's alliance with the body appeared to have led in the opinions condemned at Paris and Oxford in 1277.[5] These included many Aristotelian and at Oxford some Thomist propositions concerning the intellect's dependence upon the senses; in particular both before and after these condemnations one of the issues most heatedly debated was precisely St Thomas Aquinas's definition of the soul in Aristotelian terms as the body's form. The subsequent response to such ideas was to reaffirm the older Augustinian doctrine of the complete ontological separateness of body and soul as distinct beings each having its own separate knowledge.

---

the rejection of it by Duns Scotus and Ockham for direct intuitive knowledge of individuals see S. Day, *Intuitive Cognition: A Key to the Significance of the Later Scholastics* (St Bonaventure, New York, and Louvain, 1947).

[2] Day, *op. cit.*, 26; *Summa Theologiae*, I, q. 86 a, l; text quoted in Day.

[3] *De Anima*, III, ch. 7, 431 a, 15.

[4] Day, *op. cit.*, 129–30.

[5] See C. Bérubé, *La Connaissance de l'individuel au moyen âge* (Paris and Montreal, 1964), and my *Paris and Oxford Universities in the Thirteenth and Fourteenth Centuries* (New York, 1968), 222–38.

Duns Scotus developed this to mean that the intellect had two forms of simple or immediate apprehension, one of the existence of individual things and their species, which he called intuitive knowledge, and the other abstractive knowledge by which the individual was known not in itself but by means of an intelligible species or representation in which it is contained.[6] His justification of intuitive knowledge was on the double grounds of experience and the superiority of the intellect over the senses. By the first, intellectual knowledge of individuals was a fact; by the second, the intellect must be able to know individuals because a superior power is capable of whatever an inferior faculty is capable of. He accordingly re-interpreted Aristotle's axiom to mean that whereas the senses can only know individuals, the intellect can also know universals.[7] Ockham did likewise; but, as we shall discuss presently, he modified the meaning of intuitive and abstractive to make them both immediately of what was known, whether individuals or universals, rejecting the notion of an intelligible species and all universal essences and natures in abstractive knowledge. With Duns Scotus Ockham agreed that intuitive and abstractive knowledge differed as modes of knowing, not over what was known: intuitive knowledge was existential; abstractive was indifferent to existence or non-existence. But Ockham went beyond Scotus in abolishing the independent standing of all general concepts which for Ockham were the mind's response to knowing many individuals. At the same time both of them went beyond St Thomas Aquinas's notion of abstraction to the source of concepts, in the intellect's immediate apprehension of individuals.[8] Cognition began there, and not with abstraction from the images previously converted from sensory experience. What therefore for Aquinas had been the pre-cognitive phase preceding the intellect's formation of concepts, for Scotus and Ockham belonged to the intellect's own cognitive activity. It was coterminous with awareness of existence; but whereas for Ockham that awareness preceded all other knowledge, for Duns it could be merely independent of other knowledge.

Finally, Ockham went further still in transforming the status of abstraction from ontological to conceptual. Since for him there was no essence or common nature to abstract from things, what constituted a universal concept was merely the mind's recognition of similarity among a number of individuals: according to their degree of likeness, as we shall consider in chapter three, individuals were of the same species or genus: neither was an essence inhering in things but a concept predicable of fewer or more individuals. Abstraction therefore becomes the intellect's response to experience of individual existence as opposed to the disengagement of some universal quality or form which has its own—higher—ontological status.

Ockham's break with universal natures was thus complete. It meant, as we shall see, the virtual rejection of the medieval neoplatonised conception of Aristotle of which St Thomas Aquinas was the outstanding representative: at virtually no

---

[6] Day, op. cit., 58.
[7] Ibid., 59–60, 117–18, together with Scotus's text.
[8] Cf. Day's remarks (ibid., 35).

point either epistemologically or ontologically is there any real rapport between Ockham and Aquinas; and the attempt to find it in their doctrine of abstraction and individual experience of being does so by ignoring the entirely different import which both being and cognition have for the two thinkers.[9] Nothing could be more misconceived than to believe that sensory experience of individuals means direct cognition of individuals: as we have just seen, it does not. Similarly abstraction of an essence is at the opposite pole to identifying individual likeness which ontologically remains inseparable from the individuals themselves constituting it. One is real, the other remains a concept. As we shall see in the following chapters, Ockham devoted himself to purging Aristotle's categories of the metaphysical meaning with which so many thinkers from the time of Porphyry and Boethius in the fourth and fifth centuries had invested them: above all the protean distinction between essence and existence which in the case of St Thomas Aquinas was of pivotal importance.

From one standpoint Aquinas and Ockham can be regarded as two different responses to Aristotle whose own unresolved Platonism—exemplified in his theory of abstraction which assumes the inherence of forms in individual things—added to the ambiguity which the accompanying neoplatonist interpretations so enormously increased; their resonance with a Christian conception of being, as deriving from the archetypes or essences of things transmitted by God, gave them an almost unshakeable hold which was strengthened rather than weakened by the application of Aristotelian metaphysics in the thirteenth century. A world of essences, whether self-subsisting and known only in the soul or embodied in individuals and reached through the senses, must give rise to an epistomology of essences. Duns Scotus was no exception; the change which he initiated concerned the way in which the individuals belonging to those essences were known: the essences remained. And it was partly the continued duality between individual and essence which prevented Scotus from reaching the same systematic resolution between intuitive and abstractive knowledge which Ockham achieved. On the one hand intuitive knowledge in being of individual existence was more perfect than abstractive knowledge which was only of an individual in an intelligible species—what Duns called a diminished likeness stopping short of the individual itself. On the other hand, for that very reason, abstractive knowledge was alone necessary to conceptual and universal knowledge which could not be of actual existence.[10] Such a view allowed of no rapport between the two kinds of knowledge: they merely represented different modes of knowing individuals non-discursively, one directly in themselves, the

[9] The prime example is E. A. Moody's *The Logic of William of Ockham* (London, 1935; reprinted New York, 1965). This pioneering study of Ockham's logic, to which I am indebted, suffers from attempting on the one hand to make Aristotle an Ockhamist and on the other Ockham a Thomist. Moody's book was written before Day's and from a strictly logical standpoint; it fails to recognise how completely Ockham's doctrine of intuitive individual knowledge separates his outlook from that of Aquinas, and indeed Aristotle. In the case of Aquinas, far from Ockham's epistemology being reconcilable with his, Ockham rejects intelligible species which Aquinas upholds, and upholds direct intellectual cognition of individuals, which Aquinas rejects.

[10] Day, *op. cit.*, 74-5.

other indirectly in their species or likeness. The first could not enter into discursive knowledge; the second could not draw upon the first for evident support.

Ockham overcame these limitations by taking direct intuitive cognition of individual existence as the point of departure of all other knowledge, abstractive, discursive, individual, universal, contingent, necessary, and as we shall see in chapter four, self-evident. All were founded upon evident knowledge of individuals because, naturally, individuals were the only reality. Accordingly as Duns Scotus had dispensed with the Thomist conversion of images,[11] Ockham dispensed with the Scotist intelligible species. All non-discursive cognition must be direct whether intuitively of individuals or abstractively of their representations in the intellect. The two modes were therefore directly related to one another as phases of immediate knowledge. They differed as evidential and inevidential; and for Ockham the problem of knowledge resided precisely in their difference, namely, according to whether or not something known in the mind could also be shown to exist outside it. If it could it was evident knowledge; if it could not it was abstractive as some form of apprehension or belief or opinion. Intuitive knowledge alone can tell because it alone gives knowledge of real existence. Hence the validity of any knowledge depends upon intuitive knowledge: it is the focus of an outlook which centres upon what can be known evidently, namely the individuals to which all knowledge must be reducible.

We must now consider both intuitive and abstractive knowledge more closely, and their relation to one another and to the images in the imagination which are derived from the senses.

I INTUITIVE AND ABSTRACTIVE KNOWLEDGE

The connection of intuitive and abstractive knowledge with evident knowledge can be seen in the opening question of the Prologue of the *Ordinatio*, where both are treated in the context of how evident knowledge is possible. By evident knowledge Ockham means knowledge of a true proposition caused directly or indirectly by knowledge of its terms; as such, evident knowledge is wider than strict or scientific knowledge (*scientia*)—as well as wisdom and what Aristotle called intuitive reason or knowledge of first principles (*intellectus*)[12]—in being of what is contingent and not confined to necessary propositions.[13] Evident knowledge is therefore of whatever can be known to be true; unlike self-evident knowledge which is immediately engendered from knowledge of the terms of a proposition, to know the

---

[11] Nec est alia conversio ad phantasmata nisi quod intellectus intelligens universale imaginatur singulare eius (*Opus Oxon.*, I, d. 3, q. 6, n. 19, quoted in Day, 116.

[12] Which together with art form the intellectual states, or habits, of the soul, *Ethics*, bk. VI, 1138 b–1145 a.

[13] Dico quod notitia evidens est cognitio alicuius veri complexi, ex notitia terminorum incomplexa immediata vel mediata nata sufficienter causari . . . Ex isto sequitur quod notitia evidens est in plus quam scientia vel intellectus vel sapientia, quia propositio contingens potest evidenter cognosci, et tamen illa notitia nec est scientia nec intellectus nec aliquis illorum habituum quos ponit Philosophus VI Ethicorum [ch. 3, 1139 b, 16–17] (*Ordinatio*, Prologue, q. 1, 5–6).

terms of an evident proposition does not suffice for evident knowledge: merely to have concepts of Socrates and whiteness without also knowing the existence of whiteness in Socrates does not enable us to know as true the proposition 'Socrates is white'. For that we have also to know it in fact. The difference is between abstractive and intuitive knowledge.[14] By the first only the terms of a proposition or their concepts are known; by the second the existence of the things for which they stand are known.

Abstractive and intuitive knowledge are thus different ways of knowing in-complexes (*incomplexa*), that is, concepts or terms like 'man', 'run', 'dispute', 'lion', 'white man', as opposed to complexes which are propositions.[15] As incomplex knowledge each is distinguished from complex, i.e. propositional, knowledge in being an immediate apprehension of the object known and not a judgement on its truth or falsity. Acts of judgement can only be of propositions and are made precisely on the basis of what has been apprehended, as we shall consider in detail in chapter four.[16] Hence, naturally, judgement—as an act of assent, dissent or doubt over a proposition—presupposes apprehension, namely intuitive or abstrac-tive knowledge of its terms. And it is precisely over the evidence or inevidence of the latter that a proposition formed from them will be judged true or false or neither. The distinction between intuitive and abstractive knowledge therefore is designed to answer the question, Why are some propositions judged to be evident and others inevident? The reply is that if only the terms are known—abstractively—without also knowing the existence of what they signify—intuitively—as in the example of Socrates and whiteness, then the proposition will only be known abstractively and inevidently. Abstractive knowledge—as apprehension of the terms —is the condition of propositions at all; but intuitive knowledge—as the apprehension of things as well—is the condition and the guarantee of their truth. One is non-existential, the other is existential.

Ockham defines them as follows:

Abstractive knowledge can be understood in two ways; by one it is in respect of something abstracted from many singulars; and thus abstractive knowledge is nothing else than know-ledge of a universal, of which more will be said later. And if a universal is a real quality really existing in the intellect as can probably be maintained, then it would have to be conceded

[14] Dicendum quod propositio per se nota est illa que scitur evidenter ex quacumque notitia terminorum ipsius propositionis, sive abstractiva sive intuitiva. Sed de propositione contingente non est hoc possibile, quia aliqua notitia terminorum sufficit ad causandum notitiam evidentem veritatis contingentis, scilicet intuitiva, sicut post patebit; aliqua autem non sufficit, scilicet abstractiva. Unde si aliquis videat intuitive Sortem et albedinem existentem in Sorte, potest evidenter scire quod Sortes est albus. Si autem tantum cognosceret Sortem et albedinem existentem in Sorte abstractive, sicut potest aliquis imaginari ea in absentia eorum, non sciret evidenter quod Sortes esset albus, et ideo non est propositio per se nota (*ibid.*, 6–7).

[15] Cf. the definition in the Commentary on the *Categories*: Primo modo dicitur incom-plexum simplex dictio, hoc est una dictio sine additione alterius dictionis, sicut 'homo', 'currit', 'disputat', 'leo'; et per oppositum dicitur complexum omne compositum ex diversis dic-tionibus. Secundo modo dicitur incomplexum terminus propositionis, sive sit una dictio sive plures sicut 'homo albus' ... Per oppositum dicitur complexum compositum ex nomine et verbo faciens aliquem intellectum in animo audientis (*EA*, 40 b).

[16] *Ordinatio, ibid.*, 16.

that a universal can be seen intuitively, and that the same knowledge is intuitive and abstractive taking abstractive in this (first) sense . . . By the other sense, abstractive knowledge is taken for what abstracts from existence and non-existence and the other contingent circumstances which concern a thing or are predicated of it. Not that something is known by intuitive knowledge that is not known by abstractive knowledge, but the same thing is totally and in every identical aspect known by both kinds of knowledge. They are however, distinguished in this manner: because intuitive knowledge of a thing is knowledge in virtue of which it can be known whether a thing is or is not, and so that if it is, the intellect immediately judges it to be and knows its existence evidently, unless impeded by the imperfection of this knowledge.[17]

Now it will be observed to begin with that it is in the second sense of knowledge which abstracts from existence and non-existence that Ockham opposes abstractive knowledge to intuitive knowledge. In the first sense, of a universal concept abstracted from many singulars, abstraction is compatible with intuition if what is abstracted is regarded as really existing in the intellect as opposed to being merely an image or object of thought. The distinction is important both as it affects abstractive knowledge and Ockham's notion of a concept. We shall consider the latter in the next chapter. For abstractive knowledge it means that the distinction from intuitive knowledge is, as we have said earlier, over how an object is known, not over what is known: as Ockham also says in the preceding quotation, whatever is known intuitively is also known in the same respects abstractively. Each of is the same incomplex objects; but where abstractive knowledge is never of existence or non-existence, intuitive knowledge enables the intellect to judge as evident what by abstractive knowledge will always remain inevident.[18] By the same token, intuitive knowledge gives knowledge of a real relation between things, such as the inherence of one thing in another (for example, whiteness in Socrates), the distance between things and so on.[19]

Far then from Ockham's doctrine of intuitive knowledge implying a world of merely discrete individuals, as it has often been represented,[20] it ensures knowledge of their interconnection. Intuitive is thereby the means of distinguishing the real from the mental both among things and in the relations between them which, as we shall discuss in chapter three, to be real must be known by reference to real

---

[17] Ibid., 30–1. Ockham also adds that if perfect intuitive knowledge of a non-existent were conserved by God, it could be known that something does exist. We shall consider this facet later.

[18] Et universaliter omnis notitia incomplexa termini vel terminorum, seu rei vel rerum, virtute cuius potest evidenter cognosci aliquia veritas contingens, maxime de presenti, est notitia intuitiva. Notitia autem abstractiva est illa virtute cuius de re contingente non potest sciri evidenter utrum sit vel non sit. Et per istum modum notitia abstrahit ab existentia et non existentia, quia nec per ipsam potest evidenter sciri de re existente quod existit, nec de non existente quod non existit, per oppositum ad notitiam intuitivam (ibid., 31–2). Also Quodlibet v, q. 5.

[19] Similiter notitia intuitiva est talis quod quando alique res cognoscuntur quarem una inheret alteri vel una distat loco ab altera vel alio modo se habet ad alteram, statim virtute illius notitie incomplexe illarum rerum scitur si res inheret vel non inheret, si distat vel non distat, et sic de aliis veritatibus contingentibus (Ordinatio, ibid., 31).

[20] By the present writer included.

existence and not just known abstractively. Intuitive knowledge is accordingly the ·
source of all experimental knowledge both of what is contingent and what is
necessary.[21]

Ockham resumes the difference between intuitive and abstractive knowledge in
five negative conclusions[22] framed as answers to the alternative explanations of
Duns Scotus for whom their difference lay elsewhere than in that between evident
and inevident knowledge.

The first conclusion is that it is not because abstractive knowledge is indifferently
of what exists and does not exist, or is present and absent, whereas intuitive knowledge is exclusively of what exists and is present. The reason, which we shall discuss
more fully in connection with intuitive knowledge of non-existents below, is that
God can supernaturally conserve the intuitive vision of something which is not
immediately existent or present.[23] Nor, secondly, do the two kinds of knowledge
differ, because only intuitive knowledge seizes the object perfectly in itself, with
abstractive knowledge confined to knowing it in a diminished likeness which Duns
identifies with an intelligible species. As Ockham has already said, and repeats
again, both intuitive knowledge and abstractive knowledge are wholly of the same
object known under the same object for both. For there is nothing—*in rerum natura*
at least—the existence and nature of which cannot be doubted when known intuitively; anything therefore known intuitively can also be known abstractively in
not being of existence or non-existence.[24] The third difference advanced by Duns
is equally untenable: namely that the causes of intuitive and abstractive knowledge
are formally distinct, with the object the direct cause of intuitive knowledge but
intelligible species as the medium in which the object is known abstractively. That
they do not have distinct causes can be proved by the same argument from God's
power employed in answer to the first of Duns's arguments; that is, God could himself totally cause either kind of knowledge without an object.[25] That applies equally
to the fourth and fifth conclusions. The fourth is that intuitive and abstractive knowledge do not differ because intuitive knowledge has a real and actual relation to the
object while abstractive knowledge may have only a potential relation and not ·
necessarily a real one. To Duns's assertion to the contrary, Ockham's reply is that
since according to Duns a real relation cannot have non-being for an object, and
God could cause intuitive knowledge of a non-existent, intuitive knowledge could

---

[21] Igitur isti termini, vel res, una alia notitia possunt cognosci quam sit illa virtute cuius
non possunt cognosci tales veritates contingentes, et illa erit intuitiva. Et ista est notitia a qua
incipit notitia experimentalis, quia universaliter ille qui potest accipere experimentum de
aliqua veritate contingente, et mediante illa de veritate necessaria, habet aliquam notitiam
incomplexam de aliquo termino vel re quam non habet ille qui non potest sic experiri (*ibid.*,
32–3).

[22] *Ibid.*, 33–4.

[23] *Ibid.*, 35–6.

[24] Hoc patet, quia nulla res est, saltem in istis inferioribus, nec alia ratio sibi propria sub qua
potest res intuitive cognosci quin illa cognita ab intellectu possit intellectus dubitare utrum
sit vel non sit, et per consequens quin possit cognosci abstractive. Igitur omne idem et sub
eadem ratione quod est obiectum intuitive notitie potest esse obiectum abstractive (*ibid.*, 36–7).

[25] *Ibid.*, 37.

equally be without a real relation.[26] From that follows the fifth conclusion that the presence of the object known does not distinguish intuitive knowledge from abstractive knowledge where the object is contained in a perfect representation. Once again, God could cause intuitive knowledge of what is not present, thereby eliminating the distinction.[27]

Accordingly intuitive and abstractive knowledge differ in none of these five ways posited by Duns Scotus, but in themselves (seipsis). Where naturally intuitive knowledge cannot be without the existence of the object which is its efficient cause, immediate or indirect, there can be abstractive knowledge when the thing known is destroyed.[28] If Duns's differences are intended to have this meaning then Ockham accepts them here, although as he promises there remain other differences.[29] The outstanding ones are over intuitive knowledge of non-existents and the presence of intelligible species in abstractive knowledge. We shall consider each of them in due course. Here we need only remark that they have been the main source of disagreement in Ockham's five conclusions. Together they radically alter Ockham's conception of both intuitive and abstractive knowledge. On the one hand the possibility of direct intervention by God in causing knowledge of what does not exist or is absent means that any distinction between intuitive and abstractive knowledge based upon the existence of what is known becomes purely contingent, as Ockham's replies to the first, third, fourth and fifth of Duns's arguments show: in each case the distinction posited by Duns between the two kinds of knowledge falls to the ground. Something more is therefore needed to define intuitive knowledge; and this, as we have repeatedly seen, is that it is evident: enabling the object to be known immediately as it is, regardless of whether it is present. Although naturally only what is present can be known evidently, supernaturally, as we shall see, it need not be. Hence intuitive knowledge, secundum se et necessario, is equally of existence and non-existence.[30] It is that which makes it different from abstractive knowledge: where the latter is defined by its indifference to existence and non-existence, intuitive knowledge is precisely of what exists and does not exist; it is therefore existential in the full sense, negatively as well as affirmatively, because it is of what is contingent, which by definition concerns non-existence as well as existence. The difference is that naturally non-existence cannot be known intuitively but only, as we shall see, by God's omnipotence. Hence pro statu isto as it concerns man's capacity, in contradistinction to the nature of intuitive knowledge

[26] Quartum patet per idem, quia relatio realis secundum istos [i.e. Duns Scotus, Quodlibet, q. 13, n. 14–15], non potest terminari ad non-ens; obiectum autem notitie intuitive potest esse non-ens . . . (ibid., 37).

[27] Ibid.

[28] Ideo dico quod notitia intuitiva et abstractiva se ipsis differunt et non penes obiecta nec penes causas suas quascumque, quamvis naturaliter notitia intuitiva non possit esse sine existentia rei, que est vere causa efficiens notitie intuitive mediata vel immediata, sicut alias dicetur. Notitia autem abstractiva potest esse naturaliter ipsa re nota simpliciter destructa (ibid., 38).

[29] Ibid.

[30] Et ita notitia intuitiva, secundum se et necessario, non plus est existentis quam non-existentis, nec plus respicit existentiam quam non-existentiam, sed respicit tam existentiam quam non-existentiam rei, per modum prius declaratum (ibid., 36).

in itself, *secundum se et necessario*, intuitive knowledge is always of what exists here and now. Logically, however, it bears equally upon existence and non-existence, which is how Ockham always defines it.[31]

This represents another conception of intuitive knowledge from that of Duns Scotus, in the face of which neither Gilson's statement that Ockham's inclusion of non-existents wrecked the Scotist view of intuitive knowledge,[32] nor Day's that Ockham's was the logical continuation of Scotus,[33] seems particularly pertinent. Ockham was saying something that Scotus did not say and had apparently had not intended saying; that Ockham said it on the basis of what Duns did say does not of itself make Ockham either the betrayer or the continuator of Scotus, any more than pouring new wine into old bottles means that it should be or need be the same as the old.

That again can be seen in Ockham's treatment of abstractive knowledge on the other hand; he equally changed its import by making it also directly of the same aspect of the same object known intuitively; he thereby at once made the two kinds of knowledge convergent upon the same object and eliminated from abstractive knowledge any kind of intermediary, such as the intelligible species or similarity under which it was known, posited by Duns Scotus. Abstractive knowledge accordingly becomes the non-existential complement of existential intuitive knowledge, with all the other Scotist impedimenta of formally distinct causes and diminished perfect similarities left behind.

Ockham confirmed these differences in his replies to a series of queries or doubts (*dubia*) raised in the same first question of the Prologue of the *Ordinatio*. To begin with, he repeats that intuitive and abstractive knowledge are distinguished in themselves as different kinds of knowledge with different natural—as opposed to supernatural—causes. In doing so, Ockham for the first time briefly indicates the relation of abstractive to intuitive knowledge: where naturally intuitive knowledge is caused by the thing known, the efficient cause of abstractive knowledge is intuitive knowledge or a habit inclining to abstractive knowledge as he will afterwards explain.[34] For the moment we too shall leave the matter there, only observing that it is not merely in the formal enumeration of their differences that Ockham diverges from Scotus over intuitive and abstractive knowledge; but also in their different relation of the kinds of knowledge to one another and their different roles

[31] E.g., Quia notitia intuitiva rei est talis notitia virtute cuius potest sciri utrum res sit vel non (*ibid.*, 31). Also *Reportatio*, II, qq. 14–15, E.

[32] 'En fait, Ockham a hérité de Duns Scot les mots *cognitio intuitiva* et *cognitio abstractiva*, mais loin d'avoir reçu de lui la notion de connaissance intuitive, il l'a ruinée, et avec elle la distinction même, en proposant cette monstruosité aux yeux de Duns Scot: l'intuition de quelque chose qui n'existe pas'; E. Gilson, *Jean Duns Scot* (Paris, 1952). As we shall discuss below, intuition of a non-existent is not the same as knowledge of non-existence: by God's absolute power the intellect could equally know that something does not exist and know something which did exist or is absent, but not nothing as something, which would be contradictory.

[33] *Intuitive Cognition*, 145; also 146, 172.

[34] Tamen naturaliter loquendo iste notitie habent distinctas causas effectivas, quia causa effectiva notitie intuitive est ipsa res nota; causa autem effectiva notitie abstractive est ipsamet notitia intuitiva vel aliquis habitus inclinans ad notitiam abstractivam, sicut alias dicetur (*Ordinatio, ibid.*, 61). The reference is to the *Reportatio*, book two, qq. 14 and 15.

in knowing as a whole: as we shall also see, the primacy which Ockham gave to individual cognition makes intuitive knowledge the prerequisite of all other knowledge. At the same time however he reaffirms that even if the two kinds of knowledge did not have different objects they could still be of different species, for it is possible for an infinite power—namely God—to produce different effects in the same subject.[35] Hence, as Ockham has already said and will say again, there can be intuitive knowledge even without the existence of the object.

The second part of the same doubt presents Ockham with the problem that Duns had to face: namely that intuitive knowledge is of individuals but the intellect knows only universals; moreover the intellect abstracts from what exists here and now, but intuitive knowledge is of what is here and now. How then can the intellect be said to know intuitively?[36] Ockham's response is not only to reaffirm that the intellect has intuitive knowledge of singulars, but as he will show, it knows the individual first as the first object of knowledge by primacy of cognition.[37] Nor does Aristotle deny the fact; his concern was to distinguish between the intellect and the senses. Hence if the intellect knows not only the individual but also the universal, and the senses only what is individual, it follows that they are distinct, which was the meaning of Aristotle's contrast.[38] Like Duns Scotus, then, Ockham interprets Aristotle's reference to the intellect in an inclusive sense:[39] that in addition to knowing singulars it also knows universals, although Ockham adds that for Aristotle the intellect, in knowing the individual first, does not know it precisely.[40] What, if any, difference that makes to the intellect's knowledge Ockham does not specify.

To the other objection that the intellect abstracts from present existence (*hic et nunc*) Ockham replies that sometimes it does, and then it has abstractive knowledge; and sometimes it does not and then it has intuitive knowledge by which the intellect is able to judge whether or not something does exist and is present.[41] Ockham also directly meets the further objection raised by Aquinas's view that the intellect always first abstracts what it knows from its material conditions which, as we shall discuss in more detail subsequently, Ockham opposes for denying that the individual can be known by the intellect directly. In this context, he declares, abstraction has nothing to do with the object of knowledge; for the same thing is the object of both senses and intellect, and so no more abstract for the intellect than the senses. Where they differ is that the intellect can subsequently, after this initial cognition of an individual, which is first in the order of knowing, abstract many things from it, such as universal concepts, and know them separately from their conjunction in real beings. That is possible only for the intellect because its know-

---

[35] *Ibid.*, 61.

[36] Tertium dubium, *ibid.*, 53.

[37] Ad secundum argumentum probans quod intellectus non habet notitiam intuitivam, quia non cognoscit singulare, dico quod intellectus pro statu isto cognoscit singulare et primo, sicut patebit alias; et est primum cognitum primitate generationis (*ibid.*, 63).

[38] *Ordinatio, ibid.*, 64.

[39] Cf. Day, *Intuitive Cognition*, 59–61, 68, 117–18.

[40] *Ordinatio, ibid.*

[41] *Ibid.*

ledge is alone immaterial.[42] Ockham therefore confronted head-on the Aristotelianism represented by St Thomas Aquinas.

The relation between the intellect and the senses is made more precise in answer
to the next doubt, which is that the intellect cannot have intuitive knowledge
because it cannot know its own acts directly but only by reflexion; but intuitive is
directly of what exists outside the intellect; and since what is singular is only known
by the senses, the intellect does not know intuitively.[43] Two separate issues were
here involved. The first is over the possibility of intelligible—i.e. non-sensory—
knowledge of the intellect's own acts which Ockham has earlier treated and we
shall consider later: to this he reiterates what he has said previously, that the intellect
has direct intuitive knowledge of its own acts by which it is able to know that it
knows something similar to its acts. For that reason he does not accept that there is
properly speaking a distinction between reflexive acts by which the intellect knows
its own acts, and direct acts by which it knows other things outside it. In the broad
sense, reflexive is another way of saying that the intellect has intuitive knowledge
of its own acts.[44] As we shall see, and as Ockham once again confirms in his reply
to the next doubt, such intelligible knowledge is exclusively of the intellect's acts
and not its habits or states which in this life cannot be known directly; that applies
not only to states like those of knowledge, love, and joy, but also to those of faith
and charity which can all only be inferred from direct experience of their actions.[45]
Indeed *pro statu isto* the intellect knows nothing clearly and perfectly, including the difference between a direct and reflexive act.[46] In this context, as we shall
see when we examine the matter more closely, the influence of St Augustine is
paramount.

The second issue concerns knowledge which comes through the senses. Here
Ockham interprets both Aristotle and Averroes, quoted in support of the objection
that there is only sensory knowledge of individuals, to mean that, naturally,
sensible things are known first in this life. Hence when Aristotle says that the
intellect does not know without an image, he means merely that all intellective
cognition presupposes sensitive cognition, both exterior and interior, and not that

[42] Quia dico, sicut alias probabitur, quod idem totaliter sub eadem ratione a parte obiecti
est primum obiectum sensus exterioris et intellectus primitate generationis, et hoc pro statu
isto; et ita obiectum intellectus in illa intellectione prima non est magis abstractum quam
obiectum sensus. Potest tamen postea intellectus abstrahere multa: et conceptus communes,
et intelligendo unum coniunctorum in re non intelligendo reliquum. Et hoc non potest competere sensui. Si autem illa abstractio intelligatur universaliter, intelligenda est a parte intellectionis, quia illa est simpliciter immaterialis; non autem sic cognitio sensitiva (*ibid.*, 64–5).

[43] Quartum dubium, *ibid.*, 54.

[44] Ad quartum dubium dico, sicut probatum est prius, quod intellectus noster pro statu
isto intelligit aliquod mere intelligibile in particulari et intuitive. Ad primum in contrarium
dico quod proprie loquendo et stricte nulla est intellectio reflexiva, quia reflexio stricte sumpta
includit necessario ad minus duo, sicut patet in motu locali reflexo. Accipiendo tamen reflexion-
em large, concedo quod illa intellectio est reflexa, et tamen cum hoc stat quod sit intuitiva
(*ibid.*, 65). Also *Quodlibet* II, q. 12 for much the same opinion.

[45] Ad quintum, *Ordinatio, ibid.*, 69.

[46] Intellectus autem noster pro statu isto nihil cognoscit intuitive clare et perfecte, et ideo
non potest discernere illud a quolibet alio. Et propter hoc non potest discernere inter actum
rectum et reflexum, et sic de aliis, quamvis possit discernere ab aliquibus aliis (*ibid.*, 68).

the intellect can only know individuals by means of images or phantasms.[47] Again, if it is said that intuitive knowledge in being primary does not presuppose any other knowledge—i.e. that sensory knowledge suffices for intuitive cognition of individuals—the reply is that it does not presuppose anything else in the same faculty, but it does in another faculty: for example intellectual knowledge of whiteness presupposes sensitive cognition of whiteness, as intuitive knowledge of intellection, feeling or happiness presupposes knowledge of their objects.[48] Similarly, Aristotle's saying that nothing is known by the intellect unless it was previously in the senses applies not to everything in the intellect but only to sensibilia existing outside it.[49] Intuitive knowledge, therefore, is equally of intelligibles. Whatever may be laid at Ockham's door, it cannot include reducing all knowledge to sense perception.

Ockham's account of intuitive and abstractive knowledge in the Prologue of the *Ordinatio* shifts the emphasis, compared with Duns, from the contrast between perceptual and conceptual knowledge to that between evidential and inevidential. The change is apparent in two main respects: in the possibility of intuitive knowledge of non-existents, and in the direct causal relation between intuitive and abstractive knowledge where nothing else is required to explain abstractive knowledge than previous intuitive knowledge and the habit their conjunction engenders. We shall examine them in turn, taking intelligible intuitive knowledge as an annexe to the questions raised by intuitive knowledge of non-existents. Both the main issues take us beyond the Prologue of the *Ordinatio*, above all to book two of the *Reportatio*, questions fourteen and fifteen, where Ockham treats each *ex professo*. In the case of intuitive knowledge of non-existents we shall refer also to the *Quodlibets* where several questions are expressly devoted to the problem.

II INTUITIVE KNOWLEDGE OF NON-EXISTENTS

So far we have been considering intuitive knowledge as it occurs naturally. We must now turn to see it as it could be by God's absolute power. To do so is not to introduce a different kind of intuitive knowledge, but, as we have said before, to exhibit it in itself *secundum se et necessario* unqualified,[50] and so detached from its present contingent circumstances, where it is, naturally, inseparable from an object which is ontologically extrinsic to it. Since their interdependence is the result of God's free concausation, he could as freely suspend it, enabling intuitive knowledge, as anything else which is distinct in kind, to exist in its own right. Such a change, however, is a theological not a philosophical one, entailing a shift from the plane

---

[47] Ad aliam auctoritatem *De memoria et reminiscentia* dico quod nihil est intelligere sine phantasmate, quia omnis notitia intellectiva presupposit pro statu isto necessario cognitionem sensitivam tam sensus exterioris quam interioris (*ibid.*, 67).

[48] *Ibid.*

[49] Ad aliam auctoritatem *De sensu et sensato* dico quod non est de intentione Philosophi quod nihil intelligitur ab intellectu nisi prefuit sub sensu, sed quod nullum sensibile extrinsecum intelligitur ab intellectu nisi quod prefuit sub sensu (*ibid.*, 67–8).

[50] This is stressed by Day, *Intuitive Cognition*, 163–4, 167–8, who calls it 'the key to Ockham's insistence on the possibility that God can cause intuitive cognition of non-existents'.

of natural causation to that of divine omnipotence; it is one of the keystones of Ockham's outlook and takes the stress of his individualist ontology in a contingent universe. On the one hand there are the different species of individuals which God has freely created; on the other, there is the particular mode of operation and existence which he has ordained for them. Just as he could have not created them, so he could suspend their natural sequence; conversely he could preserve one without the other.

In the hands of Ockham's followers and successors this contrast between what was *de facto*, and what could be *de possibili*, became one of the most disruptive elements in the intellectual life of the mid-fourteenth century, certainly in northern Europe, where it was frequently little more than a device to discard the accepted order of theological or natural truth. Ockham more than anyone undoubtedly helped to bring it into vogue by his own repeated use of the distinction. Yet that does not of itself implicate him in the abuses to which it was subsequently put. If invoking God's absolute power became in the end a mere device for expressing extreme paradoxes, such as are to be found for example in the writings of Robert Holcot, the early Thomas Buckingham, John of Mirecourt and Adam of Woodham,[51] for Ockham it was a device for keeping God firmly at the centre of creation. The appeal to God's omnipotence served to liberate men from their misconceptions over the nature of being and their knowledge of it; it reduced both to the individuals constituting them. In that sense, Ockham was at the farthest remove from a naturalistic self-sufficiency. Although he rejected demonstrative knowledge of God's nature and all exclusively theological truths—which as we shall see in chapter five must be held on faith—his acceptance of them as a Christian formed his frame of reference for all knowledge, including—as we shall see in the third and fourth chapters—logical truth where it concerns what is necessary and certain. However we may evaluate Ockham's outlook, its foundation was the dialectic between what can be known in virtue of being human and what must be believed through being a Christian. Ockham differed from his predecessors in the rigour with which he pressed the distinction, and from his successors in the control with which he applied it.

Central to it was the role of divine omnipotence as the touchstone of what was essential to God's dispensation. Since for Ockham this reduced itself to a relation between creator and creature, the invocation of God's omnipotence became the principle of divine economy. Granted the existence of a creature, its only necessary accompaniment was the presence of the creator; no other creatures were necessary because God could, if he so willed, do directly what he had ordained to be done through secondary causes. That was the logic of God's omnipotence: the displacement of secondary causes by his own direct intervention as concause or conserver, as we shall repeatedly encounter.

Ockham's conception of divine power rests upon two assumptions, neither peculiar to Ockham who was not their originator any more than he invented his mistermed 'razor'. The first was the long-accepted distinction between two different

---

[51] See my *Bradwardine and the Pelagians* (Cambridge, 1957), part two.

connotations of God's power: his absolute power (*potentia absoluta*) and his ordained power (*potentia ordinata*).[52] The invocation of such a difference went back at least to Peter Damian (d. 1071), and had recently been revived by Henry of Ghent and Duns Scotus. Ockham in his *Quodlibets* defined it as follows:

> God can do some things by his ordained power and some by his absolute power. This distinction is not to be taken to mean that there are really two powers in God, because God's power is the same in God as outside him, and is himself in every way. Nor should it be so understood that God can do some things ordinately and some absolutely and not ordinately; for God can do nothing inordinately. Rather his power to do something is sometimes to be accepted according to the laws which he has ordained and instituted; and this way God is said to be able to act by his ordained power. Alternatively his power means his ability to do all that does not include a contradiction, whether he has ordained that it should be done or not, because God can do many things that he wills not to do, according to the Master of the Sentences [Peter Lombard], book one, distinction forty-three; and this is called his power by his absolute power.[53]

God's absolute power therefore represents his omnipotence unqualified and uncircumscribed by reference to his decrees as creator. It represents God himself as supreme being and supremely free and omnipotent. As such Ockham rests his distinction upon the twin supports of faith and logic. The first is contained in the words of the creed: 'I believe in God the father almighty'. The second is logically entailed from it, namely that God can do anything that does not impair his power, i.e. everything that is not contradictory.[54] It is important to stress that the limitation here is a logical one; for it is precisely the application of the criterion of non-contradiction that was to make the notion of God's absolute power so destructive of traditional theology. Unless taken in conjunction with the concept of God as *summum bonum*, which defined his being and so all his actions as those of a being supremely good as well as supremely free, it could too easily lead to subsuming God's nature under the attribute of mere omnipotence. In consequence, his power to do rather than his purpose in doing became the criterion of his actions, which was the very danger inherent in invoking his absolute power: it too easily led to a disjunction between means and end, or more strictly, the means, in this case the testing of the ramifications of God's power, became the end. It was not, however, true of Ockham as we shall see.

That brings us to the second element in his notion of God's absolute power,

[52] On the origin of the distinction see J. Miethke, *Ockhams Weg*, 141ff.

[53] Circa primum dico quod quedam potest deus facere de potentia ordinata et quedam de potentia absoluta. Hec distinctio non est sic intelligenda quod in deo realiter sint due potentie quarum una sit ordinata et alia absoluta, quia unica est potentia in deo ad extra que omni modo est ipse deus. Nec sic est intelligenda quod aliqua potest deus ordinate facere et aliqua absolute et non ordinate, quia deus nihil potest facere inordinate. Sed est sic intelligenda quod posse aliquid aliquando accipititur secundum leges ordinatas et institutas a deo; et illa deus dicitur posse facere de potentia ordinata. Aliter accipitur posse pro posse facere omne illud quod non includit contradictionem fieri, sive deus ordinavit se hoc facturum sive non, quia deus multa potest facere que non vult facere, secundum Magistrum libro 1 Sententiarum dist. 43; et illa dicitur posse de potentia absoluta (*Quodlibet* VI, q. 1).

[54] Credo in deum patrem omnipotentem. Quem sic intelligo quod quodlibet est divine potentie attribuendum quod non includit manifestam contradictionem (*ibid.*, q. 6).

its application. Here again Ockham was not only within a recognisable tradition, but a strongly Augustinian one, which had become explicit as a reaction to the naturalism condemned at Paris and Oxford in 1270 and 1277.[55] It is expressed by Ockham in the phrase—again not original, at least in intent—'Whatever God can produce by second causes he can produce and conserve immediately.'[56] From one point of view it can (as we have already suggested) be regarded as the application to God of the principle of economy—that a plurality should not be assumed unnecessarily (*pluralitas non est ponenda sine necessitate*). As a general principle it goes back to Aristotle, and was taken up at Oxford in the thirteenth century by Robert Grosseteste as first of a line extending through Roger Bacon, Duns Scotus, Ockham and beyond.[57] But however important as a methodological precept, the principle of economy also represented a fundamental theological truth. This was that God as sovereignly free creator was not dependent upon creatures for his effects. As first cause of their production and concause in their conservation, without him nothing could be and with him nothing else need be. In that sense, as interpreted by Ockham, God's absolute power is either the reversion to God of the power which ordinarily (*ordinate*) he has conferred upon creatures or its manifestation in actions which fall outside what he has ordained. It is here that Ockham departs from a merely causal explanation of creation: unlike St Thomas Aquinas he denies to the relations between second causes any internal necessity.[58] Instead he makes omnipotence and freedom of God as first cause not only the *raison d'être* for how things are but for the possibility that they could be different. At the same time—and this is where Ockham differs from some who were to follow him— Ockham always conceived God exclusively as creator; the exercise of his absolute power is not just an exercise in seeing how far God can go in doing differently from what he has decreed: it is directed to sustaining the same order by different means. Hence for Ockham the logic of God's absolute power lay in substituting a wholly divine for a partially divine concausation; it represented God's direct intervention in actions ordinarily performed by creatures and conserved by him. It thereby meant suspending the relations between secondary causes while conserving their own separate existence as independent beings. In that sense God's absolute power was only reducing creation, or a particular aspect of it, to irreducible individual being and its two constituents of substance and quality, which, as we shall see in chapter three, are alone absolute and so capable of independent existence.

[55] Interesting light is thrown upon this point in the recently published *Disputed Questions* of Peter de Falco, 3 vols, edited by A.-J. Gondras (Louvain and Paris, 1968) who uses the phrase *frustra fit per plura quod potest fieri per pauciora*, to stress God's direct rapport with creatures even at the expense of second causes.

[56] Preterea in illo articulo fundatur illa propositio famosa theologorum: quidquid deus producit mediantibus causis secundis potest immediate per se causare et conservare (*Quodlibet, ibid.*).

[57] See A. C. Crombie, *Robert Grosseteste and the Origins of Experimental Science* (Oxford, 1953; reprinted 1966).

[58] E.g. Confirmatur, quia in individuis eiusdem rationis non est ordo essentialis quin quando realiter distinguuntur unum possit fieri sine alio si neutrum sit pars alterius. Sed deus vidit ista factibilia ab eterno, et vidit quod neutrum potest esse pars alterius; ergo potest facere quodcumque istorum sine alio (*Ordinatio,* d. 17, q. 7, D).

'Every absolute (i.e. individual) being', Ockham declares, 'which is distinct in place and subject from something else absolute can exist by divine power after the other absolute is destroyed.'[59]

These are the theological grounds upon which Ockham upholds the possibility of intuitive knowledge of non-existents by God's absolute power. However close this was subsequently to come to scepticism in doubting everything, two things stand between Ockham and such a position. The first is that God does not mislead the intellect; there is therefore no question of his causing it to err in knowing what does not exist.[60] The second is the principle of non-contradiction, which precludes knowing a non-existent as real when it is not: that would be to know nothing as something. What, however, God's power does call into question is the order in which intuitive knowledge can occur. Thus, while naturally it precedes abstractive knowledge—so that for example someone born blind cannot possess the concept of colour[61]—God could himself by his absolute power produce both kinds of knowledge independently of the other.[62]

The reason is to be found in the same possibility of intuitive knowledge of non-existents, which could lead to three different states: knowledge of what is absent; vision or apprehension of something without an accompanying judgement of existence; and conversely, the belief in the existence of what does not exist. The discrepancy in each case arises from the distinction between apprehension and assent. As we shall consider more fully in chapter four they are really distinct from one another whether they concern incomplexes (things or terms) or complexes (propositions).[63] Apprehension is an immediate awareness of something tout court without a judgement of existence (in the case of incomplexes) or of truth (in the case of complexes). Such a judgement belongs to assent or dissent or doubt over what has been apprehended or perceived. For that reason, while naturally there can be apprehension without assent, assent presupposes apprehension; that is to say they are really distinct and can be either separate, or in conjunction as the elements in any act of judgement, incomplex or complex, where naturally they are inseparable.

Now on the principle already enunciated, that what is distinct naturally can be conserved separately by God supernaturally, it follows that there can be not only apprehension without assent to what is apprehended, but assent without ap-

---

[59] Preterea omnis res absoluta distincta loco et subiecto ab alia re absoluta potest per divinam potentiam existere alia re absoluta destructa (Quodlibet VI, q. 6). For its ramifications see M. A. Pernoud, 'Innovation in William of Ockham's references to the Potentia Dei', Antonianum 45 (1970), 65–97.

[60] Et sic nullo modo ponit intellectum in errore (Reportatio, II, q. 15, EE).

[61] Nulla res potest cognosci abstractive in se a nobis ex puris naturalibus nisi ipsa precognoscatur intuitive . . . Secundum ostendo, quod nihil potest cognosci a nobis ex puris naturalibus in conceptu simplici sibi proprio nisi ipsum in se precognoscatur. Ista patet inductive; aliter enim posset dici quod color posset cognosci a ceco a nativitate in conceptu proprio coloribus (Ordinatio, d. 2, q. 9, 314).

[62] Quia deus per idem totaliter potest causare utramquam notitiam, nec requiritur quod res moveat in propria existentia et obiective (ibid., Prologue, q. 1, 37).

[63] 245–55 below. The main references to Ockham's discussions are Ordinatio, Prologue, q. 1; Reportatio, II, q. 15, q. 25; Quodlibet III, q. 8; IV, q. 17; V, q. 5; VII, q. 4.

prehension; and it is precisely their varying relations of independence that explain the different ways in which non-existents can be known: namely as apprehension of existence without assent; assent to existence without apprehension of existence; or dissent from an apprehension of existence, so that knowledge and belief are in conflict.

Ockham explored these different ways in the Prologue of the *Ordinatio*, the second book of the *Reportatio* and the *Quodlibets*, on each of the occasions that he discusses intuitive knowledge: an indication that he regarded them as inherent facets of intuitive knowledge. Before turning to the details of what he said it is important to emphasise that the question at issue is intuitive knowledge of a non-existent, that is, of something which is either apprehended or assented to, when it is not present, and only indirectly of non-existence when the existence of the same non-existent is denied. As S. Day has rightly said,[64] a judgement of non-existence can be either supernatural, when applied to a non-existent, or natural when it merely means lack of assent to what is not known intuitively to exist: the latter is a separate consideration and only indirectly touched upon by Ockham as we shall mention.

Now the grounds for the possibility that there can be intuitive cognition without an object are given in Ockham's rejection of the first of the five reasons of Duns Scotus for their difference which he considers and dismisses in the Prologue of the *Ordinatio*.[65] This is that, contrary to Duns, the two kinds of knowledge do not differ according to whether or not they are of what really exists and is present to the intellect, for then, on Scotus's own arguments which Ockham accepts against a form in the intellect, the object would have to be either efficient or material cause. It is not efficient cause for the very reason that whatever God can do through an efficient cause he can do directly; nor is it a material cause because as independent of the intellect the object could then receive the intellect's cognition and continue to have it after the intellect ceased to have it. Conversely the object could not by definition be formal cause, nor final cause, since God is the only final cause necessary for existence as he is the only necessary efficient cause.[66] Nor is the object required as that at which the act of cognition terminates, for the same reason that it is not an essential cause by any of the four kinds of causality; and if it is not essential there can be an act of intuitive cognition independently of an object and so of a non-existent. Accordingly taken in itself, *secundum se et necessario*, intuitive cognition is not more of existence than of non-existence.[67]

---

[64] Day, *Intuitive Cognition*, 174–5.

[65] *Ordinatio*, Prologue, q. 1, 33–5.

[66] *Ibid.*, 35.

[67] Si dicatur quod obiectum requiritur in ratione obiecti terminantis, contra: aut obiectum in quantum terminans habet rationem alicuius cause essentialis, aut non. Si sic, arguo sicut prius. Si non, tunc arguo sicut isti arguunt alibi: Omnis effectus sufficienter dependet ex suis causis essentialibus, ita quod illis positis, omnibus aliis circumscriptis, potest sufficienter poni effectus. Igitur si obiectum in quantum terminans non habet rationem cause essentialis respectu notitie intuitive, si obiectum in quantum terminans simpliciter destruatur secundum omnem existentiam sui realem, potest poni ipsa notitia intuitiva; igitur ipsa re destructa potest poni ipsa notitia intuitiva. Et ita notitia intuitiva secundum se et necessario non plus est exis-

Only naturally must it be immediately of existence; supernaturally it can be of either state according to whether what is known is nothing real or something whose existence is beyond the natural range of the intellect, for example, something at Rome known immediately by someone not in Rome.[68] Each is a non-existent in that neither is present to the intellect; but only the first has non-existence. Hence a non-existent is defined in relation to the intellect and not by its own non-existence, since it may equally exist. Knowledge of it arises solely from God's power to cause and/or conserve knowledge which naturally is from an object. Although such knowledge can only be supernaturalis engendered, where, however, God conserves an initially intuitive cognition of a real object, the resulting cognition of a non-existent will be natural by causation and supernatural by conservation,[69] as the assent to what is known supernaturally can also be natural.[70]

Whichever God's precise role, as cause or conserver or both, such knowledge will be neither contradictory nor illusory. It is not contradictory first because God himself, as omniscient, has intuitive knowledge of all non-existents as well as existents;[71] and second, because as we have said before, whatever is distinct in place and subject from something else can by God's absolute power continue to exist without the other, as the vision of a star could be conserved by God after the star's destruction.[72] Such knowledge is not illusory or the source of error for the very reason that it is not the same as a judgement of existence or non-existence; and, by God's absolute power they can, as we have said, be separated from one another. Accordingly, on the one hand, there could be a vision of something non-existent without any act of assent to its existence or non-existence;[73] and on

---

tentis quam non existentis, nec plus respicit existentiam quam non-existentiam sed respicit tam existentiam quam non-existentiam, per modum prius declaratum (ibid., 35–6). Also Reportatio, II, q. 15, E.

[68] Reportatio, II, q. 15, E; Quodlibet v, q. 5. Aureole on the other hand held there could be intuitive knowledge of non-existents naturally. See P. Boehner, 'Notitia Intuitiva of non-existents according to Peter Aureoli', FcS 8 (1948), 388–416.

[69] Si primo de aliquo obiecto causetur cognitio intuitiva naturaliter, et post ipso obiecto destructo deus conservet cognitionem intuitivam prius causatam, nunc est cognitio naturalis quantum ad causationem et supernaturalis quantum ad conservationem. Tunc est idem dicendum per omnia sicut si illa cognitio esset supernaturaliter causata, quia per istam possum iudicare rem esse quando est, quantumcunque distet obiectum cognitum, et non esse quando non est posito quod obiectum corrumpatur. Et sic potest aliquo modo concedi quod per cognitionem naturalem intuitivam iudico rem esse quando est et non esse quando non est, quia per cognitionem naturaliter causatam, licet supernaturaliter conservatam (Reportatio, ibid.).

[70] Ordinatio, Prologue, q. 1, 70; Reportatio, II, q. 15 E.

[71] Preterea deus per eandem notitiam videt rem esse quando est, et non esse quando non est; ergo ita potest esse in proposito sine repugnantia (Quodlibet v, q. 5); also Ordinatio, Prologue, q. 1, 39.

[72] Sed visio intuitiva, tam sensitiva quam intellectiva, est res absoluta, distincta loco et subiecto al obiecto. Sicut si videam intuitive stellam existentem in celo, illa visio intuitiva, sive sit sensitiva sive intellectiva, distinguitur loco et subiecto ab obiecto viso; igitur ista visio potest manere stella destructa; igitur etc. (Ordinatio, ibid., 39); also Quodlibet vi, q. 6.

[73] Ad aliud concedo illud principium et conclusionem, et totam deductionem, quia non est contradictio quod visio sit, et tamen per illam visionem nec iudicem rem esse, nec non esse, quia deus potest facere visionem sine omni tali assensu. Sed per naturam hoc non potest facere (Quodlibet v, q. 5).

the other there could be assent to the existence or non-existence of a non-existent without evident knowledge of it.[74] In neither case is there any contradiction because different kinds of knowledge are involved.

Thus to begin with God cannot cause in us evident knowledge that something is present when it is absent; that would be contradictory because evident knowledge by definition tells us of what is present; otherwise it would not be evident.[75] God can, however, cause a creditive act by which we could believe that something absent is present; but then such a belief would be abstractive since it would not be evident.[76] Conversely God could conserve the vision of something seen so that it could be seen intuitively and yet not judged to be or not to be;[77] for once again evident knowledge is distinct from an act of assent or dissent or doubt. By the same token the intellect could believe that what it sees evidently does not exist.[78]

The distinction, then, is between knowledge of appearance and of existence. Only the first is compatible with non-existence; and when it is the accompanying knowledge is abstractive not intuitive, because inevident and based on belief. As Ockham says,

God cannot make evident assent of this contingent proposition 'This whiteness is' when this whiteness is not, on account of the contradiction which follows, because evident assent denotes that it thus exists in fact as signified by the proposition ... I concede, however, that God can cause assent which is of the same kind as evident assent ... but this assent is not evident because what is assented to is not as it is in fact.[79]

---

[74] Ad secundum potest dici probabiliter quod notitia incomplexa terminorum et apprehensio complexi et iudicium sequens distinguuntur realiter et quod quodlibet istorum per potentiam divinam est a quolibet separabile ... quia de nullo absoluto realiter distincto ab alio absoluto debet negari quin possit fieri sine eo per divinam potentiam absolutam nisi appareat evidens contradictio. Sed non apparet evidens contradictio quod iudicium sequens apprehensionem sit, et tamen quod apprehensio non sit; nec quod apprehensio complexi sit, et tamen quod notitia incomplexa terminorum non sit; igitur etc. (*Ordinatio*, Prologue, q. 1, 58–9).

[75] Ad primum istorum dico quod deus non potest causare in nobis cognitionem talem per quam evidenter appareat nobis res esse presens quando est absens, quia hoc includit contradictionem, quia cognitio talis evidens importat quod ita sit in re sicut denotatur per propositionem cui fit assensus. Et per consequens cum cognitio evidens huius propositionis 'Res est presens' importat rem esse presentem, opportet quod sit presens; aliter non esset cognitio evidens (*Quodlibet* v, q. 5).

[76] Tamen deus potest causare actum creditivum per quem credo rem esse presentem que est absens. Et dico quod illa notitia creditiva erit abstractiva, non intuitiva. Per talem actum fidei potest apparere res esse presens quando est absens, non tamen per actum evidentem (*ibid.*). A. Maier, 'Das Problem der Evidenz', *Scholastik* 38 (1963), 188, regards Ockham's position here as a change towards scepticism. See also R. C. Richards, 'Ockham and scepticism', *New Scholasticism* 42 (1968), 345–63, T. K. Scott, 'Ockham on evidence, necessity and intuition', *Journal of the History of Philosophy* 7 (1969), 27–49, and M. A. Adams, 'Intuitive cognition, certainty and skepticism in William of Ockham', *Traditio* 26 (1970), 389–98. Such criticism overlooks that creditive knowledge is no longer evident; moreover, that, absolutely, no knowledge of existence is necessary and so can never attain absolute certainty.

[77] Quia non est contradictio quod visio sit, et tamen per illam visionem nec iudicem rem esse nec non esse, quia deus potest facere visionem sine omni tali assensu. Sed per naturam hoc non potest facere (*Quodlibet, ibid.*).

[78] Ad secundum forte non est inconveniens quod res intuitive videatur et tamen quod ille intellectus credat rem non esse, quamvis naturaliter non possit hoc fieri (*Ordinatio, ibid.*, 70).

[79] *Quodlibet* v, q. 5.

That also helps to explain why God could not alone cause evident assent without an object, for that would be a fallacy of a figure of speech: assent connotes an object in the same way as merit connotes the created will.[80] Each without the other would be contradictory; and God's power cannot be invoked to sustain contradictions. In Ockham's words again: 'It is a contradiction to see something and for what is seen not to be an effect or not to be able to be . . . But it is not a contradiction that what is seen does not really exist outside the mind so long as it can be seen in an effect or did at some time exist in nature.'[81] Hence God is never more than a partial cause of an act of assent, as the vision of what is assented to is also only a partial cause;[82] and as, naturally, assent to what is seen depends upon the presence of what is seen, together with the concurrence of all the other requisite causes, so supernaturally each of the remaining partial causes depends upon the concurrence of the others. It is that which guarantees the infallibility of intuitive knowledge since it can only be of what evidently exists or does not exist when it exists independently of where and how it is known.

Finally, from that there follows the answer to perhaps the most serious objection brought against these arguments, that there can be no cause of evident knowledge of non-existence and so no such knowledge. The cause cannot, the objection runs, be the intellect or its intuitive knowledge because both remain unchanged independently of any change from existence to non-existence on the part of the object. They cannot therefore be of themselves the cause of opposing judgements about the object. Nor can the cause be the object which as non-existent will be nothing, and nothing cannot be the efficient cause of something.[83]

Ockham's reply is that the cause of these opposing judgements lies in intuitive cognition of the object. Just as intuitive knowledge that an object exists when it exists leads to a judgement of existence, so intuitive knowledge that something does not exist when it does not exist leads to a judgement of non-existence. The difference therefore is in the different partial causes, which engender different effects: to a judgement of existence when the object is known intuitively to exist, to a judgement of non-existence when the object is known intuitively not to exist. One is *cum re*; the other is *sine re*.[84] Judgement is thus in each case over intuitive knowledge of the object's existence or non-existence as partial cause of the judgement. For that reason God cannot deceive, for only if a non-existent is known

[80] *Ibid.*
[81] *Quodlibet* VI, q. 6.
[82] *Quodlibet* V, q. 5.
[83] *Ordinatio*, Prologue, q. 1, 56.
[84] Ad septimum dubium dico quod per notitiam intuitivam rei potest evidenter cognosci res non esse quando non est vel si non sit. Et quando queritur a quo causabitur illud iudicium, potest dici quod potest causari a notitia intuitiva rei. Et quando dicitur quod illa habet causare effectum oppositum si res sit, potest dici quod non est inconveniens quod aliqua causa cum alia causa partiali causet oppositum effectum et tamen quod illa sola sine alia causa partiali causet oppositum effectum. Et ideo notitia intuitiva rei et ipsa res causant iudicium quod res est. Quando autem ipsa res non est tunc ipsa notitia intuitiva sine illa re causabit oppositum iudicium. Et ideo concedo quod non est eadem causa illorum iudiciorum quia unius causa est notitia sine re, alterius causa est notitia cum re tamquam causa partiali (*ibid.*, pp. 70–1), also *Quodlibet* V, q. 5.

intuitively to be or not to be can there be evident—as opposed to creditive or false—assent to what is known. In that respect therefore there is no difference between an evident judgement naturally or supernaturally, since in each case it depends upon the existence or the non-existence of the object. The difference is that supernaturally it can be of a non-existent and of non-existence as well as existence, whereas naturally we can only know intuitively what exists and therefore can have neither knowledge of a non-existent nor make a judgement of non-existence. In Ockham's words:

By intuitive knowledge we judge a thing to be when it is; and this (holds) generally whether caused naturally or supernaturally by God . . . In the same way in intuitive knowledge I can judge that a thing does not exist when it is not. But this cognition cannot be natural, because there is never such knowledge nor is it conserved naturally unless the object is present and exists. If such knowledge does remain after the destruction of the object it is then supernatural in its conservation, although not in its causation.[85]

Does that mean that intuitive knowledge of non-existence—as opposed to a non-existent—is exclusively supernatural? As direct knowledge, the answer must be 'yes', for the reasons already given, namely that there can only be intuitive knowledge of what does not exist when such knowledge is conserved or caused by God. Indirectly, however, as Day has said, we can know that something does not exist through intuitive knowledge of what does exist: in Day's example, that Socrates is not black if we know that Socrates is white.[86] Such knowledge is however accidental, confined only to the absence of some quality in what already exists; it is therefore, as Day acknowledges,[87] conditional on preceding intuitive knowledge of existents. Indeed for that reason it is questionable whether it can be properly called intuitive knowledge at all and not an inference from what is known intuitively, in which case it is complex knowledge, as assent to a proposition (i.e. 'Socrates is not black'). Certainly that is so where it concerns knowledge of absolute non-existence with the object not known at all: say, 'Socrates is not' or 'There is no Socrates'. For then we have no means, naturally, of distinguishing intuitively— as opposed to inferring or believing—non-existence from absence. If something is beyond the range of the intellect's apprehension it is simply not *known* immediately, regardless of whether or not it exists. Hence intuitively we can never know that something absolute which we do not apprehend does not exist: only that it is absent. Such presumably is the reasoning behind Ockham's restriction of intuitive knowledge of non-existence to non-existents. But they are not his reasons because as we have said the question of whether, and if so how, we can know non-existence naturally and can distinguish it from existence is not his question. Ockham did indeed discuss non-existence, as we shall consider in chapter four, but for its inferential role in demonstration, not as a matter of natural experience: its value lies precisely in its non-existential import which removes it

[85] *Reportatio*, II, q. 15 E; also *Ordinatio*, Prologue, q. 1, 31.
[86] Day, *Intuitive Cognition*, 178; also 175.
[87] *Ibid.*, 175.

from the contingency of time and place. It is therefore knowledge of a different order from that of existence.

What, then, of the implications of Ockham's notion of intuitive knowledge of non-existents? Does it, as many recent critics have averred,[88] open the way to scepticism by removing natural certainty? Not, I think, if we adhere to Ockham's own discussion. To begin with, as we have just concluded, knowledge of non-existence, the main bone of contention, arises only in the context of supernaturally engendered knowledge of non-existents. Secondly the basis of knowledge of non-existence is the distinction between intuition or apprehension and assent, dissent or doubt over what is apprehended, which again can only be separated supernaturally. In the third place, whatever their different combinations, the certainty of what is evidently known is assured because only that can be evident which is of what really exists: God could not be implicated in a contradiction. Accordingly judgements of existence and non-existence will be evident if existence or non-existence is real; if not they will be abstractive. Intuitive knowledge is therefore distinguished from abstractive knowledge epistemologically and psychologically by the certainty of existence—and at the supernatural level—non-existence in virtue of which it is evident. There can be no other test than that of experience and the principle of contradiction.

In this connection it is worth considering the doubts of L. Baudry[89] who spoke from as intimate a knowledge of Ockham's writings as any modern commentator. The first is that there is no means of knowing when God causes in us abstractive knowledge by which we believe what does not really exist to exist. The answer must surely be that since such a belief could only occur supernaturally the means of identifying it would also be through God's power; and just as naturally man can be said to have faith in what he does not know evidently, so he could supernaturally. Baudry's query does, however, raise the question of the precise relation of assent to apprehension, and we shall return to it at the end of this discussion.

The second objection is over what Baudry regards as the incomplete reconciliation between the notion of such a false belief and Ockham's statement in the Prologue of the Ordinatio that something could perhaps be seen intuitively and yet the intellect believe that it does not exist.[90] That, however, is only the other side of the same coin, namely the separability of intuition from judgement by God's absolute power. In each case there can be a false judgement which is independent of what is evidently known; in the first it is in default of intuitive knowledge; in the second it is a misconstruction of intuitive knowledge. In neither does misplaced judgement produce evident knowledge which is erroneous. The certainty of intuitive knowledge would thus appear to remain unimpugned in face of both doubts.

[88] Cf. Boehner, 'Notitia intuitiva of non-existents', Collected Articles, 288–92; Day, Intuitive Cognition, 160 ff.

[89] L. Baudry, Lexique Philosophique de Guillaume d'Ockham (Paris, 1957), 177. This is an invaluable instrument in the study of Ockham and I express my gratitude for it.

[90] Forte non est inconveniens quod res intuitive evideatur et tamen quod intellectus ille credat rem non esse, quamvis naturaliter non possit hoc fieri (Ordinatio, Prologue, q. 1, 70).

The third doubt is of a less direct nature and brings us to the final problem raised by intuitive knowledge. Ockham, says Baudry,[91] maintains that awareness of our own interior states gives the most certain of all knowledge, which allows of no doubt. How, then, he asks, are we to interpret intuitive knowledge of external things? Are we to suppose that while interior knowledge is infallible, external knowledge is open to doubt? The question then is, What is the nature of this interior knowledge and how does it differ from exterior knowledge?

Ockham's point of departure here is St Augustine's doctrine of intelligible knowledge contained in *De Trinitate*. From it Ockham establishes two main propositions. The first is that the mind knows intelligibles as immediately as it knows sensibilia; and the second, that this knowledge enables us to know intuitively our own interior states.[92] Both are supported by St Augustine's definition of faith (*De Trinitate*, book twelve, chapter one) as the presence within us of things which are absent, eternal and unseen. Ockham takes this to mean that while some things are not seen (intuitively) but only known abstractively, faith, itself, by which they are believed, is actually seen and not merely known abstractively.[93] Faith accordingly enables us to know things individually and naturally rather than in a general concept, because according to St Augustine it is known differently from other things and can be of what was previously sensed and is now absent. Hence faith is knowable intuitively whereas things alone which have been known in the past can only be known abstractively when they are no longer present.[94] Faith, however, is not concerned with sensible things; it belongs as St Augustine said to the heart, not the body; it is within us, not outside; and it is seen not in others but by each one in himself. From this Ockham concludes that we know faith by two kinds of incomplex knowledge: that which belongs to us and is known evidently; and that which is not ours which we cannot know evidently, whether it exists or not.[95] Although the second does not have to be known in a general concept, it is of a different kind from faith known evidently.[96]

Now of all the contingent truths known more certainly and evidently by the intellect, intelligible truths come first, as both experience and St Augustine confirm, when in book fifteen, chapter twelve of *De Trinitate* he declares that one may doubt sensibilia but not such intelligible truths as 'I know that I live', 'I know that I wish to be blessed', 'I know that I do not want to err'. The firmest of all these which no one can doubt is 'I know that I live'.[97] Some of these have been sensed

---

[91] Baudry, *ibid*. Also raised by Hochstetter, *Studien zur Metaphysik und Erkenntnislehre*, 61.

[92] *Ordinatio, ibid.*, 41–2.

[93] Ex ista auctoritate patet quod quamvis res alique non videantur sed tantum cognoscantur abstractive, ipsa tamen fides qua creduntur videtur et non tantum cognoscitur abstractive (*ibid.*, 41).

[94] *Ibid.*, 41–2.

[95] Ex quo patet quod aliam notitiam incomplexam habet de fide propria per quam evidenter cognoscit eam esse, et aliam de fide aliena per quam non potest evidenter cognoscere utrum sit vel non sit (*ibid.*, 42).

[96] Et per consequens aliam notitiam secundum speciem etiam haberem de fide alterius et de fide mea (*ibid.*).

[97] Sed veritates contingentes de istis mere intelligibilibus inter omnes veritates contingentes certius et evidentius cognoscuntur a nobis, sicut patet per experientiam et per beatum

first, some have not, but intelligibles remain the most evident of all contingent truths so that anyone knowing them by his own faith cannot doubt them. As more evident than anything else they do not presuppose other truths by which they are known. Accordingly they require their own intuitive knowledge.[98]

It is here, needless to say, that Ockham departed from St Augustine who did not of course employ the concept of intuitive knowledge; nor was he concerned with the status of evident knowledge in Ockham's sense. It does, however, show that Ockham as a Christian could not be content only with knowledge of what exists outside the mind; and that where the soul—as a spiritual being—is concerned, Ockham tends towards St Augustine, as we shall again have occasion to observe in the next chapter, over his original explanation of concepts: this is a relation which has been rather overlooked in assessing Ockham.

For interior intuitive knowledge itself—as of course for intuitive and abstractive knowledge as a whole—it is to Duns Scotus that Ockham is beholden. At this point he cites Scotus *in extenso* from the *Opus Oxoniense*[99] to show that the soul has intuitive knowledge of its own acts which derive from its recollective or memorative power, a topic to which we shall return at the end of this chapter. Here the arguments quoted by Ockham stress the capacity of the intellect to record acts which are entirely independent of the senses as well as all that comes through the senses. If it were unable to do so we could not repent evil volitions or refer to what is known as past or future. The ability to do so belongs to the intellect in virtue of its recollective power; without it we should in many ways be power-less;[100] with it we can know both immediate and remote objects and reason discursively and syllogistically.[101]

Ockham expresses something of his ambivalence towards Duns Scotus when he adds, 'And if it is said that elsewhere he says the opposite, that weighs little with me because I do not regard him as an authority, nor do I cite this opinion because he stated it but because I consider that it is true'.[102] These are hardly the words of a disciple—which is how it has been the tendency of recent Franciscan writers like Boehner and Day to present Ockham's relationship to Scotus. Rather Duns's ideas served as an anvil for many of Ockham's. In this case they are the basis for Ockham's opinion that intelligibles can be known intuitively; and as intuitive, such knowledge must be prior to all others; for if we are able to know the acts of our own intellect and will, such as happiness and sadness, and this knowledge is contingent, it cannot follow from any knowledge which precedes it.[103] As we have previously

Augustinum xv *De Trinitate*, cap. 12, ubi declarat diffuse quod quamvis posset dubitare de istis sensibilibus, non tamen de talibus: scio me vivere, scio quod volo esse beatus scio quod nolo errare '. . . animi autem quasdam firmissimas per se ipsum perceptiones rerum verarum, quale est illud quod dixi 'scio me vivere', nequaquam in dubium vocare potuerunt' (*ibid.*, 43). See also *Reportatio*, II, q. 20 F., *Quodlibet* I, q. 14.

[98] *Ordinatio, ibid.*, 43–4.
[99] *Ibid.*, 44–7.
[100] *Ibid.*, 45–6.
[101] *Ibid.*, 46.
[102] *Ibid.*, 47. On the other hand see also Ockham's tribute to Scotus, *Ordinatio*, d. 2, q. 6, 161.
[103] *Ordinatio, ibid.*, 40.

remarked, Ockham only accepts that this knowledge is reflexive in the broad sense, since it is also intuitive; and strictly speaking the intellect cannot distinguish reflexive from direct knowledge.[104] In knowing anything, as St Augustine says, we also know that we are: there is therefore no need to posit an additional act of knowing which would in turn require another and so on infinitely as had been objected. The first intuitive act of knowing our own acts suffices.[105]

As we have also seen, the intellect only knows sensible things through the senses; for interior intelligible knowledge of acts of intellection or feeling no preceding sensitive knowledge is required.[106] Such direct knowledge does not, however, as we have remarked, enable us to know our own acts perfectly and distinctly; in our present state, we can do that for nothing, including discern a reflexive from a direct act of cognition. As St Augustine has said, the mind can know itself and yet not differentiate itself from others.[107] By the same token the mind cannot have intuitive knowledge of all the intelligibles present to it but only of its acts.[108] Experience shows that its habits or states cannot be known immediately, for we can be directly aware of knowing or loving or being joyful but not of the inclination towards such acts as a habit or state within us. We can only come to know the latter discursively from knowing their acts. Thus no one sees faith or charity as such, but from the acts of belief and love which they elicit he can infer the presence in the soul of their habits.[109]

The traits that thus distinguish intelligible or interior knowledge are first that it is of the soul's own acts, independently of and distinct from sensory perception of external things; and second that it is prior to or more certain than any other knowledge. It is not, however, perfectly distinct or of the soul's states. Can we then resolve Baudry's opposition between such intelligible knowledge and sensory knowledge of things existing outside the soul? Is the first to be regarded as infallible but the second merely dubitable?

To begin with, the issue is not between certainty or infallibility on the one

---

[104] *Ibid.*, 65. Ad quartum dubium.

[105] Quia si cognosco aliquam rem qualitercumque, possum scire me intelligere illam rem; et ulterius secundum beatum Augustinium xv *De Trinitate*, cap. 13, possum scire me scire intelligere hanc rem, et sic adderem quartum et quintum et innumerabilia. Tunc quero de causa secunde intellectionis: quare illa intelligitur? Et quecumque detur, consimilis potest dari de tertia et quarta, et sic de aliis. . .

Ideo dico pro omnibus quod standum est in primo: quod prima intellectio intuitive videbitur . . . Quod tamen ita sit, per experientiam novimus, nec aliter scire possumus, sicut alias dicetur (*ibid.*, 65-66).

[106] Similiter notitia intuitiva intellectionis vel affectionis vel delectationis presupponit notitiam obiecti illius intellectionis vel affectionis vel delectationis, et sic de aliis . . . Per hoc quasi innuens quod mens potest sentire—hoc est intuitive cognoscere—aliqua que exterius sunt; et similiter potest intuitive cognoscere aliqua que interius sunt, cuiusmodi sunt actus intellectus et voluntatis et delectationes et huiusmodi sine sensu, hoc est sine notitia intuitiva sensitiva illorum, quamvis notitia intuitiva aliquorum necessario presupponatur (*ibid.*, 67-8).

[107] *Ibid.*, 68-9.

[108] Ad quintum dubium dico quod notitia intuitiva pro statu isto non est respectu omnium intelligibilium, etiam equaliter presentium intellectuii, quia est respectu actuum et non respectu habituum (*ibid.*, 69).

[109] *Ibid.*

hand and uncertainty or doubt on the other. Ockham does not say that intelligible
knowledge is certain; only that it is *more* certain and *more* evident; nor, as we have
already seen, is it perfectly distinct. The difference between intelligible and sensory
knowledge is therefore only a relative one between different degrees of certainty.
In the second place, nothing that is known intuitively is *ipso facto* certain because
secundum se et necessario the existence of anything can be doubted, which is another
way of saying that it can also be known inevidently by abstractive knowledge.[110]
As we shall discuss in chapter four, only what is self-evident is indubitable; but
anything known intuitively can only be known contingently, because intuitive
knowledge is of existence and non-existence; and all existence other than God's—
which cannot be known intuitively[111]—is contingent: that applies equally to
intuitive knowledge of the soul's actions which, as we have also seen, Ockham
describes as being of contingent truths. From that it follows that intuitive knowledge, of its nature, is not, as Boehner asserted,[112] infallible, from the very fact
that some things known intuitively can be doubted or appear less than certain.

Where, however, does the uncertainty lie? It cannot be in the existence of the
object which is the condition of all naturally engendered intuitive knowledge. It
must therefore be in the knower, for whom something is inevident or less immediately knowable than something else. At this point Ockham does not specify
how that can occur. What he does say, which is of the utmost importance, is that
the nature or concept (*ratio*) under which something can be known intuitively
can be doubted to exist;[113] and it is that which he subsequently illustrates in the
third distinction of the *Ordinatio* when he argues that there can be confused knowledge of individuals since they are composite beings.[114] Hence we can have intuitive
knowledge of the existence of something known only indirectly and generically—
say as an animal—in the distance before we are able to recognise it as an individual
man. For that reason we can have intuitive[115] knowledge of existence and doubt
the nature of what exists. And Ockham in comparing interior with exterior
knowledge does not seem to be saying more than that: namely, our own acts are
more immediate and certain than the existence of other things.[116] St Augustine
had, as we saw, said the same long ago, and it had become one of the truisms of
Augustinian thought. Unlike St Augustine, however, Ockham did not linger over
its psychological accompaniment; and it is a defect in Ockham's epistemology

---

[110] Quia nulla res est, saltem in istis inferioribus [i.e. sensible things] nec aliqua ratio sibi
propria sub qua potest res intuitive cognosci quin illa cognita ab intellectu possit intellectus
dubitare utrum sit vel non sit, et per consequens quin possit cognosci abstractive (*ibid.*, 36).

[111] See chapter 5, 359–60 below.

[112] 'Notititia Intuitiva of non-existents' (*Collected Articles*, 280 ff.).

[113] Note 110 above.

[114] Quarta conclusio est quod solum singulare potest cognosci confuse, quia solum compositum cuius aliquid latet potest cognosci confuse (*Ordinatio*, d. 3, q. 5, 475).

[115] *Ibid.*, q. 6, 497–8.

[116] By implication also such knowledge in being of our own acts could not be known as
non-existents, as external things can be. As the scribe of the Munich MS. CLM, 8943 wrote in
the margin, 'Nihil est in intellectu nisi prius fuerit in sensu est de rebus extra, non de actibus
eius' (f. 37 b) (Hochstetter, *Metaphysik und Erkenntnislehre*, 50).

that for most of the time he is not concerned to go beyond a naive realism in his desire to establish the cognitive primacy of individual existence in all knowledge. To that extent Baudry was drawing attention to a genuine inadequacy, in Ockham's failure to integrate assent and apprehension. What is it that enables the intellect to doubt what exists or to err or to believe that something is or is not what it is? Is it simply incomplete evidence of existence? In that case why do we disagree over things on whose existence we are all agreed? Lack of consideration of the discrepancy between intellect and senses, or between knowledge of existence and judgement of the nature of what exists, is inherent in Ockham's doctrine of intuitive knowledge which is founded upon their correspondence: disagreement is the result of an impediment in either apprehension or assent and is not of their nature. Ockham's is therefore an optimistic view of the capacity of the intellect so far as natural experience is concerned. Although as we shall see, logically, he is fully able to account for the asymmetry between terms and propositions on the one hand and things on the other, psychologically he allowed no place for the discrepancies between judgement and experience other than as a malfunctioning of the machinery. Few would now regard that as adequate.

Far then from giving us cause to doubt the reliability of intuitive knowledge, Ockham endows it with as great a certainty as any contingent truths can give. That is not the same as infallibility, as we have said; but it is at the opposite pole from scepticism. Naturally we can know the existence of all that we can experience; the limitation is in the completeness of that knowledge, which cannot extend to non-existence or what is not immediately known. But if that circumscribes intuitive knowledge, it makes what is known more certain in being of here and now. Supernaturally the limitations of existence are overcome; but they no more imply scepticism than the restraints of time and place. Intuitive knowledge must still be evident and so can only be of what actually exists or does not exist. There is thus no possibility of deceit by God: a deceiving God would also be a contradictory God.

Nevertheless in so far as God could cause an illusion by separating assent from apprehension Ockham was introducing an element of uncertainty. Theologically justification was on his side; the possible discrepancy between natural and supernatural was the legitimate expression of a believer in an omnipotent God. Lack of natural certainty in that sense is inherent in faith, and Ockham was in the direct line of descent from St Augustine, including Duns Scotus, in putting certainty in God's power before certainty in nature. For that very reason it must also weaken the force in the natural dependence of intuitive knowledge upon the existence of what is known. Ockham did not attempt to do so; but many of his successors did. That does not identify him with their doctrines, but his qualifications to the natural order gave a leverage to those who were to be more concerned with uncertainty than certainty.

We must now turn to the relation between intuitive and abstractive knowledge, which excludes any place for species.

III   THE RELATION OF INTUITIVE AND ABSTRACTIVE
KNOWLEDGE

The relation between intuitive and abstractive knowledge is exhibited by Ockham in his account of what, following Duns Scotus, he calls recollective or imperfect intuitive knowledge of past existence. Unlike perfect intuitive knowledge which—naturally—is dependent upon the existence of the object known and is therefore always of the immediate present, imperfect intuitive knowledge is of what no longer exists. On the other hand it differs from abstractive knowledge in being temporal—of what has existed—where abstractive knowledge is without reference to existence and non-existence. It is not therefore exclusively identifiable with either kind of knowledge. How then is it caused? And more specifically, at what point does knowledge of existence become knowledge of past existence, with the object no longer present and yet its previous existence known?

Ockham's reply is in the same question (14–15) of the second book of the *Reportatio* in which he has just previously discussed intuitive knowledge of non-existents. It is in two variants each based upon the same principle that imperfect knowledge is the result of a habit in a sequence which begins with perfect know-ledge.[117] They differ over the role of abstractive knowledge. By the first variant, in order of its appearance, the habit is due to abstractive knowledge as its partial cause; by the second, intuitive knowledge is alone partial cause. Now according to Boehner[118] the first version (as it appears in the text) originated after the second, which it superseded. Whether or not the order should be reversed is less clear since Boehner bases his belief upon the assumption that the only other place where the second version occurs, in question twelve of the fourth book of the *Reportatio*, was earlier than the present question 14–15 of the second book, which I find difficult to follow. But there is every reason to accept that the first version was the one adopted by Ockham, for he both reinforces it[119] and repeats it in the same question,[120] and restates it in question three of distinction twenty seven of the *Ordinatio*, as we shall mention later.

Much less tenable, however, is Boehner's explanation of the two versions which he attributes to Ockham's fear of challenging Aristotle's axiom that a habit is produced by similar acts and inclines to similar acts.[121] Quite apart from imputing to Ockham the unsupported inferences against which, coming from others,

---

[117] Cognitio autem intuitiva imperfecta est illa per quam iudicamus rem aliquando fuisse vel non fuisse; et hec dicitur cognitio recordativa. Ut quando video aliquam rem intuitive, generatur habitus inclinans ad cognitionem abstractivam, mediante qua iudico et assentio quod talis res aliquando fuit, quia aliquando vidi eam (*Reportatio*, II, q. 14–15 G; all citations from Boehner's edition in 'The Notitia Intuitiva of non-existents according to William Ockham' *Traditio*, I (1945), 245–275, at 250.

[118] 'Notitia Intuitiva of non-existents' (*Collected Articles*, 272–4).

[119] *Reportatio*, II, q. 14–15 G (Boehner, *Traditio*, at 251, beginning 'Ponendo cognitionem intuitivam habere semper).

[120] *Ibid.*, U.

[121] His words are 'Ockham does not dare challenge this axiom'. 'Notitia Intuitiva' (*Collected Articles, ibid.*, 272–3).

Boehner so vigorously defended him, it makes nonsense of Ockham's whole case against species: namely that they are rendered superfluous by habits. That the psychology of habits is fundamental to Ockham's theory of cognition should become apparent. At the same time Boehner needlessly inflates the difference between the two views—which he calls theories[122]—as a closer examination will show. For that we shall reverse the initial order and begin with what, following Boehner, we may assume to have been the original version (which appears as the second one in Ockham's text). It runs as follows: 'Otherwise it can be said that a habit is produced from intuitive cognition as partial cause, and abstractive knowledge which is produced together with intuitive knowledge denied.'[123] That is to say since there is not an act of abstractive knowledge accompanying perfect intuitive knowledge, the habit inclining to imperfect knowledge of what has been known must be from perfect intuitive knowledge alone as partial cause in conjunction with the intellect. In support of this view is experience or rather the absence of any experience of knowing abstractively what is known intuitively. That follows from the opposed conditions of the two kinds of knowledge: intuitive depends upon the existence of an object whereas all abstractive knowledge can be of what does not exist. Accordingly only repeated acts of intuitive knowledge of present existence seem to be needed for a habit leading to imperfect intuitive knowledge of past experience, which in being of what no longer exists is also abstractive.[124] That means that acts of one kind (intuitive knowledge) can engender habits of another kind (abstractive knowledge), and raises the problem of how such a conclusion can be reconciled with Aristotle's axiom already mentioned that similar acts produce similar habits. Ockham's reply—described unwarrantably by Boehner as taking refuge in weak evasion[125]—is that it only holds for total causes but intuitive knowledge is here only a partial cause. He himself seems to be dissatisfied with this answer describing it as 'less incompatible' than the alternative of admitting the co-existence of abstractive knowledge with intuitive knowledge in the generation of a habit, which seems contrary to experience.[126]

It is this alternative that he adopts in the first opinion, thereby jettisoning the

[122] *Ibid.*, and following him Day in his on the whole unexceptionable account (*Intuitive Cognition*, 180–8).

[123] Aliter potest dici quod habitus generatur ex cognitione intuitiva sicut ex causa partiali et negari [Edition 1494 has 'ex illa cognitione' instead] cognitio abstractiva, que simul ponitur cum intuitiva (*Reportatio, ibid.*, K; *Traditio*, 253).

[124] Tum quia nullus experitur quod simul et semel cognoscat eandem rem intuitive et abstractive, et hoc loquendo de cognitione abstractiva rei in se, immo potius experitur homo oppositum, maxime cum ille cognitiones habeant aliquas conditiones oppositas; tum quia omnis cognitio abstractiva potest manere destructa intuitiva; ista autem que ponitur, non potest manere, quia tunc per eam iudicaret intellectus quod illa res cuius est illa cognitio, aliquando fuit . . . Igitur, ut videtur, cum cognitione intuitiva perfecta non manet cognitio abstractiva eiusdem, sed ex cognitione intuitiva frequentata generatur habitus inclinans ad cognitionem abstractivam sive intuitivam imperfectam (*ibid.*).

[125] 'Notititia Intuitiva' (*Collected Articles*, 272–3).

[126] Minus enim inconveniens apparet quod habitus inclinans ad cognitionem abstractivam generetur ex cognitione intuitiva tamquam ex causa partiali quam quod cum intuitiva maneat semper cognitio abstractiva generativa habitus, cum tamen experientia non sit ad hoc, sed potius ad oppositum (*Reportatio, ibid.*, K; *Traditio*, 252–3).

very reasons with which he sought to vindicate the second opinion. Whether or not the change had anything to do with his more explicit recognition of the purely abstractive nature of imperfect intuitive knowledge one can only surmise; but immediately following his previous justification of intuitive knowledge as a partial cause of an imperfect intuitive habit, he considers how imperfect intuitive knowledge is at once intuitive and simply abstractive. It is intuitive in so far as it is temporal by referring to past existence; to that extent it differs from abstractive knowledge of what has never been seen, such as an individual known in a universal concept the existence or non-existence of which remains unknown. At the same time it is purely abstractive knowledge in being of what no longer exists; it is therefore one kind of abstractive knowledge which is none the less abstractive for being imperfectly intuitive.[127]

That brings us to the other—first—opinion, which is, it may be recalled, that 'together with intuitive cognition of something I also have at one and the same time (simul et semel) abstractive knowledge of the same thing. And this abstractive knowledge if the partial cause acting together with the intellect in producing a habit inclining to imperfect intuitive knowledge by which I judge that something has existed (fuisse)'.[128] This differs then from the second opinion in positing (a) a concurrent[129] act of abstractive knowledge with perfect intuitive knowledge, and (b) that the habit inclining to imperfect intuitive knowledge of the object is produced by this act of abstractive knowledge and not by perfect intuitive knowledge as in the second opinion. Abstractive knowledge, accordingly, replaces intuitive knowledge as partial cause of the habit. The reasons are as we have said the reverse of those for the second opinion: namely that like acts produce like habits; but perfect intuitive and imperfect intuitive knowledge are unlike because the latter is purely abstractive; therefore an act of one cannot lead to a habit of the other.[130] Any habit engendered by perfect intuitive knowledge would incline to perfect intuitive knowledge; hence a habit of imperfect knowledge will be from abstractive knowledge which is simultaneously of the same object as perfect intuitive knowledge. That is shown by experience; for if someone has perfect intuitive knowledge of an object, he can, immediately after it has vanished or no longer exists, form a proposition, to which he evidently assents, that 'This thing existed'. And it is the intellect's readiness to elicit such an act of past knowledge

---

[127] Ideo licet illa cognitio per quam iudico rem aliquando fuisse sit simpliciter abstractiva, quia tamen mediante ea assentio et iudico rem aliquando fuisse et non mediante aliis duabus cognitionibus, ideo respectu earum potest dici cognitio intuitiva, imperfecta tamen (ibid., M).

[128] Ibid., G; Traditio, 250.

[129] Boehner, 'Notitia Intuitiva' (Collected Articles, 273) calls it 'concomitant'; but as Day, Intuitive Cognition, 187, n. 91, says, that suggests that one cannot be the cause of the other; Ockham's intention here is that both intuitive and abstractive knowledge exist together after abstractive has been caused by intuitive.

[130] Cuius ratio est quia habitus semper generatur ex actibus inclinantibus ad consimiles actus eiusdem speciei; sed huiusmodi non est cognitio intuitiva, quia intuitiva perfecta et imperfecta sunt cognitiones alterius rationis, quia cognitio intuitiva imperfecta est simpliciter cognitio abstractiva; nunc autem intuitiva perfecta et abstractiva sunt alterius rationis; ergo etc. (Reportatio, ibid.).

where before it had none, which is evidence of a habit inclining to such imperfect, intuitive knowledge.[131] Such an inclination can only be from an act of abstractive knowledge concurrent with perfect intuitive knowledge of what is initially known. It must be abstractive as already said because it is of what no longer exists; and concurrent because the inclination to such knowledge follows immediately on the disappearance of the object and so cannot be caused by an act of abstractive knowledge which is subsequent to perfect intuitive knowledge.[132]

We have thus the sequence (1) perfect intuitive knowledge of an object leading as partial cause to (2) concurrent abstractive knowledge of the same object which in turn is partial cause of (3) a habit of imperfect intuitive knowledge inclining the intellect, immediately the object no longer exists, to (4) knowledge of its past existence.[133]

Does this explanation eschew experience for 'Aristotelian *a priorism*' as Day believes,[134] on the grounds first that it gives no reason for intuitive knowledge as the cause of abstractive knowledge and second that Ockham denies experience of either abstractive knowledge 'which is concomitant with intuitive knowledge' or its causation by intuitive knowledge? The answer must be that this is to invert Ockham's position: the causal primacy of intuitive knowledge is for him an evident principle known from experience; and like all that is known immediately —whether by experience or self-evidently—it is indemonstrable, as we shall discuss in chapter four. Hence no other reason is needed than the fact, known from experience, that all knowledge begins with intuitive knowledge of existence. On the other hand we have no experience of abstractive as the accompaniment or the effect of intuitive knowledge. We therefore need a reason, which is supplied by the principle that like acts lead to like habits. That excludes perfect intuitive knowledge as the cause of imperfect intuitive knowledge because they are different

---

[131] Ergo si habitus inclinans ad cognitionem intuitivam imperfectam generetur ex aliquo actu cognitivo, illa cognitio erit abstractiva, et illa erit simul cum cognitione intuitiva perfecta, quia statim post cognitionem intuitivam perfectam, sive obiectum destruatur sive sit absens, potest intellectus eandem rem, quam prius vidit intuitive, considerare et formare hoc complexum: 'Hec res aliquando fuit' et assentire evidenter, sicut quilibet experitur in seipso. Ergo oportet ponere aliquem habitum inclinantem ad istum actum, quia ex quo intellectus potest modo prompte elicere istum actum post cognitionem intuitivam, et ante non potuit; ergo nunc est aliquid inclinans intellectum ad istum actum quod prius non fuit. Illud autem vocamus habitum (*ibid.*; *Traditio*, 250–1).

[132] Sed ille habitus sic inclinans intellectum non potest causari a cognitione intuitiva perfecta, sicut ostensum est, nec ab aliqua cognitione abstractiva sequente cognitionem intuitivam, quia ille est prima per propositum, que habetur post cognitionem intuitivam; ergo oportet necessario ponere aliquam cognitionem abstractivam simul cum cognitione perfecta existente que est causa partialis cum intellectu ad generandum istum habitum sic intellectum inclinantem (*ibid.*, 251).

[133] Ponendo cognitionem intuitivam habere semper necessario abstractivam incomplexam, tunc cognitio intuitiva erit causa partialis illius cognitionis abstractive; et illa abstractiva est causa partialis respectu habitus inclinantis ad aliam cognitionem abstractivam incomplexam consimilem illi cognitioni, ex qua generatur habitus sic inclinans. Et tunc intellectus formato hoc complexo, 'Hec res' cuius est hec cognitio intuitiva abstractiva, 'fuit', potest virtute illius cognitionis incomplexe evidenter assentire quod hec res fuit, et sic debet intelligi (*ibid.*). This is the interpolated passage and summarises his view here.

[134] Day, *Intuitive Cognition*, 187–8.

in kind.[135] At the same time perfect intuitive knowledge cannot be the cause of a perfect intuitive habit because only actual knowledge of an existing object is properly intuitive and nothing else. We must therefore conclude on rational grounds that only abstractive knowledge can produce a habit because habits are only of abstractive knowledge; and since a habit of imperfect intuitive knowledge immediately follows the cessation of perfect intuitive knowledge, abstractive knowledge must be concurrent with it.[136]

Ockham has not then superseded experience; he has supplemented negative experience by reinterpreting it in the light of principles drawn from reason. He thereby brought the two into alignment, where in the second opinion he modified the principles to conform to lack of experience. There seems little doubt that he regarded the first version as the proper one; apart from repeating and amplifying it he attempts to resolve a problem which the second opinion could only acknowledge. In consequence there is now an established relation between what Ockham later in the same question calls first and second abstractive knowledge:[137] the first concurrent with intuitive knowledge, which together with the object and the intellect is a partial cause; the second which is produced as the result of a habit engendered from first abstractive knowledge as partial cause. We can therefore identify second abstractive knowledge with the habit leading to imperfect intuitive knowledge of what has existed, making all past knowledge abstractive.[138]

Having established a habit as partial cause of both second abstractive knowledge and imperfect intuitive knowledge, Ockham is now in a position to prove the superfluity of species. This he does in three conclusions, having first defined the principle of knowing in one of three ways, as whatever is prior to the act of intellection as partial cause—such as the intellect or the object known or God—

---

[135] Licet ille habitus nec ponatur propter inclinationem nec propter experientiam, tamen ponitur propter rationem evidenter inducentem ad hoc; sed in cognitione intuitiva nec inducit experimentum nec ratio evidens ad ponendum ibi habitum, ergo etc (*Reportatio, ibid.*, K).

[136] Respondeo quod ex nulla cognitione intuitiva sensitiva vel intellectiva potest generari habitus. Quia si sic, aut ille habitus inclinat ad cognitionem abstractivam vel intuitivam: non abstractivam, propter causam iam dictam, quia sunt alterius speciei, nec intuitivam, quia nullus experitur quod magis inclinatur ad cognitionem intuitivam post talem cognitionem frequenter habitam quam ante omnem cognitionem intuitivam, quia sicut prima cognitio intuitiva non potest naturaliter causari sine existentia obiecti et presentia, ita nec quecumque alia, nec plus inclinatur ex tali cognitione frequenti quam in principio. Sed de cognitione abstractiva aliud est, quia post primam cognitionem intuitivam habitam experitur quis quod magis inclinatur ad intelligendum illam rem, quam prius vidit, quam ante omnem cognitionem intuitivam; sed hoc non potest esse per habitum generatum ex cognitione intuitiva, ut probatum est; ergo generatur ex cognitione abstractiva simul existente cum cognitione intuitiva (*ibid.*, G-J; 252).

[137] *Ibid.*, PP; 270; also II: see next note.

[138] Loquendo vero de notitia abstractiva, tunc aut loquimur de illa que semper consequitur intuitivam, aut de illa que habetur post corruptionem intuitive. Si primo modo, sic ad illam requiritur obiectum et intellectus et cognitio intuitiva tamquam cause partiales. Quod probatur sicut prius, quia illud quo posito etc. Si secundo modo loquimur, sic ad illam requiritur intellectus et habitus generatus ex cognitione abstractiva elicita simul cum intuitiva; et non requiritur obiectum in ista secunda cognitione abstractiva tamquam causa partialis, quia illa potest haberi, etsi obiectum annihiletur. Et est utraque istarum notitiarum abstractivarum incomplexa. Et ista secunda est causa partialis notitie complexe qua iudico quod res aliquando fuit (*ibid.*, U; 258).

or is the efficient cause of the act of knowing in contrast to the possible intellect, or is necessary to the act of intellection in addition to the possible and active intellects.[139] We shall have more to say in the last section of the chapter on what Ockham means by the possible and active intellects.

The first conclusion is that for intuitive knowledge nothing—certainly not a species—is required besides the intellect and the object known.[140] That follows from the principle of economy that it is vain to do by more what can equally be done by fewer;[141] but neither by experience nor self-evident reasons is it necessary to posit anything other than the intellect and the object known.[142] Nor is intuitive knowledge merely visual, as many mistakenly suppose; it includes all immediate experience of what exists, interior as well as exterior; hence knowledge of what cannot be seen is not of a different kind from intuitive knowledge of what can be seen. Finally if a species were necessary to intuitive knowledge as its efficient cause, it would mean that the species could be conserved in the absence of the thing known, thus giving intuitive knowledge of what was not present, which is false and contrary to experience.[143]

Abstractive knowledge, on the other hand, does require something other than the intellect and the object known. That is the second conclusion.[144] The reasons are those already given in explaining the genesis of imperfect intuitive knowledge: namely that the intellect in having abstractive knowledge is now able to know something which it did not know previously. Since this additional knowledge comes through intuitive knowledge, as partial cause, abstractive knowledge must be the result of something left by intuitive knowledge.[145] Thus Aristotle in *De Anima* distinguishes a thing's essential powers from its accidental powers where something else is added. That applies equally to the senses where the image or phantasm of the thing perceived intuitively can remain in the imagination—as

---

[139] *Ibid.*, N; 253.

[140] Prima est quod ad cognitionem intuitivam habendam non oportet aliquid ponere preter intellectum et rem cognitam et nullam speciem penitus (*ibid.*, 254, O).

[141] In this case expressed as 'Quia frustra fit per plura quod potest equaliter fieri per pauciona' (*ibid.*). This principle with its variants mistakenly called 'Ockham's razor' of course goes back to Aristotle and was employed well before Ockham among others by Duns Scotus. Ockham did undoubtedly make much more extensive use of it, above all to excise unnecessary concepts; in that sense it was a razor but not the only or principal one; the next note provides another example of economy.

[142] Day, *Intuitive Cognition*, 189–90 has pointed to Ockham's inversion of Scotus's argument for an intelligible species, which was that where an agent acts directly upon an object, together they suffice to produce an effect, and this, in the case of cognition, is the receipt of an intelligible species in the possible intellect. Ockham on the other hand used the same argument of the concurrence of agent and object to prove the minor that they suffice to produce intuitive knowledge as the effect *without the need of anything else* (*Reportatio, ibid.*, O).

[143] *Ibid.*, P; 254.

[144] Secunda conclusio est quod ad habendam cognitionem abstractivam oportet necessario ponere aliquid previum preter obiectum et intellectum (*ibid.*, Q; 255).

[145] Sed intellectus habens notitiam intuitivam potest in cognitionem abstractivam et non habens eam non potest manente obiecto equaliter in se post notitiam et ante; ergo habita cognitione intuitiva aliquid relinquitur in intellectu, ratione cuius potest in cognitionem abstractivam, et prius non potuit; ergo preter obiectum et potentiam necessario est ponere aliquid aliud ad habendam cognitionem abstractivam (*ibid.*).

the repository of sensory images—after the thing known is no longer there.[146]
Both the intellect and the imagination therefore have—essentially—the same
power of abstractive knowledge which is only realised—accidentally—as the
result of intuitive knowledge.[147] The change in the case of the intellect—as in
that of the separated soul—is due to something left from intuitive knowledge.[148]

The third conclusion is that what is left is a habit and not a species, because, to
begin with, habits follow acts whereas species precede them.[149] Here we reach the
heart of the matter supported by more arguments than the first two conclusions
combined. Among them, that an accidental capacity to elicit an act is explained by
what is accidental; and where there is a habit inclining the intellect to knowledge
the intellect has such an accidental power; hence there is no need to posit anything
else beyond a habit in the intellect in such cases. That too is confirmed by De
Anima where in the third book Aristotle speaks of the mind's having a different
potentiality after the acquisition of knowledge from before. Which is interpreted
by Ockham to mean an accidental potentiality to perform a similar act elicited
through the presence of a habit.[150] For that reason no one experiences that ability
until after an act of knowledge; even a thousand species before or without such
preceding cognition will not lead to an (accidental) inclination to a further act
of (abstractive) cognition. Where, on the other hand, there is a preceding act, the
intellect immediately knows itself to have the capacity for a further act of knowledge, hence this can only be from a habit left by a previous act.[151] If species
sufficed, it would follow that however many species there may have been, if none
remained, a further act of knowledge would be impossible since there would be no
further means of knowing, which is absurd. Nor does it help to assume that species
would be increased by repeated acts of cognition and with them a greater inclination to acts of cognition; for that would make habits superfluous, which contradicts
their universal acceptance. Accordingly it must be species which are superfluous.[152]

Of the five grounds on which species can be posited—assimilation, representation, causation, potentiality, and union—Ockham rejects each in turn.[153] Species
cannot assimilate the object to the intellect, for assimilation will be either by the

---

[146] Ibid. The reference is to book, II, probably ch. 5, 417 a, 5–417 b, 1. 2, where Aristotle
discusses the different kind of potentiality.

[147] Ergo eodem modo est de intellectu qui ante cognitionem intuitivam est in potentia
essentiali ad cognitionem abstractivam, sed ipsa habita est in potentiali accidentali, ita quod
potest in cognitionem abstractivam, et prius non potuit; ergo etc. (ibid.).

[148] Ibid.

[149] Tertia conclusio est quod illud derelictum non est species sed habitus. Hoc probatur,
quia illud quod derelinquitur ex actibus sequitur actus; species autem non sequitur sed precedit;
ergo etc. (ibid., R).

[150] Ibid.; the reference appears to be to De Anima, III, ch. 4, 429 b, 2–10.

[151] Unde numquam experitur aliquis se esse in potentia accidentali respectu cognitionis
nisi post intellectionem. Si enim ponantur mille species previe actui intellectus, si nullum actum
habeat intellectus, non plus est nec experitur se esse in potentia accidentali quam si nulla sit
ibi species et si non ponatur aliqua species in intellectu. Et tamen si actus intelligendi ponatur,
statim intellectus experitur se esse in potentia accidentali respectu alterius cognitionis. Et hoc
non potest nisi per habitum derelictum in intellectu ex primo actu (ibid., 255–6).

[152] Ibid., S; 256.

[153] Ibid., T; 256–8.

intellect of the object or the effect of the cause. Neither needs a species: not the intellect of the object because if the intellect knows an object its assimilation of it will be in virtue of the intellect's own nature as a substance rather than of the species as an accident inhering in the intellect; for an accident is less assimilable to a substance than a substance to a substance. Nor will assimilation be by the intellect as the recipient of the act of intellection caused by the object, since that is achieved immediately by the act of intellection; while to posit a first species to assimilate the object to the intellect would entail an infinity of species, each necessary to assimilate the preceding species. Finally intuitive knowledge requires assimilation no less than abstractive knowledge; but no species is required for intuitive knowledge; therefore it is not for abstractive knowledge.

That applies also to representation, for which neither abstractive nor intuitive knowledge requires more than the object and the act of intellection, and so not a species. Furthermore nothing can give knowledge of something else unless what is represented is already known, as only someone who has seen Hercules previously knows Hercules by his statue. But a species is said to be prior to every act of knowledge; it cannot therefore, in coming before the object known, represent it to the intellect. If it did, the consequence would once again be an infinity of species, since it would mean that an object could not act upon the intellect at a distance, causing it to know, without first engendering a species; and that would in turn require a previous species to bring the object to the intellect to be known by another species, and so on infinitely. The alternative is that a distant object can immediately cause a species in the intellect without a previous species; and in that case it can immediately cause an act of cognition without any species at all representing the object.

The argument is no better founded for a species as the cause of intellection; it is that the corporeal and material cannot act upon the spiritual. But that holds not only for the possible—i.e. passive—intellect as a spiritual quality, in arguing that it cannot be acted upon by material things; but also for the active intellect which as equally spiritual cannot therefore have a material image as partial cause upon which it acts in producing an intelligible—i.e. immaterial—species. This is Ockham's reply to the classic Aristotelian–Thomist justification of abstraction from the material images converted in the imagination,[154] alluded to at the beginning of the chapter. If it is said that it is the intellect's nature to need what is material to produce species, then, *tu quoque*, the material is needed for acts of intellection.[155] Equally the species is unnecessary to determine the potentiality of the object, because that can be done by the object and the intellect alone as the agents.

Finally there is no place for species in uniting the mover (the object) with the moved (the intellect), since that would once again lead to infinite species, the uniting species in the intellect requiring a further species to unite it with the object and so on.

[154] As Day remarks (*Intuitive Cognition*, 194).
[155] Si dicis quod natura intellectualis requirit materiale ad producendum speciem, ita dicam ego de intellectione (*Reportatio, ibid.*, 257).

Species then are superfluous for both intuitive and first abstractive knowledge; only with second abstractive knowledge is something besides the object known and the intellect required; and that is a habit inclining to a proposition—and thereby complex knowledge—by which something is known to have existed: it represents the principle (ratio) of knowing in both the angelic and human intellects.[156] The sequence is from intuitive knowledge of individuals apprehended immediately by the senses and the intellect; far from the intellect not being able to know individuals intuitively on the—time-honoured—grounds that it can only know by abstracting from the material conditions of here and now, Ockham in the first of his replies to five dubia[157] reaffirms its power to have such knowledge. It can do so moreover in all the conditions and more in which the senses can apprehend corporeal individuals, first because the intellect is superior to the senses and the superior power can do everything that an inferior power can do, and second because to know hic et nunc is to know more perfectly the nature of what is known than when it is not thus known;[158] both arguments, it will be recalled, are to be found previously in Scotus, from whom Ockham probably took them. In consequence the intellect always knows individuals intuitively through the senses,[159] in time and place and in all their material circumstances: the opposite of Aquinas's position.

By material knowledge Ockham means either such knowledge of what exists corporeally here and now and from which the intellect can abstract, or knowledge of matter as an object; and then such knowledge is not accessible to the senses but confined to the angelic and human intellects. Matter itself, however, impedes intellection which can only be achieved in abstraction from it. [160]

To the second doubt, that if the intellect had intuitive knowledge it would err, Ockham replies that that can happen only supernaturally.[161] That, contrary to the third doubt, it can know individuals both intuitively and abstractively, is due to such knowledge being produced by one particular cause and not another, that is to say by one object leading the intellect to know it rather than another object. That has nothing to do with assimilation either by the intellect or a species.[162]

Ockham devotes most of his answer to the fifth and last doubt—that if the senses know intuitively and yet have prior species so must the intellect—to glossing

---

[156] Ibid., x; 259.

[157] Ibid., z; 260–1.

[158] Ad primum istorum dico quod intellectus primo intelligit singulare intuitive, tum quia intellectus intelligit illud quod est in re intuitive; sed nihil est tale nisi singulare; tum quia hoc convenit potentie inferiori, puta sensui, et est perfectionis; ergo etc. Item, illud quod cognoscit aliquid ut est hic et in hoc situ et in hoc nunc et sic de aliis circumstantiis, perfectius cognoscit et est perfectius nature quam illud quod non sic cognoscit; si ergo sensus sic cognoscat et intellectus non, intellectus esset imperfectior sensui. Ideo dico quod intellectus cognoscit intuitive singulare ut hic et nunc et secundum omnes conditiones secundum quas cognoscit sensus, et etiam plures (ibid., AA; 262).

[159] Quia naturaliter nihil intuetur intellectus nisi mediante sensu existente in actu suo (ibid., BB).

[160] Ibid., CC; 262–3.

[161] Ibid., DD; 263.

[162] Ibid., EE; 263–4.

the supporting passages from Aristotle which accompany it. The most important is his interpretation of Aristotle's use of the term 'species' in *De Anima* book two, to mean act or habit; the authority for this he finds in Averroes who always has the word 'form' instead of 'species' as a synonym for intellection or habit. Hence when Aristotle says that the soul is the place of species that is to be understood as the subject of acts and habits.[163] To this he adds that the intellect has no need of phantasms as extrinsic cause of an act of knowledge, rejecting, with Duns Scotus, the conversion of phantasms: they are rendered equally superfluous by species and habits.[164] Where they are necessary is in giving the body and all its powers,[165] including the imagination, the necessary disposition to an act of knowing without which there can be no knowledge, as in the case of children and madmen.[166]

Ockham, however, goes beyond Duns Scotus in denying the presence of species, as the condition of knowledge, in the intellect at all. He concludes this same question by countering Duns's arguments for species both as universal concepts and as distinct from sensible species in the imagination. His arguments show how far removed his own reliance exclusively upon direct cognition of individuals was from that of Scotus, for whom, as we have said, all non-intuitive knowledge was by means of species and who also believed as we shall see again, that the intellect first grasped the nature or species of something before knowing it individually. Here Ockham begins by opposing Duns's argument that there must be a species in the intellect from the presence there of universals: if universals were only in the intellect to say that they would then be species begs the question; if they existed outside the intellect, that would be impossible because then the same thing would be universal and individual and so opposed, for everyone agrees that what exists outside the intellect is singular; and as according to Duns the same thing cannot be represented to be both individual and universal so it cannot actually be both universal and individual. The remaining alternative, that it could be a composite of species and individual, is equally precluded, because that would be the consequence of an act of intellection whereas a universal is supposed to precede it. There is therefore no basis for Duns's conclusion that the object present to the intellect is a species; for if the object is purely mental, as a representation or image (*fictum*), it will be caused by an act of cognition and not a previous species;

---

[163] Ad omnes auctoritates Philosophi dico quod quod accipit speciem pro actu vel habitu. Hoc patet, quia Commentator numquam nominat speciem, sed semper ubi Philosophus dicit speciem ipse nominat formam, et accipit formam pro intellectione vel habitu. Et quando dicit quod anima est locus specierum, verum est, quia subiectum intellectionum et habituum (*ibid.*, FF; 265).

[164] Ad aliud dico quod ita concludit contra ponentes speciem sicut contra me. Unde sicut ipsi dicunt quod preter speciem non requiritur alius motor extrinsecus ad actum intelligendi, ita dico ego quod preter habitum non requiritur alius motor extrinsecus tamquam causa partialis respectu actus intelligendi nec phantasma nec aliquid in sensu, et hoc in cognitione abstractiva, licet forte sit oppositum in cognitione intuitiva. Et ideo nulla talis conversio ad phantasma requiritur tamquam ad causam partialem in cognitione (*ibid.*, HH; 266).

[165] Day, *Intuitive Cognition*, 196, renders 'omnium virtutum' as 'all the cognitive powers'; but coming between 'dispositio corporis' and 'phantasie' it seems more likely that it refers to corporeal powers as the prerequisite for intellectual activity.

[166] *Reportatio*, II, q. 14–15, *ibid.*, HH; 266.

if it is a real object then it can be present immediately to the intellect as it is present to the senses without any species.[167]

This reply of Ockham exhibits the logic of intuitive knowledge when made the prerequisite, as partial cause, of all other knowledge, a step which Duns Scotus did not take. For that reason Ockham does not accept a distinction between the knowledge provided by a species in the imagination and what is known by the intellect, but reiterates what he has earlier said in reply to the first doubt that the intellect can know *hic et nunc* as well as the senses, employing a similar argument to that just used to show the untenability of holding that a sensible species knows under the aspect of singularity and an intelligible species under the aspect of universality.[168] Indeed from Duns's view that the nature of a thing is known first it follows that the same thing is represented by an intelligible and a sensible species.[169] In fact, however, no species in the imagination itself is adequate to know anything.[170] To have intuitive knowledge—intelligible and sensible— what is required is the intellect and an object; to have first abstractive knowledge, the intellect and intuitive knowledge; and to have second abstractive knowledge, a habit. Nor is a phantasm necessary in itself for abstractive knowledge, but only accidentally for this life: that is to say a separated soul can see a thing as it is immediately without any images.[171] As to the effect of the active intellect upon the possible intellect, what it causes is a concept; and when Duns says that it knows the universal actually as its object, that again is not possible either for what it knows in the mind, which would then be a species, or for what exists outside it, which is only singular. Hence there is no more reason for saying that the object of the intellect is universal than that the object of the senses is; for if the intellect could only know what is similar indifferently that would apply equally to the senses: for example if Socrates existed here and his likeness at Rome, one could not be represented without the other, which is of course not the case.[172] Accordingly the action of the intellect is real since it gives real intuitive knowledge of what exists.

Finally, there is the role of the active intellect which, Ockham corrects Duns, is not—according to Aristotle and Averroes—to make potential knowledge actual, but the possible or passive intellective active so that it now actually knows where previously it had the potentiality of doing so. That is confirmed by Averroes; and, when he says that abstraction is the work of the active intellect, that can be understood in two ways: the first is that the active intellect together with the object or habit partially causes intuitive or abstractive knowledge, since such knowledge is immaterial. The other meaning is of abstraction of a universal concept as a some-

---

[167] *Ibid.*, MM; 268.

[168] *Ibid.*, NN–OO; 269–70.

[169] Tum quia secundum eum natura primo videtur et per consequens primo representatur, et ex hoc sequitur quod idem representatur per speciem intelligibilem et sensibilem, et sic non oportet ponere distinctas species (*ibid.*, OO; 270).

[170] Ad rationem respondeo quod sola species in phantasia non sufficit ad cognitionem alicuius rei (*ibid.*, PP).

[171] *Ibid.*

[172] *Ibid.*, RR; 271.

thing purely mental. By the first mode the active intellect is a necessary accompaniment; and would be even if, as Plato held, the essences of things were abstracted from matter. But by the second mode it would not be necessary for then universals would exist independently of the intellect.[173]

The conclusion Ockham draws is that the active intellect has no such role towards phantasms or the possible intellect of purifying, illustrating, irradiating, removing, abstracting, or withdrawing which is wrongly attributed to it; it does not cause species either by removing something from them—or by engendering something in them.[174] Ockham thereby at once dispenses with the traditional conception of abstraction and of the intellect's activity in attaining it; it now becomes identified with the intellect's ability to know *tout court*, whether individuals outside the soul or their images or general concepts within the soul. Each of these is equally in abstraction from matter since the intellect is by definition immaterial. Accordingly abstraction is nothing more than the intellect knowing and so knowing intelligibly and immaterially in contradistinction to the material nature of sensory knowledge. In consequence Ockham has freed simple cognition[175] from dependence upon conversion of images, and with it removed the onus of explaining abstraction from them. Instead, as we shall see more fully in the next two chapters, cognition, whether sensory or intellectual, consists in a perfect similarity with the object, which in being of what is known is more perfect than knowing a species. In the case of intelligibles they can also be known not only actually but by a habit as well; hence a habit, also, is as perfect a similarity as an act or species.[176]

Ockham has therefore excluded all intermediaries between the intellect and its object: whether it knows intuitively or by first and second abstraction, or what might be called third abstraction, namely universals, the intellect knows immediately, regardless of the existence or non-existence of what is known. The full force of the blow falls upon species which as prior to the act of knowing and able to inhere independently of what is known, both before and after the latter's presence,[177] would, if permitted, mean the pre-existence in the intellect of forms informing it. For Ockham that would have been tantamount to a denial of individual cognition, since nothing could then have been known directly in itself, whereas his own position is expressed in the phrase taken from Aristotle, 'the soul

---

[173] *Ibid.*, xx; 273.   [174] *Ibid.*

[175] That is how I interpret Ockham's statement, *Reportatio*, IV, q. 12, s, where he appears to say the opposite: Ad primum principale dico quod licet pro statu isto intellectus non intelligat nisi propter conversionem ad phantasmata, et hoc forte propter peccatum, quia deus non vult concurrere ad actum intelligendi concurrente actu phantasiandi, tamen in anima separata non valet, quia tunc sunt omnia principia sufficientia ad actum, et deus vult concurrere sine tali actu. Here Ockham speaks of 'intelligere', to understand, and of principles rather than cognition of things; and in that sense they would have to be elicited from the individual things known immediately by the senses. See note 47 above.

[176] Et utraque cognitio est ita perfecta similitudo obiecti et perfectior quam species. Sed differentia est in hoc, quod sensus non est sensibilia nisi per cognitionem actualem, sed intellectus est omnia intelligibilia per actualem et habitualem. Unde habitus ita perfecte est similitudo rei sicut species vel actus (*ibid.*, zz; 274).

[177] Hic primo suppono quod species sit illud quod est previum actui intelligendi, et potest manere ante intellectionem et post etiam re absente (*ibid.*, c; 245).

is in a way all existing things':[178] by sensitive cognition all sensible things and by intellective cognition all intelligibles.[179] The effect is to deny species and to subsume all cognition under the intellect's own actions and habits elicited by what is known.

What, then, is the nature of the intellect which enables it to know both sensibles and intelligibles; more particularly what does Ockham mean by the active and possible intellects? Not two separated intelligences, which was Averroes's interpretation of Aristotle's distinction in *De Anima*. For Ockham as a Christian there could be no question of accepting Averroes's view that the two souls acted as two external powers moving man rather than as spiritual faculties belonging to man's own being; but Ockham also went further than the majority of Christian thinkers in rejecting any distinction between the active and possible intellects; they were terms signifying the same thing but having different connotations, the active intellect as the soul knowing actively, the possible intellect as the soul knowing passively in receiving the knowledge engendered in its active state. Each therefore describes one and the same thing under its different aspects.[180]

Ockham, as we have seen, still further reduced the role of the active intellect to that exclusively of an efficient cause in any act of knowing, without any of its traditionally ascribed powers of illumination of the possible intellect or purification of the images present to it. Its power of abstraction therefore, as we have said, means either the soul's own capacity to know, intuitively or abstractively, or to form universal concepts.[181]

In the *Ordinatio*[182] Ockham, as we shall see in the last part of this chapter, opposes the entire Thomist doctrine of abstraction in its assumption that the individual cannot be known directly by itself but only through reflexion upon the universal which is alone known directly to the intellect. As in his arguments against Duns Scotus, that also involves the rejection of species,[183] and with it the view of the active intellect's role as the source of universal knowledge through its powers of abstraction. In the latter connection, Ockham again restates his definition

---

[178] *De Anima*, III, ch. 8, 431 b, 20.

[179] Ad aliud dico quod anima est quodammodo omnia per cognitionem omnium, nam per cognitionem sensitivam est omnia sensibilia et per cognitionem intellectivam omnia intelligibilia (*Reportatio*, II, q. 14–15, ZZ; 274).

[180] Ideo dico quod non est ponenda pluralitas sine necessitate, quia intellectus agens et possibilis sunt omnino idem re et ratione. Tamen illa nomina vel conceptus bene connotant diversa, quia intellectus agens significat animam connotando intellectionem procedentem ab anima active. Possibilis autem significat eandem animam connotando intellectionem receptam in anima; sed idem omnino est efficiens et recipiens intellectionem (*ibid.*, q. 24; Q).

[181] Respondeo quod actus intellectus agentis est tantum causare intellectionem, et hec intuitivam vel abstractivam . . . et nullam aliam actionem habet circa phantasmata sicut alii imaginantur, quia nec depurationem nec illuminationem etc., sicut dictum est supra (*ibid.*, R). Also *Ordinatio*, I, d. 3, q. 6, 520: Ad aliud dico quod duplici de causa ponitur intellectus agens; ponitur enim ut sit causa effectiva intellectionis cuiuscumque, quia, sicut teneo, intellectus agens nullo modo distinguitur ab intellectu possibili, sed idem intellectus habet diversas denominationes. Ponitur etiam intellectus agens non tantum ut causet intellectionem sed etiam ut causet aliquo modo improprie universalia abstracta, illo modo quo habent causari.

[182] *Ordinatio*, d. 3, q. 6, 488–92.

[183] *Ibid.*, 489.

of the active intellect, this time in reply to Henry of Ghent's contention[184] that just as Averroes says we should not need an active intellect if, as Plato held, essences could be known in themselves, so we should not need one if individuals could be known in themselves. The active intellect can mean either the intellect as efficient cause of any act of intellection and is then merely another way of describing the intellect as a whole with no distinction between the active and possible intellects. Alternatively, it can be used in an improper sense for knowledge of universals abstracted by the intellect, whether or not the act of intellection is itself regarded as real—a matter to which we shall come in the next chapter. By the first connotation we should still need an active intellect even if Plato were correct; but not by the second.[185] In other words the intellect knows individuals independently of the universals which it may abstract from them.

So far as the process of intellection itself is concerned, then, the crucial distinction is between images as the principles of cognition and as the product of cognition; Ockham rejects the first and accepts the second, where they constitute some kind of abstractive knowledge, first, second or of universal concepts. As dependent upon an initial act of intuitive knowledge (which for all that exists outside the intellect comes first through the senses), abstraction in any of these three modes and beyond, to all subsequent abstractive knowledge, third, fourth, fifth and so on, is ultimately dependent upon intuitive knowledge as partial cause; and if each preceding abstractive habit were destroyed the latest abstractive knowledge would depend directly upon the intuitive knowledge.[186] For that reason the soul knows more perfectly in conjunction with the body than alone; and so do angels.[187] The only intermediary between the corporeal and the spiritual is not the imagination, which is itself material being extended in space, but the intellective soul,[188] which in knowing is also the active intellect. That is how the designation by Averroes of the active intellect as light should be understood. As light is the partial cause, together with colour, in an act of sight and yet does not inhere in the object seen, so with the active intellect: as partial cause of an act of knowing, it acts upon the object and does not work within it in the different roles traditionally ascribed to it.[189] Hence the active intellect is the intellect knowing

---

[184] *Ibid.*, 488.   [185] *Ibid.*, 520.

[186] Potest dici quod sicut prima abstractiva necessario et naturaliter presupponit intuitivam tamquam causam eius partialem, ita secunda, tertia, quarta, quinta, et sic deinceps posito casu necessario presupponit intuitivam. Nam si habitus derelicti a prima abstractiva, secunda, tertia et quarta corrumpuntur per oblivionem, sicut est possibile, tamen ad hoc quod quinta abstractiva eliciatur naturaliter necessario presupponit intuitivam tamquam causam eius partialem (*Reportatio*, II, q. 16, Y).

[187] Et dico quod non est precisa causa quare corpus potest agere in animam nostram quia est coniuncta corpori; sed causa est precise quia anima non potest de se habere omnem perfectionem ad quam est in potentia mediante corpore et quam potest habere a corpore. Et hec eadem est causa quare agit in angelum . . . (*ibid.*, CC).

[188] Similiter quando dicit quod fantasia est medium etc., falsum est; sed si ponatur aliquod medium inter mere corporale et spirituali erit anima intellectiva, nam virtus fantastica est extensa in materia cum materialibus conditionibus, et est pure materialis et corporalis (*ibid.*, DD).

[189] *Ibid.*, EE.

an object; no other metaphysical or psychological principle is involved. As Ockham also glosses Averroes in his earlier replies to Duns Scotus, it is the same intellect variously described according to its different dispositions, as active, material, possible, speculative and adept.[190]

IV SENSORY EXPERIENCE

So much for intellectual cognition. There is a parallel order in sensory experience from the thing perceived to its image in the senses; the difference is that the image is impressed both in the sensory organ, as the exterior sense, and in the imagination as the interior sense, remaining in each after perception of the object.[191] That something is impressed in the exterior senses beyond the act of sensation is shown by the many examples cited by Aristotle in *De Somno*. Thus to begin with, if someone after looking at the sun or other bright object turns away to where there is less light he will not see or will see less well. That must mean a change in the senses since it cannot be in the medium or the object; and the change consists in the impression of something in the organ not previously present as opposed to the loss of something already there. A similar conclusion is reached from the effect of gazing at something white or from closing one's eyes after seeing the sun or from the change involved in looking at something moving slowly after something moving fast: in every case what first seen will continue to be seen.[192]

Now such additions are both invisible and visible: they are invisible in not being the object of vision or its principle or an act or a species, but consist rather in an alteration to vision as the result of an act of sight, which is now weaker or stronger than before. Thus after seeing colours we can continue to see them either more or less brightly. The change comes from colour itself as the object sensed, and not from the destruction of an existing habit, because it is due to receiving something which was not previously in the organ of sight. For that reason the latter's altered disposition is not accidental: like blindness which impairs vision it remains independently of any act and so of a species as the principle of an act. By the same token the change cannot be in the object or light. Hence it must be a non-sensible quality which is impressed in the organ at the moment when the object—in this case colour—is seen, remaining there for a longer or shorter period, and sometimes for life.[193]

---

190 *Ibid.*, q. 14–15, xx; 273.
191 Sunt ergo duo articuli. Primum est quod in sensu exteriori est species. Secundus est quod in sensu interiori est species. (*ibid.*, q. 17 c).
192 *Ibid.*, D; Ex hiis patet quod preter actum videndi est aliquid impressum in sensu exteriori, quia aliter post actum videndi remaneret eque dispositus ad actum respectu cuiuslibet obiecti sicut prius. Also *ibid.*, M.
193 Secunda conclusio quod in visu derelinquitur aliquid quod non est visibile, nec est obiectum visionis, nec principium, nec actus, nec species. Quod probatur, quia postquam aliquis cessaverit ab omni visione remanet visus aliter dispositus quam ante . . . ergo est ibi aliquid impressum quod nec est sensibile nec species nec actus nec est sensibile a se nec ab alio, sed est quedam qualitas impressa in organo visus que aliquando est confortativa, aliquando debilitativa et imprimitur effective a colore et simul cum actu videndi. Nec est previa actui, nec etiam principium eius; nec generatur ab actu sed a colore simul cum actu videndi in organo visus imprimitur; et manet illa qualitas aliquando usque ad finem vite, aliquando per maius spacium, aliquando per minus (*ibid.*, E).

Impressed visible qualities are the principles of vision, as Aristotle's examples show: thus, in moving from a bright to a dark place the form of light is lost; but it can be regained on closing our eyes, which shows that there is now some added quality in the eye enabling it to see as a real object what no longer exists as an object outside it. Unlike the latter, what it now sees as an appearance of the original object—seen in itself—does not enable the organ to know that the object really exists. The object is the total cause of the quality but only partial cause of the act of seeing. Like an invisible quality, a visible quality is immediately impressed when the object is seen; and once impressed the visible quality in turn becomes partial cause of a less perfect but intuitive act of seeing the object's appearance: the latter is the object of a real act of vision but not of a real thing.[194] Accordingly we can say that whether visible or invisible something is impressed in the sense organ itself and not the sensory faculty alone. As Averroes said, it is in the organ, composed of form and matter, that the increased or diminished power resulting from this quality inheres.[195]

The act of sensation also leaves something in the imagination, as the interior sense, enabling it to act subsequently in the absence of an object, where previously it could not. Therefore something left by the first act must incline it to further acts;[196] and as the quality impressed in the organ weakens or strengthens it, so does that in the imagination, which is conserved and strengthened by the body.[197] But the impressed qualities themselves are distinct because the quality in the imagination elicits from it a further act, whereas that in the organ provides an object to be sensed.[198] Both imagination and organ as interior and exterior senses have the same object, but what is impressed in the imagination is not the same as the original object of the senses because it is no longer the actual thing sensed—whether a sound or colour. Moreover, no object of the imagination can itself be increased, but what is impressed into the imagination can. Therefore only the latter can incline to an object.[199]

Both the exterior and interior senses, then, receive two impressed qualities.

---

[194] Tertia conclusio est quod in visu imprimitur aliquid quod potest videri et esse principium visionis . . . Unde illa qualitas imprimitur in visu a sensibili simul cum actu primo videndi; et non est obiectum illius primi actus, sed post primum actum terminatum ad aliquod sensibile excellens, quia visus aliquem actum imperfectiorem qui vocatur apparitio et est cognitio intuitiva tantum. Et respectu illius actus est illa qualitas obiectum et causa partialis. Quod probatur, quia ille actus est verus actus videndi; ergo est aliquid terminans illus actum; sed non-ens non potest aliquem actum terminare naturaliter; ergo etc. (*ibid.*, F).

[195] *Ibid.*, G.

[196] Secundus articulus est de sensu interiori, puta de fantasia. Et hec est prima conclusio quod aliquid ibi remanet post actum sententiendi, quia prima potentia aliter est reducibilis ad actum post primum quam ante, quia ante non reducitur ad actum nisi in presentia sensibilis realiter. Et post primum actum potest reduci ad actum in absentia; ergo necessario aliquid requiritur inclinans ad actum post primum actum quod prius ante primum actum ibi non fuit (*ibid.*, H).

[197] *Ibid.*, I–K, conclusions two and three.

[198] Tertia conclusio est quod aliquid imprimitur in illa potentia ut distincta contra organum, quia aliquid ibi ponitur ut eliciat actum et non ut terminet. Ergo illud se tenet ex parte elicientis non terminantis (*ibid.*, K).

[199] *Ibid.*, K–M.

In the organ one inheres invisibly strengthening or weakening it; the other is an attribute which can be seen and is of the same nature as the object experienced outside the senses. Both the qualities are impressed at the same time as the object is sensed; but the second is the subject of a further act of seeing the appearance of the object after it is no longer present.[200] In the imagination correspondingly, one quality increases or diminishes its power; it is not of the same nature as the object and is received from the sensory organ; the other quality is not from the organ, but a habit engendered from a preceding act of imagination inclining it to further acts in the absence of the object.[201] As such it is comparable to second abstractive knowledge in the intellect. Like abstractive knowledge its object is not a likeness of the object; but the same individual images—as the prophets, saints and doctors call them—are themselves sensible things which have been previously sensed (*sensibilia prius sensata*) and afterwards imagined. They are not the species of things known.[202] Thus it is the same man whom I first saw and now imagine. As in the case of divine ideas, the images are of actual individuals and not of their species, with the individual equally the object of sensory perception, imagination and abstractive knowledge; no species is therefore involved. Both in God and among creatures, the term 'idea' or 'concept' signifies principally the created individual thing and connotes the act of knowing; similarly the word 'image' signifies principally the created individual thing and connotes the act of imagining.[203] Hence the commonly held opinion that a species has its own image is false; the truth is that there are as many images as there are individuals imagined.[204] They are caused partly through seeing the object physically and partly by the imagination, where the object's presence is no longer required and indeed the vision of it could —as we discussed earlier—be preserved after it had ceased to exist.

What is indispensible, however, is intuitive knowledge itself; without an immediate vision of the object which the exterior senses have intuitively, there can be no act of imagination in the interior senses.[205] Since both together constitute one faculty the intuitive knowledge received in the sensory organs suffices for

---

[200] *Ibid.*, M–N.

[201] Sed quantum ad sensum interiorem, puta fantasiam est duplex qualitas: una impressa ab obiecto confortativa vel debilitativa organi; et illa est alterius rationis ab obiecto extra, sicut illa in visu. Et est alia generata per actum generandi, que non est subiective in organo, ut distinguitur contra potentiam precedens qualitatem, sed est subiective in potentia, ut distinguitur contra organum sicut ipse actus fantasiandi. Et illa qualitas secunda non est alicuius actus sed est habitus generatus per actum fantasiandi indinans sicut causa partialis ad actus consimiles in absentia rei sensibilis, sicut posui prius in intellectu . . . (*ibid.*, N).

[202] Ita quod post primum actum si ipsum sensibile destruatur potest potentia phantastica cum illo habitu generato ex primo actu elicere actum fantasiandi terminatum ad idem sensibile numero quod prius vidi, sicut cognitio abstractiva intellectus terminatur ad idem singulare numero quod vidi intuitive in intellectu; et non terminatur ad aliquam similitudinem vel imaginationem, sicut imaginantur aliqui et false. Quia omnia illa que a prophetis, sanctis et doctoribus vocantur fantasmata, simulacra, idola sunt ipsamet sensibilia prius sensata et post fantasiata, et non species sensibilium (*ibid.*).

[203] *Ibid.*

[204] Et sic commune dictum est falsum quod species habet tantam unum fantasma, quia tot sunt fantasmata quot individua (*ibid.*).

[205] *Ibid.*, N–O.

abstractive knowledge in the imagination; both the principle of economy, that knowledge in one part of something having the same form suffices for knowledge in its other parts, and the nature of the imagination in not referring to existence or non-existence, together lead to the conclusion that the imagination has abstractive knowledge only.[206]

The sequence leading to such knowledge in the imagination is thus parallel to that in the intellect: namely, from intuitive experience of an individual by the sensory organ, a concurrent act of abstractive knowledge of the same individual can be produced; like the sensory organ this initial act can weaken or strengthen the power of the imagination, but where the effect upon the organ is towards retaining its initial sensation of the object, in the imagination it is towards a further act of imagination, the object itself never having been directly experienced.

Whatever we may think of the tenability of either of these distinctions—between the two different effects of sensation or imagination upon the exterior and interior senses, and the different responses by these different senses—Ockham has made them an exclusively individual affair, entirely debarring species from any of them: the individual is the first object both of what is sensed and imagined. In his own words,

This is the order of proceeding naturally: that first the sensible thing—though by God's power it could be otherwise—causes the act of sensation intuitively. Second, the same object causes and terminates the intuitive act of the intellect; and afterwards the intellect without any immediate causation by the thing (known) can have abstractive knowledge of the same thing at the same time as it has intuitive knowledge of it. And finally it (the intellect) can abstract universal concepts and compose them (into propositions) of which there can be an immediate act of apprehension and after it an act of judgement.[207]

All judgement, as an act of assent or dissent over a proposition, is from the intellect even though over what exists the senses appear to be making it; for only the intellect can form propositions; and since it can do so immediately it has intuitive knowledge of the same thing perceived by the senses, it is the closeness of the connexion between the two faculties which makes the difference between them imperceptible.[208]

Here we have the sequence from immediate intuitive experience, sensory and intellectual, to complex knowledge, leading as we shall discuss in chapter four not only to individual and contingent propositions but also to universal and

---

[206] *Ibid.*, O–R. For that reason I do not discern a change in Ockham's view of the status of the imagination between the *Ordinatio* and the *Reportatio* (II, q. 16, IV, q. 12) which Hochstetter does (*Metaphysik und Erkenntnislehre*, 39–41).

[207] *Ibid.*, q. 18, I. My rendering of the passage has been free.

[208] Credo enim quod omnia iudicia que attribuuntur sensui respectu aliquorum obiectorum sunt actus intellectus, quia statim quando sensus habet operationem circa sensibile habet intellectus cognitionem intuitivam respectu eiusdem, qua habita potest intellectus complexa formare et de eis iudicare per actum assentiendi vel dissentiendi. Et quia iste operationes sunt; et quia iste operationes sunt ita connexe, ideo non percipitur utrum iudicium tale sit actus sensus vel intellectus. Mirabile enim est quomodo sensus potest iudicare, cum iudicare sit actus complexus terminative . . . quod non potest fieri per potentiam sensitivam (*ibid.*, P).

necessary propositions. Whichever they are, intuitive experience of individual existence is their foundation as it is of imagination: in one case it comes through the intellect, enabling it to know abstractively and conceptually; in the other through the exterior senses acting upon the imagination to form images. In both cases the source is in individuals previously sensed, from which both knowledge and imagination begin.

Now just as there is no room in such a process for species, either in the intellect or the imagination, equally there is none in the relation between sensible things. Ockham rejects the common view that species inhere in the same medium as their qualities, for example the species of colour in a coloured object: if that were so, species would then be either of the same nature as the object causing them, which would mean that contrary qualities belonging to the species—say black and white as individual colours—would coexist, which is contradictory; or that the species would be seen before the quality, which is false. Alternatively if the species were of a different nature from the object they would then themselves be qualities, which again is contrary to experience.[209] In fact an object causes nothing of a different kind in a medium, but only what is of the same nature, as colour causes colour; and when colour is produced—say when the rays of light pass through a red window—what is seen is real colour and not the species of colour.[210] Neither experience nor reasons drawn from experience or which are self-evident lead to the conclusion that there are species; hence they should not be posited.[211] If there were any reason in support of species it would be the one universally employed by Averroes—of the direct contact between mover and moved—to prove their existence.[212] That, however, is disproved by the sun's actions which are evidence that a mover can act at an extreme distance upon what is moved without any medium between them.[213]

Not only, then, are there no species in the intellect, senses, or nature, but both intellect and senses experience their (individually derived) objects directly. The immediate nature of intuitive cognition is a theme to which Ockham returns in distinction twenty-seven, question three, of the *Ordinatio* which he revised after coming upon Peter Aureole's theory that the intellect knows every individual by means of a mental representation of appearance (*esse apparens et intentionale*) formed of the object.[214]

According to Aureole this mode of knowing is universal, and applies equally to the senses and the intellect; each has as its immediate object the thing itself known in a concept, which is also the word in the mind, as we shall discuss later.[215]

209 *Ibid.*, c.   210 *Ibid.*, E.   211 *Ibid.*   212 *Ibid.*   213 *Ibid.*, D.

214 Quia tamen pauca vidi de dictis illius doctoris; si enim omnes vices quibus respexi dicta sua simul congregarentur non complerent spacium unius diei naturalis, ideo contra opinantem istum nolo multum arguere . . . Possent autem contra istam conclusionem adduci aliqua argumenta que feci distinctione XXVI huius libri de esse cognito, quam materiam tractavi, et fere omnes alias de primo libro antequam vidi opinionem hic recitatam. Predicta argumenta querat ibidem et applicet hic qui voluerit (*Ordinatio*, d. 27, q. 3, H). According to Boehner, *Collected Articles*, 123, d. 27 is as far as Ockham took his revision of the *Ordinatio*.

215 Prima est quod in omni intentione emanat et procedit non aliquid aliud, sed ipsamet res cognita in esse obiectivo, secundum quod habet terminare intuitum intellectus . . .

Aureole's arguments as cited by Ockham at some length fall into two parts. The first concerns the senses and consists in eight 'experiences' showing that all sensation terminates immediately at a concept (*esse obiectivum*) of the thing itself sensed; for if that is how the senses perceive, so by the same token that is how the intellect must know, since it is not less able to form representations than the senses.[216] Among the more prominent of Aureole's examples taken up by Ockham the first is of trees which appear to be moving to someone carried past them on the water. Now this movement seen mentally in the eye cannot be the act of vision itself; otherwise vision would be the object of vision and so reflexive (i.e. of nothing other than itself). Nor can the movement be really in the trees or the river bank because then they would themselves be moving; and it cannot be in the air since movement is not attributed to the air but to the trees. Therefore movement exists only conceptually or mentally in what is seen and judged to exist:[217] that is to say, as a concept in the mind. Similarly with the second experience, of the sudden movement of a stick describing a circle in the air, where the circle appears to be made by the stick. Of the possible explanations, the circle cannot really exist in the stick because the stick is straight, or in the air because the air cannot contain a defined and coloured circle, or in the vision itself for the same reason as before, or in the eye because neither the vision nor the eye is in the air. There therefore only remains that it has the appearance of a circle in the air while not existing really outside the senses.[218]

The final example we may mention is contained in the sixth experience of images in a mirror which appear diversely both within it and outside it. Such images cannot be real species or real things, since nothing is really in the mirror; nor can they be something seen merely in the eye, for the very reason that they appear in a mirror and elsewhere outside the eye. Once again, then, they must be appearances known only in the senses.[219] These and other examples led Aureole to the same conclusion that there must be appearances of real things in the senses, and *a fortiori* in the intellect, since to deny them would be to fall into the error of treating all appearances as real existences.[220] Nor can they be said to be due to mistaken vision, for there is no means of distinguishing the appearance from the

---

Primam, propositionem probat iste alibi sicut ipsemet dicit hic, videlicet, quod in actu intellectus de necessitate res intellecta ponitur in quoddam esse intentionali conspicuo et apparenti (*Ordinatio*, *ibid.*, c). An *intentio* is a concept in the mind, which as we shall discuss in the next chapter, and shall have an example of in this, can be interpreted as either an image or representation (*fictum*) or the act of intellection itself. *Esse obiective* and *esse subiective* have the opposite of their modern connotations: 'obiective' means what is known mentally as an object existing only in the mind; 'subiective' means real, whether it exists as part of the mind or as something outside it. Hence whatever the intellect knows as an object it knows only as a non-existent i.e., an image or figment in the mind; whatever it knows subjectively it knows as an existent having real being, mental or material or spiritual.

[216] *Ibid.*   [217] *Ibid.*   [218] *Ibid.*   [219] *Ibid.*

[220] Et universaliter qui negat multa habere esse intentionale et apparens tantummodo, et alia que videntur esse extra in rerum natura, negat omne ludificationem et incidit in errorem dicentium quod omnia que apparent sunt ... Cum inquam ita sint de sensu interiori et exteriori relinquitur multo fortius quod intellectus ponit res in esse intentionali et apparenti (*ibid.*).

thing itself; the real thing known by the mind coincides with its appearance, so that it knows everything through its appearance: as St Augustine said, such is the power of thought that the mind can only see itself by thinking.[221]

Secondly, according to Aureole it is in the nature of the mind's activity to know by a formal similarity to the thing known; and this can only be mentally through a representation or an appearance, since all understanding is a certain formal appearance in the same way as vision consists in a certain appearance in the eye.[222] That can again be proved, first (and *a priori*) because, granted that knowing consists in the closest likeness to the thing known, either that likeness is of something real or merely an expression; it cannot be an expression, for what is in the mind is not simply an expression in the way that, say, Caesar is expressed in a picture without himself being present as he appears. Rather by an act of knowing, in its similarity with what is known, the thing itself is known in a concept or in its appearance.[223] The same conclusion can be reached *a posteriori* from experience of knowing a rose. Of the possible explanations of what is known when we know a rose,[224] only that of knowing it immediately in a concept or mental appearance is, says Aureole, tenable. Among the others, species are excluded, because if we knew the rose by its species, then nothing real existing outside the intellect would be known; nor indeed is a rose a species. Equally the immediate object cannot be the intellect's own act of knowing, for the same reason as before, that the rose's appearance would then only be known indirectly; it would also lead to Averroes's error of a single possible intellect for all mankind in having only one rose to know, since the appearance of the rose cannot, according to Aureole, be multiplied (why, it is not clear). In any case, an act of intellection does not itself make something real; if the intellect's knowledge consisted in its own acts there would be no knowledge of real things, and propositions would not be true since their terms would no longer stand for the same things. By the same token the object cannot be a concept preceding what is known since that would lead to the Platonic notion of self-subsisting ideas which would remain independently of the destruction of the things they represented; there could then be a concept of a rose where no rose existed, all of which violates what Aristotle says about knowledge and the relation of first and second substances.

Accordingly for Aureole the solution lies in the presence in the intellect of a single representation of a rose which stands for all roses; and the intellect in seeing the representation thereby sees every individual rose, not distinctly but immediately and as real. In that way the correspondence between what is known in the mind and what exists outside it is ensured and real knowledge safeguarded.[225]

---

221 *Ibid.*; the reference is to *De Trinitate*, bk. IX, ch. 6; but it seems more likely to be to bk. x, ch. 4.

222 Sed constat quod intellectus non est aliud quam apparitio quedam formalis, sicut enim visio est quedam apparitio in oculo consistens (*ibid.*).

223 *Ibid.*   224 *Ibid.*, C–H.

225 Ergo relinquitur ut detur ultimum, videlicet quod non habeat nisi esse apparens et intentionale, ut sic omnes rose que in esse reali distincti sunt ponantur in esse non reali sed intentionali una totalis rosa, et sic salvantur omnia que inducta sunt. Nam rosa illa est idem cum

Aureole then like Ockham sought also to establish the immediacy and the individuality of intellectual cognition; but in a manner too different to be compatible with that of Ockham who rejected both Aureole's conclusion and his arguments.[226]

To begin with, the notion of a mental representation (*esse apparens et intentionale*) must either be merely conceptual or real, that is, something existing outside the mind as an absolute—i.e. individual—being. It cannot be purely conceptual because then a real quality would never be apprehended by the senses, or two different qualities, one real and the other mental, would be apprehended; and so in either case the mental representation would not be the means of knowing what is real. If on the other hand the representation is real, it cannot be a concept but will then be a substance or an accident into which—as we shall consider in chapter three—all real being is divided. Again if it is through a representation that we see, say whiteness, the representation and whiteness will either be the same, which they are not, because then every time the representation is seen whiteness must exist, since, as Aristotle says, whatever is the same is produced and destroyed at the same time; or if they are different there could be a representation with nothing to see and so whiteness without vision. As they are not really the same they must be totally different, one as a concept, the other as an absolute—i.e. individual —thing; and since whatever is totally different can, by God's absolute power at least, be conserved separately, the absolute thing—whiteness—could be apprehended immediately by the intellect as its object without also apprehending the *esse apparens*. Accordingly, the latter is superfluous. Again, either whiteness itself really appears to the senses or it does not; if it does not, it is therefore not seen, which is manifestly untrue. If it does and in addition it also has a representation, it will then have two representations. From that it can be argued that whenever something has two appearances, the reason for one will be the reason for the other; therefore if whiteness has an additional distinct appearance, by the same token that appearance can have another appearance and so on infinitely, which is obviously untenable. Nor is this overcome by saying that the representation itself appears to the intellect directly, for that will equally apply to whiteness itself, again rendering a separate appearance unnecessary. The same conclusion also follows from the fact that the same thing apprehended successively first without one thing and then without another can by God's power be apprehended without both, as whiteness can be known first without a true representation and then without a false representation, as Aureole himself shows.[227] Finally the immediate object of any act of apprehension does not require any medium between it and the apprehending power.[228]

---

omnibus rosis, quia illa conspecta conspiciuntur omnes rose ut unum, non ut distincte, et ita scientia est de rebus et propositio et diffinitio et res cognoscuntur directe (*ibid.*, G).

[226] Istam opinionem quantum ad conclusionem pro qua rationes priores sunt adducte videtur nihi falsa (*ibid.*, H).

[227] *Ibid.*

[228] Preterea quod immediate terminat actum alicuius potentie non requirit aliquod medium ad hoc quod apprehendatur a potentia; sed albedo immediate terminat actum videndi; ergo non requirit tale esse apparens medium (*ibid.*).

That is Ockham's own position, reaffirmed in three propositions. First, that the object of intuitive knowledge, sensitive or intellective, is never known in a medium but always immediately in itself, in the same way as there is no medium between God as a creator and what he creates. Second, that by first abstractive knowledge the object is also known immediately, because the same thing is totally the object of both first abstractive knowledge and the intuitive knowledge with which it is concurrent and by which it is known directly. Third, that for abstractive knowledge which is a universal concept in the intellect, there can probably be said to be both a medium and no medium, according to whether the concept is regarded as a representation (*fictum*) or really part of the intellect as an intellection (*intellectio*).[229] These alternatives represent the two different theories of the nature of concepts which, as we shall discuss in detail in the next chapter, Ockham at this time held to be more or less equally tenable. In either case the universal stands confusedly for all the individuals confusedly represented by it, but only in the second case are they known directly. Aureole by his notion of the *esse apparens* sought to have the best of both worlds, namely of direct individual apprehension by means of a universal representation. It was for that above all that Ockham criticised him here. This applies equally to the senses to which nothing is added as the result of apprehension, save perhaps a description or statement of what is apprehended; but that is merely a matter of predication, and as such the work of the intellect not the senses.[230]

Nor do Aureole's arguments drawn from experience prove that there is a representation in the senses or the intellect. The first example of trees appearing to move does not hold because the trees are not really moving; all that has happened is that the intellect can now form and assent to a proposition that the trees are moving. But if the proposition is taken to mean that such movement is really experienced by the senses, then it is false. If on the other hand it means that there is now an apprehension in the senses eliciting similar actions to those which can be experienced physically by the body, then the proposition can be accepted; for that does not entail the presence of real movement in the senses, but merely of equivalent apprehensions to those produced by movement. Aureole's fallacy has been to argue 'The trees appear to be moved; therefore there is a concept of movement in

---

[229] Unde dico primo quod in nulla notitia intuitiva nec sensitiva nec intellectiva constituitur res in quocumque esse quod sit medium aliquod inter rem et actum cognoscendi . . . Nec plus est aliquod medium inter rem et actum propter quod dicatur res videri quam est aliquod medium inter deum et creaturam propter quod dicatur deus creator. . . .

Secundo dico quod per notitiam abstractivam immediate sequentem notitiam intuitivam nihil fit, nec aliquod capit esse preter ipsam notitiam abstractivam, quia idem totaliter et sub eadem ratione est obiectum notitie intuitive et abstractive immediate sequentis; ergo sicut nihil est medium inter obiectum intuitive cognitum et ipsam notitiam intuitivam, ita nihil est medium inter obiectum et notitiam abstractivam. Tertio dico quod quando est aliqua notitia abstractiva qua habetur universale in intellectu, potest probabiliter utrumque teneri . . . Si ponatur medium potest probabiliter dici sicut dictum est prius quod illud medium non est nisi quoddam fictum commune omnibus singularibus quod intelligitur; et tunc illa intellectione nullum singulare intelligitur. Vel potest dici quod est quedam intellectio anime habens esse subiectivum in anima distincta realiter ab omni alio obiecto anime. Potest etiam dici probabiliter quod nihil tale est medium . . . (*ibid.*, 1). Cf. also *Reportatio*, II, q. 14–15, O.

[230] *Ordinatio, ibid.*

the mind'; but that is no more true than to say that when there is real movement, there is real movement in the intellect, which no one would accept. Accordingly real movement does not produce either real movement or an appearance of real movement in the intellect but merely the apprehensions of movement equivalent to those really elicited by movement. Where there is no such movement, as in Aureole's example, no movement is seen, but only the trees without any medium, successively and in diverse distances, from the eye of someone who is moving. Nothing more is implied.[231]

Much the same holds for the second experience of a circle formed in the air by a stick; no circle actually appears to the eye, but the intellect believes it to be true in assenting to the proposition 'A circle is in the air' through the equivalent responses which its appearance engenders. As with the sixth experience of images in the mirror what has changed is not in the advent of something not there previously, but in a judgement which the intellect now makes and previously did not have. Only if by an *esse apparens* is meant that something—moving trees, a circle, or what is seen in a mirror—appears, will Ockham accept it; that however does not give it the conceptual status of a direct representation which Aureole intends for it, since nothing more is involved than a judgement by the faculty concerned.[232] Far then from Aureole's contention holding that to deny an *esse apparens* would be to deny all illusions, the reverse is true. The discrepancy between what appears and what exists is not due to any medium but variously to faulty apprehension or judgement by which something appears to be as it is not; and that, no less than a correct apprehension, occurs without any medium.[233] As to the similarity of the intellect to its object Ockham, as we have seen earlier, accepts this Aristotelian notion of their near identity; but that does not mean that the intellect thereby creates what it knows or seizes something from the object, any more than a portrait of Caesar seizes something of Caesar or contains his presence. Rather something appears to the intellect as an object solely because the intellect knows it for such, and nothing more.[234]

There remains Aureole's example of a rose:[235] on either of the two probable explanations of a concept as a *fictum* or as an intellection, it is inadequate to the role Aureole assigns it of knowing all roses. As a *fictum* the concept of a rose would not be of real roses outside the intellect; as an intellection it would be only of external roses and not the concept of a rose standing for all roses. In the second case, therefore, roses themselves would be the immediate object of the intellect, and knowledge of them would be without a medium. The third alternative is that the intellect knows things as they really exist.[236] Many of Aureole's own arguments against the alternatives to an *esse apparens* are also inconclusive, in particular his rejection of species which many hold are the means of knowing external things,

[231] *Ibid.*, K.

[232] L–P. E.g. quia res modo iudicatur esse intra speculum et prius non, non propter hoc quod rei aliud adveniat, nisi forte per denominationem extrinsecam, sed propter hoc quod illud iudicium modo est in potentia et prius non . . . Si autem intelligas quod apparet esse ibi, concedo. Sed ad hoc sufficit quod sit iudicium realiter in potentia (*ibid.*, P).

[233] *Ibid.*   [234] *Ibid.*, X.   [235] *Ibid.*, AA–DD.   [236] *Ibid.*, Y–Z.

his assertion that there can be only one rose which stands for all roses, as well as a range of replies concerning subject, predicate, propositions, definitions and real knowledge. We shall pass over Ockham's comments on these matters here since they form much of the subject of chapters three and four.[237]

Over the question of knowing a rose, we are presented by Ockham with a choice between knowledge of a real rose existing outside the mind or knowledge which is not of a real rose. If it is not of a real rose, then by Aureole's reasoning knowledge is not of real things and neither definition nor propositions will be true. Moreover, if this rose which is known in the mind is really the same for all roses, as Aureole asserts, it is not really engendered and so does not really exist. It will then be known not to exist because Aureole has himself said that what is seen truly belongs even more to an *esse apparens* than what is seen falsely; but as this rose will be falsely seen to be real it will also be truly seen not to be of real roses. If, on the other hand, the rose in the intellect were not distinguished from real roses there would then be nothing else known beyond the intellect and particular roses. Hence if these roses now appear because of an act of the intellect, the latter will be extrinsic to the roses, and not their cause; to say therefore that this rose now appears will itself be merely an extrinsic description and not a representation of the rose in the intellect. Correspondingly if this rose seen in the intellect is the same as particular roses and really exists, it cannot be merely conceptual. Nor does it make them conceptual to say that they appear in the intellect, for by the same token it could also be said that God in creating has conceptual being of what he creates, an argument to which we shall return in chapter six. Furthermore if this rose is of particular roses which really exist although they do not appear to the intellect, the rose which appears to the intellect is not caused by its appearance. Finally, according to Aureole, the rose in the intellect is not a particular rose but as the same for everyone cannot be multiplied. From which Ockham—contrary to Aureole— concludes that it is not of particular real roses.[238]

So much then for Aureole's attempt to unite what appears in the senses and the intellect with what exists really outside them. He did so, as we have said, in the same interest of direct individual cognition as Ockham; but with very different results. To Ockham the notion of an *esse apparens* could only lead to the consequence Aureole sought to avoid, that of interposing a medium between the senses or intellect and the object known. Unlike Aureole, Ockham began from the opposite assumption, of the discrepancy between the mental and the real, and the need to keep them distinct. Only at the immediate level of intuitive and first abstractive individual cognition is there a direct correspondence between apprehension and existence, and evident experience of it is the only means of testing the validity of a concept or an expression with claims to be of what is real. Ockham's mode of argument thus revolves around reducing all concepts to their individual import in the way we have just encountered; it recurs again and again throughout his work and might be called the *reductio ad unum* of separating what has real (i.e. individual or absolute: the terms are interchangeable) signification

237 *Ibid.*, AA–CC.   238 *Ibid.*, CC.

from what is merely mental or terminological. We shall discuss the full ramifications of this view in chapter three. Here we need only remark that for Ockham only what is individual is real; and only what is real can exist independently and absolutely of anything else. It is to distinguish the real, underpinned by God's omnipotence, from the non-real and, ontologically, superfluous, that Ockham's arguments are designed; all claims to reality have to meet the simple test of whether what is so designated can exist independently and individually; if it cannot because of purely mental status, it is to be denied not in itself but as a constituent of being. Far, then, from Ockham's epistemology being one of mere correspondence between the real and the conceptual it is founded upon their discrepancy and thus the need to look beyond mental appearances to ontological reality. In that way he sought to restore the rightful boundaries between them, as we shall have ample occasion to see.

V MEMORY AND THE WORD

Ockham's discussion here is an extension of his treatment of the word in the soul, to which we may briefly turn. It consists in bringing to order St Augustine's—as the author of the concept—varied usage over the word; and a large part of Ockham's question is taken up with extended quotations from *De Trinitate*. From these he is able to show that Duns Scotus's restriction of the word to a purely declarative role of something else, and not itself productive of first simple knowledge, is contrary to St Augustine.[239] The problem of what the word is, Ockham regards as mainly terminological. Everyone, he declares, accepts that there is something in the mind and engendered by it, which is a likeness or an image of things, in the way described by St Augustine.[240] Whether it has merely mental status as an object or really exists as part of the mind, Ockham passes over here. Certainly it is not a species.[241] The question is how Augustine understands this likeness.

In reply Ockham distinguishes five different ways in which Augustine employs the term. First, in the broadest sense as an act of knowing; second, as a proposition, true or false; third, in a strict sense as the true word; fourth, in a stricter sense still as the true word engendered by love; and fifth, as a mental concept, whether understood as an object in the mind and whether or not distinguished from an act of cognition.[242] It follows therefore that doubtful propositions, accepted as neither true or false, are not the word, because they do not constitute knowledge;[243] St Augustine's word is thus not every word.[244] But every act of knowing is the word, and so in a certain manner it is an act of both will and intellect.[245]

The complexities of the word are accordingly resolved with no concession to species or other additional presences beyond concepts within the intellect. The psychological mechanisms by which the mind forms concepts belongs to the next chapter. Of immediate interest here is the relation of the word to memory, as the

239 *Ibid.*, d. 27, q. 2 B.   240 *Ibid.*, L.   241 *Ibid.*, K.   242 *Ibid.*, M.
243 *Ibid.*   244 *Ibid.*, CC, U.   245 *Ibid.*, Z–BB.

remaining element to be considered in simple cognition. It is raised in this context
by Ockham as a doubt over the role of memory in the generation of the word for
which St Augustine frequently insists memory is necessary. Ockham meets it by
defining memory according to St Augustine as either an intellectual habit derived
from intellectual acts, or the sufficient principle of the word.[246] In either case it is of
the soul's own nature. The knowledge which it causes is not therefore something
additional and habitual beyond the rest of the soul's knowledge; nor is it to be
distinguished from the soul's actions. Rather memory is the knowledge by which
the soul knows itself before it thinks; and it is able to do so because it already
possesses knowledge in the memory from its previous acts of knowing. Memory
for Augustine is the parent engendering the word as the offspring of the soul's
previous knowledge, which—since memory and the soul are the same—means the
soul as the parent of its own knowledge.[247]

The identification of memory with the soul forms the basis of Ockham's
own account of memory contained in the fourth book of the *Reportatio*. There in
question twelve he gives two other definitions of knowledge. The first is a more
general statement—with which Ockham does not expressly associate himself—
similar to St Augustine's two definitions just mentioned. By it, memory has three
connotations: as the habit inclining, as partial and efficient cause, towards an act of
intellection; as the sufficient principle of intellection, whether from the soul or the
object or anything else; and as the principle of the act of recollecting the past
as past, in such propositions as 'I have done that' or 'I was there'.[248]

Finally from the first and third components of this definition Ockham produces
a more precise version of his own. By this, memory is either a power, or faculty,
having a quality or habit left by a previous act, which enables it to produce a
similar act independently of an external object. Alternatively it can be understood
as the power or faculty which is the cause of memory in the strict sense of referring
to the past as past; this also is by means of a habit but concerns propositions not
incomplexes (terms or things), because memory here consists in acts of recalling
what has been seen or heard.[249] As such this second sense differs from the first
sense in probably being exclusively of the intellect; for unlike the incomplex
images of things past, which can belong to both the sensitive faculty and the
intellect, there can be no memory of propositions in the senses.[250] The reasons are

---

[246] *Ibid.*, R.   [247] *Ibid.*
[248] *Reportatio*, bk. IV, q. 12, B.

[249] Dico quod memoria dupliciter accipitur. Uno modo pro potentia habente aliquem
habitum vel qualitatem derelictam ex actu preterito virtute cuius potest talis potentia in aliquem
actum consimilem et eiusdem rationis cum actu perterito, qui quidem actus preteritus aliquid
requirit ad suum esse quod non exigitur ad esse secundi actus, puta obiectum extra. Alio modo
acciptitur pro potentia que potest in actum recordandi proprie dictum mediante habitu genito
ex actibus preteritis, non quidem incomplexis sed complexis; puta ex eis intelligo me nunc
audire hoc vel videre hoc (*ibid.*, 1). Also *Quodlibet* I, q. 13.

[250] Primo modo accipiendo memoriam dico quod memoria reperitur in parte sensitiva et
intellectiva, quia certum est quod in utraque derelinquitur aliqua qualitas mediante qua potest
in aliquem actum in quem prius non potuit in actum similem primo actui . . . Secundo modo
loquendo de memoria dico tanquam certum quod est in parte intellectiva, sed non est ita
certum quod est in potentia sensitiva (*Reportatio, ibid.*).

obvious. To begin with, the senses cannot perceive their own acts. Nor can they have propositions for an object; that includes the act of memory which is the work of the intellect in distinguishing what cannot be really perceived outside the mind (*in re*), past and present. Finally, acts of the senses are not reflexive; but a past act entails reflecting upon one's actions. For the senses, however, everything experienced internally must first be perceived externally: a position which would have to be reversed for the senses to be able to reflect.[251]

Although the senses then are not themselves the means of a strict act of memory, they are nevertheless its prerequisites as the beginning of a sequence which have already encountered in the formation of imperfect intuitive knowledge from individual experience to an act of recollection stated in a proposition. Thus in order to have an act of memory, we must first have seen or heard something in the senses intuitively; otherwise such past knowledge of what is no longer present would be indistinguishable—as Aristotle says—from hope or opinion.[252]

Now the act of memory, as the recall of a past act, consists of two interdependent acts: the initial act of memory, and the commemorative act by which that act is apprehended as partial object, independently of whether it remains in the mind or not. Thus the first object of an act of memory is an act of recall which is prior to the act of recalling the object actually remembered.[253] Together they enable the past to be known as past. Ockham opposes this view of memory as past knowledge to that of Aquinas by which it is present knowledge to the intellect and past only to the senses. The cause of the difference lies once again in the Aristotelian doctrine of the universal character of the intellect's knowledge, so that it does not apprehend the particulars experienced solely through the senses. Ockham in reply reaffirms the intellect's ability to know individuals and thus what has been experienced in the past as past equally with the senses.[254] Ockham has just previously invoked the support of Duns Scotus for his claim that the intellect has intuitive knowledge of individuals, including Scotus's argument that since the intellect, as the superior power, can know all that the senses know, it can therefore have past knowledge of the same (individual) objects experienced by the senses, which the intellect, equally with the senses, experiences intuitively. At the same time the intellect can also know its own acts and those of the will, which the senses cannot do. Accordingly the intellect is able to know past as past and to recall whatever—and more

---

[251] *Ibid.*

[252] Ideo dico quod ad actum recordandi requiritur sensualis experientia, puta quod hoc vidi, hoc audivi, quia aliter non distingueretur a spe et opinione (*ibid.*, F).

[253] Dico quod actus iste recordandi est respectu alicuius actus precedentis at preteriti inquantum precedens est . . . Sed quia actus qui est obiectum actus recordandi sit precedens actum recordandi tempore, sive continuetur sive non, ita quod ad recordationem requiruntur duo actus. Primus est actus recordantis precedens qui est obiectum partiale actus recordativi. Secundus est actus recordativus quo apprehenditur primus actus, sive primus actus maneat sive non (*ibid.*).

[254] *Ibid.*, H. Contra istam opinionem, quia sicut spes est respectu futuri vel opinionis, sic memoria est respectu preteriti; sed spes vel opinio sunt in intellectu; igitur eodem modo memoria. Preterea intellectus potest cognoscere preteritum sub ratione preteriti . . . Preterea ratio adducta non concludit, quia non tantum sensus cognoscit singulare sed intellectus, immo sicut prius dictum fuit, singulare primo intelligitur (*ibid.*, F).

than—is known and recalled by the senses; in each case such recollection is of individual objects first known intuitively.[255]

For Ockham, then, memory rests upon intuitive cognition of individuals and of the soul's own acts. The act of memory itself, however, as a proposition about past experience, is complex;[256] it is thereby the work of the intellect which in turn forms such a proposition about the past from imperfect intuitive knowledge, with its partial cause in a habit derived from first abstractive knowledge in the way earlier discussed. Memory is thus the final product of imperfect intuitive knowledge, as a proposition about what has been, which has its source in perfect intuitive knowledge. Ockham enumerates these features—that it is from a habit, that it is complex, and that it is the result of the intellect's activity—in the subsequent discussion. Since we have already encountered them all at different times —and just recently discussed the third—we need not linger over them.

So far as the first is concerned, since memory can occur independently of the existence of the thing remembered, it must be caused by something in the soul.[257] That something is a habit engendered, as we have seen before, by first abstractive knowledge as partial cause together with the intellect (and of course God). The arguments in favour of a habit are similar to those which we met previously in Ockham's rejection of species in the intellect. There can, following Aristotle, only be acts, habits and passions in the soul; of these only habits are necessary to memory because there can be an act of memory in the absence of either acts or passions.[258] Species on the other hand would precede any acts from which a habit of memory is derived; they would also be indifferent to time, whereas memory is of past time.[259] To the objection that a habit caused by an incomplex act cannot incline to a complex, which memory constitutes, Ockham replies as he did in the *Reportatio*, book two, questions 14–15, that incomplex habits incline partially and indirectly to an act of recollection, and so to a complex habit which follows such an act; but only a complex habit can directly incline to an act of recollection because the latter is complex and dissimilar habits can only indirectly lead to similar acts.[260]

That such knowledge of the past is complex is proved because only intuitive and abstractive knowledge are simple, and an act of recollection is neither of these; therefore it must be complex. Moreover, complex knowledge has for its object a proposition containing distinct things, or more properly terms standing for them, which can only be joined by a verb, in the way that every complex or proposition comprises subject, predicate and copula, as we shall discuss more fully in chapter four. In the case of an act of recollection the verb or copula is always in

---

[255] *Ibid.*, E.

[256] *Ibid.*, H.

[257] Nihil extra animam est causa respectu actus recordandi . . . Sed positis rebus extra vel destructis nihilominus potest poni actus recordandi; igitur etc. Ideo dico quod causa actus recordandi est aliquid existens in anima (*ibid.*, G).

[258] Quod autem habitus concurrat, patet, quia, sicut sepe dictum est, nihil est in anima nisi actus vel habitus vel passiones consequentes actus . . . Sed nec actus nec passio potest esse causa actus recordandi, quia actus recordandi habet esse quando neutrum est (*ibid.*).

[259] *Ibid.*

[260] *Ibid.*, P. Ad quintum dubium.

the past tense; it is also always in the first person of the form, 'I have seen or heard or known this'. It is therefore always a complex. It consists on the one hand of a partial object which is an act of simple recollection, intuitive or abstractive, in the intellect, senses or appetite, of some past act by the person making it. The total object, on the other hand, is a proposition in which the predicate, as the other extreme, is joined to the subject as first extreme by a verb in the past tense and the first person: for example 'I heard John lecture on such a day'.[261] Hence the subject must always be the first person who remembers, since the recollection derives from his own past experience.[262] For that reason not all past knowledge belongs to memory. There is all the difference between a statement recalling an experience such as the proposition, 'I heard a master lecture in the schools' and a statement about a past occurrence based upon memory but not itself remembered, for example the proposition 'A master shouted while disputing and sat down in his chair': the second proposition is not from the experience of the person making it, and his memory of it cannot be a partial cause. In that sense memory, strictly understood, must always record as partial cause what has been directly and evidently encountered in the past by the subject of the proposition recounting it.[263]

To a doubt whether such knowledge is intuitive or abstractive Ockham replies that as complex it is abstractive; which is an instance of a further but less common use of abstractive for any knowledge that is not intuitive.[264] It is nonetheless evident since it consists in assent to a proposition known by imperfect intuitive knowledge and so presupposes perfect and evident intuitive knowledge.[265]

The third issue of whether memory belongs to the intellect or the senses has already been answered in Ockham's definition of memory; it is reinforced by what has just been said and in his reply to the eighth and last doubt, that only the intellect can form propositions and judgements which are distinct from incomplex apprehensions.[266] Memory therefore is firmly located as past knowledge in the intellect, in a progression from intuitive and first abstractive knowledge, through a habit formed by the latter to imperfect intuitive knowledge as partial object of a proposition about what has previously been experienced. Its starting point is therefore individual cognition, sensory and intellectual, or intellectual alone; and Ockham stresses that *pro statu isto* all intellection is by means of the images

---

[261] *Ibid.*, H; also P.

[262] Non enim obiectum partiale immediatum est actus alterius a recordante, puta actus loquendi vel disputandi vel scribendi alterius hominis, quia de talibus non recordor nisi quatenus me recordor audivisse vel vidisse eum talia facere (*ibid.*, H).

[263] *Ibid.*

[264] Ad sextum dubium dico quod actus recordandi est abstractivus, quia est actus complexus, qui est abstractivus et non intuitivus (*ibid.*, Q).

[265] Ad aliud dico quod illud complexum est evidenter notum; et dico quod illa notitia est evidens notitia qua intellectus evidenter assentit huic complexo: 'Hoc vidi, hoc audivi, hoc intellexi'. Causatur ex notitia intuitiva terminorum; sed intuitiva duplex est, sicut alibi patuit: quedam perfecta, quedam imperfecta . . . Tunc dico quod notitia evidens predicti complexi causatur ex notitia intuitiva imperfecta terminorum, et hec presupponit naturaliter loquendo intuitivam perfectam (*ibid.*).

[266] *Ibid.*, K, R.

derived from individual experience: he also uses the term 'conversion of images'[267] which, as we shall consider in the next chapter, belongs to his earlier interpretation of conceptual knowledge as occurring through images of individuals previously sensed (intuitively). All knowledge derives from intuitive cognition of individuals; and memory, as past knowledge, from past, i.e. imperfect, intuitive cognition. Hence memory is governed by the same processes as all evident knowledge and made accessible to the intellect by a habit which like all habits is conserved in the soul through the requisite dispositions of the body.[268] In consequence memory loses any independent metaphysical status as a separate—or higher—source of awareness and is assimilated, by means of imperfect intuitive knowledge, to perfect intuitive knowledge, which begins with individuals.

VI SIMPLE ANGELIC COGNITION

Ockham's doctrine of simple cognition is resumed in question sixteen of book two of the *Reportatio*, where he extends it to angels, in opposition to two contrary opinions, one that angelic knowledge is exclusively spiritual and owes nothing to material things;[269] the other that it is non-discursive. He rejects the first opinion on the grounds that angels are no less dependent for their knowledge than men upon the prior existence of the object known as partial efficient cause.[270] The second opinion is untenable because it would mean that an angel in knowing a premise would thereby know all the conclusions following from it, which is false since a premise can have an infinite number of conclusions. Angels on the contrary can be ignorant of something and later come to know it. They therefore know discursively in passing from apprehension of a premise to knowledge of a conclusion previously unknown.[271]

From this Ockham enumerates six characteristics of angelic knowledge all of which parallel that of the human intellect.[272] The first is that angels can gain intuitive knowledge from material and immaterial objects alike as partial cause. Second, they can have abstractive knowledge of things: first abstractive knowledge from intuitive knowledge with the object known intuitively as partial cause; second abstractive knowledge from a habit produced by first abstractive knowledge as partial cause in the absence of the object known.[273] Third, angels can know universals through abstraction from individuals and form concepts in the same way as the human intellect can. Fourth, they can derive contingent complex knowledge (i.e. propositions about the existence of things) from intuitive and

---

[267] Ad primum principale dico quod licet pro statu isto intellectus non intelligat nisi propter conversionem ad phantasmata, et hoc forte propter peccatum, quia deus non vult concurrere ad actum intelligendi, non concurrente actu fantasiandi, tamen in anima separata non valet quia tunc sunt omnia principia sufficientia ad actum (*ibid.*, s). In other words the intellect must abstract from individuals in order to understand them, which is what Ockham says in the *Ordinatio*, Prologue, q. 1, 67. Also notes 47, 175 above.

[268] *Reportatio, ibid.*, C.

[269] Utrum angelus accipiat cognitionem a rebus spiritualibus an a corporalibus. (*Reportatio*, II, q. 16, A).

[270] *Ibid.*, B–C.   [271] *Ibid.*, E (–F).   [272] *Ibid.*, G–N.   [273] *Ibid.*, I, X, GG–II.

abstractive knowledge, and assent to or dissent from its propositions. Neither angels nor men can have evident knowledge or evidently assent to it unless on the one hand the extremes of a proposition—subject and predicate—or rather that for which they stand, really exist, and on the other they are known intuitively, in the way that evident knowledge of the proposition 'The wall is white' depends upon the actual whiteness of the wall and intuitive knowledge of the fact. A cognitive habit cannot be generated merely from abstract and complex knowledge of such a proposition because—in default of intuitive knowledge—no one will feel more inclined to assent to a proposition about what does not exist after knowing the proposition than before. Conversely if that to which assent has been given in a proposition no longer exists, assent turns to dissent: for example if God conserved intuitive cognition of a wall, after it had been destroyed, it would then be false to say 'This wall is white'; and the proposition would be rejected. In other words, there can only be evident knowledge and assent to it when there is both individual existence and intuitive knowledge of it; in Ockham's words, 'Therefore for the angelic intellect to have evident cognition of an affirmative contingent proposition by which it judges what it knows to exist, there must necessarily be existence of the extremes and intuitive cognition of them.'[274] A negative proposition to be known evidently only needs knowledge of the extremes leading to a denial that they—or what they stand for—really exist.[275] That is at the centre of Ockham's doctrine of evident knowledge; intuitive cognition alone—naturally—guarantees existence and non-existence and is therefore the foundation of abstractive and complex knowledge, including necessary propositions, the ability to form which is the fifth feature of angelic knowledge. Whether in fact angels do derive in-complex or complex knowledge, contingent or necessary, from things cannot be known by us, because that depends upon God's will which in all things is freely and contingently exercised.[276] Finally, angels can know discursively for the reason stated at the beginning, that they can come to know what is not initially known, as well as be mistaken: thus it is the accepted opinion of the authorities that a bad angel cannot know the hidden secrets of the heart and can misconstrue an external sign, such as taking a smile to mean joy when it does not. Similarly, it is generally held that many angels do not know of the Incarnation and yet freely assent to its truth, just as demons, according to St Augustine and others, are able over a long period to know much of what previously they were ignorant. By the same token it would be extraordinary if the devil were to know everything. Hence angels like men can proceed from the known to the unknown discursively.[277]

---

[274] *Ibid.*, M.   [275] *Ibid.*, N.

[276] Ergo ad hoc quod intellectus angelicus habeat cognitionem evidentem de aliquo con-tingenti complexo affirmativo, qua iudicatur hoc esse, requiritur necessario existentia extremorum et notitia intuitiva eorum. Et hoc dico naturaliter, non loquendo de potentia divina. Sed ad habendum notitiam evidentem de aliquo complexo contingenti negativo quo negatur hoc esse, ad hoc vere sufficit notitia intuitiva extremorum; et illa necessario requiritur naturaliter, et non existentia rei (*ibid.*, L).

[277] *Ibid.*, M.

With the doubts which these conclusions raise over the possibility of the material acting upon the spiritual we are not directly concerned, but we may briefly remark that Ockham resolves them principally by treating what is material and corporeal as partial cause of the angels' own spiritual knowledge;[278] the latter differs from human understanding in not depending upon the imagination which, in having physical extension, angels do not possess.[279] Similarly an object does not have to be in direct physical contact with the angelic intellect to cause knowledge but must merely have spiritual and virtual contiguity, in coming within the intellect's range.[280] Like the human soul, however, the angelic soul does not have the same powers which it has in conjunction with a body (in its case spiritual).[281] The difference is that for men all knowledge is in origin corporeal, of what exists (or does not exist) absolutely as substance or quality, and is discernible physically to the senses and/or intellect. For that reason all human knowledge originates in individual experience; and it is this facet of simple cognition which we must now finally consider.

VII   THE PRIMACY OF INDIVIDUAL COGNITION

Ockham's claims for the primacy of the individual as first in the order of what is known (*primitate generationis*) is made directly in response to the contrary views of St Thomas Aquinas, Henry of Ghent and in a more restricted sense, Duns Scotus. In questions five and six of the third distinction of the *Ordinatio*, he argues firstly against the primacy of something more general than the individual, and secondly against the Aristotelian doctrine—or what he considers to be the misrepresentation of Aristotle's doctrine—of indirect cognition of individuals through abstraction. Only the first concerns Duns Scotus who while, as we have seen, upholding direct individual cognition did not accept that the individual was the first object known. Instead Scotus argued that the first object of confused or indistinct knowledge is the *species specialissima* or lowest species coming immediately above the individuals belonging to it, as man is the *species specialissima* of individual men; and the first object known distinctly is the concept of being as the most universal and absolutely simple of all concepts. By confused knowledge Duns meant knowing an object merely by name as opposed to its definition; and when an individual is experienced by the senses it is the name of the individual's *species specialissima* which is first known to the intellect as a result.[282] That, for Ockham, is to say that the intellect cannot know the singular as singular (*sub propria ratione singularitatis*), a position

[278] *Ibid.*, N–Z, especially Ad 4[m], 5[m], 6[m], 9[m], 11[m].
[279] *Ibid.*, Q–R, EE. Ad 4[m] and 9[m].   [280] *Ibid.*, Q, Ad 1[m].
[281] Ad aliud dico quod non est inconveniens quod corpus agat in spiritum causando intellectionem sui partialiter sicut potest causare in anima coniuncta corpori. Et dico quod non est causa precisa quare corpus potest agere in animam nostram, quia est coniuncta corpori; sed causa est precise quia anima de se non potest habere omnem perfectionem ad quam est in potentia mediante corpore quam potest habere a corpore. Et hec eadem est causa quare agit in angelum, quia ipse potest habere aliquam perfectionem posito corpore quam non potest habere destructo corpore (*ibid.*, CC).
[282] *Ordinatio*, d. 3, q. 5, 443–4.

which Duns initially adopted but later amended.[283] Among Duns's reasons is that based upon the action of natural causes which, if not impeded, immediately produce the maximum effect of which they are capable; that applies to an act of cognition which, as a natural cause preceding any act of will, has as its most perfect effect a concept of a *species specialissima*; any other concept would be less perfect because according to Duns the more universal is always included in the less universal; and as the part is less perfect than the whole so any concept more universal than the *species specialissima* as the least universal of all is related to the latter as part to the whole.[284] This relation of the more universal to the less universal also explains why being is the first object of distinct knowledge; for as the most universal and absolutely simple of all concepts it is contained in all other—less universal—concepts and itself contains none. But since nothing can be known distinctly, according to Duns, unless everything essential to it is also known, distinct knowledge of everything must include distinct knowledge of being as its prerequisite. Therefore being must be the first object distinctly known.[285] Duns also adds that the sequence of knowing is always from confused and indistinct to distinct.[286]

Ockham disagrees. To begin with, the concept of being as alone absolutely simple carries the implication that nothing else is absolutely simple which, as we shall consider in chapter three, is not so. Similarly it would mean that a genus or a *species specialissima* would be composite including among their parts the concept of being, which Duns denies, as well as all those concepts which constitute their definition as species or genus: that would be to make a definition and what is defined the same terms, which again Duns denies. Ockham also rejects the distinction between knowing something indistinctly by its name and distinctly by its definition, on the grounds that anything conceived as a whole and according to any part is known distinctly; and that can be without a definition as in the case of a species.[287]

That a *species specialissima* is not the first object known can be shown by Duns's own argument that the first object of knowing—specially that which is first in order of origin—is present to the knower in the aspect in which it is known before the act of knowing; and that is not as a *species specialissima*. Moreover, an individual thing is known in some way as singular or it is not known at all, in which case we could not ask anything about it. It must therefore be knowable, and if, not in an individual concept proper to it alone, in a common concept. But according to Duns every non-essential concept presupposes an essential, or quidditative, concept; therefore there must be a concept of individual difference which must be known immediately in itself.[288] Nor do Duns's reasons hold for a *species specialissima* as the most perfect effect of an act of knowing. Not only do all causes not immediately engender the most perfect act of which they are capable, but whatever can cause a less universal concept suffices for a more universal concept; hence a *species specialissima* cannot be produced without producing a more universal concept.[289]

[283] *Ibid.*, 444. [284] *Ibid.* [285] *Ibid.*, 445. [286] *Ibid.*, 446. [287] *Ibid.*, 446–9.
[288] *Ibid.*, 449–50. [289] *Ibid.*, 449–53.

At the same time, on Duns's own arguments, the singular is known before a *species specialissima* because, as he says, whatever the senses can experience the intellect also knows; but what is sensed in singular; so therefore is what is known, and a singular concept is more perfect than a concept of a *species specialissima*. Moreover, if Duns's major premise is true the singular will be known immediately—as the most perfect effect of the intellect's act—and an individual concept produced immediately.[290] If therefore, the singular were, as Duns says, known under a *species specialissima*, the same thing would either be known in the same real aspect by both senses and intellect or it would not. If in the same real aspect then it cannot be said that the *species specialissima* is first really known to the intellect while its individual is immediately apprehended by the senses; for both intellect and senses would first know the *species specialissima*. If on the other hand intellect and senses know the same object differently, since according to Duns the individual thing exists in nature before any act of knowing, the individual will be the immediate object of an act of sensing; and so the first object of the intellect will also really be individual, although known in its nature rather than its individual difference:[291] in other words, even if known otherwise than in its individual difference, it will still be the individual which is first object of the intellect, as it is of the senses.

As to the first object of distinct knowledge, Duns's contention that it is the concept of being is groundless; for any object can be known distinctly without knowing what is not essential to it; but a concept of being is not included essentially in a *species specialissima* or in any individual coming under it; therefore they can each be known without a concept of being.[292] The notion of being, as Duns acknowledges, is merely conceptual; hence it is not part of the nature of anything which really exists outside the mind, as we shall discuss in chapters three and five. Here we need only observe that when distinct things are brought under the same concept, if one can be known independently of their common concept so can the other; that applies to both God and creatures when considered under a concept of being.[293] Furthermore no concept is known intuitively;[294] when therefore

[290] Preterea, quando accipitur in minore quod conceptus perfectissimus in quem possunt est conceptus speciei specialissime, hoc non debet concedi secundum istos, quia illud idem est intellectum quod est sensatum; sed sensatum est singulare; igitur singulare est intellectum, et conceptus singularis est perfectior conceptu speciei specialissime. Igitur si maior eorum sit vera, singulare primo intelligetur, et conceptus eius primo producetur. Confirmatur ista ratio, quia singulare sub ratione singularis est sensatum a sensu; igitur singulare sub ratione singularis est intellectum a intellectu. Consequentia patet, quia in quodcumque obiectum potest sensus, in illud idem sub eadem ratione potest intellectus, maxime secundum istos [i.e. Duns] (*ibid.*, 453–4).

[291] *Ibid.*, 454–5.

[292] Contra secundum articulum in quo ponit quod ens necessario est primum distincte cognitum primitate originis, hoc est simpliciter falsum, quia omne obiectum potest distincte cognosci, non cognito illo quod non est de ratione eius essentialis nec includitur essentialiter in eo; sed conceptus entis non includitur essentialiter nec in specie specialissima nec in aliquo inferiori reali; igitur unumquodque eorum potest cognosci distincte sine cognitione entis communissimi (*ibid.*, 458).

[293] *Ibid.*, 458–9.

[294] Sed notitia intuitiva non est respectu alicuius conceptus; igitur erit ibi notitia intuitiva distincta sine cognitione talis conceptus (*ibid.*, 459).

something is known distinctly its knowledge will not include knowledge of the concept of being. And just as the senses can know one thing distinctly without knowing anything else, so can the intellect.[295]

That also answers Duns's other contention that confused knowledge precedes distinct knowledge, because both the senses and the intellect can know something distinctly at once. In fact confused knowledge can follow distinct knowledge, for example a concept of many genera, which depends upon prior knowledge of diverse individuals of different species.[296] By the same token distinct knowledge does not always depend upon a definition of what is known; for sometimes there can be distinct intuitive knowledge of something before any definition. All definition is by means of general terms which are not of a thing's essence whereas intuitive knowledge is. That is not to say that definition does nothing towards providing knowledge of what is defined; it does, as we shall have ample occasion to see in chapters four and five; but it is knowledge less of the thing in itself than of its attributes or of what is known in a concept or as enabling us to investigate the parts of the thing defined.[297] It is not, however, the condition of distinct knowledge, which comes through intuitive knowledge.

Ockham's criticism of Duns Scotus centres here principally upon the anomalies which arise from combining intuitive individual cognition with an order of cognition which does not begin from the individual. St Thomas Aquinas, also, reaches a similar conclusion but from a different, Aristotelian, standpoint, based largely upon what Aristotle says in the *Physics*:[298] namely that we always advance from generalities to particulars, beginning with what is confused, as exemplified by children who at first always call all men 'father' and all women 'mother'. Aquinas interprets this as a progression from potential incomplete knowledge to actual or complete knowledge; only complete knowledge is perfect. Hence the sequence is always from imperfect to perfect knowledge, by which the object is known distinctly. That applies equally to the senses; they too begin from the more universal both in place and in time: in place because something is first indistinctly seen from a distance; in time as children first distinguish between men and other beings rather than among different individuals. The reason in each case is that we begin from indistinct knowledge, and in knowing indistinctly we are potentially able to know distinctly, as to know a genus is to have potential knowledge of individual differences. Accordingly distinct knowledge is the medium between potential and actual knowledge. From that Aquinas concludes that singular knowledge is prior to universal knowledge as sensory knowledge precedes intellective knowledge; in both the more common comes before the less common.[299]

For Ockham Aquinas's opinion is false first because it would mean there could only be less universal knowledge if everything more universal were first known. In fact many *species specialissimae* are known to us while their genera remain

---

[295] *Ibid.*, 460.   [296] *Ibid.*   [297] *Ibid.*, 478–80.
[298] *Physics*, I, ch. 1, 184 a, 21–184 b, 14.
[299] *Ordinatio, ibid.*, 464–5.

unknown.[300] Moreover Aquinas himself says that universals do not exist independently of their individuals; therefore nothing real is known save the individual or many individuals.[301] That is confirmed because the object of a first act of cognition is something real existing outside the soul, or a concept, or a combination of both. It cannot be either of the latter two, because the first object must precede the act of knowing and so must be in a real relation to the knowing power which depends upon the presence of the object for its knowledge. A concept or the product of what is at once conceptual and real are both subsequent to the act of cognition; they cannot therefore be its first object, which accordingly must be something real, whether one individual or many.[302]

Secondly, to say that the intellect proceeds from potential to actual knowledge is obvious if taken strictly with the corollary that when the first act of knowing is of an individual it is more perfect. If, however, it is meant metaphorically as the sequence from imperfect to perfect knowledge, then it begs what has to be proved; nor is it universally true, for first knowledge can be more perfect than subsequent knowledge, as knowledge of the principles is more perfect than knowledge of the conclusions, and knowledge of cause more perfect than knowledge of an effect. It is equally false to posit a universally intermediary incomplete phase between what is potential and what is actual, because one follows immediately from the other, as the will immediately passes from non-loving to a complete act of loving and the sun immediately illuminates the air,[303] Indeed the entire notion that a complete act constitutes perfect knowledge is false and contradicts what Aristotle says in the *Posterior Analytics* that a universal demonstration is a more perfect than and prior to singular demonstration as we shall consider in chapter four.[304]

Finally there is no parallel order in sensory experience between the more and the less universal because the senses only apprehend what is singular and nothing else. If they could distinguish between the more and the less universal there would have to be a distinction between them. Now a distinction can be real or formal or mental. It cannot, in this case, be real, for according to St Thomas whiteness is not composed of really distinct parts; nor is it formal since St Thomas denies that there is such a distinction; and if it were simply mental it would be the result of the intellect's activity and so not prior to an act of sensation, which it must be to be apprehended by the senses. Accordingly the senses cannot know something as more and as less universal, just because there is no real distinction between, say, colour and whiteness or anything else for them to perceive.[305] In maintaining that there is, St Thomas is merely contradicting what he says also about the singular as that which is first known; for the singular cannot both be known first and be the completed act which follows a prior incomplete act of what is known more generally and confusedly.[306]

Ockham's own conclusion, that the singular is the first object known, is proved

---

[300] *Ibid.*, 465–6.

[301] Preterea secundum istos, universalia non sunt aliqua distincta a parte rei ab ipsis singularibus; igitur nihil unum reale potest cognosci ab intellectu nisi singulare vel multa singularia cognoscantur, et per consequens non universale (*ibid.*, 466).

[302] *Ibid.*   [303] *Ibid.*, 466–7.   [304] *Ibid.*, 468–9.   [305] *Ibid.*, 469–70.   [306] *Ibid.*, 470–1.

from the general principle—conceded by his opponents—that what is first known by some power is present to that power before the act of knowing and in the aspect in which it is subsequently known. But only the singular precedes the act of knowing; therefore the singular is the first object known.[307] It can moreover only be known in itself, because if it were known only accidentally it would not be known by a distinct act from that which is known essentially. Hence a singular could only be known in knowing a universal, which is false. And if the singular is known essentially it does not presuppose knowledge of a universal because whenever the intellect has a concept of many things, knowledge of any one suffices for knowledge of the rest; the intellect does not need to know anything else to have knowledge of the singular.[308]

The same conclusion can be persuaded by the argument that where a prior power ends, a posterior power begins; but the sensitive faculty ends in cognition of the singular; therefore the intellective faculty begins with individual cognition.[309] Again, a familiar argument where powers are related as superior and inferior over the same object, what the inferior power can do the superior can do; that applies to senses and intellect. Since the senses can immediately experience an individual, so can the intellect.[310]

It will be observed that Ockham's mode of arguing adheres to the accepted Aristotelian conception of demonstrative knowledge as universal and necessary. Although Ockham does not call any of these arguments more than proofs and some only persuasions—since as we shall see in chapter four he recognises the severe limitations upon attaining universal and necessary knowledge—the order is always deductive from a general principle as the major premise. Ockham did not attempt to go beyond Aristotle's framework; his innovations came from the rigour with which he sought to test concepts and propositions in conformity with experience. Nothing could be more misconceived therefore than to believe that Ockham renounced universal concepts, terms or propositions; what he denied was the assumption that universality existed in its own right without reference to the individuals to which it was always reducible. That should become more apparent over the next three chapters.

From the primacy of the individual as the first object known Ockham concludes in the second place that it can be known distinctly. The proof lies in the previous argument that everything known distinctly by the senses can be known distinctly by the intellect.[311] It is supported by what Ockham has also said earlier in reply to

---

[307] His visis dico ad questionem, et primo quod communissimum non est primum cognitum a nobis primitate generationis. Circa quod primo ostendam hanc conclusionem, quod primum cognitum nobis primitate generationis est singulare. Hanc probo, quia illud quod primo cognoscitur ab aliqua potentia sub aliqua ratione, sub illa ratione precedit actum illius potentie; sed solum singulare sub ratione illius quod est singulare precedit actum potentie; igitur etc. ibid., 473). Also *Quodlibet* I, q. 13.

[308] *Ibid.*, 473–4.   [309] *Ibid.*, 474.   [310] *Ibid.*

[311] Secunda conclusio est ista, quod primum cognitum distincte cognitum potest esse singulare. Hoc probatur, quia omne distincte cognitum a sensu potest esse primum distincte cognitum ab intellectu; sed singulare potest ante omnem actum intelligendi esse distincte cognitum a sensu; igitur etc. (*ibid.*).

Duns Scotus: that anything can be distinctly known by the intellect without knowing what is inessential to it; but a universal is not of the essence of any singular as we shall discuss in the next chapter. Therefore the individual can be known distinctly without knowing the universal.[312] That also follows from Ockham's own definition of distinct knowledge as that in which everything essential to everything known is present to the knower.[313] It does not, however, mean that every individual is always known distinctly: Ockham's third and fourth conclusions are that something other than the individual can first be distinctly known, and conversely only an individual can be known indistinctly.[314] The reason in the first case is that if the senses perceive an individual only confusedly the intellect can do so, too; and if so, it can then abstract an absolutely simple concept of what is known before it knows any other individual. This concept will be the first object of distinct knowledge because any simple concept contains nothing that is not known when the concept is known. An individual, on the other hand, is composed of essential parts—substance and accidents and when material form and matter—which may not all be known when the object is known; and when they are not, knowledge of the object, in not including all its essential parts, will be confused.[315] That does not apply to a composite concept which although composed of a number of concepts is also distinctly known since a concept by definition is that which is known. Therefore each concept composing the whole must be known and nothing remains unknown.[316]

Finally Ockham rejects the order from confused to distinct knowing, for sometimes as we have seen an individual is distinctly known.[317]

Ockham has therefore distinguished a first object of knowledge, which is always without exception an individual, from whether it is known distinctly; in the second case the individual does not have to be first object known because, unlike a concept which can only be known distinctly, an individual can also be known indistinctly. Hence although a concept cannot be absolutely the first object known, it can be the first object of distinct knowledge. The two poles are therefore the individual as first known and the universal as distinctly known. They thereby reverse the order, upheld by both Scotus and Aquinas, from the more to the less universal and modify the invariability from the confused to the distinct.

In the case of Aquinas, however, this is part of a further and fundamental

---

[312] Ibid., 475.

[313] Ibid., 471; also 417, e.g.: Ad primum principale dico quod quando simplex cognoscitur in se, aut totaliter cognoscitur aut totaliter ignoratur, quia nihil potest illius latere quin totum lateat (d. 3, q. 2).

[314] Tertia conclusio est quod aliquid aliud a singulari potest esse primum distincte cognitum ... Quarta conclusio est quod solum singulare potest cognosci confuse (ibid., q. 5, 475).

[315] Ibid.; Ockham defines confused knowledge thus: Cognitio confusa obiecti est illa qua aliquid patet potenti et aliquid latet illam potentiam ipsius obiecti, ita quod non quidlibet illius obiecti apprehendatur (ibid., 471-2).

[316] Ibid., 476.

[317] Quinta conclusio sequitur ex predictis quod non semper totus ordo confuse concipiendi precedit totum ordinem distincte cognoscendi, quia aliquando primum cognitum primitate originis est distincte cognitum, sicut quando aliquid distincte est sensatum illud idem potest esse primum distincte cognitum ab intellectu (ibid., 476).

difference over what it is that the intellect knows. Whereas Ockham and Duns agree that the intellect has direct cognition of the individual, intuitively, but diverge over how the intellect becomes cognisant of the individual, Aquinas diverges from both in denying the intellect direct knowledge of the individual at all. For him there is no such thing as intuitive knowledge of individual existence; the intellect comes to know individuals indirectly through the images of things converted in the imagination from the senses, as we have mentioned earlier. Such a doctrine of indirect intellectual cognition ran directly counter to the doctrine of intuitive cognition as the foundation of Ockham's epistemology. In the next question, six, he took up its challenge, expressed in the opinions of St Thomas Aquinas and Henry of Ghent. His discussion there represents his response to the Aristotelian doctrine—or as we have said for Ockham its misrepresentation—of abstraction; it is at once a refutation of indirect intellectual cognition and a justification—supported from his own gloss of Aristotle's texts—of direct intuitive cognition. This question, therefore crystallises the difference between intuitive knowledge and abstraction.

The view of Aquinas which Ockham opposes is that the intellect cannot know directly material individuals, on the grounds that their principle is matter; it therefore only knows them indirectly by abstracting an intelligible species from matter; and since what is abstracted from matter is universal, the intellect knows only the universal directly and the individual indirectly through reflecting upon the universal. It does so moreover not by knowing the individual thing but its image into which it is converted; this is supported by the statement earlier referred to in *De Anima*[318] that the soul never thinks without images.[319]

Henry of Ghent's standpoint is similar, contrasting direct intellectual cognition of the universal abstracted from the image of an individual with indirect cognition of the individual known in the intelligible species which has been abstracted. The intellect therefore first knows the universal species in the image and then the species in its singular aspect.[320] Both opinions are supported by a multiplicity of citations from Aristotle and Averroes.

To St Thomas, Ockham begins by repeating what he has said in the last question, namely, that Aquinas's conception of indirect individual cognition contradicts his view that only the individual really exists outside the mind. His reasons for abstraction apply no more to matter than to form; if therefore it contradicts the intellect to know anything material directly, it will equally contradict it to know directly any form.[321] Moreover, that which is abstracted when the intellect knows, say, an ass or the earth will be either something existing outside the mind—and so by abstraction a real individual will be known—or it will exist only in the mind and will then either precede the act of knowing or be subsequent to it. If subsequent it will not be the first object known; if previous to the act of knowing, an intelligible species will be the first object known, which St Thomas denies. Nor

[318] III, ch. 8, 430 a, 16–17.
[319] *Ordinatio*, d. 3, q. 6, 483–4.
[320] *Ibid.*, 484–5.   [321] *Ibid.*, 488.

can it be argued that what is abstracted is something represented by an intelligible species before the latter is known; for the same could equally be said of a sensible species (for example, whiteness), which is as representative of all the individuals coming under it in virtue of their similarity (being white) as an intelligible species is.[322]

As for the process of abstracting a universal from a material individual, that can mean either knowing one thing without knowing something else or knowing something common to many things. The first is impossible because only the most individual whiteness is abstracted from something white if the whiteness is known apart from the matter in which it is present. Moreover the senses can perceive one thing without another, and by that mode they can also abstract; which would mean that they too would know universals. If on the other hand something common to many things is known by abstraction it follows that it will be common only to matter in being derived from material things; forms and composites of form and matter would then be known only indirectly by some kind of reflexion.[323]

Conversely the intellect does not know the individual only indirectly because, on the one hand, if individual and universal were known separately, the universal, in being known directly, would be known before the individual, which St Thomas denies. If on the other hand they are known by distinct acts, that of knowing the individual will be caused by an image or something in the senses, or an intelligible species or the same act as that by which the universal is known. By each of the first three modes the individual could be known first: by the fourth, cause and effect have to be present simultaneously, and then, despite St Thomas, there would be two distinct acts of cognition.[324]

Ockham's rejoinder to Henry of Ghent is that his account of abstraction would also make sensory experience of individuals indirect; in consequence the senses would know the same thing twice, first in its sensible species and then as an individual. That in turn contradicts what Henry has said about abstraction leading the intellect first to cognition and then to reflexion upon what is abstracted; for when a universal is abstracted from an individual phantasm there must be a change either in the intellect or the senses: otherwise there will be no abstraction and so no—what Henry calls—direct line from the intellect to the universal. The change cannot be to the senses or a part of them because then the universal would be in the senses. It must therefore be in the intellect and in something prior to both the act and the habit of knowing which according to Henry are subsequent to the change. That must be an intelligible species, which Henry denies; hence his explanation depends upon positing what he rejects.[325] It also leads to indirect cognition of the universal by the intellect, since for Henry the intellect knows the universal as an object, which occurs only as the result of reflexion.[326]

Ockham thus dismisses the claim for indirect cognition of individuals through universal cognition. Not all his arguments are equally convincing, especially those directed against the notion of abstraction upon which Ockham equally

322 *Ibid.*, 488–9.   323 *Ibid.*, 489–90.   324 *Ibid.*, 490–1.
325 *Ibid.*, 491–2.   326 *Ibid.*, 492.

depends to explain genera and species as common to individuals of the same
degree of similarity: if one could only abstract the concept of matter from material
beings, there would be no means of knowing specific properties such as whiteness
or rationality. Nor does it follow that there is any more reason for abstracting the
concept of matter from individuals than that of their whiteness or rationality.
Again the change of which Henry of Ghent speaks could as well come from the
intellect itself as from any species.

Ockham's own counter-position is stated in three conclusions: that the individual is known, known intuitively and known before anything else.[327] They
take us to the heart of his justification of individual cognition. So far as the first
conclusion is concerned, if the individual were not known that would be due to
either the intellect's imperfection or its perfection; it cannot be imperfection
because the senses are more imperfect than the intellect and they perceive individuals. Nor can it be due to its perfection, which would be for one of three
reasons: that it would not know something as imperfect as a material individual,
that it could not be changed by something material or that it does not receive
anything material.[328] The first does not hold, because a universal abstracted from
material things is no more perfect than a singular and yet it is known; therefore
a singular can be known.[329] The second similarly applies as much to an individual
as to a universal; for if—according to St Thomas and Henry of Ghent—the
intellect is moved by the active intellect to cognition of a universal so it is moved
to cognition of an individual; and if—again according to them—the intellect
receives determinate knowledge of a universal from an intelligible species and
phantasm, it must also thus receive determinate knowledge of an individual.
Moreover in the same way as the intellect can know an individual after knowing a
universal it can know an individual before the universal, because in each case it
knows this individual rather than that, whereas in knowing a universal it knows no
particular individuals.[330] Hence knowledge of an individual does not depend upon
knowledge of a universal; and, in reply to the third reason, the intellect is no less
able to know an individual immaterially before knowing a universal than after.[331]

The last issue was in many ways the central one as more than any other responsible for the attempt to overcome, by some kind of indirect or intelligible
cognition, the problem of the material acting immediately upon the immaterial
and spiritual. For Ockham as for Scotus the prospect held no terrors. Both equally
rejected the until then almost immutable Greco-Christian belief that knowledge
of universals is superior to that of individuals (as opposed to the greater demonstrability of universal propositions with which it must not be confused); and

[327] Ideo dico aliter ad questionem. Et primo quod singulare intelligitur. Secundo quod
prima notitia singularis est intuitiva. Tertio quod singulare primo intelligitur (*ibid.*, 492).
[328] *Ibid.*
[329] Primum non impedit, quia universale abstractum a meterialibus non est perfectius ipso
singulari, et tamen intelligitur (*ibid.*, 492–3).
[330] *Ibid.*, 493.
[331] Nec tertium impedit, tum quia non plus repugnat huic singulari recipi immaterialiter
quam universali; tum quia cognitio singularis sequens post cognitionem universalis reciptiur
immaterialiter; igitur non repugnat sibi primo recipi immaterialiter (*ibid.*).

Ockham here directly extends the argument to the distinction between immaterial and material knowledge, which he equally rejects. If, he replies, the universal is known immaterially, as St Thomas and Henry maintain, that is because of the immaterial nature of the intelligible species and the intellect by which the universal is known. In that case the individual will also be known immaterially for it is also, according to them, known by the same means. Nor is it any more contradictory for the individual to be known immaterially than the universal, both of which are received in our intellect as well as in the separated intellect.[332] Conversely, if it contradicted the intellect to know a material individual it would be equally contradictory for it to know a material universal abstracted from material individuals.[333]

Ockham has thus established direct cognition of individuals largely by turning the arguments of his opponents against them to show the untenability of any distinction between the intellect's mode of knowing individuals and universals.

The second conclusion, that the individual can be known intuitively, is the condition of all contingent knowledge as prior to abstractive knowledge.[334] Hence the sensible individual must be known absolutely first, both by the senses and the intellect immediately. It therefore always comes first in the order of knowing *pro statu isto*, with same individual sensed and known under the same aspect, unless there is some impediment.[335] The superiority of the intellect over the senses does not mean that it must know the individual more eminently as universal and abstract rather than individual and concrete. In the first place it does not apply to an object which is more imperfect; but the universal is absolutely more imperfect than the singular and known subsequently to it; therefore the intellect does not know more eminently as universal what to the senses is individual.[336] In the second place the distinction made by St Thomas between the abstract as universal and the concrete as individual is 'an absurd and fatuous way of talking'. Whiteness as abstract no more signifies a universal than a concrete white thing. As we shall consider fully in chapter three, abstract and concrete differ exclusively as terms having different modes of signification. As such they both belong to the intellect.[337]

That completes what we may call the epistemological basis of individual cognition. The remaining two thirds of the question (six)[338] are devoted to detailed

[332] *Ibid.*, 493–4.

[333] *Ibid.*, 496.

[334] Secundum probo, quia notitia singularis aliqua potest esse intuitiva, quai aliter nulla veritas contingens posset evidenter cognosci ab intellectu; sed notitia intuitiva rei non est posterior notitia abstractiva; igitur notitia intuitiva rei singularis est simpliciter prima (*ibid.*, 494).

[335] Tertio dico quod notitia singularis sensibilis est simpliciter prima pro statu isto, ita quod illud idem singulare quod primo sentitur a sensu idem et sub eadem ratione primo intelligitur intuitive ab intellectu nisi sit aliquod impedimentum (*ibid.*).

[336] Contra: quando cognitum a potentia superiori est simpliciter imperfectius cognito a potentia inferiori, tunc superior potentia non cognoscit modo eminentiori illud quod cognoscitur a potentia inferiori; sed universale est simpliciter imperfectius et posterius ipso singulari; igitur intellectus non cognoscit obiectum sensus modo eminentiori (*ibid.*, 495).

[337] *Ibid.*, 495–6.

[338] *Ibid.*, 496–520.

exegesis of passages, principally from *De Anima* and the *Physics* together with the Commentaries of Averroes upon them, which appear to confirm the standpoint of St Thomas and Henry of Ghent that the universal is known directly and first. In the course of his explanation Ockham distinguishes between the intellect's inclination to know the universal first and actual knowledge of individuals which is presupposed in any awareness of universals. There is thus a contrast between the psychological order, of consciousness, and the real order of knowing: the first begins with the universal, the second from direct cognition of individuals which precedes the first. The distinction, independently of whether or not it was forced upon him by his authorities, also expresses Ockham's central preoccupation with reconciling the discrepancy between the nature of what is known and how it is known. It is that which constitutes the problem of universals in a world of individuals, as we shall discuss in the following two chapters. Here Ockham is concerned only with explaining why the mind should seem to know universals first.

Most of his discussion is prompted by Henry of Ghent's citations in support of his preceding account of universal cognition. Ockham begins by amplifying the statement in *De Anima* that children begin by calling all men father and all women mother. Far from this proving that the universal is known first, it would, if taken as evidence of universal knowledge, prove that the individual is the first object to be sensed because the same lack of discrimination is found among lambs. The inability to discern individuals has therefore nothing to do with universal cognition, for it occurs in those who, like children and animals as well as madmen and fools, do not have the use of reason, and so cannot have knowledge of universals. Nor, however, is it confined to those who are without the use of reason, since men who know both universals and individuals can also fail at first to differentiate one man from another, calling several by the same name. The cause thus lies not with the intellect or with the priority of the universal over the individual but with the capacity of the senses to distinguish only what is dissimilar. Hence although the individual is always immediately perceived, it is not immediately known distinctly unless it is in some way differentiated from similar individuals, whether by colour or shape or position or in some other manner.[339]

Confused knowledge is therefore due to nothing more exalted than the limitation of the senses. Moreover, it has no bearing upon the order from the more to the less universal of which Aristotle and Averroes speak in the *Physics* and the Commentary on it; for they are referring to the procedure to be followed in that and other works on nature, where the universal terms belonging to universal propositions are known before the propositions. That applies to any body of knowledge (*scientia*); it is easier for most men to go from the more to the less universal once they have apprehended one or more individuals, as movement can be known from experience of something sensible, and colour from two intermediate species of colour such as white and black; and these being known there is no need to have immediate or proper knowledge of all the individuals or species belonging to the genus or species. Thus every man can have a concept of animal and know the

[339] *Ibid.*, 497.

properties of animals without encountering every animal in each different region or having strict knowledge of them. All such universal knowledge, however, always begins from direct experience of individuals: those who learn about animals in Greece, for example, will first know the animals in Greece which may not be the same as those in Italy or France or England. Accordingly the greater facility which most men have in knowing universals is not the same as knowing them first.[340] That is the sense of Averroes's remark that the composite individual is not the principle of demonstrative knowledge—which as we shall see in chapter four must be a universal and necessary proposition—and yet is the principle of acquiring knowledge of a universal which is the principle of demonstrative knowledge. For knowledge which is universal, whether simple or complex, is preceded by knowledge of individuals.[341]

Secondly, when Averroes says that the confused is better and more certainly known he means by confused what is composite, which in having really distinct parts can be known as a whole before its parts are known. Similarly his assertion that individuals should come to be known through knowing universals as more easily known refers to the universal properties common to all the individuals coming under a universal, which are more easily known of the universal; and in being known of the latter can help towards knowledge of individuals.[342] At the same time less is needed to know what is whole and more universal than less universal and a part; which explains why Averroes declared that the whole is better known by the senses.[343] Conversely the universal is more known by the intellect because only reason can apprehend universals. That does not mean, as we saw at the beginning of the chapter, that the intellect does not equally know the singular. Once again Ockham stresses that Aristotle and Averroes, in affirming that the intellect knows universals and the senses individuals, are not denying that the intellect also knows individuals: they are simply pointing to the difference between what the two powers can know.[344] Nevertheless the difference between omitting and including mention of the intellect's ability to know individuals became by Ockham's time precisely the difference between indirect and intuitive knowledge of the individual, which Ockham's glosses are perforce designed to overcome.

---

[340] Ibid., 500–2.   [341] Ibid., 503–4.   [342] Ibid., 504.

[343] Ad tertiam auctoritatem dico per idem quod sicut totum secundum sensum est notius, quia pauciora sufficiunt ad notitiam totius ut totum discernatur ab alio toto quam ad discernendam unam partem unius ab alia . . . ita est de universaliori quod multa sunt que divisim sufficiunt ad notitiam universalioris, et tamen non sufficiunt, vel nulla, vel aliqua, ad notitiam minus universalis (ibid.).

[344] Ad secundum concedo quod universale est notius secundum rationem, quia sola ratio potest apprehendere universale et nullo modo sensus . . . Per idem ad aliud concedo quod universale est comprehensibile ab intellectu et singulare ab sensu, et cum hoc stat quod non tantum universale est comprehensibile ab intellectu sed etiam singulare. Propter quod advertendum quod Philosophus et Commentator frequenter dicunt quod sensus est particularium et intellectus universalium, ut innuant differentiam esse inter sensum et intellectum. Nunc autem ita est quod ita contingit arguere intellectum differe a sensu si sensus sit precise apprehensivus singularium et intellectus sit apprehensivus singularium et universalium sicut si sensus esset precise apprehensivus singularium et intellectus precise universalium. Et ideo ad intentionem eorum sufficit quod intellectus sit apprehensivus universalium et non sensus (ibid., 505).

To Averroes's statement that the intellect is brought to actual knowledge by universal things existing in the mind, Ockham's reply is that from Averroes's usage universal things can be understood as universal habits; and that they move the intellect to its ultimate perfection of strict or scientific knowledge, which is solely by means of universals, whether terms or propositions. Confirmation can be found in different places among Averroes's writings where he says that only habits, acts or passions really inhere in the mind; hence even if species are added, as they are by Aquinas and Scotus among others, they have no more claim to be considered universals than the others. For that—rather unconvincing—reason Ockham concludes that it is not inconvenient for habits to be identified with universal things leading to universal knowledge.[345]

Over the way in which the intellect knows the substantial form of an individual thing, neither Aristotle nor Averroes can be interpreted as holding that the form is known separately as a universal and through it, indirectly, the individual. On the contrary, both philosophers speak of individual and form as two objects each apprehensible by the same power in different ways, one perfectly in itself, the other in dependence upon other knowledge and dispositions. The first applies to many of the objects known by the common sense which can know diverse individual objects, while for others it must rely upon additional support through some defect in the other senses.[346] Both the universal and a substantial form, on the other hand, can only be known from previous individual knowledge. Accordingly knowledge of a universal or a substantial form is the result of diverse powers and dispositions: it begins with sensory experience of the individual in turn causing intellectual cognition of the same individual, from which the intellect is then able to know its form independently of the individual. Which is just what Averroes says in distinguishing the individual and its form as the two kinds of being into which all sensible being is divided; each is known by a different power when known singly for itself, and their difference by a single power acting diversely.[347] In other words, both the senses and the intellect know the individual, and the intellect knows both its form and the difference between it and the individual. Averroes's division is not therefore to be taken either as that between an individual and a universal or between real beings; for strictly no being is subdivided into other being. Rather he means that sensible beings are individuals which have both a substantial form and matter, and that the first is known as the result of knowing the second through its sensible accidents, although neither is part of the other or essential to it.[348] Only the intellect can distinguish between them, for it alone has the power of judgement. But in order to recognise difference it must know the extremes that constitute the difference. Hence it is not enough to say that the senses knows the singular and the intellect the form; the intellect must equally know both, and from such knowledge it is able to judge the difference between them.[349]

In conclusion Ockham takes the account of abstraction given in *De Anima* and

---

[345] *Ibid.*, 507–8. [346] *Ibid.*, 509–11. [347] *Ibid.*, 511–12. [348] *Ibid.*, 514.

[349] Sed quando comprehendit alietatem, tunc necessario iudicat per unam vitutem, quia sola una virtus est iudicativa illius alietatis, quia sola una virtus comprehendit utrumque

by Averroes to mean that it is the individual which is known directly and the universal indirectly by reflexion. For the images from which the universal is abstracted are themselves—as we have seen—of individuals previously sensed; and the intellect in knowing them thereby knows the images of these individuals directly. From its apprehension of the individual it can directly abstract the common concept which indicates the nature or essence of the individual—but which is not itself of the individual's essence—and from that arrive at its substantial form. It thus returns by complex or second, or propositional, knowledge, to what it first knows immediately. Subsequently it may enquire into the nature of the substantial form, whether it is simple or complex until it reaches its essence. Thus beginning with whiteness or heat previously sensed the intellect then abstracts many concepts including those of being and quality together with other connotative concepts,[350] such as 'to depend upon', 'to inhere in something else', and so on. Similarly with man, beginning with whether he is composed of matter and form, the nature of man's form, whether it is simple or composite, man's simple form or essence is finally reached, so that it is understood not in itself but in some common concept, as we shall discuss in chapter five.[351]

The coda to this question and Ockham's discussion of the primacy of individual knowledge is provided by Ockham's reply to the next, whether the individual can be known distinctly before knowing being or any other universal.[352] He answers it in one brief sentence: 'I say to the question, as before, that distinct knowledge of the individual does not necessarily require distinct knowledge of any universal for the reasons previously given.'[353] These as we have seen allow no room for the primacy of the universal because the universal, as the work of the mind, has no independent standing and must therefore always be the result of what is known independently, which is always singular.

That completes our examination of simple cognition. It rests upon the primacy of the individual known first intuitively in its existence by both the senses and the intellect, and then abstractively in the intellect alone, as the source of all evident human knowledge, individual and universal, contingent and necessary, present and past, in man's present state. In the course of establishing it, Ockham makes knowledge of the material individual at once directly accessible to the intellect and more perfect than that of a universal concept or image itself derived from

---

extremum illius alietatis, scilicet intellectus et non sensus. Et ideo non est talis processus, quod primo singulare sentitur et postea intelligitur forma, et tertio iudicatur alietas inter illa, quia omnis virtus cognitiva alietatis inter aliqua ita presupponit notitiam unius sicut alterius et ita est cognitiva unius sicut alterius . . . Est igitur iste processus, quod sensus primo sentit singulare sensibile; secundo intellectus intelligit illud idem singulare sensibile; tertio intellectus intelligit formam vel universale; et quarto iudicat differentiam inter illa, quia precognoscit utrumque; sensus autem quia non precognoscit utrumque sed alterum tantum, ideo non iudicat illam alietatem (ibid., 515–16).

[350] See chapter three, 141-3 below.
[351] Ordinatio, ibid., 516–20.
[352] Ibid., q. 7, 521.
[353] Ibid.

knowledge of individuals. He thereby reverses both the traditional Augustinian belief in the independent non-sensory origin of intelligible knowledge, as coming exclusively from the intellect, and the Christian Aristotelian—predominantly Thomist—view of universal knowledge as primary and the proper object of the intellect. In each of these he was preceded by Duns Scotus; but he surpassed Duns in making the individual alone real and always the first object known, regardless of whether or not distinctly known, and denying any role to species in its attainment. Ockham's doctrine of simple cognition thus for the first time directly contrasted individual existence with the universal nature of the concepts and knowledge to be derived from it. How he sought to explain it belongs to the next three chapters.

CHAPTER TWO

Concepts and Universals

CONCEPTS

HAVING CONSIDERED simple cognition, both of individual things and their representations in the intellect, we must now inquire into the nature of concepts and their relation, as universals, to individuals. So far as the first in concerned, we are confronted with one of the few areas of uncertainty in Ockham's system; it arises over the possible alternative explanations of a concept, above all between treating it as an image or representation (*fictum*) in the mind and as the act of knowing or intellection itself (*intellectio*). By the first it had merely conceptual status as an object of thought (*esse obiectivum*); by the second it really existed as the part of the mind sharing its being (*esse subiectivum*). We have already encountered references to these different notions in Ockham's discussion of Aureole's *esse apparens*. Ockham continued to veer between these and other interpretations intermediate to them in the *Ordinatio* before coming down finally in favour of the *intellectio* in his later works—the *Logic, Quodlibets* and Questions on the *Physics*.

Of itself the issue of the status of concepts in the mind is secondary to their status, above all as universals, in relation to what exists outside it. But the matter has a direct bearing—one of the very few—upon the chronology of Ockham's speculative and non-political writings. For that reason the sequence between his preferences for one theory over the other has been taken as one of the main pointers to the sequence of his works, receiving, in the recent study of Ockham, a prominence that is disproportionate to its intrinsic importance. We have to remember that on the main issue of the exclusively mental status of concepts Ockham never wavered; while even as a chronological guide much uncertainty remains—and will probably remain—inviting a multiplication of hypotheses hardly appropriate to their subject.

From the standpoint of chronology the main problem concerns the sequence between the books of the Commentary on the *Sentences* and the four Logical Commentaries—on Porphyry's *Isagogue* (or Introduction to Aristotle's *Categories*), Aristotle's *Categories, Interpretation*,[1] and *Sophistical Questions*. Although there is

---

[1] These three works have become known as the *Expositio Aurea*, the title to them given by Mark of Benevento, who first published them at Bologna in 1496. We shall treat them as separate treatises—as they were written.

some disagreement over the place of the Commentary on the *Physics* as well as of the order between the *Logic* and the *Quodlibets*, there can be little doubt that Ockham completed his main speculative writings before fleeing from Avignon in 1328.[2] In case of the Commentary on the *Sentences* and the Logical Commentaries, the question of which came first is further complicated by the relation between the books of the Commentary on the *Sentences* themselves. As the outcome of lectures given in the theological faculty they would, as we have said in the introduction, take two forms: an *ordinatio* consisting of the lecturer's own text revised by him for publication, and a *reportatio*, lecture notes by one of his auditors which may or may not have been corrected and authorised by the lecturer. As an *ordinatio* a commentary was fuller and more considered as well as more authoritative than a *reportatio*; it enabled an author to develop and modify his ideas where the summary and often second-hand nature of a *reportatio* held the danger of garbling them. An *ordinatio* of its nature as an author's own work lent itself to subsequent revision, some texts, such as Durandus of St Porciano's, passing through several editions or versions: a factor that could make for complications no less than the absence in a *reportatio* of an author's guiding hand.

Ockham's Commentary on the *Sentences* consisted of both forms, sharing these different traits. Book one is an *ordinatio*, in places later modified by subsequent additions; the other three books are *reportationes* of uncertain reliability and badly in need of editing.[3] We have therefore to treat the Commentary less as two different books in three different editions, as Boehner suggested,[4] than according to two and sometimes three different levels or layers; that principally entails inverting the chronological order between book one and books two to four, and secondarily distinguishing the earlier and later versions of the *Ordinatio*. The latter until recently have tended to be regarded as two different editions, a complication which in turn made the question of chronology more complicated.[5] That has now been eliminated by the editors of the first volume of the collected edition of Ockham's works, who for two redactions have substituted the distinction between an incomplete and complete version of the same text of the *Ordinatio*. The incomplete version exists in only a single manuscript (Florence, Bib. Naz., Conv. Soppr. A. 3 801); the other manuscripts contain in varying degrees the completed versions

---

[2] Three recent attempts to date Ockham's non-political writings (which as has been said came before 1328 when he fled to the Emperor, Ludwig of Bavaria) are by L. Baudry, *Guillaume d'Occam*, ch. 1 and appendix IV; P. Boehner in *Collected Articles on Ockham*, especially 99–107, 146–8, 168–74, and C. K. Brampton, 'The probable order of Ockham's non-polemical works', *Traditio* 19 (1963), 469–83, who closely follows Boehner. An exception to the division between the non-polemical and polemical periods (after 1328–*c.* 1349) must it will be recalled be made for the two shorter *Summae logicae*, discovered in Munich and Assisi. Cf. Boehner, *op. cit.*, 70–96.

[3] That applies both to the text and the authenticity of certain parts of it. Cf. Boehner, *op. cit.*, 24, 295–8. Although he considers bk. II, q. 25 to be a foreign element, he nevertheless utilises it (*ibid.*, 101), in arguing for the temporal priority of the *Sentences* over the four Logical Commentaries (on Aristotle's *Logic*).

[4] Boehner, *Collected Articles*, 112; also 100ff. and 119ff.

[5] Cf. Boehner, *ibid.* and Brampton, *art. cit.*

on which the 1495 Lyon printed edition was also based.[6] Ockham indeed made not just one series of additions, but several, so that to call any of these a redaction would mean talking of four or five redactions, a course at which the editors rightly jib, not least because it creates a false perspective of greatly modified texts. In fact, from the codiographical studies so far made on the *Ordinatio*, it remains essentially the same work in all its manuscripts, the greatest difference being precisely the introduction of the *intellectio* theory of concepts into question eight of the second distinction and brief interpolations of it elsewhere in the Prologue and among some of the other questions of the first twenty-seven distinctions of the *Ordinatio*.[7]

Of the order between the *Ordinatio* and the *Reportatio* it can be accepted that the *Ordinatio* as the revised and full edition of Ockham's lectures is subsequent to the *Reportatio*, whose books never received the same finished form. We have therefore to distinguish between them and to take each separately both in relation to the other and to the Logical Commentaries.

So far as that between the *Ordinatio* and the Logical Commentaries is concerned, there is ample evidence that the *intellectio* theory was interpolated into each. The evidence is more clear-cut for the *Ordinatio*, and we shall consider it later. Among the Logical Commentaries it occurs in the Commentary on *Perihermenias* where the matter is complicated by the confusing state of the text.[8] Ockham begins by asking whether a concept is something which exists outside the mind or an image (*fictum*) in the mind or some real quality in the mind. He then recounts four opinions of which only one, on *ficta* incompletely treated, properly corresponds to these initial questions. He then begins his answer again with three new opinions, this time reponding to the three initial questions, and concludes by replying to the objections raised against the fourth opinion of the first group which had remained unanswered. We thus have two sets of opinions, each addressed to the same problem of the nature of concepts and cutting across one another.

Boehner's explanation[9] of the discrepancy seems most likely, namely that the second group, of three opinions, was originally the first, and that the first group of four opinions was added later, though whether, as Boehner believed, because Ockham wanted to establish the *intellectio* theory as the most likely is more open to doubt, as we shall see. Boehner's reversal of the order between the two groups would seem to explain why the replies to the *fictum* theory put forward in the first group of four opinions are only resolved in the second group of three. For, if the latter had come first, then both the objections and the replies would already have been made before the four additional opinions were interpolated. That would also help to explain why the *fictum* theory in the second group of three

---

[6] *OT* I, Introduction, 19* ff. In this they were preceded by Baudry, *Guillaume d'Occam*, 267–8 who also saw no fundamental change in the original text.

[7] Boehner, *Collected Articles*, 99–105.

[8] Baudry, *Guillaume d'Occam*, 35, has noted the asymmetry; but it was Boehner, *Collected Articles*, 56 and 172–4 (text edited in *Traditio* 4 (1946), 319–35) who concluded that this was the result of an addition to the existing redaction: one wonders why he did not reach a similar conclusion from the additions to the text of the *Ordinatio*.

[9] *Collected Articles*, 172.

(on Boehner's hypothesis the first group) appears unannounced; namely, because Ockham incorporated the first part of the *fictum* theory—its exposition and objections to it—into the new group of four opinions of which it was fourth, leaving only the resolution of the objections in the original group. Even so, the outcome can hardly be called symmetrical; it takes many readings and indeed the tenacity of Boehner to give it coherence; and any student of Ockham must be grateful to Boehner for the light that his zeal has shed here and elsewhere.

Yet it has also carried with it an excess of commitment, evinced here in his arguments for the (temporal) priority of the *Reportatio* and what he took to be the first redaction of the *Ordinatio* over the Logical Commentaries. As he says, in neither the *Reportatio* nor the *Ordinatio* did Ockham consider the *intellectio* theory as a possible alternative to the *fictum* theory, the *Reportatio* not mentioning it, and the first redaction of the *Ordinatio* dismissing it. Only with the second redaction of the *Ordinatio* did Ockham recognise the claims of the *intellectio* theory, but only then, Boehner opines, equivocally. In the Logical Commentaries on the other hand, he believes that the balance of favour had tilted towards the *intellectio* theory, although Boehner also, perhaps inconsistently, concedes that the second redaction of the *Ordinatio*, despite Ockham's equivocal attitude, could have been produced after the Logical Commentaries.

Much therefore in Boehner's arguments depends upon accepting his interpretation of tone together with certain ambiguous references which—as they stand—cannot, I believe, be taken as conclusive. Before considering them mainly in juxtaposition to Baudry's counter-view that not only all four Logical Commentaries but also the *Exposition on the Physics*[10] were written before the Commentary on the *Sentences*, I should perhaps say that I agree with Boehner's rather than Baudry's chronology, both from the internal evidence and even more because the normal sequence in the scholastic career of a religious such as Ockham would have been from bachelor of the *Sentences*, when they were commented, through the second and last part of his career in the theological faculty commenting the Bible, to his own responsibilities as a teacher in a house of studies (in Ockham's case not known) belonging to his order: it is there that as a graduate in theology (although not in his case as a master) he would then have lectured on Porphyry and Aristotle.[11] That the Logical Commentaries were lectures is clear from their characteristic form of a close and inevitably repetitious exposition of the text discussed, with its division into numerous brief passages. It is difficult to see how Ockham could have been in a position to lecture on these works until he had completed his own training in theology, which would have included a Commentary on the *Sentences*. Moreover, the different circumstances of the Commentary

[10] Baudry, *Guillaume d'Occam*, 44–8. Brampton has, however, shown convincingly ('Probable order', 476) that the references to an earlier work *in logyca* in the Prologue to the Exposition on the *Physics* are to the *Summa Logicae* not to the *Expositio Aurea*, a title—as said in note 1 above—unknown in Ockham's time.

[11] Cf. my *Paris and Oxford Universities in the Thirteenth and Fourteenth Centuries* (New York, 1968) 35–6. Brampton, 'Probable order', 480–1, also thinks that Ockham lectured on Porphyry and Aristotle after he left the theological faculty.

on the *Sentences* and the Logical Commentaries would account for their different styles; what Baudry regards as the diffuseness and lack of precision as well as the calm tone of the Logical Commentaries compared with the tautness of expression in the Commentary on the *Sentences*, exaggerated as these contrasts are, spring from the two different kinds of exercise and milieux, and so cannot be treated as an index of maturity and chronology.[12]

More specifically, the main evidence for the difference between these works lies in the change from sole recognition of the *fictum* theory in the last three books of the Commentary on the *Sentences*—the *Reportatio*—to its acceptance as probable in the *Ordinatio* and the Logical Commentaries. That is enough to establish the anteriority of the *Reportatio* independently of whether or not one believes with Boehner that the degree of acceptance by Ockham of the *intellectio* theory is the measure of a work's maturity, with the greater the acceptance, the later the work.[13] The *Ordinatio*, however, is another matter, since, as we have said, it does contain references to the *intellectio* theory which are clearly in the form of additions.

For Boehner the problem of which came first, the *Ordinatio* or the Logical Commentaries, was overcome by positing two redactions of the *Ordinatio*, so that the absence of any mention of the *intellectio* in the first redaction (Florence, MS. A. 3. 801) was for him evidence that it was produced before the Logical Commentaries. That in itself would still hold, even with no subsequent redaction of the *Ordinatio*; for even if it is only incomplete, it remains true that the first redaction was written before Ockham had come to recognise the claims of the *intellectio* theory. Unfortunately this factor is counterbalanced by Boehner's equally strong case for the interpolation of the *intellectio* with that of the additional four opinions into Ockham's initial exposition in the Commentary on *Perihermenias*. Any weight therefore that we give to the additions made to the *Ordinatio* must fall equally upon those to the Commentary on *Perihermenias*. Hence we must look elsewhere for evidence of their chronology.

Here we are confronted with a number of possible cross-references in both works. The least ambiguous are two, one in the *Ordinatio*, the other in the Commentary on *Perihermenias*. The first comes in the addition to the end of distinction two, question eight to which we have already referred; there Ockham declares how he has stated elsewhere what could be said for the *intellectio* theory and how objections to it might be answered.[14] Since that does not occur earlier in the same

---

[12] *Guillaume d'Occam*, 25.

[13] 'If there is a work in which Ockham does not consider these two theories as probable and not only does not accept the "*Intellectio*-theory", but strongly embraces the "*Fictum*-theory" and rejects the other, then we must concede that such a work belongs to the first period of Ockham's philosophical and theological activity, and that such a work must have been composed prior to those in which he considers both theories at least probable' (*Collected Articles*, 100).

[14] Et posset ista opinio declarari et possent argumenta solvi contra eam, sicut alibi declaravi (*Ordinatio*, d. 2, q. 8, 291); but Boehner (*Collected Articles*, 170) is wrong to say that Ockham had earlier dismissed the *intellectio* in the same question; he only says 'Contra istam opinionem potest argui' (*Ordinatio*, ibid., 268), whereas he calls the next opinion that a universal is a species 'false' (*ibid.*, 269).

work, the obvious place would be the Commentary on *Perihermenias* where alone at this time such a discussion is to be found. The second reference, pointed out by Boehner,[15] is in the second logical Commentary, on the *Categories*: in the chapter on relation, Ockham refers to *multa alia* which he has said elsewhere on the topic; that place, correspondingly is, as Boehner rightly, I think, says, in book one, distinction thirty, question three of his Commentary on the *Sentences* which contains just such an extended discussion of the matter. The alternative is to multiply entities beyond necessity and posit a still earlier work than either the Commentary on the *Sentences* or the Logical Commentaries, since the first and preceding Logical Commentary on Porphyry does not of course treat relation.

Among the other references, two are more ambiguous but still, I think, point to priority of the *Sentences*, at least in their original form as lectures. Both are to be found in the fourth and still unpublished Logical Commentary on the *Sophistical Questions*. One is in the future tense, bracketing the Commentary on the *Sentences* with an unwritten Commentary on the *Metaphysics*. Such future reference was not uncommon with Ockham who *inter alia* envisaged commenting all Aristotle's philosophical books, only his four Logical Commentaries and three additional works on the *Physics* being completed.[16] The reference in the future to the Commentaries on the *Sentences* and *Metaphysics* reads: 'Ista responsio super metaphysicam et librum sententiarum diffusius ostendetur'. Baudry, who first noticed it, has taken it as evidence that the Logical Commentaries must have been written before the Commentary on the *Sentences*.[17] But Boehner has, with equal force, replied that the word in future tense there, *ostendentur*, 'it will be shown', refers not to the composition of the *Sentences* which he maintains Ockham had already lectured on, but to their publication in *Ordinatio* form, and more specifically to the fourth book where the matter in question, on accidents, was customarily treated.[18]

Here again, on the main issue, Boehner's explanation seems the more plausible expecially when taken in conjunction with the previous two references. The same must be said of the last reference, found also in the Commentary on the *Sophistical Questions*. This time it is to works of philosophy and to the *Sentences*. The issue turns on whether or not the word 'speak' is in the first person perfect tense (*locutus sum*) or the third person plural, present tense (*loquuntur*). Boehner, the protagonist of the first interpretation, has found this version in three of the earlier manuscripts;[19] Baudry, who upholds the second reading, takes his from only one manuscript.[20] Let us try each of them in turn. By Boehner's version we have: 'And thus I have frequently spoken of connotative terms when lecturing on both (*super*) philosophy and the *Sentences*'. By Baudry's: 'And thus they frequently speak of connotative

---

[15] Boehner, *ibid.*, 107.

[16] Baudry, *Guillaume d'Occam*, 26 ff.

[17] *Ibid.*, 32 and 262–3.

[18] Boehner, *Collected Articles*, 108–9.

[19] *Ibid.*, 108.

[20] Baudry, *Guillaume d'Occam*, 263–4. Baudry is also prepared to read *either* 'he/one speaks' (*loquitur*) *or* 'I speak': in the latter case he appears to me to concede Boehner's case, for Ockham must then be using the present historic tense to refer to what he has *already* been saying.

terms when lecturing on both philosophy and the *Sentences*'.[21] Even allowing
for the greater weight of Boehner's manuscript evidence, it is difficult to see the
point of the statement in Baudry's version, which is devoid of any real content,
and for that reason alone is out of character with Ockham's style. Baudry, it is true,
attempts to save his rendering by taking it in conjunction with the previous
reference in the future to the *Sentences*. As he says, it is hardly tenable to believe that
in so short a distance[22] Ockham moved from past to future. That would be true
enough, but only if we assume that Ockham had not yet lectured on the *Sentences*.
It is precisely that assumption which none of the references warrants.

On the contrary, what these references point to is an overlap between the
Commentary on the *Sentences* and the Logical Commentaries which is best explained by accepting an interval between Ockham's lectures on the *Sentences*,
represented for the last three books by the surviving *Reportationes*, and his redaction
of the first book as an *Ordinatio*. It would then be plausible to see the Logical
Commentaries as coming closely upon, perhaps concurrently with, the *Ordinatio*,
the very interaction between them leading Ockham to modify his view on the
nature of concepts first in the Commentary on *Perihermenias* and then in the
Ordinatio. On that showing we should be able to explain more satisfactorily the
contrast between the incomplete and complete redactions of the *Ordinatio*, not as
two set stages, but as the result of a continuing dialectic between what he had
written in his *Ordinatio* and the philosophical texts on which he subsequently
lectured. That would help to account for the frequent additions—often running,
the editors of the first volume in the new collected edition of his works say,[23] to
three and four—which he made to his *Ordinatio*.

Such a view does not differ substantially from Boehner's conclusion 'that while
he was preparing this [the *Ordinatio*] he started commenting on the philosophical
works',[24] except, of course, that it does not share Boehner's belief that there were
different redactions of the *Ordinatio*. The divergence is rather over Boehner's
approach. More often than not he has reason on his side; but in establishing his
case he too often seeks to press the evidence into too clear-cut a shape, ignoring
the nuances of which Baudry had so just an appreciation.

That is to be seen in two main respects. The first, which bears directly on the
preceding discussion, is Boehner's graduation of Ockham's commitment to the
intellectio theory in an ascending scale of 'successively as probable, more probable
and finally as the only acceptable theory'.[25] The middle stage is apparently that
of the Logical Commentaries, above all on *Perihermenias* and the Commentary on the
Physics, where 'both theories are considered to be more or less on an equal ground,
although it is safe to say that the "*intellectio* theory" is definitely preferred since it

---

[21] Et sic $\left\{ \begin{array}{l} \text{locutus sum} \\ \text{loquuntur} \end{array} \right\}$ de nominibus tam super philosophiam quam super Sententias
(*ibid.*).

[22] The references in Baudry's MS., Paris B.N. Lat. 14721, come on f. 119 d and 119 c.

[23] *OT*, I, Introduction, 20*.

[24] Boehner, *Collected Articles*, 99.

[25] *Ibid.*, 100.

now always appears in the first place'.[26] Elsewhere Boehner characterises Ockham's acceptance of the *intellectio* theory as 'still weak'.[27] Before we consider whether the comparison is justified, it must be said that if it is, Boehner would have damaged his own argument which rests upon his contention that the Commentary on *Perihermenias* is stronger in support of the *intellectio* theory than the *Ordinatio*. But if, as Boehner himself acknowledged, the addition to the *Ordinatio* was made after the Commentary on *Perihermenias*[28] and to which—as we have seen—the addition in the *Ordinatio* refers, it is incompatible to hold both (a) that the *Ordinatio* is weaker than, and so prior to, the Commentary on *Perihermenias*, and (b) to acknowledge that this very addition in the *Ordinatio*, characterised as weaker, refers to and so must be posterior to the Commentary on *Perihermenias*. Since (b) is an accomplished fact, (a) must be jettisoned as irrelevant. Is it also groundless?

Let us begin with the two texts which Boehner has here juxtaposed. In the Commentary on *Perihermenias* the decisive text which according to Boehner gives precedence to the *intellectio* theory contains this passage—of which his is only one of two versions: 'There could be another opinion that a quality of the soul [i.e. a concept] is the act of understanding itself. And because this opinion seems to me more probable than all those which make these qualities really exist in the soul, I shall thus first state the more probable way of supporting it.'[29] The other reading is that which Baudry bases upon the earlier Florence manuscript Bib. Naz. 1618—used but not followed by Boehner—and the Paris manuscript Bib. Nat. Lat. 14721. This version has the word 'of' (*de*) between 'probable' and 'all those', thus rendering the passage, 'and because this opinion seems to me the more probable of all those ...'. This second interpretation, as Baudry says, makes much better sense, for it expressly includes the *intellectio* theory in the same category as the other opinions which treat concepts as real qualities in the soul. Even if one prefers the first version, which is to say the least is obscure, since it contraposes the *intellectio* theory to all theories holding that concepts are real mental qualities, the opposition is still to those theories and not to the *fictum*. The passage cannot therefore be read in either sense as making the *intellectio* theory more probable than that of the *fictum*. Ockham's lack of preference becomes explicit when a little later he adds, 'These opinions [of *intellectio* and *fictum*] appear to me probable. Which is true and which is false let the learned discuss'.[30] There is nothing here, then, which can be justifiably construed to favour the *intellectio* over the *fictum*.

That is equally apparent in the addition to distinction two, question eight of the

---

[26] *Ibid.*, 170; also 100, and 170 where he says, 'The Commentary on *Perihermenias* ... explains both theories for the first time *in extenso*, giving, however, preference to the "*Intellectio*-theory"'.

[27] *Ibid.*, 170.

[28] *Ibid.*, 'For in an edition to this second redaction [i.e. the present complete edition as printed at Lyon in 1495] we have a reference to his Commentary on *Perihermenias* (d. 2, q. 8 T [Q]). Cf. also note 26 above.

[29] Quoted in Baudry, *Guillaume d'Occam*, 264 and discussed in appendix IV, 264–6.

[30] *Ibid.*, 265, and the Commentary on *Perihermenias*, 90d where, as Baudry points out, the equivalent expressions applied to *ficta* occur three times.

Ordinatio which opens with the words, 'He who does not like this opinion of *ficta* could equally hold that a concept exists in the soul as a quality belonging to its subject'.[31] To Boehner, we have seen, this indicated a weak reinforcement of the *intellectio* theory. But he omitted to notice that it shares its main strength or weakness with the very passage in the Commentary on *Perihermenias* which, Boehner affirmed, favoured the *intellectio* theory over the *fictum* theory; for in the addition to distinction two, question eight of the *Ordinatio*, Ockham expressly considers an *intellectio* as one of three ways in which a concept could be a quality in the soul; the other two are as the sign of a real thing existing outside the soul and as something distinct from and subsequent to the act of understanding (presumably a habit).[32] This confirms Baudry's reading, just previously discussed, that Ockham's stated preference for the *intellectio* theory in the Commentary on *Perihermenias* was one of a number of alternative notions of the concept as a quality in the soul. Hence its greater probability is only as it refers to other interpretations of a quality and is not to be set over a *fictum*. Only within the context of the *intellectio* as a quality therefore can Boehner's contention be accepted; where Ockham in the Commentary on *Perihermenias* prefers the *intellectio* theory, in the addition to distinction two, question eight of the *Ordinatio*, Ockham remains undecided between the three opinions.[33] But that is as far as Ockham's commitment extends; it has no bearing upon the *fictum*, and so Boehner's claim for a shift towards the *intellectio* theory in the Commentary on *Perihermenias* is unfounded.

More important, however, is his interpretation of Ockham's thinking on universals exclusively in terms of the antinomy between the *fictum* and *intellectio* theories. To begin with, it wrongly identifies its evolution with the progressive elimination of the *fictum* by the *intellectio*. What we have just considered disproves that; in his discussion in the *Ordinatio*, which on Boehner's showing was added after that in the Commentary on *Perihermenias*, Ockham reverted to a position of neutrality over the *intellectio*; his development cannot therefore be measured by its progressive acceptance. The same passage in the *Ordinatio* also helps to dispose of Boehner's second main misconception, namely that there were only two theories which Ockham ever seriously considered as probable. For here we have two additional theories, of a concept as a quality, which he is prepared to accept or reject equally with the *intellectio* and *fictum*. The same holds for the Commentary on *Perihermenias* where in the second group of three opinions Ockham accepts as probable an opinion that the concept is a quality in the soul, which he does not identify with an act of understanding (*intellectio*). The full ramifications should emerge in what follows. As a preliminary we can say that the issue was more than *fictum* versus *intellectio*; it was rather the concept as an object of thought—a mental construct—or as a real property of the mind existing as part of it: as such it could be the act of knowing or some other quality; and it took an extended discussion

---

[31] *Ordinatio*, *OT*, II, 289.

[32] Aliter posset poni quod ista qualitas esset aliquid aliud ab intellectione et posterius ipsa intellectione (*ibid.*, 291).

[33] Quamlibet istarum trium opinionum reputo probabilem, sed que earum sit verior relinquo iudicio aliorum (*ibid.*).

before Ockham decided in favour of the act of knowing. Even then, as we shall see, more was involved.

We must now turn to Ockham's discussion in more detail and first to the Commentary on *Perihermenias*, where he fully broached the problem of concepts. He did so expressly, coming in a logical commentary, as a digression into metaphysics. He begins with Aristotle's—whose text he was commenting—definition of a concept as an attribute of the soul (*passio anime*) which is neither a written nor a spoken word and is predicable of something else. The question to be answered is whether this concept exists as a thing outside the mind or as something real in the mind or merely as an object of thought in the mind (*ens fictum*).[34] We shall follow Ockham's order of discussion first of four opinions and then of three, recalling that the second group of three seems to represent the answers to the initial alternatives posed, and so originally to have come first.

By the first of the four opinions it could be held that a concept really inheres in the soul as a quality which is distinct from the intellect and the act of intellection but is at the same time the object of the act of intellection through which alone it exists. Such a quality is a true likeness of a real thing and so is naturally able to represent it, in the way that words are instituted to stand for real things.[35] This stress upon the concept is a natural sign, engendered naturally in the mind, as opposed to words which are conventional signs arbitrarily chosen, is central to Ockham's notion of a concept, however variously he at different times defines it. Over the truth or falsity of this opinion Ockham does not commit himself; but the difficulties which he raises tell against it; and, as we shall see, he prefers other explanations. One difficulty is that this quality would not correspond to any of the three qualities in the soul enumerated by Aristotle in the *Ethics*, book two, chapter five: that is to say it is not a habit, a passion or an act.[36] The other difficulty is that such a quality could not be an object of the intellect, because concepts are meant to correspond to words; but in this case the quality of say animal would be distinct from what the word animal signified; rather than being the object of the intellect it would be an accident even more separate, as a spiritual quality, from an animal than whiteness or heat are from physical bodies.[37]

---

[34] Secundo videndum est quid sit ista passio. Et est sciendum quod passio accipitur aliter hic et aliter in libro Predicamentorum . . . Sed in proposito accipitur passio anime pro aliquo predicabili de aliquo quod non est vox nex scriptura, et vocatur ab aliquibus intentio anime, et aliquibus vocatur conceptus. Qualis autem sit ista passio, an scilicet sit aliqua res extra animam, vel aliquid realiter existens in anima, vel aliquod ens fictum existens tantum in anima obiective, non pertinet ad logicum sed ad metaphysicam considerare. Verumtamen aliquas opiniones que possent poni circa istam difficultatem volo recitare (All references to Boehner's edition of this text in *Traditio* IV (1946), 320–335, at 321).

[35] *Ibid.*

[36] This does not correspond to Aristotle's terminology by which the things found in the soul are 'of three kinds—passions, faculties, states of character' (*Nichomachean Ethics*, bk. II, ch. 5, 1105 b, 19-20). More to the point, Ockham's inclusion of a habit as one of the things that this quality is not means that Boehner (*Collected Articles*, 56, 71-2) was mistaken in calling it a '*habitus*-theory'; Ockham did not mention a '*habitus*-theory' in either group of opinions in his Commentary on *Perihermenias*. He reiterates the argument against the next opinion.

[37] *Ibid.*, 321-2.

The second opinion that the concept could be a species in the mind—not surprisingly in view of what was said in the last chapter—Ockham rejects as more irrational than the first both on the same grounds of economy—that nothing should be posited in the soul beyond habits, passions and acts—and because these qualities could inhere in the soul, and so could propositions, without causing cognition.[38]

He finds the two more probable explanations of concepts in the third and fourth opinions. The third identifies the concept with the act of knowing (*intellectio*), thereby going beyond the first opinion; and Ockham regards it as the more probable of all those opinions which treat the concept as a real quality in the soul.[39] In its more tenable form this opinion of an *intellectio* holds that the intellect in apprehending an individual produces in itself exact cognition of this very individual as a concept: like a name (say, Socrates), it can stand for actual things; but whereas a word receives its meaning from convention, a concept is a natural sign. Once engendered, it enables the intellect to form other concepts standing for no individual in particular, like the word 'man', for example, which does not signify Plato more than Socrates.[40]

The properties of these different signs belong to the next chapter. Here, as they concern the nature of concepts, Ockham replies to possible objections. To the first, that an intellection could not be of all the individuals belonging to it—including those never known—he affirms that there can be knowledge of individuals by means of general concepts: thus the concept 'man', while referring to no individual in particular, is sufficiently like all men to enable the intellect to know that an individual man is a man and not an ass.[41] The second objection is that an act of knowing would be inadequate to form a proposition in the soul, which composed of at least subject, predicate, and copula, must originate either in things outside the soul or in other acts in the soul. Here Ockham has a number of things to say which we shall encounter in chapter four. One is that a proposition is in one sense a composite in the mind of many acts of intellection where what is stated is known confusedly: for example, the proposition 'Man is an animal' which is an act by which all men are known indistinctly by one act and all animals indistinctly by another act. It could also be regarded as an act equivalent to three acts existing together in the intellect; in that case a proposition would not be really composite but only equivalent to what is composite. The difficulty of distinguishing between the different component propositions could be met by treating them all as part of a single act of intellection equivalent to one all-embracing proposition.[42] There

---

[38] *Ibid.*

[39] Boehner's edition in *Traditio* has only, 'quia ipsa opinio videtur mihi probabilior omnibus opinionibus' (*ibid.*); so has the 1496 Bologna edition.

[40] Dico ergo quod qui vult tenere predictam opinionem potest supponere quod intellectus apprehendens rem singularem elicit unam cognitionem in se, que est tantum illius singularis que vocatur passio anime, potens ex natura sua supponere pro illa re singulari, ita quod sicut ex institutione hec vox 'Sortes' supponit pro illa re . . . ita ipsa intellectio ex natura sua sine omni institutione supponit pro re cuius est. Sed preter illam intellectionem illius rei singularis formabit sibi intellectus alias intellectiones que non magis sunt istius rei quam alterius, sicut hec vox 'homo' non magis supponit pro Sorte quam Platone (*ibid.*, *Traditio*, 322).

[41] *Ibid.*, 323–5.   [42] *Ibid.*, 324–5.

could be other variations on the same theme of one total act of intellection embracing the whole proposition composed of particular acts of intellection.[43] Finally, Ockham differentiates between the act of knowing a proposition and the act of apprehending it; the latter is equivalent to forming the proposition and so belongs to the proposition more than the act of knowing it. Accordingly what is understood in the mind by this proposition is neither simple nor composite; rather is it the act of understanding by which the mind apprehends confusedly, as in the proposition 'Every man is an animal', where what is understood is not composite but many.[44] Moreover, mental propositions unlike those spoken and written, which are composed of subject, predicate, and copula, are not invariably composite, but merely equivalent to what is composite. In that sense it would be more true to say that a proposition is not always understood when it is in the mind but only when it constitutes the act by which many things or concepts are understood, that is, when it is itself the act of knowing.[45] The act of knowing a proposition, however, is different; for then two simultaneous acts are involved: that of the proposition itself and the act of knowing it. Such a distinction does not, Ockham says, conflict with what Aristotle says and he who wishes could hold it.[46] The most appropriate way of doing so is to treat all propositions, syllogisms, concepts and everything that belongs to the mind as real beings really inhering in the mind in the way that whiteness is present in a wall or heat in fire. Then the distinction between real being outside the mind and mental being would be only one between being as a mental quality and other being.[47] This is an almost identical statement with the second opinion in the second group of three, which, as we shall see, Ockham also regards as probable.

Before we reach that, we have to consider the fourth and last opinion of the first group—that of the *fictum*. According to this, a concept is a term able to serve as either subject or predicate in a mental proposition corresponding to the same terms in a spoken proposition (*in voce*); all concepts would then be mental propositions or syllogisms or their parts.[48] But by this opinion they could be considered not as real qualities actually belonging to the mind but merely as thoughts or representations (*ficta*) or images (*idola*) without real existence.[49] On this view,

---

[43] *Ibid.*, 325–6.   [44] *Ibid.*, 326.

[45] Et ideo secundum istum modum dicendi verius esset dicendum quod propositio non semper intelligitur quando est in anima sed est quo intelliguntur res vel intellectiones anime, hoc est actus intelligendi, quia tunc propositio est actus intelligendi (*ibid.*, 327).

[46] Nec unquam invenitur ab Aristotele quod negaret duos actus intellectus posse simul esse in intellectu . . . Sic igitur qui vellet, posset tenere istam opinionem quod passiones anime de quibus loquitur Philosophus sunt intellectiones; que est opinio probabilis et concordat in ista conclusione communi cum precedentibus quod passiones anime sunt vere qualitates mentis (*ibid.*).

[47] *Ibid.* The 1496 Bologna edition is particularly unreliable here, misrepresenting 'intellectiones' by 'intentiones' throughout this opinion and replacing 'tenere' by 'negare'.

[48] Boehner, *Traditio, ibid.*

[49] Sed posset poni quod talia non sunt qualitates mentis vere, nec entia realia existentia subiective in anima; sed tantum sunt quedam cognita ab anima ita quod esse eorum non est aliud quam ipsa cognosci; et potest vocari idola secundum modum loquendi aliquorum vel ficta secundum modum loquendi aliorum (*ibid.*, 327–8).

when the intellect apprehends an individual it conceives a mental equivalent which, although not existing any more than the image in the artificer's mind of the castle he is to build exists, nevertheless possesses something which is also present in that to which it refers outside the mind.[50] The image is thereby able to stand for the thing from which it has been conceived. It can be called an attribute (*passio anime*) of the mind because it is the work of the mind; it can also be called a concept (*intentio anime*) because it has only intentional or conceptual being (*esse intentionale*) which Ockham again contrasts with the real being of a habit in the soul. As such, a *fictum* is that at which the act of knowing terminates as an object in the mind when there is no external object.[51] When common to a number of individuals it can be called a universal, referring equally to all that from which it is abstracted and enabling the mind to form propositions which give knowledge of it.[52] Unlike the first opinion of this group, the fourth treats concepts not only as objects in the intellect but also as thought objects or images devoid of real being.

The objections against this opinion carry us into the second group of opinions; before considering them we must establish their sequence. Ockham ends the fourth opinion and the first group having only posed the difficulties against the *fictum* theory; their resolution comes only at the end of the second group. In between are the three opinions which, prefaced by Aristotle's definition of a concept, reopen the entire question of its nature. Of these the *fictum* theory is the last and the only one which strictly corresponds to any of the four opinions in the preceding group; furthermore, the two treatments are given continuity by sharing the same objections and replies, since there can be little doubt that the replies at the end of the third opinion fit the objections at the end of the fourth opinion. There is a further point which would help to explain their separation in less fundamental terms than Boehner's.[53] It is that Ockham in his statement of the *fictum* theory in the third opinion refers to what he has already said about it (*sicut tactum est*);[54] this must mean in the previous opinion where, as we shall see, his first three arguments against the concept as a quality were counter-claims for the concept as a *fictum*. By the time, then, he came to the latter in the third opinion he had already argued the case for and against it at length; that would account also for the brevity of its treatment in the third opinion. It would also have enabled him to transfer the objections against it to the subsequent—fourth opinion in the first group—where it should be added, he expounds it a good deal more fully without impairing its

---

[50] *Ibid.*, 328.

[51] Et propter istam causam potest supponere in propositione pro re ex qua fingitur, et potest vocari passio anime pro eo quod non habet nisi per operationem anime; potest etiam vocari intentio anime, pro eo quod non est aliquid reale in anima, ad modum quo habitus est aliquid reale in anima, sed tantum esse intentionale scilicet esse cognitum in anima (*ibid.*).

[52] *Ibid.*

[53] *Collected Articles*, 172–3. I also find it hard to understand why Boehner (*ibid.*, 173) also claims that his view that the four opinions were added afterwards—with which I agree— explains why a quotation from Averroes on the *Metaphysics* was omitted in the first opinion of the second group of three (o in his edition) but given later (s in his edition): for both of them came in the same second opinion and so have no bearing upon the other group of four opinions.

[54] Boehner's edition (*Traditio* 4), 334.

intelligibility; for the third opinion in the second group is really an addendum to what has been said in the second opinion, knowledge of which it already presupposes. That is not to pretend that the abstraction of the objections from the third opinion is anything but unsatisfactory and muddling; but in itself it does nothing to sustain Boehner's belief that Ockham had thereby demoted the *fictum* theory and was no longer particularly concerned to defend it. Moreover such a view is also inherently improbable: firstly, because Ockham's preceding discussion of the competing claims of the *fictum* and *intellectio* theories in the second opinion shows how closely balanced he found the arguments for and against the two theories. Secondly, the *fictum* theory was the only one which he treated twice in almost identical terms: hence, the very fact that he was prepared to make use of the same arguments in favour of the *fictum* on both occasions must lead to the opposite conclusion from Boehner's, namely that Ockham continued to adhere to his original position—as appropriate a reason as any for its retention unchanged.

Let us begin with the objections stated at the end of the fourth opinion; they are of two main kinds: the first is over the difficulty of reconciling *ficta* known by a real act of knowing with their non-existence in whole or in part as either substances or accidents in the real world. The second objection concerns the difference in kind between *ficta* as mere thought objects (*ens rationis*) and as real things (*ens reale*) which *ficta* are supposed to represent: *ens rationis* and *ens reale* differ more completely than any two real things can differ. Therefore a *fictum* is much less able to stand for a real thing, and so will be less universal than an *intellectio* which has real being as part of the soul. From this it could be argued that a *fictum* is superfluous, since an *intellectio*, in being closer to real things, is better able to provide the knowledge of them ascribed to *ficta*.[55]

Before considering Ockham's replies, let us look at the arguments in favour of *ficta* with which he opposed the quality theory in the preceding second opinion. That *ficta* exist independently of what exists outside the mind is, he says, a fact shown by the mind's ability to conceive imaginary beings (*figmenta*) like the chymera or stag-goat or golden mountain which have no correspondence to anything real; similarly, a builder can devise a castle in his mind before he has built it. In the second place, being can be divided into that which is in the mind and that which is outside it; the latter can be in turn subdivided into the ten categories. But what of the former? Either it can be accepted for a real quality belonging to the mind itself; it would then come under the category of quality and so be among the ten categories into which—as we shall discuss in the next chapter—all being outside the mind is divided. Or it can be taken for what is not really in the mind but only for what is known: as such it can be an object of thought in which case it is a *fictum*. Or again it is really in the soul of the knower, in the way that any real being exists, from which it would then be indistinguishable, contradicting the proposition that mental and real being differ. That also contradicts what Averroes says in his Commentary on the *Metaphysics*, book six, that acts of forming propositions in the intellect are not found in being outside the

[55] *Ibid.*, 328–9.

intellect which is divided into ten categories. Hence the two are not the same.[56]

That is as far as Ockham takes the arguments in favour of *ficta* in the second opinion; we shall consider shortly his counter-arguments. But first we must return to the third opinion and to the remaining answers there to the other objections against the *fictum* theory. In support of his preceding contention that there can be images of non-existents, such as the chymera or a golden mountain, Ockham distinguishes between *ficta* to which there can be no real correspondence outside the mind and *ficta* which are or can be similar to real things; *ficta* of the second kind are called universals. On the basis of this distinction Ockham then answers the second objection that *ficta* differ more from real things than real things differ from one another. He agrees; even so a *fictum* when also a universal is closer to a real thing in this respect, that if it could be realised, it would be like something which was real. Accordingly, it can stand for real things better and more universally and intelligibly than any other quality.[57]

So much for Ockham's defence of *ficta* which as we have stressed is unchanged for both groups of opinions. The case against them is also the case for the concept as a quality in the soul: that constitutes the second opinion of the second group. Ockham regards both these opinions as probable, having dismissed as absurd and destructive of all philosophy and knowledge the first opinion that the concept was a real thing which could exist outside the mind as a universal.[58] In the second opinion Ockham does not yet specify what this quality in the soul is; and Boehner is probably right in supposing that only subsequently did Ockham come to a more precise conception, substituting three alternative opinions of a quality in the first group for the single opinion in what was originally the second group.[59] In this form Ockham likens a quality in the soul to the whiteness inhering in a wall or coldness in water:[60] it will be recalled that he employed the same analogy between concepts as qualities and physical properties in the third opinion of the first group. In the second opinion the analogy is supported by reference to Averroes on the seventh book of the *Metaphysics*,[61] that universals are mental qualities which when not written or spoken are in themselves numerically one and simple and are universal only by predication and representation.[62] This opinion would have the opposite implications from those of the *fictum*: by it, nothing would be conceivable unless it were or could be real.[63]

In meeting the opposing arguments—just adumbrated—in favour of *ficta*, Ockham distinguished the ways in which a term could stand in a proposition. We shall discuss his theory of supposition in the next chapter; as employed here

---

[56] *Ibid.*, 330–1.   [57] *Ibid.*, 335.

[58] Sic igitur ultimas opiniones reputo probabiles (*ibid.*). For an almost identical reading, cf. Baudry, *Guillaume d'Occam*, 35, n. 5. The 1496 Bologna edition has 'Illas tres opiniones reputo probabiles', which of course makes nonsense of the preceding rejection of the first opinion, as 'omnino absurdam et destruentem totam philosophiam Aristotelis et omnem scientiam et omnem veritatem et rationem, et quod est pessimus error in philosophia' (Boehner, *ibid.*, 329).

[59] *Collected Articles*, 172–3.   [60] Boehner's edition, 329.   [61] *Ibid.*, 327.   [62] *Ibid.*, 330.

[63] Et si tenet istam diceret quod nihil est imaginabile nisi sit ens reale vel possit esse vel aliquid aggregans talia que sunt vel esse possunt entia realia (*ibid.*).

he pointed to the different meaning that a word like 'chymera' could have accord-ing to whether it was taken for itself (*suppositio materialis*) as a word, or for a concept (*suppositio simplex*), or as signifying something real which was a chymera (*suppositio personalis*). Only in the last case is a chymera nothing; as a word or a concept it exists as a physical sound or in the mind. Accordingly in both these senses concepts could really inhere in the mind and not merely as objects of thought as the *fictum* theory maintained.[64] Without dwelling on Ockham's use of supposition, this is one example of the central role it played in his attempt to establish the appropriate level of discourse, above all in differentiating between the conceptual and the ontological.

Strictly speaking, then, every figment is a real thing as even a lie is real, when taken for the word itself or for a mental act of understanding. What distinguishes figments and lies from real things is that they do not correspond to what exists *in re*; it is in that sense that they are untrue.[65]

That Ockham was already thinking of the concept in terms of an *intellectio* can be seen both from this reference to an act of understanding and from his reply to the second argument previously, where he says that to conceive a castle in the mind is to produce particular intellections.[66] But he had not yet differentiated it as the clear alternative which it becomes in the other group of four opinions.

The replies to the other objections are mainly alternative glosses on Averroes's texts. Thus Ockham interprets the image of a castle in the artificer's mind not as an object but as his knowledge of a castle and his ability to build one, which on Averroes's analogy of health (*Metaphysics*, book seven) is a form existing in the mind as well as a habit in the body. Similarly, in the division between mental and external being, the former can be understood as being which really exists in the mind as a concept or other quality under which category all the other categories are contained. In that way all mental concepts, propositions, and syllogisms, are both real and yet mental qualities which belong to the mind as their subject.[67]

The Commentary on *Perihermenias* thus presents Ockham almost equally divided between the claims of *fictum* and *intellectio*. What he says there alone hardly justifies the view that the *intellectio* theory was yet in the ascendant: merely that—in the likelihood that the group of four opinions represented his final view—it had ousted alternative explanations of the concept as a mental quality. Only when we relate this development to the whole tendency of his thought to economy and to the establishment of the *intellectio* theory in his later works can we read more into the emergence of the *intellectio* in the Commentary on *Perihermenias*. We can then see that the *intellectio* provided Ockham with the best means of overcoming

---

[64] *Ibid.*, 331–2.

[65] Ad istud potest dici quod potest concedi de virtute sermonis quod omne figmentum est vera res, sicut omne mendacium est vera res, quia si sit mendacium vocale, est vera vox vel voces. Similiter si sit mendacium mentale est vera intellectio vel intellectiones vel alias qualitates ... quia una res magis dicitur figmentum quam alia non quando sit vera res positiva, sed quando tali non correspondet aliquid in re quale denotatur sibi correspondere (*ibid.*, 333).

[66] Quando aliquis fingit castrum vel huiusmodi non aliter fingit nisi quia elicit talem vel tales intellectiones (*ibid.*, 332).

[67] *Ibid.*, 333.

the problem of *ficta* as simply images and yet also as representations of real things, as well as keeping the mind clear of anything which could be misconstrued as intelligible species. At the same time, Ockham also recognised that the mind could know—abstractively—what no longer exists; hence it must possess images. The question was whether it knew things existing outside the mind through images inhering in the mind as objects of thought, or directly by an act of intellection as itself the natural sign for real things, in the way described by the third opinion of the second group of four. By either mode, however, concepts were exclusively mental as the work of the mind; to that overriding truth all other considerations were subordinate.[68]

Turning now to the *Ordinatio*, distinction two, question eight, where Ockham treats concepts as part of the problem of universals, we find, as we have said, a similar development to that in *Perihermenias*. Originally four opinions were considered and dismissed in favour of the probability of a *fictum* as a concept. Subsequently three more opinions of a concept as a quality, including an *intellectio*, were added. These did not displace the *fictum* but were presented equally as probable, leaving the question—once again—open.

Of the four opinions—for the most part variations upon those previously encountered—the first is that of a concept as an *intellectio*, by which as a universal it represents what is known confusedly; and the more indifferent its knowledge the more universal it is. Against this opinion Ockham argues that a concept or universal[69] so defined would refer to nothing outside the mind and so could be about nothing; nor does it meet the accepted definition of a concept as the object of the intellect's act of knowing, for it could be anyone's object.[70] The second opinion, and the one most abhorrent to Ockham, is that the universal could be a species in the intellect and called universal because it bears equally upon everything individual; moreover in itself it too is singular but universal by representation. Ockham denies that a species can be a concept on two counts. The first is that a concept is known by abstraction, but a species, if known, could only be known in itself intuitively or in something else; in that case, that in which it was known would in turn be a universal in relation to a species, and this second universal could then itself only be known in relation to a further universal, and so on infinitely. The alternative is that a species is not a universal.[71] Secondly, in not being abstracted, a species would be generated, since it would be a real quality in the intellect, a conclusion which Ockham does not accept.[72]

---

[68] Que tamen sit vera et que falsa studiosi discutiant. Hoc tamen apud me est omnino certum quod nec passiones anime nec universalia aliqua sunt res extra animam et de essentia rerum singularium sive sint concepte sive non concepte (*ibid.*, 335).

[69] *Ordinatio*, d. 2, q. 8, 267–8.   [70] *Ibid.*

[71] Sed ista opinio videtur esse falsa, quia sicut alias declarabitur, talis species non est necessaria. Secundo quia universale ponitur illud quod intelligitur per abstractionem intellectus, sed illa species non sic intelligitur, quia aut intelligitur in se, et sicut alias patebit, tunc necessario primo intelligitur intuitive, aut intelligitur in alio; et per consequens sicut alias patebit, illud aliud est universale respectu illius. Et tunc quero de illo sicut prius, et ita vel erit processus in infinitum vel species non erit universalis (*ibid.*, 269).

[72] *Ibid.*

That leads to the third opinion, that a universal is a real thing which results from an act of intellection. Ockham does not call this thing a quality, though it corresponds closely to the quality theory stated in the second opinion of the second group in the Commentary on *Perihermenias*. He does, however, expressly deny that it is a habit, despite Boehner's designation of it as such, 'because everything that is in the intellect is an act or a passion or a habit, but this thing cannot be any of these'.[73]

Where all these three opinions agree is in treating the universal as something real and singular in itself but common to real things outside the mind through a natural similarity, in virtue of which it could, like a statue, stand for real things indifferently, not engendering knowledge of one thing rather than another. That would apply equally to a species or a habit as well as to an intellection. Ockham does not believe that they can be easily proved or disproved, unlike those against which he argues elsewhere—presumably those which treat universals as real things existing in *rerum natura*.[74] Indeed, at this initial stage, before he revised his opinion about the *intellectio*, he was clearly predisposed against any tendency to treat the concept as real, even as an attribute of the intellect. On the other hand Ockham was not a nominalist. The distinction between natural and conventional signs was fundamental to his thinking; and for that reason he does not accept the fourth opinion, that a universal is a conventional sign, a word which unlike a thing is predictable of many individuals and so a universal. If that were true, Ockham replies, nothing would be naturally genus or species; and God himself, or any natural thing, could as well be a universal as something in the mind.[75]

His own preference is for the final opinion, that the concept is a *fictum* inhering in the mind as an object of thought without existence either in the mind or outside it. As such it arises through the formation in the mind of an image of something seen outside it; so that if the mind had the power to reproduce it as real, the image would be of the same kind as the thing seen, differing from it only numerically.[76] In that respect the process is analogous to the way in which a builder constructs a house, beginning with the image in his mind derived from houses already in existence, and realising his own conception in an actual house which will differ from other houses only as one more of the same kind. In each case the *fictum* acts as the exemplar of individual things; it can be called a universal just because it refers indifferently to all individuals which share a common likeness and for which it can stand. For that reason it is a universal by abstraction and not by generation.[77]

The strength of Ockham's commitment to the *fictum* at this stage can be seen

---

[73] *Ibid.*, 269–70.   [74] *Ibid.*, 270.   [75] *Ibid.*, 271.

[76] Ideo potest aliter dici probabiliter quod universale non est aliquid reale habens esse subiectivum, nec in anima nec extra animam, sed tantum habet esse obiectivum in anima, et est quoddam fictum habens esse tale in esse obiectivo quale habet res extra in esse subiectivo. Et hoc per istum modum quod intellectus videns aliquam rem extra animam fingit consimilem rem in mente, ita quod si haberet virtutem productivam sicut habet virtutem fictivam, talem rem in esse subiectivo—numero distinctam a priori—produceret extra (*ibid.*, 271–2). Also d. 13, q. 1, 1.

[77] *Ordinatio, ibid.*, 272.

both from the space he devotes to discussing it[78] and in the stress upon its exclusively conceptual nature, which is what distinguishes it from the other opinions. His thinking displays a markedly Augustinian cast in the attention he gives to the formation of concepts. Some of his arguments we have already met. Thus he takes Aristotle's division between mental and extramental being to show the inapplicability of the ten categories to concepts in the mind. As Aristotle himself declared, the categories refer only to being which is outside the mind.[79] If, however, intellections had real being they would then fall under the category of quality and, together with all accidents in the mind, would be real qualities informing the mind in the way that heat and whiteness inform physical bodies. The same would hold for figments in the mind: chymera and stag-goat would then be real things; so would mental propositions and syllogisms, and all images, whether those in the mind of an artificer or ideas of creatures in the mind of God before they were created. There would correspondingly be no distinction between first and second intentions and all distinctions of reason which are commonly not regarded as real. Concepts must therefore be *ficta* which exist only as objects in the mind.[80] It is thus as an object of the act of knowing that the mind knows a concept as a universal, since it is certainly not a real thing. Similarly it is as an object that a concept can remain invariable and so able to stand for a number of species in virtue of not being any of them.[81]

Psychologically a universal concept could be regarded as the mental counterpart of a universal term in a proposition which is written or spoken. Just as the latter is instituted by convention to be the subject of a proposition, without standing for something real, so can a concept be naturally the subject of a mental proposition and stand for nothing real existing outside the mind: the difference is that a concept is formed through abstraction from individual things previously known.[82] Unlike spoken or written words it is not a real thing.

At this point Ockham turns for confirmation to St Augustine's *De Trinitate*.[83] This excursus shows the Augustinian foundation of Ockham's *fictum* theory. Once abandoned he no longer had recourse to the psychological explanation of the formation of images which St Augustine's insight provided. Nowhere is it more in evidence in Ockham's outlook than here before he subsequently abandoned its impedimenta for the simplicity of the *intellectio*. In the first place, Ockham takes over from St Augustine the notion that the mind always forms images of things of which it has knowledge but does not actually encounter. The image may bear a true likeness to the real thing, although more often it does not. But in any case it is derived from experience of real things and bears equally upon all individuals of the same kind as an object in the mind. Thus in Augustine's example from book eight of *De Trinitate*, someone hearing or reading the words of St Paul conjures up a picture of a living man from a concept of man in the soul gained from previous

---

[78] *Ibid.*, 271–81.   [79] *Ibid.*, 273.   [80] *Ibid.*, 273–4.   [81] *Ibid.*, 274–5.

[82] Posset igitur dici quod sicut vox est universalis et genus et species, sed tantum per institutionem, ita conceptus sic fictus et abstractus a rebus singularibus precognitis est universalis ex natura sua (*ibid.*, 276).

[83] *Ibid.*, 276–89.

experience of individual men. The same applies to the image of Christ as a man drawn from the same concept we have of man as a species, or to a town that we have never seen but only heard of; the details formed from our own conception will not agree with many of the real details, but the man or town will be recognisable as such.[84]

In the second place, Ockham interprets these examples to mean that the *fictum* stands not for itself but for the thing imagined. Thus someone who forms the concept of whiteness from something white does not regard the image itself in his mind as white, nor attributes to it the properties of whiteness, such as colour and so on; rather, just because he cannot conceive of everything which is really white he employs an image to stand for all white things.[85]

In the third place, then, St Augustine treated all mental concepts as representations of real things, calling them variously image, likeness, picture, phantasm, species.[86] Ockham takes this to mean that to St Augustine *ficta* were objects known by the intellect; they could therefore be the universal terms in a proposition standing for all the things to which they were common.[87] Finally, *ficta* as mental images reside, according to St Augustine, in the memory immediately inclining the mind through a habit to know them; they therefore approximate to potential knowledge, since from their presence in the mind the intellect can bring them into conceptual existence. That is not possible for things outside the mind.[88]

Thus Ockham on Augustine. He completes the discussion of *ficta* by replying to five objections.[89] The first two are familiar from the Commentary on *Perihermenias*. To the first, that whatever is known in the mind as a mental object (*esse obiectivum*) must really exist in nature, since everything must be either substance or accident, he says that the intellect can imagine non-existents just as God before their creation had the ideas of beings which did not yet exist. The categories of substance and accident belong only to what is outside the mind. The second objection, that *ficta* have no real similarity with things outside the mind and less than that of substance and accident, Ockham acknowledges; nevertheless the intellect can produce concepts with a likeness to things just as it can conceive what has no likeness. That helps to answer the third objection that *ficta* are not universals, because if translated into reality, like the architect's image of a house, they would be singular, numerically distinct from other houses and only common in kind. As concepts *ficta* are not of the same nature as the things they represent: the image of a man or an animal is not a real man or animal, just because it is in the mind. That does not, however, mean that universals are mere figments with no correspondence to what is real; a *fictum* is a universal in virtue of its likeness to real things.

On the other hand, they have to be distinguished from logical terms, cathegorematic, syncathegorematic, connotative, negative, which are also universals. These

---

[84] *Ibid.*, 276–8.

[85] Unde quia non potest omnem albedinem extra cogitare, utitur illo ficto pro omni albedine *ibid.*, 277).

[86] *Ibid.*, 279; also 281.   [87] *Ibid.*   [88] *Ibid.*, 279–81.   [89] *Ibid.*, 281–9.

are the work of convention not nature; and so are not derived, as the fourth objection maintained, from things in the way that *ficta* are abstracted from real individuals. We shall consider the logical role of universals and other terms in chapter three. A similar distinction applies to the fifth objection, that words cannot be universal for then they would be genera and species, so destroying the whole order of categories. Ockham replies that a word can itself be a universal by institution, and thus a genus or a species equally able to signify what is true or false or necessary or impossible, as it is true to say that man is an animal and impossible that man is an ass. To deny that would be to deny that we could speak or write truth or falsity and other absurdities abhorrent to all human association.

This is Ockham's most complete discussion of the *fictum*; in relation to the preceding four opinions there can be little doubt that initially he favoured it of all possible explanations. But he never identified himself with it, never calling it more than probable and always employing the third person and subjunctive to speak of it.

Subsequently, however, as we have said, he added another section restating the quality theory. That, too, is far from being an unqualified affirmation, least of all of the *intellectio*, which is only one among three alternatives each declared equally probable.[90] That is largely compensated for by the references to his fuller discussion elsewhere,[91] which as we have seen earlier, must mean the Commentary on *Perihermenias*. Even so, there is nothing at this stage to indicate preference for the *intellectio* theory; indeed the main part of the addition is devoted to stating the case for the concept as a natural quality in the soul, which Ockham appears to consider opposed to either of the two alternative theories.[92] By it the concept or universal could be regarded as a real quality of the mind and a natural sign for things outside it, as a word is a conventional sign; and just as some words signify real things, so do some concepts. This attribute seems no more unlikely than the capacity of both men and animals to make sounds which denote certain things. The difference is that whereas the latter represent merely their own feelings and what is particular to them, the mind by its greater power can produce qualities which refer naturally to everything. Hence this opinion would accept that any universal or general genus was in itself something singular and determinate, and only universal by predication in being able to stand for other things. The categories of substance would then consist of qualities related as superior and inferior according to whether they stand for more or fewer individuals, as genera and species do naturally, and words do by convention. Moreover, so long as substance is itself taken as a concept or term and not as a real thing, then it is true to say that it is a real quality.

So much for the revised quality theory, which it will be seen, has important logical ramifications which we shall again meet in the next chapter. At this point

[90] *Ibid.*, 289–92. A pointer to its later derivation is in the use of the word 'concept' where previously he had employed only 'universal'.

[91] *Ibid.*, 291.

[92] *Ibid.*, 289–91.

Ockham sets against it the *intellectio* theory and the earlier third opinion namely that a concept is a quality distinct from and subsequent to the act of understanding. Neither is developed; each is equally probable; and all three could be used to answer the *fictum* by the alternative view that a concept is a quality in the soul, as he has argued at greater length elsewhere.[93]

Ockham's position at the end of this discussion is comparable to that reached in the Commentary on *Perihermenias*, except that in the latter work he reduced the different versions of a concept as a quality to an *intellectio*. That both these works, however, contain additional restatements indicates the fluctuation in Ockham's views at this time. His own closing words on the matter in the *Ordinatio* express both his uncertainty over the exact nature of concepts and his certainty that whatever else they may or may not be, they do not exist independently of the mind:

> I consider any of these three opinions [i.e. on the concept as a real quality] as probable; but which one is more true I leave to the judgement of others. This, however, I do maintain, that no universal, save perhaps by convention (*per voluntariam institutionem*), is something which exists in any way outside the soul, but that all which is naturally predicable of many is in the mind, whether as part of it (*subiective*) or as an object (*obiective*) and does not belong to the essence or nature of any (other) substance. The same holds for the other conclusions rejected in previous questions. In reply to the principal argument, I say that what first moves the intellect is not a universal but an individual, and so the individual is first known by primacy of generation as will be later shown.[94]

Ockham did not reach a resolution between *fictum* and *intellectio* or its variants in the *Ordinatio*. As we saw in the preceding chapter, he continued to pose them as equally plausible in questions two and three of distinction twenty-seven at which his revision of the text ended. Moreover, neither there nor in any of the earlier parts of the *Ordinatio* did the addition of an *intellectio* or quality as alternatives to a *fictum* modify the argument into which they were interpolated—which is perhaps the best indication of the peripheral nature of the problem.

What then led Ockham to change his mind in favour of concepts as intellections? Perhaps the clearest explanation comes in the *Quodlibets*, where in common with the *Logic* and the *Questions on the Physics* Ockham unqualifiedly rejects a *fictum*. The *fictum*, he says in the fourth *Quodlibet*, impedes knowledge; it is not cognition nor something known outside the intellect nor both together, but a third thing, coming between cognition and the thing known. Hence if a *fictum* is known, the thing outside the intellect is not known; and when we form a mental proposition—

---

[93] Verumtamen ista opinio posset diversimode poni: uno modo quod ista qualitas existens subiective in anima esset ipsamet intellectio; et posset ista opinio declarari, et possent argumenta solvi contra eam, sicut alibi declaravi. Aliter posset poni quod ista qualitas esset aliquid aliud ab intellectione et posterius ista intellectione. Et tunc posset responderi ad motiva pro opinione illa de fictis in esse obiectivo sicut tactum est alibi, ubi magis expressi istam opinionem de intentione anime seu conceptu, ponendo quod sit qualitas mentis (*ibid.*, 291).

[94] *Ibid.*, 291–2. Ockham's final explanation of *intellectio* was almost the same as Walter Chatton's, who attacked the *fictum* explanation. It may have influenced Ockham. See G. Gál, 'Gualteri de Chatton et Guillelmi de Ockham Controversia', *FcS* 27 (1967), 191–212.

say, that God is three and one—we do not know the thing itself (God) to which the proposition refers, but the *fictum*—an absurd conclusion.[95] Ockham thus came to regard *ficta* in much the same way as Aureole's *esse apparens*, as an intermediary between the intellect and its object. He accordingly rejected it on many of the same grounds, above all of superfluity, which he states in the *Logic* as follows:

> But what is this thing in the mind? What is such a sign? It should be said that there are diverse opinions over this matter. Some say that it is nothing but something conceived (*fictum*) by the mind. Others say that it is a certain quality really existing in the mind distinct from the act of knowing. Others say that it is the act of knowing, and for these the reason is this, that it is vain to do by more what can be done by fewer. But everything that is saved by positing something distinct from the act of knowing can be saved without such a distinction, so that to stand for something else and signify something else can as well belong to the act of knowing as to another sign. Therefore nothing else beyond the act of knowing should be posited.[96]

This summary dismissal of the alternatives to an *intellectio* constitutes the whole of Ockham's discussion of the nature of concepts in the *Logic*.

In the other two works just mentioned his discussion is fuller. In the fourth *Quodlibet* he begins his case against *ficta* along similar lines. If, he says, two things suffice to verify a proposition, a third is superfluous; but all agree that propositions such as 'Man is known', 'Man is a subject', 'Man is a species', which contain a mental object (*esse fictum*) are verified of real things and so must be true; for if knowledge of a man is posited in the intellect, the proposition 'Man is known' cannot be false. The same applies to other propositions.[97] More specifically, *ficta*, in addition as we have already said to impeding knowledge of things, would, as concepts, be eternally inseparable from knowledge of things, which would mean—falsely—that God could not destroy them. Nor is a *fictum* to be posited as the condition of a subject and predicate in a universal proposition. An act of knowing suffices for that, because an individual known both in itself and as a representation by a *fictum* is also known by an act; otherwise a *fictum* could be known independently of an act knowing it as an object of thought, which is impossible.[98] Accordingly, whenever a *fictum* is posited, so is an act of knowing. For that reason, in virtue of the dependence of a *fictum* upon an act of knowing, God could cause an act of knowing without a *fictum*, but not *vice versa*.[99] This shows clearly the distinction between the presence in the mind of *ficta* as objects of thought, which Ockham never denied, and their directly representational character, which Ockham did now deny. As we have seen in both the Commentary on

---

[95] Preterea tale fictum impedit cognitionem rei; ergo non est ponendum propter cognitionem. Assumptum probatur, quia illud nec est cognitio nec albedo extra cognita nec ambo simul, sed quoddam tertium medium inter cognitionem et rem. Ergo si illud fictum intelligitur tunc res extra non intelligitur; et tunc quando formo hanc propositionem mentalem, 'Deus est trinus et unus', non intelligo deum in se, sed illud fictum; quod videtur absurdum (*Quodlibet* IV, q. 35).

[96] *SL*, I, ch. 12, 39.   [97] *Quodlibet* IV, q. 19.   [98] *Ibid.*

[99] Preterea non est contradictio quod deus faciat cognitionem talem sine tale ficto essentialiter, sed contradictio est quod ponatur in intellectu quando [following MS. Bib. Nat. 17841 (q. 19)] aliquid intelligatur; ergo non est ponendum propter intentionem communem (*ibid.*).

Perihermenias and in the *Ordinatio*, the arguments against a *fictum* had been its non-existence, as merely an object of thought, and hence its lack of correspondence with things which did exist. It is this descrepancy that now disqualifies *ficta*, as exclusively mental, from directly representing what is real. Instead the act of knowing has the attributes of signifying all things of the same nature with which earlier Ockham—under the influence of St Augustine—had endowed a *fictum*. In his own words, 'So I say that both a first and second intention [i.e. concepts][100] are really an act of knowing, because by an act [of knowing] everything can be saved which is saved by a *fictum*. For an act [of knowing] in being the likeness of a subject can signify and stand for real things, can be subject and predicate, genus and species and so on, as a *fictum* can'.[101]

The same conclusion is reached in the *Questions on the Physics*, probably the latest of Ockham's speculative writings and his most systematic discussion of concepts. Of the first seven questions devoted to them, five restate the arguments against concepts as *ficta*[102] or as real things outside the intellect[103] or as species or habits[104] or as the object of an act of knowing.[105] The arguments are familiar from the preceding discussions. Those in the first question against *ficta* are the most comprehensive. A concept is not a *fictum*, first, because all propositions can be verified by one mental act; second, because a *fictum* would impede knowledge; third, because there would be an eternal order of infinite species; fourth, because there can be subject and predicate without a *fictum*; fifth because God can cause an act of knowing without a *fictum* (Ockham here refers to what he has said in the fourth *Quodlibet*); sixth, because it is hard to conceive how there can be a real act of intellection by a concept which itself is without real existence; and seventh, because an image differs more from anything else than things differ among themselves; hence it is less assimilated to real things and less able to stand for them and has less universality than a concept, as a natural sign, has.

A concept as an act of knowing on the other hand is also a mental quality: that does not reduce it to the same status as something purely imaginary, like the chymera or golden mountain or the house in the architect's mind or a lie, because, as Ockham has replied before in the Commentary on *Perihermenias* and the *Ordinatio*, the latter stand only for themselves without real signification; they therefore have only simple or material supposition whereas concepts have real signification and stand in personal supposition for what exists outside the mind.[106] *Ficta*, therefore, unlike concepts, can be said to be qualities only to the extent that they are words. If for no other reason, as we shall see in the next chapter, Ockham's adoption of the theory of supposition would have precluded him from being a nominalist in the eleventh- and twelfth-century sense of regarding words merely as physical sounds (*flatus vocis*). It is precisely their representational quality which distinguishes concepts from mere mental pictures. As Ockham expresses it in the fourth question, 'Not every likeness in the mind is a concept of a thing but only of that which is

[100] See chapter 3, 128–30 below.
[101] *Quodlibet* IV, q. 19.   [102] *Questions on the Physics*, q. 1.
[103] *Ibid.*, q. 2.   [104] *Ibid.*, q. 4.   [105] *Ibid.*, q. 5.   [106] *Ibid.*

actual knowledge or at least requires actual knowledge'. That can only be achieved by an act of knowing which, as itself a concept, does not have a quality for an object any more than it has a *fictum*.[107] When the concept is common to many individuals one individual is not better known than another; they are merely distinguished as members of one class from those of another class, as the concept 'man' distinguishes a man from an ass but not one man from another. A singular concept on the other hand gives proper knowledge.[108]

In the seventh and last question on concepts Ockham describes how a concept is an act of knowing. When the intellect apprehends a mental sign (*intentio*) which stands for something real, it thereby gains intuitive knowledge of the thing itself. Thus just as a word—say, Socrates—denotes an individual man, so that in hearing or seeing the word the intellect knows that it is affirmed of Socrates, so the intellect in having a concept of Socrates knows Socrates. The difference is that a concept signifies things naturally where a word does so by convention. Similarly from individual concepts the intellect can form common or universal concepts of many individuals belonging to the same or different species. Hence concepts of both genus and species are caused in the same way as individual concepts, from intuitive knowledge of individuals.[109] The logical consequences of this standpoint will become apparent in the next chapter where genus and species directly signify only individuals and not universal natures or essences.

That completes discussion of the nature of concepts; its resolution, received in the later three of the five works over which it extends, consists in identifying concepts with the act of knowing and subordinating *ficta* to mere objects of thought, which may or may not bear a likeness to real things, but are not their natural signs. That is reserved for acts of knowing what is real. Accordingly, unlike *ficta*, which have purely mental status as what is known in the intellect, concepts are real in virtue of signifying what exists outside the intellect.

The difficulty with this explanation is that it does not distinguish between knowing a concept and knowing a thing. If, as Ockham stresses, a concept is neither something real outside the mind nor an image in the mind, but the act of knowing in itself as a natural sign, either the sign must be known before the thing signified; in which case it will be known in the mind as a likeness. The *concept* would then be a *fictum*, which Ockham denies. Alternatively, if the thing signified is known directly, every act of knowing something real will be equally a concept; there will then be no difference between knowing a concept and intuitive knowledge of what is known, with the consequence that all concepts would be real things including individual concepts. That would destroy the distinction between mental and real which is the foundation of Ockham's epistemology. The only solution is to acknowledge what Ockham by implication admits—the mental status of a

---

[107] Ad argumentum principale dico quod assumptum est falsum, quia conceptus non terminat actum intelligendi, quia tali qualitate destructa per potentiam dei, adhuc habemus verum conceptum rei, et per consequens talis conceptus terminans non est conceptus (*ibid.*).

[108] *Ibid.*, q. 7.

[109] *Ibid.*

concept both as subject of an act of real knowledge and as an object known in the mind; for unless a sign is known as a sign, it cannot signify.[110] Hence it differs from a mere image not in the way that it is known—as an object—but in the knowledge that it gives as the subject of an act of knowing. Where knowledge of a *fictum*, as a mere object of thought, ends at the *fictum*, that of a concept terminates in a real object known by the concept as an act of knowing. Their difference is one of signification.

That this is what Ockham means is suggested by his account in the seventh of the *Questions on the Physics*, cited above, of how Socrates or man are known through apprehending the concept of either as a natural sign in the intellect. Now a sign, as Ockham never tires of reiterating, as we shall see in the following chapters, is not a thing. Therefore it must be known in abstraction from real things outside the mind, and the only way—as we saw in the first chapter—in which the intellect can know in abstraction is by a habit left from a past act of knowing, and inclining it to a further act of knowing what is not immediately present.

The dependence of intellectual acts (as opposed to acts of will) upon habits is affirmed in the third *Quodlibet*.[111] Although in the fourth of the *Questions on the Physics* Ockham dismisses the claims of habits—together with species—to be concepts, on the grounds that there can be a habit in the intellect without any act of knowing, he nevertheless stresses in the *Quodlibets* that an act of knowing something already known must in itself presuppose a habit. Without a habit the intellect would be no more disposed to know something after previously knowing it than before and so would remain in the same state of potential knowledge towards everything. Which is false, since the intellect can continue to know some-thing after it is no longer present, as Aristotle showed in the third book of *De Anima*. There must therefore be a habit from a preceding act.[112]

The full implications of this doctrine have already been treated in the previous chapter over imperfect knowledge. We need only observe here that it must equally apply to concepts as natural signs of what is already known. Hence while it is true that Ockham rejects the notion of a concept as a habit *tout court*, a concept as an act of knowing carries with it the presumption of a habit.[113] For that reason it is

---

[110] Cf. Ockham's own definition in the *Logic*: 'signum' duplicitur accipitur: Uno modo pro omni illo quod apprehensum aliquid aliud in cognitionem facit venire . . . Et sic vox naturaliter significat . . . Aliter accipitur 'signum' pro illo quod aliquid facit in cognitionem venire et natum est pro illo quod supponere vel tali addi in propositione (*SL*, 1, ch. 1, 9–10). Whether taken in the first sense as a natural sign or the second sense as a word imposed by convention its function is the same of *making someting other than itself known*. Hence as Boehner has said (*Collected Articles*, 203), knowledge of a sign 'implies two cognitions which are distinct and two objects which are known'.

[111] *Quodlibet* III, q. 17.

[112] Quarto dico quod in intellectu necessario ponitur habitus, quia aliquis post frequentiam actuum intelligendi redditur promptus et inclinatus ad consimiles actus et nullo modo redditur promptus et inclinatus ante omnem actum. Tum quia aliter intellectus esset eodem modo in potentia ante omnem actum, et post, quod est falsum, quia post primum actum intelligendi destructo obiecto aut absente potest intellectus in aliquod actus in quos non potuit ante primum actum; et ista est ratio Aristotelis 3 *De Anima* ad ponendum habitus intellectuales, quia cum habitu intellectus destructo obiecto cum volumus intelligimus (*ibid.*).

[113] That is expressly stated of all natural signs in the *Logic*: quamvis [signum] non faciat

misconceived to oppose them as sharply as Boehner and Brampton do. It is more accurate to say that concepts are the way in which the mind knows real things in abstraction through a habit; it is that which distinguishes them from mere objects of thought which are merely known in the mind: their logical import belongs to the next chapter.

II THE STATUS OF UNIVERSALS

Ockham's systematic treatment of universals, in which he examines and rejects the arguments that they are real things or the essences in things, or are the same as things but are not concepts, occupies questions four to seven of the second distinction of the *Ordinatio*;[114] having established that universals are concepts he then examines the nature of concepts in the eighth question, as we have recently discussed.

He begins with the opinion misattributed to Duns Scotus that[115] universals really exist outside the mind as the essences of individual things in which they inhere, at once distinct from the individual itself and from other universals, as the universal 'man' is really and distinctly in every individual man and distinguished from the universals 'animals' and 'substance'. Hence according to this opinion there are as many universals in an individual as there are distinct things in it, each universal remaining one and the same in every individual of the same species, not multiplied in the way individuals are.[116] In support of this opinion are Aristotle's statements in the seventh book of the *Metaphysics* that definition and essence belong primarily to substance and only secondarily to accidents,[117] and that there is neither definition nor demonstration of sensible individual substances which, as material and destructible, are capable of being and non-being.[118] Therefore, immediately definable substance must be distinct from individual substance; it is not however separate from a sensible individual because Aristotle also says that a separated substance cannot exist apart from individuals.[119]

Moreover, according to this opinion, substance is defined strictly by genus

---

mentem venire in primam cognitionem eius, sicut alibi est ostensum, sed in *actualem post habitualem* [my italics] euisdem. Et sic vox naturaliter significat, sicut quilibet effectus significat saltem suam causam, sicut quilibet effectus significat saltem suam causam, sicut etiam circulus significat vinum in taberna. (1 ch. 1, 9). Hence a sign as denoting what must have been previously known gives only secondary knowledge—i.e. imperfect intuitive or recordative knowledge through a habit.

114 There is also a much more summary treatment in the *Logic*, 1, chs. 14–16.

115 Ockham himself in the next question, five (*Ordinatio*, *OT*, 11, 154), says that this opinion is attributed by some to Scotus; according to the editors (*ibid.*, 100) Ockham probably had in mind Henry of Harclay who in question three of his *Disputed Questions* seems to imply Duns as the author. For the affinities between Ockham and Harclay over universals, see G. Gál, 'Henricus de Harclay: Quaestio de significato conceptus universalis', *FcS* 31 (1971), 178–234.

116 *Ordinatio*, d. 2, q. 4, 100–1.

117 *Metaphysics*, bk. vii, ch. 4, 1030 b, 4–14.

118 *Ibid.*, ch. 15, 1039 b, 28–31.

119 *Ibid.*, 1040 a, 8–27; *Ordinatio, ibid.*, 101–2.

and difference;[120] and these must be either things or concepts. If things, then a genus will be a universal thing because no individual thing is a genus; it will also be of the essence of the species which it defines: otherwise the definition would not be intrinsic to the species. Accordingly if a genus is a thing, there will be a universal thing in addition to individual things. That genus is a universal thing and not a concept follows from what Aristotle says in the *Metaphysics*, namely, that a substance is only defined by substances. Therefore both genus and difference are both substances.[121] Again a definition is immediately of what is defined; but no definition is immediately of an individual, for it would not then be of any other individual; nor is it of something extrinsic to an individual; it must therefore be of something which is not an individual and yet intrinsic to an individual. That can only be a universal.[122]

The other arguments for this opinion[123] all share the same premises that only a real thing can give real and so immediate knowledge, and that an individual is inadequate to give knowledge of more than itself. Hence real knowledge is of universal things; universal terms (i.e. those universally predicable of only one thing) like 'man' stand for real things which are distinct from their individuals; and the intellect can know 'man' without knowing individual men. Similarly, only a real universal thing is the adequate object of the intellect or the senses, the first subject of an attribute or the object of a natural agent. These conclusions are reinforced by the authority of Aristotle and Porphyry.

To Ockham this opinion is false and absurd.[124] In the first place, nothing—other than the divine essence—can be at once numerically one and also in different individuals, even when they are created simultaneously. Therefore universals are not the essences in real things.[125] That is proved because whenever two things are distinct from one another, whether equally simple or not, each will be numerically one; but by this opinion, an individual and a universal are really distinct. Hence if an individual thing is numerically one, its universal will be so also. That a universal cannot be composed of more—i.e. be less simple—than an individual can also be shown, because if more things were intrinsic to a universal than to an individual, these would be either universals or individuals. Not universals, for that would in turn pose the same alternatives, leading to an infinite regress. Nor individuals save as whole and part; which is impossible even for the advocates of this opinion, for whom the individual, in containing the universal and something else, is the whole and the universal the part. But if the part is numerically one and distinct, the whole will be one and distinct as well. Consequently this opinion, by affirming that whatever is included in the universal is included in everything coming under it, such as that whatever is essential to man is essential to Socrates, is affirming that neither individual nor universal includes more than the other; hence each is equally one and simple, if the singular is numerically one.[126]

The objection that a universal includes many things which are extrinsic and

---

[120] Discussed in the following chapter, 186ff. below, and again in chapter four.
[121] *Ordinatio, ibid.*, 102–3.   [122] *Ibid.*, 103.   [123] *Ibid.*, 103–6.
[124] *Ibid.*, 108.   [125] *Ibid.*   [126] *Ibid.*, 108–10.

so not numerically one does not hold, because many things—God, matter, any cause—contain many things which are really distinct, and yet each of these is numerically one.[127] Nor again does the argument that only a universal is really communicable to many things, in which it inheres, so that although they do not contain intrinsically more than singulars, universals are not numerically one. Whether communicability is taken to mean identity through multiplication or distinctness through invariability between what is communicated and that to which it is communicated, neither implies a plurality in universals. By identity and multiplicity a universal is the same as the individuals to which it is communicated, which is really to say that things are communicating themselves. Moreover, if universals were multiplied beyond the multiplication of individuals there would be as many universals as individuals, and so none of them would be universals, which contradicts this opinion that universals remain invariable and yet really exist in many individuals. By this second mode the same thing can be successively —as opposed to simultaneously—in different things, while retaining its numerical identity, as the same matter or form can belong successively to different individuals.[128] Other examples include—somewhat inappositely—Averroes's 'fictitious' possible intellect which is the same for all men and yet numerically distinct from every individual in which it is present.[129] The import of all such instances is that they show that a universal is itself numerically one, and so singular like everything else which is only one.

That too follows from this opinion in upholding the separate identity of universals; for everything which constitutes a number with something else really distinct from it is either numerically one or a plurality. That applies to a universal and singular: either they are one or several. They are not several, since they would then be many individuals, which this opinion denies; therefore a universal is numerically one and singular.[130] Its singularity moreover will consist not only in being numerically one as opposed to many but in being distinct from everything else, neither inhering in many things nor signifying a continuum containing many, as an angel or the soul is one, distinct and non-continuous.[131]

In the second place, whatever is prior to and really distinct from something else can exist without it; but that is the case with a universal according to this opinion; therefore there can be a universal without an individual. Correspondingly, if something can exist separately from something else naturally, and does not depend essentially upon it, it can by God's power exist independently when they

---

[127] *Ibid.*, 110.   [128] *Ibid.*, 110–11.   [129] *Ibid.*, 111–12.

[130] Et ita per consequens, cum omnis res una numero sit vere res singularis, omnis res universalis erit vere res singularis. Tota ratio precedens confirmatur sic: omnis res faciens numerum cum alia re realiter distincta est una res numero vel plures res numero; sed talis res universalis, si ponatur, vere facit numerum cum re singulari; igitur ipsa est una res numero vel plures res numero; sed non est plures res numero, quia tunc esset plura singularia, quia secundum istos et secundum veritatem omnis res una numero est singularis; igitur plura res numero sunt plura singularia; sed nulla res universalis est plura singularia secundum istos, quia secundum istos distinguitur realiter ab omnibus singularibus. Igitur est una numero. (*ibid.* 113). Cf. also *SL* I, ch. 15, 46–8.

[131] *Ordinatio, ibid.*, 114.

are joined. That too applies to a universal which by this opinion can really exist without any individual; it is confirmed by the same opinion that an individual adds something beyond its nature, making it one with a universal, since otherwise the individual would be neither substance nor accident. Hence it would not be contradictory for God to conserve this addition alone—which is absurd.[132]

In the third place, an individual of a species can be created *de novo* regardless of how many individuals belonging to it already exist: and since all creation is absolutely from nothing, with no essential part of what is created already in being, that excludes universals as the distinct pre-existing essences of individuals; for such essences would precede all individuals, which would not then be created since they would not be *de nihilo*. Hence there is no need to posit something common to individuals. This is confirmed by the ontology of individual existence.[133] Since every individual that does not depend upon another individual for its existence can be annihilated without the destruction of any other individual, God could annihilate one man without annihilating another; and with his annihilation nothing intrinsic to him or in any way real would remain of him. Therefore no such common thing exists; otherwise its annihilation in one individual man would entail the annihilation of all men in having the same essence.[134] This individual ontology is at the opposite pole from the later extreme realism of Wyclif, and carries the opposite implications. For Ockham one of the decisive arguments against the real inherence of essences is that it would entail an all-embracing annihilability, from which nothing sharing the same nature would escape and which God himself could not mitigate. For Wyclif, this—for Ockham —false conclusion becomes his major premise and leads to the opposite conclusion, namely, that nothing can be annihilated, because then not even God as the source of the essences of all beings could escape destruction.

Conversely, since this opinion denies that the individual is the essence of the universal on the grounds that otherwise the universal man could not exist without the individual Socrates, it must follow that neither is the essence of the other. Either therefore they constitute one thing; and then Socrates would not be an individual but a part of something which is a unity, leaving him no more essentially a man than matter is the form in conjunction with which it constitutes an individual. Alternatively, if universal and individual are not one thing or one an accident of the other, each will be self-subsisting in the manner of a Platonic idea; they will then coexist together with many other such beings, which Ockham regards as only one of the absurdities resulting from this assumption.[135] They are not obviated by positing that the universal is only part of the essence of the in-

---

[132] *Ibid.*, 115.   [133] *Ibid.*, 115–16.

[134] Praeterea omnis res singularis potest adnihilari sine adnihilatione vel destructione alterius rei singularis a qua in nullo dependet; igitur potest iste homo adnihilari a deo nullo alio homine adnihilato vel destructo. Sed in adnihilatione nihil intrinsecum rei remanet nec in se nec in alio quocumque in esse reali; igitur non est aliqua talis res communis utrique, quia tunc illa adnihilaretur, et per consequens nullus alius homo remaneret secundum totam essentiam suam, et ita quilibet homo saltem corrumperetur, quia adnihilata quacumque parte destruitur totum (*ibid.*, 116).

[135] *Ibid.*, 117–18.

dividual as its essential part. To begin with, the individual would not be more singular than universal because the whole would not be connoted more by one essential part than another, as a composite of form and matter is not called form more than matter, or conversely, although form is the principal part. Secondly, the individual and the universal would then be in the relation of matter to form or *vice versa*, with the singular added to the universal if they were not to be either identical or disparate. Thirdly, there would then be as many distinct things in a singular as in a universal, so that Socrates would be of a different nature from Plato, since every accident would be composed of a universal nature and something added to it of a different nature.[136]

Lastly, everything which exists outside the mind comes under the category of substance and as such is capable of admitting contrary qualities, as we shall discuss in the next chapter; that would also apply to a universal if it were a real substance. But no universal is capable of sustaining contrary qualities. Therefore no universal is a substance and so not a real thing. If it were, individuals of contrary natures could belong to the same species, which is impossible.[137] Theologically it would lead to the absurd consequence that something intrinsic to Christ could be both blessed and damned in deriving from a nature common to Christ and all men informed by both beatitude and misery. Similarly, the same thing could be simultaneously in diverse places. In every such case a substance containing contraries would not be subject to one rather than the other.[138]

Every attempt, then, to identify a universal nature with an independent essence really inhering in an individual reaches the same impasse: if one is distinct from the other, each can exist without the other and so the universal can be reduced to singularity; if on the other hand they are the same, the universal or the individual loses its identity as part of the whole which they constitute—which is again individual. Neither logically nor ontologically, therefore, is the independent inherence of universals in individuals tenable.[139] The only reason to posit them would be for the essential predication of one by the other or for knowledge of things and their definition in the way Aristotle describes Platonic ideas (*Metaphysics* XII, ch. 4, 30–7). They are not necessary for predication because if universals were intrinsic to individuals and yet really distinct from them, they would be part of individuals, and a part cannot be predicated essentially of a whole, as neither matter nor form can be affirmed of something composed of both; hence if a universal is affirmed of something, it must stand not for itself but for an individual. But that can be achieved by something entirely extrinsic to the thing of which it is affirmed, standing for neither the thing nor its part, as animal can be affirmed of man or Socrates in the propositions 'Man is an animal', 'Socrates is an animal': here 'animal', 'man', and 'Socrates' are not essentially part of the other, nor does each stand for something which exists independently as something real.[140] Rather,

---

[136] *Ibid.*, 118–19.   [137] *Ibid.*, 119–20.   [138] *Ibid.*, 120–1.

[139] Ideo dico aliter ad questionem quod nulla res realiter distincta a singularibus rebus et intrinseca eis est universalis vel communis (*ibid.*, 122).

[140] *Ibid.*, 122–3.

as we shall see in the next two chapters, not all knowledge is immediately of real things; it can also be of terms standing for real things. And of whichever it is, any knowledge can only be expressed in propositions whose truth or falsity depends upon the conformity of their terms with what exists. That precisely depends upon their supposition, so that where universal terms are employed they can only be true if they stand not for themselves but for the individuals which come under them.[141] Accordingly, whether in a proposition or a definition, subject and predicate, definition and what is defined, are neither the same things nor the same terms, but they stand for the same thing.[142] Thus if in the proposition 'Man is a rational animal', 'man' stands for anything other than individual men, it is false, for no such being is conceivable; correspondingly the definition of man as a rational animal will also be false, since it can only be affirmed of this or that individual man.[143] Universals therefore, as should become apparent, are such by predication in virtue of being terms affirmed of the individuals coming under them and not as the essences inhering in things.

That brings us to the next question, also imputed to Duns Scotus, whether a universal exists really and distinctly in an individual, not as the same in each but multiplied and varied by a contracting difference from which it is equally distinguished.[144] This again Ockham regards as false, since everything really distinct from something else is so either by itself or by something intrinsic to it. But according to this opinion the humanity in Socrates is really distinguished from the humanity in Plato; it must therefore be distinguished by itself or something intrinsic to it. Leaving aside their contracting differences, since their distinction cannot be as species, it must be numerically as different individuals. Hence they are distinguished by themselves, without any contracting difference.[145] That holds whether or not their humanities exist independently without the same species, because two forms, even when separated from their matter, are still distinguished numerically, even if they do not subsist independently.[146] It is not altered by invoking a contracting difference. Thus, if the humanity of Socrates is distinguished from the humanity which is its species by a contracting difference, the difference would be due either to humanity itself or to the contracting difference. It cannot be the contracting difference, because nothing is distinguished from something else by the thing from which it is distinguished; rather something derives its likeness from something else. Therefore humanity must in itself be distinguished from a contracting difference, as two distinct things: which is only possible if they are numerically different. Hence they owe their difference to humanity itself and not to a contracting difference. In that case the humanity of Socrates would also be distinct from the humanity of Plato in having its own contracting difference.[147] Their humanities would then be really distinct, by themselves and not their contracting difference, which proves Ockham's case. So does the alternative that

---

[141] *Ibid.*, 124–7, 134–8.
[142] E.g. Ad primum istorum dico quod nunquam definitio et definitum sunt eadem res ... hoc tamen non obstante pro eadem re supponunt et precise pro eadem re (*ibid.*, 130).
[143] *Ibid.*, 129.   [144] *Ibid.*, q. 5, 154.   [145] *Ibid.*
[146] *Ibid.*, 154–5.   [147] *Ibid.*, 155.

they are not really distinct, since, to be one, they would have to constitute a real
composition as really distinct parts. Again by God's omnipotence at least, each as
an absolute could be seen without the other; hence there could be intuitive knowledge of the humanity of Socrates without its contracting difference and similarly
with the humanity in Plato; which again proves their real difference from one
another.[148]

A second consequence of this opinion would be that if humanity were thus
diversified there would be as many *species specialissimae* as individuals, entailing
the absurd conclusion that there would then also be as many general genera. For
if humanity is a *species specialissima* it is the humanity of Plato or Socrates or something which is neither. If of Socrates or Plato, it will not be more of one than the
other and there will then be two humanities, each a *species specialissima*. If of
neither, it must be either of something real existing outside the mind, which has
already been disproved in the preceding question, or only in the mind; and then
universals will not be outside the mind.[149] The same alternative recurs if man is
taken as a species: either he stands for something existing outside the mind or in
the mind. If outside the mind, he will either exist undifferentiated and undiversified
in all individual men, which has been disproved; or multiplied into as many
species as there are individuals which is equally impossible, for individuals are not
species as they are not common beings. There remains then a universal as something
only in the mind:[150] a conclusion reinforced by the very opinion that a common
thing like humanity belongs only determinately to individuals and not indifferently
to many individuals. Consequently it is only to be found in individuals, and
nothing universal exists outside the mind. It is no answer to say that a contracting
difference does not contradict a universal, as in itself common and indifferent to
many individuals but determinate to a particular individual only through something extrinsic to it. Nothing that is not really and positively common to many
things can belong to them; if therefore the thing which is in Socrates cannot be in
something else it will not only not be common: it will be less common than form
or matter which can by God's power be successively in different things. A contracted nature—e.g. the humanity in Socrates—will also be less common than an
individual contracting nature—Socrates—when it is joined, as it can be, to a more
common nature which according to this opinion is present in the individual as
the genus and species of each of its parts.[151]

Accordingly there is no universal nature in an individual, which is at once
distinct from the individual and from a contracting difference, because such a
nature could only exist as an essential part of an individual. In fact there is always
a proportion between the whole and the part such that, if the whole is singular,
any part of it will be correspondlingly singular, with no part more singular than
another.[152] This opinion, too, then cannot be sustained.

---

[148] *Ibid.*, 156.   [149] *Ibid.*, 156–7.   [150] *Ibid.*, 157.   [151] *Ibid.*, 157–8.

[152] Ideo dico ad questionem quod in individuo non est aliqua natura universalis realiter
distincta a differentia contrahente, quia non posset ibi poni talis natura nisi esset pars essentialis
ipsius individui; sed semper inter totum et partem est proportio, ita quod si totum sit singulare

With the third opinion we come to the view of Duns Scotus himself, 'the subtle doctor who excelled all others in the subtlety of his judgement', to whom Ockham himself attributes this opinion. It is that there exists in an individual, and outside the mind, a nature which is the same as the contracting difference which determines an individual, but is formally distinct from it; and that this nature is itself neither universal nor particular, but incompletely universal in things outside the mind and fully universal in the mind.[153] This is Duns's celebrated formal distinction with which he sought to reconcile an individual and a common nature. As with so many of Duns's leading ideas, Ockham, as we shall now see, recounts it at length and often verbatim in order to present Duns's 'whole opinion' before proceeding to criticise it at length: a further indication of how seriously he takes Scotus's doctrines.

Ockham begins with the four points of comparison from which a qualified, or contractible, universal nature can be regarded: namely in relation to what is singular, to a numerical unity, to a universal being, and to a lesser than numerical unity, which according to Duns this nature is.[154]

Compared with something singular this nature does not exist by itself but only together with an added individual substance to which, like any essential nature and as the individual's ultimate nature, it is naturally prior and indifferent. Each is therefore distinguished from the other not as real beings but formally within the same being, as matter and form or a composite of both are not really distinguished from their being. Hence any determinable—i.e. reducible to an individual— nature although itself one, can be formally distinguished as common and individual. From which Duns concludes that individual difference is not itself essential or quidditative; that a (common) nature is naturally prior to an individual contracting difference—i.e. that which reduces a common nature to an individual; that as indifferent to particular individuals which are naturally subsequent to it such a nature is not contradicted by what contradicts a particular individual; that nature and individual are distinguished only formally, as not the same as the other, so that although really different they do not exist separately. Every substance therefore which exists does so either by itself or by something proper to it by which it becomes an individual. As such it is distinguished from every other substance, as the substance of Socrates is distinguished from that of Plato.[155]

From the second aspect, of numerical unity, a contractible nature is only numerically one in virtue of belonging to one individual; it is neither one in itself nor can it be in more than one individual. It thus receives its numerical unity from the individual unity into which it is contracted, itself remaining only poten-

---

non commune, quelibet pars eodem modo est singularis proportionaliter, quia una pars non potest plus esse singularis quam alia (ibid., 158–9).

[153] Ibid., q. 6, 161; cf. SL I, ch. 16, 49–51 for a much more cursory treatment of Scotus's opinion.

[154] Ordinatio, ibid. For the Scotist distinction see A. Wolter, The Transcendentals and their Function in the Metaphysics of Duns Scotus (Washington, 1946), 20–30.

[155] Ordinatio, ibid., 161–3.

tially one, as a species, say, colour, is one as part of something else white and not through being a species.[156]

Thirdly, in comparison with a universal being, a common nature is, as Duns has already said, completely universal only in the intellect. Although of itself more common than singular it lacks the unity by which a real universal being is indifferent to any individual in particular; for outside the mind it exists only determinately in one individual rather than another. Hence, while in itself a common nature is not more compatible with one individual rather than another, in its real existence, as part of a determinate individual, it is, and cannot therefore be identified equally with any individual of the same nature as a real universal can.[157]

That leaves the fourth aspect, of a common nature as a unity which is less than a numerical unity and included in a numerical unity. It is expressed in Avicenna's saying that equinity—as the nature of a horse—is only equinity, in itself neither one nor many.[158]

This is Duns's principal conclusion.[159] He argues for it on diverse grounds:[160] of inherence, so that what is independently in one thing must be included in everything that includes that thing; of contradiction, by which what belongs to one opposite cannot belong to the other, as something numerically one cannot be more than one; of the priority of an object to an act of knowing, where the singular is always prior to what is known as universal in the intellect; and finally because a real, proper and sufficient unity is less than a numerical unity, as the nature in a stone is a unity less than the numerical unity of this or that stone. That follows since nothing is of itself one by a unity greater than is sufficient for its unity; and if a proper unity is less than a numerical unity, then a numerical unity is not its proper unity: otherwise the same nature would at once have a greater and lesser unity, which is contradictory. Moreover, if there were no unity less than the numerical unity of what is singular, and every unity other than that of singularity or specific nature is less than a real unity, there will be no real unity less than its numerical unity. That this is false Duns shows[161] first from the real unity of a genus in which, according to Aristotle in the *Metaphysics*,[162] one is the measure of all its individuals. It must be real, because mental being—i.e. what is known only in the mind— cannot be the real measure of real being; and it must be other than singular, because what is singular cannot be the measure of all that is in a genus with no order of priority among individuals of the same species. The real unity of a species equally can be shown from what Aristotle says in the *Physics*[163] about the comparison of the attributes of a species which must be of the same nature. That cannot apply to a genus which does not have the same unity (i.e.

---

156 *Ibid.*, 164–5.   157 *Ibid.*, 166.   158 *Ibid.*, 166–7 and 173.

159 Et est de intentione istius doctoris quod preter unitatem numeralem est unitas realis minor unitate numerali, que convenit ipsi nature que est aliquo modo universalis. (*ibid.*, 161).

160 *Ibid.*, 167–8.

161 *Ibid.*, 168–73.

162 *Metaphysics*, bk. x, chs. 1–2, 1052 a, 15, 1054 b.

163 *Physics*, bk. vii, ch. 4, 249 a, 2–5.

where everything is of the same nature). If therefore it only existed in the mind it could be equally affirmed of genera. Again, relations of identity, similarity, equality and opposition are founded on a real identity which is not numerical because nothing can be compared with or opposed to itself. Nor is the object of an act of sensation numerically one, although it has a real unity; for the senses do not distinguish between numerically different objects of the same real unity, for example one ray of sun from another. Finally if all real unity were numerical, then all real diversity would be numerical, which would—falsely—mean that all diversity, in being numerical, would be equal and there would no longer be anything common for the intellect to abstract from diverse individuals. A universal would then be a pure figment of the intellect.

For all these reasons Scotus maintains the distinction between a numerical and natural unity and with it a formal distinction between an individual and its common nature.

Ockham's reply is first that it is impossible for something in creatures to differ formally unless it is really distinguished;[164] hence if a nature were in some way distinguished from a contracting difference they would differ as real things or mentally or as what is real and what is mental. The first two alternatives are excluded by Duns himself; therefore they could only be distinguished as something real and something in the mind, and then any such distinction will be mental and not real. That follows because if a nature and its contracting difference were not the same in all respects, something could be truly affirmed of one and denied of the other. But that is not possible for anything created, which is the same as itself; accordingly it can only be of what is more than one. To say otherwise would entail the end of any way of proving a real distinction among created things in which the way of contradiction is pre-eminent. All contradictions are equally contradictory, including the contradiction between being and non-being. Their contradiction is not overcome by positing a real non-identity instead; for the same syllogistic form holds in every case, so that if A is B, and C is not B, then C is not A. Consequently if all individual difference is of itself proper to a particular individual and its nature is of itself not proper to the same individual, it follows that the nature is not really the same as the individual difference.[165] It is not mitigated by the exception of the divine nature which surpasses all understanding and is held on the authority of the Bible.[166] Nor by the converse, that the contracting difference is not the common nature although not really distinguished from it; for by the principle of contradiction they will then be the same, as shown by the syllogism: they are not really distinguished; each is a thing; therefore they are really the same and one is the other.[167] As we shall see in chapter four, syncategorematic terms like 'of itself', 'really', 'formally' and so on, when regulated, as here by the *dictum de omni et de nullo*, produce valid conclusions. Logically therefore the formal distinction—in violating the principle of contradiction—is untenable.[168]

---

[164] Contra istam opinionem potest argui duplici via: primo, quia impossibile est in creaturis aliqua differre formaliter nisi distinguantur realiter (*ibid.*, Ordinatio, 173).
[165] *Ibid.*, 173-4. [166] *Ibid.*, 174-5. [167] *Ibid.*, 176-7. [168] *Ibid.*, 175-6.

In the second place, even granting this distinction, it is still not true. To begin with, whenever one of an opposite agrees with something, the other will disagree and will be absolutely negated by it. Yet according to Duns everything existing outside the mind is really singular and numerically one, although something is singular of itself and something is singular only by what is added to it. Therefore nothing outside the mind is really common or one by a unity opposed to that of singularity. Hence the only real unity is singular.[169] Nor does it help to say that these two unities—of a nature and an individual—are not really opposed, as singularity and community are not opposed: for if they are not really opposed then they could really and immediately agree in all respects and so be one by both unities, with singular and common the same in all respects.[170]

Moreover to say, as Duns does, that a common nature is less than a numerical unity is contradictory, for whenever the antecedents contradict one another, so do the consequents. But these are contradictory: A (as a common nature) is compatible with a numerical multiplicity; A is not compatible with a numerical multiplicity. So therefore are these: A is one by a lesser unity; A is one by a greater unity. But that is what Duns says in holding that a common nature is numerically one; i.e. one by a greater unity, and one by a lesser unity: therefore the second of these is false; and a common nature is not a lesser unity.[171] Moreover, Duns's own statement that 'A lesser unity is compatible with and does not contradict a plurality opposed to a greater unity', besides being contradictory contradicts what he also says: namely that a common nature and individual difference do not really differ; for when two things are really the same, by God's power whatever one can be the other can be. But an individual difference cannot be numerically more than one really distinct thing; nor therefore can the nature which is really the same as this contracting difference, or anything else beyond this contracting difference. Hence a common nature is not compatible with a plurality.[172] That is confirmed because every universal, whether complete or not, is really common or can be common to many things; but no real thing is really common to many; therefore no real thing is in any way a universal. If it were and something real corresponded to say man, it would have to be the nature in Socrates or Plato or something which is neither. It cannot be in Socrates or in Plato because what is singular cannot be in more than one thing; nor be something which is not singular, since according to Duns everything outside the mind is really singular. If moreover something common did really exist outside the mind it could by God's power be communicated to many things; but that is not possible for what is not common to many things and singular.[173] Nor is this in turn overcome by positing something added to a nature, making it one by real identity although not inhering in many things; that would be merely a negative community of non-contradiction. Hence only a numerical unity is positive. A negative unity on the other hand can for that reason be attributed to what is individual since it is not of itself numerical; in that sense it is true when Duns owns that it does not contradict individual difference

169 *Ibid.*, 179.   170 *Ibid.*, 177–8.   171 *Ibid.*, 178.
172 *Ibid.*, 179.   173 *Ibid.*, 179–80.

to be in many, just as its opposite is false, that this individual difference is absolutely and essentially one.[174]

Furthermore the existence of a common nature would entail as many genera and species as individuals, since the nature of each individual would be a species. That would mean two natures—and so two species—in each individual, with the lesser unity the attribute of the numerically individual nature: and as the individual nature is multiplied among all its individuals, so will the lesser unity which is also common to them. There would thus be as many common natures as individual natures, which is absurd.[175]

It is not overcome by saying that a universal exists only completely in the intellect, because a universal is either something real outside the mind, which would support what has just been said and contradict Duns's own view that only singulars really exist independently of the intellect; or it is entirely mental, and then nothing real is universal, completely or incompletely. The third alternative is that a universal is both real and mental, and once again it will follow, as it does from the first alternative, that there will be as many genera as individuals, since there will be as many things inside the mind as outside it.[176]

Furthermore, according to Duns, a complete universal is in and of many things and predicated of them: but so is a common nature; it therefore meets all the requirements of a complete universal and will, as genus or species, be as numerous as the individuals belonging to it. It would then follow that, if the nature that is in Socrates were really common, the destruction of Socrates would be accompanied by the destruction of something essential and common; but in fact it is certain that something common remains in the continuance of individuals. To overcome this contradiction Duns has to acknowledge a real distinction between them. Therefore one is not really the other and they are more than one. Their unity is not saved by positing a contracting difference between them, because for Duns this community belongs to a nature existing outside the intellect. Hence this nature must be something real, and either singular or common; it cannot be common because Duns says that such a nature is really numerically one and singular. Accordingly it is singular and there is no real common nature.[177]

In the third place, if the humanity in Socrates and the humanity in Plato are really distinguished, each is numerically one and neither common to the other. The explanation that their difference is due to a difference added to each, without which they would not be singular, cannot be sustained; for everything is distinguished essentially from everything either by itself or by something intrinsic to it. That applies to the humanity in Socrates and the humanity in Plato. Just as Socrates is not distinguished essentially from Plato by an ass, similarly he is not distinguished by something else which is extrinsic, a view confirmed by Aristotle and Averroes that being is the same as unity and not from something added to it.[178] Nor does it carry the implication of dividing and contracting.[179] That follows

---

[174] Ibid., 180–1.   [175] Ibid., 181.   [176] Ibid., 182–3.   [177] Ibid., 183–4.
[178] Metaphysics, bk. IV, ch. 2, 1004 b, 24.
[179] Ordinatio, ibid., 184–5.

because if the humanity in Socrates is not common it is not essentially common; and whenever something is said negatively to agree essentially with something else—as a creature is called non-being or matter a privation which are equivalent to negative statements, that a creature is not essentially this or that or matter is not of itself formed—they must be able to belong together, at least by God's power, even if actually they do not. Thus as a creature can be non-being and matter can be deprived of a form, so by the same token the humanity in Socrates should be able to be common to many men; but that is impossible. Therefore a common humanity in Socrates is impossible. The reason is that, in creatures, when things are the same, one cannot be really the same as something else unless the other is also the same; that in a certain manner is also true of God, where although it is false to say that the Father is the Son, the being of one is nevertheless the being of the other. In the case of Socrates, since his humanity is really the same as the contracting difference and can be the same as the contracting difference in Plato, both can be one and the same; one thing would then be in both which is contradictory.[180]

Again according to Duns whatever is really distinguished from something else, as not formally the same, can be seen intuitively without the latter. Therefore the humanity in Socrates can be seen without its contracting difference, and correspondingly the humanity in Plato. Which would not be possible if they were distinguished by their contracting differences. They must accordingly be distinguished numerically of themselves.[181] Nor can the contracting differences be included in their distinct humanities as formally distinguishing them, because whenever things are really distinct in any way a term can be made to stand for one and not the other: otherwise there would be no propositions denoting their differences.[182]

If a contracted nature were really distinct from every difference contracting it that nature would of itself be one, as already proved in question four; it is not therefore less than one in virtue of being really the same as a contracting difference. This is confirmed by Duns himself when he says that things distinguished in any way have the same order as when they are really distinguished. A contracted nature and its contracting difference would then be distinguished as potentiality and act in the same way as any two things (i.e. matter and form) constituting a numerical unity.[183] The same consequence can be seen from the relation of genus to specific differences: if, say, the nature of colour were really the same as whiteness and blackness and yet as natures they were distinguished, they would be both more and less perfect in themselves and the same, as they exist here and now in conjunction, which is contradictory.[184] It would also follow that if a common nature were communicable to many individuals, an individual difference would be equally communicable, and is indeed communicated to many universals. That, however, contradicts a nature subject to individual differences.[185] Moreover a nature and a difference, in being of the same individual, must be of the same kind; but then it will not be more of one individual than another.[186]

<hr />

180 *Ibid.*, 185–6.   181 *Ibid.*, 186.   182 *Ibid.*, 187–8.   183 *Ibid.*, 188–9.
184 *Ibid.*, 190.   185 *Ibid.*   186 *Ibid.*, 190–1.

Finally, if a nature could be contracted by a contracting difference, from which it was distinguished only formally, there would correspondlingly be a real univocity between God and creatures derived from something real common to each, as there is among creatures. Duns denies such a real univocity; but it is no more inconsistent when founded upon a formal distinction with God's simplicity than a formal distinction between the divine essence and the divine persons is.[187] Hence it is Duns who is inconsistent.

So much for the untenability of a formal distinction between a common contracted nature and the individual difference by which it is contracted or individuated. As to Duns's arguments, Ockham begins by challenging a number of his formulations.[188] First that a nature precedes a being as the condition of its existence; that it is untrue because by the same token since there is—by Duns's conception—a formal distinction between essence and relation, the essence would be prior to relation. In fact, according to Duns himself, every nature prior to another can by God's power come into being without the other nature; but that would be impossible for a contracted nature since it is really the same as its contracting difference.[189] Nor secondly does it seem correct to say that individual difference is not quidditative or essential, understanding by quidditative all that is of the essence of something existing in itself; for individual difference is precisely of an individual's own existence. No such real being is communicable save as form is communicated to matter or in such a way as one distinct being is communicated to another.[190]

The remaining objections[191] principally concern the contradictions inherent in the notion of a contracted nature, making it at once indifferent in itself and yet individually differentiated, numerically one and yet common, and endowing what exists outside the mind with both community and singularity. Indifference cannot be non-indifference, just as to predicate a numerical unity of a whole which includes a common nature is to include the common nature in the numerical unity; and conversely a less than numerical unity affirmed of a common nature will be also affirmed of the individual difference as its attribute. Hence on Duns's argument a complete individual will be connoted by both a numerical and a less than numerical unity. An actual universal similarity cannot be called an indifferent unity either logically, when it will not exist in things but will be predicated of them, or ontologically where having existence it would have a unity.

That in turn answers the first of Duns's arguments that a common nature— e.g. 'man'—can inhere in an individual; for 'inhere in something' can either be taken as real inherence and then it is false; or it can mean inherence by predication in which a term is affirmed of a subject, for example 'Socrates is a man'. If 'man' here is understood significatively as standing for real individual men (i.e. in personal supposition) then such a proposition is true; if, however, 'man' is taken to stand for itself (as a concept, in simple supposition) then it is false, for no such thing as 'man', in contradistinction to individual men, really exists. As we shall see in the

---

[187] *Ibid.*, 191–2. [188] *Ibid.*, 192–5.
[189] *Ibid.*, 192–3. [190] *Ibid.*, 193–4. [191] *Ibid.*, 194–5.

next chapter, to confuse suppositions and to treat a concept as itself having real
signification—instead of standing for all the individuals coming under it—is to
commit the fallacy of a figure of speech, of which Ockham indicts Duns here.[192]
The same applies to Duns's second argument that what contradicts a nature
contradicts a numerical plurality: it is true when 'nature' stands in personal supposition for real individuals but not when it signifies only itself as a concept.[193]
Ockham reserves his discussion of the primacy of a universal until the next distinction, which we have already considered in the previous chapter.

To Duns's arguments for the difference between a numerical and less than
numerical unity, Ockham distinguishes between unity which is precisely one
and numerical, and a unity which is collective, such as genus or species; in the
latter sense a unity is not necessarily numerical, but neither is it in any way distinct
from the individuals comprising it.[194] As we shall discuss in the next chapter,
genus and species to Ockham are quidditative terms immediately signifying their
individuals and not standing significatively for themselves as independent qualities
or entities. It is the opposite of the Scotist conception and leads Ockham to re-
interpret Duns's references to Aristotle's use of genus and species in a contrary
sense, substituting an individual for a universal unity.[195] He also denies Duns's
view that relation has a real foundation, independent of what is related, a matter
which we shall again consider in the next chapter.[196] Similarly, he affirms that the
object of an act of sensation is numerically and not collectively one, and that the
senses can know one thing from another although, as we saw in the last chapter,
it is the intellect which properly discerns like objects as distinct from one another.[197]
Moreover, just as all real unity is numerical, so is all diversity, including specific
and generic diversity which is the result of numerically different species. That does
not mean that everything which is numerically diverse is equal, nor that if all
diversity were numerical there would be nothing common which the intellect
could abstract from individuals, leaving universals mere figments. Although
Socrates and Plato are numerically diverse as distinct individuals they are also
men. They therefore agree as like being where neither is of the same nature as an
ass or whiteness. At the same time their community is as individual men and not
from some third thing called man existing independently of each.[198] Conversely
while Socrates and Plato differ immediately only as individuals they differ indirectly from an ass or whiteness as belonging to different species and genus. Hence
both similarity and difference—as opposed to mere diversity or otherness—are as
Aristotle says in the Metaphysics[199] by reference to something common, namely
genus or species:[200] which for Ockham is simply whether or not the same common
term can be affirmed immediately and essentially of different individuals; if it
can, as 'man' can be affirmed of Socrates and Plato, they belong to the same
species, and similarly with generic terms like 'animal'; if it cannot they do not.[201]

[192] Ibid., 198–200.
[193] Ibid., 200–1; to confuse supposition also leads to the fallacy of equivocation in using a
term in more than one—unspecified—sense.
[194] Ibid., 202–3.   [195] Ibid., 203–18.   [196] Ibid., 205–8.   [197] Ibid., 209–10.
[198] Ibid., 210–12. [199] Bk. x, 1054 b, 20–30. [200] Ordinatio, ibid., 212–18. [201] Ibid., 219–20.

All of this belongs to the next chapter; here it is designed to expose the difference between the exclusively individual import of a common term when used significatively.

The great division between Duns Scotus and Ockham, then, over the formal distinction is essentially over the principle of singularity. For Duns it can only be through a medium, namely a contracting difference added to the common nature by which that nature becomes individuated. For Ockham the individual is itself individual. Nothing else therefore is needed to explain it. That is the first of two conclusions; it follows because singularity belongs immediately to what is singular and so cannot belong to itself by means of something else.[202] Correspondingly a universal is universal by its own universality; neither therefore can become the other by something added to it.[203]

The second conclusion is that, as we have seen, whatever exists outside the mind is really singular and numerically one, since everything outside the mind is either simple or composite. If simple it does not include a plurality of things and so it is numerically one; if composite it must contain a determinate number of parts, each of which will be numerically one, and so their aggregate will be a numerical unity: otherwise they would be numerically distinct and each numerically one. Moreover all that is numerically one is equally one, with one thing not more indifferent than another, save perhaps on account of superiority, as an angel is superior to an ass.

For Ockham there is thus no problem of individuation. The individual exists in its own right. It does not have to be explained; that is reserved for a universal and what is common which do not really exist formally distinct from an individual.[204] In his own words: 'It is not the cause of individuation that should be sought, save perhaps the extrinsic or intrinsic cause of something composite; but much more it should be asked how something can be common and universal.'[205]

Ockham accordingly countered the Scotist, and Avicennan, notion of being founded upon common natures or essences—like humanity and equinity—with that of individual being in its most thoroughgoing Aristotelian form of actual existence. As such it is defined by its own intrinsic properties and not as a manifestation of a common prior nature. That sets Ockham at the furthest extreme from an Augustinian ontology of a world of essences into which Duns sought to integrate the individual by means of a contracting difference, thereby making the individual the most immediate expression of a common nature. Unlike Duns, Ockham had no such commitment to the separate identity of essences in a world of individuals. He was therefore freed from having to account for each as beings,

---

[202] Ideo dico aliter ad questionem. Et primo ostendo istam conclusionem quod quelibet res singularis se ipsa est singularis. Et hoc persuadeo sic: quia singularitas immediate convenit illi cuius est; igitur non potest sibi convenire per aliquid aliud; igitur si aliquid sit singulare, se ipso est singulare (*ibid.*, 196).

[203] *Ibid.*

[204] Respondeo igitur ad formam questionis, quod illud quod est universale et univocum non est aliquid realiter ex parte rei distinctum formaliter ab individuo. (*ibid.*, 197).

[205] *Ibid.*

which need had hitherto been amongst the central problems of Christian thought. Since, for Ockham, whatever was real was individual, there could be no real difference which was not of individuals. Under the inescapable alternatives of real difference or real identity Ockham dissolved the formal distinction like snow in the sun.

Finally there is what Ockham calls the common conclusion, that there is some kind of universal nature in individuals, if only potentially and incompletely, although opinions differ whether it is distinguished really or formally or mentally.[206] It can be argued in support of this opinion[207] that whatever is really divided into real things and is of their essence, as genus and species are, must itself be real; therefore universals are real. There is also a real identity communicable to individuals which must be universal. Finally since all being is, as Aristotle says divided into ten categories, which includes genus and species, genus and species must be real beings.

This opinion like the others preceding it is untenable because no substance exists outside the mind except perhaps as a conventional term for the purposes of discussion. To begin with, all agree that universal and singular are opposites; they therefore conform with what is opposite and distinct; but not formally or really as has already been proved, nor mentally since an individual is real. They must accordingly be distinguished as mental and real with the universal only in the mind. In the second place, the same thing cannot be really and formally singular and universal as the three previous questions have shown. A universal can be predicated of many things; a singular cannot. Hence they are not the same. Their difference is not due merely to a mental act of composition by which what is singular in itself can be predicated of many, for it would be contradictory to say that something is not only predicated of many and is not predicated of many. A universal is predicable of many before any activity of the intellect, whereas the singular is not and cannot be predicable in the same way.[208] Moreover all that Aristotle and Averroes say on the question of first and second substances confirms that universals are not proper substances.[209]

As to the arguments for this opinion, the difference between a real being divided into its essential parts, as a body is, and things divided into genus and species, is that the latter are only signs; they therefore remain undivided, in the same way as any word signifying many, which is not really part of the term signifying it.[210] Similarly, a more universal or superior term is never of the essence of what is included under it, as less common or inferior, as we have seen in the first chapter in the case of being and shall discuss further in the next chapter.[211] Nor is anything other than the divine essence communicable to individuals by a real identity, as

[206] *Ibid.*, q. 7, 225–6.

[207] *Ibid.*, 229–35. The editors point out (*ibid.*, 229, n. 2) these arguments are from Ockham rather than a particular author he is opposing.

[208] *Ibid.*, 235–7.

[209] *Metaphysics*, passim; *Ordinatio*, *ibid.*, 237–40.

[210] *Ordinatio*, *ibid.*, 255.

[211] *Ibid.*, 255–8.

not everything belonging to the ten categories is itself real being for the reason already mentioned: that all universal terms like genus and species when taken significatively stand immediately and essentially not for themselves but for the individuals coming under them.[212]

So much for the common opinion generally. Of the three variants in which Ockham also considers it, the first, held by St Thomas Aquinas and Harvey Natalis, is that in individuals there is a form which in its actual existence is singular and without unity, and only as conceived by reason is a unity. It does not therefore subsist of itself in any individual, whether as a genus which needs the addition of another form, namely a species, or as a species which is itself one and universal and independent of another species but outside the mind particular, divided among its individuals.[213]

Ockham rejects this opinion on familiar grounds: if a universal is distinct from the individual which designates it, they must be distinguished either as real things, which has already been disproved; or in the intellect, and then one of them will be only the work of the intellect, because nothing is really distinguished from something else unless they are real, just as nothing real is the same as something else simply according to the intellect.[214] In fact there is no such difference among creatures because whatever is distinguished formally—as not the same as something else—must be distinguished in reality, and nothing created can be the same and yet something else.[215]

The second of these opinions is that the same thing is singular as it exists outside the intellect and universal in the intellect, so that it is both singular and universal in different states of existence.[216] Ockham's reply is that, since universality must be the work of the intellect, by the same token anything singular can be known as universal, say Socrates or the divine essence which in itself is supremely singular. The absurdity of such a consequence is confirmed by the principle that whenever something of its nature contradicts something else they cannot be reconciled by anything extrinsic. That applies to singular and universal: regardless of how it is known, a singular can never become a universal.[217]

Lastly there is the corresponding view of Henry of Harclay that the same thing known under one concept is singular and under another universal, so that as Avicenna said, singular and universal are but different aspects of the same thing. On the one hand everything outside the mind is singular; on the other it can move the intellect to know it both distinctly and confusedly: in the latter aspect it is universal in being indistinguishable from something else, as Socrates known confusedly—as a man rather than as Socrates—is not distinguished from Plato. From that Henry concludes that universal terms like man, animal, body, signify the same thing as the particular term of which they are affirmed. Hence the proposition 'Socrates is a man' is only another way of saying 'Socrates is Socrates'. All such distinctions between superior and inferior terms are accordingly solely from the intellect.[218]

---

[212] *Ibid.*, 258-9.   [213] *Ibid.*, 226-7.   [214] *Ibid.*, 240; and q. 2, 64-5.
[215] *Ibid.*, 240 and q. 1, 19.   [216] *Ibid.*, 227.   [217] *Ibid.*, 241.   [218] *Ibid.*, 228.

This opinion, like the other two to which it belongs, and unlike the opinions preceding them, thus makes no real distinction between universal and singular save in the intellect. Where they all agree, however, is in regarding universals as really part of individuals and so in some way real.[219] They are therefore equally false, and Henry's both false and unintelligible, because if a thing indistinctly conceived is universal it will be common to something else and predicated of the latter as superior of inferior. Socrates would then be Plato known indistinctly and likewise God, who is not known distinctly, would be a creature. That follows whether a common term is taken significatively for something real in personal supposition or for a concept in simple supposition; in both cases a common term like 'animal' will make that of which it is affirmed the same as something else of which it can be affirmed, so that if Socrates or Plato or an ass is each an animal known confusedly, each will be the other. It is equally nonsensical to attribute superiority and inferiority to things as conceived by the mind; for nothing, however it is considered, is superior in the same way as it is not indifferent. It also contradicts Henry's other statement that nothing existing outside the mind is common or indifferent.[220] For that reason it is false to say that the same thing under one concept is singular and under another is universal, since a thing that is itself singular is in no way universal: whenever an antecedent is qualified but not restricted or diminished, the conclusion will follow without qualification, as it does in the propositions 'A thing under such a concept is universal; therefore the thing is universal'. But the conclusion is false, for there is no such thing; so therefore is the antecedent, and nothing under a certain concept is universal.[221] It is also impossible for the same thing to have both singular and common meaning as in the proposition 'Some man is a species or a universal' where 'some man' can only stand for an individual man. To attribute both singularity and universality to man as an individual is thus to commit the fallacy of equivocation in using the same term in more than one sense; and conversely when 'man' is taken in a universal sense, he cannot have individual signification. All such cases of conceiving individuals differently according to their different aspects implies that they can be unqualified without any determinations: they would then lose any identity, with the result that a man under one concept could as well be called an ass, and under another an ox and under a third a lion, absurdities which would negate any rational means of discourse.[222]

Universals then do not exist outside the mind either by themselves or by something real or mental added to them, no matter how they are considered.[223]

---

[219] Sic ergo omnes iste opiniones ponunt quod universale et singulare sunt eadem res realiter, nec differunt nisi secundum rationem; et in hoc discrepant a tribus opinionibus recitatis in tribus questionibus precedentibus. Onmes tamen in hoc conveniunt quod universalia sunt aliquo modo a parte rei, ita quod universalia sunt realiter in ipsis singularibus (ibid., 229).

[220] Ibid., 241–3, 249–50.

[221] Ibid., 244–7; cf. SL I, ch. 16, 51, where the same argument is employed against Scotus.

[222] Ibid., 247–8.

[223] Ideo aliter dico ad questionem quod nulla res extra animam nec per se nec per aliquid additum, reale vel rationis, nec qualitercumque consideretur vel intelligatur, est universalis (ibid., 248–9). Cf. SL, I, ch. 15, 46–8.

The only exception is perhaps a word employed as conventional sign, for example 'man', in itself singular but with a universal import.[224] Otherwise it is as impossible for a real man to be universal as it is for him to be an ass. Nor does any universal exist in the individuals to which it is universal any more than a word is part of what it signifies.[225] Just as, according to Averroes,[226] definitions are not the substances of things but their signs, so substances are individuals composed not of universals but form and matter. Universals are such only by predication, not inherence, as the minds response to what exists outside it.[227] As Ockham expresses it,

Nature works unseen in universals, not in producing universals outside the mind, but because by producing its knowledge in the mind unconsciously (*quasi occulte*)—whether directly or indirectly—it produces these universals as a natural process. And so all that is in common is in that sense natural and comes from outside the mind, but it can be [produced] in the mind.[228]

Universals are thus the result of the mind's activity; and what occurs in the mind does not affect what exists outside it. When it knows universally it does not make anything real universal: it merely knows what can only exist individually in another way. How it does so belongs to its own nature and must be taken as given; and with it the discrepancy between the mental and the real which is the foundation of Ockham's epistemology. Far therefore from seeking to deny an independent conceptual order, Ockham is concerned to stress its autonomy and to rescue what really exists from its confusion with what only exists in the mind. However we may wish to describe his outlook, it is as antithetical to a crude nominalism—in its eleventh- and twelfth-century sense of denying any meaning to universals—as it is to a realism which assigns them independent existence. Ockham for the first time since Abelard, though for quite different reasons, reverted to a psychological explanation of universals as the mind's natural signs—whether as *ficta* or as acts of intellection did not affect their mental status—and not as real being or in real being. That enabled him in turn to redefine their logical role as conventional signs, or terms, which we shall consider in the next chapter. In each aspect their significance is precisely in denoting real things, however divergently.

It is among the purposes of logic is to identify these different modes of signification. That can be done only by reference to actual being which as exclusively individual means that the individual becomes the criterion of all existential import. What that implies for logical and scientific discourse should become apparent over the rest of this book, and first as it concerns terms themselves.

224 *Ibid.*, 249.
225 *Ibid.*, 252.
226 *Commentary on Metaphysics*, bk. VII, (*Opera Omnia*, ed. Iuntina (Venice, 1574), VIII, f. 93 r).
227 *Ordinatio, ibid.*, 252–3.
228 *Ibid.*, 261.

CHAPTER THREE

Terms and their modes
of signification

HAVING CONSIDERED the source of the intellect's knowledge and the concepts which it forms, we now turn in the next two chapters to the logical disposition in terms and propositions of what is known. That takes us in the third chapter to the different modes of simple signification—namely, the diverse ways in which terms can stand in propositions as signs for real things and for other signs—and in the fourth chapter to complex—i.e. propositional—forms of knowledge as statements of what is true or untrue or doubtful and of their inferential relation in syllogisms and demonstrations. Together these two chapters represent the most systematic part of Ockham's thought and the one where—apart from the smaller scale of the uncompleted *Summulae Physicorum*, to be considered in chapter nine—we can talk of a system. It was achieved in the *Logic* (*Summa Logicae*), which can as I have said before be regarded as Ockham's master work; it is the basis of what follows here complemented by the Logical Commentaries, the two smaller later logical treatises, the Prologue to the Commentary on the *Sentences*, with certain questions from its *Ordinatio* and *Reportatio* and from the *Quodlibets*. The change in form from the preceding chapters will be apparent; although there are areas of polemic—over quantity, relation, essential definition among others—for the most part the discussion is expository, concerned with stating and establishing the rules of logical discourse. That does not mean that much of what Ockham said was not controversial: it was, and wherever ontological import was concerned. Formally Ockham was not a logical innovator; beyond the adoption of the terminist category of supposition—and a mention of the category of appellation—his one departure from the traditional Aristotelian framework was his treatment of consequences, which we shall not consider. It was the exclusively individual import which he gave to all terms and propositions that distinguishes his logic from that of his predecessors. What they had for the most part regarded as metaphysical categories he treated as logical categories; he did so not because he was a logician who reduced philosophy and theology to logic, as he has in the past been depicted, but because his logic and his philosophy, and by extension of what could naturally said of theology, were founded upon an ontology of individual existence and an epistemology of individual cognition. It is that which makes his logic central to his outlook; for it was there that he systematically sought to resolve the discrepancies between the exclusively individual nature of all being and the universality of all proper knowledge. He thus began from the opposite of the traditional neo-platonically-inspired assumption—which had hitherto dominated medieval thought—of a direct rapport between being and thinking. For Ockham it was the discrepancy between individual things and our concepts of natures and essences that required investigation. And logic was the instrument, in the ways we shall now consider.

I TERMS AND SIGNS

Ockham defines the subject of logic at the beginning of the *Logic* (*Summa Logicae*). It is, he says, concerned with arguments or syllogisms, propositions, and terms, each reducible to the other. Terms form the basic constituents of propositions, in the relation of subject and predicate; arguments or syllogisms rest upon propositions.[1]

Now so far as terms are concerned they are not all of the same kind: they can be spoken, written or mental, as concepts in the mind (*concepta*).[2] Until the time of Duns Scotus, Boethius's interpretation of this threefold division had been the accepted one, deriving from Aristotle's remark at the beginning of *Perihermenias* that spoken words are the symbols of concepts and written words are the symbols of spoken words.[3] Boethius took that to mean that concepts directly signify the object whereas words, as the signs of concepts, only signify indirectly through concepts.[4] Ockham, however, followed Duns Scotus in treating words themselves, written and spoken, as direct signs, reinterpreting Boethius's statement that words are subordinated to concepts to mean not that words strictly stand for the concepts themselves, as their signs, but that they signify the same as concepts signify. It is in that sense that words are subordinated; for the word is a conventional sign imposed to signify what is already known naturally in the soul as a concept. Accordingly, the meaning of a word is dependent upon the meaning of the same thing which has been signified in a concept; and if the latter were to change so would the signification of the word, without changing its form. Hence whatever a word signifies directly and primarily it will always signify a concept secondarily.[5]

Ockham had already stated the same doctrine more emphatically and at greater length in distinction twenty-two of the *Ordinatio*.[6] There he took the accepted division between words of first and second imposition—to be mentioned later—to show that some words signify things, others concepts, and others mental states. Whichever the case, all words have been instituted to signify that for which

---

[1] *SL*, bk. I, ch. I, 8.
[2] *Ibid.*, 8–9.
[3] *Perihermenias*, ch. I, 16 a, 4–7.
[4] Boehner, *Collected Articles*, 218 ff.
[5] Sic etiam intendit Boethius quando dicit voces significare conceptus; et universaliter omnes auctores dicentes quod omnes voces significant passiones vel sunt note earum, non aliud intentunt nisi quod voces sunt signa secundario significantia earum (*SL, ibid.* 9).
[6] *Ibid.*, C–G.

they stand—their significates. When a word stands for a concept, that is because it does not signify the things of which it is a concept. Although there can be a concept of whatever is known, that does not mean that everything is known through a concept; indeed the knowledge of a concept which comes through a spoken word itself derives from previous knowledge of an individual thing. It will be seen therefore that Ockham's notion of direct signification by terms rests upon the primacy of intuitive knowledge in all that is directly known. That will become more apparent.

Immediately, the distinction between natural and conventional terms is that a conventional term can always change its meaning whereas a natural term cannot.[7] The absence of limitation upon a conventional term accounts, as we shall see, for the way in which it can be imposed upon several concepts to give equivocal predication as it can also be instituted to stand for one concept alone.

Just as there are natural and conventional terms, so there are natural and conventional signs by which terms are able to signify. A sign in its broadest—and natural—sense is that which, in being known, makes something else known; it does so not directly but through habitual knowledge already present in the intellect, as we have considered in the first chapter.[8] As Boehner says, such knowledge implies two cognitions—of the sign and of the thing known by means of the sign; which means that knowledge engendered by the sign was previously in the intellect as second abstractive knowledge.[9] The importance of this view is that, for Ockham, as we have again seen in the first chapter, no sign can give primary or actual knowledge of something else; it can only call to mind what is already known and inheres in the mind as a habit. Only if at source we have already known something can its sign enable us to know it again, in the way that a barrel hoop (circulus) signifies wine in the tavern and thus knowledge of the fact.[10]

Here, too, Ockham's position derives from what he considers to be the correct order, from immediate intuitive cognition to conceptual knowledge; we shall consider in chapter four how it leads to demonstrative knowledge; in passing we may remark that its condition, namely that all demonstrative knowledge must be founded upon intuitive or self-evident knowledge, in no way entails the scepticism associated with successors of Ockham such as Nicholas of Autrecourt. Ockham only denied that incomplex knowledge of one thing could be had from simple knowledge of another incomplex thing,[11] which he expressly contrasted to the actual, i.e. scientific, knowledge of another thing only gained through complex knowledge, by means of propositions. Far from denying inference from one thing to another, or evidence of causality, Ockham was restating the conditions for

---

[7] Inter autem istos terminos alique differentie reperiuntur. Una est quod conceptus sive passio anime naturaliter significat quidquid significat; terminus autem prolatus vel scriptus nibil significat nisi secundum secundariam institutionem. Ex quo sequitur alia differentia, videlicet, quod terminus prolatus vel scriptus ad placitum potest mutare suum significatum; terminus autem conceptus non mutat suum significatum ad placitum cuiuscumque. (SL, ibid.).

[8] Ibid., 9–10.

[9] Boehner, Collected Articles, 203–4; Boehner calls it second recordative knowledge.

[10] SL, ibid., 9.

[11] As Boehner stressed (Collected Articles, 203–4).

valid deduction by which, in default of immediate experience of one thing, we can infer it from experience of another. In Ockham's own words:

But for something to lead to knowledge of something else can be understood in two ways, either as causative of knowledge of something else . . . so that knowledge of it is the cause of knowledge of the other or immediately without [any other] knowledge, as the intellect as cause leads immediately to knowledge of whatever is intelligible. The first way has two modes giving rise either to first knowledge (or cognition) or only to recollection of something known habitually. By the first of these modes singular knowledge is the cause of universal knowledge, and knowledge of the premises is the cause of knowledge of the conclusion. But this way incomplex knowledge of one thing is never the cause of first knowledge of another incomplex, as stated in the Prologue, and especially not the sufficient cause, together with the intellect and others required by the intellect . . . By the second mode one incomplex by means of its knowledge can be the partial cause of remembering something else (already) known habitually, so that such habitual knowledge acts as partial cause. What is thus known can be called representative of another thing, and nothing else is strictly representative.[12]

Thus, to repeat an earlier example, to see a statue of Hercules without already knowing Hercules, is no more to know him than to know Achilles or Socrates through seeing the same statue.[13] An image or sign is only representative of what is already known habitually; it can then as partial cause enable us to know through recollection something else actually, where of its own nature it would not represent one individual more than another.[14]

These characteristics of a natural sign are the pendant to what Ockham has said about terms. As constituting second abstractive knowledge, natural signs cannot give direct knowledge of things which they signify; they cannot therefore serve as the invariable intermediaries between conventional terms and the things signified. On the contrary, as we shall see, they can as natural terms have no signification in the strict sense, as well as be without reference to anything real outside the mind. Ockham does not, however, employ sign in this wide conceptual sense; he takes it in its other meaning of linguistic term, such as verbs or syncathegoremata (i.e. terms not having any definite signification), which belong to propositions and can stand for things by imposition, but not naturally.[15]

Similarly, of the three ways in which a term can be understood, Ockham usually takes it, as he has in the previous discussion, in the second sense of any incomplex word contained in a proposition, not only subject and predicate (cathegoremata) but verbs, adjectives and all indefinite terms (syncathegoremata) which do not stand for anything.[16] This is in contrast to the first sense of 'term' as a group of words (oratio) including sentence or proposition, and the third sense

---

[12] Ordinatio, I., d. 3, q. 9, OT II, 544–5. See also Prologue, q. 9: Et ideo notitia illuis singularis erit causa notitia illius communis, tamen notitia unius singularis nunquam est causa sufficiens—cum intellectu—notitie alterius rei singularis que non est communis sibi (OT I, 254; also 255).

[13] Ibid. [14] Ordinatio, d. 3, q. 9, 545–6. [15] SL, I, ch. I, 10.

[16] The division between cathegorematic and syncathegorematic terms is between words which have a definite signification, like 'man' or 'white', and words which taken alone do not —'every', 'none', 'some', 'only'—but when added to a cathegorematic term do stand for something, e.g. 'every man': cf. SL, I, ch. 4, 15–16. The terms antedate Ockham and medieval logicians.

where it is identified with the subject or predicate when they stand for something else.[17]

No part of Ockham's thinking has been more widely misrepresented than his theory of terms. With the honourable exception of a few pioneers, above all Moody, Baudry, Boehner, Vignaux, it has, like his logic as a whole, been treated as mainly a doctrine of terminism. In fact, as Moody first showed over thirty years ago,[18] the only category which Ockham adopted from the thirteenth century terminist logicians was the distinction between signification and supposition. That it was fundamental to Ockham's thinking we shall shortly see in more detail; and for the very reason that it was not merely logical but also conceptual and epistemological. Far from reducing one to the other Ockham's theory of terms was an intricate analysis of the discrepancies and interaction between concepts as natural signs, words as conventional signs, and things as exclusively individual.

Thus to begin with, all conventional signs (*signa ad placitum instituta*) are, as we have seen, secondary to concepts which are the primary signs. Independently of whether we take them as *ficta* or *intellectiones*—Ockham had, it will be recalled, adopted the latter as the explanation by the time of the *Logic*—concepts are natural signs designed to signify something for which they can stand, independently or as part of mental propositions.[19] It is precisely over the relation of concepts as natural signs and terms of mental propositions to the corresponding role of conventional signs that Ockham's theory of signification and supposition is best understood. Although there is no direct correspondence between them, just because natural signs lack the variety and multiplicity of grammatical accidents possessed by conventional signs,[20] natural signs provide the *raison d'être* of conventional signs. If the intellect had no concepts of things there would be nothing for words to signify. But words can also be used non-significatively to express both concepts and themselves. Accordingly the great distinction is between terms which signify something else and those which refer only to terms as words and concepts. This entails not only an asymmetry between signification and supposition, but between concepts as natural signs and words as conventional signs, expressed in the distinction between first and second imposition.

Imposition, as the naming of signs and objects by convention, or arbitrarily, is itself defined by reference to natural signs or concepts. We shall therefore be able better to discuss imposition when we have considered natural signs. Natural signs or concepts are divided into terms of first intention and second intention; together these determine the nature of all signs, that is terms which stand for something distinct from themselves. Both first and second intentions can be understood in a broad and a strict sense. Ockham discusses them in three works,

---

[17] *Ibid.*, ch. 2, 10–11: Aliter accipitur hoc nomen 'terminus' secundum quod distinguitur contra orationem: et sic omne incomplexium vocatur terminus (*ibid.*, 10). An *oratio* can be either, in a broad sense, any grouping of words, or more strictly a sentence or proposition (Commentary on *Perihermenias*, ch. 3, *EA*, 96(a)–97(b)).

[18] *Logic of William of Ockham*, 189.

[19] *SL*, I, ch. 12, 39.

[20] *Ibid.*, ch. 3, 11–15.

the *Ordinatio*, the *Logic*, and the *Quodlibets*,[21] without any noticeable variation. He defines terms of first intention as signs for real things as opposed to their signs, though the latter can also be included with the things signified: man, animal, Socrates, Plato, whiteness, white, being, true, good are all examples.[22] Taken broadly, a first intention can include every natural sign which does not stand for any other sign, in whatever sense—broad or strict—sign is understood. That means verbs, syncathegoremata, and all other incomplex terms which alone do not stand for anything else, but which when joined to a cathegorematic—i.e. definite term which does stand for something else—can signify things: thus the term 'every' added to 'man' can designate individual men, as in the proposition 'Every man runs'.[23]

Terms of second intention on the other hand are the signs of first intentions, that is, signs of signs or concepts such as genus, species and so on. Thus where a first intention like the term 'man' is predicated of every individual man, terms of second intention like 'species' are predicated of the term 'man'.[24] In its broad sense a term of second intention signifies not only concepts, which are natural signs of first intention in the strict sense, but also conventional signs in so far as they signify mental syncathegorematic signs. How far there are such signs is open to question: and in opining that perhaps they are only words,[25] Ockham was expressing the same doubt just adverted to, over the exact degree of correspondence between words as conventional signs and concepts as their natural counterpart in the soul. That does not affect his broad definition of second intentions as all those signs in the soul which can signify first intentions. Taken in their strict sense, second intentions are concepts which exclusively signify first intentions as natural signs. They can thereby stand for the latter in a proposition, as 'species', as a term of second intention, can take the place of 'man' as a term of first intention, because a second intention thus understood is the natural sign of a first intention which is in turn the natural sign of real things.[26]

By the time he came to write the *Quodlibets* Ockham, as we have seen, identified a concept with an act of intellection. He accordingly answered affirmatively the question whether first and second intentions are distinct.[27] This helps to clarify

---

[21] *Ordinatio*, d. 23, q. 1, C, *SL*, I, chs. 11 and 12. *Quodlibet* IV, 19 and VII, q. 16.

[22] E.g. Nomina autem prime intentionis vocantur omnia alia nomina a predictis [terms of second intention], que videlicet significant aliquas res, que non sunt signa nec consequentia talia signa, cuiusmodi sunt omnia talia: 'homo', 'animal', 'Sortes', 'Plato', 'albedo', 'album', 'ens', 'verum', 'bonum' et huiusmodi, quorum aliqua significant precise res que non sunt signa nata supponere pro aliis, aliqua significant talia signa et simul cum hoc alias res (*SL*, I, ch. 11, 38).

[23] *Ibid.*, ch. 12, 40; *Quodlibet* IV, q. 19; *Ordinatio, ibid.*

[24] Intentio autem secunda est illa que est signum talium intentionum primarum, cuiusmodi sunt tales intentiones 'genus', 'species' et huiusmodi. Sicut enim de omnibus hominibus predicantur una intentio communis omnibus hominibus . . . ita de illis intentionibus, que significant et supponunt pro rebus, predicatur una intentio communis eis sic dicendo: 'Haec species est species', 'illa species est species' et sic de aliis. (*SL*, I, ch. 12, 40); also *Ordinatio, ibid.*; *Quodlibet*, IV, *ibid.*; and *SL*, III, iii, ch. 45.

[25] *SL, ibid.*, *Quodlibet* IV, q. 21.

[26] *Ibid.*, especially *Quodlibet* IV, q. 19.

[27] *Quodlibet* IV, q. 19. Utrum intentiones prime et secunde realiter distinguantur.

the difference between intentions as natural signs, which govern all significative terms, and imposition.

Imposition is also divided into first and second, each understood broadly and strictly. Both kinds constitute conventional signs; but whereas terms of second imposition refer to names of conventional signs, and so are names of names, terms of first imposition are conventional signs for all terms of first and second intention: that is, the names of natural signs. In Ockham's own words: 'Names of second imposition are names imposed to signify conventional signs (*ad placitum instituta*) and those contained by such signs, provided they serve as signs.'[28] These are grammatical terms like 'noun', 'verb', 'participle', 'case', and so on. In the broad sense, a name of second imposition is every word which signifies a conventional sign regardless of whether it corresponds to a natural sign, or concept, in the mind, such as those just instanced. These come essentially within the province of the grammarian who uses them exclusively for the parts of speech but only significatively. That excludes all names which can be used non-significatively, even though they can also signify a term: thus words like 'quality' or 'sound' are not names of second imposition because they can be imposed without having to signify another name.[29] It is in that sense that 'name' is a word of second imposition, because it can only be called a name when it is imposed upon another name say 'man': until then it is not a name since it has no name—such as man—which it can signify.[30] That is why only a name denoting a name is a term of second imposition. Strictly, this means only conventional names, as opposed to all concepts, applying to words like 'conjugation' and 'figure' which have no equivalent natural signs in the mind.[31]

Names of first imposition are in the broad sense all those which do not belong to second imposition, and include all syncathegorematic words like 'every', 'none', and so on. Strictly, however, they apply only to cathegoremata, of both first and second intention.[32] They therefore differ from names of second imposition in signifying both words and concepts as words of first and second intention, which together combine both conventional and natural signs in the way we have already considered.[33]

[28] *SL*, I, ch. 11, 36; also *Ordinatio*, I, d. 22, q. 1, C; *Quodlibet* VII, q. 10.

[29] Et vocantur ista nomina 'nomina nominum', quia non imponuntur nisi ad significandum partes orationis, et hoc non nisi dum iste partes sunt significative. Illa enim nomina que predicantur de vocibus, ita quando non sunt significative sicut quando sunt significative, non vocantur nomina secunde impositionis. Et ideo talia nomina, 'qualitas', 'prolatum', 'vox' et huiusmodi, quamuis significent voces ad placitum et verificentur de eis, quia tamen ita significarent eas, si non essent significative, sient nunc ideo non sunt nomina secunde impositionis. (*SL*, *ibid.*, 36–7). Also *Quodlibet* VII, q. 16, where the text is almost identical.

[30] *Ibid.*

[31] Stricte autem dicitur nomen secunde impositiones illiud quod non significat nisi ad placium instituta, ita quod non potest competere intentionibus anime, que sunt naturalia signa, cuiusmodi sunt talia: 'figura', 'coniugatio' et huiusmodi (*SL*, *ibid.*, 37); also *Quodlibet* VII, q. 16.

[32] *Ibid.*

[33] Stricte autem accipiendo nomen prime impositionis sic solum nomina cathegorematica sunt nomina prime impositionis. Sed illa sunt in duplici differentia, quia quedam sunt nomina prime intentionis et quedam sunt nomina secunde intentionis (*Quodlibet* VII, q. 16); also *SL*, *ibid.*

Ockham resumes these different kinds of signs as follows:

Certain names signify solely conventional signs and only when they are signs (these are of second imposition); others signify both conventional and natural signs (these can be both signs of first imposition and second imposition);[34] others again stand exclusively for things which are not signs or terms in propositions (first intention); and yet others indifferently signify the such real things and also signs, like 'being', 'something' and so on (again first intentions).[35]

To this we may add signs which stand for these signs of real things, which are second intentions.

As we shall see, despite the inevitable intricacy of these distinctions when so defined, the main divisions are twofold: between natural and artificial signs (or concepts and words), and between signs for real things and the signs for those signs. Although they overlap, as we have seen, the first division is broadly between intention and imposition, and the second between first and second intention.

II SUPPOSITION AND SIGNIFICATION

So far we have been concerned with the different modes in which signs can signify, and the different kinds of terms which correspond to those modes. We must now distinguish between such signs and those which have no significative function, merely standing for themselves as either natural or conventional signs. The importance of this distinction lay in establishing the truth of a proposition, which, as Boehner remarked, is when subject and predicate stand for the same thing.[36] That was the purpose of supposition, a device introduced by the thirteenth century terminist logicians, Peter of Spain and William of Sherwood, and effectively, as we have said, the only one taken over—with modifications—by Ockham from them and their successors.

Supposition concerns the relations of terms as subject and predicate; it therefore only applies to terms in propositions. By it, according to Ockham, a term could stand in a proposition in one of three different ways: significatively in personal supposition (*suppositio personalis*) for some thing or sign other than itself, or non-significatively either as a concept, when it is in simple supposition (*suppositio simplex*), or as a word and then it is in material supposition (*suppositio materialis*). That is to say, according to whether the predicate stands for something other than

[34] Baudry, *Lexique*, 114, equates these with second imposition in the broad sense; that is true only negatively in that it does not exclude natural signs, but positively their inclusion comes under first imposition (cf. preceding note) and second intention (see note 24). Boehner on the other hand (*Collected Articles*, 229) recognises second intentions but omits first imposition.

[35] Ex quibus omnibus colligi potest quod quedam nomina significant precise signa ad placitum instituta, et non nisi dum sunt signa; quedam precise significant signa tam ad placitum instituta quam signa naturalia. Quedam precise significant res que non sunt signa talia, que sunt partes propositionis; quedam indifferenter significant tales res que non sunt partes propositionis nec orationis, et etiam talia signa, cuiusmodi sunt talia nomina: 'res', 'ens', 'aliquid' et huiusmodi (*SL*, ibid., 38).

[36] *Collected Articles*, 232: cf. *SL*, I, ch. 63, 176. Est igitur una regula generalis, quod nunquem terminus in aliqua propositione, saltem significative accipitur, supponit pro aliquo nisi de quo predicatur vere.

the subject, or for the subject itself as either a concept (i.e. a second intention) or a word, written or spoken (i.e. a term by second imposition) the subject of which one or other of these is affirmed will be in personal, simple or material supposition. These represent the three different ways terms can stand in propositions.

Before we consider them more closely we need to recognise the asymmetry between personal supposition on the one hand, and simple and material supposition, on the other. The difference between them is not between standing for real things as opposed to concepts and words; it is between terms which *signify*, no matter what—not only things, concepts, words, but anything imaginable—and terms which do not, standing only for themselves. For that reason supposition and signification are in turn asymmetrical: all signification implies supposition but not *vice versa*, since by definition simple and material supposition are non-significative.[37] The importance of this distinction is precisely that it overcomes terminological confusions, such as those which lead to the paradox of the liar, by showing how a term is being used, above all whether significatively or non-significatively. As Moody has written: 'Thus in the statement "What I am saying is false", the subject term stands either for itself as a term (in which case the predicate "false" can not signify anything that is not a proposition) or else it stands for something other than itself (e.g. for "What I have just said") in which case there is no vicious circle.'[38] We shall return to that in the next chapter.

We have in effect already seen this distinction at work in the preceding chapters. Earlier medieval writers had distinguished between formal and material supposition:[39] in material supposition a word stood for the term itself, in formal supposition for something represented by it. William of Sherwood and Peter of Spain had further subdivided formal supposition into personal supposition and simple supposition. But the threefold division adopted by Ockham seems to have been that of Raymond Lull, although it also has affinities with Sherwood.[40] Ockham employed it in the Logical Commentaries making up the so-called *Expositio Aurea*, and in the Commentary on the *Sentences*: but he did not first formally define supposition until the second and fourth distinctions of the *Ordinatio*, and again in the Commentary on *The Sophistical Questions* with his fullest treatment in the *Summa Logicae*, to which must be added the recently discovered and edited *Elementarium Logicae* and the briefer *Tractatus Logicae Minor*. Neither of these alters Ockham's previous positions found in the *Summa Logicae*, which is the basis of what follows; apart from certain precisions—to be noticed—in the *Elementarium*, the one obvious difference is the formal one, that both the lesser works treat supposition after propositions and not before as in the *Summa Logicae*. But in all three works Ockham is equally clear that supposition belongs to terms in propositions, where, as we have said, it can alone occur.[41]

[37] Cf. Boehner, *Collected Articles.*, 232 ff.; Moody, *Logic of William of Ockham*, 41–4, 189.
[38] Moody, *ibid.*, 43.   [39] For what follows see Moody, *ibid.*, 41–2, n. 1.
[40] Boehner, *Collected Articles*, 236.
[41] Dicto de significationibus terminorum, restat dicere de suppositione que est proprietas conveniens termino sed nunquam nisi in propositione. (*SL*, I, ch. 63, 175).

Taken in the broad sense in which it is not distinguished from appellation—another terminist category mentioned only in the two lesser treatises and nowhere else employed by Ockham—supposition etymologically means the substitution of one term in a proposition for another, either as what is predicated (subject) or that which predicates (predicate).[42] Thus, for 'Socrates is an animal' we could substitute the pronoun 'this' so that in the proposition 'This is an animal', 'this' supposits for 'Socrates'.[43] But whatever the case, a term in any proposition—certainly when used significatively—must be true if it is to stand for another. For that reason it is wrong to say, as some who are ignorant do, that a concrete term predicated of something stands for its abstract counterpart, so that 'white', as predicate, denotes 'whiteness'.[44] As we shall consider shortly, concrete and abstract terms do not always have the same significations and cannot then be treated as synonyms.

That brings us to the different forms of supposition, which arise just because terms can have different meanings. Personal supposition is 'when a term stands for what is signified, whether what is signified is a thing outside the soul . . . or a word or a concept, or something written, or anything else imaginable, so that whenever the subject or predicate of a proposition stands for its significate, so that it is held significatively, it is always personal supposition'.[45] That applies to a proposition like 'Every man is an animal', where 'man' stands for every individual man, as opposed to something common,[46] and equally to propositions such as 'Every spoken word is part of a sentence', or 'Every species is a universal', or 'Every concept is in the soul'; in each case the subject stands for something other than itself. A term is thus in personal supposition when it is a sign for something, regardless of whether what it signifies is a real thing or a term or a concept.[47]

Simple supposition is 'when a term stands for a concept but not significatively'.[48] Thus, in the proposition 'Man is a species', 'man' stands for the concept, that is, for itself, and so it does not strictly signify a concept, in not signifying something other than itself. Both word and concept are consequently subordinated to signifying the same thing, namely the kind of sign which it is; its meaning does not extend beyond what it is.[49] It is here that Ockham departed from tradition in denying simple supposition independent signification. In contradistinction to

---

[42] Est autem sciendum quod suppositio accipitur dupliciter, scilicet large et stricte. Large accepta non distinguitur contra appellationem, sed appellatio est unum contentum sub suppositione. Aliter accipitur stricte, secundum quod distinguitur contra appellationem. Sed sic non intendo loqui de suppositione, sed primo modo tantum. Et sic tam subiectum quam predicatum supponit; et universaliter, quidquid potest esse subiectum propositionis vel predicatum, supponit. Dicitur autem suppositio quasi pro alio positio, ita quod quando terminus stat in propositione pro aliquo . . . supponit pro illo (*ibid.*, 175–6). Also *Ordinatio*, d. 2, q. 4, 134–7, and d. 4, q. 1, E–F.

[43] *SL, ibid.*, 176.   [44] *Ibid.*   [45] *Ibid.*, ch. 64, 177.

[46] Non enim proprie significat aliquod commune eis, sed ipsosmet homines (*ibid.*).

[47] *Ibid.*   [48] *Ibid.*, 178.

[49] Verbi gratia sic dicendo: 'Homo est species' iste terminus 'homo', supponit pro intentione anime, quia illa intentio est species, et tamen iste terminus 'homo' non significat proprie loquendo illam intentionem, sed illa vox et illa intentio anime sunt tantum signa subordinata in significando idem (*ibid.*).

Roger Bacon and later Walter Burley, Ockham, against whom Burley's treatise
De Puritate Artis Logicae was written,[50] allowed simple supposition no more real
import than material supposition; one was affirmed of a term as a concept, the
other of a term as word. And Ockham expressly warned against the common
misconception that in simple supposition the term stands for its significate; in
that case a concept would be a real thing instead of just a concept.[51] From that we
can see that it is in virtue of his ontological principles, and not through being a
terminist logician, that Ockham holds to this interpretation. The non-existence of
anything else than individuals entails that simple supposition, in being of concepts,
is of nothing real outside the mind. Hence it does not have real signification.

The same applies to material supposition where in Ockham's words, 'A term
does not stand significatively but for what is either written or spoken'.[52]. For
example in the propositions ' "Man" is a name', ' "Man" is written', 'man' stands
for the word itself without signifying it.[53] The difference is that in material supposition the subject can stand for any part of a proposition, not only complex and
incomplex, significative and non-significative, but for any words, spoken or
written, whether adverbs, verbs, pronouns, conjunctions, propositions, inter-
jections, or participles, as well as propositions and expressions, for example ' "Man
is an animal" is a true proposition' or ' "Man runs" is an expression', ' "Reading"
is a participle', ' "If" is a conjuction', and so on. Both in material and simple
supposition, however, a term sometimes does not stand for itself but for a word
or concept in another construction or case; but it remains non-significative.[54]
In the *Elementarium Logicae* Ockham makes this distinction more precise: if a term
stands for itself in a mental proposition it is then in simple supposition, as opposed
to material supposition in a written or spoken proposition, since the term is then a
concept, and not a word.[55] He also adds that a term which stands for another term
non-significatively is not in material or simple supposition by the strictest mode;[56]
and correspondingly a term is only in personal supposition improperly when it
stands for conventional signs significatively.[57]

Now ordinarily a term will always be in personal supposition save when it is
limited to one of the other two kinds by voluntary imposition: namely when the
predicate is a concept or word.[58] In other words, in personal supposition a term
signifies naturally or by imposition; in simple or material supposition it is only
through imposition. For that reason personal supposition as the natural mode of
employing a term in a proposition, namely to signify something else—whether a
thing or a natural or conventional sign—is primary; only when the intention of

[50] S. F. Brown, 'Walter Burleigh's *Treatise de Suppositionibus* and its influence on William of
Ockham', *FcS* 32 (1972) 21–6. Ockham opposes Burleigh's opinion, *Ordinatio*, d. 4, q. 1, F.

[51] *Ibid.*   [52] *Ibid.*   [53] *Ibid.*   [54] *Ibid.*, chs. 67 and 68, 186–7.

[55] *Elementarium*, 204.   [56] *Ibid.*, 208.   [57] *Ibid.*, 205.

[58] Notandum est etian quod semper terminus, in quocumque propositione ponatur, potest
habere suppositionem personalem, nisi ex voluntate utentium artetur ad aliam ... Sed terminus
non in omni propositione potest habere suppositionem simplicem vel materialem, sed tunc
tantum quando terminus talis comparatur alteri extremo quod respicit intentionem anime vel
vocem vel scriptum (*SL*, 1, ch. 65, 179).

the user is otherwise and the predicate signifies either a concept or a word does it cede to simple or material supposition.[59]

The distinction between them is the difference between signification and predication which lies at the centre of Ockham's treatment of predicables and categories, as we shall discuss. Far from subject and predicate both standing for real things, they can stand merely for themselves, or cognate terms, as concepts or words. Consequently there is no necessary and intrinsic correspondence between words and things. The recognition of the difference, in the diverse ways terms can stand in propositions, is the condition of the latter's truth. For what can be false by one mode can be true by another, as the proposition 'Man is a species' is false when 'man' is taken in personal supposition, but true in simple supposition when 'man' stands for a concept.[60] It then states a conceptual as opposed to an ontological fact, as a term in material supposition states what is grammatically or semantically true. Accordingly supposition is the means of establishing the appropriate level of discourse by distinguishing between a term's ontological, conceptual, and grammatical import, whether or not it is employed significatively.

For Ockham the distinction between them is quite independent of the names given to these different suppositions, which are merely a matter of convention whose origin he does not pretend to know.[61] Of these three modes, personal supposition as the natural form receives the greatest attention. To begin with, in being significative, it is solely of cathegorematic terms standing for determinate things, or concepts or words, unlike terms in simple and material supposition, which, as we have said, can be of expressions, sentences and propositions, and in the case of material supposition of syncathegorematic terms—verbs, adverbs, conjunctions and so on—as well. Personal supposition can moreover be further divided into significative, discrete, common, determinate, confused, and improper supposition.

Significative supposition—which in the *Reportatio* Ockham calls a fourth mode of supposition—is applied to accidents in substances such as whiteness in Socrates. When the substance alone is signified, personal and significative supposition are the same.[62] Ockham mentions significative substance only once, and in passing, in the *Reportatio*, book two. By the time of the *Logic* it appears to have been incorporated into improper supposition.

The most general division in personal supposition is between discrete and

[59] Potest igitur regula dari, quod quando terminus potens habere predictam triplicem suppositionem comparatur extremo communi incomplexis sive complexis, sive prolatis sive scriptis, semper terminus potest habere suppositionem materialem, et est talis propositio distinguenda. Quando vero comparatur extremo significanti intentionem anime, est distinguenda eo quod potest habere suppositionem simplicem vel personalem. Quando autem comparatur extremo communi omnibus predictis tunc est distinguenda eo quod potest habere suppositionem simplicem, materialem et personalem (*SL*, I, ch. 65, 180).

[60] *Ordinatio, ibid.*; *SL*, I, ch. 68, 187. In this connection Boehner's argument can be accepted that Ockham's use of *de virtute sermonis* (by virtue of expression) means to treat a proposition in its proper supposition (*Collected Articles*, 248–53). See also *SL*, I, ch. 77, 213–14 and note 72 below.

[61] *Elementarium*, 208.

[62] *Reportatio*, II, q. 12, TT–UU.

common supposition. Discrete supposition is when a proper name or demonstrative pronoun is signified, giving rise to a singular proposition, such as 'Socrates is a man' or 'This man is a man'. Common supposition is when a common term stands as the subject of a proposition such as 'Man runs' or 'Every man is an animal': it can in turn be subdivided into determinate and confused common supposition.[63] It is determinate when it can descend by disjunctions to singular propositions, so that it can be true of determinate individual cases independently of any others. Thus for the proposition 'Man runs' to be true it suffices that it can be verified of only one man, even if it is false for another man. For that reason, although usually most or all its other instances will be true, such a proposition established of one individual has determinate supposition.[64] Accordingly in the proposition 'Man is an animal', both extremes—subject and predicate—have determinate supposition, since it follows from the statement that 'Man is an animal' that this or that or that individual man is this or that or that animal'.[65]

Confused supposition is that which is not determinate, and can be either simply confused (confuse tantum) or confused and distributive. It is simply confused when only the predicate is disjunctive and the subject as a universal term is not reducible to its individual members. Hence in the proposition 'Every man is an animal', 'animal' remains simply confused because it cannot be broken down into the proposition 'Every man is this or that animal', but only into 'Every man is some animal', the same for all. Supposition is distributive and confused when the universal term as subject can be taken conjunctively to include each of its individual members. The proposition 'Every man is an animal' then signifies that this man and that man and that man is each an animal, with no need to infer one from the other as they each must be inferred in discrete supposition.[66] On the other hand their con-

[63] SL, I, ch. 70, 189–90.

[64] Est igitur regula certa quod quando sub termino communi contingit descendere ad singularia per propositionem disiunctivam et ex qualibet singulari infertur talis propositio, tunc ille terminus habit suppositionem personalem determinatam (ibid., 190).

[65] Ibid.

[66] Ibid., 190–1. Also Ordinatio, d. 2, q. 4, 146–7. In this connection W. and M. Kneale, The Development of Logic (Oxford, 1962) write: 'Clearly what he means by descent in each of these cases is a transition to an equivalent statement which does not contain the original general term but contains instead singular terms linked either conjunctively or disjunctively. It is impossible, however, even in principle to make such a descent. For if every general term [my italics] were merely an abbreviation for a list of proper names linked by 'and' or by 'or', every statement would be necessarily true or necessarily false, which is absurd. When we say 'Socrates is a man' we do not mean 'Socrates is either Socrates or Plato or Aristotle . . . ' On the contrary we mean that he has a certain character, and our use of the word 'man' to signify or express that character is logically prior to our use of the word to stand for any individual man'. (268).
This would appear to commit the very confusion that supposition was designed to avoid. Ockham is here considering only personal supposition in which a term like 'man' is used significatively; as the authors add, Ockham was concerned here 'to show how general terms may be said to stand for individuals'. (ibid.). But that is not the only function of general terms, nor is it logically prior to the concept formed of them, as the authors would have found had they turned to what Ockham said about first and second intentions, and (in the Quodlibet IV, q. 6) about univocal and equivocal predication. For the difference between terms of first and second intention, as of those which are univocal and equivocal, consists precisely in standing for things or for concepts; and as Ockham also explains (see below), we are only able to predicate a common term because of the similarity which has been previously abstracted from them by the

junction also to some extent (*aliquo modo*) represents a descent to individual cases; but it is not invariable. There can be exceptions to a universal subject expressed by such propositions as 'Every man except Socrates runs', which descends by conjunction to propositions affirming that every other individual, Plato, Cicero and so on, is running. When that occurs, confused and distributive supposition is said to be mobile; when it is invariable it is called immobile.[67] Ockham completes his discussion of these distinctions by stating rules for recognising when a term stands discretely, commonly, confusedly, and/or distributively.[68] They hold not only for what is present but also past, future and possible.[69] Since, moreover, it signifies the subject not the predicate its tense or modality (as possible or necessary) refers to the subject, which must accordingly be correctly signified to avoid the confusions that arise from failing to distinguish the subject or its pronoun from its predicate. Thus for the proposition 'White was black' to be true, it need never have been true that 'White is black'. But its truth depends upon its having been true that 'This is black', where 'white' stands for 'this' in the proposition 'White was black'. Similarly a term can also signify negatively, for example in the proposition 'There is no white man', which can have one of two causes, either the non-existence of any man, and so of no white man, or because there are men but no man who is white.[70]

By the same token it is important to distinguish inexact or loose supposition (*improprie*) from strict supposition. That can be in a number of ways, whenever a term does not stand precisely for what is signified: for example, by the use of a proper name to describe what is represented (antonomastically), substituting the part the whole (by synecdoche) or by metaphor, taking the term under which something is contained for the content, or the abstract form for the subject. They therefore only apply to conventional terms.[71] Since these occur throughout the writings of the philosophers and authorities, either through common usage or the intention of the author, few are free from equivocal expressions, which should

---

intellect and formed into a concept. The question therefore of a concept's verisimilitude is distinct from its significative function; the second concerns its truth, the first its cognitive role. The Kneales appear to have confused the two and thereby denied that one can be separated from the other, which would be to identify logic with psychology.

Ockham himself anticipated just this objection in the *Elementarium* (207), namely that the proposition 'Every man is an animal' cannot signify real men because 'man' cannot stand for Socrates when Socrates is dead. Ockham replied by distinguishing between to 'signify' taken not only in the present but in all tenses and modes—possibly, contingently, affirmatively, and negatively—when it can be true of Socrates both before and after he is a man. See also J. Swiniarski, 'A new presentation of Ockham's theory of supposition', *FcS* 30 (1970), 206–8, who rightly, in my view, points to the Kneales' confusion of specific people with discrete concrete terms: the latter are not logically equivalent to proper names, as Ockham again declares in the *Elementarium* (218). See also *SL*, I, ch. 72, 195 (also note 69 below).

[67] *SL*, ibid., 191–2.
[68] *Ibid.*, chs. 71, 73, 74.
[69] Pro quo est intelligendum quod tunc terminus supponit personaliter quando supponit pro suis significatis vel pro his que fuerunt sua significata vel erunt vel possunt esse (*ibid.*, ch. 72, 194–5).
[70] *Ibid.*, 195–6.
[71] *Elementarium*, 218.

not be treated as univocal[72] and given only one meaning—one of Ockham's repeated cautions.

In the *Elementarium Logicae*[73] Ockham elaborates these permutations to show first that a term has determinate supposition when its proposition is neither universal nor negative, for example 'A man is an animal' and 'Some man is an animal' where both subject and predicate are determinate, as opposed to 'Every man is an animal', where neither term is determinate, and 'A man is not an animal', where only the subject is determinate. But in 'Some non-animal is a man' and 'Some non-animal is a non-man', where only the terms—as opposed to the proposition—are negative, they are determinate. Secondly in universal propositions, affirmative and negative, the terms have confused supposition, the subject distributively confused, the predicate purely confused, as in 'Every man is an animal' and 'No man is an animal'. That also applies to the predicate in negative singular propositions, such as 'Some man is not an ass' where the subject is determinate. Finally he repeats the rule for negation:[74] that whatever added to an immobile term makes it mobile, makes a mobile term immobile. Hence 'not' added to 'Socrates is a man', where 'man' is immobile—i.e. cannot descend conjunctively alone—becomes mobile in 'Socrates is not a man'. Conversely, 'man' changes from mobile in the proposition 'Socrates is every man' to immobile in the proposition 'Socrates is not every man'; and similarly with negative terms like 'except'.[75]

Closely connected with these differences in supposition, is the distinction between an *actus exercitus* and an *actus significatus*.[76] It arises again from the need to differentiate the proper supposition of a term. In an *actus exercitus* the term has existential import, implying the verb 'is' or an equivalent; it thus not only signifies that something is predicated of something else but also 'exercises' this predication to make it real in propositions like 'Man is an animal', 'Man disputes' or 'Man runs'.[77] Its terms are therefore taken in personal supposition, with the terms standing for something other than themselves. An *actus significatus*, on the other hand, treats the terms for themselves, not for their significates. They therefore carry no existential import, but express only a relation of terms, implied by words like 'to be predicated of' or 'to be made the subject' or 'to be verified of' or 'to belong to'.[78] Thus in the proposition 'Animal is predicated of man', 'animal' is not actually predicated of 'man' as something which exists; for 'animal' here is not the predicate but the subject: that is to say, it stands for nothing but itself as a concept and so this proposition does not mean the same as 'Man is an animal'. The latter taken significatively is false because one term is multiple (i.e. a genus) and the other is

---

[72] *Ibid.*, ch. 77, 213–14. Both here and in ch. 66, 182, Ockham uses the term *de virtute sermonis* to contrast the strict meaning of an expression in its proper supposition from its verbal, and inexact, supposition. Cf. note 60 above.

[73] *Elementarium*, 209–14.   [74] *SL*, I, ch. 74, 207–8.   [75] *Ibid.*

[76] Treated in *SL*, I, ch. 66, 182–4, *Quodlibet* VII, q. 15 in almost identical terms.

[77] Est autem actus exercitus qui importatur per hoc verbum 'est' vel aliquod huiusmodi, quod non tantum significat aliquid predicari de aliquo, sed exercet predicando unum de alio, sic dicendo: 'Homo est animal', 'homo disputat', 'homo currit' (*SL, ibid.*, 183).

[78] Actus autem significatus est ille qui importatur per hoc verbum 'predicari', vel 'subiici' vel 'verificari' vel 'competere' vel huiusmodi, que idem significant (*ibid.*).

not. Nevertheless Aristotle himself and many others take one for the other, which leads a great number into error.[79] To be true, both 'man' and 'animal' must be in simple supposition. To translate (exercise) an *actus significatus* into terms which are real and true, sometimes involves a double *actus exercitus*. Thus Aristotle's proposition in the *Posterior Analytics*, where he did not distinguish between these different senses, that 'Man is immediately risible' is true as an *actus significatus* where both 'man' and 'immediately' (meaning 'predicated exclusively and universally') are concepts in simple supposition, but false by an *actus exercitus*, where 'man' as a common term cannot smile at all. It can, however, be true when exercised as two separate acts to mean 'Every man is risible' and 'Nothing but man can smile'; for 'man' then stands in personal supposition for every individual who can smile.[80] Accordingly as Ockham says in the *Quodlibets*: 'a term in an *actus significatus* supposits simply, but in an *actus exercitus* it supposits personally'.[81]

Supposition, then, is concerned with the proper use of terms by distinguishing the sense in which they can be legitimately taken. It therefore acts as regulator in identifying which meaning a term may have in a proposition, above all, whether it can be verified in experience, if it is supposed to represent something other than itself. That for Ockham made supposition of universal applicability. In itself supposition does nothing to terms; it merely takes them in their particular forms and asks what they represent when they stand in propositions. The great innovation which supposition, and Ockham's employment of it, constituted was in the distinction between terms taken significatively and non-significatively even though it is questionable whether personal supposition effectively applied to terms as well as things. This recognition by Ockham, more than anything else, transformed virtually the entire philosophical and theological vocabulary of scholasticism. Whether or not we attribute it, as Moody does, to Ockham's return to Aristotle's own usage of his terms appropriated by Christian thinkers, it meant the reduction to logical or conceptual status of terms which had long enjoyed ontological status, above all abstract terms like being, essence, whiteness and so on, which had come to be treated as self-subsistent realities. As we shall see Ockham reached this position from the grammatical and logical forms a term could have, enabling him to identify its significative or non-significative function. In that sense his use of supposition rested upon the analysis of propositions into their terms; he did not invent these distinctions but merely gave them a new application by bringing them to bear upon what had for long been regarded as ontological categories. The effect of translating them back into their appropriate logical and grammatical forms could, in the circumstances, hardly fail to be revolutionary.

III ABSOLUTE AND CONNOTATIVE TERMS

Central to Ockham's purpose of identifying the correct import of terms and to his whole outlook was the distinction between those having real definition (*quid rei*) and those with only nominal definition (*quid nominis*). By means of it he was able

[79] *Ibid.*   [80] *Ibid.*   [81] *Quodlibet* VII, q. 15.

to classify terms and their signification as absolute or connotative and so to distinguish between those standing for real things, either as substances or qualities, and those which either corresponded to nothing real but consisted in verbal expressions (*orationes*) or which had indirect or relative or negative signification, in denoting something real. In that way he was able to explain the difference between concrete and abstract terms, as well as non-existents like chymera and negative terms like incorruptible thereby breaking the neoplatonic spell that every name must represent something real. More specifically, a real definition in its strict sense seizes the essential nature of the thing defined, briefly and without reference to anything extrinsic to it. It can be natural or metaphysical.[82] A natural definition is when a thing is defined through its essential parts, for example 'man' as 'a substance composed of a body and an intellective soul'. Here the terms of the definition stand for man's essential parts of body and intellective soul; the latter therefore signify man indirectly, or obliquely, since it is through them that man is defined.[83]

In a metaphysical definition, on the other hand, the terms directly signify what is defined through its genus and essential difference. Here all the parts—instead of being signified for themselves and only indirectly through them for that to which they belong—directly stand for the latter as the subject in the way that 'white stands not for whiteness but for the white subject in which whiteness is present.[84] 'Man' is thus defined as 'a rational animal' or 'an animated, sensible, rational substance', in which the differences, or parts, 'animated', 'sensible', 'rational', stand for 'man' who is each of these: they therefore directly signify part of man as concrete terms.[85]

There are no other real definitions beyond these two. Moreover, these do not represent two different kinds of being; there is not a natural and a metaphysical man, but merely two different ways of considering the same thing. That is possible because while a definition signifies what is defined they are not identical: a definition is an *oratio* or group of words, mental, spoken or written; what it defines is something real.[86] Nor is a real definition, although it expresses essential nature, necessarily true of the present. Whereas it is necessary as a hypothetical or possible definition that 'If man exists, a rational animal exists', and conversely, a merely

[82] Aliter accipitur hoc nomen definitio [quid rei] stricte; et sic est sermo compendiosus exprimens totam naturam rei, nec aliquid extrinsecum rei definite declarans (*SL* I, ch. 26, 77). Also *Quodlibet* v, q. 19; *Reportatio* IV, q. 1, B; *Ordinatio*, Prologue q. 5, 170–3, and d.2, q.4, 127–34.

[83] Nam quandoque in tali sermone ponuntur casus obliqui exprimentes partes rei essentiales, sicut si definiam hominem sic dicendo: 'Homo est substantia composita ex corpore et anima intellectiva', isti enim obliqui 'corpore' et 'anima intellectiva' partes rei exprimunt. Et ista potest vocari definitio naturalis (*SL, ibid.*) cf. also *Quodlibet* v, q. 15.

[84] Alia est definitio in qua ponitur nullus casus obliquus, sed ponitur genus in recto, et similiter ponitur in recto differentia, vel ponuntur differentie exprimentes partes rei definite ad modum quo 'album' exprimit albedinem; et ideo sicut 'album', quamvis exprimat albedinem, non tamen supponit pro albedine sed tantum pro subiecto albedinis, ita differentie ille, quamvis exprimant partes rei, non tamen supponunt pro partibus rei, sed precise pro toto composito ex partibus illis (*ibid.*). Also *Quodlibet* v, q. 15.

[85] *Ibid.*

[86] *SL, ibid.*, 78–9. *Quodlibet* v, q. 15.

affirmative categorical proposition of the present is merely contingent; for if no man exists now, it cannot be true that 'Man is a rational animal'.[87] Ockham adds that Aristotle would regard such propositions as necessary.[88] The significance of these differences between contingent and necessary truth, according to whether it is existential or possible, and between Ockham and Aristotle on the matter, will become apparent in the next chapter.

Nominal definitions, on the other hand, state explicitly what is merely implied by a conventional sign (dictio). Thus the word 'white' is equivalent to the expression 'something having whiteness'.[89] Such definitions do not therefore directly signify things as real definitions do; for that reason they can also be of what is impossible as well as possible—'vacuum', 'non-being', 'infinite', 'chymera', and so on—as they can be of verbs, conjunctions and adverbs, like 'where', 'when', 'how many?', and any other syncathegoremata. In all these cases the verb 'to be', if included in the definition, is without signification: that is, it merely joins the terms. For example the definition of 'chymera' is 'an animal composed of goat, [lion], and man', where all the terms have material supposition (i.e. as words): it is therefore true quid nominis as an expression whose words stand only for the word 'chymera' and not for anything real, when it would be false.[90] This substitution of one sign for another is not new; and Ockham quotes the example of Priscian's first book of Constructions.[91] For Ockham, however, its importance lies in such definitions having no real or absolute import taken in themselves. Hence no nominal definition can stand directly for what exists undividedly.

The distinction between real and nominal definition is expressed precisely in the difference between absolute and connotative terms. Absolute terms are those signifying something real—or absolute—completely and undividedly, by means of words like 'animal', 'man', 'goat', which directly stand for real things.[92] Connotative terms, in contrast, have nominal definitions signifying one thing primarily and another secondarily. They therefore do not stand directly for an undivided thing but connote it obliquely through signifying something else. Thus 'white' is defined as 'something informed by whiteness' or 'something having whiteness', in which the thing which is white is signified directly and the whiteness inhering in it indirectly.[93] The same holds for all such concrete terms (i.e. those which

---

[87] SL, ibid., 79; Quodlibet v, q. 15.

[88] SL, ibid.

[89] Definitio autam exprimens quid nominis est oratio explicite declarans quid per unam dictionem importatur. Sicut aliquis volens docere alium quid significat hoc nomen 'album' dicit quod idem significat quod hec oratio 'aliquid habens albedinem'. (SL, ch. 26, 80). Cf. also Quodlibet v, q. 19; Reportatio IV, q. 1, B; Ordinatio, Prologue, q. 5, 173–4.

[90] SL, ibid.; Quodlibet, ibid.

[91] SL, ibid.; Quodlibet, ibid.

[92] Nomina mere absoluta sunt illa que non significant aliquid principaliter et aliud vel idem secundario, sed quidquid significatur per idem nomen eque primo significatur . . . Et its est de nominibus mere absolutis, quod stricte loquendo nullum eorum habet definitionem exprimentem quid nominis. Talia autem nomina sunt huiusmodi: 'homo', 'animal', 'capra' . . . (SL, I, ch. 10, 33–4). See also Ordinatio, d. 3, q. 3, 428.

[93] Nomen autem connotativum est illud quod significat aliquid primario et aliquid secundario. Et tale nomen proprie habet definitionem exprimentem quid nominis; et frequenter

denote an actual thing) and also relative terms: they denote one thing directly and connote something else obliquely or secondarily inhering in it by means of a nominal definition.[94] We shall presently consider concrete terms. For the moment we must observe that all terms like 'white', 'just', 'animated', 'human', signify one thing by means of consignifying another, so that neither part stands exactly for the word itself as 'whiteness' does not stand for 'white'.

As we shall see in due course, for Ockham, as for Aristotle, only the categories of substance and quality signify real independent beings; they alone therefore have absolute terms.[95] All that comes under the other categories—of quantity, relation, and so on, including some qualities—are facets of substances or qualities, and have connotative or relative terms. Thus it is the characteristic of connotative terms and relative terms that they do not signify substances or qualities undividedly or independently. In the case of connotative terms, some principally signify a substance and connote secondarily a determinate quality, as in the earlier example of white; others, however, signify substance or quality without connoting anything determinate, and these do not need verification through the existence of something in addition to what is signified. Such terms belong to the category of quantity; hence to know that, say, wood is a quantity does not require the existence or knowledge of anything else.[96] The same applies to all other terms which fall under quantity, like 'body', 'figure', 'longitude', 'latitude', and indeed under all the other categories, save substance and some qualities. Since that also includes relation, relative terms are also connotative taken in its broadest sense; but the converse does not hold that all connotative terms are relative for the very reason that connotative terms are more universal.[97] As terms they differ in what they connote: a connotative term signifying something determinate like white, at the same time obliquely signifies its abstract, whiteness; but a relative term standing for something concrete connotes obliquely something which is distinct from what is determinately signified, as 'master' or 'father' connotes 'servant' or 'son'; without such connotation an individual would be neither master nor father.[98]

---

oportet ponere unum illius definitionis in recto et aliud in obliquo, sicut est de hoc nomine 'album'; nam habet definitionem exprimentem quid nominis in qua una dictio ponitur in recto et aliud in obliquo. Unde si queras quid significat hoc nomen 'album', dices quod ista oratio tota, 'aliquid informatum albedine' vel 'aliquid habens albedinem' (*ibid.*, 34). Also *Reportatio*, III, qq. 4, 5.

[94] *SL, ibid.*, 34–5.

[95] *Ibid.*, 35. And: Ad primum istorum et pro sequentibus sciendum est, sicut alias dictum est, quidam sunt termini absoluti qui significant sua significata eque primo uno modo significandi. Et istorum terminorum quidam important substantias, sicut homo, animal, quedam qualitates, sicut albedo, nigredo. (*Quodlibet* VI, q. 16).

[96] *Quodlibet*, VI, q. 16.

[97] *SL, ibid.*, 35; *Quodlibet* V, q. 25.

[98] Sed differunt in hoc: quandocumque conceptus connotativus vere predicatur de aliquo convenienter potest sibi addi suum abstractum in obliquo solum, quia nihil est album nisi sit album albedine . . . Sed quando conceptus relativus predicatur vere de aliquo, semper potest sibi convenienter addi obliquus casus qui non est eius abstractum. Exemplum est de domino, patre et sic de aliis, quia Sortes non est dominus nisi sit alicuius servi dominus; nec potest esse pater nisi sit alicuius filii pater (*Quodlibet* V, q. 25).

Accordingly relative terms signify substances or qualities principally and connote determinate things secondarily. Such terms, in contrast to connotative terms of the second group, must be verified of the things connoted: only when something else than what is signified is known to exist is a term relative. To be called 'similar' or 'cause' or 'effect' one thing must be similar to another, or cause or effect of another. For that reason in the case of relative terms the existence of the thing to which something is related must be known.[99] As with all connotative terms, however, and in contradistinction to absolute terms, relatives have only nominal definition, because the term 'father' or 'master' cannot itself stand for the part which it connotes, namely 'son' or 'servant': a father is not a son, but has a son.[100]

It will be noticed that the differences between these various terms largely turn upon the distinction between concrete and abstract terms which—in Ockham's systematic exposition of terms in the *Summa Logicae*—precedes his treatment of absolutes and connotatives. The reason should now become clear.

Ockham defines concrete and abstract terms as nouns having the same root (*principium*) but different endings, as 'just' and 'justice', 'animal' and 'animality', 'strong' and 'strength', and so on have. In addition to having usually more syllables than a concrete term, an abstract term is a noun and a concrete term an adjective.[101] Their logical relation, however, is not so simple, for they can be both synonymous and have different meanings.[102] From what Ockham has previously said we can extrapolate two preliminary explanations of why that is. The first is that concrete terms signify what we encounter immediately through intuitive cognition; as they stand—before analysis—they are the terms of what is known intuitively: 'white', 'hot', 'man', 'animal' are the signs of individual things immediately given without explanation of what they are. For that we have to go beyond the things signified as 'white' or 'hot' or 'man' to their meaning; which must lead either to a real or to a nominal definition, according to whether what is being defined is an absolute or not. From that follows the second and principal consideration: that strictly speaking, in the case of absolute terms, concrete and abstract terms are synonymous since they refer to the same complete and undivided thing; they differ only where they do not stand wholly for the same thing, one either signifying one part and the other the whole, or one the accident and the other the subject as we have already seen in connotative terms. Consequently, it is over the latter that concrete and abstract terms differ.

The importance of this for Ockham's analysis is that it reduces all distinctions between concrete and abstract terms so far as they concern real things (absolutes) to verbal distinctions; he thereby cut the ground from under the majority of his predecessors and contemporaries who treated the division as an ontological one

---

[99] *Quodlibet* VI, q. 16.

[100] Cf. Moody, *Logic of William of Ockham*, 96.

[101] *SL*, I, ch. 5, 16; also *Ordinatio*, d. 5, q. 1, K–M.

[102] Nominum autem concretorum et abstractorum multi sunt modi. Quandoque enim concretum aliquam rem significat vel connotat sive importat seu dat intelligere, pro qua etiam supponit, quam abstractum nullo modo significat, nec per consequens aliquo modo supponit pro eadem, sicut se habent iustus et iustitia, album et albedo (*ibid.*, 16–17).

between essence and existence, universal and individual: an outlook exemplified for Ockham above all in Duns Scotus's formal distinction which Ockham never ceased to combat. The corollary of Ockham's position was that where there is a discrepancy in meaning between concrete and abstract terms it can only be grasped by translating the connotative terms into its nominal definition. Its true signification can then be discerned, whether as a form of words, like chymera, or standing for something determinate like white.

Let us consider these terms in more detail. And first those cases where they are not synonymous, so that concrete and abstract cannot stand for the same thing in a proposition. Thus, 'just' really signifies a man but 'justice' only a quality. One cannot therefore be predicated of the other.[103] Ockham states three forms which these differences can take. The first is where the concrete term stands for the subject or substance and the abstract for the accident as a real quality or form inhering in its subject; or *vice versa*. Here each represents something independent (i.e. two absolutes), exemplified in the familiar pairs, whiteness–white, heat–hot, where one cannot stand for the other. The same holds for the converse, so that an abstract term, 'fire', can represent substance and a concrete term, 'igneous', its quality or form. Secondly, concretes and abstracts can differ through one standing for a part and the other for a whole, again interchangeably. For example in the pair 'soul-animated' (*anima–animatum*) a man can be animated but he cannot be a soul: 'animated' therefore signifies the whole (man) and 'soul' the part (inhering in man). In each of these first two groups, the concrete term can be taken equivocally to signify either the whole (as in 'animated') or the subject which receives the part (in their case body) and so itself represents another part of the total composition—subject and accident—of an actual (physical) individual. The third mode of difference is for both concrete and abstract to signify different things, neither of which is subject or part of the other. That can occur in a number of ways: as cause and effect, when a work is called 'human' but is not a man; or as sign and what is signified, so that the essential difference in any man is not the same as his essence; or again as a place and provenance, by which we call a man 'English' but not 'England'. As in the two previous subdivisions the roles of concrete and abstract term can be reversed, each acting as part or form, whole or substance, cause or effect.[104]

In addition to these ways in which concrete and abstract terms can be opposed, there are some concretes having no abstract counterparts, for example the word 'studious'. Moreover, although he does not give examples, Ockham says that the same word for diverse things could be concrete or abstract.[105]

That brings us to concrete and abstract terms as synonyms, taking synonym in the broad sense of signifying the same in all respects. Failure to recognise this

---

[103] *Ibid.*, 17.

[104] *Ibid.*, 17–18. Ockham also, *SL*, I, ch. 9, 32–33, gives a further way in which they can differ: abstracts can be collective—populace, army—and so stand for many individuals; but concretes can only stand for individuals—'of the people' or 'plebeian'.

[105] Similiter etiam non est inconveniens quod idem nomen respectu diversorum sit concretum et abstractum (*ibid.*, ch. 5, 18).

criterion leads to the misconception that concrete and abstract terms mean different things, the name 'God' standing for the whole, and 'deity' for its part.[106] Concretes and abstracts are synonyms when they stand for absolutes in the category of substance signifying individual beings—'man', 'animal', 'house'—undividedly and not as part or whole, accident or subject, in disjunction. As 'God' and 'deity' mean the same, so do 'man' and 'humanity', 'animal' and 'animality', and so on.[107] Moreover, Ockham points to the absence of abstract forms for many concrete substantives and indeed to the ancients' disregard of them—save for literary or metretricious purposes—even where they do exist:[108] all of which serves to underline their lack of independent signification as abstract terms. That applies equally to those in the category of quantity and relation. Where they are synonymous with their concrete counterparts they do not stand for anything distinct: thus 'quantum' and 'quantity', 'long' and 'longitude', 'father' and 'paternity', 'cause' and 'causality' mean the same.[109] The difference between terms in these two categories and terms belonging to substance is that terms of quantity and relation do not signify distinct beings absolutely, but the accidents or attributes of substance and quality, which can alone be denoted independently.[110] For that reason, only quality, as really distinct from substance, cannot be signified synonymously by concrete and abstract terms.

A concrete term by definition denotes something determinately either as substance or as an accident inhering in substance; it does not therefore directly signify quality as such—which is, as we have seen, abstract in form—but only as part of substance. Accordingly quality can either be denoted by an absolute term undividedly for itself, when it will be abstract in form like 'whiteness' or 'heat' or 'sweetness';[111] or it can be connoted by a concrete term denoting a substance, such as 'white', or 'hot', or 'sweet', which signifies something in which whiteness or heat or sweetness are present. Concrete and abstract terms cannot then be synonyms in the category of substance because quality can only be independently and absolutely signified by terms of abstract form.

But even where they are synonymous, concrete and abstract terms frequently

[106] Large dicuntur illa synonyma que simpliciter significant idem omnibus modis, ita quod nihil aliquo modo significatur per unum quin per reliquum eodem modo significetur, quamvis non omnes utentes credant ipsa idem significare, sed decepti existimant aliquid significari per unum quod non significatur per reliquum, sicut si aliqui existimarent quod hoc nomen 'deus' importaret unum totum et 'deitas' partem eius. Isto secundo modo intendo uti in isto capitulo et in multis aliis hoc nomine 'synonyma' *SL*, I., ch. 6, 19).

[107] Sub isto modo nominum concretorum et abstractorum secundum intentionem Philosophi et Commentatoris comprehenduntur omnia nomina substantiarum et abstracta ficta ab eis, que nec pro accidente nec pro parte nec pro toto illius quod importatur per nomen concretum secundum formam nec pro aliquo re disparata ab eo supponunt, cuiusmodi secundum eos sunt 'animalitas', 'equinitas' et huiusmodi (*ibid.*, 19–20). Or, as he later says (*ibid.*, cf. ch. 72, 202), they are synonyms if abstract terms are names of first intention.

[108] *Ibid.*, 19.

[109] *Ibid.*, 20.

[110] E.g. Quod quidam sunt termini absoluti, qui significant sua significata eque primo et uno modo significandi. Et istorum terminorum quidam important substantias sicut 'homo', 'animal', quidam, qualitates sicut 'albedo', 'nigredo'. (*Quodlibet* VI, q. 16).

[111] *SL*, I., ch. 10, 34.

cannot be predicated of one another in propositions. Thus we can say 'Man runs' but not 'Humanity runs', although man and humanity are synonyms. Does that mean, as his opponents would object, that since these terms and many more cannot stand for one another indifferently, that they are not really synonyms? The answer to this question is given by Ockham at two different levels. The first is ontological, by which he excludes, on Aristotle's authority, anything from *rerum natura* which is not composed of form and matter, essentially or accidentally. At this level, there can be no real distinction between 'man' and 'humanity', for 'humanity' cannot signify less than the unity of intellective soul and body by which man is an independent being.[112] Ockham therefore dismisses once again— this time as contrary to Aristotle—Duns Scotus's notion of a common, specific nature—humanity—to which the contracting or individuating nature 'man' is added to become an individual. The relation of man to humanity, replies Ockham, is that of Socrates to 'Socratesness'; and just as there is nothing in Socrates which is not shared by his nature, so there is not in 'man' and 'humanity'. If there were, it would be either a specific nature which must be common to each or to none, or it must be matter or form or composite or accident, which is denied by the exponents of this distinction. The only other alternative, that Socrates and his nature are distinguished by individual difference, again could not be upheld according to Duns's doctrine which is founded precisely upon the addition of an individuating nature to a common nature, and so must belong both to Socrates and his nature. Otherwise there would be no distinction between Socrates and Plato; and they would each have the same nature which belonged to all humanity.[113]

Theologically the identity of man and humanity must be qualified by Christ, who is both man and God. Instead therefore of the proposition 'Every man is humanity', it is restricted to 'Man is humanity';[114] but once again with qualifications. This time they are logical and represent the second level. In one sense the logical problem may be said to arise directly from the ontological, or rather from the apparent irreconcilability of one with the other. If 'man' and 'humanity' together with all other concrete and abstract synonyms really stand for the same thing, why cannot they stand for one another in a proposition? The reason is to be found in the structure of certain abstract terms. Where they do not denote an absolute quality—whiteness, heat and so on—they have, as we have seen, nominal definitions. They do not therefore directly signify something absolute. Accordingly it is for the logician to discover to what such terms are equivalent by resolving them into their constituent parts which in effect is to reduce them to real definitions; he is then able to judge according to the established rules of discourse whether an abstract term forms part of a valid proposition.[115] When taken in conjunction

---

[112] *SL*, I., ch. 7, 22.   [113] *Ibid.*, 23–24.   [114] *Ibid.*, 23–25.

[115] Dicendum quod ad sciendum an aliquis discursus valeat, oportet presupponere significata vocabulorum, et secundum hoc iudicandum est de discursu, an sit bonus vel non . . . De omni tamen discursu posset logicus iudicare an valeat resolvendo terminos in suas definitiones exprimentes quid nominis; quo facto potest per regulas certas evidenter cognoscere quod de eo est dicendum (*ibid.*, ch. 8, 31).

with the preceding reduction of synonymity to real, i.e. absolute terms, this means their correlation with the real equivalent—through a nominal definition—of an abstract term. It can then be seen whether the proposition in which the abstract term stands is true.

Now it is a peculiarity of some abstract terms to include syncathegorematic or adverbial terms in their definition so that they are equivalent to a statement containing a concrete, or other, term joined to a syncathegorematic or other sign or signs. Hence, by imposition, one conventional word can stand for several, as letters of the alphabet can stand for terms or expressions. For that reason, it is possible for concrete and abstract terms to stand for the same thing and yet not to be predicable of one another, because they have different equivalents.[116] Thus in the case of the abstract term 'humanity', the presence of a syncathegorematic term (i.e. every) makes it reduplicative to mean 'man in so far as man'. It does not therefore signify anything else than man; but, unlike its concrete term, it is equivalent not determinately to an individual but to every man taken conjunctively. Hence concrete and abstract cannot predicated of one another, although signifying the same reality. While it is true that 'Man runs', to say 'Humanity runs' is equivalent to saying 'Man in so far as he is man (i.e. every man) runs', which is not true. It therefore represents a universal statement where the concrete can be taken as singular.[117]

The same applies to all the other propositions in which an abstract term, although having the same signification as a concrete term, cannot stand for its concrete counterpart. Thus accepting that quantity is not something distinct from substance or quality, it yet remains wrong to say 'Substance is quantity' or 'Quality is quantity', because when reduced to its nominal definition, 'quantity' means the equivalent of 'necessarily quantum in its actual existence'. It can then be seen that this holds neither for substance nor for quality. To predicate quantity of substance is equivalent to the proposition 'substance is necessarily quantum in its actual existence', which is false, as it is false to predicate quality of substance.[118] In that way the seeming absurdities of all such propositions, 'Matter is privation', 'The soul is sin', including as we shall consider in chapter six those applied to God, for example 'God knows by his will', can be resolved. They are terminological, not real, and so the concern of logic.

It is through failure to realise this that 'those ignorant of logic uselessly fill innumerable pages creating a problem where none exists and turning away from the problem which they should investigate'.[119] The classic instance of this is Avicenna's dictum that 'Equinity is only equinity' (*equinitas est equinitas tantum*) by which he meant that nature of a horse or any other being logically comes before, and is formally distinct from, its determinations in individual horses and as a universal concept in the mind. Duns Scotus adopted as we have seen the same interpretation to explain universals. Ockham in contrast treats the same statement according to his rules of nominal definition which, not surprisingly, yield a very different result. It is that neither singular nor universal terms, in the

---

[116] *Ibid.*, 28.   [117] *Ibid.*   [118] *Ibid.*, 29.   [119] *Ibid.*

mind or outside it, enter into the definition of horse, and that the term 'equinity' is merely a verbal expression equivalent to a nominal definition and not something real, either in the mind or outside it. It does not therefore stand, as Duns Scotus (true to Avicenna) had interpreted it, for a common nature independent of any determinations.[120]

These divergencies between Ockham and Duns Scotus (and Avicenna) show particularly clearly what was at issue. To Ockham, Duns treated a logical problem as a metaphysical problem; he took the diversity arising from different terms for a real diversity and transposed it into that between different natures. Duns therefore at one and the same time violated the ontology of individual existence and the logic of real and nominal definitions. As Ockham said elsewhere: 'It is an absurd and fatuous way of speaking to say that to know something concretely is to know what is singular, and to know abstractly is to know what is universal, because concrete and abstract are conditions or properties of words or signs, and perhaps concepts.'[121]

The implications of Ockham's position are to be seen throughout his system. However he may interpret the outcome, we are compelled once again to recognise that they have their source in the opposite of nominalism. It was Ockham's sensitivity to the nuances of language which led him in precisely the other direction of refusing to equate forms of expression with specific counterparts in the real world. The main agent in differentiating them was the distinction between connotative and absolute terms, and so between nominal and real definitions. Abstract terms thereby were reduced to their linguistic components. What that meant for the traditional modes of thought, beyond Ockham's denial of Duns Scotus's notion of a common nature individuated by a contracting difference, may be seen from a passage in the Prologue of the *Ordinatio*.[122] Replying to John of Roddington's (Reading's) contention that risibility is a quality that inheres in man as an aptitude for laughter, Ockham declares that it is really something distinct from man but not as something real (*a parte rei*). The mistake of treating it as real arises from failure to recognise a connotative term, thereby attributing to it a real instead of a nominal definition. The effect is to equate risibility with real beings, like man or whiteness, which is false: an aptitude for laughter is equivalent to a complex expression with that very meaning, namely, 'something can laugh'.[123] In all such cases it is the nominal definition which must be investigated in order to establish not what the expression is but what it signifies. That applies equally to negative terms, 'privation', 'infinite', 'vacuum', and so on, and to connotative terms like 'creativity' attributed to God. None of these stands for a real thing but a statement, as 'creativity' states that 'There is something that can create *de nihilo*'.[124] To confuse these with real definitions is to commit the fallacy of a figure of speech which happens frequently through mistaking a connotative for an absolute term;[125] though Ockham

---

[120] *Ibid.*, 29–30.   [121] *Ordinatio*, d. 3 q. 6, 495–6.

[122] *Ibid.*, Prologue, q. 3, 138–41.   [123] *Ibid.*, 139–40.   [124] *Ibid.*, 140.

[125] Et ideo in multis argumentis est fallacia figure dictionis, sub nomine simpliciter absoluto accipiendo nomen connotativum (*ibid.*, 141).

in a subsequent interpretation concedes that philosophers often employ terms like 'risibility' and 'aptitude' equivocally so making them synonymous with their concrete counterparts.[126] That does not, however, affect the need to observe the distinction between absolute and nominal definition which, as we shall see, underlies virtually every aspect of knowledge in the proper sense.

IV PREDICATION: UNIVOCITY, EQUIVOCATION AND ANALOGY

Ockham's distinction between signification and supposition, on the one hand, and absolute and connotative signification, on the other, meant that terms could not of themselves be taken to correspond to real substances. In contrast to Porphyry, who made no distinction between predication and signification and thereby helped to neoplatonise Aristotle's categories,[127] Ockham made predication depend upon signification. To predicate one term of another we must first know whether it signifies at all in Ockham's sense of having personal supposition, and if so whether it does so absolutely or connotatively. To that extent predication is founded upon the differences between absolute and connotative terms. Both can in turn be either univocal or equivocal according to whether one or more than one concept is intended. We shall first consider the difference between absolute and connotative, or, as Ockham also calls it, denominative predication; and then between a concept used univocally and equivocally.[128]

Absolute predication (*in quid*) is exclusively of an absolute or whole subject without reference to its parts or what is extrinsic to it, in the way that something affirmed absolutely of man is of man and nothing else, and of man simply as a being, independently of whether he can smile or has a rational soul. Accordingly predication *in quid* answers the question of what something is (*quid sit aliquid*). For that, it is not enough to reply that say 'Socrates is rational', because 'rational' does not state directly and undividedly what Socrates is but only signifies a part of his nature indirectly—namely rationality—by means of a concrete term. The answer 'animal' on the other hand does suffice since it can itself be absolutely predicated of Socrates as a man wholly and undividedly with no other connotation. 'Having animality', in contrast, would not do so, since it would again be indirect, connoting what inhered in Socrates, and not Socrates absolutely as a man.[129]

---

[126] *Ibid.*

[127] Moody's point (*Logic of William of Ockham*, 67 ff.).

[128] On Ockham's theory of predication see M. M. Menges, *The Concept of Univocity* (New York and Louvain, 1952). This is a helpful comprehensive study, marred only by the tendency to say for Ockham what he does not himself say. On the difference between Menges's and Baudry's interpretations of Ockham's conception of univocal being, see Baudry, *Lexique*, 287, with which I largely agree.

[129] Quarto notandum quod predicari in quid de aliquo est predicari vere de aliquo et non importare aliquod extrinsecum competere illi de quo predicatur, nec significare determinatam partem illius de quo verificatur. Per primam particulam excluditur quod 'asinus' non predicatur in quid de 'homine' nec e converso. Per secundam particulam excluditur omnis predicatio passionis et importantis aliquid extrinsecum illi pro quo supponit; sicut 'risibile' non predicatur in quid de 'homine', quia hoc nomen 'risibile' importat actum ridendi qui nec est homo nec pars

The distinction is also, as we shall discuss, between affirming genus and difference: genus is affirmed absolutely of a whole, difference connotatively or denominatively of a part.[130] For that reason, we shall see, only genus or species, or transcendental terms like being and one, can be predicated absolutely in denoting individuals undividedly and whole.

The converse is true of denominative predication (*in quale*), which is indirect and partial. It can be either necessary or accidental according to whether it connotes what is intrinsic or extrinsic to the subject of which it is affirmed. Denominative predication answers the question of what kind or quality something is.[131] Hence it is legitimate here, as it is not over predication *in quid*, to say that man is rational or laughing; for the reply is directed not to what man is, as an absolute being, but what is distinctive to him, essentially or accidentally. Similarly, by predication *in quale* a raven can be called black—which Ockham regards as accidental.[132] The distinction is of the first importance, since upon whether the essential definition of something can be known depends the possibility of a strict demonstration of its attributes, as we shall discuss in the next chapter.

Now predication can be essential by one of two different modes, as we shall also consider in the next chapter. By the first essential mode (*per se primo modo*) the predicate either necessarily defines the subject, as 'rational' defines 'man', or the subject comes under the predicate as an inferior, i.e. less universal, term is contained in a superior, i.e. more universal, term: for example in the proposition 'Man is an animal', where the subject (man) is included under its genus (animal). By the second essential mode (*per se secundo modo*) the order is reversed, and the subject or superior term defines or enters into the definition of the predicate or inferior term. Thus the proposition 'Man is risible' belongs to the second essential mode because the subject (man) is included in the definition of 'risible': for to be able to laugh is an attribute of man; hence to laugh is defined by reference to man. Similarly 'creativity' as the attribute of God is by the second essential mode, since the capacity to make something from nothing belongs to God; he therefore enters into the definition of 'creative' which is affirmed of him. By this second mode, also, the predicate or inferior term, in contradistinction to the first essential

---

hominis. Per tertiam particulam excluditur differentia, quia omnis differentia essentialis importat determinate unam partem illius pro quo supponit, et non aliam; sicut 'rationale' quod supponit pro Sorte et Platone quando ponitur in propositione, importat determinate animam intellectivam; non sic autem importat aliam partem correspondentem. Et ideo illud quod importat totum et non importat partem nec aliquid extrinsecum predicatur in quid, quia querendo quid sit aliquid, puta quid sit Sortes, convenienter respondetur quod est animal, non quod habet animalitatem (*Expositio*, 22–3).

[130] *Ibid.*

[131] Quia illud predicatur in quale et non in quid, per quod respondetur ad questionem factam per quale, non per quid. Sed ista sunt huiusmodi; nam si interrogatur qualis est homo, convenienter respondetur quod est rationalis; et ita respondetur per differentiam (*ibid.*, 29).

[132] *Ibid.*, 23, 29; also 78–9, and *SL*, I. ch. 23, 68. Moody (*Logic of William of Ockham*, 103) and Baudry (*Lexique*, 125) both employ the term *quale quid* to express essential definition but it is not contained in the texts to which they refer. (*Expositio*, 78–9 and *SL*, I., ch. 23).

mode, can stand for something distinct from the subject, as 'creative' is by reference to what is created, i.e., a creature.[133]

From this it follows that predication *in quid* will always be necessary by the first essential mode, not in the absolute sense that it is necessary that man is an animal—for nothing is necessary other than God—but in the conditional sense that granted a man exists he belongs to the genus animal, and so animal is essentially predicated of man.[134]

Essential predication *in quale*, on the other hand, can be by either the first or second mode. When the predicate defines the subject as its inseparable accompaniment, as 'rational' defines man, it is by the first essential mode; for then the predicate signifies man through what is intrinsic to him and does not express anything additional to him as man.[135] When however the predicate is either separable from or in some other way subsumed under the subject so that the subject or superior term is part of the definition, as in the examples already given of 'risible' or 'creative', predication is by the second essential mode;[136] it is still necessary even though it signifies something really distinct from the subject, for granted that man exists, it is necessarily true that man is able to smile—independently of whether he does smile: we shall consider the implications of this in due course. Similarly if God is creator God is creative—i.e. able to create, independently of what he creates; each of these attributes is therefore an essential part of man or God.[137]

We are now in a position to examine how by any of the above modes absolute or denominative terms can be employed univocally or equivocally. The feature of Ockham's view of univocity and equivocation is that he reduces all universal signification to one or other mode. That applies equally to absolute and connotative terms, which must be either univocal or equivocal when used significatively according to whether they stand for one or more concepts. Hence, as we shall see, Ockham allows no place for analogy. More specifically we can say, firstly, that terms can only be univocal or equivocal when they are universal, that is signify more than one thing; these modes do not therefore concern particular terms, standing only for one individual.[138] In the second place, univocal terms are dis-

---

[133] *Ordinatio*, Prologue, q. 6, 180, and especially *SL*, III, II, ch. 7. See also Menges, *The Concept of Univocity*, 52–5 for a clear summary.

[134] *SL, ibid.*; also I, ch. 24, 73 and 286 ff. below.

[135] Stricte dicitur differentia que per se primo modo predicatur de aliquo et non indicat aliquid extrinsecum rei pro qua supponit illud de quo predicatur (*SL*, I., ch. 23, 68). Also: Secundo sciendum quod ad rationem differentie non sufficit predicari in quale precise; sic enim accidens predicatur in quale; sed simul cum hoc requiritur quod non exprimat aliquid extrinsecum illi pro quo supponit (*Expositio*, 78).

[136] Et sic nihil predicatur per se primo modo nisi per se superiora et partes intrinsece rei, vel importantia precise partes rei. Per se autem secundo modo dicitur illud quod importat aliquid distinctum realiter ab importato per subiectum, sicut hic: 'omnis homo est risibilis', 'deus est creativus' et sic de aliis (*Ordinatio*, Prologue, q. 6, 180). Ockham adds that, following Grosseteste, it can also be said that whenever the predicate is the cause of a subject that it is *per se primo modo* whether intrinsic or extrinsic; and by the converse it is *per se secundo modo*.

[137] *SL*, III, II, ch. 7, and chapter four, 286 ff. below.

[138] Si predicetur unus conceptus de uno conceptu, si uterque sit conceptus simpliciter

tinguished from equivocal terms in denoting only one such common concept, in contrast to equivocal terms which signify more than one universal concept. In the third place, while strictly speaking a univocal concept is a word, improperly understood it can also be a concept. An equivocal term, on the other hand, in standing for two or more concepts, can only be a word, since only a word can signify more than one concept, as opposed to things.

Taking a univocal term first, strictly or properly, it is defined as a univocal word which is not equivocal or denominative. Broadly, or improperly, it is a concept because a concept can be of only one concept, which is why a concept can only be univocal and never equivocal.[139] In either definition a univocal term is one predicated of many things. When it is a word it does so in subordination to a concept through whose natural signification of many things it signifies many by convention.[140] A univocal word is therefore an artificial sign imposed—by first imposition—upon a concept which is a natural univocal sign for each of the individuals whose likeness it bears through abstraction: a point to which we shall return. Each of these distinctions can in turn be divided into strict and denominative definition, so that while univocal in the strict and proper sense applies only to a word strictly predicable of one common concept, it can in fact also be taken in three other ways—denominatively as a word, or strictly and denominatively as a concept. We can therefore for the purposes of discussion treat strict and denominative univocity as holding for both words and concepts.[141] The difference between them is expressed most succinctly in the fourth *Quodlibet*, question sixteen, although the same import is contained in the *Ordinatio*, distinction two, question nine, and the *Reportatio*, book three, question nine.

A term is strictly univocal when it signifies the things for which it stands by a single word by means of one concept and one grammatical mode of signifying. It is then predicated absolutely and *in quid*, as 'animal' is predicated absolutely of man and horse, where 'animal' stands directly for all that is signified by it as a word and a concept.[142] A term is univocal in the broad sense when it is still by

---

proprius alicui singulari, tunc est predicatio discreta nec equivoca, nec univoca, nec denominativa proprie loquendo, quia Philosophus et alii auctoritates tractando de istis predicationibus tractabant solum de predicatione termini communis (*Quodlibet* IV, q. 16).

[139] Circa primum dico quod 'univocum' proprie accipitur pro voce univoca, quia accipitur secundum quod distinguitur contra equivocum vel denominativum . . . Et ita extendendo nomen univoci, potest improprie dici quod aliquis conceptus est univocus . . . sed nec proprie nec improprie debet dici quod aliquis conceptus est equivocus (*Ordinatio*, d. 2, q. 9, 306–7); also d. 2, q. 4, 139–40.

[140] *Ibid.*, *SL*, I., ch. 13, 42; *Quodlibet* IV, q. 16.

[141] Tamen proprie loquendo non est univocum nisi significet vel natum sit significare plura eque primo . . . ita quod sit signum subordinatum in significando uni signo naturali, quod est intentio seu conceptus anime . . . Ex predictis colligi potest quod non semper univocum habet unam definitionem, quia non semper proprie definitur (*SL*, *ibid.*, 42–3). See also *Ordinatio*, *ibid.*, 307–10.

[142] Pro istis et aliis distinguo de univoco, quia aliquando accipitur stricte quando scilicet subiectum et predicatum significant illa pro quibus supponunt unica impositione et mediante uno conceptu, et uno modo significandi logicali et grammaticali. Et sic omnis predicatio univoca est predicatio in quid. Sic enim 'animal' predicatur univoce de homine et de asino et in quid (*Quodlibet* IV, q. 16).

means of a single word and concept but not a single direct mode of signification; instead it signifies indifferently both *in recto* and *in obliquo*, one thing principally and another secondarily. It is then denominative.[143] As we mentioned earlier, a denominative term is comparable to a connotative term. Broadly, a term is denominative when its concrete and abstract forms signify the same thing, independently of whether or not the abstract stands for an independent quality in something: thus the concrete 'producing' does not denote something distinct corresponding to it in that which produces. Taken in that sense, all relative terms are denominative (as they are also connotative). Strictly, however, a denominative term is one in which the abstract counterpart does signify something totally different inhering in its subject, as when it is said that matter is informed by form; in the strictest sense the different thing signified by the abstract term is an accident, that is a quality inhering in the subject.[144] This is the sense in which Aristotle and Boethius used the term, where 'just' or 'strong' connote 'justice' and 'strength'; it is also the sense employed by Ockham who discarded the strict sense in the *Summa Logiae*.[145] Denominative predication is not, however, a distinct kind of predication, but is univocal or equivocal according to whether a term is predicable of many things corresponding to one concept or several.[146] Thus the term 'white' is univocally predicated of man and an ass because it signifies them both by a single word corresponding to one concept; but it is also denominative in signifying the subject man or ass directly and the quality of whiteness inhering in them indirectly. It does not therefore signify the same subject equally and undividedly.[147] Now it is a characteristic of denominative predication in its broad sense that it must be verified of that part which is represented by the indirect grammatical form. Thus for the predication of a man as white to be true, it must also be true that whiteness inheres in a man. Accordingly, denominative predication entails two propositions, in one of which predication is direct (a man is white), and in the other indirect (whiteness inheres in a man). In another sense, however, the indirect form suffices for denominative predication.[148]

By denominative predication, then, either the subject and predicate terms do not stand for the same, one being *in recto* and the other *in obliquo*; or if the terms do stand for the same, as in the proposition 'A man is white', its truth depends

---

[143] Aliquando accipitur univocum large, quando scilicet subiectum et predicatum significant illa pro quibus supponunt unica impositione mediante uno conceptu et indifferenter uno modo significandi vel diverso. Et sic predicatio univoca non est predicatio in quid sed denominativa (*ibid.*).

[144] *EA*, 39 d. Moody, *Logic of William of Ockham*, 126.

[145] *SL*, I., ch. 13, 43. E.g. scilicet stricte, et sic terminus incipiens, sicut abstractum incipit, et non habens consimilem finem et significans accidens dicitur terminus denominativus, sicut a 'fortitudine' 'fortis', a 'iustitia' 'iustus'.

[146] E.g. Notandum quod etiam predicatio denominativa non est aliquid simpliciter distinctum a predicatione univoca et equivoca, sed quedam est univoca et quedam equivoca (*EA*, 39 c). See also *Quodlibet* IV., q. 16; *Ordinatio*, d. 2, q. 9, *ibid.*

[147] *Quodlibet* IV, q. 16.

[148] *Ordinatio, ibid.*, 309–10. Also *SL*, II, ch. 11, 253. Unde sciendum est quod quandocumque in propositione ponitur concretum cui correspondet abstractum importans rem informantem aliam rem, semper ad veritatem talis propositionis requiruntur due propositiones.

upon a further oblique proposition, 'Whiteness inheres in man', where the terms do not signify the same. Otherwise, where they do stand for the same thing independently and completely by means of one term, predication is absolutely univocal, as it would be equivocal if each term had its own imposition.[149]

Ockham's specific definitions of denominative predication undergo some modification between book three of the *Reportatio* and the second distinction of the *Ordinatio*. In the *Reportatio* he gives three senses of denominative. By the first and broad sense it includes something entirely distinct from the subject but to which it is related as an effect, for example 'God is creative', where 'creative' is an action distinct from God but at the same time the result of his activity. Secondly and strictly, it occurs where the predicate signifies a material or formal part of the subject in being attributed to the whole—Aristotle's definition in the *Categories*. Thus man is called 'mortal', or 'rational', or 'living'; for these are properties which are intrinsic to him as subject. The third and strictest sense of denominative predication is the converse of the first: here something which inheres in the subject is predicated of it, as whiteness of man, in the proposition 'Man is white'.[150]

In the *Ordinatio* we are presented with four definitions.[151] Of these the second in each group, and the third in the *Reportatio* and the fourth in the *Ordinatio*, more or less agree, and need not concern us further. The others are more discrepant. The first definition in the *Reportatio* in its original form disappears, but the third sense in the *Ordinatio* seems in effect to replace it. This follows closely the initial broad definition of a denominative term which we met at the outset, namely one in which concrete and abstract terms stand for the same accident in a subject so that there is no abstract counterpart or perhaps no abstract term at all, as when we say that 'A man is studious'. In other words there is no quality inhering in the subject which is denoted by an abstract term, a position very similar to the first sense in the *Reportatio* expressed in the proposition 'God is creative'. The difference is that their relation is not now causal but has instead been made a logical one of subject and accident. Only the first definition in the *Ordinatio* has no counterpart in the *Reportatio*: it consists in the broadest (*largissime*) sense of denominative, which we have also recently considered, namely when subject and predicate do not stand for the same but do not signify equivocally.[152]

These divergencies are due to a more refined approach in the *Ordinatio*. By then Ockham had come to see the question of predication as one of the relation of terms, and treated it according to the appropriate logical and grammatical forms, above all those of direct and indirect signification and of concrete and abstract terms. None of these finds a place in his earlier discussion in the *Reportatio*. They only appear with the Logical Commentaries, making up the *Expositio Aurea*. From then onwards they form the framework of his successive discussions. If, therefore, the change is evidence of anything, it is of a greater logical sophistication and awareness first apparent in the Logical Commentaries, which would

---

149 *Ibid.*, 310; also 316.   150 *Reportatio*, III, q. 9, D.
151 *Ordinatio, ibid.*, 330–1.   152 *Reportatio*, III, q. 9, Q.

seem to suggest that they came later than the *Reportatio* in the chronology of Ockham's writings.

The importance of denominative predication for Ockham is that it makes possible the notion of univocal predication of what does not exist concretely. It thereby extends univocity to what would otherwise be equivocal in involving more than one concept. How that affects univocal predication of God will be shown in chapter five. It also has a direct bearing upon Ockham's whole conception of individual being in preserving the ontological unity of concrete and abstract: either by treating them as a logical and grammatical relation or as synonyms or as subject and accident constituting a single being in the case of quality— Ockham's only concession to the separate identity of something signified by an abstract form. In all of these cases the abstract has no separate identity as a nature or an essence. It can therefore be reduced to the same term as its concrete counterpart, which would not be possible if 'human' and 'humanity' really stood for different beings.

Ockham's stress upon univocity thus flows directly from his conviction that any common or universal concept denotes only individuals and not a common nature; and the same must apply to the term representing the concept. Hence, we shall later see in more detail, as the concept 'animal' stands for real individual animals, so does genus to which animal as a term belongs. More immediately, it means that so long as individuals can be seized in a common concept they can be predicated univocally. Accordingly there can be univocal predication in varying degrees of abstraction in proportion to the degree of similarity between individuals brought under the same term. The two main ones are those of species, taken in its strict and most specific sense (*species specialissima*), and genus. Each of these corresponds to what can be abstracted from real determinate individuals; they therefore can be said to be taken concretely. There is in addition a further degree of univocity which is exclusively abstract in that there is no real likeness to which it corresponds determinately.[153]

A *species specialissima* is last in the order of universal terms; beyond it come particular terms. Correspondingly, as the most restricted in its membership, it has the greatest real identity, based upon what Ockham in the *Reportatio* calls perfect similarity, amended in the *Ordinatio* to greatest similarity, among its individuals. Its feature is that they are specifically of the same nature so that although they do not constitute a single whole—i.e. one single common nature—if they were to do so such a nature would not contain more of the species than the individual comprising it.[154] For that reason the ancients regarded a *species specialissima* as a form, unlike a genus, whose members do not possess such real unity.[155]

In the *Reportatio* Ockham adumbrates this similarity: it is in both substances and accidents so that even when the accidental forms of say whiteness vary in

---

[153] *Ordinatio*, d. 2, q. 9, 310–11.

[154] Et ita dico quod universaliter quod illa que sic sunt univoca quod sunt simillima, si per possibile vel impossibile possunt facere unum per se, illud unum erit eiusdem speciei cum illis, et non plus esset illud per se contentum sub specie quam reliquum (*ibid.*, 311).

[155] *Ibid.*

degree they remain without dissimilarity just as individuals of the same nature do not differ in kind.[156]

The perfect or complete similarity of the *species specialissima* is contrasted with the imperfect similarity of the genus which forms the second degree of (imperfect) univocity. Here the individuals, substance or accidental qualities, are not of the same nature and so are also dissimilar; or as Ockham expresses it they are 'neither entirely similar nor entirely dissimilar, but similar in some respects and dissimilar in others'. Their similarity also differs from that of perfect similarity in being either extrinsic or intrinsic.[157] Thus man and ass can belong to the same concept of 'animal', as their genus, because while differing in their own natures as species they have matter which is of the same nature. Similarly man and angel meet in the same univocal concept of 'substance': although not agreeing in anything intrinsic to them they have the same accidental qualities of intellection and volition. So do black and white, which share the same subject of colour but intrinsically have no connection, differing in all other respects. Because of these dissimilarities, Ockham explains, Aristotle treated genus as equivocal, in saying that it contained many equivocations.[158] Here Aristotle was taking as equivocal everything that was not univocal by perfect similarity. For Ockham, however, univocity belongs to all that can be brought under a single concept; for that there must be real similarity, independently of the degree of perfection. Univocity in the case of genus comes through predication of individuals *in quid*, i.e. absolutely, as we shall discuss more fully later. In being reached through abstraction, genus denotes not a universal nature but merely those aspects of individual being, intrinsic or extrinsic, which have the same formal nature. It is that which makes possible imperfect univocal being.

By the same token the one exception is the divine nature which alone is one common being. For that reason there can be neither perfect univocity, based upon complete identity of species nor imperfect univocity, derived from diversity, between God and creatures, since there is no ontological similarity, intrinsic or extrinsic, between the divine and the created. There can, however, be a conceptual similarity between them corresponding to nothing actual. This constitutes the third mode of univocity. Unlike the other two, similarity by the third mode is neither essential nor accidental; those of whom it is predicated therefore have nothing real in common and are dissimilar in all real respects, as God and creature are in their natures, essence, wisdom, goodness, and so on.[159] For that reason both the *sancti* and the philosophers accepted only this third—conceptual—way of univocity as applicable to God and creatures. As John of Damascus, following the

---

[156] *Reportatio*, III, q. 9, Q.

[157] Que nec sunt omnino similia nec omnino dissimilia, sed in aliquibus similia et in aliquibus dissimilia, vel quantum ad intrinseca vel extrinseca (*ibid.*).

Secundo modo dicitur univocum omne predicabile de pluribus differentibus realiter, que non sunt una res nec etiam sunt simillima, ita quod conceptus unus in quid predicatur de eis; et isto modo genus est univocum (*Ordinatio*, d. 2, q. 9, 311).

[158] *Reportatio, ibid.*

[159] *Ibid.*

Pseudo–Dionysius said, God is not wisdom but superwisdom, not good but supergoodness.[160] Accordingly, as we shall see in chapter five, God and creatures share only the notion—as opposed to the reality—of wisdom, goodness and so on which, in being predicable of each, is univocal to them. That, however, is not the same as saying, as Menges does, that 'Although Ockham does not say this expressly, he leads us to the assertion that *there is a common genus between God and creature*'.[161] As we shall again see in the same chapter Ockham expressly denies that God can be predicated in genus.

For our present purposes we can say, then, that Ockham's three categories of univocity represent similarity in ascending degrees of abstraction. The first two belong to determinate individuals; the third is an exclusively abstract concept, and indeterminate. However this last is to be interpreted, species and genus are univocal in virtue of real individual similarity, which is abstracted in a common concept and predicated of individuals, not a common nature.[162] When there is no such similarity there is no univocal term, and predication will be equivocal,[163] as we must consider.

Ockham defines equivocation as occurring when a word signifies many things by means of more than one concept. Only a word can therefore be univocal, because as we said earlier concepts as natural signs can only have one meaning, which is defined from signifying things, not other concepts. A word, on the other hand, is an artificial sign which can change its meaning and so have more than one meaning. Thus for a term to be equivocal, i.e. to have more than one meaning, it must be a word, either spoken or written.[164]

Ockham takes over the two accepted senses of equivocation, *a casu* and *a consilio*. Equivocation *a casu*, as the expression suggests, occurs when the same word is imposed on some individuals and not on others, in the way that the same proper name is given to different individuals each of whom answers to it.[165] Such words can be equivocal or univocal. They are equivocal in having diverse meanings according to their different impositions; but they are univocal when they signify the same for all who understand them by a particular imposition. That applies to the same word rendered differently in different languages: in Ockham's example

[160] *Ordinatio, ibid.*, 311.

[161] *The Univocity of Being*, 83; Menges's italics.

[162] Circa secundum dico quod nullum univocum est de essentia suorum univocatorum, nec ponit aliquid in eis realiter, nec facit compositionem cum eis nec cum aliquo quod est in eis, quia omne univocum est universale vel saltem commune predicabile de illis de quibus predicatur coniunctim acceptis in numero plurali, sicut 'Socrates et Plato sunt homines' et 'homo et asinus sunt animalia' (*Ordinatio, ibid.*, 312).

[163] Est autem vox illa equivoca que significans plura non est signum subordinatum uni conceptui, sed est signum unum pluribus conceptibus sue intentionibus anime subordinatum (*SL*, I., ch. 13, 41). Also *Reportatio* III, q. 9, U; *Quodlibet* IV, q. 16.

[164] Secunda conclusio est quod equivocatio non est in conceptu, sed tantum in voce vel scripto. Hoc probatur, quia ad equivocationem requiritur unitas signi et pluralitas significatorum . . . sed nihil significat mediante uno conceptu vel pluribus nisi vox vel [in] dicto vel in scripto quia nec conceptus sic significat nec potest sic significare, tum quia vox non significat mediante conceptu, sed [significat tantum] vox vel scriptum; tum quia conceptus naturaliter significat quecunque significat vox ad placitum sicut significat equivocum (*Reportatio*, III, q. 9, F).

[165] *Quodlibet*, IV, q. 16; *Ordinatio, ibid.*, 326–7; *SL*, I, ch. 41.

'dog' in Latin means an animal which barks; in Greek it refers to a constellation of stars.[166] *A casu*, therefore, a term is equivocal without reference to another term. That is its difference from equivocation *a consilio*, where the various meanings of the same word derive from an observed relation of similarity between them. Thus the word 'man' originally denoted any rational animal and all that came under the term: from that it was extended to include any likeness to man (as in a statue) because of the similarity of one to the other. The word thereby became equivocal, signifying both man and representations of him, with the second meaning dependent upon the first on account of the proportion between them.[167]

In the *Ordinatio* Ockham amplified the characteristics of equivocation *a consilio*. It can be the result of a deliberate act of will or through similarity of proportion. An example of the first is the decision by someone to call three different individuals by the same name: equivocation will here consist in the different impositions, or meanings, which the name has in each of the three cases; that is to say a term is equivocal because it signifies by different concepts. Hence it will be no less equivocal in signifying individuals of the same species if each is known by a different concept upon which the same word is imposed.[168] By its other mode, that of similarity, a term can be equivocal *a consilio* either absolutely, in the example already given of 'man', or connotatively. Here in contrast to the word 'man', which whether it signifies a real man or representation has the same direct grammatical form, a word like 'healthy' is at once absolute and connotative as well as equivocal. It is absolute when it directly signifies the quality of health formally inhering in an animal. It is connotative when predicated of, say, food or urine, for it then signifies each, both directly and indirectly, in a nominal definition equivalent to 'food that is productive of health' or 'urine which denotes health'. Finally, it must be equivocal when predicated of both food and urine, which in not having the same formal character cannot be signified by a single concept; and so 'healthy' requires separate impositions for each of them.[169]

From this we can see that univocity and equivocation are not in themselves mutually exclusive. In certain circumstances the same word can be both univocal and equivocal, as Ockham makes explicit in the *Logic*. What is not possible is for the same word to be univocal and equivocal of only one thing: the same man can be both father and son but not of the same person, just as something can be similar and dissimilar but not the same thing.[170] It is that which makes the difference between a univocal and an equivocal term.

---

[166] *Ordinatio, ibid.,* 327.

[167] *Quodlibet* IV, q. 16; *Ordinatio, ibid.,* 327; *SL, ibid.,* 41–2. E.g. Equivocum a consilio est quod imponitur pluribus impositionibus ad significandum plura mediantibus pluribus conceptibus et imponitur uni quia prius imponitur alteri; et hoc propter aliquam similitudinem causantem proportionem (*Quodlibet* IV, q. 16).

[168] Equivocum a consilio dupliciter potest accipi . . . alio modo quando sola voluntate idem [nomen] diversis [impositionibus], non propter identitatem conceptus, diversis imponitur . . . si aliquis ex deliberatione imponeret hoc nomen Sortes ad significandum tres homines determinatas. (*Ordinatio, ibid.,* 327). Also *ibid.,* q. 4, 139.

[169] *Ordinatio,* 327–8.

[170] Est autem intelligendum quod ista divisio terminorum per equivocum et univocum non

The most notable consequence of Ockham's conception of univocity and equivocation, which as we have said arises directly from his notion of individual being, is that he rejects analogy as a separate mode of predication. The reason is that both univocity and equivocation are founded upon similarity and embrace all its degrees. On the one hand univocal similarity stands for what is formally of the same nature, whether perfectly in a *species specialissima* or imperfectly in a genus; but in either case only if the things signified share the same nature in whole or in part, essentially or accidentally. On the other hand equivocation represents a further degree of abstraction where the concept of similarity, as in the third degree of univocity, is no longer of determinate and concrete similarity but is wholly abstract, since there is no direct correspondence between an equivocal term and that for which its different concepts stand. A word like 'man' which can be predicated equivocally of man and his likeness cannot signify something determinate which is both man and his likeness, but only two different determinate things of which the univocal term is compounded. Ontologically, beyond the level of abstraction represented by genus, real similarity—and with it univocity—breaks down: which is another way of saying that the limit of a concept as a natural sign of second intention has been reached. At that point any remaining similarity is similarity between concepts, which can be either univocal in the third sense or equivocal according to whether the word imposed upon them can stand for the same concept (which as we shall see in chapter five only properly applies to God and creatures in common concepts such as 'wisdom'). Either way, they are united by the term; no longer ontologically. Formally, then, the difference between a univocal and an equivocal term lies in the discrepancy between intention and imposition. Where there is a direct correspondence between them, the concept is univocal; where there is not, and one word stands for more than one concept— or, as Ockham says, where the word is the same and the meaning is diverse[171]— a term is equivocal. Between them there is no room for analogy.

Ockham does not treat analogy as a separate consideration, but everywhere reduces the claim for it to either univocity or equivocation in varying degrees. Neither a concept nor a word, written or spoken, can, he argues, be analogical because any common term predicable of many—the condition of all univocal and equivocal predication—will always be shown to be either univocal or equivocal. To take a concept first, if it is predicated in a proposition of something else, as in the proposition 'Man is white', where the predicate (white) has at least to be a common term, it will be univocal. The alternative is for several concepts to be predicated of another concept or of several other concepts. That, however, will lead either once again to univocal predication, this time by a composite term, with

---

est simpliciter per opposita, ita quod hec sit omnino falsa: 'Aliquod equivocum est univocum', imno vera est, quia vere et realiter eadem vox est equivoca et univoca sed non respectu eorundem, sicut idem est pater et filius, non tamen respectu eiusdem; et idem est simile et dissimile, non tamen eidem per idem (*SL*, I, ch. 13, 42).

[171] Quia quando vox est eadem et intentio est diversa, tunc est equivocatio (*Reportatio*, III, q. 9, U).

one predicate absolute and the other denominative, as in the proposition 'Socrates is a white man', or to a proposition which is contradictory and so unintelligible ('Socrates is a man ass') or irrelevant ('Socrates is a white grammarian'). Either, then, the predicate determines the subject and so is univocal, or it does not and has no meaning.

The same holds for words, which must also be common terms predicable of many and significative. Now a word can signify either by one imposition and by means of one concept, in which case it will be univocal, or by means of several impositions and concepts, when it will be equivocal. Once again there is no third way.[172] If, on the other hand, equivocation is not taken generally, both *a casu* and *consilio*, but *a consilio* only, then Ockham considers that analogy and equivocation are the same; it is then the third term between univocity and equivocation *a casu*, imposed neither by means of one concept nor several merely arbitrarily but according to similarity of proportion between different things. Thus 'healthy' is predicated analogically of animal, food and urine in not being predicated univocally, denominatively or equivocally *a casu*.

In one sense this changes nothing so far as it affects analogy or equivocation as modes of predication: equivocation *a consilio* remains what it was and analogy does not become something independent. At the same time, however, their identification produces an asymmetry in relation to univocity. Negatively, it is true that analogy is reduced to univocity or analogy, so that, as Menges has said, 'analogy is either univocity or equivocation'.[173] But positively analogy is equivocation *a consilio* in a way that it is not correspondingly univocal, once Ockham had gone beyond what he wrote in the *Reportatio*, as we shall shortly see. By the time of the *Ordinatio* and *Quodlibets* we can say that relation of analogy to univocity is disjunctive: analogy is either univocal or equivocal, whereas the relation of analogy to equivocation is also categorical: analogy is equivocation *a consilio*.

That is the position as stated in *Quodlibet* four, question sixteen. Previously Ockham had discussed analogy more briefly in the *Reportatio* (book three, question nine) and the *Ordinatio* (distinction two, question nine) where he reaches definitions which cannot as they stand be reconciled. In the *Reportatio*, having stated the case against analogy in similar terms to those which we have just examined in the *Quodlibets*, he subsequently replies to an objection—to which we shall return—that Aristotle had used the term in the *Posterior Analytics* (book two). Ockham does not reply to that directly, contenting himself with giving two definitions of analogy both of which reduce it to univocity in all three modes. By the first definition, univocity consists in a univocal concept in the third sense of univocal, which is called analogical because it has neither perfect similarity nor imperfect similarity, and so it is held to be intermediary between univocity and equivocation. By the second definition, analogy can be univocal by either of the other two modes of univocity, either as perfect similarity (of a *species specialissima*) or as imperfect similarity (of a genus). Analogy in either degree is had through the proportion

---

172 *Quodlibet* IV, q. 16; and *Reportatio*, III, q. 9, E (also U).
173 *The Concept of Univocity*, 130.

between four terms related as two pairs in the same degree: thus man is to animal as whiteness is to colour (second degree of imperfect similarity), and Socrates is to man as whiteness is to white (first degree of perfect similarity). It is the relation between these terms which is analogical, for otherwise there would be no proportion between the terms of the two pairs.[174] Thus Ockham in the *Reportatio*.

When we turn to the *Ordinatio*, the question to be answered is whether by then Ockham had changed his mind about analogy or whether, as Menges implies, by omission of anything to the contrary,[175] Ockham was addressing himself to another problem. The two are not necessarily exclusive, because it was again over the same issue of what Aristotle had meant by analogy that Ockham considered it. But the different interpretation which he this time put upon Aristotle's text and the two definitions which he now brought to it, make their reconciliation with his previous treatment in the *Reportatio* in turn depend upon assuming what has to be proved: namely that Ockham had not rejected his earlier definitions but had turned his attention to another aspect of the problem. Not only does this not form a basis of valid argument but the evidence seems to me overwhelmingly against it.

To begin with, as Menges himself shows, Ockham in the *Ordinatio* applied himself directly to Aristotle's text, while in the *Reportatio* he had merely introduced the objection which his two definitions were designed to meet with the words: 'There seems to be analogical predication because according to the Philosopher, if the attribute is analogous the middle term will be analogous'. The main weight of Ockham's replies to this and the accompanying objections was upon establishing the validity of univocal predication of God and creatures; and he did not bother to pursue the meaning of Aristotle's text, or even cite it or its references. As we have seen, he interpreted analogy in both definitions as univocal. In the *Ordinatio*, by contrast, Ockham gives two very different definitions of analogy. The first is taken directly from the *Posterior Analytics* book two, chapter seventeen, where he defines analogy proportionately according to which the likenesses between different things alternate. In Aristotle's words:

The cause of likeness between colour and colour is other than that between figure and figure; for likeness is here equivocal, meaning perhaps in the latter case equality of the ratios of the sides and equality of the angles; in the case of colours identity of the act of perceiving them, or something of the sort. Again, connexions requiring proof which are identical by analogy have middle terms which are analogous.[176]

In view of what we have just previously said we can make two comments. The first is that likeness is taken by Aristotle to be equivocal, which is how Ockham paraphrases him, namely that 'likeness is equivocal in every respect'. The second is that from its last sentence we can see that this is the passage to which Ockham referred in the *Reportatio*; it is therefore inconceivable that Ockham was thinking of a different question from that raised by Aristotle when he gave his second

[174] *Reportatio*, III, q. 9, R.
[175] *The Concept of Univocity*, 131.
[176] *Posterior Analytics*, II, 17; 99 a, 11–16.

definition in the *Reportatio*:[177] it, too, was framed around four terms in a relation of likeness, but they were then treated univocally. When we come to the *Ordinatio*, Ockham has accepted Aristotle's suggestion that terms in a relation of proportionality are equivocal. Accordingly, we must conclude that Ockham changed his opinion over the same issue, from defining analogy univocally to defining it equivocally, which is how we meet it in his latest discussion of the subject in the *Quodlibets* examined earlier.

Whenever the change first came to Ockham (perhaps as the result of commenting on Aristotle's logical works) it is firmly recorded in the *Ordinatio*, as we can see if we look at it more closely. There he once again gives two definitions in answer to the same objection that Aristotle held relations between terms to be analogous. The first definition is based upon the passage referred to in the *Posterior Analytics*, this time cited as well as summarised. According to this, Ockham defines analogy as a word imposed upon many things because of a similar proportion which they have to one another, in Aristotle's example of colour and figure. Such analogy, he declares, 'is absolutely equivocal not *a casu* but *a consilio*'; and that is what Aristotle said.[178] The second definition of analogy is denominative and equivocal, as in the example already considered, of 'healthy' predicated of 'animal', 'food', and 'urine'. It is predicated thus of diverse things not by means of a common concept but because of some likeness to a thing first signified by a term, in virtue of which likeness other things can be brought under the same term: that is to say, things can be united equivocally *a consilio* by a relation of similarity. Analogy thus defined extends as we saw to both absolute and connotative terms.[179]

Despite the undeniable distance between these definitions and those in the *Reportatio*, we must not exaggerate their importance. Ockham nowhere accepted analogy in its own right: he merely came to more precise and sophisticated terms with it by following Aristotle's lead in the *Posterior Analytics*. He was thereby able to reconcile his own position with Aristotle's, something that exercised him in the *Reportatio* and *Ordinatio*, and again in the *Quodlibets*. That involved him in changing the definition of analogy from univocity to equivocation *a consilio* by the time of the two later works. Even so it remained only a change in definition, which had no other implications. Upon the one area where the role of analogy or its equivalent was of real importance, namely knowledge of God, it had no real bearing. For Ockham, as we shall see in chapter five, this remained exclusively the preserve of a

---

[177] It is here that Menges (*op. cit.*, 131) produces a non-sequitur which leads to the inference that Ockham was no longer concerned with Aristotle's view of analogy, when he says with no reason, 'Instead, he at once gives the *second* way he understands analogy, and this is proportionality'. If that is not the issue raised by Aristotle's discussion it is hard to know what it was. The difference, as Menges says a page later, is that Ockham in this second definition in the *Reportatio* treats proportionality as equals and so dependence provides no basis for comparison. For that reason the difference relates to the *same* problem.

[178] Sed de analogo potest distingui, quod uno modo accipitur secundum quod est aliquod nomen impositum multis propter consimilem proportionem quam habent diversa ad illa, sicut ponit Philosophus exemplum quod sicut se habet color ad colorem ita figura ad figuram ... Ad propositum dico quod analogum primo modo est equivocum simpliciter, non tamen a casu sed a consilio (*Ordinatio*, d. 2, q. 9, 328–9).

[179] *Ibid.*, 328–30.

common univocal concept in the third mode of univocity. Such a concept was the only means by which the real dissimilarities between God and creature could be overcome in univocal abstract terms like 'being' and 'wisdom'. From that point of view Ockham's identification of analogy with equivocation *a consilio* helped to demarcate knowledge of God from knowledge of created things: while the former was univocal, the latter—in both the *Ordinatio* and *Quodlibets*—concerned only the natural order. The contrast between the two kinds was indeed made explicit in the same question sixteen of the fourth *Quodlibet*. Once again it arises over the way in which Aristotle understood analogy; and once again Ockham identifies it with equivocation *a consilio*, explaining this time that Aristotle was following Greek usage in employing the term 'analogy' for equivocation. Ockham now, however, extends Aristotle's use of equivocation to include the ten categories of being[180] on the ground that 'being' is predicated equivocally of substance and the other categories in the same way as 'healthy' is predicated equivocally of animal, food and urine: in both cases the terms 'being' and 'healthy' signified one thing—'substance' and 'animal' directly—and accidents or attributes—categories in the one, food and urine in the other—secondarily; only 'substance' and 'animal' could strictly be identified with their predicates, the others being nominal definitions signifying the property or quality of being or health.[181] We shall consider the ten categories presently. Their interest in this context is that they can only be seized by an equivocal term when they are predicated concretely of determinate beings, which are not united as genus or species.

It is different, however, when 'being' is predicated of God; for although Aristotle understood being in this sense equivocally *a consilio*, as predicable of both God and creatures, that is not, says Ockham, the Christian meaning. Being as applied to God is univocal, signifying everything directly (*in recto*), as substance and quality are also predicated absolutely.[182] Each of these terms, 'being', 'substance', 'creature', 'quality', as well as 'quantity' and 'relation' and the other categories is predicated univocally in the strict sense when they are considered for themselves.[183] It is when being is predicated of the ten categories that it is equivocal; for, as we shall consider in detail, only substance and quality among them are absolute terms standing for what can exist independently: the others are connotative. Hence being when predicated of the latter cannot signify them by means of a single concept, although when taken for itself it is univocal, as a concept in the third degree of univocity standing for nothing determinate. That is how it

---

[180] Sic enim secundum opinionem Philosophi ens predicatur equivoce de decem predicamentis anologice, quia nec predicatur proprie secundum eum univoce, nec proprie equivoce a casu, sed medio modo, quia predicatur equivoce a consilio. Et hoc quia talis fuit usus loquendi tempore suo in lingua greca. (*Quodlibet* IV, q. 16).

[181] *Ibid.*

[182] Ad aliud dico quod licet secundum intentionem Philosophi ens dicatur equivoce equivocatione a consilio de deo et creatura, de substantia et accidente, non tamen secundum usum nostrum loquendi quia ut nos utimur hoc nomine 'ens' significat omnia sua significata una impositione et uno conceptu et uno modo significandi, quia omnia entia significat in recto. Ideo dico quod ens de deo predicatur univoce (*ibid*). Also *Quodlibet* V, q. 14.

[183] *Ibid.*

is predicated of God, without reference to its real dispositions signified by the ten categories.

V   TRANSCENDENTALS, PREDICABLES AND CATEGORIES

That completes our examination of the different modes of predication and brings us to the terms of which they are predicated. These are of three main classes, transcendentals, predicables and categories or predicaments. Each of these is a universal: transcendentals are terms both of first and second intention, predicables are terms of second intention, and predicaments are terms of first intention.

1   Transcendentals: the concept of being

Transcendentals were so called because they signified things by both intentions. The reason is that they are convertible with being, and so at the level of existence apply to all that is, indifferently. There are six such terms: 'being, 'thing', 'something', 'one', 'true', 'good'.[184] These are in turn are divided between 'being', on the one hand, and the remaining five on the other. 'Being' alone of these is an absolute term standing for everything that is; the rest are connotative. Thus, 'one', for example, is an attribute of being, which while signifying the same as being, does so, however, indirectly by means of a nominal definition by the second essential mode of predication, namely where the subject enters into the definition of its predicate, in this case meaning 'a being which is one'.[185] Accordingly, being is the most universal of all terms, and we shall concentrate upon it, not least because it is also the touchstone of Ockham's ontology and epistemology.

The first thing to be said is that Ockham treats being exclusively as a transcendental concept: it has no separate ontological identity, apart from the diversity of individual beings. Consequently when it is predicable of God, or has the community which enables us to describe it by a concept, that is exclusively the work of abstraction. In adopting this standpoint Ockham was directly combating the entire scholastic tradition, by which being had an independent reality as the universal condition of everything which is. Not only therefore did being on this view constitute the most universal term but also the most universal nature, knowledge of which for Henry of Ghent and Duns Scotus was, as we have seen, the first proper object of understanding. Ockham therefore in affirming the purely logical status of being had also to detach it from the ontological import with which such thinkers had endowed it. We must consider it in both aspects.

Ockham defines being in the two ways just previously mentioned. By one, it can be understood as a common univocal concept predicated absolutely *in quid*,

---

[184] Primo tamen dicendum est de quibusdam communibus omnibus, sive sint res que non sunt signa, sive sint signa, cuiusmodi sunt 'ens' et 'unum' (*SL*, I, ch. 38, 98).

Quedam indifferenter significant tales res que non sunt partes propositionis nec orationis, et etiam talia signa, cuiusmodi sunt talia nomina: 'res', 'ens', 'aliquid', 'unum' et huiusmodi (*ibid.*, ch. 11, 38). Also *Ordinatio*, d. 2, q. 1, 22–3.

[185] *Ibid.*, ch. 37, 97.

and transcendentally, of every thing and every term.[186] As more universal than anything else it can be predicated of everything else in the way that we can know that Socrates is, without knowing that he is a man or an animal.[187] In that sense, as we said earlier, being is independent of its different modes or dispositions.

By its second definition, however, being is equivocal because it is predicated absolutely and indifferently of everything that is, no longer by means of one concept, but diversely by diverse concepts.[188] Being is here a common term by imposition, corresponding to a number of concepts each with its own signification. That is how it is predicated of the ten categories some of which, like substance and quality, denote real things independently (*divisim*) for themselves, while the others signify in conjunction (*coniunctim*), with one term dependent upon another. This division corresponds once again to absolute and connotative concepts, though in the Commentary on *Porphyry* where it occurs Ockham does not use the expressions. Thus substance stands for what exists independently as individual substances. But in the proposition 'This white thing is similar', 'similar' cannot stand for an individual thing taken in itself but is only verifiable of two or more individuals taken together. For that reason the ten categories do not all represent distinct beings, but the same individuals considered differently: as we shall see in due course, the same substance or quality—Socrates and whiteness—can be conceived equally from the standpoint of relation, quantity, action, passion, and so on, although then not absolutely and for itself. Hence being is never predicated univocally of the ten categories, because of this conceptual diversity.[189]

In the same way the distinctions between substance (*ens per se*) and accident (*ens per aliud*), and between potential and accidental being, are due to different ways of signifying individual things, not different kinds of being. In one case, since whatever exists must be individual, to call it substance or accident is to signify an individual being either for itself absolutely or in terms of something else con-notatively. In the other case, since only what exists has actual being, to say that something has potential being is to say that it can exist as a proposition in the mode of possibility:[190] something to which we shall again return.

From this it can be seen that these different modes of predication arise from the universality of being as a concept; it can refer to anything that is or can be conceived of as being. That applies no less to its abstract forms of 'existence' and 'essence'. Not only do these not for Ockham constitute distinct levels of being, whether of actuality and potentiality in the manner of Thomas Aquinas and the Christian

---

[186] Circa 'ens' autem est primo sciendum quod 'ens' dupliciter accipi potest. Uno modo accipitur hoc nomen 'ens' secundum quod sibi correspondent unus conceptus communis omnibus rebus predicabilis de omnibus in quid, illo modo quo transcendens potest in quid predicari (*SL*, I, ch. 38, 98). Also *Quodlibet* v, q. 14.

[187] *SL, ibid.; Quodlibet* v, q. 14.

[188] Tamen non obstante quod sic sit unus conceptus communis omni enti, tamen hoc nomen 'ens' est equivocum, quia non predicatur de omnibus subiicibilibus quando significative sumuntur, secundum unum conceptum, sed sibi diversi conceptus correspondent (*SL, ibid.*, 99). Also *Quodlibet* v, q. 14 and *Expositio*, 45.

[189] *Expositio*, 45–6.

[190] *SL, ibid.*, p. 99.

thinkers who adapted Aristotle's categories, or as the contrast between immaterial essences or forms and their created determinate states in *rerum natura* in the Augustinian tradition; he also regarded the terms 'being' and 'to be' as interchangeable, save when 'being' stands for an individual being. So far as essence and existence are concerned, they cannot be two distinct things, for then they would have to be either substance or accident. Existence is not an accident because, if it were, the existence of a man would be a quality or quantity, which it is not; nor is it a substance which is either matter or form, or a composite of both, or immaterial. Hence if existence is supposed to be distinct from any of these it cannot be any of them—which would be absurd. In the same way, if existence and essence were distinct they would either constitute a distinct being or not; if they did, one would have to be act—and form—and the other potentiality and matter which again is absurd. Alternatively, if they were not a unity they would be a mere aggregation, or one would be the accident of the other. God could, then, if they were distinct, conserve one independently of the other. Which is impossible. Consequently essence and existence are not two things but two words signifying the same thing, one as a noun the other as a verb. For that reason they cannot be conveniently interchanged, for they have different functions. 'To be' (*esse*) can be used as a copula joining two terms as in the proposition 'Man is an animal', whereas 'thing' or 'entity', as nouns, cannot. 'To be' therefore signifies the thing itself. 'Being' on the other hand signifies either the first simple cause, which is God, or secondary causes, which are dependent upon the first cause and in virtue of which they can be said to be. In no sense, then, can essence be said to be indifferent to existence or non-existence any more than essence can be said to be indifferent to non-essence. With Grosseteste Ockham therefore affirms that essence and existence are in no way two things. Far from expressing the difference between God and creatures, what distinguishes God's essence is its complete simplicity and independence of anything else; conversely the dependence of creatures upon God's essence does not mean something additional in their essence: it merely denotes the difference between contingent being through another and necessary being which is being itself.[191]

We have pursued this distinction—or for Ockham absence of distinction—between essence and existence beyond the immediate limits of being as a concept, to show the break with tradition to which it led him. It came from a refusal to identify grammatical and logical forms with ontological realities. It also shows that Ockham, even here, was also writing as a Christian believer, who was prepared to draw theological conclusions, positive as well as negative, from the order of dependence between beings, even while rejecting the attempt to do so from their internal relations. As such it is a further example of the same arguments by which Ockham rejected the formal distinction; in each case, however the terms are

---

[191] *SL*, III, II, ch. 27. Both Moody, *Logic of William of Ockham*, 266–7 and Boehner, *Collected Articles*, 389–92, print translations of the text. Moody's on the whole is the better translation and slightly fuller, but Boehner's is accompanied by the Latin text, though his omission of 'essentia' (390, para. 4, 6) seems to me mistaken.

predicated, and whatever their grammatical form, significatively they are only of real individual beings.

From that follows the further conclusion of the utmost importance for Ockham's outlook: that individuation, as Moody has said,[192] far from occurring from a common nature, which has by definition common being, is achieved in the order of knowing by the use of the verb 'to be'. In the example given above, when 'to be' is used as a copula—'is', 'are'—it individualises a universal, as in the proposition 'Socrates is white' or 'Socrates is an animal' where a genus or species is predicated of an individual to give a particular proposition. Thus in opposition to the main Christian tradition from the time of St Augustine, Ockham treated being as a term predicable of individuals and not a universal essence. To say that 'Socrates is white' is to make both terms stand either for real individuals or the properties of real individuals. Abstract forms therefore remain universal only so long as they remain indifferent or indeterminate, without existential import; so soon as they enter into a proposition significatively they become finite and individual. It is that which makes universal knowledge proper knowledge as we shall discuss in the next chapter; for unless universals are reducible by real definition to individuals, the propositions of which they are part will be false, as it is false to say 'Every man is an ass'.[193]

That has a direct bearing upon the meaning of 'being' itself. As the most universal of all terms the question is whether it is also the first adequate object of knowledge under which knowledge of everything else is contained. Duns Scotus held that it was.[194] Ockham opposed him on the grounds that to make 'being' the first term of all other knowledge would be to destroy its univocity as the one common concept embracing all created being and uncreated being alike. His arguments, as we shall now see, are an extension of the preceding ones: that is, significatively a universal can only stand for individuals of which it is predicated, either absolutely or denominatively. Hence to give knowledge, it must refer to some individuals directly or indirectly; there is no other way in which terms can have independent ontological import.

Now a first object of the intellect can be understood in one of three ways: by primacy of generation as that which is first known as the object of an act knowing; or by primacy of correspondence (adequatio), when the object is predicated of everything which is itself intelligible; or thirdly by primacy of perfection as the most perfect object which can be known. Only in this last sense is God first object of the intellect.[195] Ockham's rejection of the first two ways as providing direct knowledge of God belongs to chapter five. But his denial that a concept of being

---

[192] Logic of William of Ockham, 174. See also G. Bergmann, 'Some remarks on the ontology of Ockham', Philosophical Review 63 (1954), 561 ff., who, rightly in my view, says that Ockham accepted not only the real existence of individual objects but individual instances of qualities present in them.

[193] E.g. quia omnes propositiones universales equaliter inducuntur ex suis singularibus . . . igitur ad verificandum tales propositiones universales a parte rei sufficiunt singularia (Ordinatio, d. 2, q. 4, 143).

[194] For Duns's doctrine of being as first adequate object see Wolter, Transcendentals, 58–99.

[195] Ordinatio, d. 3, q. 1, 388–9.

can be the first object of the intellect (*primum cognitum*) as it refers to God is the main issue here between Ockham and Duns Scotus, who held the contrary view. In rejecting it, Ockham was principally concerned with a first object in the second sense of adequation as predicable of all that comes under it, rather than in its other connotation of perfect correspondence between the object and the act of knowing.[196] From this standpoint a first adequate object has two meanings: absolutely in which everything coming under it is known for itself individually and can only be known thus in virtue of such predication. Alternatively the first object can be the most universal (*communissimum*) among all that is knowable, and the means by which everything else coming under it is known. By the first mode, being cannot be known naturally as the first object of the intellect because there is no means of knowing that what it subsumes is naturally knowable. By the second mode, being can be known as the most universal concept (*communissimum*), but again without knowing that everything contained under the concept is naturally knowable individually and distinctly.[197]

This definition in the *Ordinatio* is paralleled and amplified by that in the *Reportatio*, book four. When being is a concept abstracted from everything of which it can be predicated *in quid*, it can be the natural and adequate object of the intellect, since it is predicable of all that can be known absolutely. But when being is extended to include everything that can come under the term, then it cannot be the natural and adequate object of the intellect in its present condition, for being includes many things, individually and in themselves, such as all material and immaterial substances and many accidents, which are beyond the intellect's natural powers.[198]

In other words, being as *communissimum* can only be the intellect's adequate and natural first object when it consists of a univocal term in the third mode; it thereby brings together in an abstract concept beings that cannot be known determinately and *in quid*, including God and spiritual natures. For Ockham, unlike Duns, the condition of such a univocal concept as the most universal is that it does not give real knowledge of everything that comes under it; if it did, it could not be *communissimum* just because not everything is naturally knowable. Unknowability is the price of universality; to refuse to pay it is to deny the one means of bringing together God and creatures in a common concept. Hence a concept can only be the most universal if it is not the first and adequate object of the intellect.

---

[196] *Quodlibet* I, q. I.

[197] Ad tertiam dico quod aliquid esse obiectum primum alicuius potentie—et hoc loquendo de obiecto primo primitate adequationis—potest intelligi dupliciter: vel quia illud cuius quodlibet contentum est in particulari et sub proprie ratione apprehensibile ab illa potentia, et nihil est sic apprehensibile a potentia nisi de quo illud predicatur; vel quia est communissimum inter omnia que possunt apprehendi ab aliqua potentia, nec potest aliquid apprehendi ab illa potentia nisi de quo ipsum predicatur. Primo modo dico quod non potest naturaliter cognosci quod ens est primum obiectum intellectus, quia non potest naturaliter cognosci quod quodlibet contentum sub ente est sic cognoscibile ab intellectu. Secundo modo est possibile, sed tunc non est naturaliter notum quod omne contentum sub tali primo obiecto est naturaliter cognoscibile distincte et in particulari a tali potentia (*Ordinatio*, d. I, q. 4, 436–7). Also d. 2, q. 4, 140–I.

[198] *Reportatio*, IV, q. 14, C.

That is the basis of Ockham's criticism of Duns Scotus's view that being is the first adequate object of the intellect. There are three main arguments. First, univocity is not something real communicated to what is univocal: hence there is no real identity between individuals which come under the same concept, but merely community by predication. For that reason the universal does not inhere in the individual as its essence.[199] Second, that applies equally to terms: Duns Scotus's view displays the common misconception that every inferior, i.e. less universal term, always contains its superior, i.e. more universal term, and that the former is directly predicable of the latter, as, on this view, species is directly predicable of genus absolutely. That also leads to the further fallacy that the less general a concept, the more composite it is, in including the more general.[200] Here again, as we have seen, the relation of inferior to superior is one of predication and has no bearing upon its composition; a *species specialissima* can be absolutely simple.[201] Third, the relation between terms does not imply a corresponding relation between beings. According to whether they are taken significatively or non-significatively they can have divergent meanings. There is all the difference between knowing that a man is an animal when 'animal' has personal supposition and when it is in simple supposition: by the first, knowledge of man carries with it knowledge that he is an animal; by the second, when animal is a concept, it does not, since we can know that someone is a man without knowing that he is an animal. Similarly if being is not predicated of a man personally but in simple supposition as a concept, man can be known independently of knowing that he is being.[202] Thus in every proposition containing universal terms we must distinguish between whether they stand for themselves or for the things from which they are abstracted and of which they are verified. If a term like being is to stand for real beings then it cannot stand for a concept.[203]

On these grounds Ockham opposed Duns Scotus's arguments for being as the first object of the intellect both by primacy of generation and adequation. By the first of these Duns, as we saw in chapter one, contended that while a *species specialissima* is the first object of the intellect, known through one of its individuals moving the senses, it is known only indistinctly because, like a genus or higher species, it is a composite concept whereas only an absolutely simple concept can be known distinctly. Being, on the other hand, is an absolutely simple concept; for it is included in the essence of everything else; and since nothing can be distinctly conceived unless everything belonging to its essential nature is known, being must be first known distinctly if anything else, as inferior to it, is to be known. Thus, whereas nothing else can be known without being, being can be known independently of anything else.[204]

---

[199] *Ordinatio*, d. 2, q. 7, 258; d. 2, q. 9, 312.

[200] *Ibid.*, q. 9, 320–1.

[201] *Ibid.*, d. 3, q. 5, 446–8; d. 8, q. 1, G–H.

[202] *Ibid.*, d. 2, q. 7, 257.

[203] Igitur ens, quod est precise univocum entibus realibus, univoce et in quid predicatur de ente reali et de ente rationis, sed tunc illud ens rationis non supponit pro se sed pro re (*ibid.*, 259).

[204] *Ordinatio*, d. 3, q. 5, 443–5.

We have considered the ramifications of these arguments as they concern the order of knowing in chapter one, where, as we have seen, for Ockham the individual comes first in the order of knowing by primacy of generation; but not always as first object of distinct knowledge. Nor did he accept that a species or genus is not an absolutely simple concept. Contrary to Duns Scotus, a *species specialissima* can never be known indistinctly; for only what is composite can give confused knowledge, and only individuals are composite.[205]

On the main issue of being as first object of the intellect by primacy of origin, Ockham dismisses Duns's contentions as completely false. Any object can be known distinctly without knowing what is inessential to its nature or is not included essentially in it: the case with the concept of being which is not necessary to a *species specialissima* or anything real which comes under it. Hence the latter can be known independently of the concept of universal being.[206] The minor is confirmed by Duns himself when he said that the concept of being is not something real; therefore it is only in the intellect and not of the essence of anything existing outside the soul. Moreover if one thing which belongs to a concept can be known distinctly from it, so can other things belonging to the same concept. But God—as being—can be known independently of the concept of being which is predicated of him *in quid*; so therefore can a creature of which being is equally predicated absolutely.[207] In the same way whatever can be known by the senses without knowing anything else can be known also by the intellect; and as the senses have no need of the concept of being, nor has the intellect.[208]

Accordingly not the *communissimum* by primacy of generation but the singular is the first object of knowledge,[209] save when a universal has been previously abstracted from individuals and can be known before another individual is known. In any case concepts, because they are formed from abstraction, are always simple and can be absolutely simple; only individuals, in being composed of different parts, are known confusedly.[210]

The second group of arguments, for being as first and sufficient (*adequatum*) object of the intellect—discussed by Ockham in question eight of the same third distinction as the preceding arguments—begins with St Thomas Aquinas's definition of an adequate object.[211] It is that an object is sufficient when it is proportionate to the cognitive power whose object it is. In the case of the human intellect, dependent upon the senses for its understanding, its adequate object is the form which it identifies and abstracts from an individual material being and knows as a phantasm or image in the mind. Ockham's criticism of this view, which we

---

[205] *Ibid.*, 446–58.

[206] Contra secundum articulum in quo ponit quod ens necessario est primum distincte cognitum primitate originis, hoc est simpliciter falsum, quia omne obiectum potest distincte cognosci, non cognito illo quod non est de ratione eius essentiali nec includitur essentialiter in eo; sed conceptus entis non includitur essentialiter nec in specie specialissima nec in aliquo inferiori reali; igitur unumquodque eorum potest cognosci distincte sine cognitione entis communissimi (*ibid.*, 458). Also 478–9.

[207] *Ibid.*, 458–9.   [208] *Ibid.*, 460.   [209] *Ibid.*, 473.   [210] *Ibid.*, 475.

[211] *Ibid.*, d. 3, q. 8, 525. Ockham does not deny that the object is proportionate to the subject but that they shared the same mode of being (*ibid.*, 541).

have seen extends well beyond the question at issue here, is that it is not a definition of a sufficient object. A first and sufficient object, he says, must engender knowledge —though not first knowledge—of everything else necessarily contained under it, as, say, colour, as first and sufficient object of vision, must enable all colour to be of itself visible. But a form known by abstraction from an individual thing cannot be such as object and so nothing common to it will be first and sufficient object of the intellect as indeed nothing else is a common first object of the intellect.[212] That is to say, for Ockham, what is abstracted is known first as a singular and not universal; and as singular it cannot serve as first object common to everything else.[213]

Duns Scotus, however, identified being as first and sufficient object because he held that it was included in all that was intelligible either essentially—in the case of genera, species, individuals and their essential parts—or virtually, where it could not be known essentially, in the case of ultimate differences and their properties. Accordingly, while in neither aspect alone could being be predicated of all things, it could when taken under this double primacy.[214] In that way colour, for example, could, according to Duns, be the first object of sight by which all colour could be seen—in its properties and differences as well as for itself and in all its species and individuals—because where it was not included essentially it could still be inferred as belonging virtually to its properties and differences.[215]

Ockham, it need hardly be said, did not accept such a doctrine: above all because, by neither primacy, could being be extended to include intelligible beings. As terms of second intention they are different in kind from real beings and so they do not share a common univocal term.[216] Nor could they be brought under it virtually, since such a primacy is confined to real beings. That is shown by the fact that intelligibles can be known independently of knowing real beings; therefore they are not contained virtually in knowledge of real beings. For that reason Duns's arguments do not suffice to establish being as first and sufficient object of the intellect.[217] Their inadequacy is confirmed from the example of God, who is included essentially or virtually in knowledge of everything else which can be known for itself, and yet he is not first and sufficient object of the intellect.[218]

Ockham's own solution is noteworthy for its subsequent modification in a later revision of the text in the *Ordinatio*. While not altering his essential position,

[212] *Ibid.*, 525–6.

[213] Preterea quod dicit quod 'obiectum proportionatur potenti cognitive', hoc concludit eque faciliter oppositum principaliter intenti, quia si obiectum proportionatur potentie, igitur potentia singularis et una numero habebit pro obiecto singulare et unum numero, igitur universale abstractum non erit primum obiectum . . . Preterea quecumque potentia intelligit illam formam que est individualiter in materia, sive intelligat prout est in materia sive non, intelligit vere illud quod est individuum et singulare (*ibid.*, 527–8).

[214] *Ibid.*, 529–30.

[215] *Ibid.*, 530.

[216] Ens non habet alteram primitatem respectu alicuius per se intelligibilis; igitur non est primum obiectum et adequatum . . . quia ens rationis et respectus rationis sunt per se intelligibiles et intentiones secunde, et tamen ens neutram primitatem habet respectu talium (*ibid.*, 530).

[217] *Ibid.*, 2, 530–1.

[218] *Ibid.*, 531.

he qualifies it to become less unequivocal. We shall best discern the difference by taking the original statement first. By this Ockham replied as follows:

Therefore I say otherwise to the question. First that there is no sufficient object of the intellect. The reason is that a sufficient object is that which of itself is common to everything apprehensible by this power (i.e. the intellect). But there is no such thing in respect of intelligibles. Therefore there is not an adequate object. The major premise is evident because neither virtual nor essential inherence suffices [for such an object] as has been said. The minor is clear because second intentions, what is false and impossible, and all propositions, can of themselves be known by the intellect and yet nothing is univocal to them; and so they have no common term.[219]

It will be seen that this rejection of a sufficient object is made upon the assumption that all mental concepts are *ficta* which do not have real being: it is the same distinction between real and intelligible which underlay the first two arguments against either kind of primacy posited by Duns Scotus for being.

When, however, Ockham came to make his addition, he introduced two changes. The first is that he no longer treated this view as his but as an opinion which he was reciting. The second is that he now put forward the alternative explanation based upon interpreting a concept as a real quality in the mind; by this, intelligible being would be real being, and so being would be the sufficient object of the intellect, because it was common to all being, in the mind or outside it. Under it would be included all second intentions, false and impossible notions, and propositions, which the original opinion excludes; for everything known by the intellect would *eo ipso* be being[220]—even the properties of which being is predicated when they are taken in simple supposition, as concepts: a statement that clarifies an earlier argument that the attributes of being when predicated absolutely by the first essential mode—by which the predicate defines or subsumes the subject—do not stand for anything distinct from the subject, as the concept 'man' stands for all men.[221]

It would be difficult to reconcile these two positions. They rest upon two different conceptions of intelligible being; according to whether it is taken as real or not, being can or cannot be the first and sufficient object of the intellect. But opposed as these two alternatives are, they do not, in fact, change Ockham's fundamental standpoint which is expressed in his other conclusion. That stood unchanged in the form that we have frequently encountered it, as follows: 'That the most universal term (*communissimum*) that can be apprehended by us is being which is univocal to all real being; for otherwise, we could not have any real knowledge of God or substance'.[222] In other words being remains the most

---

    [219] *Ibid.*, 533.

    [220] Istam conclusionem dico recitative, secundum opinionem que ponit quod conceptus sive intentiones anime habent tantum esse obiectivum et nullum esse subiectivum. Quia secundum opinionem que ponit quod conceptus sive intentiones anime sunt vere qualitates, id est subiective existentes in anima, est dicendum quod ens est obiectum adequatum intellectus nostri, quia commune univocum omni per se intelligibili . . . nec est aliquid quocumque modo apprehensibile ab intellectu quin de eo ens per se predicetur (*ibid.*, 533–4).

    [221] *Ibid.*, 534 and d. 2, q. 9, 322.   [222] *Ibid.*, 534.

universal of all terms, predicable of everything that can be known, regardless of whether that includes intelligible being or not. The status of being as a univocal term, common to all creatures and to God, remains therefore unaffected by the status of intelligible being. Only its status as a sufficient object is in question.

To decide where it stands after Ockham's amendment we must recall his earlier definition of an adequate object. It could be either *communissimum* as a concept, extending only to what is known, or it must include absolutely knowledge of everything which comes under it. Ockham rejected the second alternative as naturally unattainable. Now when we compare these definitions with the conclusions we have just considered, it is clear that what Ockham has said about being as *communissimum* in his second unamended conclusion—namely that as a univocal concept of all real being it can be apprehended by us—agrees with his earlier definition of being as an adequate object taken as *communissimum*. He now, however, does call being, as *communissimum*, an adequate object: in other words, once being extends to intelligibles it is not only the most universal but it also includes everything that can be known, real and intelligible.

This amended conclusion agrees with what he has previously said in distinction one, question four of the *Ordinatio*, as well as in book four of the *Reportatio* where, certainly in the latter, there is every reason to think that he identified concepts with *ficta*: namely that being could be the first and adequate object of the intellect, without enabling us to know more than that being is predicated of all that comes under it. Why then, did Ockham in question eight of the second distinction of the *Ordinatio* initially deny that there was an adequate object? One can only surmise that whereas he was initially prepared to include *ficta* in a definition of being as a universal concept (since—though not themselves real—they stood for what was real), when he came to challenge Duns Scotus's arguments for being as virtual and common, he was then confronted by the very discrepancy between real and intelligible being which led him to reject by either mode univocity between them.[223] Hence he rejected being as an adequate object if concepts were *ficta*. Later with the second interpretation of concepts as real acts of intellection he reinstated them under being which, in again including everything, could be a first adequate object in the sense of being universally predicable of anything. He was thus able to explain the predicative primacy of being while showing its inadequacy to give determinate knowledge of anything coming within it, God included. This final position is therefore mark three, designed to overcome what would otherwise have been the inconsistency of having first accepted and then denied that being was an adequate first object. It should not be exaggerated; the ambivalence was, as throughout where concepts were concerned, over definition, not the nature of existence or what could be known of it. However being was defined, it did not permit greater or less knowledge of that which came under it; as a univocal term in the strict, i.e. absolute, sense, it still had to be predicated absolutely of everything which could be known to be. By the time Ockham came to write the *Logic* its nature as a transcendental term made being predicable of

[223] Above, 165.

everything and every other term. In the *Ordinatio* its status does not seem to have been entirely resolved.

That seems apparent from Ockham's replies to the doubts and objections which follow his conclusions in question eight, distinction two. To the first doubt, whether something can only be known when it is contained under a univocal concept of real being, he prefaces his reply by saying that this can be accepted as true if concepts are understood as real qualities, but false if they are taken as *ficta*. Without committing himself to the truth or falsity of either opinion he then answers it according to the original interpretation of concepts as *ficta*. On this view, intelligibles can be known independently of real being by a real act of intellection, provided that such cognition derives from a previous act in which something real was known.[224]

It is in relation to the primacy of the individual as the foundation of real cognition that Ockham's remaining discussion is best considered; for it is precisely upon whether it can engender such knowledge of real individuals that the claims for a common univocal term as the sufficient object of knowledge rest. We shall therefore first take the replies which deal with the role of individual cognition before the long discussion in the second *dubium* of Duns's treatment of an adequate object. The key to Ockham's position is contained in his reply to the third *dubium*, whether the intellect has a sufficient object which moves it.[225] Ockham declares that this object is the individual, and it is in this light that being as *communissimum* can be understood as first object (note that Ockham does not say first sufficient object). For then being will be first object in virtue of its primacy as the most universal term. As such it is predicable of everything which can be known by the intellect and can move it to an act of intellection, although being as a univocal term will not itself do so. Once again Ockham qualifies this statement with the words 'according to one opinion'. Discounting that for the moment, the original import is plain: when such a concept of being is taken in personal supposition, as standing for real beings, it can be called the real mover of the intellect, but not when being stands in simple supposition; for then being is not the real mover of the intellect. Ockham also makes the same qualification to the final statement in this third doubt: namely that while it is true to say that 'all being is the mover of the intellect', it is quite false to say that 'the being common to every mover of the intellect is its motive': in other words that intellect does not know everything else through first knowing being.

How then do these three—and subsequently added—qualifications affect the original view? As interpolated on each of the occasions where real being is opposed to being as a concept, they therefore reverse the previous position that a concept is not real and cannot act directly upon the intellect. To that extent they amount merely to another way of saying that, if it is a real quality, the concept of being as the most universal could be a sufficient object of the intellect. But, once again, that also leaves unaltered Ockham's fundamental position that being as a univocal concept is predicable *in quid* of the individuals which come under it, and that it is

---

[224] *Ordinatio, ibid.*, 536–7.   [225] *Ibid.*

abstracted as a concept from intuitive knowledge of individual being.

That is underlined by his reply to the fourth doubt: that what moves the intellect to knowledge of itself *pro statu isto* is a sensible quality existing outside the soul together with its own acts and passions, and perhaps the intellective soul itself, if it should see itself intuitively. But, he continues, what is open to question is whether these different movers are united in a common term which can be predicated absolutely of them. That doubt remains unqualified. Which is of itself significant in pointing to where the divergence between the two interpretations of a concept lies. It does not affect the role of a univocal concept, nor its formation, both of which come through predication of and abstraction from real individuals originally known intuitively. The point at issue is rather whether the concept as a concept is real or exclusively representational. In its bearing upon being as a univocal concept that means the difference between a first object and a sufficient object but not in what comes under being itself or what the intellect can know as being.

We can now turn to the second *dubium* where Ockham argues this point at some length against Duns's notion that the first and sufficient object of the intellect is naturally attainable.[226] By that Duns meant that the intellect naturally inclines to being, although it does not fully attain it in not knowing everything included under being as first object.

Ockham opposes Duns because a first object of the intellect is predicated of everything that can be known in itself, which, on Duns's view, would mean everything which is the subject of natural knowledge—what Duns calls metaphysics. Nor does Ockham accept Duns's reply—made not of course to Ockham's objection but over the distinction in the meaning of a natural object—that this is to commit a fallacy of a figure of speech by treating being as something in itself and not as that which is included in all things: that is to say absolutely *in quid* instead of connotatively *in quale*. For it is just this juxtaposition which to Ockham appears contradictory. If on the one hand being is, as Duns says, univocal to everything, created and uncreated, because it is included in all things, and it is understood naturally, it must then be naturally known as a single intelligible in a single act of intellection. On the other hand, Duns says that being as included in everything is not naturally known and yet the intellect naturally inclines to it. In that case being must stand either for this common univocal term which is a single intelligible or for something contained under it. If the first, and being is naturally knowable, then the being contained in all objects is equally attainable; if the second, then it is not, because in whatever way it stands, confusedly, distributively, or determinately, it will always be false to include being in everything, because it is false of any singular; being will then be predicated as first adequate object of whatever is falsely contained under it, in which case it would then be better to say that everything is the first object of the intellect rather than that being is included in everything.[227]

Being, then, cannot be known naturally as it is present in everything, for not

[226] *Ibid.*, 536-40.   [227] *Ibid.*, 536-8.

everything which is being can be known by itself; it can be known only in so far as all that can be known is known. Hence, even granted that it could be the intellect's natural object, being would still not extend to everything coming under it; for although to know everything contained by an adequate object would suffice for knowledge of it, it would not contain knowledge of what was included in another adequate object,[228] just as to know the content of an adequate object is not always to know the adequate object itself. Thus, as we saw in the first chapter, the intellect can know a whole without knowing the parts of which it is predicated when they are the object of the senses. Knowledge of one does not presuppose knowledge of the other as it does not of an adequate object and its individuals. To reconcile Duns's belief, then, that being is first adequate object of the intellect and also naturally attainable, being would have to be predicated not of the concept which constituted the intellect's adequate object—and to which according to Duns the intellect naturally inclines—but of the being which it can understand naturally.[229] That is, since the intellect can only attain naturally to the beings which it is able to know naturally, it cannot have, as a natural adequate object, a single univocal term which embraces everything whether knowable or unknowable to the intellect. These are the alternatives which confront Duns's views. Ockham does not regard them as contradicting Duns's own principles; indeed if Duns is interpreted in this second sense where being stands for what the intellect can know naturally, then his position can be accepted. If on the other hand he means that all being is naturally attainable by the intellect, then, Ockham declares, he contradicts himself.[230]

Ockham, then, unlike Duns Scotus, was treating being not ontologically but logically and conceptually. It was not a real universal property or nature present in all that exists, but the most universal term in a definition of what is real, and itself denoting a concept derived in abstraction from individual beings. As such it is predicable of all real things, absolutely and univocally, but not of what constitutes them. That was the difference between the two thinkers: it was fundamental.

Ockham throughout regarded being as a defining term; like any other; of itself it neither gave nor presupposed real knowledge. It was not, as we have seen included quidditatively in what comes under it, as no superior is included essentially in its inferior.[231] In the same way no definition—contrary to Duns's contention— necessarily provides distinct knowledge of what is defined, because things can be known intuitively and distinctly before any definition. Moreover, every definition is composed of certain common terms which do not belong to the essence of the

---

[228] Ideo dico quod posito quod ens esset obiectum adequatum intellectus, adhuc obiectum adequatum posset naturaliter attingi, non tamen oportet quod omne contentum possit naturaliter attingi. Cuius ratio est quia tunc ad intelligendum naturaliter obiectum adequatum intellectus sufficeret quodlibet per se contentum sub obiecto adequato, non tamen sufficeret ad intelligendum unum aliud contentum (ibid., 538-9).

[229] Ibid., 539 and 532.

[230] Ibid., 539-40.

[231] Ibid., d. 3, q. 5, 458 and 478.

thing defined. Consequently distinct knowledge is not dependent upon a preceding definition; and conversely a definition may add little to knowledge of something, save when it is by means of a subject's properties. But these in turn presuppose prior distinct cognition of the subject, in order to give such knowledge.[232] Above all, some things are not known in themselves at all but in a common univocal concept, whether simple or composite.[233] Which as we shall see is the only way in which God can be known. It is in this abstract sense that being as *communissimum* is predicable of everything; it does not give real knowledge of being as a distinct quality, but affirms being as a universal and abstract term of everything indeterminately. It cannot in its univocal form be reduced to concrete being because as a single concept being cannot embrace all that comes under it. Once it is reducible to what is determinate, which can of course only be in relation to created beings, it then becomes an equivocal term predicable of the ten categories. As a transcendental term it does not permit differentiation or exclusion.[234]

In one aspect Ockham's entire discussion can be interpreted as concerning status of abstract terms. In his arguments against Duns Scotus in particular, he sought to show that being as an abstract term does not correspond to a universal quality or nature, an error which we have seen he castigates as absurd and foolish. Abstract terms may or may not—as the definitions to which they belong may or may not—denote real things; if they do then these must be singular; if they do not they can only represent a concept indeterminately without concrete ontological import. What they cannot do is to denote a concept which is also real so that it at once inheres as a real essence or property and yet is also a term predicable of itself independently. For that reason Ockham criticised Duns in making being both a univocal abstract term and univocally real by concrete inherence. From that point of view Ockham's notion of being serves as a paradigm for universals generally, as we shall now see in his discussion of the five predicables, of genus, species, difference, property and accident, as terms of second intention.

2. *Predicables*

Here, too, Ockham was concerned to establish for predicables what he argued for being (although chronologically his treatment of predicables, as we shall consider

---

[232] *Ibid.*, 478; also d. 2, q. 4, 127–34 where Ockham distinguishes the meanings of universal adequate definition. When taken as convertible with what is defined it cannot apply to substances but only to concepts. But in the negative sense of defining individuals through their parts, without reference to any particular individual, there can be a universal definition of substance. Thus 'rational animal' defines man but not Plato more than Socrates. On the other hand it is only in having personal supposition that such a definition can be true, signifying this and that and that individual man; where taken simply for rational animal in itself it would be false for 'rational animal' as real is only individual. As we have just seen, to define something by predication does not provide distinct knowledge of what is defined, for it is known confusedly and by means of distinct parts. But it remains essential definition.

[233] Similiter, aliquando res non est cognita in se sed tantum in conceptu aliquo simplici communi, vel composito proprio, et tunc aliquando definitio facit ad notitiam rei, quia tunc non est cognoscere rem quam cognoscere definitionem rei, illo modo quo dictum est prius deum cognosci in aliquo conceptu composito sibi proprio (*ibid.*, d. 3, q. 5, 479–80).

[234] *SL*, I, ch. 38, 99.

presently, comes first): namely that they were terms predicated significatively of individuals and not of qualities or essences of which individuals were the contingent expression. That is to say, predicables were terms denoting individuals to which they were related logically by predication and not essentially. In that way Ockham was attempting to restore what he conceived to be Aristotle's own meaning which had been largely neoplatonised and lost in the tradition inaugurated by Porphyry's *Isagogue*.[235]

That work was designed as an introduction to Aristotle's *Categories*; for although Aristotle did not treat predicables in the *Categories* but in the *Topics*, he specified in the latter that the predicables were each included in each of the ten categories as their defining elements. Porphyry however gave them a quite different import from Aristotle.

In the *Topics* (book one, chapters four to ten),[236] Aristotle had enumerated four predicables of definition, property, genus and accident, which in his own words 'every proposition and problem indicates', and from which every proposition and problem is formed.[237] Together they state what a thing is, and so presuppose the ten categories which are classes of predicates signifying a thing in its different aspects. In other words before we can discuss, say, man by reference to his substance, quality, and quantity, and so on, we must be able to define him as a being by identifying his essence, genus and property as a man and his peculiarity or accidents as an individual.

Porphyry in the *Isagogue* altered both the number of predicables and their meaning. Where Aristotle had omitted species and included difference under genus, Porphyry instated them both as predicables and omitted definition. More important he made both genus and species stand no longer absolutely for individuals *in quid* but connotatively, so that they are equivalent to the attributes of individuals, predicated necessarily as universal natures, and contingently for the individuals in which they inhere. Predicables thereby become identifiable with essential qualities, and individuals simply with their occasion; predicables therefore lose their significative function, no longer standing for all those individuals which come under them by predication, but for independent universal qualities which are known connotatively through the individuals in which they inhere, as the term 'man' connotes the humanity in individual man and not the individual men signified absolutely and *in quid* for themselves.

This was the first and decisive step in the long tradition, culminating in Duns Scotus's formal distinction, of treating abstract terms as the expression of universal natures, to be identified in their concrete individuals. By that, as Moody has said, 'Porphyry insisted that Aristotle's analysis of modes of signification could only be understood in the light of his analysis of the ways in which one term can be related to another in predication. Thus he reversed the Aristotelian order, bringing the

---

235 Cf. Moody's illuminating discussion of Porphyry's divergence from Aristotle (*Logic of William of Ockham*, 67–75).
236 *Topics*, 101 a, 11–104 a, 44.
237 *Ibid.*, 101 b, ch. 4.

very instrument of Aristotle's criticism of Plato into the service of the Platonic dialectic'.[238] To which we can add that Ockham in his turn reversed Porphyry's order, by maintaining the significative primacy of both predicables and categories as directly denoting individuals. He did so first and most obviously in his own Commentary on Prophyry's *Introduction* which forms the first of the three logical treatises. For that reason we shall take it as the ground plan of Ockham's exposition of predicables and categories adding whatever is necessary from the *Ordinatio* and the *Logic* in particular.

In his Commentary on Porphyry's *Introduction* Ockham had the double task not only of expounding Porphyry's text but also of restoring Aristotle's meaning as he saw it. He did so by the accepted medieval practice of reconciling rather than juxtaposing his authorities. In this case with the cleavage between them so deep, that could only be at the expense of Porphyry's meaning. Even so Ockham did not make any simple and complete return to Aristotle; he accepted Porphyry's number of five predicables, and he related the discussion to his own medieval Christian tradition as well as to immediate issues, above all in criticising what he regarded as the contemporary confusion of logical terms with universal essences. Since that had begun with Porphyry himself, Ockham also had to broach metaphysical issues in what should have been an exclusively logical treatise.

Thus he expressly opens his Commentary on Porphyry with a prologue in which he treats the three questions, raised but not answered by Porphyry, on the nature of universals, because of the numerous errors of logic into which so many moderns have fallen through ignorance of the difference between logic and metaphysics. For that reason, 'these must be briefly considered and what should be taught stated according to Aristotle's opinion and the truth'.[239] The three questions were whether genus and species exist independently outside the mind or only in the intellect; whether they are corporeal or incorporeal; and whether if they are incorporeal, they are separable from sensible things or included in them.

We can take Ockham's answer to these questions as the point of departure for his view of the way in which universals can be used significatively. To the first he replies that genera and species are solely in the intellect as intentions or concepts formed to signify the nature of things; and as the signs of the latter they are not the same as what they signify. Nor are they part of real things but predicable of them, standing not for themselves as genera and species by simple supposition but in personal supposition for the individual things which belong to them, as in the proposition 'Socrates is an animal', where 'animal' stands not for itself but for the individual being which is Socrates. From that it follows in reply to the second question that genera and species as concepts, as opposed to words, are incorporeal since they are only in the intellect, and for the same reason, in answer to the third question, that they are not in sensible things or of their essence or part of them.[240] That is what Averroes means when, in his Commentary on the

---

[238] *Op. cit.*, 67.
[239] *Expositio*, 10.
[240] *Ibid.*, 14.

Metaphysics, he says that universals are not themselves substances but declare the substances of things as signs declare what they signify; there must therefore be a distinction between them.[241]

Positively, universals are terms of second intention predicable of many.[242] As concepts they are natural signs of real things through abstraction from them; by this Ockham does not, as we have seen earlier, mean the isolation of an essence within things, but the formation of a concept which is common to other things by similarity. Knowledge is founded upon similarity of the object: *intellectus est similitudo obiecti*.[243] Epistemologically the difference between singular and universal is the difference between knowing determinately and knowing indifferently, for the very reason that only singulars are real and determinate.[244] For the same reason, as we have also had ample occasion to remark, universals can never be real, that is, first substances:[245] whether Ockham's view, that as second substances they are only terms, is consonant with Aristotle's notion of second substance we shall leave for later.

So far as the general characteristics of the predicables are concerned, Ockham outlines them in both the Prologue to the Commentary on Porphyry's *Introduction* and the *Logic*.[246] They have substantially the same import, but there is some shift in emphasis. To take the later work first, Ockham's main distinction in the *Logic* is between those predicables which signify individuals absolutely *in quid* and those which do not. Those which do, reply to the question 'what?' applied to something and can be either a *species specialissima* where all the individuals of which it is predicated are of the same kind, or a genus where they differ as species. That is when species and genus are taken strictly. In their broad sense they can also be connotative, when the reply to the question 'what is something?' cannot be answered by an absolute term or its corresponding pronoun. For example, the question 'what is white?' demands a nominal definition that it is coloured; and that cannot be rendered by an absolute term or the pronoun 'this' or 'that'. This refinement is introduced into the *Logic*,[247] and is not found in the Commentary on Porphyry's *Introduction*. Nor does it have a substantive part in Ockham's discussion of the predicables. The other group, again following the *Logic*, has three cases where

---

[241] *Ibid.*, 14–15.

[242] E.g. Dictum autem est quod termini secunde intentionis sunt tales: 'universale', 'genus', 'species' etc. Ideo de illis que ponuntur quinque universalia est modo dicendum (*SL*, I, ch. 14, 44). Also *Quodlibet* IV, q. 19: Stricte accipiendo dicitur intentio secunda conceptus qui precise significat intentiones naturaliter significativas, cuiusmodi sunt genus, species, differentia et alia huiusmodi.

[243] *Reportatio*, II, q. 15, EE.

[244] Confirmatur ista ratio, quia omne universale realiter, sive sit complete universali sive non, est realiter commune pluribus ... sed nulla res est realiter communis pluribus; igitur nulla res est universalis quocumque modo. Maior manifesta est, quia per hoc distinguitur universale a singulari quod singulare est determinatum ad unum; universale autem est indifferens ad multa illo modo quo est universale (*Ordinatio*, d. 2, q. 6, 179–80).

[245] E.g. *SL*, I, ch. 15, 45–8 and ch. 16, 51.

[246] *Expositio*, 15–16; *SL*, I, ch. 18, 56–9.

[247] *SL*, *ibid.*, 57–8.

universals are not predicable *in quid*. The first is when they denote a part and not the whole, but the part is intrinsic to the whole, as 'rational' is the term denoting man's form but not his material nature; this is the predicable of difference. The second and third both concern what is extrinsic to the thing in question and so not a part of it. If this addition is essential it is a property; if contingent it is an accident.

In the Commentary on Porphyry, Ockham's main division is not between predication *in quid* and *in quale* (he does not use the latter expression in the passage just resumed but simply says 'not *in quid*'); it is between extrinsic and non-extrinsic predication. Genus, species, and difference belong to the latter; property and accident to the former. Difference, moreover, occupies a more prominent place. It constitutes the other subdivision of non-extrinsic predication and is predicated connotatively of the whole, which it signifies indirectly, and directly of the part. It thus fulfils exclusively the function which, in the *Logic*, Ockham appears also to assign to genus and species in their broad sense, of connoting individuals by nominal definition, as the difference 'rational' consignifies 'man', and 'white' consignifies the subject of whiteness. The later change in the *Logic* seems to be one of more precise definition than any change in the role of either genus and species or difference: in both works, as we shall see, one of Ockham's main contentions is that difference does not represent the form of a thing, and genus the material part, but that difference is predicable equally of form and matter. Finally in the Commentary on Porphyry, Ockham treats property and accident under extrinsic predication in terms very similar to those in the *Logic*.

Before we consider the five predicables we must pause to examine what Ockham understands by signify. In the *Logic* and *Quodlibets*[248] he distinguishes four meanings. By the first and strictest of them, 'to signify' denotes the direct physical presence of a thing which can be expressed by a pronoun, as when we point to a man and say 'He is white' or 'He is rational'. The second sense is the opposite of the first and is when a term can stand in any proposition for a thing, whether it is present, past, future or only possible, so that regardless of contingent circumstances it will always signify the same thing univocally and *in quid*: the proper sense of universal signification. The third and fourth senses are both connotative: the third in its accepted meaning of signifying one thing by a concrete term directly and another thing by its abstract term indirectly, as 'white' principally means something white and secondarily the whiteness by which it is white, although white cannot itself stand for whiteness. The fourth sense is the widest of all and extends to both direct and indirect, positive and negative, signification; here signify can belong to a proposition, a part of proposition or an expression without any of these standing for anything distinct. Under this mode are included all negative and privative terms like 'blindness' and 'nothing', which consignify something positive as blindness does sight (of which it is the absence) and nothing signifies negatively something (of which it is the negation). All universals signify in the first two senses, although by the first a term loses its meaning the moment what

[248] *SL*, I, ch. 33, 87–9; *Quodlibet* v, q. 16.

it signifies is no longer present;[249] and genus and species as absolute terms can only signify in the first two senses. The other predicables can also signify in the other two senses through not standing for whole things.[250]

A term then for Ockham is universal because of the many things it can signify; taken for itself as a word or concept it is singular like anything else.[251] Universality is therefore a logical, not an ontological attribute; it rests upon predicability of many individuals by a term and not a real inherence in them by a nature. All correct discourse about predicables depends upon observing this distinction. It was a distinction which Porphyry ignored, turning logical into metaphysical relations, and one which Ockham in reply was determined to restore. For him the so-called tree of Porphyry as a descending order of predicables in which the superior was predicated of the inferior, as genus is of species, was an exclusively logical one. Terms were related as genus and species not because one was really of a different nature from the other, but in virtue of their greater or lesser universality in signifying more or fewer individuals. Accordingly the relation among universals rested upon their degree of predicability: superior and inferior were measures of universal predication, not part of a natural hierarchy of natures.[252]

That is the light in which Ockham interprets Porphyry's ways of expressing the relation between predicables and things: 'to participate in', 'to be of', 'to be present in', 'to be absent from' all suggest a real relation; and this metaphysical sense had predominated in the discussions of universals during the middle ages until the time of Ockham: although Abelard, Aquinas and Ockham all came to a similar conclusion over the psychological role of abstraction in the formation of universals, they diverged fundamentally over the ontological nature of what was abstracted.[253] For Aquinas, as we mentioned in the first chapter, it was the essence or form of the thing which the intellect identified and freed from its material accompaniment, thereby exhibiting it in its pure intelligible and universal form; whereas for Abelard[254] and Ockham it was merely the likeness which the mind recognised in things of the same genus or species: it did not stand for any quality

[249] Omne enim universale vel significat plura primo modo vel secundo, quia omne universale predicatur de pluribus, vel in in propositione de inesse et de presenti, vel in propositione de preterito vel de futuro vel de modo (SL, ibid., 88).

[250] Sed universale quod est genus vel species quod predicatur de pronomine demonstrante aliquam rem non significat nisi primo modo vel secundo modo accipiendo 'significare'. Reliqua autem universalia significant plura primo modo vel secundo, et aliqua etiam tertio modo vel quarto, quia omne aliud universale significat plura in recto et aliquid in obliquo, sicut patet de 'rationali' et 'risibili', 'albo' et sic de consimilibus (SL, ibid., 89).

[251] Dicendum est igitur quod quodlibet universale est una res singularis, et ideo non est universale nisi per significationem, quia est signum plurium (ibid., ch. 14, 44).

[252] Notandum quod ordo predicamentalis non componitur ex rebus extra, sed componitur ex conceptibus sive intentionibus in anima que non habent aliquem ordinem nisi quod unum est communius et dicitur de pluribus, et illud vocatur superius; et aliud est minus commune et dicitur de paucioribus, et illud est inferius (Expositio, 37-8).

[253] For that reason I cannot agree with Moody (Logic of William of Ockham, 50-1, n. 2) when he argues that it is hard to see how Ockham's theory differs in any important respects from that of Aquinas. See also 165-72 above for Ockham's criticism of Aquinas.

[254] On Abelard's theory of universals see P. Vignaux, 'Nominalisme', Dictionnaire de Théologie Catholique, xi, cols. 717-84.

which was distinct from individuals themselves. Hence, as we have already said, a universal corresponded to nothing which could be identified with an independent essence or nature.

This refusal of an ontological status to universals set Ockham apart from the main medieval tradition, which Porphyry had helped to inaugurate; in countering it Ockham was also expressly opposing the received interpretation of his own time. Towards Porphyry himself Ockham put a logical gloss upon his metaphysical language, denuding it of metaphysical implications. Thus he explained Prophyry's statement that 'a species contains individuals' as follows: 'Thirdly it must be observed that a species contains individuals not as some whole to whose essence individuals belong in the way that man contains a body and a soul; but "contain" here means to be predicated of many and "to be contained" is to be predicated of fewer. None of these however, is a part or essence of the other.'[255] Again when Porphyry says that 'Many men are one by participation of the species', that is not to be taken as literally true; nor does he, or many of the other authorities, mean that there is one man over and above individual men, for that would be contradictory. Rather 'participate' should be construed as 'to be predicable of' in virtue of a more common term—in this case the species 'man'—containing a less common term—here individual men. The same holds for 'to be in' which also stands for the predication of an inferior by a superior term. Similarly the properties attributed to individuals—as risibility is to man—are not to be treated as really inhering in them.[256] In all these instances the widespread error of confusing predication with inherence arises from ignorance of the equivocal meaning of phrases like 'to be in'.[257] Ockham's repeated need to invoke it in order to save Porphyry's text was what doubtless led him at one point to declare that the *Introduction* was intended less as a discussion of five universals than of 'five equivocal words'.[258] For Ockham they were equivocal because of the different ways in which, as universals, they could be predicated significatively of individuals, as we shall now consider more closely.

So far as genus and species are concerned, we have seen that they are the two universals which can only signify univocally and *in quid*. Both are concepts, which as terms of second intention are predicated not of themselves but of the signs for real things.[259] They therefore stand in personal supposition[260]—*non pro se sed pro*

[255] *Expositio*, 42.

[256] *Ibid.*, 53 and 57.

[257] Et ignorantia istius equivocationis de 'esse in' est causa multorum errorum in exponendo auctiontates philosophorum et aliorum (*ibid.*, 57).

[258] Sciendum quod nec hic nec in aliquo alio loco istius libri invenitur quod acutor dicat se velle de predictis quinque determinare tamquam de quinque universalibus ... sed determinatio sua principaliter est de quinque vocabulis equivocis (*ibid.*, 100). Moody, *Logic of William of Ockham*, 66.

[259] Ista autem intentio que est genus non predicatur de rebus extra animam quia ille non subiiciuntur, sed predicatur de signis talium rerum (*SL*, ch. 20, 61).

[260] Secundo notandum quod quando genus vel species predicatur de pluribus ... in talibus genus et species non supponunt pro se, quia tunc omnes tales essent false, sed supponunt personaliter et pro contentis suis (*Expositio*, 27).

rebus—denoting things really and absolutely, independently of anything extrinsic or essential. It is that which distinguishes genera and species from the other three predicables which can connote something other, or less, than the whole individual.[261] For that reason genus and species are neither part of the individual things which they signify nor of each other, for in each case their relation is a logical one of predication and signification. In the first place, if they did not stand for real things, genus and species could not be predicated of one another. The proposition 'Man is an animal' can only be true when both 'man' and 'animal' signify something other than themselves as terms; if they stood only in simple supposition the proposition would be false, since as concepts 'man' and 'animal' are not the same and so one can not be predicated of the other.[262] In the second place, however, they can stand only for real individuals, because, as we have already seen, there is nothing which corresponds to 'man' or 'animal' or any other universal in *rerum natura*. Accordingly genus and species do not signify wholes which are independent of the individuals which belong to them.[263] In the third place, genus and species are distinct concepts; therefore they cannot be part of one another, since they have no common essence in which they inhere.[264] For the same reason one cannot be the principle or cause of the other; and when Porphyry says that genus is the principle of species, that is to be understood not in the sense that genus is intrinsic to species but that it is more common[265]—an indication of how far Ockham had stretched Porphyry's meaning to gain nominal agreement.

Genus and species, then, are predicated of individual things. That leads to the overriding consequence that when they are predicated of one another, they are predicated of the same things; for as absolute terms when they signify jointly they will be signifying the same individuals of which both are predicable.[266] Hence the terms 'man' and 'animal' in the proposition 'Man is an animal', in denoting not separate essences but individual men and animals, must as universal terms refer to every man who is also an animal: that man and that man and that man and so on.[267] Conversely, if genus and species are united by what they signify, they differ

---

[261] *Ibid.*, 22–3; *SL*, ch. 20, 61.

[262] Et ita vox vere predicatur de voce, sicut in hac propositione prolata, 'Homo est animal'; sed in ista propositione voces non supponunt pro seipsis, quia tunc esset propositio falsa, sed supponunt pro ipsis rebus extra, immo pro eisdem pro quibus supponunt genus et species que sunt intentiones in anima (*Expositio*, 20). Also 22.

[263] Similiter, sicut genus non predicatur de speciebus pro se sed pro rebus quas signficat, ita species non predicatur de pluribus pro se sed pro rebus. Ipsa enim species non est plura, quamvis predicetur de pluribus(*SL*, I, ch. 21, 64).

[264] Ita genus non est de essentia speciei alicuius, nec species est de essentia generis, quia genus et species sunt due intentiones in anima distincte (*Expositio*, 20).

[265] *Ibid.*, 19; *SL*, I, ch. 20, 61–2; *Ordinatio*, d. 8, q. I R, q. 2, K–L, q. 4, S.

[266] Et tamen illud quod est genus predicatur in quid de illo quod est species non tamen pro se, quia neuter terminorum supponit pro se tantum supponit pro ipsis singularibus(*Expositio*, 20). Secundo notandum quod genus non predicatur in quid de specie . . . quia ipsam speciem non significat; sed predicatur in quid de specie pro contentis sub specie (*ibid.*, 34). Also *SL*, I, ch. 20, 61–2.

[267] Notandum est tertio quod sicut genus non est de essentia speciei nec pars eius, ita species non est de essentia individui nec pars individui, sed est quedam intentio in anima significans ipsa individua et predicabilis de eis non pro se sed pro ipsis individuis(*Expositio*, 35).

by what they do not signify; in each case the criterion of absolute individual predication is the same, so that genus and species are distinguished according to how much they can signify. Whereas genus can be predicated of individuals of diverse species, species can signify only individuals of the same kind. Hence they are related not as whole to part but according to their degree of universality: genus can be predicated universally of species but species only particularly of genus as in the proposition 'Every man is an animal' but not 'Every animal is a man'. 'Animal' as genus signifies more individuals and more diversely than 'man' or species does.[268]

This forms the basis of all comparisons between them. Their similarities and peculiarities flow from their function as terms predicable of individuals. It enables us to explain the various ascriptions made to them. Thus when genus is sometimes called, improperly, by the authorities, the matter of things, that means that it is part of a material definition in which it comes first, as matter comes first in material being composed of matter and form; but not that simple things, which have no matter, have no genus. They do; for example 'colour', which is common to all colours and yet is not a composite of matter and form.[269] Again, genus is prior to species by a logical not a natural priority; and when it is said that if a genus is destroyed the species will be, that too refers to a logical not a real dependence.[270] Nor is the relation between genus and species invariably a necessary one: the proposition 'Man is an animal' is a contingent proposition whose truth rests upon the necessary truth of the conditional proposition 'If man is, animal is':[271] an issue to which we shall return in the next chapter.

For its part, species has various definitions: as the form of the thing, the corporeal form, the intelligible species in the mind, or the act and habit, which is Aristotle's usage in *De Anima*.[272] Ockham, however, treats it here as a predicable which like genus remains invariable as the absolute term for other things; even in relation to its genus, a species is not always divided from it by essential difference (as 'rational' divides man from other animals) but only where it signifies composite beings (that is of form and matter).[273] In the *Ordinatio*, distinction eight, Ockham takes issue with what he calls the common opinion that every species is divided into its genus and difference, and conversely that every genus is divided by its differences into species. For Ockham this is a further example of accepting as received truth a belief which has no real foundation.[274] He opposes it because if it were true all simple beings would then also consist of genus and difference, which is false, since they are without matter and so cannot be differentiated. Hence if such beings are differentiated in the mind that must mean either that the different concepts denoting them are synonyms for the same thing, in which case it is not composite;

[268] *SL*, I, ch. 21, 63 and ch. 22, 65; also *Expositio, ibid.,* and *Ordinatio,* d. 2, q. 4, 150–1.
[269] *SL, ibid.,* 62.   [270] *Ibid.,* ch. 22, 66–7.   [271] *Ibid.,* 65–6.   [272] *Expositio,* 32.
[273] Quarto notandum est quod non semper dividens genus in species dividit per differentias essentiales, quia sole species per se definibles et significantes res compositas habent differentias essentiales; species autem significantes res simplices non habent differentias essentiales (*ibid.,* 49).
[274] *Ordinatio,* d. 8, q. 3, B.

or that they do have separate import, in which case they do represent a composite being.[275] In no case is a species dependent upon essential difference any more than it is upon accidental difference; as an absolute term it is predicated directly of an individual substance undividedly, and not of its parts. It does not therefore differentiate between them. As Aristotle says, a proper definition is of the substance, not the accidents;[276] and just as one can exist without the other, so can one be known without the other, as a creature can be defined without knowing God.[277] Moreover, as both Aristotle and Averroes agree, a proper definition is of composite beings; simple beings which—like substantial form, angels and material substance —lack any parts cannot therefore be the subject of a strict definition.[278] Species then are composite or simple according to whether they are predicated of composite or simple beings. That, too, is a further consequence of Ockham's definition of them as absolute terms; for they can never be taken in separation from the individuals which they signify. Only if concepts are identified with mental qualities can genus and species be said to have being; but that is intelligible being and has no import outside the mind.[279]

Finally we must examine what it means to say that something is in or comes under a genus (in genere). There are two senses. Either the expression refers to individuals, as alone real, and so excludes all genera and species unless they are to be considered as real in virtue of being mental qualities really present in the soul. Alternatively, it can mean that a genus is predicated in personal supposition by the first essential mode (primo modo dicendi per se), that is, with the predicate wholly defining or subsuming the subject. By this mode genera and species are included in the genus of substance, not as real substances, but as terms which are included in the definition of individual substances coming under the same genus of substance. There is then a descending order from substance as the most universal generic term (genus generalissimum)[280] through genera and species as the intermediary terms directly predicable in quid of the individuals belonging to substance. Each more general term is included in the definition of the inferior, i.e. less universal term. This order of substance is therefore a logical one of predication, in which, again, only individuals are real.[281] It is in this same sense that Aristotle is to be understood when he says that genus is a part of species, by which he means that it is part of the definition of species.[282]

Now not everything can belong to a genus, notably being itself, God, and certain natures. The reason is that genus, as we saw earlier in the discussion on univocity, demands a certain relation between its members so that it is not wide enough to extend to everything. In the same distinction eight, question two, of the Ordinatio, Ockham states the conditions for inclusion in a genus: namely

---

275 Ibid., c.   276 Ibid.; Expositio, 49.   277 Ordinatio, ibid.   278 Ibid., D–G.
279 Ibid., H; Expositio, 52.
280 Following Aristotle both genus and species are subdivided: genus into the most universal of all (genus generalissimum) and a middle genus (genus medium), and species into a middle and a most specific (specialissima), under which come only individuals.
281 Ordinatio, d. 2, q. 7, 260; Expositio, 39–40.
282 Ordinatio, d. 8, q. 2, L.

that it must be predicable *in quid* of things of different species which have a determinate proportion to one another and do not constitute the essential part of some
other whole.[283] Although angels come under this definition,[284] being and God
do not. Of the reasons why they do not, the first is common to both of them. It is
that although being as a concept can be univocally predicated *in quid* of God and
creatures, as we shall consider in chapter five, there is no determinate proportion
between God's infinite perfection and the limited perfections of everything else.[285]
Ockham does not regard this as a demonstration but as a persuasion.[286] So far as
being is concerned there is a further argument which does not allow any uncertainty that it is not in a genus: namely that whereas each genus is separated from
every other genus, being, as predicated of everything, is not.[287] In other words, as
we shall again discuss in relation to God, being as *communissimum* is too universal
to be contained in a genus, and God as infinite being is too perfect, contrary to
Duns Scotus. The soul, form, and matter, on the other hand, do not each belong
to a separate genus because they are the essential parts of complete beings with
their own essential natures. They are not, therefore, predicated *in quid* but connotatively, *in quae*.[288] To be in a genus, then, has nothing to do with the nature of a
being as either simple or composite, as it has nothing to do with belonging to a
species. The criterion of both genus and species is predicability *in quid* of individuals
which are ontologically similar. That distinguishes them from the other predicables which signify not individuals themselves but what subsists in them,
although, as a term, no predicable itself inheres in real things.[289]

Of the three remaining predicables, that of difference is to be understood as a
term signifying the nature of a thing, not a real difference between things. It can be
essential or accidental, which in the *Ordinatio* corresponds to what is intrinsic or
extrinsic.[290] In the Commentary on Porphyry and again in the *Logic* Ockham
begins from Porphyry's three distinctions in which accidental difference is subdivided
into what belongs to something as an accident and what belongs to something else
as a real difference. In the Commentary on Porphyry's *Introduction* Ockham
excludes both of these as not pertinent to difference as a predicable; their inclusion
makes difference an equivocal term since it then contains accident and property
as well as difference in its proper universal sense. Thus it is an accident when

---

[283] Quia omnis conceptus predicabilis in quid de pluribus differentibus plus quam sola
numero [sc. specie] habentibus certam proportionem secundum prefectionem inter se quorum
nullum est pars essentialis alicuius per se unius est conceptus generis (*ibid.*, B).

[284] *Ibid.*

[285] Sciendum quod, sicut declaratum est, quamvis aliquis conceptus, puta conceptus entis
predicatur de deo et aliqua creatura in quid, quia tamen ista contenta non habent certam proportionem secundum perfectionem inter se, ideo non est genus (*ibid.*). Also *ibid.*, q. 1, L.

[286] Tertio dico quod deus non est in genere. Hoc tamen difficile est probare. Verum tamen
persuadeo magis per viam narrationis quam per viam probationis (*ibid.*, q. 1, L).

[287] Sed ens non est genus, cuius ratio est, quia omne genus separat illud cuius est genus ab
alio . . . sed nihil potest negari ab ente in negativa immediata, cum ens predicatur de quolibet,
ergo ens non est genus (*ibid.*). Also *ibid.*, q. 2, P.

[288] *Ordinatio*, d. 8, q. 2, B.

[289] *Expositio*, 125.

[290] *Ordinatio*, d. 8, q. 4, B.

something differs from something else in being black or in sitting; but it is a difference of property for something to be risible. Only if difference is taken in Porphyry's third sense as specific difference can it be properly regarded as a universal term and one of the five predicables.[291]

In the Commentary on Porphyry's *Introduction* Ockham has naturally to stay more closely with Porphyry's text, disengaging as he goes along the proper meaning from the equivocal. In the *Logic*,[292] however, where he is able to follow his own sequence, Ockham makes a clear-cut distinction between difference in its proper and accidental senses. The latter he subdivides into three of increasing breadth. Taken broadly, difference corresponds to property, as that which is necessarily predicated of something and which cannot belong to other things, as 'risible' is the difference of man, because it is necessary to him and not possible to others. More broadly, difference is an inseparable accident, so that it cannot be successively affirmed and denied of the thing of which it is predicated. In the broadest sense of all, difference extends to anything predicable of one thing and not of another, corresponding to Porphyry's first and general definition where it is a separable accident: for example if Socrates is white and Plato is black, 'white' is the difference of Socrates.[293] Ockham excludes each of these three senses, confining difference in its proper meaning to specific difference; it is then a universal term predicable of something necessarily and intrinsically by the first essential mode.[294] In this sense difference is not an essence but a concept denoting connotatively (*in quale*) what something contains. Difference is thereby a middle term leading to a negative conclusion (*medium concludendi negativam*) through which the difference of one thing is the means of differentiating it from something else, as 'rational', the difference of man, enables us to deny that he is an ass or anything else that is not a man. This we do by arguing syllogistically—that every man is rational; no ass is rational; therefore no ass is a man.[295]

From that it can be seen that difference serves as a connotative term, dividing

---

[291] Circa istam partem est primo notandum quod differentia quam dividit hic auctor non est aliquod quinque universalium; nam sub isto hic diviso continetur tam proprium quam accidens, sicut manifeste patet per exempla sua: Nam 'esse nigrum', 'esse sedens' est differentia communiter dicta; similiter 'esse risibile' est differentia proprie dicta; et ita non dividit hic differentiam que est unum quinque universalium, sed differentiam que est equivocum ad ista tria universalia, scilicet differentian et accidens et proprium. Nam differentia magis proprie dicta est ista que est unum quinque universalium . . . (*Expositio*, 60).

Sed differentia magis proprie dicta est illa qua aliquid differt ab alio differentia specifica (*ibid*.).

[292] *SL*, I, ch. 23.

[293] *Ibid*., 68.

[294] Stricte dicitur differentia que per se primo modo predicatur de aliquo et non indicat aliquid extinsecum rei pro qua supponit illud de quo predicatur. Et sic est unum quinque universalium, de quo in hac parte loquendum est (*ibid*.).

[295] Et est intelligendum quod differentia non est de essentia rei, sed est quedam intentio anime predicabilis de contentis non in quid. Que intentio ideo dicitur differentia, quia, cum non predicetur in quid, est tamen medium concludendi negativam, in qua negatur illud cuius est differentia ab alio. Sicut 'rationale' est medium concludendi negativam, que negat hominem ab asino at aliis que non sunt homines, sic arguendo: 'Omnis homo est rationalis, nullus asinus est rationalis, igitur nullus asinus est homo' (*ibid*., 68).

one species from another, and is not something intrinsic; if it were, it could not be a universal term but would be either form or matter or a whole composed of both. In fact, difference, as belonging to one species and not to another, is called essential not as the essence of something but in expressing an essential part of something.[296] That part can be either form or matter: as 'rational' expresses the intellective soul, so 'material' expresses matter.[297] Hence the opinion of many moderns is mistaken, if taken literally, that difference stands only for form. It is rather that, while able to signify matter equally with form, the role of difference in a definition is comparable to that of form in a being; each is added to what already exists, and presupposes it: difference to genus, and form to matter. That, however, applies to difference when it expresses matter no less than form. Thus in the definition of body as 'a material substance', 'substance' as genus comes first with 'material' as difference added to it, by which it implies matter principally. The corollary is that in species of simple beings, as we have seen before, there is no essential part and so no proper definition, whether it is of a substance or not.[298]

Ockham summarises his notion of difference in the *Logic* under the following heads. First, it is a concept predicable connotatively of a determinate part whose whole is signified absolutely and convertibly by a species.[299] Second, it is a concept because it is a universal which is a natural sign. Third, it expresses a part because if it signified the whole it would be indistinguishable from a species; and it is intrinsic because otherwise it would be a property or an accident. Fourth, it is determinate because difference is always expressed by a concrete term to which an abstract term corresponds, signifying a part of the thing, as whiteness corresponds to white. Thus, as we have discussed earlier, the abstract term must always stand for the part and the concrete for the whole composed of this part and something else—as a white thing is that in which whiteness is present.[300] By the same token difference is predicated *in quale*, connotatively, because it answers the question, 'what kind (*quale*)?': thus if we ask, 'What kind of being is a man?,' it can be replied that he is rational or material. Either term is predicated of the same being of which the species 'man' is predicated; they are therefore convertible with one another not for themselves but for what they signify.[301]

Despite the contrasting comparatively succinct form of the *Logic* with the line by line emergence of his standpoint in the Logical Commentaries, where he had to

---

[296] *Ibid.*, 68–9.

[297] Unde differentia de qua nunc est sermo semper exprimit partem rei. Et aliqua differentia exprimit partem materialem, aliqua partem formalem. Sicut ista differentia hominis 'rationale' exprimit animam intellectivam . . . Hec autem differentia 'materiale' consimiliter et proportionaliter exprimit materiam . . . (*ibid.*, 69).

[298] *Ibid.*

[299] Est igitur differentia quedam intentio anime exprimens determinatam partem rei predicabilis in quale de eisdem de quibus species cum qua convertitur predicatur in quid (*ibid.*, 70).

[300] *Ibid.*

[301] Quod autem differentia predicatur in quale, patet, quia per differentiam non respondetur ad questionem factam per quid de aliquo sed per quale. Si enim queras qualis est homo, convenienter respondetur quod est rationalis vel materialis; predicatur igitur in quale et de eisdem predicatur de quibus predicatur species, quia convertibilis est cum specie (*ibid.*, 71).

disengage both the predicables and the categories from their traditional meta-physical associations, Ockham's view here as elsewhere remains fundamentally unchanged. Central to it in the case of differences is that difference is the means of concluding that one thing is not something else.[302] That holds whether difference is taken in its proper sense as intrinsic or in its broad sense as accidental; hence it remains the means of differentiating one thing from another whether by necessary or contingent propositions. Difference is therefore not a term predicable *in quid*, standing for a thing itself, but, for a part, essential or accidental.[303] Nor as a term is it itself the reason for the difference between different things, but the sign which enables us to conclude that one thing cannot be assimilated to another; and when they differ intrinsically as species, by a strict definition, difference then signifies what it is in something which leads us to conclude that it is essentially different from anything else, as 'rational' is man's essential difference. Difference in itself, then, alters nothing;[304] it neither informs something nor enters into its com-position.[305]

Secondly, Ockham had also to stress that difference plays no part in differenti-ating a species from a genus. Specific difference can only be among substances (namely of what is in the category of substance), because only substances are composed of parts which are of different natures. Hence only specific differences are real differences; they do not, however, of themselves constitute a species from a genus, but merely make something containing an essential part convertible with species, in the way we have just mentioned.[306] The role of difference in the for-mation of species is in providing a definition through signifying the same thing which is signified by a species but connotatively, as 'rational' defines man as a species, denoting all the individual men who in virtue of being men are rational.[307] But here, too, Ockham had to reiterate that not all species had essential differences and so were not all susceptible of strict definition.[308] Nevertheless what distin-guishes difference from the accident and property is precisely that it is not only predicable *in quale*: they are, too; it is that it does not express anything extrinsic, but consignifies by its abstract term the quality which is the essential constituent of the whole signified determinately by its concrete term, as 'white' signifies directly something white and secondarily the whiteness by which it is white.[309] That does not, however, mean that difference is related to species as part to the whole, just because one is not composed of the other; rather they are related as distinct concepts in a definition, not in a real composition, as is proved because a

---

[302] E.g. *Expositio*, 61, 64, 82, 113.

[303] Et ita patet quod differentia de qua est hic sermo non est nisi quoddam predicabile non in quid de aliquo, quod est medium concludendi ipsum differre ab alio, et hec sive ex pro-positionibus necessariis sive ex contingentibus (*ibid.*, 61). Also *ibid.*, 31.

[304] *Ibid.*, 64. I.e. that cannot be something else as opposed to not being (contingently) something else.

[305] *Ibid.*, 65.   [306] *Ibid.*, 66, 79.

[307] *Ibid.*, 74.   [308] *Ibid.*, 75–6.

[309] Tertio sciendum est quod ideo differentia predicatur in quale, quia non exprimit primo totum—hoc est, non est concretum abstracti exprimentis primo totum, sed suum abstractum precise significat unam partem rei et non aliam (*ibid.*, 78–9); also 86.

species can be known without knowing its difference.[310] Conversely, if species were really composed of genus and difference there would then be no distinction between species and definition which is also composed of genus and difference. In fact a definition is of a species because only terms are included in either; and together they are predicable not of themselves but of real individuals. It is in that sense that we are, once again, to understand the comparison between difference and form. It is not a real one, but arises from the role of difference in a definition of species; difference is then the term affirmed of its essential part or nature (*in quale*); it thereby stands in the same relation as form; that is, as what is added to what is already given—in this case genus—in the way that form is added to pre-existing matter and the part is added to the whole. Difference, as we saw in the *Logic*, has the same role in definition whether it is predicated of form or matter, as 'material' expresses the essential difference of body as a species.[311] As part of the definition of species, difference must denote the nature of a substance, which alone, as we have said, has strict definition.[312]

In both the *Logic* and the Commentary on Porphyry, Ockham was as we have said concerened to disengage the logical import of difference as a predicable from any metaphysical implications, and to show that, as in the other predicables, all such expressions as 'intrinsic', 'divide', 'part of', 'flow into', 'separable', 'inseparable', depicted a logical relation between subject and predicate. As we should expect, this task was far more protean in the Commentary on the *Introduction* where Ockham has directly to confront Porphyry's strongly metaphysical imagery. In addition to the arguments already considered, we may briefly mention three others. The first is that properly speaking nothing can differ from itself either essentially or accidentally. To describe the same man in youth and in age, or the same thing in movement and at rest, as different from itself, is a fallacy of consequence, since each is not the same at the time when it is different.[313] Although Ockham does not extend the argument here to the formal distinction and contracting difference his arguments against each of them rest upon a common denial that real being is reducible beyond individual substance as the measure of what can exist absolutely and independently. The second argument is devoted to explaining that the correct meaning of separable and inseparable difference is as predicables which can or cannot cease to be predicated of their subjects according to what they signify: a difference is separable when it need no longer be predicated of something, as 'moving' is not predicable of Socrates when he is not moving; it is inseparable when it is dependent upon the existence of its subject so that it can only cease when the subject ceases to be, as 'snub-nosed' cannot be without a nose.[314] But even so, an inseparable accident does not, as we have seen, constitute an essential difference.[315] Thirdly, there is the neoplatonic image of Porphyry that 'difference is that by which a species flows from a genus'. Here, once again, Ockham saves Porphyry's text only by the broadest of interpretations by which this becomes 'to

310 *Ibid.*, 79.   311 *Ibid.*, 80–1.
312 *Ibid.*, 85.   313 *Ibid.*, 61–2.
314 *Ibid.*, 68.   315 *Ibid.*, 68–9.

have some predicate truly predicable of a species by a universal sign which is not also predicated of genus'.[316] But that only applies to species of composite beings, which alone have essential parts and of which alone difference is properly predicated.[317] It then completes a definition which differentiates one species from another.

Ockham's treatment of the remaining predicables, property and accident, is also designed to establish their universality as terms, in addition to their being equivocal words, which are predicable of many individuals as genus, species and difference are. What distinguishes property and accident from the other three, is that they signify something extrinsic which is either common to all members of a species—property—or can be predicated necessarily or contingently of individuals of different species, as an accident.[318]

So far as property is concerned, it is a universal only in the fourth of the four senses in which it can be understood. By this it is defined as what belongs necessarily and exclusively to everything coming under the same common term—usually a species—of which it is predicated and with which it is convertible. Thus 'risible' is the property of man in belonging to all men without exception, such that no one can be a man who is not also capable of laughter, and conversely a being capable of laughter is a man.[319] In that way property differs both from difference which is intrinsic, and from the other three senses of property in all of which it is an accident and an equivocal term, as either not belonging to every member of a genus or species (as to be a grammarian does not apply to every man) or as not confined only to the members of one species (as biped is not) or as common to all its members at some time (as greying belongs to old age but not to youth).[320] In its proper sense, then, property belongs to every individual of which it is predicated, all the time and invariably. It is not something real which either inheres formally in things or exists as an absolute *in rerum natura*; nor does it always stand for something real; indeed it can imply something extrinsic which is distinct from the subject, affirmatively or negatively. Thus 'calefactive' or 'creative' are not part of their subjects but denote something that can be produced by a subject, just as negative terms like 'immortal', 'incorruptible', and 'immaterial' stand for what a subject can be. Sometimes, again, properties can denote attributes which inhere in subjects, such as the capacity to be white or to change.[321]

---

[316] *Ibid.*, 75–6; *SL*, I, ch. 23, 70.

[317] *Expositio*, 75–6.

[318] Sed de proprio et accidente potest aliter dici, quia predicabile quod importat aliquod extrinsecum aut est proprium individuis unius speciei, et sic vocatur proprium, aut est commune pluribus individuis diversarum specierum, sive predicatur contingenter vel necessario, et sic est accidens (*ibid.*, 100).

[319] Quarto modo dicitur proprium omne illud quod convenit alicui communi universaliter sumpto et nulli alii nisi illi communi et contentis sub illo ita quod est convertibilis cum illo, necessario predicabile de eodem, saltem si esse existere predicatur de illo. Et proprium sic acceptum est unum de quinque universalibus. Alia autem magis continentur sub accidente. Et sic 'risibile' est proprium homini; sic enim competit omni homini et soli et semper, quia deus non posset facere aliquem hominem existere quin ipse esset risibilis (*SL*, I, ch. 24, 72).

[320] *Ibid.*, 71–2; *Expositio*, 88.

[321] *SL*, *ibid.*, 72–3; *Expositio*, 89–90.

It will be seen that in all these cases property is predicated in terms of what is possible for a subject. It is its feature as a necessary universal term that it is always predicated in the mode of possibility, as 'risible' is equivalent to 'able to laugh'. Otherwise property would be predicated of its subject's existence in a contingent proposition; as such it could always be false since God in his omnipotence can separate one created thing from another. That is the difference between saying 'A man is laughing' and 'Every man can laugh'; the first is contingent depending upon the existence of an act of laughter; the second is necessary as an essential attribute of man,[322] which as we shall discuss in the next chapter, is conditional only upon the existence of man, so that, granted that man exists, every man is capable of laughter. Accordingly every property as necessary is equivalent to what is possible for its subject. For that reason property does not have actually to exist in *rerum natura*; it can simply be predicated of what can be known in a mental proposition, just as it can be negative.[323] The same applies to other attributes all of which, together with property, are equally preicable of genus in the same way as they are of species, that is to say of all the individuals coming under them; they are moreover predicated essentially by the second mode, by which the subject is part of the definition of the property in a nominal definition.[324]

Accident, on the other hand, as the fifth universal is predicated contingently. Its physical meaning must be distinguished from its logical role. Physically an accident is a quality which is really distinct from its subject, both able to inhere in it actually and to be separated from it without the destruction of the subject, as white can be in a wall and then cease to be, the wall remaining. In this physical sense accident cannot be a predicable, for it is a term of first intention standing for real things and not a universal standing for a term.[325] When accident is taken as a predicable the phrases 'to be present' and 'to be absent' receive a correspondingly logical meaning. Here, once again, Ockham had to interpret Porphyry's use of them equivocally, this time translating 'to be present' as 'to be affirmed of' and 'to be absent' as 'to be denied of'.[326] In the *Logic*, Ockham states three ways in which accident as a predicable can be understood: it can be in the sense first given where it can be predicated and not predicated of a subject; or it can be successively affirmed and denied of the same subject through a change in the subject or through one caused by something else; or finally, it can be affirmed of something in a subject which is not an absolute (such as quantity) because of a change in the subject.[327] Whichever way an accident is predicated it will always be contingently predicated; for as defined by the philosophers, 'an accident is what can be present or absent without the destruction of the subject'.[328] That applies even when an

---

[322] Unde quelibet talis est contingens . . . 'Homo ridet', et sic de aliis. Sed tales propositiones . . . 'Omnis homo est risibilis' necessarie sunt sic quod non possunt esse false cum veritate propositionis, in qua enuntiatur esse existere de subiecto, et equivalent propositionibus de possibili. Sicut ista; 'Omnis homo est risibilis equivalet isti: 'Omnis homo potest ridere' . . . Ratio autem quare alie propositiones sunt contingentes ita quod possunt esse false simul cum veritate propositionis in qua enuntiatur esse de subiecto, est quia deus potest omnem rem creatam facere sine alia, saltem priorem sine posteriore (*SL*, ibid., 73). *Expositio*, 92–3.

[323] *SL, ibid.*   [324] *SL, ibid.; Expositio*, 93–4.   [325] *Expositio*, 94–5; *SL*, I, ch. 24, 74.
[326] *Expositio, ibid.*   [327] *SL, ibid.*, 74–5.   [328] *SL, ibid.*, 74. *Expositio*, 94.

accident is inseparable from the subject, and its removal would mean the destruction of the subject; although the philosophers would deny this, by God's absolute power any accident without exception could be separated from its substance and the latter remain in being.[329] That helps to explain why an inseparable accident differs from a property. While an inseparable accident cannot be naturally removed from the subject in which it inheres, an accident of the same nature could be withdrawn from another subject without destroying the latter, as black is inseparable from a raven but not from Socrates. A property, however, can never be separated from any of its subjects without destroying them.[330] It is the difference between contingent and necessary attribution.

That completes Ockham's treatment of the five universals. Throughout it, in both the Commentary on Porphyry and the *Logic*, it has been informed by a central theme expressed in Ockham's final summary at the end of the chapter on accident in the latter work:

Any universal is a concept (*intentio anime*) signifying many which can stand for what is signified. And so each distinct concept is predicated of another not for itself but for the thing which it signifies. Hence in those propositions where one concept is predicated of another, one does not denote the other, but frequently what is meant by one is meant by the other. In that sense universals are not things existing outside the soul, and so not of the essence of real things nor parts of things, but certain beings in the soul distinct both among themselves and from external things, some of which are the signs of those things, and some the signs of their signs, as the name 'universal' is common to all universals and consequently the sign of all other universals than itself. It can thus be conceded that the universal which is predicable of the five universals, standing not for itself but for the other universals, is in the relation of genus to universals, as a word (*dictio*) predicable of all words is a noun and not a verb or a participle or a conjunction etc.[331]

Before turning to the ten categories, as terms of first intention, we must briefly notice the term *passio*. Ockham devotes a separate chapter to it in the *Logic*, and it comes into the other main works, notably the Commentary on the *Sentences*[332] and *Quodlibets*.[333] Of all the terms it is the least precise, or if preferred the most equivocal, Ockham at one point in the Commentary on the *Categories* (the second Logical Commentaries), enumerating seven different meanings: although most of these concern physical, mental, and sensitive, rather than logical, attributes, even as a logical term *passio* is not clear cut. As defined in both the Prologue to the Commentary on the *Sentences* and the *Logic* it is equivalent to a property, predicable of the subject by the second essential mode; it thereby enters into the subject's definition, as 'risible' helps to define 'man'.[334] Ockham does not, however, define *passio* in the same strict way as one of the five predicables, although both *passio* and property are necessarily predicated of their subjects which they signify connotatively in a nominal definition. *Passio* thus appears to have a less deter-

---

[329] *SL, ibid.*, 75; *Expositio*, 96–8.   [330] *SL, ibid.; Expositio*, 98.   [331] *Ibid.*, 75–6.
[332] Eg. Prologue, q. 3 and q. 4, 133–6, 144, 150–2, 233–60; d. 2, q. 4, 140–2.
[333] v, q. 18; vi q. 16; ii q. 15.
[334] *EA*, 73 b.

minate meaning, standing for all that property stands for, but also for any attribute which can be predicated of a subject.[335] Both in the Prologue of the *Ordinatio* and in the *Logic*, Ockham gives four ways in which it can stand in a proposition; they are not identical. The two works, however, take them in the same context of attributes which are demonstrable or indemonstrable of their subjects as they concern propositions. Of the four definitions of *passio* the first two are indemonstrable and the second two are demonstrable. In the *Ordinatio* the two pairs are stated in summary form as follows: 'There are some which imply absolute things really distinct from their subjects and formally inhering in them, such as "capable of learning", "heat-giving" and so on. Some imply movement and change such as "risible", "mobile", "changeable" and so on. Some are connotative, and some negative or privative.'[336] In the *Logic* the first pair corresponds to that in the *Ordinatio*, where in one *passio* implies the subject directly and a form really inhering in it indirectly, and in the other the subject directly and something distinct from the subject, in which it is not inherent, indirectly. In both cases the *passio* represents what belongs to the subject potentially. In the second pair, by the third definition, *passio* is specified as that which signifies directly the subject and indirectly not only its parts but also something distinct such as two right angles to which the three angles of a triangle are equivalent. Finally by the fourth mode, *passio* is signified indirectly and negatively in such terms as 'corruptible' which directly signifies substance and indirectly that it can cease to be.[337] In the next chapter we shall consider in detail how attributes can be known in these four ways and in which of them they can be demonstrated of a subject. So far as the discrepancy between the third definitions in the *Ordinatio* and the *Logic* is concerned, it is more apparent than real.[338] They are both of a connotative form; but where the *Ordinatio* does no more than state the fact, the *Logic* specifies its appropriate meaning in a context which is the same for both works, as we shall see when we come to propositions in the next chapter.

Finally there is evidence for the diverse usage of *passio* in the fourth *Quodlibet*, question thirty-seven (in the 1491 Strasbourg edition) where it has three senses: as a term predicable of a subject by the second essential mode, as 'risible' is of 'man'; as that which is indirectly implied by a term, as 'risible' implies the act of laughter; and as that which stands for the same as the subject stands for. In the last sense subject and *passio* are always inseparable; in the other two senses they could be separated save in the first sense when *passio* is in the mode of possibility: for if a man can exist he must, as we have said before, be risible.[339]

We have said enough to show that *passio* is equivalent to whatever can be predicated of a subject, and therefore has as many connotations as there are modes of affirmation. Its real import, in its relation to a subject, will become apparent when we consider demonstration.

[335] *Ordinatio*, Prologue, q. 3, 133–4, q. 9, 244; *SL*, I, ch. 37, 96; *Quodlibet*, v, q. 18.
[336] *Ordinatio*, Prologue, q. 4, 144.
[337] *SL*, III, II, ch. 12.
[338] Baudry, *Lexique*, 192.
[339] *Quodlibet*, IV, q. 37.

3 Categories

We can now turn to the ten categories, which we shall consider here only in their logical aspects, leaving their physical aspects for chapter nine. Ockham's discussion of them follows from what he has said about predicables. Like the latter, they are predicated significatively. Both sets of terms therefore stand for real individuals. But where predicables do so indeterminately, the categories do so determinately. They differ as terms of second and first intention. The five predicables taken together provide the necessary elements in the definition of a thing's nature; they do so as universal terms of second intention which signify individual things through the signs which stand for them. The categories on the other hand are terms which signify things directly, as terms of first intention, that is of individual substances which together with their qualities or essential differences alone constitute absolute things. Categories therefore state the specific conditions under which real things can exist, while predicables state the requisites for indentifying the class to which they belong. As such categories represent all the possible ways in which an individual thing can be apprehended in its specific determinations, of quantity, quality, time, place and so on. They thereby signify the ten different ways in which something can exist. Unlike the predicables these are concerned with a thing's existential import both in its essential and its contingent facets. In that sense the categories may be said to take up the analysis of individual things from the point at which the predicables have identified them. In both cases they do so formally in abstraction from the real existence of things.

In the Prologue to his Commentary on the *Categories*, Ockham defines the object of the work in the following words:

In this work the intention is first to discuss names and words signifying things not according to any property and figure but in so far as they are significative . . . And ignorance of Aristotle's purpose in this book leads many moderns into mistakenly believing that much here refers to things which in fact he wanted to be understood only in connection with words and intentions or concepts in the mind. The value of this book lies in knowing which names signify which things, and that is necessary in any argument, since every dispute presupposes knowledge of the signification of words. This knowledge is especially useful in recognising fallacies of figure of speech, unawareness of which confuses many; for some words may signify things absolutely and others signify them in comparison with others, connoting other things. Accordingly to argue from first words to second words, that is from words signifying things absolutely to things in comparison with others by connoting them, is to commit a fallacy of a figure of speech . . . and such sophisms are believed by many to be demonstrations.[340]

In this connection we may begin by recalling Ockham's remark in the preceding Commentary on Porphyry's *Introduction*, that the ten categories are not principles corresponding to the essences in things which belong to the categories, but are to be understood as principles universally predicable of the things contained under them.[341] Moreover, because the categories do not all signify things in the same way they are predicated of being equivocally: some, like 'substance', denote

340 *EA*, 37 a–b.   341 *Expositio*, 44.

things absolutely; others do not signify them absolutely but in conjunction with other things, as 'similarity' depends upon the relation of different things.[342] The different categories do not therefore always imply distinct things but rather stand for the same thing, whether as really distinct constituents as substance and quality are, or what is relative or connotative in the case of the other categories like relation or action. For that reason being is not predicated univocally of the categories, since they themselves signify being equivocally, that is by ten different concepts.[343] Thus in the same way as 'animal' could be made—by imposition— to signify all men univocally and yet the concepts 'man' and 'men' would still be equivocal in not being the same, so 'being' can be predicated univocally of all that is; but not of the ten categories which, as ten different ways of signifying being, are not univocal.[344]

Ockham develops this theme in the first part of the Commentary on the *Categories*. The categories are terms which are neither really distinct things outside the mind nor stand for the things which are really distinct. Not only is there not always a direct correspondence between concepts, words and things;[345] the categories are not all terms of the same kind: some are nouns, some verbs, some adverbs, as Aristotle says. The category of substance, a noun, contains an order from more to less general which has no place in the category 'when' (*quando*), just as the latter does not have a co-ordinate division between species and essential difference to be found in substance (other than simple substances). This divergence between the categories arises precisely from their signifying the same thing;[346] if they signified different things they would then stand for themselves as common natures which existed outside the mind and were of the essence of everything coming under it; the quality of whiteness would then contain at least the common nature of whiteness and colour, as well as the *genus generalissimum* of quality, with impossible consequences.[347]

Since, however, individual substances alone exist absolutely, the categories must all signify individual substance.[348] For that reason as Ockham explains in the *Logic* the categories all answer questions raised by the category of substance.[349] They are therefore categories in virtue of signifying substance; and in denoting it equivocally they are by definition not reducible to one another. Each is concerned with substance in a different aspect; 'where' does not ask the same question as 'when' or 'quality' as 'quantity'. By the same token many moderns, unlike the

---

[342] *Ibid.*, 45–6.

[343] Ideo de predicamentis non dicitur 'ens' univoce, quia de talibus numquam aliquid univoce predicatur. Cum hoc tamen stat quod de omnibus rebus potest aliquid univoce predicari, quamvis non predicatur univoce de omnibus predicabilibus quocumque modo de rebus omnibus (*ibid.*, 46).

[344] *Ibid.*, 47.   [345] *EA*, 42 a–b.   [346] *Ibid.*, 42 c.   [347] *Ibid.*, 42 b.

[348] Istis non obstantibus dicendum est simpliciter quod nulla est substantia realiter extra animam nisi solum substantia particularis, et quod ista est divisio incomplexorum ex quibus componuntur propositiones, et ex quibus lince predicamentales componuntur (*ibid.*, 40 d).

[349] Et sufficiat scire quod omne incomplexum per quod respondere potest ad aliquam questionem factam de substantia, est in aliquo predicamento sive illud sit adverbium sive verbum sive nomen sive prepositio cum suo casuali (*SL*, I, ch. 41, 108).

ancients, make the mistake of treating all categories as independent realities, adverbs like 'when' and 'where' becoming 'wheness' and 'whereness' as abstract terms standing for the essential differences in things.[350] Neither Aristotle, a philosopher, nor John of Damascus, a theologian, was guilty of that error; both recognised in the categories a diversity of terms which signified not different things but the same things in different aspects.[351] More precisely, as we shall see, the only real distinction among categories as terms of first intention is that between substance and quality; they alone are absolute terms; all the others are accidents signifying what these two signify.

The distinction, however, between substance and quality is not a metaphysical one, but of different modes of signification. Both substance and quality denote individual things; but where substance does so absolutely, quality does so connotatively. Their difference corresponds to Aristotle's division between those terms 'which are stated of a subject but are not present in it' and those 'which are not stated of a subject but are present in it'. These together with the other two members of Aristotle's quadripartite classification—namely that which is both predicated of a subject and present in it, and that which is neither predicated nor present—are treated by Ockham exclusively as terms. He has therefore to reconcile this interpretation with that of Boethius who saw in it a fourfold division of things corresponding to universal and individual substances and universal and individual accidents. This Ockham does by explaining that by 'things' Boethius means concepts and words as well as real things outside the mind. This fourfold division accordingly resolves itself into universal and singular terms standing for substances, and their accidents standing in conjunction or discretely.[352]

It is in that sense, too, of terms standing in personal supposition for real individuals, that Ockham understands Aristotle's two rules, again in modification of Boethius's interpretation. The first is that 'When one thing is predicated of another, all which is predicable of the predicate will be predicable also of the subject'.[353] In order to avoid the fallacy to which this can lead, namely of predicating genus or species of an individual—for example that because man is a species, Socrates is a species—Boethius confined the application of this rule to absolute predication *in quid*, that is, of real substances and not their accidents. Ockham by taking 'substance' to include essential difference (in composite beings) extends this to connotative predication of what belongs to a substance as well.[354] He thus treats substance for the equivocal term which he has previously declared it to be.[355] He also adds two conditions which exclude such fallacies. The first is that the subject must be in

<hr />

[350] *Ibid.*, ch. 41, 105.

[351] *Ibid.*, 106. E.g. Et isti duo auctores, unus sanctus et alius philosophus, sufficiant ad probandum quod per predicamenta non intelligunt nisi quedam incomplexa continentia sub se diversas voces vel intentiones anime, de quibus tamen non predicantur predicatione propria et in recto (i.e. not invariably as absolute terms).

[352] *EA*, 40 c–41 b.

[353] *Categories*, ch. 4, 1 b, 10–14.

[354] *EA*, 41 b–c.

[355] Nec est plus inconveniens quod substantia sit nomen equivocum ad veras substantias et ad incomplexa veras substantias importantia . . . (*ibid.*, 41 a).

personal supposition; it is then false to say that 'Man is a species', a statement which can only be true when man as subject is taken in simple supposition, as a term. The other condition is that in a universal proposition the middle term must be distributed so that it is predicated necessarily of all that comes under it: because both man and stone are coloured it is fallacious to say that 'everything coloured is a stone'.[356]

Aristotle's second rule is that, 'If genera are different and co-ordinate, their differences are themselves different in kind . . . But where one genus is subordinate to another there is nothing to prevent their having the same differences: for the greater class is predicated of the lesser'. This Ockham takes as a relation between terms, related by predication and not by essence, as of greater or lesser universality in the way we have already discussed.[357]

'Category' itself is a term of second intention which can mean either the whole order of terms in a category related as more or less universal (superior and inferior); or it can mean the first and most universal term (the *genus generalissimum*) of a category. In this second sense categories are terms of first intention signifying things in the different modes of the ten categories. In the first sense, however, category includes terms of both first and second intention.[358]

The expression 'to be in a genus' also has two senses here. The first is where category denotes real things as individual substances and qualities, the latter always imported by universals signifying substances. In the second sense category is the first and most general genus signifying what comes under it; that includes genus and species which are in the genus of substance: hence we can say 'Animal is a substance', 'Man is a substance', and so on.[359]

(a) *Substance.* That becomes clearer in turning to substance as the first of the ten categories. Ockham, in both the Commentary on the *Categories* and in the *Logic*, follows Aristotle closely, but he is above all concerned to stress Aristotle's distinction between first substance and secondary substances. First substances as individual things are alone real; secondary substances are genera and species which are only predicated of individual first substances. Ockham is convinced that Aristotle did not regard the latter as having any reality outside the mind; although this view has been contested it seems to me to be tenable from what Aristotle says in the *Categories*.[360] Whatever the standpoint adopted, however, it is with Ockham's interpretation that we are concerned here. He takes in turn each of the

---

[356] *Ibid.*, 41 c.
[357] *Categories*, ch. 4, 1 b, 16; and *EA*, 41 d.
[358] *SL*, I, ch. 40, 102.
[359] *Ibid.*, 102–3.
[360] E.g. 'All substance appears to signify that which is individual. In the case of primary substance this is indisputably true, for the thing is a unit. In the case of secondary substance, when we speak, for instance, of 'man' or 'animal' our form of speech gives the impression that we are here also indicating that which is individual, but the impression is not strictly true; for a secondary substance is not an individual but a class with a certain qualification; for it is not one and single as a primary substance is; the words 'man', 'animal', are predicable of more than one subject. (*Categories*, ch. 5, 3 b, 10–17).

attributes of substance treated in the *Categories*, beginning with the difference, already mentioned, between the first and second substance.[361] In the Commentary on the *Categories* Ockham develops a proof that second substances are not real things existing outside the intellect, nor of the essence of individual things; for if genus and species were real things, it would then, among the other impossible consequences, follow that individuals were composed of a universal nature and something added to it, so that the universal would not be more universal than the individual.[362] The division into first and second substances is thus one according to degrees of universality under the *genus generalissimum*; it therefore includes terms (second substances) as well as real substances (first substances).[363] That can also be shown on the principle of the *dictum de omni et de nullo*, namely that whatever is universally denied of everything contained under a universal term will be denied of the universal term as well. By that no universal can therefore be a substance; for 'secondary substance' is denied of everything which 'substance' signifies; it is therefore universally denied of the term substance. Hence as no substance is a second substance, no second substance is a substance, corporeal or incorporeal.[364]

The difference between first and second substances, as terms, is the difference then between terms of varying universality: terms of first substance are peculiar to only one substance; terms of second substance, like genera and species, common to many substances. The latter are also in the category of quality; in the category of substance they signify individuals and do not stand for themselves as universals, as the term 'man' signifies individual men.[365] In the case of first substance, Aristotle, here as elsewhere, is equivocal, sometimes meaning a term, sometimes a thing. In all such cases the correct interpretation must be gauged from his intentions. What is certain is that when substance means a thing it can never stand for another thing just as second substances must always stand for things.[366]

When Aristotle says, then, in the *Categories*[367] that 'All substance appears to signify that which is individual. In the case of primary substances this is indisputably

---

[361] Notandum est hic primo quod omnis substantia que est vera res contenta in genere substantie est simpliciter substania prima, et individua et singularis, ita quod genera et species et ipsummet genus generalissimum non sunt substantie vere extra animam, nec sunt de essentia substantiarum particularium, quia sunt quedam intentiones extra animam nullo modo existentes, vel alia signa importantia veras substantias (*EA*, 45 a).

[362] *Ibid.*, a–b.

[363] *Ibid.*, a. Also *Ordinatio*, d. 2, q. 4, 149–50.

[364] *Ibid.*, b; *SL*, I, ch. 42, 110.

[365] Et ideo dicendum est quod ista divisio non est nisi divisio unius nominis communis in nomina minus communia ut sit equivalens isti divisioni: nominum importantium seu significantium substantias extra animam quedam sunt nomina propria uni substantie, et illa nomina vocantur hic prime substantie, quedam autem nomina sunt communia multis substantiis, et illa nomina vocantur secunde substantie. Que nomina postea dividuntur, quia quedam sunt genera et quedam sunt species; que tamen omnia sunt vere qualitates. Et ita omnia illa nomina communia que sunt in predicamento qualitatis. . . . Omnia tamen illa sunt in predicamento substantie . . . Et ita secunde substantie non sunt nisi quedam nomina et qualtates precise significantes substantias nomina et qualitates precise significantes substantias (*SL*, *ibid.*,). Also *EA*, 45 a–b and *Ordinatio*, d. 2, q. 4, 148–50.

[366] *SL*, *ibid.*, 111–12, *EA*, 45 c.

[367] *Categories*, ch. 5, 3 b, 10; *SL*, *ibid.*, 110–11.

true', primary substances, and *a fortiori* secondary substances, must be understood as terms.[368] Only secondary substances as signifying more than one substance are predicated univocally;[369] and it is this difference between signifying one or many that explains what is meant when it is said that first substance signifies that which is (*hoc aliquid*), while second substance the nature of what is (*quale quid*). The latter does not represent something additional to the individual as a quality or a part; it merely denotes the class to which it belongs in virtue of not signifying any individual in particular.[370] Thus, in an almost Abelardian sense, to see a man from a distance is not to know he is that or that individual, Plato or Socrates, but only that he is a man indeterminately; and thus by any species or genus, individuals are signified by kind, univocally rather than for themselves. They are nonetheless signified absolutely, and not by their differences or parts.[371]

That helps to explain Aristotle's statement that a species is more a substance than a genus: by that he did not mean that one was more truly a substance than the other, but that a species in denoting fewer substances signifies them more distinctly, determinately and so more perfectly than a genus; it is therefore able more easily to answer the question 'What is this?', as it is easier to say what a man is than what an animal is.[372]

The first three properties of substance, then, are that it does not inhere in any subject, whether as a thing or as a primary or secondary term; that all secondary substances are predicated univocally of real substances; and third that whereas first substances signify determinately (*hot aliquid*), secondary substances do so indeterminately (*quale quid*).

The fourth property of substance, whether it is taken for a term or thing, is that is not the contrary of another substance. Contrary terms, like black and white, cannot be predicated simultaneously of the same subject; nor can contraries really inhere in the same subject when contraries are understood in the strict sense of each mutually excluding the other through gradual increase or decrease of one or other; for they then belong not to substances but to qualities. In the broader sense, however, of anything which is mutually exclusive, substantial forms are contraries —for example fire and air—and so composite substances containing them will also to a certain degree be contrary; but not absolutely, because strict contraries have nothing in common whereas composite substances all contain matter in common. So far as Aristotle is concerned he understands 'contrary' in the strict sense, according to which substance has no contrary.[373] He also affirms that 'substance does not admit of variation of degree'. That is its fifth property; and it means that no single

---

[368] *SL, ibid.,* 110; *EA,* 45 c.

[369] *SL,* I, ch. 43, 114; *EA,* 51 c.

[370] Secundo sciendum quod non ideo dicitur secunda substantia significare quale quid, quia significat aliquid adveniens ipsi individuo, puta qualitatem vel partem aliquid tale ... Sed secunde substantie dicuntur significare quale quid, quia non significant precise unum numero sed multa; et hoc satis innuit Aristoteles ... (*EA,* 51 d); *SL,* I, ch. 43, 114-15.

[371] *EA,* 51 d–52 a.

[372] *SL,* I, ch. 42, 111; *EA,* 47 b–c; *Ordinatio,* d. 2, q. 4, 150-1.

[373] *EA,* 52 a–c; *SL,* I, ch. 43, 115.

substance can become more or less than it is or, as Ockham states it, it cannot have
the adverb 'more' or 'less' added to that which is predicated of it, as Socrates
cannot become more or less of a man.[374] Unlike quality, substance cannot be
acquired or lose some part; if it did, it would become another substance.[375]

The sixth and last property of substance is that 'while remaining numerically
one it is capable of admitting contraries'. Aristotle calls that 'its most distinctive'
mark, peculiar to substance alone.[376] For Ockham this shows the falsity of the view
held by many moderns that Aristotle treated quantity as something distinct from
substance and quality.[377] In the *Logic* Ockham modifies this earlier statement from
the Commentary on the *Categories*. It now forms the first of two conclusions which
can be attributed to Aristotle on the basis of what he has just said, without pro-
nouncing on the truth or falsity of either. In the case of quantity it can be said that
Aristotle did not regard it as an accident distinct from substance and really inhering
in substance as the subject of corporeal qualities. That it does is a misconception of
many moderns. If that were so, it would then necessarily follow that something
absolute other than substance was able to receive contraries through undergoing
change; quantity would thereby be more immediate than substance and able
to admit contraries before substance. The second consequence of Aristotle's
position is that no accident can be the subject of another accident, at least of
accidents having a contrary. For it is Aristotle's meaning that every accident exists
immediately in a subject.[378] In that way the faculties of the soul, namely the
intellect and will, are not its accidents which themselves undergo intellections
and volitions, as the subjects of change; nor as we shall shortly see are relations
distinct things from substance, existing in quality and quantity as accidents of
substance.[379] Without exception it is substance which admits contrary qualities;
and it does so by itself changing. Statements and opinions are not proof to the
contrary, as Aristotle himself demonstrates in replying to the objection that they
too are able to change and yet are not substances. Although that is true, they differ
from substances in their mode of change; unlike that of substances, it does not come
from themselves as statements and opinions, but from the things to which they
refer, so that the truth, in first consisting in the proposition that 'Socrates is sitting'
and later that 'Socrates is not sitting', depends upon Socrates to whom the change
is due. Accordingly truth and falsity for Aristotle are not qualities inhering in
propositions, as we shall see in the next chapter, but belong to the consonance of
propositions with what they signify.[380]

That completes Ockham's discussion of substance with its stress upon the
distinction between substance as something real, when it is exclusively individual,
and as a term, when it is not. Next in Aristotle's order of categories comes quantity
followed by relation and quality. These first four together form the nucleus of the
categories, and for none more than Ockham in his conviction that only substance
and some qualities exist independently; all other categories represent aspects of

[374] *EA*, 52 c–d; *SL*, *ibid.*, 116–17.   [375] *EA*, 52 d.
[376] *Categories*, ch. 5, 4 a, 10.   [377] *EA*, 53 a.   [378] *SL*, *ibid.*, 116–17.
[379] *Ibid.*   [380] *SL*, 117–19; *EA*, 53 b–d.

substance or quality and are always—including quality—to be found in substances. This conception gives especial prominence to quality, quantity, and relation as exemplifying the main kinds of category together with substance; their nature also bears directly upon the nature of being, both created and divine. We shall reserve these natural and theological aspects for their appropriate chapters in the second and third parts. At the same time, because of the wider ontological questions which they raise, I shall change the customary order and take quality before, instead of after, quantity and relation, that we may see more clearly why Ockham denies independent standing to both of the latter.

(b) *Quality*. Of quality the first thing to be said is that Ockham normally upholds it as the only other absolute category in Aristotle's, rather than his own, name; he does so principally in defence of Aristotle's opinion against the claims of the moderns that quantity also represents something which is distinct from substance. Only in the *Quodlibets* does he dispense with such disclaimers as 'If this opinion were true, it would then follow . . . ' or 'Whether or not this opinion is true or false', which punctuate his discussions in the Commentary on the *Categories* and the *Logic*. The reason is not immediately apparent. Unlike his hesitations over the nature of concepts, Ockham seems to have had no doubt from the beginning that quantity, relation, time, place, action, passion, position, and state did not stand for separate things. Nor would the cause appear to be theological, since Ockham's doctrine of the eucharist was as we shall see in chapter nine to provide some of his most sustained arguments against treating quantity as an absolute. Without magnifying what is only a side issue, the answer is perhaps provided by Ockham's reply to the second question of the seventh *Quodlibet*, 'Whether quality differs from substance.' In one of his rare personal declarations in this context before the *Treatise on the Sacrament of the Altar*, Ockham distinguishes between the third and fourth kinds of quality enumerated by Aristotle: the third—the 'affective' qualities like sweetness, bitterness, heat, cold, whiteness, in virtue of which things possessing them are said to be such by reason of their presence—really differ, he says, from substances.[381] The fourth, however—of figure and shape, to which Ockham adds density and rarity—do not.[382] That the affective qualities are separable from their subjects can only be through the acquisition or loss of something, since it is not due to temporal or local movement: for example, Socrates can first be white and afterwards not white. Accordingly whiteness is really distinguished from man. It is not the same with the fourth kind of quality, where in propositions like 'Substance is straight', 'Substance is curved', substance alone suffices for their verification; it will be one or other according to its situation, and not because something is added to or subtracted from it.[383] As in so many of these discussions Ockham applies the test of God's absolute power here: if God, by means of it, were to separate from a straight substance every absolute accident (i.e. quality) and

[381] *Categories*, ch. 8, 9 a, 28–9 b, 10.
[382] *Ibid.*, 9 b, 10–24.
[383] *Quodlibet* VII, 97.

conserve its parts in the same place, the substance would still remain straight.[384] In other words straightness is not separable from its substance.

Ockham's differentiation here into quality which is absolute and quality which is not distinct from substance, suggests why he did not talk unequivocally of quality as an absolute. Of all the categories it is the most diverse, and for that reason it is important to know in which aspect it is being considered.

In an instructive discussion in an earlier *Quodlibet*[385] Ockham gave the ground for this distinction. It lies in the difference between an accident in the strict sense and in its broader sense. Strictly, accident is an accidental form which does not constitute a unity with the substance which it informs, as whiteness, blackness and so on are not one with their subjects. Broadly, it is any term which can be contingently predicated of something, such that it can be successively affirmed and denied because of a change on the part of one term or the other: that applies to relations of similarity, equality and so on. In the broadest sense of all, an accident is whatever is predicable contingently and successively of something else, regardless of how it is predicable. Now quantity and relation are accidents in the broad senses; but quality, as we have seen, when it stands for something absolute in its third mode distinct from substance, can be a strict (i.e. absolute) accident. It is in this sense that Ockham says later in the same question and in subsequent questions that only substance and quality are absolute terms which signify things directly and undividedly *in quid*.[386] In each of these questions he asserts the independence of quality in direct opposition to quantity, which never represents something distinct from substance and quality, and so, as we shall see, is predicated connotatively.

We can now examine quality in detail. So far as its general characteristics as a category are concerned, Ockham begins his discussion in the *Logic* with a characteristic qualification:

The fourth category is the category of quality. As in the case of the previous categories, first we must proceed according to the opinion which seems to me to be consonant with Aristotle's principles, whether true or false; and second we must consider it from a contrary opinion. It seems to me that according to Aristotle's principles it should be said that the category of quality is a certain concept or sign containing under it all that by which the question of what nature a substance is (*quale de substantia*) can be appropriately answered; it does not however state its substantial part.[387]

As we have already seen, some qualities—colour, black, white and so on—stand for absolutes really distinct from substance, and some do not; they differ according to whether they can be successively affirmed or denied because of local movement. If they can, they are not distinct from substance, as we saw in the case of straight-

[384] *Ibid.*

[385] *Quodlibet* IV, q. 30.

[386] Ad quintum dico quod consequentia non valet, quia substantia et qualitas sunt termini absoluti qui significant sua significata diversa uno modo significandi. Sic non est de quantitate (*ibid.*). Also *Quodlibet* IV, q. 26 and q. 27.

[387] *SL*, I, ch. 55, 163; *EA*, 71 d.

ness and curvedness where the change from one to the other is due to local movement of the parts of a substance: it is curved when they come together more
closely, and straight when they are farther apart. Similarly with density and rarity.
The same does not hold for colour or heat, the inherence of which in a substance
is due not to local movement but to a distinct quality.[388]

The other two kinds of quality are habits and dispositions, on the one hand, and
capacities for action on the other. Of the first pair, Aristotle says that 'Habit differs
from disposition in being more lasting and more firmly established. The various
kinds of knowledge and of virtue are habits . . . By a disposition, on the other hand,
we mean a condition that is easily changed and quickly gives place to its opposite.
Thus, heat, cold, disease, health, and so on are dispositions'.[389] Accordingly habits
are dispositions but dispositions are not necessarily habits.[390] For Ockham qualities
of this kind include both those which are really distinct from a subject and those
which are not. The first can be signified connotatively, so that the abstract term
stands directly for the quality, and not for the subject denoted by the concrete
term, as 'hot' connotes 'heat' as the quality by which something is 'hot'. In that
sense concrete and abstract terms stand each for something distinct and absolute,
the concrete for the subject, the abstract for the quality connoted by the concrete.[391]
Other habits and dispositions, however, do not represent anything distinct from
substances; for example, health, sickness, beauty, ugliness, of none of which does
the abstract term denote a distinct absolute quality. The reason is that such terms
have a nominal definition, so that while they, too, answer the question 'What
kind?' (quale), they do not correspond to something distinct. Thus to say that a
man is healthy or beautiful, connotes nothing absolute, but a particular set of bodily
dispositions. They therefore signify not one distinct thing but many in different
physical combinations which together come under the category of quality, in the
same way as all that relates to magnitude is not something distinct from substance
and yet belongs to the category of quantity.[392] This diversity among qualities is

---

[388] Ad sciendum autem quando qualitas debet poni alia res a substantia et quando non, hac
arte convenit uti, quod quando aliqua predicabilia possunt successive verificari propter solum
motum localem, non oportet quod ista predicabilia res distinctas significent (SL, ibid., 164).
Also EA, 76 a.

[389] Categories, ch. 8, 8 b, 35–9 a, 13; SL, ibid.; EA, 71 c–d.   [390] Ibid., ch. 8, 9 a.

[391] Ex illo autem sequitur quod aliqua de predicamento qualitatis important res simplices
mere absolutas sine omni connotatione ita scilicet quod quodlibet istorum de una re potest
verificari. Aliqua autem non sic important sed important plures res, nec de una aliqua re possunt
predicari. Aliqua autem important unam rem aliam connotando. Primum patet, nam si queratur
qualis est homo, convenienter respondetur quod est 'albus' vel 'niger', 'calidus' vel 'frigidus'; et
tamen calor quod est abstractum calidi de una re simplici verificatur. Nam hec est vera: 'Hec
res est calor', et sic de aliis. Et quando ita est, tunc res pro qua supponit illud abstractum est in
genere qualitatis, quod non est de genere substantie, et tale concretum et abstractum sibi correspondens simpliciter pro diversis supponunt. (EA, 71 d).

[392] Secundum similiter patet. Nam si queratur qualis est homo, convenienter respondetur
quod est 'sanus', vel 'eger', vel 'bene complexionatus' vel 'male' . . . Et tamen nullum abstractum correspondens alicui istorum precise significat unam rem, ita quod sit predicabilis de una
re simplici et per se una. Nam sanitas nec est aliqua qualitas una distincta ab aliis qualitatibus,
quia non est nisi debita vel determinata proportio humorum . . . Et ita est de multis aliis que
ponuntur in predicamento qualitatis, quod nullum eorum significat unam rem de qua possit
vere predicari sed multas, ad modum quo dictum est de aliquibus in genere quantitatis (ibid.).

one of the reasons why Aristotle said that quality has no single sense. Ockham adds that Aristotle did not intend by qualities things existing outside the mind independently as beings in their own right. Nor, by the same token, do habits and dispositions really differ; as we mentioned, for Aristotle, all habits are also dispositions. Together they comprehend not only mental qualities but also all sensible qualities and natural powers.[393]

The other class of qualities (second in Aristotle's order) is that which in Aristotle's words 'includes all those terms which refer to inborn capacity or incapacity', as when we call men good boxers or runners, or healthy or sickly; or say that something is hard or soft because it has or lacks 'that capacity of resistance which enables it to withstand disintegration'.[394] Ockham interprets this kind of quality as also coming under habits since it represents natural powers; such qualities are therefore in many cases not distinct from their subject, in the manner just mentioned.[395]

From this account of quality[396] it will be seen that something can belong to more than one kind of quality: namely to the first and second, and the first and third, while the attributes of figure in the fourth quality can also be considered as belonging to quantity.[397]

There remains to consider the different properties of quality. According to Aristotle they are: that qualities can be contrary so that the contrary of one quality must always be another quality; they can vary in degree, as one thing is more or less white than another; and it is in virtue of qualities that things are called like and unlike. This last property is peculiar to quality alone.[398]

As contraries, qualities can be taken in both the strict sense of being mutually exclusive and so unable to coexist in the same subject, and in the strictest sense where in addition they are extremes within the same genus. In this second sense, black and white are contrary qualities but intermediate colours are not. In the first, less strict sense, intermediaries as well as extremes are contraries.[399] In every case, however, contraries are terms denoting real contraries, and in that sense they refer to qualities—black and white—and not to their subjects, black and white things.[400] They also extend to qualities in the soul, like justice and injustice.[401]

The second property of admitting variation in degree can refer either to the term denoting the quality or to real qualities. In the first meaning, which is how Ockham interprets Aristotle, the adverb 'more' or 'less' is added to the concrete

---

[393] Ibid., 71 d–72 a.
[394] Categories, ch. 8, 9 a, 14–27.
[395] EA, 72 c–d.
[396] EA, 72 d–74 c and SL, I, ch. 55, 165 for the third and fourth kinds.
[397] SL, ibid., 165.
[398] Categories, ch. 8, b, 10–11 a, 20; EA, 76 b–77 b; SL, ibid., 165–6, where Ockham does not mention this last point, referring the reader to his fuller discussion in the Commentary on the Categories.
[399] EA, 76 c.
[400] Notandum est hic primo quod contrarietas vere convenit multis qualitatibus que sunt res de genere qualitatis, quia multe tales res sunt mutuo se expellentes . . . Et isto modo albedo et nigredo vere sunt contraria. Et isto modo modo album et nigrum non contrariantur (ibid., 76 b).
[401] Ibid., 76 c.

term standing for the thing in which the quality inheres, as we say that 'Socrates is whiter than Plato'.[402] But 'more' or 'less' can also be applied to things themselves so that they have more or less of a certain quality through the addition or subtraction of a part of the same kind; thus someone can be called more just or more white than before through an increase in justice or whiteness. The same cannot, however, be said of triangular or quadrangular, as Aristotle observed.[403]

Similarity and dissimilarity belong strictly to quality, although in a broader sense they can be ascribed to things. For Ockham they are important in confirming what he has already argued over relation: namely that it is not an absolute, distinct from substance or quality. Hence relatives, like the two preceding properties, belong to quality by predication not inherence.[404] He has the full support of Aristotle who, in the *Categories*, said that quality as a category contains many relatives including habits and dispositions, and that in practically all such cases the genus is relative but not the individual. Thus knowledge as a genus means knowledge of something, but not individual branches of knowledge.[405] Ockham extends this to cover all genera and species in the category of relation as well as the individuals of which they are predicated absolutely. When, however, genus and species are in different categories, one cannot be predicated absolutely of the other. At the same time, while certain things can come under only one category, as black and white belong only to quality, others can be included in more than one, in the way that habits and dispositions can be at once qualities and relatives.[406]

That concludes Ockham's discussion of quality. In form it is faithful to Aristotle; but as in his treatment of all the categories Ockham was concerned with another issue: to show that thay did not stand for anything distinct from individual things. Hence his stress here upon the exclusively individual import of quality, directly or in a nominal definition.

(c) *Quantity*. Nowhere is Ockham's purpose more marked than in his discussion of quantity, where he was combating the received wisdom that quantity was an absolute term standing for something distinct like quality. Although preceded in this view by Peter John Olivi, whose rejection by Richard of Middleton Ockham cites verbatim in the first of his two treatises on the eucharist,[407] Ockham gave it much more sustained advocacy, relating the problem of quantity to that of the eucharist, as we shall see in chapter nine. It led to the inclusion of his opinions on the eucharist among Lutterell's articles for censure at Avignon.[408] Although Ockham vindicated his views in the treatises on the eucharist written almost

---

[402] Intelligendum est hic primo quod Philosophus principaliter loquitur hic de nominibus intendens quod aliquibus concretis potest convenienter addi illud adverbium 'magis' et 'minus' ... ut convenienter dicatur quod Sortes est magis albus quam Plato (*ibid.*, 76 d).

[403] *Ibid.*, 77 a.

[404] *Ibid.*, 77 b.

[405] *Categories*, ch. 7, 6 b, 1–6; ch. 8, 10 b, 30–11 a, 3 b; *EA*, 77 c.

[406] *Ibid.*, 77 d.

[407] A. Maier, 'Zur einegen Problemen der Ockhamforschung', *AFH* 46 (1953), 178–9.

[408] See chapter 9 below.

certainly after 1323,[409] in response to Lutterell's censure, he may well have felt some uncertainty over his position; for while he speaks in his own name in the *Quodlibets*, in the *Logic* he argued according to what he declared to be Aristotle's opinion, regardless of whether it was 'true or false, catholic or heretical'.[410] His own position he expresses in question twenty-five of the fourth *Quodlibet* (the second of eleven questions devoted to quantity[411]) as follows:

Quantity is predicated essentially and in *quid* of its individual (thing) or of a connotative term of an individual, in such propositions as 'This line is a quantity' or 'This surface is a quantity'. But it is not predicated absolutely of an absolute term standing for its individual, for example in propositions like 'Socrates is a quantity', 'This piece of wood is a quantity', 'Whiteness is a quantity'. In confirmation I say that they are not similar because quantity signifies a substance and connotes parts extended in space; for substance can be quantity but it is not the same as quantity. Unlike quantity, both substance and quality do not connote something else. Therefore there can only be substance and quality (as real things).[412]

Accordingly although substance, quality and quantity are distinct categories, quantity does not signify something absolute, distinct from the other two, because they are terms for the same things, but signifying them differently. Substance always signifies directly, but quality and quantity do so both directly and indirectly. While both denote substance, they differ in what they connote: quantity that it has extended parts (which are not distinct from substance), quality an accident inhering in a substance which is distinct from it.[413]

We shall leave for chapter nine the physical implications of Ockham's notion of quantity, above all in relation to the eucharist, confining ourselves here to his formal consideration in his Commentary on *Categories* and his more summary treatment in the *Logic*. In both he again follows the main divisions of Aristotle.

In the *Categories* Aristotle begins by distinguishing quantity as discrete or continuous, that is to say where 'Each part of the whole has a relative position to the other parts' or where there is no such relation between the parts. 'Instances of discrete properties are number and speech; of continuous, lines, surfaces, solids, and, besides these, time and place'.[414]

For Ockham, these definitions show that Aristotle did not, in contradiction to the moderns, regard quantity as standing for something distinct from what comes under the categories of substance and quality.[415] That is demonstrated from the

---

[409] The evidence from MS. Vat. Ottob. 179, f. 108 b, which has 'Sanctus Thomas'—canonised in 1323 by John XXII—is not conclusive, since other MSS. including Vat. Borghese 151, Balliol College 299, and Merton College 137, have 'beatus'. See Miethke, *Ockhams Weg*, 43–4.

[410] *SL*, I, ch. 44, 122.

[411] Among them, whether Aristotle (q. 32) and the *sancti* (q. 33) held quantity to be something distinct.

[412] *Quodlibet* IV, q. 30. Also q. 32: Ad propositum dico quod substantia, qualitas, quantitas sunt distincta predicamenta, quamvis quantitas non significet rem absolutam distinctam a substantia et qualitate, quia sunt distincti conceptus et voces easdem res diversimode significantes.

[413] *Quodlibet* IV, q. 32.

[414] *Categories*, ch. 6, 4 b, 20.

[415] Ad evidentiam totius partis precedentis et istius capituli est intelligendum quod non est

example of point, line and surface, none of which can be separated from substance and quality. For if a point were independent of a line, it would be either part of the line, which it is not since, as Aristotle says, no line is composed of points. Or alternatively, a point would not belong to a line; each would then be totally distinct from the other. But if a point is not part of a line, it is not part of anything else and so must be self-subsisting. It would then belong to its own category as something absolute, which it does not. It is not therefore a distinct thing. Nor is it an accident, because as indivisible a point could only be wholly in the whole of a subject and not as a part of a part; that would mean that there could be no other point in the same subject. Accordingly, a point does not really exist outside a substance or in it.[416]

This last argument also holds for line and surface; to say that they really inhered in a body or a substance would entail an infinite number of each as parts in a whole having no connection with one another; which violates Aristotle's principles.[417]

Ockham also denies any separate existence to a body on the grounds of super-fluity: every composite substance both has quantity and is a body. Therefore there is no need to posit either quantity or a body in addition to substance. That follows from the definition of quantity as that which has parts extended within a defined space. To have parts is the property of substance and owes nothing to quantity or a body.[418] As we said earlier it is just because quantity is dependent upon substance but not synonymous with it, that substance can be without quantity as the eucharist proves. In that sense therefore Ockham was at the opposite pole from the modern view which would regard substance as extension in space. Only as denoting that the parts of a substance are effectively extended from one to another need quantity be invoked; but not as their formal cause inhering in a subject.[419]

In the same way, time and place are not real, as we shall discuss more fully in their physical aspects in chapter nine. Time is not real either as an accident or in its own right. It is not an accident because it cannot really exist in a subject, indivisibly or divisibly: it is not indivisible since it is divided into past, present and future; nor divisible, as none of its parts is real, and therefore there is not one rather than another which could inhere as a part in a part of a subject. By the same token in not being real, it does not exist *per se*.[420] Space similarly is nothing real for the same reason as a surface is not something distinct.[421]

---

intentio Aristotelis quod quantitas sit quoddam predicamentum importans rem absolutam realiter et totaliter distinctam a rebus in genere substantie et in genere qualitatis [text, quantitatis] sicut communiter tenetur. Sed est intentio sua quod nulla res importatur per genus quantitatis quin sit realiter substantia vel quantitas (*EA*, 54 b). Also *Quodlibet* IV, q. 32.

[416] *Ibid.*, 54 c–d; *SL*, I, ch. 44, 122–3.
[417] *EA*, 54 d–55 a; *SL*, *ibid.*, 124–5.
[418] *EA*, 55 a.
[419] Si etiam dicatur quod partes substantie non sunt distantes nisi per quantitam. Contra: quamvis hoc esset verum, hoc non esset per quantitatem nisi effective, sicut partes istius substantie non distant nisi per generans effective quamvis formaliter se ipsis sine omni re addita distent. Igitur non oportet ponere quantitatem talem rem aliam nisi ut faciat effective partes substantie distare. Sed hoc posset facere quamvis non informet (*ibid.*).
[420] *Ibid.*, 55 a–b.   [421] *Ibid.*, 55 b.

In the *Logic* Ockham reinforces these naturally-based arguments by the argument drawn from God's omnipotence. By this, as we have seen on a number of occasions, he can separate one absolute from its accidents or from other absolutes to which it is ordinarily connected by the laws of creation. Thus he could conserve a substance in the state in which it existed before it underwent local changes by destroying the effects of the latter. Accordingly, if quantity were really something inhering in substance, and substance is prior to quantity, God could then conserve substance unchanged and destroy its quantity. It would then follow that if the substance continues to exist in space, quantity as something additional to it is superfluous; granted the possibility, there is no other alternative.[422]

The same applies to point and surface; if one is really distinct from the other then God could conserve the line and destroy the point, and so the line (since it is not infinite) will be finite without need of a point to terminate it. A point is therefore unnecessary to the existence of a line which will be a continuous quantity independently of it. That also holds for surface. Hence neither point nor surface exists independently of one another or of bodies.[423]

Again, the example of the eucharist shows that quantity is not an independent medium between substance and quality. If it were, then the qualities in the host after consecration would not be independent of it, but would really belong to quantity and so to the host. That would contradict Peter Lombard who said that such qualities as colour, weight and taste, subsist independently after consecreation. For by the continued inherence of quantity these qualities would continue to inform the host.[424]

None of these terms associated with continuous quantity, then, signifies something distinct, added to or inhering in a substance. In every case they are like quantity itself, connotative terms signifying substance according to different spatial dimensions. Thus a point is a term or concept which denotes the limits of a line; it stands for nothing which itself is the common boundary joining the parts of a line but signifies that the line itself is of a certain length. A line does not terminate by means of a point but according to how long it is as a line; the point signifies its boundary. Similarly a line is not something real, distinct from a substance, but signifies the length of something, which is due to the local movement of its parts (as we have seen) and not to something absolute added to it to give it length. The same holds of surfaces and bodies, which are terms denoting substance in its different dimensions.[425] As different species of quantity these terms must not

---

[422] *SL*, I, ch. 44, 123–4.   [423] *Ibid.*, 124–5.   [424] *Ibid.*, 124.

[425] De quo est dicendum quod punctus non est aliqua res absoluta distincta realiter ab omni substantia et qualitate. Sed punctus est nomen vel intentio importans non ulteriorem pertransitionem secundum longitudinem. Unde cum dicitur 'punctus est finis linee' importatur quod illa substantia non ulterius protendatur secundum longitudinem. Et ideo linea nunquam finitur alia re sed se ipsa finitur formaliter . . . Secundo dico quod linea non est talis res alia, sed est notans aliquid esse longum. Nam si substantia realiter habeat partes distinctas possibile est quod ille partes longiori corpore coexistant et breviori, quantumcunque corpori eque lato coexistant, sicut patet in rarefactione et condensatione. Et ita ista substantia non erit longa propter aliquam rem absolutam sibi advenientem . . . Eodem modo dicendum est de superficie, quod non importat aliam rem . . . Sic etiam dicendem est de corpore (*EA*, 56 a–b).

be confused with species as absolute terms signifying real things determinately and *per se*. Propositions such as 'Substance is a line' or 'Substance is quantity' when taken significatively in personal supposition are true, because then concrete and abstract terms stand synonymously for real things and are not connotative: 'line' then means 'something which is long'. As so often the confusion arises from the equivocal way in which these terms are used. Aristotle employs abstract terms as synonyms with their concretes, sometimes taking them as standing for real things, and at others as signifying concepts; they are then not predicated significatively.[426]

Discrete quantity—number, speech, and so on—equally does not constitute something real, distinct from substance and quality. Number, for example, does not exist independently of things which are numbered, either as substance or accident. Three dogs, for example, do not contain the number three as something really inhering in them, because then the same accident would be in different subjects, which is not possible. Nor can 'threeness' be divided between the three dogs; for then it would not be one thing and so could not exist as something real. There can be no unity whose parts are separated spatially from one another by other things. If those things were of the same nature in virtue of being triune, it would lead to the absurdity that each of them was triune in the same way as the parts of fire are fire. If they were not of the same nature, their unity would depend upon number as something additional making them of the same nature. That would lead to impossible consequences—that number was at once form and matter and that it constituted a unity in each separate part as well as being the means of a common triune nature. It cannot therefore be something distinct.[427] Nor can the parts of speech because they are inseparable from words as the qualities constituting discourse. These exist neither as substance nor as accidents.[428]

Quantity, then, according to Aristotle is always predicated of a substance or quality; and in one of two ways: either of something which consists of different parts or of different things which are taken together.[429] That brings us to the second way in which Aristotle divides quantity, that is, according to whether or not its parts bear a relative position to one another. Where they do, as in the case of lines, planes and space, each part lies somewhere so that its position and its relation to the others can be stated. Where they do not, as in number or time or speech, none of the parts has a permanent existence but they are related to one another as prior and posterior. Thus the number one is prior to the number two as words in speech are prior to each other without in either case having a fixed spatial position.[430]

For Ockham there is also a distinction between essential predication (but still

[426] *Ibid.*, b–c; *SL*, I, ch. 45, 129–30.
[427] *Ibid.*, 55 b–c.
[428] *Ibid.*, 55 c.
[429] Ex predictis patet satis quod non est verum nec est intentio Philosophi ponere quantitatem esse aliam rem absolutam et per se unam et totaliter distinctam ab alius rebus. Sed intentio Philosophi fuit assignare differentiam nominum et predicabilium intentionum que non predicantur nisi de aliquo habente diversas partes, vel de rebus diversis et distinctis coniunctim sumptis (*ibid.*, 55 d).
[430] *Categories*, ch. 6, 5 a, 15–37; *EA, ibid.*

contingent upon the existence of a substance[431]) and accidental predication as well as between the different meanings of quantity. To take the latter first, when quantity is predicated of the parts of a substance, such as a body, it can vary according to position of the parts: it is greater when they are more extended and less when they are closer. That does not hold for quantity predicated of different things; two dogs and two men remain the same number regardless of their position.[432]

The other difference is expressed in the two senses that number (and part) can have. Strictly, it can only be predicated of what is itself a unity, which corresponds to a substance having continuous parts, that is, continuous quantity. Thus form and matter composing a substance are not separate things but the parts of something which is a unity. In this sense, then, number can only apply to that which has continuous quantity. In the broad sense, however, its meaning can extend to whatever can be distinguished from something else, whether an independent entity or not. That can include—although Aristotle does not—collective things such as populace, city, army, crowd, and so on, none of which stands disjunctively for specific individuals. In the same way we can talk of Socrates and Plato as a pair. In all such cases the parts contained under the term do not have permanent position.[433]

The distinctions of quantity accordingly arise from how it is predicated of substance or quality. It is continuous if the parts of a unity are not separated, and discrete if they are.[434] But whatever the case it is also as a term predicated contingently in a nominal definition of something that exists, i.e. a substance, that quantity is invoked in answer to the question 'How much?' or 'How many?'. In this view Ockham goes beyond Aristotle, as he himself declares.[435] Even so, he adds, if Aristotle did sometimes say that substance is not quantity, or quality, what he meant was that it is not a necessary proposition that 'Substance is quantity' as it is not necessary that 'Quality is quantity'. The reason is that continuous quantity connotes extended parts, whereas substance does not.[436]

So far as its properties are concerned, Aristotle enumerates three. The first is that definite quantities have no contraries: nothing is the contrary of 'two cubits long' or of a surface. Although terms such as 'big' and 'small' can be called contraries, these are not definite but relatives. Ockham takes this as evidence that for Aristotle quantity—like the other seven categories—is a term and not a thing. If it were something real then Aristotle's statement would be false; for something which

---

[431] E.g. Quamvis esset possibile quod non haberet partes habentes distinctam positionem (*EA, ibid.*). Also 58 c.

[432] *Ibid.*, 55 d–56 a.

[432] *Ibid.*, 56 a, 57 c–d, 58 b. It can also be called accidental in Aristotle's secondary sense (*ibid*) when something such as white is called large or an action lengthy. (*EA*, 58 b; *SL*, I, ch. 45, 129–30).

[434] *EA*, 57 a; *SL*, I, ch. 45, 130.

[435] Quarto sciendum quod quamvis quantitas non sit alia res a substantia et qualitate, tamen contingenter predicatur de substantia, ita quod quantum est ex forma predicationis et ex forma quid nominis ipsius substantie non repugnat ipsam esse et non quantam, licet aliter sit secundum intentionem Aristoteles. (*EA*, 58 c); *SL*, I, ch. 45, 132.

[436] *SL*, I, ch. 45, 132.

is black and three cubits long is the contrary of something white and three cubits long. Anything real will have the properties of substance, foremost among them its capacity to receive contrary qualities. Accordingly quantities can only be without contraries if they remain terms and not things.[437]

The same goes for the second property of quantity, namely that it does not admit of variation of degree; for things which are quantities can be greater or less than other such things, as something can be more or less white than something else.[438] Only as terms, then, are quantities constant.

The third and 'most distinctive mark of quantity', according to Aristotle, 'is that equality and inequality are predicated of it'. Unlike the two previous properties the third also applies to things, which can be said to be unequal and equal quantitatively, as one white thing is equal to another. Strictly speaking it is not quantity itself which is equal or unequal; it is its property to make other things equal or unequal. For that reason equality and inequality are accidental to substance and quality, as quantity is itself.[439]

That completes discussion of quantity, which has been characterised by Ockham's insistence upon its nominal status. As a connotative term it stands only for substance or quality in their aspect of extension, whether as magnitude if continuous, or number if discrete.[440] Hence quantity is not included in the definition of either substance or quality, neither of which, as we shall see in chapter nine, is essentially a quantity.[441]

(d) *Relation*. The category of relation was almost as vexed for Ockham as that of quantity. Although it did not have the same repercussions, it raised the same question, namely whether relation existed in its own right or whether it signified individual substances and qualities, in particular conjunctions, by themselves and not through the addition of something called relation. Ockham adopted the second explanation that relation expressed a real relation between things and was neither something really distinct from what was related—what Duns Scotus, whom Ockham opposed for taking the contrary view, called its foundation—nor merely the work of the intellect (Peter Aureole's opinion). The difference is that, unlike his position over quantity, Ockham's standpoint over relation approximated to the commonly accepted one, including that of Aquinas. As should become plain, the older claim advanced by P. Doncoeur[442]—and convincingly refuted by G. Martin[443]—that Ockham's theory of relation was nominalist, is groundless.

---

[437] *EA*, 59 b–d; *SL*, I, ch. 47, 137.   [438] *EA*, 60 a; *SL*, ibid., 137–8.

[439] *EA*, 60 b; *SL*, ibid., 138–9.

[440] Ex predictis etiam colligi potest quod prima et essentialior divisio et distinctio illorum que sunt in genere quantitatis sumitur per hoc, quod illud per quod respondetur ad interrogativum factum per 'quantum' large accipiendo 'quantum' vel est expressivum plurium, et sic est numerus, vel est expressivum unius compositi ex pluribus, et sic sumitur magnitudo (*SL*, I, ch. 46, 135).

[441] Moody, *Logic of William of Ockham*, 151–2, was the first, in this as in so many other respects, to state the true position; he rightly criticised De Wulf, as others have subsequently done, for the mistake of confusing substance and quality with quantity in Ockham's doctrine.

[442] P. Doncoeur, 'Le Nominalisme de Guillaume d'Occam: La théorie de la relation'. *Revue Néo-scholastique* 23 (1921), 1–25.

[443] G. Martin, 'Ist Ockhams Relationstheorie Nominalismus?', *FS* 32 (1950), 36 ff.

Ockham's was a universe of individuals; but not of discrete individuals. In the absence of common natures and intelligible species the only connecting links were precisely those of relation, above all of similarity and causality. One provided the ontological connexion expressed in the diverse degrees of univocity among individuals, united in species and genera; the other the intelligibility of their connexion, in their dependence upon one another and enunciated in the definitions and principles governing things. We have already encountered instances of both; they should become more apparent in the succeeding chapters. The role of relation in Ockham's outlook is not therefore confined to its formal treatment in what follows, where I shall first consider Ockham's main definitions in his logical works and then his polemics refuting the opinions of Duns Scotus and others that relation either exists independently or only in the intellect.

An interesting light is thrown on the evolution of Ockham's thinking by a remark in the *Logic*. After stating Aristotle's opinion that relation is not something outside the mind as something really and completely distinct from individual things, he continues: 'Others, however, hold that relation is a definite thing which is not more real than a man is an ass, but is really and totally distinct from a real thing. And there are many theologians of this opinion, which I once believed was that of Aristotle. But now it seems to me that the opposite one (i.e. the first) follows from his principles.'[444] When and where Ockham held this opinion there is no indication; but a certain ambivalence over the exact status of relation as a term remains: while Ockham has no doubt that relation is neither a substance nor quality, he seems less certain whether it should, according to Aristotle, be regarded as a term of first or second intention. Doubt is expressed openly in the sixth *Quodlibet*, question twenty-two, over whether Aristotle treated relation as a first or second intention. Ockham acknowledges the opinion in favour of a first intention as both reasonable and one which he himself had earlier held (*Quodlibet* five, question twenty-one); he now, however, thinks that the other alternative is correct; and that Aristotle understood relation as a second intention.[445] In that earlier question, which is concerned with the categories generally as first or second intentions, Ockham includes relation among the rest as a first intention when category is taken in its first and most general sense. A category then signifies many things, as opposed to signs, even though it can, as in the case of quality, also signify signs. When, however, category means the whole order of terms related as more and less universal, it then, as we have seen before, includes terms of both first and second intention, as genus comes under both quality and relation as categories.[446]

The change between these two quodlibetal questions does not represent a shift in Ockham's own notion of either the categories in general or of relation in

---

[444] Alii autem ponunt quod relatio est quedam res que non plus est res absoluta quam homo est asinus, sed est distincta realiter et totaliter a re absoluta et a rebus absolutis. Et de ista opinione sunt multi theologi, quam etiam aliquando credidi fuisse opinionem Aristotelis; sed nunc mihi videtur quod opinio contraria sequitur ex principiis suis (*SL*, I, ch. 49, 140–1). Also for a similar statement, *ibid.*, ch. 54, 161.

[445] *Quodlibet* VI, q. 22.

[446] *Quodlibet* V, q. 21.

particular; it is rather the latest instalment of the problems posed by the ambiguity of relation as a term. As we shall shortly see, from his earliest discussions of relation in the Commentaries on the *Categories*, and the *Sentences*, Ockham repeatedly asked the same question raised in the sixth *Quodlibet*: whether relation was a term of first or second intention. That arose from its very definition as denoting one thing by reference to another (*ad aliquid*). It could not therefore stand for only one thing as substance or quality could, nor connote one or other as quantity could. In other words there was nothing which is a relation in the way that something is substance or quality; nor can something have relation as it can have quantity as a physical attribute. From that it can be seen that the problem of relation springs from its status as a term; in signifying more than one thing, without itself corresponding to anything as such, it cannot stand for something real which is a relation *in se*. Hence its ambiguity.

Since Ockham's discussion of relation is in extent the widest ranging of that in any of the categories—including a lengthy distinction (thirty) of five questions in the *Ordinatio* and over a dozen questions in the sixth *Quodlibet*, in addition to the two expositions in the Commentary on the *Categories* and the *Logic*—we shall first take its more formal treatment in the two latter works and then consider the further issues which it raises.

According to Aristotle,[447] 'Those things are called relative, which, being either said to be *of* something or else *related to* something else, are explained by reference to that other thing'. For example, 'superior' means superiority over something else, and 'double' is double of something else, and so on. A relative term therefore, always indicates a reference to something else in an oblique case—genitive, dative, or ablative—by means of a preposition added to it. Thus something is similar *to* something else, or big *in comparison with* something else. Although not all relatives can be modified or have contraries, they all have correlatives. That is their distinguishing mark *par excellence*; it applies in all cases where relative terms have been properly defined, that is, reciprocally connected such that, say, a slave is related to a master and not to a man, or biped, where there is no reciprocity of definition. Although primary substances, such as an individual man or an individual ox, or wood as a substance, are not relatives, some secondary substances, such as 'head' or 'hand' which form parts of primary substances are defined by reference to that to which they belong. These are not, however, relatives in the complete sense in which relation to an external object is the necessary condition of existence; for in apprehending a hand, it does not follow—as it does in a necessary relation—that we thereby apprehend that to which it is related in the way that knowing something is double, we must know of what it is double. In definite relation, then, relative terms have correlatives.

That briefly is Aristotle's text to which Ockham addresses himself in the Commentary on the *Categories* and in the *Logic*. As in the case of quality and the remaining categories, his initial and primary concern is to establish that relation is solely a term; there is no such *thing* as relation, and when used significatively it

[447] *Categories*, ch. 7, 6 a, 36–7 b, 15.

denotes, not itself, but individual substances or qualities. Accordingly, Aristotle is not here talking about things in first substances, in the manner of heat or whiteness; he is employing conventional terms which signify things or the signs of things. As words they also belong to the category of quality. 'Father' or 'double' is not something really inhering in that which is a father or double; as relative terms their relativity (*ad aliquid*) consists in their dependence upon something else so that it cannot be verified of one thing without also being verified of its correlative. Hence relative terms like father or man cannot stand alone. Something is only a father if he has a son or double if there is a half.[448] For that reason, as we have seen, a relation always refers to something else by means of an oblique case.[449] That is clear evidence thay are only terms, since only terms, not things, can have an oblique case. Moreover double is not a real thing, since, for Aristotle, number is not real.[450]

That relations are not absolutes or accidents can be proved. They are not absolute; otherwise there would be an infinite number of relations in any real thing, which contradicts Aristotle. Nor are they accidents, because they would then like accidents, have to exist in both a whole and in every part, which would mean that, on the one hand, 'equality' or 'double', by inhering in the whole would be equal to or double a whole to which they belonged; and on the other that each part would be the same as the whole. Both are impossible.[451]

In the *Logic*, as in the *Quodlibets*, Ockham adds the theological arguments, derived from God's omnipotence, which are characteristic of all his writings— after the early logical Commentaries—and are perhaps, in parenthesis, a pointer to their chronology. In the *Logic* these arguments are two. Both uphold God's power to do directly what is done naturally through secondary causes. By the first argument Ockham applies that principle to efficient causes: if the relation of an efficient cause were distinct from the efficient cause itself, God could then cause the relation without the cause. But that is impossible because as anything is white in virtue of whiteness, so any efficient cause would be efficient in virtue of a relation. There would therefore still be an efficient cause in addition to God. Relation then cannot be distinct from that to which it is related. The second argument follows from God's power to conserve one absolute thing without another; so that he could produce something *de novo* without the other having existed. Hence paternity and filiation were real things, one could not exist independently of the other, with the result that there could be a father who had never had a son. Again God in

---

[448] Circa primum sciendum est quod non est intentio Philosophi describere huiusmodi res existentes extra animam in substantiis primis ad modum quo albedo et calor sunt extra. Sed intendit tantum describere nomina significantia res et signa rerum vel alorium, ita quod ipsa nomina que sunt vere voces significative ad placitum et sunt quedam qualitates absolute de genere qualitatis vere sunt ad aliquid, secundum quod hic loquitur Philosophus. Unde hoc nomen 'pater' vere est ad aliquid, et similiter hoc nomen 'duplum', et sic de aliis. Et non est aliqua res subiective existens in illo qui est pater vel in illo quod est duplum que sit ad aliquid et non sit res absoluta quia secundum intentionem Pholosophi, in illo qui est pater nulla est res imaginabilis quin sit vera substantia vel vera qualitas (*EA*, 63 d).

[449] *Ibid.*, *SL*, I, ch. 49, 141.

[450] *EA*, 64 a; *SL*, *ibid.*, 142.

[451] *EA*, 64 a; *SL*, 145; also *Ordinatio*, d. 30, q. 1, M.

his absolute power could create one man *de nihilo* before other men and produce in him something to be found in other men; that could include being a son. Accordingly, if relation were a real thing, filiation could inhere in someone who had never been a son, which is again impossible.[452]

Relation, then, is not an independent thing but a term expressing a relation between things. Something is similar in virtue of being like something else, and not because of something in it as a similarity. It is this dependence of one thing upon another for its definition that distinguishes relation from the other categories; it alone is in respect of something else. As Ockham expresses it in the *Logic*, 'Therefore according to Aristotle relation (*ad aliquid*) is a noun whose meaning is such that it cannot suitably stand for what it signifies unless an oblique case can be added to it'.[453] This analysis, he declares a little later, conforms to Priscian's usage, namely that relation is a word which can only be known when it is known to what it refers, as 'son' or 'servant' must be defined by reference to 'father' or 'master'.[454]

Relation therefore always signifies more than one thing. That is where it differs from a connotative term. Unlike the latter, the oblique case of a relative term refers not to its own abstract term, connoting a part of the same thing denoted wholly by its concrete term, but to something else.[455] On the other hand, like a connotative term and unlike an absolute term, a relative term is in a nominal definition, standing for nothing which is a relation as such, a point reiterated in the *Ordinatio* and *Quodlibets*.[456] As in the case of all the other categories, save substance and quality, what belongs to relation also belongs to substance or quality. While only one or other of the latter can be predicated absolutely of any one thing, since otherwise there would be more than one thing, all the other categories also connote substance or quality. Thus relation, like quantity and the remaining six categories, stands for substance or quality in an extrinsic mode. As quantity signifies substance according to extension, and not because of something absolute which is

---

[452] *SL*, 146–7. Ockham also employs here arguments already encountered over quantity, namely those of divisibility and indivisibility and of form and matter (*ibid.*, 145–6).

[453] *SL*, 142; *EA*, 64 a–b.

[454] *SL*, 144–6.

[455] Circa quod dicendum quod predicamentum relationis distinguitur ab aliis in hoc: quod nomina aliorum predicamentorum non dicuntur ad aliquid sive non sunt aliorum. Non enim si Sortes sit homo oportet quod sit alicuius homo. Quod tamen oportet in predicamento relationis. Nec si albedo sit qualitas oportet quod albedo sit separata a subiecto . . . Nam albedo est abstractum albi et per se in predicamento qualitatis . . . (*EA*, 64 a–b). Also 65 c. Also: Conceptus autem relativus concretus maxime habet predictas conditiones quas habet conceptus connotativus. Sed differunt in hoc: quandocunque conceptus connotativus vere predicatur de aliquo, convenienter potest sibi addi suum abstractum in obliquo solum, quia nihil est album nisi sit album albedine . . . Sed quando conceptus relativus predicatur vere de aliquo, semper potest sibi convenienter addi obliquus casus qui non est eius abstractum (*Quodlibet* v, q. 25). Cf. also *SL*, I, ch. 52, 156–7.

[456] Ex predictis patet quare secundum intentionem Aristotelis unum relativorum diffinitur per reliquum, quia secundum eum relativum non habet diffinitionem exprimentem quid rei sed tantum habet diffinitionem exprimentem quid nominis (*Ordinatio* d. 30, q. 3, 1).

And: Ad secundum concedo quod relativum in quantum relativum diffinitur per terminum diffinitione exprimente quid nominis, non autem diffinitione exprimente quid rei (*Quodlibet* vi, q. 24).

quantity, so relation considers substance or quality in comparison with some other substance or quality, and is not through the inherence of something which is relation. To call a man 'father' connotes nothing new in him by which he is changed into a father in the way in which whiteness makes Plato white; but it connotes the appearance of another being which is his son.[457] For that reason, relation and quantity and the remaining six categories do not have personal supposition for what corresponds to them as categories: significatively they denote substance or quality which are alone absolutes; materially or simply, they stand for themselves as words or concepts, when they can be regarded as qualities in the way that all terms and concepts are.[458]

That raises the question of whether 'relative' is a term of first or second intention. Ockham in both the Commentary on the Categories and in the Logic seems to be in no doubt that taken for itself it is a term of second intention. The reason follows from what has just been said. Since relative or relation does not, personally, stand for itself as an individual substance or quality, it cannot signify things but only terms as the signs of things. That is how Ockham interprets Aristotle; it explains why the proposition 'Man is a relative' does not follow from 'Man is a father' in the way that 'Man is a quality' follows from 'Man is white', and 'Man is a substance' follows from 'Man is an animal'. In each of the latter two cases quality and substance stand for real things because they are both predicated absolutely. Relation, on the other hand, like the other six categories, is not. The difference therefore consists precisely in their connotative character.[459] From that Ockham concludes in the Commentary on the Categories that as conceived by Aristotle relatives are principally names and do not constitute things.[460] In the Logic he is more explicit; relation or a relative is, he says, according to Aristotle, a term of second intention or second imposition and not of first intention. Thus 'man' or 'whiteness' cannot be called a relation, but 'father' can; for father is a relative term which stands for 'man' as a term of first intention. In other words, the terms which come under relative are terms of first intention but not the relative terms themselves.[461] That is confirmed by the oblique cases taken by all relative terms, which, as we have already seen, are only applicable to terms. This view is in keeping with Aristotle's statement in the Categories that 'neither wholes nor parts of primary substances are relative'.[462]

---

[457] Et ita est universaliter in omnibus relationibus secundum intentionem Aristotelis, scilicet quod relatio non importat aliquam rem que non sit de genere substantie vel qualitatis, et tamen de nulla re predicatur in quid, sicut 'simile' non predicatur in quid nec de homine nec de albedine.... Et sicut est de quantitatite et relatione, ita est de omnibus sex generibus aliis (EA, 64 c).

[458] Ibid.

[459] Ibid., 64 d–65 a; SL, 141–2.

[460] Ex istis manifeste patet quod relativa, de quibus loquitur Aristoteles principaliter hic, sunt nomina et non res extra que non sunt signa, sicut moderni dicunt (ibid., 65 c).

[461] Tamen puto quod Aristoteles nihil posuit relativum nec ad aliquid nec relationem nisi solum nomen ex quo nata est propositio mentalis, vocalis vel scripta componi. Et ideo secundum opinionem Aristotelis, ut estimo, relatio sive ad aliquid, sive etiam relativum erat nomen secunde impositionis vel nomen secunde intentionis, et non nomen prime intentionis (SL, I, ch. 49, 141–2).

[462] Categories, ch. 7, 8 a, 15.

The problem of the status of relation, then, is of a term which always refers to two or more things in conjunction, but which, at the same time, (unlike substance and quality) does not denote them absolutely. Accordingly, there has to be a distinction between concrete relative terms which can stand in personal supposition, such as 'mover' and 'moved', 'father' and 'son', and the abstract terms 'paternity' and 'movement' which refer indifferently to both. Ockham's argument shows that it is relation as a universal abstract term which is of second intention, a view that is made explicit in Quodlibet six, question twenty-two, referred to above. The reason is that the abstract term always stands for both parts of the relation and so, like any universal term cannot itself be a term of first intention. In that, relation differs from the other categories where the abstract term has a different role of connoting the same substance as the concrete term. That leads to the further characteristic that in relation, there is an order of superior to inferior, from second to first intentions, which involves not just the most universal term of the category, such as quantity or relation taken for itself as a term, but the whole range of abstract terms under which the concrete terms come. Thus 'movement' is a term of second intention which stands for nothing as such, independently of or distinct from absolute things, but consignifies the relation between 'mover' and 'moved' as terms of first intention. It is the latter which signify real substances. And Ockham's entire argument for relations and relatives as terms is based upon the distinction between those which stand in personal supposition for substances or qualities and those which are exclusively terms and so of first intentions. That is once again illustrated by the case of movement; if it were of itself something real, then everything which moved could only do so by means of new movement added to it, which Ockham rejects as contrary to Aristotle as he rejects all the other claims for the self-subsistence of relation.[463] The same holds throughout the natural order and for philosophical knowledge of it; but not for theological truth where the relations between the divine persons are self-subsistent and not the signs for real things.[464]

Following Aristotle it is necessary to distinguish true relative terms, where the correlatives are reciprocal, from seemingly relative terms, where the correlatives are not reciprocal. Only the first are properly called relatives because, in Aristotle's words, 'Relation to an external object is a necessary condition of existence'.[465] Thus we can only know that a man is a father if we also know that he has a son, or a slave if he has a master; and if one of the two correlatives is withdrawn, then the other will cease to exist in relation to it. When, however, the correlatives are not reciprocal, one can be known without the other, the case with parts of substances like head or hand belonging to something else; in knowing them 'it does not necessarily follow that we should know to which they are related'.[466] Ockham only differs from Aristotle here in calling these distinctions by their scholastic names of relation secundum esse, where the correlatives are reciprocal, and relation secundum dici where they are not. Like Aristotle Ockham does not regard the latter as proper relative terms, expressly excluding them from consideration as such in both the

[463] EA, 64 r.   [464] SL, ch. 49, 141.   [465] Categories, ch. 7, 8 a, 33.   [466] Ibid., 17–20.

Commentary on the *Categories* and in the *Logic*.[467] Where he does differ (as he acknowledges in the introduction of the terms *secundum esse* and *secundum dici*) is in positing the further distinction between necessary and contingent relation; this does not correspond to the preceding division, since a determinate relation between correlatives is still contingent—in the way that it is contingent that a man is father; it rather refers to the terms in a relation, like that of effect to cause, where one cannot be denied without denying the other.[468] Ockham does not press this one; and it does not appear in the *Logic*. Indeed it is hard to see how it can be validly maintained in contradistinction to a proper determinate relation (*secundum esse*). In the *Logic* he describes verbs together with their participles in the category of action and passion, such as heat-giving and hot, causing and caused, as belonging to the second mode of relation.[469] In the *Quodlibets* as we shall see, he discusses relation in its different modes.

Over the properties of relation, Ockham is concerned to distinguish between where they refer to terms and where to things. For the first property of relation, namely that relatives can have contraries such as virtue and vice, there are two senses of the term 'contrary'. Strictly when contraries stand for real things belonging to the same category which are mutually exclusive; since things can only be contrary because—as we have seen—of their qualities, in the strict sense contrary relations are the signs of contrary qualities. In the other broader sense terms are contrary when they cannot be simultaneously predicated of the same thing. Accordingly when relatives are said to be contrary (and not all are: for example, there is no contrary of 'father' or 'triple') they are signs for what is either really contrary or contrary by predication.[470] In the *Logic* Ockham only gives the second sense, an indication of his view of relation as exclusively a sign.

The second property, that some but not all relatives admit variation of degree, is similarly due to variation in quality and not to more or less of a relation. That again can be taken in two ways. It can mean that something real, namely a quality, is augmentable by the addition of a part; or that 'more' or 'less' are adverbs added to terms predicable of things to make them relative terms, so that we say that Socrates is more white than Plato: which is how Ockham interprets Aristotle's meaning.[471]

The third property of relation, that its correlatives are reciprocal, distinguishes relation from the other categories, as we have said. It is common to all relatives, and, for Ockham, overwhelming evidence that relation is a term. Although usually expressed by the interposition of a preposition in an indirect case between the two correlatives, the same word can also serve for both, in the direct and the oblique

---

[467] Secundo est notandum quod [Aristoteles] non intendit distinguere de relativis quod quedam sunt relativa secundum esse et quedam secundum dici, quia nec tali modo loquendi utitur Aristoteles. Sed intendit dicere quod aliqua sunt nomina que possunt de aliquo verificari respectu alterius et que possunt verificari de aliquo non respectu alterius sibi addito in obliquo; et talia nomina non sunt vere de capitulo relationis, et talia sunt hec: manus, caput, pes, et huiusmodi (*EA*, 69 a). Also *SL*, I, ch. 52, 156–7.

[468] *EA*, 69 b.   [469] *SL*, I, ch. 52, 158–9.

[470] *EA*, 65 a–b; *SL*, I, ch. 53, 159–60.   [471] *EA*, 65 b; also *SL*, 160.

cases. Thus we can say that 'Everything similar is similar by what is similar'. The same construction applies here as in the case of dissimilar words like 'father' and 'son'.[472] In the Commentary on the *Categories*, in which here as throughout the discussion is appreciably fuller, Ockham also clarifies Aristotle's statement that exact designation of a correlative excludes all that is not essential to its definition, so that 'master' and not 'man' is the correlative of 'slave'. That does not mean that 'man' is an accident in the categorical sense of not being a substance but only that in this context it is misplaced as a relative term and cannot act as the correlative of 'slave'. It is therefore not predicable essentially by the first mode as defining the subject.[473]

The difference between these three properties is that whereas the first and second refer to things as well as terms, the third belongs exclusively to terms as the signs of things, because the being which is 'father' is not itself the correlative of the being which is 'son' but only of their terms.[474] The same would apply if it were held that relatives themselves really existed; for if 'paternity' were something real it would no more be the correlative of 'filiation' than 'father' is of 'son' when each is a real being; but as 'father' stands for him who is a father and not for a son, so 'paternity' would stand for what was paternity and not for filiation. In the same way Ockham rejects as un-Aristotelian the notion of Duns Scotus that a relation is founded in what is real; that would mean either that a relation stood for something which really existed as such or for a name. Neither is tenable, the first because there is no such real thing as a relation; the second because strictly a name cannot be founded in a thing, while it is precisely the metaphorical sense of such expressions which impedes the simple from attaining real knowledge. The correct way of expressing the status of relation is that it is predicated of something real and stands for what really exists (but not as a relation).[475]

The fourth and last property of relatives is that many correlatives come into being simultaneously; that is applicable to both terms and things. It does not mean that they actually coexist and are of the same duration, as father and son are not; nor that relative terms really exist simultaneously. Rather, Aristotle's meaning was that if one correlative is said to exist, it entails saying that the other correlative also exists. Accordingly, there is a formal relation between them, such that if the proposition 'He is a father' is true, then the proposition 'He is a son' will also be true. Whenever, then, existence is verified of one it must be verified of the other, and conversely when correlatives are negated. This must not be confused with actual dependence, because although they are correlatives, father and son as real beings can exist separately and independently of one another, like all absolutes. It is as

---

[472] *EA*, 66 a; *SL*, 160.

[473] *EA*, 66 c.

[474] Ultimo circa totam istam partem est notandum quod prima proprietas relationis non tantum competit nominibus relativis sed etiam ipsis rebus pro quibus nomina relativa supponunt, sicut tactum est prius. Similiter secunda proprietas aliquando convenit ipsis rebus et etiam ipsis nominibus modo ibidem esposito. Sed ista tertia proprietas convenit tantum nominibus et signis rerum et non ipsis rebus que non sunt signa, quia illa res que est pater non dicitur ad convertentiam, nec illa res que est filius, et sic de aliis (*ibid.*, 67 a).

[475] *Ibid.*

relative terms, not things, that they are simultaneous, so that understood literally it is false to say that they come into being at the same time. Aristotle says the same when he declares that the object of knowledge or perception can exist independently of knowledge or perception of it.[476]

That completes Ockham's treatment of relatives in the Commentary on the *Categories* and in the *Logic*. In being principally directed to Aristotle's text in the *Categories*, Ockham only indirectly touched there upon the contemporary debate. He thus explicitly omits two issues which occupy a considerable place in the Commentary on the *Sentences* and the *Quodlibets* neither of which is found in Aristotle.[477] These are first, the difference between a real relation (*relatio realis*) and a mental relation or relation of reason or logic (*relatio rationis*), and, second, whether in the terminology of Duns Scotus a relation is independent of its foundation (*fundamentum*), as that to which it belongs or refers. The latter is an extension of the same argument which forms the thread of the discussion in the Commentary on the *Categories* and in the *Logic*. In the other two works it is more pointed and polemical, framed as a reply to opponents like Henry of Ghent, Duns Scotus, and Peter Aureole.

Ockham's acceptance of the distinction between a real and a mental relation makes the question of whether his theory of relation is 'nominalist' or not, peculiarly pointless. For, as we have seen and shall see in this connection, Ockham regards relation in the same way as the other seven categories which are not substance or quality. Namely, that they do not stand for what is independent of substance or quality, but signify one or other in its different aspects. To call such a doctrine 'nominalist' would be nearly as misleading as to call it realist (in the medieval sense): relation for Ockham expresses a real relation between real things but not something real in its own right. It is not therefore a thing, but nor is it merely a name: it is a sign for the actual way in which real substances and qualities are ordered in respect of one another, as quantity or action or passion signify them according to other modes of existence. Each of these categories, then, has a real signification, deriving precisely from the real existence of what they signify. Only, then, on the assumption of extreme realism that something is real only if it exists as some self-subsistent nature which answers to a concept in the mind, is it tenable to call Ockham's doctrine of relation nominalist. But that would be to destroy the very distinction between what is in the mind and what exists *in se*, a distinction which to Ockham was the indispensable safeguard to any proper understanding of either. In this context a term like nominalism, as G. Martin[477a] recognised, would equally embrace certain aspects of Aquinas's theory of relation, and can serve no purpose.

That can be seen from Ockham's definition of a real and mental relation. A real relation is when something is denoted by a relative term independently of the

[476] *EA*, 67 b–c; *SL*, 160–1.

[477] *EA*, 69 a; see *SL*, 158, for real and mental relations. In both Ockham says that Aristotle made no distinction between a real and a mental relation; he also, *SL*, I, ch. 54, 162–3, refers to the opinion of others who do distinguish one from the other, but without comment.

[477a] 'Ist Ockhams Relationstheorie Nominalismus?', 39–44.

intellect's operations, as the whiteness by which two white things are similar owes nothing to the mind's activity. The same applies to 'father' and 'son' and other relations for which a relative can stand as a term of first intention.[478] A relation of reason on the other hand is the work of the intellect, without which there would be no relation, as subject and predicate are related through a mental act and not of themselves[479] In the *Ordinatio* Ockham amplifies the meaning of a relation of reason. It can be understood either as the word or concept which signifies something which is a relation, such as 'sign' or 'payment'. Or it can be taken for the things themselves signified by those terms; these can only be absolutes, which exist actually, potentially or even—according to one opinion upon which Ockham does not pronounce, which seems to have been that of Peter Aureole—as concepts. They are denoted as relatives through an act of intellect and will, and not because they signify something other than the absolutes to which they refer. In other words a relation of reason is through an act of imposition by which a conventional meaning is given to a word which would not otherwise bear it naturally, as 'man' is used to designate men, or 'Socrates' a particular man. Relative terms of reason therefore can be either nouns themselves expressing a relation, like 'knowledge', 'knowable', 'subject', 'predicate', in every case connoting an act of reason. In the other sense they signify absolute things in relation, through an act of intellect or will; without such a mental act, the extremes—i.e. the two terms related—will continue in being but not longer in relation. Thus, terms like 'sign', 'payment', 'dominion', 'servitude', are all the work of convention, since without the intervention of the intellect and will there would be only natural signs of absolute things: what is signified by 'number' as opposed to 'payment' or 'money', or by 'man' instead of 'Socrates'.[480]

Real relation is a different matter. To begin with, Ockham regards it as conforming to the proper philosophical sense of relation, certainly as understood by Aristotle, in whose works Ockham declares he has not anywhere found mention of a relation of reason. Ockham accordingly treats the two as distinct from one another.[481] In the second place, in the *Quodlibets*[482] he identifies real relation with each of the three different modes enumerated by Aristotle in the *Metaphysics*: numerical (as double is to half), active and passive, (as capable of giving heat is to capable of being heated), and measurable, knowable, or thinkable (as knowable is to knowledge).[483] None of these, he says, stands for something distinct from

---

[478] Sed quando res est talis qualis denotatur esse per relationem vel per concretum relationis sine omni operatione intellectus, ita quod operatio intellectus nihil facit ad hoc, tunc potest dici relatio realis modo supra exposito, sicut quia unum album est simile alteri albo sine omni operatione intellectus comparantis vel non comparantis (*Ordinatio*, d. 30, q. 5, H). Also *Ordinatio*, d. 31, q. 1, B; d. 35, q. 4, H; *Quodlibet* VI, qq. 25, 27, 28, 29, 30.

[479] Potest dici quod relatio realis distinguitur a relatione rationis per hoc, quod quando sine operatione intellectus non est talis qualis denotatur esse per relationem vel per concretum relationis, tunc est relatio rationis. Verbi gratia, quia nihil est subiectum nec predicatum sine operatione intellectus, ideo iste relationes dicuntur relationes rationis (*Ordinatio*, d. 30, q. 5, H). Also *Ordinatio*, d. 31, q. 1, B; d. 35, q. 4, E, H; *Quodlibet* VI, qq. 28, 29, 30.

[480] *Ordinatio*, d. 35, q. 4, E.

[481] *Ibid.*, d. 30, q. 5, H; *Quodlibet* VI, q. 30.

[482] *Ordinatio*, d. 30, q. 3, P–Q; *Quodlibet* VI, q. 30.

[483] *Metaphysics*, IV, ch. 15, 1020 b–1021 b.

absolute things, according to Aristotle: and each is an equally real relative, having reciprocal correlatives independently of the mind's actions. They differ in that, by the first two modes, correlatives are simultaneously in the mind and in nature but by the third mode they are first in nature. Thus something must be knowable before there can be knowledge of it and perceived before there can be perception of it; but something does not have to be measurable before there is measurement, or to be heat-giving before there can be heat. Accordingly, where by the first two modes the extremes of a relation are simultaneous, by the third mode they are not. But they are equally real by all three modes: knowable and knowledge are true correlatives, such that one entails the other; for if something is knowable it is knowable by knowledge; and if it is knowledge it is knowledge which is knowable.[484]

The question whether a relation terminates at another relative or at an absolute depends for its answer upon how the terminal extreme is defined. When taken strictly as a correlative, it will be a relative, and then one relative term will refer to another, as 'father' has 'son' for its correlative and not 'man' or 'animal'. In that sense a relation does not have another terminus since it is not something distinct from real things. But in the other broader meaning, the terminus of a relation is something absolute, because it then stands for what the relative term signifies. Thus 'creator' as the terminal extreme of 'creature' is not itself a relative but an absolute, namely, God, denoted by a relative.[485]

As this concerns a real relation it means that the extremes which—at least as terms—are numerically distinct, need not be verified of more than one and the same thing. That applies whether the extremes are taken strictly, as themselves the correlatives, or broadly for what they signify. In the strict sense they will differ as numerically different terms and be in a different grammatical case even if they are reduplicative. Thus one and the same thing which is self-moving will be expressed in a relation between mover and moved: the extremes will be numerically different although the thing to which they refer will be the same. In the second broader sense they will be verified only of the same thing; and in this sense there will be no real distinction between extremes although they will still express a real relation. Accordingly, for a real relation, the extremes do not have to be really distinct, even though they must always differ numerically.[486]

The distinction arises because relatives as such have nominal definitions by which their correlatives must be known reciprocally but which do not thereby stand for real things distinct from absolutes, as 'son' is not a separate being from 'man'. For that reason two correlatives need only express one and the same thing, as 'father' and 'son' in different grammatical cases can refer to the same man.[487] Ockham declares that Aristotle conceived relation in exactly this manner as reciprocally defined by its correlatives so that to know one is to know the other.[488]

[484] *Quodlibet* VI, q. 19; also qq. 17 and 18.
[485] *Ibid.*, q. 24.
[486] *Ibid.*, q. 27; *Ordinatio*, d. 31, q. 1, H.
[487] *Quodlibet* VI, q. 24.
[488] *Ibid.*

By the same token they express a real relation in connoting absolutes which, like two white things, are really related independently of the intellect.[489] All that the intellect does is to express these terms in different ways (*diversimode*): thus it can form an absolute concept, say that Socrates or Plato is white; and from that it can make these terms into a relation by stating that Socrates and Plato are similar in virtue of each being white. Thus it arrives at a real relation by means of a relative concept like 'similar'; it is the latter which only exists in the mind.

From that it follows that we have to differentiate accepted usage from strict meaning. By the first relative terms like 'similarity', 'equality', and so on, signify absolutes; but they are not themselves absolutes, nor are they predicated absolutely of absolutes because usage does not permit us to say, 'Whiteness is a similarity' (for reasons which we have discussed in connexion with concrete and abstract terms previously). We can only signify 'whiteness' connotatively by a concrete relative term like 'similar'. In their strict sense, however, the abstracts of relatives such as 'similarity', 'equality' and so on should be first intentions; this too could be interpreted in different ways. Thus it could be argued that while the concretes stand for a single absolute thing, their abstracts are universals standing for a number of individuals as collective nouns, like 'crowd', 'army', and so on. 'John' and 'Richard' would then be individually companions but collectively a 'society', as one white thing would be 'similar' but two or more 'similarity'. Ockham concedes that this could probably be maintained for equiparate words such as those just cited, but not for those which were disparate, where it would not be correct to say that 'God' and 'creature' are 'active creation', or that 'father' and 'son' are 'paternity'. Accordingly, as we have seen earlier,[490] when concrete and abstract signify exactly the same thing and by the same logical and grammatical mode, and provided no syncathegoremata are included to make them reduplicative, they are predicated of the same thing.

That is the case with concrete and abstract relative terms like 'similar' and 'similarity'; neither signifies something not signified by the other. There are therefore no grounds for holding that they differ as singular and universal. It is usage which prevents our saying that 'Socrates is a similarity' but it means the same as 'Socrates is similar'.[491]

One of the common misconceptions over relatives is to compare their concrete and abstract forms with those of absolute terms and so conclude that they each have the same signification. Thus a pair of relatives like 'similar' and 'similarity' is equated with a pair like 'white' and 'whiteness' in which 'whiteness' signifies a real quality where both terms stand for the same thing. But relatives do not stand for things themselves but for the names or the signs of things; and of no specific thing can the term 'relation' be predicated. Failure to recognise that leads to the fallacy of predication in supposing that there are as many real things as there are terms

[489] *Ibid.*, q. 25; *Ordinatio*, d. 30, q. 5, E, G.

[490] E.g. *Quodlibet* V, q. 9 to which Ockham refers here in *Quodlibet* VI, q. 25; also *Ordinatio*, d. 31, q. 1, 1.

[491] *Ordinatio, ibid.*; *Quodlibet* VI, q. 25.

regardless of their logical and grammatical form. Thus syncathegoremata like 'by' or 'yesterday' are given their own abstract terms like 'byness' and 'yesterdayness' which are taken to signify something absolute.[492]

For that reason relative and relation are terms of second intention and do not themselves signify anything absolute. Nor are they related to one another as concrete and abstract. A relative stands for real names or signs predicable of individual things, like 'father', 'son', 'similar', 'equal' and so on; whereas relation stands for names or signs that cannot be really predicated of anything, such as 'paternity', 'filiation', 'similarity', 'equality'. In neither case, then, do they denote real things as substances or qualities: we cannot say 'Man is a relative' or 'Man is a relation' in the same way as we can say that 'Man is a father'.[493]

A real relation, therefore, has nothing to do with the independent existence of something which is a relation. It refers to what is really related, whether one thing or many, whether in abstraction or concretely denoted by relative terms standing for actual things.[494] In none of these forms does relation add anything to what is related, either among creatures themselves or between God and creatures, where creation is a real relation but not something distinct from one or the other.[495] Only where theological truth is concerned is relation a term of first intention as it applies to the relation between the divine persons; even here, however, as we shall consider in chapter six, relation is not really distinct from the divine persons, as they are not really distinct from one another.[496]

A verbal difficulty arises when non-being is related to real being as in the case of matter which is potential and form which is actual. Many call that a potential or aptitudinal relation. In the Ordinatio[497] Ockham appears to accept this where a real relation is taken strictly to mean a relation between actual things; for clearly such a relation between, say, matter and form cannot be a real one thus defined. In the broad sense of real relation, however, by which things are really related, whether they are potential or actual, it is a real relation, since the relation of form to matter is no more the work of the intellect than a relation between actual things. By the time of the Quodlibets, while giving substantially the same explanation Ockham seems to have discarded the notion of a potential relation as intermediate between a real relation and a relation of reason.[498]

So much for Ockham's view of real and mental relations; it derives from the same principles which informed his discussions in the Commentary on the Categories and in the Logic. That also applies to the other and more far-reaching question of whether relatives have a real foundation: an issue raised by Duns Scotus in both the notion of a foundation and its real distinction from a relation. This, as Ockham explained briefly in the Commentary on the Categories, to which we have

[492] Ordinatio, ibid., L.
[493] Ordinatio, ibid., I; Quodlibet VI, q. 27.
[494] Ordinatio, d. 30, q. 5, P.
[495] Ordinatio, ibid., q. 4, F; Reportatio, II, q. 2, C–G; Quodlibet VI, q. 27.
[496] Ordinatio, q. 1, P(i); also q. 5, E; d. 33, q. 1, B–D, and d. 35, q. 4.
[497] Ordinatio, d. 30, q. 5, I.
[498] Quodlibet VI, q. 25; also q. 18.

already alluded, was an attempt to uphold the independence of relation as being founded in something absolute. On that view relation is something real which exists in a real thing. Ockham dismisses this notion as untenable and un-Aristotelian. It would mean that relative terms like 'paternity' and 'filiation' were not correlatives because instead of referring to one another, as 'paternity' refers to 'filiation', each would be related to itself as father or son in which it was founded. Only terms can therefore be relatives because they alone can be correlatives, as Aristotle said; nor did he ever talk of a foundation for terms or things. It is possible for neither, and so false for both; even when used metaphorically of relation as a term it impedes many from a proper understanding of the truth.[499]

In the *Ordinatio* (distinctions thirty, thirty-one and question five of distinction thirty-five), the *Reportatio* (book two, questions one and two), and the *Quodlibets* (questions ten, eleven, twelve of the sixth *Quodlibet*) the problem of a foundation engaged Ockham much more closely. There, from the same standpoint, and over much the same ground just encountered in the two logical works,[500] Ockham met the issues raised above all by Duns Scotus, as well as by Henry of Ghent and Peter Aureole among others still to be identified. These went beyond the logical status of relation to its metaphysical and theological import: whether relation was an integral part of being and whether God could dispense with it. The further question of relation within God's own essence we shall leave to chapter six.

It is within this wider context that the question of the existence or non-existence of a foundation arises. Ockham rejects it on the major premise common to his whole outlook that only absolute can exist independently and of themselves, whether naturally or by God's absolute power, and the minor premise that relation as a term is neither really distinct from nor identical with absolutes. As a nominal definition it does not directly stand for anything as such.[501] I shall therefore, at the risk of some repetition, attempt to place Ockham's discussion within that framework.

To begin with, Ockham opens the question of whether relation is something which really exists in something (*a parte rei*) by declaring that it is—at the natural level—a matter of reason, not authority[502] Its nature is made more open by the

---

[499] Et si dicatur quod verum est quod res absoluta in qua fundatur relatio non dicitur ad convertentiam, sed illa relatio in re absoluta fundatur ad convertentiam, hoc non valet, quia secundum istos paternitas est relatio, sed illa paternitas non dicitur ad filiationem. Non enim, dicitur quod paternitas est filiationis paternitas, nec filiatio est paternitatis filiatio; sed magis dicitur quod paternitas est ipsius patris et filiatio est filii. Patet igitur quod talis res poneretur non diceretur ad convertantiam . . . Nec iste modus loquendi quod relatio fundatur in re absoluta invenitur, in dictis Aristotelis sicut nec invenitur quod nomen fundatur in re que significatur. Et ideo non debet dici . . . quia si relatio fundatur in re, aut relatio ibi supponit pro re, et hoc est falsum, quia nulla talis res que est ibi posset sic fundari. Aut supponit pro nomine, et hoc est falsum, quia nomen non fundatur in re nisi metaphorice loquendo, et certe locutiones metaphorice multum impediunt simplices ab acquisitione vere sciente (*EA*, 67 a).

[500] For his interpretation of Aristotle see especially *Ordinatio*, d. 30, q. 3, G–X, q. 5, C–D, I–L, and *Quodlibet* VI, q. 21 and more generally qq. 8–30, and *Quodlibet* VII, qq. 1–2; he again dismisses foundation as un-Aristotelian. *Ordinatio*, d. 30, q. 3, I, and *Quodlibet* VI, q. 11.

[501] *Ordinatio*, d. 30, q. 3, I; q. 5, N; *Reportatio*, bk. II, q. 1, G; *Quodlibet* VI, q. 15.

[502] Circa istam questionem primo sciendum pro intellectu quod non est questio de veritate quid secundum veritatem sit tenendum, sed est quid teneret volens precise initi rationi possibile pro statu isto et nolens aliquam sectam vel auctoritatem recepire (*Ordinatio*, d. 30, q. 1, B).

difficulty of resolving the opposing arguments; among them four, by which the unity of the universe, the existence of composite beings, the maintenance of causality and of mathematical relations are made dependent upon the independence of relation.[503] In reply Ockham points to the consequences which would follow if relation were independent. It would mean first that it could be known in itself without our having to know that to which it was related. Then if one were to know the similarity of Socrates and Socrates himself without any corresponding similarity by which he was similar, it would follow that it could be at once known that Socrates was similar and yet doubted whether he was similar to something else; in the same way someone could be known to be a father without knowing that he had a son. Hence there could be intuitive knowledge of similarity without previous knowledge of anything else similar. The latter could then only be deduced, as the cause is deduced when only the effect is known.[504] In consequence to know a relation independently of anything else would entail ignorance of that to which it was related. Nor does it help to alter the major premise and allow that relations must be known by reference to one another; for, as Ockham's opponents concede, the divine essence can be known without knowing its relation which is the same as itself. Conversely, absolutes which are more dependent upon each other, as creatures are upon God, than any relation is upon another relation, can be known separately; but relations cannot be so known because they are not absolute.[505]

In the second place, the extremes of a relation can be at the furthest distance from one another and each remain unaffected by what happens to the other. Thus if they were real things, say one black and the other white, the black could by God's absolute power become white without what was white being changed; and in virtue of their mutual whiteness they would now be similar. That shows that relation is not a real thing since the original white thing has become similar without alteration.[506]

Thirdly, as God can make anything absolute exist without anything else, he could make two white things each white and each exist singly. They would then have no additional relation between them, but they would nevertheless be similar in both being white. Relation again cannot therefore be an independent thing:[507] the invocation of God's absolute power to conserve absolutes is one of the features of Ockham's discussion in these works.[508] Fourth, if relation were really distinct from absolute things, that would include not only relations like similarity, equality, paternity, filiation, but also those like diversity, distinction and others of the same kind; but the latter are not real things. Nor therefore are the former. If diversity and difference were real, it would mean an infinite regress, for each would be distinguished absolutely from the absolute things to which, as relatives, they referred; they would therefore need a further relation of difference or diversity to

503 *Ibid.*, D.
504 *Ibid.* [No. E].
505 *Ibid.* [No. E].
506 *Ibid.*, F.
507 *Ibid.*, G; also *Reportatio*, bk. II, q. 2, G.
508 E.g. *Reportatio*, II, q. I, N; q. 2, F, G, Q; *Ordinatio*, d. 30, q. 4, C.

enable them to refer to those things from which they were absolutely separate; and the same need would again arise for this second relation: it too, in being separate from absolute things, would in turn require a further relation by which it too could be related; and so on to infinity.[509]

It is at this point in all three works that the concept of a foundation properly appears as part of Duns Scotus's defence of the independence of relation, distinct from absolute things. As interpreted by Ockham, Duns's view was that many foundations, in being absolutes, are really distinct from their relation when not related to something else, as something can be white and not similar when there is no other white thing to which it is similar. Conversely when there is something to which it refers, a foundation is then inseparable from a relation as that at which the latter terminates and by which it is related.[510] Duns is mentioned by name in connection with this opinion only in the *Reportatio* where it is the last of four in favour of relation as a real thing;[511] but both there and in the *Ordinatio* and *Quodlibets* (in abridged form) his is the one view strenuously contested from both these facets. On the one hand Ockham is concerned to demonstrate the impossibility of treating a relation as really inseparable from a foundation, and on the other the untenable consequences—above all of infinite regress—which would follow from their real separation. Each shares the same fallacy of treating relation and its foundation as real things which can be joined or separated.

It is their inseparability which arises first, invoked in the previous connection to counter the arguments of an infinite regress. Duns's grounds for making them the same are that it would be contradictory to have one without the other, since a foundation is that by which a relation is related: both together therefore constitute the extremes of any relation with the foundation as the 'otherness' to which a relation must refer in virtue of being a relation. They must accordingly, in being inseparable, be the same.[512] Their identity in turn breaks an infinite regress; for a relation in terminating at a foundation as its other extreme, will, in the usage of the time, be 'terminated in the second', namely the foundation as its other term. There is thus no need to posit a further relation by which it is related.[513]

On this view, then, a foundation, as something real, is at once the condition for a relation's independence and its relativity. For Ockham although with some variation between the *Reportatio* and the other two works which we shall in due course remark, it is neither.

In the first place, relation cannot be identical with a foundation thus defined, because a relation in referring to something else (*ad aliquid*) consists of two distinct terms. Accordingly if a foundation is the terminus of a relation as that by which a

---

[509] *Reportatio, ibid.,* H.

[510] *Ordinatio,* d. 30, q. 1, C; *Reportatio,* II, q. 2, E.

[511] For the other three opinions see *Reportatio, ibid.,* B–E and notes 533, 552, below.

[512] Ad istud dicit predictus opinans quod relatio seipsa refertur ad fundamentum. Non enim potest fieri sine fundamento vel absque se sine contradictione. Ipsa enim existente et fundamento simul ambo sunt sunt extrema huius relationis, scilicet alietas que est ad fundamentum (*Ordinatio, ibid.,* I) Also *Quodlibet* VI, q. 11, where the arguments throughout follow those in the *Ordinatio* very closely; and *Reportatio, ibid.,* F.

[513] *Ordinatio, ibid.,* K; *Quodlibet, ibid.; Reportatio, ibid.*

relation is related to something else (its otherness), it must by the same token be other than the relation whose extreme it constitutes. Every relation has immediately only one other term. As the other term of the similarity or paternity in Socrates is the whiteness in Plato or a son, so the term of otherness by which a relation is other than its foundation—and so is a relation—is the foundation itself: thus if the similarity in Socrates is distinguished from that in which it is founded, say his whiteness, whiteness itself as the foundation will be the term by which similarity is other than whiteness. They therefore can no more be same than the similarity in Socrates and the whiteness to which it refers in Plato. Therefore a relation and its foundation are really distinguished.[514] This is tantamount to denying that there is such a thing as a foundation; and, as we have mentioned, Ockham does deny it elsewhere.[515] Here, however, he is concerned to expose the claim, that a relation is inseparable from its foundation, as part of the same fallacy that a relation can exist independently of absolute things. He accordingly seeks to show that if a foundation belongs to a relation the two must be distinct.

It must then follow in the second place that there will still be an infinite regress. For if the similarities of Socrates to Plato and of Plato to Socrates are really distinct, then the first similarity in either will be similar to a second and a second to a third, and so on infinitely.[516] Nor does the reply hold that the first will terminate at the second. That rests upon the argument that if Socrates and Plato are mutually identical, the identity in each must belong to their common identity. Thus whereas Socrates and his identity are distinct and can remain independent of the other, and so can Plato and his identity, their mutual identity cannot, for they must exist simultaneously. Each is therefore inseparable from their common identity which is their foundation, and in referring to one another they are also referring to their foundation. There is therefore no infinite regress since each relation has both a foundation and a term at which it terminates.[517]

Ockham does not accept this proof (which he states algebraically), first because, although the identity between Socrates and Plato must be mutual, it is not the same identity as that between John and Paul. Hence each identity is really distinct from the other. But since they are also of the same nature, if one refers to something by a distinct relation so will the others. Therefore if the identity of Socrates and Plato refers to the identity of John and Paul by a distinct relation, it will also refer to the identity of Plato and Socrates by another distinct relation, and so one will not

---

[514] Contra istam responsionem arguo primo sic. Ubicumque sunt distincti termini aliquarum relationum, ibi sunt distincte relationes, quia relatio secundum istos est ad aliquid; ergo ad distinctum est distincta, quia unius relationis est primo unus terminus tantum, sicut illius similitudinis in Sorte vel illius paternitatis in Sorte terminus est filius vel aliud album. Terminus autem istius alietatis qua ista relatio est alia a suo fundamento est ipsum fundamentum; ergo ista relatio et ista alietas realiter distinguuntur (*Ordinatio, ibid.*). Also *Quodlibet* VI, q. 11 which is more explicit, e.g. Sicut similitudinis in Sorte terminus est albedo in Platone. Terminus autem illius alietatis qua similitudo est alia a fundamento est fundamentum similitudinis in Sorte, puta albedo in Sorte. Ergo albedo in Sorte et sua alietas a suo fundamento distinguuntur realiter.

[515] E.g. Similiter dico quod relatio non habet fundamentum (*Quodlibet* VI, q. 10). Also *EA*, 67 a (note 499 above); *Ordinatio*, d. 30, q. 1, R; q. 3, I. See 233 ff. below.

[516] *Ordinatio, ibid.*; *Quodlibet, ibid.*

[517] *Ordinatio, ibid.*, K; *Quodlibet, ibid.*

terminate at the other but lead to new distinct relations infinitely. As in a continuum there will always be a further distinct relation.[518] Secondly, accepting the above opinion that Socrates and his identity can be really distinct but that his identity cannot be distinct from the identity in Plato, it would also follow that Socrates could be distinct from the otherness by which he is distinct from his identity and his identity from him. Therefore there will be an additional intermediate relation between Socrates and his identity and this again will recur infinitely. Nor will it do to say that while this applies to the distinction between Socrates and his identity it does not hold for his identity taken in itself where its otherness its own foundation and so the same as his identity. That would be to negate a real relation which, even if it were to be granted that it is the same as its foundation, cannot be the same as its terminus, but must by definition be something other than itself. For that reason identity and its otherness cannot both terminate at the same identity.[519]

This is also another argument against a foundation, in denying the very premise on which it is based, namely that what is the same as a relation can serve as its other term: if it is contradictory for a relation to be without a foundation, it is also contradictory for the foundation to be the other term without which there can be no relation.

In the third place, Ockham argues from Duns himself that the relation of God to a creature does not really differ from a creature, because, on the grounds of the *dictum de omni et de nullo*, whatever can be stated of one thing belonging to a term must be stated uniformly of everything else belonging to it, and whatever is stated of nothing can only be stated of nothing. Now if creation were really distinct from what is created, it would be uniformly stated of everything other than God. Thus if a stone were related to God as an effect to a first cause, the relation of cause and effect in being distinct from a stone would itself—as something real and so other than God—be related as an effect to a first cause, in turn engendering a further relation of effect to first cause and thus to infinity. Creation as a real relation could not then be predicated of anything but its own foundation.[520] Thus in reply to Duns, Ockham enlists the same argument against the independent existence of identity. It must be stated uniformly of every—as opposed to no—identity since each identity belongs by definition to something. But if each identity were real it would need a further identity added to it to be the same as the identity to which it belongs, and this would again continue infinitely as first argued. It is not enough to reply that identity is not uniform and that each separate identity can be of the same identity by means of another identity which is distinct from it but the same as their common identity. On that analogy it could then equally be said that the relation of an effect to a first cause does not uniformly refer to every creature because it belongs absolutely to a creature by means of a relation as a separate thing. In fact they are the same in both cases.[521]

Finally Ockham invokes another argument from Duns Scotus, namely that as a contradiction is the way of inferring a distinction, so identity tells us that a real

[518] *Ordinatio, ibid.; Quodlibet, ibid.*
[520] *Ordinatio, ibid.*, K; *Quodlibet, ibid.*
[519] *Ordinatio, ibid.; Quodlibet, ibid.*
[521] *Ordinatio, ibid.*, K–L; *Quodlibet, ibid.*

contradiction is impossible. Applied to the mutual similarity of Socrates and Plato it means that it must be the same for both, since one without the other would be contradictory. But Socrates's similarity to Plato is not really in either Plato or Socrates; it cannot therefore be really anywhere, and so is neither a substance nor an accident. Nor, as Duns held, can it inhere in one or the other; for then in being in one it would be really distinct from the other, which is contradictory, as it is also contradictory or begs the question or concedes the same point, to claim that their similarities coexist simultaneously depending on how simultaneous existence is understood.[522] The only exception to this rule is where contradictories can be verified successively of the same thing when they refer to its local movement or time or production and destruction, because here they are relatives, not absolutes.[523] That can be seen from God's power to keep separate, without local movement, what is naturally joined, such as accident and subject, and form and matter. In then being subsequently united by him, something new would be successively verified of them without signifying the addition of anything new.[524]

In the connection one of the features of Ockham's reply to Duns Scotus, in both the *Ordinatio* and the *Reportatio*, in his substitution of local movement and proximate causation for what Duns attributes to a relation.[525] Thus terms such as 'union' and 'composition' do not stand for the relation between two absolutes but signify that nothing is interposed between them; they do not therefore express a relation but a negation, namely, the absence of intermediaries impeding the action of one thing upon another. Since that requires their proximity, there is no need to invoke a causal relation as the cause. That again can be illustrated from God's omnipotence: he could suspend the action of one proximate thing upon another so that when it did occur it would do so without any mediating relation.[526] In the same way it would be irrational to suppose that the existence of a white thing in Rome entails the presence of something positive in a white thing in England; in every natural action the agent must be within range of what it acts upon.[527] If these or the other categories, such as action, passion, place, and time, were real things, even to move a finger would fill the universe with infinite relations because such movement would then have a different position from before in relation to every other part. Thus if place as a relation were a real thing, there would be as many relations in heaven as there are parts, which are infinite, since they would extend over its entirety.[528] Equally if action were something real, every agent in acting would be changed by

---

[522] *Ordinatio, ibid.,* L.

[523] Unde pro omnibus istis est una ratio solum que est ista: impossibile est contradictoria successive verificari de eodem nisi propter motum localem alicuius, vel propter transitionem temporis vel propter productionem vel destructionem alicuius (*Ordinatio,* d. 30, q. 4, E).

[524] *Ibid.*

[525] *Ordinatio,* d. 30, q. 1, P; *Reportatio* II, q. 2, G–H. E.g. Tunc nullum respectum oportet ibi ponere, quia omnia per motum localem salvarem que tu salvas per respectum, quia tunc unio non significat nisi ipsa extrema connotando negationem medii intercepti. Et ideo quando illud medium est interceptum non est unio . . . Alii autem respectus qui ponuntur, scilicet approximatio, unio partium, ordo universi, et sic de aliis possunt salvari per negationes (*Reportatio, ibid.,* H).

[526] *Reportatio, ibid.,* G.

[527] *Ibid.*   [528] *Ibid.*

engendering in itself action as something real:[529] in the case of the sun it would newly receive as many things as it heated, which would be infinite, as in heating a piece of wood which consists of infinite parts.[530] The category 'when' likewise in having time as its termination would contain both yesterday and tomorrow, thereby destroying future contingents.[531] All these and other absurdities would result, such as that any movement would engender something new in everything, spiritual and material, and that every angle in being separate from each infinite part of a continuum, would itself contain infinite parts.[532]

These arguments apply to any claim for the independence of relation, regardless of whether it belongs to a foundation or is distinct from one. They were, as we have said, directed principally against Duns Scotus for holding that either was possible.[533] Ockham's opposition rests upon the fundamental principle that a relation cannot be separated from the correlatives which define it and act as its extremes. Since these are terms, relation itself is the product of reciprocal terms signifying things simultaneously. In that sense it is equally misconceived to treat relation as really separable or inseparable from a foundation; for it is not a thing which can be isolated from or joined to other things. Although all three works unite in this same standpoint, the *Reportatio* stresses the consequences which follow from treating relation and foundation as really separable, where the other two works put more stress upon the consequences of inseparability. The arguments do not differ in essentials since in each case the issue, of the independence of relation, is the same.

Thus in the *Reportatio* Ockham reduces Duns's assumption, that a relation is something real in itself and distinct from a foundation, to mean that a relation could exist without its foundation and extremes—that is, without being related and in not referring to something else—which would negate it as a relation.[534] Again, Ockham argues that if relation were something real apart from its foundation, then he would go beyond Duns Scotus and declare the same for every relation without exception, because whenever one thing is compared with another it is either really the same or really different. For Ockham there are no ontological half-way houses like the formal distinction.[535]

---

[529] *Ordinatio*, d. 30, q. 2, C.

[530] *Ibid.*, q. 1, M; *Quodlibet* VI, q. 12.   [531] *Ibid.*, q. 2, C.   [532] *Ibid.*

[533] E.g. *Reportatio* II, q. 2, E: Quarto est opinio quod alique relationes distinguuntur realiter, alique non, que est Scoti. Primum probatur multipliciter per separabilitatem relationis ad fundamentum. Cf. *Ordinatio*, d. 30, q. 1, C where this is the minor of the opinion quod relatio est alia res ab omni re absoluta et ab omnibus absolutis, ita quod sicut substantia et qualitas sunt res distincte quarum neutra est de essentia alterius, ita substantia et relatio sunt distincte res realiter, et neutra de essentia alterius.

[534] Sed relatio est aliquod positivum preter fundamentum per te, et potest fundamentum existere sine relatione. Igitur potest relatio intelligi sine fundamentis et extremis, quod falsum est, cum eius diffinitio et cognitio dependeant ex diffinitione extremorum. Igitur nihil est preter extrema (*Reportatio* II, q. 2, G).

[535] Sed si tenerem quod relatio esset aliqua res, dicerem cum Iohanne quod esset res distincta a fundamento, et discordando dicerem quod omnis relatio differt realiter a fundamento, et ita creatio passio sicut quecumque alia. Cuius ratio est quia quecunque creatura alteri comparata vel est eadem sibi realiter vel differt realiter, quia non pono distinctionem formalem in creaturis (*ibid.*, H).

That does not, however, commit Ockham to accepting a real diversity between relation and its foundation. He begins his reply to Duns's opinion in the second question of book two of the *Reportatio* by again showing that such a real distinction would mean an infinity of distinctions.[536] Further on he rejects the main assumption in Duns's argument that inseparability entails identity, and conversely that what is distinct is separable, in the way that, according to Duns, something can be white and not similar.[537] Such a view confuses absolutes, which are distinct, with a relation between them, which is reciprocal. Thus equality and inequality are really distinct from their foundations of two differing quantities, and yet as relations they are inseparable, as double is from half, each of which at the same time stands for something absolute and distinct from the other. A relation is therefore at once separable and inseparable from its foundation in virtue of referring to real things which are at once distinct and reciprocal; if a relation were founded in a relation, as similarity in similarity, the result would be infinite similarities.[538] There is no contradiction in absolutes being related: every creature is dependent upon God, and every accident belongs to a subject, yet they remain absolutes.[539]

We can now identify foundation: it is that to which a relation is related not as something real but as a name which is applicable to something real; one is connected to the other by predication as opposed to inherence.[540] Both are therefore terms; one does not contain the other; and far from being the same they are distinct, as Socrates is not his similarity.[541] The reason is that relation is a connotative term signifying one thing principally and another thing secondarily. For that they have to exist concurrently; if one is destroyed the relation lapses, since the meaning of each term depends exclusively upon its reciprocity with the other. Their correlation alone constitutes a relation; it has nothing to do with something distinct which is a relation, as two white things are similar by their mutual whiteness, not by some additional quality of similarity; and if they cease to be similar through the disappearance of one of the two, the other still remains white but no longer similar, as something can be white and not similar.[542] That is what Aristotle meant when he said in the *Physics* that a relation comes about without any accompanying alteration to that which is related.[543] For him a relation had a nominal definition, since one term was defined by the other, which is impossible in real definitions. Accordingly Aristotle did not use the expression 'foundation' because relatives are names, not

---

[536] *Ibid.*, F.

[537] *Ibid.*, E and I.

[538] *Ibid.*, I.

[539] *Ordinatio*, d. 30, q. 1, P.

[540] Et si dicatur quod omnis relatio fundatur in aliquo fundamento, dico quod si accipiatur fundamentum realiter pro inherere, et non pro denominare in predicatione, quod hec est simpliciter falsa, sed aliter est vera (*ibid.*, R).

[541] Quia relatio realis differt realiter a fundamento vel ab illo quod refertur (*Reportatio*, II, q. 1, C). Also: Sed dico ad minorem quod fundamentum non continet per identitatem, nec simul nec successive tales relationes, quia hec est falsa: 'Sortes est realiter simultudo' ... et ideo non pono quod relatio est idem realiter cum fundamento (*Ordinatio, ibid.*).

[542] *Ordinatio*, II, q. 2, H. Also F.

[543] *Ibid.* Ockham's reference is to book V, but it seems to correspond more to book VII, ch. 3, 246 b, 11.

something real founded in real things.[544] Moreover, as part of a nominal definition one relative term is not prior to another as one term is prior to another in a real definition.[545] On all these counts, then, it is false to say that there can be one or more relations in the same foundation or that they are the same as their foundation or that they can belong to the same subject. All relative terms are mental concepts signifying a number of absolutes; they are not independent of them.[546] All relation is in virtue of absolutes in themselves and of nothing else.[547]

The order between relation and foundation is thus between absolute and relative terms. It rests upon two principles, which Ockham stated in all three works. The first is that relation always follows its termination and foundation, that is to say the other term in a relation. Although terminus and foundation can be the same, they cannot be the same as a relation. The second principle is that the mutual correlatives in a relation must exist and be known together. The first principle can be shown from the example of cause and effect: in any relation between them the effect, as that which is related to the cause, acts at once as foundation and as that at which the cause terminates. In each of these respects therefore relation is subsequent to the real things that are cause and effect. The second principle follows from the first: since mutual relations must exist simultaneously, both in the mind and in nature, whatever is prior to one will be prior to the other. But it has just been shown that an effect is prior to a foundation in it: it must therefore also be prior to the foundation in a cause.[548]

These two principles crystallise Ockham's view that a foundation represents what is related. It is neither a real thing nor a relation, as Socrates is not his similarity; but rather that by which something is related, as Socrates, in being similar to Plato, and Plato to Socrates, are at once the foundation of their mutual similarity and the termination of the similarity of the other, and correspondingly two white things are each the foundation of their similarity and that at which the other's similarity terminates.

[544] Ex predictis patet quare secundum intentionem Aristotelis, unum relativorum diffinitur per reliquum, quia secundum eum relativum non habet diffinitionem exprimentem quid rei, sed tantum habet diffinitionem exprimentem quid nominis, et in talibus non est inconveniens unum diffiniri per reliquum, et e converso. Sed de diffinitionibus exprimentibus quid rei est hoc impossibile. Ex predictis etiam patet quod relatio de qua Philosophus loquitur in Predicamentis non est realiter ipsum fundamentum . . . quia relatio non fundatur in illo sicut reale in reali, sed tantum . . . est quoddam denominabile (*Ordinatio*, d. 30, q. 3, I).

[545] *Ibid.*, N. •

[546] *Ibid.*, q. I, R; also *Reportatio* II, q. 2, Q.

[547] *Ibid.*, P; also *Reportatio*, II, q. I, D–E, G; q. 2, F.

[548] Preterea suppono ista duo fundamenta vera, etiam secundum alios. Primum est quod respectus est essentialiter posterior suo fundamento et termino. Secundum quod respectus mutui sunt simul natura etiam in intellectu. Ex primo fundamento arguo sic. Effectus productus est fundamentum vel terminus cuiuslibet respectus qui est inter causam et effectum, quia est fundamentum respectus effectus ad causam, et terminus respectus cause ad fundamentum. Ergo isti respectus mutui sunt posteriores natura tam causa quam effectu. Ex secundo fundamento arguo sic. Respectus mutui sunt simul natura et in intellectu; ergo quidquid est prius natura uno illorum est prius altero. Sed effectus est prior respectu fundamento in eo; ergo effectus est prior natura respectu fundamento in causa (*Quodlibet* VI, q. 12). Also *Ordinatio*, d. 30, q. I, M; *Reportatio*, II q. 2, N–O.

The real relation of absolutes is thus the pre-condition of a relation founded upon them and terminating reciprocally at them. In Ockham's own words: 'Therefore the order is first the absolute in the cause and then that which follows in the effect, and then, if there are such, these relatives. From which it follows that there can well be cause and effect, producer and what is produced without any relation of reason, because cause and production signify an absolute nature which is a cause and connote an effect; and conversely with an effect and that which is produced.'[549] This passage comes as close as any to stating Ockham's doctrine of relation. To be real it must be founded in real things so that its terms stand in personal supposition for what is real.[550] A relation is therefore always subsequent to the extremes and foundations by which things in a real relation are related.[551]

The question, then, whether Ockham's theory of relation is nominalist can only be intelligibly answered in the context of his conception of the categories as whole. If to ask it means, 'Did Ockham deny the independent existence of relation as something real in its own right, distinct from absolute things?' the answer must be 'yes'. Ockham opposed especially Duns Scotus, and in passing Henry of Ghent and Peter Aureole,[552] for upholding in different ways the separate identity of relation as real or mental. For Ockham, in contrast, no matter what the particular relation between things—whether of similarity, causality, identity or whatever— they are related by themselves (seipsis) as absolutes and by nothing else. Hence the question put in that way is largely meaningless. Ockham was saying of relation

---

[549] Reportatio, ibid., O.

[550] Ibid., q. 2, R. Debet sic inteligi quod quando de aliquo termino vel aliquibus terminis supponentibus personaliter verificantur extrema contradictionis, scilicet esse et non esse, necesse est quod inter illa pro quibus termini supponunt sit distinctio realis.

[551] Ibid., Q.

[552] Baudry, Lexique Philosophique, 232. Of the four opinions which Ockham cites in the Reportatio, book II, q. 2, Henry of Ghent is named in the text as the author of the first and Duns Scotus as the author of the fourth. No names are given for the other two. Baudry attributes the second to Aristotle and surmises that the third may be that of Harvey of Nedellec. The attention Ockham devotes to the three other than Duns's should not be exaggerated. They are only briefly mentioned in the Reportatio, whereas the issues raised by Duns Scotus recur in all three works. Of the other opinions, the first, by Henry of Ghent, divides each category into a first intention which concerns its mode of predication and distinguishes one category from another. In the case of relation as a first intention it is the same as its foundation but as a second intention they are distinct. (Reportatio, bk. II, q. 2, B). Ockham in reply (ibid., K–O) denies that any category is separated into a second intention, as the example of quantity or quality shows; nor does he accept the identity of a relation with its foundation but follows Duns Scotus that even if several relations had the same foundation they would still differ as species. He also adds that the reason why two similar things are distinguished lies in themselves and not in something extrinsic. With Duns he is also prepared to concede that there is an accidental composition between relation and foundation.

To the second opinion—according to Baudry, of Peter Aureole—that a relation is something absolute distinct from its foundation (ibid., C) Ockham declares (ibid., P, where it is wrongly called the third opinion) that this involves a superfluity by multiplying relations infinitely. Relation is not the cause of anything absolute; only an absolute is. The third opinion (ibid., D) is that relation is something absolute distinct from its foundation, in which it is not really present, since it is added to its foundation without engendering any change in the latter. Thus a stone which is seen is distinguished from one which is unseen, and Socrates coexisting with someone else is distinguished only by a relation not in him. This, too, Ockham regards as untenable because it would make relation a substance.

only what he said of quantity and all the other categories, save substance and quality: namely, that they do not exist in themselves but only by reference to substance and/or quality.[553] In that sense the reality or non-reality of relation, as of any of the remaining seven categories, does not arise: they all stand as terms of first intention for absolutes in a nominal definition. His concern is precisely to show how they can be said to be real; to that end he sought to substitute not terms for things but diverse modes of signification for a diversity of things. He therefore reversed the traditional scholastic order. Where previously thinkers like Duns Scotus looked for a correspondence between terms and beings, Ockham reduced all concepts to different ways of signifying the same individual beings as substances and/or qualities. He therefore made a radical disjunction between logical and grammatical forms on the one hand and ontological import on the other. The causalities were abstract terms, including eight of the ten categories;[554] in being returned to what Ockham regarded as their properly conceptual status, they lost their metaphysical status as autonomous natures.

The focus of Ockham's theory of terms—as of his epistemology as a whole— is the asymmetry between terms and things, and with it between connotative and absolute terms on the one hand and supposition and signification on the other. Far from being a theory of direct correspondence of what is known to what exists, its point of departure is their discrepancy, and its novelty the attempt to reduce all forms of knowledge, incomplex and complex, to individual existence. In the case of incomplex knowledge as this chapter has shown that is principally through identifying the content of a term, as either connotative in a nominal definition or absolute in having a real definition, and the sense or supposition it can have, as a term of first or second intention, employed naturally or conventionally by imposition. Through these means it becomes possible to grasp the truth function of all terms by reference to real individual existence, and thereby their appropriate mode of predication—univocal, equivocal or connotative—when more than one individual is signified. The effect upon incomplex knowledge was, as we have seen, to deny independent standing to all universal terms taken for themselves, and to confine real signification to individual signification, since what cannot be conceived individually cannot be taken to exist. Not only is truth not, as it was for St Augustine, a quality in the mind; it cannot for Ockham go beyond the aggregation of possible individuals signified since, as we shall now consider in the case of complex forms of knowledge, it is in the relation of what is affirmed or denied to what is signified that truth consists.

---

[553] In that connection I fail to see the force of Bergmann's contention 'The Ontology of Ockham', 571, that Ockham's theory of relation lacked provision for something in each instance not localised in space as individual substances and qualities are. Ockham derived their relation from similarity or causality abstracted from individuals having likeness or dependence.

[554] Ockham, except in *Quodlibet* VII, qq. 1–7, does not treat the remaining categories separately; the same principles apply to them as to relation, as we have seen above, because they represent variations of relation.

CHAPTER FOUR

Propositions, syllogisms and demonstrations

Having examined the concepts and terms (*incomplexa*) which arise from simple —i.e. intuitive and abstractive—cognition, we pass to complex knowledge, which is of propositions. This as we have already said differs from incomplex knowledge in being of statements containing at least a noun and a verb. For Ockham, as for Aristotle and scholastic tradition, the intellect gains its understanding through propositions.[1] Hence, as we shall see, knowledge in the proper sense belongs not to things but to statements about them; propositions alone enable us to judge what is true and what is false. In Ockham's own words, 'There is no assent in respect of a thing because nothing is said when I assent to a stone or an ox'.[2] Only when we have formed what we apprehend into a proposition (*complexum*) are we in a position to assent to it or dissent from it as being or not being the case. All knowledge accordingly arises from the ways in which assent can be gained and the degrees of certainty which such assent carries. These form the object of Ockham's enquiry into propositions, syllogisms, and demonstrations.

It should thus be unnecessary to reiterate what Moody, Baudry, Boehner and others have already shown, that Ockham in confining real existence to individuals was not thereby reducing all knowledge to individual cognition. As the Prologue to the *Ordinatio*, the whole of the second and third parts of his *Logic*,[3] as well as important questions in the *Ordinatio*, *Reportatio*, and *Quodlibets*, show, Ockham was precisely concerned with establishing the different kinds of propositions and the conditions which govern strict, demonstrative knowledge. Far from denying or neglecting the universal nature of all necessary knowledge he more than any other previous medieval thinker systematically explored its scope and limits. If he was more impressed by the latter than the former, that was the result of the rigour with which he demarcated necessary from probable and merely contingent

[1] Per oppositum dicitur complexum compositum ex nomine et verbo faciens aliquem intellectum in animo audientis (Commentary on the *Categories*, *EA*, 40 b).

[2] *Quodlibet* IV, q. 17 (translated in R. McKeon, *Selections from Medieval Philosophers* (New York, 1958), II, 386).

[3] Excluding here his elaborate analysis of conditional propositions (*consequentiae*) in the third section of the third part of the *Logic*; and similarly his treatment of fallacies in his fourth logical commentary, on the *Sophistical Questions*.

knowledge. It is here that the primacy of individual cognition in knowledge is paramount, not in undermining its universality but in helping to restrict its demonstrability to what is neither indemonstrable nor contingent. Intuitive knowledge is by definition both: it is indemonstrable in being of individual existence which is its immediate and irreducible condition; it is contingent because it is of individuals as they are here and now. Whether and how such knowledge can enter into universal necessary propositions will depend upon the kinds of deductions that can be made from it. At the other extreme there are self-evident propositions; they too are indemonstrable, because also immediately known, but they are also necessary in being immediately known through their terms, so that given the terms, the propositions to which they belong must be evidently known. The diversity which lies between these two poles of immediate, and so indemonstrable, knowledge provides the focus for Ockham's analysis of propositional forms and the knowledge they engender. For the purposes of discussion we can treat it under three main heads: the role of propositions in general and their formation from incomplex knowledge; the different kinds of proposition; and finally the kinds of knowledge they yield, in syllogisms and demonstrations.

I PROPOSITIONS

So far as the first is concerned, we may best begin with Ockham's distinction between real and rational knowledge; this is the difference between propositions whose terms are of first intention and propositions whose terms are of second intention. In both cases knowledge is of terms, not directly of things. Hence real and rational knowledge differ not because one is of things and the other is of terms, but as propositions composed of different kinds of terms. Whereas first intentions stand, as we have seen in the previous chapter, in personal supposition for real individuals, second intentions stand for concepts or other terms (in simple or material supposition). The divergence between the two kinds of knowledge is thus according to whether its terms stand for what exists outside the mind or for what belongs solely to the mind.[4]

It was by this distinction, as we have also seen, that Ockham rejected universals as real, since they are terms which stand only for concepts or other terms in the mind.[5] Paradoxically, then, for those who regard Ockham as a nominalist, he

---

[4] Nunc autem ita est quod scientia aliquarum talium propositionum prolatarum est realis at aliarum rationalis, et tamen ists scita et omnes partes istorum vere sunt voces. Quia tamen partes aliquarum supponunt et stant non pro se ipsis, scilicet vocibus, sed pro rebus extra, puta pro subiectis, ideo illarum propositionum scientia dicitur realis; alie autem partes aliarum propositionum stant pro ipsis conceptibus mentis, ideo scientia illarum potest dici rationalis vel logicalis ... Quia tamen termini aliquarum propositionum stant et supponunt personaliter, scilicet pro ipsis rebus extra ... ideo talium propositionum dicitur esse scientia realis. Termini autem aliarum propositionum supponunt simpliciter, scilicet pro ipsis conceptibus ... ideo talium dicitur esse scientia rationalis (*Ordinatio*, d. 2, q. 4, 136–7).

[5] E.g. Nihil igitur refert ad scientiam realem an termini propositionis scite sint res extra animam vel tantum sint in anima, dummodo stent et supponant pro ipsis rebus extra; et ita propter scientiam realem non oportet ponere aliquas tales res universales distinctas realiter a rebus singularibus (*ibid.*, 137).

arrived at his 'nominalism' through treating knowledge as the property of terms in propositions. In his own words, 'Any knowledge is solely of propositions as of that which is known, because only propositions are known'.[6] For that reason things themselves or their parts cannot enter into real knowledge but only the terms which stand for them. It is real, as opposed to rational, in virtue of not being of universals which have no real significance as substances existing outside the mind, as the proposition 'Every body is composed of individual matter and individual form' refers only to individuals.[7]

The difference, then, between real and rational knowledge is between propositions composed of singular terms and propositions composed of universal terms. It is in the second sense that references to universal knowledge are to be understood, in denoting universal predicables of things, not universal things themselves. That is how Ockham interprets Aristotle, so that to say, 'Every man is risible' or 'Every man is capable of learning', constitutes real knowledge in virtue of being of real individuals, while to say 'Genus is predicated absolutely of different species' is rational knowledge, in not standing for real things.[8]

I   *Truth and falsity*

From this it follows that as knowledge belongs to propositions, so also do truth and falsity. That does not mean that truth and falsity are purely mental relations (*respectus rationis*) just as they are not absolutes. Rather they connote what a proposition signifies: if that corresponds with what exists *in re* it is true; if it does not it is false.[9] True and false accordingly can be said to have three properties. First, they are not themselves absolute but connotative terms which stand not for propositions themselves but their meaning.[10] As Ockham puts it, 'Therefore I agree with Aristotle, and say that the truth and falsity of a proposition are not distinct from a true and a false proposition. Hence unless these abstract terms "truth" and "falsity" include syncathegorematic terms [i.e. indefinite terms like any, some, all, none] this must be accepted absolutely, that truth is a true proposition and falsity a false proposition.'[11]

Accordingly, truth and falsity are not really present in propositions any more than subject and predicate are. For an affirmative proposition to be true, subject and

---

[6] *Ibid.*, 134.

[7] *Ibid.*, 137–8.

[8] Breviter igitur ad intentionem Philosophi est dicendum quod scientia realis non per hoc distinguitur a rationali quia scienta realis est de rebus, ita quod ipse res sunt propositiones scite vel partes illarum propositionum scitarum, et rationalis non est sic de rebus, sed per hoc quod partes, scilicet termini propositionum scitarum scientia reali, stant et supponunt pro rebus, non sic autem termini propositionum scitarum scientia rationali, sed illi termini stant et supponunt pro aliis (*ibid.*, 138). Also d. 27, q. 3, AA.

[9] Ad aliud dico quod veritas et falsitas propositionis non dicunt parvos respectus rationis, sed sunt conceptus relativi significantes ipsas propositiones non absolute. Sed veritas sive iste conceptus veritas ultra propositionem quam significat connotat quod ita sit in re sicut importatur per propositionem. Et falsitas importat quod non sit ita in re sicut importatur per propositionem (*Quodlibet* VII, q. 4.)

[10] *Ibid.*; also *SL*, I, ch. 43, 120.

[11] *Quodlibet* v, q. 24; *SL, ibid.*

predicate must stand for the same thing; but they do not have to be really the same, nor has one to inhere in the other or to be in some other way united. To say 'Socrates is a man' or 'Socrates is an animal' does not entail the existence of something called 'humanity' or 'animality' in Socrates, or that one or other is his essence or his quiddity.[12] We have seen in the third chapter the absurdities which result from treating predicates as real qualities distinct from the subject,[13] instead of recognising them as terms which are affirmed of the same thing as that for which the subject stands. In the second place, then, truth depends upon conformity between what is known in the intellect with what exists outside it *in re*. This is not a simple relation: both the act of knowing and what is known have to enter into a proposition, which, as we shall shortly see, can only be by means of an act of assent. Hence each is only a partial cause of the truth which results. The thing known can be called the measure of truth not in virtue of its own substance but according to what can be attributed to it through a complex act. That is the sense in which Ockham interprets Aristotle and Averroes, that the measure is prior—in being and cognition—to the measured: the existence of the thing guarantees the truth of the act of knowing it, by which there is assent to the thing as true. To that degree the knowable is the measure of knowledge, the truth of one leading to the truth of the other; but it cannot be the whole truth and so not the total cause, since the truth of what can be known lies in more than the thing's existence.[14]

That may help to explain the absence, upon which Baudry has remarked,[15] of any reference by Ockham to the classic scholastic definition of truth as 'the correspondence of thing and intellect' (*adequatio rei et intellectus*); the word 'correspondence' occurs nowhere in that context. Now since truth consists in more than a simple term, like 'white' or 'man', it cannot correspond exclusively to a simple thing; rather, as we have just seen, the truth in a thing can be the cause of truth in the intellect, which means being able to affirm or deny something of the thing. That requires the conjunction in a proposition of subject and predicate through a copula, so that any true statement must contain at least three terms.[16] Its truth is, as we saw, conditional upon subject and predicate standing for the same thing. But that does not make them the same; subject and predicate by definition are distinct as terms and have distinct meanings. Thus for the proposition 'Man is an animal' or 'Man is capable of laughter' to be true, 'man', 'animal' and 'capable of laughter'

---

[12] *SL*, II, ch. 2, 224–5.

[13] Rehearsed, *ibid.*, 225–7.

[14] Tunc ad Philosophum et Commentatorem dico quod res extra non est mensura actus intelligendi; sed veritas in intellectu mensuratur veritate que est in re, quia in eo quod res est vel non est etc.; et non est res mensura actus assentiendi secundum substantiam suam sed solum secundum quod denominatur cui assentit. Et veritas in re distinguitur a veritate in intellectu sicut res a ratione; et veritas similiter in intellectu (dico complexa) distinguitur ab actu intelligendi. Et potest dici mensura actus assentiendi veritas in re quatenus certificat de veritate actus intelligendi, quia ex hoc quod cognosco sic esse in re, ex hoc cognosco quod actus per quem rei assentimus est verus. Unde scibile est mensura scientie, vel quia scibile est causa partialis scientie, vel quia veritas in scibili est causa veritatis in scientia. Et aliter non est mensura, quia per veritatem in re ducor in cognitionem veritatis in scientia (*Reportatio*, II, q. II, M).

[15] *Lexique*, 292.

[16] *SL*, II, ch. I, 217.

must all be able to stand for the same thing. They do not thereby become tautological, since their community lies in what they stand for, not their own signification as terms.[17]

'Subject' can be taken as a term or as something real; in this second sense it
means strictly the subject of real accidents which inhere in it but of which it can
exist independently as a substance, and broadly anything—including matter—
which is really the subject of accidents inhering in it. As a term, subject is the part
of a proposition which precedes the verb as 'man' is the subject of the proposition
'Man is an animal'. Subject in this sense can broadly belong to any proposition,
true or false; strictly only to a true proposition; and more strictly to the conclusion of a demonstration, when it can also be the subject of a particular branch of
knowledge, as we shall discuss in the next chapter. There is also a final and strictest
sense by which subject can mean that which is first among subjects; but common to
all of these is that a subject in virtue of predication.[18] We can add, though Ockham
does not say so explicitly, that subject is therefore a term of second intention
denoting other terms. Much the same applies to 'predicate' as the other term (or
extreme) in a proposition and the one following the verb or copula. It can belong
to false or true propositions, in the latter by direct predication as 'animal' is the
predicate of 'man', but not of 'stone'. Strict predication includes each of the five
(four for Aristotle) predicables as universals, when it concerns strict knowledge;
for as we shall discuss later only universal propositions constitute strict knowledge.[19]

As we shall also consider in due course it is in being able to affirm or deny an
attribute of a thing that knowledge of any kind consists. More immediately it
indicates the complex nature of all knowledge which makes the traditional formula
of correspondence inappropriate. Truth as a connotative term does not signify
any one thing, and in its negative aspect it lies in the discrepancy between subject
and predicate over the same thing.[20] Ockham's own definition of knowledge as
the similarity of the object (*intellectus est similitudo rei*)[21] would seem to confirm
this view. It springs from his disjunction between concepts, which can be universal,
and being which is only individual. Ontologically, their similarity is in inverse

---

[17] Sed ex hoc non sequitur quod propositiones non sunt vere, quia non sequitur, subiectum
est alia res a predicato, ergo propositio non est vera. Nam per talem propositionem 'Homo est
animal', vel 'Homo est risibilis' non denotatur quod subiectum sit predicatum sed quod stant
pro eodem; et ideo est propositio vera (*Ordinatio*, d. 27, q. 3, AA). Also: Et si dicatur quod si
in tali propositione subiectum et predicatum supponerent preo eodem, tunc idem predicaretur
de se, dicendum quod non sequitur: quia quamvis idem sit pro quod supponit tam subiectum
quam predicatum, tamen illud quod supponit non est idem ... et hoc quia illud quod sub-
iicitur non est idem cum eo quod predicatur, quia aliud est quod supponit et pro quo supponit
(*SL*, II, ch. 3, 231–2). Also *Reportatio*, III, q. 9, A; *Quodlibet* III, 95.

[18] *SL*, I, ch. 30, 84–5.

[19] *Ibid.*, ch. 31, 85–6.

[20] Et ad veritatem talium [propositionum] sufficit quod subiectum et predicatum supponant
pro aliquo eodem, si sit propositio affirmativa ... Sed si talis sit negativa, requiritur quod
subiectum et predicatum non supponunt pro omni eodem, immo requiritur quod subiectum
pro nullo supponat vel quod supponat pro aliquo pro quod predicatum non supponit ...
(*ibid.*, II, ch. 3, 229).

[21] *Reportatio*, q. 15, EE.

proportion to a concept's degree of universality: as we saw in the last chapter, the more individual or specific a concept, the truer its likeness to what it represents. Logically, however, their correspondence is one of supposition, not real likeness; any term imposed upon a thing or a concept or another term can be said to re-present it regardless of whether or not they are really like one another.[22] That is the difference between a conventional and a natural sign: it holds not only for terms but also for propositions whose signification, and so level of truth, will be according to whether its terms are of first or second intention and the supposition they are in.

There is therefore an asymmetry between truth and being. On the one hand, ontologically, they are, to quote the *Logic*, 'convertible'; 'truth', like 'intelligible' or 'good', is a transcendental term, predicable of every other term and connoting being which can be known by the intellect.[23] Its foundation is the existence or non-existence of that denoted by a proposition; hence truth is always *a parte rei*. As the Commentary on the *Categories* expresses it, 'A proposition is called true because it signifies the thing as it is'.[24] In terms of being, then, the order is always from what is to how it is known; never the other way.[25]

On the other hand truth as a connotative term is known through propositions; it signifies the proposition and connotes what the proposition signifies. It therefore depends upon conformity between proposition and significate. In the words of the Commentary on the *Categories*, 'Truth and falsity are terms predicable of pro-positions and denote that what is signified is or is not as signified by the proposition acting as its sign'.[26] Now this is essentially a matter of supposition; according to whether a proposition stands for itself or for something else it will be neutral, true or false. Strictly speaking incomplex terms cannot be true or false; but they can be taken significatively in personal supposition, and in one of two different ways. Either the terms are of first intention and signify real things, in virtue of which they can be judged true or false: for example the proposition 'Man is an animal' is true if subject and predicate both stand for the same thing, namely man as he is an animal. Alternatively, the word 'proposition' or an equivalent incomplex sign, such as the letter 'A', can stand personally for the same proposition; it can then similarly be designated true or false because in each case the proposition is under-stood significatively. In the first, 'Man is an animal' stands for what exists outside the proposition; in the second, 'proposition' or 'A' stands for 'Man is an animal' as a

---

[22] That presumably is the sense of Boehner's statement that universals 'are in a relation of similarity, that there is a correspondence between them and a representation of the one by the other' (*Collected Articles*, 162).

[23] Et eodem modo dicendum est de 'vero' et 'bono', quia 'verum' quod ponitur convertibile cum 'ente' significat idem quod intelligibile (*SL*, I, ch. 10, 36).

[24] *EA*, 53 c.

[25] E.g. Quia ex re dependet veritas propositionis, quamvis non econverso; immo ad hoc quod homo sit asinus vel non sit asinus, nihil facit intellectus. Sed quod hec propositio 'Homo non est asinus' sit vera non sufficit quod homo non sit asinus, sed requiritur quod ista propositio, 'Homo non est asinus' sit (*Ordinatio*, d. 24, q. 1, o).

[26] Sed veritas et falsitas sunt sunt quedam predicabilia de propositione importantia quod est ita vel non est ita a parte significati, sicut denotatur per propositionem que est signum (Com-mentary on *Perihermenias, EA*, 91 d). See also Commentaty on the *Categories* (*ibid.*, 53 c). As will be seen this is not a literal translation.

proposition, and is true or false according to whether man is or is not an animal. Hence we can say 'A is true' when we know that man is an animal.[27] There are thus two levels of truth corresponding to the level of intention; but whether it is first or second, the proposition to be true or false must always have personal supposition; which means that it must always signify something other than itself, either another proposition or the things or terms for which its terms stand, in the way just described. That precludes a proposition from having simple or material supposition, although its terms can. There is all the difference between 'A' when it stands significatively for 'Man is an animal' and when it stands only for itself as 'proposition', understood either as an incomplex term or word. Only in the first sense where it has personal supposition does it stand for something else and so can be true or false. To say 'A is true' when A stands only for A is meaningless, since it has no signification.[28]

This distinction overcomes apparent insolubles of the kind of the paradox of the liar by which, in its medieval version, Socrates declares that what he says is false: to the sophist it must follow that, since this is Socrates's only sentence, in saying something false he is speaking the truth; and conversely if he is lying he is also speaking the truth. Ockham's reply is that one proposition alone without reference to anything else cannot be true or false, for the reasons we have just examined: namely, that something other than the proposition itself must be signified. To say 'This proposition is false or true' (in simple supposition) is equivalent to saying that Socrates does not say something true or false beyond the proposition in which 'true' or 'false' occur as terms: in other words 'true' and 'false' are here part of the proposition. They are not predicated of it; nor as parts can they at the same time be predicated of the whole. As predicables of propositions, 'true' and 'false' must by definition be logically higher (i.e. predicable of more) than the propositions which they signify; only if the logically higher can stand for the logically lower can there be a valid consequence from one to the other. If in the proposition 'Man is an animal', 'animal' cannot stand for 'man' it cannot follow that, if Socrates is a man, Socrates is also an animal. In the same way, in the proposition 'Socrates says something false', 'false' does not stand for the entire proposition, and so the proposition cannot be called either false or true. It remains a single statement without reference to anything save itself.[29]

[27] Sciendum quod aliquod incomplexum supponens respectu veri vel falsi potest habere suppositionem simplicem vel personalem. Si simplicem vel materialem sic nullum incomplexum est verum vel falsum; et sic etiam hoc predicatum 'verum' vel 'falsum' non predicatur vere de aliquo incomplexo. Si habeat suppositionem personalem, sic de aliquo incomplexo vere predicatur hoc predicatum 'verum' vel 'falsum', sic de hoc termino 'propositio' verificatur quod aliqua propositio est vera vel falsa ... Similiter si A instituatur ad significandum hanc propositionem: 'Homo est animal', tunc hec est vera, 'A est verum', si A supponat personaliter, et falsa si supponeret pro se. Et isto modo in respondendo frequenter utimur una dictione pro propositione et pro uno complexo, et ita ista dictio neque est vera neque falsa; sed illa propositio pro qua utimur illa dictione est vera vel falsa (Commentary on the *Categories*, ibid., 43 d; also 53 c).

[28] *Ibid.* First part of text from Boehner's version (*Collected Articles*, 255, n. 31).

[29] Text quoted (in translation) by Boehner (*ibid.*) from the *Logic*, for which he gives no reference.

That leads to the third aspect of truth and falsity: that they can belong to the same proposition if its signification changes. For that the proposition does not have itself to change; nor can it be both true and false at the same time. Rather it loses its original connotation and acquires another through no longer signifying the same situation, as it can be first true to say 'You are sitting', while you sit, and afterwards false when you are no longer sitting. It is in that sense that a proposition can have successively (as opposed to simultaneously) contrary meanings: further evidence that truth and falsity are not real qualities in the way that black and white are. Nor do they inhere in propositions, but are terms predicable of propositions according to what the latter signify.[30]

2   The formation of propositions: apprehension and assent

Next we must examine how the intellect gains knowledge through propositions. That involves distinguishing the elements which lead to a judgement that something is or is not the case—knowledge in the proper sense. There are three: incomplex cognition of a proposition's terms (Socrates and white); complex knowledge of them as a proposition (Socrates is white); and assent to or dissent from or doubt over the proposition by which we judge it to be true or false or neither. The main distinction is between the first two acts, both of which constitute apprehension, and the third which is judgement or assent (or dissent). Just as apprehension concerns anything known by the intellect, incomplex or complex, so assent can only be towards an incomplex or complex; in the first case it is to existence; in the second to what is true and false since only propositions can, as we have seen, be judged true or false.[31] From that it follows that every act of judgement or assent presupposes apprehension of both a proposition as a complex and of its incomplex terms.[32] Although, naturally perhaps, one is not separable from the other, they are

[30] Sed accipiendo secundo modo pro terminis et hoc large, non stricte, et suscipere secundo modo [sc. pro predicatione], sic verum et falsum sunt contraria, et propositio recipit contraria successive per predicationem, licet non simul, quia de eadem propositione numero primo predicatur ille terminus 'verum', et postea ille terminus 'falsum'. Sed per hoc nihil realiter recipitur in propositione nunc quam prius, sed ideo recipit successive predicationem illorum contrariorum quia nunc significat aliter esse a parte rei quam est, et prius significabat ita esse a parte sicut fuit. Sicut ista propositio 'Tu sedes', ponamus quod modo sit falsa et prius fuerit vera. Nunc significat te sedere et tamen non sedes, ideo est falsa, sed prius fuit vera, quia prius sedisti . . . Ideo dico quod veritas potest esse falsitas, sicut propositio vera potest esse falsa. Sed hec est neganda veritas est falsitas sicut hec propositio vera est falsa propositio. (*Quodlibet* v, q. 24). Also *SL*, I, ch. 43, 118–19, *Ordinatio*, d. 39, E and *Reportatio*, III, q. 4, R.

[31] Est igitur prima distinctio ista quod inter actus intellectus sunt duo actus quorum unus est apprehensivus, et est respectu cuiuslibet quod potest terminare actum potentie intellective, sive sit complexum sive incomplexum . . . Alius actus potest dici iudicativus quo intellectus non tantum apprehendit obiectum sed etiam illi assentit vel dissentit. Et iste actus est tantum respectu complexi, quia nulli assentimus per intellectum nisi quod verum reputamus nec dissentimus nisi quod falsum estimamus. Et sic pauet quod respectu complexi potest esse duplex actus, scilicet actus apprehensivus et actus iudicativus. (*Ordinatio*, Prologue, q. 1, 16).

[32] Ex istis sequitur secunda conclusio quod omnis actus iudicativus presupponit in eadem potentia notitiam incomplexam terminorum, quia presupponit actum apprehensivum. Et actus apprehensivus respectu alicuius complexi presupponit notitiam incomplexam terminorum, secundum Commentatorem III *De anima*, commento 21 (*ibid.*, 21).

as acts really distinct[33] and God by his absolute power could make them each independent acts.[34] This is in accordance with the order of knowing, which is from intuition of individual existence—the condition of all exterior knowledge[35]—to the terms and propositions which can be formed from it in abstraction: as we shall see the problem of demonstration is over their relation when neither experience is immediate nor a proposition is self-evident.

Now while complex knowledge does not entail incomplex knowledge, it must derive from it;[36] indeed abstractive knowledge in the wider sense of all that is not intuitive cognition must have the latter as partial cause, granted that it is in the intellect as opposed to the senses.[37] There is thus a sequence from individual experience to judgement of a complex in which each succeeding stage is dependent upon the preceding one, but not *vice versa*: incomplex knowledge can be without apprehension of a complex, and complex apprehension can be without assent, where neither complex apprehension can be without incomplex, nor assent without apprehension.[38] And in not standing naturally alone without apprehension, assent may be said to be a certain kind of apprehension.[39] That, however, is not to blur their difference. On the analogy of the relation between evidence and assent we may regard apprehension and assent as distinguished not in the act of judgement itself but as superior and inferior, where one is included in the other.[40] Like complex and incomplex knowledge they are of different species which can yet coexist without contradiction or mutual destruction.[41]

---

[33] Ad primum istorum dico quod actus apprehensivus distinguitur realiter ab actu assentiendi et dissentiendi et dubitandi, et est compossibilis cuilibet eorum, quamvis forte naturaliter non possit fieri sine quolibet eorum. Et ideo stant simul quod quicumque apprehendit aliquam propositionem assentit illi vel dissentit vel dubitat de ea, et tamen quod actus apprehensivus distinguitur realiter a quolibet eorum (*ibid.*, 57–8). Also *Quodlibet* IV, q. 17.

[34] Ad secundum potest dici probabiliter quod notitia incomplexa terminorum et apprehensio complexi et iudicium sequens distinguuntur realiter et quod quodlibet istorum per potentiam divinam est a quolibet separabile. *Ordinatio, ibid.*, 58–9).

[35] *Ibid.*, 67–8.

[36] Quia certum est quod preter notitiam complexam qua cognoscuntur termini est una notitia incomplexa cuiuslibet termini (*ibid.*, 60).

[37] E.g. *Reportatio*, II, qq. 14 and 15, E: Et tunc si ista duo, abstractivum et intuitivum dividant omnem cognitionem tam complexam quam incomplexam, tunc iste cognitiones dicerentur cognitiones abstractive, et omnis cognitio complexa diceretur abstractiva, sive sit in presentia rei stante cognitione intuitiva extremorum sive in absentia rei et non stante cognitione intuitiva. Et tunc secundum istam viam potest concedi quod cognitio intuitiva tam intellectus quam sensus est causa partialis cognitionis abstractive que predicto modo habetur. And *Ordinatio*, Prologue, q. I, 22.

[38] Dico quod naturaliter primum est separabile a duobus sequentibus, et secundum a tertio; sed tertium nullo modo est separabile a duobus precedentibus, nec secundum a primo (*Ordinatio, ibid.*, 60.)

[39] Potest dici quod non est contradictio quod aliquis intellectus assentiat alicui propositioni et tamen non apprehendat eam una apprensione distincta realiter ab illo assensu. Tamen quod assentiret et nullo modo apprehenderet includeret contradictionem. Et ideo posset dici quod assensus est quedam apprehensio (*ibid.*, 59).

[40] Et in omnibus istis patet quod evidentia in actu assentiendi non distinguitur ab ipso actu, sed distinguitur sicut superius et inferius, quia sequitur: evidenter assentit, ergo assentit, sed non sequitur e converso (*Reportatio*, II, q. 25, Y).

[41] *Ordinatio, ibid.*, 60.

This represents one of Ockham's main arguments for the distinction between apprehension and assent; it rests mainly upon a psychological explanation of how the mind elicits its different acts. Among the doubts and objections raised, he accepts the third that if apprehension and assent were really distinct it would mean that there could be diverse simultaneous acts in the intellect. Not only is that true of apprehension and assent, which have a defined order, but also of acts which do not have an order, for example the act of knowing that someone is loved where the act of loving presupposes incomplex knowledge of what is loved: there are here two different acts mediated by an act of will. In each case the intellect has diverse acts simultaneously.[42]

The second argument—not in sequence—is the familiar one that habits follow their acts and can only incline to acts of another habit if their own acts do so first. An apprehensive habit, however, inclines to a judicative act; and since it must already incline to an apprehensive act, there must be both apprehensive and judicative acts together in the intellect. By the same token an apprehensive act, in coming first, can be without an act of assent; for if someone frequently thinks of a proposition to which he is initially indifferent, i.e. treating it as neither true nor false, and then comes to assent to it, he will himself be ready to assent to it subsequently as the first act of assent. But such an inclination cannot be solely from one act of assent because only by first reflecting upon a proposition is someone then inclined to give it his assent. That is to say, the inclination is in part from a habit acquired from previous acts of apprehension.[43] The same applies to an act of doubting a proposition, which becomes assent; in each case, together with the habit of apprehension or doubt, there must be another habit inclining to assent.[44]

That in turn meets the third objection that it is not the habit of apprehension but a further principle, not previously in existence, which is the cause of the act of assent; for it is only in virtue of apprehension that such a principle is engendered. Hence the latter is only a partial cause together with the habit.[45]

In a later addition in the *Ordinatio* Ockham specified that for the intellect to assent to a complex through something else, could mean either that this additional power was the cause of the intellect's assent, and then this would be immediately through the act of apprehension; or it could mean that this other power facilitates the act of assent, in which case it will not be through the act of apprehension, although the latter remains efficient cause.[46] Whichever the interpretation, the act of apprehension is the prerequisite of the act of assent.

On the one hand, then, assent must be to a proposition already apprehended; on the other, apprehension can be neutral, and independent of either assent or dissent, so that if one or other subsequently follows it can only be through previous

---

[42] *Ibid.*, 19–20, 59–60.

[43] *Ibid.*, 17–18; also *Quodlibet* v, q. 6.

[44] Ergo quando acquirebatur habitus dubitativus, acquirebatur etiam aliquis alius habitus qui adhuc manet et inclinat ad actum assentiendi (*Ordinatio, ibid.*, 58).

[45] *Ibid.*, 19–20.

[46] *Ibid.*

apprehension.[47] These are the main grounds for keeping them two acts distinct according to an irreversible order.

From the second book of the *Reportatio*[48] and four quodlibetal questions[49] we are enabled to pursue in more detail the characteristics of apprehension and assent. Already in the Prologue of the *Ordinatio*, as we saw in the first chapter, Ockham distinguishes briefly between the judgement accompanying intuitive knowledge of something's existence or non-existence and a judgement about a proposition. Only the second can properly be called judgement in being concerned with a complex; the first is inseparable from an act of intuition and so equivalent to perception of existence or non-existence. As such it is included in intuitive cognition which by definition can be without an act of assent or dissent, as the terms of a self-evident proposition could be known without knowing the proposition.[50]

This distinction between two kinds of judgement—or rather its identification with assent to a proposition—is repeated in the *Quodlibets*[51] By the first kind nothing is strictly known in the sense—mentioned earlier—that nothing is said when we assent to a stone or an ox or an ass or white or any other incomplex, whether a thing or a term; we only know that one is not the other.[52] Hence only the second kind of judgement—as assent to a proposition—constitutes real knowledge; which conforms to the philosophers' common view that the habit of a conclusion—as the effect of a demonstration—is the object of knowledge.[53] We shall have more to say about that later. Here it means that since knowledge is assent to the conclusion of a proposition, assent will vary with the nature of the proposition apprehended; so will the agent which gives or withholds assent. According to how a proposition is known—as self-evident and necessary, contingent, doubtful, or credible—judgement will be from either the intellect or will, or both, as Baudry recognised in correcting the older view that assent was exclusively an act of will.[54]

[47] E.g. *Quodlibet* v, q. 6.

[48] Questions 15 and 25.

[49] *Quodlibet* III, 6; IV, q. 17; V, q. 6; VII, q. 6.

[50] Ad sextum dubium [de notitia intuitiva et illo iudicio quo iudicatur res esse vel non esse (*Ordinatio*, Prologue, q. 1, 55)] dico quod notitia illa intuitiva et illud iudicium distinguuntur realiter, quia illa notitia intuitiva est respectu incomplexi; illud autem iudicium est respectu complexi. Et si queratur de iudicio consequente precise notitiam intuitivam sensitivam an distinguatur ab illa, potest dici quod non distinguitur ab illa, sicut nec iudicium intellectus quod stat precise in notitia incomplexa; et ideo non est iudicium sequens nec est proprie iudicium, quia non est respectu alicuius complexi, sed tantum est iudicium equivalenter, sicut alias dicetur [*ibid.*, 139–40].

Ad primum argumentum in contrarium dico quod potest fieri illa notitia intuitiva sine iudicio consequente . . . sicut non est impossibile quod aliquis cognoscat terminos alicuius propositionis per se note et tamen non sciat illam propositionem, etiam posito quod apprehendat (*Ordinatio*, 69–70).

[51] *Quodlibet* III, q. 6; IV, q. 17.

[52] *Ibid.*

[53] E.g. Loquendo vero de actu secundo sciendi vel assentiendi dico quod ille actus est proprie actus complexivus qui habet pro obiecto complexum, quia ille actus est quo aliquid verum scitur; sed res extra non scitur . . . Et de tali actu loquuntur communiter philosophi. Dicunt enim quod effectus demonstrationis est habitus conclusionis, et per consequens actus correspondens habitui est habitus conclusionis tamquam obiecti (*Quodlibet*, III, q. 6).

[54] *Lexique*, 132–5, in opposition to Abbagnano and others.

The ways in which judgement occurs are discussed in question twenty-five of the second book of the *Reportatio*. So far as it concerns the intellect, its assent, dissent or doubt are involved in any proposition where knowledge—as opposed to faith—is involved. Self-evident, contingent, and neutral propositions, in being known, all carry the intellect's judgement. Self-evident and necessary propositions do so necessarily without any activity on the part of the intellect which in knowing such a proposition and its terms must assent to it.[55] The only other cause here as in everything else is God. Contingent propositions can receive assent or dissent in two ways: either as a first contingent proposition which is known through immediate intuitive cognition of its terms, the condition of all evident knowledge; or assent can be to a second contingent proposition derived from assent to the first (together with apprehension, incomplex and complex, of it), with the second act of assent the necessary cause of the second act.[56] When a proposition is doubtful or neutral it can be known either deductively through a middle, or in some other non-deductive way. For a proposition to be inferred from a middle, there has to be another prior and better known proposition as the middle term from which the neutral proposition can be deduced—necessarily or probably according to whether the prior proposition is necessary or probable.[57] The latter therefore serves as the premise for the neutral proposition as conclusion. That explains how there can be a wrong judgement through mistaking the prior proposition as true when it is false, or through faulty inference from it to the conclusion.[58] Assent or dissent which is non-deductive, i.e. inductive, can be necessary by means of principles drawn exclusively from experience. Thus the necessary proposition 'Everything hot is heat-giving' is derived from assent to an evident contingent proposition, namely 'This heat is heat-giving', which is known intuitively, together with a self-evident—and so universal—proposition, known also from experience, that 'All forms of the same nature can produce effects of the same nature'. Only when a proposition is contingent does the intellect assent or dissent either because of authority or of the will, which in apprehending a proposition, wishes to believe it.[59]

We can see then that the intellect is only dependent for its assent or dissent upon

---

[55] Ideo dico quod propositio cui intellectus assentit vel est per se nota et necessaria vel contingens vel neutra. Si primo modo assensus causatur sufficienter ex notitiis incomplexis terminorum et notitia apprehensiva complexa, et a deo tamquam a causa partiali sine omni activitate intellectus, quia positis istis necessario sequitur assensus respectu talis propositionis (*Reportatio*, II, q. 25, L).

[56] Si secundo modo, tunc illa propositio vel est prima contingens, vel sequitur ex prima evidenter. Si primo modo tunc ille assensus causatur ex notitia incomplexa terminorum et ex apprehensione complexi sufficienter sine omni alio excepto deo . . . Si secundo modo, tunc assensus respectu secunde contingentis causatur ex notitia incomplexa terminorum suorum et apprehensione illius complexi et assensu respectu prime contingentis, quia ille assensus necessario requiritur ad causandum assensum secundum (*ibid.*).

[57] Si sit neutra vel dubia, tunc aut habetur aliqua propositio prior et evidentior ex qua tamquam ex medio potest necessario inferri vel probabiliter, vel sophistice vel non . . . Unde assensus evidens et certus respectu premissarum causat cum aliis predictis notitiis assensum necessarium et evidentem respectu conclusionis sequentis. Assensus probabilis qui est cum dubitatione sui opposti respectu premissarum potest causare dissensum respectu conclusionum (*ibid.*).

[58] *Ibid.*   [59] *Ibid.*

the will or some authority when it is unable to recognise a proposition's truth or falsity; that occurs when it lacks self-evident or evident knowledge or the means of arriving at a necessary or probable conclusion through deduction or experience. Otherwise the will cannot command the intellect's assent or dissent; and if someone knows a proposition evidently to which he assents, only persuasion by a stronger reason—not the will—can move him to dissent unless he should forget what he knows evidently. That, however, does not occur with inevident propositions where assent can be at the will's behest; so that a theologian could obey the will, and disbelieve what study had taught him to believe, without needing to forget it first.[60] Nevertheless in both cases assent, however caused, is from the intellect not the will. At most the will directly compels assent; it does not itself give or withhold it.

That brings us to the different roles of the intellect and the will in complex knowledge. They are treated mainly and most explicitly in the same twenty-fifth question of the second book of the *Reportatio*, which is a reply to twenty-one arguments affirming the active nature of the intellect. Ockham accepts its activity but denies its demonstrability; beyond the authority of the *sancti* and the philosophers, above all Aristotle, there are only probable reasons, not proofs, for the intellect as an active power,[61] as we shall consider in chapter eight. So far as assent is concerned we have just seen that it is given or withheld exclusively by the intellect where propositions are self-evident or evident. Elsewhere the will enters into the intellect's judgement; and in three main areas. The first, which needs no further discussion, is when a proposition is at once contingent and inevident in the way previously remarked: for then the will can command the intellect's assent or dissent. The second which we have also encountered is where the intellect can assent to a proposition, initially neutral or doubtful, through deduction; and the third concerns changes in the intensity or awareness with which the intellect knows or judges what it knows. We shall examine the last two and then consider the role of the will in apprehension.

All discursive acts by which one proposition is inferred syllogistically from another through a middle term involve the will. They are not mere acts of apprehension; even if they were, that would not make the intellect active, since it would then syllogise naturally, as opposed to freely, and there would be no explanation why it should do so at one time rather than another.[62] In fact, however,

---

[60] Preterea, quicumque scit evidenter aliquod complexum, non potest dissentire illi complexo solo imperio voluntatis, sed oportet quod persuadeatur per rationem fortius moventem intellectum suum ad dissentiendum, vel oportet quod obliviscatur alicuius evidenter noti. Sed theologus quantamcumque studuerit in theologia, solo imperio voluntatis potest dissentire credibilibus etiam sine ratione fortius movente; quia nulla ratio ex falsis potest fortius movere quam ratio ex veris evidenter notis; nec oportet quod obliviscatur alicuius ad hoc quod dissentiat. Ergo non habet notitiam evidentem respectu alicuius talis (*Ordinatio*, Prologue, q. 7, 192).

[61] Sciendum est quod circumscripta omnium sanctorum auctoritate et philosophorum propter nullam rationem necessario concludentem oportet ponere intellectum activum sed solum passivum, et equaliter possunt rationes solvi ponendo unum passivum sicut activum (*Reportatio*, II, q. 25, A; also AA).

[62] *Ibid.*, N.

syllogisms result from disposing propositions in a particular mode and figure. For that, incomplex knowledge of the terms and volition suffice, together with God, as the total cause. Granted these, nothing else need be posited. There is thus no place for the intellect's activity beyond that of the will in deciding to form certain propositions from terms already apprehended.[63]

Similarly the will is the agent in all cognitive acts which entail more than simple apprehension or judgements of truth and falsity; for there is then an additional psychological element regulating the intellect's response to what is known. Thus the will is the cause of the intellect's knowing something more at one time than another: for however active the intellect may be in knowing an object its role will be that of a neutral agent whose knowledge is due to the presence of the object, granting which the intellect will continue to know as before. Hence if its knowledge varies there must be some further cause beyond the intellect and the object; this is the will freely willing to know in some other way.[64]

That applies to any variation in cognitive acts; changes in intensity leading to more or less perfect cognition, or effort or attention, come from the will alone.[65] So also do acts of comparison and reflexion.[66] The reason is the same in each case: namely that whether the intellect is regarded as active or passive it is exclusively a natural agent whose actions are consequently invariable.[67] Its knowledge therefore remains unchanging, whatever it knows. The will in contrast is a free agent able to choose what it knows and how it knows it. That is the great division between them; it applies to both sensitive and intellective knowledge of which equally the will can be the immediate cause.[68] The division is therefore essentially between different modes of knowing. The intellect responds only to what it takes to be truth or falsity; the will to what it desires to know or believe; the intellect's role is veridical, determined by the nature of the evidence; the will's role is affective, determining its act of knowing and believing. That can be seen in the way in which the will is able to know—by a reflexive act—that it loves. Its initial act of loving has the intellect for its efficient cause since the will can only love what it first knows;

[63] Ideo dico quod predicti actus discurrendi, syllogisandi etc non sunt actus apprehensivi, quia facere syllogismum non est nisi formare propositiones dispositas in modo et figura; et sic est de discursu. Isti inquam actus causantur sufficienter a notitiis incomplexis terminorum et actu voluntatis, quo voluntas vult talia complexa formare, ita quod ille notitie incomplexe terminorum et volitio integrant unam causam totalem cum deo respectu talium actuum, quia positis notitiis predictis et volitione predicta statim sine omni activitate intellectus sequitur naturaliter sicut effectus actus syllogisandi (*ibid.*, N).

[64] *Ibid.*, I.

[65] *Ibid.*, T–U.

[66] *Ibid.*, P–R. Also *Ordinatio*, Prologue, q. 1, 68.

[67] E.g. Ad aliud dico quod ita non concludit intellectum esse activum, quia si sit activus ageret naturaliter, et per consequens non causaret plus actum fidei uno tempore quam alio (*Reportatio*, *ibid.*, V. And: Ad aliud dico quod equaliter concludit contra activitatem intellectus sicut pro, quia ita intellectus est causa naturalis sicut intellectio vel obiectum (*ibid.*, Q). And: Ex hoc patet ad aliud quod est in potestate voluntatis reflectere se super actum suum et actum intellectus, et non sic est in potestate intellectus, quia est pure passivus; et si esset activus, adhuc cum naturaliter ageret non est in eius potestate plus reflectere se super unum actum quam super alium (*ibid.*, R).

[68] *Ibid.*, U.

by the same token it cannot love without knowing that it loves. To acquire such further knowledge, there has to be a second volition caused by the preceding volition and its accompanying cognition; it can then know its first volition without any further action by the intellect. In that sense both intellect and will can in turn be efficient causes of one another's actions: the intellect of the will's first volition, the will of its second act by which its first act is known.[69]

Conversely experience shows that the intellect alone does not reflect upon its knowledge: if it did, it would follow that all incomplex cognition would be immediately accompanied by acts of reflexion; that would mean an infinite series of acts each engendered by the previous one.[70] And similarly with acts of comparison or any others due to intervention by the will: the intellect alone will not know them if inevident and will know them unalterably when it knows them: any change is because of the will.[71]

Again, faith in a proposition can be acquired with or without the assent of the will but always independently of the intellect. Thus if an act of believing some proposition follows from prior faith in another proposition, the second act of faith will depend upon neither will nor intellect for assent, since to hold one belief without the other would be contradictory. When, on the other hand, there is no such pre-existing faith, an act of faith is due to the will alone, for the intellect does not—as we have seen—assent to what cannot be known self-evidently or evidently through deduction or experience.[72]

In these ways, then, assent or cognition by the will can be autonomous, just as assent by the intellect to veridical propositions owes nothing to the prompting of the will. Psychologically, however, as volition derives from cognition and only becomes autonomous subsequently, so cognition, when it is apprehension of a proposition, depends upon volition, as we must now consider.

Apprehension, like assent, is of two kinds: one is the formation of a proposition —or composition or division; the other is knowledge of a proposition already formed.[73] Composition or division consists in joining two incomplex terms by a verb—as copula—through which one term, the predicate, is affirmed (composition) or denied (division) of the other term, the subject. Although there are three terms in the formation (or first apprehension) of a proposition, two acts of cognition

---

[69] Respondeo primus actus [voluntatis] causatur a cognitione qua ille intellectus cognoscitur, quia nihil est amatum nisi cognitum a voluntate immediate; et secundus similiter. Et ita videtur esse coniunctim in istis actibus, quia actus intellectus est causa efficiens actus voluntatis, et e converso non respectu eiusdem actus sed respectu diversorum. Et it a quando quis amat non oportet quod percipiat se amare, sed statim quando voluntas vult actum suum cognosci. Secunda volitio causatur a voluntate et a prima volitione et cognitione qua cognoscitur obiectum amatum, et istis positis statim sine omni activitate intellectus sequitur naturaliter unus alius actus cognitionis quo cognoscitur primus actus amandi (*ibid.*, R.)

[70] P–R.

[71] E.g. Ad aliud dico quod quantumcunque ponatur intellectus activus non potest assignari causa quare plus cognoscit unum obiectum habitualiter notum quam aliud, quia solum esset naturaliter activus (*ibid.*, AA).

[72] *Ibid.*, X.

[73] Ockham's *ex professo* treatment, brief though it is, is in *Quodlibet* v, q. 6. Cf. also Commentary on *Perihermenias*, EA, 89 b–c.

suffice. The first is incomplex knowledge of the extremes or the concepts standing for them: for just as there can be one act of cognition in respect of many things, for example, knowing all the terms in a proposition in knowing the proposition, so subject and predicate can be known by the same act, whether they are regarded as absolute or relative terms. If absolute, there is no more reason to know Socrates than Plato in the proposition 'Socrates is not Plato'; if relative, one cannot be known unless the other is known. Such an act is due to a habit and so belongs to abstractive knowledge where the terms stand for concepts.[74] In the same way once the proposition is formed it can be known by one act through a habit engendered from an immediate act of knowing the proposition itself, as opposed to a relation, real or logical, constituted by the terms. The reason is that while there can be distinct acts of knowing each of the terms, the act which has the proposition as its object terminates not absolutely at the verb—as copula—but simultaneously at all the terms. Conversely, when that does not happen, acts terminating at the subject and predicate will be incomplex: that is, they will not be joined in a proposition by a verb.[75]

There are therefore two distinct kinds of knowledge and two different acts in first apprehension: incomplex knowledge of the extremes and complex knowledge of the copula. When the extremes are known separately from the copula they can be known by an incomplex act, intuitive or abstractive, whether or not they are of same nature, as we can see white and black—although different—at the same time. When they are known in conjunction with a copula, knowledge will be of the proposition—'White is not black'—which results: and that as we have said can be by a single complex act terminating, in this case, at the negative verb through which the extremes are immediately known.[76] In other words the verb is the means by which incomplexes become complex. Their union in a proposition changes their logical status; from being incomplex absolute terms they become also relative as subject and predicate, no longer complete in themselves but as parts which can only be understood by an act of intellection embracing the whole.[77]

[74] *Reportatio*, II, q. 15, Y–Z.

[75] Ideo dico quod sicut in prima apprehensione sive formatione complexi habeo unum actum respectu subiecti, alium respectu predicati, et tertium respectu copule, ita post primam formationem mediante habitu inclinante per unum actum numero possum ista tria intelligere, ita quod ista tria sive isti tres conceptus absoluti terminant illam intellectionem et non aliquis respectus rationis nec realis. Et ex illo actu frequenter elicito potest generari habitus unus numero. Si dicas quod in prima apprehensione per te sunt tres actus respectu complexi, et ex illis generantur tres habitus inclinantes ad tres actus forte alterius rationis quia actus respectu subiecti et predicati possunt esse alterius rationis. Ergo mediantibus istis tribus habitibus non posset elici aliquis unus habitus numerus respectu complexi, sed necessario erunt tres. Respondeo posito quod sint tres actus modo predicto, tamen actus terminatus ad copulam vel conceptum copule non terminatur ibi absolute. Sed simul cum hoc ad subiectum et predicatum, et ideo actus qui solum terminantur ad subiectum et predicatum sunt incomplexi. Sed actus terminatus ad copulam est complexus quantum terminatur immediate ad totum complexum; et iste dicitur compositio vel divisio. Et ex isto uno generatur habitus inclinans ad actus consimiles respectu totius complexi (*ibid.*, z).

[76] *Ibid.*

[77] Potest enim aliquis absolute cognocere cognitione incomplexa et hominem et animal, et tamen nec homo erit subiectum nec animal predicatum. Et hoc quia deficit ille conceptus

So far we have been considering first apprehension from its logical standpoint as the difference between incomplex and complex knowledge. We must now ask the psychological cause of the change from one to the other. The answer is the will. As we have seen, incomplex terms are themselves neither true nor false. Hence the intellect—whether regarded as active or passive—is correspondingly indifferent to them as incomplexes, and not more inclined to form them into true or false, positive or negative, propositions. If therefore the intellect and its concepts were together the cause of propositions, they would, as natural agents unable to choose, either form no propositions or propositions which were at once true and false, positive and negative. Which is against experience.[78] Someone can simultaneously apprehend contradictions but he cannot want to form them simultaneously since that would involve contradictory acts of assent.[79] Accordingly we have to look to some other agent which can decide between one proposition and another. That is the will, freely willing which proposition should be formed. It does so from incomplex knowledge of the terms; all composition and division are the result of their conjunction, such that given incomplex knowledge and an act of will over them, the formation of a proposition follows naturally, as effect necessarily follows cause.[80] Once formed, second apprehension of the complex follows.

It is then that there can be assent and so knowledge. Apprehension itself, first or second, is not knowledge; nor the same as or part of a proposition, although it could be part of another proposition: it is a distinct cognition which is the prerequisite of assent.[81] We have seen already how they differ in the case of second apprehension—of a complex; they are no less discrepant when it is first apprehension. Whereas a conclusion can be known a priori and a posteriori, by faith and opinion, or held in doubt, knowledge cannot be both a priori and a posteriori, and is incompatible with faith and opinion, when it would be at once evident and inevident, and with doubt. Yet those would be the consequences of making assent the same as first apprehension which they therefore cannot be.[82]

These then are the constituents of complex knowledge; neither in themselves nor in relation to each other are they naturally engendered. On the contrary, as we have just seen, they are the outcome of volition and cognition, and so free as

---

syncathegorematicus 'est'. Quo posito sine omni alio respectu statim homo erit subiectum et animal predicatum, et habetur tota propositio. Unde concedo quod tam subiectum quam predicatum est conceptus relativus rationis (Quodlibet VII, q. 4).

[78] Ideo dico sicut alibi dictum est quod ad causandum actum quo apprehenditur complexum qui dicitur compositio, concurrit actus voluntatis, sive intellectus sit sive non, quia notitie incomplexe terminorum et intellectus sit sive non, quia notitie incomplexi terminorum et intellectus, si sit activus, sunt naturaliter agentia at non plus inclinat ad formandam propositionem veram quam falsam, affirmativam vel negativam. Et ideo vel formaret neutram vel simul utramque, quod est contra experientiam. (Reportatio II, q. 25, K).

[79] Ibid.

[80] Et ideo actus qui apprehenditur post complexum formatur a notitiis incomplexis terminorum illius propositionis et ab actu illius voluntatis; et hoc generaliter, quia posito actu voluntatis quo vult tale complexum formari, et positis notitiis incomplexis terminorum illius complexi, necessario sequitur actus apprehendendi sive formandi illud complexum sicut effrctus sequitur necessario ad suam causam (ibid.).

[81] Quodlibet IV, q. 17.   [82] Quodlibet V, q. 6.

well as necessary acts. Both the formation of a complex and the act of assenting to what is not immediately evident—and all variations in knowledge together with faith and opinion—are through the intervention of the will. Conversely, only simple apprehension, intuitive or abstractive, and assent to immediately evident propositions are directly from the intellect. Accordingly the fundamental division in cognitive activity between the intellect and the will is not that between knowing and assenting—as it has been frequently misconceived to be[83]—but between knowledge which is gained naturally and so immediately, and knowledge which is dependent on a further act—or acts—and so is acquired freely. That means that only incomplex knowledge—as wholly natural and immediate—is entirely autonomous; all complex knowledge—beginning with first apprehension—is in some degree from the conjunction of intellect and will. Their relationship is determined by the degree of evidence—or lack of it—for a proposition which is known. If immediately evident it receives assent immediately from the intellect; if known indirectly, the assent of the intellect is indirect through the will; if inevident, only the will can cause assent. Assent, therefore, like apprehension, is over the object of knowledge and not exclusive to one faculty.

3 *Kinds of proposition*

Having considered generally the role and the formation of propositions we must turn briefly to their different types. That is the subject of the second part of the *Logic*. Both there and in the final part on conditional propositions (*consequentiae*, part three, third part) Ockham followed the terminists beyond Aristotle in the analysis of propositions and the conditions for their verification.[84] The change from the earlier Logical Commentaries should not be exaggerated; Ockham still adhered to Aristotle, especially in the first and second parts of part three of the *Logic* on syllogisms and demonstrations, as we shall see, and in part one as we have already seen. In part two he gave his own explanation for departing from Aristotle: 'And if it is asked why the Philosopher did not treat these matters [on the indifferent kinds of propositions] nor enumerated them, the answer is that in the interests of brevity—since what he said about others could be applied to these—he did not wish to say more'.[85] The *Logic*, unlike the earlier logical writings, was not a commentary upon a set text of Aristotle: Aristotle's was still the main presence but not in such concentration. Here the colophons to each of the parts of the *Logic* in the Paris manuscript BN Latin 6431 are instructive: the first two are called merely part one and part two, but the remaining three parts of part three are designated respectively Expositions upon the *Prior Analytics*, *Posterior Analytics* and *Topics*, a classification which largely corresponds to their contents. What follows in the second part, and from a somewhat different basis in the first part of the third part, is

---

[83] A misconception into which Moody appears to fall when he wrongly telescopes first apprehension and ascent, both of which he attributes to the will: i.e. 'Every act of assent or dissent is the act of forming a proposition, and the will is free to form or not to form a proposition'. (*Logic of William of Ockham*, 179).

[84] As noted by Moody *ibid.*, 185, also citing Prantl, *Geschichte der Logik im Abendlande*, III, 332.

[85] *SL*, II, ch. 1, 219.

treated only in the *Logic* and differs from anything elsewhere in Ockham's works.

Ockham's stated intention in the second part is threefold: the investigation of the various kinds of proposition; how they are verified; and the rules for their conversion. The main division among propositions is between categorical and hypothetical; categorical propositions are further divided into assertoric (*de inesse*) —affirming the existence or non-existence of something—and modal (*de modo*) by which existence or non-existence is held to be necessary, contingent, possible or impossible. Finally categorical propositions are themselves equivalent to hypothetical propositions when they contain syncathegorematic ('any', 'none', and so on), connotative, reduplicative ('in so far as'), exceptive and exclusive ('unless' or 'except'), relative, infinite, privative or fictive terms. These are called exponibles and contain two or more categorical propositions, as we shall discuss in more detail shortly. To these divisions must be added those between universal and singular propositions, and affirmative and negative propositions.[86]

For categorical propositions, the condition of truth in both particular and universal affirmative propositions is that subject and predicate must be able to stand for the same thing or things. As we have seen, that implies neither real identity or inherence, nor tautology; two terms can stand for the same thing and yet have different meanings, as 'animal' and 'man' can both signify Socrates while remaining distinct terms. They are related by predication.[87] Thus subject and predicate must have personal supposition if the proposition is to be true; but when negative the subject of such a proposition does not stand for the same as the predicate and can stand for nothing at all. For example, only if no man is white is it true that 'A white man is not a man'.[88] Conversely, indefinite propositions are not convertible when their subjects are not both in personal supposition: 'Man is a species' where 'man' has simple supposition is true and cannot become 'Some man is a species' in which 'man' is taken personally and so false.[89]

Universal propositions differ according to the sign of quantity—'all', 'every', 'any', 'each', 'none', 'both', 'neither'—prefixed to the subject by which it becomes universal. Many signs, including those just mentioned, apply alike indifferently to substances and accidents; others—adverbs such as 'everywhere' and 'always'—only to accidents. But no matter what the distributive sign, for a universal proposition to be true its subject must be able to stand for every individual coming under it, and the predicate for everything for which the subject can stand.[90] But where the

---

[86] *Ibid.*, 217–18.   [87] *Ibid.*, ch. 2, 224–8; ch. 3, 231–2.

[88] *Ibid.*, ch. 3, 229–31. E.g. Sed quid sufficit ad veritatem talis indefinite, si sit indefinita? Dicendum quod ad veritatem talis sufficit quod pro eodem supponant subiectum et predicatum si sit affirmativa, vel quod non supponant pro eodem, si sit negativa, sicut hoc sufficit ad veritatem propositionis singularis (*ibid.*, 231).

[89] *Ibid.*

[90] Est igitur primo sciendum quod ad veritatem talis propositionis universalis non requiritur quod subiectum et predicatum sint idem realiter, sed requiritur quod predicatum supponat pro omnibus illis pro quibus supponit subiectum, ita quod de illis verificetur; et si ita sit—nisi aliqua causa specialis impediat—propositio universalis est vera. Et hoc est quod communiter dicitur quod ad veritatem talis propositionis universalis sufficit quod quelibet singularis sit vera (*ibid.*, ch. 4, 234).

predicate is universal, neither predicate nor subject can stand for more than one thing, which is the same thing, if the proposition is to be true, as 'Every man is every animal' holds only if there is one animal which is one man. In indefinite and particular propositions, however, there is no such restriction; if there were only one man and many animals it would be true that 'Some animal is a man'.[91]

As we shall consider when we come to demonstrations, universal categorical propositions only of the present are never necessary propositions, holding only for what exists here and now and not for what has been or can be. To be necessary a proposition must be invariable, and so true not merely existentially but also potentially. It must therefore be timeless, in abstraction from all determinate and contingent circumstances. For that reason the formalism of propositions and syllogisms must be independent of changes in things; and Ockham opposes the older terminist distinction, made among others by William of Sherwood, by which a proposition can only be universal if the term 'every' (omnis) signifies at least three individual things. As we shall see, the only way to overcome the contingency of universal categorical propositions of the present is to treat them conditionally in the mode of possibility: then 'An animal is an ass', can be false but 'If an ass exists, it is an animal' is true.[92] Similar considerations apply to past and future propositions save that the predicate must be verifiable not only of the subject as it is, but as it was or will be. Neither here, nor in his treatise on future contingents—as we shall mention in chapter six—is Ockham concerned to reconcile the indeterminateness of future propositions with God's foreknowledge.

Modal propositions are treated by Ockham exclusively for the two ways in which modal terms govern them; he does not analyse the different kinds of modal proposition. A modal term can act either as predicate or as an adverb. In the first case it is cum dicto and the proposition is taken a composite sense (in sensu composito); in the second it is sine dicto and understood in a divided sense (in sensu divisu). Ockham did not originate these distinctions; but they were of the first importance to him, as to many other fourteenth-century thinkers for the nuances they brought to a proposition's meaning, and especially in Ockham's case to the conversion of modal propositions. When a proposition is cum dicto, i.e. taken in a composite sense, the modal term is always predicated of the proposition and so verified of the proposition. Thus in the proposition 'It is necessary that every man is an animal', or 'Every man is an animal is necessary', 'necessary' is verified of 'every man is an animal' the latter, as the dictum or predicable, being in the accusative and infinitive.[93] When sine dicto the modal term refers only to the copula which it modifies as its adverb, giving as the corresponding proposition 'Every man is necessarily an animal'. It follows therefore that in a proposition sine dicto the modal term is verified of the subject, and to be true it must hold for every individual or demonstrative pronoun for which the subject stands: in this case that every

[91] Ibid., 238.
[92] Ibid., 235-7.
[93] Ibid., ch. 7, 242-4.

individual man is necessarily an animal.[94] Conversely in a proposition *cum dicto* since the modal term is predicated of the whole proposition, it can be necessarily true regardless of whether any particular thing is false or contingent. Thus *cum dicto* in a composite sense it is true and necessary that every true contingent is true, and yet any singular can be false; by the same token it would be false to say *cum dicto* that 'It is necessary for this contingent to be true' just because a contingent can be false.[95] Accordingly propositions *cum dicto* in a composite sense are not covertible with propositions *sine dicto* in a divided sense; and one can be true while the other is false: for example in a composite sense the proposition 'It is necessary that every man is an animal' is true, but false in the divided sense that 'Every man is necessarily an animal', since it does not apply to every individual man.[96] From that it can be seen that propositions in *sensu divisionis*, like assertoric propositions, are existential, true, necessary, or contingent only if they hold for every individual coming under the subject term or its equivalent. Similarly, again like assertoric propositions, a singular proposition in *sensu divisionis* can occasionally be true although its unversal is false, as one of two contradictory courses may be possible for Socrates and so necessarily true for him but not true universally.[97]

Ockham regards these distinctions as according with Aristotle; his only modification is to suggest that *cum dicto* the proposition of which the modal term is predicated has material supposition, i.e. stands for meaning of the proposition's own words, whereas *sine dicto* the proposition is taken significatively, denoting the individuals for which the subject stands in personal supposition.[98]

Finally there are exponible propositions, that is, categorical propositions which are equivalent to hypothetical propositions because their truth depends upon the truth of one or more other propositions. In part two of the *Logic* Ockham devotes the longest part of his examination of propositions to them.[99] He had previously in his Commentary on *De interpretatione* (*Perihermenias*) touched upon the question discussed by Aristotle in chapter eleven of propositions whose subject or predicate

---

[94] Et est primo sciendum quod aliquando dicitur propositio de modo, quia accipitur dictum propositionis cum tali modo, sicut patet de istis: 'Omnem hominem esse animal esse necessarium; 'Hominem currere est contingens'. Alia autem propositio dicitur modalis in qua ponitur modus sine tali dicto propositionis.

Propositio modalis primo modo dicta semper est distinguenda secundum compositionem et divisionem. In sensu compositionis semper denotatur quod talis modus verificatur de propositione illius dicti, sicut per istam, 'Omnem hominem esse animal est necessarium' denotatur quod iste modus 'necessarium' verificatur de ista propositione 'Omnis homo est animal', cuius dictum est hoc quod dicitur 'Omnem hominem esse animal', quia dictum propositionis dicitur quando termini propositionis accipiuntur in accusativo casu et verbum in infinitivo modo. Sed sensus divisionis talis propositionis semper equipollet propositioni cum modo sine tali dicto, sicut ista: 'Omnem hominem esse animal est necessarium', in sensu divisionis equipollet isti: 'Omnis homo de necessitate vel necessario est animal' (*ibid.*, ch. 9, 245–6).

[95] *Ibid.*, 246–7.

[96] *Ibid.*, ch. 10, 248–9.

[97] *Ibid.*, 249. In this connection Moody (*Logic of William of Ockham*, 199) adds: 'In most cases a singular modal proposition in *sensu diviso* is equivalent to a singular proposition *in sensu composito*'.

[98] *SL*, III, I, ch. 20, 375–6.

[99] *Ibid.*, II, chs. 11–20, 252–87.

cannot form a unity: i.e. those where what is affirmed or denied is of or by disparate things, which one proposition does not suffice to express. In Aristotle's example, while we can unite man and biped, or man and white, into single propositions ('man is a biped' or 'man is white'), 'yet if a man is a shoemaker and also good, we cannot construct a composite proposition and say that he is a good shoemaker'.[100] For Ockham the explanation lies in the diverse significations of the propositions: 'man' and 'white', or 'man' and 'biped' form a unity because they stand for a real unity, but 'good' and 'shoemaker', or 'white-complexioned' and 'musical', do not, and so cannot be combined to stand for what is not really one.[101]

In his Commentary on *Perihermenias* Ockham observed that Aristotle was as concerned with inference from separate propositions to a composite proposition as he was with propositions containing other propositions.[102] But it was to the second problem that Ockham addressed himself in the *Logic*. Such propositions were those, as we have said, containing connotative, relative, privative, infinite, fictive, reduplicative, exclusive, exceptive, and similar terms.

Connotative and relative terms, as we know, have nominal definitions by which they signify one thing principally, and consignify something else secondarily, as 'white' or 'hot' denote something having, or informed by, whiteness or heat. Now just as such propositions have, through their abstract counterparts, a double signification direct and oblique, so their presence in propositions correspondingly entails two propositions, direct and oblique. One proposition directly signifies existence; the other the inherence of the quality, predicated of the subject by the connotative term. Thus 'Socrates is white', to be true, requires the truth of these two propositions: 'Socrates is' and 'Whiteness inheres in Socrates'.[103]

Relative propositions depend equally upon other propositions affirming the existence of that by which things are related: hence if 'Socrates is similar to Plato' is true, Socrates and Plato must each have a common quality—say being white—which makes them similar. 'Socrates is similar to Plato' accordingly presupposes 'Socrates is white' and 'Plato is white'.[104]

These considerations, it will be seen, apply to propositions denoting existence;

---

[100] *De interpretatione*, ch. 11, 20 b, 35. Cf. Moody, *op. cit.*, 199–200, whose references I have followed.

[101] *EA*, 118 b–c.

[102] Notandum est hic quod Philosophus non loquitur precise de propositione que est plures, sed etiam indifferenter de propositione que est plures et de aliqua quando non semper valet consequentia a divisis ad coniuncta (*ibid.*, 119 a). Moody (*op. cit.*), 200 interprets this passage somewhat differently to mean that Aristotle, according to Ockham, 'is concerned chiefly with the question of the conditions under which the truth of two propositions, taken separately, allows us to infer the truth of a simple proposition in which the two subjects or predicates are combined as a single composite expression.'

[103] Unde sciendum est quod quandocumque in propositione ponitur concretum cui correspondet abstractum importans rem informantem aliam rem, semper ad veritatem talis propositionis requiruntur due propositiones que possunt vocari exponentes ipsius, et una debet esse in recto et alia in obliquo. Sicut ad veritatem istius, 'Sortes est albus', requiritur quod hec sit vera: 'Sortes est', et quod hec sit vera: 'Sorti inest albedo' (*SL*, II, ch. 11, 253).

[104] *Ibid.*, 253–4.

they are therefore exponible just because they are existential and of the present.[105] For that reason they are contingent, and so it is not strictly correct to say as Aristotle does in *Perihermenias*[106] that 'it is possible to predicate a term simply of any one instance and say that some one particular man is a man' when it is understood as necessary predication (*per se* and *in quid*). For strictly, any proposition of individual existence is only contingent. Hence whether a connotative or relative term is predicated of only a demonstrative pronoun—'This is white'—or a common term signifying essential nature is predicated of an individual—'Socrates is a man'— neither of them is necessary in signifying only present existence.[107] In the broader meaning of direct and absolute predication, however, in which nothing extrinsic to the subject is connoted, the second case can be called necessary in the sense in which Aristotle holds 'This man is a man' to be an example of necessary predication.[108]

Propositions with privative, infinite, and fictitious terms similarly presuppose two or more propositions to explain them, since they, too, are connotative and have nominal definitions. Thus 'immaterial' is defined as 'something which does not have matter' and blind as 'something that lacks sight and was born to see'.[109] Privative terms are distinguished according to whether they are equivalent to infinite terms or not. When they are, terms like 'non-man' and 'immaterial' have two propositions as exponibles, one of them affirmative. 'An ass is a non-man' then corresponds to 'An ass is something' and 'An ass is not a man'; and 'An angel is immaterial' to 'An angel is something' and 'An angel does not have matter'. The negative proposition in these cases stands for nothing, unlike the negative in the proposition 'God is uncreated'.[110] Propositions where privative terms do not correspond to an infinite have more than two exponibles such as in 'He is blind', which consists of the following propositions: 'He is something'; 'He is born to see'; 'He is naturally unable to see'. There can be more according to the proposition.[111]

Fictitious terms like negative and privative terms, in having nominal definitions, gain their meaning not from anything they themselves signify but through positive terms which define them. But whereas negative and privative propositions can denote real things, fictitious propositions cannot, for their terms are always without real signification. Hence if a fictitious term, like chymera, is taken significatively in an affirmative proposition it will be false in having a false exponible: as 'Chymera is a non-being' is strictly speaking false because it is equivalent to the propositions

---

[105] Istis suppositis sciendum est quod quelibet propositio que habet talem terminum est habens exponentes exprimentes quid importatur per talem propositionem. Sed diverse propositiones habent diversas exponentes propter diversos terminos connotativos vel relativos (*ibid.*, 253). For that reason it is not quite correct to say as Moody does (*op. cit.*, 205) that exponibles here apply only to propositions denoting existence.

[106] Ch. 11, 21 a, 18–20.

[107] *Ibid.*, 254–5. E.g. Sicut si hec sit per se et in quid: 'Sortes est homo', ita erit hec per se et in quid: 'Iste numerus est numerus' ... Tamen intelligendum est quod proprie et stricte accipiendo predicari per se et in quid, quod scilicet est necessario predicari, sic nulla talis species 'homo', 'asinus', 'numerus' et huiusmodi predicatur per se de aliquo per se et in quid, maxime in propositione de inesse et de presenti, et hoc quia nulla talis est necessaria 'Sortes est homo'.

[108] *Ibid.*, 255.   [109] *Ibid.*, ch. 12, 255–6.

[110] *Ibid.*, 256.   [111] *Ibid.*, ch. 13, 258.

'Chymera is something' and 'This is non-being', the first of which is false. That applies wherever a non-being is taken to signify being and thus to all fictitious terms.[112]

The relative pronoun 'who' in a proposition acts as a copula and so involves more than one proposition. When such a proposition is particular or indefinite and singular, it is always equivalent to two propositions: for example 'A man who is white is running' has as its exponibles 'A man is white' and 'He is running'. As a universal proposition, however, it can be understood in one of two ways. Either in the sense, parallel to that of *sensus compositionis*, where the principal verb ('is running') is predicated of all that precedes it ('every man who is white') to give 'Every man is white' and 'Any such man is running': i.e. any man who is white also runs. The other sense is to predicate 'white' and 'running' of 'every man'; this will then correspond to the propositions 'Every man is white' and 'Every man is running', so that all men both are white and are running.[113]

Reduplicative propositions, containing the term 'in so far as' (*inquantum*) or its equivalents, when they are affirmative are so either by concomitance or by cause. If by concomitance, they always have four exponible propositions; if by cause, five through the addition of a causal proposition. In the first case the proposition 'Socrates in so far as he is a man is coloured' has the following propositions: (1) 'Socrates is coloured', (2) 'Socrates is a man', (3) 'Every man is coloured', (4) 'If a man exists, he is coloured'. Upon the last of these, as conditional, depends the truth of the reduplicative proposition. Where a proposition is reduplicative by cause, the fifth proposition states the cause. Thus in the proposition 'Man in so far as he has an intellective soul is capable of learning', to have an intellective soul is the cause of his capacity to learn and will constitute the fifth proposition stating its cause. The distinction between a causal and a concomitant reduplicative is illustrated by the proposition 'A man is able to laugh (*risibilis*) in so far as he is capable of learning': as a statement of cause it is false, since a capacity to learn is not the cause of a capacity to laugh; but by concomitance as a statement of the conditions for a man's capacity to laugh it is true.[114] That in turn helps to explain *sophismata* like 'Things in so far as they differ agree'; while causally such a proposition is false, concomitantly in making existence (and so agreement) the condition of difference it is true.[115]

Certain rules can be deduced from reduplicative propositions. One is that when affirmative the reduplicative proposition always implies its logical antecedent as one of its exponibles. If 'Man in so far as he is an animal is sensible', it follows that 'man must be sensible'.[116] Another rule is that the principal subject term undistributed (i.e. without the prefix 'every', 'any', and so on) implies its higher term undistributed, as 'Socrates in so far as he is a man is able to laugh' has as its consequence 'An animal in so far as it is a man is able to laugh'; and similarly for the predicate. That, however, does not apply to the term coming under the distributive: i.e. 'Socrates

---

112 *Ibid.*, ch. 14, 259–60, and ch. 12, 256–7.
113 *Ibid.*, ch. 15, 260–1.   114 *Ibid.*, ch. 16, 262–3.
115 *Ibid.*, 264.   116 *Ibid.*

in so far as he is man . . . ' does not enable us to infer 'Socrates in so far as he is an animal . . . ', although it is sometimes done improperly.[117]

Negative reduplicative propositions can be either of the whole proposition or of the reduplicated term. If of the whole proposition, say 'A man in so far as he is rational is not an ass', it will, like a corresponding affirmative proposition, have four or five terms, with two negative exponibles if concomitant, and three if causal. Where the reduplicative term is negated, it suffices for only one of the exponibles to be negative, as the proposition 'Socrates is not a man in so far as he is white' will be true if any of the following is true: 'Socrates is not a man', 'Socrates is not white', 'Something white is not a man', 'If this is white it is not a man'.[118]

Finally, just as the expressions 'according to', 'as', 'in the nature of' can be reduplicative, so 'in so far as' (inquantum) can be employed to express the characteristics (specificative) belonging to something, as 'hot' is affirmed of 'fire' in 'Fire in so far as it is hot is heat-giving'. Such a proposition will not be reduplicative, and its truth will not depend upon the proposition 'Everything hot is heat-giving' as its logical antecedent. Instead it requires that 'hot' implies 'heat' as the principle by which fire is heat-giving. That is to say when not reduplicative the principal predicate does not have to be affirmed universally of that which is added to the subject (i.e. heat-giving of hot) because one implies the other more than either implies the subject; hence it is in virtue of heat-giving being hot that fire, as hot, is also heat-giving.[119] The same holds when reduplicatives are equivalent to temporal adverbs.[120]

Propositions are exclusive when the terms 'only' and 'alone' are taken syncathegorematically, as adverbs; cathegorematically they merely qualify the subject, denoting that it is solitary. 'Only Socrates is running' applies to Socrates alone and can be true although many others are running; for it says no more than that Socrates, who is alone, is running. Exclusive propositions vary according to whether their terms are accepted in their usual meaning (ex primaria institutione), i.e. in their real signification, or secondary, indirect, sense (ex secundaria institutione), as the word 'man' can be made to stand for a statue or an image of a man rather than for a real man which is its primary signification in ordinary usage.[121] By the latter exclusive propositions in which the exclusive term qualifies the subject have two exponibles. For affirmative propositions denoting that the predicate belongs to that subject and to none other, one exponible is affirmative and one negative. 'Only man is an animal' has again these propositions: 'A man is an animal' and 'Nothing other than a man is an animal'. When the proposition is negative both exponibles are negative and signify that the predicate belongs to every subject save that negated in the proposition. 'Only a man is not an ass' means 'A man is not an ass' and 'Everything other than a man is an ass'.[122]

Where the subject is taken in its secondary meaning there can be three kinds of exclusive proposition, all universal or of a plurality: namely, propositions in which the predicate does not have a greater distribution than the subject; propositions

---

[117] Ibid., 264–5.   [118] Ibid., 265–6.   [119] Ibid., 266–7.
[120] Ibid., 267.   [121] Ibid., ch. 17, 268. [122] Ibid., 269.

which include nothing not signified by the subject and its parts; and propositions which do not contain a numeral greater than the number expressed by the subject. Ockham gives rules for all such propositions distinguished according to their strict and proper senses.[123]

This distinction also applies to propositions in which an exclusive term is added to the predicate. In the strict sense, a predicate is then affirmed of its subject and of nothing of which the subject is not verified, as 'Man is only an animal' denotes that man is an animal and nothing else than an animal. In an improper sense, the exclusive term modifies the verb of the proposition, thereby excluding any other verb from belonging to the subject. Thus 'A man only sees' (and nothing else) means that a man does not hear or move or do anything other than see. For that reason exclusives in this second sense can be false in debarring all other predicables, including accidents, from their subjects.[124]

Similarly there are different rules for the supposition of terms according to whether the exclusive qualifies the subject, predicate or the proposition, whether they are taken strictly or improperly and whether they are in a direct or an oblique case.[125]

Exceptive propositions result from the inclusion of the terms 'except' or 'unless', the latter also being hypothetical if it is consecutive, as in 'Socrates cannot run unless he has feet'.[126] The condition for an exceptive proposition is the removal of the predicate from what does not belong to the subject and its inclusion in whatever else comes under the subject (with the converse for negative propositions). Such propositions require two exponibles, one negative, the other affirmative. Thus 'Every man except Socrates runs' corresponds to 'Socrates does not run' and 'Every man other than Socrates runs', both of which must be true. Since neither of these predicates is affirmed of Socrates, the inferior term (Socrates) does not in this case follow from the superior distributed term (every man other than Socrates) nor the singular from the universal. Hence if the exceptive proposition is true its unmodified antecedent must be false (i.e. every man runs); and only if the antecedent is universal can the exceptive proposition be understood in its proper sense, which lies (when affirmative) in the incorporation of predicables into a subject of which they are not initially predicated. For it is the feature of exceptive propositions that the exceptive term must be brought under the subject and so is never wholly universal.[127]

Lastly, there are propositions with the verbs 'begin', 'end', and 'become', all of which have two exponibles taken in conjunction, as 'Socrates begins to be white' is equivalent to 'Socrates is white' and 'Socrates was not white immediately before'.[128] Here, as throughout, Ockham's interest is in the logical relation between propositions, not their real import; he therefore rejects any distinction between propositions of movement and propositions of rest. Such propositions of this kind can

---

[123] Ibid., 269–72.   [124] Ibid., 273.   [125] Ibid., 273–5.
[126] Ibid., ch. 18, 277–8. This seems to be a *petitio principii* since the second proposition is itself exceptive.
[127] Ibid., 278–80.   [128] Ibid., chs. 19 and 20, 280–7.

be understood either strictly or broadly; there are also cases of ambiguity, when 'begin' and 'end' are not used in an exponible sense.[129] Care must be taken especially over the supposition of their terms. Any term employed significatively, whether it is determinate, confused or distributive, can be either represented by a demonstrative pronoun which can stand alone in signifying an absolute, in the way that 'that runs' can stand for 'that man runs' and, if distributive, for 'man runs'. Alternatively the demonstrative does not stand by itself but requires another term which, if distributive, is a common term. It is this second connotation that applies in propositions of beginning and ending; the demonstrative does not stand for something which is absolute (*hoc aliquid*) but for a quality (*quale quid*) predicated of the absolute undergoing the change. Thus if 'Socrates begins to be white', 'That is white' stands for Socrates who is becoming white and not for some other white thing in addition to Socrates. Mistaking a connotative for quidditative predication leads to the fallacy of a figure of speech.[130]

Nor again, when supposition is determinate, does the predicate always ascend from the lower to the higher, as it does not follow that if Socrates begins to be white he begins also to be coloured. The reason is that an antecedent negative exponible does not entail a consequent negative exponible: in this case 'Socrates was not white' does not imply that 'Socrates was not coloured'; and so beginning to be white does not entail beginning to be coloured. Hence from inferior to superior does not hold in propositions of beginning and ending but leads to the fallacy of accident, as in the first figure of the syllogism there is a fallacy of accident when the major is affirmative and the minor negative.[131]

That completes the different kinds of propositions. The concluding chapters of the second part of the *Logic* (chapters twenty-one to thirty-seven) state the rules for their conversion, which can be confined here to the salient conclusions.

Conversion, or the transposition of subject and predicate, can occur with or without any change in the words themselves. It can be simple, accidental or by contraposition. Conversion is simple in the strict sense when both antecedent and consequent are of the same number and in the less strict sense if the conversion is mutual although the quantities are different: thus it does not follow that 'No ass is Socrates', therefore 'No Socrates is an ass'; but it does hold that therefore 'Socrates is not an ass'. Conversion is accidental which is neither mutual nor of the same quantities; for example 'Every man is white; therefore something white is a man' is true; but not the converse. Conversion by contraposition is when finite terms become infinite.[132]

In categorical, assertoric propositions of the present, conversion varies according to whether the proposition is direct or oblique; if the latter, the predicate is modified by the addition of a present participle. 'No man is in the house' becomes 'Nothing existing in the house is a man'.[133] In past and future categorical propositions the subject in personal supposition must be equivocal, in both the tense of the proposition and in the present tense.[134]

[129] *Ibid.*, 281–2.   [130] *Ibid.*, 283–4.   [131] *Ibid.*, 284–5.
[132] *Ibid.*, ch. 21, 287–8.   [133] *Ibid.*, 290.   [134] *Ibid.*, ch. 22, 291.

Exponible propositions similarly are convertible with all their constituents when they are in the same mode, or with only some if they are in different modes. They are not, however, converted into the same kind of proposition. A reduplicative proposition will be convertible with a proposition the subject of which is composed of the predicate of the antecedent proposition together with the part modified by the reduplicative term and mediated by the pronoun 'which'. Thus 'An animal in so far as it is a man is capable of laughter,' becomes 'Something which, in so far as it is a man is capable of laughter, is an animal' and not 'Capable of laughter in so far as it is a man is an animal'. Correspondingly, in exclusive propositions, the exclusive term is converted not into another exclusive term but into a universal, so that 'Only an animal is a man' becomes 'Every man is an animal'. And also with exceptive propositions, and propositions of beginning and ending.[135]

Conversion of modal propositions is governed by the distinction between *sensus compositionis* (*cum dicto*) and *sensus divisionis* (*sine dicto*). In *sensu compositionis* they convert like categorical propositions; and for necessary propositions follow the rules, in simple conversion, that if one of the convertibles is necessary the other is necessary, and, in accidental conversion, that if the antecedent is necessary so is the consequent. Thus if 'No man is an ass' then 'No ass is a man', and if the first is necessary the second is also. That applies to all propositions taken *in sensu compositionis*. In *sensu divisionis*, however, the terms must also be modified, as their transposition alone does not suffice for conversion, in the way that from 'A white man is necessarily a man' it does not follow that 'A man is necessarily a white man'. To overcome this disability the expression 'something which is' must be added with the modal term to the subject of the converted proposition (which was the predicate of the antecedent proposition). This then enables, say, 'Everything impossible is necessarily untrue' to become 'Something which is necessarily untrue is impossible'. Strictly, therefore, an existential proposition of the present which is necessary *in sensu divisionis*, or its equivalent, is convertible with another existential proposition rather than a necessary proposition.[136]

Of the other accepted modal propositions, possible propositions follow the rules for necessary propositions and, so with amendment, do impossible propositions.[137] Contingent propositions, however, are more involved. Those taken *in sensu compositionis* are converted as assertoric propositions when conversion is simple; but when it is accidental, they cannot be converted through direct transposition of the same terms, since that would falsely imply that from the contingent the contingent follows, whereas the contingent leads to the necessary. Hence the contingent proposition 'Every substance which actually exists is God' becomes the necessary proposition 'God is a substance which actually exists'.[138]

In *sensu divisionis* the distinction is between propositions where the subject— whether a common term, a participle, a proper noun or demonstrative pronoun— stands for what is, and those where it stands for what may be. In the first case, the proposition is converted not into another contingent proposition but into one that

[135] *Ibid.*, ch. 23, 294–6.   [136] *Ibid.*, ch. 24, 296–8.
[137] *Ibid.*, chs. 25 and 26, 299–302.   [138] *Ibid.*, ch. 27, 303.

is assertoric and possible, with the addition of the words 'which happens to be' to the subject of the second proposition. To establish that, Ockham employs an expository syllogism, that is a syllogism in the third figure,[139] formed from two singular propositions and leading to a particular or a singular or an indefinite conclusion. By this means we can prove that God is contingently creator and therefore something which is contingently creator is God, as follows: This is God. This is contingently creator. Therefore something which is contingently creator is God. No further proof is required. Amongst other things Ockham regards this as the vindication of the expository syllogism, frequently dismissed by contemporary theologians.[140] It enables us to state as a general rule that when propositions are exclusively assertoric and of the present, and the subject and predicate are un-qualified, there is never a fallacy of accident.[141] Hence when the subject of a contingent proposition stands for what exists it is converted into a proposition which is assertoric and possible. When, however, the subject stands for what can be, then the proposition is convertible with another contingent proposition, as 'Some man can run' has as its consequence 'Something running is a man'; both subjects are contingent, so that something which is contingently running is contingently a man.[142] Contingent propositions are also convertible by opposite qualities in *sensu divisionis*; that is, an affirmative proposition can become a negative pro-position; for if it is contingent that B is A, it is also contingent that B is not A. The negative in such propositions qualifies the verb, not the contingent, which is affirmed of both propositions, as the negative of 'Every man is contingently run-ning' is 'Every man is contingently not running', and conversely. None of this holds in *sensu compositionis* because the conclusion in being contingent would be false.[143]

The second part of the *Logic* ends with an examination of five different kinds of hypothetical propositions—conditional, copulative, disjunctive, causal, and temporal.[144]

It hardly needs saying that this analysis of propositions has been logical not metaphysical. Their diverse forms and relations, as those of terms discussed in our previous chapter, have been taken for different ways of representing the same things whether categorically, conditionally, or hypothetically. The same individual can be conceived as existing here and now or as past, future, necessary, possible or im-possible; he may be white or running or what he is in virtue of his species or some other conditions or causes. It is precisely in those last respects that Ockham's insistence upon the formal relation between propositions, as between terms, was so important; it meant as we have seen that expressions like 'humanity' and 'whiteness' were ways of affirming attributes or qualities of individuals, not the existence of self-subsisting beings or universal natures. In that sense Aristotle's categories can be regarded as the sinews of Ockham's metaphysics, as well as his logic, but hardly of his ontology as a whole. That involves elements which cannot be ascribed to Aristotle, namely the doctrine of intuitive and abstractive cognition

---

[139] For syllogisms, see 267 ff. below.   [140] *SL, ibid.,* ch. 27, 303–5.
[141] *Ibid.,* 305.   [142] *Ibid.,* 306–7.   [143] *Ibid.,* ch. 28, 308–9.   [144] *Ibid.,* chs. 29–37.

and Ockham's Christian faith. No one reading any of Ockham's logical, or indeed other, works can be in doubt of the central place of either. So far as the first is concerned, it explicitly reduces all general terms to expressions of individual existence; hence, however Aristotle may have regarded them—and it is doubtful whether he denied general natures any independent existence—in Ockham's hands all such, by then, metaphysical terms as being, substance, genera, and species were exclusively conceptual and referred only to individuals. In that, explicitly at least, his entire emphasis was different from Aristotle's. For Ockham recognition of individual existence was the criterion of any truth having existential import. But at the same time for Ockham as a Christian such truth was of contingent existence and therefore only contingent; hence truths about things, whether individuals or natures, could not have the indestructible eternal quality which Aristotle attributed to them, while the presence of an eternal creator meant the inapplicability of what held for finite beings to an infinite being.

II SYLLOGISMS

These basic tenets differentiate Ockham from Aristotle just as their application to Aristotle's categories differentiates Ockham from scholastic tradition. Before we can consider their bearing upon Ockham's theory of demonstration, confined between intuitive evident knowledge and self-evident knowledge of what can be known necessarily, we must follow his discussion of syllogisms in the first part of part three of the *Logic*. As in the previous part Ockham's analysis is formal, applying to different kinds of proposition the rules for their combination in logical discourse. Once again, their truth and falsity are a matter of valid inference independently of the real existence of things signified. To establish the relation between the latter is work of demonstration which has as its prerequisite knowledge of the correct forms of implication and deduction.

Ockham divides syllogisms into those which are necessary, those which are topical (i.e. probable), and those which are neither. A demonstrative syllogism is one in which first knowledge is gained through propositions known evidently. A topical proposition, in contrast, has for its premises only probable propositions; these appear to be true to all or most people or to those (the wisest) versed in natural reason, because they are true and necessary, but not self-evident, or known or demonstrable through experience. Accordingly probable propositions can be defined as necessary truths which are neither principles nor the conclusions of a demonstration but which appear true and are true.[145] They therefore exclude all

---

[145] Secunda distinctio est quod syllogismorum quidam sunt demonstrative, quidam topici, quidam nec topici nec demonstrativi. Syllogismus demonstrativus est ille in quo ex propositionibus necessariis evidenter notis potest acquiri prima notitia conclusionis. Syllogismus topicus est syllogismus ex probabilibus. Et sunt probabilia que videntur omnibus vel pluribus vel sapientibus et de his que videntur vel omnibus vel pluribus vel maxime sapientibus. Et est ista descriptio sic intelligenda, quod probabilia sunt illa que cum sint vera et necessaria non tamen per se nota nec ex per se notis syllogisabilia nec etiam per experientiam evidenter nota nec ex talibus sequentia; tamen propter sui veritatem videntur esse vera omnibus vel pluribus, etc. (*SL*, III, I, ch. I, 327).

that is contingent and false, as well as certain necessary truths—namely those of faith—which appear false since they are neither probable nor appear necessary by natural reason, nor are they the principles or conclusions of a natural demonstration. A topical syllogism is therefore always valid both materially and formally; and no one can normally know evidently and demonstratively that a syllogism is a topical syllogism although he can believe it to be one, for it can engender firm faith as well as doubt and fear. Hence topical syllogisms can be held as certainly as demonstrative syllogisms.[146]

Syllogisms which are not demonstrative or topical have either probable or improbable premises; if the latter they are erroneous. Error itself can be formal or material.[147]

There is a further division, between uniform syllogisms, where the propositions are all in the same mode and mixed syllogisms, where the modes of the propositions are different, as for example categorical and necessary.[148] But beyond these differences, the definition of syllogism common to all syllogisms is that it is 'a discourse (oratio) in which from two premises, disposed in mode and figure, a conclusion necessarily follows'. This is independent of the truth or falsity of the premises. What can, however, be stated as a general rule is that if the conclusion is false the premises cannot be true, although the converse can hold. In other words as a method of reasoning from premises to conclusion the validity of a syllogism rests upon correct inference of the conclusion from the premises regardless of the truth of the latter. A syllogism can therefore be valid if the conclusion is valid, and yet false; and both false and invalid when its conclusion, as well as its premise, is false.[149]

Ockham follows the accepted division of propositions into assertoric (de inesse) and modal. Every syllogism consists of three propositions—two as premises, one as conclusion—and three terms, and is classified according to mood and figure.[150] The major term is the predicate and the minor term the subject of the conclusion, while the middle term appears in each of the premises but not in the conclusion. Although the major premise—i.e. that to which the major term belongs—is usually stated before the minor premise—that to which the minor term belongs—the order is not invariable. The essential requisite is that major and minor terms are connected through the middle term in the conclusion, as in the following: Every man is an animal; Socrates is a man; Therefore Socrates is an animal, where 'man' is the middle term joining 'Socrates' and 'animal'. The mood of a syllogism is governed by the quantity—every, none, some—and the quality—affirmative or negative—of the premises and the conclusion. The figure depends upon the position of the middle

[146] Ibid., 327–8.
[147] Ibid., 328.
[148] Ibid.
[149] Sciendum est tamen quod definitio communis omnibus predictis est ista: Syllogismus est oratio in qua ex duabus premissis dispositis in modo et figura de necessitate sequitur conclusio. Et ad istam definitionem nihil refert an premisse sint vera vel false. Hoc tamen est generale quod numquam premisse sunt vere et conclusio falsa, quamvis possit esse econverso (ibid.).
[150] Ibid. ch. 2. 329.

term in the premises.[151] Ockham, in common with the majority of scholastic thinkers, recognised only three figures.[152] In the first figure, the middle term is the subject of the major premise and the predicate of the minor (as in the example above); in the second the middle term is the predicate in both premises; in the third the middle term is the subject in both premises. The fourth figure is an inversion or the first, on which grounds Ockham discounted it as separate. Of categorical syllogisms in the first figure the major premise must be universal and the minor affirmative; it is the figure in which a rule (the major) is stated, applied to a case (the minor), and a deduction made concerning the rule.[153] In the second figure the case is this time denied so that the major premise is universal, and the minor and the conclusion are negative, thus: 'Every ... No ... Therefore No ...'. For the third figure the minor premise must be affirmative and the conclusion particular so that whatever is the case is in virtue of something particular and not as the application of a general principle, thus: 'Every/No ... Some ... Therefore some ...'.

In addition to these rules for the different figures there are the rules which hold for all figures: (i) The rules of distribution already mentioned: that the middle term must be distributed to be in both premises, and a term can only be in the conclusion if it is distributed in the premises. (ii) The rules of quality: that at least one premise must be affirmative; that if one is negative, the conclusion will be negative; and if both premises are affirmative the conclusion will be affirmative (iii) The rules of quantity, that at least one premise must be universal, and if either is particular, so will the conclusion be.

Now it can be seen that of the first three figures only the first is unqualifiedly universal and affirmative; the second and third are either negations of or exceptions to a rule stated universally. Hence for Ockham as for Aristotle the first figure alone is directly governed by the *dictum de omni et de nullo*, defined here as 'when nothing is included under the subject, of which the predicate is not also affirmed'.[154] For the other figures this can only be established by reducing them to the first figure, that is deducing them from a first figure syllogism which is alone assumed to be valid without the need for further proof.[155] That can be done either directly by converting the propositions or transposing the premises, or indirectly through reduction to impossibility so that if the conclusion is not true at least one of the premises must be false, failing which the original syllogism is true. We need not concern ourselves with the particulars. For us the central point here is that the *dictum de omni et de*

---

[151] For good accounts of the syllogism see A. N. Prior, *Formal Logic* (second edition, Oxford, 1962), 110–25; W. and M. Kneale, *The Development of Logic* (Oxford, 1962), 67–96; and S. Stebbing, *A Modern Elementary Logic* (fifth edition, London, 1954), ch. IV.

[152] *SL, ibid.*

[153] Following Prior, *Formal Logic*, 111–12.

[154] Est autem dici de omni quando nihil est sumere sub subiecto quin de eo dicatur predicatum. (*SL, ibid.*, 330).

[155] Tertium preambulum est quod omnis syllogismus immediate vel mediate regulatur per dici de omni vel per dici de nullo. Syllogismi enim in prima figura regulantur immediate per dici de omni vel per dici de nullo. Syllogismi autem secunde et tertie figure reducuntur in syllogismos prime figure vel per conversionem vel per impossibile vel per transpositionem propositionum, et ideo mediate regulantur per dici de omni vel per dici de nullo (*ibid.*).

nullo is regarded by Ockham as the condition of a valid syllogism, whatever the mood and figure. In Moody's words the *dictum de omni et de nullo* is 'the principle by which a syllogism can be distinguished from an arrangement of terms and propositions that is not a syllogism'.[156] That does not mean that the major term (predicate) must be really predicable of everything of which the middle term (subject) is predicable, for then there could be syllogisms only of true propositions; rather it denotes that in a universal affirmation the predicate can stand for everything for which the subject can stand, and conversely for the *dictum de nullo*.[157] So far as the first figure is concerned that reduces the number of valid combinations, of universal affirmative, universal negative, particular affirmative, and particular negative propositions, to four out of a possible sixteen as only they can be regulated by the *dictum de omni et de nullo*.[158] Moreover their validity can only be proved dialectically not demonstratively since the truth of a conclusion from two universal affirmative premises, such as 'Every man is an animal' and 'Every man is able to laugh' depends upon the truth of the instances of which the propositions are generalisations. That is to say, their universality presupposes the *dictum de omni*, and is not deduced from it; it must therefore be established inductively from the truth of the conclusion since if the conclusion is true the premises will be true, in this case 'Everything able to laugh is an animal'.[159] Accordingly syllogisms in the first figure are regulated immediately by the *dictum de omni*. It is the criterion of validity, and not the signification of the terms involved; hence it is mistaken to say, as Boethius did, that terms can stand only for substances. They can stand for accidents, qualities, quantities, or anything else. The only further condition for their doing so is that they are not employed equivocally; that leads to the fallacy of equivocation by which a syllogism in one sense of a term—say, 'man' in simple supposition—will be false in another if 'man' is taken significatively in personal supposition.[160] Similarly an adverb or other modification employed consistently in the major and the conclusion will not invalidate an otherwise valid syllogism, for example 'Every divine person is necessarily God; The Creator is a divine person; Therefore the creator is necessarily God'.[161] But if the additional term is in the minor premise, making it either negative or exclusive or exceptive or the equivalent, then categorical syllogisms in the first figure will not hold; for then the rule of the *dictum de omni et de nullo* that the subject must stand for everything for which the predicate stands is violated, as in 'Every man is an animal; Only man is able to laugh; Therefore only something able to laugh is an animal'.[162] In the same way abstract terms

---

[156] *Logic of William of Ockham*, 214–15.

[157] *SL, ibid.*

[158] *Ibid.*, chs. 3 and 4, 331–42.

[159] Ista narrata non possunt probari nisi per modum quo probat Aristoteles ea, probando scilicet quod quatuor modi sunt utiles per hoc quod non contingit inferre instantiam. Unde servando talem modum arguendi ex duabus universalibus affirmativis: 'Omnis homo est animal, omne risibile est homo, igitur omne risibile est animal', impossibile est invenire instantiam ubi premisse sunt vere et conclusio falsa (*ibid.*, ch. 4, 333).

[160] *Ibid.*, 333–4.

[161] *Ibid.*, 334–5.

[162] *Ibid.*, ch. 5, 343; that applies also to hypothetical propositions (*ibid.*, ch. 7, 349).

which include syncathegorematic words will invalidate propositions and syllogisms in which they are treated as concrete terms. Thus 'humanity' which is equivalent to 'necessarily man'—cannot stand in the proposition 'Humanity runs'.[163]

Each of these cases is governed by the *dictum de omni et de nullo*, illustrating what Ockham has just previously said, that it is concerned not with the truth of what is predicated but with its predicability as a form of affirmation (or, if the converse, of negation). Hence in every syllogism regulated by the *dictum de omni et de nullo* the term can be indifferently of substances, accident, or anything else provided they can be combined in universal discourse.[164]

Ockham's analysis of the different figures is for the most part traditional; in the first figure his one departure is in holding that the major premise can be singular, on the ground that whether affirmative or negative it will be true if subject and predicate stand or do not stand for the same thing. Such a proposition is regulated in the same way as a univocal proposition by the *dictum de omni et de nullo*, the subject in each standing actually for all that it signifies, even if it is only one thing. Thus we can say 'Socrates is an animal; Only a man is Socrates; Therefore only a man is an animal'.[165] That only applies to syllogisms composed of direct propositions; oblique, modal and mixed propositions all have their own peculiarities, which Ockham analyses separately, in each of the figures. As we mentioned earlier, Ockham includes in the third figure the expository syllogism formed from two singular propositions producing a singular conclusion, which can be particular or indefinite. The minor premise must always be affirmative; otherwise, to say 'Socrates is an animal; Socrates is not Plato; Therefore Plato is not an animal', is not a valid syllogism. The major on the other hand can—as predicate in the conclusion—be in the negative, thus: 'Socrates is not an accidental whole; Socrates is a white man; Therefore a white man is not an accidental whole'.[166] This is consistent with Ockham's admission of a singular major premise in the first figure and is connected with his theory of signification; if a term has personal supposition it can be said to conform to the *dictum de omni et de nullo* provided it signifies whatever it stands for, even one individual. That in turn enables Ockham to argue that in the second figure both premises can be affirmative when the middle term is either singular or universal, the first because it can be converted with an expository syllogism, the second because it is convertible into a syllogism of the first figure, each of which is regulated by the *dictum de omni et de nullo*. He justifies these exceptions by interpreting the rules of the second figure to mean that one should not always (rather than never) argue from affirmative or particular premises;[167] but does concede that this is not found in the *Prior Analytics*.[168]

---

[163] *Ibid.*, ch. 4, 341–2.

[164] Sic igitur breviter omnis syllogismus regulatus per dici de omni vel de nullo est simpliciter bonus et de se evidens nec indigens aliqua probatione. Et non refert quale sit illud quod sumitur sub in minori, sive sit terminus substantialis sive accidentalis, sive dicat quale sive quantum sive ad aliquid sive ubi sive quodcumque aliud (*ibid.*, 342).

[165] *Ibid.*, ch. 8, 350. [166] *Ibid.*, ch. 16, 367–9.

[167] *Ibid.*, ch. 13, 361. [168] *Ibid.*, ch. 16, 369.

He also of course diverges from Aristotle, but not from medieval logicians, by taking modal propositions in both their composite and divided senses as well as briefly analysing hypothetical propositions according to his earlier categories of reduplicative, exclusive, exceptive and other forms. These, together with mixed syllogisms, are all treated according to the rules already enunciated for such propositions and the different figures of the syllogism, which it would be tedious and not particularly rewarding to recapitulate. Ockham's examination was exhaustive rather than original or particularly influential; its main interest is technical and indeed antiquarian since it occupies no significant place in the history of logic. Much the same can be said for the final third part, part three of the *Logic* devoted to *consequentiae* and fallacies, although probably here Ockham's influence was greater; for especially *consequentiae* became one of the main fields of logic in the fourteenth century as it has become in the twentieth century, known as the logic of propositions or propositional calculus. In Ockham's time, true *consequentiae* or implications were concerned with inferring the propositions implied by other propositions. For Ockham the construction of such propositions was by means of abbreviated syllogisms, or enthymenes, where the full premises are not stated. Here, as throughout what he says about propositions, Ockham distinguishes between consequents which hold absolutely (*consequentia simplex*) and consequents which are contingent as true at a certain time (*ut nunc*).[169] Ockham's use of 'now' has nothing in common with Aristotle's in his celebrated conundrum of tomorrow's sea battle.[170] Unlike Aristotle, Ockham was not concerned with the truth value of a proposition in the present about a future event, but with the implicative relation of one proposition to another which he believes can be temporal as well as exclusively logical.

Ockham's other main distinctions are between consequents which hold by an intrinsic middle and consequents holding by an extrinsic middle, and between formal and material consequents. By an intrinsic middle an antecedent is formed from the same terms as the consequent: for example 'Socrates is running; *therefore* a man is running' has 'Socrates is a man' as its middle. A middle is extrinsic when it is a general rule not peculiar to the terms of the propositions which it connects, as 'Only a man is an ass; *therefore* every man is an ass' holds by the rule 'An exclusive proposition is convertible with a universal affirmative proposition when the terms are transposed'. All syllogisms hold through extrinsic middles; so indirectly do consequents with intrinsic middles; but whereas the latter hold more immediately by what is intrinsic to them as propositions, propositions connected through extrinsic middles need supplementing by further premises.[171] It has been remarked that Ockham's inclusion of intrinsic middles is inconsistent with his initial definition of *consequentiae* as enthymenes; certainly this had the serious result that

[169] *Ibid.*, III, III, ch. I.

[170] W. and M. Kneale, *Development of Logic*, 289, which associates the two. The problem of the sea battle is in chapter nine of *De interpretatione*, discussed and corrected with sledgehammer blows in Kneale, 46–54. These are two instances of the condescension towards many of the earlier thinkers which, especially in early chapters, is a blemish on this excellent book.

[171] *SL*, III, II, ch. I.

he made no allowance in his rules for propositions related by the two kinds of middles.[172] Both are also included under formal consequences, an intrinsic middle immediately, an extrinsic middle mediately, regardless of the import or nature of the propositions. A material consequence, on the other hand, has no necessary connection between its propositions, but holds merely on account of the meaning of the terms, by which the consequent is true if the antecedent is true. Thus 'A man runs; therefore God exists', where 'God exists' is necessary.[173]

After stating the rules for the different kinds of *consequentiae*[174] Ockham devotes the major part of this final section of the *Logic* to a similar exercise for predicables involved in arguments.[175] This follows closely the method of the *Topics* for identifying genus (sixty-nine rules given), difference, property, and accident, as well as restating from the same dialectical standpoint the meaning of definition and the terms 'same' and 'diverse'. Ockham also touches briefly upon inferring universal from singular propositions, and gives rules—again drawing upon the *Topics*—for identifying equivocation.[176] What appears to be the genuine part of the work ends with general rules for *consequentiae* as a whole.[177]

III DEMONSTRATION

Here we shall leave these formal topics and return to the preceding second part of part three of the *Logic*—and in places in the Prologue to the *Ordinatio*—in which Ockham treats demonstration. Unlike the first and third parts of part three, this concerns the application of the rules for terms, propositions, and syllogisms to the relation between real things, as substances and qualities. Hence the conditions for valid demonstration consist not merely in the formal requirements for correct implication but in the ontological truth of what is demonstrated.

Ockham's theory of demonstration is governed by the epistemological scope and limits of what can be known self-evidently and absolutely by intuitive cognition; since this is confined to individuals, and their existence as immediately given is indemonstrable, strict demonstration is confined to what can be necessarily adduced from individual existence in abstraction from its contingent circumstances of existence. It is to overcome this seeming paradox that Ockham's theory of demonstration is directed; its consequence is to reduce drastically the area of demonstrable knowledge; together with Ockham's Christian belief that makes for important divergencies from Aristotle, while still adhering to the framework of the *Posterior Analytics*. Once again, as in his theory of terms, Ockham gives to Aristotle's principles an individual import; in this case it has as its accompaniment the primacy of experience over demonstration, both as the precondition of

---

[172] Kneale, *ibid.*, 289.

[173] *SL*, III, II, ch. 1 and ch. 37.

[174] *Ibid.*, III, chs. 3–16.

[175] *Ibid.*, chs. 17–28. For a brief account see Moody, *Logic of William of Ockham*, 290–3.

[176] *Ibid.*, chs. 31–35.

[177] *Ibid.*, chs. 36–37. The final short discussion on obligations and fallacies seems to have been tacked on. Cf. Moody, *Logic of William of Ockham*, 294.

demonstrative knowledge and the predominant form of knowledge. It is the price of an individual ontology in which, as we said earlier in this chapter, the truth of propositions depends upon the existence of that on which they bear.

Before we turn to demonstration, it is worth remarking that even in the most formal contexts of the *Logic*, to say nothing of all his other works, Ockham writes as a theologian as well as a logician or philosopher. In each of the preceding parts, as we have sometimes had occasion to mention, Ockham repeatedly points to the implications of the logical issues under discussion for the truths of faith or for God. Thus in part one of part three on syllogisms, much of what Ockham says on the *dictum de omni et de nullo* is devoted to showing the inapplicability of the *dictum* to God as a single being containing three persons, and so to what is both numerically one and plural.[178] Comparable discrepancies arise, as we shall see, in demonstration over the necessity which belongs to God and necessary truths which do not. From this it seems that Ockham at least was not after all so far removed in awareness of the distinction between natural and divine truth from Nicholas of Cusa who rejected Aristotelian categories in the name of transcendental truth. As so often justification for a break with the past was from much the same foundation as what was broken with.

Ockham's systematic treatment of demonstration is in the *Logic*. We shall therefore take that as our basis, supplemented from certain questions in the Prologue to the *Ordinatio*, where demonstration was considered principally in connection with God's existence and theological truth—to be discussed in chapter five below. Since Ockham's theory of demonstration derives from Aristotle's in the *Posterior Analytics* we may best begin with a brief resume of the matter there.

Aristotle defines demonstration as 'a syllogism productive of scientific knowledge';[179] it is therefore more than a mere syllogism, namely a syllogism in which knowledge of the conclusion is derived from pre-existing knowledge—whether of a term's meaning or a fact—in the premises. That means first that all new knowledge presupposes old knowledge; and second that, in order to prevent an infinite regress, the premises, as cause of the conclusion, must be true, primary, and indemonstrable in being immediate propositions to which no others are prior. Hence demonstration is from the indemonstrable (the premises) to the demonstrable (the conclusion); for that reason not all knowledge is demonstrable.[180]

The object of demonstration is to establish the necessary connection between a subject and its attribute (i.e. that which belongs to the subject), so that the attribute must in every case be true of the subject. For that there must be a necessary, and so universal, demonstration, the prerequisite of which is a necessary middle term by which no other conclusion is possible. The distinctive character of a demonstration lies in its necessity.[181] In Aristotle's words, 'Demonstrative knowledge must be knowledge of a necessary nexus, and therefore must clearly be obtained through a

178 *SL*, III, I, ch. 4, 337–8, 340–1.
179 *Posterior Analytics*, I, ch. 2, 71 b, 17–18.
180 *Ibid.*, ch. 3, 72 b, 18–24.
181 *Ibid.*, ch. 4, 73 a, 26; ch. 6, 74 b, 5–18.

necessary middle term; otherwise its possessor will know neither the cause nor the fact that his conclusion is a necessary connection'.[182]

Demonstration accordingly establishes the inherence of essential attributes in things; it does so either because the attributes are elements in the essential nature of their subjects or because their subjects are elements in their attributes' essential nature;[183] here we have the source of the distinction between essential by the first mode (*per se primo modo*) and essential by the second mode (*per se secundo modo*) which we shall frequently meet throughout the rest of this work. Such knowledge is scientific because as necessary and universal—when predication is not of the same subject it is accidental and so not demonstrative[184]—it is knowledge of causes. In Aristotle's words, 'We suppose ourselves to possess unqualified scientific knowledge, as opposed to knowing it in the accidental way that the sophist knows, when we think that we know the cause on which the fact depends, as the cause of that fact and no other, and, further, that the fact could not be other than it is'.[185]

Demonstration is therefore a syllogism that proves the cause of a thing, giving what Aristotle calls knowledge of the reasoned fact, as distinct from knowledge of the bare fact which is only of what is particular at a definite time and place.[186] Knowledge of the fact can be by perception, but knowledge of the reasoned fact never; it is the difference between knowing that there is an eclipse of the moon and knowing that it is an eclipse through the interposition of the earth which excludes the sun's light.[187] By the same token demonstration, which is of what cannot be otherwise, is incompatible with opinion which can be equally of what is true and what is false.[188] Neither knowledge of the bare fact nor opinion is reached through the cause as a necessary middle—the condition of a necessary conclusion and so demonstration.[189] Now since such a conclusion of a demonstration is always of an attribute inhering essentially in its genus (i.e. nature), the attribute which belongs essentially to the subject must also belong essentially to the genus of the subject.[190] From that it follows that both existence of the genus and the definition of essential nature contained in the premises must be indemonstrable; although there are different ways in which definition can be understood, in a strict demonstration the existence and sometimes, as in arithmetic, the nature of what is defined must be assumed.[191] Although definition of essential nature can be deduced it can never be demonstrated; only exhibited in a demonstration.[192] Accordingly definition depends upon existence: 'We cannot apprehend a thing's definable form without apprehending that it exists, since while we are ignorant whether it exists we cannot know its essential nature'.[193] To know the nature of a thing therefore is also to know that it exists. For that reason a purely nominal definition which does not posit essential nature is circular, because demonstration is of the essential nature or being of something, and must assume its existence. That is the difference between

[182] *Ibid.*, ch. 6, 75 a, 12–15.   [183] *Ibid.*, ch. 22, 84 a, 11.
[184] *Ibid.*, 83 a, 23–5.   [185] *Ibid.*, ch. 2, 71 b, 8–11.
[186] *Ibid.*, ch. 24, 85 b, 23.   [187] *Ibid.*, ch. 31, 87 b, 39–88 a, 1; II, ch. 16, 98 b, 20–5.
[188] *Ibid.*, I, ch. 33, 88 b, 30–5.   [189] *Ibid.*, ch. 6, 75 a, 4.
[190] *Ibid.*, ch. 6, 75 a, 27–ch. 7, 75 b, 52.   [191] *Ibid.*, II, ch. 9, 93 b; also chs. 2–10.
[192] *Ibid.*, II, ch. 8, 93 a, 15.   [193] *Ibid.*, 16–20.

knowing human nature, which entails knowing that man exists, and knowing the name 'goat-stag' which is without essential nature. Neither of these names gives proof of existence: one of them assumes knowledge of existence, the other does not and cannot, unlike the first, form the starting point for a demonstration.[194]

Three terms, then, enter into demonstration: subject, attribute and definition as middle term. Since demonstrative knowledge consists in knowing the cause of a thing, each of the four causes can act as middle term; for example the answer to the question 'Why do I take a walk after supper?'—that it is for the sake of my health—expresses the final cause, that the reason is preservation of health.[195]

Aristotle distinguishes four different kinds of questions which can be asked about things corresponding to the different things that can be known. The answers therefore constitute our knowledge. The first question is whether the connection of an attribute with a thing is a fact (in medieval terminology *quia est*); second, what is the reason of the connection (*propter quid*); third whether a thing exists (*si est*); fourth, what is its nature (*quid est*).[196] The answers to the second and fourth questions depend on those to the first and third, for only after ascertaining the existence as a fact of both a connection and a thing can we ask the reason of the connection and the nature of the thing. These two pairs therefore represent two different kinds of questions about middles: one and three, whether there is a middle; two and four, what the middle is; in all of them the middle is the cause.[197] This is exemplified by Aristotle as follows:

Thus, 'Does the moon suffer eclipse?' means 'Is there or is there not a cause producing an eclipse of the moon?' and when we have learnt that there is, our next question is, 'What, then, is this cause?'; for the cause through which a thing *is*—and the cause through which it is—not *is* without qualification, but *is this or that* as having some essential attribute or some accident—are both alike the 'middle'. By that which *is* without qualification I mean the subject, e.g. moon or earth or sun or triangle; by that which a subject *is* (in the partial sense) I mean a property, e.g. eclipse, equality or inequality, interposition or non-interposition. For in all these examples it is clear that the nature of the thing and the reason of the fact are identical: the question 'What is an eclipse?' and its answer 'The privation of the moon's light by the interposition of the earth' are identical with the question 'What is the reason of the eclipse?' or 'Why does the moon suffer eclipse?' and the reply 'Because of the failure of light through the earth's shutting it out'.[198]

That is to say, demonstrative knowledge is not of existence in the unqualified sense that something is, but of the nature of existence in the qualified sense of what something is. Such knowledge is demonstrative when of the reasoned fact (*propter quid*) and presupposes knowledge of existence (*si est*) and the connection of subject and attribute as a fact (*quia est*), but not the converse.[199] Only in the case of mathematics (Aristotle's mathematical examples are drawn from arithmetic and geometry) can both the existence and the nature of what is defined be assumed: a characteristic which Ockham, like Grosseteste, stresses. In a demonstration,

---

[194] *Ibid.*, ch. 3, 90 b, 27, and ch. 7, 92 b, 4–18.   [195] *Ibid.*, ch. 11, 94 b, 7.
[196] *Ibid.*, ch. 1, 89 b, 1.   [197] *Ibid.*, ch. 2, 89 b, 1–90 a, 5.
[198] *Ibid.*, 6–18.   [199] *Ibid.*, II, ch. 8, 93 a, 15–30.

existence of both subject and attribute is given in the definition as the middle term joining them in a necessary conclusion. It is from the necessary order of these three terms that the truth of demonstration springs. On the other hand, as we have also seen, knowledge of existence entails awareness of what is known, incomplete though it is; indeed we can still be aware of the nature of something through apprehending only an accidental element, such as thunder by its noise, or an eclipse through privation of light. Thus, while the definition of essential nature is indemonstrable, we can arrive at its elements by division: that is, enumerating the constituent species into which the genus, as primary term, can be divided.[200] This is not a demonstration but what Aristotle in the *Prior Analytics* calls a weak syllogism, begging what has to be proved.[201] Nevertheless by taking the universal nature and its attributes as necessary we can work through the properties belonging to their species. At the same time we can begin from individuals of distinct species, but of the same genus and observe what element each group of specifically identical individuals has in common; when discovered that will be the definition of the genus.[202]

These are the principles—modified and, in the case of definition, made considerably more precise—adopted by Ockham. He begins his discussion of demonstration in the *Logic* by defining it with Aristotle as a syllogism productive of knowledge. For Ockham this is a nominal definition; of syllogism which he has just discussed no more need be said. But knowledge may, among its diverse meanings, be understood in three ways: as evident comprehension of a truth which can be either necessary or contingent in the way one can know that one is sitting or beginning to move; as comprehension of a necessary truth, when it is a proposition which cannot be false; or as comprehension of necessary truths in a syllogism, through a conclusion deduced from two premises, which is the sense in this definition. Demonstration accordingly must have three terms, although like any definition it cannot itself be demonstrated.[203]

Not every term, however, can enter into a syllogism but only those which engender necessary knowledge. That excludes all contingent terms of existence giving affirmative existential terms of the present (*de inesse et de presenti*). Here we come to one of the fundamental divergences between Ockham and Aristotle, and to some degree Ockham's scholastic predecessors, over the meaning of necessity. As we have seen, 'necessary' for Aristotle is what cannot be known to be otherwise and applies to things in *rerum natura*, such as the reason for the moon's eclipse. For Ockham as a Christian on the other hand only God is necessary, and everything else, as dependent upon his will, contingent. Necessity and eternity

---

[200] *Ibid.*, ch. 13.
[201] *Prior Analytics*, I, ch. 31, 47 a.
[202] *Posterior Analytics*, II, ch. 13, 97 b, 7 to the end of chapter.
[203] *SL*, III, II, ch. 1. Omnes enim recte loquentes de demonstratione intelligunt syllogismum quod ex duobus premissis necessariis notitiis per quas scitur conclusio que aliter ignorata ... Quamvis igitur demonstrari non possit quod demonstratio est syllogismus faciens scire modo exposito, sicut nec significatum vocabuli nec diffinitio exprimens quid nominis probari possit, nec per usum loquentium et fundamentum est tamen pro fundamento quod demonstratio est syllogismus faciens scire.

cannot be attributed to generable and corruptible things but only to the truths of necessary propositions which remain unchanging. Such necessity is therefore logical, never ontological; it can only be of things in so far as they are abstracted from existence and so made independent of the present. For that, we have seen, propositions must be conditional, or hypothetical, in the mode of possibility, or negative.[204] They can then be necessary because existence is either presupposed or denied; but in neither case affirmed significatively. Thus if a man exists he is necessarily a rational animal, not because his existence is necessary, but because rationality is necessary to man such that, given the possibility of man's existence, his rationality is a necessary consequence. Contingency is thereby overcome and the same attribute is universally predicable of everything that can be a man, regardless of actual existence. By the same token such propositions in being necessary are not exponible, as a necessary proposition cannot be equivalent to categorical propositions of the present.[205] Hypothetical and conditional propositions thus fulfil the conditions of the *dictum de omni* by assuming the existence of whatever an attribute is affirmed. As we shall see that does not of itself suffice for a strict demonstration but it enables the terms of contingent things to enter into necessary propositions.

Necessity—other than God's—is therefore on Ockham's view exclusively logical, and consists in the relation of subject to predicate. It is at this point that he also deviates from scholastic tradition by which universals, whether as essences or forms, were the necessary and essential constituents of all created being, contingent though it was in itself. Ockham's divergence from this conception will become apparent above all over the two questions of the nature of an attribute and the relation of essence to existence, to each of which Ockham conceded only logical status.

Necessity, with universality, is the property common to all parts of a demonstration, premises as well as conclusion; for if the conclusion is necessarily true, the premises must be true as well.[206] Ockham acknowledges that this restriction of the meaning of necessary to propositions conflicts with Aristotle for whom it

---

[204] Non autem possunt omnes termini demonstrationem affirmativam ingredi de propositionibus de inesse et mere de presenti. Illi autem termini de nullo possunt predicari nisi contingenter vel false ipsis sumptis significative esse partes demonstrationis talis ... quamvis in demonstratione negativa possunt, quia in negativa possunt de aliis necessario predicari. Similiter quamvis tales termini, 'album', 'nigrum', 'calidum' et huiusmodi non possunt esse partes propositionum necessariarum mere de inesse et depresenti affirmative, quia tamen possunt ingredi esse partes propositionum de possibili necessariarum, ideo talem demonstrationem ingredi possunt (*ibid.*, ch. 2).

[205] Nec valet dicere quod ista: 'Homo est animal rationale' equivalet 'Si homo est, homo est animal rationale', quia ista est conditionalis et non cathegorica; et ita stat primum dictum quod nulla propositio mere de presenti et cathegorica est necessaria ... Hoc tamen non obstante dicendum est quod multe propositiones composite ex talibus terminis possunt esse principia et conclusiones demonstrationis, quia propositiones et conclusiones de possibili et eis equivalentes possunt esse necessarie (*ibid.*).

[206] Una enim proprietas communis omni propositioni requisite ad demonstrationem est necessitas. Nulla autem requisita ad demonstrationem est contingens et possibilis sed hec est necessaria. Quod autem conclusio sit necessaria patet per diffinitionem demonstrationis, quia demonstratio est syllogismus faciens scire propositionem necessariam. Igitur conclusio erit necessaria ... ergo premisse propter quas scitur conclusio sunt necessarie (*SL*, III, II, ch. 5).

included all being as perpetual. But that, as we have seen, means for Christians what is generable and corruptible and so contingent. Hence, other than God, necessity can only belong to propositions.[207] The same applies to universality, the other common requisite of a demonstration, the condition for which is that everything signified by the subject must also be signified by the predicate at all times and without exception.[208] Necessity and universality together distinguish a demonstration from a syllogism; the latter to be valid must be universal, but the former must be universally and necessarily true. This distinction is in keeping with the two different definitions of the *dictum de omni* to be found in the *Prior Analytics*, where it merely means universally predicable, and the *Posterior Analytics* where universally predicable must be also universally true.[209]

Ockham thus narrowed the area of demonstrability by narrowing the meaning of necessity; he did so moreover as a Christian rather than as an Aristotelian. The effect from both standpoints should become apparent in what follows. We shall first consider the knowledge (of propositions and terms) requisite to a demonstration; next, the respects in which it has to be necessary; and finally Ockham's response to Aristotle's four questions above all in relation to strict demonstration.

Ockham's conception of demonstration starts from the same axiom as that which opens the *Posterior Analytics*: 'All instruction given or received by way of argument proceeds from pre-existent knowledge'.[210] That is, demonstrable knowledge depends upon preceding indemonstrable knowledge as its condition. For that there have on the one hand to be the propositions which belong to demonstrations—giving the three terms of subject, attribute and definition—and on the other, additional propositions which are not themselves part of a demonstration but are presupposed by those which are. These are first principles which are always indemonstrable. They are of two kinds: those which are universal and underlie all scientific knowledge, such as the principle of the excluded middle or the principle of contradiction; and those which belong to a particular science—geometry or physics—which is the subject of a demonstration.[211] The latter can be known as

---

[207] Secundo etiam sunt perpetue et incorruptibiles. Quod non est intelligendum quod ille propositiones sint quedam entia necessaria et perpetua. Hoc enim falsum est. Solus enim deus est hec. Propter quod sciendum quod perpetuum, necessarium et incorruptibile dupliciter accipiuntur. Uno modo dicitur aliquid necessarium perpetuum et incorruptibile, quia per nullam potentiam potest incipere et desinere (esse); et sic solus deus est talis. Aliter diciter perpetua, necessaria et incorruptibilis propositio que non potest esse falsa . . . Ex quo patet quod quamvis repugnet dictis Aristotelis, tamen secundum veritatem nulla propositio de illis que importat precise res corruptibiles mere affirmativa et mere cathegorica et de presenti potest esse principium demonstrationis vel conclusio, quia quelibet talis est contingens (*Ibid.*).

[208] Alia conditio tam premissarum quam conclusionis demonstrationis est ista quod tam premissa quam conclusio potest esse de omni. Est autem esse de omni non quando predicatum competit alicui contento sub subiecto et alicui non, sed quando predicatum competit omni tempore et omni contento sub subiecto (*ibid.*, ch. 6).

[209] *Ibid.*

[210] *Posterior Analytics*, I, ch. 1, 71 a, 1.

[211] Est autem sciendum quod propositionum ad demonstrationem requisitarum quedam sunt partes demonstrationis, sicut premisse et una conclusio; quedam non sunt partes demonstrationis et vocantur dignitates et maxime, vel suppositiones quia sub propria forma non ingrediuntur demonstrationem. Virtute tamen illarum aliquo modo sciuntur premisse

axioms or by experience; either way they are indemonstrable. Thus the principle 'All heat is heat-giving' is presupposed in, but not demonstrable of, the proposition 'Everything hot is heat-giving' because in being known only immediately through experience it is contingent; this second proposition can, however, be part of a demonstration as major premise independently of the first proposition which it presupposes: for example to demonstrate that fire is heat-giving. Similarly with mathematical or physical principles concerning number or movement.[212]

First principles can also belong to demonstrations as premises. For Aristotle and Scholastics the two were interchangeable. But whereas first principles are always indemonstrable, premises which can also be the conclusions of other demonstrations are to that extent demonstrable.[213] The conclusion must always be demonstrable; it must also be dubitable, since only what is not known immediately—whether through experience or as self-evident—can be known through a middle term, which is what distinguishes demonstrable from indemonstrable knowledge. Both in the *Logic* and in the Prologue to the *Ordinatio* Ockham stresses that demonstration is a syllogism productive of knowledge just because it makes known what was previously not known or doubted or appeared false.[214] In the *Ordinatio* he states as the three conditions of demonstration that it must be a necessary proposition, initially dubitable and made evident through deduction. The first condition excludes immediate propositions known only through experience and so liable to be false; the second condition excludes self-evident propositions whose truth in being immediately known cannot be doubted; the third condition excludes both previous kinds of proposition in being indemonstrable.[215] Thus a proposition

---

demonstrationis . . . Propositio autem requisita ad demonstrationem non tamquam pars sub-dividitur, quia quedam est talis quod necesse esse quemlibet docendum eam habere. Cuiusmodi sunt tales: 'Quodlibet hec vel est vel non est', 'de quolibet est affirmatio vel negatio'. Quedam sunt tales quas non est necesse quod hoc quamlibet docendo eam habere . . . (*SL*, III, II, ch. 4).

212 *Ibid.*

213 Propositio autem que est pars demonstrationis subdividitur, quia quedam est premissa tantum que scilicet est indemonstrabilis; quedam est conclusio tantum, que scilicet est demonstrabilis sed non potest esse principium demonstrandi aliquam propositionem. Quedam est premissa et conclusio, que potest demonstrari per diversas alias premissas et potest esse principium demonstrandi aliam conclusionem. Alia divisio potest poni quod propositionum requisitarum ad demonstrationem quedam sunt principia, quedam sunt conclusiones. Principia dicuntur ille propositiones que non sunt conclusiones et tamen requiruntur ad demonstrationem, sive sint partes demonstrationis sive non. Et vocantur principia prima que subdividi possunt, quia quedam principia sunt per se nota, quibus scilicet intellectus statim assentit ipsis terminis apprehensis, ita quod si sciatur quid significant termini statim sciuntur. Quedam autem sunt principia prima que non sunt per se nota sed tantum per experientiam sunt nota, quia non possunt demonstrari, sicut est de ista: 'Omnis calor est calefactivus', et de multis aliis que non possunt fieri note nisi per experientiam . . . (*ibid.*).

214 Omnis conclusio demonstrationis est dubitabilis ita quod non est per se nota. Cum enim demonstratio est syllogismus faciens scire, et nihil facit scire aliquid prescitum, necesse est si apprehendatur conclusio sine premissis quod illa conclusio potest ignorari, et per consequens potest de ea aliquis dubitare, cum non possit sciri esse falsa (*ibid.*, ch. 9); also *Ordinatio*, Prologue, q. 2, 76–7.

215 Circa primum dico quod propositio scibilis scientia proprie dicta est propositio necessaria, dubitabilis, nata fieri evidens per propositiones necessarias evidentes, per discursum syllogisticum applicatas ad ipsam (*Ordinatio*, Prologue, q. 2, 76). Also *ibid.*, 87–8.

can be indubitable and still not necessary, such as 'heat is heat-giving' or 'gravity pulls downwards', which are known by experience and so not self-evident, but neither, as immediately known, demonstrable.[216]

Both principles and conclusions can be known by experience and also doubted;[217] but only conclusions can be demonstrated.[218] That distinguishes them from first principles, which are first and indemonstrable because known immediately. Only if they are also self-evident are they necessary as well; for as we have seen,[219] propositions known immediately by experience are not necessary, nor do they enter into demonstrations.[220] Hence it is their immediacy—not necessity—which makes propositions first principles, and many first principles are not necessary.

To call a proposition a first principle is not however the same as saying that it has no proposition prior to it; as Aristotle shows, a negative proposition can be a first principle and so is subsequent to one that is affirmative. It is rather that a first principle is first in order of demonstrability as that beyond which there is no regress.[221] In the same way there can be other principles prior to first principles in the order of contingency, since the meaning of the terms of an indemonstrable proposition—that, say, Socrates is a man—assumes the existence of what is denoted —that Socrates is.[222] There is therefore a double order of priority—logical and ontological—each governed by its own sequence but depending for its truth upon the order of being. Among terms priority belongs to the more universal term or that from which another term follows; among propositions to the more explanatory or the more universal or the proposition from which another proposition is deducible; among things to that which is first in time.[223] And before any of these can become knowledge, what they signify must be known.[224] In that sense all knowledge which is not self-evident derives from the—contingent—order of being; for only if there is prior knowledge of existence of the subject can attributes

---

[216] *Ibid.*, 77–8, 83–4.

[217] *Ibid.*, and *SL*, III, II, ch. 9.

[218] Dicendum quod potest esse consimilis modus adquirendi notitiam aliquorum principiorum et aliquarum conclusionum. Sed preter istum modum communem est unus proprius notitie conclusionum, scilicet per demonstrationem, que nullo modo potest competere notitie principiorum primorum quorumcumque (*Ordinatio, ibid.*, 90).

[219] *Ibid.*, 83–6; *SL*, III, II, ch. 4.

[220] Ex hoc autem quod principia possunt esse prima, sequitur quod dicuntur esse immediata et indemonstrabilia (*SL*, III, II, 14). Oportet autem scire quod quamvis principia demonstrationis sint prima, sic quod non sint demonstrabilia, tamen aliqua propositio non necessaria, que non est principium alicuius demonstrationis, potest esse prima (*ibid.*, ch. 13).

[221] *SL*, III, II, ch. 13.

[222] Unde sicut est ordo inter propositiones necessarias quod aliqua est prior et alia posterior, ita est ordo inter propositiones contingentes quod aliqua est prior et alia posteriora, sicut ista, 'Sortes est' est prior ista, 'Sortes est homo', quia sequitur tamquam a priori . . . (*ibid.*).

[223] *Ibid.*, ch. 14.

[224] Aliter potest intelligi illud dictum universaliter de omnibus principiis: quod congnoscuntur cognitis terminis, excludendo alias propositiones necessarias, priores eis, ex quibus syllogistice possunt inferri et per eas sciri. Non tamen sufficit quecumque notitia terminorum, sicut est de notitia propositionis per se note . . . sed requiritur notitia intuitiva saltem alicuius termini vel alicuius importati per terminum, et forte requiruntur frequenter multe notitie intuitive (*Ordinatio, Prologue, q. 2*, 86–7). Also *SL, ibid.*, ch. 13.

be affirmed or denied, which is why God's nature, in not being known intuitively, cannot be proved. The problem of demonstration for Ockham as for Aristotle is to pass from what the *Posterior Analytics*[225] call primary truths—whose existence is assumed—to necessary knowledge of secondary truths which can be attributed to them but whose existence is either not known or if known is known as a fact and not as reasoned fact. Experience alone, in giving knowledge only of existence, can do neither.

There is, however, a third way between indemonstrability and demonstration, that of induction, described by Aristotle in the *Posterior Analytics* and the *Metaphysics*. By this mode the mind can reach the universal, as the principle of all art and science, syllogistically from experience of individuals. In Aristotle's words quoted in the Prologue to the *Ordinatio*,[226] 'So out of sense perception comes to be what we call memory and out of frequently repeated memories of the same thing develops experience. From experience again—i.e. from the universal now stabilised in its entirety within the soul, the one beside the many which is a single identity with them all—originate the skill of the craftsman and the knowledge of the man of science'.[227] Ockham, for whom like Aristotle, the intellect has only acquired as opposed to innate knowledge, states it as the principle of induction that whatever is predicated of one thing is predicated of all its genus, so that the genus can be inferred from its species.[228] With this general principle as middle term, knowledge of the universal can then be grasped inductively. For example if we know that a certain herb cures a certain complaint and also the general principle that every cause of the same species has effects of the same species, we can then by means of this principle conclude that every such herb cures.[229] Such a proof as we saw before is by an extrinsic middle.[230]

The conditions for such inference depend upon the universality of the term to be inferred. If it is a *species specialissima*, it suffices to know one individual coming under it in a singular proposition, for example that fire heats, because there is no reason why fire should be more heat-giving in one case than in another; if it is a genus, then each of its species must be known through their individuals in singular propositions. But any universal proposition, including one with a *species specialissima*, requires knowledge of many individuals, as it takes more than one act of

[225] *Posterior Analytics*, I, ch. 10, 76 a, 30–5.

[226] *Ordinatio*, Prologue, q. 2, 85.

[227] *Posterior Analytics*, II, ch. 19, 100 a, 1. 3. Also *Metaphysics*, I, ch. 1, 980 a.

[228] Sed tenebit per illus medium 'quando aliquid competit cuilibet contento sub aliquo genere, competit universaliter illi generi'. Et ita tale principium de genere vel de aliquo communi ad plura alterius et alterius rationis accipietur per experientiam et aliquo modo per inductionem, scilicet inferendo unam universalem de genere ex omnibus universalibus, de omnibus speciebus contentis sub genere (*Ordinatio*, Prologue, q. 2, 93).

[229] Per notitiam tamen evidentem alicuius contingentis et notitiam unius veritatis necessarie, non ordinatas in modo et figura, potest accipi notitia evidens conclusionis demonstrabilis per modum declaratum. Quia scilicet scietur evidenter conclusio necessaria per unam contingentem evidenter notam, ex qua contingente sequitur formaliter conclusio illa demonstrabilis. Sicut sequitur formaliter: hec herba sanat, igitur omnis herba eiusdem speciei sanat (*ibid.*, 91).

[230] pp. 272–3 above.

apprehension to know whether this herb or the physician cured a certain invalid. As we have frequently seen, one effect can have many causes.[231]

The basis of all such induction is the intellect's capacity to know immediately—by intuitive knowledge—what is perceived by the senses and apprehended in the imagination (as the sensitive faculty). That enables the intellect to form evident contingent propositions—[232] e.g., 'This hot thing is heat-giving'—from experience of heat by which it can know that something is hot and can transmit its heat. Such propositions can in turn be universalised in the way just described by means of a universal principle.[233] The resulting propositions may be necessary but they do not follow necessarily in formal demonstration, regulated in mood and figure, because they are reached through an extrinsic middle and from a contingent proposition—'This herb cures' or 'This heat is heat-giving'—which cannot be the premise of a demonstration. Accordingly, although the middle here is a necessary truth it is not a necessary middle since there is not a necessary nexus making the conclusion necessary, in which true demonstration consists.[234] As Aristotle says, 'When the conclusion is necessary the middle through which it was proved may yet quite easily be non-necessary. You can in fact infer the necessary from a non-necessary premise just as you can infer the true from the not true'.[235]

We can say then that the difference between induction and demonstration is the difference between knowing the fact and the reason of the fact. They differ as kinds of knowledge but they can produce knowledge of the same kind, as other causes of different natures can produce effects of the same nature, for example heat produced by the sun and by fire.[236] Consequently a conclusion known by experience can also be known by demonstration; and to know it first by one mode and then the other is not thereby to gain new knowledge. Indeed experience can be a stage in demonstration as an indirect partial cause.[237] That it can never be a direct cause is due to the nature of each; as we have said, only a necessary proposition can be the premise of a demonstration, a condition unattainable by what is known only by experience, which is from intuitive knowledge. For demonstration,

---

[231] *Ordinatio*, Prologue, q. 2, 92–3 and *Logic*, III, II, ch. 10.

[232] Unde sciendum quod est quod sensu apprehendente aliquid apprehensibile potest virtus fantastica illud idem imaginari; et non solum fantasia sed etiam intellectus potest illud apprehendere. Quo apprehenso potest intellectus aliquas propositiones contingentes cognoscere . . . (*SL*, III, II, ch. 10).

[233] *Ibid.*

[234] Dico quod intentio Aristotelis est quod necessarium non potest demonstrari per contingens tamquam per aliquam premissam in demonstratione. Per notitiam tamen evidentem alicuius contingentis et notitiam unius veritatis necessarie, non ordinatas in modo ex figura potest accipi notitia evidens conclusionis demonstrabilis per modum declaratum . . . Et tenet ista consequentia non per aliquod medium intrinsecum quo adiuncto esset syllogismus, sed tenet per medium extrinsecum (*Ordinatio*, Prologue, q. 2, 91–2).

[235] *Posterior Analytics*, I, ch. 6, 75 a, 1–18, to which the above reference is.

[236] *Ordinatio*, Prologue, q. 2, 90–1.

[237] Est autem ista notitia intuitiva causa partialis tantum, quia ista notitia non sufficit nisi evidenter sciatur quod omnia individua eiusdem rationis sunt nata habere effectus eiusdem rationis . . . Et si primo sciatur conclusio per experientiam et post eadem conclusio sciatur per demonstrationem non causabitur nova scientia distincta specie, sed fiet unum ex gradu precedente et sequente (*ibid.*, 91).

on the other hand, the premises have to be known as the cause of the conclusion.[238]

That brings us to the requisites for the premises. At the beginning of the third part of the *Logic*, it will be recalled, Ockham specifies that a demonstrative proposition is one reached through evidently known necessary premises; by that it seems he can only mean self-evident premises, for he contrasts demonstrative propositions with probable, or topical, propositions which are neither self-evident nor reached from self-evident premises.[239] He is more explicit in the *Ordinatio* (Prologue) when he says that 'some conclusions are demonstrable from self-evident principles and some can stand with principles which are not self-evident but can only be known by experience'.[240] As the latter can never be part of a demonstration they cannot fulfil the first and third of the conditions—previously stated—of a demonstration, namely that it must be necessary and shown to be such syllogistically; while the second condition that it must be dubitable applies to the conclusion, not the principles.[241]

Unlike Aristotle, then, Ockham's logical conception of necessity excludes any but logically necessary premises, which can only be those which are self-evident. Here as elsewhere it is the notion of necessity which differentiates Ockham's criteria from Aristotle's. Just as Aristotle never expressly formulates the graduations of demonstration, so he has no place for the distinction so central to Ockham between self-evident principles which are indemonstrable and indemonstrable principles which are not self-evident and so not necessary. It is not too much to say that Ockham's theory of demonstration hinges upon their difference. In consequence Ockham, while accepting Aristotle's requirements for premises—namely that they must be true, primary, immediate, better known, and prior to the conclusion, which is related to the premises as effect to cause—diverged in his conception of primary and immediate.[242] For Aristotle a primary proposition is an immediate proposition, or basic truth, to which no other proposition is prior;[243] he did not differentiate kinds of immediate proposition or distinguish orders of priority in the way in which we have seen Ockham do so.

Of Aristotle's other requisites, the stipulation that the premises must be better known than the conclusion follows from the meaning of demonstration, since what is less known or unknown cannot give knowledge of what is either better known or unknown. Moreover, temporally as well as demonstratively, either premise can be known before the conclusion; only when both major and minor are known together is the conclusion also known, whereas if the conclusion is known in-

---

[238] Quia respectu omnis conclusionis demonstrabilis sufficit notitia aliquarum premissarum, ergo non requiritur aliqua alia causa nisi que requiritur ad notitiam premissarum. Minor probatur inductive, quia quantumcumque habeatur notititia abstractiva tam de subiecto quam de passione tali, nisi intuitive videatur aliquod contentum sub subiecto et aliquid importatum per talem passionem virtute cuius cognoscatur evidenter quod hoc inest huic nunquam evidenter scietur talis propositio universalis (*ibid.*, q. 4, 147).

[239] *SL*, III, I, ch. I, 327.

[240] *Ordinatio*, Prologue, q. 2, 85.

[241] *Ibid.*, 76–7.

[242] *Posterior Analytics*, I, ch. 2, 71 b, 20.

[243] *Ibid.*, 71 b, 22–72 a, 8.

dependently of a demonstration, it is known by knowledge which is not peculiar to it but common to every proposition which is similar.[244] This condition explains the last one, that the premises must be related to the conclusion as cause to effect. Ockham here interprets cause in diverse senses. Premises can be called efficient causes in producing knowledge of the conclusion; or for making known the reason of what is known in the conclusion; or because they enable the conclusion to be inferred from them as a natural consequence; or because the conclusion is composed of terms drawn from them, which is how Aristotle understands material cause.[245] Each of these connotations refers to a proper demonstration *a priori*; in an *a posteriori* demonstration, as we shall see, the sequence is reversed, and begins from the conclusion as effect.

Finally, we must consider the first condition upon which all the others depend, namely that the premises must be true. For that the meaning of each term must be known in order to know whether an attribute can be necessarily affirmed or denied of a subject, to achieve which is the object of demonstration.

Accordingly in any demonstration, the definition (*quid est*), real or nominal, of all the terms must be known and in most instances the existence of what they stand for (*quia*) as well. In the case of the subject, that entails knowing its signification, and in all affirmative propositions where it does not have to be proved, its existence; that is to say, the subject when taken significatively in an affirmative proposition must denote what can exist: only in negative propositions can the subject stand for what is impossible. The existence of the attribute must similarly be known in affirmative categorical propositions but not those which are conditional or hypothetical. The reason is the same for both subject and attribute, namely that an affirmative proposition cannot be true if the existence of what is stated in the premises implies a contradiction; hence to be true, being must be possible both for the subject and what is attributed to it. For the same reason the definition as the third term, in being of real things, must also be real:[246] that as we shall see does not mean it cannot in certain cases be a nominal definition. Ockham refers for support to Aristotle's distinction between basic truths—the subject—whose existence has to be assumed and their attributes of which existence has to be proved.[247] The difference of course is that Aristotle did not make the distinction between categorical and hypothetical propositions. Here as throughout Ockham's is a dual point of departure, not only in Aristotle but in scholastic tradition which

---

[244] *SL*, III, II, ch. 16.

[245] *Ibid.*, ch. 15; also *Ordinatio*, Prologue, q. 2, 95–6, and q. 8, 222.

[246] E.g. Breviter ergo dicendum est quod secundum principia Aristotelis de subiecto in propositione affirmativa tam categorica quam (hypothetica et) in demonstratione composita ex una cathegorica et alia hypothetica conditionali, quod oportet precognoscere de subiecto quid significat et quia est; (et) hoc est quod sibi non repugnat esse, ita quod propositio predicans esse de illo subiecto non includat contradictionem. De passione autem in demonstratione simpliciter cathegorica et affirmativa, oportet precognoscere tam quia est quam quid est, propter eandem rationem propter quam oportet de subiecto precognoscere quia est; sed in aliqua demonstratione non oportet precognoscere de passione quia est. De (eius) diffinitione autem oportet precognoscere quia est, propter eandem rationem quam de subiecto (*SL*, III, II, ch. 3).

[247] *Ibid.*; *Posterior Analytics*, I, ch. 10, 76 a, 30–5.

carries almost invariably non- or extra-Aristotelian implications. That should become apparent shortly when we consider how these terms can be known in response to Aristotle's four questions. But first we must complete the preliminaries by examining how the terms have to be essentially true and the different kinds of demonstrations which result from different degrees of necessity and universality.

The requirement that demonstrations be essentially true is entailed by these other two requisites of universality and necessity. It means that the attribute must belong essentially to the subject. As defined by Aristotle, 'Essential attributes are (1) such as belong to their subject as elements in its essential nature (e.g. line thus belongs to triangle, point to line . . .): (2) such that, while they belong to certain subjects, the subjects to which they belong are contained in the attribute's own defining formula. Thus straight and curved belong to line . . . '[248] This is the source of the distinction between the two different modes of essential predication, mentioned in chapter three. By the first essential mode (*per se primo modo*) the predicate essentially defines the subject or a term superior to the subject absolutely and *in quid*, for example, 'Every man is a rational animal' or 'Every man is rational' where the predicates 'rational animal' and 'rational' define 'man', so that if such propositions are necessary they are always essentially true. Similarly in propositions like 'Every man is a body' 'Every man is composed of matter and form', the predicate is affirmed essentially of a term superior to the subject and so of the subject in coming under the superior term, although the predicate defines only the latter. By the second mode of essential predication (*per se secundo modo*) the subject or a term essentially inferior to the subject enters into the definition of the predicate or a term essentially inferior to the predicate, as 'man' is part of the predicate 'able to laugh' in the proposition 'Man is able to laugh': that is to say, 'able to laugh' is defined by reference to man. The same holds for a superior term, as in the proposition 'Every man is receptive of contraries', where substance is the subject of 'receptive of contraries'; accordingly man as inferior to substance must be part of the definition of a predicate inferior to 'receptive of contraries', namely 'receptive of such contraries' as less universal.[249] By either mode propositions which are universal and necessary are essentially true because they express through the relation of subject to predicate the essential nature of what is signified. Aristotle states the connection as follows: 'I term "commensurately universal" an attribute which belongs to every instance of its subject, and to every instance essentially and as such; from which it clearly follows that all commensurate universals inhere *necessarily* in their subject'.[250]

For Ockham, however, these are not invariable accompaniments: propositions can be essential which are not necessary, and *vice versa*. That can be seen from the meaning of 'essential' which as it refers to propositions—as opposed to being when it applies only to God as self-subsistent, or to substances in contradistinction to accidents, or efficient and final causes to the exclusion of material causes—has a broad and strict sense. By the first it extends to every proposition in which subject

[248] *Posterior Analytics*, I, ch. 4, 73 a, 34–40.
[249] *SL*, III, II, ch. 7; *Ordinatio*, Prologue, q. 6, 178–80.
[250] *Posterior Analytics*, I, ch. 4, 73 b, 26–30.

and predicate are related *per se primo modo* (when the predicate defines the subject) or *per se secundo modo* (when the subject enters into the definition of the predicate) in the way just described. In the second strict sense a proposition which is essential by either mode had also to be absolutely necessary, such that it cannot be false. Consequently by this sense, not every essential proposition is necessary: that is to say, all categorical assertoric propositions of the present denoting generable and corruptible things. Once again this is the dividing line between Ockham as a Christian and Aristotle as a pagan philosopher. Where Aristotle accepts as necessary a proposition like 'Every man is an animal' in which 'animal' is predicated essentially of 'man', Ockham regards it as contingent because man is not a necessary being. Only if man exists can he be an animal; hence to become part of a necessary proposition man's animality must be stated in the mode of possibility or another hypothetical or conditional equivalent.[251]

Conversely, a necessary proposition is not essential when the inferior (i.e. less universal term) is predicated of the superior (more universal) in a particular case, for example 'Some man is an animal'. To be both necessary and essential, predication must be strict and direct, which excludes particular propositions. A proposition is then necessary and universal. It is in this strictest sense of essential that propositions can enter into demonstrations.[252] A negative proposition can also be essential when the position is reversed, and subject and predicate do not enter into the definition of the other by either mode. They are also necessary when the terms stand only for absolutes and so can be denied of one another.[253] Thus if it is true and necessary that no man can be an ass and that every man is able to laugh, it is true and necessary that no ass can laugh. As with affirmative propositions, predication must be proper to the term concerned; otherwise it will not be essential.[254]

That brings us to the final requisite for a demonstrable proposition: that as well as being universal, necessary and essentially true it must be primary. In Aristotle's

---

[251] Preter istos modos dicendi per se sunt aliqui alii modi dicendi per se, scilicet quando aliquid predicatur per se de altero; et sunt duo modi. Unus est quando predicatum ponatur in diffinitione subiecti. Aliud est quando subiectum ponitur in diffinitione predicati. Circa istos modos est primo advertendum quod iste terminus 'per se' vel quod predicatur de propositione, dupliciter dicitur, scilicet stricte et large. Large dicitur propositio per se quando subiectum cadit in diffinitione predicati vel e contrario, vel per se superius ad unum sicut quando unum diffinit reliquum vel diffinitur per reliquum. Et isto modo hec est per se: 'Omnis homo est animal' . . . Aliter accipitur 'per se' stricte, et sic cum prioribus conditionibus ad hoc quod propositio sit per se requiritur quod ipsa sit simpliciter necessaria ita quod nec potuit nec poterit esse falsa. Et sic accepto 'per se', quamvis secundum opinionem Aristotelis qui ponit generatio et corruptio rerum est eterna, multe propositiones cathegorice et de inesse et de presenti sunt per se, tamen secundum veritatem tales de terminis importantibus precise res corruptibiles sive creatas non sunt per se, quia non sunt necessarie. Unde sic accepto 'per se', hec non est per se: 'Omnis homo est animal', quia potest esse falsa puta, posito quod nullus homo sit. Verumtamen propositiones de possibili et eis equivalentes composite ex talibus terminis sunt per se. Unde ista est per se: 'Omnis homo potest esse animal' sumpto subiecto pro eo quod potest esse (*SL*, III, II, ch. 7).

[252] *Ibid.*

[253] Nam alique negative sunt per se in quibus tamen predicatum non diffinit subiectum, nec econverso. Est autem sciendum quod omnis negativa necessaria in qua terminus subiectus et predicatus sunt mere absoluti et non relativi nec connotativi est per se. Unde hec est per se, 'Omnis homo non est asinus' (*ibid.*).

[254] *Ibid.*

words, 'An attribute belongs commensurately and universally to a subject when it can be shown to belong to any random instance of that subject and when the subject is the first thing to which it can be shown to belong'.[255] Ockham calls such a proposition immediately true (*primo vera*); he defines it as one in which the predicate does not belong more immediately to any other subject which is more general than its own subject or to a subject which is not predicable of its own subject. The predicate which thus belongs immediately and exclusively to its subject is universal in relation to its subject, and the subject is the first subject of the predicate if it is predicable in the second mode of essential predication.[256]

These conditions obviate the mistake of treating propositions as primary and universal when they are not. The first—that there must be no term more universal than the subject—avoids the three ways of possible error enumerated by Aristotle.[257] When the subject is individual and unique—like the sun—and so treated as universal; when the subject belongs to different species whose genus is excluded because it has no name; and when the subject is only a part but is taken for the whole. The first condition therefore ensures against attributing to the less universal term (species) what belongs to the more universal term (genus).[258] The second condition—that the attribute does not belong more immediately to a subject which is not predicable of its subject—prevents misattributing to a concrete what belongs more immediately to its abstract; for example heat-giving, which is predicable of heat before it is of something hot, since only if there is first heat can something become hot through calefaction. Accordingly, as we saw in connection with first principles, the proposition 'Every hot thing is heat-giving' presupposes as a further principle the proposition 'All heat is heat-giving'; both are indemonstrable, but only the second is immediately true. Negative propositions can also be immediately true when the predicate cannot be denied of a term more general than the subject, such as the proposition 'No corporeal substance is an incorporeal substance'.[259]

In the Prologue of the *Ordinatio* Ockham defines this relation between a first subject and its attribute by which a proposition is *primo vera*. 'I call a first subject that to which the attribute can belong, with everything else excluded and nothing of the attribute excluded' (*omni alio circumscripto, et nulli ipso circumscripto*). Thus, 'capable of learning' has the intellective soul as its first subject because it belongs exclusively to it, such that the soul alone can learn and nothing without the soul.

---

[255] *Posterior Analytics*, I, ch. 4, 73 b, 32–3.

[256] Est autem propositio primo vera quando predicatum nulli subiecto communiori illo subiecto nec alicui subiecto non predicabili de illo subiecto, prius competit quam illo subiecto. Et tale predicatum respectu talis subiecti vocatur universale, et tale subiectum vocatur primum subiectum illius predicati, saltem si sit predicabile secundo modo dicendi per se (*SL*, III, II, ch. 8).

[257] *Posterior Analytics*, I, ch. 5, 74 a, 4–11.

[258] Per primam particulam excluditur a primo subiecto omne inferius demonstrandi... Istis modis peccatur attribudendo universale alicuius communioris minus communi (*SL*, III, II, ch. 8).

[259] Per secundam particulam excluditur concretum alicuius abstracti cui primo competit. Unde si nihil sit calefactivus nisi calor tunc hoc predicatum 'calefactivum' non primo competeret calido, quia hec non esset primo vera 'Omne calidum est calefactivum' sed hec est primo vera 'Omnis calor est calefactivus'... (*ibid.*).

Man is also the subject of the same attribute, but not the first subject just because the soul is still capable of learning if man does not exist;[260] the same applies to the accidents which belong to a whole through its parts. Because an attribute belongs to it first subject immediately it is not demonstrable, for as Aristotle says, an indemonstrable proposition is one to which no other proposition is prior, as we have considered. Only if subject is taken in the sense of a term of which something can be predicated—as opposed to that which stands for everything of which something is predicable—can an immediate proposition be demonstrable through an immediate subject: that is to say when the subject has a nominal definition as a connotative term.[261] That applies especially to mathematical propositions as we shall consider before long. By the same token when a subject is not a first subject it can be demonstrated; for, as more or less universal than the first subject it is not known immediately and can thereby be known through a middle term.[262]

Does that mean that essential propositions are demonstrable? St Thomas Aquinas and Duns Scotus denied that they could be doubted, because they took essential propositions to be self-evident.[263] For Ockham, however, as we have seen, propositions can be essential without being necessary, and they can be both necessary and doubtable. Hence when he raises the question in the Prologue of the *Ordinatio*[264] his reply is not unequivocal. The difference between the two modes of essential predication is that by the first mode the predicate signifies nothing extrinsic to the subject or its superior term and its intrinsic parts; but by the second mode something distinct from the subject is denoted as in the proposition 'Man is able to laugh' where the capacity to laugh is something additional to man.[265] By this second mode most propositions are demonstrable; some are also demonstrable by the first mode but the demonstration will then be *a posteriori* through an extrinsic middle.[266] The reason, not given here, is to be found in what Ockham had said elsewhere about immediate propositions (which all essential propositions by the first mode are): either they are self-evident and cannot be doubted or they are known by experience and so dubitable; only the latter can therefore be demonstrated.[267] But since they are known through experience they can never be

---

[260] *Ordinatio*, Prologue, q. 4, 144–5: Et voco subiectum primum illud cui potest competere omni alio circumscripto et nulli ipso circumscripto. Verbi gratia: anima intellectiva est primum subiectum respectu 'susceptibilis discipline', quia omni alio circumscripto adhuc potest anima suscipere disciplinam, et nihil potest suscipere disciplinam circumscripta anima intellectiva. Sed homo est subiectum illius passionis; non tamen primum sed magis secundarium, quia homine destructo adhuc potest anima suscipere disciplinam.

[261] *Ibid.*, 145–6. [262] *Ibid.*, 147–8.

[263] D. Webering, *Theory of Demonstration*, 48.

[264] *Ordinatio*, Prologue, q. 6, 177: Utrum sola propositio per se secundo modo dicendi per se sit scibilis scientia proprie dicta.

[265] Et tunc dicitur 'per se primo modo' quando nihil importatum per predicatum tamquam predicabile de illo predicato universaliter . . . est totaliter extrinsecum subiecto. Et sic nihil predicatur per se primo modo nisi per superiora et partes intrinsece rei, vel importantia precise partes rei. Per se autem secundo modo dicitur illus quod importat aliquid distinctum realiter ab importato per subiectum, sicut hic: 'Omnis homo est risibilis. . . . (*ibid.*, 180).

[266] *Ibid.*, 181–2.

[267] E.g. Et ita prima principia in arte et scientia adquisita per experientiam sunt dubitabilia, et per consequens non sunt per se nota (*Ordinatio*, Prologue, q. 2, 86).

necessary. Hence they are demonstrable *a posteriori* in the way that we have seen when we learn that fire is heat-giving or that a certain herb cures.[268] In consequence propositions which are essential by the first mode are never strictly demonstrable and when they cannot be doubted they are self-evident and necessary. Thus it is by the second mode of essential predication that propositions are strictly demonstrable—although not all are—in the proper sense that the premises are not only true, primary, immediate, better known than, and prior to the conclusion, but are also its cause.[269] Otherwise the proposition known will be a principle and not a conclusion.[270]

That brings us to the different kinds of demonstration. These are of two kinds, *a priori* and *a posteriori*. As we have mentioned before *a priori* demonstration is from cause to effect and *a posteriori* demonstration from effect to cause. Hence only *a priori* demonstration can fulfil the conditions of proper and demonstrative knowledge *propter quid*. Although they are often interchangeable, there are as we shall see exceptions: and whenever knowledge is not *propter quid*—i.e. the result of necessary demonstration which cannot be doubted—it is *quia*. The most perfect kind of demonstration is a *demonstratio potissima*. Ockham defines it in the Prologue of the *Ordinatio* as

that which is *propter quid*, universal by both kinds of universality [i.e. in respect of things and time], and affirmative. From this it follows that it is in the first figure [i.e. where the middle is the subject of the major and the predicate of the minor] and therefore *propter quid*. And because it is *propter quid* it follows that it is known through the cause (*per causam*). Similarly because it is affirmative it is ostensive [i.e. direct].[271]

A *demonstratio potissima* is therefore the strictest kind of demonstration *propter quid*. Ockham's definition is more explicit than Aristotle's statement that a universal proposition is superior to a particular proposition and an affirmative proposition is prior to and better known than a negative proposition.[272] But that does not lead him to follow Aristotle in restricting the middle term to the formal and essential definition of the first subject. The nature of the middle term—upon which the nature of any demonstration depends—is discussed in question five of the Prologue. There Ockham considers where and when it is a formal definition and which term it defines. So far as the first is concerned, Ockham concedes that generally the formal definition is middle term of a *demonstratio potissima*; but even here there are exceptions.[273] For example 'capable of learning' as the attribute of man cannot be demonstrated through the definition of man, because—as we have discussed in a

---

[268] In the Prologue, q. 6, 181, Ockham gives us an example, 'Every ass is an animal' which can be doubted *per se primo modo* and can be syllogised through the middle term 'Everything that moves is an animal'.

[269] Et ideo si premisse fuerint vere et prime et immediate et notiores et priores, et tamen non fuerint cause conclusionis—hoc est notitia premissarum non fuerit causa notitie conclusionis—non erit demonstratio (*ibid.*, 182).

[270] *Ibid.*, q. 4, 147.   [271] Prologue, q. 5, 165.

[272] *Posterior Analytics*, I, chs. 24 and 25, 85 a–87 a.

[273] Secundo dico quod demonstrationis aliquando medium est definitio et aliquando non (Prologue, q. 5, 165).

previous context—rational soul is the first subject of capable of learning. Hence it cannot be the definition of man as a first *a priori* indemonstrable principle from which a *demonstratio potissima* is formed, since it depends upon a prior principle, namely 'The intellective soul is capable of learning'.[274]

Following Aristotle, Ockham understands by a formal definition what is intrinsic and essential to the thing defined, and by a material definition, what is extrinsic to it.[275] A formal definition is such not because it expresses the form of a thing but rather its essential principles. In the strict sense a formal definition can be only of composite substances, but in the broad sense it can apply to anything which has distinct parts of the same nature, and includes many mathematical definitions: for example the definition of a triangle is of a figure bounded by three lines where the lines do not differ in kind.[276] When there are other causes they give an extrinsic definition, following Aristotle's division between a cause which is either identical with the essential nature of a thing or distinct from it; in the latter case an essential nature is proved through another essential nature: that however is not a demonstration but a dialectical proof.[277] In both cases, for Aristotle, the definition acts as the middle we seek in all our enquiries.[278] Ockham agrees that cause and middle are the same when cause is understood as everything to which it immediately belongs and without which it could not belong to something else.[279] But an extrinsic cause has only nominal definition; otherwise it would be indemonstrable, because a definition is convertible with what it defines. Accordingly if the latter were inferred from a real definition it would be from something intrinsic and so not from an extrinsic cause; indeed by God's absolute power at least it could be without a cause.[280]

Now no nominal definition can be the middle term of a proper demonstration. As we have mentioned and shall consider in more detail, in a proper demonstration both subject and attribute have to be known in a real and a nominal definition;[281] the only exceptions are certain mathematical propositions of which more will be said in a moment. In all other cases a nominal definition as middle term will lead not to a demonstration but a *petitio principii*, as in the inference 'Everything productive of heat is heat-giving; Heat is heat giving; Therefore all heat is heat-giving', which is circular because knowledge of the minor premise is not distinct from and prior to knowledge of the conclusion. It therefore fails to fulfil the condition of a demonstration, that the meaning of both subject and attribute must be known before the conclusion;[282] otherwise if the conclusion is known in a nominal

---

[274] *Ibid.*, 166.
[275] Dico ergo quod definitio formalis datur per intrinseca et essentialia, hoc est per conceptus exprimentes principia intrinseca. Definitio autem materialis datur per extrinseca rei cui primo competit definitio (*ibid.*, 171).
[276] *Ibid.*, 169–70.
[277] *Ibid.*, 170–1; *Posterior Analytics*, II, ch. 2, 89 b–90 a, and ch. 8, 93 a, 1–15.
[278] *Posterior Analytics*, II, ch. 2, 5–6.
[279] Prologue, q. 5, 176.
[280] *Ibid.*, 170–1.
[281] *SL*, III, II, ch. 4, and ch. 12.
[282] *Ibid.*, ch. 12; also chs. 18 and 34.

definition at the same time as the minor premise—i.e. that in which the subject is defined—it cannot be doubted, and so not demonstrated. For example if we know that 'creative' means to produce something from nothing, we cannot both know the proposition 'God produces from nothing' and at the same time doubt that God is creative. Hence the syllogism 'Everything which produces something from nothing is creative; God produces something from nothing; therefore God is creative' begs the question in being from a definition to what it defines.[283]

That is not to say, however, that nominal definitions do not enter into essential definition as part of the middle in a *demonstratio potissima*. On the contrary they are themselves the middle in reaching the definition of all composite terms which include those signifying all artificial things like house and saw—to use Ockham's examples—most mathematical terms, and some natural terms. These all have in common subjects with one or more essential parts, or other things to which they refer, which are knowable independently of their subjects. Hence their terms are always connotative in the same way as attributes which are predicable of their subjects by the second essential mode (*per se secundo modo*). The difference is that here the subject is the connotative term and its nominal definition is the middle in its complete definition. For reasons which we shall later elaborate, an essential definition is never demonstrable because it is always immediate;[284] hence demonstration of a definition is only possible where the essential definition is not given or is known only incompletely.

Now as we have discussed in chapter three connotative terms signify one thing directly and consignify something else obliquely, or, as Ockham puts it in the *Logic*, the same thing diversely or diverse things, as 'white' signifies a substance directly and consignifies the quality of whiteness inhering in it indirectly, and 'creative' God directly and what he can create—a creature—indirectly. Connotative terms always have a nominal definition, but in some cases it is exclusively nominal and in others it is the essential definition as well. A definition is exclusively nominal when it denotes only the term which it defines, and has no real signification because like 'chymera' or 'goat stag', it stands for what is impossible and so contradictory to existence.[285] It has essential definition when it signifies what can exist; it is in this second sense that definition is demonstrable, when one part can be the means of inferring the other. That occurs when the formal definition is immediately known and can act as the indemonstrable premise of the material definition. It therefore applies to terms in which one part can be known in an independent definition from another part, enabling the definition of the latter which is not immediately given

---

[283] *Ordinatio*, Prologue, q. 2, 116–17.

[284] Dico quod definitio exprimens quid rei nunquam potest demonstrari de definito, quia semper illa propositio est immediata (*Ordinatio*, Prologue, q. 5, 173).

[285] Non solum autem ista diffinita absoluta diffiniuntur, sed etiam diffinita connotativa, et illa sunt in duplici differentia. Quedam enim sunt talia de quibus significative sumptis impossibiliter predicatur 'esse', cuiusmodi sunt, 'chymera', 'hyrocervus' . . . Alia sunt de quibus possibiliter predicatur 'esse', cuiusmodi sunt 'album', 'nigrum' . . . Prima habent precise diffinitiones exprimentes quid nominis, nullo modo exprimentes quid rei, sicut 'chymera' habet diffinitionem exprimentem quid hoc nomen 'chymera' significat sed non habet diffinitionem exprimentem quid est illa res quam 'chymera' significat quia nulla talis res est nec nullus talis res esse potest.

to be deduced from the former. Which is another way of saying with Aristotle that such terms have ' "a middle", i.e. substantial cause other than that being itself', as opposed to terms whose essential natures are immediate and must be assumed or known other than demonstratively.[286]

In the *Posterior Analytics* Aristotle stated two alternative ways of knowing the definition of a thing's nature. One is as a statement of the meaning of the term, or an equivalent nominal formula, which tells us nothing of its existence. The other is by a quasi-demonstration exhibiting a thing's essential nature, which differs from a strict demonstration in showing what, as opposed to why, a thing is.[287] Ockham related one mode to the other through the relation of formal to material definition; their meaning underwent some modification between the *Ordinatio* and the *Logic*, probably to align them more closely with the terminology of the four causes employed in the *Posterior Analytics*; but their import remained the same. Thus in the *Logic*, formal definition becomes the formal and/or final cause, and material definition the material and/or efficient cause.[288] At the same time the *Logic* makes explicit what is more implicit in the Prologue of the *Ordinatio*, namely that the formal definition is both exclusively nominal (*quid nominis tantum*) and the only proper and strict definition. At first sight this appears paradoxical since an exclusively nominal definition denotes only the term as an expression and not the essential nature of anything. The Prologue of the *Ordinatio*, however, gives two senses of 'nominal', the first of which is the same as the first of Aristotle's senses, mentioned above: namely that it is a statement of a word's meaning which as a purely nominal expression is indemonstrable.[289] It is just this sense which corresponds to that of formal definition given in the *Logic*: i.e. that it is an indemonstrable statement of a thing's nature from the meaning of the terms defining it. Since, however, it is also the one strict and proper definition, it must also be a nominal definition of what is essential; this is confirmed in the *Ordinatio* where a formal definition is said, as we have seen, to be of the essential elements of the thing defined.[290] The formal definition is therefore the strict and proper meaning of a thing's nature known solely in a nominal and indemonstrable statement.[291] The material definition it will be recalled is also a nominal definition; but in this case

---

Alia autem connotativa, hoc est illa que significant diversa vel idem diversimode, hoc est affirmative vel negative, in recto vel obliquo, vel in aliquibus talis modis diversis, possunt habere duplicem diffinitionem, scilicet unam que exprimat quid nominis tantum et aliam que exprimit quid rei (*SL*, III, II, ch. 33).

[286] *Posterior Analytics*, II, ch. 9, 93 b, 26.

[287] *Ibid.*, 94 a, 1–10.

[288] Et iste diffinitiones que sumuntur a causa finali et formali vocantur diffinitionis formales, et ille que sumuntur a causa efficiente et materiali vocantur materiales (*SL*, III, II, ch. 34).

[289] Sed loquendo de definitione exprimente quid nominis, distinguo de ea, quia dupliciter accipitur. Vel pro aliqua oratione quam omnes loquentes de nomine intelligunt per nomen; vel pro oratione cuius veritas sequitur ex veritate prioris rationis (*Ordinatio*, Prologue, q. 5, 173).

[290] *Ibid.*, 170.

[291] Illa que exprimit quid nominis tantum est propriissima diffinitio, propter quod vocatur a non nullis diffinitio formalis et diffinitio secundum speciem. (*SL*, III, II, ch. 33). And: Et est dicendum quod generaliter diffinitio exprimens quid nominis non potest demonstrari de diffinito, sed illa presupponitur omni demonstrationi et omni syllogismo (*ibid.*, ch. 34).

because it is of what is extrinsic. In the *Logic* Ockham makes its relation more precise: a definition is material of one thing when it is essential (*quid rei*) of something else. Hence a material definition is not a proper definition of the same thing. For that reason in being the essential definition of another thing it can only be the nominal definition of that which it defines materially and so improperly.[292]

These differences are illustrated in the example of a saw. Its formal definition expresses its final cause in the statement that 'A saw is something by which we can cut wood'; this tells us only what is essential to its nature as a saw and nothing of how its purpose is fulfilled. Hence we can know that a saw cuts wood without knowing whether it is made of air, water, wood, or precious stone. That further knowledge of its constituents—namely metal—belongs to its material definition. The latter is equally integral to its complete definition; but it is not its proper definition for the reason that to be metallic is not peculiar to being a saw; if something other than metal could achieve the same end of cutting wood, that too would be a saw. Hence the material definition is less universal than the formal definition and comes under the latter.[293] When the two definitions are juxtaposed, the material can be inferred from the formal as its middle term. That follows from what has already been said: for if the formal cause is immediate and indemonstrable it serves as the principle, and the material cause, in not being already known, becomes known as the conclusion. Thus if the formal definition of house is 'something which excludes cold, wind, rain and heat' expressing its final cause of affording shelter, we can infer the material condition that it must be composed of materials like wood and stone which give protection, in the following syllogism: 'Everything which excludes cold, wind, etc. is composed of wood and stone; A house is a shelter which excludes cold, wind, etc.; Therefore a house is composed of wood and stone.'[294] This differs grammatically from a proper demonstration in being reached through only part—the formal part—of the definition and yielding the other part—the material part—as its conclusion. Although it is *a priori*, it produces knowledge not of the attribute but of a subject's complete definition. For that reason as Aristotle said it is a quasi-demonstration.[295]

In such cases as these, then, formal and material definition are of what is ontologically integral but logically separable.[296] Which occurs where a thing has

---

[292] Illa autem que exprimit quid rei non est propriissima diffinitio talis diffiniti, propter quod frequenter dixi quod tale connotativum non habet diffinitionem nisi exprimentem quid nominis tantum, et ideo non diffinitionem quid rei, quia talis diffinitio non est propriissima diffinitio talis diffiniti, immo forte non est diffinitio sua. Et propter hoc vocatur ab aliquibus diffinitio materialis (*ibid.*, ch. 33).

[293] *Ibid.* Also ch. 17.

[294] Et iste diffinitiones sic se habent quod diffinitio materialis potest demonstrari per formalem diffinitionem. Verbi gratia supposito significato istius termini, scilicet 'domus', et per consequens presupponatur diffinitio exprimens quid nominis, qua nota, acquiritur sine demonstratione. Et diffinitio sumpta a cause finali domus est ut sciatur 'cooperimentum prohibens nos a frigore, vente et pluvia et caumatibus. Quo facto potest demonstrari quod domus componitur ex lignis, lapidibus et aliis, per talem argumentum 'Omne prohibens a frigore etc.' componitur ex talibus . . . (*ibid.*, ch. 34). Also ch. 17.

[295] *Ibid.*

[296] Est etiam notandum quod in hac parte non solum vocatur causa materialis aliqua pars

logically determinate parts knowable independently of one another, so that the definition is composite and not immediately known in knowing the subject.[297] For Ockham as for Aristotle, that means that the subject has a cause other than itself, enabling its attribute to be elicited by any of the four causes.[298] It is in such cases that the nominal definition acts as middle term.

The other area in which it does so is mathematics. The difference is that here their demonstrations can be *potissima* because they are of the first subject through an essential definition. This is due to the two distinctive characteristics of mathematical terms. The first is that their subjects, as we have briefly remarked before, are connotative in having distinct essential parts separately definable and yet do not connote a composite substance as an absolute composed of subject and accidents.[299] The reason is that mathematical subjects are non-existential and although their primary terms, such as unit and magnitude, do denote real things, terms like triangle can be known without knowing whether they exist. Hence their definitions can be essential (*quid rei*) without having existence (*si est*). It is in this connection that Aristotle refers to the arithmetician 'who assumes both the nature and the existence of unit';[300] and for Ockham it is of mathematics that Aristotle's statements about *a priori* demonstration of a first subject through an essential middle must be understood.[301] In all other demonstrations, even where the attribute is a negative connotative term, existence must first be posited. For example a negative term like 'corruptible' whose nominal definition is that 'one part of a material substance is separable from another', must in order to negate its subject first presuppose its existence. It can therefore only be part of a necessary demonstration, that a material substance is corruptible, if it has as a prior indemonstrable principle a hypothetical proposition of existence, namely 'If such a material substance

---

realiter a forma componens cum causa ea ipsam recipiendo; sed causa materialis vocatur hec pars integralis rei quomodo ligna et lapides vocantur materia domus, et due premisse et conclusio vocantur materia demonstrationis (*ibid.*).

[297] Patet quod est maior ratio quod una passio sit demonstrabilis quam alia, quia aliqua passio presupponit subiectum suum habere partes realiter distinctas sine quibus nullo modo possit sibi competere, et per distinctam notitiam illarum partium devenitur in notitiam passionis de subiecto, et ideo illa est demonstrabilis per definitionem exprimentem illas partes tamquam per medium (*Ordinatio*, Prologue, q. 4, 157–8).

[298] *SL*, III, II, chs. 34, 35, 39.

[299] Similiter definitio aliquando datur per principia essentialia vel per declarantia principia essentialia . . . Large tamen accipiendo potest competere alicui habenti distinctas partes eiusdem rationis; et tali definitione difiniuntur multa mathematica, sicut triangulus, quadrangulus, et sic de aliis (*Ordinatio*, Prologue, q. 5, 170).

[300] *Posterior Analytics*, II, ch. 9, 93 b, 24–5.

[301] Postea autem cognitio cuius et quales nunc sunt sue partes, sine ulteriori experientia de passione, potest eadem passio sciri de subiecto; et hoc per diffinitionem exprimentem illas partes que in obliquo vel negative importantur per passionem. Et tales demonstrationes sunt mathematice propter quod de eis in parva vel nulla requiritur experientia, et demonstrantur de eis semper vel frequenter per diffinitionem subiecti tamquam per medium. Et quia in paucis scientiis habemus diffinitiones proprie a priori, nisi in mathematicis ubi communiter de termino demonstratur passio de suo subiecto primo per diffinitionem subiecti tamquam per medium, ideo frequenter dicit Aristoteles quod passio est demonstrabilis de suo subiecto proprio (*SL*, III, II, ch. 12).

composed of separable parts exists . . . '.[302] A mathematical demonstration, on the other hand, can be *potissima* without such a condition.

That explains the other feature of mathematical demonstration, that the essential parts defining the subject do not constitute a strict definition in the accepted sense which it has for absolute composite things, namely as expressing genus and essential difference. Instead the different parts can be enumerated through separate demonstrations, each producing as a conclusion its own definition. That is how many authors interpret the *Posterior Analytics* in what is said there about a *demonstratio potissima* (an expression not employed by Aristotle) reached through a definition of the subject.[303] In such cases a demonstration can be said to be from necessary and indemonstrable premises only in the broad sense, because not every syllogism productive of knowledge is from necessary and indemonstrable premises.[304]

On the other hand, to infer the nominal definition of an attribute already demonstrated of a subject, say risibility of man, does not give a *demonstratio potissima* but a description containing what is accidental to the subject (as risible is to man) or a concrete term connoting a form inhering in the subject. Such a definition is therefore only partial and not of a thing's essential nature. As such it can be the middle in a definition of an attribute when it connotes that part of the subject to which the attribute as an accident or form belongs, together with its efficient cause.[305]

Mathematical propositions then are demonstrable for the same reason as any proposition having for a subject a connotative term; namely that its attributes are dubitable, in the way that the sum of the angles of a triangle is equal to two right angles can be doubted, and its parts may initially be unknown.[306] That means that no proposition whose subject is composite, mathematical any more than non-mathematical, is tautological. The difference between one and the other is rather that mathematical demonstration is of a first subject by means of a nominal definition of essential nature in the sense already stated: that its terms have no real or independent signification.

It can be said therefore that whether the definition as middle term is strictly of the first subject or a superior term, or broadly of it, as in the case of mathematics, it is always of the subject as a formal definition of essential nature. Among Ockham's contemporaries, however, Richard of Connington held that the definition was of the attribute;[307] and in the Prologue of the *Ordinatio* Ockham states his reasons for opposing him. If, he replies, the definition were of the attribute, it would be of what is either intrinsic or extrinsic. It cannot be intrinsic, because there are many attributes, namely those denoting absolute subjects, which do not

---

[302] *Ibid.*, ch. 40. Ockham here does not compare negative connotative terms of existence with mathematical terms, but merely states this condition for the former. See also ch. 26.

[303] Verumtamen sciendum quod talis diffinitio talis subiecti non semper est propriissima diffinito, qualis est substantiarum precise. Sed frequenter est diffinitio indicans partes integrales rei, quales sunt demonstrationes mathematicorum; et de tali demonstratione potissima per quam demonstratur passio de suo subiecto primo, per diffinitionem subiecti tamquam per medium, intelliguntur multe auctores Aristotelis in libro Posteriorum (*ibid.*, ch. 40).

[304] *Ibid.*   [305] *Ibid.*   [306] *Ibid.* and ch. 26.

[307] *Ordinatio*, Prologue, q. 5, 159–62.

have intrinsic definition, that is they are indemonstrable. Nor can it be extrinsic, because such a definition would either include the subject, which is impossible, since no middle term can contain another term, whether the major or the minor premise; or it would include something other than the subject, which precludes it from belonging to a universal demonstration, for the reason already given, that an extrinsic cause—as the material definition—cannot be the middle term of a proper *demonstratio potissima*. Again according to Richard of Connington the definition of the attribute is demonstrated *a priori* from its subject, but a *demonstratio potissima* is from indemonstrables; therefore the attribute cannot be the principle of a strict demonstration. Nor, finally, is the definition really distinct from what it defines; hence again as we have considered, one cannot be the cause of the other and so not the middle of a demonstration which, as Richard of Connington himself says, is through its causes.[308] Richard's mistake, like that of Duns Scotus, to be examined in another context, is to regard the inherence of the attribute in the subject as the result of a formal cause; a simple form however inhering in a subject as an accident is itself the form of something else, and thus can have only an efficient or a final cause. It cannot therefore be defined by its form or demonstrated by a formal cause; and far from the middle being the definition of the attribute as its formal cause, the middle must demonstrate that the subject is the cause of the attribute through defining the subject.[309] Here as throughout Ockham understands the formal definition as expressing not an inherent form but the essential principles of what is defined.[310] Hence when Richard of Connington says that the middle is the formal cause of the attribute, he cannot mean that it is the cause of its inherence in the subject because then the subject and attribute would be equally the cause and so both constitute the middle term. The only alternative is to regard the middle as the cause of the attribute, in which case it must be of the subject, expressed through its definition.[311] Accordingly whenever the middle term is a definition, it is of the subject.[312]

These, then, are the requisites for a *demonstratio potissima*; they are only fulfilled in the first figure, which is universal, affirmative, direct, and *propter quid* because known necessarily through the cause. That excludes negative syllogisms in the second figure, which although *a priori* are indirect and so *quia*,[313] as well as particular demonstrations in the third figure which are not *de omni* either because the attribute is not predicable of everything coming under the subject or because it holds for only a limited time.[314] In practice, despite Ockham's qualification,

---

[308] *Ibid.*, 162–3.   [309] *Ibid.*, 167.

[310] Ad illam declarationem quod definitio formalis est medium demonstrandi, dico quod verum est: quando definitio est medium in demonstratione universali tunc definitio formalis subiecti est medium. Sed ista definitio non includit precise formam rei, sed dicitur formalis quia includit principia essentialia rei (*ibid.*, 169).

[311] *Ibid.*, 167.

[312] Tertio, dico quod quando medium est definitio, est definitio subiecti non passionis. Hoc patet, quia talis definitio debet exprimere causam et aliquid necessario requisitum ad hoc quod passio predicetur de subiecto. Sed tale est definitio subiecti, quia exprimit partes subiecti sine quibus impossibile esset passionem illi subiecto competere (*ibid.*, 166).

[313] *SL*, III, II, ch. 19.   [314] *Ordinatio*, Prologue, q. 4.

demonstratio potissima is always by means of a formal definition containing genus and essential difference, or a mathematical definition expressing essential parts of the same kind. Before we examine its nearing upon Aristotle's four questions we must first consider the characteristics of demonstration *quia* and *propter quid*.[315]

To begin with, they differ, it will be recalled not over what is known but over how it is known: that is to say the same thing, for example an eclipse (which Ockham takes from Aristotle as his main illustration of the differences between the two kinds of demonstration) can be known both *propter quid* and *quia* in different syllogisms, one giving knowledge of the reasoned fact, the other merely of the fact. In the first case, knowledge of the conclusion depends absolutely upon prior knowledge of the premise as its cause, and not at all upon prior experience of the conclusion which can be previously unknown, as it can be unknown that the moon is eclipsed until demonstrated in a syllogism such as: 'When the moon is in a certain position it is eclipsed; The moon is now in such a position; Therefore the moon is now eclipsed'. The conclusion is here deduced *a priori* from the premises and owes nothing to its own knowledge as a fact.[316] In a demonstration *quia* on the other hand it does; for the moon can then be known to be eclipsed without knowing its cause. Hence instead of knowledge of the effect following from the premises necessarily and unconditionally as a reasoned fact, it is better known than the cause, and forms the premise in a syllogism in which the cause is the conclusion. The process is therefore reversed from an *a priori* demonstration *propter quid*, and in form parallels demonstrations of a definition; the difference is that *a posteriori* demonstration infers not one part of a demonstration from another but establishes the connection between the particular and the general, both known inductively. That means, as Aristotle said, relating the major premise to the middle by the minor premise, as opposed to relating the major to the minor by the middle in an *a priori* demonstration.[317] The distinction is tantamount, as Aristotle remarked, to having no middle term in induction;[318] for what is demonstrated is precisely the definition of the middle, as in the following *a posteriori* syllogism of an eclipse: 'When the moon is eclipsed the earth is interposed between the sun and earth; The moon is now eclipsed; therefore the earth is now interposed between the sun and earth'. Here the interposition of the earth explains this eclipse, so that the conclusion is clearer than the premise in being directly derived from experience. But that is not the same as better known, because it is known only as fact through knowing an eclipse as a fact instead of as the conclusion of a demonstration. We can therefore continue to ask why the earth is interposed between the sun and the moon after knowing that its interposition is the cause of an eclipse.[319] To be

---

315 *SL*, III, II, chs. 17–23.   316 *Ibid.*, chs. 17 and 19.
317 *Prior Analytics*, II, ch. 23, 68 b, 8–36.   318 *Ibid.*, 31–33.
319 Pro quo sciendum quod illa vocatur demonstratio propter quid, que est ex propositionibus necessariis prioribus, qua habita cessat omnis dubitatio et omnis questio circa conclusionem, sicut si scirem quod luna eclipsatur, per hoc quod scio quod terra interponitur inter solem et lunam, cessat omnis questio de iste conclusione: luna eclipsatur. Nec queritur utrum luna eclipsatur nec queritur quare eclipsatur. Demonstratio quia est illa que non est ex prioribus propositionibus, vel qua habita non cessat omnis questio circa conclusionem (*SL*, III, II, ch. 19). Also 17 and 20.

propter quid, and resolve further doubt, the order of the terms would have to be through the middle term as definition thus: 'When the moon is eclipsed the earth is interposed between the sun and the moon; The earth is now interposed between the sun and moon; Therefore there is now an eclipse'. Here the fact of an eclipse is no longer the middle but the conclusion, reached necessarily from the premises through the definition of the eclipse as the middle. It therefore explains not only what an eclipse is but why it has occurred.[320]

An *a posteriori* syllogism can nevertheless be called a demonstration because it is productive of knowledge, which like that of a definition can become the starting point for necessary knowledge through a rearrangement of the terms in the way just illustrated. By the same token it is not demonstrative when it does not provide knowledge; hence a syllogism can be at once demonstrative for one person and non-demonstrative for another according to whether knowledge is or is not acquired.[321] As Ockham has said in the Prologue of the *Ordinatio,* there can be knowledge of the same kind from both demonstration and experience; so that if something is known first by experience and then by demonstration it does not represent new knowledge of a different nature.[322]

Demonstration is *quia* not only when it is strictly *a posteriori,* with the cause stated in the conclusion, but also when the cause is remote and indirect. Such a syllogism will then be negative and in the second figure:[323] for example proving that something is not an animal as follows: 'Nothing that does not breathe is an animal; A plant is not an animal; Therefore a plant does not breathe'. Here, again, the fact—that a plant does not breathe—is demonstrated but not the reason, this time because the middle is not immediately convertible with the major: that is, not being an animal is not equivalent to being a plant; hence inability to breathe cannot be the immediate cause of plant and so does not give scientific knowledge. Where on the other hand the major and middle reciprocate, the demonstration will be *quia* because the conclusion contains knowledge of the cause not expressed in the premises; it is therefore more explanatory than the premises. That holds even

---

[320] Ockham's comparison is taken from Aristotle's other example (*Posterior Analytics,* I, ch. 13, 78 a, 30–78 b, 3) of planets which do not twinkle as evidence of their proximity to the earth. *SL,* III, II, ch. 19.

[321] *SL,* III, II, ch. 17.

[322] It is not clear whether this remark applies only to *a posteriori* demonstration, which is how Moody, *Logic of William of Ockham,* 253, interprets it, or whether Ockham envisages that knowledge equivalent to *a priori* knowledge could be acquired non-demonstratively.

[323] . . . differt demonstratio quia a demonstratione propter quid, et hoc dupliciter in eadem scientia sicut tactum est in precedente capitulo. Uno modo quia demonstratio quia licet sit per prius, non tamen per causam immediatam: hoc est non est per medium convertibile. Aliquando tamen demonstratio quia est per posterius, ita quod in premissis non accipitur aliquid importans causam quare sic denotatur esse per conclusionem, sed magis e converso . . . Et ita universaliter quando propositio prior scitur evidenter per hoc quod premisse posteriores sciuntur evidenter, est demonstratio quia, immo etiam sufficit quod una premissarum sit posterior conclusione. Similiter quando demonstratur effectus non per causam immediatam sed per remotam est demonstratio quia. Sed advertendum quod semper talis demonstratio est negativa in secunda figura ita quod affirmative non contingit sic demonstrare . . . (*SL,* III, II, ch. 20).

if only one of the premises is known evidently; for the sequence remains from existence to cause.[324]

There is one further respect in which knowledge *quia* and *propter quid* differ, and that is as different branches or sciences. Here, however, one does not act formally as premise and the other as conclusion; rather they are related accidentally as subalternating and subalternated knowledge by which the principles of the former are appropriated by the latter in the way that knowledge of geometry enters into the study of optics or the mathematics into physics.[325] We shall have more to say on this topic in the next chapter.

That brings us to Aristotle's four questions. From what has been said it will be apparent that they revolve principally around the questions of existence (*si est*) and the nature of what exists (*quid est*), as these concern both subject and attribute. For it is directly in response to these two questions that the demonstrability, whether of a subject or its attributes, arises; and, as we have repeatedly seen, that is possible only if there is a middle term. Accordingly, Ockham agrees with Aristotle that every question of demonstration is a question of a middle, whether in establishing existence (as in questions *si est* and *quia est*) or the nature and cause of what exists (in questions *quid est* and *propter quid est*). Only in the second case is this a syllogistic middle, when it is almost always a definition of essential nature; in *a posteriori* and inductive demonstration on the other hand experience can be the middle if it leads to knowledge of what was previously unknown, which is the sense in which any middle should be understood.[326] The nature and possibility of demonstration therefore revolves around the middle term; and since the difference between demonstration *propter quid* and *quia* demonstration consists in the presence or absence of an essential definition—itself indemonstrable—as middle term, the problem of definition is central to that of demonstration. Ockham, however, unlike Aristotle in part two of the *Posterior Analytics*, does not treat definition as a question apart,[327] but submits it to the same inquiry of whether and how it can be known according to Aristotle's four questions. That occupies the latter part of the section in the *Logic* devoted to demonstration, which is a more systematic development of the discussion in part two of the *Posterior Analytics*. Of these four questions *propter quid* stands apart from the other three; for, as we have just seen, the latter can constitute a demonstration *quia* independently of giving the reason or cause *propter quid*. To establish the connection between subject and attribute in an *a posteriori* demonstration we need only know the existence and definition of the subject and the nominal definition of the attribute; the cause is another matter requiring separate demonstration. Thus, as we have seen from the example of the

---

[324] *Ibid.*, chs. 19 and 20.   [325] *Ibid.*, ch. 21.

[326] Ex predictis patet quod omnis questio vel querit si est medium deveniendi in notitiam prius quesiti, sicut questio quia et questio si est, vel querit quid est illud medium, sicut questio quid est et questio propter quid est. Ex quo patet quod omnis questio est quodammodo questio medii. Sed sciendum est quod medium hic sicut dicit Lincolniensis non accipitur hic pro medio syllogistico sed vocatur hic medium omne illud per quod decurrit ratio in notitiam prius ignoti; et ita experientia potest vocari medium hic, quia quandoque aliquis per experientiam cognoscit illud quod prius ignoravit (*ibid.*, q. 23).

[327] As Moody observes, *Logic of William of Ockham*, 260.

moon's eclipse, *quia est* answers the two questions, whether the connection between subject and attribute is a fact, and whether there is a middle by which the fact can be known. Such knowledge, however, does not give knowledge of the cause; that is provided by demonstration *propter quid*, which answers the question, what the strict and proper middle is. Hence demonstration *propter quid*, as knowledge of the reasoned fact, presupposes knowledge of the fact, whether known demonstratively (*quia*) or through experience and induction.[328] Like Aristotle, Ockham groups *quia est* with *si est*, and *quid est* with *propter quid est*; the first two ask if there is a middle; the second two what the middle is,[329] understanding middle as cause in every case. Correspondingly when the question is simply one of existence, unqualified by the connection with an attribute, it is confined to the fact of existence (*si est*) and the nature of what exists (*quid est*), but the division is still between asking whether there is a middle and what the middle is.[330] For the object of each of these questions is, as Aristotle said, to know the cause.[331]

It can be seen then that demonstration depends upon knowing *si est* and *quid est*; only if the existence and the nature of both subject and attribute are known can the connection between them be established. In the case of the subject, both, as we have previously said, must be assumed since it is of the subject that an attribute is demonstrated. The attribute on the other hand is what has to be proved; nothing else than its nominal definition need therefore initially be known, as it must be known of every term which enters into any kind of discourse. With this knowledge we can then put all four questions of the attribute, so that if we know that there is a moon and what it is and we know what the word eclipse means, we can ask whether the moon is eclipsed, or why it is eclipsed, or if there is an eclipse, or what is an eclipse. Here *propter quid* and *quid est* are the same thing because the essential definition—as Aristotle said[332]—of the attribute contained in the answer to *quid est* is also the

---

[328] Omnis enim demonstrator, si dubitat aliquid quod debet scire, vel dubitat de aliqua propositione in qua predicatum importat aliam rem vel eandem rem alio modo ab illo quod importatur per subiectum, sicut potest dubitare de tali propositione 'Luna est eclipsabilis', et tunc potest tripliciter querere circa talem propositionem. Primo enim potest querere an talis propositio sit vera. Secundo potest querere, supposito quod sit certum apud eum quod est propositio vera, quid est medium per quod potest fieri notum quod propositio illa est vera. Et istos duos modos querendi comprehendit Aristoteles sub questione 'quia est'... Scito igitur quod est vera, sicut scito quod luna eclipsatur, et scito quod est aliquod medium per quod certificari potest quod luna eclipsatur, et scito quid est illud medium, utpote scito quod est aliquis effectus vel aliquid aliud per quod certificari potest quod luna eclipsatur, contingit ulterius querere quare et propter quid luna eclipsatur. Unde potest aliquis scire evidenter quod luna eclipsatur . . . tamen potest ignorare causam quare luna eclipsatur. Et ista est alia questio, scilicet propter quid; et tunc queritur propriisimum medium per quod potest sciri quod luna eclipsatur (*SL*, III, II, ch. 23).

[329] Ex predictis patet quod omnis questio vel querit si est medium deveniendi in notitiam prius quesiti, sicut questio quia et questio si est, vel querit quid est illud medium, sicut questio quid est et questio propter quid est (*ibid.*).

[330] *Ibid.*

[331] *Posterior Analytics*, II, ch. 2, 90 a, 5: to 'We conclude that in all our enquiries we are asking whether there is a "middle" or what the "middle" is: for the middle is precisely the cause that we seek in all our enquiries'.

[332] *Ibid.*, 14. 'For in all these examples it is clear that the nature of the thing and reason of the fact are identical'.

explanation of the reason or cause why the attribute belongs to the subject provided by the answer *propter quid*. This, however, is only reached through first knowing the connection between subject and attribute as a fact derived from experience.[333] The order is therefore from knowledge of the subject and a nominal definition of the attribute to the fact of the attribute's existence and its essential nature. That known, we can then ask whether the attribute is predicable of the subject, and what the middle term is (*quid est*) which in turn, given this knowledge, enables us to know the reason in a demonstration *propter quid*. The latter is only a special case of *quid est*, as *quid est* is itself more specific than the nominal definition of the attribute with which we begin. Each delimits the attribute still further until we know not only its nature but its nature as the cause of its connection with a specific subject. Which is why Aristotle said they are almost the same.[334]

The difference between demonstration *quia* and *propter quid* is therefore the difference between the middle known as a fact and the middle known as the reason for the fact; each expresses the cause, but *quia* does so from the effect where *propter quid* exhibits it as the cause syllogistically and necessarily. We must now enquire how we come to know the terms in a demonstration in response to these questions.

The first, *si est*, concerns a thing's existence; it is answered when it can be shown that being, either actual or possible, can be predicated of something as its attribute. Now there are two kinds of subjects, absolute affirmative terms denoting individual things which exist *per se* and independently; and connotative, negative or relative terms.[335] The existence of the first, as we have repeatedly discussed, can never be demonstrated because knowledge of absolutes is intuitive through experience. They therefore have no middle term by which they can be known, as we can only know whiteness through knowing something white. Accordingly, in all such cases, the answer to the question *si est*, of whether something exists, is experience: in perceiving that something is, we also, as Aristotle says, perceive what it is; and conversely in knowing what something is we know that it is.[336] In this onto-

---

[333] *SL*, III, II, ch. 23.

[334] Patet autem in isto processu quod diffinitio exprimens quid nominis passionis presupponitur in omni questioni, et quod prima questio est questio si est de passione, que querit medium, id est viam deveniendi in notitiam passionis que est possibilis: hoc est quod 'esse' de ea possibiliter predicatur. Secunda autem questio est questio quid est de passione, quid sicut illud quod diffinitio sua explicat in generali, tertia questio querit magis in speciali, quod quidem quesitum est generale ad illud propter quid luna eclipsatur, quia corpus opacum est commune ad terram. Scito autem si est et quid est et sicut in speciali de passione, queritur ulterius an passio sit predicabilis de subiecto isto et quod est medium deveniendi in notitiam illius quesiti, quo scito queritur in speciali causa propter quam competit passio isti subiecto. Et ita quid et propter quid querunt idem. Sed questio quid est de passione querit magis in generali, et questio propter quid querit magis in speciali, quamvis forte aliquando possibile est quod utreque querunt idem etiam in speciali. Et propter ista vult Philosophus quod in tali processu questio quid est et propositio propter quid quasi idem sunt, et quod medium et causa idem sunt, quia medium syllogisticum explicat causam frequenter in tali processu . . . (*ibid.*).

[335] *Ibid.*, ch. 25.

[336] Et ita talis propositio si est non potest terminare nisi per experientiam, hoc est nisi per notitiam intuitivam que est principium experientie, et de tali loquitur Philosophus cum dicit 'Qui ignorat quid est, nesciat si est; quemadmodum habemus quia est, sic habemus quid est'. Unde quantum aliquis scit de aliquo tali quid est, tantum scit si est et e converso (*ibid.*). Cf. *Posterior Analytics*, II, ch. 8, 93 a, 18–20. Also, *Ordinatio*, Prologue, q. 5, 175.

logical identity of being and nature, where being is conceived as exclusively individual, we have the quintessence of Ockham's outlook: on the one hand it reduces all logical terms and propositions to ways of describing individual things; on the other it excludes from demonstration, because from knowledge, what cannot be known intuitively, i.e. individually, for which reason as we shall discuss, no demonstration of God is possible. The distinctiveness of Ockham's standpoint lies precisely in the individual import which it gives to Aristotle's logic, so that the source of all knowledge is not merely intuition of being but of individual being, and knowledge of essence or nature knowledge of individual existence. This view receives explicit statement in Ockham's rejection of any distinction between essence and existence, including God; but where in him they signify absolutely simple being, in creatures they denote beings which have a cause other than themselves.[337] 'To be' and 'thing' mean the same; they differ only as verb and noun. Hence being or essence far from signifying what is independent of existence, and need not exist (the classical scholastic view), is always individual existence.[338] To exist therefore is to be an individual; and as Ockham explains in the Prologue of the *Ordinatio* to know *quid est* entails knowing *si est* in the sense that it ensures that the nominal definition is of what can be and so does not contradict the possibility of existence.[339]

With negative, connotative and relative terms, however, *si est* is not immediately known through experience, for which reason some are demonstrable. When existence is predicated of such terms they form propositions in which an attribute other than that of existence is predicated of its subject. Thus the proposition 'There is an eclipse' is equivalent to 'Something is eclipsed' and 'It is hot' to 'Something is hot'. Some of these can be demonstrated when the subject is a term more universal than the first subject, i.e. when the subject is not an absolute term, in which case the definition of the subject is the middle (as we saw in demonstrating that man has a rational soul). But in the strict sense these are not demonstrations, in not being of the first subject, while those subjects which are immediately known, as say heat and something hot, are indemonstrable.[340] We shall defer a full examination of such terms to demonstrability of attributes since it is to that category that they belong. For the rest we can say that *si est* of an absolute subject can only be known intuitively, and that, as giving knowledge of existence, it entails knowledge of what is known. That, however, is not the same as complete knowledge; to obtain it we have to turn to essential definition (*quid est*).

Quid est answers the question of what something is with a complete definition of essential nature. It therefore, as we have said, goes beyond the nominal definition which accompanies knowledge of every term, as the prerequisite of all discourse

---

[337] *Ibid.*, ch. 27.

[338] *Ibid.*

[339] Dico quod non potest sciri 'quid est' sine 'si est'. Hoc est, non potest sciri 'quid est' sine notitia qua scitur hoc esse vel fuisse vel futurum esse, quia aliter naturaliter non potest sciri esse possibile in rerum natura, et quod 'quid nominis' non includit contradictionem (*Ordinatio*, Prologue, q. 5, 175).

[340] *SL*, III, II, ch. 26.

but not real knowledge of what it defines.[341] We have already discussed definition of connotative terms which we saw could be either strict demonstrations through a nominal definition as the middle, when as with mathematical terms, the subject consists of a series of essential principles each carrying its own nominal definition; or an *a posteriori* demonstration by the means of one or more of the four causes, especially where the definition of the subject term contains, as the definition of all those signifying *artificialia* does, a final cause: its nominal definition can then be the middle in a syllogism giving the complete definition. In all these cases definition is by the second mode of essential predication (*per se secundo modo*) which in this case defines it. The definitions of such subjects are demonstrable because they are connotative terms which can be known through a nominal definition.[342]

Absolute terms, however, must be known through their essential definitions. These can be of two kinds: essential definition in the strictest sense (*propriissime dicta*) which is exclusively of what belongs to the subject as an independent substance, and essential definition *per additamentum* which in addition to being of what is intrinsic to the subject connotes something extrinsic to it. Thus where 'rational animal' is an essential definition exclusive to man expressing genus and difference, the definition of the soul as 'the act of the body' is *per additamentum* in including 'body' which is not a part of the soul. In both cases, however, essential definition is always of absolutes.[343] But only in the first, that of intrinsic essential definition, does the attribute define the subject *per se primo modo*, which as we know is indemonstrable. Definition *per additamentum* in also connoting what does not belong immediately and essentially to the subject has at the same time one or more terms which define the subject *per se secundo modo*; and these are in some cases demonstrable. Accordingly, the ways in which the two kinds of definition can be known vary.[344]

Intrinsic essential definition (*propriissime*) is of genus and essential difference, the genus standing for the subject, as we saw in chapter two, absolutely as an independent whole, and the difference or differences connoting the essential part

---

[341] Sed ignorata diffinitione exprimente quid nominis non potest quis cum alio disputare. Et ideo quando quilibet addiscit significata vocabulorum tunc addiscit diffinitionem quid nominis quamvis non addiscat diffinitionem exprimentem quid rei. Non est igitur diffinitio exprimens quid rei necessaria disputanti, quia talis diffinitio non tantum exprimit quid significat nomen sed exprimit etiam quid res est (*ibid.*, ch. 28).

[342] *Ibid.*, chs. 33 and 34, and above.

[343] Talis autem diffinitio est duplex: quedam est diffinitio talis que non importat aliquid extrinsecum rei alio modo quam importat rem vel partem rei; et talis diffinitio vocatur diffinitio propriissime dicta, que non potest esse nisi substantiarum vel nominum substantiarum ... Talis est diffinitio, animal rationale, cum sit 'animal' genus et 'rationale' differentia, quia 'animal' importat totum hominem et 'rationale' importat partem hominis sicut suum abstractum. Alia est diffinitio importans quid rei, que simul cum hoc quod importat rem importat vel exprimit aliquid aliud quod non est de essentia rei, sicut diffinitio 'anime' que est ista: 'Anima est actus corporis physici organici' ... que importat animam et aliquid quod non est pars anime, puta corpus, quod non est anima nec pars anime. Et ista vocatur diffinitio per additamentum, et tales diffinitiones importantes quid rei convertuntur cum nominibus mere absolutis affirmativis (*ibid.*, ch. 28).

[344] Diffinitio data per additamentum non solum explicat essentiam rei sed etiam simul cum hoc explicat aliquid aliud ... Et ideo talis diffinitio non solum componitur ex aliquo predicabili per se primo modo sed etiam componitur ex aliquibus predicabilibus secundo modo, que sunt passiones diffiniti (*ibid.*, ch. 32).

or parts. Neither genus nor difference is ever demonstrable *a priori* because each is known immediately in knowing the absolute thing whose essential nature they constitute and from which they are inseparable. Hence there is no middle between the thing and its parts; they are given together in the same act of knowing what they define. That means that genus, in signifying the subject as an essential unity, is always indemonstrable; for the subject cannot be known in an essential definition apart from its genus, as for example in the definition of man as an animal.[345] Here both 'man' and 'animal' denote absolutes by concepts formed in the mind from experience of individual men and animals, and common to all men and animals, in the way already familiar to us and recounted here.[346] From their combination into propositions (through the verb 'is') the intellect can then in seeing a man know that man is an animal. It does so through knowledge of what the terms stand for and not by demonstration. Hence every proposition in which the genus defines the subject (that is by the first mode of essential predication) is indemonstrable because known self-evidently, through its terms.[347]

This restates what has been said earlier in the *Logic* and the Prologue of the *Ordinatio*, that predication *per se primo modo* is indemonstrable and self-evident; but with the amplification that this is because both genus and species are concepts which signify univocally and essentially all the individuals coming under them. Ockham underlines the immediate nature of the definitions which they give in considering three objections. To the first that we can in fact form *a priori* syllogisms, demonstrating, say, that man is a substance, he reiterates that a syllogism is only a demonstration when it makes known what was previously not known, which is not the case here. To the second objection that we can doubt propositions such as 'Man is an animal' Ockham distinguishes mental propositions, composed of simple and proper concepts like these, and spoken and written propositions. The first can never be doubted because they are immediate; but the second can, because words are conventional terms imposed upon concepts and they may not correspond to a simple and proper concept. When they do not, they will be of a composite concept instead, that is one composed of simple concepts of other things none of which is proper to the meaning of the word. In that case the signification of the word will not be self-evident because it will not be of what has been known immediately and intuitively. Thus if someone has never seen a lion, but only knows of it through the reports of others, he will form a notion of a lion composed of concepts taken from his experience of other animals; and although he

---

[345] Diffinitio exprimens quid rei non data per additamentum semper continet pro prima parte aliquod genus diffiniti, et pro alia parte vel aliis partibus continet differentiam vel differentias essentiales vel aliquos obliquos significantes per se et primo partes rei. Et iste partes sunt diverse. Nam genus importat totum; alie vero partes significant determinatas partes rei. Prima pars diffinitionis, puta genus, nec a priori nec a posteriori potest demonstrari de diffinito, sicut quod homo sit animal demonstrari non potest, sed propositio talis sine syllogismo acquiritur mediante notitia intuitiva (*ibid.*, ch. 29).

[346] *Ibid.*

[347] Et ita quelibet talis propositio, in qua predicatur genus de diffinito propriissime dicto, habetur sine omni discursu; et hoc est universaliter verum de omni genere respectu speciei que est mere absoluta; quia talis propositio per se cognoscitur statim cognitis terminis (*ibid.*).

can believe that a lion is an animal he can also doubt the fact until he himself has had the experience of seeing a lion. After that he can then from his concept of an animal, as the major premise, identify what he has seen as a lion, and so conclude that it is an animal; and in that broad sense, such an inference can be called a demonstration.[348]

Each of these two replies reaffirms that genus and species are simple and proper concepts of absolute things known intuitively. So does the reply to the third objection which is that, as we can first doubt and then know that something seen from a distance is animal, we can demonstrate that it is an animal. Ockham concedes its dubitability but not its demonstrability, on the ground that demonstration is universal but this case is of an individual. Even, however, granting that it could be demonstrated it would still not be of a simple concept, for the same reason as in the case of the lion: only when it is known intuitively can there then be a proper concept of it; and once it is known its definition cannot be demonstrated in a proper demonstration.[349]

Genus, therefore, is indemonstrable by any mode. Difference, on the other hand, can be demonstrated of a species a posteriori because, as we saw in chapter three, it is a connotative term signifying one part of the subject indirectly.[350] That enables it to be demonstrated by its effects. Thus a man equipped with a concept of his own sensitive soul and the meaning of sensitive derived from his own experience, could recognise the same attributes from the sensitive actions in another being of which he also had a simple concept. From these effects he could conclude, what he previously did not know, that all such beings also have a sensitive soul. The effect of being sensitive, accordingly, serves as the middle in deducing sensitive soul (connoted in the term 'sensitive being') as the essential difference in a species. Which is again how Aristotle proves that all material substances have matter as their essential difference.[351]

Even so it is not a complete definition because the genus always remains indemonstrable and so does a species when it is a simple absolute concept. There can therefore never be a priori demonstration of essential definition because there is no middle by which the complete definition (quid rei) of genus and essential difference can be known before what is defined.[352] That applies to all simple and absolute

---

[348] Ibid.   [349] Ibid.

[350] Quamvis propositio in qua predicatur genus absolutum de specie mere absoluta composita de conceptibus simplicibus demonstrari non possit nec a priori nec a posteriori, tamen propositio in qua predicatur differentia de specie tali a posteriori demonstrari potest. Nam differentia, sicut dictum est prius, importat unam partem in obliquo, et ideo quia per effectus demonstrari potest talem rem habere talem partem, ideo per effectus demonstrari potest differentia talis de specie tali (ibid., ch. 30).

[351] Ibid.

[352] Ex predictis potest patere quod diffinitio a priori demonstrari non potest de specie diffinita. Diffinitio enim de nullo potest per prius et notius predicari quam de diffinito; et per consequens per nullum medium potest demonstrari de diffinito a priori. Nec etiam potest talis diffinitio demonstrari a posteriori de specie que sit conceptus mentis simplex et proprius significatis causatis per speciem precise, quia quamvis una pars talis diffinitionis esset demonstrabilis a posteriori de subiecto, tamen alia pars non est demonstrabilis de subiecto tali nec a priori nec a posteriori (ibid., ch. 31).

concepts of genus and species which signify individuals immediately *per se* and *in quid* in the manner discussed in chapter three. On the other hand where we know something immediately without knowing its complete essential definition *quid rei* we can arrive at its definition either by abstraction or by an *a posteriori* inference. By abstraction we begin with its essential parts from which we form a concept of the whole. This becomes the complete definition once the concept of genus is abstracted from the individuals coming under the definition. It can be applied to other individuals and concepts; and like any complete definition known immediately of the individuals which belong to it, it will be indemonstrable. By an *a posteriori* demonstration the order is reversed with the whole as a generic concept known first and the parts, not at first known, deduced from it; in that way the definition will be at once from experience and inference, and by both ways the genus will—as always—be indemonstrable.[353]

Finally there is Aristotle's method of division which, as we saw earlier, is not demonstrative but designed to elucidate the logical order of the parts contained under the genus already known.[354] For Ockham both the modes in which it can be done depend upon immediate knowledge of the genus acquired in one or other of the two ways just described. By the first of Aristotle's modes the genus is divided into its essential difference, giving rise to a new genus which is in turn divided, yielding a further genus and so on until a complete description of the terms is had through a series of diverse genera and differences. For example if man is known to be a substance, substance can be divided into corporeal and incorporeal, of which corporeal can be attributed to man. Corporeal substance, or body, then becomes the next genus and is divided into animate and inanimate with animate as the next attribute. Animate is then divided into sensitive and non-sensitive being, leading finally to rational and irrational as the division of sensitive which is equivalent to animal. The final definition of man is then a corporeal, animate, sensitive, rational substance.

The other mode of division confines enumeration of differences to the same genus, as in Aristotle's example of 'triad' where the genus 'number' is divided first into 'odd' and then into 'prime'. The complete definition of 'odd prime number' is for that reason indivisible; for unlike the previous method, where not only the whole definition but also the last difference (rational) can define the subject (man), it contains no second or third genus compounded of the previous genus and difference, each separable from the other. By neither mode, however, can the definition be taken significatively of what it defines, since it is of second intentions standing not for real things but concepts, and so presupposes the existence of that which it describes.[355]

---

[353] *Ibid.* The restatement of this position in *SP*, I, 5 misled Brampton into believing that it made universal cognition primary, on which grounds he denied the authenticity of the *Summulae* (*Isis* 55 (1964), 418–26). Also ch. 29, *Ordinatio*, d. 3, q. 6, 497, and *Quodlibet* I q. 13.

[354] *Ibid.*; the reference here is to the *Topics*, VII (ch. 3, 153 a, 6–154 a, 12) and the *Metaphysics*, VII, but Aristotle also treats division in the *Posterior Analytics*, II, ch. 13, 96 a, 24–97 b, 5.

[355] In primo processu non solum tota oratio est convertibilis cum diffinito sed etiam

Essential intrinsic definition therefore, as *per se primo modo*, is neither demonstrable from existence nor demonstrates existence, save in the qualified and partial manner discussed. When it is *per additamentum*, however, the extrinsic part, which is always defined by the second mode of essential predication, can sometimes be demonstrated *a priori* and sometimes *a posteriori* according to whether or not there is a middle. Thus the definition of whiteness 'as the colour most dazzling to the sight' is indemonstrable because whiteness as well as its genus colour can only be known from experience intuitively. 'Incorruptible' on the other hand, as a negative connotative term which cannot be known of anything significatively and immediately, is demonstrable *a priori* through an essential definition of 'angel', although the genus substance remains indemonstrable as the major premise thus: 'Whatever is an incorruptible substance is without parts; An angel is a simple being without parts; Therefore an angel is in an incorruptible substance'.[356] A case like this is the nearest we can come to a proper demonstration of essential definition and it always remains incomplete. Accordingly the question *quid est* is always answered in part and often completely by experience; by demonstration no definition can be known completely and only sometimes is known in part.

Next comes the question *quia est*, of how the attribute is known. Now demonstration centres on the relation of subject and attribute; hence the nature of demonstration will be conceived according to how that relation is conceived. This has two facets: the first, treated in the Prologue of the *Ordinatio*, concerns the meaning of attribute; the second, the diverse ways in which it can be predicated of a subject.

In the Prologue of the *Ordinatio* Ockham discusses whether an attribute is really distinct from its subject.[357] He begins with John of Reading's opinion, taken over from Duns Scotus, which he rejects, that they are really the same but formally distinct, since to have one without the other, when one is necessarily predicated of the other, would be contradictory. To this Ockham replies that apart from the impossibility of a formal distinction in creatures, if it were true of subject and attribute, the attribute, in being inseparable from the subject, would then be known immediately together with the subject and so indemonstrable of it.[358] Instead an attribute is by definition always really distinct from its subject, whether it is taken

---

ultima differentia est convertibilis cum diffinito . . . In secundo processu nulla pars diffinitionis est convertibilis cum diffinito, sed quelibet erit in plus, et tota oratio est convertibilis. Hoc tamen generale est quod nihil scitur de diffinito per divisionem, propter hoc quod primus intellectus non componit talem diffinitionem sed quicquid scitur de diffinito scitur per aliam viam. Hoc tamen haberetur in fine, quia scitur quod hec oratio est diffinito talis diffiniti; non tamen per hoc scitur quod hec diffinito significative sumpta predicatur de diffinito significative sumpto. Et hoc vult Aristoteles quando probat quod per divisionem non syllogizatur nec demonstratur diffinitio de diffinito inquantum explicat quid est diffinitum secundum quod eum exponit Lincolniensis. Unde per talem artem diffiniendi non cognoscitur diffinitio de diffinito significative sumpto, in quantum scilicet explicat quid est res, sed hoc potest precedere artem diffiniendi; sed per artem diffiniendi partes diffinitionis debite ordinantur (*SL*, ibid.).

356 *Ibid.*, ch. 32.
357 *Ordinatio*, Prologue, q. 3.
358 *Ibid.*, 130–2.

for a real thing, in which case it is an accident or a form inhering in a subject, or for a concept. It is in the latter sense that it is employed in demonstration as a term predicable *per se secundo modo* of a subject as another term. As such they are by definition distinguished from one another.[359] It is in their logical relation as terms— and not as John of Reading held in their ontological unity as different facets of the same thing—that their necessary connection lies. As terms an attribute differs from a subject in always being predicated by the second essential mode, where it signifies the subject directly and consignifies something additional to the subject indirectly, as 'risible' signifies man together with the act of laughing, and 'creative' God together with what is created.[360] For that reason an attribute is of what is distinct from and accidental to the subject. Hence far from being of what is necessarily the same thing, which was John of Reading's mistake, involving the contradiction that something necessarily one can be known to be different from itself, subject and attribute represent different things in a real distinction; they signify not the necessary inherence of one thing or form in another but the predicability of one absolute as an accidental quality or form of another.[361] Their separateness is thus the condition of their demonstrability; for only if one can be known without the other, and so their necessary connection doubted, can it be demonstrated.

That brings us to the second aspect of how that can be done, discussed in the next question—four—of the Prologue and in the *Logic* (part three, second part) as the third of Aristotle's four questions. Like the answers to the previous two, the answer to *quia est* turns on the distinction between what can be known immediately, and as such is indemonstrable, and what in not being known immediately can be known through a middle demonstratively. Now since, as we have just said, an attribute is a connotative term predicated of the subject and something else (i.e. by the second essential mode)[362] its demonstrability will depend upon whether this additional something can be signified separately from the subject: that is to say upon how the subject is connoted by it. Ockham distinguishes four main kinds of such attribution, two indemonstrable and two demonstrable, according to whether or not the subject has determinate parts really distinct from the subject.[363] If it has, they can be known independently of and prior to the subject; and then through a definition of the subject's essential parts (for example the three angles of a triangle), an attribute can be demonstrated of a subject (that the angles of a triangle are equal to two right angles). If the subject has no distinctive parts, the attribute will be indemonstrable because nothing belonging to the subject can be known prior to and independently of it, but only immediately that the subject is known immediately through experience. There will therefore be no middle between attribute and subject, which is the case either when the attribute, in addition to signifying the subject directly, connotes a form inhering in it or another absolute extrinsic to it: for example, 'calefactible' and 'creative'. As their nominal definitions

[359] *Ibid.*, 133–4.   [360] *Ibid.*, 134–5.   [361] *Ibid.*, 136–8.

[362] Et hoc est quod in sciendo quomodo propositio per se secundo modo dubitabilis potest evidenter cognosci (*SL*, iii, ii, ch. 35).

[363] *SL*, iii, ii, ch. 12.

show, one part cannot be known without knowing the other: for knowing that something can be hot entails also knowing that heat inheres in it, which can only be known immediately from experience.[364] Similarly, to know that something is able to create something else is to know that something is a creature. Neither heat nor creature, therefore, is known prior to or better than its subject from which each, whether intrinsically or extrinsically, is inseparable.[365]

That is where they differ from the two kinds of demonstrable attribute, the subjects of which are connotative terms whose parts are separable. In the first of these the attribute signifies the subject directly and its essential parts, together with something which is extrinsic, indirectly in the way that the attribute 'having three angles equal to two right angles' denotes triangle as the subject, and connotes three angles as its essential parts, together with two right angles, which are extrinsic to them. The second kind of demonstrable attribute is a negative connotative term signifying the subject directly and negating its parts indirectly, as 'corruptible' signifies substance and connotes that its parts can cease to be or can be separated.[366] We have already seen the way in which both kinds of attribute can be demonstrated of a first subject through the subject's definition: that holds almost without exception, and includes virtually all mathematical attributes. What distinguishes these subjects from the two previous kinds, which are indemonstrable, is that we can doubt whether they are composed of parts. Hence if we know, say, that every substance composed of parts is corruptible because the parts are separable, and we then encounter something which is composed of parts we can arrive at a *demonstratio potissima* that all such things are corruptible. In the same way we can demonstrate that every triangle has three triangles equal to two right angles, except in this case, as we have also already considered, we do not have to posit the existence of what is being demonstrated as we do in all propositions with the terms of natural

---

[364] Ad argumentum principale patet quod est maior ratio quod una passio sit demonstrabilis quam alia, quia aliqua passio presupponit subiectum suum habere partes realiter distinctas sine quibus nullo modo posset sibi competere, et per distinctam notitiam illarum partium devenitur in notitiam passionis de subiecto, et ideo illa est demonstrabilis per definitionem exprimentem illas partes tamquam per medium. Aliqua autem passio, quantum est ex se, nullam presupponat distinctionem partium quin simpliciter potest poni quacumque illarum partium circumscripta, et ideo nihil est exprimens quecumque intrinsica suo subiecto cui prius vel notius conveniat quam subiecto, et ideo talis non est demonstrabilis (*Ordinatio*, Prologue, q. 4, 157–8).

[365] Est ergo sciendum quod aliqua propositio in qua predicatur passio de suo subiecto primo est indemonstrabilis et aliqua non. As cuius evidentiam est sciendum quod aliqua proprie passio importat in recto precise idem quod importatur per subiectum et aliquam formam realiter sibi inherentem in obliquo. Alia autem passio precise importat in recto illud idem quod importat subiectum et in obliquo importat aliam rem non sibi inherentem nec essentialem nec accidentalem ... Exemplum primi, 'calefactibile' respectu sui primi subiecti, nam 'calefactibile' non importat nisi quod importatur per calorem et subiectum in obliquo. Quod patet ex diffinitione exprimente quid nominis quod 'aliquod poten shabere calorem'. Examplum secundi, 'creativum', nam 'creativam' nihil importat nisi deum in recto et creaturam in obliquo, ut patet ex diffinitione exprimente quid nominis illius, que est ista: 'Aliquid potens creare aliquid' ... De passione primo modo dico quod universaliter quod nulla talis potest demonstrari de subiecto suo primo, quia talis passio si primo ignoretur de subiecto suo primo potest non sciri de eo nisi per experientiam tantum, ut patet inductive. Unde dicendum est de passione secunda propter eandem rationem (*SL*, III, II, ch. 12). Also *ibid*., ch. 35, and *Ordinatio*, Prologue, q. 4, 144–7.

[366] *Ibid*., and ch. 35.

things for their subject. Accordingly, as we have frequently said, granted the condition that something with determinate parts exists, attributes both affirmative and negative can be demonstrated of it.[367]

That does not mean, however, that no attributes can be demonstrated of absolute subjects or of connotative subjects whose parts cannot be known independently of it. There are two main ways in which they can. The first is when the subject is qualified; for then the attribute is no longer known immediately of the subject but only according to certain conditions. Thus there is no means of demonstrating the sun's illumination of the moon because it can only be known by experience; but once it is known as fact it is then possible to qualify it by specifying the circumstances in which the moon is illuminated.[368] From that we can infer its subsequent illuminability in the syllogism, 'When there is no opaque body between them, the moon is illuminated by the sun; But when the moon is in that position there is nothing between them; Therefore when the moon is in that position it will be illuminated by the sun'. This, as we shall recall, is not an *a priori* demonstration because it is not by an intrinsic middle as the cause but by an effect derived from a particular instance. For that reason it is not *de omni*, demonstrable of every individual at all times, but only of a certain time and so is only of temporal difference.[369]

The second way in which both kinds of indemonstrable attributes are demonstrable is when they are not of the first subject, but the first subject is the middle, as described earlier in the example of 'man' and 'intellective soul' where 'capable of learning' is demonstrable of man as non-first subject. Here 'man' and 'intellective soul' are related as whole and part, one of the three possible combinations enumerated in the Prologue of the *Ordinatio*, where Ockham discusses the meaning of a non-first subject.[370] The other two are either as a term superior or inferior to the first subject, as triangle is to isosceles or figure is to angle; or alternatively when the first subject is included in the non-first subject as a form, attribute or other accident in the manner in which heat is included in fire. In any of these connotations an attribute can be demonstrated of a non-first subject through the first subject as middle; where the first subject is a term inferior to the non-first subject, demonstration will be particular in the third figure, because the first subject as middle will be the means of concluding its attributes of a particular non-first subject: as three angles can be demonstrated of an isosceles triangle through triangle as their subject.[371]

In the case of an attribute connoting an inherent form it can be demonstrated of a non-first subject which is inferior to the first subject through prior knowledge

[367] *Ibid.*, ch. 40. Also *Ordinatio*, Prologue, q. 4, 146–7, 151–2.

[368] Quamvis autem omnis passio talis non possit demonstrari de suo subiecto primo sine omni determinatione, specificante seu modificante poterit tamen demonstrari de suo subiecto primo mediante aliqua determinatione, sicut si 'illuminabile' sit passio prima lune, quamvis non potest demonstrari. 'Luna est illuminabilis', hec tamen potest demonstrari: 'Si luna est in tali situ luna erit illuminata a sole' . . . (SL, III, II, ch. 36). Also *ibid.*, ch. 35 and *Ordinatio*, Prologue, q. 4, 154–5.

[369] *Ibid.*, and *Ordinatio*, Prologue, q. 4, 155.

[370] *Ordinatio*, 148–9; also SL, III, II, chs. 37 and 38.

[371] *Ordinatio, ibid.*, and SL, III, II, ch. 35.

of both premises, as we can prove that man is an alterable body through first knowing that every body is alterable and knowing that man is a body.[372] By this means, too, we can demonstrate attributes of God, for example 'being', in the syllogism, 'All being is one; God is one; Therefore God is being'. The difference here is that no attribute can be said to inhere in God who is absolutely simple.[373]

Attributes which connote something extrinsic to the subject, as cause or effect or in some other manner, can also be demonstrated of a non-first subject as a term inferior to the first subject from prior indemonstrable knowledge of the attribute's connection with the first subject.[374] Thus if we know immediately as the major premise that heat is heat-giving or that the rational soul is capable of learning, together with corresponding intuitive knowledge of the non-first subject as the minor, we can then demonstrate the attributes, known immediately of the first subject, of the non-first subject, for example fire or man as terms inferior to heat and rational soul. When the first subject is a quality or form connoted by a concrete term—like hot or animate—it will be the middle of such a demonstration. That applies to both the second and third kind of non-first subject specified in the Prologue of the *Ordinatio*, namely where it either contains the first subject as part of a whole, as rational soul is part of man, or as an attribute or form or other accident of an already complete whole, as heat-giving belongs to fire which is its own subject. In the *Logic* Ockham states a different method of demonstrating an attribute of both these kinds of non-first subject by means of the concrete of the first subject as the middle.[375] Thus from intuitive knowledge both of hot as the concrete of the first attribute of calefactive (i.e. heat-giving) and of fire as hot, where hot is the concrete of the first attribute of fire (i.e. heat), we can demonstrate heat-giving of fire through hot, as follows: 'Everything hot is heat-giving; Fire is hot; Therefore fire is heat-giving'. Here the immediate connection of first-subject and non-first subject with their attributes constitutes the indemonstrable premises, the concrete of the first subject being the attribute of the non-first subject as an instance of the third kind of non-first subject just mentioned. (The order between the second and third is reversed in the *Logic*.) Similarly with the second kind of non-first subject, say, 'animate' signifying man directly and 'rational soul' as his part, or form, indirectly: from prior intuitive knowledge that what is animate is capable of learning, as major, and that man has a rational soul, as minor, we can demonstrate that man is capable of learning through rational soul.[376]

---

[372] *Ibid.*, ch. 37.   [373] *Ibid.*

[374] *Ibid.*, ch. 38 and *Ordinatio*, Prologue, q. 4, 149–50.

[375] Quamvis aliter non possint demonstrari de suis subiectis primis, tamen quando subiectum primum alicuius talis passionis est nomen forme informantis reliquum, tunc potest demonstrari de illo de quo primo predicatur concretum illius subiecti . . . Quando autem talis passio predicatur de toto sive de nomine totius, tunc debet demonstrari de illo per concretum significans totum in recto et formam in obliquo, sicut 'esse susceptibilis discipline' debet demonstrari de homine per animatum, quia debet significare animam in obliquo et hominem in recto . . . Quando autem illa passio non predicatur de toto sed de subiecto, tunc debet demonstrari de illo per concretum importans subiectum in recto et formam in obliquo, sicut exemplificatum est de calefactivo (*SL*, III, II, ch. 38).

[376] *Ibid.*

The same considerations hold for attributes connoting matter instead of form, as well as for God's attributes like 'creative', 'immortal', 'eternal' and so on, save that of God we have no simple and absolute knowledge *pro statu isto*.[377]

We can conclude then that the demonstrability of an attribute, as a term always predicable by the second essential mode,[378] depends upon whether what it connotes in addition to the subject belongs immediately to the subject or is known by a middle term; only in the second case is an attribute demonstrable of a subject through a real distinction between them, so that in knowing one the other is not immediately known. For that to be possible the subject must have determinate parts which can be known independently of it, whether affirmatively or negatively. Whenever they cannot, and knowledge of the attribute is contained in knowledge of the subject, the attribute is indemonstrable unless determinations can be introduced into the subject, so coming between knowledge of it and knowledge of the attribute. A considerable part of Ockham's treatment of the question *quia est* in the *Logic* is directed to showing how that can be achieved, by the two means of either qualifying the attribute temporally and/or spatially—as in specifying the time and place at which an eclipse can occur—or through making it demonstrable of a non-first subject. By the first mode, demonstration will be *quia*, as it will be also where the first subject is a term inferior to the non-first subject; for in both cases it will not be *de omni*. But by the second mode, where the non-first subject is a term inferior to the first subject, whether the latter is a part of the non-first subject or merely an attribute, demonstration can be *potissima* through the first subject as middle. Here, too, however, it will not be of the first subject as such. Hence we must say that a strict demonstration of an attribute of a first subject is confined to subjects which have distinct essential or negative parts.

It is clear, then, that demonstrability arises only in the absence of immediate knowledge; and since for Ockham as for Aristotle all knowledge originates in experience, it is only when our knowledge is incomplete and the connexion between things already known is unknown or can be doubted that we have recourse to inference or deduction. In that sense demonstration is called in when experience, it is only when our knowledge is incomplete and the connection only as an extension of what is already known from experience. That is the difference between Ockham and his scholastic predecessors. He restricts demonstrability precisely to what can be deduced from what is already given intuitively. Hence to establish the connection between subject and attribute we must first know of the existence of each, and what they are, and that they are connected, before we can either demonstrate their connection as a fact or the reason for it; and since, as we have seen, knowledge of both existence and nature can by only of individuals known intuitively, the scope of demonstration is confined to those cases where the connection with—but not the existence of—their attributes is not also immediately known. Accordingly Ockham's restriction of demonstrability has nothing to do with the restriction upon knowledge as such—and even less to do with scepticism—but with its exclusively individual source in natural experience,

---

[377] *Ibid.*   [378] *Ibid.*, ch. 35.

where, that is, it concerns the external world. It is the pre-eminence of intuitive knowledge which gives first principles and self-evident propositions their pre-eminence over the conclusions which can be drawn from demonstration. If the latter is the summit of human knowledge,[379] its very difficulty of attainment is due to its conditions of universality and necessity which remove it from contingent experience of the natural order. For that reason only when the relation between beings which are ontologically contingent can be shown to be logically necessary is strict demonstration possible. We must therefore invert the not uncommon assumption applied to Ockham that the denial of demonstrative certainty represents a denial of natural certainty; rather it is the derivation of all knowledge from individual experience, immediately accessible to man for all that he encounters in the contingent world, that restricts demonstration to what cannot be known immediately and must be known necessarily. Ockham's outlook cannot therefore be judged by the scope it allows to demonstration.

That is confirmed by his answer to the last of the four questions, *propter quid est*, which occupies one brief final chapter of the treatise on demonstration in the *Logic*.[380] As we have frequently mentioned, to give the reason is to exhibit the cause. But the cause itself can only be known intuitively and from experience, or *a posteriori*. In the first case it is entirely indemonstrable as either self-evident, known through its terms, or immediately given. By the second it can be inferred through the effect as an extrinsic middle in the way we have encountered from the example of an eclipse given here, or from knowledge that a herb cures, where the conclusion is reached inductively from one or more instances.[381] Such knowledge of the cause can then become the first principle or premise of further demonstration; which may or may not be *a priori* according to whether or not it is universal and *de omni*.

The regress therefore ends in intuitive knowledge of individual being; and it is the need to reconcile it, as the source of all knowledge, with the universality and necessity of demonstrative knowledge that is the hallmark of Ockham's theory of demonstration, distinguishing it from that of virtually every other scholastic before him. For unlike both Aquinas and Duns Scotus, who in different ways made knowledge of the individual the first point of departure for universal knowledge, Ockham denies the latter, expressed in universal natures and essences, any ontological identity. Demonstration is for him concerned with what can only exist individually; it therefore depends upon establishing the necessary and universal logical conditions which hold for beings which ontologically are neither universal nor necessary. Since that entails terms freed from existential import, the problem of demonstration revolves around disclosing what these are and how and where they arise. As we have seen, that is when the terms themselves are

---

[379] Here I must disagree with Webering, *Theory of Demonstration*, 177, when he says that first principles and self-evident propositions are more perfect than demonstration: for demonstration, at least when it *potissima*, gives necessary understanding of *why* a proposition is true.
[380] *SL*, III, II, ch. 41.
[381] Ockham defines extrinsic middle or cause in the Prologue of the *Ordinatio*, q. 4, 155, as that which is only the cause of a thing in being of its effect.

self-evident (*per se primo modo*) or non-existential as in the case of mathematical or negative terms, or when they are abstracted from existence (*de inesse*) and made hypothetical or conditional (*de possibili*), with varying degrees of universality and so necessity, or when the demonstration is not of a first subject but something included under it. In only a minority of these, however, is demonstration *propter quid* and *potissima* in being *de omni*, affirmative, and direct, as well as *a priori*. In the majority of cases knowledge is immediate and indemonstrable. That applies both to the existence and nature of all absolutes, and to their attributes, save those not known immediately, i.e. which are connoted. Similarly with first principles, which are known either immediately through experience or self-evidently through knowing the terms.

Here we come to one of the most significant features—or rather lacks—of Ockham's theory of demonstration, the subordinate place of self-evident knowledge. To begin with he rarely gives example of self-evident propositions: among the few that he does give is that of knowing that man is an animal as a mental proposition by the first essential mode.[382] To that we can add certain universal principles, such as that the whole is greater than the part and that all forms of the same kind can have effects of the same kind.[383]

Now the question is, whether beyond the latter any knowledge is self-evident independently of initial experience of the individuals for which the terms stand. It is a striking fact that Ockham never explicitly discusses the matter. Unlike Grosseteste, for whom there was a threefold order between metaphysical, mathematical and sensory knowledge, with mathematical knowledge *sui generis* and of a superior kind,[384] Ockham makes no such distinction. For him mathematical propositions are distinguished in being non-existential and so freed from the contingency of all other knowledge which depends upon experience of real existence. Accordingly mathematical terms do not, as we have seen, have real definition in the strict sense, in not consisting of genus and difference. That enables them to be demonstrated *a priori* in a *demonstratio potissima*. To that extent they give the most certain demonstration. But for that very reason they are not self-evident. It is here in Ockham's total reliance upon experience for all that is known— whether immediately or indirectly, of sensory or non-sensory objects—that his theory of demonstration, as indeed his whole epistemology, diverges from previous tradition and particularly that of Grosseteste.

In establishing the rules for strict demonstration his concern, like Aristotle's, was with what could be inferred through essential definition of things, knowledge of which began in experience. But, unlike Aristotle, Ockham refused to accept anything directly given in experience as necessary knowledge. Hence only if it were removed from direct dependence upon knowledge of existence could it be in varying degrees necessary, as conditional or hypothetical or possible: in the case of

---

[382] *SL*, III, II, ch. 29; see note 385 below.
[383] *Ibid.*, ch. 4.
[384] Cf. A. C. Crombie, *Robert Grosseteste and the Origins of Experimental Science* (Oxford, 1953; repr. 1971), chs. 4 and 5.

self-evident propositions, that entailed assenting immediately to the truth of a
proposition through knowing the real as opposed to the nominal *meaning* of a
term: in other words, where essential definition is contained in the term without
having to know it in experience or independently of the term first. For that in
effect meant that it could never be of a first subject, in presupposing knowledge of
a preceding proposition, as 'Everything hot is heat-giving' is self-evident because
it presupposes knowing that 'All heat is heat-giving' which to be evident must be
known in experience and so is irreducible. That makes it at once indemonstrable
and contingent, and thereby prevents it from entering into a demonstration.
'Everything hot is heat-giving' on the other hand demands no recourse to immediate experience or knowledge of anything beyond the meaning of the terms; which
is derived from evident knowledge of the first proposition. Hence it can be self-
evident. That also applies to knowing that man is an animal, from preceding
experience of individual men. In each case, the sequence is from inductive knowledge of individuals to the formation of their concepts, knowledge of which can
be assented to in propositions such as 'Man is an animal'.[385] That only occurs in
propositions by the first essential mode, and in all mental propositions, where, as
we have seen, genus is affirmed of an individual or species. It does not hold for
propositions by the second essential mode because the predicate can remain distinct
from the subject. The connection is thus not immediately given and so can be
doubted; hence their demonstrability, where genus is indemonstrable.[386]

For Ockham, then, the criterion of self-evidence is the pragmatic one of whether
terms give immediate knowledge. He does not distinguish between different kinds
of self-evidence or consider whether self-evident propositions are merely tautologies. As in the whole of his system he assumes a norm of intelligibility, the
ultimate test of which is conformity with real being. Self-evidence is not therefore
a short-cut to knowing anything not already known. That is shown in his one
ex professo treatment of the matter, which comes not in the parts of the Prologue
of the *Ordinatio* or of the *Logic* devoted to demonstration but in the third distinction of the *Ordinatio* on the possibility of self-evident knowledge of God.[387]
Beyond restating the meaning of self-evident knowledge—without example—his
arguments are negative. The first is that self-evident knowledge of what is compos-

---

[385] Sed iste est processus, quia primo cognoscat hominem aliquo sensu particulari; deinde
ille idem homo cognoscitur ab intellectu. Quo cognito habetur una cognitio generalis et communis omni homini . . . Deinde apprehenso aliquo animali ab homine vel aliis animalibus,
elicitur una notitia generalis omni animali et ista notitia generalis est omni animali . . . Quo
[conceptu] existente in anima potest intellectus componere istum conceptum cum tali conceptu
priori. Quibus compositis ad invicem hoc verbo 'est' mediante, statim intellectus assentit illi
complexo sine omni discursu. Et ita quelibet talis propositio in qua predicatur genus de diffinito
propriissime dicto habetur sine omni discursu. Et hoc est universaliter verum de omni genere
respectu speciei que est mere absoluta, quia talis propositio per se cognoscitur statim cognitis
terminis (*SL*, III, II, ch. 29).
[386] Verbi gratia, ista propositio 'calor est calefactivus' est necessaria et dubitabilis, quia si
aliquis intellectus apprehenderet calorem intuitive solum per intellectum et nunquam videret
nec sentiret calorem calefacere . . . ita posset dubitare an calor posset producere calorem (*Ordinatio*, Prologue, q. 2, 78). Also q. 6, 178–81.
[387] *Ordinatio*, d. 3, q. 4, 432–42.

ite does not give knowledge of its parts, whether by an essential definition which is intrinsic or by a definition *per additamentum*.[388] The reason is that in both cases the connection of the whole and parts is contingent, and in the second also accidental, so that self-evident knowledge of the part does not follow from self-evident knowledge of the whole.[389] In other words there cannot be evident—i.e. incomplex—knowledge of one thing from incomplex knowledge of something else. Hence to know something by the first essential mode, such as man is an animal, does not itself give essential definition, that man is a rational animal. Secondly, for that reason, too, universal knowledge of a term does not suffice for self-evident knowledge of that for which it stands, although the authorities sometimes improperly call self-evident a universal proposition deduced from other universal propositions.[390]

We must therefore conclude that whatever is known self-evidently must be known in itself, and for that there must be preceding intuitive knowledge. The problem of self-evident knowledge thus crystallizes that of demonstrability in general, which for Ockham revolved around the need to reconcile Aristotle's notion of the universal and necessary character of demonstrative knowledge through essential definition with the individual and contingent nature of all created being. It is just that which cannot be provided by the majority of propositions, whether by the first essential mode which in composite beings is only of genus and not difference, or mathematical definitions which as nominal are the result of a series of preceding demonstrations. Even if the latter come closest to strict demonstration, they do so improperly. In effect that reduces necessary premises to tautologies, with no minor premise, in being of what is determinate, genuinely necessary unless in the mode of possibility. Ockham's is thus a valiant effort to preserve Aristotle's doctrine from the logic of his own fundamentally different—Christian and individual—view of being. More clearly than any other scholastic he showed the limitations of demonstration in a contingent world, which could only in certain instances be overcome by qualifying the meaning of propositions out of actual existence into possible existence. The result was a radical restatement of the role of demonstration. In retrospect it could be said, logically, not to have been radical enough; for however far Ockham was prepared to go epistemologically and ontologically, in logic he remained bound by Aristotle's system. Rather than discard Aristotelian principles of demonstration he largely rendered demonstration inefficacious. That, in the circumstances of his time, was radical enough; but in assessing Ockham's impact we should recognise that it came not from logic alone nor was it upon logic, where its effect was comparatively slight. Rather it meant the reinterpretation of virtually the whole of scholastic discourse in terms of his revised categories of being and knowing, as we shall now see further when we turn to theology.

---

[388] Nunquam predicatum est per se notum de aliquo subiecto composito nisi sit per se notum partes suas uniri, sed de nulla definitione potest esse per se notum partes illas uniri; igitur nulla talis potest esse per se nota (*ibid.*, 435).

[389] *Ibid.*, 435–6.   [390] *Ibid.*, 439.

PART TWO

The theological order

CHAPTER FIVE

Theology and knowledge of God

I SCIENTIA

Ockham's view of theology is developed in the Prologue of the *Ordinatio*, its customary place, and in its customary context of its relation to knowledge. It has two main aspects: the subject, or content, of theology, and the status of theological truths. Both have their point of departure in Ockham's conception of knowledge (*scientia*) as a body of truths; their application to theology can be regarded as a special case of the principles which govern any science, taking the term in its traditional sense as a discipline or a defined branch of knowledge. We shall therefore begin with the latter before turning to theology, and first the meaning here of *scientia*.

In the opening question of the Prologue the term received two senses. By the first, and the operative one, *scientia* is a collection of knowledge of many kinds, complexes, incomplexes, principles, conclusions, corrections of errors, solutions of faulty arguments, brought into unity either through pertaining to the same thing or through having a determinate order among themselves.[1] This definition also therefore includes written works on subjects like the *Physics* and *Analytics* constituting unified disciplines. Their unity does not however make them numerically one and the same knowledge; each such *scientia* contains many different habits or states which differ not only as species but also in genus. What gives them their unity and distinguishes them from other knowledge is the special order peculiar to them alone. Consequently the same truth can belong to one or more different sciences, whether as the same conclusion reached by different means, or as a conclusion in one and a principle in another, in the way that being is treated both by metaphysics and theology, with knowledge of the former contained in the latter. Similarly with physics and metaphysics which in Averroes's example are related to being respectively as the study of separate beings and being as such.

[1] Ad primum istorum dico quod scientia ad presens dupliciter accipitur. Uno modo pro collectione multorum pertinentium ad notitiam unius vel multorum determinatum ordinem habentium. Et scientia isto modo dicta continet tam notitiam incomplexam terminorum quam notitiam complexorum, et hoc principiorum et conclusionum; continet etiam reprobationes errorum et solutiones falsorum argumentorum; continet etiam divisiones necessarias et definitiones, ut frequenter. (*Ordinatio*, Prologue, q. 1, 8–9). See also the Prologue to the Exposition on the seven books of the *Physics* translated in *Philosophical Writings*, 3–17.

It is in the first sense that, as we shall subsequently see, theology can appropriate natural knowledge.[2] That does not, however, apply to the second sense of *scientia* by which it is merely a habit as one mental quality among others, such as understanding and wisdom; it does not therefore utilise other knowledge because by this connotation *scientia* is only of one conclusion and so numerically one and not many as it is by the first definition.[3]

The difference between these two senses then is of *scientia* as an ordered multiplicity and as a single conclusion. Each is complex knowledge. The first in its totality as a unified whole which includes incomplex parts; the second in itself as a single proposition to which, as Ockham later specifies in the case of metaphysics, the intellect inclines from previous immediate knowledge.[4] It is therefore as the object, what is known as opposed to how it is known, that *scientia* is to be understood here. Provided that a body of knowledge has unity, whether collective or individual, the manner in which it becomes knowledge is not germane. For that reason, as we have previously said, and Ockham again stresses, different disciplines can overlap and a habit be both theological and metaphysical in the same way as the same man can belong to an army or to a city.[5]

Now it is this notion of *scientia* as complex knowledge which leads Ockham to identify it with the conclusion rather than the subject taken alone. In this he was to be opposed by Gregory of Rimini on the ground that the conclusion could not be known without also knowing the other parts of a proposition, so that the object of knowledge was not the conclusion but the total signification (*significatum totale*).[6] In retrospect this seems either pedantry or a wilful misrepresentation of Ockham's position, which is that knowledge of the conclusion is only possible through knowing all the parts of the whole to which it belongs. Thus, as we have considered in Part One, a conclusion can be known either evidently through knowing the subject and predicate evidently, in the way that from intuitive knowledge of Socrates and white, we can conclude—by means of a proposition—that Socrates is white;[7] or it can be known demonstratively through a syllogism, whether as a *demonstratio potissima* or not. By whichever of these modes, the conclusion is of a complex, as one or more propositions, and cannot—as Gregory of Rimini imputed to Ockham's position—be seized directly, in dissociation from the terms involved.

---

[2] *Ibid.*, 9.

[3] Alio modo accipitur scientia pro habitu existente per se in genere qualitatis, distincto contra alios habitus intellectuales, scilicet contra intellectum, sapientiam etc. Et isto modo eadem veritas non pertinet ad distinctas scientias, quia unius conclusionis non est nisi una scientia isto modo dicta, quia quelibet talis scientia est una res numero, non continens notitiam plurimarum conclusionum (*ibid.*, 11).

[4] *Ibid.*, q. 7, 198–9.

[5] *Ibid.*, q. 1, 11–14.

[6] See G. Leff, *Gregory of Rimini* (Manchester, 1961), 55 ff.

[7] E.g. dico quod notitia evidens est cognitio alicuius veri complexi, ex notitia terminorum incomplexa immediate vel mediate nata sufficienter causari. Ita scilicet quod quando notitia incomplexa aliquorum terminorum ... in quocumque intellectu habente talem notitiam sufficienter causat vel est nata causare mediate vel immediate notitiam complexi, tunc illud complexum evidenter cognoscitur (*Ordinatio*, Prologue, q. 1, 5–6).

The effect was therefore the very opposite of that proclaimed by Gregory of Rimini, in making knowledge of the conclusion knowledge of the whole; only if each of the parts is known can the conclusion be known. That in turn was the outcome of Ockham's rejection of Duns Scotus's contention that a *scientia* is defined by its subject through which its elements can also be known. For Ockham on the contrary, a *scientia*, whether as knowledge of one conclusion or many, is the product of knowing a complex. It must therefore include not only the subject but each of the terms entering into a proposition. Ockham's argument against the self-sufficiency of the subject is the opening of his attack upon Dun Scotus's conception of virtual knowledge underlying the *distinctio formalis*.

To begin with—although not in order of discussion—Ockham contrary to Duns treated the subject as an incomplex term which taken by itself could not yield knowledge. For that it had to be joined to a predicate in a proposition in virtue of which it could then become the subject of a conclusion, and as such the subject of knowledge. It is therefore as the subject of a conclusion that there is a subject of knowledge, because, of the terms in a proposition, only the subject can be the subject of a conclusion, as only the conclusion can be the object of knowledge.[8] That holds whether the subject is of a complete or a partial *scientia*; it is as inseparable from the subject of knowledge as the principle of acting is from action.[9]

That means in the second place that the subject is never directly known in the way that the conclusion is known; for only the latter is the object of knowledge as that at which, in Ockham's words, knowledge immediately terminates. The subject as part of the conclusion can never therefore be more than a partial object.[10]

By the same token it can only be a partial cause, together with the predicate, of knowledge reached in the conclusion. Neither, however, is contained virtually in knowledge of the other.[11]

That, in the third place, takes us to the heart of Ockham's position, namely that knowledge is derived from the conjunction of subject and attribute coming through knowledge of the subject and the attribute both known independently. Far from knowledge of the attribute coming through knowledge of the subject, in which the attribute belongs virtually, each must be known in its own right. The

---

[8] Ideo dico quod de ratione subiecti scientie non est aliud nisi quod subiciatur respectu predicati in propositione scita scientia proprie dicta, ita quod universaliter idem et sub eadem ratione est subiectum scientie et subiectum conclusionis scite. Hoc declaratur: quia aut subiectum scientie et subiectum conclusionis sunt idem simpliciter, et habetur propositum; aut non sunt idem. Sed hoc est impossibile, quia impossibile est scientiam haberi sine notitia illius scientie . . . Confirmatur, quia omne subiectum alicuius scientie est aliquod incomplexum. Sed preter subiectum conclusionis et predicatum nullum est incomplexium nisi medium. Et non est predicatum conclusionis, nec medium; ergo etc. (*ibid.*, q. 9, 247–48). Also 259.

[9] *Ibid.*, 248–50.

[10] Ex isto sequitur tertium quod differentia est inter subiectum scientie et obiectum scientie, quia subiectum scientie est subiectum conclusionis, sed obiectum scientie est illud quod scitur et terminat actum sciendi. Huiusmodi autem est ipsa conclusio scita. Et ita subiectum est pars obiecti; et si sit obiectum, non est nisi obiectum partiale (*ibid.*, 266). Also 258.

[11] Ad secundum, quod subiectum non est causa adequata totius habitus sed ipsa notitia subiecti se habet ad habitum sicut causa partialis ad effectum . . . Ita, dico, est in proposito quod notitia subiecti et notitia predicati sunt due cause partiales, et tamen neutra continetur virtualiter in alia, sed utraque continet per propriam rationem (*ibid.*, 262–3).

consequence is that it is the attribute equally with the subject which defines a *scientia*, since there are as many conclusions as there are attributes predicated of subjects, and correspondingly as many sciences as there are conclusions or collections of conclusions.[12] For that reason the same subject according to its different attributes constitutes different *scientiae*, as knowledge of bodies from the standpoint of movement produces physics and from the standpoint of quantity mathematics. The subject remains unchanged; and as in the case of accidents the difference will be due to the attributes, since it is from them rather than the subject that it arises.[13] That is not to say that different subjects do not constitute different knowledge; they do. Indeed strictly speaking no *scientia* has merely one subject, but there are as many as there are subjects of conclusions. That applies to any discipline like metaphysics or physics or mathematics or logic. Their unity as we said earlier is collective from some kind of order among the different subjects, which can be one of predication, from superior to inferior, or of perfection, or of whole to part, and of which there can be a first subject. The latter again is not strictly first, but the result of a corresponding primacy, none of which is exclusive to all the parts of the subject, as for example in the *Physics* the first subject is natural bodies but they are not the subject of every part; and similarly with the syllogism as the first subject of the *Prior Analytics*.[14]

The relation among the subjects of a *scientia* thus may be likened to that between the kings of individual kingdoms and a king of the world or Christendom; the latter does not exist as such, but sometimes there is an order among individual real kings when one is wealthier or more powerful than the others. In the same way there is no one subject of the whole of say metaphysics, but diverse subjects for its different parts which nevertheless have an order among themselves giving them a unity.[15] Accordingly the distinction between different knowledge depends upon either subject or predicates, as opposed to the subject alone; for the latter cannot be considered for itself apart from its attributes in a conclusion.[16] As

[12] Et ita quot sunt conclusiones etiam habentes idem subiectum et tamen diversa predicata tot sunt scientie. Et non plus variatur scientia secundum numerum ad variationem subiecti quam ad variationem predicati, quia scientia ita respicit predicatum sicut subiectum; quia primo respicit ipsam conclusionem cuius subiectum et predicatum sunt partes (*ibid.*, q. 8, 225).

[13] Ex isto patet quod idem subiectum sub eadem ratione a parte subiecti—que ratio debet presupponi passioni—potest esse subiectum diversarum passionum. Sicut idem sub eadem ratione a parte subiecti potest esse subiectum diversorum accidentium, quamvis propter diversitatem accidentium consequantur diverse denominationes; sed illa sic denominata magis habebunt rationem passionum quam subiectorum . . . Et ita est de mobili, de quanto et omnibus huiusmodi respectu substantie quod ille rationes—propter quas ponunt multi quod de eodem subiecto sub alia et alia ratione sunt distincte scientie—sunt distincte passiones illius subiecti. Sicut de corpore, inquantum mobile, est scientia naturalis, de corpora inquantum quantum, est mathematica, quia iste rationes, scilicet esse mobile et quantum, sunt passiones corporis. Ex isto sequitur propter disinctionem passionum, sine omni distinctione a parte subiecti, possunt esse distincte scientie de eodem subiecto (*ibid.*, q. 9, 242–3). Also 246, 260–1, 268.

[14] *Ibid.*, q. 9, 255–8.

[15] *Ibid.*, 259.

[16] Et ita non est proprie dictum quod diversus modus considerandi causat diversitatem scientiarum, et quod idem modus considerandi causat identitatem scientiarum, sed semper distinctio scientiarum requirit distinctionem subiectorum vel predicatorum (*ibid.*, 261).

Aristotle says, knowledge is always in respect of a proposition; hence its meaning can only differ if the subject does not have the same import either because it or its attributes are not the same.[17]

Accordingly, the subject of knowledge, as opposed to that of the intellect, belongs to the object of knowledge as part of the conclusion, whether subject is understood in its proper sense of a term or concept, or improperly as that for which it stands.[18] A predicate can therefore belong to a subject in a proposition regardless of whether or not it actually belongs to one immediately.[19] In other words subject and attributes stand for different terms which to become knowledge must be known in a proposition. Hence neither can be more than a partial cause of the conclusion, and so the object of knowledge; and both must be known independently of the other, by the modes discussed in Part One.

It is on these grounds that Ockham opposes Duns Scotus's opinion that a first subject contains virtually knowledge of all truths belonging to its habit, as the state of knowledge which it engenders.[20] Duns's reasons were, firstly, that the first object contains immediate propositions because their subject contains the predicate and so knowledge of the whole proposition; and since immediate propositions contain the conclusion, the subject contains all the truths belonging to its habit. Secondly, the object is related to the habit as cause to effect;[21] but an adequate cause must contain the whole effect virtually, where adequate, following Aristotle's definition in the *Posterior Analytics* (book one, chapter four), means universal, and virtual means to contain something else. Therefore the subject contains all its truths virtually, while as first subject it is contained in nothing else; for there has to be something absolutely first in everything having an essential order, which in the case of knowables is a first simple subject as the principle of all other knowledge, without itself being known from anything else.

In reply Ockham denies that it is of the nature of a subject to contain virtually either knowledge of its attribute or the attribute itself.[22]

So far as the first is concerned, a cause no less perfectly contains its effect than a subject its attributes, and yet a cause does not contain knowledge of its effect. Nor therefore does a subject contain knowledge of its attribute, even if it were the attribute itself. The minor premise is confirmed by what Duns Scotus himself says, namely that knowledge of distinct natures (*quidditates*) requires distinct concepts of each; hence distinct knowledge of only one nature will not give knowledge of another nature of which there is no proper concept.[23] Again on Duns's own argument when a number of things is each known in its formal nature, none is the first object of knowledge by any primacy over the other; accordingly knowledge of one does not contain knowledge of the remainder. But that applies to subject

---

[17] *Ibid.*, 261–2.   [18] *Ibid.*, 266.   [19] *Ibid.*, 271.

[20] *Ibid.*, q. 9, 227–8 from Scotus, *Ordinatio*, I, qq. 1–3.

[21] This sentence is excised (Vatican edition, I, 97).

[22] Contra istam opinionem, quod non sit de ratione subiecti continere virtualiter notitiam passionem; secundo quod nec de ratione subiecti est continere virtualiter passionem (Ockham, *Ordinatio*, Prologue, q. 9, 229).

[23] *Ibid.*

and attribute which according to Duns are frequently distinct things. Moreover any absolute thing which is formally distinct moves the intellect, because, when something is the adequate object of a faculty, whatever is contained under it also moves the same faculty. Since, for Duns, the adequate object of the intellect is being, that includes everything. There is therefore no first object which has primacy over something else.

That is shown from the fact, supported by Aristotle, that the intellect is dependent upon the senses for intuitive knowledge of sensible things. The senses can, however, be moved by accidents; so therefore can the intellect. Consequently the intellect could know an attribute without knowing its subject. Conversely where knowledge from one sense is dependent upon another sense, as colour and taste depend upon experience of tangible qualities, if the dependent sense is lacking, its experience will also be lacking, as colour cannot be experienced without sight however perfectly developed the tactile sense. Hence knowledge of the latter as cause does not contain knowledge of colour as the effect.[24] Secondly, on Duns Scotus's first argument, it would follow that what contains perfect knowledge of something else also contains imperfect knowledge of it; but knowledge of the subject does not give even the most imperfect knowledge of the attribute because it lacks even a nominal definition of the latter. The subject therefore cannot be said to contain such knowledge virtually.[25] The third argument against Duns's view is that any virtual knowledge should be attributed to the middle as the cause of the connection between subject and attribute. Knowledge of the subject alone can go together with ignorance of the attribute, through not knowing its extrinsic cause, in the way that the moon can be known abstractively without knowing whether it is eclipsed because the extrinsic cause of an eclipse—the interposition of the earth—is not known. Once again this disproves virtual knowledge of the part of the subject.[26]

Fourthly, according to Duns, only what is contained virtually and essentially can lead to knowledge of something else. But many attributes are relative or connotative terms and as such known only through something outside the subject and really distinct from it. That includes all attributes by the second essential mode of predication (*per se secundo modo*) which include something additional to the subject. Only therefore if we can know beatitude, or form or charity and so on independently, can we know that blessedness or charity is an attribute of a rational being or that something can receive a form. Ockham does not immediately add that many such attributes are naturally inaccessible to man in this world. He does, however, employ them against a further argument of Duns Scotus that the more imperfect cannot contain knowledge of the more perfect; for qualities like beatitude and charity are more perfect than man and so cannot be contained in knowledge of man, and similarly with other attributes more perfect than their subjects.[27]

Fifthly, virtual knowledge of the attribute through knowledge of the subject would result in knowing the attribute upon knowing the subject. The consequence

[24] *Ibid.*, 231.   [25] *Ibid.*, 232.
[26] *Ibid.*, 232–3.   [27] *Ibid.*, 233–4.

would be a chain reaction, knowledge of the attribute giving knowledge of the premise and knowledge of the premises knowledge of the conclusion. It would then be possible to have evident knowledge of the theological truths previously mentioned, for example that man can be blessed or can have charity. Which proves the falsity of Duns's contention. There are many attributes of creatures which are naturally unknowable.[28]

Finally by Duns's opinion any attribute of being would be known self-evidently from knowing being, because according to him distinct knowledge of the subject together with knowledge of the predicate leads immediately to a proposition, and being is known in a distinct absolutely simple concept. Therefore any knowledge of being's attributes is self-evident. The falsity of this conclusion is apparent. Duns Scotus himself acknowledges that many things are not evidently knowable to man in his present state. The source of Duns's error is to regard virtual knowledge as the property of something simple, so that knowledge of one incomplex can engender knowledge of another incomplex. That is the division between the two thinkers. Their opposed standpoints rest upon divergent conceptions of how incomplex knowledge is gained. For Duns it can be virtually, through another incomplex. For Ockham it is exclusively through direct intuitive experience of each individual thing which is known. Hence, as we discussed in the previous chapters, concepts can only stand for the individuals which they signify and not for what is contained only virtually or formally but not really within the same thing—the basis for Ockham's rejection of the Scotist notion of the formal distinction. Since the only absolutes are substances and qualities, all knowledge, whether incomplex or complex, immediate or discursive, must derive from intuitive knowledge of one or other. Hence an attribute must be known independently of a subject, whether as an absolute or connotative term.

Accordingly, Ockham also denies that the subject virtually contains the attribute. To do so the subject would have either to be the cause of something distinct which inhered in it, or of a concept of something distinct. It cannot be the cause of a concept for the reasons already given against the subject's virtual knowledge of the attribute. Nor can it be the cause of something really distinct because many attributes such as 'creative', 'true', 'good', are not absolutes and so not distinct things, while others stand for what is more perfect than their subjects and cannot therefore be contained virtually in them.[29]

Ockham expresses these different arguments in three negative conclusions. The first is that incomplex knowledge of something existing outside the mind is

---

[28] *Ibid.*, 235-6.

[29] Contra secundum, quod subiectum non semper includat virtualiter ipsam passionem. Quia si sic, hoc non est nisi vel quia causat aliquam rem realiter distinctam sibi inherentem, vel quia causat conceptum illius rei. Non potest dici secundo modo, quia nunquam potest causare conceptum rei nisi causet notitiam rei. Sed non est causa notitie, sicut probatum est; ergo nec conceptus. Nec potest dici primo modo, quia non semper passiones ille sunt res absolute realiter distincte, secundum istos, quia creativum, verum, bonum et huiusmodi sunt passiones aliquorum et tamen non sunt res ab eis distincte. Preterea, aliquando passio importat aliquid perfectius subiecto, sicut esse in potentia ad formam importat formam que est perfectior ipsa materia. Sed perfectius isto modo non continetur in imperfectiori (*ibid.*, 239-40).

never the sufficient cause of incomplex knowledge of another such thing.[30] That is proved from experience because, as he has frequently said, however much something is known intuitively, that knowledge does not suffice for intuitive knowledge of something else if it is itself not already known. All incomplex knowledge, both abstractive and that which is of an individual thing, presupposes prior intuitive knowledge, save by God's absolute power; and intuitive knowledge can only be had as the effect of what is known, whether immediately or indirectly. For that reason there can be no clear and proper notion of anything not already perceived by the senses or the intellect, as intuitive knowledge of a substance does not provide knowledge of a particular accident.[31] This represents the epistemological foundation of Ockham's case against Duns Scotus's doctrine of virtual knowledge. To know something therefore as the subject of an attribute, far from being the cause of knowing the attribute is the result of previous knowledge of the attribute. It is the independence of one from the other which enables the same subject to have different attributes as the same body can be hot and cold.[32]

The second conclusion repeats what Ockham has previously said about attributes which are connotative and relative terms, and so not contained virtually in a subject.[33]

By the third conclusion not all distinct and immediate knowledge of a subject and attribute contains virtual knowledge of an immediate proposition:[34] in other words they are not self-evident, because someone as we have seen can know heat intuitively and also know distinctly that the sun gives heat, and yet, if he has never had experience that heat produces heat, not know that heat is heat-giving any more than that whiteness produces whiteness. Accordingly as we have also seen intuitive knowledge is frequently required for knowledge of contingent truths as the condition of a universal and necessary proposition; only if a man and his ability to laugh are both known by experience can it be known that a man is capable of laughter.[35]

It is not therefore in the nature of a subject to contain knowledge of the attribute or to determine *scientia*, as a particular conclusion or a body of knowledge, or indeed its own dignity as a subject; these all come from separate knowledge of the attribute upon which the subject depends for its diversity, as exemplified in the different sciences like mathematics and physics, and differing degrees of nobility between, say, man as the subject of both blessedness and of risibility.[36]

[30] Ideo quantum ad istum articulum dico primo quod universaliter nunquam notitia unius rei extra incomplexa est causa sufficiens. etiam cum intellectu, respectu prime notitie incomplexe alterius rei (*ibid.*, 240).

[31] *Ibid.*, 241.

[32] *Ibid.*, 242–3.

[33] Secundo, dico quod subiectum non continet semper virtualiter passionem, quia frequenter passiones sunt quidam conceptus respectivi, secundum aliquos, vel connotativi secundum alios, et important aliqua que non continentur virtualiter in subiecto; et ita nec illi conceptus continentur virtualiter in subiecto (*ibid.*, 244–5; also 240).

[34] Tertio dico quod etiam non semper notitia distincta subiecti et notitia distincta passionis immediate continent virtualiter notitiam illius propositionis immediate (*ibid.*, 245; also 240).

[35] *Ibid.*, 245–6.

[36] Circa quartum [quid sit de ratione subiecti primi?] dico quod non est de ratione subiecti

Hence ontological causality does not entail epistemological causality; for knowing something as cause of something else does not mean knowing the effect through the cause or conversely. Thus even if the subject did contain the attribute virtually, knowledge of the subject would still not contain virtual knowledge of the attribute, as knowing that the sun is the cause of heat or worms does not thereby give incomplex knowledge of either heat or worms.[37] There are three ways of knowing one thing from another each of which presupposes incomplex knowledge of individuals and none which gives individual incomplex knowledge. They are: inference, from knowledge of the premises to knowledge of the conclusion; composition, from knowledge of incomplex terms to knowledge of a proposition; and abstraction, from knowledge of individuals to knowledge of a common concept formed from them which can only be of the individuals to which it is common.[38] For that reason similarity only gives knowledge of what is known habitually through previous intuitive knowledge: for example, a statue of Hercules, we will recall, only recalls Hercules to someone who already knows Hercules; otherwise he will no more recognise Hercules than Achilles or anyone else he has never before encountered.[39]

Ockham's rejection of the claims for a first subject's virtual knowledge of what comes under it springs then from treating subject and attribute as separate terms which must be known independently. For that there has to be intuitive knowledge; or rather intuitive knowledge is the condition of all evident knowledge as we have seen in the first chapter. It is that which invalidates any analogy between causal primacy and primacy in the order of knowing. As we have seen not every order is one of causality, least of all efficient causality.[40] So far as knowledge is concerned, comprehension of all the causes will still not give incomplex knowledge of an effect;[41] hence we can know that heat is heat-giving and yet not know whether calefaction is due to the sun or to fire or to God acting alone. Only that which depends upon another being is related as effect to cause; but a habit engendered by a conclusion does not incline to knowledge of the premises.[42] In other words causality in knowing is from the object known; cause as Ockham says in the *Logic*, is used equivocally as applied to things and to propositions.[43]

We can say then first that the subject of knowledge has only partial primacy

---

continere virtualiter passiones, sicut declaratum est. Nec etiam quod ab ipso determinetur et specificetur scientia, quia subiectum potest esse simpliciter idem re et ratione, et tamen scientie esse distincte scientie propter distinctionem passionum. Nec est de ratione subiecti quod a subiecto scientia habeat suam dignitatem ... Sicut scientia qua scio quod omnis homo est beatificabilis est nobilior illa qua scio quod homo est risibilis, et tamen subiectum est idem, sed una passio est nobilior quam alia (*ibid.*, 246).

[37] *Ibid.*, 252–3.

[38] *Ibid.*, 253–4.

[39] *Ibid.*, 254.

[40] E.g., *ibid.*, 255–8, 264.

[41] Ad secundum dubium dico quod notitia omnium causarum simul non sufficit ad causandum notitiam incomplexam ipsius effectus (*ibid.*, 255).

[42] *Ibid.*, q. 8, 213.

[43] *SL*, III, II, ch. 20.

in virtue of belonging to a proposition as the subject of a conclusion; second, that *scientia*, whether as one conclusion or many, is the product of both subject and attribute known independently through intuitive knowledge, whether direct or indirect, and joined in a proposition; and third, that the subject alone as an incomplex term gives or contains knowledge of nothing beyond awareness of itself as something known, because all knowledge in the proper sense is of complexes.

Finally there is the connection between the sciences, only touched on in the Prologue and formally treated in the *Logic* and the *Exposition on the Physics*.[44] There are two facets. The first concerns subalternating and subalternated knowledge traditionally conceived as the order between a superior and a dependent body of knowledge. As we shall shortly discuss, it is in this manner that St Thomas Aquinas, for example, regards the relation between faith and theological knowledge, the former providing the principles in the light of which the truths of theology can be known as *scientia*. For Ockham, on the other hand, one science is subordinated to another when it appropriates the latter's conclusions for its own principles. That is not the same as saying that the same conclusion known *a priori* in a subalternating science is known *a posteriori* in a subalternated science; although different sciences can have the same conclusion that does not relate them as subalternating and subalternated. Nor does it mean that knowledge of the conclusion in the subalternated science goes with ignorance of the principle in the subalternating science, or conversely, in the way that a sailor can be ignorant of an astronomer's principles, while utilising his conclusions, and correspondingly an astronomer ignorant of a sailor's conclusions.[45] Rather in a broad sense a science which depends upon the conclusions of another is subalternated to it, whether in whole or in part; consequently in any science, as a collection of habits, one part can be dependent upon one science, and another part upon another, as one part of perspective, but not every part, is subalternated to geometry. By the same token, one part can be subordinated to a number of different sciences and different parts to different sciences, as part of physics to geometry and part to arithmetic. But generally a science because it has an order is not said to be subordinated to another science save as a whole or where the greater part of it is concerned.[46] In almost every case subordination is due to the superiority, i.e. the greater universality, of the principles derived from the subalternating science, which to enter a demonstration

---

[44] *Ibid.*, ch. 21.

[45] *Ibid.*

[46] Oportet autem scire quod, cum scientia subalternans et etiam scientia subalternata sint quedam collectio multorum habituum habentium determinatum ordinem, non est possibile quin aliqua scientia secundum unam partem subalternetur uni scientie et non secundum aliam partem, sicut perspectiva secundum aliquam sui partem subalternatur geometrie et non secundum omnem partem sui. Similiter possibile [est] quod una scientia secundum eandem partem diversis scientiis subalternetur . . . Sciendum etiam est quod una pars unius scientie potest subalternari uni scientie et altera alterius scientie potest subalternari uni scientie et altera alteri scientie, sicut una pars scientie naturalis potest subalternari geometrie et altera arithmetice. Verumtamen una talis scientia non dicitur subalternari alteri scientie propter unam conclusionem vel paucas nisi tota vel pro maiori parte sibi sit subalternata (*ibid*).

in the subalternated must be qualified in the manner discussed in the last chapter making them less universal.[47]

Subalternation in the broad sense then means that a conclusion, usually universal, belonging to one science or some part of it, is known in the whole of another science—taken as a collective unity—so that they are not related as more and less universal in the same body of knowledge but as different sciences.[48] Thus, in Aristotle's example, medicine through that part of it which contains the conclusion that circular wounds heal more slowly than oblong wounds, is subordinated to geometry for knowledge of the principles leading to that conclusion.[49] In this general sense, also, both logic and metaphysics, as the two universal sciences, can be said to be subalternating through the appropriation of certain of their parts by the particular sciences. That does not probably apply by the second strict meaning of subalternation by which a principle is known by one science and a conclusion by another and are only related accidentally as superior and inferior:[50] that is, that the conclusion of the subalternating science is the point of departure as the principle of that which is subalternated, without at the same time being intrinsically more universal. Ockham gives no example here, but it would not seem an unreasonable inference that this second sense applies to knowledge taken as a single conclusion as opposed to a collection.[51]

That brings us to the second aspect of the relation among the sciences, namely of logic and metaphysics on the one hand and the particular sciences on the other. We can best discern the differences between them by examining first logic and then more briefly—because Ockham wrote no specific work on it metaphysics. Ockham's fullest statement of the nature and purpose of logic comes in his Prologue to the Exposition on Prophyry, where he considers it under five heads.[52] The first concerns its nature, which like any science, consists not in one habit but a

[47] Est autem advertendum quod semper vel frequenter principium cognitum in scientia subalternate est ex terminis universalioribus, ex illo debeat quis demonstrare conclusionem scitam in scientia subalternata . . . non accipiat illud principium in sua communitate sed addit alicui termino alium terminum ut compositum ex istis duobus sit minus quam prius (ibid.).

[48] Et est sciendum quod hoc nomen scientia subalternans et similiter hoc nomen scientia subalternata dupliciter accipitur, scilicet large et stricte. Large dicitur scientia subalternans vel secundum se vel secundum aliquam sui partem quandocumque aliqua scientia cognoscit principium universale alicuius conclusionis vel principia propria et alia scientia totalis cognoscit conclusionem; ita tamen quod ille scientie non constituant unam scientiam totalem, per quod excluduntur scientie de per se inferiori et per se superiori (ibid.).

[49] Ibid.

[50] Isto modo non est inconveniens quod logica et metaphysica secundum aliquas sui partes subalternent sibi aliquas, scilicet partes particularium scientiarum. Scientia subalternans stricte accipitur quando per unam scientiam scitur principium et conclusionem per aliam, et simul cum hoc subiectum unius scientie est per accidens inferius ad subiectum alterius . . . et sic forte logica nullam aliam scientiam sibi subalternat nec forte etiam metaphysica (ibid.).

[51] This is clearly not Moody's view (Logic of William of Ockham, 255–7) who quite unwarrantably includes the example of circular wounds which Ockham gives for the broad sense of subalternation under the strict sense, as well as adding a series of embellishments to explain the meaning in this context of accidental subordination which corresponds to nothing in Ockham's text. He also adds again wrongly that 'logic and metaphysics are not related to the discursive sciences in either of these ways' (ibid., 257).

[52] Expositio, 1–6.

collection, having in common the syllogism. One part considers the syllogism and its attributes, another the demonstrative syllogism, another a proposition, and so on, each with its different attributes which together constitute an ordered whole in virtue of belonging to the same principle. Second come the essential causes, which in logic as in any science are only two, efficient and final; for unlike composite things which have all four causes, because they contain both form and matter, knowledge is simple and so has no distinct intrinsic parts. Its causes are therefore extrinsic. Of these the efficient cause, in the case of logic, is Aristotle himself whose writings provide the basis for its study, while the final cause is immediately the act of knowing, from which logic as a collection of habits is engendered, and mediately or ultimately knowledge of some aspect of nature. As such it is therefore the instrument of the sciences, but, as Moody remarks,[53] not of metaphysics, for reasons which we shall suggest shortly. Thirdly, there are the uses of logic which are many. They include the capacity to distinguish between truth and falsity, to know self-evident propositions and to reach conclusions from them, to reply to arguments by recognising and denying what is contradictory and solving what is fallacious, all of which depend upon knowing the rules that goven logic as an art. Not for the last time Ockham adds that ignorance of the rules of logic leads to confusing sophisms with genuine demonstrations.

Fourthly, the hallmark of logic, distinguishing it from the other sciences, is that its knowledge derives from concepts which are exclusively the product of the mind. Consequently they and all to which they give rise—syllogisms, propositions, terms—are the mind's work, or fabrications as Ockham calls them, and not of anything outside it. For that reason logic is called the science of reason (*scientia rationalis*), as opposed to all the other sciences, which are of real things (*scientia realis*), and independently of whether its concepts are to be taken as really existing in the mind or not, which is a problem for metaphysics to decide. Logic therefore treats all that depends upon reason, and without it there is no reason. That in turn supplies its final characteristic, namely that its knowledge is practical rather than speculative in coming—following Avicenna's definition of practical (*Metaphysics*, book one, chapter one)—from our own actions. In this case these are internal, and only secondarily of what is external. In the Prologue to his Commentary on the *Categories*, however, Ockham states that some part of the logic treated in that work —in his view the least practical of all Aristotle's writings—is speculative in not being from human actions: namely the things for which our terms and concepts stand.[54] In other words in its significative as opposed to its formal aspect, logic is dependent upon what exists independently of the mind's fabrications, as indeed it must if it is to be more than a purely mental process.

---

[53] *Logic of William of Ockham*, 32. Once again it has to be said that Moody's account of Ockham's view of logic (*ibid.*, 30–8) based on some of the Prologue to the *Expositio* goes far beyond anything in Ockham's text, as his later discussion of Ockham's view of metaphysics (118–22) also does. In both instances Moody attempts to make Ockham an Aristotelian without reference to what Ockham says, which in the case of the nature of metaphysics is virtually nothing.

[54] *EA*, 37 a–b.

As we shall see over theology, 'speculative' for Ockham does not, as it does for Aristotle, mean knowledge which is simply theoretical but of what is not from human powers. In that sense the practical sciences are the subjects of the *trivium*, logic, grammar and rhetoric, as Ockham says in the Prologue of the *Ordinatio*; for they are all the outcome of voluntary acts of understanding and so of human actions.[55] Now practical knowledge can be of two kinds: dictative (*dictativa*) in declaring what should and should not be done; in this moral connotation none of these three subjects, nor indeed any of the mechanical arts, is practical. They are, however, in its ostensive sense of showing how something may be achieved; they then provide the knowledge by which the will and intellect can act together if they so decide.[56] That also makes them directive, having an object of praxis rather than praxis as an object in itself, as the art of building is directed to a house as opposed to its own activity of building.[57] Therefore the practical nature of logic lies not in knowing the things themselves dignified by its terms and propositions but in the modes of signifying them. That applies to all conclusions which are composed of first and second intentions, such as 'Man is an animal' or 'Man is a species'. If these all belonged to logic it would mean that before the logician could understand their signification he would have to know them as facts; hence the logician would depend for his knowledge upon first knowing all the other sciences.[58] He does not, because he is concerned only with their formal aspects, and so only uses them as examples, not for the knowledge which they constitute. Logic is therefore the instrument of all the other sciences for gaining knowledge of their own particular conclusions, while itself treating conclusions only in general; it does not provide the principles of their existence.[59]

That belongs to metaphysics, in virtue of which it is the other universal subject. Precisely how is not fully clear. Ockham it seems did not write his projected Commentary on the *Metaphysics* and he left no other work on the subject. His references to metaphysics in the *Ordinatio* and the *Logic*, particularly as they concern the notion of being, present a very incomplete picture. Before, however, we are led to conclude that the absence of any developed theory of metaphysics leaves a gap in Ockham's system, it is as well to examine what he does say and whether he

[55] Aliud sequitur quod logica rhetorica et grammatica sunt vere notitie practice et non speculative, quia vere dirigunt intellectum in operationibus suis que sunt mediante voluntate in sua potestate, sicut logica dirigit intellectum in syllogizando, discurrendo, et sic de aliis (*Ordinatio*, Prologue, q. 10, 316). Also 301.

[56] Potest tamen distingui de practica, quia quedam est dictativa et quedam tantum ostensiva. Prima est illa qua determinate dictatur aliquid esse faciendum vel non faciendum . . . Et isto modo nec logica nec grammatica nec rhetorica est practica, nec etiam ars quecumque mechanica, quia nulla istarum dictat aliquid esse faciendum vel fugiendum . . . Secunda notitia practica est tantum ostensiva, quia non dictat aliquid fugiendum aut prosequendum, sed tantum ostendit opus quomodo fieri potest; virtute cuius notitie si intellectus dictet illud esse faciendum et voluntas velit, statim potest recte operari . . . Et eodem modo logica et alie artes sunt tantum ostensive et non dictative (*ibid.*, 316–17).

[57] *Ibid.*, 317.

[58] *SL*, III, II, ch. 22.

[59] Dico quod ad logicam non pertinet scire consequentias in particulari sed tantum naturam consequentiarum in generali. Et ideo omnis scientia utitur logica tamquam instrumento, quo mediante cognoscit suas consequentias in particulari (*Ordinatio*, Prologue, q. 7, 201).

has any place for a full-fledged independent metaphysics. If we begin with his view of being it may be recalled that he treated the concept of being on the one hand as a transcendental term which when understood univocally was the most universal of all concepts; as such it had no real signification since it refers to nothing in particular. On the other hand, being could be predicated equivocally of real individuals by means of the ten categories; it was then signified by the ten different ways in which individual beings could be denoted. In consequence, Ockham correspondingly rejected on the one hand the view of Duns Scotus—and also Henry of Ghent and Avicenna—of being as a universal nature which both had primacy in the order of being and was the first object of the intellect; and on the other hand the Thomist distinction between essence and existence. Like Duns Scotus he did not conceive the different modes of being, such as the relation of matter to form and potentiality to actuality, under metaphysics; but unlike Duns he did not seek to transcend being's individual determinations, which were the province of the different sciences like physics, just because all being was individual and in space and time for this world. Ockham therefore cut the ontological link between being as universal and individual being, uniting them only in the univocal concept of being as a transcendental term. Hence, as we have seen, both being as a transcendental and the categories lost their metaphysical status and became logical terms of second and first intention, in the same way as essence and existence were merely the abstract and concrete forms of the same term, denoting the capacity to be an individual being. Ockham, as we have also considered, thereby reduced all significative terms to the same ontological import of individual being and made their differences exclusively logical and grammatical.

It is in this context that the question of what remains to metaphysics arises. Although it is not directly raised by Ockham, he has an instructive passage on the role of metaphysics, in the same chapters in the *Logic* just previously alluded to, where he discusses the relation of logic to the real sciences. Just as logic does not depend upon or provide the principles of the particular sciences like physics, neither do they depend upon logic for their knowledge; otherwise they would be subalternated. Such principles are known, he continues, either under metaphysics or jointly under the particular subject to which they belong and logic, together with any other particular sciences to which they are subalternated for their knowledge.[60] Thus given both a knowledge of the particular science and logic, the conclusions deriving from such knowledge can easily be reached, so that if there is proper knowledge of say man's nature and logic, it can easily be known whether or not 'rational' constitutes his essential difference. It is for that reason that the philosophers did not write special treatises on these different individual sciences.[61]

---

[60] Et ideo dicendum est quod tales propositiones vel pertinent ad metaphysicam, sub cuius intentione cadunt tam intentiones prime quam secunde, quibus utitur logic adupliciter: secundum quod logica est modus sciendi et etiam accipiendo propositiones consideratas in logica. Vel tales pertinent ad aliquam scientiam specialem ita quod alique pertinent ad unam scientiam specialem et alique ad aliquam, que quodammodo subalternantur tam logice quam etiam aliis scientiis pertinentibus . . . (*SL*, III, II, ch. 22).

[61] *Ibid.*

This clearly suggests that the special sciences together with logic can serve the same purpose traditionally ascribed to metaphysics in combining universal understanding with knowledge of specific being.

That Ockham restricts metaphysics to a conceptual role is also suggested by his different remarks in the Prologue of the *Ordinatio*. To begin with while being and its attributes all pertain to metaphysics as a *scientia* they also belong to their particular sciences as the study of real beings.[62] Now it is this very duality of all beings which deprives metaphysics of specific content since specific beings form the subjects of the particular sciences of nature. In the second place metaphysics like any other *scientia*, as a body of knowledge is not one subject but a collection of many; in that strict sense Averroes however is wrong to call being the subject of metaphysics. It can however be accepted in the broader meaning that being comes first among the many subjects of metaphysics, by primacy of predication: that is to say as the most universal term.[63] Hence the relation of metaphysical being to actual being is a logical not an ontological one, whether of perfection, as Duns held, or of causality, which was more the notion of St Thomas, or of whole to part which is inherent in any ontological conception. As Ockham expresses it a little later, ' . . . metaphysics, which considers being, can exhibit all the attributes of being for everything coming under it, and in so far as these attributes are common (to all beings) metaphysics is of every particular nature, since no other science considers these attributes'.[64] Ockham does not specify what these attributes are; and it is at this point that logic and metaphysics appear to encroach upon one another, above all over the ten categories which are at once metaphysical, as facets of existence, and yet do not constitute distinct ontological principles in being predicable precisely of the same individuals. Both logic and metaphysics have thus here the same ontological import. But for Ockham, unlike Aristotle, who treated them from both standpoints, they pass from logic not to metaphysics but to the particular sciences under the aegis of which the study of real being—above all physics—falls. Hence, as we have seen, Ockham acknowledges both that the subjects of metaphysics are also those of the particular sciences and that the latter in conjunction with logic can know what metaphysics knows. The consequence is that metaphysics would seem to lose any defined area which is not shared by logic and the sciences of nature. It is the price of denying any ontological identity to being as a universal state or nature: metaphysics has to cede to logic as the one universalising science since only its concepts and the terms and propositions derived from them are universal. To that extent metaphysics is displaced not by nominalism but by the conjunction of logic providing terms of second intention,

---

[62] Ad confirmationem concedo quod ille sunt passiones entis, et ideo pertinent ad metaphysicam; sed cum hoc stat quod pertinent ad alias scientias (*Ordinatio*, Prologue, q. 1, 12).

[63] Et ita de virtute sermonis dictum Commentatoris est falsum quando dicit quod ens est subiectum metaphysice, quia cum ens non sit subiectum omnium partium . . . non potest dici quod sit subiectum totius, de virtute sermonis. Tamen secundum intentionem suam ens est subiectum metaphysice, quia per istam propositionem, 'Ens est subiectum metaphysice', intelligit istam propositionem 'inter omnia subiecta diversarum partium metaphysice ens est primum primitate predicationis' (*ibid.*, q. 9, 258–9).

[64] *Ibid.*, 274.

and the real particular sciences concerned with terms of first intention. If there is a lacuna in Ockham's system it is not in the failure to account for metaphysics but to account for the effect upon metaphysics of his shift away from them as traditionally conceived.

It is perhaps here above all that the divergence of Ockham from Aristotle lies. Even the absence of a specific work on the subject will hardly explain the marginal place Ockham allows to metaphysics. They have nothing of the same priority for him as for Aristotle, beyond the categorical primacy of being as the most universal of all terms. Even Aristotle's assertion that metaphysics is a kind of wisdom Ockham glosses to apply to all demonstration *propter quid*, so that it is not to metaphysics itself as a body of knowledge but to particular first principles and their conclusions that wisdom belongs.[65] Accordingly the role of metaphysics is as a subalternating science whose principles are appropriated by the other sciences and generalised by logic. It therefore stands outside demonstrative knowledge, and is best understood as the starting point of experience, which is the province of the particular sciences whose subject is real—i.e. individual—being. We may add finally that metaphysical knowledge is speculative because it treats what is outside human agency. Only if taken in Aristotle's definition of a natural theology can that part of it which is moral be called practical but that does not hold for metaphysics in its strict sense.[66]

So much then for the different sciences. We have now to place theology among them.

II THEOLOGY AND KNOWLEDGE

The difference between theology and the other sciences concerns not only its subject but also its status, namely whether theology is knowledge as they are. These two issues, involving the nature at once of knowledge and theology and the relation between them, largely came by the end of the thirteenth century to be the focus of the Prologue to a Commentary on the *Sentences*, a practice observed by Ockham, whose own Prologue opens with the question, 'Whether someone in this world (*viator*) can have evident knowledge of theological truths', and almost at once involves the distinction between evident, intuitive, and abstractive knowledge, as it had in the case of Duns Scotus. I shall accordingly begin with—though not follow in strict sequence—the ways in which theological truths can be known; and then discuss the subject of theology.

Ockham defines theological truths as those necessary to man for his salvation. Some can be known naturally, for example that God is, that he is wise, good, and so on; others are only known supernaturally, such as that God is divine, is incarnated, and similar truths for which there is no natural reference among created beings.[67] As we shall mention again, not all supernaturally knowable truths are

---

[65] *Ibid.*, q. 7, 198–9, and q. 8, 223–4.   [66] *Ibid.*, q. 12, 364–5.

[67] Circa tertium dico quod omnes veritates necessarie homini viatiori ad eternam beatitudinem consequendam sunt veritates theologice ... Ex isto sequitur quod alique veritates naturaliter note seu cognosci biles sunt theologice, sicut quod deus est, deus est sapiens, bonus etc, cum sint necessarie ad salutem; alique autem, sunt supernaturaliter cognoscibiles. sicut deus est trinus, incarnatus et huiusmodi (*Ordinatio*, Prologue, q. 1, 7).

necessary truths;[68] but if that precludes those that are contingent from constituting scientific knowledge it does not thereby make them evident, because, as we have seen, an evident proposition is one which is known through incomplex knowledge of its terms indirectly or directly. For that it must be either self-evident or from what is self-evident i.e. by demonstration; or the result of experience through intuitive knowledge. None of these modes is possible for the truths of theology since they are all matters of belief (credibilia). It is that which distinguishes theology from the other sciences and prevents its truths from being equally accessible to the unbeliever: without the need for faith everything known by the faithful would also be known by the infidel, whether self-evidently, demonstratively or by experience.[69] It would also follow that necessary theological truths could be known evidently, which is false, since no one can know naturally that he is in charity or that Christ is present in the eucharist.[70]

Theology thus differs from the rest of knowledge not as another kind of knowledge but in resting upon faith. Faith is thus the barrier between what is believed and what is known evidently and/or demonstratively, regardless of whether one or other is necessary or contingent. To the claim then for the primacy of theology among the sciences Ockham replies that 'it is not first or last or middle because it is not a proper science in this respect'.[71]

This is in the course of his discussion of three opinions all of which he opposed for affirming in varying degrees that theology is proper knowledge. The first is that of St Thomas Aquinas and Richard of Middleton; it holds that there are two kinds of knowledge: one which proceeds from principles known in the natural light of the intellect, for example the principles of geometry, and the other which derives from principles known in the light of a superior science, as perspective takes its principles from geometry, to which it is therefore subalternated. Theology is of this second kind; its first principles are held on faith but the conclusions which follow from them are knowledge in the proper sense. Accordingly theology is knowledge in the light of principles drawn from superior knowledge, namely that of God and the blessed; and as music accepts the principles transmitted by arithmetic, so theology believes in those revealed by God. To say otherwise would derogate from the dignity of theology as well being contrary to truth; for theology excels all other sciences in certainty and in its subject-matter. Unlike the other

---

[68] Quia quedam veritates theologice solum supernaturaliter cognoscibiles sunt necessarie et quedam contingentes que nec naturaliter nec supernaturaliter possunt scientifice cognosci (ibid., 15). Also 50.

[69] Omne quod est evidenter notum, aut est per se notum; aut notificatum per per se nota; aut per experientiam mediante notitia intuitiva, et hoc mediate vel immediate. Sed nullo istorum modorum possunt ista credibilia esse nota. Quia non sunt per se nota, manifestum est; tunc enim essent nota infidelibus. Nec notificantur per per se nota, quia tunc quicumque infidelis ordinate interrogatus de eis assentiret secundum beatum Augustinium I Retractationum cap. 8. Nec sunt nota per experientiam notitia intuitiva mediante, quia omnem notitiam intuitivam quam habet fidelis habet infidelis; et per consequens quidquid potest fidelis scire evidenter mediante notitia intuitiva et infidelis, et ita infidelis posset evidenter scire ista credibilia (ibid., q. 7, 187–8).

[70] Ibid., 188.

[71] Ibid., 205.

sciences it cannot fail those who embrace it, and its truths exceed the powers of human reason. Hence the other sciences are called its handmaids and are judged by it.[72]

The second opinion—partly of Francis of Marchia, partly of Duns Scotus—goes further than the first in regarding both the conclusions and the principles of theology as true knowledge, so that its principles are known by faith and also in the light of the active intellect in the soul. The reason is that theology is distinct not only from understanding of first principles (*intellectus*), practical wisdom (*prudentia*), and art, but also from faith, since they are distinct habits with distinct acts: that of faith is to assent at the command of the will and without evidence, whereas the act of theology is to defend and strengthen faith, according to St Augustine. That theology is knowledge is proved firstly because whatever is not impossible can be known, but theology is of what is possible; therefore it can be known. Second—Duns Scotus's argument—when the concept under which something is known as a subject contains all the knowable truths belonging to the subject, these can themselves be really known. That is the case with God known under the concept of the divine nature, which contains all theological truths knowable abstractively by the human intellect. Thirdly, the first in any genus is the greatest; and among the sciences that is theology; if it were not, the theologican's state would be no better than an old crone's.[73]

Henry of Ghent's is the third opinion which is also that both the conclusion and the principles of theology constitute knowledge, but only in the light of a superior understanding at once beyond that of faith and natural knowledge, and between faith and glory. It is this further light that enables us to know one matter of belief more firmly and clearly than another. Like Duns Scotus, Henry of Ghent cites the same passage from St Augustine's *De Trinitate*,[74] that knowledge strengthens faith, to show that faith and theology are not always the same.[75]

Ockham, as we have seen, rejects the scientific status of theology on the very ground that the first opinion upholds it, namely that it presupposes faith. There cannot be two different habits of judgement over the same object because different habits incline to different acts. Hence one does not necessarily presuppose the other; even if it did, that faith would not be infused faith since the habit of the latter would incline to the same object of faith as acquired faith; hence it would be from acquired faith—directed towards knowledge—that theology would derive,[76] thereby excluding all that is supernaturally infused.

More specifically, in reply to the first opinion, the principles of any science must not only be known if the conclusions are to be known; they must be better known than the conclusions. That applies equally to opinion. Moreover, whoever knows a conclusion evidently from its premises must know it necessarily; hence he must know the principles evidently.[77] As to the two different kinds of knowledge, they are true of subalternated knowledge known in the light of principles from a superior science, but only when the conclusions are known from experience

[72] *Ibid.*, 184–5.   [73] *Ibid.*, 185–7.   [74] *De Trinitate*, bk. XIV, ch. 1, n. 3.
[75] *Ordinatio, ibid.*, 187.   [76] *Ibid.*, 188–9.   [77] *Ibid.*, 189–90.

or from evidently known premises. It does not, however, follow that one person knows conclusions because he believes someone else knows the principles; nor by the same token that there is knowledge of theological conclusions because God knows the principles which are believed by those to whom he reveals them.[78] It derogates no more from theology to say that its conclusions cannot be known evidently than it does from its principles on the same grounds. Since neither can be known evidentially, the certitude in which theology excels all other sciences must be understood as that of adhesion not evidence. It is for that greater certainty that the other arts are called the handmaidens of theology; and the *sancti* call theology knowledge in leading to knowledge and wisdom. Nor does Aristotle in the *Ethics*[79] include faith among the five veridical intellectual habits, because it can be of what is false as well as true. As it concerns theology, however, it is a veridical habit.[80]

That also answers the first argument of the second opinion that faith and theology are distinct acts; for only what is independent of faith can be known veridically and apprehensively.[81] Moreover to say that they are different acts does not prove that theology is knowledge; for as a separate act it would then be open to an infidel, enabling him to defend and strengthen faith, as opposed to knowledge. On the other hand, if theology were knowledge then, as said before, its truths could be known naturally without a supernaturally infused habit of faith.[82]

To the first proof for this opinion, that that is known evidently which is not impossible, Ockham adds that which is evidently known not to be impossible; here however what is to be known is a matter of belief and so there is no question of knowing it evidently. For that reason theological arguments are not susceptible to the same evident correction as other propositions on the grounds of logical or material error: for example 'The divine essence is the father; The divine essence is the son; Therefore the son is the father', which is formally incorrect but cannot evidently be known to be so from natural experience, just as no one can know naturally that one absolute being is several persons. Conversely an argument can be false materially and yet its falsity not be evidently known, such as 'God is immortal; No man is God; Therefore no man is immortal'. Here the minor premise is false, but it can only be believed to be such.[83] The second proof, that God under the concept of the divine nature contains all the theological truths that can be really known, is treated and rejected in the subsequent question, which we shall consider when we come to the subject of theology.[84] We shall also see that Ockham denies that we can have a proper concept of the divine nature, as he denies the third opinion of Henry of Ghent that there is a habit naturally acquired which inclines towards an act of knowing *credibilia*. Once again it would lead to the same consequence, that it would then be attainable by the infidel as well. Furthermore the intellect has evident knowledge of all its acts; therefore of this one

[78] *Ibid.*, 199.
[79] *Nicomachean Ethics*, VI, ch. 3, 1139 b, 16–17.
[80] *Ordinatio, ibid.*, 200–1.   [81] *Ibid.*, 190–1.
[82] *Ibid.*, 202–3.   [83] *Ibid.*, 202.   [84] *Ibid.*, 202–3, Prologue, q. 9.

if it exists. In that case no theologian could doubt that he knew as knowledge what he believed, whereas in fact many do doubt it. Just as no one can believe without the certainty that he believes, so no one can know without knowing that he knows. What remains open to doubt is whether one act is really distinguished from another, so that someone can know he feels both love and delight without knowing where they differ.[85] Finally, as we have observed in another context, the difference between theology and true knowledge is to be seen in the contrast between dissent from what is known evidently and dissent from what is believed: in the first case, it is due to reason or forgetfulness; in the second, to the will's behest no matter how well versed in theological study the person concerned.[86] Here as throughout the dividing line is faith.

The view of theology with which Ockham does agree is that expressed by William of Ware, namely that while *credibilia* may be known they cannot be known by man in his present condition under the existing dispensation; hence theology is not properly knowledge as it concerns matters of belief although it could be knowledge of some things. Ockham's own solution to the nature of a theological habit is in two parts.[87] Negatively there can be no habit which excludes faith and is exclusive to a believer, because a habit of conviction derives either from what is known or from the authority of the Bible: if the first, it is also known by an infidel; if the second, it concerns only matters of belief and so belongs to faith.[88]

The second part is that the habit of theology is a habit of acquired faith either preceding the study of theology, which then augments it, or if the habit does not previously exist, leads to its acquisition. The possession of such a habit distinguishes the believer from the infidel.[89] Nevertheless beyond such acquired faith both the heretic and the infidel, as well as the believer, engaged in the study of theology, acquire many other scientific habits which could be derived from other sciences and also many scientific conclusions which belong to no particular science. For all of them—regardless of whether they are complex or incomplex, propositions or conclusions, to be known or believed—the pursuit of theology yields an apprehensive habit. From their combination the theologian is able to preach, teach, strengthen the faith and perform all the other duties in its defence.[90] That a theological habit is not one of proper knowledge is shown by its dependence upon faith for assent to truths which are matters of belief and not shown evidently. That is not to

---

[85] *Ibid.*, 191–2. [86] *Ibid.*, 192.

[87] Alia est opinio que ponit quod quamvis credibilia possint evidenter sciri, non tamen a nobis pro statu isto de communi lege. Et ideo theologia, secundum quod communiter addiscimus eam, non est scientia proprie dicta respectu talium credibilium, quamvis respectu aliquorum posset esse scientia. Et istam opinionem reputo veram. Ideo circa istam opinionem primo ostendam quod omnem habitum preter fidem quem acquirit theologus fidelis potest acquirere etiam infidelis; secundo est videndum qualis habitus acquiritur in theologo preter fidem (*ibid.* 193).

[88] *Ibid.*, 194.

[89] Ideo dico ad istum articulum quod theologus respectu credibilium augmentat habitum fidei acquisite quando fides acquisita precedit studium suum; quando autem non precedit tunc acquirit fidem acquisitam, si sit fidelis. Et talis habitus non est in infideli (*ibid.*, 196–7).

[90] *Ibid.*, 197.

say that no supernatural knowledge is necessary to man beyond infused faith; it is, but it can only be evident supernaturally and outside the present dispensation: within it infused faith suffices.[91]

Ockham opposes his view of a theological habit to that of Peter Aureole who describes the habit gained from the study of theology as declarative rather than adhesive: that is to say it does not cause assent but represents what Aristotle in the *Ethics* calls philosophic wisdom as 'the most finished of all forms of knowledge', combining intuitive reason of first principles with scientific knowledge of the highest objects.[92] To Aureole this is what the *sancti* mean by light and intelligence; as such, theology represents an additional habit to faith, first because it is caused by the active intellect and the propositions expressing it, both subsequent to faith; and second because theology employs reasons to defend and enhance faith. Moreover unless something further were acquired from the study of theology it would be in vain; but this cannot be a habit of adhesion, for it would then constitute opinion. Ockham accepts that a further habit is acquired, but it is not one of wisdom; otherwise it could be had by an unbeliever, since, as Aristotle says, there is no wisdom without understanding and knowledge, whereas on Aureole's own arguments a declaratory habit can be without either. On the one hand he says it can be of faith alone, but on the other in treating such a habit as knowledge he opens it to an unbeliever, who in possessing it would at the same time know and err over matters of faith. Wisdom, however, cannot err.[93] Accordingly a theological habit can be declaratory, as it can be adhesive (which is not the same as opinion), but not wisdom; for it depends upon faith whose truths cannot be known evidently by man's natural powers.[94]

The role of a theological habit is thus to augment acquired faith. Unlike knowledge or wisdom, which is an evident veridical habit of necessary truth, most of theology is an inevident veridical habit which concerns faith and includes some habits which are exclusively apprehensive, as we have seen. Taken as a whole the habit of the theologian is more perfect than that of a layman, although not always over particular matters of belief.[95]

We have next to consider whether theology is one habit or many. As we should expect, Ockham comes down for the latter in the course of rejecting the arguments of St Thomas Aquinas and Henry of Ghent for its numerical unity.

According to St Thomas theology is one because the unity of any science depends upon the formal nature of its object. The object of theology consists in what is divinely revealed. Therefore everything divinely revealed belongs to the same formal object of theology.[96]

Ockham does not however recognise that a habit or faculty owes either its unity or distinction from others to the formal unity or distinction of its object.

[91] *Ibid.*, 197–8.
[92] *Nicomachean Ethics*, VI, ch. 7, 1141 a, 9–1141 b, 7.
[93] *Ordinatio, ibid.*, 196.
[94] *Ibid.*, 198–9.
[95] *Ibid.*, 206.
[96] *Ibid.*, q. 8, 208.

If it did, the same thing could not be the object both of the senses and the intellect, or of intuitive and abstractive knowledge, or of knowledge, opinion and error, of all of which it can be without entailing a separate formal concept, and so a distinct thing, as the object of each different habit or faculty. Conversely there can be distinct objects of the same faculty, as white and black can both be the objects of sight. Nor will he accept the distinction between particular colours as material objects and colour itself as a formal object, on similar grounds to his rejection of a formal distinction within the same thing: namely that a particular colour is itself colour, either as the subject of colour or as contained under the formal nature of colour; in neither case therefore can one be distinguished from the other. If they were, colour would be something distinct as a universal, apprehensible only to the intellect; which it is not, just as whiteness is not a particular form belonging to colour: for they would then be really distinct as things, which is contrary to St Thomas who denies a formal distinction. Finally St Thomas's definition of the object of theology is also false: it cannot be what is revealed, since that would include any conclusion of geometry which is also from God, as well as God, who according to St Thomas is the subject of theology under the concept of the divine nature.[97]

The same conclusion, that theology is one, is held by Henry of Ghent. His reasons are that in theology, as in any science, there is only one habit because there is but one subject, which unites all its different attributes under the same formal mode of conceiving it as a concept. That gives a science like theology or metaphysics the same simplicity as an affective habit like temperance or whiteness and applies to every part of it. If there were no such single habit the principles of a science could not be better known than the conclusions, or one conclusion better known than another. Furthermore, as Aristotle says, 'Of a single thing *qua* single there is single scientific knowledge',[98] and in whatever is essentially ordered there must be a first subject.[99]

To this Ockham replies firstly that to attribute unity to a formal concept it must follow that it is due either to the intellect or to the object. It cannot be the intellect since there can be diverse modes of considering the same term or concept and yet they will not give rise to distinct sciences, according to Henry of Ghent, since for him the same conclusion cannot be at once mathematical and metaphysical. Nor can the mode of considering a subject be from the object, because the presence there of distinct concepts would signify distinct things, which is false according to Henry of Ghent, for whom there is no such real distinction within things.[100]

There must therefore be distinct habits for principles and conclusions and different conclusions, on the established grounds that habits incline to acts of the same nature; and the habits of principle and conclusions and different conclusions

[97] *Ibid.*, 208–11.
[98] *Posterior Analytics*, II, ch. 3, 90 b, 20.
[99] *Ordinatio, ibid.*, 211–12.
[100] *Ibid.*, 212.

are not of the same nature. Hence a habit engendered from a thousand acts of knowing a principle will not lead to the same effect as a habit generated from only two acts of knowing a conclusion.[101] Furthermore, as Duns Scotus has argued, in a subject like geometry knowledge of some principles and conclusions can go with ignorance of other conclusions; but there cannot be contrary habits over the same propositions; therefore the habit of knowing is not the same as the habit of error.[102] To the objection that this is a difference in degree not kind, Ockham replies that whenever something in the most perfect degree can coexist with another thing but not with something else of the same degree as itself, they must be of different species in the way that whiteness and sweetness can both be present in milk but not white and black, which are contrary natures. That applies equally to perfect knowledge of one principle and conclusion and error over another conclusion; they cannot coexist over the same conclusion because like any contraries they formally contradict one another as different in kind. Correspondingly different sciences and sciences with diverse conclusions are or contain different species of knowledge. In the case of theology this diversity is manifest, comprising as it does necessary and contingent knowledge and evident and inevident knowledge. In that aspect it cannot therefore be said to be a single habit.[103]

So far as habits in general then are concerned, they are always proportioned to their acts; as the invariable outcome of acts, habits are always identical or diverse according to the identity or diversity of their acts. Thus while distinct acts of knowing principles and conclusions give rise to distinct species of habits, there can also be one act for a number of principles and conclusions, and so one habit, as in a syllogism. Similarly in any science, as a collection of habits, there can be a multiple order among the conclusions as of the subject or the attribute or both.

In the case of theology there is a distinction between infused and acquired faith. By the first, theology is one habit because, as Ockham explains in the third book of the *Reportatio*, infused faith has for its immediate object a proposition which can be a premise and partial principle—i.e. cause—in inferring every article of faith. The proposition in question is that everything revealed by God is true: from it as a habit of belief, we can infer that God is triune, was incarnated, and suffered, in being all true articles of faith. This first proposition, therefore, as the immediate object of infused faith, inclines indirectly to each particular act of belief in each article of faith by means of such conclusions.[104] Both the other supernatural

---

[101] *Ibid.*, 213.   [102] *Ibid.*, 215.

[103] *Ibid.*, 216–17; also *Reportatio*, III, q. 8, I.

[104] Quantum ad secundam difficultatem quomodo potest esse una fides omnium articulorum fidei, potest dupliciter dici. Uno modo quod fides infusa habet aliquod complexum pro obiecto immediato, quod potest esse premissa et principium partiale inherens omni articulo fidei. Et istud complexum, 'Omne revelatum a deo est verum', sicut revelatur esse verum. Nam istud potest inferre omnem articulum fidei. Potest enim sic argui respectu cuiuslibet articuli, 'Omne revelatum a deo est verum' . . . sed deum esse trinum et unum et incarnatum et passum etc. Unde sicut istud complexum est principium inferens omnem articulum in speciali, ita habitus fidei infuse, cuius hoc complexum est immediatum obiectum inclinat mediate ad actum elicitum circa omnem articulum in virtute speciali huius complexi; et sic est una fides omnium articulorum fidei mediate, sed non immediate (*ibid.*, I).

virtues have a corresponding proposition as their immediate object: of hope it is that future blessedness is to be conferred on man for his merits; and of charity that God wishes to be loved from charity.[105] Like any habit of knowledge these propositions can incline immediately to knowing the principle and indirectly to knowing the conclusion; in that way the immediate object of infused faith is the indirect and partial cause of every article of faith.[106] But not the immediate cause; hence the habit of infused faith does not of itself suffice for particular acts of faith. For that it must be completed as concause by acquired faith, through reading or speaking. That can be seen from the example of a baptised infant who, without instruction in the articles of faith, although having infused faith, would remain in ignorance of them.

All specific acts of belief thus require the conjunction of infused and acquired faith.[107] Their relation can be likened to that between an equivocal universal cause and a univocal particular cause, comparable to that between the sun and its many indirect effects. That is to say, infused faith is not the immediate cause of any act of belief but a partial cause of every act, as the cause of the cause by inclining towards it. And as infused and acquired faith are of different species so are particular acts of belief in the different articles of faith. There cannot thus be one single act of belief, because there are as many acts of acquired faith as there are articles of belief, each with its own habit.[108] God, can however, create a habit of faith inclining a believer immediately to belief in all the articles of faith, assuming the possession of acquired faith in each of them, just as there can be a habit of wisdom which, as Ockham argued in the Prologue,[109] is of the whole demonstration, not merely of either the principles or the conclusion without the other. Such a habit would not be impaired by conflicting individual articles of faith, for example over whether Christ's death is in the future or past, according to when it is believed; for these differences concern acquired faith, whereas infused faith always remains constant as the partial cause of every act of belief.[110] Thus in the example just given, the discrepancy between belief in Christ's death as a past or future event is not over belief in its truth; that is shared as an article of faith by all believers: it arises over the time at which it was held, either before or after Christ died. Whenever that was, adherence to its truth is the outcome of the same habit of infused faith in the truth of all revelation as its immediate object.[111] The articles of faith accordingly differ as propositions but not in the infused habit of faith that informs their

---

[105] *Ibid.*, G. [106] *Ibid.*, J.

[107] Sed alio modo inclinat fides ad actum credendi articulos in speciali, et alio modo habitus principii ad actum de quo supra dictum est, quia fides infusa sic inclinat ad actum fidei elicitum circa articulos in speciali quod nec habitus fidei infuse nec actus potest cum intellectu esse principium sufficiens ad eliciendum actum credendi circa articulum aliquem in speciali. Patet, nam parvulus baptizatus nutritus solitarie alicubi ubi nunquam instruitur in articulus fidei ille habet fidem infusam et usum rationis; et tamen nullum actum credendi circa quemcumque articulum potest elicere; igitur ad actum eliciendi circa articulum specialem necessario requiritur fides acquisita circa illum articulum, puta per auditem . . . vel per visum (*Ibid.*, L).

[108] *Ibid.*, M–O; also *Quodlibet* III, q. 7, where the same analogy is employed.

[109] *Ordinatio*, Prologue, q. 8, 222–3.

[110] *Reportatio*, III, q. 8, P; also N.

[111] *Ibid.*

acceptance by every believer. For that reason someone can lose acquired faith over a particular article because the principle or conclusion changes but not his infused faith, which is unchanged.[112]

That explains the difference between them. Infused faith is a prerequisite of acquired faith in engendering belief in the truth of all its articles; acquired faith is over the different articles which may or may not be known or known wrongly. For that reason acquired faith is not numerically one habit but consists in as many different habits as there are articles of faith. That they are of different species is, as Duns Scotus says, proved by the coexistence of truth and error in the acquired faith of the same believer; which is the cause of heresy. If all the articles were of the same species such divergencies could not coexist since they would contradict one another; and as Ockham has already said in the Prologue and repeats again here in the third book of the *Reportatio*, contraries of the same degree negate one another.[113] In the same way there can be faith over the principles of a demonstration and knowledge over the conclusion just as there can be evident knowledge of one and error over the other. What is not possible is to have contradictory acts simultaneously over the same object.[114]

What, then, of the relation between faith and knowledge? Are their different habits compatible? Ockham makes a threefold distinction (a) between a habit and an act, (b) between acts and (c) between habits. In the first case there is generally no contradiction between them; hence a habit of faith can coexist with an act of knowledge or clear vision; for they are not more exclusive of one another than an act of error and a habit of knowledge over the same conclusion, or a habit of temperance and an act of intemperance. Thus someone knowing a conclusion in geometry can forget it, and instead choose some other act towards it. It cannot be an act of knowing because that requires knowledge both of principles and from experience; the alternatives are an act of belief or doubt or error. Whichever of these is adopted it will nevertheless stand with the habit of knowing the same

---

[112] Et ex hoc apparet quare aliquis potest habere demonstrationem circa aliquos articulos fidei, et tamen non perdere fidem infusam licet perdat fidem aquisitam . . . (*ibid.*, N).
And: ita quod fides infusa est semper eadem, sed acquisita variatur (*ibid.*, P.). In *Quodlibet* III, q. 7, however, Ockham says that only authority can decide whether error over a particular article also destroys infused faith in relation to it.

[113] Quantum ad primam [difficultatem] sunt due conclusiones. Prima quod quilibet articulus habet fidem acquisitam distinctam. Secunda quod ista fides non tantum distinguitur numero sed specie. Prima probatur per rationem Johannis in Metaphysica de scientie unitate. Quia quando aliquis potest habere actum et habitum credendi circa unum articulum et non circa alium, immo potest errare circa alium, necessario illi actus credendi illos articulos et habitus generati ex illis sunt distincti. Sed aliquis potest habere fidem acquisitam circa unum articulum et non circa alium, sed circa alium errare, sicut hereticus . . . Secunda conclusio probatur, quia quando cum uno contrariorum stat unum et aliud non stat, sed sibi repugnat illud quod stat cum uno contrariorum et aliud quod non stat, necessario distinguuntur specie . . . Sed fides acquisita circa unum articulum stat cum errore circa alium. Patet de heretico. Sed acquisita fides et error non stant circa eundem articulum. Ergo fides acquisite circa unum articulum et alium sint distincte specie, quia si essent eiusdem speciei, tunc sicut error repugnat uni, ita repugnat alteri, et sicut stant cum uno, et ita cum altero. Et per istam viam tenent rationes Johannis in questione predicta (*ibid.*, K).

[114] *Ibid.*, N.

conclusion derived from the now forgotten act of knowledge. And the same with an act of intemperance which can be performed by someone who has acquired a habit of temperance. In each case the inclination may be less positive than a dis-inclination towards its opposite.

As to the second and third distinctions, Ockham dismisses the contention that habits are mutually compatible regardless of the nature of their acts. Rather their relation depends entirely upon that of their acts. If they are contrary, as those of temperance and intemperance are, their habits will also be contrary; conversely if their acts do not conflict, neither will their habits. Those of knowledge and faith can coexist because if someone first knows the conclusion of a demonstration and later forgets it, he can then believe that he knows it: there can thus be knowledge and faith over the same conclusion. The act of faith by which he does so is acquired; and the first object of his belief is not the habit of knowledge but the act of having known it: for it is in virtue of past knowledge of the conclusion, to which the habit left by it inclines him, that he believes the conclusion to be true. The habit of knowledge is therefore only the indirect object of his belief in leading him to the act as the object of his faith.[115]

From that it can be seen that theology from the standpoint of acquired faith consists in a collection of habits, which, as we have seen, include evident habits both of propositions and conclusions together with apprehensive habits of all that comes under theology, complex and incomplex. Acquired faith, as opposed to infused faith, cannot therefore be numerically one habit because its acts, and so its habits, are of different kinds, as in the example of a heretic in whom acquired faith over one article goes with error over another. That also applies to apprehensive habits, which are separable from one another; there can accordingly be a strong inclination to reflect upon one article but not upon another.[116]

The difference between infused and acquired faith then is between a habit of assent indirectly to all the articles, through immediate assent to the truth of re-velation, and direct assent to particular articles; for both, the object of assent must be a complex, as it is in knowledge, since only propositions, as opposed to things or terms, can be true (or false).[117] Whether assent is to one or all the articles, however, only faith not knowledge is acquired, because whatever is of faith is by definition inevident.[118] For that reason it is not the same to know that there is a first mover and to believe in The Trinity; the second can never follow from the

[115] *Ibid.*, Q–R.

[116] Circa secundum principale [de habitu theologie] dico quod theologia uno modo includit fidem infusam. Et theologia secundum istam partem est una unitate numerali, quia fides infusa est una numero ... Alio modo theologia includit fidem acquisitam et aliquos habitus evidentes tam propositionum quam consequentiarum, et'habitus apprehensivos omnium, sive complexorum sive incomplexorum; et isto modo non est una numero. Quod enim fides acquisita non sit una numero patet ex predicitis, quia actus credendi distinguuntur specie, ergo habitus generati ex illis actibus. Similiter hereticus habet fidem acquisitam circa unum articulum et errorem circa alium, circa quem tamen potest habere fidem acquisitam. Similiter habitus apprehensivi sunt distincti quia unus potest separari ab alio; potest enim aliquis esse inclinatus multum ad cog-itandum de uno articulo et non de alio (*Ordinatio*, Prologue, q. 8, 220).

[117] *Quodlibet* III, q. 6.

[118] *Quodlibet* IV, q. 10.

first, because it is neither self-evident nor deducible from what is self-evident. Hence to apply natural reason to faith leads to the fallacy of expression in misusing the terms, as in the syllogism, 'God is three persons; God is the father; therefore the father is the Trinity'. The falsity here arises from the articles of faith—that the father is not the Trinity—not the mode of reasoning, which is therefore inapplicable to matters of belief. The source of their incongruity is the absence of evident knowledge of the terms employed; that can be either, as we know, from demonstration in the case of composite terms, or experience when the terms are simple. Neither can be had of God because we have no simple cognition of him as middle term; that is reserved to the blessed.[119] As we shall consider presently, we can know God in a composite or negative concept but that does not give evident knowledge of him. Hence, as *viatores*, we can only believe in him.[120]

That does not however mean that the believer does not use concepts which can be understood by reason and in certain cases give knowledge. He can, as is shown both in his relation to pagans and to the blessed as *comprehensores* of the truths of faith. So far as the first is concerned, pagan and believer can only contradict one another, say, over God's triunity because they both know the meaning of the terms 'God', 'three' and 'one', and so possess the same concepts. The same conclusion can therefore be the object of diverse sciences, even if it is not believed or is understood differently, which is the case with theological and non-theological truths,[121] and also theological truths believed by the *viator* and evidently known by the blessed.[122] Although a creditive and a demonstrative middle are of different kinds as composite and simple concepts, their conclusions can be the same and known in the same intellect, as the same conclusions can be known by demonstration and authority and by demonstration and experience.[123] Once again therefore diversity of cause does not entail diversity of effect.[124] It is this principle which explains at once the divergence of theology from the other sciences and its rapports with them.

III   THE SUBJECT OF THEOLOGY

That brings us to the subject of theology. We may best begin at the end of question nine of the Prologue where it is considered. There theology is defined in two ways. By the first it is a habit necessary in this life for eternal life. By the second it is every theological habit regardless of whether it is necessary and should be known or not; in this second sense it concerns all incomplexes but not all complexes,[125] because

---

[119] *Ibid.*, II, q. 3.

[120] *Ibid.*

[121] *Ibid.*, v, qq. I and 3.

[122] Utrum aliqua veritas theologica eadem numero vel specie sit credita a viatore et evidenter scita a comprehensore . . . Ad istam questionem dico breviter quod sic (*ibid.*, q. 3).

[123] *Ibid.*, q. 3; also q. 2 for a conclusion known by demonstration and experience.

[124] Quia si cause sint alterius rationis, non oportet propter hoc quod effectus sint alterius rationis (*ibid.*, q. 3).

[125] Sed tunc est dubium: de quibus est theologia? An scilicet sit de omnibus, vel de aliquibus, et de aliquibus non? Ad hoc potest dici quod theologia potest accipi dupliciter: vel pro habitu

there is no incomplex which has not some theological attribute: for example, creatable, annihilable, perpetuable, and so on, all of which belong exclusively to theology as predicated of God's effects. Hence as metaphysics considers being as such, theology is concerned with what derives from God as universal cause of creation; and those attributes which are common to all beings, as his effects, are theological. In that aspect therefore theology is of all incomplexes; but not all complexes since many—with different attributes—bear no relation to theology, for example, the proposition, 'Every triangle has three angles'. Neither all complexes nor all incomplexes belong to theology in the first sense; indeed there is scarcely time enough to know those which are necessary to salvation.[126]

Where then among them do we find the subject of theology? And more specifically is it God under the proper concept of the divine nature? That raises the question of the nature of the first subject in any science. Ockham as we have seen, resolves it by treating the subject as a term in a proposition and making the subject of the conclusion the subject of knowledge. The subject can then be either a term which stands for something else or, imprecisely, that for which the term stands, as in the proposition 'Every man is able to laugh' where 'man' is a term common to all men, whether a concept or not, but that for which 'man' stands can only be an individual man. Sometimes the two meanings of the term can be the same.[127] So far as theology by God's present dispensation is concerned—as opposed to what is possible for us by his omnipotence—God under the proper concept of the divine nature is not the subject of theology, where the subject is a term standing for something else. For God is not the term of a conclusion; if he were he would be the immediate object of an act of intellection. God, however, can only be known— as we shall see—indirectly through a concept proper to him but which is not the same as God. That concept is the subject of theology. But when a subject is taken improperly as that for which the subject of the conclusion stands, then God is the subject of theology in so far as the concept of the divine nature refers to him in particular aspects, such as in relation to the divine persons or creation. The term 'God' does then denote God himself, for example when we say that 'God creates' or that 'God is the father, or the son, or the holy spirit'.[128] It follows therefore that

---

qui est nobis necessarius pro statu isto ad vitam eternam consequendam . . . Aliter accipitur theologia pro omni habitu simpliciter theologico sive sit nobis necessarius pro statu isto et investigandus sive non. Secundo modo, dico quod theologia est de omnibus incomplexis sed non de omnibus complexis (*Ordinatio*, Prologue, q. 9, 273).

[126] *Ibid.*, 273–4.

[127] *Ibid.*, 265–6.

[128] Et dico primo quod accipiendo subiectum pro illo quod supponit, quod deus sub ratione deitatis non est subiectum theologie nostre. Hoc patet, quia subiectum isto modo dictum est terminus conclusionis. Sed deus non est terminus conclusionis, quia illud est terminus conclusionis quod immediate terminat actum intelligendi, vel est actus intelligendi. Sed deus in se non immediate terminat actum intelligendi sed mediante aliquo conceptu sibi proprio, nec est conceptus. Igitur ille conceptus, non deus, erit subiectum theologie nostre. Secundo dico quod accipiendo subiectum pro illo pro quo supponitur, sic respectu alicuius partis deus sub ratione deitatis est subiectum, et respectu alicuius partis pater vel filius vel spiritus sanctus, et respectu alicuius creatura (*ibid.*, 268–9).

the different parts of theology have different subjects and that theology is not one subject.[129] These are the same both for this world and for the blessed, in having the same propositions; where they differ is that in those which have God for their subject he can be known by the blessed in himself as well as by means of a concept; he therefore both stands for whatever the subject stands for and is that for which the subject stands. That holds equally for necessary and contingent propositions which as we mentioned earlier both belong to theology.[130] Only if predicables are treated as concepts really existing in the mind can God not be taken as a subject which has supposition; in that case the blessed have a concept proper to God as a subject which will be simple or composite in different propositions.[131]

Viewed according to these definitions most of the opinions on theology's subject can, Ockham believes, be reconciled even if it is not what their author intended. That of St Thomas, that its subject is God under the aspect of the divine nature, is true when the subject is understood as that for which the subject stands; the subject is then also first by primacy of nature and cause, but not in containing virtually knowledge of all truths which are known by the created intellect in knowing the first subject, for the reasons fully discussed earlier. Nor, for the same reason, is the divine nature the first subject of every part of theology, namely of that part which is predicated of the divine persons individually, or of creatures; for these are themselves the first subjects to which their attributes belong immediately, as the father is first subject of the proposition 'The father generates'. Similarly the view held by Grosseteste and Bonaventure among others that the first subject of theology is Christ can be in a very imprecise sense upheld through his union with both the divine persons and with creatures; that gives him a certain primacy as subject. Again things and signs can be called the subject of theology in the manner in which St Augustine and Peter Lombard point to God and creatures as things and to the sacraments as signs; that does not, however, apply to all things and signs. Where Ockham does draw the line is at relative terms, such as 'glorifier', taken by Giles of Rome to describe Christ as the subject of theology; for these are all predicates which are affirmed of subjects, and are not subjects at all. He therefore dismisses them as completely groundless.[132]

Theology then on the one hand has as many subjects as there are theological propositions, whether they bear upon future salvation or any other article of faith; they can therefore be equally of the divine persons or creatures as well as of God, who himself cannot be known by a *viator* in a simple concept. On the other hand the subjects of theology can belong to other sciences, either appropriated from them or by them, as the proposition 'God is first cause' belongs to both metaphysics and theology.[133] As we have seen that, however, does not involve them as sub-

---

[129] *Ibid.*, 269.

[130] *Ibid.*, 269–70.

[131] *Ibid.*, 269. This is another of Ockham's later interpolations which arise from his view of the nature of concepts; once again it makes no substantive difference to his position.

[132] *Ibid.*, 271–3.

[133] Ad primum argumentum principale patet quod deus non est subiectum cuiuslibet partis theologie, sed alicuius partis est una persona subiectum et alterius partis alia persona, et

alternated and subalternating sciences, because theology is demarcated from the other sciences by faith which makes its propositions matters of belief, not knowledge. Its truth therefore depends upon faith not demonstration; and it utilises the conclusions of the other sciences and natural experience to express in propositions truths which remain independent of natural experience.

IV THEOLOGY: SPECULATIVE OR PRACTICAL?

Before we enquire into if and how God can be known, there remains the question of what kind of pursuit theology is, namely speculative or practical. Once again we have to begin with the meaning of these terms, which we have so far only touched upon in passing. A measure of the importance Ockham attaches to this topic may perhaps be gauged from the length of his discussion over three questions running to nearly one hundred pages in the new edition of the Prologue.[134]

The first of these questions concerns the faculty to which practice belongs and more particularly whether it is the sensitive faculty. Ockham considers two opinions. The first by Robert Cowton identifies practice with the work of the practical intellect as that of an exterior or inferior power to the intellect and will. His reason is that the practical intellect is concerned with our contingent actions as the outcome of a moral choice; and such activity distinguishes the active from the contemplative life.[135]

Ockham rejects this on the grounds that every action which is the object of practical knowledge is practice and that includes interior actions, not just those directed outside, as the first opinion holds; otherwise we should have only speculative knowledge of our internal actions. In fact all the authorities, including Aristotle in book six of the *Metaphysics*, concur in distinguishing practical knowledge as that which is of our own actions. That also explains the role of the will, whose operations are in our power; and since they cannot themselves constitute either practical or speculative knowledge—the province of the intellect—they must be practice.[136] Accordingly there can be no place for a faculty inferior or external to the intellect and will.

Nor does Ockham accept the second opinion—of Duns Scotus—that practice is the act of the will in conformity with right reason and so naturally subsequent to the intellect on whose knowledge it depends. That such acts must be both from a faculty other than the intellect and subsequent to it Duns proves first because

---

alterius aliqua creatura, secundum quod diverse passiones de istis considerantur . . . Ad tertium patet, in prima questione, quod non est inconveniens idem esse subiectum in aliqua veritate pertinente ad diversas scientias, propter diversa principia per que concluditur eadem conclusio. Similiter patet prius quod non est inconveniens idem esse subiectum diversarum scientiarum propter diversitatem passionum. Ita est in proposito: quia ista veritas 'Deus est prima causa', pertinet ad metaphysicum et ad theologicum, quia forte ex diversis principiis concludit istam unus et alius (*ibid.*, 275–6).

[134] *Ibid.*, qq. 10, 11, 12, 276–370.
[135] *Ibid.*, q. 10, 277.
[136] *Ibid.*, 279.

the intellect cannot extend its understanding to itself but only to other faculties, while its own discursive activities cannot be called practice; for then logic would be practice. His second reason is that only vegetative and other sensitive acts do not follow those of the intellect and these cannot be called practical.[137] Ockham in reply repeats what he has just said to Robert Cowton, that understanding can be called practice; moreover, Duns himself says the same.[138] That must include knowledge of the intellect's own speculative activity which is at once the result of our own action and is known to us. Hence the work of the intellect is also practice. So too is every act of intellect which the will directs, such as the decision to study say theology; the intellect decrees and the will executes its decision. The conjunction between the two faculties can hardly be denied. Thus when Duns says that the intellect cannot extend to knowledge of itself, he is restricting the meaning of extension as commonly used by philosophers. It is enough to recognise that practical knowledge extends to our activities as its object, and so whatever knowledge is from our powers is practice or the object of practice. That includes any intellectual habit which has an act—but not another habit—as its object, as well as every act directed to a desired end or performed at the will's command, both those in conformity with right reason, which are morally virtuous, and some which are without moral worth in following false reason. All such acts as the result of choice made from knowledge thereby make such knowledge practical.[139] Unlike Duns Scotus, therefore, Ockham does not confine practice to virtuous acts but to any which come from the will through an act of intellection.[140]

For Ockham the problem of where to locate practice is more one of words than substance. Almost all agree that it consists in understanding, which states the end and the means of attaining it, and volition and counsel to pursue the end. There is thus a sequence from knowing what should be done and how, to choosing to do so and how, as an invalid can know that he needs health and what must be done to gain it, and the will decides to comply and chooses which course to follow of those presented by the intellect, say walking or medicine. The question of practice is not therefore what it is but what can be called practice.

Here Ockham turns to the four part division of Eustratius in his Commentary on the *Ethics* as expressing both Aristotle's and Averroes's views. The first two distinctions treat practice as activity, either broadly as the action of any power, natural or free, or strictly as the result of some kind of cognition or desire or feeling of joy or sadness; in both these senses practice is some form of energy. By the other two definitions, however, it refers to what is in our own power, either in the third and stricter of the preceding definitions, as any such action whether virtuous or vicious which is from us, or in the fourth and strictest definition of all, as actions which exclusively conform to the precepts of reason and follow from the choice

---

[137] *Ibid.*, 280–1.

[138] Scotus, *Ordinatio*, Prologue, qq. 1–2 (Vatican ed., I, 155–83).

[139] Ockham, *Ordinatio*, Prologue, q. 10, 281–5.

[140] E.g. confimatur: quia qua ratione actus elicitus conformiter rationi recte est praxis, eadem ratione elicitus conformiter rationi false erit praxis. Igitur non omnis praxis est nata elici conformiter rationi recte (*ibid.*, 285).

of the will.[141] Only these two definitions are germane to the present discussion as the way in which practice is commonly understood, the third in being sometimes applied to the practical intellect, and the fourth in always denoting the deliberative intellect.[142] Ockham considers these two senses, beginning with the difference between the practical and deliberative intellects.

The practical intellect is concerned with practical principles and practical conclusions. Its first principle is a complex stating the end to be pursued, because the will acts only on account of an end either dictated by reason or chosen freely of its own volition;[143] hence every act of will, even that with no end, necessarily presupposes volition of an end.[144] The practical intellect is directed both to the principles and the conclusions, because all truth belonging to a right action is practical. The deliberative intellect on the other hand refers only to the best means of fulfilling an end already decided upon by the intellect and will in conjunction; it is therefore only concerned with the practical conclusions, not the principles, as in the example just given of an invalid seeking health; once decided upon by the intellect and the will, the deliberative intellect inquires into and advises upon the best way of gaining health. Its deliberate role thus lies in concluding how an end —already determined—is best achieved.[145] That makes the same intellect at once practical and deliberate and speculative; each of these terms is a nominal, as opposed to a real, definition.[146] Thus 'speculative intellect' means the intellect in so far as it can consider what is not in its power; the 'practical intellect' stands for the intellect as it is able to know what is in our power; and similarly with the 'deliberative intellect'.[147]

From that it follows that when practice is understood in the third sense, as that which is simply in our power regardless of its worth or lack of it, every act of willing and knowing, as well as every exterior act, is practical. Practice in this third sense always applies first to volition, because an act of will is both immediately in our power and the means by which any other action can be in our power. The term 'practice' therefore belongs immediately to acts of will which can be either good or bad according to whether or not they conform to right reason;[148] for only an act of will carries moral judgement: otherwise it would be merely necessary

---

[141] *Ibid.*, 287–90.   [142] *Ibid.*, 290.

[143] Circa primum dico quod intellectus practicus est respectu principiorum practicorum et etiam respectu conclusionum practicarum. Et ideo intellectus practicus est respectu finis, quando scilicet de aliquo fine iudicatur quod est appetendus vel prosequendus. Et hoc est intelligendum quia est respectu unius complexi quod affirmat aliquem finem esse appetendum, et istud est primum principium practicum in operando ... Et ratio huius est quia voluntas nihil agit nisi propter finem, et hoc vel propter finem dictatum a ratione vel propter finem quem ex libertate sua sibi prestituit (*ibid.*, 290–1).

[144] *Ibid.*, 291.

[145] *Ibid.*

[146] Et ita patet quod respectu quorumcumque est intellectus consiliativus respectu eorundem est intellectus practicus. Unde sciendum est quod idem intellectus numero est practicus et speculativus et consiliativus. Tamen isti termini distinguuntur et habent distinctas definitiones exprimentes quid nominis (*ibid.*, 291–2).

[147] *Ibid.*, 292.

[148] *Ibid.*, 292–3.

(*naturalis*) as outside our free power and so morally neutral.[149] This distinction between free and natural acts, although in no way peculiar to Ockham, was extended by him to all human actions, so that as we shall see in chapter seven merit becomes inseparable from free will. Here, Ockham draws the following corollaries. First, that knowledge does not have to conform to right reason in order to be practical, because we can act wrongly in opposition to right reason, say in hating an enemy—which violates God's precept. Second, there can be practical acts which are indifferent to right reason, such as an act of will which is in response to an object presented by the intellect as neither true nor false. From that it follows in the third place that practice does not formally signify an act as such but an act connoting the will freely and effectively producing it. Hence the same act, certainly in kind and perhaps in number, can be first practical and then not practical, as first freely produced by the will and then conserved by God independently of the will, in which case it would not be in the will's power.[150]

By its fourth and strictest meaning practice can be regarded as the work of the will, the intellect, and an external action; for it is the outcome of the will freely choosing to follow the guidance of the deliberative intellect, as in the example of health given above. To attain its end the will could as well decide upon an external as an internal action, just as it can upon an act of pure speculation; each will be practical provided the will acts in response to the intellect; and conversely whenever the will follows its own imperatives its actions will not be practical in this strictest sense because they will not conform to right reason.[151] It follows then that practice is not merely the act of the sensitive or an inferior faculty.[152]

That enables us to distinguish Robert Cowton's conception of practical knowledge as what is within our power and contingent, which Ockham accepts, from the object of practical knowledge which need not be within our power or contingent. For that reason pure speculation and love, in being from our own powers, are practical and constitute practical knowledge, even though their objects are not practical.[153] Accordingly many arts such as the mechanical arts and music are

---

[149] Ista autem praxis dividitur in praxim virtuosam et vitiosam, quia utraque istarum est in potestate nostra . . . quia nulla operatio que non est existens in potestate voluntatis est virtuosa sed magis naturalis (*ibid.*, 293).

[150] *Ibid.*, 293–4.

[151] Circa tertium dico quod praxis ultimo modo dicta est omnis operatio existens in potestate voluntatis, consiliata ab intellectu, respectu cuius est electio voluntatis. Et isto modo praxis dicitur vel potest dici tam de actione voluntatis quam de operatione intellectus quam etiam de operatione exteriori . . . Et ita concedo quod pura speculatio potest esse praxis isto modo dicta quia de ipsa potest esse consilium, et respectu ipsius potest esse electio. Ex isto sequitur etiam quod operatio exterior imperata a voluntate non est semper praxis isto modo dicta, quia quando operatio est prestituta a voluntate tamquam finis, tunc non est consiliabilis nec eligibilis, et per consequens nec est praxis isto modo dicta secundum Aristotelem dicentem III *Ethicorum* (*ibid.*, 294–5). Also 298–9.

[152] *Ibid.*, 295.

[153] Ad primum argumentum prime opinionis respondeo quod bene invenitur quod notitia practica est circa opera nostra et circa contingentia operabilia a nobis, sed nunquam invenitur quod praxis sive opus, de quo est notitia practica, sit circa contingens aliter se habere, nec circa aliquid quod est in potestate nostra . . . Et ideo pura speculatio et similiter dilectio, quia sunt

practical without being the result of our actions, save the instruments by which they are operable.[154] The efficient cause of practice in the strictest sense is always a choice made by the will both towards an act of pure speculation, from the intellect, and towards an external act; for before we decide any action we can doubt which course to follow in the light of the intellect's counsel.[155]

That raises the next question of whether practical and speculative knowledge are distinguished according to their ends or their objects. The answer of Henry of Ghent was according to their ends on the grounds that as a science is ordered according to its end as knowledge, so the knower orders his knowledge to the end of knowing. The distinction between them is the difference between the necessary and the accidental ends of knowledge; the necessary end arises from the nature of a body of knowledge, the accidental from the interests of the knower. Only the first, necessary, sense can knowledge be called speculative or practical, because it leads either to truth (in which case it is speculative) or to the achievement of the good (and then it is practical). For Henry that proves that speculative and practical knowledge are distinguished by the essential end of knowledge, first because every effect is distinguished by its more noble cause, and the final cause is the noblest of all causes; and second because a science is distinguished either by its subject or its end, and since speculative and practical knowledge cannot be distinguished by their subject they must be distinguished by their end.[156]

Ockham disagrees. Not only do practical and speculative knowledge not differ over ends; they can have the same end, because knowledge and knower have the same end, and so have an agent and a corresponding action. Moreover the essential cause of anything is that on which it depends for existence; but knowledge depends upon the end of the knower without which there would be no knowledge. Therefore the end of the knower is the essential, and final, cause of knowledge *propter quid*.[157]

Ockham instead distinguishes end as that which is loved, either from desire or from friendship: by the first, something is loved on account of something else as health is the end of walking; by the second, the end is loved for itself, for the sake of which the previous end is produced, as man in loving himself desires health and the means (walking) to achieve it, or love of God above all is the end of all other actions. In the first sense, an end desired by concupiscent love is usually less noble than the act, or at least the agent achieving it, because as prior in intention and last in execution it is the effect of such an action; but an end informed by love of friendship comes before the action directed towards it, and when informed by right reason is not inferior to the action.[158]

Now in the case of knowledge its end is properly speaking that which is loved by the inquirer, by either of these modes. The same end is thus the final cause of both knowing and knowledge, not in the sense that the final cause of knowledge

---

operabiles a nobis, quamvis non habeant talia pro obiectis, vere sunt praxes, et de ipsis vere erit notitia practica (*ibid.*, 296); also 298.

[154] *Ibid.*, 296–8.   [155] *Ibid.*, 299–300.

[156] *Ibid.*, 303–4.   [157] *Ibid.*, 304–6.   [158] *Ibid.*, 306.

is thereby also the final cause of knowing, but rather because what the knower desires in acquiring knowledge is the final cause of his knowledge. Accordingly someone who learns for the love of friendship he bears himself, and for which he desires love or money, is himself the final cause of such knowledge, which depends essentially upon him. Correspondingly, money or the equivalent can in some way be the final cause of knowledge if it provides the reason *propter quid* someone learns. The difference, however, is that the money will not be the final cause of the knower himself since he does not depend upon it essentially, as his knowledge depends upon him.[159]

There can be two kinds of final cause in knowledge: one is the strict meaning just discussed where it is that on account of which knowledge is sought and which moves the agent to action. The other is as that which should be freely intended according to right reason; by this mode the end of practical knowledge is a work or an action, and of speculative knowledge it is deliberation. If it is neither of these they will not be final causes, for no knowledge will depend upon them.[160] Conversely there can be several final causes of knowledge as there can be of heat and as there can be several effects of the same efficient cause, each different in kind and numerically.[161]

The reply then to the question of how practical and speculative knowledge differ is that they are formally and intrinsically distinct in themselves and causally distinct by their different ends and agents. They can also be distinguished according to their objects—i.e. conclusions—but never by their subjects,[162] because, as we have discussed, the subject does not itself constitute knowledge or its essence.[163] Hence the subject cannot be the cause of distinct knowledge and indeed can belong to different knowledge, as the same subject in having some attributes which denote what is in our power is practical, and others denoting what is not in our power is speculative. Thus to know the earth as round or dry or heavy is to have speculative knowledge of its properties as beyond our powers, whereas to know the same earth as arable or cultivable is to know what we can do to it and so gives practical knowledge. Nor is it an objection to say that this would be to deduce practical conclusions from speculative principles, for the latter can act as at least indirect or partial causes of the former in the way that, from speculative knowledge that the earth is hard, we can draw the practical conclusion that it needs something hard to plough or break it.[164] That applies universally because there is no speculative principle from which some practical conclusions cannot be drawn, and so those principles commonly regarded as purely speculative are in that sense also virtually

[159] *Ibid.*, 307–8.   [160] *Ibid.*

[161] *Ibid.*, 309–10.

[162] Ex his respondeo ad questionem quod iste scientie se ipsis distinguuntur intrinsice et formaliter, sed per fines vel per finem distinguuntur causaliter, sicut causaliter distinguuntur per causam efficientem. Sed per subiecta scientie nullo predictorum modorum distinguuntur necessario ... Sed isto ultimo modo [tamquam per aliqua sibi propria] distinguuntur per obiecta, hoc est per conclusiones scitas (*ibid.*, 310).

[163] Quod enim non distinguantur per subiecta formaliter et intrinsice manifestum est, quia subiectum nec est ipsa scientia nec est de essentia eius (*ibid.*, 312).

[164] *Ibid.*, 313–14.

practical:[165] even the proposition 'Every triangle has three angles' has practical application in the mechanical arts.[166] For that reason practical knowledge is sometimes subalternated to speculative knowledge, as music is to arithmetic; that would not be possible if practical conclusions could not be resolved into speculative principles.[167] That also explains how practical knowledge and speculative knowledge are distinguished by their conclusions; for they are one or other according to whether they state what can or cannot be performed by us. Both kinds of knowledge are therefore complex, and the object of practical knowledge will be a conclusion stating what can or should be done by us; such a conclusion will be more indicative of our power, and so more practical as knowledge, than any incomplex term belonging to it. On the other hand, there can also be speculative knowledge of either complex or incomplex knowledge which is not ostensive or directive—the two modes, as we have discussed, of practical knowledge.[168]

It can thus be said that speculative and practical knowledge are distinguished by their ends both causally and formally as proper to them as distinct kinds of knowledge with different objects.[169]

That brings us to the question whether a habit or state of theology is speculative or practical. Ockham here confronts two different sets of opinions. The first, held in common by Henry of Ghent, Robert Cowton and William of Alnwick among others, is that a theological habit is purely speculative, for, as a moral habit is practical in being concerned with good actions, a theological habit is speculative since all its actions are directed to the speculative, and the active life is subordinate to the contemplative. Hence while many things in theology could be called practical, it must, as wisdom, be called speculative because it considers temporal things in the light of eternity. Among the arguments advanced in support by one or other of these authors are that as the will's love of God is not practical, the knowledge concerning it is not; that if love of God were practical then metaphysics would also be practical since the object of such love would be essential not personal, but metaphysics is more concerned with essences than theology; that metaphysics considers God under the concept of goodness and so what is to be loved: if therefore the latter is practical knowledge, so is metaphysics, which it is not; that the knowledge man can naturally acquire about love of God, which for theologicans is supernatural, cannot be practical because it would then be nobler than all other knowledge, which contradicts Aristotle in the *Ethics*, and the *Metaphysics*; and finally that practical knowledge is only of what is contingent, but theology is not of the contingent.[170]

For Ockham, however, many theological truths are practical, for example the injunction to worship God, which with many more belongs exclusively to theology. Moreover they are not concerned only with contemplation of the eternal,

---

[165] Potest tamen dici quod illa principia sunt aliquo modo virtualiter practica, tamen secundum modum communem loquendi sunt simpliciter speculabilia, quia aliter nullum principium esset pure speculativum, quia nullum penitus est principium quin aliquo modo possit se habere ad praxim (*ibid.*, 314).

[166] *Ibid.*   [167] *Ibid.*, 314–15.   [168] *Ibid.*, 315–16.

[169] *Ibid.*, 321.   [170] *Ibid.*, q. 12, 325–8.

for, as he has already argued, theology is not one subject but many truths which can be known or not known independently of one another. The distinction between one proposition and another is absolute; they cannot be regarded as being heterogenous parts of a single whole because they are of different species. Even if a science were contemplative that would not make it speculative; its acts are no less practical because their object is one of contemplation, for as Henry of Ghent himself acknowledges all practical knowledge has activity (opus) as its object, and that holds regardless of the subject. In fact, theology considers what is in our power, including love of God, which is practical in so far as it is from the will, and of which there is thus practical knowledge.[171] Metaphysics however, is not practical, for it only considers God speculatively as incorruptible, simple, perpetual, the cause of all things, and so on, none of which refers to our actions, although they can be the principles of practical knowledge: as, for example, from knowing that God is the cause of everything we can conclude that he is to be loved and honoured above all. But then it is no longer metaphysical knowledge but of some moral science from which metaphysics like theology is distinct.[172]

Knowledge of love of God, however, in being practical is not thereby superior to a speculative habit; indeed as the conclusion of a speculative principle it will be inferior to it, as every conclusion is less necessary and so less perfect than its principle. Conversely not all propositions of theology are practical, just as only part of it concerns what is contingent.[173] Ockham therefore also opposes the second group of opinions, held by Peter Aureole and Duns Scotus, that theology is only practical.

Aureole argues that any knowledge is purely practical whose object is attainable by nobler acts than the act of merely knowing; for then it is the object not only of speculation but of our own activities. Thus as medicine and its activities are practical because they have as their object the attainment of health, which is more noble than to have knowledge of health and yet remain ill, so theology is practical in having God as the object of our actions which are nobler than merely to know belief.[174]

Duns Scotus's view is that practical knowledge consists in conforming to practice according to some natural priority; which for theology consists in love of God. That is shown because right willing is virtually the first object of theology at once determining the created intellect to right knowledge of theological acts and the will to their performance as its end.[175]

Each of these opinions omits to recognise that not all theological truths are either within or beyond our power. They are therefore both practical and speculative,[176] as we have practical knowledge that God should be loved or honoured, which are actions we can perform, and speculative knowledge that God is three persons or that he is omnipotent, which are truths over which we have no con-

---

[171] Ibid., 328–33, 362–3.   [172] Ibid., 364–6.
[173] Ibid., 366.   [174] Ibid., 333–4.
[175] Ibid., 334–5.
[176] Ideo aliter dico ad questionem quod theologia non est una notitia vel scientia, sed habet vel continet plures notitias realiter distinctas quarum alique sunt practice simpliciter et alique speculative (ibid., 337).

trol.[177] To this Duns had replied that the latter are themselves practical truths since to know that God is triune is also to know virtually that the divine persons should be loved virtuously. If, however, that were true it would follow that there was no speculative knowledge because, again according to Duns, there cannot be practical and speculative knowledge of the same subject. But there is no proposition which does not also include knowledge of right willing: to know for example that man is made in God's image is at the same time to know that a man should be loved more than an ass. On Duns's argument, however, such knowledge is practical and so cannot be speculative. Hence no knowledge would be speculative. Similarly metaphysics would be practical. Not all of theology, however, is concerned with love of God, and so knowledge of him gives rise to speculative as well as practical principles.[178]

To Aureole's contention that a practical habit is always from a nobler act than a habit of knowledge, Ockham rejoins that practice has nothing to do with the nobility of its act, which can be greater or less, but only with whether it is in the will's power. That is the sole criterion of practice, which sometimes, as in the actions of mechanics, is inferior to knowledge of those actions, while in those parts of theology which are practical God is the object of our actions and not something upon which we can act, as Aureole wrongly says.[179] What Ockham does concede, in reply to a doubt over the relative worth of a speculative and a practical habit, is that if they are both equally evident a speculative habit will be the nobler because of its subject. To know that God is infinite and the highest good is more noble than to know that we should love him.[180] That, however, is not invariable.[181]

In reply to another doubt about the relation of practical and speculative habits to the practical and speculative intellects, Ockham confutes at length Aureole's view that a theological habit belongs only to the speculative intellect;[182] Aureole's reason is that the practical intellect knows only from experience and so its knowledge is confined to singulars. The speculative intellect on the other hand understands universals through deduction; it is therefore theoretical and ratiocinatory where the practical intellect is experimental, the one concerned with universals, the other with singulars.[183] Ockham's reply is first that as practical and speculative are conventional terms for the same intellect, as Aureole concedes, there can be a practical habit in the speculative intellect and *vice versa*. Secondly, universal habits, practical and speculative, can be acquired from experience, and so there will be universal speculative habits in the practical intellect. It is therefore absolutely false to say that the practical intellect does not possess universal habits, because the practical and speculative intellects are entirely one for all habits and acts; their diversity refers to the different habits which can be added to the intellect.[184] Accordingly, as we mentioned earlier in connection with the practical and deliberative intellects, the practical intellect is only the intellect having or able to have a practical act or habit and the speculative intellect is the same intellect in relation to a

---

[177] *Ibid.*, 335–8.   [178] *Ibid.*, 336–8, 369.   [179] *Ibid.*, 367–8.
[180] Ad 5[m] dubium, 358–9.   [181] *Ibid.*, 370.   [182] Ad 4[m] dubium, 348–57.
[183] 348–9.   [184] 349–50.

speculative act or habit.[185] If, however, speculative and practical are taken to mean an act and not a power, then it can be accepted that a practical habit is in the practical intellect without necessarily being in the speculative intellect, and conversely; in other words there can be a speculative habit without a practical habit and a practical habit without a speculative habit; but when the intellect has both then each exists in the intellect of the other. In that sense each is accidental to the other.[186] Which answers the reference to Aristotle's statement in the *Ethics* that the practical—or as he calls it there the deliberative—intellect is about variable or contingent things; for strictly speaking it is about those which are necessary and purely speculative, in being the same as the speculative intellect, as the speculative intellect is similarly about the acts which we are able to perform. Beyond that, however, Aristotle's intention is that when the intellect is practical it is immediately concerned with what we can do, which concerns individual and contingent things; but that does not mean that the practical intellect only knows individuals, because it is frequently of universals, as we have already said; nor does it only know by experience but it can also have habits derived from self-evident knowledge which are practical. The speculative intellect, however, can be exclusively of universals.[187]

That completes our examination of theology. From it we can draw two main conclusions. The first is that for Ockham what distinguishes theology from any of the sciences is its exclusiveness to the believer. All its propositions rest upon faith for the very reason that they are naturally inevident. Theology cannot be called a science because assent to its truths is a matter of belief alone independently of what can be known naturally by experience or as self-evident. Ockham's uncompromising refusal to allow theology any dependence upon evident knowledge shows a Christian awareness as great as any of the scholastics and a rigour greater than all of them: he repeatedly reduces previous attempts to establish an evidential bridge between theology and knowledge by the argument that theology would then be open to the unbeliever and believer alike. That does not however lead him to reduce theology to a mere act of belief. Which brings us to the second conclusion: that if on the one hand faith makes theology inaccessible to natural knowledge, on the other hand it makes natural knowledge accessible to theology. As we have seen Ockham distinguishes between theological truths which can be known naturally, such as that God exists, that God is good, wise, and so on, and others such as God is triune or incarnated which are only knowable supernaturally. The first, that is to say, can be conceived in terms of non-theological—usually metaphysical—knowledge where the second have no natural equivalents. Their com-

---

[185] Ideo dico aliter quod cum intellectus nullo modo distinguatur sed sit simpliciter idem respectu omnium habituum et omnium actuum, intellectus speculativus et intellectus practicus nullam ponunt distinctionem a parte intellectus, sed sunt diverse denominationes accepte a diversis habitibus qui adduntur ipsi intellectui. Et ideo quia intellectus practicus non est nisi intellectus habens habitum practicum vel actum vel saltem natus habere, et intellectus speculativus est intellectus habens actum vel habitum speculativum vel natus habere, de virtute sermonis potest concedi quod habitus practicus est in intellectu speculativo et habitus speculativus est in intellectu practico, quia simpliciter idem est qui est intellectus speculativus et practicus (*ibid.*, 351).

[186] *Ibid.*, 352–4.   [187] *Ibid.*, 355–6.

munity and their difference are explained by the distinction between infused and acquired faith. The former unites theology into one habit which is the prerequisite and partial cause of all individual acts of belief which constitute the habits of acquired faith. These can vary in number and kind and—in the case of a heretic —assent, without impairing the habit of infused faith which is the condition of all acts of acquired faith. Theology can therefore draw upon all the sciences and every kind of knowledge, necessary, contingent, complex, incomplex, to increase faith, just because assent to all theological truth is from pre-existing faith. That is the difference between knowing the same proposition as a believer and as an unbeliever. Whatever the lacunae or errors in his acquired faith a believer through his habit of infused faith accepts all theological truths, whether they can be known naturally or not, as matters of belief, not knowledge. In that way theology is safeguarded and the sciences are put at her disposal: a position not so very different from the traditional conception of theology which Ockham is sometimes supposed to have destroyed.

V KNOWLEDGE OF GOD

We must now consider knowledge of God. There are two aspects: how we know God and the evidence we have of him. They are distinct from one another and Ockham does not treat them systematically together. The first concerns the concepts which denote God; the second the proofs that can be given for his existence. Nor should either be confused with what we can say about his nature or attributes; these are given in revealed truth and so form the point of departure for all discussion of him. The question of God's knowability therefore proceeds from belief in him; and the degree in which we can know what we believe has nothing to do with the truth of our belief. It accordingly no more derogates from God not to be able to know him naturally than it derogates from any other truth of theology; for as Ockham replied to Thomas Aquinas, theology is not knowledge, because it is founded on faith. And as the inability to demonstrate what we know immediately from experience or self-evidently does not impugn the certainty of what we know, so the inability to know what we believe does not make our belief any less real. It is in that context that we should regard Ockham's treatment of God; his rejection of evident knowledge of him is no more a confession of agnosticism[188] than the indemonstrability of whatever is not known immediately or self-evidently means scepticism. The object of theology is faith, not knowledge; Ockham's arguments are designed to keep them distinct and thereby overcome the past ambiguities which have resulted from their confusion.

So far as knowledge of God is concerned, the point of departure must be that while by his absolute power God could be known both intuitively and abstractively

---

[188] Thus Menges, *The Concept of Univocity*, entirely misses the point when he says—without any foundation—'Ockham's attitude is that, if we deny univocity of being, we fall into ag-nosticism, because we have no intuitive or abstractive knowledge of God' (153). A believer does not need knowledge to be certain of God.

or only abstractively,[189] by man's power *in statu isto* he cannot have intuitive knowledge of God, nor therefore abstractive knowledge which, naturally, intuitive knowledge of the same thing must precede.[190] That applies to both contingent and necessary theological propositions, evident knowledge of which depends upon intuitive knowledge of one of the extreme terms. Thus for contingent propositions—i.e. those which refer to God's actions *ad extra*—such as 'God creates' or 'God is incarnated' or 'The blessed will be resurrected'—to be evident, there must be intuitive knowledge of them or his actions. Similarly with necessary propositions having connotative predicates known evidently through intuitive knowledge of some further contingent truth as partial cause, for example 'God can be incarnated'. Such a proposition, to be necessary, must, it will be recalled, be demonstrable from one of the premises known intuitively in the way that we arrive at the conclusion 'Every such herb cures' from intuitive knowledge that this herb cures together with an extrinsic middle—that all causes of the same kind lead to effects of the same kind.[191] Naturally, however, neither God nor such truths as they refer to creatures can be known intuitively, and so not evidently. Again where the predicates are absolutely simple concepts—or perhaps things—there must also be intuitive knowledge, so that if a thing (for example the father) is predicated of God it must be known really to be God, in the same way as whiteness is known distinctly to be a colour or a quality.[192] In all these ways, then, intuitive knowledge is the condition of evident knowledge of theological truths, which cannot thereby be known naturally by a *viator*.

Now the natural inaccessibility of knowledge of God under the proper concept of the divine nature means in turn that we cannot deduce the divine attributes. Hence they too cannot be known naturally. That is the next stage—or perhaps more accurately the first full stage—in the consideration of God. Here as so often it is against the arguments of Duns Scotus that Ockham's own are principally directed. According to Duns, God's attributes and all concepts referring both to himself and to what is outside him are demonstrable *propter quid* and *a priori*. His reason is that there is an order of concepts, with essence absolutely first, under which God can be conceived. For just as there would be a real order among things really distinct, which if they were essential qualities would be subsequent to essence as first among them, so there is a conceptual order among essential concepts ordered under essence. Thus from an infinitely perfect immaterial nature, there follows a perfect immaterial intellect and from that a perfectly proportioned knowledge both of itself and secondary objects, enabling us to demonstrate *propter quid* that a perfect immaterial nature has also perfect understanding. The order here, unlike that of a demonstration *quia*, is from what is nearest to the cause to the effect most removed from it; all those conclusions which can be derived

---

[189] *Ordinatio*, Prologue, q. 1, 48–9.

[190] *Ibid.*, 5, 72. This is expressed succinctly in *Quodlibet* v, q. 14: Quia nec cognoscimus deum cognitione intuitiva nec abstractiva. De intuitiva patet. De abstractiva probatur, quia quelibet talis notitia abstractiva presupponit intuitivam.

[191] Prologue, q. 2, 90–1.

[192] *Ibid.*, q. 1; *ibid.*, 50–1.

from the effects belong to the cause, and so in the case of God's attributes as the effects of his nature. Similarly with God's relation to what is outside him, we can demonstrate that he is omnipotent, creative and so on, because there is a necessary middle from the distinction between his nature, intellect and will, by which we can conclude that he has the power to be omnipotent and creative.[193]

Such a distinction is just what Ockham denies. No quidditative—i.e. essential—concept can be demonstrated *propter quid* of that which is immediately contained under it for the very reason that it is an immediate proposition, as Aristotle says in the *Posterior Analytics* (I, ch. 3, 72 b), and so one is not prior to the other. That applies to every concept which is common to God and creatures, as we shall see shortly. Moreover, as we shall also subsequently discuss, there is no distinction real or rational between God's nature and his intellect and will. Hence any concept, like that of goodness, is quidditative and cannot be demonstrated of God.[194] To Duns's contention that there can be several concepts—both quidditative and connotative—of the same simple thing, Ockham replies that there can only be one real concept of any one thing; for if of the same thing there was more than one concept there would be no more reason to suppose one rather than the other was quidditative. If, however, there is (as Duns holds) no real distinction between the divine nature and intellect or the act of intellection, there can be no means of expressing them more by one concept than another; therefore both or neither will be quidditative. Nor again can they be said to express the same thing in a different way; for a quidditative concept by definition expresses the nature of one thing and not another; to express something in another way would be to express something else.[195]

All quidditative concepts therefore in being immediately predicated have no middle, and, with perhaps the exception of some attribute of being demonstrable through the concept of being, are indemonstrable of God. That holds equally for the relations between the divine persons and between God and creatures; in each case there is no middle, either something real or as a mere concept, since the attribute concerned belongs more immediately to the subject—as omnipotence does to God's essence—than to anything else.[196] For the same reason omnipotence could not be—as Duns held it could—demonstrated of one of the divine persons, as that would be to know that the divine essence itself was omnipotent and yet to doubt the omnipotence of a divine person.

[193] *Ibid.*, 98–102.

[194] Contra istam opinionem, quantum ad aliqua dicta in ea, arguo primo quod attributa non possunt de deo demonstrari propter quid, et hoc de deo distincte cognito, quomodo loquitur doctor iste. Quia nullus conceptus communis quidditativus potest demonstrari demonstratione propter quid de illo quod immediate continetur sub eo, quia talis propositio est immediata, secundum Philosophum I *Posteriorum*, et per consequens illa non est altera prior. Sed omnis talis conceptus est communis deo et creatura, ut suppono nunc, quia postea probabitur. Et est conceptus quidditativus, quia suppono ad presens, et postea probabitur, quod inter divinam essentiam et divinum intellectum vel voluntatem nulla est distinctio, nec realis nec rationis. Igitur conceptus bonitatis vel quicumque talis est quidditativus, et per consequens nullus talis potest de deo demonstrari (*ibid.*, 103).

[195] *Ibid.*, 103–4.

[196] *Ibid.*, 104–5.

Nor is the contradiction avoided by positing a formal distinction between God's attributes, from which Duns argues for a distinction between quidditative and connotative concepts. To begin with, that contradicts Duns's own claim that the distinction of concepts is independent of a formal distinction between essence and attributes, on the grounds that a thing can contain virtually connotative (or as he calls them denominative) concepts which the intellect is able to distinguish from a quidditative concept. Even however granting a formal distinction here, it would still not follow that one concept was quidditative and another denominative; for if, say, the intellect were denominative and the essence quidditative, the intellect would be denominative either of the essence or of something including essentially both essence and intellect. Concepts denoting really distinct parts of the same thing, like form and matter, are not more denominative or quidditative than the other; nor are concepts standing for what is only formally distinct. If they were, a denominative concept of essence would be derived from a quidditative concept of intellect, and the concept of essence would be quidditative of whatever formally was not essence, which is impossible because the same concept includes essence and all the divine attributes. By the same token they are still one if they are related as subject and attribute; for as matter and form are one, so much more so are qualities only distinguished formally and really the same.[197] That, too, is confirmed on Duns's own principles that what is formally distinct has the same order as what is really distinct. If then essence and intellect were really distinct the intellect would come, in order, after essence, with neither included in one or more essentially and formally than in the other or with a quidditative concept more of one than the other. Accordingly the concept of intellect is as quidditative as that of essence.[198]

Ockham's own solution is to distinguish between things which can be predicated of God (if indeed things can be predicated), by which he means the activities of the divine persons, and concepts. The first cannot be known naturally; the second can, because they are only concepts which are neither really nor formally the same as God.[199] Ockham's discussion of them was originally conducted in terms of concepts as *ficta*, i.e. merely objects of thought. Subsequently, however, he added the qualification that they can also be conceived as real mental qualities, in which case their role would be proportionate to things predicable of God;[200] that does not imply that they would thereby become naturally unknowable because, as we shall now consider, the concepts predicable of God are those derived from what is naturally knowable. This is expressed in six conclusions.

The first is that nothing intrinsic to God can be demonstrated of the divine essence such that the latter is both subject and predicate.[201] That is clear because it is impossible to know distinctly—abstractively as well as intuitively—that something is the same and yet doubt its identity; and indeed a self-evident proposition consists chiefly in predicating the same of what is really the same. But the divine

---

197 *Ibid.*, 105–7.   198 *Ibid.*, 108.   199 *Ibid.*, 109–10.
200 *Ibid.*, 110–11.

201 Secundum hec, ad istam questionem prima conclusio erit ista: quod nihil intrinsecum deo potest de divina essentia demonstrari ita quod divina essentia in se subiciatur et aliquid quod est realiter divina essentia predicetur in se (*ibid.*, 111).

essence is really the same as God; therefore if we have distinct knowledge of him, we cannot doubt—and so demonstrate—their identity. Moreover whenever something is demonstrated of something else it is first predicated of something other than that of which it is demonstrated as a middle. Nothing, however, really the same as God can be first predicated of something other than the divine essence, save a divine person or divine relation; and that does not enable us to demonstrate, say, that the divine essence is the father because if we know both in themselves we cannot doubt their identity to begin with.[202] Such knowledge is not, however, open to man *pro statu isto*; he has therefore neither the terms nor propositions by which it is self-evident, but only certain concepts common to believers and un-believers alike. These—as we shall mention presently—are not of God and the divine nature *in se* but stand for the terms which constitute human propositions about God. They are therefore distinct from those which distinctly signify God and the divine nature in themselves—a conclusion for which Ockham was censured by the Avignon Commission.[203] Thus we can doubt the proposition 'God is God' because we know him in only a nominal definition whose meaning is equivalent to 'the highest and infinite being'; and in not knowing God as God we can doubt his predication of himself, as we can doubt that a white man is white if we do not know that there is a white man. In each case the proposition could be false.[204]

From that follows the second conclusion that nothing can be demonstrated of the divine persons, because of their real identity with whatever is predicated of them, which if known could not be doubted. That indeed applies equally to self-evident propositions about creatures.[205]

The third conclusion is that common concepts predicable absolutely (*in quid*), as opposed to connotatively, of God and creatures cannot be demonstrated *a priori* of God's nature nor of a simple concept proper to God, if there is such a concept.[206] The reason is once again that all such common concepts are immediately predicable of that into which they are directly divisible, in this case God and creatures. Thus 'wisdom', 'knowledge', 'goodness', and so on are as common concepts each at once uncreated and created; in immediately belonging to God and to creatures they cannot therefore be demonstrated *a priori* of either. It is not, for example, a demonstration to argue 'All being is good; God is being; therefore God is good', where 'good' is predicated absolutely of 'God'; for then 'good' and 'being' are completely synonymous. If, however, 'good' connotes determinate

---

[202] *Ibid.*, 112.

[203] Sed nos pro statu isto non possumus habere illam propositionem sicut nec terminos eius, sed habemus unam aliam. Quia in nostra propositione, nobis possibili de communi lege, sunt termini conceptus quidam communes fidelibus et infidelibus; in illa autem propositione quam haberet talis intellectus, unus terminus est essentia el alia paternitas, et pro istis supponunt termini propositionis nostre, non pro se. Et ideo sicut termini sunt distincti, ita propositiones sunt distincte; et ideo potest una illarum esse per se nota et alia simpliciter dubitabilis et forte demonstrabilis (*ibid.*). See above.

[204] *Ibid.*, 112–13.

[205] *Ibid.*, 113–14.

[206] Tertia conclusio est ista: quod conceptus communes predicabiles in in quid de deo et creaturis non possunt de divina essentia in se demonstrari a priori nec de conceptu proprio sibi et simplici, si talis sit possibilis (*ibid.*, 114).

being, in the way that 'able to will' connotes the will, the demonstration can be in some way *a priori* but 'good' will not then be predicated of God absolutely.[207]

By the fourth conclusion, on the other hand, connotative and negative terms which are common to God and creatures can be demonstrated of the divine essence when God as known in himself can be doubted.[208] All such concepts in being predicable adequately of something common can through the latter as middle term be demonstrated of all that comes under it. That holds for what is common to God and creatures, for example the concept of being, which can be syllogised to give perhaps some kind of *a priori* demonstration, namely 'All being is good; God is being; Therefore God is good'. The conclusion must constitute knowledge in the strict sense since it is not understanding or wisdom, although it is not the result of a *demonstratio potissima*.[209] Nor is it of God's essence in itself; connotative and negative concepts, like 'creative', 'omnipotent', 'eternal', 'infinite', and so on, are not demonstrable of God himself because they cannot belong to a middle before they belong to God.[210] That is the fifth conclusion; it is proved because an *a priori* demonstration is one where the middle belongs to the predicate (as the more universal term) before it belongs to the subject; but neither a thing nor a term can belong to anything prior to God. Therefore no term can be demonstrated of him known in himself, as opposed to a concept of him which is common or composite.[211] As we have discussed in the previous chapter, a syllogism where the middle is a nominal definition is a *petitio principii* with the conclusion already stated in the premises, and so cannot be doubted. Thus it is no proof to argue 'Everything productive of something from nothing is creative; God is productive of something from nothing is creative; God is productive of something from nothing; Therefore God is creative'; for to know that something is productive from nothing is also to know that it is creative.[212]

The converse, however, is true, and stated in the sixth and last conclusion: namely that where God's essence or distinct knowledge of him or a common concept including him is the middle, connotative and negative concepts can be demonstrated of him, for they then belong first to him.[213] That applies to all that can be predicated of God: divine relations and persons which are part of his essence; negative and connotative concepts proper to God himself; and those

---

[207] *Ibid.*, 114–15.
[208] Quarta conclusio est quod conceptus connotativi et negativi communes deo et creaturis possunt de divina essentia demonstrari; et hoc si aliquii tales sint de divina essentia in se cognita dubitabiles (*ibid.*, 115).
[209] *Ibid.*
[210] Quinta conclusio est quod conceptus connotativi et negativi proprii deo non sunt de divina essentia in se demonstrabiles a priori. Et ideo esse creativum, esse omnipotens, esse eternum, infinitum, immortale, et sic de aliis, non sunt de divina essentia in se demonstrabiles ... Sed talia predicata nulli possunt competere per prius quam deo quod possit esse medium ... (*ibid.*, 116).
[211] *Ibid.*   [212] *Ibid.*, 116–17.
[213] Sexta conclusio est quod omnia predicabilia de deo in se, que sunt dubitabilia de conceptu composito proprio deo qualem nos habemus de facto, sunt de illo conceptu demonstrabilia per divinam essentiam in se tamquam per medium, vel per cognitionem distinctam deitatis, vel per aliquod commune tamquam per medium (*ibid.*, 117).

attributable to him under a common term, such as true, good, and one.[214] Only in the first two cases, however, can there be proper *a priori* demonstration, and then only through God's direct intervention. Thus a *viator* can doubt God's existence, because he cannot know of it naturally, but afterwards receive intuitive or abstractive knowledge of God from God himself enabling him to demonstrate that God exists. A common concept of God does not, however, carry knowledge of him in himself or of the divine nature and cannot therefore be the middle in an *a priori* demonstration of either; for that there has to be intuitive or abstractive knowledge which can come only from God.[215] Consequently we have no demonstrative knowledge of God *in statu isto* because no distinct knowledge of him.

That limitation is not overcome by Duns Scotus's notion of an order of essential perfection, with essence first, which can be demonstrated *a priori* of God. Any demonstrative order must be one or other of superior and inferior, or subject and accident, or whole and part, or subject and attribute, through an essential definition. God's attributes correspond to none of these. Nor is there a formal distinction among them which corresponds to a real distinction among really distinct things.[216] The fallacy of this view is shown from a comparison between man and whiteness as real things, and man and animal as concepts. The first are related as subject and accident; the second as superior and inferior. If, therefore, the second had the same order as the first, genus and species would belong as subject and accident and one would no longer be predicable of the other by the first essential mode (where the superior as predicate defines the inferior as subject), which is manifestly false.[217] The same applies to God and being which would then be distinguished as act and potentiality, and to God and divine nature, which would differ as perfect and more perfect with neither predicable of the other.[218] Conversely, among distinct things there is no order of superior and inferior as there is among concepts.[219] Finally, it is not enough for things to be distinct in order to be demonstrable; they have to be related in one of the ways just adumbrated.[220] Hence however much the divine nature, intellect and will were really distinguished there is no such order among their concepts which makes them demonstrable of one another; if there were,

[214] *Ibid.*, 117–18.

[215] Verumtamen ille due premisse [Deus est *and* essentia divina est] non sunt nobis possibiles. sed tantum possunt apprehendi ab intuitive vel abstractive intelligente ipsam deitatem in se. Et ideo soli tali sunt ille conclusiones in se demonstrabiles a priori que non possunt demonstrari de deo per aliquod commune tamquam per medium (*ibid.*, 118).

[216] *Ibid.*, 119–21.

[217] Similiter ista propositio adhuc est falsa intelligendo est false intelligendo eam sic quod 'qualem ordinem haberent aliqua si essent distincta realiter, talem ordinem habent rationes vel conceptus correspondentes illis rebus si essent, qui tamen conceptus non sunt una res; quia non est semper consimilis ordo in rebus et in conceptibus correspondentibus.

Exemplum: homo et albedo ordinantur sicut subiectum et accidens, non tamen sic ordinantur conceptus correspondentes. Similiter, homo et animal si distinguerentur realiter unum esset potentia et aliud actus, et neutrum esset de altero predicabile primo modo per se sed tantum secundo modo, nec unum esset de intellectu alterius (*ibid.*, 121).

[218] *Ibid.*, 121–2.

[219] *Ibid.*, 122.

[220] *Ibid.*, 122–4, 126.

omnipotence would not then belong immediately to the divine intellect, as it does, but to the intellect or will, which it cannot, since omnipotence is predicated immediately of the divine essence and thereby indemonstrable. Similarly if the divine nature alone were able to know and will and yet were really distinct from the intellect and will, whatever was predicated of one would be predicated of the other, which is not the case, for the divine essence is not the same as every act of knowing.[221]

It is perhaps paradoxical that it should be Ockham, so often regarded as a reductionist and nominalist, who corrected Duns Scotus for the very fault of holding to a direct correspondence between the real and conceptual orders. If there is one theme which informs Ockham's writings it is of the discrepancy between things on the one hand and their logical and grammatical forms on the other. Which means not that there is no correspondence between them but that the only real counterpart to any terms and concepts is that of individual things. Accordingly the distinction is not between different kinds of being but between different kinds of knowing what is real and invariably individual; far from denying the intellect its own freedom Ockham grants it more fully than any other scholastic, because he distinguishes more clearly than any other between an *ens rationis* and *ens realis*. Thus to the objection here that there can be several different concepts of God notwithstanding his simplicity, such as 'being', 'one', 'true', 'good', all of which represent distinct notions with a corresponding real distinction, Ockham replies that a difference between concepts must always be founded upon a difference between or within things in whatever it may consist. In this case terms like 'one', 'true', and 'good' connote different acts of knowing and willing; otherwise they would not be distinct concepts: similarly those which differ as superior and inferior do so because they stand for more or fewer things as more or less universal. That holds for all different concepts such as 'definition' and 'defined',[222] which, as he explains elsewhere, are never the same as terms yet always stand for the same thing.[223] Accordingly, the connotative concepts which can be had of God all signify the divine essence principally and consignify its different activities, so that, as the sixth conclusion has explained, the divine intellect and the divine will are both the divine essence as it knows and wills; neither is synonymous with the essence but both are the same.

The reason why then we are left with connotative and negative concepts of God's attributes is that on the one hand we have no distinct knowledge of God and on the other that there is no distinction between his essence and attributes which enables us to distinguish between them; in belonging immediately and intrinsically to him they are indemonstrable and God unknowable in himself. Consequently the only kind of knowledge we can have of them is the knowledge that we can have of him naturally, namely of concepts abstracted from knowledge of creatures. For that reason all our knowledge of God is by reference to what we

[221] *Ibid.*, 124–5.
[222] *Ibid.*, 119, 127–8.
[223] *Ibid.*, d. 2, q. 4, 130.

can know from creatures, and although it can be exclusive to him it cannot be exclusively of him,[224] as we shall now examine.

Concepts can be either simple or composite according to whether they are one or more, as being is composite if it consists of form and matter.[225] Now there are four ways in which we can know things: in themselves, in a simple proper concept, in a proper composite concept, or in a common simple concept. By the first two God cannot be known naturally, since each presupposes intuitive knowledge, which can only be had when we cannot doubt the existence of something.[226] We can no more have such knowledge or a concept which derives from it of God than someone born blind can have much knowledge of a colour he has never seen.[227] By the other two modes, however, God can be known naturally. In a simple concept common to him and creatures, because the same concept abstracted from creatures can be applied to God, for example, the concept of being which includes all that is, God as well as creatures, or of wisdom or of goodness, and many others, all of which extend to what is both uncreated and created. When these different simple concepts are combined they give a composite concept proper only to God, enabling us to conclude that there is a being which is at once wise, good, loving, just and so on. This fourth mode therefore differs from the third in simultaneously predicating of God a number of simple concepts which in him are one but are separate among creatures where they do not stand for the same thing. Accordingly when compounded in a single concept, being, wisdom, goodness, love, and so on, cannot extend to creatures but are proper only to God. To have such a concept is not to know him really just because these are concepts derived singly from creatures; and as they do not represent him in a simple concept common to him and creatures, nor do they when combined to connote him alone.[228]

[224] *Ibid.*, 116; this passage which belongs to the fifth conclusion was cancelled from three of the collated manuscripts, but it has remained undisturbed in the heavily annotated MS. Bib. Mazarine 894.

[225] Tertio distinguo de conceptu, et dico quo quidam est simplex qui non includit plures conceptus, et quidam compositus qui non est simplex et includit plures conceptus modo suo, sicut compositum includit actualiter realiter plures res reales, scicilet materiam et formam (*Ordinatio*, d. 3, q. 5, vol. II, 472–3).

[226] *Ibid.*, d. 2, q. 9, 312–14.

[227] Secundum ostendo, quod nihil potest cognosci a nobis ex puris naturalibus in conceptu simplici sibi proprio nisi ipsum in se precognoscatur. Ista patet inductive; aliter enim posset dici quod color posset cognosci a ceco a nativitate in conceptu proprio coloribus, quia non est maior ratio quod deus cognoscatur in conceptu sibi proprio sine precognitione ipsius in se quam color . . . sed manifestum est quod a tali non potest concipi color in conceptu sibi proprio; igitur nec deus (*ibid.*, 314–15); also d. 3, q. 2, 402–3.

[228] Secundum patet, quia sicut creatura potest cognosci in conceptu aliquo communi simplici, ita potest deus, quia aliter nullo modo esset a nobis cognoscibilis. Sed nunc est ita quod quando sunt multa communia simul habentia aliquod idem contentum, omnia illa communia simul accepta faciunt unum proprium illi, quia ex quo sunt distincta communia, oportet quod aliquod contineatur sub singulo quod sub nullo aliorum continetur; igitur omnia illa communia simul accepta nulli alii possunt convenire. Sed nunc est ita quod sunt multi conceptus simplices naturaliter abstrahibiles quorum quilibet est communis deo et alicui alteri; igitur omnes illi simul accepti facient unum conceptum proprium deo, et ita cum possit cognosci quod ille conceptus de aliquo verificatur deus in illo conceptu cognoscetur. Verbi gratia ab entibus potest abstrahi conceptus entis qui est communis deo et omnibus aliis entibus. Similiter potest abstrahi conceptus sapientie qui est precise communis sapientie increate et sapientie

Simple and connotative concepts therefore differ as quidditative and connotative; by the latter God's being is conceived determinately as absolutely first or creative or as first cause or immortal or indestructible and so on, each signifying principally being and secondarily the quality or attribute which makes it peculiar to God.[229] Simple concepts on the other hand are quidditative; if they were merely denominative or connotative there would then, as Duns Scotus showed, be an infinite regress because a connotative concept—like that of 'creative'—must be ultimately attributable to a quidditative concept, in this case a concept of being, previously known. Moreover, as common to both God and creatures, it must be predicable of both by the first essential mode, that is absolutely and immediately; which in turn means that it must be univocal, denoting the same for all that comes under it. As we discussed in chapter three, such univocity, as far as it concerns God and creatures, is by the third mode where all that they have in common is the same concept, without any real similarity as either species (the first mode) or genus (the second mode). Neither in essence nor wisdom or indeed any other attribute, is there any real comparability between God and creatures, save conceptually.[230]

At the same time different quidditative concepts in standing immediately and absolutely for distinct things or qualities have by definition distinct significations; and as absolute things are not—except for form and matter—communicable, so quidditative concepts standing for things of a different nature are not interchangeable.[231] That applies to distinct simple concepts of God, like essence and wisdom, which as we have seen are quidditative of both creatures and God. Contrary to Duns Scotus, Ockham, as we have also seen, rejects the view that there can be quidditative and connotative concepts of the same simple thing;[232] and since the simple concepts common to God and creatures are abstracted from both, they cannot be quidditative of one and not of the other. So far as they concern God such concepts as essence and wisdom each stand for the divine nature itself without connoting anything else; each must therefore be at once quidditative and conceptually distinct: otherwise they would not be convertible and so the same concept. Among composite beings, however, there can be diverse quidditative concepts of

---

create. Similiter potest abstrahi conceptus bonitatis ... et omnes isti conceptus simul non poterunt verificari nisi de solo deo, ex quo, per positum, nulla sapientia creata est bonitas creata nec a converso. Et ita cum possit concludi quod aliquod ens est bonitas et sapientia et sic de aliis, que vocantur attributa, sequitur quod deus isto modo cognoscitur in conceptu composito sibi proprio. Et hoc non est aliud nisi a creaturis abstrahere multos conceptus communes deo et creaturis, et concludere particulariter de uno conceptu simplici communi sibi et aliis unum conceptum compositum proprium deo, sicut contingit abstrahere conceptum entis, conceptum bonitatis, sapientie, caritatis, et sic de aliis, et contingit de ente particulariter sumpto concludere quod est bonitas, sapientia, dilectio, iustitia, et sic de aliis, et hoc est cognoscere deum in conceptu composito sibi proprio (*ibid.*, d. 3, q. 2, 403–4); also d. 2, q. 9, 315.

[229] *Ibid.*

[230] *Reportatio*, III, q. 9, Q. Walter Chatton opposed these arguments for a common univocal concept on the grounds that (a) they could equally apply to God and a chymera (non-existent), and (b) they could lead to an infinite regress. N. A. Fitzpatrick, 'Walter Chatton on the Univocity of Being', *FcS* 31 (1971), 98–100, 156–8.

[231] E.g. *Ordinatio*, d. 2, q. 6, 193, 212–13.

[232] *Ibid.*, d. 2, q. 9, 271–2; d. 3, q. 3, 428–9.

the different parts which in some way will be also of the whole and to that extent interchangeable.[233] The diversity of quidditative concepts of God does not impair his unity any more than that of connotative concepts does, because no universal concept can have a perfect similarity to him whom we cannot know other than in a concept.[234]

The grounds for Ockham's position, that we can only know God from a concept formed from knowledge of what is not him, are that God cannot be the first object of the intellect by either primacy of generation or adequation but only by primacy of perfection. That is to say he is not the first object known by the intellect, nor that which is predicated of all others that can be known, which, it will be re-called from chapter three, is the second of the two modes—namely of predication—by which an object is said to be adequate to the intellect.[235] He is not the first object because as we have repeatedly seen there cannot be intuitive knowledge of God *in statu isto* and so knowledge of God either in himself or in a concept proper to him, which derives from it, is impossible to us. That holds equally if a concept is taken to be an act of intellection rather than a mental object, for God in being immediately known to us would then be known self-evidently, which is no more possible naturally than as an object.[236] He is not an adequate object because—as we discussed in chapter three—no object of the intellect contains knowledge actual or virtual of all that comes under it.[237] The only adequate object possible to man naturally is the concept of being abstracted from all that can be known individually and affirmed of individuals. It is therefore confined to knowledge of individuals unlike Duns Scotus's double primacy—of community and virtuality—which extends to everything conceivable, including universals. Such a notion violates Ockham's individual conception of being and his axiom that incomplex knowledge of one thing does not lead to incomplex knowledge of something else. Even if all concepts are identified with acts of understanding, and so have being, that is not equivalent to having real knowledge of all that exists outside the mind; nor does the concept of being as an adequate object contain real knowledge of everything coming under it because there are many beings—God and substance included—

---

[233] Ad septimum et ad omnes auctoritates, dico quod deo et creature non est aliquid univocum sic quod aliquid essentiale creature vel accidentale habeat perfectam similitudinem cum aliquo quod est realiter in deo. Et talem univocationem negant omnes sancti respectu dei et creature; non tamen negant univocationem conceptus predicabilis de deo et creatura in quid et per se primo modo (*ibid.*, d. 2, q. 9, 335–6).

Also: quia cognoscere aliquid 'quid est' vel quidditative potest intelligi dupliciter. Vel quia ipsa quidditas rei vel aliqua pars quidditatis in se cognoscitur, et sic non est possibile deum cognoscere quidditative nec finem ultimum. Vel quia aliquis conceptus quidditativus cog-noscitur, et sic potest deus cognosci a nobis 'quid est' et quidditative (*ibid.*, d. 3, q. 2, 414).

[234] Ideo dico quod respectu dei possunt esse plures conceptus quidditativi, non tamen erunt plures conceptus quidditativi convertibiles . . . Ista ratio procedit de conceptibus respectu rei simplicis, cuiusmodi est deus, quia de re composita propter diversitatem partium possunt formari diversi conceptus convertibiles (*ibid.*, d. 3, q. 3, 419–20).

[235] Secundo dico quod deus non est primum cognitum a nobis, nec a primitate generationis nec primitate adequationis, sed est primum primitate perfectionis (*ibid.*, q. 1, 389).

[236] *Ibid.*

[237] *Reportatio*, IV, q. 14, C; chapter three, 170–6 above.

which we cannot know by either of these modes of adequation.[238] Adequation does not then have the role for Ockham which it had for Duns Scotus; and the contrast between them throws into relief the difference in outlook between the two thinkers.[239]

There remains in consequence only the third way of knowing God, by primacy of perfection through a concept in the way discussed above. We are thus able to conceive God as the most perfect being and to attribute to him in an eminent degree all the perfection appropriate to the highest being.[240]

Knowledge of God is therefore by means of univocal concepts with the concept of being, as the most universal, its foundation. Ockham establishes this exclusively conceptual notion of being in opposition to the views of St Thomas Aquinas, Henry of Ghent, and Duns Scotus above all. In a series of questions mainly in distinctions two, three and eight of the *Ordinatio* he disputes with them—so far as knowledge of God is concerned—over four main areas: of univocal and analogical predication, the role of being, the first object of knowledge, and whether God can belong to a genus. His relation to these thinkers is complex; he frequently shares their conclusions, especially those held on faith, and he diverges from all of them in the primacy he gives to individual knowledge and his denial of any but individual being. As the same time, however, he has a special relation to Duns Scotus which distinguishes him from the other two. Where his attitude to the latter is one merely of opposition, he largely defines his own position as the obverse of that of Duns. That is particularly apparent over the notion of universal being which they have in common against the doctrine of analogy maintained by St Thomas Aquinas and Henry of Ghent, although Ockham only discusses Henry's. Correspondingly Ockham's view of being as the most universal concept is a refinement of Duns's from which all ontological reality and virtual knowledge are excluded. As the foundation of Ockham's standpoint here I shall begin with his discussions of univocity and analogy.

Over univocity, the principal source of contention is Duns's denial that being is predicated absolutely and quidditatively of what he calls ultimate differences —i.e. those distinguishing individuals from their species—and the attributes of being. If according to Duns it were so predicable, that would introduce being as something diverse into what is one and the same; it would also mean that being could be predicated of itself, because an attribute is predicated of its subject *per se secundo modo* as something additional to the subject. Accordingly being cannot be predicated essentially of either ultimate differences, which must be without further differences, or its own attributes which cannot be different from it.[241] Ockham's

---

[238] *Ordinatio*, d. 3, q. 8, 529–42; *ibid.*, d. 3, q. 1, 390.

[239] That would seem to be the obvious conclusion rather than that of Baudry, of neglect by Ockham's expositors, a view based on the importance that adequation had for Duns Scotus (*Lexique*, 184).

[240] Tertium patet, quia deus est ens perfectissimum; igitur cum sit aliquo modo cognoscibilis a nobis, sicut in sequente questione patebit, erit intelligibile perfectissimum (*Ordinatio*, d. 3, q. 1, 390).

[241] *Ibid.*, d. 2, q. 9, 295–8.

reply is that being is not more univocal to non-ultimate differences than to ultimate differences, because everything necessarily either belongs to a genus or is an essential part of something which belongs to a genus. Moreover for Duns the essential difference is not something real outside the mind; therefore it should be either included in a genus or be an essential part joined to another part really distinct from it. Either way, by Duns's view, being is predicated *in quid*; hence it must be also univocal, since there is no real distinction, at least among creatures, which does not correspond to a real distinction among things. Again, any ultimate difference between one thing and another will be less than that between a thing and God; but on Duns's principles ultimate differences both agree (as species) and differ (ultimately); and as that which is common to God and creatures is predicated *in quid*, so *a fortiori* must that which is common to ultimate differences. On Duns's principles, too, the intellect can be certain of one thing and doubtful of another from the juxtaposition of which it can form a neutral concept. But someone can be certain that A is being and yet doubt whether or not there is an ultimate difference, which shows once again that there is something common to ultimate and non-ultimate differences.[242] To this Duns had replied that although the intellect could be certain that something is being it cannot be certain that it is essentially being but only accidentally; that such a concept is absolutely simple and must be wholly known or unknown; and that concepts which are certain can be univocal with those which are doubtful, not quidditatively but as determinable and determinate, or denominable and denominated, since to know absolutely simple concepts quidditatively would be contradictory.[243]

These reasons do not suffice for Ockham. The first would apply equally to quidditative concepts of God, who could then only be known connotatively and negatively—Henry of Ghent's position. In fact ultimate differences do constitute real being because whenever one component of something really exists, so does the other; therefore if that to which ultimate difference belongs is really and essentially being, by the same token the ultimate difference will be real being as well. Nor does the second reason of absolute simplicity hold more for ultimate difference than for God; but God can be known in a univocal concept, although not known in himself; so therefore can any ultimate reality. That also answers Duns's third reason; simplicity of ultimate difference does not exclude absolute being. For either ultimate difference is absolutely simple so that if being cannot be predicated absolutely of it, neither can it be predicated of that to which it is added; and then humanity or intellective soul could not have being predicated of them univocally and *in quid* which Duns denies. If, on the other hand, difference is composite with that to which it is added, we have again the same alternatives of simplicity versus compositeness, and so on infinitely. Furthermore, for Duns, whatever can be really communicated to other things is quidditative; that must include ultimate differences, which are not self-contained but are solely of ultimately different individuals. Hence anything affirmed of individual ultimate differences is affirmed absolutely.[244] That applies to all the individuals coming immediately under a

[242] *Ibid.*, 300–2.   [243] *Ibid.*, 302–3.   [244] *Ibid.*, 303–5.

common term like 'intellective soul';[245] they are signified by it absolutely and
univocally in the way discussed of genus or species in chapter three. That ultimate
difference is not self-contained follows from what has just been said. If, for example,
a common term like 'man' is not absolutely simple, then one part of the whole
constituting him will be in turn either absolutely simple, in which case (according
to Duns) being will not be predicated absolutely of it, or it will be composite; and
then the same question arises again, and so on either to infinity, or ending at a first
absolutely simple thing which is not self-contained but communicable to other
things. That will be the ultimate difference. Similar arguments hold for the attributes of being which are also univocally included under being.[246]

The That is the difference between Ockham and Duns. For Ockham being is a
common univocal term extending to whatever exists outside the mind, predicable
of it absolutely and by the first mode of essential predication, for the simple
reason that such beings, at least those which are creatures, are in some way distinct things. By the same token being can be common to God as well.[247] Strictly,
therefore, ultimate differences cannot be said to include being, as no inferior
includes its superior or anything includes what is univocal to it; for all differences
are due to the differences between things in themselves, and likewise among
different species. That does not, however, prevent ultimate differences as well as
any other differences from having being affirmed of them, just as the same species
and genus can be affirmed of numerically different individuals, and God and
creatures, who are totally distinct, can share the same univocal concept.[248] In all
three cases the superior is a term predicable of what is inferior, not of something
contained in the latter.

The mistake of Duns Scotus was to think that one is contained in the other.
Accordingly all his arguments in this connection arise from the misconception
that the inferior concept always includes the superior quidditatively and univocally,
and that therefore the inferior must be more composite than the superior. That
applies both to his notion of individual ultimate difference and to the properties
of being.[249] The latter he further fallaciously imagines as simple things, as if goodness were something really distinct from being, which cannot therefore be predi-

---

[245] Omnis realitas que non est de se hec, est de se communicabilis pluribus; sed nihil quod est
de se communicabile pluribus communicatur primo nisi suis per se inferioribus; igitur differentia
ultima anime intellective communicatur primo suis per se inferioribus et primo contentis sub ea
(ibid., 305).

[246] Ibid., 305–6.

[247] Circa quartum principale dico quod quibuscumque existentibus extra animam ens est
commune univocum, predicabile de eis in quid et per se primo modo. Cuius ratio est, quia
omnia que sunt extra animam, saltem in creaturis, si sint aliquo modo distincta, sunt res realiter
distincte; sed omnibus rebus ens est commune univocum eadem ratione qua est univocum deo
et creaturis; igitur etc. (ibid., 317).

[248] Ibid., 318–20; also d. 8, q. 1, N.

[249] Unde dico quod conceptus speciei non includit conceptum generis nec conceptum entis,
et tamen uterque predicatur de eo univoce et in quid. Unde omnes iste rationes procedunt ex
falsa imaginatione, scilicet quod semper conceptus inferior includit conceptum superiorem,
predicabilem de eo per se et quidditative et univoce, et quod conceptus inferior est universaliter
compositior conceptu superiori, ita quod includat conceptum superiorem et aliquid plus; que
et omnia consimilia sunt simpliciter falsa (ibid., 320); also 332.

cated of it absolutely, since being does not include goodness formally or essentially. In fact, as we have discussed fully in previous chapters, for Ockham properties have no independent existence outside the subject to which they belong. Accordingly being is part of their nominal definition as in that of say goodness whose meaning is equivalent to 'being which is desirable to the will', or a similar expression; here being is signified directly (*in recto*) and something additional to it indirectly (*in obliquo*). In this connotation it is perhaps true to say that being is not predicated by the first essential mode (where as predicate it defines the subject), in such propositions as 'White is being', although nothing is really signified by 'white' other than being predicated of it absolutely. And of all simple non-connotative concepts, like 'man', being is always predicated absolutely.[250] For that reason the notion of being is not contained in what comes under it, as Duns wrongly imagined.

A univocal term, then, corresponds to nothing real, as thinkers like St Thomas Aquinas, Henry of Ghent and Thomas of Sutton who denies its applicability to God, mistakenly believed. That does not, however, imply that a univocal concept is merely imaginary (*fictivum*), because while it corresponds directly to no one universal thing, it is predicated absolutely of many individuals which answer to it, as the concept of 'man' corresponds to every individual man.[251] Moreover a univocal term, although not prior logically or naturally to what comes under it, can be called prior consequentially, as more common than that from which it is abstracted. In that sense a word can be said to be prior to God, for example in the statement 'A is God; therefore A is being'; in all such cases the converse does not hold, since the univocal term is more universal than that of which it is affirmed. It is precisely in that way that a term is univocal to God and creatures; as common to diverse things, it cannot, by definition, be simpler than that to which it is univocal.[252]

That also explains the notion of parity (*parificatio*) as it concerns what is univocal. To the objection that nothing can be univocal to God and creature because they are unequal, and to be univocal is to be equal in fact as well as in name, Ockham distinguishes two senses of parity. If it means that two things are really equal because of what is intrinsic to them, then God and creatures are equal in nothing; but if it means that they have something in common which is intrinsic to neither of them, then they can be said to be equally related to it, which is the case with a univocal concept signifying both God and creature immediately. Unlike the first sense, no such concept is of the essence of either.[253]

---

[250] *Ibid.*, 321–2.
[251] *Ibid.*, 331–2.
[252] Ad secundum [argumentum tertii dubii] dico quod nullum univocum est prius realiter vel natura illis quibus est univocum, sed tantum est prius prioritate consequentie, quia scilicet ab univocato ad univocum est bona consequentia et non convertitur; et quod aliquid tale sit prius tali prioritate ipso deo non est inconveniens. Isto enim modo potest dici quod etiam aliqua vox prolata est prior deo, quia in voce etiam est ista bona consequentia, '*a* est deus, igitur *a* est ens', et non e converso; igitur illa vox communior est quam deus. Et quando dicitur quod univocum est simplicius univocatis, patet per predicta quod hec est simpliciter falsa' (*ibid.*, 332).
[253] *Ibid.*, 333.

This then is the foundation of Ockham's doctrine of univocal knowledge of God as a purely conceptual community between him and what can be known from creatures. It will be seen that it is far from being a confession of ignorance. Nor can it be said to close previously open doors upon God. Rather it seeks consistency in keeping conceptual what can only be known through concepts. To that end most of Ockham's criticism of Duns Scotus is directed to purging his arguments of their non-conceptual elements. In stressing that there can be no real or distinct knowledge of God *in statu isto* Ockham was taking up a traditional position; his innovation, if such it can be called, lies only in the rigour with which he pursued it, even at one point cautioning Duns Scotus for seeming to imply that what exists in creatures could also be in God.[254] As in the rest of his epistemology it is Ockham who shows a distrust for uncanonical refinements and a commitment to what he considers to be established truths.

Ockham and Scotus do nevertheless agree upon univocal knowledge of God, and with it recognition that God is not the first object of knowledge, differently though—as we have seen in the preceding part—they interpret the first object, a point to which we shall return. Ockham and Henry of Ghent on the other hand are opposed on both questions. Over the latter, Henry of Ghent held that the concept of God is naturally the first object of knowledge, together with that of being, because all knowledge proceeds from the indeterminate and univocal to the determinate and the particular—the reverse of Ockham's standpoint. Deductively, however, God is the final object of knowledge as he is the end and principle of being; and as nothing can be perfectly known unless God is perfectly known, so nothing can be imperfectly known unless God is known imperfectly; the same applies to being. Accordingly knowledge of a universal attribute in God, like being or goodness, is the means of knowing its created counterpart; the order must be always from God to creature and so from absolute to finite; the other way, God cannot be distinguished from creatures as he cannot be known from what is derivative and finite.[255]

Ockham rejects both the conclusion and the arguments. God cannot be the first object of knowledge, for then one of two alternatives would follow. Either the first object would exist outside the intellect as something real or it would belong to the mind as a univocal concept. In the first case it would be God himself, whose nature would then be known in itself, which Henry denies is possible. On the other hand if it were a universal concept it cannot be the first thing known (*primum cognitum*) because a concept must be preceded by something real. Nor is it enough for Henry to argue that the first object is God himself known under a general notion and not in himself. That would entail the further alternative of a distinction between God and such a concept or their identity. If they were distinct, the concept would then not be part of God but, on Henry's own arguments, the work of the intellect; and since according to Henry also, the first action of the intellect is not to know distinctly or to distinguish clearly between concepts, there must be an act prior to this act, which is the first act of the intellect. If on the other hand,

[254] *Ibid.*, 300.   [255] *Ibid.*, d. 3, q. 1, 381–4.

God and the concept were the same, then—once again—God would be known in himself under his own nature and not in a general concept. Moreover, for Ockham, whenever there is a mental distinction between things, one or other of what is distinguished will be a concept (*ens rationis*); hence if a general concept is distinguished from God, it will be caused by the intellect since God cannot be its first object; that will be the act of knowing it presupposes.[256]

For Ockham, on the contrary, *pro statu isto* we know a creature before we know God because it is the first object of our knowledge. It therefore gives us knowledge of an individual thing before anything else as we have seen in chapter one.[257] If the reverse were true, as Henry of Ghent holds, and we knew creatures through first knowing God's nature, God would be either the cause of knowing a creature by itself or by its knowledge. Henry denies the first, as that is the way God is known by creatures; the second is untenable for such knowledge would be purely created and imperfect; and as incomplex knowledge of one thing does not give incomplex knowledge of another it could not be the cause of all created knowledge. Accordingly, while a creature cannot be known from a concept of God, the converse is possible, as we have seen: for if we have a concept we have a first object.[258] Such a concept, however, is always of an individual as the first thing known, for the very reason that the intellect always proceeds from the particular and determinate to the general and indeterminate; the latter as merely conceptual is not necessary to knowledge of the former in the way that knowledge of individual being does not presuppose knowledge of being in general.[259]

Such concepts, however, are univocal not analogous. That again contradicts Henry of Ghent who, while accepting God's unknowability in himself, maintained that he can be known in universal concepts analogical to him and creatures. These were the result of abstracting such notions as goodness from created things and joining them to an analogous concept derived from God's attributes in a notion of goodness, common to both and of neither in particular, which could be of varying degrees of generality.[260]

To Ockham no concept is analogical, but, as we saw in chapter three, either it is univocal or there is more than one concept. That applies to Henry of Ghent's common concepts. If they are univocal, as predicated absolutely of all that comes under them, they cannot be of God's essence nor, in being concepts, are they the first object of knowledge, which contradicts Henry's view that God's essence is the first thing known. If, on the other hand, there are several concepts one will be proper to God and another to creatures which would have the anomaly of enabling God to be known in himself.[261] To the objection that something is only known in a proper concept if it is known distinctly, Ockham cites the example of something

---

[256] *Ibid.*, 384–6. [257] *Ibid.*, 386. [258] *Ibid.*, 386–7.

[259] Ad ultimum dico quod aliquod ens particulare potest cognosci, quamvis ille intentiones generales entis et unius non cognoscantur, quia ille intentiones non sunt nisi quedam entia rationis, vel saltem non sunt de essentia rei; et ideo cum quidlibet reale possit cognosci non cognito aliquo ente rationis vel non cognito aliquo sibi extrinseco, ideo potest res cognosci talibus intentionibus non cognitis (*ibid.*, 392).

[260] *Ibid.*, q. 2, 394–6. [261] *Ibid.*, 396.

seen from a distance, where it appears both particular and confused in its parts. That would apply much more to a simple being like God.[262]

A simple and proper concept of God cannot be sustained on the basis of analogy any more than of univocity. If, as Henry of Ghent maintains, there is such a concept it would be either really of the divine nature and we should then know it in itself which is impossible; or it would be really distinct from God either as something real, and so a creature (instead of God), or as a concept, and then not as *primum cognitum*. Moreover there is nothing to say how such a proposition could be had from creatures, without which it is valueless.[263]

Now since, according to Henry of Ghent, it is not univocal, and it cannot, according to Ockham, be analogical, a simple concept proper to God, if such there were, must be particular to God alone, on the principle that whatever can be known distinctly alone can be known distinctly when known together with something else. If therefore God can be known distinctly and in particular without a creature, he can be equally known distinctly and particularly with a creature.[264] In fact, however, a common concept must be univocal to all that comes under it, which by definition cannot be known distinctly;[265] so that far from knowing God, as Henry avers, in a threefold order of generality, when we know him in a common concept like goodness he is known no more clearly than an ass is known.[266] That is the only way we can know God, not for himself but in a concept. Accordingly these concepts can never stand personally for him but only in simple supposition as terms; and when we say that 'God is' we do not thereby signify God's being but merely a concept which stands for it.[267]

By the same token since God cannot be known distinctly no concept proper to God can be a simple univocal concept but, as we discussed earlier, it must be composite. For that reason the assertion of Duns Scotus that the concept of infinite being is simpler and more perfect than that of any other attributable to God is unfounded. It is not more perfect because as a negative concept it is not formally more perfect than any affirmative concept. Nor is it more simple, but on the contrary, when affirmed of being, it is a composite concept; if it were simple it would then, as quidditative, be convertible with God, which Duns denies. Indeed as a concept composed of both a negative and an affirmative term, 'infinite being' is more composite than one, like 'highest being', composed of two positive terms.[268] Finally 'infinite' is as much an attribute or property of God as any other, and not as Duns says an intrinsic mode of being, of the subject itself, as intense whiteness is intrinsic to whiteness and not accidental in the way that visible whiteness is.[269] That, however, is to misconceive infinite for something real; it is in fact an attribute like any other, as whatever is demonstrable of something else—which Duns holds infinity is of God—and predicable of its subject by the second essential mode— which infinity as a negative term must be—is an attribute. It cannot therefore be

---

[262] *Ibid.*, 396–7.   [263] *Ibid.*, 397.   [264] *Ibid.*, 397–8.

[265] Preterea quandocumque omnis res quocumque modo correspondens conceptui est simpliciter una et indistincta, conceptus erit univocus et eiusdem rationis (*ibid.*, 398).

[266] *Ibid.*, 399.   [267] *Ibid.*, 412–13.

[268] *Ibid.*, q. 3, 421–3.   [269] *Ibid.*, 421.

immediately intrinsic to God, since only what is predicable by the first essential mode is immediately intrinsic; but among all the connotative concepts which can be attributed to God it expresses most fully his complete perfection.[270]

The division between Ockham and his adversaries over knowledge of God springs above all from their different conceptions of intellectual knowledge. Henry of Ghent and St Thomas Aquinas, and in a lesser degree Duns Scotus make the universal the object of the intellect, where for Ockham it is the individual which must be always known first. Duns like Henry of Ghent follows Avicenna in holding that being is first in what is distinctly known to the intellect, in order of origin. The reason as we saw in chapter one, is that nothing is distinctly conceived unless all that belongs to it is known distinctly; but being is included in all other—inferior—quidditative concepts; therefore before these can be distinctly known being must be known distinctly.[271] Ockham rejects this view as he does also Duns's contention that a *species specialissima* moves the intellect first, and its individual the senses.[272] No universal, however, specific or general can be the first object, whether known confusedly or distinct, because only what belongs essentially to something is known with it. That does not include the concept of being, which as the work of the intellect is not something real outside it, as Duns agrees; and what belongs only to the intellect cannot be of the essence of anything else. Furthermore, as we have seen, if one of the things contained under a common concept can be known distinctly without at the same time knowing their superior, so can the other; but being is predicated absolutely of God and a creature, and as God can be known distinctly without knowing being,[273] a creature can equally be known distinctly. Similarly whatever can be distinctly known by the senses without knowledge of something else can be distinctly known by the intellect in the same way; and since sensible objects can be known by the senses without having a concept of universal being they can be known in themselves by the intellect too. For that reason also, Duns's assertion is untrue that distinct knowledge is always preceded by confused knowledge.[274] If we could not know the singular as singular, we should never be able to know it.[275]

That holds also for St Thomas Aquinas's opinion that the intellect always knows the more universal before the less universal so that the most universal is *primum cognitum*. As such it is intermediate between potential knowledge and a perfect act of knowing distinctly and completely; for the more universal in containing many things known distinctly, gives imperfect knowledge.[276] Ockham, as we have also seen, dismisses this reasoning. If, he replies, the more universal were

[270] *Ibid.*, 423–4.
[271] *Ibid.*, q. 5, 445.
[272] *Ibid.*, 443–4, 446–58; see chapter two above.
[273] This has nothing to do with the contingent order of our knowledge but is a formal statement of God's absolute simplicity so that if he could be known intuitively he would be known distinctly, on the principle—derived from Aristotle (*Metaphysics*, IX, ch. 10, 1051 b, 17–26)—that something simple is either totally known or totally unknown (*Ordinatio, ibid.*, 459).
[274] *Ibid.*, 459–60; 478.
[275] *Ibid.*, 449.
[276] *Ibid.*, 464; the reference is to *Physics*, I, ch. 1, 184 a, 23–184 b, 14.

known before the less universal we should then only know the latter through the former, which is false; for many genera remain unknown whose species are known, at least confusedly. Moreover, according to St Thomas, universals do not exist independently of individual things; therefore the only real things that can be known are individuals. Individuals, not universals, must be therefore the object of the intellect. By the same token they will constitute the first object of the intellect but known immediately and perfectly by their singularity, not through the mediation of what is first known more universally, and imperfectly. The whole notion of a sequence from imperfect to perfect and incomplete to complete knowledge is without foundation when taken as a general rule. To know the premises is more perfect than to know the conclusion, as to know the cause is more perfect than to know the effect and each is prior to that which it excels. Correspondingly in nature the illumination of the air by the sun is a process from potential to actual yet it does not presuppose an incomplete stage of actuality between them, nor does the will in performing an act of loving.[277] The same applies to the senses, which contrary to what St Thomas says, do not have a parallel order of experience from more universal to less universal which he imputes to the intellect. For each the singular is always the first object.[278]

That does not however, as we have seen, mean that it is always the singular that is first distinctly known: the first distinct object can equally be a concept, which when it is absolutely simple, can only be known distinctly in order to be known at all. Conversely only a singular can be known confusedly, for only a singular is a composite not all of whose parts need be known; and when they are not all known it cannot be distinctly known, which is the sense in which Ockham here takes confused knowledge.[279] In contrast each of the concepts belonging to a composite concept must be known because there is not a concept unless it is known; and so all concepts, simple or composite, must be distinctly known, although they need not stand for something distinct, as we have seen in the case of universal concepts.[280]

The limits for Ockham of a univocal quidditative concept are apparent. Although it can be the first object distinctly known it is neither in itself of what is distinct, nor does it precede cognition of the individual things from which it is abstracted. It cannot therefore be quidditatively included in the latter. Hence, as we saw in the first part, the whole structure of virtual knowledge on which Duns

[277] *Ibid.*, 465–7; also conclusio quinta, 476.

[278] *Ibid.*, 469–71; 473–4. E.g.: Igitur in omne obiectum in quod potest sensus, intellectus potest in illud idem: sed sensus potest primo in singulare, igitur et intellectus (474).

[279] Tertia conclusio est quod aliquid aliud a singulari potest esse primum distincte cognitum . . . potest intellectus abstrahere aliquem conceptum simpliciter simplicem ante cognitionem cuiuscumque alterius rei singularis . . . Sed simplex non potest cognosci nisi distincte, quia non est possibile, eo ipso quod est simplex, quod aliquis eius lateat et aliquid pateat; igitur primum cognitum tunc distincte erit aliquid universale quod non est singulare. Quarta conclusio est quod solum singulare potest cognosci confuse; quia solum compositum cuius aliquid latet potest cognosci confuse; sed huiusmodi est precise singulare includens multas partes; igitur etc (*ibid.*, 475). Also 471–2.

[280] *Ibid.*, 475–6. The difference is expressed in the distinction between knowing something confusedly—i.e. when not all the intrinsic parts are disclosed—and knowing something confused, which can be a universal concept containing a number of different things (*ibid.*, 472).

Scotus built his conception of univocal knowledge of God falls to the ground with Ockham. To call it destructive is beside the point: Ockham was not denying conceptual knowledge of God; he was denying that it could be anything other than conceptual. Indeed conceptually he was prepared to go further than Duns in treating univocal concepts of God as quidditative, or at least as having absolute import in the absolute simplicity of God's being, where Duns Scotus treated those attributed to God's being as connotative. Ockham drew the line at the point at which the conceptual passed over into the ontological. Hence his criticism of Duns Scotus's inclusion of the concept of being in knowledge of everything else, and his opposition to the primacy given by all three of his opponents to universal cognition over singular.

The coda to these problems comes in the question of whether God can belong to a genus. We have discussed the meaning of the expression *in genere* in chapter three.[281] Here, as it concerns God, Ockham treats it in relation to the opinions of St Thomas Aquinas and Duns Scotus. Both agree with him that God is not in a genus; he takes issue with them over what constitutes genus and species. Against St Thomas he argues that they can be of simple substances like angels (as St Thomas himself acknowledges) and accidents as well as composite beings. Accordingly it is not, as St Thomas holds, because of God's simplicity that he is not in a genus.[282] Nor because nothing can be more universal than God, for—as we have seen in his discussion of univocal concepts—something can be more common than God, by predication, as opposed to something more real or more perfect.[283] He also rejects St Thomas's other arguments, based on the identity God's being and essence (which we saw in chapters three and four is for Ockham merely a grammatical distinction), that if God were in a genus, his genus would be that of being in signifying his essence absolutely (*in quid*); but according to Aristotle (*Metaphysics*, book three) being cannot be the genus of any difference; God cannot therefore be in a genus. To that Ockham replies that the same argument would be true for angels which for St Thomas are in a genus.[284]

Duns Scotus's reasons centre upon God as infinite being, the foundation of his epistemology of God. There can be a common univocal concept of God and creatures but it cannot be a genus because it is indifferent to the distinction between infinite and finite contained under it. That would not be possible if it were a genus, for genus must signify what is potentially divisible into difference—i.e. it must be differentiable into species; otherwise genus would completely define what belonged to it without any differentiation into species. Nothing infinite, however, can be potential to anything; hence God cannot be in a genus, whereas every species in belonging to a genus is composed of genus and difference.[285]

Once again, Ockham opposes the notion that a species must be composite,

---

[281] See 186, 199 above.

[282] *Ordinatio*, d. 8, q. 1, B–C.

[283] Ultima ratio non valet, quia non est inconveniens aliquid esse principium prius deo prioritate conclusione, quia scilicet est communius deo; et isto modo precise deus est prius illis que sunt in genere, non secundum rem nec secundum perfectionem (*ibid.*, F). Also Q–R and q. 2.

[284] *Ibid.*, E.   [285] *Ibid.*, G.

having, in Duns's terminology, two realities, one of genus, the other of difference. If, as Duns himself accepts, there are many distinct individuals which do not contain distinct things, that is even more true of species; and as species are related to individuals, so are genera to species. That individuals are not constituted of these two realities can be proved, because, if they exist, they will either be of the same kind and then belong to a common universal concept abstracted from them, which Duns denies. Or they will be of diverse kinds and so their individuals will not be of the same species; for they cannot be of different species from their differences. Furthermore, it is untenable to say as Duns does that a specific nature is potential and perfectible, because nothing can be potential to itself. That cannot be overcome by positing a formal distinction between them, for it would then also apply to God with either his essence potential to his relation (among the divine persons) or *vice versa*. Since, however, there is always composition wherever there is both potentiality and actuality, God's infinite perfection would then be composite, which is absurd. In fact, nothing is potential to something unless really distinct from it.[286] Nor is there any ground for positing with Duns Scotus not only a species but its intrinsic mode of contracting individuals into the same species. That would in turn be to assume something contracted, distinct from the individuals which it united and additional to genus and difference; which is untenable and against Duns himself. The fallacy comes from Scotus's assumption that genus is intrinsic to species in helping to constitute it.[287]

For Ockham, then, genus is not confined to what is composite, but can include what is absolutely simple, as angels are absolutely simple and in a genus. Nor does it depend merely upon the compatibility of different things, although that is a condition, because if there was only one species, say 'man', there could not be a genus 'animal'. So far as God is concerned it cannot be demonstrated that he is not in a genus but arguments can be stated to persuade that he is not.[288]

The first is that if he were in a genus, other things would be in a genus with God; that would mean that being or something else common to God and creatures was a genus, which is false. Being is not a genus; for a genus separates what belongs to it from what does not; but being, as predicable of everything, can be negated of nothing, which is how Aristotle is to be interpreted in the *Metaphysics* (book three) when he says that every genus is really negated by difference, but not being. That applies also to something—other than being—common to God and creatures; a genus which is predicated of greater differences is also predicated of lesser differences, which would not be the case of something including God.[289] Secondly, everything in a genus has a certain proportion and perfection; but God infinitely exceeds everything else; therefore he is not in a genus with anything else. That is supported by St Augustine who says that God is neither in a genus nor a species; although Augustine was concerned here only to prove that God's essence was not a species, the argument also applies to genus because things belonging to a genus or species are always said to be more perfect when taken together than alone. That

286 *Ibid.*, H.   287 *Ibid.*, and R.
288 *Ibid.*, K–L; also R.   289 *Ibid.*, L.

is possible only if they have a certain proportionate perfection to one another, which cannot include God whose perfection is infinite. Duns Scotus, too, can be interpreted in the same sense when he says that everything in a genus is less perfect of itself than with something else. That excludes God who alone is not more imperfect in himself than with something else. The minor, however—which is proved from the fact that God unlike a substance which alone is less perfect, does not have accidents—implicitly contradicts Ockham's repeated insistence that compositeness is irrelevant to being or not being in a genus.[290]

That is as far as argument will take us; there is no sufficient proof that God is not in a genus because it cannot be established from his necessity, simplicity, or infinity, or from a univocal concept of being. Ockham's reasons differ from those proffered by St Thomas and Duns Scotus in attempting less and claiming less. Unlike those two thinkers Ockham eschews any ontological explanation of genus and species, confining them neither to composite beings as St Thomas does nor making one potential to the other as Duns does. As related directly to the individuals which come under them the only criterion of both genus and species is the relation of individuals to one another. Provided they have a certain proportion based upon similarity, as we saw in chapter three, they can be classified under one or other. It is precisely that which is lacking in the relation of what is not God to God; but because there is no way of demonstrating that genus derogates from God's own nature, Ockham refuses to regard that argument as decisive. In view of the charges often made against Ockham of destructiveness we can begin perhaps to appreciate where it lay: not in denying the possibility of discourse, whether about God, or, as we shall see in the following chapter, other matters of belief; nor in denying most of the traditional questions, but of the false claims made for answers based either upon *ignorantia elenchi* or a mistaken conviction in their certainty.

That is exemplified in the preceding discussion of God. Ockham denies virtually all the metaphysical arguments advanced by previous thinkers for the very reason that, in his view, they rest upon a confusion between the conceptual and the ontological. If one can hardly fail to be impressed by his remorselessness in stripping away unfounded distinctions, one can hardly fail equally to be struck by the moderateness of his own position which he substitutes. He accepts the traditional way of conceiving God not in himself but by concepts; he allows that these can be concepts univocal to God and creatures through abstraction and that they can be predicated absolutely of God. At the end God still remains God together with the means of identifying him. What we cannot do is to know him in himself because we have neither intuitive nor self-evident knowledge of him.[291] As Ockham expresses it in one of the *Quodlibets*, 'A *viator* cannot of his own natural powers have knowledge of God which is absolute not connotative, affirmative not negative, simple not composite, proper not common, before composition and division (i.e. forming a proposition) because he cannot know God alone without knowing something else'.[292] Hence he can either be known in a simple common concept or a

[290] *Ibid.*   [291] *Ordinatio*, d. 3, q. 4; *Quodlibet* I, q. I.
[292] *Quodlibet* IV, q. 18.

composite proper concept. The condition of any univocal concept other than being—which is the foundation of our knowledge of him—is that it must be abstract and not concrete; otherwise if it were concrete it would be equivocal for it would then refer to different modes of actual being. Whereas anything predicated of God, as absolutely simple being, is identical with his being and so affirmed absolutely, it is connotative when predicated of a creature. Thus to say God is wise means that he *is* wisdom, but to say the same of a creature means that it *has* wisdom. In order to overcome this real disparity, wisdom or any other quality must be taken in its abstract form—i.e. wisdom as opposed to wise—without reference to actual being.[293] Correspondingly when being is predicated of God univocally with creatures, it is abstracted from its infinite and finite modes; when 'infinite' is added to being it then becomes, as we have seen, a composite term proper to God alone and thereby loses its univocal character.

VI PROOF OF GOD'S EXISTENCE

That helps to explain Ockham's rejection of Duns Scotus's use of the concept of infinity, not only to distinguish divine from created being, by which he sought to prove, as we have just discussed, that God is not in a genus, but also to establish his existence. In a series of quodlibetal questions, Ockham returns to the same problem of whether we can prove that God is intensively—as opposed to extensively—infinite: that is to say, is infinite in a perfect degree—as a quality or state of his being—rather than in having the power to know or produce an infinite number of effects. Ockham's discussion of this issue brings us to the final aspect of knowledge of God: whether we can prove God's existence from natural reason and experience. As we shall see Ockham's predominantly negative conclusion is merely the conclusion to our previous discussion; it denies not that we can know God but that we can do so directly, which is the basis of all that he has said about knowing God by means of concepts. For that we have to assume his existence: far from our knowledge of God standing or falling by whether or not God can be proved, it takes its starting point from his existence in the full range of his perfections. Discourse about him is therefore defined, not nullified, by lack of evidence for his existence. If that marks a break from the immediate past in the systems of St Thomas Aquinas and Duns Scotus, who gave a central place to proofs for God, it is consonant with a continuous Christian tradition of God's unknowability, into which the hundred and seventy or so years of scholastic efforts to show that God exists, was a brief incursion. That Ockham was instrumental in ending it is not more remarkable than that he still sought ways of continuing it, albeit in a restricted and modified form. Whether we choose to regard Ockham's treatment of knowledge of God as essentially the work of a logician, it is undeniably that of a Christian logician for whom the truths which he discusses are the basis of his discussion.

There are three facets to Ockham's consideration of God's existence: infinity, causality and conservation. Only the last offers a way of establishing it.

[293] *Ibid.*, q. 2.

In the case of infinity it is treated, as we have remarked, in the *Quodlibets* from a number of different standpoints with Ockham concluding from each that it does not give proof that God is intensively (i.e. perfectly) infinite. Following the order in the *Quodlibets*, his infinity cannot be proved from natural reason, for that would be to conceive it from the standpoint of its effects. All that we can achieve by this mode is to show that an effect could be of infinite duration, or that God could cause an infinite effect or effects, simultaneously or successively, or that he knows infinite things. None of these bears on God's infinity: the first is inadequate because, as we shall mention again, we cannot demonstrate that God is the efficient cause or mover of all things; even if he could be known to be first mover, infinite movement does not entail God's infinity, for that could as well be due to an indestructible agent; and even then it requires no greater power to make something endure for a thousand years than for one day, since what can last one day could last to infinity if there were nothing to prevent it. As for infinite effects they are only possible in the third sense, that is successively. But that can be from a finite cause, as the sun or fire can produce infinite heat in different things; similarly the created intellect could know infinite diverse knowledge from a succession of different objects.

Again, as we shall mention when we consider God as cause, it cannot be proved that God is immediate cause of infinite effects, nor by the same token, that he knows infinite things or indeed knows or wills what exists outside him.[294] That does not mean, however, that it is not more reasonable to hold that God does in fact know and will what is outside him or that he knows and moves heaven and everything else just because he is the most perfect being. For that reason Ockham accepts that he does; it is rather that there is no need to posit such perfections from the point of view of natural reason.[295] The distinction is fundamental to Ockham's entire discussion; there is no question of denying the truths of faith, for the question is not of their truth but their demonstrability. And as the circumscription of demonstration does not impair the certainty of natural experience or self-evident truth attained naturally, nor does it lessen conviction held on faith. Ockham did not confuse either with demonstration which for him was—as we saw in the last chapter—weaker than knowledge and—as we have seen in this one—irrelevant to faith.

To say, as Ockham does, that from the point of view of natural reason we cannot prove that a first mover acts on account of a desired end, or a first efficient cause acts according to its chosen end, or that the contingency in things is due to the contingent actions of the first cause, or that God's infinity, or of a first being, does

---

[294] *Ibid.*, II, q. 2.

[295] Ad primum istarum dico quod non potest sufficienter probari quod deus intelligat aliquid extra se, aut vult extra se, quia nulla videtur necessitas ponendi quod intelligat aliqua extra se, cum non possit probari sufficienter quod deus sit causa sufficiens alicuius. Cum tamen hoc videbatur precise rationis efficacia ad ponendum deum intelligere aliquid extra se, ut cognoscat illud quod agit et sic rationabiliter agat. Dico tamen quod sicut rationabiliter ponitur quod est movens celum effective, ita rationabiliter ponitur quod intelligit celum et omne aliud corpus quod movet, quia est ens perfectissimum, et per consequens movet intellectualiter et rationabiliter (*ibid.*).

not contradict intensive infinity, merely points to the limits upon natural certainty. That would apply even if we could prove some or all of these.[296] It holds equally for each of the possible ways open to demonstrating infinity of God. Thus by that of God as immediate efficient cause of all things, which he also knows, we do not prove more than that God can produce an infinity of finite things—since all his effects are finite. Moreover both confused knowledge on our part of all God's effects and distinct knowledge of them will be finite; for we have only finite knowledge and God will know what is only finite.[297]

Here we come to the contrary position of Duns Scotus, whose proof for God's infinity Ockham examines in the seventh Quodlibet. By that from efficient causality Duns argues first that a cause having infinite effects by its own active power is infinite; that includes a cause which of itself has infinite movement. Second, an agent which can be in many effects is more perfect than one which can have only a few; therefore that which can have infinite effects is of infinite power. Third, a cause which can have infinite effects simultaneously is infinite, which is the case with the first cause in containing eminently the causes of all possible causes. Lastly, the first efficient cause to which a second cause adds no further perfection is infinite; otherwise it would be finite. For Duns, all of these are applicable to God and thereby prove his perfect infinity.[298] They are rejected by Ockham for the reasons already given in the previous question (in the third Quodlibet).

To begin with, what Duns says about a first mover cannot apply to God because to be infinite he would have to move instantaneously, but according to Aristotle that is possible only if an infinite power is in matter as well as outside it, which excludes God. Hence there is no sufficient way of proving God's infinity by efficiency. As to Duns's individual arguments, the first and second—derived from infinite effects—could as well be of a finite first mover, which could equally be more perfect than its effect and of infinite duration through producing its effects successively. Accordingly something which is the cause of infinite effects does not itself have to be infinite, provided infinity is understood numerically and not as of infinite species; the latter does not arise here, and even if it did, it would not necessarily imply an infinite first cause, for the same reason that a finite cause could produce an infinite number of distinct species. The third argument includes a contradiction because, if a first cause contained formally and distinctly the causality of all possible causes, it would be infinite; but it is then contradictory to say that it could produce them because they would already pre-exist in the first cause. Nor is it true to say that the first cause would more perfectly contain them formally than really, which is a fallacy of a figure of speech. In the fourth argument, 'more perfect' can mean either nobler or more powerful. In the first sense it is true as Duns says that finites in aggregate are more perfect than alone, but it is not true that an infinite first cause and a second cause cannot produce a more perfect effect than a first cause acting alone. When more perfect is understood as more powerful,

[296] Ibid.
[297] Quodlibet III, q. 1.
[298] Quodlibet VII, q. 17.

then the reverse is true: combined finite causes do not increase the perfection of their action, but an infinite and a finite cause do.[299] For Ockham, the distinction is between simultaneous infinite effects, which argue an infinite first cause, and successive infinite effects, which do not. It is that which Duns's arguments from efficient causality do not establish.[300]

Nor do they do so by his other approaches. The next, from cognition, where Duns reasons that an intelligence knowing all things infinitely, actually and simultaneously, must itself be infinite, for Ockham only proves that its infinity is extensive, by reference to what is infinite, not in itself, intensively.[301] The third way, of simplicity, is based upon Duns's proof that God as infinite and absolutely simple cannot be in a genus of substance with what is finite and composite. As before, Ockham refuses to accept that only God is absolutely simple: hence Duns's arguments could as well apply to the intellective soul, which is finite. Furthermore, God can be in a genus of substance when substance is understood transcendentally (i.e. as beyond its generic determinations), for it is then not a proper concept of genus but a transcendental concept used for convenience in place of a proper concept. God is also in a species in the sense that if there were more than one God a concept of species could be predicated of each divinity as it could be of more than one sun. Since, however, there is only one God it would be contradictory to affirm a concept of plurality of what is unique. It does not follow either that if God is under the genus of substance he must also be in a species of categories like quality, when a term like 'wisdom' (which belongs to the category of quality) is predicated of him; for in every case he is transcendental being and so above all categories.[302] Ockham in denying Duns's arguments has appeared to sail very close to the wind in giving the widest possible interpretation to genus and species compared with what he has said in the Ordinatio. The difference, however, is more in the brevity and pointedness of expression, which are in the nature of the quodlibetal form,[303] and can make the unexceptionable appear paradoxical: perhaps it was that which led De Wulf to misconstrue Ockham's first question of the first Quodlibet into a denial that God's existence could be proved[304]—a point to which we shall return.

Resuming our proofs for God's perfect infinity, Ockham rejects the remaining two ways[305]—of final causality and eminence—adopted by Duns Scotus. By the first of these Duns reasoned that the human will inclines to infinite good as that which it desires beyond everything finite; and since perfect infinity does not contradict the highest good if it is infinite, perfect infinity is compatible with the most perfect being which is the will's end. Ockham dissents on the ground that the philosophers deny that the will can desire infinite good; for it can only rightly

---

[299] Ibid.

[300] Ad principale dico quod infiniti effectus simul producti arguunt infinitam causam, sed infinit effectus successive producibiles non arguunt causam infinitam (ibid.).

[301] Ibid., q. 18.

[302] Ibid., q. 19.

[303] Cf. my Paris and Oxford Universities in the Thirteenth and Fourteenth Centuries, 171–3.

[304] See Boehner, Collected Articles, 150–1.

[305] He does so briefly in Quodlibet III, q. 1.

follow the judgement of reason—although as we shall see in chapter seven it is of course free to dissent from it—and that cannot be of infinite good. Nor is it in the power of the will to desire what is perfectly infinite; even if the will could desire something greater than anything finite, which Ockham denies, the result would perhaps be extensively—i.e. eternally—infinite, through choosing between imaginary greater and lesser goods, but not intensively infinite.[306]

The way of eminence for Duns Scotus enables us to prove that since there cannot be anything more perfect than the most eminent being, such a being must be infinite. Among the arguments he employs to show that perfect infinity and perfect being are not contradictory is that drawn from Anselm's ontological proof that a being than which nothing greater can be conceived without contradiction is infinite.[307]

Ockham replies first that it cannot be sufficiently proved that God is the most eminent, and second that the most eminent could be finite, for there is no evidence to the contrary. In Anselm's ontological argument, Ockham distinguishes between a true thought and non-contradictory thought; while every true thought is non-contradictory, not every con-contradictory thought is true, as we can think that there is a star both without contradiction and truth. Applied to the notion of a being than which no higher can be conceived, its freedom from contradiction is no guarantee of its truth. A true thought and a non-contradictory thought are equally thinkable; they differ therefore not as thoughts but according to whether what is thought exists also *in re*, and is true, or only in the intellect as a fiction. Hence a non-contradictory thought of a being than which nothing greater can be conceived does not prove its existence.[308] Moreover such a being can be understood either as existing actually (*de facto*) or conditionally, as that which if it existed would be greatest. Ockham interprets Anselm in the first sense, to mean that nothing which does not actually exist can be greater than that which does not actually exist: in other words only that which actually exists can be conceived as greater than anything else, and this, for Ockham, presupposes that there cannot be an infinite regress.[309]

That hardly bridges the gulf between them, which is precisely over the self-consistency—i.e. non-contradictoriness—of of a thought as the criterion of its truth. The ontological proof assumes their identity; it is thereby self-evident, since knowledge of the terms carries assent to their truth, namely, that in virtue of our ability to conceive a being than which no greater can be conceived, such a being

---

[306] *Quodlibet* VII, q. 20.

[307] *Ibid.*, q. 21.

[308] Et ad primam probationem dico quod aliquid esse summe cogitabile potest intelligi dupliciter: vel vera cogitatione, vel cogitatione non includente contradictionem, quia non omnis cogitatio non includens contradictionem est vera cogitatio, sicut cogitare me super astra esse non includit contradictionem . . .

Et ultra dico quod illud quod est in re non est magis cogitabile non includens contradictionem quam illud quod est in intellectu tantum. Sed bene est magis cogitabile vera cogitatione, et ideo non probatur tale cogitabile summum existere quo maius non potest cogitari cogitatione non includente contradictionem (*ibid.*).

[309] *Ibid.*

must exist: what is conceivable without contradiction must—so far as it concerns God—by definition be true. That is the opposite of Ockham's position where truth consists in the relation of what is thought to what exists; it is not therefore self-contained within the terms of a proposition unless the terms have ontological import; which can only be known intuitively. For that reason a self-evident proposition must be one that is universally true, such that whenever one term is predicated of another, we assent to their conjunction. That in practice means, as we discussed in the previous chapter, when a genus is predicated (universally) of its subject by the first essential mode, giving an essential definition. Hence in virtue of knowing man and animal, through experience, we can define man as an animal in a self-evident proposition. That is just what we cannot do of God, in having neither intuitive knowledge of him nor a genus under which he can be defined, other than in transcendental terms. Our knowledge of him is therefore neither self-evident nor intuitive because it surpasses natural experience.

We are not, however, left with nothing in consequence. On the contrary, all believers share with Anselm the same conception of God as a being than which there is no better, prior, or more perfect;[310] and as we shall shortly consider, it is on that same foundation that Ockham himself proves God's existence, though not by Anselm's way.

Before turning to that aspect, however, we must complete what cannot be demonstrated of God which, as we have said, extends to all his attributes, for the reason that we have no evident or self-evident knowledge of him. Ockham concludes his discussion of God's infinity with Aristotle's and Averroes's interpretation of the matter. Where Duns Scotus understands them as holding that perfect—intensive—infinity is demonstrable of God, Ockham confines it to extensive infinity. For Scotus God's infinity is intensive because God as first mover can move by infinite movement and so has infinite powers. For Ockham, on the other hand, this movement is infinite only by duration, and it does not require greater power to make an effect last for a thousand years than for one day; for as we have said where there is no contrary power, the same effect will continue indefinitely. Nor can Duns's inference, that God as infinite mover has thereby infinitely intensive power, to be drawn from 'Aristotle's words in the *Physics* (book eight); to Ockham they are designed to show that a first mover, in moving infinitely, is indivisible and without the magnitude: for a magnitude cannot be infinite and there cannot be infinite movement of what is finite.[311]

That God is actually infinite by perfect infinity is certain by faith; it can also be persuaded by reason because God can make a more perfect species than any which exists, and that cannot be done by a finite power, which is circumscribed; God must therefore be infinite in his own nature. Nor is his infinity proportionate to anything finite, whether as mover to what is moved or as measure to what is measured; such a proportion holds only among finite beings in virtue of having a limit beyond which they cannot go.[312]

[310] *Quodlibet* I, q. I.
[311] *Quodlibet* VII, qq. 22 and 23.　　　　[312] *Ibid.*, q. 24.

This is as far as Ockham is prepared to go in proving God's infinity. Throughout his discussion he has argued according to the criteria of the philosophers, not because he has renounced the role of theologian, nor, as Guelluy more than once suggests, because he argues as a logician,[313] but for the very opposite reason, that arguments—initially not his—involving philosophical and logical criteria must be judged philosophically and logically. Ockham's novelty did not lie in inventing such arguments, as his criticism here of Duns Scotus, for one exemplifies; he came to a tradition of nearly two centuries' standing of theological propositions reached from logical and philosophical grounds. Ockham met them on those grounds. He differed not as a philosopher among theologians but in the consistency with which he distinguished philosophical from theological truth. He did so from a more rigorous and circumscribed view of reason's scope than the majority of his predecessors; which explains the paradox that his radicalism was not due to allowing natural reason to run riot but to denying it access to what had traditionally been taken to be within its purview.

That brings us to causality, which offers the only way of proving anything about God, namely his existence as the source of everything else. It is perhaps an irony that Ockham as the thinker most associated with undermining Scholasticism through his supposed denial of cause should have not only employed it throughout his system, from demonstration to nature, but also treated it as the one means of inferring God's existence. That does not, however, apply to every kind of cause; of the three that could be predicated of God, Ockham disregards formal cause and denies the demonstrability of final cause; there therefore remains only efficient cause which we shall shortly see, can give proof, although not in a *demonstratio potissima*, of God. First, however, let us examine the reasons for the inadequacy of final cause.

Ockham defines final cause as something for love or desire of which an action or actions are performed. It must accordingly be distinguished on the one hand from what is merely loved or desired without leading to an action on its account, and on the other from something real which has actually to exist in order to be a final cause. It is the feature of a final cause that it can be a cause and yet not be, because it suffices to act for a desired end—which may be merely in the mind—to have a final cause.[314] From that it follows that by its nominal definition, at least, a final cause is distinguished from the nominal definition of an efficient cause, which can be described as that from whose being or presence something else follows. Whether they are really distinct can only be known on faith, by which it can be held that sometimes they are the same, as God is both the efficient and final cause of many effects. By natural reason, however, the same cannot be proved either from self-evident knowledge or from experience because a final cause cannot be proved

---

313 E.g. *Philosophie et Théologie chez Guillaume d'Ockham*, 76: 'Au probleme religieux c'est substitué un problème de logique'.

314 Circa primum dico quod causalitas finis non est aliud nisi esse amatum et desideratum ab agente efficienter, propter quod amatum sit effectus . . .
Ex quo patet ultra quod finis quandoque est causa, quandoque non est, quia aliquando finis desideratur quando non est, quia non est aliud esse causam finalem quam desiderari vel amari modo predicto (*Quodlibet* IV, q. 1).

of any effect.[315] We are therefore left only with immediate experience of what is desired or loved. By the same token God cannot be proved the final cause as the end of something, whether 'end' is taken to mean either what the will loves or determines in advance, or an effect or action intended by an agent; in this second sense, where what is first in intention is last in execution, God can never be the end or final cause of anything; if he were, he would then be of no greater power than anything else; for nothing which is produced excels in power that which produces it. By the first sense, which is how Ockham understands the question, there can only be a final cause where actions are freely willed; those which are from natural necessity, as invariable and uniform, cannot be proved or known either self-evidently or intuitively to be on account of a final cause decreed by the will.[316]

Thus qualified the question is whether created—or as Ockham calls them here second—intelligences can be proved to have God as their final cause. The answer is once again negative. God cannot be proved the final cause either of a created intelligence in itself or its effect, because a created intelligence either acts from knowledge and freely or from necessity; if freely it can itself be the end decided by its will, and so there is nothing to say that it acts on account of God. If on the other hand it acts from necessity, then it cannot be proved that it has other than a natural end to which it is determined unknowingly. Nor can it be demonstrated that God is the final cause of a second intelligence's being, for it cannot be shown as self-evident or by experience that it is the effect of something which can produce it; experience can tell us only of inferior beings. That applies to an efficient as well as a final cause of a created intelligence. Even if it could be evidently proved that God were the final cause of the effects of a second intelligence, it would still not follow that he was their efficient cause, for the reason, as we have just seen, that a final and an efficient cause cannot be proved to be the same.[317] We can, however, know from experience that God can be the final cause of effects produced by a second intelligence. Moreover, anyone can have the experience of performing works in honour of God as the total end,[318] as we shall see in chapter seven.

That is as far as we are able to go in experience of God naturally. As immediate to those who possess it, it cannot be regarded as either evident or demonstrable knowledge, though it is none the less real for that, as with so much else that is not demonstrable. In this case the lack of demonstrability springs from the very nature of a final cause in being freely willed; for that reason it is not invariable and so is

---

[315] Nam primo modo loquendo dico, quod secundum veritatem fidei, non quilibet effectus habet causam finalem distinctam ab efficiente, quia quandoque idem est causa finalis et efficiens, sicut deus quandoque est efficiens et finis multorum effectuum, saltem semper debet esse causa finalis secundum rectam rationem. Secundo vero modo loquendo dicerem, si nullam auctoritatem reciperem, quod non potest probari ex per se notis nec per experientiam quod quilibet effectus habeat causam finalem distinctam ab efficiente, quia non potest probari sufficienter quod quilibet effectus habeat aliquam causam finalem. (*ibid.*). Also II, chs. 4 and 6.

[316] *Quodlibet, ibid.*, q. 2; *SP, ibid.*

[317] *Quodlibet* IV, q. 2.

[318] Quia quilibet experitur quod potest facere opera propter honorem dei tamquam propter totalem finem. Tertio dico quod potest evidenter sciri per experientiam quod deus potest esse causa finalis effectuum productorum (*ibid.*).

not entailed from the effect. Thus there is nothing to say that if God were not the final cause of everything many things would be necessary, because there is no means of establishing that any final end is necessary or uncreatable or that that upon which all things do not depend as their final end is imperfect, or that the universe is ordered in dependence upon one principle. Indeed by natural reason it can only be demonstrated that there are two or more ends of the same thing, as for example when someone who goes to a tavern to eat and drink, both eating and drinking can be equally the final cause of his visit; even if there can only be one end for one effect, there can be diverse ends of different effects.[319] Accepting, however, that God as first intelligence is the final cause of a second intelligence in itself, as opposed to its effects, he can then also be proved to be its efficient cause; for if the second cause has a final cause, it must also have an efficient cause. Since this cause cannot be posterior to the second intelligence it must be the first intelligence, assuming that there is only one, as that which is alone prior to it.[320] But there is no way of proving God's final causality.

Nor his efficient causality of all things. On the one hand there is nothing to prove that many things, namely separated substances like the celestial bodies and the intellective soul, are not their own sufficient causes of their own effects, which would make a first cause of such causes otiose. On the other hand, if it could be proved that God were the sufficient cause of all things else, and not a partial or insufficient cause, all other things efficient causes would be superfluous. Accordingly whether as total and immediate or partial and indirect cause, God's efficiency cannot be proved.[321] In other words there is no evidence for one first cause: the only primacy which Ockham acknowledges in this connection is that of perfection not causality, because God is different in kind from all other causes.[322] From that standpoint it is our inability to establish God's unicity that prevents us from proving him first cause by efficiency. Not that it cannot be persuaded by reason that God is efficient or moving cause of an effect; otherwise it would be purposeless to speak of efficient causes if something in the universe could not cause something effectively.[323]

That persuasion can be on the assumption that everything depends essentially upon God, which would be untrue unless God were cause of everything. If he were not, then either something else than God would be uncreated or there would be an infinite series of causes. Now if this other cause were uncreated there would be the

---

[319] Ibid.; also SP, II, ch. 4, 37 a. E.g.: Ex quibus apparet quod eiusdem rei possunt esse plures cause finalis, et non solum insufficientes sed etiam sufficientes.

[320] Quodlibet IV, q. I.

[321] Secundo dico quod non potest probari naturali ratione quod deus sit causa efficiens alicuius effectus . . . Ex istis sequitur demonstrative quod non potest probari quod deus sit causa mediata alicuius effectus, quia si posset probari quod deus esset causa mediata respectu unius effectus, posset probari quod esset causa immediata respectu alterius in genere cause efficientis. Sed secundum non potest probari; ergo nec primum. Ex hoc sequitur quod nec potest probari naturaliter quod deus sit causa efficiens totalis cuiuscumque effectus nec partialis (Quodlibet II, q. I).

[322] Inter illa prima tamen est aliquod efficiens simpliciter primum respectu aliorum, non in causalitate quacumque sed in perfectione, quia oportet quod differant specie (ibid.).

[323] Ibid.

same infinite regress which would follow if God were not first cause; but if it is created then God is its cause. God is therefore first cause. He is moreover the immediate cause of all things, because everything other than God depends no less upon him than one creature depends upon another creature, which it does as its immediate cause. Therefore God must also be the immediate cause of any creature.[324] The main impediment would be actual sin on the creature's part, but that does not prevent the same act from being caused unculpably by another cause, namely God, as the same act of will has both a natural cause (from cognition) and a free cause (from the will).[325] As universal efficient cause, God's causality extends to mental or logical beings as well; for by the time of the *Quodlibets* Ockham had embraced the *intellectio* theory of concepts, by which all mental acts were really part of the intellect. Thus the truth of fictitious terms like 'chymera' or propositions such as 'God creates nothing' lies in their existence as words and propositions not in their real signification (i.e. in their personal supposition) as we have considered in chapter three.

That these conclusions are only persuasions, not demonstrations, is due to their assuming what cannot be demonstrated: namely that everything depends upon God. Among these assumptions is God's unicity as the unique source of everything else. It forms the subject of the opening questions of the first *Quodlibet*. As indicated earlier it has gained perhaps disproportionate significance through the redoubtable Boehner's defence of Ockham's views there against the misrepresentations of De Wulf. Its interest is that it forms, as Boehner implicitly recognises,[326] the logical—as opposed to temporal—transition to Ockham's proofs for God by primacy of perfection in the Questions on the *Physics*. That is achieved through the second of the two definitions discussed in the first *Quodlibet*, which in not positing God's unicity is for that very reason demonstrable of God. Even so we must remember that Ockham stated the same proof for God's existence in the *Ordinatio* as that later found in the Questions on the *Physics* before either that work or the *Quodlibet* was written.

Of the two definitions of God in the first question of the first *Quodlibet*, one is an affirmative statement of God as something nobler and better than everything else; the other is the Anselmian negative of God as that than which nothing is better or more perfect. By neither can we prove God's unicity: by the first we have no evident or self-evident knowledge of God so defined; if we had then his unicity could also be made evident, for there could not be two or more Gods, each at once more perfect than the other, without each being also more imperfect than the other, which is a manifest contradiction.[327] The second definition similarly does not prove God's unicity, but it can prove his existence. For that, as we shall now discuss, nothing more is required than to establish the necessity for a

[324] *Quodlibet* III, q. 3.
[325] *Ibid.*
[326] *Collected Articles*, 149–51, 399–420. The text of the first question of *Quodlibet* I is edited with abridgements on 406–7, and the relevant question (126) from the Questions on the *Physics* on 408–9; both are translated in *Selected Writings*, 136–40.
[327] *Quodlibet* I, q. I.

first efficient being, from the impossibility of having an infinite regress of actual beings and so the need to stop at a first being to which no other is prior or more perfect. That, however, is not the same as saying that there is only one such being. Hence to prove the existence of such a being is not also to prove its unicity.[328] The condition of proving God's being therefore is precisely to dissociate being from unicity as indeed from omnipotence,[329] or any other of God's attributes save the notion of primacy by perfection in its negative connotation. Anything else entails evident knowledge which is not at the disposal of a *viator*. For that reason in the same quodlibetal question Ockham rejects all of Duns Scotus's seven ways—without discussing Duns's arguments for God's unicity. His own proof for God's existence do, however, take their point of departure in those of Duns Scotus from a first efficient cause. To these we must now turn.

As we have said, Ockham's discussion of God's existence is to be found in both the *Ordinatio* and the Questions on the *Physics*. It largely takes the same form in both, of analysing and replying to Duns's arguments on three main problems, which are stated as separate questions in the Questions on the *Physics*: Whether in causes ordered essentially (1) the second cause depends upon the first, (2) the higher is more perfect, and (3) whether essentially ordered causes must be simultaneous in order to produce an essentially ordered effect. From these follow the two central questions of the relation of production to conservation in proving a first efficient cause. In this sequence, which is largely his response to the arguments of Duns Scotus, Ockham as in his discussion of univocal concepts of God, surpasses what Duns says in a new resolution rather than merely demolishing it.

Taking the discussion of Scotus's arguments in *Ordinatio* as our framework, each of Ockham's first three questions in the Questions on the *Physics* represents Scotus's conclusions cited in the former work. They are established in support of Duns's initial argument that there must be a first being which has a threefold primacy as efficient cause, final cause and most eminent. If there were no such being there would be an infinite regress; for since being which is effectible cannot be caused by nothing or by itself, it must be caused by something else. It must therefore have a first cause or there will be an infinity of causes.[330] The latter is impossible. Therefore there must be a first cause.

These three conclusions of Scotus were in response to the objection that Aristotle had accepted an infinite regression in generation.[331] They were designed to explain the difference between accidental causes and essential causes. Whereas, Duns held, among accidental causes there is merely the comparison between cause and effect, in causes essentially ordered, one is the cause of the other by its own nature, leading

---

[328] Tertio dico quod unitas dei non potest evidenter probari accipiendo deum secundo modo . . . Sciendum tamen est quod potest demonstrari deum esse secundo modo prius dicto, quia aliter esset processus in infinitum, nisi aliquid in entibus quo nihil esset aliquid prius nec perfectius. Sed ex hoc non sequitur quod potest demonstrari quod tantum est unum tale; sed hoc fide tantum tenetur (*ibid.*). Also *Ordinatio*, d. 2, q. 10, 356–7.

[329] *Ibid.*

[330] *Ordinatio*, d. 2, q. 10, 338.

[331] *De generatione et corruptione*, II, 338 b, 5–12.

to the three characteristics of dependence, difference in perfection, and simultaneity in causation. That these preclude infinity Duns sought to show by further proofs to which Ockham replies in the Questions on the *Physics*;[332] Duns also argued that the first being must be both necessary and one.[333]

Ockham does not accept these conclusions as they stand. In the *Ordinatio*, he argues against the notion itself of a distinction between essential and accidental causes in the form expressed by Duns. For example it is true to say that hot necessarily heats, but not that white heats necessarily, and yet sometimes white and hot can accidentally be the same thing; in that case both white and hot can be said to give heat necessarily. But from that it does not follow formally that if heat heats then white heats because, as Ockham is sure Duns himself understood, this holds only in *sensu divisionis*, where the predicate (heat) is affirmed contingently of the subject (white) and not of the truth of the proposition as a whole (in *sensu compositionis*).[334]

An accidental cause is one which acts by something distinct, additional to the whole in which it acts, as fire can be said to heat accidentally or man to think accidentally; for should fire cease and heat remain, heat would continue to heat, as the intellective soul would continue to think if no longer joined to a human body. Accordingly the action of heating or thinking in belonging essentially to the part belongs only accidentally to the whole. An essential agent or cause, on the other hand, is such of itself and not by something else really distinct, in the way that heat itself is the cause of heat without which there would be no heat; and similarly with the intellective soul and thinking.[335]

Of Duns's three differences between essential and accidental causes the first does not hold because it would mean that the second cause depended always upon the first cause for its effects when frequently the first is as dependent upon the second, as the sun depends upon its inferior causes for its effects. Alternatively it would mean that the second cause depended upon the first for its being, and that would apply to every cause, including accidental causes, which Duns denies; in fact, God can conserve an effect without its cause. Or finally Duns's statement could imply that a second cause received its active power or other influence from the first cause, which is again untenable, since that could only be by local movement or a substantial or accidental form, none of which is received by a second cause from a first. Furthermore Duns himself says that an object and the intellect are two partial causes in an act of knowing with neither dependent upon the other; but if they each act by their own separate power they are not always mutually dependent.[336]

To the second difference—of superiority—Ockham replies that the superiority of the first cause can be understood as that of either perfection or power, namely lack of limitation. The first begs the question whether such causes are of a different

---

[332] *Ordinatio, ibid.*, 338–40; Questions on the *Physics*, 135, discussed 395–6 below.
[333] *Ordinatio, ibid.*, 340–2.
[334] *Ibid.*, 342–4.
[335] *Ibid.*, 344–5.
[336] *Ibid.*, 347–8.

order. The second implies that what is more unlimited is more perfect than what is more limited, which is simply false; for sometimes the converse is true: for example, according to Duns's own example, an inanimate celestial body is more imperfect than an animate being, say an ass or other animal, and yet the former is more unlimited as a cause.[337]

The third difference, that essentially ordered causes must always act together, similarly cannot be maintained, as is shown by Duns's own example that some animals, generated by propagation through the concurrence of a celestial body and a particular cause, could be produced through putrifaction by the first universal cause acting alone.[338]

In the Questions on the *Physics*, Ockham goes further than these replies in stating his own position on each of these issues. He amplifies the last just discussed in three conclusions. The first merely adds the example of a worm produced by the sun alone without the concurrence of another worm. The second is that a universal cause can as well produce alone a perfect effect which it produces with other causes, when the effect is indivisible, such as a substantial form; otherwise, however, the effect is perfect when the causes act together as in the case of heat generated from both sun and fire. But thirdly, a general cause can only produce the same effect in kind, never the same numerical effect: if that was Duns's meaning, he was correct, but he said otherwise.[339]

In the second question, on the greater perfection of a first cause, Ockham substitutes for his previous distinction between more perfect and more powerful two other distinctions. The first is between a total and a partial cause; the second between something which is more perfect because it is absolutely perfect in its own nature, and more perfect because of a more perfect condition or predication. Here, too, there are three conclusions: first, that a total superior cause—such as the sun or God—is more perfect than an inferior cause; second, that a partial superior cause is not usually more perfect than a second cause, when perfection is understood absolutely in the first sense, because the sun as a superior partial cause in man's generation is not in its own nature more perfect than man. In the second sense of perfection, however, the superior partial cause is more perfect. That is the third conclusion; it is supported by Ockham's previous reply in the *Ordinatio* to the first of these questions, namely that while a second cause alone cannot produce an effect of its own kind, the superior cause can act without it, as the sun can produce a man without Socrates and with Plato; hence the sun is more independent than either, and in that sense more perfect.[340]

Finally Ockham's answer to the first question brings us to the threshold of the proof for God; in it he distinguishes between existence and conservation as they concern essentially ordered causes. Socrates depends for his existence upon Plato, his father, since a son cannot be naturally caused without a father; but he is not

[337] *Ibid.*, 349–50.
[338] *Ibid.*, 350.
[339] Questions on the *Physics*, q. 134.
[340] *Ibid.*, q. 133.

conserved by Plato; for once in existence Plato can live without Socrates.[341] Not only does that prove how a second cause is independent of a first; it also indicates the difference between establishing a first efficient cause from production as opposed to conservation. In the Questions on the *Physics* this forms two separate questions: whether a first efficient cause can be sufficiently proved from production as distinct from conservation; and whether a first efficient cause can be sufficiently proved from conservation.

In the first of these Ockham takes Duns Scotus's eight arguments which are in the affirmative.[342] They are, first, that essentially ordered effects have a cause; therefore there must be one cause that does not belong to the totality of ordered causes; otherwise it would be the cause of itself. Second, the totality of what is caused is dependent upon something which is not itself part of that totality; if it were, the same thing would then be dependent upon itself. Third, no efficient first cause would mean an infinity of essentially ordered causes at the same time, since those which are essentially ordered all concur in the same effect. Fourth, what is prior is nearer to the first principle; therefore where there is no first principle nothing is essentially prior. Fifth, a superior cause is more perfect in its mode of causation; hence an infinitely superior cause is infinitely perfect. Sixth, efficiency does not imply imperfection; hence it can be in something without imperfection; but if it is in nothing dependent without imperfection a first cause would be impossible. Seventh, if there were not a first efficient cause, an infinity of accidentally ordered causes would be impossible, because such an infinity can only be successive, not simultaneous; and for that there must be a being of infinite duration. Eighth and last, perpetual deformity depends upon something permanent which is independent of the succession of things; for successive things are all of the same kind. There is therefore something upon which everything successive depends, and which is different from the proximate cause that is part of the succession. Accordingly while all that belongs to the succession is caused, the cause preceding it is separate and uncaused.

For Ockham these arguments are inadequate to prove a first efficient cause from production alone; and from the first, second and last it could equally be concluded that God could not make the world perpetual: for as there cannot, according to Duns, be a cause beyond the totality of causes, there could not be a day beyond the multitude of future days, or indeed a point beyond the multitude of points in a line, or a reflexive act beyond the multitude of reflexive acts.

More specifically, to the first of Duns's reasons, Ockham concedes that the totality of things is itself caused; but even so by natural reason there could still be an infinity of causes among them, as Aristotle shows in the case of accidentally ordered causes, where one cause can exist and be the cause of another, in the way that one man is caused by another. The contrary cannot be proved from production. Nor does it follow that the same thing is the cause of itself for the very

---

[341] *Ibid.*, q. 134.

[342] *Ibid.*, q. 135. As we mentioned (see note 332), most of these are given in the *Ordinatio*, q. 2, d. 10 (338–40), but Ockham does not there reply to them individually.

reason that the totality of these causes is not through one cause but through each cause causing the other. The second argument similarly cannot be proved from production, by which there would again be an infinity of causes: for once produced, one cause no longer depends upon another save by conservation, which Duns denies. Hence the multitude does not depend upon one cause but only upon itself in the sense of each of its causes. Conservation likewise will only prove the third argument; whereas everything which conserves coexists mediately or immediately with what is conserved, the same does not hold for everything which produces. There could therefore be an infinity of things produced, although they are actually finite.

Of the remaining arguments the fourth and the sixth are inadequate for the same reason, and the fifth has previously been met. Neither the seventh nor the eighth can be sustained on the basis of production, because there can be an infinity of accidentally ordered causes, as we have seen in the first reply, without requiring an infinite nature or which their succession depends. By production, therefore, there is no means of showing why one cause need be dependent upon a cause other than that which immediately causes it, and hence why an infinity of causes is impossible so long as one cause can cause another. It is just this infinite regress that arguments from production cannot disprove. As Ockham expresses the problem in the *Ordinatio*,

It seems that the primacy of an efficient cause can be more evidently proved by the conservation of a thing by its cause than by production, accepting production to mean that something receives being immediately after non-existence. The reason that it is difficult or impossible to prove against the philosophers that there is not an infinite procession in causes of the same nature, in the manner in which they have stated that man generates man infinitely. It is also difficult to prove from production that one man could not be produced by another as his total cause. And if these two (propositions) were true it would be hard to prove that such an infinity was impossible unless there was one eternal being upon which this infinite totality depended.[343]

Ockham's proof of such a first being by conservation runs as follows: Whatever is really produced by something is really conserved by something as long as it remains actually in being. But this effect is produced. Therefore it is conserved by something as long as it remains in being. Now this conserver can either be produced by something else or not. If it cannot, it is the first efficient cause in virtue of being the first conserving cause; for every conserving cause is an efficient cause. If, on the other hand, this conserver is produced by something else, then the same alternative recurs; and we have to ask again whether its cause is uncaused or caused, and so on infinitely, or to stop at some being which conserves without in any way being conserved. Such an efficient cause is the first efficient cause. But there cannot be an infinite procession in conserving causes, because there would then be an actual infinity, which—following Aristotle[344]—is impossible. The reason is that whatever conserves something else, whether indirectly or directly, coexists with

---

343 *Ordinatio*, d. 2, q. 10, 355.
344 *Metaphysics*, II, ch. 2, 994 a, 1–994 b, 31, cited in *Ordinatio*, 356.

what is conserved. Hence everything conserved requires the actual existence of everything which conserves. That is not the case with what is produced. Accordingly while an infinite succession could be upheld in productive causes without an actual infinity an infinity cannot be maintained in conserving causes which is not an actual infinity.[345]

The difference then between an infinity by production and by conservation is twofold. In the first place, conservation demands the existence of what conserves simultaneously with what is conserved, so that the existence of the latter always presupposes the former; in productive causes, on the other hand, what is produced can—once produced—exist independently of what produces it. In the second place therefore, an infinite succession in what is conserved must mean an actual infinity, since it entails equally the actual existence of all that conserves, as opposed to only the possible existence of what can be produced in an infinite succession. Accordingly it is on the impossibility of an actual infinity of causes, which follows necessarily from conservation, that the proof of a first cause—at which the process stops, or rather from which it begins—is founded.

Ockham's own position depends upon the assumption that production both entails conservation and can be distinguished from conservation by natural reason —as opposed to faith where God is the conserving cause of all that exists. That this is contradictory can be shown as follows. If production entails conservation and a thing once in existence is independent of its producer, it is by the same token independent of its conserver, since from natural causes the opposite cannot be proved: for if, as Ockham argues, Socrates can continue to exist after the non-existence of Plato who produces him, he can continue to be conserved after the non-existence of Plato. The alternative is to posit a conserving cause other than Plato; but if this cannot be proved from the production of one thing by another, as man generates man, it cannot be proved from their conservation, because if the totality of essentially ordered causes does not always act together in production, what natural evidence is there that it does so in conservation? And as the totality of productive causes known by natural reason is not through one cause but through each cause causing the other, the same must apply to conservation which accompanies production. If on the other hand, conservation can be distinguished from production, then this must be either in what causes the cause or in something

---

[345] In ista questione dico breviter quod sic. Quod probabtur: quia quidquid realiter producitur ab aliquo, realiter vel ab aliquo conservatur, quamdiu manet in esse reali, manifestum est; sed ille effectus producitur, certum est; igitur ab aliquo conservatur, quamdiu manet. De illo conservante quero: aut potest potest produci ab aliquo, aut non. Si non, est efficiens primum sicut est conservans primum, quia omne conservans est efficiens. Si autem istud conservans producitur ab aliquo, de illo alio quero sicut prius; et ita vel oportet procedere in infinitum, vel oportet stare ad aliquid quod est conservans et nullo modo conservatum; et tale efficiens est primum efficiens. Sed non est processus in infinitum in conservantibus, quia tunc aliqua infinita essent in actu, quod est impossibile; nam omne conservans aliud, sive mediate sive immediate, est simul cum conservato; et ideo omne conservatum requirit actualiter omne conservans. Non autem omne productum requirit omne producens actualiter, mediate vel immediate. Et ideo quamvis posset poni processus in infinitum in productionibus sine infinitate actuali, non potest tamen poni processus in infinitum in conservationibus sine infinitate actuali (Questions on the *Physics*, q. 136, edited by Boehner, *Collected Articles*, 408–9). The proof in the *Ordinatio*, d. 2, q. 10, 355–6, is almost identical.

else: it cannot be in what causes the cause for the same reasons already given, that one thing can continue to exist after its cause no longer exists. It must therefore exist in another conserving cause, and then we can ask of Ockham, as Ockham asked of Duns, is this cause created or uncreated? with the alternatives of a first conserving cause or an infinite regress. If the latter, then there is no more reason why there should be an actual infinity than in the case of a first efficient productive cause; for if conservation cannot be proved of causes acting naturally, and production implies an infinity of possible causes, then either conservation must also imply a possible infinity, or it will be contradictory to posit an actual infinity for one and not for the other.

If Ockham does not appear to overcome the limitations he saw in the argument for a first efficient cause from production, the interest of his own arguments lies as much in his attempt to improve upon it by conservation as in how far he succeeded. It is the final testimony that, far from rejecting either causality or, in some degree, God's demonstrability, he accepted both and sought to derive one from the other.

Ockham then did not close the path of either demonstrable knowledge of God's existence or conceptual knowledge of his nature; he merely narrowed it to conservation on the one hand and univocal predication on the other. In each case knowledge of God, however circumscribed, remained. The effect therefore of Ockham's activity was an attempt to strengthen and redefine the natural supports of theological truth rather than their wholesale dismantling. Whatever else Ockham left it remained a recognisable theological structure, not a series of *disjecta membra*.

CHAPTER SIX

God's nature

The previous chapter has shown the essentially inferential non-scientific nature of theological discourse. As inevident truths held on faith, the propositions of theology are neither demonstrable nor known intuitively through experience. That makes the procedure of theology different from that of the sciences. In theology the role of knowledge is only illustrative or analogical, not demonstrative; and ratiocination is accordingly restricted to establishing legitimate conclusions from premises which are themselves neither evident not self-evident. Theological enquiry is therefore governed by what must at once be believed and what can be deduced from belief, whether of God or man.

Now it was his stress upon both these facets that distinguishes Ockham's treatment of the central questions of theology. On the one hand it has its point of departure in the exclusively creditive status of all theological propositions, whose creditibility must be judged by their consonance with the articles of faith. On the other hand, for that very reason, theological inference can transcend the *de facto* limits of the present dispensation or its compatibility with natural experience; for the foundation of all such inference is the first article of the creed, of belief in one omnipotent God, creator of heaven and earth, and of all things visible and invisible. If oneness, necessity, and infinite perfection define God's own nature as supreme being, infinite freedom, flowing from his perfections, characterises his actions towards what is not God; and whatever is not God is in turn characterised by the very absence of those perfections upon which it is dependent in God. The relations of God to himself and to his creatures are thus the two poles of theological discourse; they represent the dichotomy between necessary and contingent being: all therefore that must be said of God need not be said of his creatures in the name of the same theological truth of his omnipotence. We have already discussed its grounds in chapter one, and seen both there, especially over intuitive knowledge of non-existents, and subsequently, its application to a range of epistemological questions. Its full theological import will become apparent when we reach the subject of grace, merit and justification in the next chapter. But no matter what its application, its justification is solely theological; so, therefore, is its logic which has as its middle term an essential definition of God as omnipotent, where omnipotent means the capacity to do whatever is not contradictory (whether of God's actions or his nature). By its means there can be an indefinite series of conclusions that God can do differently from how he has ordained, above all in conjunction with the premise that as first cause he can do immediately whatever he does normally through second causes. All such actions refer to God's actions *ad extra*, just because they are of what is mutable and contingent and exist only at all in virtue of his willing. Towards God's own nature, however, the same principles do not hold: logic cannot be applied to explain God's triunity, and it can only be invoked to exclude all diversity from the relation between his essence and attributes, as we shall see in both cases shortly.

There are therefore two different levels of theological discourse, as they concern God in himself, and God as creator: only in the latter aspect can anything be said which is not itself expressly held on authority; and that is only possible on the basis of what is expressly held on authority of God. Nothing, on the other hand, can be inferred from his own nature about his own nature because he is unknowable beyond the definition and names of him received as revealed truth. Accordingly the distinction is between God's ineffability in himself and his self-relevation through his creatures; and Ockham is distinctive for the rigour with which he differentiates one from the other and his acceptance of their divergent implications. He is the first scholastic thinker systematically both to deny any order between God's essence and his attributes and to pursue the theological consequences of God's omnipotence upon human acts and their relation to the supernatural virtues. Each was to be among his most potent legacies to the later middle ages, and each was many times to be taken—as his restriction of evident knowledge to intuitive experience of individual existence was to be taken—to extremes which in Ockham's own terms constituted a *reductio ad absurdum*. For Ockham himself the differences between these aspects sprang from the nature of theology itself as a collection of habits embracing both the divine and the created. We must therefore distinguish between the theological consequences which follow from his view of theology and the wider doctrinal consequences to which these consequences were to lead. Only the first is our immediate concern here.

This chapter will consider God's nature, both in relation to its attributes and to the divine persons together with his knowledge of everything through divine ideas; and the next chapter God in his omnipotence as creator and his relation to what is created, especially human acts.

I ESSENCE AND ATTRIBUTES

The problem of God's attributes is precisely whether they correspond to anything real in God which can be distinguished as part of his essence. For Ockham there is no such distinction. His grounds are the familiar ones, that of no simple being can there be more than one simple concept, and of God, as supremely simple, there can be no proper simple concept at all in this world. The first follows from the principle, discussed in chapter three, that nothing simple has essential difference; its terms are therefore synonyms in always signifying the same thing in the same way with no distinction between one part and another; and correspondingly its concepts will be of the same thing and themselves of the same kind.[1] In the case of God we saw in the last chapter that while there can be quidditative concepts of him—since a denominative or connotative concept like 'creative' in turn presupposes a quidditative concept of a creative being[2]—they cannot be proper to him because God cannot be known in himself *pro statu isto*. We thus have neither intuitive nor abstractive knowledge of him as he is, but can either form composite concepts which are proper to him or simple concepts such as those of being and wisdom which are common to him and creatures.[3] Consequently on the one hand there is no order in God by which one term is more proper to him than another; and on the other hand the terms proper to him, as composite, are not synonymous with him or one another, whether synonyms are taken strictly as being absolutely the same or broadly, as signifying and connoting the same. In this second sense, where nothing is connoted by one term which is not connoted by the other, many concrete and abstract terms are treated by many, including Aristotle, as synonymous with pairs like 'God' and 'divinity', 'man' and 'humanity', 'animal' and 'animality', each signifying substances as opposed to one standing for the whole and the other for a part.[4] In the *Logic* where he first states the distinction Ockham, as we have seen, accepts synonyms in this second sense, but not in the *Ordinatio* into which he subsequently interpolates it.[5] Neither in this wider sense nor in the first strict sense does he allow that these are synonyms of God, for the very reason that our concepts of God are not simple; they do not therefore correspond to one and the same thing, but one part can stand for something for which the other part cannot. That applies to terms like 'God' and 'deity' each of which is formed from two concepts in a nominal definition, such as 'being which knows' or, more abstractly, 'being which is wisdom or goodness' and so on, neither of which corresponds to the other. As Averroes says, the intellect can have two concepts, one concrete one abstract, of a composite being because of their likeness and yet not know whether one can be truly affirmed of the other. Thus someone can know the meaning of the words 'God' and 'deity' and yet doubt whether God is deity, or whether absolutely first being is simple or composite, as he can doubt whether whiteness is white. None of these is synonymous just because of synonyms their signification

---

[1] E.g. Hoc patet quia nullius rei simplicis possunt esse duos conceptus convertibiles et simplices, quia sicut nomina importantia simpliciter eandem rem et eodem modo sunt nomina synonyma, ita conceptus eodem modo importantes omnino eandem rem sunt unus conceptus, hoc est eiusdem rationis vel synonymi (*Ordinatio*, d. 8, q. 3, D) . . . Et ita simplex nunquam habet distincta nomina convertibilia, quorum neutrum significet nec connotet vel consignificet aliquid distinctum ab illa re simplici, et multo magis nec habet tales duos conceptus simplices et convertibiles et proprios (*ibid.*, F). See chapter three, 144–7 above.

[2] *Ibid.*, d. 2, q. 9, 315–16. There can, however, be a distinct name for God imposed by convention to denote him and nothing else, even though God himself is not known distinctly, because a word can have a distinct meaning without knowing its significate (*ibid.*, d. 22, I).

[3] *Ibid.*, 312–17, and *Quodlibet* IV, q. 18 and V, q. 7.

[4] *SL*, I, ch. 6, 18–21; *Ordinatio*, d. 2, q. 3, 88.

[5] *Ordinatio, ibid.*

cannot be known without also knowing that one is predicable of the other.[6]

Accordingly, the terms we have of God, in never being of God himself, differ not only as terms or words, as all distinct terms including synonyms, must; but also as concepts. Although they stand for God, when taken significatively, they do not signify him in the same way but by different composite concepts like 'infinite being', 'supreme goodness' and so on. We must therefore distinguish between the diverse ways of conceiving God and his own absolutely simple being which is without diversity. Any diversity is from our terms and concepts and not in God; they are thus the result of a mental distinction not a real distinction. That applies to the divine attributes which are different predicates or, as the saints and doctors, like St Augustine, Anselm, and Peter Lombard called them, names for the same undifferentiated God.[7] In being distinguished only by reason, the divine attributes represent diverse definitions or descriptions of God which are distinguished only among themselves and not by what they signify. Each corresponds to God so that, as St Augustine said, the same God is many by reason; which is to say that his diverse attributes are merely mental, vocal or written terms designed to stand for him.[8] They are therefore really distinct from one another—as terms—and the same by reason in standing for God.[9]

Such terms are like second intentions in signifying not an actual being but concepts which when taken significatively stand for real things. As a genus predi-

---

[6] Ad primum istorum potest dici uno modo quod illa nomina que habemus de deo, scilicet deus et deitatis, non sunt synonyma, quia nomina aliqua sunt quibus correspondent aliqui conceptus simplices vel aliquis conceptus simplex. Et si idem conceptus simplex correspondeat, possunt dici nomina synonyma. Aliquibus autem nominibus correspondent compositi conceptus, et talia nomina non oportet quod sint synonyma, et hoc propter distinctionem repertam in illis conceptibus compositis cuius una pars potest alicui competere cui alia pars non competit. Et ita est de deo et deitate; secundum enim quod a nobis imponuntur eis correspondent duo conceptus proprii deo, quia nullus conceptus simplex nobis possibilis est proprius deo, et una pars illius conceptus competit alicui cui altera pars non potest competere. Sicut deus dicit aliquod ens intellectuale vel intelligens et sic de aliis que competunt deo . . . deitas autem dicit omnia illa magis in abstracto, et de illis aliquod abstractum competit alicui cui non competit concretum et e converso, ut descriptio exprimens quid nominis deitatis sit ista: ens quod est sapientia, bonitas et huiusmodi. Aliter potest dici secundum ultimam auctoritatem allegatam [Averroes, Commentary on *Metaphysics*, XII, f. 151 v] quod talia nomina que imponuntur secundum assimilationem concreti et abstracti ubi significant realiter distincta non sunt nomina synonyma, quia precise imponuntur secundum assimilationem istorum que non sunt nomina synonyma . . . Et ratio huius potest esse quia aliquis potest scire significatum utriusque vocabuli et tamen ignorare utrum unum predicatur de reliquo, sicut aliquis ignorans utrum ens simpliciter primum sit simplex vel compositum potest scire quid intelligitur per hoc nomen 'deitas' et etiam per hoc nomen 'deus' et tamen dubitare an deitas sit deus, sicut potest dubitare an albedo sit alba . . . Et ideo talia nomina taliter disposita non sunt nomina synonyma, quia de nominibus synonymis non potest sciri quid significant et tamen ignorare utrum unum vere predicatur de reliquo (*ibid.*, 85–7). Also d. 3, q. 10, 562.

[7] *Quodlibet* III, q. 2.

[8] Et sic deus dicitur distingui ratione, quia correspondet diversis rationibus sive conceptibus sine omni distinctione ex parte sui. Et sic idem deus realiter est multiplex ratione, sicut dicit Augustinus . . . Ex predictus patet quid sit dicendum ad questionem. Dico ergo quod attributa divina distinguuntur ratione, quia attributa non sunt nisi quedam predicabilia mentalia, vocalia vel scripta, nata significare et supponere pro deo, que possunt naturali ratione investigari et concludi de deo (*ibid.*).

[9] *Ibid.*

cated significatively of a species stands not for the species itself but for the individuals coming under it—as animal is affirmed of a real man, Socrates or Plato—so 'infinite being' taken significatively (in an *actus exercitus*) denotes an infinite being by which we also understand God. Its actual import however is 'infinite being' as opposed to 'God', which is only a name (in the absence of any simple proper concept of God). Only if taken simply for itself as a concept (in an *actus significatus*) can it be affirmed of 'God' as a name, in which case it will not be understood significatively.[10]

The whole problem of concepts of God centres upon this distinction between terms taken significatively in an *actus exercitus* and for themselves in an *actus significatus*;[11] what holds by one does not hold by the other. By an *actus significatus* it is true that 'Animal is predicated of man' or 'Genus is predicated of species' but not that 'Animal is man' or 'Genus is species'; it is the converse by an *actus exercitus* where the terms are taken significatively in personal supposition: for nothing existing outside the mind can be predicated of something else, but it can be something real, as a man is really an animal.[12] Both Aristotle and the other authorities frequently interchange these different senses, so that strictly speaking many of their statements are false although true in intent: for example the propositions that 'A triangle has three angles' or that 'Colour is the first object of sight', which have the form of an *actus exercitus* but are meant as an *actus significatus* to denote the subjects as terms not things. That applies equally to God: when he is taken as a concept, a concept can be properly affirmed of him, such as 'being', 'goodness', and so on.[13] Accordingly our terms of God can be employed—in an *actus exercitus* —to signify what he is; they will then always denote the different things which can be affirmed of him in composite concepts, such as 'infinite being', since these are the nearest we can ever come to signifying him.

For the same reason that God is absolutely simple with no correspondence to what exists in this world we cannot affirm concrete concepts, such as 'wise' and 'good', both of him and of creatures univocally. They have different significations. Whereas in creatures 'wise' and 'good' are connotative in a nominal definition consignifying their abstracts, namely 'having wisdom or goodness', in God they

---

[10] Ad argumentum dico quod deus predicatur de conceptu die, sed non debet sic exerceri, 'Conceptus ille est deus', sed sic: 'Ens infinitum est deus', ubi predicatur deus de isto conceptus dei non autem pro conceptu sed pro re significata per conceptum, puta pro ipso deo. Sicut hec est vera: genus predicatur de specie non pro sed sed pro supposito, puta pro isto homine et illo, quia homo est vere animal . . . . Ad formam [questionis] dico quod deus vere predicatur de deo sed deus non predicatur de conceptu dei, verum est quando supponit pro se, sicut dicendo 'Iste conceptus est deus', sicut 'Nullum nomen est deus'. Sed quando conceptus dei stat significative tunc predicatur de deo non in actu significato sed in actu exercito. (*Quodlibet* VI, q. 5).

[11] *Ibid.*, and *Quodlibet* VII, q. 15; also *Ordinatio*, d. 6, q. 1, D.

[12] *Quodlibet* VII, q. 15.

[13] *Ibid.*; and *Quodlibet* VI, q. 5: Ad tertium dico quod nulla est contradictio dicere quidquid predicatur de deo predicatur de conceptu dei terminis in propositionibus acceptis significative, et tamen ille conceptus non est deus. Et hoc quia predicatio non debet sic exerceri, 'Conceptus est deus' sed sic: 'Ens infinitum est deus' ubi accipitur conceptus non pro conceptu sed pro deo, cuius est conceptus.

are predicated absolutely to denote God himself as wisdom or goodness.[14] Hence what for a creature represents the inherence of an accidental quality, for God represents his own being.

The foundation of Ockham's view of the divine attributes is that real difference or identity—as anything real—has to correspond with what exists outside the mind and cannot be merely conceptual. As he expresses it in the third of the three questions of distinction two in the *Ordinatio*, where he systematically treats the subject, 'Nothing real can be mentally (*a ratione*) distinguished from or be the same as something (else) real, so that as mental distinction and identity are mental, real difference and identity belong to real beings, perhaps not excluding formal distinction and identity, where it should be held [i.e. among the divine persons as we shall see]. Therefore I say that nothing can be distinguished from itself or something else or be the same by reason.'[15] The proof is that if something did differ from itself or from something else merely by reason, that would be either because of different concepts of the same thing, or things, or because the intellect conceived the same thing differently. Neither constitutes a real difference. Just as something can have really distinct parts without being really distinct from itself—as milk is both white and sweet, each different from the other and from milk without milk being different from itself—so there can be different concepts of the same thing while remaining the same thing. Similarly the same thing conceived differently either remains the same in all respects although the ways of seizing it are multiplied; and then the conclusion will be the same as that just reached, since the same thing can be known differently not only by the intellect but also by the different senses and yet remain the same. Alternatively it can be what Duns calls a number of formal objects and so multiple. Such a multiplicity will be either real (*ex natura rei*), and not conceptual; or conceptual, with the same consequences as before.[16] Accordingly, save for a formal distinction or non-identity—which concerns only the divine persons and is only to be held where faith compels it—the only real distinction is between real things and is independent of the intellect. Conversely a mental distinction is only between what is in the mind and excludes equally real distinction and real identity. In between there can be composites of each which are strictly neither real nor mental distinctions.[17]

Now it is precisely the absence of any real distinction in God which makes all attempts to discern some real correspondence with his attributes—or more strictly

---

[14] *Quodlibet* II, q. 4.

[15] *Ordinatio*, d. 2, q. 3, 75.

[16] *Ibid.*, 75–8.

[17] Ideo dico quod excepta distinctione vel non-identitate formali que est ex natura rei et que est difficillima ad intelligendum et que non est ponenda nisi ubi fides compellit, nihil distinguitur ab aliquo nisi sicut ens reale ab ente reali; et omnis talis distinctio est distinctio realis, nec plus dependet ab intellectu quam ipsa entitas dependet ab intellectu. Vel distinguitur sicut ens rationis ab ente rationis; et omnis talis distinctio est distinctio rationis, que identitatem realem simpliciter excludit sicut ens rationis non potest esse ens reale. Vel distinguitur sicut ens reale ab ente rationis vel converso; et ista distinctio stricte et proprie nec est realis nec rationis . . . Vel distinguitur sicut aggregatum ex re et ratione . . . et ista distinctio—sicut nec precedens—nec est proprie et stricte realis nec rationis . . . (*ibid.*, 78).

the names or terms attributed to him—otiose and misguided. That applies both to those—above all Duns Scotus and followers like William of Alnwick—who uphold a formal distinction between attributes and essence, and those who while accepting that the distinction is the work of the intellect nevertheless seek a real foundation for it either in God or outside him among creatures.

In the case of a formal distinction, as cited from Duns it goes, we will recall, beyond any mental distinction, whether of different ways of considering the same formal (i.e. conceptual) object or among different formal objects in the intellect, in belonging to what is known and so preceding knowledge of it. Thus wisdom and goodness exist *in re* as part of the nature of what is wise or good; and one cannot be the other. That applies equally to infinite wisdom and infinite goodness each of which has its own essential definition which does not include the other; otherwise they would not be formally distinct or non-identical, an interpretation which Duns finds confirmed by the ancient doctors including John of Damascus and St Augustine. Moreover if there were no such real distinction in God, which preceded a distinction between the emanations of the divine persons, there would not be different modes of their production, a point to which we shall return in the next section.[18] Similarly William of Alnwick argued that there must be formally distinct principles in order to produce a plurality, as the intellect and will are formally distinct in producing diverse persons in the divine nature.[19]

Ockham's general reply is the same for both Duns Scotus and William of Alnwick; namely that wherever there is a distinction or non-identity, contradictions will always be verified of what is distinguished, whether the distinction is of real things or in the mind or both; and if it is real it will not be mental.[20] But that is the position of the two thinkers for whom a formal distinction is from the nature of what is distinguished; hence what is formally divine wisdom is verified of divine wisdom and denied of divine goodness.[21] Moreover contradictions are equally contradictory, of God and non-God, or being and non-being, as well as of ass and non-ass or soul and non-soul. Therefore the same principle of contradiction applies to all of them, whatever the kind of distinction, real or mental; if it did not that would mean the end of proving any distinction or non-identity. In that case, just as his opponents hold that something can be truly denied of divine wisdom and truly affirmed of divine goodness, despite their real identity, so Ockham could equally assert that being and non-being can be universally verified of A and B on account of their formal distinction although they are really the same.[22] That cannot be mitigated by a syncathegorematic qualification like

[18] *Ibid.*, q. 1, 4–8.
[19] *Ibid.*, 8–14.
[20] Contra istam opinionem arguo per unum argumentum quod est equaliter contra distinctionem vel non-identitatem formalem ubicumque ponatur. Et arguo sic: ubicumque est aliqua distinctio vel non-identitas, ibi possunt aliqua contradictoria de illis verificari; sed impossibile est contradictoria verificari de quibuscumque nisi illa vel illa pro quibus supponunt sint distincte res vel distincte rationes sive rationis vel res et ratio; sed si omnia illa sint ex natura rei non sunt distincte rationes nec res et ratio; igitur erunt distincte res (*ibid.*, 14).
[21] *Ibid.*, 14–15.
[22] *Ibid.*, 15–16.

'formally' because if one thing is not formally another they still remain contradictories from which distinction or non-identity can be inferred.[23]

Accordingly because the divine attributes are really identical with the divine
essence in all the modes by which the divine essence is the divine essence, there is
absolutely no distinction or non-identity in God himself. Although a formal
distinction between them could be posited, as it is among the divine persons, since
it is the most difficult of all distinctions to maintain anywhere, it should not be
held except where it follows evidently from what is to be believed in the Bible or
from the determination of the church to whose authority all reason is subject.[24]
Since neither is flouted by denying any distinction between essence and attributes,
Ockham denies it completely in creatures as well as in God, while accepting that
the natural reasons for holding to a trinity of persons apply as well as to creatures
as to God, a statement for which he was censured at Avignon.[25]

Ockham's position is clear enough; the absence of natural evidence for a formal
distinction makes it exclusively a matter of belief; *pro statu isto* no arguments can
satisfy the proof for a plurality of infinite persons any more than for a plurality of
finite persons. Since only the first is to be held on faith there is no reason why
anything else, including God's essence and attributes, should be held to be formally
distinct.[26] As with Olivi's censors, we can only wonder in retrospect whether
Lutterell and the Masters at Avignon were condemning Ockham for what they
could not or would not understand. That applies also to two other statements
made in the same context, also condemned, that a thing is a divine idea produced
outside God and that his essence expressed in the son must also constitute the
father.[27] Ockham's distinctions here as throughout are not concerned with re-
formulating, let alone challenging the tenets of faith, but to state them more
precisely and unequivocally. Their import will be considered later.

As to a formal distinction it can only occur where there is a real distinction so
that one thing is truly said to be what another is not, as the essence which is the
father is not the essence which is the son. In its nominal definition then, one thing
absolute or relative is formally distinguished from another thing which is not the
same, although of the same essence. Only in such a case should a formal distinction

---

[23] *Ibid.*, 16–17.

[24] *Ibid.*, 17–18; also 25.

[25] *Ibid.*, 18; and note 2. J. Koch, 'Neue Aktenstücke', *Recherches* 8 (1936), 195; F. Hoffmann,
Die Schriften des Oxforder Kanzlers, Johannes Lutterell, 71.

[26] Ita enim credo facile tenere trinitatem personarum cum unitate essentie in creaturis
sicut in deo propter quascumque rationes in oppositum, quia credo quod pro statu isto eque
posset satisfieri rationibus probantibus non esse tres personas in una essentia in creaturis sicut in
deo. Nec potest evidenter cognosci quod plus facit infinitas ad hoc quod sint plures persone
in una essentia quam finitas; quia tamen unum est expressum in scriptura et aliud non, et
videtur repugnare rationi, ideo unum est ponendum et aliud est negandum. Ita dico in proposito quod quia ex traditis in sacra scriptura evidenter sequitur quod essentia divina non est
formaliter relatio, sicut post patebit, et non sequitur ex istis nec ex determinatione ecclesie nec
ex dictis sanctorum quod essentia non est formaliter sapientia nec ratio hoc concludit, ideo
simpliciter dico quod essentia est formaliter sapientia et omnibus modis sapientia, bonitas etc.,
quia nulla talis distinctio media est ponenda nisi precise propter tradita in scriptura (*ibid.*, 18–19).

[27] *Ibid.*, 25 and note 1.

be posited; it does not therefore hold either for the relation between God's essence and attributes or for creatures: not in God, because they are identical and can only be distinguished grammatically or logically; not in creatures, because nothing created is at once simple and several distinct things or any one of them, as the divine essence is three persons and each of them. It is thus a fallacy of accident to argue on the one hand 'Essence is the father; Essence is the son; Therefore the father is the son', since one essence is also really several distinct persons; and on the other hand that 'Socrates is a man; Plato is a man; Therefore Plato is Socrates', because 'man' here is predicated of many distinct individuals univocally.[28] Hence in natural terms, Ockham excludes a formal distinction or assimilates it to a real distinction as we have seen in preceding chapters.[29]

For that reason Ockham while accepting with Duns that 'infinite' added to 'wisdom' or to 'goodness' does not destroy the formal notion of either, denies that they are formally distinct, since they both stand for the same being, which is God. Hence despite their diversity as terms they do not denote diverse concepts, to which 'infinite' is added, but being which is itself infinite, namely God; only if taken in simple supposition for themselves is it true that infinite wisdom is not infinite goodness.[30] Again, as we have seen in the last chapter, it does not follow that whatever is contained under one common term is in some way distinct from all that is contained under another common term, so that all that comes under wisdom is distinguished from all that comes under goodness. As Aristotle says in the *Topics*, whenever one species falls under two genera one is embraced by the other, as prudence is contained under virtue and knowledge.[31] Consequently 'divinity' can come under different quidditative concepts such as wisdom and goodness, in the way discussed in chapter five, without either being subordinated to the other but with both subordinated to the concept of being as the most universal of all.[32] That does not mean that there is an order among concepts by which one is nearer to God than another, for no name can be affirmed of God enabling us immediately to apprehend him; but only that some terms are better affirmed of him than others.[33]

It is therefore entirely untrue to say, as Duns does, that if infinite wisdom and infinite goodness were definable they would be different definitions; on the contrary both would be included in the same definition,[34] greater than any part and equal to the whole, as John of Damascus said; whose expression *Qui est* as the most proper to God Ockham also interprets to include God's attributes equally with his essence, and not as Duns held to the exclusion of his attributes.[35] Only as nominal definitions are expressions like 'infinite wisdom' and 'infinite goodness' distinct, but in their essential definitions—of what they denote—they are the same.[36]

---

[28] *Ibid.*, 19–20; also *Quodlibet* I, q. 2.
[29] *Ibid.* Also note 17 above.
[30] *Ordinatio, ibid.*, 26–7.
[31] *Topics*, IV, ch. 2, 121 b, 29–30.
[32] *Ordinatio, ibid.*, 29–30.
[33] *Ibid.*, 33–4.   [34] *Ibid.*, 30.
[35] *Ibid.*, 31–3.   [36] *Ibid.*, 31–6.

Thus as we have said before, God's attributes differ as names, where they can be said to have real non-identity, and not to be synonyms in the way that oblique and direct terms and any terms with different nominal definitions are distinct.[37]

The only real distinction among the divine attributes then is as diverse terms; and just as they do not denote a formal distinction in God so they do not correspond to any other distinction in him or in relation to him. Ockham accordingly rejects the attempts of thinkers, like St Thomas Aquinas, Richard of Middleton, Thomas of Sutton, and Godfrey of Fontaines, to find some basis for the distinction between essence and attributes outside the mind, either in God or among creatures, while accepting that it is a purely mental distinction. Thus Godfrey of Fontaines locates it in a comparison with what is really distinct in creatures, on the grounds that any mental distinction of a plurality requires not only the thing which is distinguished as its foundation, and apprehension of it in the intellect as its condition, in being only from the intellect; but also some real diversity to which the thing can be compared, because alone it would be conceived only as one. That applies to God because as the most simple being of all, considered only by himself he would he known only as the one and most simple being. Since, however, his attributes are not distinct in themselves, but are only contained virtually in his essence as the source of all perfections, they can only be known in comparison with what approximates to them; that is achieved by the intellect's recognition of the similarity in a limited and determinate degree between the forms and qualities among creatures, which derive from divine ideas, and their perfections in God.[38]

Henry of Ghent, on the other hand, sees the source of the distinction by the intellect in the virtual distinction between essence and attributes in God and not in their comparison by reference to creatures. To seek the explanation in what can be discerned from creatures, he contends, would make goodness and wisdom in God dependent upon their existence in creatures, which is manifestly false. Hence the divine attributes differ solely by an internal relation of reason, as the divine persons are distinguished by a real relation among themselves and not through what is external to them.[39]

Ockham's general reply is that if the divine attributes are distinct in God they will be distinguished either formally and really or mentally. In the first case their distinction will be independent of the intellect and solely from God's own nature. In the second case they will not be really in the divine essence but merely in the intellect; and on Henry of Ghent's argument, that these attributes are the product of the intellect, it could be said that they are not of the essence at all but only of the intellect. Creatures themselves would be then in God—in being known in his intellect—while goodness and wisdom and the other attributes would not be part of his nature.

The alternatives then are either that the intellect forms these attributal ideas and then they are the product of its own reasoning and purely mental; or that it finds them in real being and then the intellect no more makes them attributal than

[37] Ibid., 23.   [38] Ibid., q. 2, 50–2.
[39] Ibid., 53–4.

it makes the divine essence itself.[40] They apply to every attempt at once to keep the distinction purely mental and to make them the same as God. Thus when St Thomas says that the wisdom and goodness are different forms or ideas Ockham ripostes that they either stand for something real in which case they will be different things, or for concepts and so nothing real in God. The impasse is not overcome by confining the distinction to the intellect, as its work, for the very reason that when something remains the same both before and after an act of the intellect, it is always distinct or never. Knowing of itself causes no change in what is known, as Ockham has repeatedly stressed. Therefore divine wisdom and goodness are always divine wisdom and goodness. Nor can the intellect distinguish what is the same; if it could do so between divine wisdom and divine goodness, it could also do so between essence and essence or wisdom and wisdom.[41] Since the divine attributes are the same as God there cannot be any distinction, real or of reason, between them as attributes, but only as concepts or terms: nothing that is really God can be distinguished by reason from what is really God.[42]

Notwithstanding the claims of his opponents to the contrary Ockham recognises no other reason than the intellect's own activity for the distinction among God's attributes: they are founded neither in God himself nor in a comparison with himself or anything else, because as one he cannot be more than one; the only multiplicity is of acts of cognition.[43]

So far as Godfrey's arguments are concerned, when things are distinguished only by external relations one cannot be without the other. If therefore God's attributes were known from comparison with creatures it would then be impossible to know God without a creature or for God to be wise without the wisdom of a creature. By the same token God could then be compared with created whiteness and could as well be called whiteness as wisdom.[44] Nor is it true that the one most simple being cannot be considered according to diverse quidditative concepts; for the terms 'beginning' and 'end' are applied to a point and 'right' and 'left' to a column.[45] As for Henry of Ghent's arguments they equally prove that the divine attributes are not distinguished by the operations of the intellect; just as divine goodness and wisdom are independent of any relation to creatures, correspondingly they are distinguished without reference to what is known in the intellect. Such qualities are equally absolute in God and creatures. Moreover a real distinction does not presuppose a mental distinction, but since according to Henry the distinction between the divine persons presupposes a distinction of attributes, the latter must be really distinguished.[46] If, on the other hand, as concepts they were not the same in every respect, that must be either from some distinction in their foundation or as terms, which again contradicts Henry's view, that their distinction is from God and yet there is no distinction in him.[47]

---

[40] Ibid., 54–5.   [41] Ibid., 56–7.

[42] Igitur nihil quod est realiter deus distinguitur secundum rationem ab aliquo quod est realiter deus; et ita per consequens attributa non sunt realiter divina essentia et tamen distincta inter se secundum rationem (ibid., 58).

[43] Ibid., 58–9.   [44] Ibid., 60.   [45] Ibid., 69–70.

[46] Ibid., 60–61; also 72–3.   [47] Ibid., 57.

The correct distinction is as we have seen before between attributes—or attributal perfections—taken absolutely for the perfection which is God himself and for terms predicable of God and the divine persons separately or together. By the first mode there is only one perfection undifferentiated by a real or mental distinction, which cannot properly and strictly be said to be in God or in his essence because it is in every respect God's essence. By the second mode the attributes are concepts or signs which can be predicated of God, and these should more properly be called concepts or names rather than perfections since they are neither things nor perfections.[48] As terms they can be stated of God absolutely and affirmatively (for example, will and intellect) or connotatively (creating or creative) or negatively (indestructible or immortal). But by none of these modes are they the same as God; for they depend upon the intellect whereas God's essence does not.[49] And as the divine essence cannot be distinguished from its attributes formally or really, it cannot be distinguished from them mentally because, as Ockham has already said, nothing that is really the divine essence is really distinguished from the divine essence solely by the intellect. Hence if the attributes are really the divine essence they are not really distinguished among themselves.[50] The proof for the antecedent is the same as before, namely that to be the same or distinct is affirmed immediately of something; therefore if something is in any way distinguished from something else each will be always distinguished from the other. That applies to one attribute distinguished by reason from another. If therefore each is also really the divine essence, both will be distinguished not only by the intellect but independently of the intellect.[51] Although the intellect can vary in what it knows, its own notions of identity or distinction follow what it knows to be the same or distinct; and if these are really one or the other, nothing that occurs in the intellect alters them. Therefore what is distinguished in this case are the attributes—as the work of reason— from God who is real.[52]

In this distinction between the mental and real we have the source of Ockham's opposition to all attributal distinctions in God, as to every other distinction which is not founded really in being. In his own words,

As mental being is to what is really the same or distinct, so real being is to what is mentally the same or distinct. Therefore as no concept (*ens rationis*) is really the same as or distinct from

---

[48] Ideo dico aliter ad questionem quod perfectio attributalis potest accipi dupliciter: uno modo pro aliqua perfectione simpliciter divina que sit realiter deus; alio modo pro aliquo predicabili vere de deo et de omnibus tribus personis coniunctim et divisim. Primo modo dico quod non sunt plures perfectiones attributales, sed tantum est ibi una perfectio indistincta re et ratione que proprie et de virtute sermonis non debet dici esse in deo vel in divina essentia . . . Secundo modo dico quod non sunt nisi quidam conceptus vel signa que possunt vere predicari de deo, et magis proprie deberent dici conceptus attributales vel nomina attributalia quam perfectiones attributales, quia proprie perfectio non est nisi res aliqua, et tales conceptus non sunt proprie res, vel non sunt perfecte, quia saltem non sunt perfectiones simpliciter (*ibid.*, 61–2). Also 71–2 and d. 6, q. 1, D–E.

[49] *Ibid.*, 62.

[50] Et hoc adhuc probo sic: nihil quod realiter est divina essentia distinguitur ratione a quocumque quod est realiter divina essentia; igitur attributa non distinguuntur ratione inter se et a divina essentia si sint realiter divina essentia (*ibid.*, 63).

[51] *Ibid.*, 63–4.   [52] *Ibid.*, 64–5.

any other concept, so nothing real is mentally the same as or distinct from anything real; therefore the divine essence is mentally neither the same as nor distinct from anything real and so from nothing that is really the divine essence. In the same way wisdom which is really God is not mentally distinguished from goodness which is really God.[53]

Conversely, as diverse, attributes are not God but concepts distinguished among themselves mentally—unless concepts are taken to be real—and in any event really from God, as real being outside the intellect. Hence neither really nor formally are they the same as the divine essence.[54]

All diversity in God's attributes then is from our different concepts of God and corresponds to nothing distinct in him. It is accordingly misconceived to call their distinction a relation of reason, not only because—as we discussed in chapter three—Ockham does not acknowledge such a relation but also because, even if he did, it would be accidental and extrinsic to God's attributes, unconnected with them formally or causally.[55] Nor can it be held, as St Thomas holds, that the divine attributes are distinguished through the intellect's inability to comprehend God totally, thereby conceiving him under particular aspects. On the contrary, God, as supremely simple, can only be apprehended totally or not at all, and our concepts of him are never immediate.[56] For that reason, also, Aureole's opinion is inapposite, that God's attributes are distinguished by what they connote. Not all our terms for God are connotative, as we have seen: nor are they distinguished by what they represent, since they cannot be verified of the divine essence, which does not itself signify one thing directly and consignify something else indirectly. For that a term has to be of something distinct from the divine essence.[57]

There is thus no way in which we can establish a direct correlation between the diversity of the divine attributes and God; for whenever we attempt to distinguish one perfection from another the distinction is in the intellect, not in God. We have therefore to employ our terms of God, as the ancients did, as different names for the same absolutely one and indivisible being. Once more it is against recent innovations that Ockham took his stand.

II THE DIVINE PERSONS

The divine persons, unlike the divine attributes, are distinguished formally. This is the only distinction which Ockham recognises in God and as we have said the only instance in which he recognises it. It forms one of the main threads in his extended discussion of the Trinity which in keeping with tradition occupies the greater part of the first book of his Commentary on the Sentences (the Ordinatio). Whatever their subsequent change in character may owe to Ockham with its twin emphases upon the logical niceties of what had been theological questions, particularly those concerning the Trinity, and their resolution—or as many would hold violation—by reference to God's absolute power, Ockham himself stood at the parting of the ways. On the one hand, each of these new developments is

[53] Ibid., 65–6.   [54] Ibid., 66.   [55] Ibid., 67.
[56] Ibid.   [57] Ibid., 68–9.

apparent, the first particularly as it concerns God, the second in the relation of
God to man. On the other hand, neither can be said to have been to the exclusion
of theological content. Indeed they may be said to have been the outcome of what
is closer to a theological fundamentalism. For all the talk about a 'Nominalist
Theology' the alteration was not to theology but in the attitude towards its truths.
Ockham adhered completely to the articles of faith, none of which he ever questioned. But just as he accepted the disparity between what is known in the mind
and what exists outside it, so he accepted the disparity between what is held on
faith and what can be known by reason. Where so many of his predecessors had
attempted to reconcile both, Ockham started from their difference. In theology
it meant treating much that is held on faith as discrepant from, and in the case of
the Trinity irreconcilable with, natural reason and experience. But that did not
diminish their certainty as theological truths: rather it is the role of reason which
was diminished, limited to elucidating, often no more than terminologically, the
meaning of theological propositions whose truth for a believer is unassailable.
The level of discourse is therefore theological, in taking as given the certainty of
what is under discussion, whether it concerns God himself, what he has ordained,
or what is possible to him in his omnipotence. Whichever it is, it rests upon faith
either as defined by the church or by God's omnipotence. Any questioning springs
therefore from its import for reason. If Ockham gave a new emphasis to the latter
he did not dissociate it from the object of belief. That, as so much else, was to come
with Ockhamism, Ockham's successor but not his legatee.

    His discussion of the divine persons, as of the divine attributes, is principally
over the relation of their diversity to God's unity; but whereas there is no distinction of any kind, other than as terms, between essence and attributes or among
the attributes themselves, the divine persons are at once the same and distinct.
As we have seen, such a juxtaposition passes human experience: its acceptance is the
condition of its explanation; and the more probable explanation, that of Duns
Scotus, of a non-identity between person and essence. Neither a mental distinction,
as posited by St Thomas Aquinas, nor a real distinction between essence and
relation is tenable for the reasons discussed in the previous section.[58] A formal
distinction, however, is, because, as we have also seen, whenever things are the
same in all respects whatever can be affirmed of one can be affirmed of the other,
save where there is a logical or grammatical difference; but accepting that there is
none between the terms 'father' and 'essence' it remains true that essence is the
son and father is not the son. Hence the same thing denied of father is affirmed of
essence; and since they are not logically or grammatically discrepant the difference
must lie in some non-identity between them. They are therefore non-identical in
themselves; otherwise the terms signifying them would be synonyms and it would
be true that the father is the son, which he is not.[59]

    That does not, however, mean as William of Alnwick averred, that there would
then be several essences or natures in God any more than there are several things
in him; for if essence and its reality are not formally distinct but the same, it will

_____

[58] *Ibid.*, d. 2, q. 11, 359–64.   [59] *Ibid.*, 364–6.

follow that whatever is denied of essence will be denied of its reality; and so when William of Alnwick says that the nature of essence is not the same as the nature of relation (i.e. between essence and person) it would also follow that the reality of essence is not the nature of relation. There would then be something in God which was not the divine nature, an impossibility. If on the other hand the reality of essence were not in every way the same as the nature of essence, as formally distinguished but really the same, the essence of that reality must be in turn distinguished from the reality, and so on infinitely. Alternatively things can be formally distinct without more than one essence or reality, which is the case with the divine persons.[60] Nor is there any need to have recourse to the 'most false of all opinions' to explain their formal distinction, namely that it is by means of something else, because as just shown that can only lead to an infinite regress, whether in God or creatures. Accordingly essence of itself, without any real distinction within it, is at once really the same as the persons and distinguished formally from them; and conversely.[61] That holds universally of whatever is distinguished from something else: it is distinguished in itself or by something intrinsic to it and not by what is other than itself.[62]

A formal distinction, as unique to God and held, or as Ockham puts it compelled, by faith,[63] is not exclusively of what is real or mental; nor, as Harvey of Natalis believed, is it of forms; but rather of one thing which is distinguished mentally as not formally the same as what remains. Thus a formal distinction states that there is something, whether absolute or relative, and something which remains which is not that thing, as the divine essence is really the son, and the father is not the son. Such a distinction arises when one thing has not the same meaning as something else, or something can be affirmed in one way of one thing and not in the same way of another. It can only be of God where both really belong to the same being.[64] Accordingly a formal distinction presupposes a real identity, where a real distinction presupposes a real distinction.[65] That concedes the objection that a real distinction cannot be inferred from a formal distinction; only the converse is valid, that from a real distinction between the persons, and their real identity with essence and relation, can the formal distinction between essence and relation be inferred. Hence the real distinction between essence and persons is not from their formal distinction as paternity, filiation and spiration, but because they are real relations really distinguished.[66] Moreover a real identity, unlike a formal identity, is compatible with non-identity or some negation of identity. It is then not an absolute negation and allows both contradictories to be verified of what in a real distinction would be absolutely denied.

[60] *Ibid.*, 368–9.

[61] Dico, sicut frequenter dictum est prius quod illud principium aliquorum, quod nihil convenit realiter cum aliquo et differt realiter nec formaliter ab eodem per idem sed per aliud et aliud aliquo modo distinctum, est falsissimum et in deo et in creaturis, quia tunc, sicut probatum est, oporteret ponere processum in infinitum tam in deo quam in creaturis. Et ideo dico quod essentia se ipsa sine omni distinctione a parte sui, est eadem realiter cum relatione et distinguitur formaliter, et eodem modo est de relatione (*ibid.*, 369).

[62] *Ibid.*, 369–70.   [63] *Ibid.*, 370.   [64] *Ibid.*, 370–1.
[65] *Ibid.*, 372.   [66] *Ibid.*, 372–3.

Only in God where a formal distinction is alone possible, so that it is both true that 'paternity is not communicable' and 'paternity is that being (i.e. essence) which is communicable', is contradiction not the most potent way of proving a real distinction. For that reason there can be a formal distinction only in what is really the same;[67] and it implies nothing distinct from what is distinguished any more than a real distinction does. 'Formally', like 'really' or 'necessarily', is a syncathegorematic term qualifying the proposition to which it is applied; and as 'necessarily', in, say, the proposition 'Man is necessarily not an ass', does not denote a real necessity independent of the other terms, so 'formally' does not denote a 'formality' distinct from the terms of which it is qualified.[68]

Ockham summarises his conception of the distinction between essence and persons in the second question of the first *Quodlibet*, where he interprets it in an improper sense. By that, one term stands for something which is relatively three persons and another for what is not three persons relatively, as opposed to denoting one thing which is not another. Hence while something is truly predicable of essence which is not also predicable of paternity, when each is taken significatively in personal supposition, it is untrue that one is not really the other understood significatively; for taken personally, paternity and essence are not distinguished in both denoting the same real thing. At the same time essence stands for something which is three persons and paternity for what is not three persons.[69] Here, then, is the antinomy which governs a formal distinction and one that can only be resolved by accepting it as a supernatural truth held on faith, in violating both logic and natural experience.

For the rest, Ockham's discussion of the Trinity consists in interpreting the relations between its members according to the same principles of a real diversity within a real identity; all such expressions as identity, similarity, and equality are of a real relation in God not as something distinct from essence or persons but in stating something real about him in the same way as 'creator' states that God creates.[70] As we discussed in chapter three, a real relation—which is the only one recognised by Ockham—is not distinct from its foundation, as Socrates and Plato are related by nothing other than themselves or what is intrinsic to them. Strictly then the divine relations should not be described as springing from the divine nature since they do not exist independently apart from God.[71] Nor does his unity or triunity which, like all number, is not something distinct from that of which it is affirmed. Whatever is simple is one through the absence of parts and without the addition of something else; so therefore is God as the most simple being of all.[72] Oneness taken significatively does not differ from being save as one being differs from another;[73] and correspondingly with numbers greater than one, which in the case of a trinity of persons denotes simply three persons subsisting in God and nothing more.[74]

---

67 *Ibid.*, 373–4.   68 *Ibid.*, 375–6.
69 *Quodlibet* I, q. 2; also *Ordinatio*, dd. 33 and 34.
70 *Ordinatio*, d. 31, q. I, B–E; and *Quodlibet* VI, q. 26.
71 *Ordinatio, ibid.*, E.   72 *Ibid.*, d. 24, q. I, K.
73 *Ibid.*, N.   74 *Ibid.*, q. 2, Y.

The two questions in which Ockham treats unity and triunity are characteristic of much of his—and subsequent—theological discussion, in considering them predominantly as logical or ontological issues, which is not, as we have said before, to discount their theological content. That is also apparent over the production of the divine persons. From the truth that there are three persons in one essence which is really the same as each of the persons, and that the father produces the son, the first question is whether the proposition 'God produces God' is literally true. For Ockham this is principally a problem of supposition, and most of the question is devoted to exposing its three different modes. So far as the proposition itself is concerned, if 'God' is taken as a term strictly denoting a person, as St Thomas Aquinas also holds, then the proposition can be accepted in its literal sense. When on the other hand 'God' stands for the divine essence, which is how Henry of Ghent understands it, then it cannot be accepted as it stands; for although many of the *sancti* use the proposition improperly in this latter sense, it also enables heretics to mislead those of simple faith in claiming that for God to generate God would mean more than one God.[75] Correct supposition here as elsewhere thus obviates error in theology no less than in logic. For Ockham, logic far from supplanting theology comes to its aid, and where it cannot, as in the formal distinction, theology remains inviolate. Even in the case under discussion, supposition has its limits; for formally 'God' as person can stand also for the son or the holy spirit, and then it will be equally true that God does not generate God.[76] Conversely when God stands for the divine essence it is true that God is the divine persons, on the principle that whenever things are the same in every respect, it is impossible for something to stand for one part and not for the rest. If therefore God stands for divine essence, God must also be father, son and holy spirit. Nor is God, as divine essence, God by divinity, as Duns Scotus asserted, any more than divinity is divinity by divinity; such a distinction applies only when God stands for a person as according to St Augustine God the father is God by divinity.[77]

The divine essence on the other hand neither generates nor is generated; that, too, is a matter of faith held on the church's determination, and any explanation must be compatible with its truth.[78] Ockham accepts neither that of Aquinas which is that essence cannot stand for a person or have attributed to it what is proper and distinctive to a person; nor the more elaborate argument of Duns Scotus that generation cannot be truly affirmed of essence by the first essential mode (where the predicate defines the subject), which is the only way in which anything can be formally predicated of an abstract term at the furthest degree of abstraction. To Aquinas, Ockham replies that it would be false to say that essence is paternity, because paternity is as proper to the person which is the father as generation is.[79] To Duns, Ockham rejects his assumption, because Duns accepts as true the proposition 'The divine essence is communicated to the son'; where the predicate (communicated) is affirmed formally; but that is not by the first essential mode any more than 'generation' or many other predicates. To the objection that generation

[75] *Ibid.*, d. 4, q. 1, E, G–H.   [76] *Ibid.*, I.   [77] *Ibid.*, q. 2, C.
[78] *Ibid.*, d. 5, q. 1, B.   [79] *Ibid.*, C.

expresses a real relation but 'communicate' and similar terms state only a mental relation, Ockham replies that it makes no difference; an abstract term at the furthest degree of abstraction is equally removed from mental and from real being, each of which is extraneous to it. If the former were false, not only would the latter be false, but also all those propositions affirming the divine attributes.[80] In fact, generation has to be denied of the divine essence because it would imply that essence was distinguished from what was produced (the son), which is the Lombard's reason for denying it.[81] That, and not because essence is an abstract term, or its predicate can be affirmed only formally or only by the first essential mode, is why generation cannot be predicated of essence, but solely of person to which it immediately refers.[82]

Neither essence nor relation is the formal term of production, by which a being is considered simply in its generation (coming to be) and not as the total being produced, which is the object of a total term of production.[83] Essence cannot be such a formal term any more than it can be a total term, because it does not formally or totally have being by generation. Furthermore, if essence is the elective—i.e. necessary—principle of generation and, as one opinion holds, is prior to the formal term of production, it cannot also be the formal term, as this same opinion claims, because the same thing cannot be both prior and posterior.[84] Again, generation is directly from the father; it cannot therefore be formally through essence. At the same time to communicate being by production is not the same as to be the formal principle of production. In the strictest sense of communication—which is to receive being from the generating principle which produces it, as opposed to the broad sense where what is communicated, such as form and matter, is not identical with production or what is produced, and the broadest sense of including everything which is brought into being—both essence and active spiration are communicated to the son, as we shall consider more closely.[85] The formal term of generation has therefore nothing directly to do with essence. Nor does it belong to a person, because nothing can be the term of itself; but production as we shall also see, is really and formally a relation; hence relation cannot be the formal term of production. To posit a mental distinction between them would not alter the fact; for if the intellect assigned priority to production, so that relation was the term of production, that would be either to attribute priority to God or to a mental concept. God would then either be really prior to a relation in him, which Ockham does not accept, or priority would be only in the mind and there would be no real difference, which concedes their identity.[86]

A person on the other hand can be called the formal term of generation in having its being by generation, unlike essence, and in not being formally the same as generation, unlike relation. And as formal term it is not distinguished from the total term of production since it refers to what is produced, as the father is really called 'that which generates' in relation to the son.[87] Any formal term requires

[80] *Ibid.*, D–E, Q.   [81] *Ibid.*, F, H.   [82] *Ibid.*, H.
[83] *Ibid.*, q. 3, E, (F).   [84] *Ibid.*, B.   [85] *Ibid.*, C–D.
[86] *Ibid.*, G.   [87] *Ibid.*, H and O.

some non-identity with production, when the latter is a real thing so that they are not formally the same. Hence a relation like filiation, in being the same as generation, cannot be the formal term of generation.[88]

Whether the divine essence is also the actualising or eliciting principle of generation—as that which is necessary to the production of something while remaining distinct both from production and what is produced[89]—is more open to equivocation, as the term 'actualising' or 'eliciting' is: the latter can be taken either directly to mean that something is really produced by something else, as heat is produced by fire, and as heat in fire is the principle of producing heat in wood; or it can be taken indirectly to connote something producing something else as calefaction is said to be produced by fire heating wood, where calefaction denominates fire heating wood (in a nominal definition). In this second sense the father, in being said to produce the son by active generation, is called active, eliciting generation; not in the first sense, however, because active generation is not something which is really produced, but is entirely unproduced.[90] And as the father by active generation is the eliciting principle formally producing something, so is essence in virtue of being the father; for although father does not connote essence, all generation consists in the concurrence of essence and person. If moreover, it could be accepted that all action is in the agent and not something additional to cause and what is caused, it would also follow that any change in an agent was in relation to something else and referred to nothing beyond that which was produced. In the same way, as the act of creation is said to be elicited by the essence with nothing produced beyond a creature, so it can also be said that active generation, elicited from essence, produces nothing else, and is no more distinguished from the divine essence in coming from the essence than in being founded in essence.[91] Accordingly the relation which produces is founded in essence; and while nothing can elicit itself, the formal distinction between essence and relation enables one to be the foundation of the other which produces, even though they are of the same nature.[92] Hence essence cannot be the eliciting principle save by generation; and that can only be in conjunction with a person[93] because in itself it cannot be the eliciting principle of itself.[94]

Strictly, then, the divine essence under whatever aspect, whether of an attribute or a person, is not the eliciting principle of active generation because as active generation it cannot be its own principle, as essence, father, or son. But improperly, both as what generates and is generated, essence can be the eliciting principle of

---

[88] *Ibid.*, N. [89] *Ibid.*, d. 7, q. 1, U.

[90] Ad primum dico quod equivocatio est de elicitivo vel elicito. Aliquid enim dicitur elicitum, quia est aliquid vere productum ab aliquo, et sic dicimus quod calor est elicitus ab igne . . . Similiter calor in igne est principium producendi calorem in ligno, et est principium eliciendi calefactionem qua calefacit lignum. Aliter dicitur aliquid esse elcitum illud quod denominat aliquid producere aliud, sicut calefactio dicitur elicita ab igne. Quia ignis calefactione denominatur calefacere lignum, et quia pater generatione activa dicitur generare filium, ideo dicitur generatio activa elicitiva isto secundo modo; sed non primo modo, quia generatio activa non est realitas producta, sed est simpliciter improducta (*ibid.*, Y).

[91] *Ibid.* [92] *Ibid.*

[93] *Ibid.*, II. [94] *Ibid.*, BB.

generation, which is only to say that the father generates the son. It can also be that principle under the aspect of an attribute, such as intellect, when taken reduplicatively, to denote a person as an attribute rather than as essence, for example in the proposition 'The father in so far as he is intelligence produces the son'.[95]

Just as essence cannot be its own generating principle, neither can relation—i.e. paternity or filiation or spiration—or person or generation itself as something really distinct; these are the effects of the essence's activity, and as nothing can be formally a cause without something that is caused, so what is caused cannot be prior to its cause. Hence only the divine essence in conjunction with a person can be the eliciting principle of generation and not one independently of the other.[96] Ockham accordingly dismisses all arguments which attempt to prove that relation or person is in itself the principle of active or passive generation, and on the same grounds as he denies the role to essence taken in itself: namely that nothing can be its own principle of generation. Since the divine persons are in every way the same as the divine essence, one cannot be the principle of generating the other; nor as we saw earlier can one relation be the principle of another.[97] Hence only essence, as absolute and as necessary to active and passive generation and spiration, can be the principle of generation; but because essence and persons are also really the same, whereas there is a real distinction between a principle and what derives from it, essence is not itself that which acts but that by which it acts. That is to say, it is in the father who produces and the son who is produced, both of whom in their relation as persons are really distinguished but absolutely are of the same being.[98]

In the *Ordinatio* Ockham dismisses not only arguments attempting to prove that relation is elective principle, but also a series which seeks to prove that it is not; in the latter case above all because it would follow from them that paternity was more perfect than filiation, which is manifestly false since they are really the same as essence.[99] Nor can relation be called the determining principle of generation, because the concept of determining relations is otiose and vain.[100] Equally it cannot be proved that essence is the principle of generation only in so far as it leads to the principle of property; or that the principle of generation belongs to the father rather than essence; or that the father principally generates a property, the arguments for all of which Ockham contests.[101]

Essence therefore is the absolute being which is the principle of generation. Moreover it is such under its own nature of essence and not as some say under the aspect of intellect. That follows, for as we have seen there is no distinction between essence and anything else absolute in God; hence an absolute as the principle of

---

[95] *Quodlibet* IV, q. 8; *Ordinatio, ibid.,* BB.

[96] Si autem intelligatur quod non est principium elicitivum sine supposito, verum est; sic enim nihil est causa sine causato, non tamen illud causatum est determinativum cause ad illud causatum. Unde sicut nihil potest esse causans formaliter sine causato, et tamen causatum non est elicitivum nec determinativum sed est effectus productus, ita essentia non potest esse principium elicitivum sine generatione, et ideo sine supposito, et tamen nec suppositum nec generatio nec aliquis respectus est elicitivum (*Ordinatio, (ibid.,* II).

[97] *Ibid.,* Q–T.   [98] *Ibid.,* U.   [99] *Ibid.,* CC–FF; also d. 2, q. I, 41–2.

[100] *Ibid.,* d. 7, q. I, GG.   [101] *Ibid.,* H–I.

generation must be essence.[102] All opinions then which on the grounds of distinct emanations in God posit distinct generating principles are completely false and impossible whatever their mode, as are those which maintain that the different productions—of the son and the holy spirit—are founded in different essential acts. Essence is their sole principle, in every respect the same as intellect and will and the acts of knowing and willing: any distinction between them as we have already discussed is from our diverse connotations and not from different attributes in God.[103]

For that reason father and son cannot generate by different modes, as thinkers like Duns Scotus and William of Alnwick affirmed, one producing naturally by the intellect, the other freely by the will. Every attempt to argue that they can founders upon the principle that nothing really the same can differ from itself; the only exception is the formal distinction between essence and persons. It does not, as we have seen, extend to God's attributes. Hence all claims to establish a distinction between intellect and will, understanding and willing, and to identify their differences with different persons or different kinds of activity or different causes, are false and absurd.[104] Intellect and will and their acts in so far as they are really affirmed of God in an *actus exercitus* can only be of the divine essence for reasons with which we should now be familiar; otherwise they are diverse merely as terms (in an *actus significatus*), not in what they signify. Nor is the difference between a natural and a free act as applied to God any better founded. To say that the divine nature, unlike the will, is determined to one act, is not evidence that one acts necessarily and the other freely; a natural agent like the sun can produce many effects, while a free agent, as the will is here said to be, could freely choose to perform only one action. In fact the divine will in producing the spirit acts necessarily; therefore it could equally be said that the will is the principle of producing the son who is also produced necessarily. There is accordingly no more proof by this distinction that the will is the cause of the spirit than of the son.[105]

Strictly then it is false to say that one person is produced naturally and another freely, since nothing can be produced freely unless contingently so that it could equally not be produced; but each divine person is naturally and necessarily produced. Willing in this context can only mean voluntarily, not contingently, so that God generates freely in the same way as he does in virtue of having the power to do so and of knowing and being wise and good, which is Peter Lombard's interpretation.[106] Metaphorically, and in a broad sense however, the distinction between knowing and willing can be conceded, where, as employed by the authorities, intellect and will connote the same divine essence which is generating and spirating; but that—as has been said—does not imply any distinction of

---

[102] Ideo aliter respondeo ad questionem consequenter ad precedentia quod tantum in divinis sit precise essentia, ita quod non est ibi aliquod absolutum quocunque modo ex natura rei distinctum, vel non idem cum essentia; et dictum est in precedenti questione quod aliquod absolutum est principium elicitivum. Ideo dico quod essentia sub ratione essentie est principium elicitivum generationis verbi (*ibid.*, q. 2, G; also C–D).

[103] *Ibid.*, G. [104] *Ibid.*, d. 6, q. 1, C–O.

[105] *Ibid.*, G. [106] *Ibid.*, M.

generating principles just because both signify essence as the principle of each activity.[107] Intellect and will here in addition to signifying an absolute—the divine essence—also consignify generation and spiration as concepts. Provided they are treated as such and not each as something self-subsistent, the distinction between them can be accepted in all those propositions which commonly attribute one activity to the father by way of the intellect and the other to the son by way of will.[108] These remain, however, different connotations of the same absolute being; hence if taken precisely for what they signify there is no difference in their meaning and it is as true to say that God knows by his intellect as to say that he knows by his will; and conversely: for these different terms differ only in their conventional meaning as terms, and not, when applied to God, in their real signification.[109] By the same token the lack of any such distinction in God to which these terms correspond precludes either intellect or will from itself connoting the principle of generation. There is no parallel between saying that someone is strong by fortitude and saying a divine person generates by intellect or will, any more than there is between intellect and will and whiteness. Just as intellect and will do not connote a physical property or form in God, nor do they a form or principle by which he acts. In this sense the only term which formally describes God as generating is 'generation', as God himself acting.[110]

If, then, there is no real distinction between essence and persons over generation, there is not between the substance of the persons themselves or their own relations and properties. Where essence and persons are formally distinct because something can be predicated of one, as essence can be predicated of father or son, and not of the other as father cannot be predicated of son and so not of essence whether by the first or second modes,[111] they are all of the same substance. The divine essence, as all hold, is thus common to all three persons and communicated to the son and the spirit by the father, with each constituted from its own properties and the divine essence.[112] Hence the son is generated from the same substance as the father; and with Duns Scotus, in opposition to Henry of Ghent, Ockham agrees that they are consubstantial as belonging to the same essence rather than as if they

---

[107] Ibid., d. 2, q. 1, 35–6; 45–6.

[108] Ibid., d. 7, q. 2, G.

[109] Ad aliud concedo maiorem, et ideo concedo quod quidquid convenit illi rei que est intellectus divinus, convenit illi rei que est voluntas divina, et a converso. Tamen aliqui termini possunt eandem rem principaliter importare et aliqua distincta connotare; propter que distincta connotata potest aliquid vere predicari de uno et vere negari de reliquo, sicut dictum est prius. Et ita est in proposito, quod intellectus divinus et voluntas divina, hoc est isti termini, connotant determinato modo grammaticali vel logicali aliqua distincta secundum usum sanctorum et doctorum; ideo potest aliquid convenire uni et non alteri . . . Dico quod circumscribendo omnia connotata ita quod per ista nomina 'intellectus', 'voluntas', 'intelligere', 'velle', nihil connotetur, sed precise significetur hoc nomine 'intellectus' illa res que est formaliter intellectus et hoc nomine 'voluntas' precise illa res absoluta que est formaliter voluntas, et sic de aliis nominibus, et non plus hac institutione nova facta ita erit vera 'actus dicendi est actus voluntatis' et 'deus intelligit per voluntatem' sicut hec, 'intelligit per intellectum' (ibid., d. 2, q. 1, 44–6).

[110] Ibid., d. 6, q. 1, M–N.

[111] Cf. Quodlibet I, qq. 1, 3; II, q. 4.

[112] Ordinatio, d. 5, q. 2, B.

were of the same matter.[113] At the same time, unlike Duns, whose supporting arguments of the analogy of relation to essence and potency to act in creatures he rejects, Ockham denies that essence is communicated as something pre-existing to the son; rather it is the same for both. To say that essence has being before the son, is only true in the sense that it is totally in the father, as prior in origin, before the son; but not as meaning that essence itself is totally prior to the son. For then the son would be produced from essence which is totally false, as the priority assigned by Henry of Ghent to generator over what it generates is false. The only priority is one of logical consequence of the form, 'A is filiation: therefore A is essence', and precludes all comparison with form or subject in composite beings.[114]

The only relations of priority which hold in God are thus those of logical community, where essence is common to each of the persons but no person is convertible with another,[115] and of origin or causality which applied to the father is only to say that he generates the son. As coeternal, however, the father cannot be temporally prior,[116] or by dignity or nature or dependence or any other mode.[117] That includes an order from prior to posterior, by which Duns distinguishes signs or instants of origin within God: the first sign with the divine essence and its essential generating attributes, the second with the father's generation of the son, and the third with the spirit's production. Whether as real themselves or as signs for what is real in God, these instants have no bearing upon the order of generation. If they were real they would merely be the same as the essential attributes required for generation; if signs, and they signified absolute being, there would be no difference in instants between father and son as the same absolute being, while as relative being, they would then contain whatever was essential to generation, reversing Dun's order. On the other hand, as merely conceptual they would make no difference to the real priority of the father. Even, however, if there were such instants, the father while coming first would still act with the son coming after-wards.[118] Accordingly prior and posterior, by origin, as opposed to duration, can be simultaneous.[119]

A relation of origin is what distinguishes one divine person from another, in contrast to an absolute distinction it has the advantage of being compatible with both the nature of the persons as independent substances (supposita) and with natural reason. On the principle of economy therefore it should be held, rather than invoke a miracle for which there is no warrant in the Bible: which an absolute distinction would require. That can be seen because it does not contradict some-thing incommunicable, which constitutes a single being with something else, to belong to the same being and to be distinguished from all that this being is distinguished from. But paternity is such an incommunicable being, really dis-tinguished from the persons of the son and the holy spirit and one with the divine essence. Therefore it is not contradictory for the father to be in an incommunicable being and distinguished from each of the persons.[120]

The alternative explanations, which locate the distinction variously in the

---

[113] Ibid., B–D.   [114] Ibid., E–M.   [115] Ibid., d. 9, q. 3, K.   [116] Ibid., B–E, H.
[117] Ibid., G–H.   [118] Ibid., E–G.   [119] Ibid., X–Y.   [120] Ibid., d. 26, q. 1, M–N.

persons themselves, or their real relations, or their absolute properties, or a combination of both, are all inadequate. The first in arguing from the absolute simplicity of the persons neglects that they all have a common nature; hence they are not absolutely simple nor for the same reason can they be distinguished by themselves.[121] The second opinion is from the opposite premise, that two absolute beings cannot constitute the same being, so that if the properties of the persons were absolute there would be several absolute beings in God and more than one God. To that Ockham replies that it is no more inconsistent for two absolutes to constitute the same being than for two relations to do so; if therefore there can be a real identity between essence and relation there can be one in God between essence and an absolute property. Nor, as this opinion also asserts, is it more contradictory for a relation to be without its correlative than for one absolute to be without another.[122]

The third and most elaborate opinion, of Duns Scotus, is for Ockham the most anomalous in distinguishing the persons by their absolute properties while at the same time recognising their distinct relations, unlike the fourth opinion by which there is only absolute being in God. Although not supported in the writings of the saints and fathers, or true, this view in its unqualified form (of the fourth opinion) appears to accord better with the conception of the Trinity as three persons in a single being just because it is more difficult to understand how such a being can be a relation—as something intermediate rather than absolute.[123] The third opinion in attempting to embrace both in different degrees is entirely irrational, because whenever that which is distinct is one and the same thing, each distinction constitutes that thing, since there is no more reason why it should be one rather than another. But that which includes essence and an absolute property and paternity is one being and distinct from any person; therefore this being is also a person; and so paternity—as a relation—constitutes the father and distinguishes him from the son and the spirit, both formally and efficiently. Accordingly, if relation is included in the Trinity it must, equally with property, distinguish one person from another.[124]

As to the arguments for this opinion, none of the three ways which they follow establishes it. By the first of comparing a relation with what is related it is not universally true that relation always formally refers to something, but only when something related is really distinct both from the term of the relation—that to which a relation refers—and from relation itself. When there is no such thing, and so nothing beyond a relation or what it constitutes, then it does not follow. Which is the case with essence, as really distinguished from neither a relation nor its term; it is therefore not related. Paternity on the other hand is that which constitutes a relation is distinct from its term; it is therefore related as a person or individual, but not as essence.[125] Moreover, all real relation, as we have discussed in chapter three, requires a real distinction of extremes or constitutes a real extreme or extremes; and so paternity as an extreme does not, contrary to this opinion, require a preceding distinction in God, just as in God—as opposed to creatures—a

---

[121] Ibid., B–C.   [122] Ibid., D, L.   [123] Ibid., E–I.   [124] Ibid., K.   [125] Ibid., O.

relation does not have to terminate at an absolute for the reasons just given.[126]

The second way of reasoning, from the incompatibility of relation with origin, so that only among absolutes can that which originates be prior to what is originated, is again unfounded. In God one is not prior to the other save in the sense that one is from the other. The father is father only in virtue of having a son; their origin is thus the same, in the father's having a son. There are therefore in God, as we have seen, no instants of origin or nature; and their absence, contrary to Duns, is not an argument against a relation distinguishing the divine persons. Rather such talk of instants is false or at least improper, an abuse of language which can only mislead the simple.[127] Priority in origin means simultaneity of being: far from the father coming first, it is the son, in being produced by the father, who originates in what is prior.[128]

Thirdly there are the arguments based upon the concept of something constitutive: as the formal source of a being, it must totally contradict whatever contradicts that being. If therefore, argues Duns, paternity (a relation) constituted the substance of a person's being in its incommunicable aspect, the father's communicability would contradict paternity, which is false since no essence is of itself incommunicable.[129] Ockham acknowledges that paternity of itself is singular and incommunicable, and so is any essence or form which is of itself incommunicable except perhaps the divine essence. Since, however, any relation in God is the same as essence and the two other relations, a relation cannot be called the ultimate constituent of a person, distinguishing it from the others. Hence the opposite relations, of active and passive spiration, are also the same; like paternity and divinity they are all the divine essence. No contradiction is involved because of their real identity. Moreover, as we saw in the previous chapter, a common quidditative concept as opposed to a nature can be abstracted from ultimate differences, in opposition to Duns's contention to the contrary there and again here. Accordingly there is no need to treat them as irreducibly distinct, while, as we have already seen, essence and relation can constitute one and the same thing. The distinction between them has no similarity to that between form and matter because relation is neither an accident of essence nor distinguished from it as relation, for the very reason that they are really the same. On all these grounds, it is no more impossible for relation to constitute an intellectual substance and make it self-subsistent and distinct than for substance to do so.[130]

Their relation of origin, then, distinguishes the divine persons; but relation and origin are not themselves distinct, on the principle of economy.[131] If they were

---

[126] *Ibid.*, Q–R.   [127] *Ibid.*, S.

[128] Et si dicas, si pater est prior filio, ergo in illo priori non est filius in quo tamen est pater. Respondeo quod magis debet dici econverso, quia eo ipso quod pater est prior origine filio, filius est in illo priori, et pater non est in illo priori, quia illud prius non est nisi pater (*ibid.*, S); also Y.

[129] *Ibid.*, G.   [130] *Ibid.*, S–EE.

[131] Ideo dico aliter ad questionem, et primo ostendo quod origo relatio nullo modo distinguuntur ex natura rei . . . Primum patet quod frustra fit per plura quod potest fieri per pauciora, sed omnia que salvantur ponendo aliquam distinctionem inter generationem et relationem possunt salvari ponendo omnimodam identitatem; ergo etc (*ibid.*, q. 2, H).

that would be either because paternity was necessarily founded in generation or because generation presupposed paternity or some generating or generated being (*suppositum*) as a person's constitutive property; none of which follows. Paternity, all agree, is not founded in generation because generation is itself a relation and no relation can be its own foundation, or, as we saw in chapter three, distinct from it. In this case essence is its foundation; nothing else need be posited. Nor is paternity distinct from generation, in the same way as God's act of creation is not distinct from what he creates; and if there is no such intermediary between creator and creatures, far less is there a distinction between God the father who generates, and God the son who is generated. That holds, too, for what generates and is generated, and the substance which generates and is generated; they are not distinct, for as paternity constitutes a substance and, as we have seen earlier, does not presuppose it, so could generation if it were something distinct. In none of the divine persons therefore is there any distinction between their origin and their relation to one another.[132]

That relation and origin together constitute and distinguish the divine persons can be inferred from the principle that the same thing cannot be both truly affirmed and denied of that which is absolutely the same and in no way distinct. But origin and relation are universally accepted to be really the same. Hence one cannot constitute what the other cannot constitute; and conversely if different terms, regardless of whether or not their modes of signifying differ, stand entirely for the same thing in all respects and one is truly and necessarily affirmed of that thing, the other term or terms must also be. But it is universally agreed, even by those who take a contrary view of modes of signification, that origin is relation and generation is paternity. Therefore if paternity and origin do not in any way signify something really distinct from the other origin cannot stand for something for which paternity or relation do not stand; and conversely. The terms 'God' and 'divinity' on the other hand although both denote the same being are not convertible because 'God' signifies person and essence; and as person and essence are not identical in all respects nor are the significations of 'God' and 'divinity', since the latter does not also signify person. As we have frequently mentioned, modes of signifying do not affect what is signified; and when what is signified is not itself diverse, as origin and relation are not, the diverse terms denoting them are synonyms; which is what 'relation' and 'origin' would be so far as they refer to God: only their different signification among creatures keeps them distinct. Unlike abstracts and concretes like 'man' and 'humanity' which are not convertible, although standing for the same thing, nothing is signified by relation which is not identical with that signified by origin. Accordingly we can say that origin is relation where we cannot say that man is humanity. Attempts to distinguish one from the other as presupposing or as prior to it are thus false and come from a misconception.[133]

That goes for both contrary opinions considered here, which attempt to differentiate relation from origin, the first treating only relation as intrinsic to

---

[132] *Ibid.*   [133] *Ibid.*, I–L; also *Elench.* 98 c–102 d.

the persons and the means of distinguishing them, the second isolating the productive or generative as the one real property in the father, with the others having
the power to generate, generating, and father—subsumed under it.[134] Both confuse
different modes of signifying with different significations. For something to be
intrinsic and proper to something is to distinguish it from something else; but
origin is proper to the father as active generation because it can only be affirmed of
the father. Therefore origin as active generation distinguishes the father from the
other persons, and as intrinsic to him it is in no way distinguished from paternity
as something real, nor by the same token is it as active generation either prior or
posterior to the father. If it were, the property which is prior would be distinguished
by the property which is posterior; the latter would then be a relation, and the
persons distinguished not by what is relative, as this opinion holds, but by absolutes.
If they are not distinguished one cannot be prior or posterior to the other. Any such
distinction is then the result of misconception, and will be false as any such wrong
intellection, say taking a man for an ass, will be, when it does not conform to what
really is.[135] That applies equally to the second opinion because 'generative' and the
other cognate terms all signify the same person; if therefore 'generative' really
constitutes the father so must 'father' and 'generating' and 'able to generate'.[136]
These are only distinct names and concepts which are not really in God nor themselves constitute a property but signify only the same property. The sole order
among terms is more and less universal. That does not apply here; for while it is
true that 'able to generate' is superior to 'generating', neither is a constitutive
principle; and if they, and the other terms mentioned, stood precisely for the same
divine property they would not be distinguished even as terms but would be
synonymous.[137] Only essence and relation constitute the persons; and only relation
distinguishes them, not under the aspect of relation as such taken reduplicatively
but as that by which they are also constituted.[138]

Not all the divine relations however constitute the persons in the same way.
In the strict sense, not only of being essential to something as its essence and nature
but also of distinguishing it from something else, only the three relations of
paternity, filiation, and procession are constitutive. All the other relations like
spiration are essential simply to the existence of a person without distinguishing it
from another person. That follows because the first three relations are each peculiar
to a different person, but a relation like active spiration is common to more than
one.[139] It does not however make relations like spiration any less constitutive
of the person concerned, and far from coming to a person, already constituted,

---

[134] *Ordinatio, ibid.,* B–G.   [135] *Ibid.,* E, L–M.   [136] *Ibid.,* G, N.   [137] *Ibid.,* N.
[138] Per predicta respondeo ad formam questionis. Quando queritur, an persone constituantur
et distinguantur per relationes sub ratione relationum vel secundum aliam rationem potest
intelligi quod sit una reduplicativa, et sic non constituuntur nec distinguuntur per relationes
nquantum sunt iste relationes . . . Si autem intelligatur ut scilicet ut sit equipollens uni exclusive
ut scilicet constituantur et distinguantur tantum per relationes . . . Et sic dico quod sic, quia
nihil est penitus imaginabile in persona nisi essentia vel relatio. Per essentiam autem constituuntur sed non distinguuntur; ergo per relationem precise distinguuntur, per quam tamen eo
ipso constituuntur (*ibid.,* o).
[139] *Ibid.,* q. 3, C–D.

as something added or accidental, according to one opinion, they constitute the same unity as person and essence. If they did not but were added to a person already constituted to say, paternity, they would be both posterior to paternity and prior in coming to it; and then in the way that the intellective soul comes to a composition of form and matter and together constitutes man, so could aspiration be said to constitute a person in coming to paternity and essence.[140] If therefore active spiration were really distinct from paternity there would be four incommunicable beings.[141] There are not because active spiration is as inseparable from paternity as paternity is from essence; and as essence alone does not constitute an incommunicable nature (*suppositum*) unconnected with any other, neither would essence and paternity together without spiration. Spiration is therefore essential to a *suppositum*—in this case of the father—as a real unity of all those constituents none of which is really distinct from the other.[142] They do, however, differ formally: beyond diverse modes of signifying the same thing, for example generation and paternity which are in no way distinct,[143] something can truly be verified of spiration, namely the son, which cannot be verified of the father. Hence they are not the same in all respects because paternity cannot be in the son whereas spiration can. Accordingly while each person has only one relation, there is a formal distinction between it and spiration.[144]

Person itself is an individual spiritual or rational nature (*suppositum intellectuale*). Like any *suppositum*, of which it is a species, it is self-subsistent, neither the subject of something else nor having something else as its subject.[145] That, however, is not equivalent to defining person negatively, by a double incommunicability: neither the inability to be communicated as something common to a number of similar things, as a universal is, nor to communicate something, as form is communicated, is the mark of a person, but rather of matter or even of paternity or Christ's assumed nature.[146] Person, on the other hand, stands for something positive which really exists; it is therefore a term of first intention verifiable of real things as opposed to other terms or concepts.[147] Moreover as a property of substance—coming under *suppositum*—person is predicable connotatively by the second essential mode consignifying substance and something additional, namely individual spiritual being.[148] Applied to the divine persons, however, that does not mean, as Duns Scotus held, that person signifies both essence and relation.[149]

To begin with, 'person' is not the first immediate term of a divine person because it is common to both creatures and God, and so to more than the divine persons.[150] In the second place while agreeing with Duns that something common can be abstracted from the divine persons, it is not for Duns's reasons—that there is some ultimate constituent of the divine essence absolutely simple and undeterminable of which there can be a quidditative concept, whereas there can be no such concept of ultimate difference in creatures which are determinable and so potential. Nor is it a precise concept of the divine persons themselves. Not only can

---

140 *Ibid.*, C.   141 *Ibid.*, E.   142 *Ibid.*, C, D; also d. 25, q. unica, C.
143 *Ibid.*, d. 27, q. 1, C, E.   144 *Ibid.*, D.   145 *Ibid.*, d. 23, q. 1, C; also d. 25, 1.
146 *Ibid.*, d. 23, q. 1, C.   147 *Ibid.*, D.   148 *Ibid.*, G.   149 *Ibid.*, d. 25, q. 1, B–C.

there be a quidditative concept of ultimate differences in anything created having essential unity, such as genus and ultimate difference where difference comes under the concept of its genus, but there can also be quidditative concepts of relations.[150] But there can be no such concept of the divine persons themselves; and the *sancti* did not have such a concept when using the term 'person', because, as we saw in the previous chapter, there is no simple concept of what cannot be known distinctly and in particular, and no such knowledge, intuitive or abstractive, is possible of God or the divine nature.[151] In the third place neither equivocally nor univocally does person imply essence or relation: not equivocally, for then every proposition containing the term 'person' would be equivocal, such as 'The father is a person', which is not the case; nor univocally since the nominal definition of person does not include essence or relation. Hence person formally and immediately denotes neither, whether directly or indirectly, as some hold.[152] Rather in standing for a spiritual being it signifies what is constituted by essence and relation; it therefore stands not for the latter in themselves neither of which is person but for their product.[153] By the same token it stands for what is singular both in God, where—although distinct—each person is really one and the same absolutely simple being, and in creatures where each person is an individual.[154] Hence the attempts to explain a divine person's community from a lack of determinateness are as otiose as they are unfounded.[155]

The only community which person has to three persons is as a term or word, unlike that of essence to person which is a real community; and as a common term 'person' can only be predicated connotatively by the second essential mode; for although a common concept abstracted from the persons could be affirmed absolutely by the first essential mode, we, as already said, do not possess such a concept.[156] Similarly person does not directly express a relation, although it includes a relation from which, once again, a concept of relation could be abstracted if we had direct knowledge of that—such as father—which was related.[157] Person, then, as a term can only be predicated of that which is constituted of essence and relation but of neither in itself, connotatively or abstractively. Nor does it give immediate knowledge of what they constitute because, while person is a term of first intention, it does not give proper knowledge of a being that cannot itself be known *in statu isto*.

The two principles therefore governing the relation of essence of persons and persons to one another are first, that there is no distinction within the divine essence between its different attributes such as knowing and willing, and second, that relation as that which both constitutes and distinguishes the persons is really

---

[150] *Ibid.*, C–D.   [151] *Ibid.*, E.   [152] *Ibid.*, H.

[153] Et ideo illud quod est primo et formaliter suppositum intellectuale significat per se et primo personam. Et ex hoc ultra illud quod in divinis est formaliter et primo suppositum intellectuale significabitur primo per hoc nomen persona divina, et quia nec relatio nec essentia est primo et formaliter suppositum intellectuale sed constitutum ex essentia et relatione ideo persona non plus significat essentiam vel relationem quam paternitas divina significat divinam essentiam; sed primo significat constitutum ex essentia et relatione (*ibid.*, I); also Q.

[154] *Ibid.*, I.   [155] *Ibid.*, K–P.   [156] *Ibid.*, P.   [157] *Ibid.*, R.

the same as person and so the same as divine essence. From that it follows that there can be no real distinction in either. Within essence itself the difference between knowing and willing is merely of modes of signifying its activities. Between essence and persons, and persons themselves, it consists in a formal difference of relation which is really the same as each. Both principles apply to the son and the holy spirit in the same way as we have considered for the father. Thus the son does not generate, because there is only one son and one father and so only one relation of paternity and one of filiation; if each was compossible with the other, each would be the same as the other and there would not be father or son. Such reasons are only persuasions of a truth which cannot be demonstrated but only held on the authority of the Bible.[158]

They can never be more when the premises are from faith alone; the concern therefore is not to prove them but to clarify them, more often than not by disentangling their meaning from the misconceived efforts of others at demonstration. Thus the arguments for the son's generation by the father from a first productive principle, which is perfect, necessary and self-sufficient, are inconclusive or wrong.[159] Others, as well as philosophers, would equally deny what has to be proved and is only assumed here, that God or an intelligence is productive of any knowledge, and would reply that if the intellect, from the presence of an intelligible object, did produce knowledge of what was generated, then essence and intellect would differ, which in God they do not.[160] Nor does it follow that the intellect is any more the productive principle of such knowledge than premises which normally produce conclusions or the terms of a principle which produce knowledge of a principle, none of which, many say, is distinct in God from the act of knowing.[161] Again the arguments that such a productive principle includes nothing imperfect could also be applied to God as cause, so that on the same analogy that he produces something in him, it could also be said that he causes something in him, which in being caused would be imperfect.[162] The other arguments, comparing memory and intellect, and of a first necessary product, are equally inadequate. Neither they nor any others drawn from natural reason can prove God's triunity.[163]

The answer to the question whether the son's generation is univocal or equivocal is itself equivocal. Strictly it is neither. On the one hand it is not simply univocal because for that generator and generated have to be formally the same; but paternity cannot be formally likened to filiation, as whiteness can to whiteness. Nor on the other hand are they properly equivocal, since there is nothing really different in one from the other, and what is really one cannot be generated equivocally. In consequence, because of their real identity, their generation is more univocal than equivocal, notwithstanding their formal difference.[164]

In the case of the holy spirit we have already seen that the will is not in itself the productive principle, but only as it is the divine essence, which is will as it is intellect.[165] And as the will alone is not the principle of the spirit, neither is the activity of the intellect prior to that of the will. Indeed strictly it is misconceived to

158 *Ibid.*, d. 7, q. 3, G.   159 *Ibid.*, d. 9, q. 1, B.   160 *Ibid.*, C, F.   161 *Ibid.*, F.
162 *Ibid.*, H–I.   163 *Ibid.*, G–N.   164 *Ibid.*, q. 2, C–D, N, P.   165 *Ibid.*, d. 10, q. 1.

speak of will and intellect in God; rather it should be of his willing and knowing.[166] For the same reason it is a misnomer to say that the spirit is produced freely as opposed to the son who is produced naturally. The distinction between necessary and free is more one of words than real; for if freely means voluntarily, to ask whether the will's reason can be both free and necessary is simply to ask whether the will can will something necessarily or be the necessary principle of producing something, which is just what God's will does.[167] There is thus no need to distinguish, with one opinion, between the will as necessary and an agent which acts naturally, on the grounds that a natural agent must be absolutely first or determined by what is absolutely first; and that since, according to this opinion, neither applies to the will, the first because nothing in God is dependent upon something else, the second because intellect is prior to will, the will, it is held, cannot be a necessary agent, although itself necessary.[168] As Aristotle and Averroes affirmed, there is no contradiction between acting rationally and acting freely, because an act is free only if the agent has the power to act or not to act. Nor is the divine will, as St Augustine says, subsequent to the intellect since they are in no way distinct. Therefore if God is first agent so is the will.[169]

If, then, freedom is understood strictly as a voluntary act, the spirit is not produced freely any more than the son is. But that cannot be proved as it would entail proving the definition of a word; and as we saw in chapter four, a nominal definition cannot be demonstrated. All nevertheless clearly agree that the spirit is produced both necessarily and in some way by the will; and if freedom is defined as whatever is from the will, necessarily or contingently, then it can be accepted that the spirit is produced both freely and necessarily, as being from a necessary act of will. That does not, however, apply when freedom means what is contingent or indifferent, as we have discussed before.[170] In the first case no contradiction is implied. As God, in St Augustine's analogy, is not called less than omnipotent because he cannot die or be mistaken, so his will is not less free for willing necessarily.[171]

Now because there is no distinction of any kind between intellect and will there can be no distinction between them as the principles of producing the son and the spirit. All distinctions therefore between active and passive spiration, generation and production, are real only in so far as the divine persons are formally distinguished by a real relation and not as they are themselves absolute or derive from distinct attributes in God. Consequently the different modes of generation and spiration among the persons are not from themselves as distinct but, as we have already seen in the case of the father, in virtue of belonging to formally distinct *constituta*, namely of essence and paternity in the case of the father, essence and filiation in the case of the son, and essence and procession in the case of the spirit. Hence only in their origin is there any distinction between the father and son in spirating the spirit; for, as we have seen earlier, the father is prior to the son in the sense that he produces the son. But that does not imply any order between them in

[166] *Ibid.*, P. [167] *Ibid.*, q. 2, E. [168] *Ibid.*, D.
[169] *Ibid.*, F–G. [170] *Ibid.*, H. [171] *Ibid.*, K.

producing the spirit, because, as we have also seen, there is no sign or instant in which the father is prior to the son. Spiration is common equally and immediately to both of them.[172] And as the priority of one cause over another does not prevent their concurrence as partial causes of the same effect, so the father and son act uniformly in producing the spirit.[173] Accordingly Duns Scotus's argument to the contrary based upon their diversity of origin does not hold; for if, as Duns rightly says, the father is from himself, he has nothing from anything else. Therefore he must spirate in the first instant—assuming such; otherwise if generation were in the first instant of his origin and spiration in the second, he would not spirate when the son spirates, which Duns denies. Moreover, if spiration were not in the first instant it would be necessary to posit an origin for it distinct from the father's origin, because there cannot be a prior and posterior in origin without an origin, any more than there can be prior and posterior in duration or perfection or anything else without duration or perfection. The father would then have spiration by another origin and not from himself, which Duns also denies.[174] Hence it is uniform in father and son.

That applies to all attempts to prove that the spirit is from both father and son by an order between intellect and will as productive principles or powers. The first, that the love by which the will produces the spirit is from the word by which the intellect produces the intellect, does not apply to all that is loved or necessarily to the word rather than the word's cause or principle. The second, that there is always an order in the production of many by one unless they differ only materially, is invalid because God can produce two objects of different species. So is the third of Duns Scotus that the fecundity of the intellect constitutes the father and is in some way prior to the will as the principle of love, which again falsely assumes two productive principles. None of these proves the priority of generation over spiration, first, because even if there were distinct principles or powers in God, no order between them is entailed, whether of perfection, origin, duration, or nature, as there is none between the created intellect and will; and second, because the only reason for such an order would be the priority of knowing over willing. That however does not lead to the priority of the intellect over the will, because an order among effects never formally and necessarily entails a corresponding order of causes. Indeed there can be a plurality of effects from the same cause, as the same intellect can have knowledge of premises as well as conclusions and the same will have volition of an end and the means to it; while separable and independent causes can have inseparable effects, and conversely.[175] Moreover, it is either false or irrelevant to say, as Duns Scotus does, that the will's fecundity is communicated to the son before the spirit is produced, because priority here must mean either more universal or first by origin. If more universal, to be true it will either beg the question, and imply that the will's fecundity as existing in the son is communicated to more than the spirit, or it will be irrelevant in meaning that the will's fecundity is common to more than the spirit. If on the other hand it means that the will's fecundity is communicated to the son before the spirit is produced it is false

172 *Ibid.*, d. 12, q. 3, D.   173 *Ibid.*, E.   174 *Ibid.*, C.   175 *Ibid.*, d. 11, q. 1, C–G.

or meaningless in relation to God where as we have seen there is no order of signs or instants.[176]

Ockham's own resolution of a theological problem is exclusively theological, and shows once again that the principle of economy applied to theology is more consistent with theological truth than attempts to make it accessible to reason. It is that whatever belongs to the father is also to be attributed to each of the other persons unless the contrary is expressly found in the Bible or follows evidently from its principles or from self-evident principles or from the determination of the church. But all catholics, including the Greeks against whom this question is directed, agree that the spirit proceeds from the father; nor by any of the preceding ways is it to be held that it does not proceed from the son. Therefore it must be conceded that the spirit is also from the son. The major premise is manifest because whenever something is numerically one, simple and indivisible, whatever is said of one aspect is affirmed equally of the rest. The minor follows from what is in the Bible. Anselm also used the same reasoning from God's indivisibility and simplicity to prove the same truth against the Greeks. From the fact, then, that the father spirates, it can be held that the son also spirates.[177]

In this, as in the other arguments concerning the divine persons, it is Ockham who stays most closely to the articles of faith and shows theological judgement in eschewing the temptation to translate divine operations into created terms. Repeatedly he refutes the parallels drawn from natural phenomena, both for their unsound multiplication of principles and for their inapplicability to God. Thus over the question, whether the son and the spirit would still be distinct if the spirit was not from the son, he rejects the reply that they would not in being only distinguished by opposite relations.[178] To begin with, when one thing is distinguished from another by what is proper to it, as whiteness is distinguished by whiteness from everything not having whiteness, it needs nothing else to distinguish it. But the son is distinguished from the spirit by filiation as proper to him alone. Therefore filiation suffices to distinguish them without active spiration. If filiation and spiration were the same relation the spirit would then be generated and would be the son. Nor is it true that the divine persons are distinguished by opposite relations; for that, too, would mean that the son and the spirit were the same, if filiation and passive spiration were one relation, as paternity and active spiration are the same in the father. In fact, as we have seen, the divine persons are distinguished by really distinct relations which together with essence constitute them distinct persons, as paternity and filiation are with essence the constituents of father and son. For that they have only to be distinct, not opposite or absolute or relative. When they are not distinct there is only one person, as in the case of paternity and active spiration. Moreover, not only do relations not have to be opposites in order to be distinguished; they do not have to be related any more than distinct absolutes need to be related. Contrary to the opinion under discussion relation does

---

[176] *Ibid.*, G.
[177] *Ibid.*, L–M.
[178] *Ibid.*, q. 2, B–C.

not imply distinction, because to be distinguished is wider than to be related; and something can be distinguished which is not related, as the son can be really distinguished from the spirit by filiation without being related to the spirit.[179]

The question at issue, then, is not whether it is possible for the spirit in some way to be really distinguished from the son, and not to proceed from the son, because the latter is theologically impossible; nor for the same reason whether it follows necessarily that if the spirit does not proceed from the son, it is not distinct from him. But rather whether there is in the son anything beyond active spiration which is distinguished from the spirit, in the same way as it could be asked whether, excluding his intellective soul, man could be distinguished from the angels. In man's case, the answer is by matter. In that of the son, although it cannot be shown evidently that the spirit proceeds from him, theologically it follows necessarily and formally that there is in the son something which is not entirely the same as active spiration, namely filiation, as the spirit has something which is not identical with passive spiration, namely procession. If there were nothing distinct to each, neither would be distinguished from the other, as the son if he had only active spiration without filiation would be indistinguishable from the father.[180]

In the same way the apparent paradox that, theologically, active spiration is the same in both the father and the son, and yet the father and son are distinct, does not entail accepting distinct relations of spiration; for, as we saw in chapter three, relations are only distinct if either their foundations or their terms are distinct. But the foundation of active spiration is the divine essence and its term is the holy spirit. Hence it is unique.[181]

The further difficulty of explaining how father and son can be called one spirator and one principle does not require a suggested grammatical distinction between 'spirator' as a substantive and 'spirating' as the adjective qualifying it which can be in the plural and applied to both father and son. What holds for creatures does not hold for God. When Socrates is called both musician and grammarian, these terms stand for two different sciences, but in God spirator and spirating stand for the same being. Therefore as father and son are one spirator they are one in spirating. Confused supposition does not arise, because as we also discussed in the third chapter, that occurs only over a universal or syncatheogorematic term and can never be verified of many or a plural term.[182] Nor need the father and son be distinguished in spirating, as Duns Scotus maintained. His reasons were that while both father and son spirate as one essence they do so not under the aspect of essence but of the will, with the will in turn conceived not as an absolute but as one relative property common to both persons. In this respect the will's fecundity differs from that of intellect in being in two persons; for its love unlike the wisdom which is from the intellect must be mutual and harmonious. The fallacy of this argument, for Ockham, is the superfluity of the notion of a harmonious will as something additional to essence, person and relation, which alone are in God. If it were absolute it would be distinct from the will, which is contrary to Duns's

[179] Ibid., C–F.   [180] Ibid., H–M.
[181] Ibid., d. 12, q. 1, B–C.   [182] Ibid., E–F.

contention, as it would be if it were a person; and it cannot be a relation because a relation cannot be a productive principle.[183]

Although whatever is in God must be formally and really one of these three, nevertheless a word or a concept which is not God can signify one of them principally and consignify the others; in that sense the divine will can be called the elective principle of the spirit, since will and essence are entirely the same. Moreover, harmony and concord belong as much to the love between father and spirit as between father and son; but on that account the spirit is not said to spirate. When therefore the authorities speak of the mutual love of the spirit joining the father and son they mean not some distinct mutual reality which unites them but that the father and son in loving one another produce the spirit: and their love is common to the whole divine essence, which is what Richard of St Victor says.[184] That is as far as reason can take us: there is no answer to the question why the spirit and son do not in turn produce a further person from their mutual love, beyond the probable cause that God is three persons. But that reply is made regardless of logic;[185] and strictly speaking it is false to say that the father and son produce the spirit from their mutual love because in a causal proposition the predicate of the second proposition (into which it is exponible) must be uniformly affirmed of the predicate of the first proposition. But it is universally untrue in the strict sense that whatever loves mutually produces the holy spirit. By the same token it is also untrue in the strict sense that the father and son produce the spirit either in so far as they are one or in so far as they are distinct; for in each case the reduplicatives 'one' and 'distinct' would mean that everything one or distinct would spirate, which is false. Hence the truth of all such propositions depends upon proper theological understanding contained in the Bible or the principles and authority which derive from it.[186]

The difference between generation and spiration again is due to nothing but themselves formally distinguished.[187] It can best be explained—albeit imperfectly—as that between giving birth to something totally similar to its progenitor, as the son is to the father, and making a gift, as the spirit is given in love from the father and son. Although, as we have seen, formally and really, intellection and volition, like intellect and will, are the same as essence, God in knowing himself can be said to be the productive principle of the son who is distinguished from the father not, as we have also seen, absolutely, but in being produced in total similarity to the father. The holy spirit on the other hand, as a gift, is not produced in such similarity, but is from God's willing as the principle at once of giving and producing it. The spirit is not therefore born as the son is; and that, without prejudice to more worthy opinion, is Ockham's own inadequate attempt to explain their difference.[188] It is founded upon a comparison with the created intellect and will, where the intellect, as we are by now familiar, from intuitive knowledge of an individual is able to

---

[183] Ibid., q. 2, C–E.
[184] Ibid., F.
[185] Ibid., G–I; Ad hoc respondeo non curando modo de logica (I).
[186] Ibid., I–Q.   [187] Ibid., d. 13, q. I, C.   [188] Ibid., K–L.

form a mental likeness of what was previously known, so that if it could be reproduced outside the intellect it would be of the same nature as its object: that holds also if a concept is identified with an act of knowing. The will, however, does not have the power of producing concepts, but it can make a gift to an object from love, regardless of similarity or dissimilarity.[189] Accordingly, although the divine intellect does not produce the son's similarity in the word from pre-existing knowledge, as the created intellect produces its similarities, there is in some way a proportion between them and the divine and created wills. But that is not to explain why spiration is not called generation. In statu isto there is no sufficient reason; it must be accepted on faith.[190]

The holy spirit is a gift in the strict sense of being produced from love of something; and as that in which the love of father and son unite the spirit can be called their nexus. In the broader sense of gift, however, as that which is freely given for another's possession, a gift can be said to be a property of the spirit in being from the father and son and to a rational creature which can alone receive it: that is when property is understood as something predicated necessarily and solely of spirit.[191] In the same way inascibility, when it means something which is not born or produced, as the son and spirit are, or communicated, as essence is, can be called proper to the father alone. For like a gift in relation to the spirit, it is not something real constituting the father but predicable necessarily of him, and unlike paternity, active and passive spiration, and filiation, it is not really God. Hence inascibility has only simple supposition and is predicated only of the father.[192]

Correspondingly, as the father is really paternity, the son is really the word, with no distinction between them, because all that is the word in God is generated and only the son is generated.[193] Moreover, as a distinct being independent of any other (suppositum), the son's divinity as a person is separate from his assumed human nature. The latter can therefore be discarded without affecting his divine nature. Their union, however, would then be destroyed; for like any real relation, union unites the two extremes of human and divine nature; and although it is not something distinct from either, it is additional to both. In that it differs from the relation of the word to the son or paternity to the father, which are the same. Its foundation is the son's humanity, which is imperfect and dependent. But they must not be conceived as one indivisible nature: it would be as contradictory for a human person to be divine as to be an ass. Rather the son as a man is sustained by the son in God. Like form and matter they remain distinct; but unlike form and matter they do not constitute an essential unity. Instead the human subsists in the divine as an accident, in the way that whiteness inheres in something white, and not as an independent substance (suppositum). That however is no more than a parallel with a truth which cannot be demonstrated but must be held on faith.[194]

What can be said is that the union is immediately between the son's two persons

---

[189] Ibid., I; also d. 18, q. I.   [190] Ibid., d. 13, q. I, N–O.
[191] Ibid., d. 18, q. I, F–H.   [192] Ibid., d. 29, q. I, E–G.
[193] Ibid., d. 27, q. 3, DD.
[194] Reportatio, III, q. I, B–G; also Quodlibet IV, qq. 11 and 12.

and not, as one opinion has it, between the son's human nature and the divine essence. If that were true, either the union with the son in God would be superfluous since each union would be really distinct, with that between essence and humanity prior, according to this opinion, to that between the two persons. Hence all that is said of the son will be said independently and first of essence. Alternatively there would be two unions in the son. The consequences in both cases would be heretical, because whatever can be affirmed of the divine essence without contradicting the persons can be affirmed of any person. But if essence is united with the son's human nature then any of the persons will be united; and as the son can die and be incarnated so can the father and the holy spirit, all of which is contrary to faith. Conversely, to be only of the son there need be a union only with the son. Whereas all the persons are of one essence, the persons themselves are really distinguished, so that something can be affirmed of one and not of the others.[195]

Consequently the union of the son's two natures is with the entire person of the son. Its formal term is the property constituting the son an independent being (*suppositum*); as proper only to him it is not shared by either of the other persons.[196] Hence the union is with the son. It could, however, be with the essence itself or any of the persons, as no contradiction is implied; but not with their relation, because to depend essentially is to depend totally, whether on one or more causes, which is not the case here.[197]

Only in Christ are 'man' and 'humanity' distinct because in Christ 'man' stands for the son's substance as a divine person, and 'humanity' for the human nature sustained by the son as a divine person, and really distinct from him. In that sense the two are distinguished as substance (*quod*) and form (*quo*); and Christ can be called man in virtue of the humanity sustained by him as something is called white from the whiteness in it: with 'white' and 'whiteness' in personal supposition always distinguished as substance (*quod*) and quality (*quo*). That is not true of other men where 'man' and 'humanity' stand for the same in Socrates or Plato.[198] From that point of view, then, it has nothing to do with a human person that it is assumed by a divine person; it could as well apply to an irrational nature, like a stone or an ass, as to man, because such a union depends exclusively upon the son in God sustaining another nature; which is the meaning of personified.[199]

We can therefore say that the son as a divine person is the immediate term of the union with a human person, because their union depends upon the complete person of the son. But, improperly, their union can also be said to be with the divine essence in being the same as the son.[200]

That completes consideration of the divine persons. It is perhaps the fullest testimony to Ockham's theological orthodoxy and scrupulous adherence to the articles of faith. There is none of the uncontrolled speculation either theological or naturalistic which is one of the hallmarks of the so-called nominalists. If the many distinctions devoted to the divine persons are the occasion to exercise a

---

[195] *Reportatio, ibid.,* H–O.   [196] *Ibid.,* O.   [197] *Ibid.,* P; and *Quodlibet* IV, q. 12.
[198] *Ibid.,* S; also *Quodlibet* IV, q. 11 and *Quodlibet* V, q. 10.
[199] *Ibid.,* U.   [200] *Ibid.,* BB.

range of philosophical and logical questions, on intentions, imposition, concrete
and abstract terms, number, equality, magnitude, similarity, relation, generation,
movement, causality, the predicables and the categories, it is no less true that the
foundation of his trinitarian doctrine is the formal distinction, abhorrent to both
logic and natural experience. Ockham's acceptance of the logically contradictory
truth that three persons can be the same and yet distinct, affirmed the sovereignty
of theology over reason and natural experience; far from the latter circumscribing
theology or introducing an 'alternative theology', they were enlisted in the service
of a higher understanding which they could not compass. It is theology which
limits knowledge, not *vice versa*, and knowledge which has to cede to theology. If
in the process that meant demolishing speculations insecurely founded upon
natural experience in the service of theology, the foundations of theology itself
remained unimpaired; and if a later generation confused the attack upon one with
an attack upon the other, that is only one more element in the change from Ockham
to Ockhamism.

III KNOWLEDGE AND DIVINE IDEAS

We now turn to God's relation with what is outside him; and first to his knowledge.
That God really knows can be demonstrated *a priori* in the broadest sense by which
one proposition is the formal consequence of another. For it follows formally:
God is the highest being; therefore God knows, where knowing is the consequence
of his perfection and not *vice versa*. But that is not the same as knowing the cause of
his knowledge. There is none;[201] and the attempt to explain knowing from the
immaterial nature of the knower is misconceived.[202] So are the arguments for an
order of priority between intellect and knowledge, because only what is distinct
can have an order; but as we have repeatedly seen there is no distinction in God
between essence, intellect and knowledge or any of his attributes other than as
names and concepts. Hence rather than speak of knowledge in God we should in
the strictest sense say that knowledge is God or the divine essence.[203] That applies to
Duns Scotus's arguments that the divine essence is the first object of God's knowledge because essence is first by origin, perfection and adequation.

For something to be prior by perfection, something else must be posterior; but
nothing is posterior by perfection in God, because then something in God would
be imperfect, which is impossible. That also shows the falsity of Duns's major
premise that something has the same order which it would have if it were really
distinct, since there is no distinction in God. Nor for the same reason can there be a
mental distinction either of perfection or of origin between God's attributes, as
Duns holds that there is between essence and wisdom. As to his arguments from
adequation, the divine essence cannot be said to be an adequate object in the way
in which colour could be said to be the adequate object of sight, where everything
seen would be colour or coloured; for that would mean that essence could be
affirmed concretely and abstractly of everything intelligible to the divine intellect,

[201] *Ordinatio*, d. 35, q. 1, D.   [202] *Ibid.*, B–C.   [203] *Ibid.*, F–H.

which it cannot be, either by itself or by something else. Moreover, Duns's argument that knowledge which if formally infinite must have as its adequate object what is also formally infinite, contains the—for God—false middle that all knowing depends upon an adequate object; while, as we have discussed in chapter three, an adequate object as a common term does not include formally and virtually knowledge of all that comes under it.[204]

In contrast to Duns's conception of the divine attributes as flowing from the divine essence[205] Ockham recognises only an order of origin and community among the divine persons in God and of causality and perfection between God and everything else. But so far as his knowledge is concerned, the only primacy of an adequate object is by perfection, as we saw in chapter three, because God knows himself at the same time as he knows everything else in one simultaneous undifferentiated act.[206] Hence although ontologically there is an order of origin from God's being to that of his creatures, there is none in God's knowledge of himself and his creatures, as there is none between his essence and his attributes. Ockham has thus wrought a double simplification both in God and his relation to creatures, once again freeing modes of knowing from direct correspondence with modes of being.

That also answered those who posited, on the basis of an order between God's knowledge of himself and everything else, a relation of reason between them. For if God knows everything, including himself, in a single undifferentiated act, knowledge of one cannot be subsequent to knowledge of the other and there can be no relation between them.[207] A relation of reason therefore rests upon the false assumption that God knows everything else in virtue of first knowing himself, a process in which Duns Scotus distinguishes four instants beginning with God's knowledge of his essence, then of the archetype of a creature, leading third to their comparison in relation of reason, and finally to reflection upon their relation which is therefore eternal. Apart from the misattribution of instants to God, any such relation would be either of essence to creature as real objects, and so, contrary to Duns, of eternal duration, or solely in God's knowledge and thus non-existent since he knows everything simultaneously.[208] Accordingly there are neither instants in God nor any relation between him and distinct knowledge of what is not him; and no relative terms are needed to express such knowledge.[209]

---

[204] *Ibid.*, q. 3, B–I, L–O.

[205] *Ibid.*, D.

[206] Dico primo quod deus est primum obiectum primitate perfectionis. Secundo quod non est primum primitate adequationis illo modo quo loquitur Philosophus de primitate I *Posteriorum.* Tertio quod est primum primitate adequationis secundum perfectionem. Quarto quod non est primum primitate originis . . . Quartum probo, quia quando una et eadem intellectione omnino indistincte intelliguntur plura, non prius intelligitur unum quam reliquum. Sed eadem intellectione intelligitur deus et creatura. Ergo non prius origine intelligitur deus quam creatura. Unde dico quod quamvis obiectum unum sit prius alio obiecto tam natura quam perfectione, tam etiam origine, tamen intellectio unius obiecti nulla prioritate imaginabili est prior intellectione alterius obiecti, quia est eadem omnino sine omni distinctione imaginabili (*ibid.*, K).

[207] *Ibid.*, q. 4, B–C.

[208] *Ibid.*, D.

[209] *Ibid.*, F.

God's distinct knowledge of everything outside himself cannot, however, be sufficiently proved, as its opposite, upheld by Averroes, cannot, namely that God knows nothing beyond himself. The first would depend upon showing that God as cause of all things knew his effects immediately; the second upon his supreme nobility in excess of everything else. But causality does not imply knowledge of what is caused, and God cannot be proved immediate cause of all his effects. Similarly knowledge of an object is not commensurate with its perfection or imperfection; and there is no reason why the most noble being cannot know the most ignoble. At most, it can probably be shown that God is immediate cause of an effect in virtue of which he has knowledge of what he causes.

Both the major, that something caused depends upon a first cause without which it cannot exist, and the minor, that a first cause knows its effects, are probable.[210] So is the argument for God's omniscience based upon a first efficient cause acting according to an end; it is not, however, conclusive because it does not sufficiently prove that a first efficient cause is absolutely first being or that it produces knowledge of what it causes. The same inconclusiveness applies to the argument from perfect knowledge of something to perfect knowledge of all that is connected with it, which in God's case would extend to everything; for, as we well know, incomplex knowledge of one thing does not lead to incomplex knowledge of another, and a cause can be known perfectly without knowing its effect. The third and final argument in support of God's omniscience, from the contingency of an effect to the contingent action of the first cause, does not however, hold, for reasons to be considered presently; if it did, then philosophers could be convinced of its truth, which they are not.[211]

The arguments of Averroes against God's omniscience, are false as well as contrary to scripture. Thus strictly speaking what is known does not perfect the knower, as a stone known by man does not perfect him, or God in knowing himself is not his own perfection. It should rather be said that the object which causes knowledge is the efficient cause of its perfection; but that again does not apply to God. Nor are Averroes's major premises true, that the intellect in knowing something other than itself does so not by its own substance, or that when it knows necessarily it is necessarily part of another being or that in knowing something else it is changed into something else. Nor is it ignoble to know what is ignoble when such knowledge is not caused by an ignoble object, as God's knowledge is uncaused.[212] None of these assumptions therefore in being themselves invalid has any bearing upon God's omniscience.

The full import of Ockham's simplification of God's knowledge to a single indifferentiated act by the divine essence itself with no distinction between essence and intellect on the one hand or between knowledge of God and creature on the other, or any relation between them, is to be seen over divine ideas. While accepting that God knows all that is not himself by divine ideas, Ockham denies the traditional explanations of their nature and reason. By doing so, he demotes them from their long-standing transcendental status both in God where they were regarded as

210 Ibid., q. 2, D.   211 Ibid., C.   212 Ibid., B, E.

part of the divine essence and among creatures as the source of their being. Instead they are merely the means by which God knows all that he can produce in the manner in which any craftsman must first have in his mind a picture of what he intends to construct.

The commonly held view of most doctors is that a divine idea is the same as the divine essence and only distinguished from it conceptually by reason. As interpreted by St Thomas Aquinas the difference consists in God knowing himself under another aspect, namely by imitation of creatures, so that a divine idea is simply God's essence known in relation to what is not him. The divine essence remains the principle and cause.[213]

Ockham does not accept this reasoning. If a divine idea were really essence, there would only be one idea as there is only one essence. Alternatively if it were only a relation and the relation was real it would only be one of paternity or filiation or spiration, which St Thomas denies; while if the relation is merely one of reason in God's knowledge, then it cannot as conceptual be the same as what is real and so Ockham's case is proved that essence and idea are distinct. That follows also from the remaining possibility, that an idea is a combination of essence and relation; for when an aggregate is composed of what is really distinct it is not the same as one or the other, as a composite of form and matter is not really form or matter. Divine ideas are therefore not the divine essence.[214]

St Thomas's explanation of the need for divine ideas in God fails for the same reason that they are merely conceptual and God can know everything other than himself without any such relation of reason. If he could not, he would, on Aquinas's own argument, be demeaned in gaining knowledge through an object instead of through the divine essence as sufficient mover of his intellect. Conversely, if, as Aquinas maintains, such a relation is the consequence of God's knowledge they will not, as he also maintains, be acting together any more than an effect in being caused acts upon its cause. Again if ideas are only relations of reason they are not the necessary exemplars, either in the divine or a created intellect, in knowing and producing real beings outside the mind. Nor are they necessary as the measure of perfection in creating, because if ideas and created perfections were the same in God, either they would really be God and so only one, or different and not God, which contradicts Aquinas. But only God can be the proper measure of creatures, and since according to Aquinas this perfection is the measure of creatures, the measure must be God himself, not an idea.[215]

Ockham's own solution is accordingly different. An idea is not a real thing but a connotative or relative term for something known by an intellectual principle in virtue of whose knowledge it can produce a real being outside the intellect. This definition is confirmed by both St Augustine and Seneca. It cannot be either of God or a mental relation for the reasons given, that his essence is singular and his knowledge has no such relations. But a creature does conform to this description in being known by an active intellect, namely God, that he may produce it knowingly; for without such knowledge, however much God may know his own

[213] *Ibid.*, q. 5, B.   [214] *Ibid.*   [215] *Ibid.*

essence, he would in producing a creature act from ignorance. He therefore has ideas as exemplars of real beings, as any craftsman has in knowing what he is to make; and anything that God foresees as possible is an idea.[216] An idea, then, is simply what is known by a knowing agent as the exemplar of something real which is producible. In God it signifies a creature both directly and indirectly and God's knowledge of it only indirectly; for as referring to what is known it cannot be directly affirmed of knowing or knowledge as it cannot of an exemplar.[217]

Ideas, however, are not themselves the reason for God's knowledge of creatures; there is only one reason and that is his essence which is the same in every respect as his knowledge. Nothing therefore should be posited beyond God as the cause of his own knowledge: God knows because he is God.[218] To say that ideas are the reason for knowing creatures is inapplicable to God, regardless of how the reason for knowing is understood, whether as the cause of God's knowledge, which is entirely uncaused, or the knowledge by which he knows creatures, whereas his knowledge is one and indivisible, or as the means of receiving knowledge of creatures, for the same reasons, or as necessary to his knowledge of creatures, when ideas would then be mental objects and as such unnecessary to knowing real being, as what is real is unnecessary to knowing what is in the mind. Nor should ideas be regarded as likenesses representing creatures to the divine intellect, because again in being many they cannot be God.[219] Rather to call ideas exemplars is simply to say that God knows what he produces. The reason for positing them is that God acts knowingly.[220]

It can therefore be concluded first that ideas are in God only as mental objects of what he knows can be produced and not as anything real in him. Second, that he has distinct ideas of everything which can exist as distinct beings, including form and matter and the essential parts of real beings. Third, such ideas are immediately of individuals as alone capable of real being outside the mind; they do not extend to universals, such as genus and difference, or to negation, privation and sin which do not exist independently. Finally, since God can produce an infinity of beings, divine ideas are infinite.[221]

That in turn answers the question how God knows everything other than himself by divine ideas. He does so not through ideas as the efficient cause of his

---

[216] *Ibid.*, E.

[217] Et predictis patet quid est idea, quia non est nisi aliquod cognitum ad quod agens aspicit in producendo, ut secundum ipsum aliquid simile vel ipsammet producat in esse reali . . . Unde idea importat ipsammet creaturam in recto et etiam ipsammet in obliquo, et preter hec importat ipsam divinam cognitionem vel cognoscentem in obliquo; et ideo de ipsammet creatura est predicabilis ut ipsa sit idea, sed non est predicabilis de agente cognoscente vel cognitione, quia nec cognitio nec cognoscens est idea sicut nec exemplar (*ibid.*).

[218] *Ibid.*, F, R.

[219] *Ibid.*, F.

[220] Ideo dico quod idee sunt ponende precise ut sint exemplaria quedam ad que intellectus divinus aspiciens producat creaturas. Cuius ratio est . . . quia deus est rationabiliter operans (*ibid.*).

[221] *Ibid.*, G. I have telescoped Ockham's conclusions two and three, and four, five and six.

knowledge nor as its source or the means of his knowing but as the object of his knowledge.[222]

To the objection that St Augustine repeatedly described ideas as eternally in God so that they must be really in God, Ockham distinguishes between existing eternally and being known eternally and immutably. It is in the second sense that ideas are in God, which is the difference between divine ideas and the ideas in the mind of a human creator. Ideas, moreover, connote the knowledge by which something is known, not the actual thing known, which is the way in which they are called eternal by the authorities.[223] Unlike Wyclif, then, Ockham does not endow a creature's archetype with the eternity which belongs exclusively to God's knowledge of something which can be; and when Augustine speaks of ideas as really eternal he means that they are really known eternally, as the *sancti* speak of ideas even when God does not produce something correspondingly real.[224] Although strictly the only causes are the four enumerated by Aristotle of which a divine idea is not one, a divine idea can be improperly said to be a cause as the knowledge presupposed in the production of something: in that sense, too, it is not contradictory for something to be its own cause as the condition of its realisation in actual being.[225] That is how God produces beings in knowing their exemplars; moreover, in having perfect and distinct knowledge of everything producible, his ideas, unlike those of a created creator, are of singulars as well as universals, because only individuals as we have seen are really producible.[226] For that reason divine ideas are precisely of creatures as known by God and not of God as knowing them.[227]

Again, as merely objects known, divine ideas are strictly speaking neither practical nor speculative because only knowledge can be either. But in the common and improper sense in which, as we saw in the last chapter, some principles are called practical and others speculative, as the objects of one kind of knowledge or the other, the terms can also be applied to divine ideas. The question then is whether God's knowledge of what can exist is practical or speculative. The answer is practical; for contrary to an opinion that it is speculative, practical knowledge is not defined by what should be done: logic, grammar and rhetoric, and the mechanical arts are all practical but they are not dictative. Practical knowledge, on the other hand, is concerned with what is in the will's power, which in the case of God in his power to produce a creature contingently and to act as he wills towards creatures. Hence although his will is in every way identical with him, and although strictly his knowledge of divine ideas is neither practical nor speculative, in a general sense it can be called practical in being of what he wills, as the ideas in a craftsman's mind towards his craft can be called practical.[228] So, too, can creation and conservation and similar activities, which are not real things but connotative terms signifying an absolute being concretely and consignifying a relation abstractly, to express a real relation between God and creatures but are neither God nor creatures.[229]

---

[222] *Ibid.*, H.   [223] *Ibid.*, I–K.   [224] *Ibid.*, L–M.   [225] *Ibid.*, N, P.
[226] *Ibid.*, Q–R.   [227] *Ibid.*, S.   [228] *Ibid.*, q. 6, B–E.   [229] *Ibid.*, E; also d. 30, q. 1, O.

Now just as divine ideas do not have any real being in God, neither do the perfections of creatures which he thereby knows. Hence for Ockham the common view of the doctors that these perfections are contained in God by diverse modes, perfectly, eminently, exemplarily, intelligibly, virtually and causally, is open to only one interpretation: that they refer to God in knowing them and not to their existence as perfections.[230] As merely objects known, those perfections are neither really the same as God nor really different from him or from one another, contrary to two opposing opinions. By the first of these—Duns Scotus's—it is held that in so far as they are in God perfectly, these perfections do not differ in any way from God or among themselves, even as intelligibles or representations; nor as they are contained virtually in him according to God's perfections. They do however differ in so far as they are contained virtually according to their own perfections (i.e. as belonging virtually to different creatures).[231]

Ockham confines discussion of Duns's opinion to its supporting authorities, whom he glosses in reply to mean God's knowledge when they speak of what is in God. Thus St John's statement, that all things were made through God and that life was in him refers to the productive cause and knowledge of things which are the same as God and constitute the life in him, an interpretation identical with that of Peter Lombard[232] and for Ockham confirmed by St Augustine that the visible did not exist before it became being, although eternally known in God. Again, when Dionysius says that everything is united in the One, he means that the perfections of all things are known by God in his absolute simplicity as the cause of everything else. The same applies to Anselm's celebrated remark that a creature in God is a creating essence (*essentia creatrix*). In the strict sense there can be no such thing: a creature in God is a creature. What Anselm intends however is that God is the cause of all things and knows all things. Like other authorities who call God a lion or a stone or earth he is speaking metaphorically, and in all such cases the author's intention must be distinguished from the strict meaning of his words.[233]

The second opinion, of William of Alnwick, is that the intelligible or represented being (*esse intelligibile vel esse representatum*) of a creature's perfections is not really different from God but that its represented being is the same as the form which represents it and its known being the same as the knowledge by which God knows it.[234]

To Ockham this opinion is a play on the words 'intelligible being'; and his criticism is of their misappropriation rather than of the notion of intelligible being itself. To begin with it would follow from this opinion that if a creature's intelligibility were identical with God's knowledge, its creability would be identical with his being; for as God knowing necessarily means that a creature has known being, which is the same as God's knowledge, so God as creative would mean that

---

[230] *Ibid.*, d. 36, q. unica, B.
[231] *Ibid.*
[232] As Vignaux remarks in 'Nominalisme', *Dictionnaire de Théologie Catholique*, XI, col. 762.
[233] *Ordinatio*, d. 36, q. unica, H–O.
[234] *Ibid.*, C.

a creature had creatable being which was the same as God. That in turn would make any possible being necessary, so that whatever could be would be the same as God, whether a white body or a demon, because from God's power to make something white or to damn someone, there would be whiteable or damnable being which was the same as God. These and many other absurdities occur when any compound of the infinitive of the verb 'to be' and any attribute is affirmed necessarily of something: for that is to say that it is really the same as God.[235] The reason is that the verb 'to be' must stand for real being or what does not contradict real being, which makes all such statements about a creature's represented being false in implying a real identity with God's being.[236] A creature's represented being is nothing in the sense that it does not really exist; and to say with William of Alnwick that it is positive being, on the grounds that it would still be represented by its species even if it were not known, is equivalent to saying that a demon would have damnable being without God's knowing that he could damn it. Nor is it true that represented being naturally and necessarily follows a form which represents it, because something only naturally follows something else as an effect; but known being is not really an effect eternally of God's knowing. Moreover something can only be an effect of something else from which it really differs; therefore to be the consequence of God's knowledge a creature's known being would have really to be different from God's knowledge, which this opinion denies. Logically also one does not imply the other, whether as second or third attribute. For it follows logically neither that a creature has known being because God knows it, nor that a demon has damnable being because it is damnable through God's ability to damn it. To be true, something knowable or damnable would have to exist; it is not contained in God's ability to know or to damn, which alone is eternally real.[237]

Only, then, if there is a real creature can it have real intelligible being; there cannot be one without the other. The misconception that there can arises from the false belief, expressed in Duns Scotus's example of stone's diminished being, that when something is known it acquires some kind of being. In fact, as we have discussed frequently, knowing does not entail being, whether it is of a colour in a wall or of some future being; neither thereby becomes something which it was not. Similarly with God's knowledge of a stone.[238] By the same token it can be accepted that there cannot be a representation without what is represented and yet God can know without knowing a creature, as he did before the creation of the world; for before a creature had real being it did not have intelligible being, whereas God knows eternally. Nor as possible being is a creature's intelligible being prior to

---

[235] *Ibid.*, D.

[236] *Ibid.*, O.

[237] *Ibid.*, O–P.

[238] Dicendum quod si creatura vel lapis non sit aliquid reale nec esse suum intelligibile est aliquid reale, quia impossibile est quod esse intelligibile lapidis sit aliud a lapide . . . Dico ergo quod omnia talia argumenta procedunt ex falsa imaginatione. Imaginantur enim quod per hoc quod lapis intelligitur aliquid esse quasi quoddam esse diminutum sibi acquiritur, quod est manifeste falsum. Nam per hoc quod ego video colorem in pariete nihil acquiritur nec diminutum nec perfectum ipsi colori . . . Similiter per hoc quod appeto aliquod futurum illi nihil acquiritur, ita nec per hoc quod deus intelligit lapidem (*ibid.*, S(1)).

God's will or willing or represented first in God's intellect before his will, except in so far as God knows a creature before willing it as a real or intelligible being. Contrary to William of Alnwick, therefore, a created intelligible being cannot be proper or intrinsic to God or to a creature, for the very reason that it is not anything real but merely known; and in having intelligible being only when it has real being its being is mutable as well as only possible. That, as we shall shortly see, implies nothing mutable in God's knowledge, for God always knows a creature whether it exists or not: it is a creature's being, real and intelligible, which does not always exist. It is therefore completely untrue to say that a creature's intelligible being is more necessary than its actual being, because a creature has no necessity.[239]

Ockham accordingly denies any distinction in God between a creature and its perfection;[240] if there were one it would be because a creature's perfection was its form or cause or likeness, which would then have to be in God as well as the perfection. But just as there is no matter of creatures in God, there are no such forms or causes or likenesses in him. Creature and perfection are therefore identical. But they are only in God as objects known, not real beings, in the same way as effects are contained in their causes. That in turn explains the meaning of 'contained in': it is the same as to be known by God. Hence a stone contained in him is in no way part of him but a distinct object which he knows, as by the same mode of speaking it could be said the whiteness seen in a wall is contained in the eye which sees it.[241] For that reason nothing can be contained in God eminently or virtually unless it is different from him. Hence no perfections of creatures in God are really God any more than an ass produced outside him is.[242] The only object to be known by God which is the same as himself is a divine relation (i.e. between the persons).[243] Consequently the perfections of creatures in not being the same as God are not distinguished from God eternally, and in not being eternal they are not distinguished eternally from one another; but in their existence outside him they are distinguished both from God and from one another.[244]

This radical simplification of divine ideas goes with Ockham's stress upon God's absolute simplicity. Just as there is no formal distinction among his attributes and no instants in the generation of the divine persons, there is no sequence in his activity: knowing is not prior to willing, nor knowledge of himself prior to knowledge of creatures. They all belong to the same undifferentiated simultaneous act: it is what he knows which is differentiated. Here Ockham reverses Duns Scotus's order. While both thinkers agree in rejecting the notion of St Thomas

---

[239] *Ibid.*, C, X–GG.

[240] Circo primum dico quod idem est dicere perfectiones creaturarum contineri in deo et ipsas creaturas contineri in deo. Unde non est imaginandum quod differentia sit inter perfectionem creature et creaturam ipsam (*ibid.*, E).

[241] *Ibid.*; cf. *Quodlibet* IV, q. 3.

[242] Ex predictis patet quod nihil potest contineri eminenter in deo vel virtualiter nisi sit aliud a deo; et ideo perfectiones creaturarum contente in deo eminenter vel virtualiter nullo modo sunt deus realiter plus quam iste asinus productus extra est deus (*Ordinatio, ibid.*).

[243] *Ibid.*

[244] *Ibid.*, F.

Aquinas and Henry of Ghent that divine ideas are from a relation of imitability of God to what is outside him,[245] Ockham also rejects the Scotist notion of created intelligible being in God and distinct from the real being of the creature to which it belongs. Since God knows everything past, present, and future, eternally, distinctly and perfectly, he knows what does not yet exist, as it does not exist, equally with what exists: his knowing does not endow something with being, diminished or otherwise. As Ockham repeatedly says, knowing adds to nothing to what is known: knowing is knowing and being is being; and God is omniscient precisely in knowing everything as it is, possible being as possible, no less than actual, and past being as past.

The disjunction then between knowing and being which characterises human knowledge in God is absolute. The independence of what he knows from what exists enables him to know all that can exist equally in its existence and non-existence. There is thus no need to look for ways of correlating God's knowledge with the diversity outside him; for God knows it all in the same eternal instant. Once again it is Ockham both as believer and a philosopher who has less need to multiply hypotheses.

That is to be seen again over the question of impossibility where Ockham, in addition to rejecting Henry of Ghent's explanation of it, first by reference to creatures and then to God, directly refutes the Scotist conception of intelligible beings and instants in God's knowledge. The issue as raised by Henry of Ghent was whether something is impossible because God cannot do it or whether God cannot do it because it is impossible.[246] Initially Henry attributed the cause of impossibility to creatures on the grounds that only absolute perfections can be attributed to God absolutely and immediately of themselves; all other attributions are relative in being first of creatures and only secondarily of God as their creator. Thus he is called 'lord' because temporally—as opposed to absolutely—he has creatures who are his servants. He is also called 'omnipotent' because creatures have the possibility of receiving his active power. Here, however, Henry distinguishes between God's omnipotence taken in itself (*subiective*) and in relation to its object (*obiective*). In the first sense it refers to God before anything else; it can therefore be attributed to him absolutely and immediately. In the second sense it is relative, only affirmed of God in so far as passive possibility is affirmed of creatures in relation to God. Passive possibility is therefore dependent upon active possibility and can be considered in the same ways. There are accordingly four relations between them, two active and two passive. By the first pair, God can be compared to himself and to a creature; by the second, a creature can be compared with itself and with God. The order is thus from absolute active power to absolute passive possibility and their relation, by which God's omnipotence is the correlative of a creature's dependence upon him.[247]

---

[245] Cf. A. B. Wolter, 'Ockham and the Textbooks: on the origin of possibility' in *Wilhelm Ockham, FS* 32 (1950) 75–6.

[246] Wolter, *ibid.*, 71, whose edition of Ockham's text from *Ordinatio*, d. 43, q. 2 (*ibid.*, 93–6) I have followed.

[247] *Ibid.*, B (93).

For Ockham, Henry answers himself by subsequently reversing the sequence, and attributing both what is possible and impossible to God. From that it follows that a relation with a creature is now attributed to God before it is attributed to a creature. But in fact neither priority is tenable, any more than in a relation between a creature and a created cause. Nor does it make any difference to say that the relation between God and a creature is only conceptual because it is no more contradictory for a real relation to originate from another real relation than for a conceptual relation to originate from a conceptual relation. Therefore if one does not, the other does not; indeed both really and conceptually God receives less from a creature than a created cause receives from its effect. Henry's distinction between God's two active relations is also untenable; for if something is active, however considered, it can only be active in relation to something else; and as God does not cause or act upon himself his activity must be in relation to a creature. Therefore it cannot be affirmed of God absolutely.[248]

Duns Scotus on the other hand locates the first cause of impossibility not in what God cannot do but in what contradicts existence; and that arises when incompatibles are combined. Their incompatibility is both formally from their own natures and from the principle of their natures which is God's knowledge of them in the divine intellect. Duns explains it as follows: in the first instant the divine intellect produces a nature in intelligible being; and in the second instant this nature has possible being. Now in producing possible being God thereby also produces one of the incompatibles included in what is impossible; for its incompatibility is of one formal nature with another which together cannot constitute one being or a third being composed of each. The incompatibility which these possible beings have formally from themselves they thus also derive from the divine intellect as their principle. They therefore signify what is impossible—which Duns elsewhere calls a figment[249]—and as such incapable of realisation by an agent. Impossibility stops there and does not extend to a denial of possibility in God.[250]

Ockham rejects these arguments. To begin with, it is wrong to say that God's knowledge of a creature produces it in intelligible being, because nothing but an extrinsic denomination is received through being known, whether by God's knowledge or a creature's. If knowing conferred intelligible being, God, in knowing himself, would have intelligible being of his own essence and so would anyone else really knowing God. Neither can it be from knowing what previously did not exist, because God also knows a creature when it does not exist, while the intelligibility of anything is due entirely to God's knowledge of it before which nothing is intelligible. Hence there is no possible justification for intelligible being, as there is none for a first instant in God's knowledge of a creature's nature. If there were such an instant, either a creature would be possible in which case it would be possible before God produces its intelligible being, or it would be impossible and it would then contradict being. Moreover, on Duns's argument

248 *Ibid.*, C (93–4).
249 Wolter, *op. cit.*, 76–7 (Opus Oxon., d. 43, n. 5; vol. 10, 734 a).
250 *Ibid.*, D (94–5).

that to every relation in a possible being to God there is a corresponding relation in God to a possible being, the absence of such a relation to him would imply the absence of relation in him to what is impossible. Accordingly the absence of possibility would originate in him. That follows because a relation of God to creature is conceptual in having no real foundation. Therefore as the intellect can compare a creature to God it can compare God to a creature.[251]

Ockham's own explanation is in terms neither of an ontological priority between God and what is possible or impossible nor an intelligible sequence from one to the other. Omnipotence expresses a relation between God's active power and a creature's passive possibility; like cause and effect they are correlatives which as Aristotle said[252] come into existence simultaneously. One cannot therefore be without the other or be more the cause of the other than *vice versa*.[253] Like father and son they must be taken together. Accordingly both possibility and impossibility state a reciprocal relation between God and what can or cannot be; priority lies within none of them, but one implies the other. It is therefore no more true to say that something is possible or impossible because God can or cannot make it than its converse.[254] The question is meaningless.[255]

To the objection that since God is the cause of a creature's possible being his power to produce comes before a creature's productibility, Ockham replies by distinguishing what really inheres in a creature and is from God, from what is predicable of a creature and is not real. Possible being comes in the second category: as a term it can be truly affirmed of something possible but does not itself really inhere in anything. Properly speaking, then, a creature should not be said to have possible being, but rather that a creature is possible because it can really exist.[256]

IV FUTURE KNOWLEDGE

That brings us to God's future knowledge, which Ockham discusses in both the *Ordinatio* (distinctions thirty-eight and thirty-nine) and his short treatise *On Predestination, God's Foreknowledge and Future Contingents*. The latter in addition to being fuller also considers the subject of distinction thirty-nine, whether God could know more than he does, under the wider question of whether God has determinate and necessary knowledge of all future contingents, which forms distinction thirty-eight. Conversely, where distinction thirty-eight includes Duns Scotus's opinion on the will's powers to perform opposite actions, in the treatise it is a

---

[251] *Ibid.*, E (95).

[252] *Categories*, ch. 7, 7 b, 15.

[253] Ideo aliter dico ad questionem quod generaliter omni relativo, si convenienter assignetur, correspondet aliquod correlativum, et in omnibus relativis que vocantur relativa secundum potentiam activam et passivam vel causam et effectum, semper correlativa sunt simul natura. Et ideo quia sunt simul natura et mutuo se inferant neutrum est magis causa alterius quam e converso (*Ordinatio, ibid.*, F (96)).

[254] *Ibid.*

[255] As Wolter remarks (*op. cit.*, 83).

[256] *Ibid.*

separate question. These differences make for greater coherence, and I have in the main followed the arguments of the treatise, referring where necessary to the *Ordinatio*.

Ockham's view of future contingents is essentially theological: its premises are that God is omniscient and contingency exists. The conclusion, stated in both the *Ordinatio*, distinction thirty-eight, and as the sixth supposition of the treatise forms his point of departure. It is 'that it is unhesitatingly to be held that God knows certainly all future contingents, so that he knows with certainty which part of a contradiction will be true and which false and yet all such propositions as "God knows this or that part of a contradiction" are contingent, not necessary, as said before. But it is difficult to see how he knows it, since one part is not more determined to be true than the other'.[257] In direct opposition to Duns Scotus, Ockham thus eschews any attempt to explain how God has such knowledge: it is one more truth which it is impossible to know *pro statu isto*.[258] The most that can be said is that as the created intellect can know evidently contradictory propositions from incomplex knowledge, so the divine essence in having perfect and clear intuitive knowledge of all that is past and future knows which part of a contradiction is true and which is false.[259] But that is itself a matter of faith, which must be believed on account of the authorities.[260]

For Ockham, then, God's future knowledge is given in his immediate knowledge of everything, himself included, in the same undifferentiated act.[261] On the one hand, therefore, it is through God himself knowing intuitively; but on the other it is contingent in being of what is yet to be. These are the only two terms in God's future knowledge. Unlike St Thomas Aquinas, Ockham does not attempt to assimilate God's knowledge of future contingents to the necessity of all that he knows, so that he knows them necessarily.[262] Nor like Duns Scotus does he explain the contingency of God's future knowledge by the contingency of God's will. The first would mean the necessity of whatever God knew as future, whether expressed as past, present, or future; and then, as Duns Scotus had already shown, either one or both of a pair of contradictory propositions would be necessarily true. Thus if God knew necessarily that Peter was predestined, either Peter could

---

[257] *Tractatus de Praedestinatione*, 13–14.

[258] *Ordinatio*, d. 38, L. Ideo dico ad questionem quod indubitanter est tenendum quod deus certitudinaliter et evidenter scit omnia futura contingentia, sed hoc evidenter declarare et modum quo scit omnia futura contingentia exprimere est impossibile omni intellectui pro statu isto. And *De Praedestinatione*, 15. Text of *Ordinatio*, dd. 38 and 39 edited in *De Praedestinatione* (91–103).

[259] Potest tamen talis modus assignari: Nam sicut ex eadem notitia aliquorum complexorum potest intellectus evidenter cognoscere propositiones contingentes contradictorias, puta quod A est, A non est, eodem modo potest concedi quod essentia divina est notitia intuitiva que est tam perfecta tam clara quod ipsa est notitia evidens omnium preteritorum et futurorum, ita quod ipsa scit que pars contradictionis erit vera et que pars falsa (*De Praedestinatione*, ibid.). Also *Ordinatio*, d. 38, q. unica, M (ibid., 99).

[260] Ideo dico quod impossibile est clare exprimere modum quo deus scit futura contingentia. Tamen tenendum est quod sic, contingenter tamen. Et debet istud teneri propter dicta sanctorum qui dicunt quod deus non aliter cognoscit fienda quam facta (ibid.).

[261] Ibid., 26.

[262] Boehner, ibid., 52–3, referring to *Summa Theologiae* I, 14, 13, ad 2.

not be damned and so will be necessarily saved, which denies free will; or he could be damned and then it would be necessarily true that he was both damned and saved, which is contradictory.[263]

The alternative of Duns Scotus would however impair God's future knowledge, in making it dependent upon the decision of his will. By this mode the will in one instant chooses what to realise from among all the possibilities—contingent and contradictory—already in some way known by the divine intellect indifferently in a previous instant; and in the third instant on the basis of the will's free but immutable choice the intellect in turn knows these future contingents evidently and certainly. The divine intellect would then know necessarily what was not decided by the will and contingently what was.[264] But that, says Ockham, would be in turn to subject both God's future knowledge and will to a creature's will, because either the created will is necessitated by the divine will, in which case there is no contingency, and merit and demerit are destroyed. Or the created will acts freely and then the determination of God's will does not suffice for his future knowledge, because the created will could act in opposition to it. Accordingly God will not have certain knowledge of events which are not eternal. By the same token when something is contingently determined so that it is possible for it never to have been decided, it cannot yield certain and infallible knowledge. That applies to God's willing of future contingents which, as Duns himself acknowledges, is of what is contingent.[265] Theologically as well, there is no such order of instants as Duns posits between God's knowing and willing; if there were it would imply imperfection on the intellect's part in not knowing for an instant future contingents and then receiving knowledge of them from the will.[266]

Ockham's own discussion of God's future knowledge takes as its indemonstrable premises the same propositions that Duns Scotus sought to prove, and explores their logical implications. Since the principles are held on faith the conclusions must be as well. Hence for Ockham the logic of God's future knowledge, as of divine relations, is the logic of revealed truth; it is accessible to natural reason only through acceptance of exclusively theological presuppositions: to follow those of natural reason leads to the impasse of determinism or divine fallibility, as the proofs of St Thomas Aquinas and Duns Scotus show. The tenor of Ockham's discussion is expressed in his appeal to members of the arts faculty not to confuse God's infallibility with certainty; God's future knowledge, for all its certainty, remains of what is contingent because what he knows need never have been.[267]

This initial assumption of their compatibility sets Ockham apart from virtually all the thinkers of the epoch, especially his near contemporaries and successors.

[263] *Ibid.*, 12; Ockham ends this proof 'Et illam conclusionem dicit Scotus'; hence Boehner does not seem to be correct when he says (*ibid.*, 52) that Ockham states simply that this conclusion (that any proposition concerning the future is contingent) is proved by Scotus and gives no further proof of his own.

[264] *Ibid.*; and *Ordinatio*, d. 38, D (*ibid.*, 94–5) for the fuller account.

[265] *De Praedestinatione*, 14–15. *Ordinatio*, d. 38, J–K (*ibid.*, 97–8).

[266] *Ordinatio*, d. 38, K (*ibid.*, 98); in *De Praedestinatione* Ockham confines himself mainly to the logical facets.

[267] *Ordinatio*, 239, N (*ibid.*, 99).

Where they began from the presuppositions of reason, from which they drew theological conclusions, Ockham began from theological truth and confined himself to its logical consequences. We have thus once again the paradox that it was Ockham who subordinated logic to theology, and near-contemporaries, like Durandus of St Pourçain and Peter Aureole,[268] who inverted the order and thereby helped to inaugurate a generation of theological speculation which was to become one of the hallmarks of Ockhamism. The discrepancy was one of opposed standpoints founded upon revealed or non-revealed assumptions; and the outcome is to be seen in the contrast between Ockham's formal enunciation of contingency and the speculations of thinkers like Robert Holcot, Thomas Buckingham, Adam of Woodham and John of Mirecourt over God's own knowledge of futures with its implications for revealed truth.[269]

The key to Ockham's thinking is contained in his distinction between knowledge in the broad sense of anything which may be known, incomplex, complex, necessary, contingent, false or impossible, and in the strict sense of knowing only what is true.[270] While in this strict sense God can know something which previously he did not, since it can now be true to say that 'I am in Rome' and was not before, what he knows remains constant in both senses. In the broad sense because the knowledge by which he knows is the same for everything knowable; in the strict sense because something is never true without its contradictory being false, and conversely. Hence the change of a proposition from false to true is accompanied by a corresponding change of its opposite from true to false: if it is now true that I am in Rome, it is also false that I am now not in Rome. The number of true and false propositions therefore remains constant, and God cannot know more or less than he knows; only different individual propositions which are true and false at different times.[271] Thus, as Boehner remarked, God's knowledge 'embraces two (infinite) parallel series of propositions—a series of true propositions which are known in the strict sense of *scire*, and a series of corresponding propositions of which each one is the contradictory opposite of its counterpart in the former series'.[272] Such a conception, it hardly needs saying, is based upon the principle of contradiction, so that if one part of a contradiction is true the other part must be false. Ockham acknowledges here and in his Commentary on *Perihermenias* that so far as future propositions and their equivalents were concerned, Aristotle held

[268] See my *Bradwardine and the Pelagians* (Cambridge, 1957) 179–87, and 211–16. At that time I did not appreciate the distinctiveness of Ockham's outlook (*ibid.*, 188, 213–14).

[269] *Ibid.*, 215–16.

[270] *De Praedestinatione* 16 (septima suppositio); and *Ordinatio*, d. 39 q. unica, c (101–3).

[271] Dico quod loquendo de scire et scientia dei stricte, sicut dicitur suppositione septima, quamvis deus possit aliquid scire quod modo non scit, quia cum deus isto modo nihil scit nisi verum, aliquando propositio que modo non est vera—sicut me esse Rome—potest a deo sciri, que tamen modo non scitur ab eo; tamen non debet concedi quod possit scire plura quam scit, quia nihil scitur a deo nisi verum et omne verum scitur a deo. Sed semper sunt equalia vera; igitur semper sunt equalia scita a deo. Assumptum probo, quia non est possibile quod sint plura vera in uno tempore quam in alio, quia semper altera pars contradictionis est, et nihil est verum, nisi sit altera pars contradictionis . . . dico quod accipiendo scientiam vel scire pro notititia dei qua cognoscit illas propositiones illa est eadem respectu omnium scibilium (*ibid.*, 24–5).

[272] *Ibid.*, 56.

otherwise, namely, that they could not be determinately true or false, on the grounds that the future was itself indeterminate.[273] But that has no bearing upon what must be held on faith; and Ockham's purpose in the *Tractatus* is to explain how, since God is omniscient and contingency exists, his certain knowledge of what is contingent and future is not contradictory. That involves on the one hand defining how contingent propositions can be true and false, and on the other differentiating knowledge which is certain and immutable from that which is necessary.

Any proposition about a future event is contingent, whether or not in the future tense, because its truth depends upon what is yet to happen. That applies to all propositions concerning predestination and reprobation which even when expressed as past or present propositions ('Peter was presdestined'; 'Peter is predestined') are equivalent to a future proposition. They are not therefore necessarily true, unlike categorical propositions of the present and past, which once true are necessarily true in that instant and henceforth in corresponding propositions about the event as past.[274] The contingency of future events consists precisely in the possibility that they could have not occurred. That does not mean that they are successively true and false but that in being true they could have been false. Thus Peter's predestination is contingent because before he was predestinated he could have been damned. Nor does eternity detract from contingency: that God has eternally predestined Peter remains contingent for the same reason that he could have eternally damned him;[275] indeed what is true eternally can be false temporally, as it is true eternally that the world does not exist but false at present.[276] All statements therefore which refer to future contingents, including the sayings of the prophets, are conditional in that they could be false. They only become necessarily true once they have occurred. Then it is true to say that they were always true, because there is no reason why they should then become false.[277]

In relation to God's knowledge, Ockham states these differences as follows. Over propositions of the present, as they can change from true to false and false to true, God can correspondingly first know and then not know them (in the strict sense of knowing them as true), and *vice versa*. He does so moreover without any change on his part but solely on account of the creatures and propositions which he knows, in the way that he is first called non-creating and then creating because of what is created. Similarly with our intellects: if I first believe, falsely, that Socrates is sitting when he is standing and continue to believe it when he sits I can

---

[273] *Ibid.*, 13, quinta suppositio. See Boehner's analysis of Ockham's discussion of Aristotle's view in his Commentary on *Perhermenias* (*ibid.*, 59–62) and again in the *Logic*, 62–6 (appendices II and III, *ibid.*, 104–17).

[274] *Ibid.*, 11–13. Suppositiones 1–4; also 6.

[275] *Ibid.*, 9–10.

[276] *Ibid.*, 7–8.

[277] *Ibid.*, 10–11 and 37–8: Quia sicut dictum est prius, omnis propositio simpliciter de futuro, si semel sit vera, semper fuit vera, quia non est maior ratio quare magis sit vera in uno tempore quam in alio . . . Confirmatur, quia propositiones non mutantur de veritate in falsitatem nisi propter mutationem rei, secundum Philosophum in *Predicamentis*. Sed nulla mutatio est in deo nec in Petro nec in quacumque alia re.

know unchanged what is first false and then true[278]—hardly, it must be added, a good analogy with God, who knows unchanged from omniscience not ignorance. Over future propositions, those which are exclusively future in their meaning God knows always in the same way, for so long as a proposition refers to a future time, say that Socrates will sit at a certain time, it cannot become false at any time before time A. Accordingly such propositions if once true have always been true. Those propositions which are future but refer to past or present time, so that they are spoken after the event in the future has occurred, do change their meaning: to say that Socrates will sit in A when A is tomorrow and has passed, is no longer true, as it was true before A. Hence God can know and then not know (in the strict sense) such a proposition in the same way as already discussed of present propositions. Of these some are true and become false: for example 'Socrates will sit in A' is true now until A, but false evermore after A. Others are false and henceforth become true, such as the converse of the previous proposition, where to say that 'Socrates will not sit in A' will remain false until A, but then always true.[279]

Now whether he knows these propositions as true or false God knows them definitely, infallibly, and immutably but not necessarily. That he has definite and certain knowledge of everything follows from the sixth supposition that these are truth to be held on faith. In that connection Ockham adds that one part of a proposition is definitely true because God contingently wills it to be true and the other part false.[280] As Boehner has said, that does not imply that God knows contingents through his will—against which he has just been arguing—but that they owe their truth to his willing.[281] It is therefore invalid to argue on the grounds that a possible conclusion can follow in a mixed categorical and possible syllogism, that if God knows that I shall sit tomorrow and I do not sit tomorrow, he is deceived. To begin with, if God knows something, it will be true; therefore if he knows that I shall sit tomorrow I shall sit because only what is true is known, and so its opposite that I shall not sit will be false. There can however only be a possible conclusion from mixed premises if the major is entirely categorical and remains true regardless of the minor as possible. In that case the conclusion will be the opposite of that initially posited. For from the premises 'God cannot be deceived', and 'It is possible for me not to sit' it will follow that 'Therefore God does not necessarily know that I shall sit tomorrow, but only as contingent'. In other words, to be valid syllogistically such a consequence must have as its major a categorical proposition which is held on faith, namely that God is infallible. As to the argument that what is impossible never follows from what is possible, that can only apply to a proposition's existential import not to the relation between propositions, which can be possible and yet incompatible. That is the case here: while it is both possible for me not to sit tomorrow as a real event and similarly for God to know that I

---

278 *Ibid.*, 22–3.
279 *Ibid.*, 22–4. Boehner (*ibid.*, 57–8) treats these more formally and goes beyond Ockham's text. Cf. also *SL*, III, III, ch. 31 [mistakenly 30 in text] (*ibid.*, appendix III, 114–16).
280 *Ibid.*, 16; also 18–19.
281 *Ibid.*, 55.

shall sit, the conclusion that God is therefore mistaken, is impossible because it follows from contradictory premises.[282]

Finally there is the dissociation of immutability from necessity which is central to the very conception of God's knowledge of contingents. It rests upon the distinction made in the opening question between God himself who is both necessary and immutable and what he knows which can be immutable, in the sense that its meaning cannot change from true to false, but not necessary because it could have been otherwise. Which is the case with predestination and reprobation.[283] We have already discussed the implications in the different kinds of propositions God can have of future events, so that he can both know and not know different propositions at different times without his own knowledge, which in the broad sense embraces everything knowable including what is false, undergoing any change. That disposes of all assertions that therefore God's knowledge could be increased or diminished, which in the composite sense that, say, the number of predestined could first be more and then less, is absolutely false, although it can be accepted in the divided sense that others than those now predestined could have been predestined. For, as we have previously seen, once a future proposition is true it remains as future immutably true although it could have been false. Hence to say that God's knowledge of a future proposition could change implies that God first knows it and then does not know it, which is contradictory since whatever is true God knows.[284]

It equally disposes of the arguments that therefore God's knowledge must be necessary. First, because whatever can be false when it is true is contingent and hence is known as contingent, which is how God knows all future contingents. Second, because while everything necessary is immutable, not everything immutable is necessary, which again applies to future contingents. Hence to conclude the opposite is in both cases to commit a fallacy of consequence. Third, only what is formally in God is necessary; but his knowledge of something is only predicated of him as a term or concept. It is therefore affirmed contingently, as he is called 'lord' contingently and temporally: neither is really him. For the same reason his knowledge is not an absolute perfection; hence for him not to know is not an imperfection: its cause lies in the absence of something knowable.[285] For all these reasons God's immutability and perfection do not entail necessity in what he knows. That also explains how predestination and reprobation are immutable, but their causes we shall consider separately.

There remains briefly Duns Scotus's other argument for the contingency of

---

[282] *Ibid.*, 19–21.

[283] Sed loquendo de immutabili complexo illo modo quo aliquod complexum potest mutari a veritate in falsitatem et econverso et aliquod complexum non potest sic mutari, sic non omne immutabile est necessarium, quia est aliqua propositio contingens que non potest primo esse vera et postea falsa, et econverso . . . Et causa est, quia quantumcumque sit vera et fuerit vera ex suppositione, tamen possibile est quod non sit vera et quod numquam fuerit vera absolute. Sicut hec est vera: deus scit quod iste salvabitur; et tamen possibile est quod numquam sciverit quod iste salvabitur (*ibid.*, 8–9). Also 28–9.

[284] *Ibid.*, 26–7.

[285] *Ibid.*, 29–32.

God's knowledge, which is designed to safeguard the contingency of the actions of the created will.[286] It is that, concurrently with its actual power of performing opposite actions successively and in time, so that it can first will and then not will something, the created will retains the latent non-temporal power of continuing to will and not to will the action it is performing. It therefore continues to have in the same instant in which it has decided to act the non-manifest power both to act and not to act which precedes its decision in the will's nature but not temporally. The created will's action thus also consists of different natural, but not temporal, instants.[287] Ockham denies the possibility of any such non-successive power because not even an infinite power could then make it actual; if it did, that would involve the will in the contradiction of willing and not willing at the same time. It is not overcome by the reply that if the will actually does not will in instant A then its opposite, that it does will in A, will be false and there will be no contradiction. For we have just seen that if a proposition of the present is true it will then be necessary as a proposition of the past. Once therefore it is true that the will wills in instant A, it will henceforth always be necessarily true that the will has willed something in A, and its opposite will always be false that it has not willed something in A.[288]

The power to choose between absolute opposites or between opposites non-successively is therefore not to be held in creatures, or in God save over future contingents. Contingency consists rather in the will's power either to decide freely and contingently whether or not to cause something which it precedes in time, or to cease what it is doing. But it cannot perform opposite acts at the same time.[289]

That concludes Ockham on God's knowledge. In the light of what was to follow in the next two decades his own discussion of future contingents was remarkable in keeping to the strict implications of revealed truth, here as in everything else concerning God—with the one exception of his omnipotence, as we shall now consider over God's relation to his creatures.

[286] *Ibid.*, 37–9.
[287] *Ibid.*, 32–3; *Ordinatio*, d. 38, c (*ibid.*, 92–3).
[288] *De Praedestinatione*, 33–4; *Ordinatio*, ibid., E–F (*ibid.*, 95–6).
[289] *De Praedestinatione*, ibid., 35–6; *Ordinatio*, ibid., F–G, where Ockham only states the second meaning of contingency.

CHAPTER SEVEN

God and creatures

I OMNIPOTENCE

With omnipotence the perspective changes from God in himself to God and his creatures, and with it from necessity and immutability to contingency and possibility. That is where omnipotence differs from omniscience: omniscience is knowledge of whatever is knowable; it can therefore be necessary as well as of what is contingent as we have just discussed. Omnipotence is the power to create or do whatever is creatable or possible; its necessity therefore lies only in God who acts freely and never in what he creates. Knowledge can therefore be necessary; being other than God's cannot. A proposition is absolutely necessary when its opposite includes a contradiction, for example, 'Man is capable of laughter' or 'God exists' where the converse is contradictory and untrue. It is hypothetically necessary (*ex suppositione*) when neither antecedent nor consequent is necessary but only the connection between them, so that if, say, Peter is predestined it will necessarily follow that he will be saved without excluding the opposite possibility of his damnation.[1] Ontologically, however, man's capacity for laughter is as conditional upon God's will as Peter's salvation, so that as we discussed at length in chapter four it can only be expressed as a necessary proposition if put into the mode of possibility preceded by the clause 'If man exists'.

That condition applies to all that is not God, which exists only in virtue of God's omnipotence. Thus whereas, as Ockham has repeatedly argued, God's knowledge neither implies nor confers being, his omnipotence does; it therefore has existential import in connoting what God can do.

Now it is in relation to everything outside him as its first cause that God's omnipotence manifests itself; and it is according to whether he acts together with a second cause, in the order that he has eternally but freely decreed, or immediately

---

[1] Dico quod duplex est necessitas, scilicet absoluta et ex suppositione. Necessitas absoluta est quando aliquid simpliciter est necessarium ita quod eius oppositum esse verum includit contradictonem; et sic hec absolute est necessaria 'Homo est risibilis', 'Deus est' et huiusmodi, quia contradictio est quod hec sint false et contradictiorie vere. Necessitas ex suppositione est quando aliqua conditionalis est necessaria, quamvis tam antecedens quam consequens sit contingens. Sicut hec est necessaria: 'Si Petrus est predestinatus Petrus salvabitur', et tamen tam antecedens quam consequens est contingens (*Quodlibet* VI, q. 2).

without a second cause in his absolute power to do whatever does not entail a contradiction, that his omnipotence is to be assessed. Thus, as we have said before, the distinction between God's two kinds of power does not imply any distinction or change in him, but merely expresses the truth of the first article of the creed of belief in one omnipotent God;[2] so that even if he acts in one way which can be regarded as necessarily true, granted the present dispensation, he could hypothetically have acted differently. That applies equally to theological and to natural truth where it concerns creation; and its application by Ockham to the questions of grace and merit has tended to obscure the connection between this one area of theological speculation and his essentially non-speculative theological orthodoxy in all other aspects. Both attitudes express the same concern with the strict implications of revealed truth. It is the implications—not their premises in revealed truth—which change with the change in aspect of God. Where, considered in his own nature, there is no order of perfection, there is an order of perfection and causality between God and everything else.[3]

Omnipotence thus expresses God's same perfection considered in relation to the imperfect beings which are dependent upon it: the change, to employ an analogy I have not met in Ockham, is from *esse* to *agere*; but it is the action of a perfect being whose perfection is exhibited not impugned by its power to act in different ways. The moral and theological consequences will be considered later in the chapter, and we have come upon many other examples in previous chapters. In addition to the relation of grace to merit, the ramifications of God's absolute power extend from intuitive knowledge of non-existents[4] to his relevation of future contingents,[5] the creation of infinite worlds and souls,[6] of a better world,[7] of the world and beings from eternity,[8] of matter without pre-existing form[9] and form without matter, [10] the separation of accidents from substances,[11] attributes from subject,[12] cause from effect[13] and of absolutes from one another, by not creating one without the other, or by annihilation or conservation of one without the other, through God's direct supersession of a second cause.[14] As we have said before, God's immediate intervention as first and only cause means merely the separation of what is naturally distinct but inseparable—form and matter, accident and substance, subject and attribute, cause and effect—not its negation or transformation into what it is not: though *ex suppositione* God could also create a different or better world or species, and together with a creature produce the contrary of what previously obtained.[15]

---

[2] Cf. *Quodlibet* VI, q. 1; also q. 4; and chapter one, 15–17 above.

[3] Ideo dico aliter ad questionem quod in divinis non est ordo perfectionis non plus quam ibi est ordo durationis, sed dei respectu aliorum a se est ordo causalitatis et ordo perfectionis (*Ordinatio*, d. 35, q. 3, I).

[4] Cf. chapter one above.   [5] *Quodlibet* IV, q. 4.

[6] *Ordinatio*, d. 17, q. 8, Y; d. 43, q. 1, N; d. 44, E, I; *SL*, I, ch. 23, 67.

[7] *Ordinatio*, ibid., d. 44, q. unica, E.   [8] *Quodlibet* II, q. 5.

[9] *Ordinatio*, d. 5, q. 2, H.   [10] *Reportatio*, IV, q. 7, N.

[11] *Ordinatio*, d. 9, q. 2, B.   [12] *Quodlibet* V, q. 18.   [13] *Ibid.*, IV, q. 15.

[14] *Ibid.*, and qq. 23, 25–9; *Reportatio*, II, qq. 4 and 5, D: *SL*, I, ch. 24, 73.

[15] Notes 6 and 7, and *Reportatio*, IV, q. 3, F.

Now we have mentioned before that there is no natural proof for God's omni-causality, as first immediate cause; nor that he causes freely or that his will is always fulfilled. Ockham discusses each of these facets of God's omnipotence at length both in the *Ordinatio* and the *Reportatio* (book two). So far as the first is concerned, although it cannot be demonstrated naturally it can be persuaded that God is the immediate first cause of everything, as follows: A second cause depends no less upon an absolutely first unlimited and infinitely perfect cause than it does upon a relatively unlimited and imperfect cause; but a second cause at some time does depend upon a relatively universal and unlimited cause, without whose immediate concurrence it could not produce an effect, as in the relation between the sun and its dependents. Therefore no second cause can act without the immediate con-currence of an absolutely first cause, which is God.[16] An immediate cause means an absolute being in whose absence, and despite the presence of all the other requisite conditions, there cannot be an effect, although the converse does not perhaps hold. There is no other way in which an immediate cause could be known, and it includes a universal cause like the sun equally with particular causes. In all such cases an immediate cause as the *sine qua non* of an effect is a partial cause since it is not the only efficient cause.[17] On the other hand any cause properly speaking is an immediate cause, for no cause of a cause is strictly the cause of what is caused, as a father's father is not the cause of the father's son.[18] And a remote cause is not a cause because from its presence an effect does not follow: otherwise Adam could be said to be the cause of us as his descendants, which is not true, because non-being cannot be called the cause of being.[19]

A first cause is first by primacy of perfection or lack of limitation, or by duration, either of nature or causation. God is first by all three when duration is taken in the first sense of referring to his nature. He is moreover first and immediate cause by his essence and not merely by his will, because there is no difference between his will and essence. It is therefore false to attribute God's omnicausality to his will and not to his essence.[20] As omniscience is God himself knowing and not confined to his intellect, so omnipotence is God himself willing and not the action of the will alone. Divine volition can thus either directly signify the act of God's essence or also connote that which he wills, as creation or conservation signify not only God's will but also a creature; it is in this second sense that it can be called free in being of something other than God's nature and so not necessary.[21] Hence when God is said to be everywhere and in everything by his essence, presence, and power, that is to be understood not only in the accepted sense as the cause of everything but

[16] *Ordinatio*, d. 45, q. unica, F: *Reportatio*, II, qq. 4 and 5, K.

[17] *Ordinatio, ibid.*, D.

[18] Aliud sequitur quod omnis causa proprie dicitur est causa immediata ... dico quod non semper quicquid est causa cause est causa causati, non plus quam quicumque est pater patris est pater filii ... Et ideo hoc est universaliter verum quod proprie et stricte accipiendo causam nihil est causa alicuius nisi sit causa immediata ipsius (*ibid.*, D–E); and *Reportatio*, II, qq. 4 and 5, K.

[19] *Reportatio, ibid.*

[20] *Ordinatio*, d. 45, B–C, I.

[21] *Ibid.*, d. 35, q. 6, F; cf. also *ibid.*, d. 9, q. 3, T where Ockham rejects instants in God's knowledge of creatures.

also in virtue of his knowledge of everything which is present to him and by his immediacy to everything. In addition he is present to some but not to all creatures by his grace. It does not therefore directly follow that God is in everything because he is the cause of everything, as is generally held.[22]

Although it cannot be demonstrated that God is first and immediate cause of everything the opposite view of Aristotle and Averroes and the other philosophers, that from one cause there can be only one effect, besides being heretical, is contrary to reason. Both the will and a natural power like the sun are capable of producing many effects—the will as the cause of volition, nolition, love, hate; the sun of what is generable and corruptible—and yet each remains one and undifferentiated. Moreover if to each effect there corresponded a different cause, two effects would have two causes, and those causes two more causes and so on; there would then be either an infinite series or the sequence would have to end at the first two causes; since both consequences are false the alternative would be a first cause of everything.[23] Nor does the act of creation imply any change in God for whatever reason, as the will can will now something which it intends in the future and that does not involve temporal change. Time, potential or actual, is only necessary to our will and to God's to do something previously not done, such as first the creation and then the annihilation of an angel which must take place in time.[24]

That God as first and immediate cause of everything is partial and not total cause follows from his role as principal cause in any effect produced by a second cause. For a total cause, contrary to Duns Scotus, is that which is alone required for an effect; and although God could by his absolute power be sole and total cause, from which it follows that he is free cause of the effects—a matter to which we shall return presently—de facto by the present dispensation he is not. Consequently it cannot be argued that in any joint action with a second cause both God and creature are total causes acting together. If both God and creature were to be total causes each would independently produce the same thing, which, without assertion, Ockham regards as possible: thus if God were to produce fire by means of the sun, fire would be produced in the same way as if produced directly by God and would depend essentially upon the sun as it does upon God, because it is impossible for something to depend upon something else unless caused by it.[25]

The role of God as immediate cause can be compared to that of a strong man who could carry a heavy weight by himself and yet does so together with a weak man who could not carry it alone. Because the strong man does not wish to carry the weight alone, the co-operation of the weak man is not superfluous and in vain. Similarly with God and a second cause: he is first and principal cause which if he willed could be total cause; and in acting together with a second cause he acts as immediately as he would alone.[26] For that reason it cannot be demonstrated that any effect is from a second cause, because although fire always accompanies combustion, God could himself be the cause and not fire, as he could cause directly the grace which he has ordained, with the church, should come through the

[22] Ibid., d. 38, B–E.   [23] Reportatio, II, q. 4 and 5, F.   [24] Ibid., I.
[25] Ibid., L.   [26] Ibid., Q, also Ordinatio, d. 45, q. unica, E.

speaking of certain words, or cause an angel to act in the appearance of a man as the example of Tobias shows.[27] That, however, is not Humean scepticism, because the issue is not causality as such but the possible non-existence of a second cause. Nor does it destroy the essential order between first and second cause, which lies in the dependence of the second cause upon the perfection of the first cause which conserves it and by which it is a cause.[28] As we shall mention shortly, creation and conservation are for Ockham inseparable from one another; its assumption it will be recalled underlay Ockham's proof for God's existence as first conserving cause. Consequently in acting together both first and second cause have the same end and produce one total effect.[29]

Now as nothing created can be proved to be a second cause God cannot be proved to be able to do alone all that can be done by a creature, because all, philosophers and theologians alike, agree that God does not himself produce all that can actually be produced; and in default of any means of proving that he causes contingently and freely—for reasons which we shall consider in a moment—it is impossible to prove that a necessary cause is the sole cause of everything that exists. For a necessary cause, in not acting freely, either produces everything or nothing to which it is related, since there is no more reason why it should produce one thing rather than another of the same nature; it cannot be everything as a matter of fact; therefore it would be nothing.[30]

Of Duns Scotus's four arguments designed to establish the same conclusion, Ockham accepts only two: that which he has just employed, although he observes that elsewhere Duns says the opposite in attempting to demonstrate contingency in creatures from the contingency of a first cause; and the arguments of the philosophers that nothing comes from nothing; therefore to them it did seem possible for God to act—at least in generabilia and corruptibilia—without a second cause. Even this Ockham regards as misrepresenting some philosophers for whom nothing is eternally from nothing. The other two reasons he rejects as inadequate. The first, for wrongly concluding that the philosophers did not posit a second cause as concause because of its imperfection in relation to a first cause: since Duns agrees that Aristotle held God to be the cause of everything, that would not contradict God as immediate cause but rather make him first mediate cause of everything imperfect. The remaining reason does not hold, for here Duns deduces from the philosophers' view of God as necessary cause, the negation of all causality in view of his omnipotence: in fact it would mean that God could not act upon any second cause to produce an effect.[31] Duns's first argument also raises again the issue of

---

[27] *Reportatio, ibid.,* R: e.g. Ex hoc sequitur quod non potest demonstrari quod aliquis effectus producitur a causa secunda, quia licet semper ad approximationem ignis ad combustibile sequatur combustio, cum hoc tamen potest stare quod ignis non sit eius causa, quia deus potuit ordinesse quod semper ad presentiam ignis passo approximato ipse solus causaret combustionem ....

[28] Si queras quomodo potest salvari ordo essentialis inter causam primam et secundam cum neutra sit superior sed utraque est immediata, dico quod una est superior in perfectione, puta prima, et secunda dependet a prima. Non tamen quod accipiat esse a prima, sed quia conservatur at ea, et quia non potest secunda producere nisi prima producat (*ibid.,* s).

[29] *Ibid.,* U.

[30] *Ordinatio,* d. 42, q. unica, F.   [31] *Ibid.,* B–E.

successive instants in the concausation of an effect, by which first the first cause and
then the second cause is compared to its effect. And once again Ockham dismisses
it as an improper way of speaking and the source of many errors.[32]

His own interpretation of the philosophers is that they held that an effect
followed necessarily from its cause not because of an effect's imperfection, which
they attributed equally to the cause, but of their proximity, so that one was the
accompaniment of the other; and where there was none they posited no cause.
For the same reason they held that if God as necessary cause could produce a cause
without the concurrence of another cause, he would do so before the appearance of
a second cause and its effect. Finally not only did they not say that God is not the
cause of everything, because of the priority of a first cause over a second cause, but
they never denied that he is the immediate cause of all effects, although not total
cause.[33] As for Aristotle himself, he believed that God is the cause of everything
but that he cannot be proved to be a cause *de novo*.[34] Ockham's own view is that
while it can be probably accepted that God is the cause of every effect and that he
could alone produce every possible effect, neither this nor its opposite can be
sufficiently proved by natural reason.[35]

Next there is the question of God as free and contingent cause of everything.
Ockham does not accept that this essentially theological truth is susceptible to
more than persuasion by natural reason; namely that every cause which cannot
be impeded and is in the same relation to everything or an infinity of things, if it
causes one thing in one instant and not something else, is a contingent cause,
because there seems no reason why it should do so other than by its freedom to
produce one thing rather than another. That applies to God. He is therefore first
and contingent cause of everything,[36] understanding contingency as the power to
do otherwise.[37]

The attempts of both St Thomas Aquinas and Duns Scotus to prove the same
conclusion, however, founder because contingency cannot be deduced either
from God's will as the cause of everything, which is St Thomas's course, or from
the contingency of the created will, as Duns Scotus argues. In the first case St
Thomas gives four proofs for God's freedom, all of which show that God's actions
ad extra are through his will. But to prove that God produces all creatures by his
will as the principle of his actions does not thereby entail that God acts contingently,
because according to St. Thomas's own arguments God acts both necessarily in
ordaining the end and freely in choosing its means, while from the standpoint of
natural reason Aristotle also concluded that a first cause acts by both will and
intellect and yet acts necessarily. Moreover St Thomas himself accepts that God
produces the holy spirit through his will and so naturally and necessarily. Nor is
there any means of distinguishing his necessary from his contingent act of willing or
any validity in the argument that since a nature only naturally produces what

---

[32] *Ibid.*, F.   [33] *Ibid.*   [34] *Reportatio* II, q. 6, B.   [35] *Ordinatio*, d. 42, G.
[36] *Reportatio*, II, qq. 4 and 5, E.
[37] E.g. *Ordinatio*, d. 10, q. 2, F: Ex hoc arguo quod sic: omnis potentia que valet ad opposita
contingenter agit.

is equal to it, as fire generates fire or oxen generate oxen, God acts freely in not producing what is equal to him. For the philosophers would draw the opposite conclusion that the reason God did not produce what is equal to him is that it is not producible.[38]

We have already encountered the reply to Duns Scotus's argument that the contingency of a first cause is demonstrated by the contingency of a second cause: namely that it could equally be the other way and contingency be attributed to a creature, which is how the philosophers, against whom Duns's argument is directed, would retort. Hence, according to them, however much the other causes may cause necessarily, the effects will be produced contingently. As to Duns's statement that a second cause only causes when moved by a first cause, that could mean either that the second cause depends upon the first cause for its being, and then Duns's conclusion would be invalid, or that, if the first cause moves necessarily, so does the second cause. In neither does the necessity of a conserving or a producing cause any more necessitate the action of what it produces or conserves than the necessity of an immediate and co-operating cause does: as knowing, which is a necessary cause and the condition of willing, does not destroy the contingency of willing. Hence, however necessarily God were to conserve the created will, he would not thereby necessitate it to act or not to act. If alternatively to be moved by a first cause means just that, it is still invalid, since the will is the principle of moving itself, as it is when a first cause is the immediate concause. That in turn invalidates Duns's other proof for the same conclusion that a posterior cause acts in the same way as a prior cause. The philosophers would equally reverse Duns's second argument that, if God caused necessarily, the non-existence of what he caused would imply his own non-existence, which, according to Duns, would be false on the principle that the more impossible—God's non-existence—cannot follow from the less impossible—the non-existence of what he causes. The philosophers would, says Ockham, on the contrary argue that the more impossible follows from the less impossible, and that the negation of something other than the first cause would imply necessarily the negation of the first cause because of the necessity of the first cause in causing. To say otherwise would destroy the rules of logic, namely that from one convertible to another is a valid consequence, so that if man is not able to laugh it follows that man does not exist, where the antecedent is as necessarily impossible as the consequence. Duns's third argument that if God caused necessarily sin would not exist, since the effect would necessarily receive the goodness and perfection of the first cause, rests on the assumption that God is the immediate and total cause of any effect. It does not hold if God only immediately concurs in the will's action or conserves it; then whether the will is guilty lies in the will's power and not in God. Finally in arguing that if God caused necessarily he would himself cause everything because he would act completely, begs the very question disputed by the philosophers that God could himself cause everything or is its immediate concause.[39] For them as for Ockham neither proposition can be proved by natural reason; but for Ockham as a Christian both are

[38] *Ordinatio*, d. 43, q. 1, B–F.   [39] *Ibid.*, G–L.

true: if God were only a necessary cause he would produce everything or nothing, which is absurd.[40] God can therefore cause what he does not cause because as a contingent agent he can do other than he does.[41] That is the closest to a deduction that can be made from premises held on faith.

The philosophers in contrast see God as both necessary and indirect cause conserving but not moving the created will, which of itself acts contingently.[42] The conflict of outlook is not reconcilable by natural reason but rather testifies to the latter's limitations.

From a Christian standpoint, then, God is immediate concause and conserving cause of the actions of second causes, and could equally act without them, himself producing everything produced in conjunction with second causes, or act in other ways, producing what he has not produced before. It is in that context that God could make a better world, certainly of the same kind and probably of another kind,[43] as well as act in any of the other ways mentioned before, where no contradiction is implied. God's relation to everything else is that of creator and conserver; in relation to himself the two terms are the same, for nothing can be created by him which he does not also conserve. They differ in what they connote: creation signifies something produced by God and consignifies the negation of what preceded it (i.e. its non-existence) so that it now is and before it was not. Conservation signifies the same thing produced by God and connotes its continuance, so that it exists now and it existed before, which is the negation of its interruption or destruction.[44] Consequently where creation connotes existence after non-existence, conservation connotes temporal succession and duration. But both denote the same thing produced totally by an immediate cause.[45]

That in turn distinguishes creation from generation by a natural agent. Creation is from nothing and does not require another cause or matter. Generation, naturally, needs matter. When God produces a form in matter together with a second cause, he is creating, because he could act without both matter and a second cause, but a natural agent can only produce another thing by means of matter and therefore only generates. Thus on the one hand the same thing can be both created and generated in being both from God and a natural agent;[46] and on the other God

---

[40] *Ibid.*, L–M.

[41] Ex istis patet ad solutio questionis quod deus potest facere aliqua que non facit, quia omne contingenter agens potest facere aliter quam facit; sed deus est huiusmodi; ergo etc (*ibid.*, N).

[42] *Ibid.*, O.   [43] *Ordinatio*, d. 44, q. unica, D–E.

[44] Quia creatio et conservatio per nihil positivum differunt, quis creatio significat rem connotando negationem immediate precedentem rem, et conservatio significat eandem rem connotando continuationem. Et hoc nihil aliud est quam connotare negationem interruptionis vel destructionis essentie eius (*Reportatio*, II, qq. 4 and 5, L).

And: Sed sicut creatio lapidis importat ultra deum et lapidem quod lapis [modo sit et quod prius] immediate non fuit, ita conservatio lapidis importat ultra deum et lapidem quod lapis modo est et prius fuit (*Quodlibet* VII, q. 6). Also *Reportatio*, II, q. 8, K, and q. 10, H, N.

[45] *Reportatio*, II, q. 8, K and q. 10, N.

[46] Ad aliud dico quod illud agens dicitur solum creare quod non requirit aliquam aliam causam secum concurrentem nec materia . . . Dico tunc ad argumentum quod non est inconveniens eundem effectum simpliciter generari et creari. Cuius ratio est quia illud simpliciter

could create self-subsisting absolute forms from nothing and without matter, which would therefore not be generated.[47]

In the second *Quodlibet*[48] Ockham gives four senses of 'create' (excluding the legal definition where it means promotion to an ecclesiastical dignity). The first and broad sense is that employed by Averroes on *De Anima* book three, of 'to be produced' or 'become' as the intellect creates what it knows. That sense does not apply to God as the cause of any effect. The second is the strict sense of something made from nothing or made from something made from nothing; and in that sense any effect can be said to be created by God. It can also in the third and stricter sense of something which comes into being from nothing through an agent which could produce it without any subject. But not in the strictest sense as that which is produced from nothing by God alone, independently of any concause which can only act through matter: for as we have amply seen God is not the *de facto* sole cause of any cause, simple or composite.[49]

Ockham accordingly agrees with Duns Scotus that a creature does not have the power of creating from nothing and without pre-existing matter. But unlike Duns, some of whose arguments he disputes, he does not attempt more than to persuade such a conclusion. To begin with, a creature cannot be the total natural cause of a creature because a total natural cause either produces all or none of the individuals of the same species related to it; hence if a creature could totally produce one individual of the same species it could produce an infinity of them, which is false. Nor secondly can a creature be a partial natural cause of a creature for the same reason. Finally it cannot be a free cause since that would be in virtue of an act of willing which could also be to create an infinite number of individuals, and so is equally untenable.[50]

Creation is thus a connotative term signifying nothing distinctive in either God or creation.[51] In relation to God, as active creation (*creatio actio*), it signifies himself, as divine essence, really creating; in relation to a creature, as passive creation (*creatio passio*), it signifies a creature immediately produced by God and depending

---

creatur quod producitur ab agente quod non requirit materiam concausantem, et illud generatur quod producitur ab agente quod necessario requirit materiam concausantem (*Reportatio*, II, qq. 4 and 5, Y–Z). Also *Quodlibet* II, q. 8.

[47] Quantum ad tertium dico breviter quod omnis forma que potest produci per potentiam dei sine subiecto simpliciter creatur a deo de facto; sed ille sunt tantum forme absolute ... Istud patet, quia creare est aliquid de nihilo facere ... ergo ista duo sufficiunt ad creationem, quod fiat de nihilo et quod non necessario presupponat materiam in sui factione (*Reportatio*, *ibid.*, N).

[48] *Quodlibet* II, q. 8.

[49] For that reason I disagree with Baudry, *Lexique* (69), when he interprets this as referring to forms, (a) because Ockham expressly says it applies neither to composite nor simple beings (sed quarto modo dico quod nec effectus simplex nec compositus creatur (*ibid.*)), and (b) because it refers to God's acting without other concauses which must act through matter.

[50] *Reportatio*, II, q. 7, D; *Quodlibet* II, q. 9.

[51] Ergo generaliter dico quod nec creatio activa nec passiva, nec conservatio activa nec conservatio passiva dicit aliam rem extra animam a rebus absolutis (*Quodlibet* VII, q. 6). Also *Ordinatio*, d. 26, q. 2, H; d. 30, q. 1, O.

immediately upon and related immediately to him.[52] Hence creation as a relative term can denote and stand for absolute beings, on the one hand God as active creation and on the other a creature as passive creation.[53] In that sense it can be called a real relation, as the sun's relation to its effects can be called real, with nothing conceivable thereby added to either term.[54] Not only does that exclude any relation of reason between them, but because it does not imply any medium between God and creature, Ockham initially in the *Reportatio* book two—assuming it to have been composed before the *Ordinatio*—denied that creation constituted a real relation. He modified this view in the *Ordinatio* and *Quodlibets*, but his reasoning and emphasis remained predominantly unchanged. These were mainly directed to refuting the arguments of Duns Scotus and others for a relation of reason, which we have discussed in chapter three.

As they concern creation Ockham's reasons are put succinctly in a quodlibetal question.[55] They are first that a relation of reason depends upon the created intellect. If therefore creation were a relation of reason, God could not be creator or create without the concausation of the created intellect. Creation would then depend upon the created intellect. Second, something which is really and truly signified or which really exists, does so independently of whether or not it is known or, in the case of a relation, whether the signification of either extreme is known. Hence, in the same way as a man, if he is really white, is white regardless of whether the intellect knows the fact, so God really creates; and neither God nor his creating represents anything caused by the intellect. To make God's relation as creator the work of the intellect, comparing him with a creature, would mean equally that a creature could be creator by comparing one creature with another. A relation of reason, as the act of the created intellect, can be false as well as true if it comes from a false comparison. To be true it must conform to what exists.[56] For that reason all such terms as 'creator', 'conserver', 'lord', which are affirmed of God temporally, represent a real relation between him and creatures because they are truly affirmed of God and creatures. As such they are independent of the intellect's activity.[57] God would still be creator if he created a stone with no intellect to know it.[58]

In the *Reportatio* Ockham, as we have said, also denies that creation is a real relation on the grounds that it adds nothing positive and real to what is related. That remains his view of relation throughout all his works, and, as we have also

[52] Ideo creatio actio nihil dicit vel significat preter essentiam divinam connotando vel dando intelligere existentiam creature que nullo modo potest esse nisi posita essentia divina (*Reportatio*, I, q. 1, D). . . . Quia creatio passio nihil aliud est quam creaturam immediate fieri a deo, et dependere immediate a deo, et referri immediate ad deum (*ibid.*, qq. 4 and 5, L).

[53] *Quodlibet* VII, q. 6.

[54] *Quodlibet* VII, q. 3; *Ordinatio*, d. 30, q. 5, G.

[55] *Quodlibet* VII, q. 3; *Quodlibet* VI, q. 28. Also *Ordinatio*, d. 35, q. 5, F–G.

[56] *Quodlibet* VII, q. 5.

[57] Ideo dico quod per tales terminos, 'creans', 'creativus', 'conservans', 'conservativus', 'dominus', secundum quod competunt deo, et per huiusmodi nomina que competunt deo ex tempore, nullus respectus rationis importatur nec comparatio intellectus ibi aliquid operatur plus quam in aliis relativis quibuscumque, quia ita vere et ita realiter est deus creans (*Ordinatio*, d. 30, q. 5, G; also I, P–Q).

[58] *Ibid.*, G; also *Reportatio*, II, q. 1, B–D.

mentioned, it recurs in his subsequent discussion of creation: for example, in the *Ordinatio* he declares that it is untrue that creation is really in God, for then God would really have something which previously he did not before the creation of the world, when it was false to say that God is creator.[59] In the *Reportatio* he appears to be thinking more of the absence of real diversity between a relation and its foundation and term, which it will be recalled from chapter three was the gravamen of his attack on Duns Scotus's separation of one from the other; for he expressly says that by this view of creation as the total significate of God principally and a creature secondarily, without any intervening relation real or of reason, the problems which arise from considering relations as distinct from their foundations are overcome.[60] Thus Ockham treats creation as a connotative term which he also in the same question calls a relative appellation of reason (*relativa apellatio rationis*), an expression I have not found in his other works. The difference seems to be one of terminology. Like the real relation of the *Ordinatio* and *Quodlibets* it applies to terms like 'creator', 'governor', 'conserver', which signify God directly and a creature indirectly. 'Creator' is accordingly a relative term (*ad aliud*) in denoting distinct absolutes and not a relation.[61] Its import therefore remains unchanged.

Finally if God is omnipotent and yet acts contingently and freely, can his will be impeded? This concerns the allied questions of whether God's will is always fulfilled and whether a creature must always conform to it. In keeping with tradition Ockham follows the division of God's willing into that of approbation (*beneplaciti*) and of sign (*signi*) as prohibition, precept, counsel, fulfilment, and permission. He stresses however that they do not represent any distinction in God but are merely diverse names and expressions signifying the same will which is God himself, so that to disobey God's will is equally to violate his counsel or his precept, and conversely when God is said to will something, that is equivalent to saying that he commands it. Similarly the distinction between his antecedent and consequent will is not as it is in our will, between different phases of before and after an act of volition, but represents differing nominal definitions of what is absolutely the same in every respect. His antecedent will is thus equivalent to the proposition that God gives someone the antecedents or powers to do something, in the attain-

---

[59] *Ordinatio*, d. 30, q. 1, o.

[60] Et si queras in quo est creatio actio, dico sicut supra dictum de realitate, quod quando est aliquod nomen significans plura realia non est querendum in quo est illud nomen vel conceptus sic significans, sed querendum est quid denominatur ab illo. Et dico quod essentia divina principaliter et creatura secundario et connotative, ita quod hoc nomen duo significat quantum ad suum significatum totale, scilicet unum principaliter et aliud connotative sine omni respectu medio rei vel rationis. Et ista via vitat multa inconcenientia que oportet ponere secundum ponentes relationes distinctas a fundamento (*Reportatio*, II, q. 1, E).

[61] Et est sic intelligendum quod deus est denominabilis ab istis nominbius, que significant principaliter deum et connotant existentiam creature in effectu, vel dant intelligere. Et ideo vocatur apellatio relativa, quia quando intelligo creationem, non intelligo tantum deum, sed aliud puta connotatum. Et non oportet ponere propter hoc aliquem respectum realem vel rationis. Tamen talis appellatio non potest competere sine nomine significante unum connotando aliud. Ad primum tunc dico quod nomen vel conceptus creationis est ad aliud non quod significet aliquem respectum, sed quia ipsum nomen non importat precise unum, sed cum hoc quod significat unum connotat aliud, et inter illa significata sive importata per illud nomen est distinctio absolutorum non sicut relativorum (*ibid.*, G).

ment of which he is ready to co-operate by precept or counsel provided the person concerned is willing. Only if each of these conditions is met is God's antecedent will fulfilled, as it was not in Abraham's desire to sacrifice his son, where God gave Abraham both the power and the precept to sacrifice but refused to co-operate with him in the act of sacrifice; hence it remained unachieved. In the same way God's antecedent power also excludes acts of sin in being contrary to his precepts and counsels, although giving to a sinner both the antecedent powers to sin and not withholding his own co-operation in a sinful act. God's consequent will on the other hand is that by which he wills something efficaciously.[62] Hence, while both his will as sign and his antecedent will of approbation can be opposed, his consequent will must always be fulfilled, because nothing can withstand his omnipotence, whereas by the first two God gives a creature the power to act contrary to his will.[63]

Strictly speaking, then, taken in itself, as omnipotence, God's will cannot be impeded.[64] That can be proved as follows: he who can act against his efficacious will can be sad; but God can in no way be sad; therefore whatever God wills is done in the manner in which he wills it, whether by himself or someone else. What cannot be proved is that everything willed by God is always fulfilled, because it cannot be proved, as we have seen, that God is or is not immediate cause of everything.[65]

Every created will in this life and the next must conform indirectly and habitually to what God wills by his will of approbation, when it is absolutely of all good and not on account of sin as the penalty for someone's guilt. That applies to every creature having the use of reason; its conformity is indirect and habitual, because its inclination to conform to what God wills comes through prior knowledge and is not of itself sufficient for or concurrent with an act of willing the same. Where God does not will absolutely, the created will can also will conditionally the opposite of what God wills: thus absolutely it must will that someone should be justly punished, but conditionally it can will that he is not punished. Not everyone, however, is held to conform to God's will, in willing what he wills habitually and immediately or actually, because not everyone is held to know God's will immediately; if God's will is known immediately, either as his will of approbation or as a precept, then the knower must conform, as he must in willing what God, by either of these modes, wills him to will; but not when God's will is expressed as a counsel.[66]

We shall have more to say about the relation between the divine and the created wills later in the chapter. Here, from the standpoint of God's will, we may

[62] *Ordinatio*, d. 46, q. 1, B–C.

[63] Istis distinctionibus sic intellectis dico cum aliis quod contra voluntatem dei beneplaciti nihil fit, sed contra voluntatem antecedentem vel voluntatem signi fit aliquid. Primum patet, quia contra voluntatem omnipotentem et non impedibilem volentem aliquid efficaciter nihil potest fieri . . . (*ibid.*, D).

[64] *Ibid.*, F.

[65] *Ibid.*, q. 2, B–E.

[66] *Ibid.*, d. 48, q. unica, B–G.

simply add that in the case of sin it could strictly speaking be accepted that God
wills sin, in the sense that he wills what is bad. That can be persuaded from the
example of someone wishing to give alms from vainglory. Since giving alms is
from God and vainglory is bad, God it could be argued causes a bad act. Such a
mode of inquiry Ockham only cites without judging its truth or catholicity.
But regardless of which it is, so far as the Catholic authorities are concerned, God
cannot be accepted as willing or causing sin, whether taken in the strict sense or not.
Rather to say that God wills sin means that he wills something evil justly or does
something evil justly.[67]

For Ockham, then, God's omnipotence represents God's power to act freely
and contingently but always justly in relation to everything else, since as God
himself acting there cannot be any divergence between essence and omnipotence.
Hence, in its unconditional, non-temporal expression as his absolute power, God's
omnipotence is nothing else that the God's power to do whatever does not include
a contradiction, which by definition precludes contradicting his own perfections
as most perfect being. Omnipotence is therefore less the measure of God's nature—
for which creatures can have no measure *pro statu isto*[68]—than of the dependence
of everything else upon God; so that what exists need not exist or can exist by a
different mode, and what does not exist could exist. On the other hand, even where
the present dispensation can be accepted, natural reason is too limited to give
certainty, for example over the world's eternity which in common with the
majority of Christian thinkers of the previous seventy years Ockham regards as
possible because it does not imply any manifest contradiction.[69] In the course of
considering seventeen aruments *pro* and *contra* he also discusses the meaning of
Aristotle's dictum 'That which is, must be, when it is'.[70] (*omne quod est, quando est,
necesse est esse*).

We have already alluded briefly in the section on future contingents to Ockham's
mention of Aristotle's view of the future, in the *Logic* and his Commentary on
Perihermenias. In the latter work Ockham distinguishes Aristotle's intention, namely
that if something exists at a particular time it is necessarily true that it exists at that
time, from the strict sense of the proposition, that something necessarily exists
when it exists, which he rejects as false.[71] In the question of the world's eternity in
the *Reportatio* he develops this distinction between a necessary proposition and
something which exists necessarily at a certain time. The second is false because
nothing other than God is necessary; the first is true in the sense that any proposition, of the past, present or future, is necessarily true when it cannot be false;
and its truth-value will vary according to whether it is conditional, causal, or
temporal. If it is conditional, only the relation between the antecedent and the

---

[67] *Ibid.*, d. 47, q. unica, B–F.
[68] *Reportatio*, II, q. 11, I.
[69] Dico quod utraque pars potest teneri et neutra potest sufficienter reprobari, quia tamen
non videtur includere manifestam contradictionam mundum fuisse ab eterum (*Reportatio*, II,
q. 8, A; also O).
[70] *Perihermenias*, ch. 9, 19 a, 22.
[71] *De Praedestinatione*, 109–10.

consequent has to be necessarily true, but neither need be true as a matter of fact. If it is causal, not only must the connection be true but also each part, so that the antecedent is the cause of the consequent. If it is temporal, antecedent and consequent need be true for the time that the proposition is said to be true. But, as we considered at length in chapter four, no categorical proposition about contingent being can be absolutely and unconditionally necessary because no contingent being is necessary, which is the great gulf between Ockham and Aristotle.

We return then, to our point of departure: omnipotence expresses God's free and contingent relation with what he creates. As such it is never necessary nor necessarily confined to a particular course of action, as we must now consider over predestination, grace, merit, and free will.

II PREDESTINATION

As may have been inferred from what was said about God's future knowledge, predestination and reprobation mean nothing else than God giving future eternal life or punishment to someone.[72] Neither therefore constitutes a distinct real relation in God or the recipient any more than active and passive creation do;[73] and both, like creation, are the result of a free and contingent act by God which once true is immutable because there is no change in God or those whom he has saved or damned.[74] Accordingly, as we have seen earlier, God could have not predestined Peter, so that it is possible both actually and logically that someone saved could be damned, and conversely. Once, however, God has predestined Peter, his predestination although contingent remains immutable as a proposition about the future; like any future proposition which is true, it cannot change into being false since as we have also seen there is no reason why it should be more true of the future at one time than another.[75] That applies to the proposition that it is possible for someone saved to be damned, which is true in the divided sense where subject and predicate could be changed; but not in a composite sense, where it is equivalent to saying that it is possible that someone saved is damned.[76]

As to the cause of predestination and reprobation, cause can only be understood here as a priority between propositions, not things. In that sense, of one proposition following naturally from another and related as consequent and antecedent,[77] both predestination and reprobation can be said to have a cause. For

---

[72] Circa primum dico quod predestinatio non est aliquid imaginabile in deo distinctum quocumque modo a deo et personis et deitate . . . sed importat ipsum deum qui est daturus alicui vitam eternam et ita importat ipsum et vitam eternam que dabitur alicui. Et eodem modo est de reprobatione, quod importat deum daturum alicui penam eternam et nihil adveniens (*Ordinatio*, d. 41, q. unica, F), and *De Praedestinatione*, 11, K.

[73] *Ordinatio, ibid.; De Praedestinatione*, 3–4, 11.

[74] *Ordinatio*, d. 40, q. unica, B; *De Praedestinatione*, 6, 8–10.

[75] *Ordinatio, ibid.*, c; *De Praedestinatione*, 5ᵐ dubium, 37–8.

[76] *Ordinatio, ibid.*

[77] *Ordinatio*, d. 41, q. unica,]; *De Praedestinatione*, dubium quartum, 36–7; nona suppositio, 17. Cf. Boehner's remarks (*Collected Articles*, 45–7), where he concludes that Ockham understands by a natural consequence in causal propositions their connection by *quia* or a similar term. That seems very probable.

these are valid consequences: 'He will persevere finally; therefore he will be saved', and similarly, 'He will finally sin; therefore he will be damned'. Just as God is not an avenger before someone is a sinner, he is not a remunerator before some-one is justified by grace. At the same time, however, the causes of reprobation and predestination can precede their effects in their recipients.[78] But whereas the cause of reprobation is in the sins of those who are damned, which are eternally foreseen by God, the cause of predestination is not the same for all who are saved. For some it is their own merits, so that without acting meritoriously of their own volition they would not be saved. Others, however, are ordained to eternal life not for any reason on their part but from a special grace; they are not therefore left to them-selves as others who are saved are; but like the Virgin they are safeguarded from any obstacles to eternal life. Unlike those who are saved because God foresees that they will persevere in charity to the end, as recompense for which he confers eternal life, the salvation of the second group seems to depend on nothing except God's will that they should be saved without any preceding merits, as St Paul was struck and saved with no prior merit of his own. But whether there is a reason or not, the cause of each case lies in God's will.[79]

For Ockham, then, not all are saved in the same way, although those saved on account of their merits could be saved without them, and those saved without merits could have been saved because of them.[80] Neither reprobation—wholly—nor predestination—partially—can therefore be entirely without any cause in those damned or saved, contrary to St Thomas's views that both, or predestination alone, are the total effect of God's will. That not everything ordaining someone to predestination is the effect of predestination can be seen from the example of someone in mortal sin performing good works. Although by God's ordained law his sinful state is incompatible with eternal life, nevertheless his good actions are in some way the cause of God's grace as temporal reward; hence such actions, while not in themselves strictly meritorious or deserving eternal life, can dispose a sinner towards grace and to the effects of predestination. It does not therefore follow from predestination as an effect. That applies also to preparation for grace which precedes grace and is common to those in mortal sin, and deserving of eternal punishment,

[78] *Ordinatio, ibid.,* F; *De Praedestinatione,* 36–7.
[79] Sed de predestinatione videtur esse magis dubium. Et quantum ad hoc potest dici sine preiudicio et assertione quod alicuius predestinationis est aliqua causa et ratio, et alicuius non est talis ratio vel causa. Huius ratio est, quia aliqui propter merita salvabuntur, ita quod si non voluntarie mererentur non salvarentur. Aliqui autem solum ex gratia speciali sunt ordinati ad vitam eternam, ita quod sibiipsis non sunt derelecti sicut alii sed preveniuntur ne possint ponere obicem ne perdant vitam eternam sicut fuit de beata virgine et de quibusdam aliis . . . Ita est de quibusdam predestinatis; predestinantur quia previdentur finaliter perseverare in charitate et quod deus non conferet eis vitam eternam nisi prius mererentur vitam eternam. Secundorum non videtur esse ratio quare predestinantur nisi quia deus vult ita quod quicquid dat eis dat ut consequantur vitam eternam nec permittit eis aliquid inesse quod posset eos impedire a vita eterna. Causa autem quare istos predestinat sine omni ratione et alios propter rationem non est nisi divina voluntas, sicut causa quare beatus Paulus fuit percussus et conversus sine meritis quibuscunque precedentibus et alius non sic non est nisi divina voluntas. (*Ordinatio,* d. 41, q. unica, G).
[80] *Ibid.,* H.

and those worthy of eternal life. Nor can it be replied that it depends upon divine aid—and so grace—because nothing positive can be done without divine help and yet not everything positive is the effect of predestination; while the argument that both reprobation as well as predestination are due to God's goodness, in its aspect of retributory justice, is untenable because God only punishes because of sin, and not, as he would otherwise, because he intends sin eternally of his own volition.[81] Similarly, Duns Scotus's opinion that God's end of willing predestination comes before his foreknowledge of who is saved, as the end is prior to the means, has no application to God because there is as we have seen no order of priority in his willing. Only in a creature who is predestined, not in God who predestines, is there any distinction between end and means.[82] It does not, however, follow that reprobation is something eternal which has its cause in a creature, but only as we have said as the consequent of an antecedent proposition, because nothing temporal is the cause of something eternal.[83]

III GRACE AND ACCEPTANCE

That brings us to the role of grace in merit and salvation. It can be seen from the foregoing that Ockham adheres to St Augustine's doctrine of salvation through final perseverance, as the special grace reserved for the elect regardless of the reason for its award. Without it there cannot be eternal life; hence it is independent of the temporal graces which, whether they sanctify a *viator* or enable him to act meritoriously and avoid sin, do not by themselves suffice him to follow God to the end. Ockham, however, went further, and like Duns Scotus,[84] denied any inherent place to created grace, not only in salvation but in merit of any kind, by God's absolute power. Instead the only requisite was God's acceptance of an act of will, whatever its nature. Accordingly merit and predestination could by God's omnipotence be reduced to a direct relation between the divine and created wills. On the one hand, God was free to reward as he willed; on the other, only a voluntary act, as we shall see, is meritorious or demeritorious and so alone worthy of remuneration. The principles are therefore the same as in every other case where God's omnipotence is concerned: God can do directly what ordinarily (by his ordained power) he does by second causes (in this case infused supernatural habits). Their application to created grace is not therefore, as they have so often been interpreted,[85] an attempt to undermine the certainty of revelation. Although the denial of the need for supernaturally infused habits, above all of grace, became,

---

[81] *Ibid.*, B–D.   [82] *Ibid.*, E, K.   [83] *Ibid.*, L.

[84] See W. Dettloff, *Die Lehre von der Acceptatio Divina bei Johannes Duns Scotus* (Werl, 1954), and *Die Entwicklung der Akzeptations- und Verdienstlehre* (Münster, 1963).

[85] Including my *Bradwardine and the Pelagians*, chs. VIII and XI and *Gregory of Rimini*, 20–3, and passim. For a detailed but hostile study of Ockham's doctrine of grace, see I. Iserloh, *Gnade und Eucharistie in der philosophischen Theologie des Wilhelm von Ockham* (Wiesbaden, 1956). Iserloh regards Ockham's doctrine and mode of thinking as a break with tradition and the inauguration of the change which came with the Reformation, especially in devaluing the infused supernatural virtues. For a new and more balanced perspective, see Dettloff's works cited in preceding note.

together with the uncertainties which among Ockham's successors were made to flow from God's future knowledge, the theological focus of Ockhamism, the same cannot be said of Ockham himself. For him, it is only a facet of God's relation to his creatures and is designed not as an exercise in theological paradoxes, but to stress God's freedom to act contingently in recompensing and punishing, as in everything else. Just as God could have not predestined Peter, and yet in having done so acted certainly, so he could have awarded or withheld grace without any prior condition. The issue is once again God's freedom to have acted differently; and if in the process free will is here the beneficiary that to Ockham is the very opposite of Pelagianism. Indeed it is the only safeguard against Pelagianism; for whereas, Ockham declares, Pelagius postulated that God must reward a naturally good action with eternal life, his present-day opponents go to the opposite extreme of insisting that God must reward acts performed from a supernatural habit of grace. Both therefore equally attempt to necessitate God and both therefore are equally false.[86] Moreover, Ockham later adds in the first question of the sixth *Quodlibet*, for Pelagius man could gain merit by his own natural powers (*ex puris naturalibus*) actually, by the present dispensation, but he, Ockham, says that is only possible by God's absolute power.

This is the keynote of Ockham's discussion. It is directed not against the notion of grace as divine aid; for as we have seen a creature can do nothing without God's help as concause and conserver. Nor is he denying the necessity of uncreated grace as God communicating himself or his love through the holy spirit to a rational creature. Rather it is this direct acceptance by God of someone as dear to him that Ockham opposes to created grace or charity as an absolute form distinct from the holy spirit and inhering in a rational creature. 'No such form,' he declares, 'whether natural or supernatural, can necessitate God, but it implies no contradiction for such a form to inhere in the soul for however long before blessedness and yet for God not to will to confer eternal life upon that soul.'[87]

What Ockham is contesting then is not the need for grace as such, which as God's acceptance is the condition of all merit and salvation,[88] but its created form as a supernatural habit; and then not the latter's *de facto* necessity by God's ordained power, to which he holds unconditionally as a matter of faith,[89] but the claim for

---

[86] Ut deus per nullam rem possit necessitari ad conferendum cuicumque vitam eternam. Et sic ista propria opinio maxime recedit ab errore Pelagii. Ipse enim Pelagius posuit quod si aliquis habet actum bonum ex genere, deus necessitatur ad conferendum sibi vitam eternam et non mere ex gratia sua, ita quod necessario foret iniustus si sibi non tribueret vitam eternam. Opinio autem predicta quamvis non ponat actum elicitum ex puris naturalibus sic necessitare deum, ponit tamen aliquam supernaturalem formam creatam a deo necessitare deum, quia habet ponere quod includit contradictionem quod talis forma sit in anima et quod deus nunquam dabit sibi vitam eternam (*Ordinatio*, d. 17, q. 1, L): *Reportatio*, III, q. 5, L.

[87] *Ordinatio, ibid.*, M.

[88] Unde charitas dupliciter accipitur. Uno modo precise pro quodam habitu absoluto infuso et sic non est nomen connotativum. Aliter accipitur charitas ut est abstractum respectu istius concreti 'charum', connotando aliquem cui ille est charus. Sine charitate primo modo potest aliquis de potentia dei absoluta esse charus. Non sine charitate secundo modo dicta (*ibid.*, z).

[89] *Ordinatio*, d. 17, q. 3, G; *Reportatio*, III, q. 5, N; *Quodlibet* VI, qq. 1, 2, 4.

its unconditional necessity in any action worthy of God's reward: the only sense in which God is necessitated to accept an act informed by a habit of grace is conditionally (*ex suppositione*), where by his ordained power it follows as a necessary consequence that he has ordained that such an act should be accepted; therefore he accepts it. The necessity here, as we may recall, lies neither in antecedent nor the consequent, each of which is contingent, but their connection where one cannot be true without the other.[90] The argument accordingly centres upon God's freedom to accept or reject a voluntary action by his absolute power. It is both negative in denying the indispensability of a supernatural habit and affirmative in upholding the possibility of meritorious acts without habits.

As far as the first aspect is concerned Ockham in both the *Ordinatio* and *Reportatio* begins with Peter Aureole's opinion that supernatural habits are necessary, which Ockham opposes, as Aureole had in his turn opposed Duns for the saying the opposite.[91] According to Aureole, when a form pleasing to God is present in the soul, the soul is rendered pleasing to God and thereby gratified and accepted and loved by him. Such a state is due not to God's acceptance but to the habitual love of God infused by him into the loving soul, so that without such a form, no one, even by God's absolute power, can be dear to God, and with such a form he is necessarily dear to God. To be loved by God therefore owes nothing to the soul's own natural powers.[92]

Ockham's reply is that the contrary of what is asserted here is possible, and that God can by his absolute power hold someone dear and accept him without a habit, as he can prepare and accept someone for eternal life who has never had such a habit. He is dear to God who is accepted by him; and to be worthy of eternal life means either that someone is so disposed by God according to his present dispensation (where by implication he will have created grace), or that there is no eternal life without justice; and then no one is worthy of eternal life on account of any form: for as God can temporally not confer eternal life upon someone who has a supernatural form, he could by his absolute power never do so. In the second place, both to be loved and to be detested by God are due to his will; but God can detest someone without any detestable form formally inhering in the person detested, as someone born in original sin is detestable to him and yet does not formally have a detestable form; therefore he can equally love someone without any lovable form formally inhering in the person loved. If either God's love or his hate corresponded to an inherent form of sin or charity it would follow that someone newly converted from mortal sin and baptised would be simultaneously loved and hated by God, because in addition to the habit of charity there would coexist with it a habit of mortal sin already engendered from previous acts of mortal sin. Nor indeed does God reward only acts which formally inhere through a habit; transitory actions which leave no trace, such as loving a friend for a time,

---

[90] *Quodlibet* VI, q. 2.

[91] *Ordinatio*, d. 17, q. 1, B–E; *Reportatio*, III, q. 5, A–D; where Duns (Johannis) is mentioned twice, E, H, in support. See Iserloh, *Gnade und Eucharistie*, 79–80, 86–9, and above all Dettloff, *Die Entwicklung*, 23–76, for a proper assessment.

[92] *Ordinatio*, ibid.; *Reportatio*, ibid.

or God above all, are more worthy of merit and eternal life than habits; for any acts which are in the will's power, and hence those which are purely natural, are more deserving of God's love and acceptance than habits, which are not in its power.[93]

Conversely, even accepting the presence of a purely supernatural form in the soul, it is still in God's absolute power to accept or not to accept such a soul, because when someone is hateful to someone else he does not thereby become a friend and accepted through receiving what is not in his power. That applies to a supernatural form whose infusion into a soul in mortal sin does not render it acceptable to God. God could have both redeemed the human race without Christ's Incarnation and given eternal life to the saints without any form. Moreover if a supernatural form necessarily gained God's acceptance, the reason would be either its natural good and perfection or its moral goodness. Each would make a form superfluous; if it were naturally good, a creature would then be better and more perfect naturally and so accepted by God without any such form; if it were morally good it would have to be in either a creature's power or God's, since nothing can be morally good unless in the power of someone: it is not in that of a creature because an angelic and human nature no less than any form are in God's power. No form is therefore required because of some moral goodness, as it not because of natural goodness. Nor is it in a creature's power to be disposed to receive such a form, for the very reason that it is in God's power to award it without any voluntary disposition on a creature's part, as in the case of baptised infants. Accordingly God can accept natural actions performed voluntarily which are pleasing to him, and reject those which result from the inherence of a supernatural form and are not in the power of created will.[94]

Anyone can thus be loved and accepted independently of whether or not he has a supernatural form.[95] Only God decides the worth of a person or an action, and nothing is meritorious save by God's acceptance. That does not mean that he acts arbitrarily or in defiance of his own canons. By his ordained power his saving love is reserved for the baptised who having been thus disposed to eternal life do not subsequently fall away from him into mortal sin.[96] By his absolute power he can reward any morally virtuous act performed naturally, including we shall see those of pagans. In each case his reward is for what is intrinsically virtuous, whether theologically or morally. But between such virtue and merit lies divine acceptance which can only be awarded freely as a gift, not exacted as due. Hence it will become

---

[93] *Ordinatio, ibid.* (F–G, letters omitted in text); *Reportatio, ibid.,* E, G.

[94] *Ordinatio, ibid.,* H; *Reportatio, ibid.*

[95] Ideo dico aliter ad questionem; et primo ostendo quod aliquis potest esse deo acceptus et charus sine omni forma supernaturali inherente. Secundo quod quacumque forma posita supernaturali in anima potest ipsa esse non accepta deo (*Ordinatio, ibid.,* I); also *Reportatio,* III, q. 5, G–I.

[96] Dico quod ille est acceptus et charus deo quo existente in tali statu, nisi per peccatum delinquat, deus disponit ipsum ad vitam eternam, sicut est de parvulo baptizato, quia tunc est in tali statu anime quod nisi postea peccet mortaliter deus dabit sibi vitam eternam . . . quia sive peccet postea sive non, nisi baptizetur aliquo baptismo non habebit vitam eternam (*Ordinatio, ibid.,* I).

apparent Ockham was not introducing some new radical concept of divine behaviour which overrides the difference between good and bad; he merely draws the line between their own intrinsic nature and God's acceptance of them. Even, as we shall mention, the possibility that God could reward someone for hating him is only to be conceived in terms of loving God and obeying his will. The onus is thus upon a rational creature's free will, but the reward and inclination to be rewarded are from God.

All Ockham's arguments against supernatural habits are designed to show their superfluity in what is essentially a relation between the divine and created wills. Thus if one among a number of actions, all entirely good but not worthy of eternal life, can be rewarded with eternal life, so by God's absolute power can the others. That applies to an act informed by a supernatural form and an act of loving God above all naturally, neither of which is of itself worthy of eternal life. Therefore if God can accept and reward one with eternal life he can accept and reward the other. Similarly with acts of the same kind: if God can reward and accept one elicited after the infusion of charity he can reward and accept another before the infusion of charity. As to absolute forms or qualities, whenever one can inhere in a subject independently of something else absolute, it can by God's power inhere without the other perpetually: which is the case with a supernatural habit inhering in someone temporally and independently of any beatific act. God could thus perpetually conserve such a habit without any accompanying beatific act. Again God could ordain that someone should have such a form and never be rewarded with eternal life, or that having the form, it should be annihilated and not recreated before he confers eternal life, because whatever God contingently creates he can as contingently destroy, whenever it pleases him. Moreover just as God can remit eternal punishment for mortal sin so he can will by his absolute power never to give eternal life to someone having charity as an absolute form.[97] As two effects produced by him and related to one another as prior and posterior, God can confer grace and not glory.[98]

By God's absolute power, then, no supernatural form is necessary for someone's acceptance; whomever he rewards he does so contingently, freely, mercifully and from his own grace; his actions owe no more to any gifts bestowed by him than to a creature's own natural powers, unless he so ordains that someone having the gift of created grace may merit eternal life.[99] In either event, therefore, whether God gives eternal life independently of a supernatural habit or by means of it, the decision is entirely gratuitous; and as he has freely willed one course, so he could equally have willed the other. That is the difference between his ordained and absolute powers; by the first he has contingently chosen what by the second he can as contingently not will. Thus when Aureole talks of what is pleasing to God, that must be understood here in the third of its special senses, of producing and perfecting something to its greatest possible accidental perfection, in this case con-

[97] *Ordinatio, ibid.,* K-M; *Reportatio, ibid.,* G-I.
[98] *Reportatio, ibid.,* E.
[99] *Ordinatio, ibid.,* L.

ferring eternal life upon a rational creature, as opposed to its general sense of connoting God's pleasure in relation to what is or can be good and perfect, and its other or more specific connotations of referring to God himself or to being which is nobler than other being as substance is superior to accident or an angelic nature to other natures (Aureole's sense).[100]

Far from God's pleasure following necessarily from a form which is pleasing to him, he can decide freely to accept or not to accept someone as he chooses. Moreover his acceptance can follow non-acceptance without any contradiction or change on his part, but because of some change in the person accepted, such as the inherence of a supernatural form which the latter previously did not have and which he now receives partly through his own natural powers or the independent actions of someone else. Thus God could decree that whoever should, of his own natural powers and without a supernatural form, feel grief after sinning mortally, should have his sin remitted and receive eternal life after death; and such a change from non-acceptance to acceptance would be from the person himself, not from God. In the same way through the prayers of a saint God could decide by his absolute power to accept some adult or child previously not accepted, with the change once again due not to God but to the person in whom God has decreed it. That accords with the authorities who all agree that in God there is no act or love distinct from his essence and that he will give eternal life to his servants provided it is not impeded by mortal sin.[101] Only as God loving himself does God necessarily of his nature love and find pleasing justice, charity, and the other perfections, and all creatures, especially all rational beings; but in the other senses of what is pleasing he does not necessarily love any virtue any more than he necessarily loves any angel. Nor does the necessary love which is God himself, and from which everything else flows, mean that it does so necessarily and immutably: as we have seen before, from an immutable cause there can be a contingent effect.[102]

The necessity of supernatural habits founders then upon the gratuitousness of God's acceptance and the primacy of acts over habits. That in turn explains why voluntary actions can by God's absolute power be meritorious without a supernatural habit; for only that which is in the power of an agent is meritorious or demeritorious. Hence if God were to reward a habit, that would be because of previous actions which engendered it and are acceptable to him, as he punishes sin because of actions which are sinful. A supernatural habit on the other hand is not in a creature's power; it does not therefore itself of its nature merit God's reward and need not be presupposed in a meritorious act.[103] That brings us to the role of free will in good and bad actions.

[100] In the *Reportatio* (*ibid.*, N), Ockham employs only Aureole's sense of God's special pleasure, having for its object a noble or very noble creature—such as an angel or a man—and reverses Aureole's argument that this pleasure is due to a form. It is he replies rather the greater nobility of an angelic or human nature which makes them the more immediate object of God's special pleasure than any form, which is pleasing to God only in virtue of perfecting these natures.

[101] *Ordinatio*, d. 17, q. 1, O–P.   [102] *Ibid.*, T, Y.

[103] Preterea nullus habitus reddit aliquem detestabilem nisi quia causetur ab actu detestabili et odibili; ergo similiter nullus habitus reddet aliquem ex natura habitus acceptabilem nisi quia

IV FREE WILL: VIRTUE, VICE, MERIT AND SIN

Now as we have said, Ockham's insistence upon free will as the indispensable agent in a meritorious act is, with the dispensability of created grace, the twin pole of his doctrine of merit. It brought down upon him, from both opponents like Bradwardine and Gregory of Rimini[104] and the Avignon Masters,[105] charges of Pelagianism for seeming to oust grace by free will; and there can be no doubt that the combined emphases upon the freedom of God's will and free will helped to seal a new outlook inaugurated by Duns Scotus which within a decade had gone to extremes far beyong anything held by Ockham. Yet, however we may assess Ockham's role in these subsequent developments, it should be apparent by now that his own position has a quite other import, in his own intention of (a) freeing God from the necessity of rewarding supernatural habits and (b) excluding intermediaries between God and the object of his grace. Merit is thereby reduced to God's free acceptance of an act by a rational creature freely performed. In Ockham's words, 'An act is called meritorious because it is accepted by God',[106] and it is demeritorious because God rejects it.[107] Neither therefore requires a supernatural habit; and, as we shall see, where sin is due to an act of omission it is punished for the lack of what should be.

A meritorious act then is whatever God accepts as such; regardless of whether it is with or without or prior to a supernatural habit. The only condition is that it must be freely willed. Hence the paradox that on the one hand nothing of itself is intrinsically meritorious:[108] only God's acceptance makes it so; and on the other that only an act of free will can be accepted as meritorious.[109] That means in the first place that grace and merit both converge in God's acceptance, which for Ockham is only another way of saying that the holy spirit as uncreated grace itself

---

causatur ex actu acceptabili. Confirmatur, quia nihil est acceptabile ex natura sua nisi sit in potestate habentis; ergo cum talis forma supernaturalis non sit in potestate habentis, non erit ex natura sua acceptabilis (*ibid.*, Q). Also *ibid.*, q. 2, C, and *Reportatio*, q. 5, E.

104 Cf. my *Bradwardine and the Pelagians* and *Gregory of Rimini*, in both of which I also misconstrued Ockham's notion of merit.

105 Arts 1–4 (in the second version). A. Pelzer, 'Les 51 Articles', 250–3; J. Koch, 'Neue Aktenstücke', *Recherches* 8, 82–8.

106 Quia ideo dicitur actus meritorius quia acceptatur a deo (*Reportatio*, III, q. 5, I).

107 *Ordinatio*, d. 17, q. 1, Q; q. 2, C.

108 Ideo dico aliter ad questionem quod non includit contradictionem aliquem actum esse meritorium sine omni tali habitu supernaturali formaliter inherente, quia nullus actus ex puris naturalibus nec ex quacumque causa creata potest esse meritorius, sed ex gratia dei voluntarie et libere acceptante; et ideo sicut deus voluntarie et libere acceptat bonum motum voluntatis tamquam meritorium, quando elicitur ab habente charitatem, ita de potentia sua absoluta posset acceptare eundem motum voluntatis etiam si non infundat charitatem . . . Verumtamen illum esse meritorium non est in potestate nature humane, sive habeat charitatem sive non habeat, sed est in libera dei acceptione (*ibid.*, q. 2, D); also *Reportatio*, III, q. 5, L).

109 Sed in actu meritorio nihil est acceptum quin possit esse et tamen non acceptari a deo; ergo nec in habitu caritatis, Assumptum probatur, quia nihil est absolutum in actu meritorio quin possit immediate fieri a deo nulla creatura coagente . . . et sic ille actus non esset meritorius, quia nihil est meritorium quod non est in potestate voluntatis (*Reportatio*, *ibid.*, G).

suffices by God's absolute power for eternal life without any created gift.[110] It is in that sense he interprets Peter Lombard, with grace signifying principally the holy spirit and consignifying someone worthy of eternal life. The holy spirit is then alone necessary for eternal life, but not by God's ordained power.[111] Charity by God's absolute power can thus be understood as the coexistence of the holy spirit with the created will whose action it accepts and to which it moves the will as partial cause.[112] On this view Ockham is doing no more than substitute the direct presence of the holy spirit for its created gift: as he explains in an earlier distinction of the *Ordinatio*, the holy spirit is given in its own person to a rational creature; and while ordinately that is only when a creature receives special acceptance, through habitual grace, it could also be by the inherence of the holy spirit alone.[113]

In the second place, all virtue and vice have their source in volition; and here in subsuming the worth of an action under its voluntariness Ockham was going further than any of his predecessors, Duns Scotus included. But his conception cannot be called voluntarism; far from jettisoning moral constraints in favour of the will's sovereignty, for Ockham like Duns Scotus the nature of an action is defined by the degree in which conforms to the dictates of right reason. Unlike Duns Scotus, however, for Ockham that requires more than the relation of an act to right reason: to be good or bad an act must have for its object an end which not only conforms to or violates right reason but also the requisite circumstances for its attainment; without them an act of will is merely indifferent. Every good or bad action must thus have an object outside the will, as all truth in the intellect has to accord with what exists outside it. With willing as with knowing, Ockham's outlook is at the farthest remove from subjectivism. Moral action, like knowledge, is concerned with real objects and its nature determined by its relation to them: as truth consists in the conjunction of what is known with what is, acts are good and bad through the conjunction of the will with an end; and as there can be different kinds of knowledge according to whether their conjunction is direct or indirect, so there can be different kinds of moral action.

Now as we have just seen, only acts of willing can be virtuous or vicious, because only what is in our power is laudable or culpable; and that depends upon the will's intention.[114] All actions therefore which are either involuntary or without a moral end are morally neutral; that includes interior acts of knowing and willing

---

[110] Tertia conclusio quod spiritus sanctus potest dari creature rationali sine charitate vel quocumque alio dono creato . . . Ex hoc sequitur quarta conclusio quod spiritus sanctus sufficit et non oportet ponere aliud donum ad acceptandum animam rationalem. Et hoc dico necessario (*ibid.*, K–L).

[111] *Ordinatio*, d. 17, q. 3, B–C; *Reportatio, ibid.*, E–G.

[112] Et si hec esset opinio Magistri *Sententiarum* tunc verum dicit scilicet quod charitas potest de potentia dei absoluta non esse aliud quam spiritus sanctus coexistens acceptans actum naturalem et impellens voluntatem per hunc modum sicut causa partialis ad actum illum eliciendum; sed non oportet necessario quod sit aliquod accidens inherens anime (*Reportatio*, III, q. 8, C).

[113] *Ordinatio*, d. 14, q. 2, C–F.

[114] Sed solus actus voluntatis est virtuosus. Probatur, quia solus actus voluntatis est laudabilis vel vituperabilis; igitur solus ille est virtuosus . . . Confirmatur per Philosophum III *Ethicorum*, ubi dicit quod nullus actus est vituperabilis nisi sit in potestate nostra (*Reportatio*, III, q. 10, H); also *ibid.*, q. 12, E–G; *Quodlibet* III, q. 13.

as well as all exterior acts,[115] such as walking or eating which are morally—as oposed to naturally—good or bad by reference to an interior act, namely of the will.[116] They can all be indifferently good or bad according to the will's intent.[117] Thus the act of walking to church, neutral in itself, if directed to love and honour of God is good, but sinful if done from vainglory. Similarly, to love another person for himself, without reference to any other circumstances, is a morally indifferent act which can be virtuous if love of God becomes the end.[118] All such actions not in themselves inherently good or bad are contingently good or bad by what Ockham calls an extrinsic denomination or connotation. That is to say they owe their virtue or vice to another act which is itself intrinsically and necessarily good or bad,[119] as the act of loving someone else is extrinsically good on account of a further act of loving God. An intrinsically moral act is therefore the cause of a contingently moral act; and the existence of the latter is proof of the former, since no act is contingently good or bad save by a necessarily good or bad act. Unless therefore an infinite regress of contingent acts is to be posited, for an act to be morally good or bad by an extrinsic denomination there must be a prior intrinsically good or bad act as its cause.[120]

There are accordingly two kinds of moral act related as cause and effect; and most of Ockham's extensive discussion of them in what is now the third book of the *Reportatio* and the third *Quodlibet* is concerned with establishing their different conditions.[121] The principal one is that contingent moral acts are such in virtue of their circumstances, whereas intrinsically moral acts are such because of their own nature as acts of will.[122] A contingent act can therefore vary according to circumstances, as in the examples previously cited, where the same act of loving or walking can be indifferently good or bad through the will's object in performing it. Such an act therefore when it is contingently good or bad is subordinated to the will's principal end of an intrinsically good or bad act and the circumstances needed for its realisation; and conversely the requisite circumstances cannot themselves be the object of a contingently good or bad act since they condition it. For example the act of wishing to pray to God must to be perfectly virtuous have as its circum-

---

[115] Sed actus hominis tam exteriores quam interiores, puta intelligere vel velle, secundum quod quilibet est actus indifferens, sunt contingenter virtuosi (*Reportatio*, III, q. 12, E); also XX.

[116] Ad principale dico quod actus exterior est bonus bonitate sua propria que est ipse actus naturaliter. Sed moraliter et causaliter est bonus bonitate actus interioris, quia solum est bonus quadam denominatione extrinseca. (*Quodlibet* I, q. 20). Also *Quodlibet* IV, q. 6.

[117] Quinta conclusio est quod nullus actus alius ab actu voluntatis est intrinsice virtuosus vel viciosus. Tum quia quilibet alius idem manens potest esse indifferenter laudabilis et vituperabilis; et primo laudabilis quando conformatur recte volitioni, et post vituperabilis quando conformatur volitioni viciosi (*Reportatio*, III, q. 12, F); also *ibid.*, XX; q. 10, F; *Quodlibet* III, q. 13.

[118] *Reportatio*, III, q. 10, F, O; q. 12, E; *Quodlibet* III, q. 13.

[119] Quia omnis actus aut est rectus essentialiter, aut per denominationem extrinsecam . . . Si secundo modo tunc iste actus dicitur rectus, quia causatur vel continuatur ab actu essentialiter virtuoso (*Quodlibet* III, q. 14); also *ibid.*, qq. 14 and 15; *Reportatio*, III, q. 10, P; q. 12, N, XX.

[120] *Reportatio*, III, q. 12, E; *Quodlibet* III, q. 13.

[121] I.e. *Reportatio*, III, qq. 10–13 especially 10 and 12; *Quodlibet* III, q.q 13–15.

[122] Sexta distinctio est quod aliquis actus est bonus ex genere vel malus, aliquis ex circumstantia . . . (*Reportatio*, q. 12, N). Also *ibid.*, q. 10, O.

stances the act of wanting to honour God according to the precepts of right reason, at the proper time—Sundays—and place—church. It will then have the wish to honour God as its principal object, the act of praying to him as its common object, and Sunday and church as its secondary and partial objects. From the standpoint of the will all these circumstances are the objects and partial causes of the act of praying to God. But in relation to the act of prayer itself the order is reversed: it is the common object of all these circumstances, but as an exterior act it has no circumstances for its object, whether time or place or right reason or end. It is they which help to determine its value while as an act it remains unchanged.[123]

The moral worth then of acts which are only contingently good by an extrinsic denomination is additional to the act itself. But that does not mean that good and bad acts can have the same substance, as Duns Scotus affirmed, merely differing through a relation of conformity with good or bad. Nothing positive, Ockham replies, whether absolute or relative, is added to the substance of any act. Rather goodness by an extrinsic denomination signifies a morally neutral act and consignifies a perfectly virtuous act of will as its cause.[124] Where Duns therefore locates moral worth or its absence in the relation between an act and its circumstances, Ockham identifies it with a right or wrong act of will. Hence while for Duns the act can remain the same but its relation changes, for Ockham the act is good or bad as a good or bad act of will. He devotes a separate quodlibetal question to showing that moral rectitude or difformity is inseparable from morally good or bad acts and in no way due to qualities or relations added to them. Intrinsically good or bad acts are good or bad of their substance because they cannot be other than they are; and extrinsically good or bad acts are good or bad because they are caused or continued by intrinsically good or bad acts.[125] The source of each is the will. In Ockham's own words, 'It is said therefore that difformity is not a lack of due justice or righteousness in an act but a lack of due righteousness in the will, which is nothing else than saying that the will is obliged to act according to a divine precept and does not. And so rectitude is only the act which is duly performed according to right reason.'[126]

As to intrinsically good or bad acts, they are exclusively acts of will; and in contrast to those which are good or bad by an extrinsic denomination they cannot be appropriated by the will from the intellect or senses and made contingently good or bad, as acts of pure speculation, say the study of geometry, or eating, can be good if done for a proper end.[127] Instead as we have already said they are necessarily good or bad of their own nature.[128] By 'necessarily' Ockham means here not that they are unconditionally necessary as acts: no act is, in that God could

---

[123] *Reportatio*, III, q. 10, O; q. 12, FFF; *Quodlibet* III, q. 15.

[124] *Ibid.*, q. 10, P–Q; q. 12, YY.

[125] *Quodlibet* III, q. 14; *Reportatio*, III, q. 12, YY.

[126] *Quodlibet* III, q. 14.

[127] *Reportatio*, III, q. 10, I, O; q. 12, E.

[128] Quarta conclusio est quod actus primo et principaliter virtuosus est actus voluntatis. Hoc patet primo quia ille solus est laudabilis primo vel vituperabilis. Alia autem non nisi secundaria et quadam denominatione extrinseca, puta per hoc quod eliciuntur conformiter actui voluntatis (*ibid.*, q. 12, F); Also *ibid.*, G, XX, CCC, DDD; *Quodlibet* III, qq. 13–15.

himself act immediately in its stead: and then as his act, not that of the will, it would no longer be virtuous as no longer in the will's power.[129] Rather an act is necessarily virtuous according to God's precept by which it cannot be vicious or caused by a created will which is not virtuous; it includes all such acts as loving God above all, which by God's decree cannot be bad or caused by a depraved will. They are therefore necessarily good.[130]

Now it is precisely in relation to God's command (*stante precepto divino*) that an act is morally good (or bad). God, as we have seen, is not bound by his existing dispensation, whether it concerns moral or meritorious acts. But whereas meritorious acts depend upon God's acceptance, with or without the mediation of a supernatural habit, moral acts owe their virtue to conforming to God's decrees. First among them is to love God above all, which is expressed in loving whatever God wills to be loved (and hating whatever he wills to be hated).[131] Like any essentially and intrinsically good act, it cannot be bad.[132] Consequently to obey whatever God commands is virtuous, including a command to cease loving him. Although he could give such a decree without contradiction—say, ordering someone to devote himself for a time to study and not to God—to obey would be contradictory, since the person concerned would be at once fulfilling a divine precept in not loving God above all, and violating it in loving him during the proscribed period. For that reason, then, the will could not cease to love God virtuously at God's command.[133] There is thus no question here of hating God— although as we shall see it arises elsewhere. The one absolute good is to love God, and to love God is to obey him; and to obey him freely—whether naturally according to his precepts known through right reason or in this instance through what would be outside his natural decrees[134]—is first among the virtues: even if it means ceasing to love him, in being obeyed God continues to be loved. Hence the distinction is between a precept which is not in itself necessary, and the obligation to obey, which is. In that sense the criteria of virtue and vice remain constant and necessary, namely in doing or rejecting God's will, but absolutely the acts them-

---

[129] *Quodlibet* III, q. 13.

[130] Tamen aliter potest intelligi actum esse necessario virtuosum, ita scilicet quod non posset esse viciosus stante divino precepto, aut causari a voluntate creata nisi sit virtuosus . . . Tertio dico quod ille actus virtuosus modo predicto est actus voluntatis, quia actus voluntatis quo deus diligitur super omnia et propter se est huiusmodi (*ibid.*).

[131] Tum quia ille actus est primus omnium bonorum . . . quia hoc est diligere deum super omnia, diligere deum et diligere quidquid deus vult diligi (*ibid.*).

[132] Quia amare deum super omnia est actus sic rectus quod non potest esse difformis (*ibid.*, q. 14). This contradicts Miethke's assertion (*Ockhams Weg*, 321) that to love God naturally is a morally neutral act.

[133] Dico ad hoc quod si deus posset hoc precipere, sicut videtur quod possit sine contradictione, quod voluntas non potest pro tunc talem actum elicere. Quia ex hoc ipso quod talem actum eliceret tunc deum diligeret super omnia; et per consequens impleret preceptum divinum . . . Et hoc ipso quod sic diligeret homo non faceret preceptum divinum per casum. Et per consequens sic diligendo deum diligeret et non diligeret, et faceret preceptum divinum et non faceret (*Quodlibet* III, q. 13).

[134] Iserloh, *Gnade und Eucharistie*, 49–50, recognises that hate of God is not involved, but mistakenly attributes the power not to love God to God's *potentia ordinata*. See Junghans, *Ockham im Lichte*, 251–2, n. 394, for a corrective.

selves may vary. Without right reason no act can be morally good since the will cannot then know what should be done.[135]

Now by right reason Ockham means prudence as understanding of how we should act. Although it is practical it is not synonymous with practical knowledge; for where the latter is of universals, prudence is more particular in being concerned only with our actions. Hence it is related to knowledge as experience is to art. Where art directs how something should be done according to universal principles, for example that to build a house requires the disposition of stones in a certain order, prudence dictates that a house should be built: it tells us what we should do.[136] For that reason there can be no perfect moral virtue without prudence, and the moral virtues—of temperance, continence, and so on—are connected through prudence. In that conclusion Ockham adheres to the view of Aristotle in the *Ethics*.[137] Although the will could love something worthy of love without being guided by right reason, and such an act would in its nature be good, it would nevertheless not be morally virtuous because the will would not knowingly love what should be loved. As Aristotle says, a moral act must consist in first knowing and then choosing what to do.[138]

Now the practical understanding or wisdom which constitutes prudence comes not from the formation of a proposition but from the act of assent or dissent by which, as we discussed in chapter four, a proposition is judged to be true or false.[139] Prudence thus belongs to a practical judgement of what is or is not the case, and Ockham distinguishes four senses in which it can be understood. The first is as immediate or indirect guiding knowledge of whatever is practicable, following St Augustine's definition, and is of universal propositions known both from self-evident moral principles and from experience. The other senses all derive from either or both of these components. By the second, prudence is immediate practical knowledge of particular matters as a consequence of universal self-evident principles. The third sense is as direct practical knowledge solely from experience of something practicable, the strict meaning of prudence, which is also Aristotle's by which he distinguished prudence from knowledge which is moral. The fourth sense is a combination of immediate practical knowledge, whether gained from principles or experience, as it concerns the virtuous life; and then there are as many kinds of experience as there are moral virtues each with its own prudence as an essential concomitant. That can be seen because prudence is a proposition, i.e.

[135] Similiter nullus actus est moraliter bonus vel virtuosus nisi sibi assistat actus volendi sequi rectam rationem, vel quia causatur a tali velle (*Quodlibet* III, q. 14). Also *Reportatio* III, q. 12, NN.

[136] *Reportatio*, III, q. 11, V.

[137] Dico quod virtus moralis perfecta non potest esse sine prudentia, et per consequens est necessaria connexio inter virtutes morales ad prudentia. Quod probatur, quia de ratione virtutis et actus eius perfecte est quod eliciatur conformiter rationi recte, quia sic diffinitur a Philosopho in secundo *Ethicorum*. Recta autem ratio est prudentia in actu vel in habitu (*ibid.*, x). Also *Reportatio*, III, q. 12, NN. The virtues are thus connected through prudence, a point which O. Suk, 'The Connection of the Virtues', *FcS* 10 (1950), 92, recognises but later (97) appears to ignore, when he denies any true connection.

[138] *Ibid.*; *Ethics*, III, ch. 3, 112 a, 19–112 b, 14.

[139] *Reportatio*, III, q. 11, U; q. 12, CCC.

complex knowledge, stating what should be done; it therefore varies according to the requisite action. But to know one such proposition does not entail knowing all the others: as with all complex knowledge we have abundantly seen that knowledge of one proposition can stand with ignorance of another. Hence one can know that one should live temperately and not know that God is a trinity and that one should die willingly. In this final sense, then, prudential propositions differ not only numerically but also in kind as different species of prudence.[140]

Leaving aside for the moment the different degrees of moral virtue and the relation of morally virtuous to meritorious acts, so far as prudence itself is concerned, no act can be morally virtuous without it, because as already said no act is virtuous without conforming to right reason. Prudence is therefore a necessary efficient cause together with the will and God in any virtuous act.[141] That does not however mean that prudence cannot be without a virtuous act or habit; by each of the first two connotations—where it is known from self-evident propositions—it can. Otherwise, if knowledge of prudence necessarily entailed a virtuous act, the latter would no longer be voluntary but from the intellect. No act of intellect, however, is intrinsically good or bad but only as it is in the power of the will. Therefore it would follow that if prudence alone engendered a virtuous act, the will's act would first be in the power of the intellect and would not be more free than the sensitive appetite; which is false. Hence only through the will acting according to the dictates of prudence can it be virtuous.[142] By the other two senses prudence can however be both with and without a virtuous act according to whether it is gained through experience of someone else's actions or one's own: in the latter case it is reached through a virtuous act as its partial cause, so that the act precedes prudence. For example, someone through frequently practising continence or temperance becomes more disposed to awareness and love and desire of God; he thereby comes more easily to treat with contempt incontinence and intemperance. That applies also to the fourth sense of prudence which includes the third as well as the other senses; and conversely there can be virtuous moral acts without prudence in the first two senses, for the same reason that prudence can be reached through experience without being inferred from self-evident propositions.[143]

Now the need for prudence lies in the will's freedom to act which, since it is not necessitated, can be for good or evil. It therefore requires some rule to direct it

140 *Ibid.*, q. 12, H. Corrected text in Suk, *FcS* 10 (1950), 19, n. 22–5. This differs from that in the *Reportatio* over the third sense which changes 'not immediate' into 'immediate' practical knowledge.

141 Quantum ad quartum articulum huius tertii argumenti sit hec prima conclusio. Nulla virtus moralis nec actus virtuosus est possibilis sine omni prudentia, quia nullus actus est virtuosus nisi sit conformis recte rationi . . . Et si queras utrum post generationem virtutis possit elici actus virtuosus sine actu prudentie, respondeo quod non, quia nullus virtuose agit nisi sciens agit, et ex libertate . . . Si queras de actu prudentie, in quo genere cause se habet ad actum virtuosum . . . Respondeo quod est causa efficiens necessario requisita ad actum virtuosum, sine qua impossibile est actum esse virtuosum stante ordinatione divina que nunc est, ita quod ad actum virtuosum necessario requiritur activitas actus prudentie et activitas voluntatis ita quod ille due cause sunt cause partiales cum deo respectu actus virtuosi (*ibid.*, NN).

142 *Ibid.*, OO–QQ.   143 *Ibid.*, RR–VV.

to virtue, and that is right reason or prudence.[144] The latter must be actual as opposed to habitual or potential because only actual prudence suffices for a necessarily good act. In the case of potential or aptitudinal prudence, that follows from the inability of an erring will to be virtuous when it opposes conscience or reason; for whether it does so rightly or wrongly, through culpable or invincible error, it is opposing right reason; and therefore although it may act potentially according to prudence it is without actual prudence. The intellect retains the same aptitude for prudence equally when it is in error and opposed to prudence as when it is not; the only difference is that when it is in error actual prudence is harder to attain.[145] Habitual prudence is also inadequate for a virtuous act because, as we discussed over intuitive and abstractive knowledge, one habit only inclines to the act of another habit by means of its own act. Hence before a habit of prudence can regulate an act of will, it must be preceded by an act of prudence in the intellect. Accordingly, habitual prudence does not in itself suffice for a virtuous act. Moreover no non-virtuous or demeritorious act can become meritorious or virtuous by anything merely habitual, which is not in our power. But that would be the consequence if habitual prudence could make an act of will virtuous; for the addition or destruction of habitual prudence as a purely natural quality would make the difference between a virtuous and non-virtuous act.[146]

This view of prudence as additional to an act in all other respects virtuous, is equally misconceived when applied to actual prudence. If it were true, no acts would be necessarily and intrinsically virtuous because the same act would be good or bad according to the generation or destruction of prudence.[147] Since prudence is an act of intellect, the will's virtue or vice would then be dependent upon the presence or absence of what was not in the will's power.[148] To obviate that possibility Ockham insists that prudence must be an object of the will and thereby a partial efficient cause of a virtuous act. Prudence does not then precede a virtuous act and so cannot be displaced; for although causally prior to the will, temporally prudence is simultaneous with it, as that to which an act of will is directed. Hence while there can be prudence without a virtuous action, an act cannot be virtuous without prudence.[149]

---

[144] *Ibid.*, q. 13, B.   [145] *Ibid.*, C.   [146] *Ibid.*, D.

[147] Sed quod prudentia actualis necessario requiritur potest dupliciter intelligi. Uno modo quod primo eliciatur aliquis actus voluntatis secundum omnes circumstantias requisitas ad actum virtuosum, excepta prudentia sive recta ratione; et quod post manente eodem actu in voluntate precise et nullo alio elicito per generationem prudentie fiat iste actus qui prius non fuit virtuosus propter defectum prudentie. Fiat inquam virtuosus per generationem prudentie . . . Et iste intellectus est impossibilis. Quod probatur in questione [12] de connexione virtutum, quia hoc dato nullus actus est intrinsice et necessario virtuosus, sed solum contingenter et extrinsice. Quia per generationem prudentie fieret ille actus virtuosus et per corruptionem eius fieret viciosus semper manente eodem actu in voluntate (*ibid.*, E).

[148] Against Duns's first argument, *ibid.*, q. 12, xx.

[149] Alio modo potest intelligi quod requiritur prudentia tamquam obiectum partiale et causa efficiens partialis ipsius actus virtuosi; et per consequens nihil oportet quod prudentia precedat illum actum virtuosum. Cuius ratio est sicut causa effectum vel saltem quod simul producatur cum illo actu simul dico tempore, licet de facto natura sit prior illo actu virtuoso, quia potest separari ab eo et non e converso. Et iste intellectus est bonus, verus et sanus (q. 13, E).

The difference between these two conceptions represents the difference between Duns Scotus and Ockham over the virtuous acts.[150] And it is once again a paradox that Ockham who is so often credited with being the solvent of moral values should have directed his criticism against the standpoint which made their worth less than intrinsic. For Ockham, as we have seen, an intrinsically virtuous action is one that has its object in its circumstances so that they are inseparable from an act as its cause. These include, as we have also seen, its end as principal object together with right reason and any other circumstances such as place and time necessary for its realisation. The difference between such an intrinsic act and an extrinsically moral act can be seen from the example of someone wishing to study, which as an act is good independently of circumstances. The intellect then decrees that this act of study should be continued according to all the requisite circumstances, and the will also wills its continuance in conformity with the dictates of right reason. Now it is this second—continued act—which is perfectly virtuous because it conforms to right reason, and the first which is extrinsically virtuous in conforming to the second, that is, in being performed for some higher—reason. The difference between them consists precisely in the presence or absence of prudence as partial object.[151] Prudence accordingly makes an act, in itself generically good but morally indifferent, intrinsically good in providing an end dictated by right reason. Its necessary concurrence with the will in a virtuous act is expressed in the meaning of good and bad. As connotative terms they signify an act not absolutely but together with the activity of the will and prudence. In any intrinsically virtuous action therefore one cannot be posited without the other.[152]

In opposing Duns Scotus's view of prudence, then, Ockham is concerned to establish two main contentions. First, that prudence is necessary to an intrinsically virtuous act not simply as partial cause but as the object of an act together with the other requisite circumstances; the case for prudence as an object is thus a special application of the case for circumstances in general. Second, that such intrinsic acts cannot by definition be successively good and bad or meritorious and demeritorious. His arguments are as follows.[153] Every act of will which remains entirely the same can be continued and conserved merely through apprehension of its object, since nothing more is needed than the real existence of the object together with God, the will and the object's apprehension as partial causes. If therefore these suffice to cause it, they suffice to conserve it. Now if right reason were not the object of a virtuous act, say of temperance, but only circumstances and food were, a perfectly virtuous act could then be caused without right reason, and perhaps with wrong reason; and if it could be caused without right reason it would be conserved

---

[150] *Ibid.*, and q. 12, XX.

[151] *Ibid.*, q. 12, YY; *Quodlibet* III, q. 15.

[152] Et consequens sequitur ultra quod suspensa activitate voluntatis vel actus prudentie nullo modo dicitur talis actus virtuosus. Et ratio est quia virtuosum et viciosum sunt nomina connotativa et significant ipsum actum non absolute sed connotando cum hoc activitate voluntatis et prudentie. Et quando deficit aliquod connotatum non dicitur talis actus virtuosus (*Reportatio, ibid.*, q. 13, F). Also q. 12, DDD, *Quodlibet* III, q. 15.

[153] *Ibid.*, q. 12, CCC–FFF.

without right reason after having been first caused by wrong reason. The same act would then first be virtuous and then non-virtuous or vicious, and so only contingently virtuous, not necessarily.[154] And if it is not subsequently virtuous the cause must be the absence of right reason, since all the other requisite objects are present. Conversely, if an act is virtuous and right reason coexists with it, it follows that an act previously non-virtuous is now virtuous solely through the advent of prudence. In either event only the presence of right reason as an object makes an act intrinsically virtuous; and such acts are different in kind from those which are not informed by right reason. Hence the same act cannot, contrary to Duns Scotus, be intrinsically good and then not good, or vice versa, because when it is essentially and necessarily one it cannot be the other.[155] It is not therefore good or bad through the addition of a relation of virtue or vice as something distinct; for a new relation would entail a new act as its foundation. Nor by the same token do virtue and vice inhere in an act as qualities; that could only be as a species or a habit or an act of intellection, none of which can be posited: not the first two, because they could equally stand with a contrary act, nor the third, because it is not in the will's power. The change from one moral act to another is not therefore the result of the acquisition or loss of something in the act itself but from a new act of will. Hence the same act which is intrinsically virtuous or vicious cannot also successively be its opposite.[156]

In the second place an act, contrary again to Duns Scotus, can only be intrinsically virtuous or vicious if it has prudence as its object as well as its partial cause. Otherwise if, as Duns holds, it were just a partial cause, in the way that apprehension of the object and God are partial causes, God could displace prudence as he could any second cause, leaving the will and apprehension alone as the causes of a perfectly virtuous act; which is manifestly false just because, as we have seen, by God's present ordinance no act is perfectly virtuous unless it conforms to right reason actually inhering in it. For that, right reason has to be a real object; otherwise there would be nothing to distinguish a virtuous act from any other. Moreover, to act virtuously, the will must want to follow right reason for its own sake; if it did so only for delight or some other reason, right reason would not be the object of its act, since the will would then want to follow what right reason decreed immediately it was apprehended, without recourse to right reason. It would thus not be acting virtuously because not in conformity with right reason itself. Someone can only act because of another thing if he wants that other thing; if he does not, he already wants something else for itself more than for that other thing. Therefore to want virtuously something which right reason decrees, right reason must itself necessarily be wanted; and by the same act of wanting right reason, the end on account of which right reason is willed, is also willed. Equally if time and place are also circumstances dictated by right reason, they are the object of the will's act and not the intellect's; for it is the will which elicits a virtuous

---

[154] *Ibid.*, CCC; *Quodlibet* III, q. 15.
[155] *Reportatio*, III, q. 12; CCC, EEE; *Quodlibet* III, q. 15.
[156] *Reportatio, ibid.*, XX; *Quodlibet* III, q. 14.

act.[157] Hence whatever is the object of an act of right reason is the object of a perfectly virtuous act.[158]

The two main grounds then for positing right reason or prudence as the object of a virtuous act are first that without it no act would be necessarily virtuous, and second that an act, initially non-virtuous, would become virtuous because of something not in the will's power. The first follows because without right reason an act of will would, as we have seen, depend upon the intellect's apprehension of a proposition and not from its assent to it. The will would therefore in conforming to the intellect's apprehension not be conforming to right reason and so would not act virtuously. By the second, an already existing act would be virtuous and meritorious or vicious and demeritorious solely from the presence or absence of prudence. Since, however, prudence is an act of intellect, it is not in our power. Accordingly an act would owe its moral worth to something natural, and not in the will's power; which is absurd. The only way to avoid either consequence therefore is to treat prudence as an object of an act of willing.[159]

For Ockham, therefore the identification of moral acts turns upon the will's object: where it conforms to right reason as part of the total object its act is intrinsically good; where it violates right reason it is intrinsically bad; and where there is no object an act is morally neutral in itself and extrinsically good or bad as it conforms to a morally intrinsic act of whose total object it is part.[160] An act of study is thus morally indifferent as an act without reference to circumstances; it becomes good or bad when willed for an end dictated or prohibited by right reason. It therefore owes its moral value to the end which it serves and which only the will decides in the light of reason. Where the will acts without reason, as among the demented and mad, an act is without moral value.[161] That holds for all exterior acts, whether of walking to church or lighting a candle: they are contingently good or bad in conforming to an interior act which is intrinsically good or bad through conforming or not conforming to right reason. The difference between such acts and those which are intrinsically good or bad then is that their moral nature varies with circumstances. The same contingent moral act can be virtuous or vicious according to whether it is directed to an object and with the will's intent, as an act of walking to church for love of God is good, and bad if done for vainglory. Similarly with acts like continence and temperance: if they are without reference to good and bad circumstances which are determined by right reason they are without moral value; and conversely where they have circumstances they will be good or bad according to the nature of their circumstances.[162]

Intrinsically moral acts on the other hand remain invariable; they do not there-

---

[157] *Reportatio, ibid.*, CCC–DDD; *Quodlibet* III, q. 15.

[158] Volitio dicitur perfecte virtuosa quia in omnibus conformiter elicitur rationi recte . . . et per consequens quicquid est obiectum actus dictandi rectus erit obiectum actus perfecte virtuosi (*Reportatio*, III, q. 12, DDD); *Quodlibet* III, q. 15.

[159] *Ibid.*, DDD–FFF; also XX; q. 10, R, q. 13, F; *Quodlibet* III, q. 15.

[160] *Reportatio, ibid.*, III, *Quodlibet* I, q. 20.

[161] *Quodlibet* I, q. 20; *Reportatio*, III, q. 13, F.

[162] *Reportatio*, III, q. 12, III; q. 10, N–O; *Quodlibet* I, q. 20; *Quodlibet* III, qq. 13–15.

fore strictly have circumstances, but rather objects, for it is precisely in the will's relation to a total object—of end as principal, right reason which dictates it, and the secondary objects necessary to its attainment—that an act is intrinsically virtuous. What would be circumstances in an extrinsically moral act are secondary objects in the case of an intrinsically moral act.[163] The latter cannot therefore remain the same if its object changes, since it is perfectly good or bad only in so far as it fulfils all the necessary conditions of conforming to or opposing the prescriptions of right reason. In other words an intrinsic moral act is such in virtue of its object, for it depends upon the will; and each change in object entails a new act of volition. It cannot therefore vary in any way and remain the same.[164]

Acts then are not virtuous or vicious in themselves as acts, or from anything added to them, or from a relation or their end or right reason or God's causation, none of which alone can make an act virtuous; but from the will acting virtuously or viciously, which as we have seen is the connotation of good or bad.[165] The will is therefore the determining agent in any moral act; and according to the nature of what it wills an act is virtuous or vicious: good if the object is good; bad if the object is bad, but in each case because the will conforms or does not conform to right reason.

All moral virtue accordingly resides in volition of an object, subsumed under an act of will and measured by right reason. By their direct conjunction acts are intrinsically virtuous and vicious, and indirectly and contingently virtuous and vicious through their circumstances. In that sense Ockham treats intrinsic moral virtue and vice as an interior relation between volition and reason which is realised in exterior acts such as temperance, continence and going to church. It is here that Ockham's position is in indirect opposition to that of Duns Scotus. For Duns the substance of an act remains unchanged; it is intrinsically or extrinsically virtuous or vicious according to the relation which it has to prudence or to circumstances and which in each case is additional to it.[166] On Duns's view, also, exterior acts are themselves good or bad, with their own precepts and prohibitions and circumstances.[167] To Ockham on the contrary an act's moral substance consists in the will's object; good and bad are therefore inseparable from volition.

The differences between Duns and Ockham accordingly spring from their contrasted notions of an act's substance. Ockham against Duns did not admit any distinction between substance and moral value; he therefore denied that the same act could be first extrinsically and then intrinsically good or bad or meritorious, just as he denied any independent moral status to exterior acts. To that extent he interiorised morality. But he did not dispense with moral norms.

---

[163] Ad primum argumentum secunde dubitationis dico quod non sunt circumstantie respectu actus intrinsice et necessario virtuosi, sed sunt obiecta secundaria respectu illius actus. Sed sunt circumstantie respectu illorum actuum sive sint actus voluntatis sive intellectus sive cuiuscumque alterius potentie qui solum sunt virtuosi extrinsece secundum quamdam denominationem extrinsicam per conformitatem ad actum aliquem intrinsece virtuosum (*Reportatio*, III, q. 12, FFF). Also q. 10, N.

[164] *Ibid.*, YY, FFF; *Quodlibet* I, q. 20; III, qq. 13–15.   [165] *Ibid.*, q. 10, Q–R; q. 12, YY.
[166] *Ibid.*; also *Quodlibet* III, qq. 13–15.   [167] *Quodlibet* I, q. 20.

Like any Christian thinker Ockham adhered to a hierarchy of moral justice and virtue culminating in love of God. Within it he distinguished five gradations, beginning with the wish to act justly according to the commands of right reason and the circumstances prescribed for the sake of what is to be done. The second degree is the willingness to abide by this obligation whatever the consequences, including death, if right reason so decrees, and the third degree, actually to do so once commanded. The fourth degree is the true and perfect morality, of which the saints speak, of obeying right reason for love of God. This remains a moral act since it is generated from moral virtues and inclines towards them (that is, of conforming to right reason) despite its higher—theological—end. The fifth and final gradation is heroic virtue, where the end can be indifferently love of God or everything else just, for which an act is performed in response to a formal command. Such an act is in some way either in itself or its circumstances beyond the normal course of nature or against natural inclinations, and engenders a habit distinct from the preceding acts.[168] Beyond these are the theological virtues of faith, hope and charity.[169]

Each of these gradations of moral virtue is of a different species, with its distinct partial objects. Hence the higher degree contains something not possessed by the lower, and however much the latter was intensified, even to infinity, it would not incline to the degree above it.[170] As to their connection Ockham rejects the explanations of both St Thomas Aquinas and Henry of Ghent for upholding in different ways a connection between some virtues and not others. To St Thomas the division is between the cardinal virtues common to all men and the heroic virtues peculiar to a special state of perfection. Only the first are connected, while prudence, as right reason of what can be done, is inseparable from moral virtue. Ockham regards that as contradictory, since all the virtues would not be connected through prudence. He does not, however, accept that the common virtues are necessarily connected just because there can be temperance without fortitude.[171]

Henry of Ghent distinguished between the three virtues of perseverance, temperance and fortitude, with their corresponding vices, which in their incomplete and imperfect state were unconnected, and heroic virtue, which as necessary virtue, was connected with the other virtues when complete and perfect. Ockham's rejection is as emphatic as it usually is of Henry'v views. Besides departing from Aristotle's classification of the virtues, if, as Henry maintains, there are four degrees within the same virtue, then one virtue can become heroic without another virtue. Moreover experience shows that there can be a perfectly virtuous act in the presence of incomplete vice as the opposite of another virtue. Therefore there can be a virtuous act without the corresponding virtue. Finally if Henry's account were true, many of the saints would not have had perfect virtue, because they had no occasion for acts of fortitude.[172]

---

[168] *Reportatio*, III, q. 12, K.   [169] *Ibid.*, L.
[170] *Ibid.*, K; also *Quodlibet* IV, q. 6, whose variations I have sometimes adopted in what follows.
[171] *Ibid.*, P–Q.   [172] *Ibid.*, R–S.

To Ockham the three virtues of continence, temperance (from which perseverance, following Aristotle, is in no way distinct)[173] and heroic virtue differ in kind as species because they each have a different species of right reason as their object. For continence, it is to shun the evil desires present in the will; for temperance, the same behest is wider and includes not only actual desires in the will but all occasions of concupiscence.[174] The object of heroic virtue goes furthest of all and unlike the other two is universal, not particular, in surpassing man's normal state.[175] Ockham therefore regards Duns Scotus as in error for the holding that all three virtues have the same species of object only differing in degree of perfection, with heroic virtue the most perfect. On the contrary, Ockham contends, however much the habit of continence in the will is intensified, even to infinity, it will never become even temperance, let alone heroic virtue; for each has its own distinct object, and in the case of heroic virtue not one object but many.[176] Nor by their generation in the will do these virtues generate a corresponding quality in the sensitive appetite; rather the latter generates qualities which incline to the contrary of these virtues. Hence the effect of the latter is the diminution of the inclinations of the appetite or their total destruction.[177] There is thus no need for the moral virtues to have a corresponding habit in the senses; for however many acts are produced by the senses, the flesh can always rebel against the spirit and prevent the formation of a virtuous habit, as can be seen from the example of St Paul who was both temperate and chaste. Conversely where an act of moral virtue by the will generates a corresponding act in the senses a similar habit is formed in the senses.[178] Moreover there can be a habit in the senses which is the opposite of a vice in the will, because the same act in the senses will be good or bad by an extrinsic denomination according to the nature of the will's object; so therefore will its habit which will remain the same when the nature of the will's act changes.[179]

As to the connection between the virtues, Ockham, as we mentioned earlier, locates it in certain general principles such as that whatever is good and decreed must be by right reason must be done and whatever is evil must be shunned. These can serve as the majors and the minors in practical syllogisms giving knowledge of what should be done.[180] They thereby dispose and incline someone to virtue; but they are not formally connected, for the existence of one virtue either imperfectly or perfectly does not imply another.[181] Moral knowledge is accordingly derived both from universal self-evident propositions held theoretically and from experience. Prudence on the other hand consists of universal and singular propositions

---

[173] *Ibid.*, q. 15, C and q. 12, III.   [174] *Ibid.*, q. 15.

[175] *Ibid.*, D.   [176] *Ibid.*; and q. 12, KKK.   [177] *Ibid.*, q. 15, E.

[178] *Ibid.*, q. 12, LL.   [179] *Ibid.*, MM.

[180] Ideo respondeo ad istum articulum. Et sit hec prima conclusio quod virtutes omnes generales connectuntur in quibusdam principiis universalibus, puta 'Omne honestum est faciendum', 'Omne malum est dimittendum', 'Omne dictatum a ratione recta est faciendum', quia possunt esse maiores et minores in syllogismo practico concludente particularem conclusionem, cuius notitia est prudentia in particulari directiva in actu virtuoso (*Quodlibet* IV, q. 6; *Reportatio*, III, q. 12, T). Also *Reportatio*, III, q. 11, Z.

[181] *Reportatio*, III, q. 11, Y–Z; q. 12, X. I agree here with Miethke, *Ockhams Weg*, 334, n. 692, in opposition to Suk, that there is a connection between the virtues, but not a formal connection.

each exclusively known through experience. Hence as we have seen before not all practical knowledge—i.e. that based upon general principles—is prudence, but only in so far as both are evidently known from experience. Since such knowledge can be universal as well as particular, Ockham again takes issue with Duns for confining prudence to particulars.[182]

More specifically an act of perfect virtue in the third and fourth degree namely, that which is sufficiently caused by the will and prudence, inclines to the first act of the next higher degree of virtue. That is also possible for an act of virtue in the second degree, when it is conserved by circumstances which relate to it: for example when someone defies imminent death in refusing to act unjustly, the justice of this act inclines immediately to the first act of fortitude, which consists in adhering to what by right reason he knows to be just. All three of these degrees can also incline to an heroic virtue; only the first degree of virtue does not reach higher, because the volition to act according to right reason is not incompatible with intemperance and so does not elicit the refusal to succumb to it.[183] Both the first two degrees are however compatible with a vice which is the contrary of another virtue and its appropriate right reason, as well as with incompatible circumstances. Someone can thus be temperate in the first two degrees and yet want to act unjustly and against what right reason dictates to be just. Similarly if two acts are compatible, when one of them is morally indifferent in not having circumstances, they will remain compatible if an act of the same kind has circumstances unrelated to the other act: for example the wish to be temperate without circumstances can coexist with a bad act of wanting to act unjustly, say harming one's neighbour, which has nothing to do with the circumstances required for temperance and hence can remain compatible with an act of temperance which has circumstances. By the same token temperance can coexist with error, say, the illusion that one is acting justly when acting unjustly. All this is proved from experience.[184] In the third and fourth degrees however, virtue cannot coexist with vice, although virtue in the third degree can contain error or ignorance. That is not possible in the fourth degree of justice, nor the fifth when possessed by a Christian, whose object is God; but heroic virtue in a pagan is of a different kind, and in not being directed to God can be accompanied by vice.[185]

That brings us to the relation of the moral to the theological virtues. Within the first three degrees of moral virtue there is none since they do not have God as their object. The simple pagan is able to act according to right reason and thereby acquire such moral virtue without any proper and simple concept of God, which is naturally unattainable by the present dispensation.[186] The first two degrees of moral virtue can moreover stand with what is contrary to the theological virtues, namely doubt and disbelief, and with hate of God where a virtuous man can hate Christians.[187] At this level then there is neither a greater connection nor contradiction between the theological and moral virtues and vices. But the fourth and fifth degree of moral virtue—where they concern a Christian—necessarily require,

[182] *Ibid.*, q. 15, G–H.   [183] *Ibid.*, q. 12, U.   [184] *Ibid.*, Y.
[185] *Ibid.*, Z–BB.   [186] *Ibid.*, CC.   [187] *Ibid.*, DD.

by God's ordained power, the theological virtues; for unless someone loves God above all he cannot love a creature or anything created because of loving God. That is possible only through the supernaturally infused virtues of faith, hope, and charity.[188]

The supernatural virtues then are not connected with every moral virtue; but of those with which they are, the acts of the theological virtues are the sufficient cause by the concurrence of both acquired and infused theological virtues. For as we saw in chapter five, over faith, the infused virtues do not alone suffice for a virtuous act; and by God's ordained power the theological virtues are infused into an adult having the use of reason and virtue in the fourth degree and so whose will is already disposed to good. With the addition of the infused virtues he can immediately and sufficiently do what right reason commands. Hence the theological virtues presuppose the moral virtues without which they are not long conserved; for if there is not a virtuous act immediately in response to a decree of right reason and the presence of the requisite dispositions for its realisation, failure to act will not merit the continuance of the theological virtues.[189] Correspondingly the latter are incompatible with any moral vice, since unvirtuous means contradict a virtuous end. That holds whether lack of virtue is due to avoidable error which, in not being overcome, is lack of rectitude, or to invincible error, which is not culpable, or passion or malice or any other reason, each of which would destroy righteousness because it would mean love or hate of something other than God wills to be loved or hated.[190] Habitual vice can however continue with the infusion of the theological virtues in the way a newly baptised adult still retains his inclinations to vice; but actual vice is incompatible with any theological virtues, and so is habitual vice with acquired theological virtues, which consist in acts of loving God above all and what he wills to be loved, and hating what he wills to be hated. They therefore contradict acts or habits of loving something else more than God.[191]

There can be no perfect virtue then without theological virtue; but there can be natural virtue which follows the precepts of right reason. The difference between them is precisely having or not having God as their object; and that is the difference between Christians and pagans, which as we have seen is one of kind, since God is not of the same species as any creatures.[192] What however all the virtues have in common is adherence to right reason. That is as incumbent upon the Christian as the pagan and equally open to both, as we have just seen.[193] They differ over the

---

[188] Ibid., FF–GG.   [189] Ibid., HH.   [190] Ibid., II.   [191] Ibid., KK.

[192] Ad quintum dico quod respectu obiecti supernaturalis potest esse virtus moralis, immo nulla est perfecta virtus nisi inclinet ad actum respectu obiecti supernaturalis, sicut prius ostensum est. Philosophus tamen non ponit virtutem moralem esse respectu obiecti supernaturalis sicut nos ponimus, quia non ponit quod abstinentia et continentia sint volenda propter honorem divinum tamquam propter finem. Nec talia et consimilia que sunt precepta a deo quomodo bonus Christianus ponit talia, sed solum ponit talia esse volenda, quia sunt honesta vel conservativa nature vel aliquid aliud mere naturale. Ex hoc etiam sequitur quod virtus moralis quam poneret philosophus et bonus Christianus, differunt specie non solum numero secundum predicta . . . sed deus non est eiusdem speciei cum qualibet creatura (ibid., GGG). Also q. 8, P, S; and IV, q. 3, S.

[193] E.g. note 185.

end which right reason decrees. A natural virtue serves a natural end; a supernatural virtue serves God. The first need not presuppose more than man's natural powers: the second requires the supernatural virtues and alone can lead to moral perfection. In Ockham's own words, 'There cannot be love of a creature or of something created, because of love of God, unless someone loves God above all ... But by God's ordained power there cannot be such love without infused faith, hope, and charity, nor without them in some way also being acquired'.[194] The immediate object of charity is a proposition that God is to be loved together with all that he wills to be loved; as such it is the partial indirect principle of acts of charity, both infused and acquired, performed by the will.[195] Although by God's absolute power natural habits can remain without infused habits, that is not possible by God's ordained power, where to love him above all requires the simultaneous infusion of faith and charity; through their possession someone can then merit infused charity. Consequently an infidel can by acquired faith believe as intensely as a Christian; but without infused faith he cannot love God above all.[196]

Naturally then the gulf between natural and theological virtue cannot be overcome, but only by God's agency. Hence it belongs entirely to him, not to men, to decide whether they must do so according to the order prescribed by his ordained power through the supernaturally infused virtues of faith, hope and charity, or directly by his acceptance of human actions as meritorious. For Ockham, as we have seen, the issue of whether the supernatural virtues can be superseded turns upon the alternatives open to God in his freedom, not upon man's own powers to gain his acceptance. Human actions are the beneficiary only in the sense that they are rewarded, and supernatural habits discarded; but that, as we have abundantly seen, is because merit and virtue, as with sin and vice, are inseparable from volition, which they connote. Habits on the other hand are not; only by God's ordained power are they necessary to theological virtue; and that cannot be proved but must be held on faith. The only evident reason for the existence of habits is through experience of their acts. That includes acts of faith, hope and charity, of which we also have natural experience. Hence in knowing them naturally we have evidence not of their supernatural but of their natural habits, as the example of a pagan or a heretic shows: for a pagan reared among Christians would come to believe all the articles of faith and love God above all. But he could only do so from acquired, not infused, faith and charity, as a heretic over one article of faith can believe another from acquired, not infused, faith. In each case acquired faith needs no more than settled experience, and so does not imply the presence of the infused supernatural virtues.[197] Moreover every act of volition

[194] *Reportatio*, III, q. 12, FF. In the *Ordinatio*, d. 1, q. 4, 443, Ockham says that someone can also *ex puris naturalibus sine fide* love God above all; which can be interpreted to mean without perfect virtue since such an act would be without the infused theological virtues, as we shall discuss shortly.

[195] *Reportatio*, III, q. 8, P.

[196] Quia ita intense potest unus infidelis credere sicut unus Christianus secundum fidem acquisitam, non tamen deum diligere (potest) super omnia nisi habeat caritatem et fidem, quia simul infunduntur; et ideo licet ille infidelis habeat fidem acquisitam non tamen infusam (*ibid.*, s).

[197] *Ibid.*, A–B, D.

which we experience appears to be natural; so therefore does its habit.[198] Beyond that, however, God could ordain that someone who lived according to the precepts of right reason only believing what from natural reason he concluded should be believed, was worthy of eternal life in the same way as God can accept someone for eternal life naturally without any supernatural habit and damn someone not in sin. Pagan philosophers who erred in holding heretical doctrines such as the eternity of the world could thus receive eternal life, as it was conferred on St Paul who was a sinner and without merits.[199] By the same token God could in his absolute power engender each of the supernatural virtues separately without the other.[200]

This distinction between acquired and infused habits explains the difference between merit *de congruo* and merit *de condigno*. By God's ordained power merit *de congruo* is awarded for virtuous acts performed naturally without an infused supernatural habit. Merit *de condigno*, on the other hand, is reserved for acts informed by an infused supernatural habit, and hence can only be attained by someone acting in a state of grace. Such acts are alone worthy of eternal life; and their dependence upon infused grace is a matter of authority not experience or reason for which as we have seen there is none.[201]

Now for Ockham congruous merit forms the natural bridge between the moral and the theological virtues because God by his ordained power awards such merit in response to intrinsically virtuous acts such as loving God above all and detesting sin, which the will elicits through following right reason and the other requisite circumstances.[202] These acts and their habits are at once theological in having God as partial object and moral in following right reason as partial object: they are therefore necessarily virtuous without being strictly theological, since they cannot be bad but they are not from supernatural habits infused by God alone.[203] On this

---

[198] *Ibid.*, D.

[199] *Ibid.*, C.

[200] *Ibid.*, IV, q. 3, I–K.

[201] *Ibid.*, A–B. Also: Ad primum respondeo primo quod ad ponendum charitatem respectu cuiuscunque actus quem in nobis exprimitur pro statu isto non cogit ratio aliqua nec experientia aliqua, sed hoc solum licet poni propter auctoritatem ecclesie determinantis divinam voluntatem esse talem et ordinationem eius quod nullus actus sit meritorius ex condigno nisi elicitus mediante charitate, sicut patet per Apostolum primo Ad Corinth. 13 (Ad primum dubium, *Dubitationes Addititie* appended to *Reportatio*, IV, C).

[202] Ad argumentum dico quod aliquis de congruo potest mereri gratiam ex puris naturalibus sicut aliquis diligens deum super omnia naturaliter secundum rectam rationem, et alias circumstantias requisitas ad actum meritorium, meretur primam infusionem charitatis. Sed de condigno non potest aliquis mereri gratiam et gloriam sine charitate (Ad 5ᵐ dubium, *ibid.*, AA). Also IV, q. 9, Y.

[203] Si queratur utrum ille habitus acquisitus ex actu detestandi peccatum propter deum sit virtuosus vel non, respondeo quod sic. Cuius ratio est quia inclinat ad actus conformes rationi recte, et iste actus sunt ita bona quod non possunt esse mali. Si queras an iste habitus est virtus moralis an theologica, respondeo quod potest esse theologica et moralis, ita quod potest habere diversas denominationes extrinsecas propter diversa obiecta partialia. Et dicitur theologica, quia habet deum pro obiecto partiali sicut amicitia acquisita respectu dei. Non autem dicitur sic theologia quia infunditur a solo deo. Et potest dici moralis, quia habet peccatum pro obiecto partiali et est habitus acquisitus ex actibus, et sic potest habere diversas denominationes (*Reportatio*, IV, qq. 8 and 9, X–Y).

view then the will is capable of acting virtuously to the point where God immediately rewards it with congruous merit. Indeed by his ordained power Ockham declares that God must do so.[204] That is not however the same as accepting someone for eternal life; that belongs exclusively to condign merit, which Ockham denies is concerned with grace at all, but only with blessedness.[205] Nor does it mean that in immediately infusing with grace someone who has merit de congruo, the person concerned is then able to merit de condigno. On the contrary there are many acts of merit de congruo but not de condigno; and even merit de congruo does not entail the same degree of grace for everyone, although whether that applies by God's ordained power is unclear.[206] When, however, two people do have equal grace and dispositions, if one receives glory then by God's ordained power the other must also, if other things are equal.[207]

It is the distinction between merit de congruo and merit de condigno, the one attainable without grace, and carrying no claim to eternal life, the other dependent upon grace and constituting the award of eternal life, which to Ockham marks the difference between him and Pelagius over merit. Pelagius's error was precisely that merit de condigno could be gained naturally and all sin actual and original avoided.[208] The difference is fundamental; for Ockham was claiming no more than that a man could act naturally in such a way that God rewards him with a supernatural habit. He was not however claiming a supernatural value for exclusively natural acts nor eternal life from a supernatural habit. The difference between merit de congruo and its absence was to Ockham the difference between gradations of virtue, not between blessedness and sin, for which there was no immutable order.

At the same time, though, Ockham's conception of merit de congruo and the moral virtues presupposes the capacity of men to act virtuously through understanding and adhering to Christian precepts. Although they cannot achieve perfect moral virtue of their own resources—just because they cannot naturally acquire the infused theological virtues—they are able both to know what should be done according to right reason and want to do it. This more exalted conception of human powers, which in the Aristotelian tradition endows man with the capacity for moral virtue and knowledge of the good and the right was, as expressed in Ockham's interpretation of merit de congruo, attacked as semi-Pelagian by theological conservatives like Bradwardine and Gregory of Rimini. In that there is a certain irony; for Ockham only formally treats the subject of merit in the two brief

---

[204] Si queras an ille actus detestandi sufficiat ad expulsionem culpe et infusionem gratie, respondeo ille actus est solus sufficiens ad meritum de congruo; nam habito isto actu deus statim infundit gratiam, et de potentia dei ordinata non potest non infundere (ibid., Y).

[205] Et dico quod respectu gratie nullus actus est meritorius de condigno nisi ille qui est respectu eterne beatitudinis . . . Et ideo respectu gratie non est aliquis actus meritorius de condigno, sed respectu beatitudinis potest (ibid.).

[206] Ibid. Ockham also says that the will could avoid all sins of commission or omission by suspending its actions; for whatever the will can do with charity it can do without charity, i.e. as an act as opposed to its nature (Dubitationes Addititie, AA).

[207] Ibid.

[208] Ad errorem Pelagii dico quod ipse posuit quod aliquis ex puris naturalibus potest vitare omne peccatum actuale et originale et mereri vitam eternam de condigno. Et in hoc errat (Dubitationes Addititie, AA–BB).

passages we have cited, each moreover as a reply to doubts raised, and not *ex professo*. By far the greatest part of his discussion of moral and theological virtues is concerned with the conditions for their realisation in the will's fulfilment of the dictates of right reason. Merit itself lies with God's acceptance.[209] Hence in Ockham's thinking merit, far from expressing man's ability to gain God's reward, is outside human agency, although human—or angelic—action is its prerequisite. It was precisely this distinction which Ockham's opponents as well as his successors overlooked. Ockham it is true did, like Duns Scotus, and in a different way St Thomas Aquinas, take a more favourable view of man's moral capacities, but only on the moral—i.e. natural—plane where reason, both as rational and as Christian precept, operated. With merit there is a discontinuity as there is with everything supernatural; for it lies with God; and although he has ordained the award of merit *de congruo* for intrinsically virtues acts of which God is partial object, this very decision, eternally decreed, is solely from God.[210] For that reason he can either implement it or supersede it; and whichever he does, acceptance or non-acceptance for eternal life depends solely upon him and not upon the possession of a supernatural habit of sanctifying grace. Moral virtue, then, even when converted into merit *de congruo* imposes no obligation upon God. For, as Ockham does not tire of reiterating, God is no one's debtor. Hence the asymmetry between grace, merit and sin in his rewards and punishments, as well as in their relation to the moral virtues, as the earlier example of St Paul indicates.

The charge that could be laid against Ockham is therefore the opposite of Pelagianism: that having annexed all power of decision to God over what is meritorious and demeritorious, there is an incongruity between the moral or meritorious value of an act and the value that God can put upon it. We thus have the paradox—which to Ockham is resolved in the difference between God's ordained and absolute power—that on the one hand the substance of a moral or meritorious act is inseparable from its moral or meritorious nature, which is either intrinsic or derives from another intrinsic act; and on the other hand that God can separate an act from its circumstances—through which, as we already know, it is good or bad—so rendering it morally indifferent. That is tantamount to treating it as an exterior act, since it entails taking the act for itself in dissociation from the will and its object. Correspondingly it becomes good or bad, meritorious or demeritorious, by an extrinsic denomination, as Ockham acknowledges.[211] That, as we have already remarked, is only possible by God's absolute power; and it merely underlines the conditional nature of God's present dispensation. Never-

---

[209] E.g. Sexta distinctio est quod aliquis actus est bonus ex genere vel malus, aliquis ex circumstantia, aliquis ex principio meritorio . . . Exemplum tertii: ut velle continere secundum rectam rationem et alias cirumstantias propter honorem divinum, quia talis actus est deo acceptus (*Reportatio*, III, q. 12, N).

[210] Ad 2^m dubium, *Dubitationes Addititie*, G.

[211] Si queras de conversione ad deum actu caritativo et conversione actu quo diligitur creatura quam deus non vult diligi, puta actum fornicandi, sic non repugnant illi naturaliter et formaliter inter se, sed compatiuntur se in eodem quantum est ex natura actuum. Sed solum repugnant per causam extrinsecam, puta per deum ordinantem talem creaturam nullo modo a voluntate creata diligi . . . (*Reportatio*, III q. 12, AAA).

theless as Ockham's discussion of the acts of bad angels in book two of the *Reportatio* clearly illustrates, the implication is that absolutely there are no necessary and intrinsic virtues and vices and no act is inseparable from its moral substance.

He has three principal grounds. The first is that God can cause any real (absolute) thing independently of anything else; but an act such as hating God is not in its existence, as an act, the same as its difformity by which it is sinful. Therefore God could cause the act without the difformity.[212] Secondly of whatever God is partial cause he can be total cause; that includes any act of the created will which is meritorious or sinful. Therefore God could be its total cause. But in that case such an act would no longer be sinful (as it would not be meritorious) because as we shall consider in a moment, sin connotes the will acting viciously in defying God, whereas God cannot act culpably or contradict himself. Hence acts which are sinful (or meritorious) when performed by angels or men according to his present dispensation would not be so when caused by God alone.[213] Finally by the same token acts are good and bad, meritorious and sinful, by reference to God's decree. But God is obliged to no one and whatever he does is good. Therefore he could decree differently, and acts which are now good or bad need not be so.[214] In consequence any act of sin, such as hating God or robbery or adultery, detached by God from it and circumstances, would not be sinful, and could both be caused by God and commanded by him as divine precept, when to perform it would be meritorious. Such acts would not then be called robbery or adultery or hate for the very reason that they were not contrary to God's precepts, which is what their meaning connotes.[215]

Absolutely then the criterion of good or bad is what God wills or rejects, which is *ipso facto* always for a good end.[216] This hardly represents what Iserloh regards as the displacement of an 'objective' for a 'subjective' foundation of value in the conformity of the created will to God's will.[217] While it is true that for Ockham what God decrees is ultimately the measure of all value, that is merely to transfer

[212] Et quod potest deus causare actum odiendi deum quantum ad esse absolutum in actu in voluntate creata. Probatur, quia deus potest omne absolutum causare sine omni alio quod non est idem cum illo absoluto. Sed actus odiendi deum quantum ad esse absolutum in eo non est idem cum difformitate et malicia in actu. Ergo deus possit causare quicquid absolutum est in actu odiendi deum vel nolendi non causando aliquam difformitatem vel maliciam in actu; ergo etc. (*Reportatio*, II, q. 19, F). Also M.

[213] *Ibid.*

[214] Sed deus ad nullum actum causandum obligatur, ideo quemlibet actum absolutum potest sine omni malo culpe causare et eius oppositum; et ideo sicut potest causare totaliter actum diligendi sine bonitate vel malicia morali . . . (*ibid.*, P).

[215] Ad aliud dico quod licet odium dei, furari, adulterari habeant malam circumstantiam annexam et similia de communi lege quatenus fiunt ab aliquo precepto divino obligatur ad contrarium. Sed quantum ad esse absolutum in illis actibus possunt fieri a deo sine omni circumstantia mala annexa, et etiam meritorie possunt fieri a viatore si caderent sub precepto divino sicut nunc de facto eorum opposita cadunt sub precepto divino . . . tunc non dicerentur nec nominarentur furtum, adulterium, odium etc., quia ista nomina significant tales actus non absolute sed connotando vel dando intelligere quod faciens tales actus per preceptum divinum obligatur ad oppositum (*ibid.*, o).

[216] *Ibid.*, Q.
[217] *Gnade und Eucharistie*, 64–7.

the measure from an act's being to its circumstances. Since these are determined by God, the so-called objective nature of an act is undiminished; for only in conforming to or defying God's commands and right reason is an act good or bad. The will must be the agent, but it is not the arbiter of what is good or bad. The question of subjectivism does not therefore arise beyond the accepted ethical notion which Ockham shares with the majority of his predecessors that right acting depends upon right willing and conversely; but that in turn is in response to what lies outside the will. Ockham, unlike Abelard, does not stop at intentions: rather intention for him is subsumed under the object or end which the will chooses. Nor by the same token do expressions like voluntarism and formalism, both employed by Iserloh,[218] take us much further. The first can indeed by applied to God, in the stress which it puts upon God's freedom; but that in no way frees the created will from God who can necessitate it to accept what is not in its power although not compelling it to go against its nature.[219] That is to be seen from both the confirmation of the blessed and the obstinacy of the damned who are totally maintained in their attitudes by God so that they cannot will otherwise: to do so would formally contradict them.[220] It is in this logical aspect also that one can speak of formalism but not in its ontological or ethical senses, just because, as we have abundantly seen, there is no inherent and absolute order among second causes. That is the reason why God can separate an act from its sinfulness, and supernatural habits are not indispensable.

The whole tendency of Ockham's thinking is therefore against what is fixed and inviolable; and it was precisely here that its main threat to tradition lay. Ethically is means that for virtue or vice, merit or sin, there need be nothing else than the will acting according to or against right reason and God. Neither habits nor acts such as count save in so far as they belong to the will's object. In Ockham's words, 'Difformity is not a lack of justice or necessary rectitude in an act but lack of rectitude within the will itself, which is no more than to say that the will is obliged by justice to act according to a divine precept, which it does not'.[221] The will is thus the irreducible agent in whatever is good or bad, and God can thereby dispense with everything else where sin and merit are concerned. In the process the will becomes the direct recipient of God's reward and punishment not only at the expense of supernatural habits but as sufferer as well as beneficiary. For just as God can accept the sinner without grace, dispense with baptism,[222] remit directly all sin and its penalty, including Adam's,[223] give a sinner a vision of his essence in the same instant in which he can give him grace, thus accepting him for eternal life,[224] or justify without contrition,[225] so he could also annihilate someone who loved him and all whose works were accepted by him, as Christ never sinned and yet was punished to death;[226] or inflict punishment without preceding sin, although it would not then be punishment,[227] or command someone to hate him, to obey

---

[218] *Ibid.*   [219] *Reportatio*, II, q. 19, N.   [220] *Ibid.*, F–I.   [221] *Quodlibet* III, q. 14.
[222] *Ibid.*, VI, q. I.   [223] *Ibid.*, q. 4, and *Quodlibet* III, q. 9; *Reportatio*, IV, q. 3, G.
[224] *Quodlibet* VI, q. 4; *Reportatio*, ibid.   [225] *Reportatio*, IV, qq. 88 and 9, M.
[226] *Ibid.*, q. 3, Q–R.   [227] *Reportatio*, IV, q. 3, F; II, q. 19, S.

which would constitute a worthy act.[228] At the same time not every act of loving God by the will is good, since it can be for the wrong end, of desire, instead of friendship;[229] while, as we shall in due course consider, the will can of its own accord refuse blessedness and charity.[230]

From this the distinction between Ockham and Pelagiansim is clear. These different examples—of which that of God as the cause of hate seems to be out of character with anything that Ockham has ever elsewhere said on the matter[231]— are all designed to exhibit God's omnipotence and not the will's claim upon him. Far from the will's status being enhanced when directly accepted for itself, it can equally be depressed, because God is not debtor to anyone.

How then does Ockham conceive the precise relation of grace to a meritorious act? He considers it in the first of the *dubitationes* appended to the end of the last— fourth—book of the *Reportatio*. The problem is essentially one of interpolating what must be held on authority in a matter where we have seen reason and experience have no part. But authority only says that charity is necessary for merit and nothing—especially the Bible—expressly about one as the active cause of the other.[232] Hence there is nothing to support the view that charity is necessarily required as the natural cause of merit. It can however probably be accepted as the condition—*sine qua non*—of merit in the same way as the sacraments are the *sine qua non* of grace. Although Ockham rejects such a relation among natural causes, he accepts it where the will is cause. By that mode, just as God freely infuses grace sacramentally, in response to certain exterior signs, so he ordains that an act is only acceptable when charity is present in the soul. In each case the cause is not from something natural but lies in God's will.[233]

The question then arises of reconciling this interpretation with the sayings of the authorities who use terms like handmaid and mistress, horse and rider, to describe the subservience of the will to grace. Moreover it would seem unreasonable to deny to grace as a supernatural habit the active role of cause granted to naturally acquired habits, which Ockham himself elsewhere regards as the efficient cause of their acts.[234] Should not therefore the same also be said of grace?[235] To that

---

[228] *Reportatio*, IV, q. 14, D. Preterea omnis voluntas potest se conformare precepto divino; sed deus potest precipere quod voluntas creata odiat eum; igitur voluntas creata potest hoc facere . . . Sed odire deum potest esse actus rectus in via, puta si precipiatur a deo.

[229] *Ibid.*, II, q. 19, Q.

[230] *Ibid.*, IV, q. 14, D.

[231] Cf. Iserloh's reference to Hochstetter's remarks in 'Viator Mundi', FS 32 (1950), 16 (*Gnade und Eucharistie*, 50).

[232] *Dubitationes Addititie*, ad primum, C.

[233] Respondeo sicut patet supra, licet in naturalibus non sit ponere respectu alicuius effectus causam sine qua non . . . tamen in voluntariis bene est ponere causam sine qua non respectu alicuius effectus sicut sacramenta sunt cause sine non quibus respectu gratie, ita potest dici in proposito quod charitas non necessario requiritur sicut causa naturalis respectu actus meritorii sed requiritur secundum voluntatem dei sic ordinantem, scilicet actum non esse acceptum deo nisi anime inexistat actu. Sicut factis signis exterioribus sacramenti circa aliquod deus libere infundit gratiam . . . Sic caritas secundum istam viam posset dici causa sine qua non propter divinam voluntatem libere sic ordinantem (*ibid.*).

[234] *Quodlibet* III, q. 18.

[235] *Dubitationes Addititie, ibid.*

Ockham gives two replies. The first is that charity does not itself cause an act but conserves it after it has been produced naturally; so that if someone loves God as intensely as he can in his natural state God infuses charity into him to maintain his act of love. Charity then has a comparable role to a conserving cause of an effect which could be from God alone, for example an intuitive vision without an object by someone blessed or the illumination of a dark place without the sun, where object and sun would be the means of maintaining the vision and light which God had caused immediately without them. The difference is that where these as natural effects could be conserved naturally, a meritorious act by God's ordained power could not be conserved without charity, although by God's absolute power it could be both conserved for ever without charity and charity be destroyed.[236]

The second alternative is that charity, together with the will acting naturally, causes the same act of loving God in a more intense degree than would be possible for the will acting only with natural causes. As in everything else concerning grace, its concurrence with the will is not open to experience but it can be reasonably inferred from authority. It then follows that a natural and a meritorious act can be the same both in its nature and numerically. That is when they have the same object of loving God according to the same requisite circumstances; when they do not they are not the same in either respect. Nor for such an act to be the same need it have the same causes or effects: not the same causes, because as we have frequently observed the same effect can have different causes; nor the same effect, for although different natural effects entail different natural causes, that does not apply to a contingent and free cause, in this case God, who freely ordains and accepts as worthy only an act performed in grace. It is in that sense too that the analogies of the authorities must be understood: they do not mean that grace is the principal cause of the substance of a meritorious act; the will always is. Rather that grace is mistress and the will the servant so far as God's acceptance and merit are concerned; for by God's ordained power he is more accepted who has more grace, and less accepted who has less.[237]

For Ockham then as for Duns Scotus the key term in merit is acceptance, even by God's ordained power, where grace becomes merely one of the conditions for acceptance. Moreover it is such no less by God's free decision than its dispensability by his absolute power is.

Of the two solutions, Ockham expresses no opinion which is the more feasible. Iserloh opines that it is the first in which grace is the *sine qua non*, while at the same time recognising that, by either, grace is little enhanced and is secondary to God's acceptance.[238] Indeed for that reason it seems to me that Ockham was not particularly exercised over which was the more probable mode; each represents a supernaturalising of a natural act of will, and each is compatible with his account of the connection between the moral and the theological virtues. For by both God infuses grace to carry a natural act beyond its limits, in the first case at the point at which the will has reached them; in the second in conjunction with the will. If the first approximates more to the sequence leading to merit *de congruo*, the second

[236] *Ibid.*, D–E.　　[237] *Ibid.*, E–F.　　[238] *Gnade und Eucharistie*, 111.

seems more in keeping with the relation between a moral and a theological virtue. The point should not however be pressed, for the very reason that Ockham himself refused to turn to reason and experience in what was exclusively a matter of faith.

Does that warrant Iserloh's characterisation of Ockham's view of grace as unadorned naturalism?[239] I cannot see that it does; for even if it were true, which it does not seem to be, that grace for Ockham does not carry with it the belief in inner renewal or that it has no intrinsic value, it is God's acceptance not man's self-sufficiency which transforms a man into God's adopted son. The question of whether God can do so with or without created grace does not alter man's dependence upon God but merely its mode. For Ockham, as for Duns Scotus, grace can mean either an absolute quality informing the soul and infused by God or God's accepting will. The first as habitual justifying grace or *gratia gratum faciens* is the same as sacramental grace.[240] In Ockham's own words it is given 'to render a man worthy of eternal life or to act meritoriously or to remove the faults which incline him to sin and draw him away from good'.[241] It is this grace which is in every way identical with charity, differing only as names or connotative concepts.[242] Moreover it is charity which suffices with the acquired moral virtues for a virtuous act because it immediately inclines the will to virtue; in that sense all the virtues are connected through charity, which as Gregory the Great says is the root of all precepts.[243] No act is therefore perfectly virtuous without charity; it divides not only the saved from the damned but as we have seen, the Christian virtues from the pagan, which do not, unlike those from charity, have God as their end. For that reason the philosophical virtues are not necessary for salvation nor for the deletion in baptism of the inclinations to vice which come with original sin. But equally acts which are morally virtuous could together with charity—but without their acquired habits if God should suspend them—lead to salvation.[244]

That all this can be accomplished by God directly without the infusion of charity does not detract from its intrinsic sanctifying nature; it means merely that God can do alone what ordinarily he does with a supernatural habit. For Ockham it should however be remembered that that is still by God's grace in its uncreated meaning. Only therefore if grace is to be identified with a supernatural habit or absolute quality in the soul can it be said that Ockham denies the necessity of grace. But that in turn entails the arbitrary exercise of denying the legitimacy of Ockham's

---

239 *Ibid.*

240 Ideo dico quod duplex est gratia: una est qualitas absoluta informans animam. Alia est gratia gratuita dei voluntas. Primo modo loquendo de gratia dico quod eadem est gratia gratum faciens et gratia virtutum et gratia sacramentalis (*Reportatio*, IV, qq. 8 and 9, o).

241 *Ibid.*

242 Ideo dico quod gratia et charitas sunt omnino eadem realiter, sed solum distinguuntur sicut nomina vel conceptus connotativi (*ibid.*).

243 Ad quartum dico quod preter virtutes acquisitas non sunt alie virtutes infuse necessarie [et] quod charitas sufficit cum virtutis acquisitis, quia charitas inclinat immediate ad actum cuiuslibet virtutis. Et ideo dicit Gregorius quod omnia precepta sunt unum in radice charitatis. Et isto modo omnes virtutes sunt connexe in charitate (*ibid.*, q. 3, s).

244 *Ibid.*

distinction which of course is not his but part of accepted teaching. Even were it justifiable, it would still not destroy the essential gratuitousness of God's acceptance nor, therefore, its supernatural character. The issue then is not between nature and grace, however much Ockham may be seen to vindicate natural powers at the expense of supernatural habits; it is between a God's-eye view and a creaturely view. For whatever its temporal manifestations, God's grace is the result of what he has eternally willed;[245] whether he therefore accepts and rewards, with or without a habit, makes no difference to his eternal decision upon which the efficacy or otherwise of a habit exclusively depends.

That brings us to the question of sin, which when actual, as either temporal or mortal, shares the two fundamental conditions of virtuous and meritorious acts. It is defined by reference to God's precepts and those of right reason; and it can only be through an act of the created—that is, the angelic or human—will. The difference is that it is an act against what God wills. Like 'good' or 'virtuous', 'sin' or 'bad' is a connotative term having only a nominal definition. As such it is neither something real nor the lack of something real but a name or concept signifying more than one thing, both directly and indirectly. Thus mortal sin is equivalent to saying that someone has committed or omitted an act for which he is bound to receive eternal punishment.[246] While, like all nominal definitions, sin signifies nothing in itself, it subsumes real things, namely an act, a power (the will), and future punishment. For that reason it is called a wound and sickness, from the sadness engendered in the soul, which is temporal if there is penance and eternal if there is not.[247]

Beyond that, however, sin denotes nothing, real or mental. It is not real because it neither leaves a new substance in the mind nor a species or passion or habit as accidents, all of which can cease or be destroyed and sin remain. It cannot either be said to be a privation of grace or original justice as absolute accidents, for there could be no grace together with no punishment for sin, as there was neither in the first angel and the first man, and there could be grace without original justice, as there is one and not the other in a baptised infant not in mortal sin. Nor again is sin the privation of a just act because someone lacking the use of reason cannot act rightly, but he does not thereby sin. Equally, as sin is not something absolute, it is not a relation of reason because as we have discussed in chapter three there is no such relation: a view confirmed by Duns Scotus whose analogy Ockham adopts between someone who is in mortal sin and someone who offends a prince and becomes his enemy without anything real inhering in or being added to either

---

[245] E.g. et per istum modum, quia deus ordinavit ab eterno et forte quod ille actus naturalis uno tempore non esset acceptus sine charitate; alio tempore esset talis acceptus sine omni charitate. Si solum tempus transeat ille actus esset primo non acceptus sine omni destructione vel positione cuiuscunque positivi (*Dubitationes Addititie*, Ad 2ᵐ, C).

[246] Quantum ad primum dico quod peccatum mortale non habet quid rei sed tantum quid nominis, quia nihil unum reale dicit nec positivum nec privativum vel negativum; sed dicit multa non habentia aliquam unitatem nec per se nec per accidens. Unde potest dici quod secundum quid nominis est aliquem commisisse aliquem actum vel omisisse propter quem obligatur ad penam eternam (*Reportatio*, IV, qq. 8 and 9, C); also D and S.

[247] *Ibid.*, R.

person. Otherwise, if sin were a relation of reason, dependent upon the intellect and the will, the evidence of sin would depend upon its existence in the intellect and will, the falsity of which is clear; for assuming the impossible that God did not at some time know or will and so had no relation of reason to a sinner, a man could still be in mortal sin.[248] Hence sin is not formally a mental relation as it is not substance or accident; and being none of these, but only an act of commission or omission, which—when mortal—God punishes eternally, sin neither removes nor destroys anything in the soul because it is not something present in the soul. Its lack is in the failure of the sinner to act as he should.[249]

This exclusive identification of sin with an act of will is the governing principle of Ockham's notion of sin. It thus shares the same non—or anti—metaphysical status of all connotative terms. In consequence it loses its traditional definition as lack or privation or negation of being; acting not being becomes its measure. Ockham accordingly dissociates the ontological from the conative, as he has from the conceptual and the logical; but the rejection of Christian metaphysics does not here more than anywhere else entail the rejection of Christian truth. In locating the source of sin in the will's refusal to love God above all, and love and hate what he wills to be loved and hated, Ockham is doing no more than restate a fundamental theological principle in almost identically Augustinian terms. It forms the basis both for his own analysis of the nature of actual sin and its relation to ignorance, merit, and grace.

Thus to begin with he opposes Duns Scotus's view that the sin or difformity in an act of sin is simply the absence of righteousness or justice which must be present in every good act.[250] That, it need hardly be said, is the obverse of Duns's notion that an act becomes good through the addition of prudence, where before it was in its substance morally indifferent. We have already discussed Ockham's reply. Equally in relation to a sinful act he denies that difformity exists in the act. Like righteousness, difformity as lack of righteousness comes from the will and consists in doing what should not be done or not doing what should be done, in each case contrary to God's will and his decrees. It cannot therefore be due to the lack of something in the act which before was there and now no longer is, whether something absolute or an intrinsic relation as Duns believed; for the righteousness which an act should have can only be through the will acting righteously, and that is incompatible with a vicious act where it acts unrighteously.[251] All acts are therefore sinful or righteous according to whether or not the will conforms to God's command by which it is bound.[252] Sin then is not the absence of something

---

[248] *Ibid.*, C.

[249] Ideo peccatum nihil aliud est nisi aliquem commisisse vel omisisse actum propter quem deus eum ordinavit ad penam eternam. Aliter tamen possit deus ordinare. Ex isto sequitur quod per peccatum mortale nihil corrumpitur nec tollitur in anima, quia licet tunc peccans careat aliquo actu qui deberet sibi inesse, et ad quem obligatur, tamen ille actus non corrumpitur, quia non inest nec aliquid tollitur ab anima, quia non substantia nec accidens certum est (*ibid.*, C–D).

[250] *Ibid.*, III, q. 12, XX.

[251] *Ibid.*

[252] Dico quod difformitas in actu vel peccatum in actu non est carentia rectitudinis debite inesse actui . . . sed est carentia rectitudinis debite inesse voluntati. Quod nihil aliud est dicere

real either from the act itself or from the will; its difformity lies simply in the will's opposition to God.

Now central to Ockham's conception of sin is that acts of commission and omission are not only numerically distinct but also different in kind, having different objects. They are therefore, by God's absolute power at least, separable so that there can be one without the other.[253] That has two immediate consequences one little more than a debating point, the other of fundamental importance. The first is that sin cannot be divided into a material part, which is its act, and a formal part which is the absence of righteousness. For that would mean that a sin of commission taken alone—where the will acts against right reason and a divine precept without being bound to a contrary act—would be merely material; and correspondingly an act of omission, where the will does not act when it should, would be purely formal. By the same token, only a sin of commission and omission would have both a material and a formal part, none of which is tenable.[254]

The second and important consequence is that only a sin of omission can be called privation or lacks an efficient cause, through the will's failure to act. An act of commission on the other hand has not only an efficient cause but God as partial immediate cause as concause in every created act. It therefore has a positive cause of its difformity.[255] That does not however mean that God himself sins in helping to cause an act of commission; for he is not anyone's debtor; he is thus not bound to cause this act any more than its opposite even when he does cause it. The created will by contrast is bound by God not to commit this very act; and through that obligation it sins when it does commit it.[256] That is the difference between the created will's action and God's: God is under no precept; therefore he cannot sin whatever he does or does not. The created will is under God's precept; it therefore sin's in disobeying him: if like God it were without a precept it would like God not sin.[257] That it is not, and does sin, makes a man a debtor to God.[258] The justice of all that God wills is accordingly the measure of what is just and unjust among his

---

nisi quod voluntas obligatur aliquem actum elicere secundum preceptum divinum quem non elicit et sic peccat peccato omissionis. Et ita rectitudo vel absolutum vel respectivum nihil aliud est quam ipsemet actus qui debuit elici secundum rationem rectam et voluntatem dei (ibid., YY). Also *Quodlibet* III, q. 14.

[253] *Reportatio, ibid.*, XX, q. 13, P.

[254] *Ibid.*, q. 12, YY.

[255] Ex hoc patet quomodo peccatum dicitur privatio, quia peccatum omissionis est formaliter privatio, et aliquod peccatum scilicet commissionis non dicitur privatio, sed est actus positivus quem voluntas tenetur non elicere ... Et ex hoc patet quid est causa efficiens peccati, quia peccati omissionis nulla est causa positiva, quia ipsum nihil est positivum, sed tantum habet causam defectivam. Et illa est voluntas que tenetur actum oppositum illi carentie elicere, et non elicit. Si autem loquamur de peccato commissionis, sic non solum voluntas creata est causa efficiens illius actus, sed ipse deus qui omnem actum immediate causat sicut causa secunda quecumque. Et ita est causa positiva difformitatis in tali actu (ibid.).

[256] Respondeo: deus nullius est debitor, et ideo nec tenetur illum actum causare nec oppositum actum causare nec illum actum non causare, et ideo non peccat quantumcumque illum actum causat. Voluntas autem creata tenetur per preceptum divinum illum actum non causare, et per consequens illum actum causando peccat (ibid.).

[257] *Ibid.*, IV, q. 9, E.

[258] *Ibid.*, II, q. 19, H.

creatures: and if he were total cause of acts of which he is at present partial cause, what are now sins would not be sins.[259]

That explains how sin averts the will from God; for not every sin committed is one of hating God. Someone can will to act unjustly against right reason and a divine precept and neither hate nor love God; nevertheless he turns away from God because in sinning he defies his command to do or not to do something. It is in that sense that all mortal sin is an aversion of the will from God in not loving him above all, but something else more, as grace and charity convert someone to God in causing him to be loved above all.[260]

Conversely, the will is not always right because it conforms to God's will; sometimes God wants a creature to refuse what he himself wills, for example Christ's death eternally willed by him but which he refused the Jews to want in the way in which it occurred at their hands. Similarly with the death of one's father which, as St Augustine said, God wills but does not want us to will. Hence we sin when we will something which God wills us to not will, although God himself wills it; and our sin is greatest when we will knowing that God does not want us to will. For that reason God is always partial cause of an act of sin by his conditional and consequent—as opposed to his absolute—will, because he wills it if a creature wills it, but wants a creature to want not to will it. The created will is not therefore always held to conform to God's will in what he himself wills; for in doing so it will frequently sin. Rather it has to conform over the circumstances of the object willed.[261]

That raises the question of when and how error leads to sin. From what has been said earlier it will be recalled that no act of will which is against conscience and reason, whether right or wrong, can be virtuous. If it is against right reason it then offends against God's precept and what he wills to be done according to right reason. If it is against wrong reason and conscience the cause will be ignorance either from invincible error in which case such an act will not be in the will's power, or from culpable error where the will mistakenly believes that it is opposing right reason and conscience; it thereby sins for holding reason in contempt.[262] Now a morally virtuous act of will can coexist with both invincible and culpable error over another object, as someone can virtuously want chastity and yet, as mentioned previously, be mistaken about fortitude.[263] A meritorious act on the other hand is incompatible with mortally culpable error although it can stand with invincible and venial error, for the very reason that to err culpably is to sin mortally in avoidably committing or omitting what is necessary to salvation through sloth or some similar cause.[264] Once more however it is not error which is intrinsically sinful but the will's action; hence error is culpable and vicious only by an extrinsic denomination from the will.[265] Moreover assuming that an act of omission entails an act of commission, the will, in omitting to discover what must be done for

---

[259] *Ibid.*, IV, q. 9, E; III, q. 13, O.   [260] *Ibid.*, III, q. 12, YY.   [261] *Ibid.*, q. 13, O.
[262] *Ibid.*, C.   [263] *Ibid.*, H. Conclusio prima.   [264] *Ibid.*, I. Conclusio secunda.
[265] Non quidem sic intelligendo quod [text: quia] actus istius erroris sit intrinsice viciosus, quia solus actus voluntatis est intrinsice virtuosus vel viciosus . . . sed est culpabilis et viciosus solum quadam denominatione extrinsica ab actu voluntatis (*ibid.*); and M.

salvation, sins only by commission in refusing to do so or in wanting something which contradicts the discovery of what it should know. When this act is one of mortal sin it excludes charity and thereby an act of merit; but not when it is merely venial, say when someone neglects to inquire about what he should know, or when there is invincible error in not being in anyone's power; indeed it is compatible with a just act of volition over the same object. Thus the intellect could misinterpret the general principle drawn from right reason, that anyone in extreme necessity should be helped, over a particular case where need did not in fact arise, and the will could at the same time want to help the person involved; if it did so from love of God it would be acting justly and meritoriously. So far from error in the intellect negating the justice of its act, not to want to act would be vicious and demeritorious. Accordingly right reason concurs with erroneous reason to cause a virtuous act: the error consists not in the general principle enunciated by right reason but in the minor premise and conclusion; the virtue in the will's desire to conform to right reason without which, as we have abundantly seen, an act is not virtuous; the lack of culpability in the invincibility of the error beyond the will's power. Such a concurrence here as elsewhere therefore depends upon having the use of reason.[266] Conversely the absence of these conditions precludes culpable error in the intellect and virtue in the will over the same—but not, as we have already said, a different—object; for in not conforming to right reason when it is able to, the will acts culpably. It is thus responsible for its error, which consists in failing to command the intellect to investigate the obligations which the will must fulfil. That is the difference between an invincible error which has its source in the intellect and a culpable error which is due to the will. It thereby sins both by commission in acting against erroneous reason which it—avoidably—takes to be right, and omission in not doing what it should, while if it suspends its act, its omission is doubled by not even acting erroneously. The will is thus not obliged to sin through avoidable error; it sins because it opposes what is erroneous but believes to be right.[267] In other words sin lies in the will's refusal to do what it knows should be done.

With sin then as with merit, the cause lies in the will; and as it merits by wanting to do what should be done according to right reason, so it sins for refusing what should be willed. It therefore sins not only in mistakenly rejecting the good for the bad but also for knowingly preferring the bad to the good, real as well as apparent.[268] To deny that the will could reject the good for its own sake and want the bad as its opposite would be to deny any reason for sin or merit, for it would mean that the will in acting against what—through the intellect—it knows to be right reason, could not sin or merit by refusing to do so.[269] Only where good means what is or can be willed, and bad its opposite as what is or can be refused, is it true that the will knows only the good and rejects only the bad.[270] Which is how

[266] Ibid., K. Conclusio tertia.
[267] Ibid., L–N. Conclusio quarta.
[268] Sic dico quod voluntas potest velle malum quod nec est bonum realiter nec apparenter, et potest nolle bonum quod nec est malum realiter nec apparenter (ibid., s).
[269] Ibid., s–t.   [270] Ibid., t.

the authorities are to be interpreted in saying that will cannot will anything unless it is really good or under the appearance of the good; and evil, conversely. By God's present dispensation only Christ and the Virgin could merit where the object is sinful; for all other rational creatures the consequence is demerit and sin.[271]

Ockham explicitly affirms the implication of this view, namely that the created will could refuse blessedness, whether in a universal or particular vision of its end, just because the will is free to act or not to act and so not under any compulsion to want the good either in itself or because it does not appear to bring rest.[272] Thus on the one hand it could accept a command of the intellect to refuse blessedness because of the intellect's disbelief in a final end, as someone could also reject his own existence and with it the blessedness which he takes to be its consequence. On the other hand the will can oppose the judgement of the intellect that there is a final end, since like any free power it is capable of contrary acts, able to will or refuse any object including those which bear upon God. By the same token it need not obey the decrees of right reason, although they concern its own final end; while whatever the will can deny to someone else it can refuse for itself, even blessedness. Such freedom is no less possible to the will when in a state of grace, for it still retains its use of reason which is not impeded by a supernatural habit and which enables it to reject blessedness. Moreover whatever the will can refuse for a limited time it can refuse for all time, as a mortal sinner, who refuses blessedness for the duration of sin, can do so for all this life and the next.[273]

On his part, too, God could command the will to hate him and the will could obey, as it can obey any divine precept; in doing so it would be acting rightly both in this and the next life.[274] He could also suspend fruition from blessedness since they are distinct—allowing the will to be total cause of its own refusal. Conversely if he were total cause of a beatific vision the will could not refuse him, just as it could not will perfectly something not willed by God, since both would be contradictory.[275] As we shall mention below, in Ockham's belief both the vision of blessedness and fruition of God are caused totally by him. For the moment, however, we are concerned with his conclusion that the will could itself, with the concurrence of God, refuse its own glory. In reaching it Ockham characteristically deployed any arguments which seemed germane without seeking to form them into a logically necessary sequence. More than one, such as the will's capacity to deny itself what it denies to others, or God's power to make the will hate him, seems to rest upon either questionable major premises or dubious theological

---

[271] Ibid.

[272] Sed ultra dicta ibi dico quod voluntas pro statu isto potest nolle ultimum finem sive ostendatur in generali sive in particulari . . . quia non necessario illud appetit in quo non credit se posse quietari; igitur etc (IV, q. 14, D). Also Ordinatio, I, q. 6, 503–6.

[273] Ibid.

[274] Preterea omnis voluntas potest se conformare precepto divino; sed deus potest precipere quod voluntas creata odiat eum; igitur voluntas creata potest hoc facere. Preterea omne quod potest esse actus rectus in via, et in patria; sed odire deum potest esse actus rectus in via, puta si precipiatur a deo; ergo et in in patria (ibid.).

[275] Ibid.

principles; and the invocation of God's absolute power here, taken out of context, could appear to herald the *reductio ad absurdum* of divine omnipotence which was to become the hallmark of the next generation of Ockhamists. Essentially, however, they are all designed to exhibit the created will's freedom supported by God, whether as concause or by his direct intervention, to act in contrary ways. Once again the only limit is that of logical contradiction.

It is in that sense too that Ockham juxtaposes sin to grace and merit in their different relations of compatibility and incompatibility. To begin with, as we have mentioned, sin averts from God whereas charity converts to him. Hence as acts they are incompatible when sin is taken as hating God, for it formally contradicts charity as the act of loving him above all. But it does not apply when sin means loving another creature more than God; then the act of sin, say of fornicating, is compatible naturally and formally as an act with an act of charity. They are contradictory only by an extrinsic cause, namely God's ordinance that the creature in question should not be loved by another creature.[276] The created will doing so thereby does not love God above all; if it did it would not love someone God wills to be hated or not to be loved. Accordingly the contradiction between such an act as sinful and one of charity derives entirely from God's decree; without it there would be none; and indeed, if God should decree that such a creature should be loved by another, an act which is now sinful would be meritorious. That applies only to habitual grace and sin whether as hate of God or inordinate love of another creature; they are incompatible only by an extrinsic cause, not formally, because a supernatural form does not contradict a natural form although they sometimes differ in kind. The contradiction between them therefore arises from God's decree that someone committing such an act should not receive habitual grace. On the other hand there is no incompatibility between a habit of hating God and the infusion of habitual grace, which coexist after an initial act of repentance, because one act of love does not suffice to destroy habitual sin. Indeed it requires many degrees of grace before the habit is eliminated; and at first the will is still more inclined to hate God than to love him.[277] Nor does a habit of acquired grace formally and intrinsically contradict actual sin in either of its senses: for someone having acquired grace can hate God or love a creature God wills not to be loved. Otherwise no one could sin by commission, and acquired charity would not be destroyed by hating God, as it is finally by repeated acts. Here as before the contradiction is from God's ordinance and not in the nature of the acts and habits themselves; they do however formally contradict as habits.[278]

Now with sin and grace, as with whatever is not formally and intrinsically

[276] Si queras utrum conversio ad deum actu caritativo et aversio ab eo actu odiendi eum opponuntur formaliter, dicendum est quod sic, quia diligere deum super omnia et odire deum sunt actus contrarii. Si queras de conversione ad deum actu caritativo et conversione actu quo diligitur creatura quam deus non vult diligi, puta actus fornicandi, sic non repugnant illi naturaliter et formaliter inter se, sed compatiuntur se in eodem quantum est ex natura actuum. Sed solum repugnant per causam extrinsecam, puta per deum ordinantem talem creaturam nullo modo a voluntate creata diligi (*ibid.*, III, q. 12, YY–AAA).

[277] *Ibid.*

[278] *Ibid.*, BBB.

opposed to something else through an absolute contradictory in each but simply through an extrinsic cause—in this case God's ordinance—the induction of one does not require the previous expulsion of the other.[279] And by God's absolute power the two could coexist simultaneously or inhere regardless of the other; for he could ordain differently and infuse grace without first expelling sin, as he did with the first angel and first man; and similarly as he has instituted eternal punishment as the penalty for mortal sin without the infusion of something real, so he could remit both the punishment and the sin without the infusion of anything real. That applies to sin and grace.[280] By God's present dispensation, however, first comes the expulsion of sin which must be remitted before grace can be infused.[281]

That brings us to penance as a sacrament and the conditions for its award. And first to what Ockham understands by a sacrament. Like sin and penance itself, it has only a nominal definition, meaning an efficacious sign of God's grace.[282] Although it could be predicated of both spiritual and sensible things, it is confined to the latter and, in excluding what is spiritual, it is a negative connotative concept.[283] As we have mentioned in connection with merit, the sacraments can be regarded as the *causa sine qua non* of grace, not in the natural connotation of cause, as that from whose presence the existence of something else follows, but in following from God's will as cause. In that sense, also, merit is the *sine qua non* of reward which is solely from God's will. Neither naturally nor from any power bestowed upon the sacraments themselves are they the cause of grace.[284]

Ockham opposes this view of the sacraments, as the condition instituted by God for conferring grace, without which it would not be conferred, to that of Duns Scotus for whom they were the instrumental cause of grace, not only an adornment or character, but also constituting something real in the soul to perfect it and rightly dispose it.[285] If, replied Ockham, something real were impressed in the soul by the sacraments, that would be either naturally, and then anyone could naturally attain the same grace, or supernaturally, and then it would be created and not due to the sacraments.[286] For contrary to this opinion neither can a supernatural power inhere in the sacraments nor can they be the cause of grace by their own power or instrumentally. The first contention follows, because no supernatural

---

[279] Loquendo autem de duobus que non proprie opponuntur formaliter et intrinsice, sed si opponuntur solum opponuntur per causam extrinsecam, quomodo est de culpa et gratia, quia nullum absolutum in uno repugnat formaliter alicui absoluto in alio, sed si opponantur solum opponuntur institutione divina (*ibid.*, IV, qq. 8 and 9, L). Also q. 3, H.

[280] *Ibid.*

[281] *Ibid.*, M.

[282] Ad propositum dico quod sacramentum non potest diffiniri primo modo, sed precise secundo modo; et sic dico quod oratio exprimens quid nominis est ista: 'significare efficaciter effectum dei gratuitum'. Ista autem oratio non predicatur modo de facto nisi de sensibilibus (*ibid.*, IV, q. 1, B).

[283] *Ibid.*

[284] Primo dico quod sacramenta non sunt causa gratie. Circa quod probandum primo ostendam quod sacramenta per virtutem naturalem non causant gratiam nec aliquid previum instrumentaliter gratie. Secundo quod nec per virtutem eis collatam (*ibid.*, G).

[285] *Ibid.*, C–E.

[286] *Ibid.*, E.

power belongs to a genus, whether a substance or an accident. It is not overcome by Duns's argument that incomplete being in the mind can be reduced logically to complete being; so that this supernatural virtue can be reduced to the same complete genus of quality in which as principal agent it would really be if it were not uncreated and so incomplete. Nothing, replies Ockham, is in a genus by reduction unless it is intrinsic to that which is in a genus; but this virtue is not intrinsic to anything in a genus; therefore it is not in a genus by reduction. By the same token this supernatural power cannot be reduced to grace as the maximum good, which is its end and completion, for on Duns's own previous argument it would be in the same genus as the form of the principal agent which is not that of grace. If, furthermore, they were of the same genus then all our natural acts required for blessedness would themselves be of the greatest good, and the qualities necessary to the intellective soul would be of the same genus as the intellective soul itself.

Nor can a spiritual power exist in anything corporeal, whether indivisibly, incompletely, or merely as an object known. It cannot therefore complete and perfect a corporeal thing; if it could, intellection and volition and the other spiritual perfections could also be said to exist in a stone.[287] Equally the sacraments do not act by their own power naturally; that would only be if they were an instrument which received an additional form through their own imperfection or perfection: neither need be posited. On the one hand it suffices for the instrument to be more imperfect than the form of the principal cause; and on the other the proper form of an instrument is more perfect than one added to it. Moreover, every supernatural virtue is more perfect than a natural virtue; therefore if the sacraments are a supernatural virtue they do not act naturally of their own power. Nor indeed need something always be caused before grace.[288] Lastly,[289] if the sacraments were the intrumental cause of grace they would then be moved by a principal cause which would be either a form, so subjecting them to increase and alteration, or alternatively they would be moved locally, thereby having as many distinct local movements as acts. Neither is true.

For these different reasons then the sacraments are not to be held as the cause of grace, whether in virtue of containing some supernatural power or by their own power or as an instrumental cause. They are merely the *sine qua non* of grace, as Christ also is,[290] in a relation of causality which only obtains for acts of will not natural things. As such, contrary to Duns, a *sine qua non* is more than an accidental cause.[291]

As to penance as a sacrament, it has like any other only a nominal definition meaning the absolution from sin by a priest of someone who duly repents according to the prescribed form of words and their proper meaning.[292] The act of repentance itself can be understood in a variety of senses: for the punishment

---

[287] *Ibid.*, E–G.   [288] *Ibid.*, H.

[289] This is in fact the first of the two negative conclusions in note 284 above; I have reversed the order to make the second follow directly from the preceding argument.

[290] *Ibid.*, E.   [291] *Ibid.*, C, E.   [292] *Ibid.*, qq. 8 and 9, H.

which the penitent received or the efficient cause of repentance or the act of remorse voluntarily undergone for sin committed. By the first it can be either interior, as sadness and contrition, or an exterior act experienced in the senses; and similarly by the second as displeasure at having sinned, which causes sadness, or confession which is the cause of shame expressed in penance, fasting and so on. By the third mode satisfaction can be called repentance, whether as punishment or otherwise, for example an act of loving God above all where something giving delight can be called repentance. The foregoing can be ordered as follows: first the act of detesting sin or displeasure at sin, leading secondly to confession and acts of penance; and finally acceptance of such revulsion and of subsequent sadness. The acts of detestation and acceptance themselves are distinct so that one can be separated from the other. When each of these stages has been completed then come the exterior acts of punishment which vary according to the different rules instituted.[293]

The deletion of sin itself means nothing else than not imputing a penalty to an act of commission or omission, and not the removal or separation of something absolute or relative from the sinner; it can be due either solely to temporal change, if God should decree eternal punishment for anyone committing a certain act at one time but eternal life for the same act committed subsequently, or to a new act from a sinner, as he actually remits mortal sin now, or from someone else, as he could remit sin for Christ's works. Sin could also be remitted without a new act on anyone's part.[294]

As we have previously remarked, by God's present dispensation *regulariter* sin is expelled before grace is infused, except for the angels, Christ, and the Virgin, and, according to some, also the first man. As we have seen the reason lies in God's decision and not formally in the mutual exclusiveness of sin and grace of their own nature.[295] That applies also to penance: as an external act it is never either necessary or sufficient for the deletion of sin; and as an internal act or passion, such as detestation of sin or sadness or their subsequent acceptance, it is not sufficient since it can be for the wrong end; namely repentance for the punishment alone and not for God.[296]

Beyond its own intrinsic inadequacy, however, God could himself give grace without repentance, for where an act of sin has passed there is no contradiction to grace or glory and no habit of sin. Nor is there anything in the sinner which is the necessary cause of punishment and excludes glory: that is entirely from God's will; and as he decides to inflict punishment for sin so he can remit sin without any contradiction. He does so moreover freely; otherwise if he punished necessarily he could not annihilate a sinner, for annihilation would preclude punishment. Conversely he would have to reward the sinner, who repented, with grace. On both counts of necessity God would then be powerless to annihilate someone either for not repenting or for repenting.[297]

Even by his ordained power God could remove guilt without any special penance, exterior or interior: for example in someone oblivious that he had

---

[293] *Ibid.*   [294] *Ibid.*, I; also *Dubitationes Addititie*, ad secundum, G.
[295] *Reportatio*, IV, qq. 8 and 9, L; i.e. *ex natura rei*.   [296] *Ibid.*, M.   [297] *Ibid.*

sinned and so inculpable from invincible ignorance. If he also had the use of reason —the possession of which excludes no one from salvation—and loved God above all without repenting, God could infuse him with grace because such a person would not be bound first to detest sin.[298] Nevertheless, regardless of such exceptions God has decreed that no one in mortal sin whether knowingly or not, through culpable ignorance, can have his sin remitted with an act of repentance; for he ordains that all guilt must be punished.[299]

Now first among these pentitential acts is the detestation of sin, because it is an act of the will; and just as sin is committed by the will alone, so the act of hating sin in being from the will comes before and is more essential than any other in deleting sin. Sadness on the other hand is only in the will's power as the result of an act of detestation. God could therefore suspend the former's causality, leaving detestation alone as meriting the deletion of sin and the infusion of grace;[300] for the same act of detesting sin can also be one of loving God as an act of charity.[301] An infused habit—unlike an acquired habit—can incline immediately to an act of another habit without inclining to its own act. Hence an infused habit of charity can immediately dispose someone to an act of hating sin on account of God, and do so virtuously.[302] Detestation of sin also presupposes the act of wishing to punish it, which strictly refers to an exterior act, and which by God's absolute power could be without an interior act.[303] Accordingly, first comes hate of sin, next the penalty of sadness which it engenders, then acceptance of both, and finally the wish to inflict punishment through confession or satisfaction. Their order is not properly speaking an essential one, since each can be without the other; it is rather one of efficient causality, where the three acts of detestation, sadness and acceptance lead to the will to punish sin.[304] Ockham reduces repentance itself to three acts, one interior, which is contrition, and two exterior, of confession and satisfaction.[305] That would seem to indicate that these other four acts constitute contrition as the soul's response to sin, from which the two sacramental acts follow.

In this connection, he opposes Duns Scotus for arguing that someone could receive the sacrament of penance, and with it the infusion of grace and the remission of sin, without contrition or a good impulse of the will but simply through a right intention.[306] Whilst he accepts that that could be by God's absolute power, Duns's opinion otherwise appears to conflict with the meaning of the saints, above all St Augustine, that penance consists of contrition, confession and satisfaction. Hence Ockham concludes that no sacrament can remit mortal sin in an adult having the use of free will and not in invincible ignorance, unless he is contrite.[307] As we

---

[298] *Ibid.*

[299] Tamen non obstante hoc, dico quod existenti in peccato mortali et habenti de tali peccato vel non habenti conscientiam propter ignorantiam imputabilem, non potest remitti illud peccatum de potentia dei ordinata sine actu penitentie. Et hoc quia deus sic disposuit quod nulli remitteretur culpa sine omni punitione (*ibid.*).

[300] *Ibid.*, N and U.

[301] Ita est in proposito quod eodem actu in numero aliquis odit et detestatur peccatum et diligit deum, et ideo iste actus est actus charitatis (*ibid.*, U).

[302] *Ibid.*, X.   [303] *Ibid.*, U.   [304] *Ibid.*

[305] *Ibid.*, N.   [306] *Ibid.*, P.   [307] *Ibid.*, Q.

have said before the sacramental grace that he receives is the same in every way, save as a name, as habitual sanctifying grace; and since sin is itself not to be understood either as some deficiency or something real in the soul, such grace is not, contrary to some, to be conceived as repairing a defect in the soul or its powers.[308] Nor can it be called a medicine; for a medicine cures, but sacraments, like confirmation and the eucharist, presuppose the restoration of the person already receiving them.[309]

We must now turn to original sin and its deletion by baptism. In contrast to actual sin it leaves a corrupting quality—a *fomes*—in the flesh which inclines the sensory appetite of anyone having the use of reason to sinful and immoral acts against or beyond right reason, pleasurable and sad. As a corporeal quality—as opposed to that of the intellect, will, or senses—it can remain in the body without eliciting any act; and like any quality it can be increased or diminished in different individuals. It owes its inordinateness to sin, and was not originally in Adam and Eve or ever in Christ or actively in the Virgin, whom in common with Duns Scotus Ockham absolves from any of its effects: if there ever was a *fomes* in her God mitigated and weakened it first through her baptism, so that perhaps it could have inclined her to venial sin, but never to mortal sin. And then after her second sanctification when she had conceived Christ, this carnal quality was totally eliminated or at least so diminished that it could no longer dispose her to any kind of sin or wrongdoing. Its presence in all other mankind Ockham attributes to natural causes, to which God abandoned men after Adam's sin, allowing them to engender infirmity in the same way as any other excess humour, which is what a *fomes* is. That, however, cannot be proved or disproved.[310]

The question of how the Virgin could have remained impeccable, when no act or habit can exclude every act of omission and commission, while also meriting through her own powers, is discussed in the third book of the *Reportatio*. It was due, says Ockham, to God's decision only to concur as immediate partial cause in her good acts. She was thereby able to merit from performing them, since she remained free to choose whether or not to act; at the same time she could not sin by omission because God would not co-operate. She could then be said either not to sin, in not doing what was no longer in her power, or to merit in not ceasing from this act and choosing another. By either interpretation she was not sinning.[311]

The elimination of a *fomes* can be by a habit in the will through which it is no longer inclined to act against right reason. Unlike Duns Scotus, Ockham does not consider that that can only be by means of a supernatural habit causing something more pleasurable in the will than the pleasure it experiences from an inclination produced by a *fomes*, and which it cannot of itself resist. Ockham's ground is that pleasure produced by a supernatural habit would be through an act which, in being directed to God, would be of the same nature as an act produced naturally; it

---

308 *Ibid.*, N.
309 *Ibid.*, CC.
310 *Reportatio*, III, q. 2, B; *Quodlibet* III, q. 10: which I have principally followed in the above account.
311 *Reportatio*, III, q. 2, D–F.

could therefore be equally from a habit acquired naturally. The reasons are the same as those previously given in the discussion of acquired habits produced from loving God. That does not, however, mean that someone could thereby avoid all sins; for although God could accept the same moderation from a natural as from a supernatural habit he does not do so in fact. Nor can perfect tranquility replace the rebellion of the senses save by a supernatural habit, normally the gift of impassibility.[312]

Original sin itself Ockham understands in two ways: as it is *de facto* by God's ordained power, and as it could be by his absolute power. By the first, he accepts Anselm's definition that it consists in the absence of original justice which should be in the soul. Original sin is not therefore something positive, and correspondingly original justice is something added to man's natural powers. In the second sense *de possibili*, on the other hand, original sin is not the absence of anything which should be possessed, natural or supernatural, but God's non-acceptance because of preceding demerit which could be committed naturally and is passed on to the sinner's posterity.[313] While *de facto* original sin is deleted by the infusion of created grace, by God's absolute power he could without contradiction ordain that there was no such need of justification in order to be freed from sin. For the same reason he could have enabled the Virgin to remain in original sin for only an instant, neither demanding from her original justice nor imputing to her—in the broad sense since original sin is not in someone's power—any sin subsequently. In each case no contradiction is implied in God's not wanting to punish her for her parents' derelection after the first instant of her fallen state.[314]

The penality for original sin is both eternal, as God's non-acceptance for eternal life, and temporal, as sin both voluntarily sustained and naturally inflicted. By God's ordained power baptism remits the first two, rendering a person baptised worthy of eternal life and freeing an adult—but not a child in not being responsible for its acts—from his past sins. But the third effect constitutes the disabilities common to all men, such as the need to eat and drink, which remain as part of the common course of nature.[315]

It is otherwise by God's absolute power: not only can he, as we have said more than once, remit sin, both original and actual, without created grace, or give a sinner a vision of his essence at the same instant in which he gives him grace or

---

[312] *Ibid.*, I.

[313] Circa primum est sciendum quod aliud est loqui de peccato originali de facto et [aliud] de possibili. Nam de facto dicitur peccatum originale secundum Anselm in *De concepto virginali* non est aliquid positivum in animo sed aliqua est carentia iustitie debite. Et secundum hoc dico quod iustitia originalis dicitur aliquid absolutum superadditum homini in puris naturalibus existenti. Sed loquendo de peccato originali de possibili dico quod potest fieri de potentia dei absoluta quod peccatum originale nullius diceretur carentia, nec habitus naturalis nec debitum habendi aliquid; sed solum quod aliquis propter demeritum precedens in aliquo sit supernaturalis nec indignus vita eterna. Hoc probo sic, quia aliquis existens in puris naturalibus potest acceptari a deo, et deus potest ordinare quod ipso faciente contra preceptum divinum sit indignus acceptatione divina cum omnibus posteris suis. Tunc descendens a tali peccante est in peccato originali (*Quodlibet* III, q. 9); also *Reportatio*, II, q. 26, U.

[314] *Quodlibet* III, q. 9.

[315] *Reportatio*, IV, q. 3, G.

accept him naturally for eternal life; he can also reduce him without grace to
Adam's primal state of innocence. Moreover whatever a natural cause can do to its
effect God can do to a creature; that includes reducing it to its pristine state by
alteration, as hot water can be reduced to cold. Hence God can do the same for
man. And as God has instituted punishment for sin without the infusion of anything
real into the sinner, he can equally release someone from sin without the infusion
of something real.[316] God can accordingly dispense with created grace and baptism for the remission of mortal sin.[317]

Now although baptism through the infusion of created grace removes actual
original and venial sin, such grace does not contradict original sin. That is because
when two forms are absolutely disparate the presence of one in a rational creature
does not exclude the absence of the other; but original sin is the absence of justice;
it can therefore coexist with created grace as an absolute form. Not however when
it means making someone acceptable to God with or without an infused form.
Then grace is repugnant to sin, original and actual: the former makes someone
God's friend, the latter God's enemy. Correspondingly grace as an absolute form
is as we have already discussed compatible with actual sin as a past act or liability
because they too are disparate, while the obligation to punishment does of itself
contradict grace, as the example of devil, who had both, shows; for such an
obligation is not itself something absolute in the soul distinct from an act or habit
of sin, nor is it a real relation. But it equally contradicts grace as God's acceptance.[318]

The remission of all past sin in baptism cannot then be proved naturally for the
very reason that unlike present sin there is no formal contradiction between past
sin and created grace. Past sin leaves no sinful habit, which has perhaps already been
destroyed, while the obligation to punishment which accompanies sin does not
exclude its deletion by created grace. Hence by God's absolute power there is
nothing to contradict remission without baptism. As an article of belief however all
guilt is remitted in baptism unless an obstacle is put in its way through actually
sinning, venially or mortally.[319]

Baptism thus depends upon the assent of or at least the absence of dissent, actual
and habitual from, the person baptised. Those undergoing it receive a certain
character or sign which distinguishes them from the non-baptised and remains after
baptism. Its presence cannot be proved or disproved by natural reason nor from the
Bible, but rests upon the church's authority. Accepting the existence of this
character, it is absolute rather than relative as a faculty of the soul; and assuming a
distinction between them, it is in the will rather than in the intellect, although that
again cannot be proved by natural reason. Although indelible as a sign, its indeli-
bility is not absolute because God could remove it from a person baptised as he can
separate any accident from its subject.[320] Its attributes as a character are first that
it signifies grace not of itself but by God's decree that someone baptised in some way
receives grace before such a sign, and that given such a sign he receives grace
unless he puts an obstacle in its way. Second, it disposes the recipient to grace as the

---

[316] *Quodlibet* VI, q. 4.   [317] *Quodlibet* VI, q. 1.   [318] *Reportatio*, IV, q. 3, E–F.
[319] *Ibid.*, F.   [320] *Ibid.*, q. 2, E–M.

condition *sine qua non* of its infusion; and that again is by God's institution not its own nature. It is also commemorative of the receipt of grace which God wills to be recorded, and as such of its own nature a distinctive sign of the sacrament to which it is assimilated. Finally, again by God's ordinance it signifies obligation, as a habit does in a member of a religious order.[321] These are the characteristics associated with baptism as a sacrament, signifying a *viator's* absolution from sin.

The preceding discussion leaves two uncertainties. The first is the lack of a clear explanation of how a past sin does not leave a vicious habit in the soul which, if present, could be incompatible with grace. Ockham does not go beyond saying that a habit would be destroyed once the act of sin has passed[322] without explaining why it should not be repeated, so leaving a habit in the same way as the repetition of any act. The second uncertainty is more apparent than real, and concerns what has been taken to be a discrepancy in Ockham's view over the coexistence of created grace in a state of innocence.[323] It seems to me that Ockham's position is consistently that the first man before the fall did not have created grace. There are four relevant passages: the first is where Ockham refers to the view by some that the Adam, as well as the angels, Christ, and the Virgin, had grace before the expulsion of sin.[324] Nothing warrants attributing that view to Ockham. The second is that sin cannot be regarded as a privation of an absolute accident including grace, because such a privation could be without sin, as it was in the first angel and the first man before he had sinned.[325] The third and most explicit statement is in the sixth *Quodlibet* as follows, 'Moreover not only does grace contradict sin but also the state of innocence; but there is no contradiction in a sinner being reduced to a state of innocence without grace; therefore God can remit his sin without infused grace'.[326] The seeming exception is contained in the fourth passage which, like the first two, belongs to the fourth book of the *Reportatio*. There Ockham uses the state of innocence hypothetically in the pluperfect subjunctive to illustrate that man in a state of grace would not have more grace than he would have had in a state of innocence when it would have been habitual created grace.[327]

Whichever the interpretation chosen, Ockham's concept of grace and sin and the role of the sacraments remains unaltered. It rests upon the distinction between what they are by their own nature, either as absolutes or in a nominal definition, and what God has decreed or could decree for them. By the first and third alternatives the status of grace and sin and the relation between them could be other

---

[321] *Ibid.*, M–N.

[322] E.g. *Reportatio*, IV, qq. 8 and 9, I; also C; q. 3, F.

[323] Iserloh, *Gnade und Eucharistie*, 97.

[324] *Ibid.*, qq. 8 and 9, L. (last sentence).

[325] Nec dicit privationem alicuius accidentis absoluti, quia nec privationem gratie, quia talis posset esse sine culpa. Patet in primo angelo et homine primo ante peccatum (*ibid.*, C).

[326] *Quodlibet* VI, q. 4: Preterea non tantum repugnat gratia culpe sed etiam status innocentie. Sed non est contradictio quod peccator reducatur ad statum innocentie sine gratia. Ergo potest deus sibi remittere culpam sine gratia infusa.

[327] Preterea homo pro statu gratie non habet gratiam perfectiorem quam habuisset si stetisset in statu innocentie. Sed tunc non habuisset nisi gratia gratum facientem et alias virtutes; igitur nec modo (*Reportatio*, IV, qq. 8 and 9, N).

than they are *de facto*, by the second alternative of God's present dispensation where they are held like all other theological truths on faith: among which the question of Adam's grace before the fall was undecided. The juxtaposing of these alternatives exhibits the contingency of the order God has instituted: contrasting it on the one hand with the natural affinities between grace and sin, and on the other with the possibilities logically open to God in his omnipotence. That does not of itself weaken the force of what has been decreed or the obligation upon the believer to accept its certainty: rather it shows that it is due to God as extrinsic—i.e. contingent —cause and not from any inherent necessity in things themselves. From that standpoint it could be argued that Ockham's purpose was to differentiate theological truth from natural and logical reasons, notwithstanding its opposite effect upon his successors of undermining theological truth: one is not precluded by the other.

Finally there is the question of blessedness which for Ockham like most Christian thinkers has its starting point in St Augustine's distinction between use and fruition, and opens the first book of his *Ordinatio* as it did of all previous Commentaries on the *Sentences*. By use in its most exact sense Ockham understands something which is willed by reference to something else either presented to the will or assumed in it, as a bitter draught is desired not for itself but for health, given which it would not be sought. Fruition on the other hand is an act of wanting something for itself which should be loved above all without reference to anything else.[328] In its general sense it is of what is present or absent, which is the way in which we love God in this world; in its strict sense it is the final beatific act by which the blessed love or have fruition of God in heaven. It is then perfect, bringing the will absolute tranquility, unlike the imperfect fruition of a *viator*, which is accompanied by anxiety and sadness.[329]

Now so far as use is concerned everything other than God can be the ordinate object of it; for everything else can be rejected or loved on account of a final end; but God as final end cannot be.[330] Strictly speaking, an act of use which does not have the highest being for its object is not an act of use. Use can accordingly be divided into, first, any act which is not one of fruition; second, an act which has an object caused by an act of fruition; and third, an act by which one thing is desired on account of another, thereby having as its object both an end and the means to it.[331] The same act of use can also be one of fruition, when it will be more perfect than the act of fruition, as an act of loving a creature because of God is more perfect than an act of loving God alone. That excludes fruition as a beatific act which is solely from God and more perfect than any other.[332] Unlike an imperfect act of fruition which is alone attainable by a *viator*—whether of an object obscurely or clearly seen, both of which are possible[333]—a beatific act of fruition is not actively from the will but from God alone.

That, however, can only be persuaded because the reasons are not themselves more than probable and could be denied; an opinion for which Ockham was

[328] *Ordinatio*, d. 1, q. 1, 374–5.   [329] *Ibid.*, q. 2, 396–7; q. 4, 431.
[330] *Ibid.*, q. 1, 375–6.   [331] *Ibid.*, 383–4.
[332] *Ibid.*, 385–6.   [333] *Ibid.*, q. 2, 397.

censured by the Avignon Masters.[334] These are first, that whenever two things are of the same genus and essentially ordered, and the less perfect of them is caused totally by God, so is the more perfect; that is the case with an act of beatific vision which is less perfect than an act of beatific fruition but of the same genus and caused totally by God. Therefore an act of beatific fruition is also totally caused by God. The same argument can be extended to other things supernatural, for example the habits of charity or beatific illumination which are inferior to their acts and totally from God; hence their acts must also be. Secondly, since the created will acts freely and contingently it could by God's absolute power cease to act and so cease to be blessed and confirmed in goodness, as a *viator's* will is neither blessed nor confirmed. Its blessedness must therefore be totally caused by God's will. Lastly, as God totally causes the act of will of someone damned—since if it could be from some other act of will someone could then not be damned—it is not more contradictory for God totally to cause the act of will of someone who is blessed.[335]

In the last question of the last book of the *Reportatio*[336] Ockham rebuts Duns's attempt to demonstrate the same conclusion. To begin with—contrary to Duns—the end cannot necessarily be known through the means, for the means are themselves such not from any natural necessity—to which alone Duns's argument would apply—but from God's free acceptance of them as requisite to the end. Moreover in having no natural evidence for a beatific vision the latter cannot be the means of establishing knowledge of beatific love, which, equally, cannot be known naturally. Nor again in knowing the power can we, as Duns claims, know the end to which it can be ordained, because incomplex knowledge of one thing does not lead to incomplex knowledge of another. Hence however much the will's end could be known, it does not thereby enable its particular end of beatitude to be known.

That applies to Duns's three remaining arguments which all assume that knowledge of a power's relation to its object can be deduced from knowledge of the power's attribute. The latter by the first two arguments consists in the will's perfect tranquility—as a sign of the will's beatific love of God—which according to Duns is possible only if the will is contained either entirely under its object, if it is a common object, or virtually in each of its objects, if there is more than one. In reply Ockham denies that any such common object can be known naturally: that goes also for Duns's final argument that being is man's natural object, the rejection of which we discussed in chapter five. But even if there were such an object it would not follow that the power contained in it would thus enjoy perfect tranquility: for however much the will delighted in God or was in him it could nevertheless both will and refuse many things and so feel sadness which destroys perfect peace. Although it is true that God could by his absolute power suspend the will's activity, that also cannot be proved naturally. Nor again that a power cannot be tranquil unless contained in what is perfect; for the sensitive appetite can

---

[334] J. Koch, 'Neue Aktenstücke', *Recherches* 8 (1936), 187–88, cited *OT*, I, 398.
[335] *Ordinatio*, d. 1, q. 2, 398–400.
[336] *Reportatio*, IV, q. 14, B–C; three of them are also given in the *Ordinatio*, d.1, q. 4, 432–3.

be satisfied in the sexual act without sadness supervening, and the will can follow it, rejecting reason or following erroneous reason. For these different reasons then Ockham concludes, as he does in the first distinction of the *Ordinatio*, that it cannot be sufficiently proved by natural reason that the blessedness which we expect in heaven is possible for us; but must be held on faith.[337]

By the same token it cannot be demonstrated, either, that the will cannot be satisfied and quiescent in anything other than God, or that, in being so, it could not freely want something else and not experience sadness if it did not receive it.[338] As a matter of belief, however, God is the immediate object of fruition, and not as Durandus of St Pourçain held the beatific vision of his essence; for only God is to be loved, as above everything else; and as he is the object of earthly imperfect fruition so he is of perfect fruition in heaven.[339] He alone can possess the will, because no other object excludes all anxiety and sadness; love of God is therefore the most perfect of all acts; although it is finite it cannot be achieved by any other act, from every one of which it is different in kind: only when fruition is inordinate through the intellect's mistaking the highest good, can it have another object than God.[340]

For the same reason Ockham rejects Duns's assertion that the will could without contradiction love, on earth or in heaven, God's essence and not love the divine persons, or love one person and not another. That would only be true if it meant that someone knew that he was loving the divine essence in ignorance that he was also loving a divine person. But not otherwise because everyone is obliged to love the being which is to be loved most; and that means the divine persons as well as the divine essence.[341] They can only differ as concepts, not in what they signify. As we have discussed in the previous chapter, one term—say divine wisdom— can be known without knowing another term—say divine omnipotence—although both stand for the same undifferentiated absolutely simple essence. The discrepancy lies wholly in the variation of the terms.[342] In that sense it can be accepted when Duns says that the divine essence is something conceivable which does not include the concept of relation, (i.e. divine person). But not if relation is treated as something extrinsic to essence from which it is really distinct; for then to argue that therefore only essence can be loved, and not person, or conversely only one person can be loved, or that because someone mistakenly believes that he loves only one person he is really only loving one person, is to commit a fallacy of consequence through a false implication by wrongly inferring what is not contained in the antecedent: thus from the proposition 'He believes that fruition is only of one person' it does not follow that fruition is only of one person, any more than Socrates's belief that Plato does not exist entails the truth of Plato's non-existence. In these and all other comparable cases, the truth consists not in the import of the proposition which is believed to be true but in the belief that the proposition is true.[343] Since, however, all that is true of the divine essence is true of the divine persons and *vice versa*, notwithstanding there can be a concept of one which is not

[337] *Reportatio, ibid.*, B; *Ordinatio, ibid.*, 433–4, 437.   [338] *Ordinatio, ibid.*, 434–6.
[339] *Ibid.*, 439–43, 445–6.   [340] *Ibid.*, 446–7.   [341] *Ibid.*, q. 5, 449–53, 482.
[342] *Ibid.*, 460–1.   [343] *Ibid.*, 462–4; 482–3.

of the other, whoever—assuming it was possible—loved one without the other would do so inordinately. Which is why infidels and heretics who believe that they love God and not the divine persons do not love him ordinately.[344] That they are inseparable and cannot be loved independently is an article of faith which like all others must be held on the authority of the Bible and/or the church or what can be evidently inferred from them. In this case it is open to no other construction.[345]

Now such beatific love is distinct from delight (*delectatio*) and the beatific vision, but not actually separate from either. Ockham is particularly concerned with the relation of love in general (*dilectio* and *amor*) to *delectatio*. He treats it in the *Ordinatio*[346] as well as the *Reportatio*[347] and the additional doubts appended to the last book.[348] In each his main contentions are directed against Peter Aureole's opinion that they are sometimes the same; he also criticises Duns Scotus—as well as enlisting his support—for the inconclusiveness of many of his arguments against Aureole in defence of their common belief that love and *delectatio* are really different. In the *Ordinatio* Ockham gives two formal proofs for their distinctiveness. The first follows from the general principle that whenever one thing can be without another they are really distinct; but love can remain after desire and *delectatio* are destroyed; therefore they are really distinct.[349] The second is that if love were really the same as *delectatio* it would be chiefly as a consequence of what was already loved; but since *delectatio* is not that, no love is really *delectatio*.[350]

In the *Reportatio* Ockham gives a further reason for their separability in the self-love of a bad angel who derives no pleasure from loving himself intensely. There is also another reason, again derived from the example of angels, that surpassing *delectatio* excludes all sadness, and surpassing sadness all delight. Although that appears the most powerful argument for the real distinction between delight and sadness, Ockham regards the previous one as better able to prove that between *delectatio* and love.[351] He directly opposes it to Duns Scotus's argument against Aureole, that there is a proportion between willing and *delectatio* and sadness and refusal, so that as refusal can be without sadness, willing (and love) can be without *delectatio*: thus in Duns's example someone can feel delight in refusing to sin and sadness if sin results; and conversely there can be sadness from loving if it leads to the opposite of what is willed. In each case therefore delight and sadness are separable from love and refusal. For Ockham the defect of this argument is that it does not hold universally but only in those cases where the contrary of what is willed or refused occurs. Hence it does not meet Aureole's contention that in all other instances where what is willed is loved, *delectatio* is the inseparable accompaniment of such love. And similarly with refusal and sadness.[352]   This also represents the first of the six arguments of Duns Scotus rejected by Ockham in the

---

[344] *Ibid.*, 468–9.
[345] *Ibid.*, 455–6, 482–3.   [346] *Ibid.*, q. 3, 403–28.
[347] *Reportatio*, IV, q. 14, B; he also touches upon it in III, q. 14.
[348] *Dubitationes Addititie*, ad quartum, I–U.
[349] *Ordinatio*, q. 3, 407.   [350] *Ibid.*, 413.
[351] *Reportatio*, IV, q. 14, B; also III, q. 14, D.
[352] *Reportatio*, IV, q. 14, B; III, q. 14, D.

additional doubts at the end of book four of the *Reportatio*[353] as inadequate—as this one is—or for containing a false assumption. Of the remainder, three are designed to prove the distinction between love and *delectatio* from the will's power (1) to refuse an object before its advent with the same intensity as after it, so that only change is in the subsequent addition of sadness, which is therefore distinct; (2) to refuse something freely and so without sadness; and (3) to feel pleasure in reflecting upon an act of refusal, and displeasure at any sadness. The fourth concerns God's power to refuse something without sadness, and the fifth assumes that *delectatio* could be the object of an act of love and so distinct from love.

The reason however which Ockham does accept two of Duns's arguments but they do not occur here. They are to be found in the preceding question fourteen, together with the first of the six questions which he rejects, just discussed. They are all stated by Ockham in the third person—in reply to Aureole's opinion; only in the additional doubts does Ockham after discussing Duns's six arguments himself reply directly to Aureole here—having previously done so in the *Ordinatio*—as we shall mention shortly. As to the other two arguments from Duns which Ockham by implication accepts as valid, the first is based upon the distinction between love of desire (by which something is loved because of something else) and love of friendship (where something is loved entirely for itself),[354] both of which will persist in heaven. Now *delectatio* will coexist with each but neither can coexist with the other; therefore *delectatio* is not the same as either since it is separable from both. The second follows from the difference between desire which is of something not possessed and *delectatio*: for as there can be love and *delectatio* over an object which is present to the will, there can be love and desire—without *delectatio*—over what is absent; hence love can be without *delectatio*.[355]

The reason however which Ockham finds more effective than all of Duns's is that of a bad angel's self-love, and he reverts to it in the fifth additional doubt. From this love in contempt of God, as St Augustine wrote in *The City of God*,[356] came the city of the devil, as one of the two cities made by two different loves. Now such love cannot be on account of desire because the act of desire is always principally of something not possessed;[357] but an angel is not itself present to itself as an angel; therefore its self-love does not consist in desire of something else. Nor is it *delectatio*, since there is none in a bad angel, as there is no sadness in a good angel: as Aristotle says, vehement sadness excludes any joy. Accordingly the act by which a bad angel loves himself must be distinct from any other, as an act of friendship, i.e. having no other object to love than himself, which as we have said Ockham regards as the most conclusive of all the arguments for the real difference

---

[353] *Dubitationes Addititie*, 1–Q where (1) Ockham gives a modified version of Duns's argument, but his criticism remains the same.

[354] Sic igitur patet quod Johannes facit octo rationes ad probandum distinctionem inter dilectionem et delectationem, quarum due concludunt et alie sex non concludunt, ut ostensum est prius (*ibid.*, Q).

[355] *Reportatio*, IV, q. 14, B.

[356] *City of God*, Bk. 14, ch. 28.

[357] *Dubitationes Addititie*, 1; also *Reportatio*, III, q. 14, B.

between love and *delectatio*. It is also confirmed from experience; for someone can love God ordinately and more fervently than someone else and yet have less joy than a believer who lacks his devotion. Love therefore is not inseparable from delight.[358]

That brings us to Ockham's own reply to Aureole[359] which, as far as it concerns the nature of *delectatio*,[360] centres upon his refutation of Aureole's claim that fruition and *delectatio* are the same because they derive from the same power—the will—and the same act—of loving—and the same object loved. None of these is true. They are not the same act, because only love is an act, whereas *delectatio* is a passion. Even if it were an act it would still not be true that their object was the same, for either *delectatio*, as an absolute quality following an act of will, does not have an object; or if it does the latter will be love or cognition of the object loved, because *delectatio* is always of something which is possessed. Hence they are not the same. But even if they had the same object, it would still not be true that it was of the same act; for as we have also abundantly seen, there can be diverse acts of will and intellect over the same object, namely of willing and refusing, and intuitive and abstractive knowledge. Ockham similarly rejects Aureole's further contention that love and *delectatio* are both immediately caused by an act of cognition; like Duns he replies that sensory *delectatio* could be immediately from an act of sensation without reference to the intellect, while as a quality in the will it is caused immediately by love and so only has knowledge as a partial cause. Nor conversely do they have the same immediate effect, for the reason already stated that they are not the same: far from both perfecting an action, as Aureole asserts, love is itself an act while *delectatio* as a passion follows love as its cause.[361]

Delectatio then as the accompaniment of love—in contradistinction to a sensory quality or passion where it is caused by sensory apprehension together with the sensory faculty and not by the object apprehended or the sensory appetite[362]—has its immediate cause in an act of will, not the object. The proof is that there can be *delectatio* without an object but not without an act of will: no willing, no *delectatio*.[363] Naturally then they are separable; for someone can be overborne by sadness and nevertheless will and pursue an object without delight; but someone cannot feel either delight or sadness without willing although that cannot be sufficiently proved.[364] Unlike delight in the sensitive appetite, which is immediately caused by sensory cognition, when *delectatio* is from the will, the act of volition comes between intellective cognition and *delectatio* as the immediate cause.[365] That

[358] *Dubitationes Addititie*, I.

[359] *Ibid.*, R–U.

[360] As opposed to countering Aureole's arguments drawn from other matters—for example whether a heavy body is at rest at its centre (*Ordinatio*, d. 1, q. 3, 405–13; *Reportatio*, IV, q. 14, H).

[361] *Dubitationes Addititie*, R–U; also *Reportatio*, III, q. 14, A–D for a fuller account.

[362] *Reportatio*, III, q. 14, A–D.

[363] Ideo dico quod quantum ad istum articulum quod obiectum non est causa immediata delectationis, sed causa immediata delectationis est ipse actus voluntatis (*Ordinatio*, d.1, q. 3, 415).

[364] *Ibid.*, 420.   [365] *Ibid.*, 421; *Reportatio*, IV, q. 14, H.

also explains the difference in the cause of *delectatio* and love: the first is immediately from an act of will, the second immediately from the will, in neither case totally but together with cognition as immediate concause. *Delectatio* accordingly has the same object as an act of will which like *delectatio* is not itself caused by any object.[366] That applies equally to sadness.[367] With the advent of either, desire and revulsion cease; for they are from the absence of something which is not possessed, where delight and sadness come with its possession.[368] Moreover, from the presence of the object the act of desire then becomes an act of friendship in wanting the object for itself.[369]

From that Ockham concludes that *delectatio* exists really in the will—namely as an absolute quality—as opposed to an act of will which in being able to produce a contrary act of sadness could not be the subject of contrary qualities.[370] Ockham does not explain why that should not also disqualify the will, where presumably the contrary qualities of sadness and *delectatio* must both inhere. He does however qualify this conclusion as 'more probable' and accepts that 'perhaps this could not be sufficiently proved', although it can be on Aristotle's principle that substance is susceptible of contraries.[371] Finally love is absolutely more noble than delight, a proposition which can be persuaded from the relation between their opposites, hate and sadness, where hate is worse than sadness. Again, a rational creature is superior to an irrational creature; so therefore is the accident which most distinguishes it from the latter, which is volition rather than delectation. That holds also for the love of friendship as the most perfect accident that can belong to something, as well as for the operations of the intellect and the senses, all of which are more perfect than *delectatio*.[372]

So much for *delectatio*, discussion of which—as a human passion—has unavoidably involved more than its immediate relation to fruition. Over the relation of fruition to a beatific vision Ockham was no less emphatic and much more concise in declaring that there was a real distinction between them. That follows from the rule that whatever comes after something else is separable from what precedes it.[373] Whether the absence of vision from fruition would impair perfect blessedness depends upon which of the different senses of blessedness given by the authorities is accepted. If it is understood as the union of the blessed with the object of his blessedness in perfect joy and peace, blessedness will consist principally in an act of fruition with *delectatio* as its accompaniment, but not cognition. *Delectatio* will then be the natural effect of fruition as its cause. Correspondingly fruition alone would not be perfect blessedness. If however blessedness is taken to mean a certain state of perfection for the blessed as a whole, in the way that felicity is defined, then it includes vision as well as delectation and fruition.[374] Whichever it is, both fruition and vision are caused totally by God; although that cannot be evidently proved it seems more reasonable than its contrary, because each act is the essential reward

---

[366] *Ibid.*, 421.   [367] *Ibid.*, 422.   [368] *Reportatio*, III, q. 14, B–D, P.
[369] *Reportatio*, IV, q. 14, H.   [370] *Ordinatio*, d. 1, q. 3, 422; *Reportatio*, IV, q. 14, H.
[371] *Ordinatio, ibid.*, 424–5.   [372] *Ibid.*, 425–7.
[373] *Reportatio*, IV, q. 14, C.   [374] *Dubitationes Addititie*, ad tertium, H.

conferred by God for preceding acts of merit which a creature could hardly confer upon himself. Nor can he cause, totally or partially, acts of cognition or volition in others.[375]

As to the security which the blessed have, it represents certain knowledge on their part that God wills their perpetual blessedness without interruption. Hence although not the same as either vision or *delectatio*, as a certain reflexive or indirect act which has such knowledge for its object, both fruition and vision are its partial objects. Only God, however, is its total cause. When blessedness is understood in the first sense previously given, as the immediate union with the beatific object, then security is not of its essence, as *delectatio* is not. But it is in the second sense of belonging to the state common to all who are blessed.[376]

Finally there is the nature of the beatific vision itself and of the knowledge its possessors (*comprehensores*) receive. The knowledge of the divine essence itself is, says Ockham, intuitive knowledge as more perfect than complex, and direct as opposed to indirect, since someone can be blessed without reflexive knowledge, which is complex—as we have just discussed in the case of security—or indeed without knowing that he is blessed. It does not enable the blessed to see infinites simultaneously.[377]

The *comprehensor* thus sees God distinctly with nothing concealed because the divine essence has no distinct parts; hence all or nothing of it must be revealed. Such knowledge is not however the most perfect of all by which anything can be known; that is exclusive to God's uncreated knowledge. For that reason too, beatific knowledge is not contained under knowledge of all its predicates, as God's knowledge is; nor is it related to non-beatific knowledge, as God's knowledge is to created knowledge, for unlike God's knowledge it is not infinite.[378] A *comprehensor* can in seeing God also see one creature without seeing another, because whatever is distinct from anything else can be seen separately from anything else.[379] In opposition to Duns however Ockham denies that both God and a creature can be successively seen by the same act of vision: for there cannot be a change from one thing to its contrary without the acquisition or loss of something, absolute or relative. But the beatific created intellect first seeing the divine essence and then a creature by the same act, does change from contradictory to contradictory, namely from non-vision of a creature to vision. It must therefore acquire—since it does not lose—something which it did not have before; and that must be an absolute, because seeing a creature is not a new relation when it is—as Duns avers this is—an act of intrinsically the same kind as the previous act of vision. Moreover, like any act of the will or intellect it has a primary object distinct from its secondary object; the latter will therefore be seen by a separate act, since intuitive knowledge of one thing does not—as we know—lead to intuitive knowledge of another. Accordingly the act by which someone blessed sees God is distinct from that by which he subsequently sees a creature.[380] That applies also to Duns's example of

---

[375] *Reportatio*, IV, q. 13, K.
[376] *Dubitationes Addititie*, Y; *Reportatio*, IV, q. 13, G.
[377] *Reportatio*, IV, q. 13, G–H.   [378] *Ibid.*, B.   [379] *Ibid.*, C.   [380] *Ibid.*

someone who sees something else in a mirror which previously he did not see: it too requires local movement from what was not seen to what is now seen, whether in the image or in the thing seen, and hence a new vision.[381]

In each case, then, when one thing is seen after another they must be seen by separate acts,[382] first, because one can be seen without the other, and second, because the act by which a creature is seen is different in kind from that by which God is seen.[383] However, it seems more reasonable to suppose—contrary to Duns—that God in causing a vision of his essence also causes concurrently vision of one or more other creatures in the same act. Which is how the authorities are to be interpreted when they speak of seeing many creatures in seeing the word caused totally by God. There is then no reason why one creature should be seen rather than another, so that—depending upon God's will—all or none is seen. Since by God's ordained law they are all seen on seeing his essence, it is otiose to posit either separate acts, as Duns does, or to use such analogies as a book or a mirror to describe how they are revealed; it suffices to explain their vision through the vision of his essence received immediately from God as efficient cause.[384]

Fom that it can be said that a *comprehensor* can know another creature immediately and intuitively as well as reflexively in all its facets and that he can do so more perfectly than by ordinary cognition and by the most perfect created knowledge possible; but not under all its predicates, which are not known to a creature as they are to God.[385]

That completes discussion of blessedness. It need only be added that a beatific, like a meritorious, act does not always, in its substance as an act, contradict an act of sin. For as we have seen, not all acts of sin are acts of aversion from God in refusing what God wills; some are rather from wanting other creatures, just as some acts of merit which are acts of conversion to God, in wanting and refusing what God wills someone to will and reject, can coexist with other acts whose demerit concerns creatures.[386] Accordingly their contradiction is not formally in the acts themselves, as it is in acts of willing and refusing what God wills or those which are over the same object. In the same way it is not of their substance that an act of sin and an act of charity are contradictory, but from the extrinsic cause of God's decree by which, in demeriting, grace is destroyed because it no longer

---

[381] *Ibid.*

[382] Ideo sine preiudicio et assertione potest dici quod quando aliquis beatus primo videt deum et postea creaturam quod est necessario alius actus (*ibid.*, D).

[383] *Ibid.*

[384] *Ibid.* (3rd article: letters E and F omitted).

[385] *Ibid.* (4th article: letters E and F omitted).

[386] Ad primum istorum dico quod non omnes actus peccati et actus meritorii repugnant formaliter quantum ad substantiam actus, et eodem modo de actu beatifico; sed aliqui repugnant et aliqui non. Nam per conversionem ad deum vel actum meritorium quo quis convertitur ad deum, non potest intelligi nisi actus volendi quo aliquis diligit deum vel illud quod vult deus eum diligere, vel actus nolendi quo non vult illud quod vult deus eum nolle. Per aversionem a deo intelligitur actus nolendi deum vel aliquid tale . . . Sed talis conversio et aversio non sunt in omni actu peccati, qui multi sunt actus peccati qui sunt actus volendi creaturas . . . Sed isti tres modi non salvantur in omnibus actibus peccati, quia aliquis potest deum velle meritorie et nolle aliquam creaturam, puta Johannem, demeritorie quantum ad primum modum, et

merits conservation.[387] The principle has been throughout that whatever the will can do with charity, it can do without charity—in relation to an act that is to say as opposed to the value God puts upon it; which is why it could avoid all sins of commission by suspending its action or by performing what is commanded of it, such as going to church on Sundays. For acts of both charity and sin are such because any are in the will's power.[388] To the end then—literally of the Commentary on the *Sentences*—Ockham endows a rational being with the capacity to know and want what should be done although the worth of its acts depends upon God. It is volition which God rewards as it is volition which he punishes. For all that Ockham says to the contrary this comes very close to making reason and will morally self-sufficient; for it brings within their reach as natural powers the acts informed, under God's ordained power, by supernaturally infused habits. The discontinuity between them lies not in any intrinsic difference in their operations—which are indistinguishable—but in the value God puts upon them. His acceptance alone differentiates them as extrinsic cause.

It is here that the change which comes with Ockham is principally to be found, in the shift away from an inherently fixed and certain order with clear gradations between the natural and the supernatural and within either. Ockham's theology is founded upon the disjunction between the one fixed point of certainty in God's own nature and the uncertainty of everything else which has its source in his freedom. On the one hand, God himself is outside logical categories; on the other, everything else is subject to the logic of his omnipotence bounded only by noncontradiction (and never divorced from his perfections). That did not make Ockham, as should be clear by now, the destroyer of all system any more than it led him to deny theological and rational truth; but it did introduce a tension between certainty and possibility which is the characteristic of his outlook. While God is to be conceived in almost fundamentalist terms which override the principle of both logic—in the formal distinction between his essence and persons—and creation, in his power to dispense with or supersede the present order, the latter correspondingly can be conceived in quite other terms. Ockham was the first Christian thinker who at once accepted the antinomy between what is and what could be, and systematically explored the asymmetry between them.

Already, as this chapter has witnessed, there are emerging signs of strain in reconciling a fixed moral order with God's decrees or what he could will. That applies not only to the more obvious aspect of God's power to reward acts which are either not performed in a state of grace or which could violate his precepts by his present dispensation; but also to the natural omnipresence of right reason as the guide to moral virtue accessible to all having the use of reason, pagan and Christian alike. It is here that the sovereignty given to acts, above all of volition—and

---

per unum convertitur ad deum et per alium avertitur a deo; et in istis actibus conversio et aversio non repugnant sicut nec isti actus velle deum et nolle creaturam non repugnant (*Dubitationes Addititie*, ad sextum, z).

[387] *Ibid.*
[388] *Ibid.*, AA.

allowing the same natural powers of right doing to pagans as to Christians—blurs the distinction between what is naturally possible and what comes from a divine impulsion. From each side a specifically revealed order is impaired: on one, God is not bound to uphold it; on the other, pagans, given the necessary instruction added to a natural inclination, could observe it as they already do purely natural virtues. It is not apparent than any of these is reconcilable with the others: if God can dispense with moral values they can hardly be implanted into all men as part of their natures without also destroying the present order; if right reason makes moral virtue accessible to all men—and is from God—it is not obvious where the role of revealed truth differentiates the Christian's superior knowledge of what should be done from the pagan if the latter could, as Ockham says, acquire it; and if God rewards the act of will and not the habit, what of the other supernatural virtues? They are all it is true necessary by God's ordained power; but the acts which they inform remain peculiar to the will. We have seen Ockham's reason in all these cases; but they depend upon a fine balance between nature and super-nature not maintained by his successors. Within twenty years scholasticism as a mode of reconciling them was effectively wrecked. Ockham was not the wrecker but he more than anyone pointed to the asymmetries which underminded their cohesion.

PART THREE

The created order

CHAPTER EIGHT

Man

In this last part there is a change of perspective from the principles governing natural and theological truth and what can be concluded from each, to specific facets of creation. They do not, however, stand in a uniform relation to one another; and indeed only where the physical world is concerned—the subject of chapter nine—can what follows be seen as the direct expression of the preceding parts, related as first and second order knowledge. And even there not formally; for while it is true that Ockham devotes separate works and questions to natural phenomena, their treatment—in common with that of most scholastics—is also intermingled with logical and theological questions, such as those on the categories, the eucharist, and supernaturally infused forms. For the other two chapters there is no such order. That on man is largely an extrapolation from previous discussions and does not represent any separate *ex professo* treatment on Ockham's part; his political writings in contrast are self-contained and appeal to largely separate—mainly Franciscan-inspired—principles of political and religious order. His political thinking can only therefore be juxtaposed to his speculative thinking, which temporally it displaces for the last two decades of his life.

The topics of these three concluding chapters thus form a progression in relation to the main core of Ockham's thinking. The first isolates his concept of man from the ubiquitous questions of knowing and willing and sensing which are its extension and presuppose it. It is therefore contained in his epistemological and theological presuppositions. The second is the physical counterpart of Ockham's conceptual identification of being and its categories with individual existence. It therefore represents the application of his ontological principles to nature. The third moves beyond the existing framework to a context of its own. It is therefore an excursus; and where it draws upon other of his concepts does so not as subalternated knowledge taking its principles from the conclusions of another—higher—body of knowledge but as a distinct set of practical and moral imperatives. Thus, whereas the first two chapters can be regarded as an amplification, the third must be understood in its own terms. In each case discussion of them will be comparatively summary, since they either elaborate upon what has already been discussed—as chapters eight and nine do—or are tangential to it, as chapter ten is, with the political principally examined for any connection with the speculative rather than for its own sake.

I THE INTELLECTIVE SOUL AND ITS POWERS

Turning to man, and first his soul, it can be said that Ockham like virtually every Christian thinker accepts St Augustine's view of the soul as formed in the image of the uncreated Trinity. By that Ockham understands the existence of something in man of the same univocal nature as something in God and so similar that, as in any image, the similarity in man leads to recollection of its source in God. Only a rational creature bears such a likeness to God; hence it alone is said to be an image of God.[1] Whereas it has in common with God whatever is univocally common to him and irrational creatures—for example, strength, beauty, goodness—not only as likenesses but also as properties, it has also in addition a community with God exclusive to an intelligent being: namely the power to know, will, have mercy, justice, wisdom, and so on.[2] This unique relation with God Ockham takes to be proof of a rational creature's special likeness to him beyond that of anything else. Indeed it is so close that if—as they are not—their similarities were accidents in both God and man, the latter's substance formed in the image of the accidents in God would be of the same kind as his—as a statue of Hercules owes its likeness to the accidents of colour, figure, and so on in Hercules. The image of God in a rational creature would then lead as truly to a recollection of God as a statue of Hercules leads to a recollection of Hercules.[3] The fault in this analogy is that, as we have discussed in the first chapter, according to Ockham such recollection depends upon preceding habitual knowledge; for only if Hercules is already known can we know that it is a statue of Hercules and not of someone else.[4] But God cannot himself be known; so there can be no habitual knowledge of him, regardless of the similarity between hypothetical accidents in God and creatures.

The point of the comparison however remains. More specifically, the soul's likeness to God is contained imperfectly in the soul's own substance as the source of his image; it is perfected and completed through the soul's conjunction with

[1] Circa primum dico quod—cum pateat ex predictis quod imago, secundum quod invenitur in creaturis, dicitur propter conformitatem alicuius eiusdem rationis in illo cuius est imago et in imagine, quod natum est ducere in recordationem illius cuius est imago—illa creatura maxime proprie dicetur imago dei que habet aliquid deo simillium, ita quod est precise commune univocum deo et illi creature; et quia creatura rationalis est huiusmodi, ideo ipsa sola dicetur imago dei (*Ordinatio*, d. 3, q. 10, 555).

[2] *Ibid.*, 555–6.

[3] *Ibid.*, 556–7.

[4] E.g. Per experientiam enim patet quod si aliquis nullam penitus habeat cognitionem de Hercule, si videat statuam Herculis, non plus cogitabit de Hercule quam de Sorte. Si autem primo videat Herculem et retineat notitiam Herculis, et postea videat statuam sibi similem quantum ad aliqua accidentia exteriora, virtute illius visionis statute, etiam posito quod nunquam prius eam vidisset, recordabitur de Hercule . . . *ibid.*, qq. 545).

Ockham does add here (545–6) that two things very similar can mutually represent one another, because either can indifferently cause recollection of the other, for example recollecting Socrates, already known habitually, in coming to know Plato. But that cannot apply to God who cannot become known naturally.

its acts of knowing and willing.[5] The first is confirmed by St Augustine's statement in *De Trinitate* that it is as the image of God that the soul can receive him and participate in him.[6] That can be achieved by its substance alone when understood in the sense of the soul itself possessing God or being able to do so; but not when its circumstances also connote its acts of knowing and willing as the condition of its action. That those acts also perfect it follows, because the image of God is perfected by that which enables the soul to be capable of him: namely by knowing and willing. That too is confirmed by St Augustine's words that if man had served God in the good, i.e. the image, in which God had created him, he would always have praised God with his lips as well as his tongue. Which can only be taken to mean that something has been lost in the soul as a result of sin; and that can only be an accident, namely the act of knowing or willing which previously perfected its substance.[7]

Accordingly the complete image of God consists in the soul's substance and its two acts of knowing and willing, and can also be in the conjunction of the soul's substance with the habits of its two acts.[8] As a natural trinity its operations have a parallel order to that of the uncreated Trinity. Thus as, in God, the father's fecundity leads to the generation of the son and the holy spirit, communicating to the son the fecundity by which both father and son produce the holy spirit, so from the fecundity of the soul's substance come the acts of knowing and willing, the first produced immediately by the soul, the second produced by the soul together with the act of knowing. Hence just as in the divine nature the son is from one principle and the holy spirit is from two, so correspondingly in the created trinity the act of knowing has one cause and the act of willing two. From that it can be seen how the soul as God's image is able in a certain manner to represent the divine persons in their order and origin.[9]

Ockham reinforces this unexceptionably Augustinian statement with further citations from St Augustine in replying to subsequent *dubia*. In particular he meets the objection that soul's substance, alone and undifferentiated, cannot be the image of God because, among other reasons, St Augustine employs terms standing for indistinct things to describe its nature as an image: namely the two trinities of mind–knowledge–love, and memory–understanding–will. Ockham's reply is that, to begin with, St Augustine was speaking of a perfect image; but even so, in order to establish some conformity between the parts of the soul and the divine persons, he was treating these terms connotatively. They all therefore signify the same substance of the soul of which they are thus truly affirmed, and also consignify its secondary acts. Hence they are not synonyms but they each denote something common: by 'mind', the soul's own substance; by 'knowledge', the same sub-

---

[5] *Ibid.*, q. 10, 557.

[6] *Ibid.*; *De Trinitate*, XIV, ch. 8.

[7] *Ordinatio*, *ibid.*, 557–8.

[8] Ideo dico quod completa ratio imaginis consistit in ipsa substantia anime et duobus actibus, scilicet actu intelligendi et volendi, et etiam potest consistere in ipsa substantia anime in duobus habitibus correspondentibus ipsis actibus (*ibid.*, 558–9).

[9] *Ibid.*, 559.

stance connoting the word as a secondary act which the soul's substance can produce; by 'love', again the same substance, connoting an act of willing what the substance and the word can produce; and so on.[10] Here, too, then, as we have seen frequently in chapter six, Ockham's so-called nominalism is able to reconcile the paradoxes of revealed truth by its very attention to the differences among terms. The refusal to multiply beyond necessity was not destructive of faith or knowledge but of systems which failed to identify their terms.

As to the substance of the soul itself no further distinction is needed for it to be an imperfect image of God: even alone, without its acts of knowing or willing to perfect it, it still has a greater similarity to God than any other creature, and in some way the image of both the divine essence and the divine persons. For while there is a distinction between the persons, their identity with the divine essence is as great as that of the soul's substance with itself.[11]

Ockham thus denies any distinction within the soul itself, confining it to its secondary and subsequent acts of knowing and willing.[12] He holds this view in opposition to what he calls the common opinion that the soul's own powers or faculties, of understanding, memory and will, are themselves the parts which together constitute the complete image of the uncreated Trinity. The argument for this conclusion is that it is through these powers that the soul has the attributes of greater consubstantiality, perpetuity and conformity which characterise an image. His retort is that if that were true and a distinction in its source was the reason for a distinction in the image, there would then be a real distinction between these powers—which there is not—to correspond to the real distinction among the divine persons.[13]

It is on this basis of the soul's indivisibility that Ockham considers in the *Reportatio* its powers. Before turning there we must indicate briefly in what sense he understands that there is a vestige of the Trinity in every creature. Much of his discussion concerns the similarities and differences between vestige and image. They have in common first that they differ from that whose vestige or image they are. Second, that they lead to knowledge of it: not immediate incomplex knowledge— no incomplex knowledge of one thing as we know gives incomplex knowledge of another—but as partial cause of its recollection; and for that as we remarked earlier there has to be prior habitual knowledge of what is recollected, as the recollection of Hercules from his statue depends upon having previously known Hercules. Third, when two objects are perfectly alike neither a vestige nor an image represents one more than another. Hence it is false to say, as Giles of Rome and Duns Scotus do, that an image represents an object in its individuality and a vestige represents it in its universality.[14]

---

[10] *Ibid.*, 562–3, 564–5.

[11] *Ibid.*, 561–2.

[12] Nulla est distinctio previa in ipsa substantia anime ante distinctionem actuum secondorum productorum; igitur non sunt ibi talia tria [sc. intelligentia, memoria, voluntas] que represent divinas personas (*ibid.*, 554–5). Also *Reportatio* IV, q. 2, K.

[13] *Ibid.*

[14] *Ibid.*, q. 9, 544–7.

Where they differ is first in their cause and second in the knowledge of it which they can give. A vestige is always caused by that of which it is a vestige, but an image is not, as the image of Hercules can be caused by something other than Hercules. A vestige leads not only to recollection of what it represents but also to contingent knowledge of it, so that on seeing the footprint of an ox, in addition to recalling an ox—known habitually—we can also say that an ox has passed here. Such knowledge is only contingent or founded upon belief since we can be mistaken over the source: the ox's print could have come from a severed foot. An image allows no such inference because it is not necessarily caused by what it represents.[15]

This example of a vestige corresponds to its strictest sense as the impress of a part which can lead to recollection of the whole; strictly it means the impress of something complete which is absent like that of a seal upon wax by which it can be recalled; and in its broad sense, the effect left by a cause of a species or genus the existence of which can be affirmed in a contingent proposition: for example, from smoke that there is or has been fire.[16]

So far as the relation of creatures to God is concerned, any creature can be said to be in some way a vestige of the uncreated Trinity through having in common certain properties. These when abstracted from a creature can lead to recollection of their counterpart in God, as the concept of created beauty can lead to that of divine beauty; and from that to the contingent truth that God is the cause of what exists corporeally in creatures.[17] Hence wherever properties are univocally predicable of God and creatures there can be said to be a vestige of God. Not every quality and accident is therefore included. Sometimes a vestige, as St Augustine shows, consists in a substance and distinct accident proper to each of the divine persons; sometimes in one thing which can have different connotations or common concepts leading to recollection of their source in God. By this second mode every creature—including presumably man's soul which does not have distinct accidents—can be said to be a vestige of God; but not by the first mode since not every creature has diverse accidents.[18] There is no need then for each vestige to contain three distinct qualities in order to recall the uncreated trinity; it suffices for it to lead to knowledge appropriate to the three persons.[19] As we have already discussed, that cannot be actual knowledge since it would presuppose previous habitual knowledge of the Trinity which is naturally unattainable.[20]

Ockham's treatment of the soul's powers is parallel to that of the divine attributes: just as he denies any real distinction between intellect and will, or goodness and wisdom in God so he does in man; and on the same grounds that they all connote the same indivisible substance. What are called intellect and will, in both God and man, are merely words or concepts for the same being—the divine essence or the human soul—acting in diverse ways, as we have already indicated

---

[15] *Ibid.*, 547–8.   [16] *Ibid.*, 548–9.   [17] *Ibid.*, 549–50.
[18] *Ibid.*, 550–1.   [19] *Ibid.*, 551.

[20] Ad aliud patet quod vestigium nunquam dicit in notitiam illius cuius est nisi presupposita notitia habituali ipsius, et ideo trinitas personarum, cum non precognoscatur creature, quamvis creatura non duceret in notitiam trinitatis de facto, adhuc posset dici vestigium trinitatis (*ibid.*).

in his glossing of St Augustine's trinities of mind, knowledge and love, and memory, understanding and will.

In the *Reportatio*, book two, question twenty-four, he exhibits the diverse ways in which intellect and will can be understood as nominal definitions and connotative terms, differing as words and operations but never as distinct powers either from one another or from the soul's substance. Coming to the discussion out of context it could well appear as another exercise in logical virtuosity for which Ockham has been accused of devaluing theology. But within the perspective traced in the preceding two chapters it can readily be seen as a further example of bringing logic to the aid of a defined theological standpoint. A standpoint moreover which is almost stark in its eschewal of philosophical impedimenta. Thus Ockham begins by rejecting three opinions, on the soul's powers:[21] that they are absolute accidents—i.e. qualities—superadded to the soul's essence; that they represent its relations to its different objects but add nothing distinct to it; and that they are really the same as one another and the soul's substance but differ formally from the latter as absolutes contained virtually in the soul. Ockham rejects the last two opinions—of Henry of Ghent and Duns Scotus—by the familiar arguments for disposing of unnecessary relations and untenable distinctions: the latter can only be posited where some thing or things contained in one thing is not contained in another, which as we need not discuss further, means that there must be either a real distinction or none (whether or not there is a mental distinction). There is no distinction in this case because the soul's powers are really the same as the soul. Nor is there any relation, mental or real between its powers and their objects: it cannot be one of reason because such a relation depends upon the mind's activity in comparing what already exists; hence the soul's powers exist independently of it. Equally it cannot be a real relation because according to this opinion that entails a third term as something which really exists in addition to the soul and its powers; but God can enable the soul to know and will without any object in the world; therefore knowing and willing do not imply any relation superadded to the soul.

The first opinion is more extensive and from Ockham's standpoint full of false assumptions which he rejects. These stated summarily are that power and activity are extrinsic to all being other than God; that they belong to the separate category of accident; that as the soul is not always in act its operations are potential and thus accidental, because where an essence is the principle of its operations they are always actual; that some actions are too diverse to be from the same principle but require a corporeal organ and that applies to the soul not all of whose operation are from its essence; that natural powers such as those of the soul belong to the category of quality and so are accidents; that the same thing cannot be the principle or recipient of diverse and contrary forms but requires additional absolute accidents as the soul does; that Averroes always attributes accident to substance and that includes its operations which are therefore accidents; and finally that accidents which are transitory or in flux, as knowing and willing are, are received into their substance by means of a permanent accident.

[21] *Reportatio*, II, q. 24, B–I.

The opinion epitomises the elaborate mesh of *a priori* metaphysical reasoning which had come to govern scholastic thinking. Even from this brief resumé the dependence upon assumptions, such as that operation and being are distinct, is striking. In this first argument for example it runs as follows: as being is to essence, so operation is to power; therefore by transposition, as being is to operation, essence is to power. But only in God are being and operation the same (as being and essence are the same); therefore they are distinct in everything else. Ockham in combating such modes of reasoning was attempting to restore what he regarded as the correct order of realities, namely the realisation that being, essence, power, operation, and so on, were terms which taken significantly all refer to an individual thing and not distinct entities corresponding to each, as we have amply considered in chapters three and four. It is in their diversity as terms that their difference lies: 'being' is equivocal, as either a univocal transcendental term predicable of all that is, or connoted by the categories corresponding to different facets of individual existence; 'essence' has the same signification as being (to be), but, as a noun, cannot act as a copula; it therefore has a different function as a term but not a different meaning. It is accordingly groundless to treat essence as indifferent to being, or being as accidental to essence; and correspondingly with power and operation. At the same time, since all being is individual being, its attributes must be established by an appeal to experience. Consequently between the logic of individual signification and the ontology of individual existence there was not place in Ockham's outlook for the metaphysical abstractions which had interposed themselves to the detriment of both.

More specifically he met these eight arguments principally by denying their assumptions or conclusions. The first is falsely founded, however operations is understood, whether as something produced by a principle or itself the principle of producing something or as a relation denoting the production of something: for in the first sense they are not the same in God; by the second they are the same in both God and creatures; and by the third, if as this opinion holds the relation is mental, they are the same in neither. Similarly, in reply to the second argument, power if taken as an attribute or difference of being, belongs to the same category as act, indeed they are the same; alternatively if it is taken as part of being, it is then active or passive and cannot in either aspect be regarded as an accident: in the first because this opinion concedes that an active power acts essentially; in the second because if there were no substance which was immediately receptive of the act there would be an infinite regress. Even if however an act were in the soul through an accident (i.e. if the soul's powers producing it were accidents) it would still be unwarranted to posit as many accidents as there are such acts, because knowing and willing can no less both belong to the same immediate subject than two sensible qualities of different kinds, such as whiteness and sweetness in milk, neither of which is received in the other since they are separable. That also answers the fifth argument: otherwise there would be as many powers of knowing as acts of knowing. The fourth argument, over the difference between organic and non-organic powers, is irrelevant, and the sixth confuted by the case of first matter which is the immediate principle of many diverse forms; correspondingly the same form can be generated by many diverse things without being determined by diverse absolutes. As to Averroes's statement, its meaning is that an act is always to be attributed to a substance as its subject but not necessarily as efficient or final cause. Finally a transitory accident can be received immediately into a substance: for example that of an angel which in being moved from place to place immediately receives movement as a transitory accident. That can also be said of quantity when condensed or rarefied. In fact this mode of treating knowing and willing as transitory accidents is unfounded and no more applicable to them than to a stone or an angel. Nor even if it were, and as fluxible accidents they only received their being through a fixed accident, it would again not follow that there were as many accidents in that which received them as there were transitory accidents.

In all these counter-arguments, then, Ockham bases himself not upon abstract metaphysical principle but upon definitions and principles drawn from actual being.

The difference in his approach is further illustrated in the explanation of his own position, that there is no distinction of any kind between the soul and its powers and the powers themselves, which not uncharacteristically he associates with the first part of Duns Scotus's opinion.[22] The arguments are mainly on a logical plane, beginning with the two ways in which a power can be defined. The first is as a total description expressed in a nominal definition; the second consists in what is denominated by the term power. By the first mode intellect and will are distinguished, for the definition of each contains what is not included in the other: that of intellect is 'the soul able to know'; that of will is 'the soul able to will'. These descriptions are really distinct as both words and concepts but only partially as things, because on the one hand, it is the same being which is knowing and willing but on the other, knowing and willing are really distinct acts. By the second mode, as what is connoted by power, intellect and will, they are no more distinguished than God is distinguished from God or Socrates from Socrates.

Here power stands for the soul's substance able to perform diverse acts, on account of which it has diverse denominations; it is intellect as it produces or can produce acts of knowing; and will as it produces or can produce acts of willing. The same holds for God. His power is called creative or providential or predestinatory, by an extrinsic denomination, from its effects among creatures, but it is one and the same in God. Accordingly when intellect and will are taken for what is denoted by them they are entirely indistinct from one another. If they were distinct that could only be because of either diverse acts or diverse modes of eliciting them. It cannot be diverse acts since there would then be as many different powers as acts. But in fact there are many different acts of knowing which are of different species or genera, for example those between knowing a man and knowing an ass or a man and a stone; and yet all the acts of knowing belong to the same

---

[22] Ideo dico tenendo primam partem opinionem Johannis, licet eam non teneat quod potentie anime de quibus loquimur in proposito, scilicet intellectus et voluntas, non loquendo de potentiis sensitivis nunc . . . sunt idem realiter inter se et cum essentia anime (ibid., κ). Also Ordinatio, d. 13, q. 1, 1; Reportatio, IV, q. 2, κ).

genus of quality. Hence they presuppose no distinction in the power which produces them. Nor is there any distinction from different modes of acting, because the same principle can act both necessarily and freely over different objects, as the divine will acts necessarily towards the holy spirit and freely in relation to creatures. That can also happen among creatures where the will is able to produce freely and contingently according to its own volition and to regard another creature's volition as necessary and not be impeded.

From that if follows that when the authorities talk of the soul's 'giving rise' to its powers and declare that they 'flow from it' and are its 'properties', they are to be understood in the first sense of power as a nominal definition of intellect or will; but never in the second sense when what they describe is inseparably one and the same.[23]

A power can also be regarded as an attribute if taken for a connotative term consignifying an act produced by the soul as its accident and attribute, as opposed merely to standing for an accident where its meaning either by the first or second essential mode is too limited to embrace the full signification of the term power. As a connotative term or concept however, power can be affirmed of the soul by the second essential mode—where power consignifies the soul and its power to act— in a possible proposition or its equivalent.[24] For example, that the soul is able to know or to will, or is intellective or volitional. Where the same completely un-differentiated nature is made the principle of both knowing and willing, the will can then be said to know by the intellect as well as by the will. But where each is treated essentially as the efficient cause of its own acts then each is distinct: the will wills by the will and the intellect knows by the intellect whether by the first or second essential mode. By the first, something cannot be denoted by the predicate which is not denoted by the subject. By the second, something cannot be the attribute of what it does not connote. Thus by the first essential mode the will can be volitional but not intellective, because intellective does not define the will; and correspondingly the intellect can be intellective but not volitional. By the second essential mode the soul can be both volitional and intellective because it is included in the nominal definition of both, as able to have volition or intellection; but neither of these can be the attribute of the other because the total meaning of one does not include the total meaning of the other.[25]

The other sayings of the the authorities about the soul can be similarly resolved by recourse to these different distinctions. When it is said to have a superior and an inferior part, all, including Ockham's opponents, agree with St Augustine that that is not to be taken literally; rather the terms 'superior' and 'inferior' connote

---

[23] *Reportatio*, II, q. 24, K.

[24] *Ibid.*, L.

[25] Eodem modo passio potest accipi vel pro aliquo accidente inherente subiecto vel pro aliquo conceptu connotativo. Primo modo potentia non est passio quantum ad totale suum significatum, et hoc sive accipitur primo modo sive secundo modo, quia essentia anime est de significato totali potentie. Sed accipiendo potentiam secundo modo sic est passio, quia hoc nomen potentia vel conceptus connotat aliquid quod est vere passio et accidens inherens, puta actum elicitum ab anima, qui actus potest dici vere passio et predicari secundo modo dicendi per se de anima in propositione de possibili formaliter vel equivalenter (*ibid.*, M).

the soul's different activities in turning towards the spiritual or the temporal and signify the same undivided being.[26] That also goes for the will's greater nobility than the intellect; when will denotes the same principle of volition and cognition, one cannot be superior to the other since they are entirely the same. But in its nominal definition as that by which the soul wills, the will is nobler than the intellect because it is nobler to love than to know. In this sense, too, the intellect can be said to be prior to the will; for an act of knowing connoted by the intellect is a partial efficient cause of an act of willing connoted by the will. The first can be without the second but not the converse, though priority does not imply any superiority: even when applied to the will it means not the will itself as a power but its acts and habits of loving.[27] The intellective soul is however superior to the sensitive soul from which, as we shall see shortly, it is really distinct, unlike the active and possible intellects. The latter are merely names or concepts connoting the same thing diversely as we have said in an earlier chapter: the active intellect signifies the soul and consignifies the knowledge actively coming from the soul; the possible intellect signifies the same soul, connoting the knowledge received in the soul; but the cause and the recipient of the knowledge are entirely the same. Nor, as we have also mentioned before, does the active intellect have any such role as purifying or illuminating the images presented to the soul just as it is not confined to universal abstractive knowledge.[28]

Now although it can be accepted that the intellective soul is the body's form, that the will is free and the intellect is active, none of these can be proved by reason. So far as the soul is concerned, there is nothing to say that by which we know and will is the intellective soul; for just as we attribute qualities to things idiomatically, for example calling a man who rows a rower, so we could say that the body in knowing and willing has a motor, without also positing it as the body's form. By natural reason and experience, then, the intellective soul can be regarded as a motor and not as a form.[29] That can also be persuaded.[30] But it remains a matter of belief that the soul is the body's form and an immaterial and incorruptible substance inhering whole in every part of it, which cannot be demonstrated by natural reason and experience, regardless of Aristotle.[31] Naturally, we have experience only of knowing and willing and similar acts; and from that there can be a demonstration that the body has a material and extended form, but no other kind. Such a demonstration runs as follows: Every composite being which differs as a species from another composite being does so either totally or in part; but man differs as a species from an ass, and not totally because they each have matter of the same kind. Therefore they differ by a form. From the standpoint

---

[26] Ibid., O.   [27] Ibid., P.   [28] Ibid., P–Q.
[29] Quodlibet I, q. 10.   [30] Quodlibet I, q. 11.
[31] Circa secundum articulum dico quod intelligendo per animam intellectivam formam immaterialem incorruptibilem que tota est in toto et tota in qualibet parte, non potest sciri evidenter per rationem vel experientiam quod talis forma sit in nobis nec quod intelligere talis substantie proprium sit in nobis, nec quod talis anima sit forma corporis. Quicquid de hoc senserit Aristoteles no curo, quia ubique dubitative videtur loqui. Sed ista tria solum fide tenemus (ibid., q. 10).

of faith too, according to which the intellective soul inheres in man as an immaterial and indestructible form, it is more reasonable to treat it as the body's form than solely as a motor; especially since in the latter capacity both of its functions of moving the body locally or by alteration could be achieved without it, either by the soul as its form or by corporeal agents.[32] That however raises the problems of how the soul can be said to be entire in every part of the body without being either separated from itself in the body's separate parts or being engaged in contradictory activities or informing more than one material being, as well as seeming to contradict experience.[33] To begin with, the reason that the soul must be wholly in every part of the body is that as an immaterial form without extension it must be entire wherever it is; if it were not therefore in every part of the body it could not be the form of every part, which it is. That does not however mean that it would then be simultaneously moved or quiescent, if a foot was moved but a hand remained still, since the soul can accidentally do both. Nor could it inform two discontinuous material beings save by God's absolute power. Conversely if a part of the body were severed from the rest, the soul could not, as objected, either return to the rest of the body or be destroyed; it would cease to be where it was before, as Christ's body in the eucharist ceases to be in the host when the bread and the wine are destroyed, and an angel ceases to be in a place when part of its place is no longer there. Finally it is not true to say, as a further objection does, that we experience knowing more in the head than in the feet any more than we experience seeing colour more in the eye than in the hand; in each case we are rather aware of assistance or less impediment in the head or the eye than in the feet or hands. Accordingly on the assumption—held by faith—that the soul is the immaterial form of the body, the implication that it must be present wholly throughout the body can be upheld by reason.[34]

Reason can also refute Averroes's doctrine of a single intellect for all mankind, on the grounds that it is impossible for one and the same intellect simultaneously to know and not know, love and hate, assent and dissent—as different individuals do—since these are contradictories which cannot coexist in the same subject. Hence they cannot be reconciled by arguing as Averroes does that thay are contingently caused by different images joined to the intellect, because it is from these images that such knowledge is received into the intellect. They would still therefore inhere in it as contradictories.[35] There is, then, an individual intellect in every man although reason cannot prove the spiritual nature of the soul to which it belongs.

That applies also to the intellect's activity, for which there is no natural proof by reason alone, excluding the authority of the saints and philosophers.[36] In

---

[32] Ibid.

[33] Quodlibet II, q. 12.

[34] Ibid.; the third and fourth difficulties are raised in q. 10, but their solution is postponed to q. 12.

[35] Quodlibet I, q. 11.

[36] Sciendum est quod circumscripta omnium sanctorum auctoritate et philosophorum propter nullam rationem necessario concludentem oportet ponere intellectum activum sed solum passivum (Reportatio, II, q. 25, A).

confirmation Ockham takes twenty-one opinions of Duns Scotus designed to demonstrate the intellect's activity and finds them all wanting. They are of interest in the present context for crystallising Ockham's view of the relation between will and intellect, as a brief resumé of the more germane replies may show. Of these the first bears directly upon Ockham's earlier remark that the intellect's priority over the will in an act of willing does not imply its greater perfection. Only a total cause is more perfect than its effect, and since God is partial cause in every created effect, an act of knowing, contrary to Duns, is not itself more perfect than what is known.[37]

Ockham's central argument however is that the intellect as a natural—i.e. necessary—cause can only act necessarily; hence regardless of whether it is active or passive, no change in what is known or how it is known can be ascribed to the intellect. For once it knows it will continue to know in the same way unless circumstances change; and if these are not the result of some natural impediment, or the loss of something which was previously present, they must be due to another agent which decides either to know or not to know or to know differently or more intensely or to accept or reject what is known: namely the will. In consequence all changes in the mode of knowing which are not merely natural are due to the will either wanting or refusing to know. For that reason none of Duns's arguments prove the activity of the intellect, for they could equally rest on the assumption that the intellect was passive. Thus to begin with, if an object were present equally at one time and another, and the intellect were active it would know the object present in the same way throughout; its activity cannot therefore explain the variation in knowing which must be due to the will freely wanting to know by a new act. The will is thus partial cause of such an act.[38]

Similarly an act of forming a true or false proposition—by composition or division—cannot be explained by the activity of the intellect: for if the intellect were alone the cause, it could as a natural agent indifferently compose or divide a true or false or impossible or affirmative or negative proposition; and if it caused a true proposition it could not cause a false one. The will must therefore concur in its composition and division; for although it is not contrary to experience to apprehend contrary propositions, it is contrary to experience and contradictory to assent to each. Accordingly the will is the cause why one proposition is formed as true rather than false or affirmative as opposed to negative.[39] That applies to assent to propositions which have been formed. On the one hand, wherever a proposition is self-evident or immediately known through its terms it is known independently of the intellect's activity. On the other hand, when a proposition is not immediately evident, but at first doubtful or neutral, something beyond the intellect is required to cause assent to its truth or falsity.

Neither a self-evident nor an immediate contingent proposition requires for the intellect's assent more than immediate knowledge of the terms and of the

[37] *Ibid.*, B.
[38] *Ibid.*, ad 7m H.
[39] *Ibid.*, ad 8m, H–K.

proposition which they form: assent to the first is produced necessarily (for example to the proposition that all forms of the same nature can have effects of the same nature); to the second, from intuitive experience of the terms (that all heat is heat-giving). Thus, upon knowing either, the intellect's assent follows. Where a proposition is not however immediately evident it is known either from a preceding proposition as its middle, giving a necessary or probable or sophistical conclusion according to the status of the premises, to which the intellect will give its appropriate assent; or it will be known on authority or because the will decides that it should be known and assented to.[40] Since all syllogising is itself the work of the will, in wanting to order propositions according to a certain figure and mode,[41] the will is partial cause of all inferential knowledge, as it is of the formation of propositions. Similarly with relations of reason, if they really existed, and reflexive acts. If the intellect, not the will, were their cause, every term and many things would be naturally compared as relations of reason and the intellect would reflect upon whatever it knew. Neither is true, as experience shows. Both are the result of the will wanting to compare or reflect upon what is known immediately; they are therefore in the power of the person who does so, which they would not be if the intellect were their active cause.[42] In all these cases then the will's activity has preceding cognition as partial cause: for nothing is loved unless it is first known; but something can be known and not loved or refused. For that reason knowing can be called the first activity of the intellective soul.[43]

The natural priority of the intellect as partial cause also explains why it cannot be attributed as the reason for variations in the intensity of either intellective or sensitive acts; for as a natural cause it would always act to its maximum capacity and in the same degree. A more or less intense act is therefore from the will as partial cause; and that can be interpreted either as the displacement of the previous act by a new act or, as seems more reasonable, the same act intensified or weakened. The distinction is accordingly between the initial act of cognition caused by the object and the subsequent more or less intense act caused by the object together with the will; object and will thus act together in the same act as partial causes of the second act of cognition. That the latter depends upon a new act of volition follows, because it involves a change from one contradiction to another, namely from non-intense to more—or less—intense, which cannot be explained without an act of will since the object and the intellect alone as natural agents do not suffice to cause it. In every such case, then, it is the will, in willing to continue an act and to know it more or less perfectly, which is responsible for its modification. Volition can therefore be held to be the immediate cause of renewed cognition, sensitive or intellective, on the principle that the effect sufficiently depends upon the cause; and without the will there can be no such cognition.[44]

It is also partial cause of an act of faith acquired not from belief in a preceding proposition—when assent is independent of the activity of both intellect and will— but where a proposition and its terms are known but not evidently. Assent then

[40] *Ibid.*, ad 9m, K–L.   [41] *Ibid.*, ad 11m, N.   [42] *Ibid.*, ad 13m, 14m, 15m, P–R.
[43] *Ibid.*, ad 16m, s.   [44] *Ibid.*, ad 17m and 18m, T–U.

rests with the will in choosing to believe what it knows, however inevident; for it is the characteristic of belief that it is of what is inevident. As St Augustine said, while man can refuse other things, he can believe only if he wills. Hence first assent to a proposition which is believed cannot be due to the intellect; for given such knowledge together with an act of will, and assent necessarily follows regardless of the intellect's activity; but given the latter without an act of will, and there can never be assent. Moreover assent and evidence are indistinguishable when they are over the same object known evidently, i.e. by incomplex knowledge of the terms and their proposition, or from evident knowledge derived from a demonstration *quia* or *propter quid*, or from intuitive knowledge only of the extremes. In none of these cases is the act of assent distinct from what is known evidently. They are however distinguished as more and less universal, because assent is included under evident assent, but evident assent is not included under assent. Hence someone can assent without assenting evidently, as already said.[45]

Finally for the same reasons the will is the cause of habitual knowledge of an object which is absent; for volition alone is the sufficient reason why such an object is known habitually at one time and not another,[46] as we discussed in chapter one over second abstractive knowledge and memory.

By natural reason then the attempt to prove the intellect's activity leads to the impasse that it would negate all other cognitive activity; for as a natural agent, the intellect, as also an active agent, would make all cognition invariable, with no end to what was known in the beginning and no beginning for what was known subsequently and no variations in how it was known. All of which as we have seen is against experience. But while naturally that precludes treating the intellect as an active cause, Ockham nevertheless holds to the opposite view that it is active, on the authority of the theologicans and philosophers, whose meaning like that of Aristotle in the third book of *De Anima* can only be saved by accepting an active intellect.[47]

Finally there is the will's freedom. That too cannot be proved, because every reason seeking to show that the will can indifferently and contingently cause or not cause an effect is as doubtful and as unknown as—if not more unknown than—the conclusion. But its freedom can be known evidently from experience, since however much reason may dictate what is to be done the will of anyone can nevertheless accept or reject it.[48] Assuming that the will is free, it can then be

---

[45] *Ibid.*, ad 20ᵐ, x–y.

[46] *Ibid.*, ad 21ᵐ, AA.

[47] Per predicta potest haberi occasio respondendi ad omnia argumenta que probant activitatem intellectus. Tamen tenco oppositum propter sanctorum auctoritates et philosophorum que non possunt salvari sine activitate intellectus, sicut patet de intellectu agente 3° *De Amina* (*ibid.*, AA).

[48] Circa secundum sunt due difficultates Prima est utrum possit probari sufficienter quod voluntas sit libera . . . Circa primum dubium dico quod non potest probari per aliquam rationem, quia omnis ratio probans accipit eque dubia et eque ignotum conclusioni vel ignotius. Potest tamen evidenter cognosci per experientiam, per hoc quod homo experitur quod quantumcumque ratio dictet aliquid, potest tamen voluntas hoc velle vel nolle (*Quodlibet* 1, q. 16).

proved that it is an active power; for whenever any active natural power is sufficiently close to its recipient and sufficiently disposed to act upon it, with no impediment, its action follows necessarily; but the will is also sufficiently disposed
to act, and is unimpeded, since there is nothing in the will to contradict its acting
and nothing else required for it; hence the will too is an active power. But a free
one; and in being free it does not need an extrinsic cause to reduce it from potentiality to act. It can accordingly know an object and yet choose for a time not to
act upon it, as it can equally freely then choose to act.[49]

Finally only by accepting the existence of free will can chance and fortune be
explained; for if everything other than the will acts necessarily, whatever is not
caused by the will is inevitable and unimpedible, both of which exclude chance and
fortune. Fortune can only occur from a free agent acting either with a natural
agent or another free agent, in each case beyond the agent's intention: thus someone
digging can unintentionally discover a fortune, or in going to the market place
to meet a friend be unexpectedly accosted by a creditor. Chance can arise from the
concurrence of natural causes, but always partially through a free cause, for
example if someone loads a horse with cloth and the horse carried it to some grass
where there is a fire which burns the cloth, that is by chance through an act of
free will.[50]

Not all the will's acts are wholly in its power. To begin with, it can do nothing
without God as partial cause in all that it does, although nothing created can
absolutely impede it.[51] Secondly, it is only free in relation to acts which it can
produce absolutely; that excludes many of its acts which are the result of a preceding habit, as antecedent partial cause, whether naturally acquired or supernaturally infused. Such acts are not strictly in its power, which is why the doctors
excuse from sin an act of concupiscence caused from a concupiscent habit outside
the will's control.[52] That constitutes a very big qualification, which if applied
universally would constrict the will's freedom almost universally. Ockham does
not however pursue it or indeed proceed on its assumptions. As we have abundantly
seen in the previous chapter he takes the will to be the source of all good and evil,
merit and demerit, in virtue of being the one created free power. For that reason
correspondingly, only its habits and passions are properly virtuous and vicious in
having the will as their sufficient principle. But in a broader meaning such habits
can also be acquired in the senses, although it cannot be sufficiently proved that
they result in the presence of something in the sensitive appetite not there previously
other than a corporeal quality.[53] We shall have more to say on the reasons when
we consider habits both sensitive and non-sensitive below.

[49] Ibid.

[50] Quodlibet I, q. 17.

[51] Et quando dicitur quod actus voluntatis est in potestate voluntatis, si intelligitur quod non
potest impediri, hoc nullus Christianus habet concedere. . . . Sed Christianus qui habet ponere
quod deus concurrit in omni actione immediate habet ponere quod deo non coagente cum
voluntate voluntas nullum actum elicit, quia deficit causa partialis necessario requisita. Sed tamen
actus voluntatis sic est in potestate voluntatis quod per nullum creatum potest actus suus simpliciter impediri (Reportatio, III, q. 4, L).

[52] Ibid., M–O.   [53] Quodlibet II, q. 16.

As to the passions, they too belong to the will as well as the senses. Some, like love, hope, fear, and joy, are not distinct from their acts, but others, like delight and sadness, although naturally inseparable, are, as we can see from the examples of the bad angel who loves himself without delight and the good angel who rejects sin without sadness.[54] By passion, Ockham understands some form distinct from cognition and actually present in the appetite which requires actual cognition for its existence. It thereby differs at once from actual knowledge which is not a passion and from intellectual and volitional habits and negative acts in having really to exist. As such it applies to all acts of will and of the sensitive appetite.[55] So far as the will's passions are concerned, they are either the object of the will's virtues—as temperance has volition for its object—or the operations of the will's virtues, in the way that the virtue of justice is realised by exterior acts such as distributing goods equitably, or as the proper exercise of what should be done. That holds equally for the habits of these operations. In contrast the passions of the senses as we shall see are not their objects but their acts, and their inclinations need be only corporeal qualities.[56]

Lastly, there remains the will's role in final causality. Unlike the other three causes a final cause as we have seen does not actually move an efficient cause by real movement; hence movement applied to a final cause can only be understood metaphorically.[57] The reason is that a final cause is something for love of which something else acts. Strictly such love is the love of friendship where the object loved is at least as noble as, or nobler than, the agent which acts for love of it.[58] Nevertheless as the end for which something acts, the final cause does not have to be the final action, or even the best, but what is loved.[59] On the other hand a cause is final not because it causes love in something else: it would then merely be an efficient cause. But rather because it causes something which loves it to act as the efficient cause of something else.[60] For example someone walks or drinks a bitter draught to cure infirmity because he loves health, or more properly life or himself, as the end of wanting to walk or drink to be cured. Both walking or drinking and being cured are thus related to man or life as their final cause.[61] Here final causation is expressed in the act to which love of the end leads; it can also be expressed in the will to act, which temporally precedes the act, although the action itself occurs in the same instant in which the agent is moved—metaphorically— by the end.[62]

From that it can be seen that what distinguishes final cause from the other three kinds of cause is that while many final causes do exist outside the soul as the end for which other acts are performed—in the way that health or life which causes someone to walk or fast really exists— they must always exist in the soul. In that

---

[54] *Quodlibet* II, q. 17. [55] *Ibid.* [56] *Quodlibet* IV, q. 7.
[57] *Reportatio*, II, q. 3, G, I, K, L. [58] *Ibid.*, C. [59] *Ibid.*, D.
[60] Causa finalis non dicitur causa finalis amoris quo agens amat ipsum sed dicitur causa finalis effectus causandi ab agente propter amorem finis in quantum amatus movet agens ad efficiendum, et eius motio non est nisi metaphorica et est ipsam amari. Et propter ipsam amatam aliud amari (*ibid.*, G).
[61] *Ibid.*, I. [62] *Ibid.*

sense Ockham opines that both Avicenna, who says that final cause is in the mind, and Averroes, who says that it is really present outside the mind, are both correct, and could be reconciled if the expression 'according the real existence of a final cause' is taken reduplicatively.[63] But this attempt is not particularly convincing, since the whole weight of Ockham's argument is that a final cause must always be known but need not always actually exist at the time that it is known. For nothing can be loved unless it is first known; but something can be known to be what it is even when it is absent. Hence so long as something is known as it really is, it can still move an agent to act for love of it.[64] For that reason it is a fallacy both absolutely and relatively to conclude that because the will desires an end, therefore that end actually exists, as it does not follow that when a rose is known in the mind as it exists, therefore it now exists outside the mind, or that Homer exists in opinion, therefore Homer exists.[65]

Accordingly a final cause does not owe its causality, immediately and absolutely to being loved but first to being known and loved in a single act, and afterwards to being loved by the same act; which in turn leads to love of something else expressed in an exterior or interior act. Now the will is the agent in each; and properly speaking a final cause consists in the end chosen by the will, and its effect in an exterior or interior act, which the will commands for the attainment of its end. Only when an effect is produced from loving an end can we speak of a final cause, because it owes its causality to an effect produced on its account. There cannot therefore be a final cause unless there is an efficient cause; and they must concur in simultaneously producing an effect. The effect then follows formally from the second act of willing or love which is commanded by the will because of the first act of loving or willing the end. Where two things are loved, say health and a bitter draught to achieve it, but the second is not the object of an act because of its bitterness or some other impediment, no effect then formally results from the will's imperative, and there is no actual causality from the final cause, which would be drinking the draught.[66] Where the effect is produced, the first act of loving the end is always the efficient cause of the second act of loving something else because of the first love. The second act thus always presupposes the first.[67] Not all love of an end, however, must be by love of friendship; it can also be by love of desire which as we have mentioned in the previous chapter is when something is desired from love of something else; that applies to all ends which are intermediary to an ultimate end. Thus love of health, which is the end of drinking

---

[63] *Ibid.*, L.

[64] Quia impossibile est quod moveat efficiens ut amatum nisi habeat esse in anima; et cum nihil amatur nisi cognitum, ideo sic intelligendo non movet nisi secundum esse quod habet in anima, quia sic non potest movere nisi habeat talem modum essendi . . . Dico ergo concludendo quod finis secundum entitatem eius extra animam movet agens ad agendum hoc est secundum illam entitatem ab agente. Et tamen ad hoc quod sic moveat secundum illam entitatem, hoc est ad hoc quod ametur secundum illam entitatem realem, non oportet ipsum habere actu illam entitatem realem (*ibid.*, M).

[65] *Ibid.*

[66] *Ibid.*, O.

[67] *Ibid.*, P.

a bitter draught, is itself loved by love of desire since the final end of health is love of life. Consequently even though one thing is loved because of another as its end, love of that end is still by love of desire when it is subordinated to a yet higher love.[68] That means any end is the object of two loves: of desire in being loved through something else, and of either a further love of desire, in being loved for itself as an end but not the highest end, or a love of friendship if loved as the highest end.[69] The first love of desire—in fact the second as the effect of a final cause loved for itself—can in turn be caused either freely and contingently if willed conditionally and for satisfaction, or necessarily when the will acts unconditionally and efficaciously in doing what it must to achieve its end, say, taking bitter medicine when that is the only way to fulfil its desire to regain health.[70]

There is a parallel order in rejecting a hated end. The difference is that, so far as it lies within the will's choice, it is always the result of a preceding act of volition as its final cause; for the will only refuses or hates one thing when it conflicts with something else which it already loves and wants, as death is rejected because life is loved. Love of life is therefore the final cause of hate of death as the will's first act of refusal; and as the end is also the efficient cause of the second act of volition so it is of the first act of refusal which directly follows from it.[71] Similarly as an end is the object of two acts of love, it can also be the object of an act of love and hate, as life is loved for itself and death is hated because life is loved; or two acts of hate, as death is hated for itself and illness is hated because of death. The acts by which something is rejected can also be contingently or necessarily willed according to whether they are willed conditionally or unconditionally.[72]

Now what has been said, both about loving and hating an end, has been in the context of the will's choice, which, as we have remarked, is the proper sense in which to understand final cause. For that the will must first know and love an object before it can love it for itself and, by another act, something else on its account.[73] That cannot, however, apply to the first act of loving which is by love of friendship where the object loved—namely God—cannot be first known, and loved by the will before loving him for himself. He is the first end of all created actions, whether those of intelligent beings acting from knowledge and love, or those of natural agents, as in the generation of fire, which equally are moved by God himself or what is intended by him as their final cause. By definition such an end is not intended and chosen by the created will any more than when it loves God absolutely. For that reason first knowledge and love of an end are not from the will's prior choosing but from God as superior agent.[74] That also holds for acts of refusal. Although naturally they appear to follow a preceding volition they can be directly from a dictate of reason without any previous act of will. Thus the intellect can first know that all sin is to be hated, and the will, without having willed anything before, can then hate sin as its first act of volition. The will is therefore acting in conformity with reason's decree and not in response to anything already willed.[75] The difference would seem to be between two different kinds of act;

---

[68] Ibid., Q.   [69] Ibid., R.   [70] Ibid., S.   [71] Ibid., T–U.
[72] Ibid., Y–Z.   [73] Ibid., AA, MM.   [74] Ibid., AA.   [75] Ibid., CC.

but that can only be surmised since Ockham's discussion here is tantalisingly imprecise. What can be said is that, unlike an end which depends upon the will's own prior volition, an end chosen because of reason's decree appears to be from a divine precept, if we are to go by the examples given. Second that such an end constitutes both an act from love of desire and of friendship, whereas naturally the first presupposes the second: thus in Ockham's example, to love one's neighbour, which is an act of desire (in being from love of something else, in this case God), is also to love God by an act of friendship (by which he is loved absolutely for himself), because only by loving God can one's neighbour be loved. Thirdly, in the same way, whereas naturally acts of willing and refusing can be distinct, and willing seems to presuppose refusing, they can both constitute the same act, so that to hate sin is also to love God, as its accompaniment.[76] Here we seem to be on two different planes, one natural, concerned with the operation of the will's volitions and the sequence they follow, the other moral and theological where the issue is the nature of its acts.

The difference would appear to be confirmed by a further distinction which Ockham makes between acts which are absolutely or intrinsically nobler than others, and acts which owe their greater nobility to the will in choosing them as its end. Absolutely it is more perfect to love God than one's neighbour or oneself; but by the will's acceptance one can love God on account oneself, so that, from the standpoint of the will, to love oneself is more perfect than to love God; for love of oneself will be by love of friendship—i.e. absolutely for oneself—whereas love of God will be by desire through loving oneself. Similarly one can love one's own health more than loving the doctor who ministers to it and who is therefore loved by love of desire on account of love of health: though absolutely a doctor is more perfect than health.[77] That does not however mean that when an exterior act—of the senses—is the end of an interior act—of knowing and willing—the exterior act is more perfect.[78] To begin with, an act which is directed to an end and belongs to a more perfect subject, as an interior act does, is more perfect than the act which executes its end, as an exterior act does.[79] That is to say, intention is nobler than execution. Secondly, even when the exterior act is the end of an interior act, as it sometimes is, it is rarely loved for itself but usually because of something else—whether the person willing it or God; hence it is loved by love of desire.[80]

The relation between an interior and exterior act can be seen in that between the deliberative and the practical intellects. It will be recalled when we discussed them in the fifth chapter that the practical intellect treats both the principles and the conclusions of what should be done, but the deliberative intellect concerns only knowledge of how it should be done as a conclusion reached from the principles known in the practical intellect. Thus if someone is ill and the practical intellect declares that health should be restored, the deliberative intellect, with this dictate as its principle, debates which of the possible means—medicine, walking, study and so on—should be employed to regain health. Its conclusion, say walking, con-

[76] *Ibid.*, BB.   [77] *Ibid.*, MM.   [78] *Ibid.*   [79] *Ibid.*, LL.   [80] *Ibid.*, MM.

stitutes deliberative knowledge reached discursively. Such knowledge is distinct from knowledge of the principle. Accordingly the difference between the practical and deliberative intellects is the difference between having practical discursive knowledge of both the principles and the conclusion and having knowledge only of the conclusion.[81]

Now both the interior acts of the will and the intellect and the exterior acts of the senses can be called practical in conforming to both the practical and the deliberative intellects. The intellect can dictate that someone should walk and the will want to walk and an act of walking result. Similarly the will can first want to acquire health in conformity with a dictate by the practical intellect and then, say, study geometry or drink medicine as the means of acquiring it in conformity with the conclusion of the deliberative intellect. According to the end therefore the same act can be successively practical and non-practical, and *vice versa*: for someone could first study geometry not for any practical end but simply because the will wanted the intellect to study geometry and later because the deliberative intellect concluded that geometry should be studied to gain health. The same act can therefore have diverse objects.[82]

From that it can be seen that the end is the principle of whatever is practicable, as the middle and cause of a syllogism concluding how something is to be achieved. The exterior senses can be the means or the end of an interior act of intellect and will.[83]

That completes examination of the intellective soul. It will have been observed that the intellect and will as the soul's powers are at once really identical with its substance, together forming a trinity, and have their own distinct connotations in virtue of perfecting it. The intellect as a natural power acts necessarily, giving knowledge of what is and what should be done; the will acts freely, deciding what to do. While the order is from knowing to willing, so that volition presupposes cognition but cognition can be without volition,[84] the will can in acting freely contradict the intellect: otherwise as we considered in the previous chapter it could not sin.[85] Through its powers of knowing and willing the intellective soul is the most perfect part of man and the source, as we have seen, of all his actions, natural, virtuous, vicious, meritorious, and sinful. Not the least noteworthy aspect of Ockham's discussion is the interconnection between the psychological and the theological. In what concerns the soul there can be no mistaking his Christian presuppositions.

The intellective soul is not however self-subsistent. Beyond it is the sensitive soul, to which we must now turn.

II THE SENSITIVE SOUL

The sensitive soul is distinct from the intellective soul.[86] Although that cannot be demonstrated from self-evident principles it can be proved, first, because the same

---

[81] *Ibid.*, FF.   [82] *Ibid.*, GG–KK.   [83] *Ibid.*, LL.
[84] E.g. *ibid.*, II, q. 20, E.   [85] E.g. *ibid.*, III, q. 10, C.
[86] Ad aliud dico quod in homine preter animam intellectivam est ponere aliam formam,

subject cannot have contrary qualities; but an act of wanting something is contrary to an act of renouncing something; therefore if they exist simultaneously they must exist in different subjects. Now both acts are in man whose appetite desires what his intellect rejects. Therefore their objects must be distinct in him. Moreover the same substantial form cannot have at the same time two acts of desiring the same thing, which occurs frequently in man who simultaneously desires something good by both the will and the senses. Therefore they must be different forms. Again, the same form does not produce concurrently a natural and a free act; but man can naturally and freely want the same thing. In the second place the senses are really—as we shall discuss in a moment—in the sensitive soul, directly or indirectly, and not in the intellective soul; hence the sensitive and the intellective souls are distinct. Finally the same form cannot be extended and non-extended, material and immaterial; but the sensitive soul is material and has extension, and the intellective soul is immaterial and without extension. Therefore they are not the same. The objection[87] that St Augustine condemned the notion of two souls in man can be met because he was referring to two intellective souls, one from God, the other from the devil. Nor is their distinctiveness impugned by Christ's three days in the tomb; for only God knows whether Christ's sensitive soul remained with his intellect or his body, alive or dead. Equally the distinction between the two souls does not revive the error condemned at Paris—in 1277—that when the intellective soul leaves the body, the animal part continues to live; for after the separation of the intellective soul, the sensitive soul does not remain, nor in the beginning is it introduced into the body before the intellective soul. Accordingly both the intellective and the sensitive souls are essential parts of the whole which would be incomplete without either.[88]

Correspondingly the sensitive soul and the body's form are distinguished from one another in both man and animals.[89] That again can be proved, although with difficulty: for, on the death of a man or animal, their accidents remain the same since new ones could not be caused from within or outside which would be of the same nature as the existing ones; and if their accidents remain the same so do their subjects. But the subject in neither can be first matter as it would then immediately receive its accidents if separate from them, which does not seem true. Therefore there must be another preceding form, which since it is not the sensitive soul must be the body's form. In the case of man, furthermore, if the sensitive soul and the body's form were not distinct it would mean that Christ's body in the tomb had never been an essential part of his human nature, or that God was never united with a human body in the tomb, or that the saints did not have the same body

---

scilicet sensitivam (Reportatio, II, q. 22, H). Utrum anima sensitiva et intellectiva in homine distinguantur realiter . . . Dico ad istam questionem quod sic (Quodlibet II, q. 10). Also Reportatio, IV, q. 7, F.

[87] Quodlibet II, q. 10; Reportatio, IV, q. 7, F.

[88] Ibid.

[89] Utrum anima sensitiva et forma corporeitatis distinguantur realiter tam in brutis quam in hominibus . . . Dico ad illam questionem consequenter quod sic (Quodlibet II, q. 11).

living and dead. Hence the distinction also accords better with faith. It does not however entail a further distinction between the sensitive and the vegetative forms in animals.[90]

As to the sensitive soul's powers, of seeing, hearing and so on, according to whether they are taken for whatever is necessary as partial cause of a vital act, or for the soul itself acting, they either differ among themselves and from the soul or they are the same. In the first case their difference is due to the accidental dispositions which cause one act and not another, as someone can hear and yet not see. Since one can be without the other, their dispositions must be really distinct as absolute accidents in the sensory organs; for given that the latter continue to exist, the reason why there can be an act of hearing but not an act of sight must be through the impairment or loss of the dispositions to sight, namely in the eye as the visual power. In the second sense, however, of the sensitive soul itself acting there is no distinction because it includes all its operations indifferently.[91]

The sensitive soul is therefore the subject of the sensitive powers and their operations, or sensations, directly or indirectly.[92] To say as one opinion does that their subject is something composite cannot be sustained, whether it consists in the conjunction of form and matter alone or together with other accidents. If the first, the consequence would be that, contrary to the presupposition of this opinion, different sensations could not be through different powers—as seeing is through the eye, and hearing through the ear—but from the same composite of form and matter for each. What Aristotle says would then be untrue, that an old man could see as well as a young man if he had the same eye, because if that part of the sensitive form which perfected the organ of sight were destroyed, he would not see regardless of any eye he might receive. The second alternative, that the subject is a composite of form and matter, is equally untenable since one accident has only one subject; the latter can then be composed of a substance and other accidents. Nor can the soul's powers be said, as by this opinion, to flow from the soul as their cause; for that could only be if the soul were efficient cause, which according to this opinion is impossible, since the soul cannot be the immediate principle of an accident. Accordingly for these and other reasons, including the opinions of Averroes and Avicenna to the same purport, the powers of the senses belong to the sensitive soul and not to something which is corporeal.[93]

Animals too have one sensitive form as the cause of all their sensory acts; but it is extended, with the different parts divided from one another. As with men a sensory power is that part of the soul which perfects a sensory organ, producing an act of seeing or hearing and so on. Only touch is in the whole of the soul because it can be by any part of it. Not only can one sensory power act without another, when for whatever reason the appropriate part of the sensitive soul or form fails to perfect it; but so can one part of the same power, as the pupil of one eye can see while the other cannot.[94]

A general rule for locating a real distinction between the powers of either the

[90] *Ibid.*　　[91] *Reportatio,* II, q. 26, D.　　[92] *Quodlibet* II, q. 10.
[93] *Reportatio,* II, q. 26, B–C.　　[94] *Ibid.,* E.

intellective or sensitive souls is that whenever all the external conditions for the production of an act of knowing, willing, or sensing are uniformly present and there can be an act over one object but not another, different acts will entail different powers: for example colour can be the object of sight, but for sound, another sense, of hearing, is required. Similarly someone can sense something and yet not will it. Conversely, distinct acts of knowing and desiring whether over the same or a different object belong necessarily to the same power, because naturally they are inseparable. Hence, unless God were to suspend an act of appetite, whenever something is desired it always follows naturally and immediately from an act of sensory or intellective apprehension. Really, therefore, as opposed to nominally, they are necessarily of the same power and identical. That also applies to acts of will; and there are as many distinct acts of the appetite as there are distinct cognitive acts.[95]

Finally there are the passions of the appetite. Now as we have mentioned, they are, taken strictly, in no way distinct from acts of appetite. As Aristotle said there are only powers, habits and passions in the soul; and since acts are not powers or habits they must be passions.[96] Passions in their strictest sense are acts of intensity and vehemence; in their improper sense they include pain and pleasure;[97] and in every sense they are not, as we have also remarked, the object of the virtues in the appetite but are the acts produced by the virtues and inclinations in the appetite, as we shall consider presently.[98]

Now pain and pleasure, as improper passions in the senses, differ from their counterparts in the will. Where in the will they are inseparable, although distinct, from acts of volition upon which they depend for their cause and conservation, they are exclusive of acts of appetite. The reason, as we have discussed in chapter seven, is that desire and refusal as acts of appetite can only be of what is absent and not already possessed; but pleasure and pain are only of what is present and possessed. Hence they are incompatible over the same object though perhaps they coexist over diverse objects. Where the object is the same then desire and refusal cease when pleasure and pain begin.[99] Putting aside the obvious rejoinder that desire and refusal can themselves have as their accompaniments pleasure and pain and that what is possessed can still equally be desired or rejected, it follows from what Ockham has said that neither desire nor refusal can be the cause of pleasure or pain. Nor immediately can the cause be their object because pleasure and pain can continue beyond the object—a pain from a blow can remain after the blow has passed—or they can be engendered by recalling a past object of pain or pleasure. Even when these passions depend upon the object's presence, God could conserve the sensation without the object. Consequently as with past knowledge the object

95 *Ibid.*, q. 24, T–U.

96 *Quodlibet* II, q. 15; *Nicomachean Ethics*, II, ch. 5, 1105 b, 20. Also *Reportatio*, III, q. 11, G.

97 *Reportatio*, III, q. 11, H. O. Fuchs, *The Psychology of Habit According to Willam Ockham* (St Bonaventure, New York, and Louvain, 1952), 51, 59–61, calls them secondary passions; but Ockham does not.

98 *Reportatio, ibid.*; *Quodlibet* II, q. 15, and IV, q. 7.

99 *Quodlibet* IV, q. 5; *Reportatio*, III, q. 14, B.

is not the immediate cause of pain or pleasure. Instead it is the appetite's own apprehension of the sensation which comes from the object.

Pleasure and pain are thus passions and qualities of the appetite caused by its act of apprehension together with the appetite itself and God.[100] That can be shown on the accepted principle that effects sufficiently depend upon their essential causes and dispositions; but if the object of apprehension is destroyed and its apprehension remains in the senses, pleasure and pain can continue to be caused by the appetite. Hence, as Duns Scotus averred, the object is not the immediate cause of pleasure and pain, but only indirect cause as cause of a cause.[101] There are exceptions. A madman born without the use of reason who had never apprehended anything would yet naturally hunger and thirst and correspondingly experience pleasure and pain through their satisfaction or lack of satisfaction. Again pleasure or pain could be so overwhelming that it could totally impair apprehension and the use of reason. But naturally unless there is a previous act of apprehension in the senses there is neither pleasure nor pain.[102]

How then do the passions of the senses affect the will's freedom? Strictly speaking the will only inclines to them when it wills to do so; if it refuses there is no inclination. But to overcome the inclination is not easy.[103] Nor is it easy to explain why in particular the will naturally inclines to what is pleasurable and recoils from what is painful, beyond recognising it as a fact of experience. On the one hand it cannot be due to knowing what should be done; for when that leads to pain in the senses, say the obligation to die for the republic, the will as if by nature inclines to the opposite. Nor can the cause be merely in a pleasurable object, however intense the pleasure in the appetite, because the will can again will the contrary. From that point of view the only cause is the will itself. On the other hand, pleasure or pain in the senses can be made a partial cause of the will's inclination or disinclination in disposing it to want or refuse an object more easily or at least more intensely than otherwise.

A passion of the senses then concurs with will as other partial causes do, and as an object known it is the partial cause of the intellect's assent or dissent. But it remains in the will's power regardless of such concurrence to will or refuse or not to act at all; and so again the only explanation of the will's inclinations must be the will itself.[104] Conversely the will's acts are, as we have already indicated, a partial cause of virtuous acts in the senses, such as temperance or fortitude or humility which, together with the natural inclinations of the individual concerned, can modify the passions in the senses.[105] Moreover as we briefly mentioned in the previous chapter the will can overcome the pull of the senses by directing them to a

[100] Sciendum est primo quod dolor [et delectatio] qui proprie est passio et qualitas appetitus sensitivi et ab apprehensione sensitiva causatur et non ab obiecto apprehenso sensu nec ab actu appetitus, sed solummodo ab apprehensione et potentia appetitiva et deo (*Reportatio*, III, q. 14, A). Also *Quodlibet* II, q. 17.

[101] *Reportatio*, III, q. 14, *ibid.*

[102] *Ibid.*, I–K.

[103] *Quodlibet* III, q. 19.

[104] *Reportatio*, III, q. 13, U; q. 2, G.

[105] *Ibid.*, q. 2, I; *Quodlibet* II, q. 16.

more pleasurable end. Ockham does not, however, agree with Duns Scotus that only a supernatural object can compete with the pleasure derived from the senses: according to Aristotle speculation is the source of greatest pleasure and that is to be had naturally. But even when the object is a supernatural end, the act of attaining it can be natural, on the now familiar grounds that an act over the same object without a supernatural habit is of the same nature as an act with a supernatural habit. Hence in an equally familiar example a pagan nurtured in the Christian faith can love God above all naturally and take pleasure in his love.[106] Accordingly the act produced is the same but its value is from God.

Ockham thus upholds the will's freedom towards the senses as towards everything else. Although the passions of the appetite can impede the will's acts they can also be commanded by the will. That applies to all virtuous (and vicious) acts and habits of the will which, like temperance, have the passions as their common object. The will is then their indirect cause by means of the act which it produces with the virtuous (or vicious) habit, and in turn produces a passion. At the same time the will is the immediate cause of the act of apprehension leading to the act producing the passion. That therefore is the difference between the relation of the will to the passions in the appetite and of the appetite itself to its passions, which are related to it not as objects but as its own acts elicited through its corporeal qualities.[107] From that it follows that the will, through its virtuous acts and habits, is the principle regulating the passions of the appetite, stimulating them or moderating them, as occasion demands: no passion at all would be detrimental in leaving a man vicious and insensible, for example with lack of any desire to eat; superabundant passion, leading to ceaseless eating, would be equally bad. Virtue here consists in eating when one should.[108]

It is a characteristic of the will's virtues that it can accordingly combine opposing passions, as the object of the same virtuous acts, as in the example just given or as fortitude combines fear over one thing with bravery over another, just as the same act of intellect can include knowledge of what is to be feared with knowledge of what is to be braved. Its effect upon the senses is not to produce contradictory acts of both fear and bravery as passions, but either establish a mean between them, or one passion at one time and the other at a different time.[109] Other virtues like temperance and continence are designed to quell the passions—temperance moderate desire, continence overwhelming desire. They are therefore more or less intense virtues of the same species although with different effects: where temperance can produce a virtuous act which in overcoming a bad desire also produces a feeling of greater pleasure than the preceding desire, continence cannot entirely still desire or, if it can, is accompanied by sadness rather than pleasure, and as an act is much weaker.[110] A moral virtue is in no way dependent however upon a corresponding disposition in the senses and may be completely nullified by the senses

---

[106] *Reportatio*, III, q. 2, I; also *Quodlibet* IV, q. 7.
[107] *Quodlibet* IV, q. 7; *Reportatio*, III, q. 11, M.
[108] *Reportatio*, III, q. 11, S.
[109] *Ibid.*, O–Q.   [110] *Ibid.*, S–T.

rejecting it. On the other hand, as in the case of acts of temperance and other virtues, the will can cause and conserve a virtuous inclination in the senses, which can destroy the desires in the question.[111] Indeed such virtues in the senses can survive a change from virtue to vice in the will, so that for example someone could continue to eat temperately even when the will was no longer temperate.[112]

The passions then owe their virtues and their vices to the virtues and vices in the will; of themselves, like all other acts which are not of the will, they are morally indifferent, neither conforming to nor violating right reason. They are therefore only extrinsically good or bad as the partial object—never the partial cause[113]—of an act of will which is good or bad.[114] When a passion is the object of a virtue or vice, the stronger the passion the greater the virtue or vice.[115]

In Ockham's account of the intellective and sensitive souls we can see that the will is a slave neither to the intellect nor the appetite. The keynote is man's power to act freely whether in choosing one end rather than another or a virtue rather than a vice. For Ockham that is a matter of experience, which is the foundation not only of what we can know but also what we can do. It is a paradox that Ockham's reliance upon it leads to a more restricted view of what can be known and a more exalted conception of what can be done. But in neither is experience confined merely to sense data or external stimuli; both the intelligible and the conative exist in their own right. The main reason for that is the existence of habits and inclinations; and it is to this last aspect of man's powers that we must now turn.

III   HABITS

For those who have come so far, the importance of habits in Ockham's explanation of human activity is not in need of stressing. Habit explains all knowing and willing which are not immediately occasioned by external objects. It is therefore the source of all man's non-existential awareness and volition and hence his autonomy from merely sensory or physiological stimuli. In the case of knowledge the role of habit has been so central to nearly every aspect of non-intuitive knowledge discussed in the first part that we may simply adumbrate its main areas. It is the means of second abstractive knowledge and thereby of memory and phantasy; it replaces species and later *ficta* in the formation of concepts; it constitutes a science or branch of knowledge as a collection of habits, and similarly faith; it is the means of integrating principles and conclusions in a single act of knowing a syllogism in the intellect,[116] and knowing one thing through another.

In the will habit is omnipresent, above all where virtues and vices are concerned, with acquired habits enabling the will to perform naturally acts, such as loving God above all, which in themselves are indistinguishable from acts informed by a supernatural habit. Indeed from that standpoint it is an acquired habit no less than an act of will which is opposed to the indispensability of supernaturally infused

---

[111] *Ibid.*, q. 12, LL.   [112] *Ibid.*, MM.   [113] *Ibid.*, q. 11, R.
[114] *Ibid.*, q. 10, F, H.   [115] *Ibid.*, q. 11, R.   [116] *Ordinatio*, Prologue, q. 8, 218–19.

habits: hence as we saw in the previous chapter the importance of acquired habits not only for moral but also for meritorious acts.

Now all habits are above all a matter of experience derived from the fact that when something can be done which could not be done before, or can be done more easily than before, and the change is not due to any difference in the object acted upon, some new quality must be acquired in the agent or some previous quality lost. As nothing appears to be lost something must be acquired, whether in knowledge, virtue or bodily skill.[117] It must also be a quality because only substance and qualities are, as we know, real entities—absolutes—and a habit (in existing in another substance) is not a substance. That also follows since it is the cause of a quality, namely an act, notwithstanding the opposed view of Aristotle in the *Physics* where he says that acquired states are relations and do not constitute real change; for whether or not one takes Averroes's interpretation that Aristotle was expressing Plato's and not his own opinion, what Aristotle says only holds for particular cases, such as going to church where the same act can become virtuous after having been non-virtuous, without undergoing any change.[118]

That a habit is the cause of an act can be proved by the principle of efficient causality, that something is the efficient cause of something else when the latter depends upon the former for its existence. More particularly when something can be caused in something else in which it could not previously exist it has either an efficient cause (which it did not have before) or lacks an impediment (which was not there before), as a candle can illuminate when an obstacle to its light has been removed. Now, someone before he has a habit cannot act in the absence of an object; but afterwards he can, and without any obstacle having been removed. The cause of the change must therefore be a habit. Finally when something can only be posited by positing something else the second condition must be the efficient cause of the first.[119] A similar argument to the last one is employed in the *Reportatio* to prove that an act is the cause of a habit, but there Ockham also seeks to prove the assumption that an invariable association between two events entails a causal relation between them which should only be denied if there is some reason. That cannot be done here because none of the possible grounds—that a habit is a relation, or that the power which causes the act could totally cause the habit, or that only a habit causes an act and not the reverse—can be sustained.[120] Ockham's defence of cause here is further evidence, if still needed, not only that he

---

[117] Preterea omne quod potest in actionem aliquam in quam prius non potuit et non est aliqua diversitas in passo, habet aliquam rem absolutam quam prius non habuit vel caret aliqua re absoluta quam prius habuit. Sed habens istos habitus potest in aliquam actionem in quam prius non potuit, scilicet intellectus et voluntas. Patet per experientiam, et non est aliqua diversitas in passo . . . (*Quodlibet* I, q. 18).

Potentia executiva corporalis potest post multos actus elicitos potest in consimiles actus in quos non potuit ante, vel saltem ita faciliter . . . ergo in illis potentiis est aliquid additum vel ablatum. Non apparet quod sit aliquid ablatum. Ergo est aliquid additum; et illud voco habitum (*ibid.*, III, q. 17).

[118] *Physics*, VII, ch. 3, 245 b–248 a; *Quodlibet* I, q. 18; also *Reportatio*, III, q. 4, D.

[119] *Quodlibet* III, q. 18; *Reportatio*, III, q. 4, E–F.

[120] *Reportatio*, III, q. 11, D.

did not come near to embracing a pre-Humean scepticism, such as Nicholas of
Autrecourt a generation later was to evince, but that he associated temporal
succession and efficient causality in a most un-Humean matter.

To the objection that in essential causes there is an unalterable sequence, so that
if an act is the cause of a habit it cannot in turn be the effect of a habit, Ockham
agrees so far as individual acts are concerned. One and the same act cannot first be
the cause of a habit—as the first act always is—and then be itself caused by a habit.
But acts of the same kind can be. Hence specifically the same acts can be both cause
and the effects of habits, without contradiction; for different causes can have
diverse effects of the same species, as fire and the sun can both produce heat.[121]

Strictly, then, a habit inclines a power—intellect, will, or senses—in virtue of
inhering in it as an accidental form or quality and perfecting it as partial cause of an
act.[122] It is not therefore the same as a power which in its proper sense is a form
able to produce many acts indifferently as the intellect and will can. A habit
however is limited to one kind of act, as an object also is: to that extent Ockham
concedes, in the *Reportatio*[123]—but not, expressly at least, in the *Quodlibets*[124]—
that both can loosely be called powers. But whereas a power in its proper meaning
can receive both a habit and an object, a habit cannot receive a power;[125] nor does
it precede or generate or increase a power whereas a power does all these in relation
to a habit.[126] As a partial cause of a power's disposition to act, a habit's existence
can be known from experience. Unlike an object as partial cause of an act, a habit
inclines a power to act often to the point of impelling it and sometimes in the
absence of any object. Hence its presence is felt in the power itself.[127]

From that it is plain that habits are acquired, not innate, a conclusion supported
by both Aristotle and experience.[128] If they were not acquired then, as Aristotle
says, virtues as part of nature could not incline to what is contrary to nature, which
they are able to do. Nor would it be possible to compare the intellect as Aristotle
does to a clean tablet (*tabula nuda*) on which nothing was written. But in fact even
with all cognitive habits destroyed, the intellect can still immediately—of its own
powers—assent to the proposition that the whole is greater than the part. For
Aristotle also says that habits of knowing principles are acquired from repeated
acts of knowing them through experience.[129] There is the same absence of innate
habits in the senses; bodily dispositions are not habits but physical qualities preceding any act, in the same way as there are dispositions making for health. The

[121] *Quodlibet* III, q. 18; also *Reportatio*, III, q. 4, K, q. 11, D.

[122] Tamen habitus proprie inclinat potentiam, quia est forma perficiens potentiam, et cum
hoc ut causa partialis inclinans ad actum (*Reportatio*, III, q. 4, M).

[123] *Ibid.*, I.

[124] *Quodlibet* III, q. 18.

[125] *Reportatio*, III, q. 4, I.

[126] *Ibid.*, IV, q. 2, D.

[127] *Reportatio*, III, q. 4, E, where Ockham invokes Aristotle's definition of cause in the
Metaphysics (V, ch. 2, 1013 a, 25), as that from which something comes into being, to prove a
habit as partial cause of an act.

[128] Quantum ad primum est una opinio que ponit quod virtutes insunt in nobis a natura . . .
Sed ista opinio est contra Philosophum 2º *Ethicorum* (*Reportatio*, III, q. 11, B–C).

[129] *Ibid.*, C; *Posterior Analytics*, II, ch. 19, 100 a, 9–10.

proof is that such dispositions can be stimulated or diminished artificially by medical devices, such as increasing the circulation of blood to the heart, without any preceding act and so without any preceding habit.[130] Nor can habits be regarded as existing in any power inchoately or latently as part of their nature, reaching completion through the exercise of their powers. That would be equivalent to treating habits as innate; for they would then—contrary to Aristotle and the meaning of habit—not be increased by the same power which produced them.[131] Habits are therefore by definition acquired not innate.

How then does a habit differ from an inclination? The main difference is that an inclination is something actually experienced. It is therefore itself an act added to the power or form which has the inclination and to the habit which leads to it.[132] It is also more transitory than a habit; where the same habit can remain in someone sleeping and waking there can only be an inclination in someone who is awake.[133]

Now from what has been said above it is plain that not every inclination presupposes a habit; otherwise all bodily inclinations would be from habits, which Ockham has just denied. But in the *Reportatio* Ockham, as we shall see again shortly in connection with the appetites, had not yet clarified the precise relation between habits and inclinations. For he there described an inclination as an act, particularly an act of appetite, produced by a habit as partial cause.[134] In the *Quodlibets* he merely stresses the difference between an inclination and a power and a habit, to which it is added as something real, on the same grounds, that an inclination represents a real act which was not there before. Inclination is also now made synonymous with appetite, connoting something willed or desired. In its strict sense employed in this context it means the activity possessed by a natural agent.[135] These variations would appear to indicate that inclinations are now taken to belong to the appetite rather than the will. If so, that may be partly due to the difficulty presented by the will's inclinations discussed in the *Reportatio*. The problem which they raised was whether someone having a previous habit of vice and then receiving grace could continue to have inclinations to vice. It would seem not, because if inclinations are acts, and in this case acts of mortal sin, they are incompatible with a state of grace. Yet experience says the opposite, that there can be such inclinations, not only in the senses but also in the will; and they are caused both by the will and a habit. Ockham's solution, and one that we encountered over final cause, is that these inclinations are indeed from the will, but are not caused by it freely, since its own actions had an antecedent cause in the habit inclining the will towards them.

---

[130] *Ibid.*

[131] *Ibid.*; also *Quodlibet* II, q. 18.

[132] *Quodlibet* III, q. 19; *Reportatio*, III, q. 4, M.

[133] Igitur inclinatio illius habitus est actus elicitus, et respectu huius potest poni habitus totalis causa, sicut prius positum fuit de gravitate, vel partialis causa cum apprehensione et appetitu. (*Reportatio*, III, q. 4, M).

[134] *Quodlibet* III, q. 19; *Reportatio*, III, q. 4, M.

[135] Omnis inclinatio forme importat aliquem conatum et nisum . . . Dico ad primum quod inclinatio . . . dupliciter accipitur . . . Aliter vero accipitur et hoc prout aliquid ultra addit esse in potentia receptiva, puta activitatem . . . quia sic accipiendo inclinationem nihil inclinatur nisi agens naturale (*Quodlibet* III, q. 19).

Hence the will is not culpable.[136] That it is not a particularly happy solution is in itself less important than the reason leading to it, namely Ockham's desire to reconcile experience with faith.

Inclinations are thus among the facts of experience which habit explains; indeed in the *Reportatio* Ockham calls them the principal facts, with promptness and facility in acting secondary.[137] That, however, hardly accords with his own account of the acquisition of physical skills or habits in the imagination or the intellect: in the *Quodlibets* he attributes those in both the body and the imagination to promptness or facility, while what he says about the formation of cognitive habits there and elsewhere in his explanation of abstractive knowledge and memory relies as much upon facility as upon inclination.[138] In the case of the will, to which perhaps Ockham intended his statement to apply, the presence of habits is more difficult to prove because the will as a free power can continue to act as freely as it does initially; but it can choose its first act without a habit; hence there is no reason why it cannot choose its second and third and subsequent acts freely without a habit. The will's freedom does not therefore provide an argument for habits. Nor does a comparison with the intellect, by arguing that as the intellect inclines to truth so the will inclines to the good; it is not for that reason that a habit is posited in the intellect, but because having once known an object, the intellect can then know it in its absence: which it could not before it was first known. The will on the other hand only wills what is actually known; it therefore needs the presence of an object for every act of volition, regardless of how many there have already been. A third argument, that it is more difficult for the will to will virtuously at some times than at others, is equally inconclusive: for the difference could be due to the passions or habits of the senses.[139]

Instead, a habit can be posited in the will on the evidence that it is subsequently better able or more inclined to perform the same act, after having performed it, than before. Other things being equal the change must be in the will through the acquisition of a habit. That can be seen from the example of someone who now resists his desires to which he previously submitted: since the desires remain as strongly as before in the senses, it is the will which is now inclined to remain continent, where before it was not.[140] To this Ockham later in the *Quodlibets* adds

---

[136] *Reportatio*, III, q. 4, M–O.

[137] Ad aliud dico quod non requiritur [habitus] propter facilitatem vel promptitudinem tamquam principuim activum tantum, sed propter inclinationem dicitur proprie principium activum; et propter hoc sequitur facilitatio et promptitudo, quia magis inclinatur nunc quam prius. Et ita principaliter ponitur propter inclinationem; secundario autem propter alia duo (*ibid.*, U).

[138] Circa istam questionem dico primo quod necesse est ponere habitus in corpore. Quod patet, quia potentia executiva corporalis post multos actos elicitos potest in consimiles actus in quos non potuit ante, vel saltem ita faciliter . . .

Tertio dico quod in potentia apprehensiva sunt ponendi habitus quia post frequentiam actus imaginandi redditur quis promptus ad consimiles actus . . . Quarto dico quod in intellectu necessario ponitur habitus, quia aliquis post frequentiam actuum intelligendi redditur promptus et inclinatus ad consimiles actus (*Quodlibet* III, q. 17).

In the *Reportatio*, III, q. 11, M the imagination is described as more inclined to similar acts.

[139] *Reportatio*, III, q. 10, G.   [140] *Ibid.*

the further negative reason that after repeated acts of will of the same kind the will has greater difficulty and meets more resistance in producing their contraries.[141] Thus in opposition to the arguments which he rejected, Ockham's own are founded upon the evidence of experience, that repeated acts in any power lead to the generation of habits.

The one exception is the sensory appetite to which Ockham in the Quodlibets came to deny habits, having originally upheld them in the Reportatio. In that work, after an initial uncertainty in first attributing them to the exterior as well as the interior senses, he settled for them in the interior senses and the phantasy.[142] This shift was parallel to that which led him to exclude intuitive knowledge as the direct cause of habits in the intellect: namely that the exterior senses, in being dependent upon the actual presence of an object, are no more inclined to know it differently after repeatedly knowing it than in knowing it for the first time. But in the interior senses there is such a change, inclining the appetite to produce similar acts. It is caused by the act of the sensitive appetite together with abstractive sensory apprehension. The acts of the appetite are as we have discussed identical with its passions; hence there is no distinction save grammatically between anger as a passion and being angry as an act, or the passion of hate and the act of hating; if there were, there would be two of each, which in the senses there are not. All such acts or passions belonging to the interior senses are normally produced through having abstractive sensory knowledge of the object desired as a partial cause. Where it is not a partial cause, say in a child having only appetites such as hunger and thirst but born without the use of the external senses and so without apprehension, the appetite is the total cause of its acts and they in turn of its habits.[143]

By the time of the Quodlibets Ockham had changed his mind. He still acknowledged that, after repeated acts of will, something is in the appetite which was not there before, making someone more inclined to elicit similar acts than before. But he no longer regarded this something as a habit or even that it could be sufficiently proved to be something actually in the appetite. Instead he now took it to be a quality or quantity of the body.[144] The confirmation is to be found in the way medicine can produce an inclination through bodily changes such as increasing or diminishing the body's temperature. As these can be effected without the appetite or its acts, so can other bodily dispositions. Moreover exercising the

141 Quodlibet III, q. 17; of the three arguments which he rejects in the Reportatio as inadequate to proving conative habits, the one he retains in this Quodlibet is a modification of the second that the will can only actually will something in the presence of the object willed.

142 Reportatio, III, q. 11, H, M.

143 Ibid., M.

144 Sed dubium est quid sit quod manet post tales actus. Dico quod non potest sufficienter probari quod sit aliquod ens existens in appetitu senutivo saltem quantum ad multos actus virtuosos, quia potest poni sufficienter quod sit aliqua quantitas vel qualitas corporalis que inclinat ad tales actus (Quodlibet II, q. 16). Secundo dico quod non potest sufficienter probari quod aliquis habitus sit in appetitu sensitivo ponendus, quia omnia que experimur nobis inesse post frequentiam actus appetitivi possumus experiri quandocumque in nobis per transmutationes corporales (ibid., III, q. 17). Also II, q. 18 and IV, q. 7. Fuchs, Psychology of Habit, 55–8 was the first to draw attention to the change; his characteristically balanced assessment, which I accept, is that it does not alter substantially Ockham's position.

senses can increase the strength of the passions, which would not be true if there were already virtuous habits in the appetite to mitigate them. No habit is therefore caused immediately in the appetite either by the will's virtues such as temperance or by a passion. The inclinations produced by acts of appetite are only indirect, leading not to similar acts but to other acts, in the way that someone, by eating hot food, inclines through the increased heat produced in the body not to more food but to acts of concupiscence. The precise nature however of what it is in the body that inclines the appetite, Ockham leaves to the doctors of medicine to determine.[145]

Ockham thus substituted a physiological for psychological explanation, but the phenomenon to be explained remains the same. The change from habits to bodily qualities or quantity does not therefore alter the fact that the senses have certain dispositions. Moreover the change is in keeping with the tendencies already apparent in the *Reportatio* to make bodily inclinations independent of habits as part of the body's natural endowments.[146] The framework of Ockham's discussion of the appetite's inclinations accordingly remains unaltered; it was merely given a more empirical foundation in the *Quodlibets*. And perhaps the most notable aspect of this later judgement is Ockham's distinctly unmedieval appeal for greater knowledge in order to answer the question.

Habits, then, are differentiated according to their acts which in turn are defined in relation to their objects, as acts of knowing a conclusion are distinguished from acts of knowing a principle; and their habits correspondingly.[147] That does not mean that the same object cannot engender different acts of knowing and willing; it can, as something can be known both intuitively and abstractively,[148] although only an abstractive habit can be formed. Nor that, as we have said, one habit cannot embrace diverse objects as there can be an act and a habit of knowing a syllogism and a proposition. Nor that one habit cannot incline indirectly to other acts, as a habit of knowing one conclusion can lead to knowing diverse conclusions.[149] Rather it is that an act and a habit are defined in relation to one another as being of the same nature; and that can only be in virtue of the nature of their object. There is accordingly a causal chain between object, act, and habit, with act and habit each defined in relation to the preceding link. Habit itself is the means of freeing acts from ontological dependence upon an object and thereby man's intellect and will from conformity to what exists outside him. Habit is thus the guarantee of man's cognitive and conative independence of the physical objects that surround him, enabling him to combine, in the intellect, knowledge and mem-

---

[145] *Quodlibet* II, q. 16.

[146] E.g. *Reportatio*, III, q. 4, H; q. 11, C. Pleasure and pain do not leave habits. *Ordinatio*, d. 17, q. 2, G.

[147] Et quantum ad primum dico quod tanta est distinctio actuum quanta est habituum et e converso. Tum quia distincti habitus specie sunt a distinctis actibus specie, quod non esset nisi esset equalis distinctio eorum. Tum quia distincti actus specie causant distinctos habitus specie ... Preterea nisi distinctorum obiectorum specie essent actus distincti et habitus, non posset probari distinctio specifica inter quoscumque actus vel habitus (*Quodlibet* II, q. 18).

[148] *Ibid.*

[149] *Reportatio*, III, q. 11, K.

ory of what he has learned, and in the will the virtues, above all through prudence, by which he can control his passions and seek the good.

For Ockham then man has both a sensitive and an intellective soul, which together with first matter constitute his essence as they did Christ's when a man.[150] Hence there is a plurality of forms in man, namely his two souls and his body's form.[151] Although, as we have seen, never regarding as formally conclusive the arguments for a real distinction between the intellective and the sensitive souls, because the premises are not self-evident, Ockham's discussion of man's powers nevertheless proceeds on the assumption that they are really distinct. Here as elsewhere he was less concerned with the question in its metaphysical form—in which as the alternative between a single substantial form in man or a plurality of forms it had been such a burning issue in the 1270s and 1280s—than with its empirical reality: namely of the ways in which man could act, and the relation between his different activities, cognitive, conative and appetitive. The account which Ockham produced, however destructive of the conventional meanings given to intellect, will, and memory, and their different facets, was no less accommodating to the demands of faith than the explanations of his predecessors. The difference as we have seen throughout is that Ockham sought to reconcile with faith not metaphysical definitions drawn from *a priori* reasoning, but what had to be accepted from experience. His view of man however remained as Christian as that of any other Christian thinker of the Middle Ages.

---

[150] Ideo ponendo quod in homine sunt tres res pertinentes ad eius essentiam sicut oportet necessario propter articulum puta materia prima, forma sensitiva et [forma] intellectiva, cum immediate iste sunt unite verbo sicut in triduo mortis Christi (*ibid.*, q. 1, Q).

[151] Secundum opinionem quam reputo veram, in homine sunt plures forme substantiales, saltem forma corporeitatis et anima intellectiva (*ibid.*, II, q. 9, CC).

Quod autem in homine sunt plures forme substantiales bene est difficile probare vel eius oppositum, tamen ad presens probatur sic . . . (*ibid.*, IV, q. 7, F). Also *Reportatio*, II, q. 22, H; *Quodlibet* II, qq. 10 and 11. For proofs see 547–8 above.

CHAPTER NINE

Nature

Fifty and more years ago Ockham, through the writings of Pierre Duhem,[1] was taken to be the precursor of modern science. Today he is one more scholastic who had views on a variety of physical questions—matter, form, movement, space, time, remission and intensification of forms—but not what can be called in the modern sense a scientific outlook.[2] Nor indeed did he make any distinctive scientific contribution in the manner of Bradwardine's use of proportions or Buridan's theory of *impetus* or later the mathematical calculations of Nicholas of Oresme or the Mertonians. Ockham even in the then comparatively undifferentiated state of those activities remained always a speculative thinker as opposed to a natural scientist or mathematician; he never went beyond an abstract treatment of nature, in terms largely taken over from Aristotle, to direct investigation of natural phenomena; and he brought to its consideration no new concepts, physical or mathematical.[3] In all these respects Ockham was very much of his epoch; for the most part his views on the main physical issues of the time fall into one or other of the accepted divisions, whether over the existence of a void or the way in which qualitative change occurs.

Scientific achievement is not however the appropriate criterion by which to judge Ockham's conception of nature, or its importance for subsequent thought; and in the salutary and necessary corrective to the earlier exaggerated claims for Ockham's scientific originality there has perhaps been too pronounced a contrary tendency to minimise his distinctiveness. This consists above all in reducing Aristotle's analysis of material substance, movement, and causality to that of individual being; so that while accepting Aristotle's framework—of all being as a composite of form and matter related as actual and potential being, together with his definitions of cause, movement, qualitative change, place, and time—he gives

---

[1] P. Duhem, 'Le Mouvement absolu et le mouvement relatif', *Revue de Philosophie* 12 (1908); *Études sur Leonardo da Vinci*, 3 vols. (Paris, 1909).

[2] Especially the works of A. Maier, listed in the bibliography.

[3] Junghans, *Ockham im Lichte*, 180–3, attempts to counter A. Maier's opinion (*Zwei Grundprobleme*, 48) that Ockham's approach to nature was formal and logical rather than scientific, by citing Ockham's appeal to experience. But Dr Johnson also appealed to experience when he kicked a stone to show that it existed.

it an exclusively individual import. In consequence, as we discussed in chapter three, only substance and form are real, together constituting actual being; all the other categories are the attributes of individual being neither inhering in being nor standing for independent essences or things or forms, but merely describing the different ways in which individual things can be said to exist, whether as extended in space (quantity) or in movement or in relation to other beings. This shift in emphasis by Ockham meant the dehypostasisation of nature from a universe informed by essences and universal qualities to one of individuals *tout court*, intelligible in terms of their own movement and gestation. Its significance is that it released for the first time in the Middle Ages the natural world to observation and experience for itself and not something else. Or rather for the first time it provided the justification for doing so: Grosseteste and Bacon among others had already put it into practice but within a very different—Augustinian and essentialist—conception of reality. Only with Ockham, however, did the individual cease to be the occasion for some greater and directly inaccessible reality and instead itself become the only reality through the coalescence of individual substance with individual quality or corporeal form.

This transformation was the physical counterpart of the logical distinction between predication and signification through which as we also considered in chapter three Ockham was able to demetaphysicise the predicables and the categories and all other attributes: to say that a being has quantity does not mean that something called quantity exists independently of that of which it is affirmed, any more than to say that man is an animal or risible means that animality or risibility are really distinct from man and can only belong to him by inherence. In every case where the predicate does not itself stand for something real—i.e. a quality—only the subject has real signification; and for that it must be individual, as 'man' taken significatively in personal supposition can only stand for this and that and that man, and for nothing which is not an individual man.

Applied to nature the implication is that there is no longer being beyond individual being. That effectively meant the end of metaphysics as the study of being in itself; for, as a transcendental term, as we already know, it can either be taken univocally when it is the most universal of all terms and without existential import; or it consists in ten equivocal ways of describing real individual being according to the ten categories. It then comes within the ambit of physics which is concerned precisely with individual being in its different physical modes. Since for Ockham real being is only physical—existing in time and place—it can be considered only by physics. That is the supreme consequence of Ockham's conception of the natural world. It represents the elimination of an entire realm of abstraction; for with abstract terms deprived of independent signification, the terms of metaphysics—being, essence, substance, form, matter—are either terms of second intention, where as concepts they belong to logic not to metaphysics, or they are terms of first intention standing for real things, in which case they belong to physics as a real first order science. Ockham's reduction of being to individual being therefore means the corresponding reduction of metaphysics to either logic or physics.

The importance of the change needs hardly stressing. It effectively transformed metaphysics into physics. But not directly or expressly. The scientific rethinking of the fourteenth century as of most rethinking at most times was not conceived as a break with tradition, above all with Aristotle. That was as true of Ockham as of his contemporaries and successors. They each in their different ways sought to 'save' Aristotle's explanations; and it was only through the need to bring his hypotheses— to them data, although not thinking in such terms—into alignment with the new data derived from experience or calculation that they came to modify—in the end out of recognition—Aristotle's own outlook. That did not occur in the fourteenth century. Inquiry was still pursued in Aristotle's terms; but both their meaning and the explanations given to the questions they raised were changing: as the thirteenth century had seen the proliferation of the new logic of terms, which owed nothing directly to Aristotle but was grafted on to his logic, so in the fourteenth century a series of new scientific genres, mathematical and physical, appeared in the form of treatises on proportions, new modes of quantitative calculation, and new kinematic and dynamic theories, which in turn were treated as an extension of Aristotle's doctrine of nature, but were no less distinct from it than their logical counterparts had been from his logic, and which became more distinct in the fourteenth century. At no point did those engaged in these new developments advocate a new conception of logic or nature; they regarded their activities as simply a continuation of Aristotle's principles.

That applies to Ockham in an even more marked degree. He renounced neither Aristotle nor metaphysics for a new doctrine of nature, although at his hands all that remained of metaphysics were Aristotle's metaphysical categories. The question of whether Ockham was aware of what he was doing is like most searches for motive an idle one. There is no means of knowing; and such knowledge, even if it were there, would not alter the significance of what occurred. The real unsolved question concerns the uncommented *Metaphysics*. How would Ockham have established the independent status of metaphysics between the competing claims of logic and physics? That he did not write such a commentary, but returned twice more to the *Physics* in the *Summulae* and the *Questions* after his original Commentary on the eight books, and composed three treatises on logic after the early logical commentaries, may or may not be indicative. As it was, however, he confined himself to physics and logic; and in giving them an exclusively individual import he more than anyone provided a reorientation towards the natural world which was increasingly the accompaniment of scientific change. In that sense Ockham can be said to have helped to make nature accessible to investigation by taking it in its own terms. He thereby, indirectly, at least, provided the justification for Grosseteste's experimental methodology enunciated nearly a century before. But paradoxically Ockham's own stress upon the primacy of experience did not itself further—certainly in his own thinking—Grosseteste's scientific outlook. To make the individual the measure of all natural knowledge, so that movement can be identified with an individual body in motion and quantity with an individual being which has extension, does not of itself explain movement and quantity, but it does define what they are. It is therefore a definition—in this case a re-definition—but not a scientific explanation; and that for the most part is as far as Ockham's rethinking went. That is not to minimise it; indeed such simple re-ductions of physical categories to modes of individual existence were more total and far-reaching and ahead of their time than the majority of contemporary scientific theories; but ultimately, if taken only for themselves, they were also more limited. For they remained—for all their specificity and reliance upon evident experience—at the level of abstraction: and that was ultimately the limita-tion of Ockhamism. It became one more body of categories which in their formal-ism and emptiness differed little if at all from its rival school of Scotism by the end of the fifteenth century.

The source—though not of course the accountability—can be seen in Ockham's own thinking where the most striking lacuna is the absence of any adequate consideration of mathematics and non-experimental knowledge and the con-sequently incomplete account of self-evident knowledge which we have observed in chapter four. This inadequacy was the outcome of the sovereignty given to experience. In a contingent world no existential knowledge could be regarded as necessary, including mathematical propositions which like any others had to be of what existed, whether number or a triangle. Hence apart from what appear to be tautologies like 'The whole is greater than the part' to which the intellect im-mediately assents, there are no self-evident propositions which are not in the mode of possibility and/or derived from a non-first subject. The effect was not only to diminish the number of necessary and self-evident propositions, which could be used as premises in a strict demonstration, correspondingly diminishing the possibility of strict demonstration; it was also to deny a special status to mathema-tical propositions as non-experimental.[4] That was the reverse of Grosseteste's order of certainty where mathematics were the most certain knowledge of all accessible to man naturally, and knowledge of the external world which came through the senses the least certain of all. Ockham thereby divorced himself from the Oxford tradition of which Grosseteste had been the founder. The divergence was over the intelligible or the sensible as the way to truth. Those who chose the first had from the time of Plato invariably seen in mathematics its highest natural expression. Grosseteste's successors were no exception. Thinkers like Kilwardby and Bacon and, in Ockham's own day, Bradwardine, all combined a more tradi-tional Augustinian view of reality and truth with the study or advocacy of mathe-matics; and it was they above all Kilwardby and Bradwardine, and their successors such as Bradwardine's Mertonian followers, who made the greatest advances in mathematical and physical theory. The tendency among Ockham and his followers on the other hand was more towards a classificatory attitude through logic as the instrument of ordering natural experience. The primacy given to natural experience thus led to abstraction from experience and hence confinement within what could

---

[4] In that respect I cannot agree with A. C. Crombie, *Robert Grosseteste and the Origins of Experimental Science*, 171–5, in treating Ockham as well as Duns Scotus as a continuator of Grosseteste's scientific method.

be known from it: a limitation which only mathematical thinking could transcend.

It would therefore be misconceived to see the change to a more scientific attitude in the fourteenth century as having come through the displacement of Aristotle for a new naturalism with Ockham as the agent. Matters were more complex and gradual, as well as paradoxical, than that. Neither Ockham nor his opponents or successors ever renounced Aristotle; they gradually superseded more and more of his notions, a process which was not completed until the seventeenth century. Moreover, as it was initiated in the thirteenth century by those who were theologically and philosophically traditionalists, so it came in the fourteenth century increasingly to be pursued by those who were of no fixed intellectual pedigree: and one of the most striking developments intellectually of the later Middle Ages was the emergence of a distinct body of mathematicians and scientific thinkers in their own right who did not necessarily owe allegiance to any theological or philosophical school. What emerged therefore went beyond the intentions or agency of any one thinker or outlook.

That can be seen in turning to Ockham. Virtually all his discussion of the physical world was conducted within the accepted Aristotelian framework and was for the most part directed to its elucidation. His main conclusions are resumed in the *Summulae Physicorum*, which, as mentioned in the Introduction, was among his latest speculative writings, probably contemporary with the *Logic*; and like that work written in response, so his preface tells us, to numerous requests.[5] Its actual scale however is much smaller and its scope restricted to expounding nature according to Aristotle's principles and in conformity with Catholic truth. There seems no reason to doubt either intention.[6] Despite its imperfect form, which

[5] In addition to Brampton's denial of the authenticity of the *Summula* (*Isis* 55 (1964), 418–26), Fr J. A. Weisheipl, 'Ockham and some Mertonians', *Mediaeval Studies* 30 (1968), 172–3, has also expressed doubts. They arise from what he regards as the inferior and sometimes fallacious mode of the arguments, which he regards as unworthy and uncharacteristic of Ockham, and the discrepancy between the positions adopted there on form and quantity and in Ockham's other writings. While accepting the occasional lapses in argument, I do not think they are as pervasive as Fr Weisheipl suggests, nor is it by any means true that they consist mainly in repetitions and assertions, as should be apparent from what follows. I fail also to see the grounds on which he says that Ockham throughout the *Summulae* argues on the assumption of the unity of substantial form rather than a plurality to which he holds in the *Reportatio*, II, q. 9, cc. Ockham in the *Summulae* is for most of the time treating form generically in the abstract. Nor, similarly, do I discern any real discrepancy between his view of movement in the *Summulae* and in his other works. I agree that in his discussion of movement he does not place the same stress upon its contradictory nature, but then he is not arguing polemically in the *Summulae* as he is in the *Reportatio*, II, q. 9, cc. Consequently, while accepting that there are certain anomalies in the *Summulae* compared with Ockham's other writings, the work appears to me to be a faithful expression of Ockham's main positions—as Fr Weisheipl concedes—which has the advantage for our summary purposes of presenting a systematic resumé of his views.

[6] As S. Moser, *Grundbegriffe der Naturphilosophie bei Wilhelm von Ockham* (Innsbruck, 1932), 2, does the second. This work is a thorough examination of the *Summulae* in relation to Aristotle's concepts of being, cause, movement, and time. Although at times unduly scornful of Ockham's treatment of the latter it is a valuable study. The other recent work on Ockham's physical theories is H. Shapiro, *Motion, Time and Place according to William Ockham* (St Bonaventure, New York, and Louvain, 1957); its enquiry is more restricted than Moser's but the topics are more fully treated.

suggests that it was unrevised or imperfectly recorded, I shall draw upon it for much of what follows in the first three sections to show how Ockham did interpret those principles.

I NATURAL PHILOSOPHY AS A *SCIENTIA*

To begin with, although physics or natural philosophy, like any other *scientia*, is strictly speaking not one but a collection of many habits, they constitute a unity in being of the same nature and having a determinate order.[7] Their first subject by predication—as opposed to first subject by perfection which is more perfect being, or first subject by totality, of which there is no first subject except perhaps the whole world—is natural being. That does not mean that natural being as first subject is included in every part of physics; no first subject is in every part of any *scientia*. But it remains a unity because all its attributes are of the same kind; and it is the difference in the nature of the attributes affirmed of what can be the same subject—as being is equally the subject of physics and metaphysics—which as we have seen in chapter five is the difference between one *scientia* and another.[8]

Moreover in common with every *scientia* physics has strictly only two causes, since it consists not of real things composed of form and matter but of what is abstracted from real things—namely concepts—and so is simple. Its own compositeness as a *scientia* is therefore solely through aggregation as a collection of simple intelligibles. For the same reason its causes are extrinsic, as form and matter are intrinsic causes. The efficient cause is variously said to be the intellect or the object known or the terms of all three; or indeed other things, none of which Ockham pursues. The final cause is the reason for knowing. Improperly however, four causes can be admitted, with the material cause as the thing known and the formal the mode of knowing; neither however is strictly a condition of knowledge, which can be independently of the thing known and is not really distinct from the way in which things are known.[9] Finally the knowledge which physics gives is speculative because it is wholly or almost entirely of what is not in our power— heaven, earth, the celestial bodies, the elements—and hence is not practical.[10] While it includes *a priori* demonstrations *propter quid*, its knowledge is for the most part reached by starting from the more general and knowable and proceeding to the less general and less easily known, that is, from propositions containing more general terms to those whose terms are less general.

We have considered in chapters four and five how Ockham reconciles this order with that of the primacy of the individual as the first object known. The explanation is repeated briefly here: that while the individual is always first known distinctly—if not always indistinctly—knowledge of the genus as the most universal term is more easily acquired than that of different individuals because not everyone knows the same individuals. Thus those who have experience of lions, but not horses, will know that lions are animals in the same way as those who have experience of horses, but not lions, will know that horses are animals. They will

[7] *SP*, pt. I, ch. I.   [8] *Ibid.*, 2.   [9] *Ibid.*, 3.   [10] *Ibid.*, 4.

therefore each have knowledge of animal in common without knowing the same kind of animals.[11] Ockham is thereby able to explain Aristotle's statement in the *Physics*, that the universal is the first and most obviously known but not the most clearly known,[12] by interposing an initial stage of individual cognition before knowledge of the genus. He also reiterates the meaning which he gave in the *Ordinatio* to Aristotle's remark that a child begins by calling every man 'father' and every woman 'mother':[13] that it is only of singulars, since children like animals have only sense perception and not intellective knowledge, which is alone of universals. Here, too, Ockham has given Aristotle's words an individual import; for though it is true that Aristotle does call this knowledge sence perception he in no way implies that it is not universal; rather the contrary. In both these cases then Ockham appears to have gone beyond Aristotle's meaning, or more accurately restricted it to singulars. He does so again when, as Moser has observed,[14] he effectively reverses what is, for Aristotle, equivalent to an *a priori* order from knowledge of the more universal to the less universal, by calling the more universal the effect and the less universal the cause:[15] thus implying that the more universal—the genus —is derived from the less universal—originating in the individual as the first object of knowledge.

These disparities are characteristic of Ockham's relation to Aristotle, accepting his classifications but bending his meaning to express an individual ontology. That Ockham conceived the universe in essentially Aristotelian terms is apparent even in his original plan of the *Summulae*, which was to be not only of the natural world but the celestial bodies, inanimate and animate beings—including the rational soul —animals and plants.[16] The completed work in six parts did not extend further than the first—perhaps because of Ockham's summons to Avignon and involvement presently in the affairs of his order. We must now consider what he says in more detail.

II MATTER AND FORM

So far as the natural world is concerned, all natural beings are composed of form and matter as their inseparable constituents. That cannot be proved *a priori*, either that form or matter exists or that they are distinct from one another, but it can be shown *a posteriori* from the generation and destruction of natural bodies, whether animals, plants, fire, air, or any other. For nothing can be generated from nothing; therefore something must be presupposed and it must also be intrinsic to what is generated; otherwise they would be totally distinct, and generation could not be said to be from something. On the other hand, what is presupposed cannot be the

[11] *SP*, I, 5.
[12] *Physics*, I, ch. I, 184 a, 16–25.
[13] *Ibid.*, 184 b, 12.   [14] *Grundbegriffe*, 15–17.
[15] Ordine doctrine qui incipere debet a notioribus et facilioribus communitati cui tradenda est scientia, procedendum est ab effectu ad causam, et communioribus et facilioribus ad minus communia . . . (*SP, ibid.*, I, 5).
[16] *Ibid.*, 6.

same as what is generated; for then nothing new would be generated. It must therefore be a part, which together with the part which is generated, constitutes the complete thing that comes into being. The part which is presupposed is called matter and the part which is not presupposed form. Therefore they are both included in generation and are also distinct. This proof is in turn founded upon the principle that nothing comes from nothing (*ex nihilo nihil fit*),[17] which the philosophers treat as self-evident and so do not try to prove. Its truth however can be persuaded from experience, namely that nothing is generated unless something previous is destroyed, as fire is generated from the destruction of earth or wood, and air from the destruction of fire; and where something is in something else and nothing is destroyed, as sensation is in vision or the sun illuminates air, there is no destruction. In each case the existence of something else is presupposed. Neither destruction nor non-destruction is therefore from nothing.[18]

With Aristotle Ockham calls matter and form the first principles of all actual being and becoming, as the two contraries from which everything else derives but which are not themselves derived from one another.[19] But for Ockham unlike Aristotle that is because they are the essential parts of all that exists, whether caused naturally or artificially.[20] They therefore lose the metaphysical status which they had for Aristotle as the first principles or primary contraries from which everything else, no matter what—whether musicality or the property of whiteness—comes to be or passes away;[21] and instead become the physical constituents of all actual—i.e. individual—being. The difference was both cosmic and ontological. To Aristotle form and matter were first principles in virtue of being contraries; like nearly all his Greek predecessors he believed that all being was governed by opposite or contrary principles; and he devotes two chapters of the first book of the *Physics* (four and five) to examining those of past thinkers before stating his own solution of identifying those principles with matter and form. They therefore represent the principles of being itself, in all its facets, not just as the constituents of individuals beings, which they are for Ockham in a physical world where only individual things exist. He therefore narrows Aristotle's conception of matter and form to those of merely material and formal cause, virtually ignoring their relation as contraries in other than an empirical sense: namely that something can only come from its contrary and not that to which it is merely indifferent.

Now in the case of matter and form, they are contrasted as privation and

---

[17] *Ibid.*, 7.   [18] *Ibid.*

[19] *Physics*, I, ch. 5, 188 a, 27–8; *SP*, I, 8.

[20] Eo enim quod sunt partes rei generate, sunt principia eius tam in esse quam in fieri, quia res non potest fieri nec esse sine partibus essentialibus, cuiusmodi sunt materia et forma (*SP*, *ibid.*).

[21] Compare Aristotle: 'It does not matter whether we take attunement, order or composition for our illustration; the principle [that everything that comes to be or passes away comes from or passes into its contrary or an intermediate state] is obviously the same in all, and in fact applies equally to the production of a house, a statue or any other complex (*Physics, ibid.*, 188 b, 15–18).

Compare also Moser, *Grundbegriffe*, 25–6 who was the first to point to this as well as the other numerous discrepancies between Ockham and Aristotle. But Moser exaggerates when he says that Ockham always calls form and matter the parts and never the principles.

possession; for generation consists precisely in matter's receipt of a form of which it was previously deprived.[22] It is in that broad sense as a contrary—to possession—that privation is the third principle of generation, in addition to matter and form, because there is no generation without privation. If there were, matter would already possess the form which it receives through generation; something would then be generated before generation, an impossibility. Generation therefore presupposes matter's privation of form; and the inclusion of privation as the third principle of generation is expressed in the nominal definition of generation as the existence of a thing whose matter was previously deprived of a form and now possesses it immediately.[23]

Privation is not, however, a real thing in the way that matter and form are real. That can be seen from its different meanings. By the first it is the form to be expelled by a contrary form, so that one contrary form is the privation of another. By the second it means the subject, with which it is numerically one in signifying the same deprived thing, but remains nominally distinct in having a separate nominal definition.[24] That is Ockham's interpretation of Aristotle's statement that 'the subject is numerically one, although it is two in form' while the contrary and the privation are incidental.[25] From which Ockham not unjustly concludes that privation and its subject are numerically the same, so that 'privation' can be taken for the same as that which is deprived. Where he departs from Aristotle is in distinguishing them by their different nominal definitions, which he justifies by translating 'form' to mean 'definition' or 'being'. There is nothing to suppose that that was Aristotle's meaning; and in that supposition Ockham was substituting a nominal for a real interpretation of privation. Privation and subject are thereby made equivocal by Ockham, in one sense being taken in conjunction—which he says Aristotle for the sake of brevity omitted—and so significatively; in the other for the terms themselves, where they each have a different definition, as 'man' and 'white' are really the same but differ in their definitions as terms. Ockham meets the obvious rejoinder that definitions are of things not terms by pointing to Aristotle's opening of the *Physics* as an example of the many instances in which they are of words.[26] That can be accepted while recognising that Aristotle was not talking of words in the same context as Ockham. Ockham's resolution of the relation of privation to subject here is thus one of different definitions having the same signification, with the definition signifying explicitly that which the defined signifies implicitly.[27]

The third and fourth definitions of privation involve less explanation. The third is one of the pair of contraries—privatives and positives—which Aristotle treats in the *Categories* and which are of the same subject. According to Aristotle it is 'A universal rule that each of a pair of opposites of this type has reference to that to

---

[22] *SP, ibid.*

[23] Generatio est existentia rei cuius materia prius fuit privata forma, quam nunc primo habet, ita quod ista tria, materia forma et privatio, ponuntur in diffinitione tam generationis quam generati, et propter hoc dicuntur principia (*ibid.*).

[24] *Ibid.*   [25] *Physics*, I, ch. 7, 23–8.

[26] *Ibid.*, ch. I, 184 b, 10–14.   [27] *SP, ibid.*

which the particular positive is natural', so that something is deprived when it does not have what it should have, as for example blindness refers to what should have sight.[28] Ockham however, interprets these opposites simply as opposite names or terms,[29] thereby once again excluding the ontological import which they clearly had for Aristotle. In the fourth and last definition privation is taken not strictly for the subject but for a complete expression corresponding to its meaning. Thus the statement that there cannot be a return to possession from privation must be translated, not that there is something called privation which makes such a return impossible, but that what is deprived of something cannot regain it.[30]

That privation is not something distinct from matter and form follows, because beyond matter and form nothing conceivable exists outside the soul. If therefore privation were something real it would be either matter or form or their composite. It would then, according to those who hold that it is distinct from matter and form, have to subsist in matter; but distinct privations are in relation to distinct forms; hence on the same ground it could be argued that one form introduced into matter can subsist in it without the destruction of a previous form. There could then be infinite forms in the same matter and so infinite privations, which is absurd. It would also mean that since privation is coeval with matter, matter would at some time itself be deprived of privation by the subsequent advent of a privation; and then with the coming of a form not only would a preceding form be expelled but there would also be the privation of a preceding privation, which is nonsensical. Privation then cannot be distinct from matter and it is not form, which alone is in matter. If therefore it existed independently of either it would be nothing, and then it would not be distinct from either as nothing is not distinct from anything.[31] Nor can it be in matter as a negative quality for the same reasons. It must therefore be taken, in so far as it exists outside the soul, for matter by one signification and for a form to be expelled by another signification.[32] In both senses it can variously be called the principle of generation. As standing for the form to be expelled it is an accident; and then it will not be the principle of all generation because in some accidental generation—such as the illumination of the air or sensation—no form is expelled but one is simply introduced. Where, however, generation is through the expulsion of a previous form, then privation is a principle not as cause or as a real part of generation or what is generated, but because generation begins with the expulsion of a preceding form. Hence expulsion is itself generation. This kind of generation would then be defined nominally as the form to be expelled or which is expelled, not as the essential principle constituting the essence of that which is generated, but as an accidental element contained in its

---

[28] *Categories*, ch. 10, 12 a, 26–34.
[29] Tertio modo accipitur hoc nomen privatio pro nomine privativo . . . et hoc nomen contradictorium accipitur pro nomine (*SP, ibid.*, 9), Moser, 29–30.
[30] *Ibid.*
[31] *Ibid.*, ch. 10.
[32] Dicendum est ergo quod privatio non est aliquid in rerum natura extra animam quomodocunque distinctum a materia et forma; sed privatio que est extra, vel est materia secundum unam significationem vel est forma expellenda secundum aliam significationem (*ibid.*).

nominal definition. If on the other hand privation is taken for the subject it is then the principle of generation, as the subject is the principle.[33]

How then is privation to be regarded as a third principle distinct from both matter and form, if it can be assimilated to each and is not really distinct from either? The answer is that it is a third term which is not synonymous with one or the other and which together with them must be included in a definition of generation. That was Aristotle's own intention when he said that there were three principles but only two things.[34] The reason is that one of the things namely, matter as the subject, is first deprived of form and afterwards receives it; and only in being potentially able to receive a form, but actually deprived of it, is generation possible. Privation therefore denotes matter's capacity to receive a form and so is truly included in a definition of generation.[35] Ockham thus makes privation a phase of generation, as that which precedes the introduction of a form. He thereby also reduces it to a constituent of real being—or more accurately to a temporal relation between matter and form—rather than, as Aristotle appeared to regard it, treating it as an independent principle. Once again Ockham faces the objection that Aristotle was talking about real things and not names and so for Aristotle privation was not merely a name but stood for something real. His reply is that in natural philosophy as in the other real sciences Aristotle frequently employed their terms logically: that is, as terms of second intention standing for terms of first intention, as 'animal' predicated of 'man' taken significatively is equivalent to a proposition of real natural science as 'Man is an animal'. The same applies to 'principle' predicated of 'privation' which is convertible with the proposition 'Privation is a principle'. It does not however mean that privation is something real; and when Aristotle himself declared that in some way there are three principles and in some way two, he was denying that more than two existed absolutely as real things (a parte rei) but recognising that they had three definitions.[36]

Thus Ockham resolved Aristotle's uncertainties. His resolution can hardly be credited to Aristotle's intention, which certainly was not concerned with definitions but with metaphysical principles. Privation for him was defined neither in terms of matter nor form but ontologically as that which 'in its own nature is not-being'.[37] As such it is not merely a name for something that does not exist itself, and is included in the definition of something else, but that from which—namely 'what is not'—something comes to be. Privation accordingly is for Aristotle the negative principle or state accompanying the contrary principle of non-being from which its contrary—positive being—results. It is not-being in a real ontological sense 'qua not-being',[38] and not in a nominal sense as a definition, which it is for Ockham. Ockham's justification for the discrepancy is the familiar one that Aristotle like many authors does not always use words precisely so that his meaning must be

---

[33] Ibid., ch. 11.

[34] Ockham is presumably referring to the Physics, I, ch. 7, 190 b, 35: 'The principles therefore are in a way not more in number than the contraries but as it were two, nor yet precisely two since there is a difference of essential nature, but three'.

[35] SP, ch. 11.   [36] Ibid.

[37] Physics, I, ch. 8, 191 b, 12–17, 192 a, 3–5.   [38] Ibid., 191 b, 25–6.

gauged from his intention and not solely from strict usage.[39] That includes appearing to treat terms significatively in an *actus exercitus* when their import is non- significative in an *actus significatus*. Hence just as 'risible' affirmed of man does not stand for anything really distinct from individual men able to laugh, so 'principle' affirmed of privation signifies nothing distinct from matter and form. The objection cannot therefore be upheld that privation is distinct from matter either because it is nothing and matter is something or because it is the contrary of a form and matter is the subject of contraries, of which one must therefore be privation. To say that privation is in matter is either untrue or if it is true means either that matter is deprived of form or that privation as the absence of a form is predicated of matter.[40] Similarly for matter to be the subject of contraries can mean either that it can have successively contrary forms or that successively contrary forms can be predicated of matter.[41]

Privation is not therefore some third thing. Matter, as the subject which is first deprived of a form and then receives it, remains the same subject without the presence or loss of anything called privation inhering in it as, in Aristotle's example, a man who is first musical and then unmusical remains the same man without the destruction of unmusicality. All such expressions as 'destruction' applied to privation are only metaphors for the introduction of a form into a subject which was previously without it. Accordingly when Aristotle calls privation an accidental principle[42] he means not that it is an accident distinct from matter and form but that it has a negative signification, namely of a non-existing form which can only be an essential principle of generation when it exists. In that sense privation is equivalent to a future proposition that something can be deprived of a form which it will have immediately afterwards.[43] Hence, when taken simply of present existence, privation is not true because nothing which is the principle of non-being can be essentially true.[44]

Having thus disposed of the independent existence of privation through its identification with matter and form, we must now consider how Ockham regards matter and form for themselves. They are to begin with the essential first principles of all generation and whatever is generated, included in whatever exists. But they are not the only first principles; different things have different principles and there are as many diverse things as there are principles of generation, although sometimes diverse things can have the same principle.[45] All form and matter are singular because, as Aristotle says, no universal is a substance; hence no universal can be the principle of any singular thing. Moreover only first matter, as we shall consider in a moment, precedes what is generated; form does not, but receives its own existence through generation. Universals cannot then be the first principles of being; and the genera of form and matter, as we by now should know, are merely universal names, with the individuals for which they stand each having its

<hr />

[39] *SP*, I, 12 and 13, which are devoted to reconciling Ockham's position with Aristotle's and meeting objections.

[40] *Ibid.*, ch. 13.   [41] *Ibid.*   [42] *Physics*, I, ch. 7, 189 b, 34–190 a, 8.

[43] *SP, ibid.*   [44] *Ibid.*   [45] *Ibid.*, 14.

own individual form and its own individual first matter. Therefore, while for generation as such, matter and form suffice as the two essential principles, in the generation of diverse beings there must be diverse matter and form, each distinct from the other, so that 'my first matter is not the same as your first matter'; and then it is not enough to say that matter and form are the only two principles of all generation.[46]

Now matter itself actually exists as something real which is at the same time in potency to all substantial forms (i.e. able to receive them and thereby become an actual substance) without necessarily possessing any form. Only in relation to form therefore is it potential; in itself it is always actual.[47] For that reason indeed matter is itself ingenerable and incorruptible since in being independent of any form it owes its existence to no—natural—power.[48] Hence its own existence consists in a formless—inchoate—being; and even when it does receive a form, nothing additional is engendered in matter beyond the actual being which results—through generation—as the conjunction of matter and form. No third thing is required because all substantial being is a composite of matter and form as its two essential parts. When united to a form, matter is thus transformed into a generable and corruptible with which it is numerically one.[49]

We have then to distinguish between matter in its own nature and matter as it is differentiated into individual substances. It is the same matter, which for Ockham is all first or prime matter; the difference lies in the absence or presence of a substantial form. When it is present, according to the form's nature, its matter will be that of a man or an ass or air or fire or any other body. When there is no form matter remains undifferentiated; in that state although it actually exists it cannot be known in itself either to the intellect or the senses, but only by analogy from knowledge of individual material substances.[50]

This distinction therefore is of two different modes of matter's existence. Unlike Aristotle who, in his numerous elaborations in the *Metaphysics* of the different meanings of potentiality,[51] never appeared to hold that matter actually existed independently of form, Ockham in the recent Franciscan tradition[52] does just that. He therefore differed from Aristotle in recognising that although matter

---

[46] *Ibid.*

[47] Et primo de materia. Circa quam est sciendum quod materia est quedam res actualiter existens in rerum natura, que est in potentia ad omnes formas substantiales, nullam habens necessario semper sibi inherentem et inexistentem ... Et ideo non est imaginandum quod materia sit quid in potentia tantum de se, scilicet ad essendum ad modum quo albedo futura est tantum in potentia. Sed materia est vere actu ex seipsa ita quod per nullam virtutem potest esse in potentia ad esse in rerum natura ... licet semper sit in potentia ad formam qua privatur (*ibid.*, 15).

[48] Immo ipsa [material] est de se ingenerabilis et incorruptibilis, que per nullam potentiam potest non existere et ideo esse suum proprium non habet a forma (ibid.). Ockham does not say 'natural power' here, but in the context of his outlook it must be inferred. See below.

[49] Ibid. [50] *Ibid.*

[51] E.g. bk. v, ch. 4, 1015 a, 7–10; v, ch. 12, 1019 a, 15–1020 a, 5; vii, 8, 1033 b, 5–8; viii, ch. 1, 1042 a, 27–8; ix, ch. 6, 1048 a, 25–1048 b, 17.

[52] See J. A. Weisheipl, 'Matter in fourteenth-century science' in *The Concept of Matter*, edited by E. McMullin, 151 ff.

alone is not a substance—a 'this' in Aristotle's words[53]—it is nevertheless something real which is actually *in rerum natura*. In one sense this is a more logically consistent position than that of Aristotle; for if matter is, as both thinkers agree, a primary substratum of each thing which comes to be,[54] it must have some place in the physical world in virtue of being an element in all substance. The divergence, however, lies it would seem elsewhere: namely that throughout Ockham was translating Aristotle's metaphysical principles, which do not necessarily have a direct existential import, into terms of individual existence, where they either refer to real individuals or they must be reduced to them connotatively and nominally as privation was. Consequently matter as the essential constituent of all actual being must itself exist actually: its actuality merely has different modes according to whether it is undifferentiated or differentiated into individual substances. Hence the distinction between potentiality and actuality is not for Ockham between the ability to exist—as possibility or capability, in Aristotle's scheme[55]—but between different states of actual existence.

In many ways the difference is a fundamental one; for it helps to endow matter with its own separate identity where previously, both from an Aristotelian view, by which it was dependent upon a substantial form, and from an Augustinian point of view, in having its own form of corporeity, matter's actuality was appropriated to a form. It also however presents the problem of matter's ingenerability and incorruptibility, which was not presented to Aquinas for whom, true to Aristotle, matter received its being from form.[56] Hence it was not already in existence as it was for Ockham. When therefore he says that matter as it exists is ingenerable and incorruptible he appears to be sailing close to the theological wind, and one modern commentator says expressly that he violated Catholic doctrine.[57] In view of the role that Ockham has consistently assigned to God, as creator, first cause, and concause, that cannot be sustained. But it is also true that his standpoint here does *prima facie* present an anomaly which he did not seem to recognise, probably because he took it for granted that, like everything else, first matter must be the result of God's creation, and that nature was being considered here in its own—or more strictly Aristoteleian—terms.[58]

Ockham's arguments for the actual existence of matter are founded on the rejection of an intermediate state between actual being and non-being; that is to say, all being must in some way of what actually exists. He expresses it in his first proof as follows: 'What is not cannot be a principle; but matter is part and principle of a composite being [of form and matter]; therefore it is an actual being which actually exists'.[59] His other reasons are that every substance exists outside the mind and matter is a substance as part and principle of a substance; that only what is not actual can be produced *de novo* but that cannot apply to matter which, as presupposed in whatever exists, must already exist; and finally that if matter

---

[53] *Ibid.*, VIII, I, 1042a, 27–8.   [54] *Physics*, I, 9, 192 a, 29–32.
[55] *Metaphysics*, IX, ch. 4, 1047 b, 3 30.   [56] Moser, *Grundbegriffe*, 19–50
[57] Moser, *ibid.*, 50.   [58] This is an example of the anomalies to be found in *SP*.
[59] *SP*, I, 16.

were not actual that would be because it was never without a form, and then correspondingly no form would ever be without matter, which is false.[60]

That in turn explains matter's ingenerability and incorruptibility; for whether generable and corruptible are applied strictly to a part or to a whole which newly comes into being or is destroyed—in which sense form is also ingenerable and incorruptible—matter cannot begin to be or cease to be. As Aristotle said, whatever exists exists, either as part of something else or in something else as its subject. Matter does neither, because as no being is more simple than first matter none can presuppose it; otherwise it would not be first matter or simple, but would itself have some other first matter.[61]

Now by 'actual' and 'being', which are effectively interchangeable, Ockham means one of two things: either that which informs something else or that which really exists, in contrast to what can be but does not exist. By the first meaning matter can be said to be in potency to every substantial act (i.e. form), and form can be said to give matter being *de novo*, in the sense of informing matter as an actual substance composed of matter and form. But in the second sense, of actually existing *in rerum natura* as opposed to not actually existing, matter has its being independently and before the existence of form.[62] Hence the distinction in each case is between matter's existence as a substance, when it is dependent upon a form, and its existence as part of nature, when it is not. By that means all objections to matter's own actuality can be met.

In the first place, it is only potential to form and the actual substantial being which comes with form, but not in itself; hence when Aristotle says that matter is possibility, that is to be interpreted in relation to form. Possibility thus refers to matter's own substance in its capacity to receive a form and not to any third thing which is intermediate to matter and form. For the same reason it is not a relation founded in matter; but matter itself. As a term, however, potency is relative and as such signifies matter which can have something else (namely a form) which it does not have, as man can be in potency to whiteness when he is not white but can be.[63] That potency does not exist in matter as something real can be proved; for it would then be either a substance and so precede a form in matter, or it would be an accident when it would not among other consequences survive the advent of a form. Nor would it be related to one form more than to another, and since matter can be in potency to infinite forms, it would contain an infinity of real things. Potentiality if real would also be a distinct body under the form to which matter was in potency, and then one body would be in potency to another, which is equally false and absurd. It is accordingly more exact to say that matter is potency rather than in potency since they are really the same. Moreover once matter has received a form it is no longer in potency to it. Therefore it is not always in potency, as Socrates is able not to be white when he is white.[64] Matter consequently is not simply potency. Lastly, from the same distinction between matter as actual in itself and in conjunction with form, the objection can be rebutted that, if matter

---

[60] *Ibid.*   [61] *Ibid.*, 17; also 15.   [62] *Ibid.*, 16, 17.
[63] *Ibid.*   [64] *Ibid.*

were real being, form would then be its accident, since matter only becomes a part of substance through receiving a form.[65]

The indestructibility of matter also means that the same matter, as a species, is in all things.[66] That follows both on the principle of economy and because the same matter belonging to something destroyed must be afterwards in something generated; otherwise one thing would not be immediately transmutable into something else, but only indirectly. The matter of different things must, however, be numerically distinct; for the same subject cannot simultaneously contain contraries or be in diverse places as different substances are.

Matter thus has its own unity and diversity distinct from that of form. Whereas all independent substances ultimately derive their unity and diversity as genera and species from form, matter constitutes the unity and diversity of the undifferentiated being which presupposes them and which they do not therefore owe to form.[67] It is also inseparable from physical extension. The latter is logically an accident in always being predicated of matter in the second essential mode connotatively (where matter is included in the definition of extension, which signifies matter and consignifies having extended parts). Consequently matter without extension is impossible since it must always have extended parts which whether united as those of air and water are, or more diffused, cannot all occupy the same place.[68] Extension is therefore nothing distinct from quantity, as Ockham has repeatedly emphasised in his various treatments of quantity, and as we shall consider subsequently in the final section of this chapter. Nor is it of any determinate measure but varies with the degree of quantity, which itself varies with the quantity of matter whose parts are in turn more or less extended according to the nature of the form to which it is subject: more when the form is fire, less, as we have said, when it is air or water, but always having some distance between its parts.

Accordingly matter is dimensional without being of any set dimension.[69] In this view Ockham was endowing it with its own physical characteristics; and his radical simplification, whatever significance it may or may not have had at the time, represents an important departure from medieval tradition.[70] For in refusing

---

[65] Ibid., 17.

[66] Ista autem materia prima est eiusdem rationis in omnibus compositis, sed non est una numero in omnibus compositis (ibid., 18).

[67] Ad primum istorum est dicendum quod omnis unitas et distinctio per se existentis in genere ultimate et completive est a forma ... tamen unitas et distinctio non existentium per se in genere, cuiusmodi est materia, non est a forma, immo precedit formam. Sicut enim materia tota presupponitur toti forme recepte in ea ita pars materie presupponitur parti forme (ibid.).

[68] Sciendum est autem quod licet hec sit vera per accidens, 'Materia est extensa', distinguendo 'per accidens' contra per se primo modo, hec tamen est necessaria et semper vera, et per se in secundo modo, quia impossibile est quod sit materia sine extensione (ibid., 19). Moser, Grundbegriffe, 54, is mistaken when he asserts that predication should be in the first essential mode on the grounds that first matter is simple and so cannot have an essential part. That is to confuse predication with signification: predication by the second essential mode, as by the first mode, stands only for the subject as something real, but in a nominal and not a real definition. Quantity therefore for Ockham is no more real than rationality: each describes an aspect or property— in a logical sense—of its subject and nothing internal or external to it. Moser's reaction—from the standpoint of Aristotelian orthodoxy—is perhaps indicative of Ockham's departure from it.

[69] SP, I, 19.   [70] See also Moser, Grundbegriffe, 56.

to regard the categories of Aristotle as metaphysical principles and in treating being as solely individual, Ockham annexed to matter, as one of the two components of being, quantity and extension. He thereby took a notable step in the direction of the modern conception of matter as having dimensionality and dispensing with quantity as something in itself distinct. It was still only a step; for Ockham was not able to go to the full extent of regarding matter as that which exists independently. For all his valiant efforts to give it its own actuality, it remains insubstantial and like form inaccessible in itself to the intellect or the senses. Neither can be known without the other and only by an intellectual process of composition from, as we have said, analogy with the other: in Ockham's own comparison one cannot be known without the other as a father cannot be known independently of the existence of a son.[71]

So much for matter. What Ockham has to say about form takes only one chapter to matter's six. His definition of form is either as all being that is not matter, or a composite of form and matter, namely as the other part of a composite substance, an accident, and a separated form. Alternatively it can be taken precisely for the other part of material substance, which is its sense here.[72] As such, it is like matter, a real thing. Unlike matter, it cannot exist alone but always in conjunction with matter, sometimes inhering in matter and giving it substance, sometimes not in matter and then lacking all existence, as whiteness in a body does.[73] The distinction is presumably between substantial and accidental form and is in keeping with Ockham's rejection elsewhere of the formal distinction between say whiteness and milk, to take his own example in the *Ordinatio*. Ockham does not raise the issue here, but neither does he explain how, if forms or qualities such as whiteness do not really inhere in their subjects, all qualities can be regarded as absolutes. Again form unlike matter is only ingenerable and indestructible in the strict sense—which is also Aristotle's—of that which is generated or destroyed from a pre-existing part (namely matter). But in the broader—non-Aristotelian sense—of that which comes into being or is destroyed *de novo* it is both generable and destructible. For if it could not be newly produced or destroyed both matter and form would be presupposed in the existence of everything; nothing would then be generated, and generation would be indistinguishable from aggregation and the mere addition of one part to another in the way that a house is built.[74] Form is therefore the agent in the generation or destruction of a substance. Its advent or loss determines the existence or non-existence of a substance and with it a form's own existence or

---

[71] Etiam ostendendum est quomodo materia prima non est intelligibilis sive cognoscibilis per se, id est non est intelligibilis cognitione simplici et propria . . . Oportet autem scire quod hoc non solum verum est de materia, sed etiam de forma, quia forma substantialis per aliam viam cognosci non potest; immo sicut materia cognoscitur per analogiam ad formam, ita forma substantialis cognoscitur per analogiam ad materiam (*SP*, I, 20).

[72] *Ibid.*, I, 21.

[73] Est autem talis forma quedam res que per se non potest esse sed semper est in composito adveniens materie supposite, sine qua esse non potest, que aliquando est in materia substentante eam et aliquando non solum est in materia sed simpliciter desinit esse ad modum quo albedo desinit esse in corpore (*ibid.*).

[74] *Ibid.*

non-existence. It also determines the nature of a subject. Hence, once more in contrast to matter, all forms cannot be of the same nature; if they were, all being— that is to say everything generated—would be of the same nature in having both matter and form of the same nature.[75] The final characteristic of form is that it too, like matter, has physical extension for the same reasons as matter has.[76]

This last conclusion confirms, if confirmation were needed, that Ockham's conception of form was not Aristotle's. Although continuing to regard it with Aristotle as the determining principle of being, Ockham has reduced being to individual physical substance and form to one of its two singular physical constituents. It is no longer as it was for Aristotle interchangeable with species or essence or archetype;[77] the first has become a logical concept; the second the same as an individual being; the third excluded from consideration. For Ockham then form can be generated and destroyed in the non-Aristotelian sense of coming to be or ceasing to be, because it is a physical property, whereas for Aristotle form is its own essence or substance: 'By form I mean the essence of each thing and its primary substance'.[78] It is that by which something (matter) already existing is produced.[79] Hence for Aristotle both matter and form pre-exist; and generation consists in producing in matter (in Aristotle's example, brass) a form—of roundness or a sphere—as its essence or shape, making the whole a brazen sphere.[80] Accordingly when Ockham like Aristotle argues against an additional form of the whole substance beyond the form and matter composing it[81] he is arguing for something different from Aristotle: namely for the adequacy of matter and form as the elements of any substance as opposed to Aristotle's view that the form is the form of the whole in virtue of its own wholeness and independence of the elements: in the way that the parts of a house are a house because of the presence of the essence of a house as the cause, or a syllable is not its elements.[82] The form on this view therefore stands beyond its elements.

There should be no need to labour this difference between explaining physical beings in terms of their own physical properties and in terms of metaphysical principles. Ockham effectively reduced form to an efficient cause; a momentous step theoretically, although he neither acknowledged it, as we shall see again presently in his discussion of physical cause, nor did his contemporaries or successors appear to appreciate it. Yet the abandonment of a fourfold causality is one of the fundamental differences between a medieval and a modern conception of the world.

---

[75] *Ibid.*

[76] Est autem ista forma extensa habens partem distantem a parte sicut materia habet partem distantem a parte (*ibid.*).

[77] E.g. *Metaphysics*, VII, ch. 6, 1031 b, 1–21, 1032 a, 5–6; ch. 7, 1032 b, 1; ch. 8, 1033 a, 24–5; ch. 17, 1041 b, 4–9.

[78] *Ibid.*, 1032 b, 1.   [79] *Ibid.*, 1033 a, 25.

[80] *Ibid.*, 1033 a, 1–20.   [81] *SP*, I, 25.

[82] *Metaphysics*, 1041 b, 4–end. E.g. . . . their substance [sc. of things] would seem to be this kind of nature [sc. a formal cause] which is not an element but a principle. An *element*, on the other hand, is that into which a thing is divided and which is present in it as matter; e.g. *a* and *b* are the elements of a syllable (*ibid.*, 30–33).

For Ockham, then, generation of natural beings is explained through the conjunction of matter and form occupying the same place.[83] Beyond the fact that they are related as potency and act there is no other explanation, which must therefore be accepted as irreducible, as many other things also known only from experience must be accepted without knowing their cause.[84] Experience—not metaphysics—is therefore the source of our knowledge of matter and form as of all absolute beings which they compose; and the general concepts which we have of matter and form are themselves the result of abstraction from individual experience and not from *a priori* principles. Ockham also not surprisingly rejects the notion of Albert the Great (the one scholastic named in the *Summulae*) of an inchoate form in matter, since it could in turn only be either matter or form, and so either the same as matter or presupposed by matter.[85]

Ockham comes closest to breaking with the entire Aristotelian scheme of form and matter over the generation and destruction of artificial things which he attributes solely to local movement and not to the advent or loss of a form. Thus a house owes its existence not to something new, as natural substances do, but to the assemblage of its parts in a certain order; and similarly its destruction is due to their separation and not to the cessation of something which was there before.[86] Accordingly generation and destruction are only applied improperly to artificial things to mean the verification of something's existence after its non-existence and of its non-existence after its existence.[87] The artificiality of non-natural things therefore consists in having an external agent who, although sometimes producing new accidental and substantial forms by means of natural causes, as for example in agriculture, does not do so invariably.[88] Nor is the agent itself the cause of anything new but simply of local movement as the builder of a house brings the stones and wood together but does not in ordering them as a house thereby introduce a new form.[89] Accordingly while artificial things are composed of natural things, the latter as their parts can exist independently of the whole—as form and matter cannot—and correspondingly the whole can survive the loss of a part as one member of a people can die without the whole people dying.[90] The more inconsistent of Ockham then to take the latter example as an analogy, for the unity of matter and form in a composite being requiring no other element.[91]

More germane, though, he effectively denies the Aristotelian doctrine than an artificial no less than a natural being has an essence or a form by which its parts

<hr/>

[83] Et est sciendum quod materiam et formam esse principia generationis et generati non est aliud quam materiam et formam simul in eodem in eodem loco et situ existere (*SP*, I, 23).

[84] *Ibid.*   [85] *Ibid.*, I, 24.

[86] Dicitur enim domus fieri vel generari non quod aliqua eius pars secundum se totam sit nova, sed solum quia partes per motum localem congregantur debiteque situantur, ita quod nulla res de novo advenit, sed una iuxta aliam debite vel supra aliam collocatur. Similiter per solam segregationem partium dicitur domus corrumpi (*ibid.*, I, 22). Also 25, 26.

[87] *Ibid.*, I, 22.   [88] *Ibid.*, I, 26.

[89] Quia artifex nihil agit, nisi quia movet localiter, sed movens localiter non causat novam rem sed facit tantum rem esse in loco in quo non erat prius (*ibid.*).

[90] *Ibid.*, I, 25.

[91] *Ibid.* First remarked by Moser, *Grundbegriffe*, 65.

constitute a real thing, as the parts of a house are a house because of the presence of the form of a house.[92] Although he reverses Aristotle's meaning in attributing to him the view that artificial things have in themselves the principles of movement,[93] he makes the distinction between natural and artificial things more far-reaching. For in dispensing with the need for form at all in artificial things, he was left with only matter and local movement as the elements in their generation, and the only two which have survived from Aristotle's classification. That does not make Ockham modern but it effectively takes him outside the received medieval tradition of Aristotle, by assimilating everything real to individuals composed of matter and form as the physical elements of all existence.

III CAUSALITY

From our standpoint one of the most instructive sections of the *Summulae* is that devoted to the causes of natural things. There Ockham resumes not only what he has just said about generation and destruction but his view of causes generally, which we have encountered at different points throughout this book. Although this section holds nothing new it does provide a conspectus of his own standpoint which in view of previous discussion we shall only briefly consider. To begin with it shows the tendency within his acceptance of a fourfold causality to treat efficient and final cause as the universal means of explanation. They are what he calls extrinsic causes, in contradistinction to material and formal cause as intrinsic causes;[94] a division not found in Aristotle. Of these four, material cause can be defined as that which is transmuted by an agent, whether into something real inhering in it (as matter is changed into a substantial form), its strict sense; or improperly by local movement into something which contains it: which is how Ockham defined the generation of artificial things. When matter is changed naturally by a form, a composite being exists which did not exist before, and also artificially in an improper sense, as the bronze from which a statue is fashioned is now something determinate where before it was merely bronze.[95]

A formal cause can similarly be understood strictly and properly for a distinct thing informing matter with which it constitutes a complete unity, or for an accident in a subject with which it is a unity, as a white man is both man and white; or alternatively for something which it was not before, as in the previous example of a bronze statue, where the bronze is improperly said to be the material cause and the figure can be improperly called the formal cause. Hence, although both material and formal causes have other meanings, for example for the logician or philosopher, in the case of natural philosophy each is defined in relation to the other. They must not therefore be identified with form and matter. Thus the substantial form is the form of matter, with which it is a part of the whole composed of

---

[92] E.g., 'Why are these materials a house? Because that which was the essence of a house is present' (*Metaphysics*, VII, ch. 17, 1041 b, 3–4).
[93] *SP*, I, 26; *Physics*, II, ch. 1, 192 b, 19.
[94] *SP*, ibid., II, 1.   [95] *Ibid*.

matter and form; the formal cause is of the whole, and is not itself a part. Hence it is formal cause in virtue of the conjunction of matter and form. The same applies to the material cause.[96] Ockham does not explore this distinction, which would if pursued have made formal (and by the same token material) cause into a definition as opposed to something real. Over both he was presented with the problem of reconciling what he himself called intrinsic causes with independent principles standing in some way beyond matter and form as physical elements: that is to say of how to define material and formal cause as wholes when matter and form are parts. Since for Ockham a whole which is not a real thing must be a concept, it would have meant superseding the accepted meaning of material and formal cause and indeed questioning their *raison d'être*. Perhaps that is why he had little to say about them.

No such problems arise with the two extrinsic causes. Of efficient cause he distinguishes three senses. Strictly it means something new; broadly something becoming something different as in artificial things where the parts of a house become a house; and most broadly of all for everything moving something else, however that occurs: whether by making one thing from many, or changing or withdrawing its parts or just changing its local position, in the way that the heavenly intelligence is called the efficient cause of the movement of the heavens; and then nothing new is caused in what is moved. It is however in the first sense that the real existence of an efficient cause is responsible for the real existence of something totally new and distinct: as heat is caused by the proximity of fire to wood.[97] For Ockham this meaning of efficient cause is the foundation of all knowledge of one thing as the cause of another.[98] From that he reaffirms a conclusion which we have earlier encountered more than once, that strictly there is no *sine qua non* of anything in the positive sense of an occasion or condition, although it can sometimes be conceded negatively in the limiting sense that some impediment must first be removed before a cause can act, such as opening a window—then usually without glass—to the sun's rays. Efficient cause can further be distinguished as sufficient (or some improperly call it total) and insufficient, where it cannot act without something else. Efficient cause can also be universal or particular, prior and posterior, in the meanings which we shall mention shortly. But these terms only hold for efficient and final cause;[99] and only efficient cause can be accidental when taken in relation to chance and fate as a fortuitous occurrence.[100]

Final cause we have amply considered in the preceding chapter. As that for the sake of which something acts, it must always be in conjunction with an efficient cause, but need not itself exist; and in moving something by love not change it moves metaphorically, either directly or indirectly according to whether it is the final end as God is (one of the rare references to him in the *Summulae*) or an

---

[96] *Ibid.*, 2.   [97] *Ibid.*, 3.

[98] Sic autem accipiendo causam efficientem [quando causat rem noviter existentem] sciendum est quod causa efficiens est illa ad cuius existentiam realem habet aliquid aliud esse de novo totaliter distinctum ab illa causa. Si enim ista descriptio destruatur perit omnis via persuadendi et cognoscendi aliquid esse causam alterius. (*ibid.*).

[99] *Ibid.*, 10.   [100] *Ibid.*, 8.

immediate end on account of something else, as a bitter drink is desired not for itself but for health or oneself. It is accordingly sufficient or insufficient, as efficient cause can be.[101] So far we are on familiar ground, but in the *Summulae* Ockham extends his investigation to the non-human world. He concludes that as final cause consists in the agent's intention it can also be applied to the acts of animals but not of what is inanimate, save in an improper sense as the instruments by which an end is achieved: for example an arrow shot by an archer which kills someone. In that second sense it can then be taken for what conforms to the course of nature.[102]

The difference between Ockham's conception of these two groups of causes can be seen in his discussion of what he calls their modes and conditions, namely prior and posterior, particular and universal, accidental and essential. As we have just mentioned, most of them apply only to efficient and final cause as extrinsic, and so we are concerned with the relation between independently subsisting things as opposed to their components. Ockham's concern is to show that these various modes are predicable precisely of real individuals and do not stand for anything distinct inherent in them. Thus prior and posterior can mean either that one thing is really more proximate or remote: in the case of an efficient cause always through something as the cause of the existence of something else; in the case of final cause either proximate as the end desired, or indirectly, or as that which is not the intended end (a bitter draught for health) to which a particular action (collecting herbs for a bitter draught) is directed.[103] The other sense of prior and posterior is as terms predicable first of one thing and then of another or of the same thing, as a doctor and someone skilled in healing can both be affirmed of health as its cause.[104]

There is a similar distinction between accidental and necessary cause; when it means something real, only efficient cause can as we have said be accidental as that which is fortuitous or rare. Otherwise the difference must be understood logically by reference to what can be predicated essentially of something by the first and second modes; all that cannot be, is an accidental cause as opposed to contingent. For if contingent were synonymous with accidental, nothing would be essential (other than God). Accordingly a cause is properly speaking said to be necessary when the predicate expresses the proper cause in the subject, such as in the propositions 'A builder builds' or 'A builder is the cause of a house'; conversely where the subject does not immediately state its proper cause it is accidental, for example in the propositions 'A man builds' or where the subject is irrelevant, for example 'White builds'. That does not mean that 'man' and 'white' may not stand for the same as 'builder'; and where they do their consignification can be proved in an expository (i.e. singular) syllogism—but as terms they are not synonymous in not all being immediately predicable of the same subject.[105]

Causes can also be real accidents, however, in fortuitously causing things, which is the reason why many call such causes fortune and chance. The same thing can then at once be a real absolute—i.e. independent—thing and an accident, and not merely

---

[101] *Ibid.*, 4.   [102] *Ibid.*, 6.   [103] *Ibid.*, 7.
[104] *Ibid.*   [105] *Ibid.*, 8.

accidental by predication. The problem of explaining fortune and chance is thus one of establishing how effects are caused accidentally and fortuitously, an explanation which follows that adumbrated in the previous chapter and need not be repeated here.[106]

The remaining kinds of cause are each explained according to their signification and not to different kinds of things which are causes. Thus the distinction between an actual and a potential cause is due to a different copula, actual when it is the verb 'to be', potential when it is the verb 'can be'. In the first case, cause and the subject of which it is affirmed (e.g. 'Fire is the cause of heat in wood') exist simultaneously; in the second there is no actual cause ('Fire can heat wood'). Once again where a cause has real signification Ockham is careful to emphasise that the change from cause to no cause does not entail the destruction of anything real, but merely the cessation of something having an effect and conversely something else having a cause, as something ceases to be heat-giving when it no longer has something to heat, and not through the destruction of its heat. There is no such change of existential import in potential causes, for they have none.[107]

Finally there are universal causes, which must be regarded in the same way. That is, not as real things but as names or concepts predicable in this case of a number of different individual generable and destructible things. The reasons why nothing universal is real are by now too familiar to bear reiteration. As terms, universal causes can, as we have already said, be affirmed only of efficient and final cause, when they mean universal by causation as opposed to predication, since only efficient and final cause can actually be the causes of diverse things either simultaneously or successively.[108]

This distinction effectively relegates material and formal cause to local principles of individual existence. Although they can as terms be affirmed of all like causes, they belong to the properties of individual things. That is tantamount to dispensing with Aristotle's fourfold scheme; the disparity is accentuated by Ockham's explanation of generation and destruction—the province of material and formal cause —largely in terms of efficient cause. The latter's universality together with final cause is due to the universal dependence of everything upon something else for existence and movement, as we shall consider in more detail in a moment. When interpreted in an individual as well as a Christian sense—not articulated here— the source of being must be extrinsic to the individuals which wholly constitute it. Instead of its enshrinement in four universal principles, cause in its universal application becomes for Ockham the operation of one thing upon another, either as the physical agent of its existence or movement—as efficient cause—or as their end. Although God is ultimately the cause in each sense, knowledge of natural phenonema can be universalised from experience and by deduction precisely through the universal concept of cause.

Ockham, then, so far from renouncing causality, took it—as we have seen throughout this book—as the source of intelligibility in a world of individuals. For that reason it occupied perhaps a more central place in his outlook than that

[106] *Ibid.*, 10–12. [107] *Ibid.*, 9. [108] *Ibid.*, 10.

of any preceding scholastic thinkers: in default of a world of essences, forms and intellectual species as the bearers of true being, cause was for him the unifying factor in establishing the proper order among the individuals which constituted real existence.

IV MOVEMENT, TIME, AND PLACE

Ockham's view of movement, time, and place conforms to what has gone before in seeking to reduce the accepted Aristotelian classification to individual import. At the same time he also, in the Commentary on the *Sentences*, *Quodlibets* and the other two works on the *Physics*, engaged in the by then accepted post-Aristotelian problems of projectile movement, movement in a void, and the intensification and remission of forms, the last the direct product of the question of how a habit of grace was increased. His principal concern however was to deny the independent existence of movement, time, and space in whatever aspect. Many of his arguments have been well enough rehearsed to be passed over. Their effect here as in the preceding parts of this chapter was once again to subordinate each of these concepts to individual modes of existence, in the process eliminating what can only be called their metaphysical *a priori* character, which they had not only for the majority of scholastics, but certainly so far as movement and time are concerned, for Aristotle as well.

1 *Movement*
That can be seen from the opening of Ockham's discussion of movement in the third part of the *Summulae* where he declares that 'movement is assigned the first attribute or one of the attributes of natural things because every natural self-subsisting body is mobile'.[109] Here movement is treated as the capacity of something to move or be moved; it is thereby as Ockham says an attribute of individual existence: we shall come to its specific connotations in a moment. We have only to compare this statement with that which opens book three of the *Physics*: 'Nature has been defined as "a principle of motion and change". We must therefore see that we understand the meaning of "motion"; for if it were unknown, the meaning of "nature" too would be unknown'.[110] Moreover, for Aristotle the principle of all movement is that everything moved is moved by something else,[111] either some inner principle—the form or nature of the thing moved—or some external agent pushing or pulling or in some other way impelling it.[112] That came to mean for subsequent tradition that movement was from some kind of impressed force

---

[109] *Ibid.*, III, 1. As already mentioned in n. 5, Ockham's discussion of movement in the *Reportatio*, II, q. 9, puts more emphasis upon its contradictory nature as the negation of the coexistence of contraries to infinity; he also invokes God's omnipotence to dispute that movement is either an absolute or a relation, when in either case it could be separated from other absolutes or from the terms to which it was related.

[110] *Physics*, III, ch. 1, 200 b, 1.

[111] *Ibid.*, VII, ch. 1, 241 b, 25.

[112] *Ibid.*, ch. 2, 243 a, 1–15.

(*virtus impressa*), with the velocity of what was moved in direct proportion to the power of the mover or impressed force and the resistance encountered by the medium—air—through which it was moved. Movement for Aristotle therefore always comprised one part 'that is moving and the other part that is the moved', so that nothing save the first mover was self-moving and it was eternal first movement.[113] Movement itself was the universal principle of change, not in the generation of being from non-being but as 'the fulfilment of what is potential when it is already fully real and operates not as itself but as a movable, that is in motion'.[114] In other words, all change in what exists is due to movement; and Aristotle distinguished three kinds of such movement or change: what is alterable (qualitative change), what can be increased or diminished (quantitative change) and what can move from place to place (locomotion or local movement). The fourth kind of change (substantial), by generation and destruction, is not movement since substance has no contrary into which it can change.[115] In that sense Aristotle stressed 'that there is no such thing as motion over and above the things'.[116] It consisted in the successive or continuous change from one member of these pairs of contraries to the other.[117]

By Ockham's time this conception of movement had received its own metaphysical definition, above all over the question of whether movement was flowing form (*forma fluens*) as something absolute which is continuous, or a flux of form (*fluxus forme*) as something which undergoes successive change.[118] Whether or not Ockham's position is to be identified with the latter as a special case,[119] is secondary to his express intention to reduce movement of any kind to what is in movement with no independent—impressed—force to explain its movement.

Ockham was thus presented with considerations that did not hold for Aristotle. The difference in his response can be seen in two main respects. The first characterises his entire view of natural phenomena, in making movement inseparable from the individuals which move or change in any of the three ways enumerated by Aristotle; hence knowledge of movement can only be from individual experience.[120] Its existence belongs to individual existence as one of the attributes of real things, as a universally observed phenomenon rather than as a principle. The second respect is that Ockham distinguishes between movement and change in the broad sense where it includes sudden as well as continuous or successive

---

[113] *Ibid.*, VIII, ch. 5, 257 b, 12–15; ch. 6, 258 b, 13–260 a, 10.

[114] *Ibid.*, III, ch. 1, 201 a, 28–9; also 10.

[115] *Ibid.*, 201 a, 10–15; v, ch. 1, 225 b, 9; ch. 2, 226 a, 23–226 b, 9.

[116] *Ibid.*, III, ch. 1, 200 b, 33.

[117] *Ibid.*, v, ch. 3, 226 b, 19–227 a, 32; VIII, ch. 6, 260 a, 15–16.

[118] H. Shapiro, *Motion, Time and Place according to William Ockham* (St Bonaventure, New York and Louvain, 1957, 36, n. 75). This study complements Moser's in taking Ockham within the scholastic tradition. For a discussion of these different conceptions of movement, see A. Maier, *Die Vorläufer Galileis* (reprinted Rome, 1966), ch. 1.

[119] As Shapiro says, *op. cit.*

[120] Quamvis hoc probari non possit tamen est notum per experientia, propter quod contra negantem motum non habet philosophia naturalis disputare, sicut nec aliquis habet disputare contra negantem sua principia per se nota (*SP*, III, 1).

change and in the strict sense of continuous change.[121] Aristotle did not make the distinction; for unlike Ockham, after initially including generation and destruction under change, he subsequently excluded it for the express purpose already mentioned that substance has no contrary.[122] Ockham disagreed, explicitly opposing to Aristotle's statement the evidence of contrary substances which are the result of incompatible forms, and conversely taking in the example of light something which changes successively and has no contrary. He however reconciles Aristotle's position as referring to successive change.[123] It is also Ockham's own justification for instantaneous change, although he does not give it until over twenty chapters after the initial division of change, when he also defined substance as a contrary in the broad sense of all contrary forms which can be successively in the same subject, in contradistinction to the strict sense of contrary forms which are divisible. It was in the second sense that Aristotle had denied that substance was a contrary.[124]

By both of his definitions of movement Ockham reached the same conclusion that movement is not something separate from that which moves.[125] If it were, and were something real, an infinity of real things would be destroyed whenever something moved, because there are infinite instants in any time in which something moves.[126] Here Ockham follows Aristotle's principle that anything is infinitely divisible so that potentially it contains an infinite number of divisions. Again if movement were something real it could not be destroyed either by the induction of its contrary, since it would have no contrary, nor by the destruction of its subject or cause because both remain after movement. It would therefore be indestructible. Nor does movement belong to any category: not to substance for the opposite reason that substance would be destroyed whenever movement ceased; or to any of the other categories or by logical reduction to them, since something can only be reduced to a category when it belongs to something coming under a category, either as a principle in the way that point and unity are principles of quantity, or as a part as matter and form are parts of substances. That does not apply to movement, which to be a principle must be essential and intrinsic; and if it were it would still not be self-subsisting because principles are not themselves real things, as point and unity are not real. It would also in not being a substance be accidental to substance, as quantity is.[127]

Movement then is not a thing; and the problem of what it is, is one of words rather than substantive. Whenever the terms 'change' or 'changeable' or their equivalents are used two things are involved: that which is changed as the subject of change, such as air or fire, and something which is acquired or lost, such as the illumination of the air by which light is now added to air where before there was air and no light. Beyond these two nothing else is entailed. The nominal definition of change in the broad sense, then, is equivalent to 'when what already exists and is changed has or loses another form or place which it did not have or had before'.[128]

[121] Ibid., III, 2.

[122] Physics, III, ch. 1, 201 a, 10–15; Shapiro, Motion, Time, Place, 29, points to Physics, v, ch. 1, 2 as the source, but it is not immediately obvious.

[123] SP, III, 23.   [124] Ibid.   [125] Ibid., III, 1.

[126] Ibid., III, 2.   [127] Ibid.   [128] Ibid., III, 3.

Here what already exists (*preexistens*) when it receives or loses a form is not changed or moved, in the strict sense of changing successively to another form or place or in size, but in the broader sense of becoming something else suddenly. Change in this broad sense thus means anything that is different from before through having or not having what it lacked or possessed before, as something can become white and is thereby really changed.[129] For that, only the presence or absence of one thing in another is required which was not or was there previously; nothing has to be destroyed or something transient introduced. The whole operation is between the coming or going of permanent things.[130]

Change is thus a connotative term signifying only the individual absolute thing to which the change occurs, as Ockham explains in a restatement of the distinction between absolute and connotative terms, which need not detain us.[131] Understood thus the objection that the ancient writers spoke of indivisible change can be resolved; for they meant not something distinct from real divisible things but merely non-successive or sudden movement and change. The expression 'indivisible movement' is an amphibologism, false in the sense that there is something real to which indivisible movement corresponds; true in its other sense that when something changes it does so indivisibly and simultaneously.[132]

Turning to movement itself or change in the strict sense, it occurs when something continuously and without interruption or rest acquires or loses something, in the way that something can become white successively or something is moved successively by acquiring one part after another.[133] It is no more distinct from permanent things than change in the broad sense is; if it were, as divisible it would consist of real parts existing simultaneously and would then have physical dimensions which those who regard movement as something real deny. Alternatively, it would consist of what does not exist simultaneously, which is equally invalid because what does not exist cannot be a part of something which does.[134] Ockham also gives further reasons against the independence of movement in his so called *Treatise on Successives*, among them that everything moved, including the heavenly bodies, would then be in potentiality to something real in them as well as to place, which is no less absurd.[135]

[129] Mutari est aliter se habere nunc quam prius ... Non enim aliter aliquid se habet nunc quam prius nisi quia habet formam vel locum quem prius non habuit vel caret forma vel loco quem prius habuit ... Similiter posito quod aliquod corpus informetur albedine quam prius non habuit vere mutatur (*ibid.*).

[130] *Ibid.*

[131] *Ibid.*, III, 4; also 7.

[132] *Ibid.*

[133] Et dico quod ad hoc quod aliquid moveatur, sufficit quod mobile continue sine interruptione temporis et quiete continue partibiliter acquirat aliquid successive unum post aliud, vel continue et successive seu partibiliter amittat aliquid. Sicut ad hoc quod aliquid dealbetur sufficit quod continue acquirat partes albedinis, et ad hoc quod moveatur localiter quod continue sine quiete acquirat unum locum post alium et ita quod sine quiete sit in diversis locis successive (*ibid.*, III, 6). Also *Tractatus de successivis* edited by P. Boehner, 43.

[134] *SP*, III, 5.

[135] *Tractatus de successivis*, 44–5. The *Tractatus* is a compilation of Ockham's authentic writings on movement and place taken from his Commentary on the *Physics* (see Boehner's remarks, 28–30).

Successive movement then is when contradictories can be verified of the same thing successively one after the other, so that in any instant it is true to say that a is in a particular place in which it was not before or that something has something which it did not have before or does not have what it had immediately before. Accordingly continuous movement refers only to what is permanent, that is, to something that really exists first in one place and then another, until it finally reaches its place of rest. That applies to all successive change, whether of place, alteration or increase or decrease.[136]

To the objection[137] that it is the very successive nature of movement that differentiates it from permanent things, which are not a flux or fast or slow and can be without movement, Ockham in each case returns to movement as a connotative term for permanent things in motion. Thus to say movement is a flux is only true when it means that something moved flows continuously in acquiring one place after another, and not because of something beyond its own movement as a permanent thing. It therefore remains the same thing in movement although it frequently receives additional qualities. Hence such terms as 'flux' and 'passing away' all mean that something moves successively. Conversely something is not successive when it exists simultaneously. Faster and slower, again, refer to something moving successively, so that it acquires more or less place or quantity or quality in a limited time, although Ockham adds that was not the ancients' meaning. Hence movement has parts not in the sense that it has quantity, but in successively acquiring or losing first one part and then another, which was the ancients' meaning. All such explanations are to be interpreted in a similar manner, as well as the different kinds of movement, local, quantitative and qualitative.

In his discussion of each Ockham follows Aristotle's divisions as well as many of his arguments against including them under any of the other categories than those of place, quantity and quality, and in the broad sense of change—which was not Aristotle's—substance.[138] Local movement,[139] whether as straight or circular or mixed, or natural or violent, only acquires place, wholly when it is straight and, partially when it is circular. It does not leave anything behind.

The import of Ockham's simplification of local movement to something real moving successively from place to place can be seen in his discussion of the classic problems of impulsion, and movement in a void,[140] neither of which he considers in his more formal treatment of movement's characteristics in the *Summulae*. The first arose from the apparent discrepancy which impulsion or violent movement introduced into Aristotle's principle that everything that is moved is moved by something else; for if the moved is separated from the mover, as it is when a stone

---

[136] *SP*, III, 7.

[137] *Ibid.*

[138] *Ibid.*, III, 8.

[139] *Ibid.*, III, 9–11, 31, 32.

[140] These have been considered by a number of writers including A. Maier, *Zwei Grundprobleme*; A. C. Crombie, *Medieval and Early Modern Science* (revised edition, New York, 1959), II, 47–103); E. A. Moody, 'Ockham, Buridan and Nicholas of Autecourt', *FcS* 7 (1947) 113–46 and 'Ockham and Aegidius of Rome', *ibid.*, 9 (1949), 417–42; and Shapiro, *Movement, Time and Place*, 50–62.

is thrown, how does the stone continue to move? Aristotle's reply was that its movement was sustained by the medium in which it moves, namely air or water, and ceased when the medium reached the last of its series of movements.[141] Ockham rejected that explanation because it would mean that the same air could move different things in contrary directions, for example if two projectiles thrown from opposite directions met in the same air. Nor could it be explained by the subsequent theory of Ockham's contemporary Francis of Marchia of an impressed force transmitted by the mover to the moved; for when a natural cause acts invariably it always produces the same effect; but a hand moving something slowly will not move it locally as it will when it moves something swiftly. Therefore there can be no impressed force—absolute or relative—in what is moved: a curious inference since Ockham's reasoning leads to the very conclusion that swift movement does impart movement to the moved, and by extension some power of moving. Nevertheless the purport of his argument is clear; and he reinforces it by denying that the local movement which ensues from such impulsion can be regarded as the effect newly produced and therefore newly caused, for the very reason that local movement is not an effect at all, but consists solely in a moving body coexisting in different parts of space.[142]

The problem of a movement in a void again came from Aristotle's *Physics*,[143] and received its currency from Averroes's Commentary number seventy-one, where he took issue with another twelfth-century Spanish Arabian thinker, known to the Christian West as Avempace, for offering a counter-explanation to Aristotle's. According to Aristotle the velocity of something's movement is directly proportional to the motive power and inversely proportional to the medium in which movement took place.[144] Since a void lacks any medium, movement in a void would thus be instantaneous in not encountering any resistance, which Aristotle regarded as impossible. Avempace in opposition argued that the resistance of the medium is only the accidental reason why something moves successively and not instantaneously; the real reason is the time taken to move in space. To which Averroes replied by reaffirming the distinction between mover and moved, so that something can only be moved by something else and owes its speed to the difference between the power of the mover and the resistance of the medium.

Ockham[145] adopted Avempace's standpoint on the ground that movement can only occur in time since the termini between which something moves are separated spatially. Hence what is moved cannot be simultaneously in different places at the same time, as the same subject cannot simultaneously have diverse colours. But he also accepts Averroes's contention that the speed at which something is moved follows Aristotle's formula; it is therefore not enough to posit the distance between

[141] *Physics*, VIII, ch. 10, 266 b, 27–267 a, 21.
[142] *Reportatio*, II, q. 26, M.
[143] *Physics*, IV, chs. 8–9, 214 b, 12–217 b, 28.
[144] Crombie's formulation (*Medieval and Early Modern Science*, II, 48).
[145] *Expositio super libros Physicorum* and *Questiones super libros Physicorum*, no. 92 edited by Moody, 'Ockham and Aegidius of Rome'; on the void see also *Quodlibet* I, q. 6.

the termini as the sole explanation for the time taken. He dissociates himself too from that part of Avempace's position at which he claims Averrroes directed his criticism, namely that there is not only a natural time of the distance to be traversed but an additional time of the resistance of the medium.[146] As a defence of two different positions it is hardly convincing, but it does not detract from the interest of Ockham's solution which was effectively to exclude the Aristotelian principle that all movement must be by something else.

The second kind of movement is quantitative movement. It concerns increase or decrease in either living things, when it is through the addition or loss of a like substance leading to growth or diminution, or more broadly in both living and inanimate things as extension and contraction leading to rarefaction and condensation. In the second meaning nothing new is acquired or lost; if it were, then when something was rarefied and so extended, either the preceding quantity would wholly remain or be wholly destroyed or one part would remain and not another. None of these is possible. The preceding whole could not remain because then there would be two quantities in the same subject or one would migrate into another subject. Nor could it be wholy destroyed; for that would mean that whenever something was rarefied infinite parts would be generated or destroyed from the infinite instants in each of them: in fact something of the same kind cannot destroy and then generate something else of the same kind. Nor finally is there any reason why one part more than another of a quantity should be destroyed and another remain; and if a part did remain it would—as in the first alternative— only be rarefied if the accidents went to another subject; otherwise there would— again—be two quantities. Quantity is not therefore distinct from substance; for it cannot, unlike substance, itself receive contraries. Hence as Aristotle says, nothing inheres in rarefaction and condensation, which are no more than quantity—i.e. substance—having more or less extended parts and so occupying more or less space.[147] To the objection that they do not differ from local movement the answer is that in its broad sense of acquiring or losing place, they are included in local movement as that which is moved locally; for then there is no increase in what is moved, through the extension or contraction of its parts.[148] That does not however apply to increase which comes through the addition of substance and can be either successive or by the induction of a form, when it does not differ from generation.[149]

Qualitative movement or alteration consists in the acquisition or loss of a quality, so that the subject in which the change occurs newly undergoes real alteration. It has two meanings, beyond Aristotle's division of quality into four species, of habit, powers, passions, and figure or shape, and Ockham's further subdivision between sensible qualities which are the object of a particular sense and those which belong to the interior imagination. By the first and broad definition qualitative change is any acquisition or loss of quality, whether sudden or successive,

[146] *Ibid.*, 435.
[147] *Ibid.*, III, 12 13; *Ordinatio*, d. 17, q. 8, B.
[148] *SP, ibid.*, III, 12, also *Reportatio*, IV, q. 7, L–P.
[149] *Ibid.*, III, 13.

as air is altered when illuminated or the senses altered when they sense or the intellect when it knows. By its second meaning qualitative change is successive alteration through the induction of a quality leading to a new form or a disposition to the subject's destruction, in the way that heat disposes water to be destroyed.[150] Of the four species Ockham follows Aristotle[151] in denying qualitative change to figure or to habits, the first because figure or shape is not distinct from substance and quality, as a bronze figure is still bronze, and the second because acquired states or habits of the body or the soul do not in the strict sense constitute alteration as the successive acquisition of a new quality.[152] But unlike Aristotle Ockham does concede as we know from previously that both sensitive and intellective habits are new qualities in the broad sense, in being engendered from their acts.[153] The remaining kinds of quality Ockham, with Aristotle, leaves unmentioned.

Now all sensible alteration is a matter of experience. The question is whether, when it is successive through the expulsion of one contrary form by another, the first form is totally expelled before the new form is successively introduced or whether the old one remains and receives the new one, so that both coexist in a diminished degree with the new form gradually displacing the old. This became one of the issues of scholastic debate over forms, and Ockham both in the *Summulae* and the *Sentences* at different times adopted the first explanation, because the second would entail the coexistence of contraries. This is essentially the application of a logical standpoint to nature; but one based upon a qualitative conception of nature with which it was consonant. It was also in its standpoint contrary to Aristotle; and Ockham sought to reconcile his view with Aristotle's by stressing the successive nature of the change from one form to another, so that in his own words,

in successive qualitative alteration, that which is moved does not acquire the whole of this quality simultaneously but successively; and thus while it is moved it is partly in a terminus 'from which' (*a quo*); that is, it loses part of the form which it previously had, and partly in a terminus 'to which' (*ad quem*), that is, it has some part which it did not have before. Accordingly in the change from one quality to another the subject is continuously remitted and the contrary form is expelled: and after its expulsion the other contrary quality is continuously and successively acquired.[154]

Although there are thus two movements, of expulsion and induction, they are however really one, because each is necessarily concomitant to the other; and without one there could not be the other.[155]

That leads to the cognate problem of the intensification and remission of forms. Ockham did not discuss it in the *Summulae*, but in the *Ordinatio*, over the increase

[150] *Ibid.*, III, 14.
[151] *Ibid.*, III, 15, 16; *Physics*, VII, ch. 3, 245 b, 2–248 a, 9.
[152] *SP, ibid.*, III, 17, 18.
[153] *Ibid.*, III, 19, 20, 21.
[154] *Ibid.*, III, 22; also *Ordinatio*, d. 17, q. 5, F.
[155] *SP, ibid.*, III, 30.

or decrease of grace, in which connection, as we have said, it had first been raised by Peter Lombard. The question at issue here is not the expulsion of one form by another but the mode in which an existing form is intensified or diminished in degree. The matter came to be central to any discussion of charity; and Ockham devoted five out of eight questions of distinction seventeen of the *Ordinatio* to it. Like the majority of scholastics he accepts that charity can be intensified or re-mitted.[156] But of five opinions considered he rejects them all. The first is that when charity is increased the preceding charity is destroyed and another form of charity succeeds it.[157] The second that intensification occurs not through its union with some new quality, but through its greater purification and separation from its contrary.[158] The third that it is the result not of any increase but through the participation of the form in its subject.[159] The fourth that it is through the addition of a more intense degree contained potentially in the existing degree,[160] which Ockham characterises—and dismisses—as increase by the existence of a part which is not really different.[161] The fifth that while increase is by the addition of another part it is not, as Ockham held it was, entirely of the same nature as what precedes it; for then it would be distinct from the latter. Hence according to this opinion— Peter Aureole's—the added part is only charity by reduction constituting a 'con-charity' with the existing form of charity rather than charity in its own right.[162] In relation to these opinions Ockham's solution is interesting for its exclusively quantitative explanation, namely that intensification of a form, as in quantitative increase, comes through the addition of another part of the same nature together forming a unity with what is increased.[163] For that they must be of the same nature, since when unlike things are added together none of the parts is increased. Hence one part of charity is of the same nature as the other part, in the same way as the parts of water or heat are of the same nature as their other parts. The only dissimilarity which comes with intensification is in the addition of a new part of the same kind.[164]

Ockham thus characteristically reduces intensification and remission to quantitative alteration, rejecting all modes of quasi-being less than that of substance and quality undergoing change.

He also discusses infinite intensification of a form. Here there are two considerations. The first is the distinction between an infinite series and an infinite being; one does not entail the other; hence there is no need to deny the first because of the

---

[156] *Ordinatio*, d. 17, q. 4, B. For a discussion of the problem as a whole, see A. Maier, *Zwei Grundprobleme der scholastischen Naturphilosophie*, and for Ockham's position, Shapiro, *Motion, Time, and Place*, 83–91.

[157] *Ordinatio*, ibid., q. 5, B–D, E.   [158] *Ibid.*, q. 6, B.

[159] *Ibid.*, D.   [160] *Ibid.*, G.

[161] *Ibid.*, I.   [162] *Ibid.*, q. 7, B.

[163] Ideo dico aliter ad questionem quod augmentatione alicuius forme vere aliquid reale differens realiter a priori addatur. Quod etiam postquam additur realiter distinguitur ab eodem et facit per se unum cum eo ... Ideo dico quod sicut in augmentatione quantitativa ... nihil augmentatur nisi per adventum alicuius realis distincti a priori et remanentis cum eo, ita est in augmentatione qualitatis (*ibid.*, 6, K).

[164] *Ibid.*, 7, C–G.

second.[165] The second is God's power always to increase the number of individuals beyond any conceivable limit since the only reasons why he could not do so would be because such an addition was impossible or God could not cause it or it would contradict what already existed. None of them is tenable.[166] Accordingly as God can create further individuals infinitely without creating an actual infinity simultaneously, so he can create further charity without creating infinite charity.[167] Such increase would be infinitely intensive, provided, as Ockham thinks probable, charity is separable from its subject; but forms which are inseparable from their subject probably cannot be increased infinitely.[168] Nor does it seem probable that there can be infinite increase extensively when that means rarefaction as opposed to the addition of one part to another, which can be infinite in the sense already given of successive increase indefinitely on the part of God.[169] The assumption of all such increase therefore is on the one hand an essentially Christian belief in God's power both to produce and to conserve an infinite succession of like individuals, and on the other hand that an infinity of individuals of the same nature can conconstitute a unity, without themselves ever becoming an infinity.[170]

That completes discussion of movement. One does not have to agree with Moody, that Ockham's conception made the principle of inertia philosophically possible,[171] to acknowledge its boldness. For the first time movement was conceived as bodies in motion and undergoing change, without recourse to inner or exterior principles to explain it. That was Ockham's particular contribution. He more than anyone else translated physics into the study of the attributes of real individual things acting and being acted upon in space and time.

2 Time

Much therefore that Ockham has said of movement applies also to time, in particular his argument against its independent existence[172] or that of an instant, together the view of it as something flowing (res fluens) suddenly ceasing to exist, which he equally rejects.[173] His conception of time, as of movement, is essentially empirical; its existence is a matter of universal experience which everyone shares.[174]

---

[165] Quia non est negandus talis processus in infinitum nisi ad eum sequitur infinitas aliqua in creatura (ibid., q. 8, c); also D.

[166] Ibid.

[167] Sed deus non potest facere tot charitates quin posset facere plures ... sed faciendo semper plures charitates in infinitum vel non posse facere tot charitates quin possit facere plures non infert perfectionem infinitam posse fieri a deo simul; ergo non posse facere charitatem tantam quin deus possit facere maiorem non infert deum posse facere infinitam charitatem (ibid., D).

[168] Ibid., K–M.

[169] Ibid., E–I.

[170] Ibid., F–H.

[171] 'After Ockham the discovery of the principle of inertia ... became philosophically possible' ('Ockham and Aegidius of Rome', 438). Perhaps; but that does not mean that its discovery waited upon philosophy or was owed to Ockham.

[172] SP, IV, 2. Ockham also discusses time in Reportatio, II, q. 12, more in the vein in which he considered movement in q. 9.

[173] Ibid., IV, 1.

[174] Ibid., IV, 3.

But unlike movement which is of real things moving, time is the measure of movement; and as a measure thereby dependent upon the soul. Hence although there would still be time even if the mind was not cognisant of it, time as a measure of movement is the work of the mind distinguishing movement between before and after.[175] In this broad outline Ockham's view of time agrees with that of Aristotle for whom time and movement always correspond and define one another.[176] As Aristotle put it, 'Hence time is not movement but only movement in so far as it admits of enumeration'.[177] The difference between Ockham and Aristotle was once more one of conception. Aristotle's was of time as a principle inseparable from movement as a principle, each defining the other; Ockham's was of time as another facet of individual existence, equally defining movement but only intelligible in the context of individual existence as the measure of bodies in motion. To establish that, he employed the usual distinctions between predication and signification and nominal and essential definition, of which of course Aristotle made no mention. In its more directly physical aspect, Ockham also defined time as the attribute of the first mover or movement (*primum mobile*), namely the sphere of fixed stars, the source of all movement in the universe.[178]

More specifically Ockham distinguished time as a measure in three respects. First, of movement whose quantity is unknown, to us, so that by time we certify for how long something is moved and that one mobile is moved in a longer time than another; second, of temporal things, namely that one lasts longer than another; and third, of being at rest, namely that one thing is stationary longer than another. In each case, such measurement can be either exact by employing a precise measure, or an approximate one based upon calculation from experience.[179]

Time therefore is not something composed of past, present and future, existing independently of permanent things, but an abbreviation for something moving or at rest for a longer or shorter duration. Thus the proposition 'Time exists' is equivalent to the proposition 'The intellect considering and measuring when something which is moved uniformly is first not in a certain place and afterwards is, can certify of other things how long they last or are moved or are at rest'. Time thus denotes that the same thing, without newly existing, coexists first with one place, and then another.[180] By the same token time is not measured of all movement but only of that which is uniform. Nor is it synonymous with movement since they have different definitions; and in being the measure only of movement which is uniform, time is the attribute of the first mover (*primum mobile*), which enters into the definition of time (that is, time is predicated of movement by the second essential mode) as 'man' enters into the definition of 'risible' (by the second essential mode) as his attribute. And just as 'risible' is only a term or a concept, so is 'time'. Accordingly when time is affirmed of first movement in the proposition 'First movement is time', the terms are taken significatively to denote that the first mover is moved uniformly at the fastest speed of all, enabling the intellect to gauge

---

175 *Ibid.*, IV, 16.   176 *Physics*, IV, chs. 10–14, 217 b, 30–234 a, 15.
177 *Ibid.*, 11, 219 b, 3.   178 *SP*, IV, 7.
179 *Ibid.*, IV, 3; also 6, 13.   180 *Ibid.*, IV, 5; also 10.

how long other things endure.[181] For that reason time is not distinct from first movement; for by it we know how long temporal things endure, are moved, or are at rest. One differs from the other not as real things, but because the definition of time includes the mind ascertaining what is to be said about the time of other things.[182] The same applies to an instant of time; it is not, as we have already mentioned, something real which immediately ceases to exist, but again the same as the first movement, as change is not a loss of being, but means a moving body existing somewhere in which it was not immediately before. If indeed an instant denoted something's destruction it would be either of something existing now, which it could not be since it is now, or in something else, when it would already no longer be now. Hence for something to be instantaneous is for the first movement to cease to be in one place and to be somewhere else; it is the same thing which moves but it varies in place.

Both time and instant therefore are terms having a nominal definition connoting the mind measuring the duration of things in space. In that way all propositions in which something is affirmed of time or instant as subjects, such as 'Time is a continuum' or 'An instant exists', signify something moved or at rest and consignify the mind measuring or ascertaining its duration.[183] Whoever therefore perceives time also perceives movement, and first movement, even though he has no proper concept of it, as the fastest and uniform movement.[184] As such, 'time' is a predicable of first movement, and if, *per impossibile*, there was more than one first movement there would be more than one time. Although in having a different definition from movement, time cannot be said to be fast or slow, as movement can, it can strictly speaking be called fast as the measure of the fastest—i.e. first—movement;[185] and as a measure it is not absolute but an aspect of movement.[186] In the same way duration is merely the existence of something in time and not something added to something which endures. Hence only what exists temporally, as generable and corruptible including the celestial bodies, can be measured by time;[187] and when Aristotle said that the eternal is beyond time,[188] he meant that beyond time there is no measure of duration.[189] First movement as that which the soul actually certifies, then, is only time when the soul measures it through other things which move or are at rest by enumerating them as prior and posterior. But as that which can be measured by the soul—in the mode of possibility—there can be time without the soul.[190]

Time then according to Ockham is essentially a relation between the intellect and what it apprehends in space. On the one hand it depends upon the soul's

---

[181] *Ibid.*, IV, 7.

[182] Patet ergo ex dictis quod tempus non est aliqua res alia a primo motu, quia per primum motum, onmi alio circumscripto, scimus de temporabilus quamdiu durant, moventur vel quiescunt. Et tamen tempus et primus motus differunt diffinitione, quia tempus importat animam que debet certificari, et ita non importat nisi res permanentes, quamvis importet aliquas illarum rerum permanentium moveri (*ibid.*).

[183] *Ibid.*, IV, 10; also 12.   [184] *Ibid.*, IV, 11.

[185] *Ibid.*   [186] *Ibid.*, IV, 13.

[187] *Ibid.*, IV, 14.   [188] *Physics*, IV, ch. 12, 221 b, 23–222 a, 9.

[189] *SP*, IV, 15.   [190] *Ibid.*, IV, 16.

perception of the movement or lack of movement of real things; on the other upon the existence of first movement which exists independently of the soul's awareness in the sphere of fixed stars.

3 Place

Finally the existence of place is given in the existence of movement and the perception of time, as that through which bodies, moved locally, pass and succeed one another. In Ockham's words, 'As all that is moved is moved in time, so all that is moved is moved in place'.[191] Following Aristotle he defines it as the extreme or limit of the containing body.[192] As such it is not something real distinct from real things, as movement and time are not; and for the same reasons that it is not either a substance or real accident possessing quantity or discreteness. Rather it is the same as surface, and so the same as the body of which it is the surface.[193] Place is thus that which contains another body, to the extremities, or surface, of which it is contiguous on all sides, as a vase containing water is contiguous to water. Nothing comes between them. Proper space therefore is where every extremity of that which is contained meets every part of that which contains it.[194] And when a body changes from one containing body to another, so its place correspondingly changes.[195]

Movement, time and place are therefore for Ockham all ways of describing the physical existence of individual things. They have lost any independent identity even as principles and have become the attributes of existence and change. No previous thinker had dispensed so entirely with all extra-individual distinctions. In doing so he once again gave a new meaning to the terms of the discussion.

V THE EUCHARIST

Ockham's conception of nature is completed and resumed in his conception of the eucharist. Like his predecessors he took this supreme sacramental expression of God's power to work a miracle, in making the bread on the altar into Christ's body, as the occasion for examining substance, quantity, quality, place, movement, and change, in the context of God's power to supersede their natural modes. The issues raised by the bread's change of substance were of particular importance to Ockham's belief on the one hand that only substance and quality were real—absolute—things, and on the other that God could create and/or conserve anything absolute independently of any absolute to which it was ordinarily joined in *rerum natura*.

Now by the doctrine of the eucharist, with the conversion of the bread on the altar into Christ's body, nothing of the bread remained except its accidental qualities or appearances—of colour, shape, weight, taste, touch—which now coexisted with Christ's body. Transubstantiation thus resulted in the replacement of one substance—the bread—by another—Christ's body—and the coexistence of the latter with the qualities of the previous substance while no longer having their

---

[191] *Ibid.*, IV, 18.   [192] *Physics*, IV, ch. 4. 212 a, 20; *SP*, IV, 19.
[193] *SP, ibid.*   [194] *Ibid.*, IV, 20.   [195] *Ibid.*, IV, 22.

own substance: they continued to be perceptible to the senses as bread although what they contained was not bread but Christ's body.

The central problem facing Ockham in this doctrine—beyond the traditional question of how something could exist in a place and yet not be seen and how there could be accidents without a substance and whether they could act and be acted upon in the same way as when inhering in a subject—concerned the separation of quantity from substance. For if, as he held, quantity was not an absolute as something real, distinct from substance and quality, how could there be substance without quantity—as Christ's body in the host was without quantity—or quality without substance—as the accidents of the bread were qualities with no substance? And how by the same token could God in his omnipotence separate one from the other without contradiction?

It was to answering these questions that he devoted his separate treatises *On Christ's Body* and *On the Sacrament of the Altar*, largely by-passing the more customary subsidiary issues treated in the fourth book of the Commentary on the *Sentences* and previously discussed there and in his *Quodlibets*: his return to the subject of the eucharist for a third and a fourth time is a measure of the importance he attached to his views on the subject included in Lutterell's censured articles. Throughout each of his discussions, however, there run two main threads. The first is the bread's transubstantiation: the second is the compatibility of God's power to separate quantity from substance with the nature of both indivisible beings (having no separate parts) and divisible beings (having distinct substantial parts).

This reconciliation of what God can do beyond the ordinary course of nature with what is potentially realisable naturally—though not actually realised—is the most striking testimony in all Ockham's outlook to his notion of God's omnipotence. For from being the instrument of an alternative possible theology,[196] Ockham employs the concept of God's absolute power here for the very purpose of upholding the existing dispensation. No so-called dialectic between his ordained and absolute power is involved, as indeed it is not in the greater part of his theology. Over the eucharist, as over the divine attributes, the divine persons, God's future knowledge, and predestination, Ockham's premises are taken from revealed truth and his conclusions confined to what can be deduced from them by logic and experience. If he differs from his predecessors in the rigour with which he conceives both logic and experience, he diverges from his successors in refusing to depart from the articles of faith: *pluralitas non est ponenda sine necessitate* applies as much to theology as to metaphysics, a consideration neglected by many subsequent Ockhamists.

The difference between the eucharist and the other theological and sacramental truths is that it is a miracle; as such it can only be adequately accounted for by God's omnipotence. Experience and reason can, however, point to the ways in which its occurrence can be made more intelligible, although only faith in God can make it explicable. In seeking his own explanation according to his conception of being, with which we are already familiar, Ockham, apart from the distinctiveness

[196] Or as Iserloh calls it, a 'theology of as if' (*Gnade und Eucharistie*, 279).

of his conceptions, was not doing anything fundamentally different from St Thomas Aquinas or Duns Scotus; indeed as we shall mention shortly, his view of transubstantiation itself was close to that of Duns Scotus. It is not therefore warrantable to deny Ockham an adequate spiritual understanding of the eucharist as a sacrament and a sacrifice[197] because of his notion of being and physical change. That is to misconceive his object of adducing reasons drawn from nature to support a sacrament and a sacrifice. Nor is the possession or absence of spiritual insight, assuming it could be measured, a means of measuring a doctrine which can only be judged on the nature and efficacy of the arguments employed. Unless we are to deny to Ockham the testimony of a man's own words, accorded to others, there is no more reason for denying him a comparable understanding than for doubting the sincerity of his professions of faith in the eucharist as a sacrament.

What is noteworthy about Ockham's treatment of the eucharist is rather the convergence which he sought to establish between its theological, physical and logical aspects: and it is these that we now shall consider.[198] Of the theological justification for the eucharist little further need be said, as it has been said here often enough. It consists in the application of the universal principle that God is limited only by what is contradictory—for which in the Sacrament of the Altar Ockham acknowledges Duns Scotus[199]—to the order of second causes where God can intervene directly to separate things, which normally exist in conjunction, either by creating and conserving one thing and not the other or by destroying one thing and conserving the other. No contradiction is implied because whatever is absolute is a distinct thing—as substance or accident—and can by God's power be made or remain distinct. In that way he can separate accident and substance, matter and form, cause and effect.[200] Conversely he can join what is ordinarily separate, making one thing subsist totally in another (as the intellective soul does in the body or an angel in its place) or one substance in two bodies, or two or more bodies simultaneously in the same place.[201] And he can do so in virtue of being first cause and conserver who can also be total cause, doing immediately that which he ordinarily does through created second causes. All being is therefore by his free will; and just as only if he so wills can a substance have accidents, so equally he can will a substance not to have accidents.[202]

---

[197] Ibid., 277; also 219.

[198] What follows is a brief and essentially schematic analysis of Ockham's position in relation to his main theological, natural and logical presuppositions. The two full accounts, by G. Buescher, The Eucharistic Teaching of William Ockham (New York, 1950) and Iserloh, Gnade und Eucharistie, are in many respects complementary. Buescher's, in character with the monographs of the Franciscan House of St Bonaventure, New York, tends to be over-systematised and under-critical; Iserloh's too much of a running and hostile commentary. Together they present a comprehensive and sufficiently detailed examination.

[199] De Sacramento, ch. 29.

[200] Reportatio, IV, q. 4, C, G, N, O; Quodlibet IV, qq. 26, 27, 28, 29, 37; De Sacramento, chs. 12, 13, 14, 25, 28.

[201] Reportatio, IV, q. 4, ibid.; Quodlibet I, q. 3 and Quodlibet IV, ibid.; De Sacramento, ch. 6 where he also takes the theological miracles of the Virgin birth and the bodily resurrection as further examples of God's omnipotence.

[202] Item nulla apparet contradictio quod res absoluta sine omni alio existat quod non est

Within that context the eucharist exemplifies God's creative activity besides constituting a special case of it: for it occurs on the same principle which governs all being, namely that whatever exists, exists absolutely and owes its existence whether separately or in conjunction to God's creating and conserving will. Nor is the dividing line between the eucharist and all other being absolute. On the one hand Christ's body, as we shall consider again, is present in the host in the same way as the human soul inheres in its body and an angel is located in place, each totally where it is without extension. On the other hand the separation of accident from substance enables Christ's body and the bread's appearances to remain distinct from one another. The first explains how there can be substance without quantity; the second qualities without substance.

As to the eucharist as a sacrament, Ockham affirms his interpretation of the teachings of the church in the second chapter of the *Sacrament of the Altar*: that the body of Christ is really present in the host under the appearances of the bread; that it is hidden from the bodily eye but seen by faith in the mind of the faithful; that the bread is transubstantiated or converted or changed so that its substance no longer remains; that the accidents subsist by themselves without a subject; and that body into which the bread is changed is not only of Christ as a man but the whole Christ, perfect God and real man, present in the whole host and simultaneously in every part of it, although in the strict sense transubstantiation is only of his body and not of his divinity or soul or any of his accidental qualities.[203]

While all of these truths are to be held on faith their source is not equally explicit. Only that of Christ's real presence under the bread can be found in the Bible; hence no believer can doubt it. The conversion of the bread into his body can be adduced from the fathers to whom it was revealed;[204] while the distinction between whether it refers to Christ's body or to the whole of his being depends upon whether conversion is taken strictly or improperly: in the latter sense it can also include Christ's soul and blood, although during his three days in the tomb when his soul was separated from his body it could not.[205] This distinction between the proper and improper sense of conversion replaces that in the *Reportatio* between its formal and its accidental term which Ockham adopted from Aquinas in discussing his opinion there. As in the *Sacrament of the Altar*, Ockham was concerned to modify the distinction between Christ's body as the first or formal term into which the bread was converted, and his intellect and accidents as merely accidental, which according to Aquinas were transubstantiated through their natural concomitance with Christ's body, and not from the direct act of conversion (*ex vi conversionis*), as the bread was.[206] Accidentally for Ockham could only be understood here as that which was not principally intended; thus in the three days of the

---

pars illius nec eius essentialis causa. Sed nullum accidens est causa nec pars substantialis cui inheret . . . Igitur posse per se existere. Item omne quod non est deus si esse aliud habet, oportet quod realiter a deo producatur; igitur producta substantia non potuerit esse accidens nisi deus sua libera voluntate dederit illi (*De Sacramento*, ch. 1); Also *Quodlibet* IV, *ibid*.

[203] *De Sacramento*, ch. 1.   [204] *Ibid.*, ch. 2.   [205] *Ibid.*, ch. 4.

[206] *Reportatio*, IV, q. 6, E; also q. 4, B–C for Aquinas's opinion; and Buescher, *Eucharistic Teaching*, 48, 90.

tomb, conversion would have been of Christ's body alone. Ockham indeed talks of the soul being the term of its own transubstantiation,[207] in keeping with his conception of accident which we shall mention later not as something physical but something which is only contingently predicable of its subject. Ockham's notion of accident here is thus a logical one; which is his difference from Aquinas, whose analogy between a formal term and what is accidental to it with a house and the whiteness in it, he dismisses as irrelevant.[208]

There is a comparable openness in the *Reportatio*[209] and the *Quodlibets*[210] over the question of whether Christ in the host can be seen and can see. In reply to Duns Scotus's view that neither is possible to a being without quantity, Ockham invokes the principle that when an object is present to an agent and disposed to be acted upon, an action results. Now whatever is totally present in something, as Christ is in every part of the host, is no less able to be the object of an action than something which is extended in place. But the qualities of the host can be seen as the object of an act of sight; so therefore can Christ's body which is totally present in each of them, not only in them as a medium but present to the eye. Christ could accordingly be the active and passive object of an act of vision caused by God; for if God can cause knowledge of a non-existent it is not more contradictory for him to cause vision of what exists.[211] Nothing therefore, setting aside faith,[212] prevents such a possibility of seeing Christ other than that God does not act together with these qualities to produce such an act; if he did so by his general conserving influence, as he does with other things, then those qualities containing Christ's body would be seen naturally *de facto* as other things are.[213] By the same token Christ could see corporeally as well as with his intellect all that exists in the host; and indeed by God's power his eye in one part of the host could see himself in another part as if he were extended there, because even when he is totally present in every part of it there is still sufficient distance between his parts internally for him to have corporeal vision of himself. We shall consider the physical grounds for these various assumptions presently. Here we need merely remark that Ockham is once more giving various reasons which are not contradicted by logic or the Bible; and in not implying any contradiction to what God could do, they are, he declares, more consonant with both in being consonant with his omnipotence.[214] In the *Sacrament of the Altar* however Ockham allows himself—or God—no such latitude, confining himself to the present dispensation by which it is not possible for Christ

---

[207] *Reportatio*, *ibid.*, q. 6, E; that is not however the same as saying there is a distinct transubstatiation for each separable term in Christ, as Buescher (*op. cit.*, 56) declares; to say that there is inverts Ockham's meaning, which is to distinguish between transubstantiation in its principal and essential and secondary contingent senses.

[208] *Ibid.*

[209] *Ibid.*, q. 5, C, D [misrepresented by H in Lyons 1494 edition].

[210] *Quodlibet* IV, q. 20.

[211] *Reportatio*, *ibid.*, D.

[212] Reading with Iserloh *Gnade und Eucharistie*, 255, 'sepponendo' for 'supponendo' in *Quodlibet* IV, q. 20; Iserloh, *ibid.*, 254, like Baudry, *Guillaume d'Occam* 89, also comments on the difference between Ockham's treatment in these two works and in *De Sacramento*.

[213] *Reportatio*, *ibid.*, D; *Quodlibet*, *ibid.*

[214] *Ibid.*

to be seen physically. The grounds are those of authority, and supported by two arguments: the first that what can be seen physically can be seen equally by all, but no infidel can see Christ in the host; the second that only qualities in the host perceived by the senses are sensible qualities, of touch, taste, sight and so on, which are not those of Christ.[215]

The changed tenor is plain, almost certainly occasioned by Lutterell's action. It is nevertheless in keeping with the end Ockham set himself in the Sacrament of the Altar, of defending his conception of quantity which he describes as his 'principal intent'.[216] That he wrote the treatise in the knowledge that Lutterell had included his views on the eucharist among the passages from his writings sent to the papal court for condemnation not only helps to explain why Ockham should have sought to restate them in the context of authority; but also why he modified the very question of seeing Christ. For in what became article twelve of Lutterell's list of censured extracts, 'That both continuous and discrete quantity are substance itself', Lutterell commented, 'It follows that what is seen with the bodily eye is Christ's body'.[217] In the Sacrament of the Altar Ockham excluded all reference to seeing Christ bodily. A further instance is provided by article twenty-two, 'That rarefaction and condensation, rarity and density, express nothing absolute beyond the substance of the thing rarefied'; to which Lutterell took exception for the double reason that it implies that there is no transubstantiation and that Christ is seen.[218] In the Sacrament of the Altar Ockham reiterates his concept of rarefaction and magnitude but this time claims the authority of St Augustine for it:[219] not the most obvious source for a question of Aristotelian physics.

With that we come to the second aspect of the eucharist, its physical characteristics. Here as we have said the main problems revolve upon how quantity can be separated from both Christ's body in the host and in the accidents of the bread without itself being an absolute. In consequence as we shall now see Ockham's arguments largely concern the way in which on the one hand substance can become non-quantitative and on the other how qualities can become quantitative but non-substantial.

Beginning with transubstantiation itself Ockham defines it on the one occasion he does so, as the 'succession of a substance to a substance' with the preceding substance entirely ceasing to exist in itself and the succeeding substance coming to exist under the accidents proper to the first substance of which they alone remain.

[215] De Sacramento, ch. 7.
[216] Ibid., ch. 6, A. Maier, 'Zur einigen Problemen', AFH 46 (1953), 174–6 (reprinted in Ausgehendes Mittelalter, I, 192–5), has shown that Ockham in his first and shorter treatise on the eucharist (q. 3) was opposing Richard of Middleton among the moderns, citing verbatim his argument against the independence of quantity with which Richard seems in turn to have been opposing Olivi. That does not however in my view weaken the surmise that Ockham's second treatise, with its uncharacteristic reliance upon canonical citations, was in defence against Lutterell's attacks.
[217] 'Libellus contra doctrinam Guillelmi Ockham' in F. Hoffmann, Die Schriften des Oxforder Kanzlers, 37–40. The Libellus is Lutterell's point by point reply to the fifty-six articles which he abstracted from Ockham's Sentences.
[218] Ibid., 57–8.
[219] De Sacramento, ch. 4.

Such an occurrence is possible because no contradiction is implied for God to destroy a substance and conserve the accidents, enabling them to coexist with another substance.[220] On this view of transubstantiation as succession, which is also that of Duns Scotus,[221] the connection between the bread and Christ's body is wholly extrinsic: the latter displaces the former as opposed to becoming the former through its own intrinsic conversion, which is the view of St Thomas Aquinas.[222] The difference can be seen in Ockham's interpretation of what changes substance. Of the two terms involved, only that from which the change occurs is itself changed, but the term to which the change occurs only changes place. Thus as Ockham emphasises, in his replies to the *dubia* over the same question in the *Reportatio*,[223] it is the bread which changes from being to non-being so that it is completely annihilated; Christ's body as the term 'to which' remains the same, merely changing its location to the host where the bread was before. Transubstantiation like all substantial alterations thus involves a double change,[224] deperditive (the bread's substance) and acquisitive (Christ's substance). One is not, however, dependent upon the other; even without the conversion of the bread's substance, its accidents could still have been in the host and Christ's body present under them. Contrary to St Thomas, then, Christ's body is not in the host from the conversion of the bread since the bread as a substance need never have existed.[225] By the same token and again contrary to Aquinas, Christ's body must be changed locally in now being in the host.[226] This was another of the opinions (article thirty-three for which Ockham was censured at Avignon; more it would seem because it contradicted Aquinas, who maintained that if Christ began to be in the host by local movement he would cease to be in heaven,[227] than for any direct error. Ockham contends however that Christ still also remains in heaven, so that his change consists solely in the acquisition of a new place without the loss of his preceding place.[228] The contrast in attitudes is instructive between the theologian who seeks some correlation between what is possible naturally and in God, and the theologian who posits for God what is naturally inconceivable and yet possible, provided no contradiction is involved.

---

[220] Quantum ad primum dico quod transsubstantiatio in proposito est successio substantie ad substantiam desinentem esse simpliciter in se sub aliquibus accidentibus propriis substantie precedentis. Possibilitas illius apparet, quia non repugnat potentie divine destruere substantiam in se et conservare accidentia et quod aliqua alia substantia eisdem accidentibus non eam informantibus immediate coexistat (*Reportatio*, IV, q. 6, c).

[221] For Duns's statements in this connection see the extracts in Iserloh, *Gnade und Euchariste*, 159–62.

[222] Buescher, *Eucharistic Teaching*, 29; Iserloh, *op. cit.*, 165, like Lutterell denies for that reason that Ockham had a doctrine of transubstantiation, but only of two independent changes of the bread and Christ's body. See the criticism by Junghans, *Ockham im Lichte*, 308–9, 314–15 of Iserloh's view (*Gnade und Euchariste*, 159, 160–1, 166, 202) that Ockham's philosophy was in conflict with his theology, over quantity, and that he accentuated the tendency to consubstantiation begun by Duns.

[223] *Reportatio*, IV, q. 6 F—ad 3[m], 4[m], and 7[m].

[224] *Ibid.*, G.

[225] *Ibid.*, C.

[226] *Ibid.*, C, F, G. Hoffmann, *Die Schriften des Oxforder Kanzlers*, 77–8.

[227] *Summa Theologiae*, III, q. 75, a 2, quoted in Iserloh, *Gnade und Eucharistie*, 160, n. 51.

[228] *Reportatio*, IV, q. 4, O.

However Ockham's attitude may be judged, it cannot be for lacking faith in God's power. Even so, Ockham is not unequivocal in his view of Christ's change. To begin with it is not itself successive but sudden in being directly from heaven to the host. Secondly he modifies his definition in the *Quodlibets* to that of local movement in the broad sense only, of acquiring a new place without the loss of the old; and so in the strict sense it is not local movement.[229] This seems to be more consonant with his conception of substantial alteration which it will be recalled is successive without involving local movement. In the *Reportatio* Ockham was less qualified, being concerned there to emphasise that since all local movement consists in the relation between two incompatible terms—of being in a place and not being there,—Christ in changing his place from heaven to the host is really changed, in the sense of being moved locally.[230] His intention however is plain, namely that the change which occurs to Christ is not in his own substance but in his change of place, and with it his different mode of inherence. It is upon that difference that his arguments for Christ's absence of quantity in the host turn.

Before considering them we must briefly remark upon the other term in transubstantiation, the bread. As we have already said, Ockham declares that it is annihilated not in the sense that it does not become something else, which it does, but in the sense that it is no longer anything in itself. It is thus returned to its state of non-existence which it had prior to the world's creation.[231] For that Ockham was also censured by Lutterell (article thirty-four) on the grounds that this meant not transubstantiation but annihilation,[232] despite Ockham's rider that in being annihilated the bread is converted into Christ's body 'because after the bread was here, Christ's body is, as night follows day'. Lutterell clearly wanted to eat his cake as well; for he also condemned Ockham's countervailing statement (article twenty-two) 'that fewer difficulties follow from the explanation rejected by the church that the substance of the bread remains after consecration than the church's explanation'.[233] Whereas the first of these two articles is Ockham's attempt to explain transubstantiation in accordance with the church's teaching, the second is his judgement upon one of the different possible interpretations of transubstantiation which do not entail any contradiction.[234] As such in his view it involves fewer difficulties than that held by the church according to which the accidents remain without a substance. Ockham, as against Aquinas and Lutterell, is once more arguing from the standpoint of God's omnipotence, and thereby recognising a theological paradox which they do not, namely that God in decreeing what is not naturally conceivable is still not precluded from choosing what is naturally more conceivable: the choice of one among a number of possible courses

---

[229] *Quodlibet* VI, q. 3.
[230] *Reportatio*, IV, q. 4, F, G.
[231] *Ibid.*, q. 6, ad 7m dubium, L.
[232] Hoffman, *Die Schriften des Oxforder Kanzlers*, 79.
[233] *Ibid.*, 56.
[234] Ockham states four in the *Reportatio*, IV, q. 6, D and *Quodlibet* IV, q. 30, and three in *De Sacramento*, ch. 5. In taking this position Ockham was again following Duns Scotus, whom he cites in *De Sacramento*, ch. 5.

does not negate the possibility of the others, nor is it necessarily the one most comprehensible to human reason. In the *Sacrament of the Altar*,[235] however, Ockham dispenses with these considerations, merely observing that on the possibility of consubstantiation some, like St Thomas Aquinas, hold that it is contradictory while others, like Duns Scotus, say that it is not, but it is not the actual mode by God's present dispensation. On that mode the change of tone is still more marked compared with the *Reportatio*. Nothing is now said about the bread's annihilation, merely that the substance of the bread and wine ceases to exist and only the accidents remain; nor is there any mention of the greater difficulties which such an interpretation holds. Instead Ockham defends it 'as more probable and more consonant with theological truth because it exalts God's omnipotence, denying it nothing save what evidently and expressly implies a contradiction'. This version like the entire *Sacrament of the Altar* shows Ockham's concern to comply with authority, and effectively removes Lutterell's objections, which reflect more upon the latter's limitations than Ockham's orthodoxy.

We can now turn to the other main thread of this part of the discussion, quantity as a connotative term. As such it signifies a substance and consignifies with it other extrinsic things, namely, matter, form or corporeal quality having parts extended in place, one outside the other. When thus extended the whole coexists totally with its place and the parts each with its own place and not another so that they are locally distant and there can be local movement between them. Substance and quality are then called quantity.[236] Conversely when they are not extended there is no quantity. Quantity, then, like any connotative term is convertible with an expression equivalent to 'something absolute having parts extended in place'.[237]

The significance of this view is that quantity becomes merely a term accidentally predicable of substance or quality which has extended parts. It is therefore neither included essentially in substance or quality, since it can be successfully affirmed and denied of them according to whether they have extension or not, nor does it inhere in them as something real.[238] Hence although when taken significatively, in personal supposition, quantity can mean the same as substance, they are not the same because substance, of itself and essentially, is not extended.[239]

Now it is just this distinction between substance having extended parts and not having extended parts, which is the difference between Christ's body in heaven, where it does have quantity, and Christ's body in the host, where it does not.

---

[235] *De Sacramento*, ch. 5.
[236] *Reportatio*, IV, q. 4, L.
[237] *Quodlibet* IV, q. 26; *De Sacramento*, chs. 31, 41.
[238] Dico quod dupliciter accipitur accidens. Uno modo pro aliqua re informante substantiam. Alio modo pro conceptu predicabili de substantia qui aliquando predicatur de ea, aliquando non. Primo modo secundum istam viam non est accidens, quia non est res absoluta vel respectiva alia ab substantia et qualitate. Secundo modo est accidens, quia est quidam conceptus, qui aliquando predicatur de substantia, aliquando non. Unde est conceptus connotativus significans substantiam et qualitatem, tamen connotando totum existere toti et partem parti (*Reportatio*, IV, q. 4, L). In *Quodlibet* IV, q. 30 and *De Sacramento*, ch. 32, Ockham includes a third division, which is a broader meaning of accident as a concept and does not affect the argument.
[239] *De Sacramento*, ibid. And especially *Reportatio*, ibid., ad 3ᵐ dubium, to which we shall return.

The question to be resolved therefore is how such a difference is possible if quantity is not something really distinct from substance; for if Christ's body does not lose quantity as an accident how else does it cease to be a quantum? In the *Reportatio* Ockham considers and rejects the opinions of both Aquinas and Duns Scotus. For Aquinas the bread converted into Christ's body is now separated from quantity—which is the subject of the bread's remaining accidents—and inheres in the host indirectly through the accidents by natural concomitance and not immediately itself. Ockham's reply is that it would then not be in the host without extension,[240] the reasons for which we shall consider presently. Duns Scotus distinguished between quantity as an internal order of parts within a whole, and as external position. The first is not separable from quantity; but the second is, so that there can be an order of parts without extrinsic position; it is in that sense that an absolute can be separated from quantity. Ockham however denies the distinction on the grounds that there is never an order of parts in a whole or in place without a difference between one part and another, and so extension.[241]

Ockham's own explanation can be considered under three main heads. The first concerns the arguments against quantity as an absolute; the second the way in which Christ's body is present in the host without extension; the third how the bread's accidents continue to be quanta when no longer in a substance. They all depend closely upon recourse to God's omnipotence.

The first group of arguments designed to establish that only substance which is extended is quantity is in the *Reportatio* comparatively uncomplex and familiar: first, that if quantity were an absolute distinct from substance and quality it would then have to belong to another subject, which could only be matter or form or their composite; but there is no more reason to posit them than substance and quantity; second, that whatever can exist independently of something else extrinsic to it and whose own parts are locally distant from one another (i.e. each occupy a distinct place) is a quantum, which is the case with everything composed of matter, so that all corporeal substance is quantity; third, that whatever is absolute and prior to something else God can conserve without anything posterior to it, and hence if matter were prior to quantity (as an accident) God could destroy quantity and conserve matter in its existing place without local movement or change, thereby enabling it to remain quantity. It is this third argument which underpins the more elaborate arguments in the *Sacrament of the Altar*. It not only reduces quantity but also, by implication quality, to substance, since the assumption is that substance as prior can always be conserved by God to exist alone. This is a more pronounced manner and from the opposite standpoint of divine agency expresses Ockham's tendency, remarked earlier in his treatment of substance as a natural phenomenon, to assimilate form to physical substance as one of its physical components. We must not exaggerate it, however, above all because Ockham here is talking about accidents not substantial parts; the distinction between them is crucial, as should

240 *Reportatio, ibid.*, C, D, G.
241 *Ibid.*, D, G; *De Sacramento*, ch. 29 which contains a much fuller discussion and refutation of most of the arguments which follow.

become plain, to his whole contention that nothing else need be posited than substance to explain both quantity and its absence. As he replies to the second and third doubts of the same discussion in the *Reportatio*, the change from one to the other involves the acquisition or destruction of nothing additional.[242] Substance taken in itself and essentially is without quantity; only when extended is it a quantity.[243]

In the *Sacrament of the Altar* Ockham from fundamentally the same positions takes the discussion further.[244] To begin with, there is a new emphasis upon the homogeneity of a substance which contrasts its essential parts with accidents; the parts are all of the same nature as the whole substance, so that a material substance, like wood, consists not only of its matter and form but of its integral parts extended locally each of which is itself wood. Their quantity is thus due to their own spatial relation and not to anything extrinsic. That can be shown because if some wood is divided in half no new substance will thereby be generated, nor are there now two different substances, but merely two parts of the same whole. As parts of the same substance therefore they must have occupied separate places when they were one; and equally if one of the two parts was then destroyed leaving the other, they cannot have been in the same place. That must also apply to any accident inhering in a substance; for if it is not extended throughout every part of the whole, as say whiteness is in wood, it would then have a different first subject for each part of the substance, and that in turn would lead to another first subject and so on to infinity. Alternatively it would inhere immaterially and unextended in its subject, as the soul does in man's body and an angel in its place, a topic to which we shall return in the next group of arguments.[245]

Secondly, substance together with its substantial parts, is always prior to accident; if therefore substance can be extended in space in conjunction with an accident, it can be extended in the same space by itself before the advent of an accident.[246] That holds for all material substance: it is not only extended in place independently of any separate quantity but solely because of its own extended parts. No accident can alter that fact; and any attempt to posit one as the cause of quantity can only prove that substance as prior is also quantity without it, on the principle that whenever two things occupy the same place, whatever is immediately present to one will be immediately present to the other. If therefore quantity inheres in substance and is immediately present in place, substance will be immediately present in the same place; and as prior to quantity it will be there before quantity. If it were not extended immediately it would then have to be present by the mediation of something else and then the same difficulty would again arise leading to the need to posit a further medium and so on infinitely.[247] In that way all the

---

242 *Ibid.*, K.

243 Quia substantia secundum se et essentiam suam non est divisibilis in partes loco et situ distinctas, quia hoc non competit substantie nisi quando extenditur et potest secundum se et essentialiter existere sine omni extensione, et sic potest verificari (*ibid.*, q. 4, L). Ockham does not say how it can be verified.

244 *De Sacramento*, chs. 11–14, 16, 25–30.

245 *Ibid.*, ch. 12.   246 *Ibid.*, ch. 14.   247 *Ibid.*, ch. 15.

arguments seeking to prove that quantity is an absolute can be turned against their authors, as Ockham illustrates from a modified version which substitutes the co-existence of substance and quantity for the inherence of quantity in substance. Its the grounds that God can dispense with a relation of inherence as extrinsic to substance, but the extremes, substance and quantity, will still remain. Therefore substance is quantity through the presence of quantity. That, he replies, is merely to concede that substance can be quantity without being informed by quantity, a concession reinforced by the same opinion that a relation of presence is prior to a relation of inherence. In that case God could conserve that of presence in separation from that of inherence. Hence as before if substance can be immediately extended in space by the presence of quantity, it can be extended without quantity.[248]

Conversely Duns Scotus's arguments, considered in the *Reportatio* and treated more fully with a magnanimous reference to its author's subtlety in the *Sacrament of the Altar*,[249] that something has its own essential order of position through the relation between its parts which do not however constitute quantity, in fact entails its having quantity; for something can only have position or figure if its parts are locally distant.

It is thus both superfluous and ridiculous to ascribe the cause of quantity to an accident, a course that is supported neither by reason and experience nor authority. Beyond the four causes nothing else is to be posited to explain how the parts of substance or quantity come into existence or are extended; indeed the wonder would be that one small accident posterior to a substance and its essential parts could make one part subsist outside another, where they could not do so without it. In fact no accident is needed for two parts to be locally distant from one another or for two parts to make a whole. In no case is there any more reason why an accident, added to the parts of substance and quality already in existence, should make them what they are than that they should not do so themselves. Everything then that can be saved by positing quantity as an absolute can be saved without it.[250] If quantity were really something distinct it could only be efficient or final cause in being extrinsic to them, since no accident is the formal cause of a substance or, as we have seen, of its extension. But that does not exclude the parts themselves from being extended and so constituting quantity intrinsically. And since God as efficient and final cause could extend the parts, giving a substance quantity, no additional quantity however great could be the cause of what was already quantity.[251]

Finally there is God's power to confirm the ontological priority and independence of substance over accident, and the divisibility of a substance's essential parts. All that God is able to do in separating one from the other by conservation and/or destruction is consonant with the nature of each. Only if they were inseparable would it be a violation on God's part to separate substance from accident or substantial part; but they are all absolutes, and whatever is absolute, although naturally joined to something else, is separable supernaturally. All agree, theologians and philosophers alike, that accident is not part of substance and that substance is

---

248 *Ibid.*, ch. 27.   249 *Ibid.*, ch. 29.
250 *Ibid.*, ch. 28; also ch. 37.   251 *Ibid.*, ch. 28.

composed of substances. Hence since neither substance nor accident is the essential cause of the other, each is separable from the other naturally and supernaturally,[252] as wood can exist without whiteness or many natural things can expel their accidents (in the intensification and remission of forms)[253] or a natural power can conserve a substance without an accident, as the sun can conserve wood without whiteness,[254] and similarly a substance like wood can be divided into parts.[255] Because God's power is no less than that of a created power, whatever the latter can do, he can do without contradiction. Accordingly he can conserve an extended substance in the same position and destroy all its accidents without local movement so that it remains quantity without the inherence of any accidents;[256] separate and conserve two parts of the same thing in distinct places as he could say water, with one part at Rome and the other where Ockham was writing (Oxford ?), since it requires no greater power to separate two parts of the same thing than to make two things into one substance, so that each, as we saw before, will be extended and a quantity without the advent of anything new; or denude the whole sea entirely of its accidents when it would still be extended;[257] or separate something into two parts destroying the accidents of one and not the other, with the same result of both remaining extended. The arguments all follow these same principles and need not be repeated further since they are sufficiently familiar. But their very repetition by Ockham is evidence of his concern to establish the rapport between the natural and the divine in negating the independent existence of quantity. God's power was called in not to overthrow nature but to reveal it in its true contours.

We can now turn to the explanation of how Christ's body in the host can be substance divorced from quantity. It rests upon the distinction between the two different ways in which a creature can be in a place: circumscriptively and definitively. We have already encountered the distinction in discussing the soul's inherence in man's body, which it will be recalled is totally present both in the whole body and in each of its parts; it is therefore there without extension; and whenever a being is wholly present in whichever place it is, so that none of its parts occupies its own place, it is in place definitively. That is only possible for spiritual beings, namely the intellective soul and angels. Moreover it cannot be known by experience but has to be held on faith. To be in place circumscriptively on the other hand is to be extended in place; which is the way in which we have been considering quantity, with the whole substance existing totally in its place and each of its parts having its own place distinct from that of the others, so that part is outside part.[258] Quantity is therefore synonymous with circumscriptive existence; and given one, the other follows as Ockham, notwithstanding the *petitio principii*, seeks to prove.[259] Equally the distinction between these two modes

---

[252] *Ibid.*, ch. 13. [253] *Ibid.*, chs. 14, 25. [254] *Ibid.*, ch. 13.
[255] *Ibid.*, ch. 12. [256] *Ibid.*, chs. 14 and 25. [257] *Ibid.*, ch. 26.
[258] The distinction is stated formally in *Quodlibets* I, q. 3, and IV, q. 21; see also *Reportatio*, IV, q. 4, C, N, O, P; *De Sacramento*, chs. 15, 16, 25.
[259] E.g. Item quod substantia sit quanta per suas partes substantiales intrinsecas sibi, sic ostendo. Illud quod per suas partes intrinsecas est in loco circumscriptive per suas partes intrinsecas est quantum, quia ostensum est prius quod omne quod est circumscriptive in loco est

of subsistence provides a further reason why quantity need be nothing else than substance having extended parts. For it is no more contradictory to exist circumscriptively in place than definitively. By the same token if angels and the soul as incorporeal beings can be in a place indivisibly and so without any quantity, it is groundless to argue that something can only exist in place by means of quantity as an absolute.[260]

Now it is precisely this difference that explains how Christ who is corporeal in heaven can be incorporeal in the host. Although the change is solely from God it corresponds to the modes of existence appropriate to divisible and indivisible beings; it involves nothing beyond the change from substantial parts which are extended in space to those which are not extended; nothing need be acquired or destroyed. Now the possibility—i.e. non-contradictoriness—of each is given in the analogy with divisible and indivisible beings. Among divisible beings it is to be found in the examples of condensation and rarefaction, which as we have seen involve simply the contraction or extension of a substance through the local movement of its parts either more closely together or farther apart. From that it follows that the same divisible substance can be of greater or less quantity by nothing but a change in place of its own parts, so that it is not impossible for it— through the contraction of its parts—to cease to have extension, as Christ's body does in the eucharist.[261] As Ockham expresses it, for whatever it is not contradictory to have more or less extension it is not contradictory for it to be without any extension,[262] a conclusion that appears to commit a fallacy of consequence. More to the point, however, is the congruence which it posits between natural and divine agency. That is provided on the part of indivisible beings by the examples already given of angels and the intellective human soul, which we have said are not accessible to natural experience. Accepting them as true, as all believers must, they equally confirm God's power to make the same being to exist totally in many different places, as each of these exists in every part of the place which it occupies. Hence Christ too can be in the host simultaneously and indivisibly with the whole

---

quantum. Omnis autem substantia materialis per suas partes substantiales est in loco circumscriptive, quia sicut ostensum est prius omnis substantia materialis que est extensa per suas partes essentiales est presens loco, ita quod tota substantia est presens toti loco et pars, est presens parti loci. Sed omne tale est circumscriptive in loco, et ita omnis talis substantia per suas partes intrinsecas est quanta (*ibid.*, ch. 28).

[260] Item non maiorem contradictionem includit quod substantia habens partes distinctas realiter natas distare localiter sit sine omni accidente addito sibi in aliquo loco divisibili, ita quod tota sit in toto et pars in parte, quam quod aliqua substantia carens omni parte tali sit in aliquo loco divisibili, ita quod tota sit in tota et tota in qualibet parte . . . Igitur non est contradictio quod aliqua substantia habens partes natas distare localiter sit tota in toto loco divisibili et pars in parte sine quantitate sibi addita, et sic erit quanta sine quantitate addita sibi. Confirmatur hec ratio, quia non magis includit contradictionem substantiam corpoream esse in loco modo sibi convenienti sine omni re addita sibi, quam substantiam incorpoream esse in loco modo sibi convenienti sine omni re addita sibi. Modus autem proprius essendi in loco conveniens substantie est esse in loco diffinitive . . . sine omni re absoluta addita sibi (*De Sacramento*, 26); also ch. 25.

[261] *Reportatio*, IV, q. 4, H–K; *De Sacramento*, ch. 34; *Quodlibet* IV, q. 31.

[262] Preterea cuicunque non repugnat esse sub maiori extensione et minori non repugnat sibi esse sine omni extensione (*Reportatio, ibid.*, H); also *Quodlibet* IV, *ibid.*

of his substance coexisting with all his parts.[263] Together these analogies help to explain what Ockham in the *Reportatio* calls the two difficulties: first, how the same body totally coexists in many places and second, how many parts can totally coexist in the same place.[264]

As to Christ's organic powers[265]—i.e. his bodily organs and sensitive powers which unlike his non-organic powers of intellect and will are naturally extended— they remain in his body in the host although he can no longer move organically, with part coming after part, as he can in heaven. The reason is that his organic powers no longer occupy separate places distant from one another but merely maintain the order of his being so that his eye is still in his head and not in his hand, and his foot is not his hand. For that, local distance is not necessary; only a real distinction of material dispositions, with each organ retaining its own function, as the eye and not the hand is for seeing. Spatially however they are in the same place, just as the soul is entirely in every part of man and yet is also a part of him having its own distinct operations.[266] In the *Reportatio* and *Quodlibets* Ockham concludes from that, that Christ's body can be moved locally and non-organically by his soul—namely the whole and the parts simultaneously—in the same way as an angel can be moved non-organically.[267]

From this familiar combination of what is naturally possible with what is supernaturally possible no contradiction is involved in Christ's presence in the host without quantity. He is there definitively without extended parts, a state common to indivisible beings and potentially attainable for divisible beings. Faith however is the foundation. In Ockham's words,

From the conclusion that by divine power more than by reason two parts of Christ's body can co-exist in the same place, by the same reason all the parts of Christ's body could coexist in the same place together. From this and all that precedes it the principal intent follows that if it is not impossible for God to do more than he enables us to understand, all the parts of a body can coexist [in the same place] with the same body, nor is it impossible for the whole to be in the whole and the whole in every part, as the soul and an angel show. From which it manifestly follows that it is not impossible for God to make the whole body of Christ coexist in the whole host and every part of it, which is the principal contention.[268]

Finally there are the accidents of the bread which after the consecration of the host subsist as independent qualities with their own quantity. That they are no longer part of Christ's body is clear since it is not the subject of contrary qualities as it would be if those from all the different hosts inhered in him. Nor is his body altered as it would be through the advent of each new quality. Nor does it have

---

[263] *De Sacramento*, ch. 7; *Reportatio*, ibid.; *Quodlibet* IV, q. 31.

[264] *Reportatio*, ibid.; *Quodlibet*, ibid.

[265] Organic and non-organic powers and movement are defined in *Quodlibet* IV, qq. 14, 15; also *Reportatio*, IV, q. 5, F.

[266] *De Sacramento*, ch. 6; *Quodlibet* IV, qq. 14, 15, 31; *Reportatio*, IV, q. 4, E, O.

[267] *Reportatio*, ibid.; *Quodlibet* IV, q. 31.

[268] *De Sacramento*, ch. 6. When Iserloh (*Gnade und Eucharistie*, 201) asks whether this is an ontological change, the answer is no, but a change in the ontological *mode* from extension to non-extension in the same way as any quantitative non-substantial change is.

the form of bread, and it remains unaffected by the bread's accidents through the surrounding air which separates them, for no accident can be in a different place from its substance.[269]

That the accidents themselves are both quantity and quality distinct from Christ is clear from experience as well as authority. They are quantity because they have length, breadth, depth and shape which are not those of Christ but bread; because they can be seen by the bodily eye, whereas Christ cannot; because they can be broken and separated, and Christ cannot, as all testify.[270] They are quality because nothing can be visible without being a sensible quality and because they can be perceived as the qualities of bread, not Christ, by sight, touch, taste, and so on.[271]

What then of the relation of the qualities in the accidents to their quantity? Aquinas had replied that their quantity now became their subject. For Ockham such a solution was untenable first because quantity was not itself something absolute, and so could not be the subject of anything, and second because the accidents were by definition qualities without a substance; hence they inhered in nothing, but remained qualities which were also quanta without any subject. Neither, then, can be the subject of the other. The qualities as a whole cannot be the subject of quantity for the reason that they are not numerically one subject, but only an aggregate. The same accident of quantity could not therefore be totally in all of them; nor could it be successively in each of them, which is not naturally possible when a first subject is understood as that which is adequate to the whole accident. Conversely one quantity could not be successively the subject of quantity; for when it ceased to be subject, its quantity would then be changed.[272] The remaining alternatives are all equally untenable. If each quality had its own quantity, besides being superfluous, it would mean that the bread before consecration had as many distinct quantities as qualities and so would have been simultaneously of different dimensions.[273] Conversely if only one quality is made the subject of quantity the remaining qualities will not be quanta, which is manifestly untrue, as they are all broken and divided in the eucharist. To make them the indirect subject would be no better, since they would then all belong to the quality which was the immediate subject. Which is again false; colour is not the subject of taste or *vice versa*, nor heat of colour or smell; while the destruction of one in the same subject would mean the destruction of the others.[274]

If quality cannot be the subject of quantity neither can quantity be the subject of quality. All the authentic doctors affirm that.[275] The qualities are quantity by their own extension, which can be persuaded by analogy with substance as follows. Before the bread's consecration, it had quantity; after the bread ceases to exist as a substance so does its quantity. Now either its quantity was destroyed or it was nothing distinct from the bread. The destruction of something in conversion seems to contradict the words of the authorities; therefore the quantity must have

---

[269] *Ibid.*, ch. 8.   [270] *Ibid.*, ch. 9.   [271] *Ibid.*, ch. 10.
[272] *Ibid.*, ch. 18; also *Quodlibet* IV, q. 33.
[273] *Ibid.*, ch. 19; *Quodlibet, ibid.*
[274] *Ibid.*, ch. 20; *Quodlibet, ibid.*
[275] *Ibid.*, ch. 21, especially Peter Lombard, and also the Glossa Ordinara of the Bible.

ceased to exist when the substance of the bread ceased to exist.[276] There is the further argument that quantity depends more on a substance as a subject than quality upon quantity; if quantity can be separated from a subject as it is in the host, so therefore can quality.[277] Throughout his different discussions Ockham employs analogies between them to reinforce his case. He also argues from quantity as an absolute to prove that qualities can exist without having quantity as their subject.[278]

There remains in this context the problem of what happens to the accidents after their separation, discussed in the *Reportatio*. They could still like any accidents be partial cause in generating and destroying a substance and they can be moved locally.[279]

That brings us to the final consideration, the logical aspects of the eucharist. This consists in observing the meaning of quantity as a connotative term accidentally predicable of substance and quality. That means first that quantity cannot stand in personal supposition for itself; hence it is only true significatively when what it stands for is true. Thus both these propositions are true: 'The substance of the bread is converted into Christ's body' and 'No quantity is converted into Christ's body'. For nothing is quantity in itself; and although it can be true now that substance is quantity in having extended parts, it is not necessarily true. Hence it can sometimes be true that 'Substance is quantity' and sometimes true that 'Substance is not quantity'; and similarly that 'The bread's substance is quantity' and that 'The bread's substance is not quantity', since substance itself, as we have seen before, does not necessarily have extended parts. The parallel is with a relation of similarity, which connotes two qualities of, say, whiteness existing simultaneously; when they do, it is true to say that 'Whiteness is a similarity', but there can be whiteness (as an absolute) without similarity (as a relation). It would then be true to say 'Whiteness exists' and false that 'A similarity exists'. In the case of quantity the criterion of truth or falsity can be found in substituting 'having part distant from part' for quantity.[280] Quantity as a connotative term like the other seven categories can only be necessary as its own nominal definition, namely 'Quantity is a quantum', or 'Quantity is length' and so on. For that reason to reply that if quantity can exist without substance, quantity must be something distinct, is to commit a fallacy of a figure of speech in taking a connotative term for something real.[281]

The opposite objection, that if they are really the same, wherever one is the other will be, is also false. For apart from its false implication, that what are many can really be the same, it confuses different species. Quantity as a connotative term does not have to be the same as Christ's body, because, as in the eucharist, Christ's body can be without extended parts.

Secondly, for that reason quantity as a connotative term can only truly deter-

[276] *Ibid.*, ch. 24.   [277] *Reportatio*, IV, q. 7, B.   [278] *Ibid.*
[279] *Ibid.*, H–N.
[280] *De Sacramento*, ch. 31; also *Quodlibet* IV, q. 26.
[281] *De Sacramento*, ch. 39.

mine Christ as subject and never the predicate when it is the eucharist. That can be seen from the following examples. 'The quantity of Christ's body is in the eucharist' is true, but 'The substance of Christ's body is quantity in the eucharist' is false; 'Christ's body having parts distinct from parts is in the host' is true; but 'Christ's body is in the host having parts distant from parts' is false; 'Circumscriptive substance is in the host' is true, but 'A substance is in the host circumscriptively in place' is false. In each of these the distinction is between Christ as he is in heaven and as he is in the eucharist. Hence any proposition ascribing quantity to him must qualify him as he is in heaven where he is also quantity and not as he is without quantity in the sacrament of the altar.[282]

With that we end our discussion of the eucharist and Ockham's view of nature. Enough should have been said to identify the main presuppositions in each and their implications for the rest of his outlook. Their keynote is the reduction of all real being to substance and quality and the resolution of the other categories to one or other. The effect was to give a new self-sufficiency to physical substance and to reduce form to the other material constituent of being together with matter. Change, movement, time, place and quantity (as well as action and passion) thereby become measurements of substance under which all substantial forms are subsumed. The streamlining which results can be seen in Ockham's treatment of each of these, culminating in the eucharist where economy in nature has its illustration and justification in God's omnipotence. For Ockham no less than for Aquinas, if in a quite different way, the divine did not destroy nature but completed it.

[282] *Ibid.*, ch. 41; *Quodlibet* IV, q. 26.

CHAPTER TEN

Society

That Ockham's polemical or so-called political writings—on the foundations of spiritual and temporal authority in human society—represent a distinct phase of his thought can scarcely be denied. From 1327 onwards, except for two minor logical works, he devoted the remainder of his career until his death in 1349 to the religious, ecclesiological and political issues which arose first from his order's dispute with pope John XXII over evangelical poverty, and then from the conflict, with which it merged, between John XXII, extending to his successors Benedict XII and Clement VI and Ockham's newly-found protector Ludwig of Bavaria, the German emperor. Franciscan poverty and imperial autonomy became the terms within which Ockham's thinking henceforth evolved, giving it a new orientation. To that extent there is a discontinuity with his previous thinking. It can be seen from the most cursory comparison between his speculative and political writings. The abrupt break in his career as a speculative thinker in 1327 and his entry into a world of real conflict forced upon him new considerations. On the one hand of what he had hitherto taken for granted; the inviolability of Franciscan and evangelical poverty; the inerrability of the Roman church; the unquestioned authority of the pope. And on the other hand of what he had previously, from all appearances, never considered: the violation of Christian principles by the doctrine of absolute papal power (*plenitudo potestatis*) over all men and affairs, temporal as well as spiritual; the status of the pope and the conditions in which he could be deposed; the relation of the Roman church to Christian truth and the universal church; the legitimacy of lay rulers, above all the German emperor; and the circumstances in which the intervention of laymen and ecclesiastics in the affairs of the other was warranted.

These were the themes upon which Ockham's political writings were focused beginning from his first polemical treatise, the *Opus Nonaginta Dierum* written probably in 1332. In seeking their relation to his philosophical and theological principles therefore there can be no question of attempting to deduce one from the other. Nothing in Ockham's previous outlook permits us to infer from them his later opposition to popes or his championing of emperors; indeed all the earlier indications are of deference to the former—illustrated in his doctrine of the eucharist and obliviousness of the latter. Ockham himself expresses the lack of any direct connection in his letter to the Franciscan general chapter at Assisi in 1334 when he declares that he was at the papal court for nearly four years before he recognised John XXII's heresy through fulfilling the command of his superiors to study the pope's three bulls attacking Franciscan poverty.[1] It is further confirmed by the evolution of Ockham's political ideas which apart from the uncompleted *Dialogus* and to a lesser extent the *Octo Quaestiones* and *Opus Nonaginta Dierum* are *pièces d'occasion* of varying degrees of repetitiousness and anti-papal invective rather than formal expositions in the manner of his speculative writings. Their import has to be discerned from his works taken together.

It is here that the qustion of their dependence upon his speculative writings arises; for granting a change of direction in Ockham's espousal, or at least articulation, of new principles after 1327, what part did his philosophical and theological principles play in their formulation and development and how far does his outlook as a whole share a common attitude and have comparable implications?

Here as with most questions concerning Ockham opinion is divided, beyond general recognition of the essentially Franciscan inspiration and theological character of his political beliefs: a judgement that can be accepted here and should be confirmed by the end of this chapter. The recent tendency has been to see in Ockham a political traditionalist seeking a return to a proper balance between spiritual and temporal power.[2] This view carries the implication of a dichotomy between Ockham's political and speculative ideas which Boehner makes explicit when he writes, 'Ockham's political ideas in their great outlines could have been developed, so far as we can see, from any of the classical metaphysics of the thirteenth century; for, as will be shown, they coincide with a sound Catholic political theory'.[3] Directly opposed to this interpretation is Lagarde's, which took Ockham as the bearer *par excellence* of the new 'lay spirit' that undermined traditional medieval political assumptions. While accepting, certainly in his revised volumes on him,[4] that Ockham's philosophical doctrines are rarely found directly stated in his political doctrines, Lagarde nevertheless regards Ockham as a political no less than a philosophical iconoclast through the very absence of a metaphysic which could be extended to society. Hence, according to Lagarde, Ockham unlike St Bonaventure or St Thomas Aquinas lacked any wider perspective in which to

---

[1] *Epistola Ad Fratres Minores* (*OP*, III, 6).

[2] E.g. J. B. Morrall, 'Some notes on a recent interpretation of William of Ockham's political philosophy', *FcS* 9 (1949), 335–69; P. Boehner, 'Ockham's political ideas', *Collected Articles*, 442–68.

[3] Boehner, *ibid.*, 446.

[4] G. de Lagarde, *La Naissance d' l'Esprit Laique*, new edition, vols IV (Paris, 1962) and V (Paris, 1963). These are in fact a new work compared with the original vols. IV, V and VI (Paris, 1942–6); they represent in my view the outstanding study to date on Ockham's political philosophy, less as expositions, where their arbitrariness both excludes and assumes too much, than for their intelligence and penetration. The recent study by J. Miethke, *Ockhams Weg zur Sozialphilosophie* despite its title does not, for all its thoroughness and balance, go beyond restating Ockham's known positions in philosophy, theology and politics together with their background.

On the question raised by virtually every political commentator of identifying Ockham's

comprehend human affairs and with it any philosophy of society or authority.[5]

These differing judgements are not totally irreconcilable. With Boehner we can agree that in their ordinary application, Ockham—in contrast to Marsilius of Padua—did not deny either spiritual or temporal power its traditional attributes or exalt one over the other, and that he was principally concerned with curbing what he regarded as the monstrous abuses which came from the doctrine of the *plenitudo potestatis* rather than with any attack upon papal power itself: a distinction that Lagarde recognised as clearly as anyone. But equally Lagarde is right to emphasise that Ockham's political attitudes are not detachable from his outlook as a whole. Ockham was not merely reasserting a traditional Gelasian belief in a due balance between spiritual and temporal, repeatedly as he insisted upon the observation of their mutual rights; his conception of society and authority also bears the impress of his philosophical and theological conceptions. If one facet is the negative view of which Lagarde speaks with its stress upon the limitations of power rather than its consonance with eternal principles or man's nature as a social being, it is not the only one; nor does it lack its own perspective. In what this consists I shall attempt briefly to outline in the following pages with no pretence at a full exposition.

We must begin with a distinction to which Lagarde drew attention,[6] and which helps to explain the impact of Ockham's ideas: namely the contrast between his essentially moderate conclusions and the arguments by which he supports them. It was on the way to establishing his contentions over both spiritual and temporal power that he produced a devastating critique of the traditional assumptions about the nature of each; and he did so largely by drawing upon his own wider philosophical and theological assumptions.

Foremost among them was the antinomy between the necessary and the contingent which is central to Ockham's entire outlook, whether it refers to God's own nature and his freedom as creator, or the distinction between what exists and what is possible, logically and ontologically, or between a free and a natural act. Each of these is represented in Ockham's view of society. Their most immediately obvious political expression, and in some ways his political platform, in his identification of God's law with freedom. *Lex evangelica est lex libertatis* is a phrase which first occurs in the *Contra Benedictum*, written in 1337, marking the transition to the overtly political treatises of the last decade of Ockham's life. It recurs throughout those that succeed it; but it sets the tone of Ockham's political outlook in which the same preoccupations are apparent from the beginning. As I have remarked elsewhere,[7] the affirmation of freedom was as distinctive of Ockham as its denial—to the church at least—was characteristic of Marsilius of Padua. Where Marsilius argued for the total subservience of ecclesiastical to temporal

---

own views deliberately masked in his impersonal treatises, above all the *Dialogus* and *Octo Quaestiones*, I offer no patent beyond the congruousness of his statements with his avowed views in his personal works, and, as in the case of the moral capacities of infidels, with his outlook as a whole.

[5] *La Naissance*, IV, 223. All references are to the new edition unless otherwise specified.
[6] *Ibid.*, V (old edition), 34.
[7] *Heresy in the Later Middle Ages*, II, 424.

power, Ockham sought freedom from total ecclesiastical power. Marsilius looked for unconditional spiritual submission; Ockham for mutual rights. For Ockham that was achieved by the restriction of each power to its own sphere. His conception of liberty is therefore essentially negative but no less liberating for that. It was, as Ockham himself said, to be understood 'negatively, namely that it introduced no heavy burden and that no one was made the slave of another or that only an exterior cult of God was imposed upon Christians as the Jews have submitted to it'.[8] As such, it did not mean the removal of all servitude, a crucial qualification, since every Christian must, as Paul said, accept the station to which he has been called; but rather that the perfect liberty of the gospel precludes oppression of Christians by the pope in the name of a plenitude of power.[9] The defence of evangelical liberty as the criterion of Christian authority was therefore directed against its own guardians who betrayed it: that is the erring popes who oppressed other Christians by claiming in God's name a comparable jurisdiction over all temporal rulers to that which temporal rulers exercised over their own subjects. To concede it would be to make all Christians slaves of the pope; he could then act towards temporal rulers in the manner of any other temporal ruler: intervene in their affairs, despoil them of their lands, give and sell their possessions at will, deprive them of their territories and award them to someone else.[10] All of which is the prerogative of temporal but not spiritual power.

Their differentiation into coercive and non-coercive along these lines is familiar and venerable enough; nor does Ockham carry it to the extremes of Marsilius of Padua or the Franciscan Spirituals or later Wyclif and Hus, in denying the church the spiritual sanction of excommunication as the accompaniment of an exclusively spiritual role.[11] What Ockham does is to provide a new formulation of spiritual power. Even as a slogan, *lex evangelica est lex libertatis* adds a cutting edge to the attack upon the doctrine of absolute papal power. But it is more than a slogan; it expresses the asymmetry both between spiritual and temporal power and within spiritual power.

The pursuit of this asymmetry is the hallmark of Ockham's political thinking; it has its foundation in the paradox that Ockham is the one theologian and philosopher who as a political publicist eschews any wider theological or philosophical justification for the division between temporal and spiritual as part of God's eternal dispensation. Even Marsilius of Padua—neither a theologician nor a philosopher— who would reduce the church to complete dependence upon the lay power, stressed the sacramental role of the church in ministering to man's supernatural end as the complement to man's natural end of peace and harmony fulfilled in human society. Ockham posited no such order. Certainly the function of temporal rulers was to chastise and punish wrongdoers and to defend the church from them as well. Correspondingly the church in having an exclusively spiritual role is

---

[8] *Breviloquium*, bk. II, ch. 4, 58.
[9] *Ibid.*, 58–9.
[10] *Contra Benedictum*, ch. 4, 275–6; *Dialogus*, part III, tract I, bk. III, chs. 5, 7, 8, 9.
[11] See my *Heresy in the Later Middle Ages*, II, 418–22, 516–39.

subject to a lay ruler for its temporalities and does not hold them by canon law;[12] although unlike Marsilius Ockham allowed the church its own possessions and in the case of excommunication a limited jurisdiction.[13] But that was not the same as conceiving these differences as absolute. While he did not, as John of Paris did, entirely eschew metaphors like body and soul to describe their differences,[14] temporal and spiritual were not for Ockham distinct realities which existed independently of the individuals constituting them; beyond the diverse churches and kingdoms in which they were found, spiritual and temporal power did not, as they did for most medieval thinkers, correspond to different orders, one of grace, the other of nature. In society as in the rest of creation, only the individual was real, as Ockham insisted in the *Opus Nonaginta Dierum*, rebutting John XXII's claim that the church was a fictitious person.[15] Consequently, since in Christian society spiritual and temporal were coterminous, embracing the same individuals, who were at once baptised members of the church and subject to a temporal ruler, the problem for Ockham was to establish the principles regulating the same individuals according to two different standards—of Christ and of Caesar.

It is here that the negative asymmetrical character of Ockham's political thinking lies. As it concerns the relation of spiritual to the temporal it has three main elements. The first and in many ways the most fundamental arises directly from his Franciscan conception of spiritual power. This is the distinction between the divine law governing the church and the human laws regulating the empire and secular kingdoms. Ockham develops it in his defence of evangelical poverty in the *Opus Nonaginta Dierum*. It therefore comes at the outset of the political phase of his career and can be regarded as the foundation of his attack upon the *plenitudo potestatis* in the later name of evangelical liberty.

As a Franciscan Ockham began from what can be called an apostolic view of spiritual power based upon the conception of Christ the man as a *pauper*.[16] Far from having ruled all men and things as a temporal king, Christ had in this world renounced all possessions and jurisdiction over others; he had lived on alms and exercised only a spiritual mission. Hence his power had been exclusively spiritual and non-coercive, submitting himself completely to temporal authority, as his words 'Render unto Caesar' declared, and enjoining all who wished to follow him to sell their goods and give the proceeds to the poor. This idea had underlain the Franciscan doctrine of Christ's absolute poverty, by which he and the apostles had owned nothing themselves; they had merely used what was necessary to sustain mortal life—food, drink, clothing, shelter. They did so moreover by the natural right given to all men to obtain such sustenance and not by any legal right or licence of possessions or use.

Now it was their claim to be emulating Christ and his disciples, whose life of

---

[12] *Octo Quaestiones*, q. II, 85–6, where Ockham also says that it is only in deference to the pope's spiritual office that he does not assert his lordship over the pope's temporalities. Also *Dialogus*, III, II, bk. III, ch. 7, 23.

[13] *Dialogus*, III, I, I, ch. 17.   [14] E.g. *Octo Quaestiones*, I, 58.

[15] *OND*, chs. 6 and 62; see below, p. 639.

[16] *Heresy in the Later Middle Ages*, I, ch. I.

mendicant poverty and preaching St Francis had taken as his model, in the exercise of the same natural right—later called the use of simple fact— that provided the Franciscan justification to their title of absolute poverty.[17] And it was this claim, the source of so much dissension both within the order and outside it for over three quarters of a century, that John XXII finally condemned as heretical in the bull *Cum inter nonnullos* in November 1323 as the culmination of his attack upon the doctrine. He completed the process in two subsequent bulls, *Quia quorumdam mentes* in 1324 and *Quia vir reprobus* in 1328.[18] These not only repeated his previous denial of the Franciscan distinction between use and possession and between a natural and a legal right, so that according to the pope all use was also possession and must always entail a legal right of use; they also affirmed the superiority of possessions to the lack of them. He thereby turned the Franciscans' claims against themselves. Perfection was commensurate with rights, not their renunciation, because without rights there was no justice. Hence to oppose the greater perfection of poverty—with its renunciation of all rights—to dominion and lordship—based upon rights—was absurd. Property according to the pope was the result of a divine dispensation; it had existed from the beginning of time and not just from the fall, which had led to private appropriation. Christ and the apostles had enjoyed a similar dominion over what they held, and with it rights of litigation.

This sanctifying of lordship to the exclusion of poverty represented the extension—albeit in a legal form—of the contrary doctrine of Christ's royalty which had been developed in the second half of the thirteenth century and the first years of the fourteenth by extreme papalists like James of Viterbo and Giles of Rome. On this interpretation Christ on earth had exercised all the attributes of a temporal king in virtue of his divinity; instead of the humble possessionless pilgrim and wayfarer conceived by St Francis and his adherents, Christ had been ruler of the world, king of kings, and his authority invested in St Peter and his successors.

Accordingly when Ockham came to reply to *Quia vir reprobus* with the *Opus Nonaginta Dierum* he was presented with a rival outlook which challenged Franciscan poverty by a diametrically opposed concept at once of evangelical perfection and the nature of spiritual power exemplified in the pope's condemnation of Franciscan observance; it involved the very meaning of Christ's law. Ockham treated it as such. From the beginning his defence of Franciscan poverty was inseparable from his attack upon papal pretensions, or at least those of John XXII, which in a few years crystallised into the opposition between evangelical liberty and the papal claim to a plenitude of power.

Ockham's distinctiveness was to define one in terms of the other. On the basis of his Franciscan view of Christ's purely spiritual mission—the denial of which by John XXII in the *Opus Nonaginta Dierum* he declared heretical[19]—he made non-

[17] *Ibid.*, 83–100.

[18] *Ibid.*, 163–6; for what follows, *ibid.*, 241–53.

[19] In chapter 93 Ockham described as manifest heresies John XXII's assertions first that Christ as a *viator* was king in temporal things; and second that he was lord of all *temporalia* from the instant of his conception (*ibid.*, 673, l, 101–5).

intervention, or more strictly non-involvement, in temporal affairs, the criterion of licit spiritual power. Accordingly whatever was asserted by the pope, which had been either expressly renounced or not prescribed by Christ, fell outside the pope's power. Christ's law meant abnegation of worldly power: the *plenitudo potestatis* its affirmation. That applied to spiritual and temporal matters alike; and the sequence of Ockham's political development is the extension of the contrast between what holds by divine law and what by human law to all matters where papal power was implicated—church and secular kingdoms alike. It is here that the negative import of evangelical liberty lies; as conceived by Ockham it was invoked to prise free any group or individual or institution from unsolicited intervention by the pope. Evangelical liberty consists in the absence of coercion regardless of where it may occur; and when Lagarde remarks upon the meagreness and inconsequentiality of Ockham's examples of its violation by the *plenitudo potestatis* and the lack of any recognition of the central distinction between *plenitudo* and *sollicitudo*,[20] these omissions—if they are such—are explicable it would seem by Ockham's concern with the departure from liberty and hence the violation of Christ's law rather than its specific manifestations. Christ was the exemplar of spiritual perfection in his total abdication of temporal sovereignty: judgement of legal disputes, division of hereditary lands, desire for possessions, government of others.[21] It was precisely the papal claim to act over men where Christ had exercised no such authority that constitutes for Ockham the violation of evangelical liberty in the doctrine of the *plenitudo potestatis*. To that extent Ockham's definition of the latter is as Lagarde has observed[22] of his own making, but made it must be added from Franciscan principles.

Their opposition governs Ockham's political thinking; it is expressed in the disjunction between divine and natural law on the one hand and human law on the other, with the consequent separation of what is right morally, according to right reason or divine precept, from what is legitimate according to positive human law. Neither entails the other. Acts morally good by divine or natural law can be legally indifferent by human law, which is precisely the status of the Franciscan claim to simple use of fact as a natural not a legal right. Conversely acts legitimate by human law can be ethically indifferent, although not contrary to divine or natural law. Ockham formulates the distinction in the *Opus Nonaginta Dierum* as that between *ius poli* and *ius fori*, terms taken from St Augustine.[23] *Ius poli* is natural equity and conforms to right reason whether known naturally or divinely revealed; it is independent of any positive ordinance, human or divine. Sometimes it is called natural law and sometimes divine law because, while natural law pertains to it, much that is consonant with right reason is only known by revelation, in Ockham's example that those preaching the gospel who have nothing of their own to support them are to be sustained by goods from those to whom they preach. *Ius fori* on the other hand is the result of a compact or a divine or human ordinance, and in its broad sense can be called the law of custom which is not normally to be infringed

---

[20] Lagarde, *La Naissance*, IV, 79.
[22] *La Naissance*, V, 173–203.

[21] *OND*, ch. 93, 682–3.
[23] *OND*, ch. 65, 573–5.

although it can in certain circumstances be overridden by a superior authority. That applies to granting a licence—one of the main issues between John XXII and his opponents—which if done under *ius fori* should not be revoked.

The difference between these two kinds of right then is that *ius poli* is the power to act according to right reason independently of any legal compact, whereas *ius fori* is the power derived from a legal compact to conform or not to conform to right reason.[24] The detailed application of this difference to Franciscan poverty does not concern us here, beyond recognising that it was the means which enabled Ockham to justify Franciscan poverty in natural as opposed to positive law. He thus based himself upon the very separateness denied by John XXII of one from the other arguing that the need to have the wherewithal to survive was a natural right granted to all men by *ius poli* and carried with it the right to use what was held in common, without any accompanying legal right of private ownership by *ius fori*. No one could totally renounce such right but it could be restricted to extreme need.[25] The question of receiving a licence of use only arose when what was needed was held privately by *ius fori*. A licence however did not confer any legal right upon those to whom it was granted; it merely removed an impediment to natural law which was the source of the right of use in the obligation—and— right—to maintain life.[26] That was the position of the Franciscan order; it had no positive right to the goods common to all believers but used them legitimately by a purely natural right. No laws—natural, divine, human—or any special case prohibits it; hence it is not dependent upon any legal right.[27]

The significance of this view is to be seen in its two main accompaniments, both expressly framed as Ockham's reply to John XXII's annexing of all justice and right to legal right. The first is the distinction between a licit and a just act; it rests upon a threefold meaning of justice and a just act. The first is where justice is taken as a cardinal virtue from which a just act is produced; and then many licit and meritorious human acts, such as chastity, fortitude, mercy, liberality, and others are not just because they are not from justice as a separate virtue. Second, justice can be understood in the legal sense of that which is directed to the common good; a just act then consists in wanting to obey the law. Here again not every virtuous act is a just act, because according to Aristotle there are many virtuous acts which could be just if they were decreed but may not have been decreed by human law. Thirdly, justice and a just act can mean either strictly or metaphorically what is good and consonant with true reason. It is in that sense that every licit act is a just one according to those who regard every human act as morally good or bad.[28] It is also the sense in which Ockham supports the claim of his confrères that someone can have licit and just use of goods without any legal right of use.[29] Thus when John XXII declared first that no extrinsic act could be just without the right to perform it, and second that it was absurd and false that an act of someone who had no right was more just and acceptable to God than that act of someone having

[24] *Ibid.*, 579, l. 273–6.   [25] *Ibid.*, 577–9.
[26] *Ibid.*, 578 and ch. 61, 559–62.   [27] *Ibid.*, ch. 65, 578.
[28] *Ibid.*, ch. 60, 557.   [29] *Ibid.*, 558, l. 161–6.

such a right,[30] Ockham's reply was twofold. First the pope was arguing from ignorance of the equivocal meaning of 'just' and 'unjust'; so that his assertion was only correct if just was understood in the first sense. Second, for the same reason, it would only be anomalous to say that an act was more just without justice if justice were accepted in the first sense as a distinct virtue, but not in the third sense. An act for example of loving God is just and juster in the third sense, of conforming to what is good and reasonable, than an act of paying someone for his labour, for the very reason that not every act exercised without a right is an unjust act;[31] and many acts which are not from justice as a separate virtue are neither just nor unjust.[32] Between these extremes, justice in the legal sense of conforming to what is positively decreed has only a limited application.

That is to be seen from the different ways in which temporal things can belong: by merit; necessity or honesty which accords with right reason; *ius poli*, sometimes together with *ius fori*, and good conscience; sincere conscience; and the legal rights which are exclusive to *ius fori*. Although therefore *ius poli* and *ius fori* can overlap they can also be incompatible; and something can be licit by *ius fori* yet devoid of any merit or moral worth which characterises the preceding modes. Thus by *ius fori* the avaricious have many things unworthily which are not their due and which they possess from avarice not right conscience. But legally they have a right to them.[33] In contradistinction to what holds by *ius poli*, to possess by *ius fori*, is often to possess badly. The difference lies in the relation to right reason; *ius poli* entails conformity to it; *ius fori* does not.[34]

There is accordingly no necessary connection between the different kinds of justice, as earlier it will be recalled Ockham had argued against any necessary connection between the virtues. To have a right to something can as well be from merit and right reason as from positive law; it can be merely good and not just, or morally good and just, or legally just and neither meritorious nor morally good.

It is around these different dispositions that the relations between temporal and spiritual power revolve. They make divine and natural law distinct from positive human law. The first two are virtually synonymous as Ockham declares in the *Dialogus*[35] where he distinguishes three levels of natural law: absolute precept, natural equity without reference to circumstances, and its application to circumstances in the law of nations, or other human enactments made in the light of principles derived from evident reason. As such all natural law is an extension of divine law contained explicitly or implicitly in the Bible and constitutes the general rules for each of these modes in cases where they have not been declared in scripture.[36] Not all positive human law on the other hand need conform to right

---

[30] *Ibid.*, ch. 62, 566, l. 130–5.

[31] *Ibid.*, 566–7.

[32] Quia non omnis actus exercitus sine iure quo valet quis in iudicio litigare est actus iniustus. Accipiendo enim actum iniustum prout opponitur actui elicito a iustitia particulari multi sunt actus qui nec sunt iusti nec iniusti (*ibid.*, 567, l. 160–4).

[33] *Ibid.*, 575–7.

[34] *Ibid.*, 579, l. 272–580, l. 295.

[35] *Dialogus*, III, II, bk. III, ch. 6.

[36] Hoc ideo dicunt, quia omne ius quod est a deo qui est conditor nature potest vocari ius

reason and so divine and natural law. Hence they observe different criteria; or rather positive law is not governed by the same criteria in including what is morally indifferent or bad.

This discrepancy involves Ockham in an ambiguity which persists throughout his political writings. Initially he was concerned to establish the intrinsic worth of possessionlessness by showing its consonance with right reason, and so divine and natural law independently of any legal right. At the same time he sought to explain, as we shall mention again presently, lordship and possession as the result of the fall and not as the reflection of natural and divine law. He began therefore from the formal opposition between the ideal of spiritual perfection exemplified in natural law and the *de facto* imperfection of fallen nature expressed in positive law. Subsequently he became engaged in defending not simply Franciscan poverty but imperial autonomy as well, from papal encroachment. He thus sought to reconcile temporal power in its *de facto* post-lapsarian state with the principles expressed in natural law—the purpose of the tripartite division just stated—and at the same time to debar papal intervention from wherever it had not a divine mandate. He did that by specifying in later works the nature of the pope's purely spiritual power upon which he had insisted from the outset in the *Opus Nonaginta Dierum*.

In the *Dialogus* he defined that power as to do that which must be done or omitted according to evangelical law; it had been conferred on Peter by Christ and consisted in such duties as administering the sacraments, ordaining priests, instituting and promoting ecclesiastics, and instructing the faithful in faith, divine worship and other spiritual matters. As interpreted by Ockham they did not extend beyond divine precept to counsels or supererogatory works.[37] He thereby appealed to natural law at once to uphold *de facto* temporal sovereignty which—outside the Empire at least—could be or have originated in violation of natural law, and at the very least included under its positive law provisions which violated right reason, and to prevent spiritual enforcement of counsels and works of supererogation. Characteristically, the way Ockham overcame these obstacles was by invoking cases of necessity or utility when what obtained ordinarily (*regulariter*) could be superseded. We shall have more to say about this distinction between *regulariter* and *casualiter*. But it did not alter the inherent imbalance in his outlook. Natural law applied to papal and ecclesiastical power is eternally expressed in what can and cannot be done; to that extent it is invariable although as we shall see, its means can vary. Natural law applied to temporal society can justify what does not

---

divinum. Omne autem ius naturale est a deo qui est conditor nature; igitur etc. Tum quia omne ius quod explicite vel implicite continetur in scripturis divinis potest vocari divinum ius . . . quia in scripturis divinis sunt quedam regule generales ex quibus solis vel cum aliis colligi potest quod omne ius naturale primo modo, secundo modo, et tertio modo dictum, licet in eis non inveniatur explicite, sit ius divinum (*ibid.*).

[37] *Ibid.*, III, 1, bk. 1, ch. 17: e.g., Per hoc autem quod dicit Christum dedisse beato Petro potestatem quo ad spiritualia que sunt de necessitate facienda vel de necessitate omittenda, intendit excludere a regulari potestate Petri illa spiritualia que superogationis sunt, que scilicet sunt consilii et non precepti.

express it and may violate it. It therefore operates to a double standard: towards spiritual power it limits its exercise and can be invoked to banish or overcome its transgressions, if necessary through the intervention of laymen; towards temporal power there is no such direct correlation, because what should be is not necessarily the same as what is; and although Ockham stressed the need for rulers to rule by equity and with the consent of their subjects, he recognised that they could and did rule without doing either, even if they did so without justification. In the case of spiritual power there can be no legitimate deviation from the ideal; in the case of temporal power there is no immutable ideal to deviate from.

The difference is tantamount to that between necessity and contingency. Ockham never puts it like that, if indeed he ever conceived it like that. As with his outlook as a whole, his political philosophy is less a system than a series of separate pieces of engineering. In each case he began from what was given; it is that which his politics share with his philosophy and theology. Just as the individual nature of being is *ex natura rei*, beyond which we cannot go, and theology must start from revealed truth held on faith, so politics must accept the existence of distinct temporal kingdoms not regulated by the same principles as the church. The discrepancy is built into human affairs. The former are morally indifferent in themselves; the latter are regulated by divine law accessible to all believers, through scripture and the exercise of reason. It is in that sense that the same law can also be extended to temporal kingdoms, not to justify them in themselves but to justify their independence from spiritual intervention. Hence right reason rules the church; it merely permits the existence of temporal kingdoms in relation to the church. Its application circumscribes one and liberates the other, as well as the members of both. That is the import of evangelical law.

It is hardly surprising therefore that Ockham has so little positive to say about temporal society taken for itself. The distance between the boldness of his principles and the poverty of their political application, which Lagarde rightly stresses[38] is due to the very hesitation between gratuitousness and necessity which Lagarde also, in my view rightly, discerns in Ockham's attitude to the institution of human authority.[39] In a general sense the same can be said of Ockham's outlook as a whole, not least over the moral virtues and supernatural habits. Towards society it arises directly from the need to justify a form of authority whose nature is not justified in natural law; he can therefore only apply the principles of natural law to regulate what exists independently of those principles and sometimes infringes them. To do so however is to empty of political content all those cases where the principles of natural law do not hold, namely wherever there is *ius fori* without *ius poli*. That is precisely the opposition that Ockham cannot, and does not attempt to, resolve. On the one hand there are the requisites of legitimate political authority—consent of those governed and the pursuit of the common good.[40] On the other hand there

---

[38] *La Naissance*, IV, 232–4.

[39] *Ibid.*, 223.

[40] E.g. *Octo Quaestiones*, 78, 106; *Dialogus*, III, II, bk. IV, ch. 8; bk. VI, ch. 97; III, II, bk. I, ch. 27, bk. III, ch. 6; *An Princeps*, 242, 246; *Breviloquium*, 96–7. I owe these and the details of the next note to Lagarde, *op. cit.*, IV, 228–33.

are the exceptions which limit them to a mere ideal and make it unattainable. The result is that in all temporal authority, freedom is mixed with despotism.[41] Instead therefore of a simple norm to which all men must conform there are more exceptions than rules. Thus a people can disqualify itself from the right of electing its rulers if it falls into sin or for some other cause;[42] a ruler can exercise his authority legitimately in his own interests as private lords do, without impairing it, because legitimate authority is not destroyed by its abuse any more than illegitimate authority is legitimised by good use;[43] by the same token legitimate authority can be tyrannical, and once conferred by the people it can only be retracted in the event of sin or crime by the ruler;[44] conversely a people can be deprived of its power through wrong-doing or sin;[45] its power can be ceded or transferred;[46] and finally besides consent of the people, authority can also derive from just war, purchase, donation or hereditary succession.[47] Whichever it may be, once established it must be accepted by those over whom it is exercised, for it then owes its continuance to God.

These qualifications nullify any notion of effective popular sovereignty; even if it is the source of political authority it loses its efficacy the moment a ruler is instituted, since as Ockham himself says the same authority cannot be both lord and vassal. Indeed it is essentially in such conventional terms that Ockham conceives political authority. However much he emphasises its justification in serving the common good and to preserve individual liberty, he leaves its recipients with no other power than that of submission, beyond their one action of revoking their allegiance from a ruler who acts criminally or scandalously. Only then do the principles of right reason have an application; but it is essentially a negative and limiting one. That is as far as we can speak of a political compact: a compact however based upon the obligations and rights of lord and vassal governing Ockham's own hierarchical society, as opposed to a social contract founded upon a free and revocable grant of popular sovereignty.

Ockham thus accepted the *de facto* social order in all its contingency for the very reason that he eschewed any independent system of natural law to explain its regularities or to oppose to its irregularities. In keeping with his view of reality as a whole, he recognised no mediating area of intelligibility, whether of universal principles or essences, separate from what could be derived through individual experience and revealed truth. That made all explanation ultimately theological since all existence depended upon God as conserver. In the case of human society the explanation was also immediately theological, namely Adam's sin.

Here we come to the other aspect of Ockham's separation of natural from

---

[41] Nullus enim principatus pure regalis qui est respectu liberorum non servorum inter gentes extitit institutus sed mixtus fuit cum dominativo seu despotico principatu (*De Imp*, 15).

[42] *Octo Quaestiones*, VII, 176.

[43] *Breviloquium*, bk. III, ch. 12, 133–4.

[44] *Ibid.*, bk. IV, ch. 10, 161–2.

[45] *Dialogus*, III, II, bk. III, ch. 7; *Octo Quaestiones*, I, 46; VII, 170.

[46] *Octo Quaestiones*, III, 90; IV, 141–3.

[47] *Breviloquium*, bk. IV, ch. 10, 161–2; *Octo Quaestiones*, V, 162.

human law: that all human sovereignty whether over things or people was the result of the fall. That too was part of his initial defence of Franciscan poverty against John XXII in the *Opus Nonaginta Dierum*, gradually extending it in later works to include authority as well as proprietorship. Lordship was not something eternally given to all men, infidels and believers alike, according to immutable principles grasped in the light of reason, but due to an act of contingent circumstances without which it would not have arisen. It was for Christians correspondingly a matter of theological truth and could only be understood through a correct understanding of scripture.

Ockham's point of departure is the change that came with the fall. Before it Adam and Eve had perfect power over everything; it consisted in ruling with reason and without coercion because there was then no resistance from those things which they ruled. Contrary to John XXII they possessed nothing, but together with the animals were allowed the use of certain things to meet their needs.[48] Neither then nor after the fall, however, did they have common ownership of all goods. In their state of innocence their power approximated more to that of working miracles than to any similarity with the temporal sovereignty of lordship such as that over a servant or a horse.[49] Only after they had sinned did they then acquire the power, which came with their corrupted nature, of appropriating and dividing possessions; although it did not immediately lead to appropriation and division—that happened with Cain and Abel[50]—there was henceforth no dominion in the non-proprietary sense in which Adam and Eve had originally enjoyed it. By positive law, which now regulated it, dominion was inseparable from possession;[51] and one of Ockham's charges against John XXII was of confusing dominion by positive law with the original dominion of Adam and Eve, attributing to them a proprietorship over things which they had not then had.[52] Dominion alone had been from God; lordship and possession were of human institution and will.[53]

Now what gave Ockham's theory of temporal authority its special bias was that he conceived it as the accompaniment of property—i.e. dominion with possession—engendered in the same way and for the same reason.[54] It accordingly

---

[48] *OND*, ch. 14, 432.

[49] *Ibid.*, 434-5.

[50] *Ibid.*, ch. 88, 65, l. 99-108; also *Breviloquium*, bk. III, ch. 9, 129, l. 13-17. Ockham distinguished them as different phases with dominion coming after the division of things. There were three periods: before the fall; after the fall before the division of things but with only the power of dividing them; and after the division of things and of dominion proper (*OND*, ch. 14, 438, l. 354-439, l. 367).

[51] *OND*, ch. 14, 435, l. 212-15; ch. 26, 484, l. 38-485, l. 102; ch. 88, 656, l. 94-5.

[52] *Ibid.*, 436, l. 259-437, l. 272.

[53] Secunda conclusio, quam probant, quod est primum dominium temporalium proprium post lapsum fuit iure humano seu ordinatione aut voluntate humana introductum (*ibid.*, ch. 88, 656, l. 97-9).

[54] E.g. Potestas ergo appropriandi res temporales persone et personis aut collegio data est a deo humano generi; et propter rationem consimilem data est a deo absque ministerio et co-operatione humana potestas instituendi rectores habentes iurisdictionem temporalem (*Breviloquium*, bk. III, ch. 7, 128).

showed the same characteristics: namely that it was the consequence of sin; that it was regulated by positive as opposed to natural law; and that it was of human origin. The first is implicit; the second and third are explicit: the need to reconcile them with God's dispensation for fallen man provides the tension in Ockham's doctrine of temporal authority.

Since it was principally designed in the works following the *Opus Nonaginta Dierum* to establish the independence of temporal authority from ecclesiastical sanction, its two main strands are on the one hand to demonstrate the legitimacy of temporal power in its own right as something common to all men—infidels and believers—and on the other to locate it in God's direct sanction which has nothing to do with that of the church. A comparatively succinct statement of Ockham's position is to be found in the *Breviloquium*, written in 1341 and 1342, and it will be briefly resumed here. Its most immediately obvious feature—and one representative of Ockham's entire political thinking—is its theological nature. Ockham treats the Bible as both revealed truth and sacred history which contains the evidence for the origin and development of human society. From its testimony it can be seen that God not only permitted but granted legitimate temporal jurisdiction to infidels before Christ and independently of him, whether to the kings of Sodom and Egygt in the Old Testament,[55] or to the Roman emperors in New Testament times. Christ himself as well as John the Baptist and St Paul, who also called himself a Roman citizen, all enjoined obedience to the emperor's jurisdiction; its legitimacy is further confirmed by the tribute rendered to Rome by other kingdoms.[56] The early fathers said the same; even an apostate like the emperor Julian or persecutors of Christians like Nero and Domitian were acknowledged by Augustine and Ambrose to have been true emperors.[57] Nor at that time were there laws proscribing or disqualifying heretics, so that Julian's imperial power was unimpaired by his apostasy:[58] an indication of the increasing sophistication with which the Bible was being interpreted historically by Ockham and contemporaries like Marsilius of Padua. It is also apparent in the conclusion Ockham draws. Since, he declares, true dominion and jurisdiction did exist among infidels and before there were Christians, to deny these rights to infidels would also mean denying them to Christians. For if infidels did not have them, their Christian descendants would have not legal right to inherit them; that would also disqualify every believer from such rights before baptism. The only consequence therefore of confusing the deletion of sin and the infusion of grace, through baptism, with the conferment of hereditary secular rights would be enormous injury to Christians and the infringement of their liberty.[59] It is a characteristic thrust, and one which derives its force from separating secular history from the economy of grace.

The same can be said of the second aspect of Ockham's discussion: the origin of temporal jurisdiction. Here the central distinction is between the power of appropriating possessions, and exercising temporal jurisdiction, and actual possession

---

[55] *Ibid.*, bk. III, ch. 2, 110–13.   [56] *Ibid.*, ch. 3, 113–18.
[57] *Ibid.*, ch. 4, 119.   [58] *Ibid.*, 119, l. 30–120, l. 33.
[59] *Ibid.*, ch. 5, 122–4.

and jurisdiction. The first is from God; the second is usually from man, though it can be from God, who does not relinquish the power he has granted men.[60] This qualification is again characteristic: God can always act directly and retains the same power which he freely confers on creatures. Hence, as throughout Ockham's system, the same effect can have more than one cause: the refusal to eschew exceptions helps to make Ockham's political notions at times so elusive. In this case however, God only exercised the power to confer property and jurisdiction after men had already exercised the same power given to them by him. He was not therefore the first to institute temporal possessions or rule; and Ockham insisted that nowhere does the Bible say that he was.[61] Consequently the power itself to appropriate property and to rule others was from divine law, but private possession and secular jurisdiction were sometimes—and then always first—from men and sometimes from God.[62]

Now the significance of this division is that the power of possession and jurisdiction is a natural power given by God to all men to be exercised according to right reason. It thus approximates to the *ius poli* of the *Opus Nonaginta Dierum*. It had been designed by God to overcome the greed, covetousness and neglect of the common good by all mankind, which Adam and Eve's sin had brought upon their descendants, although not all behaved in that way.[63] This power enabled men to dispose of what they held for themselves and their posterity as 'right reason commanded was necessary, expedient, decent, and useful, not only in order to live but to live rightly, both in a solitary state and politically in a perfect community'.[64]

The power then to have possessions and to appoint rulers was immediately from God without human mediation; it therefore had the force of a precept, which like every precept such as that of honouring one's parents was binding upon all, infidels equally with the faithful.[65] As an affirmative precept it is always obligatory but its fulfilment is not, where the need for temporalities and rulers does not arise. In such cases the power over both can be renounced—as the Franciscans renounced their rights to both—just as those guilty of a crime can be deprived of such power. That too applies equally to infidels; they have the same powers which they can renounce or lose in similar circumstances. Nothing in the Bible says otherwise.[66]

All property and authority thus originate in the natural power universally conferred by God on all Adam's posterity. Ockham is adamant that infidels have the same natural capacities as believers, because they all enjoy them from God,

[60] *Ibid.*, ch. 10, 130–1.
[61] *Ibid.*; ch. 9, 129–30; ch. 10, 131–2.
[62] *Ibid.*, ch. 10, 130; ch. 11, 131–2.
[63] *Ibid.*, ch. 7, 126–8.
[64] *Ibid.*, 127, l. 11–14.
[65] Duplex potestes predicta, scilicet appropriandi res temporales et instituendi rectores iurisdictionem habentes, data est a deo immediate non tantum fidelibus sed etiam infidelibus sic quod cadit sub precepto et inter pure moralia computatur, propter quod omnes obligat tam fideles quam infideles (*ibid.*, ch. 8, 128, l. 13–17).
[66] *Ibid.*, l. 21–37.

without whose mercy they would all in an instant descend into the inferno. Just as, through God, they can in their infidelity sustain life and are capable of fortitude and beauty and the other gifts and powers of body and mind, so in their infidelity they are capable of temporal possessions and jurisdiction and other secular rights and honours; if God can give them the blessings of wives and children and countless other joys, it is unthinkable that he should withhold from them all power of lordship and authority. Indeed they already have it naturally over their wives and children and possessions, of none of which can they be deprived except for sin or some other cause.[67]

The capacity to have property and authority is therefore a natural endowment of all post-lapsarian mankind. Irrespective of sacramental qualification, God has given men the requisites of naturally attaining the common good; whether they do so depends upon them. Once again as in all morally good or bad actions the issue is between the power to conform to right reason and the nature of the actions which result from the will's choice. The will is the agent in translating God's decrees into good or bad acts, as it is the agent of morally indifferent acts; but the obligation to act is from God. Hence the distinction between the power, given as a divine precept, to institute property and rulers, and their actual institution legitimised in human positive law which may not accord with right reason. Ockham has transposed the same self-sufficiency of the moral virtues to man's social and political capacities. In themselves they are not virtues in the Christian sense of leading to eternal life or making those possessing them truly just; that is reserved for those sanctified by habitual grace. But by their natural powers men can still act virtuously and legitimately, as infidels do when they marry and have dominion; not only do they not necessarily sin but even when they abuse their authority it remains—as we have already mentioned—legitimate because it is commanded by God.[68]

The right to temporal authority then is natural as opposed to sacramental; there is a corresponding separation between its natural and its supernatural justification with that between a natural and a supernatural virtue. One does not entail the other, as Ockham stresses, recurring in work after work, to St Augustine's remark that by divine law only the just can rightly possess the things of this world.[69] If the just here meant all the faithful to the exclusion of infidels, as many took it to mean, that, said Ockham, would equally exclude all those Christians who were in mortal sin; for many have true faith and are yet unjust. In that case any Christian, including rulers and kings, who fell into sin would immediately lose any right to their temporalities, a conclusion which Ockham regards as absurd. Worthiness is to be interpreted not as belonging to faith or to actual dominion, since a sinner, Christian or otherwise, would then possess justly what he had. It means being worthy of possessing or using, and as such applies only to those justified by God. That does not however prevent him from rewarding those who

[67] *Ibid.*, ch. 6, 124–5; also *An Princeps*, 237.
[68] *Ibid.*, ch. 12, 133, l. 32–134, l. 26.
[69] *Epiistula*, 93, ch. 12.

are unworthy of it with a temporal gift in this world on account of some good work.[70]

Ockham thus naturalised the right to temporal possessions and jurisdiction[71] by detaching it from any supernatural gift or sacramental qualification. A legitimate ruler need be neither sanctified by God's grace nor bound by his law; nothing beyond God's natural gift to all men of the capacity to have possessions and rulers was involved. In opposition to extreme papalists like Giles of Rome he put a very different gloss upon St Augustine's words. While lordship, it is true, was made necessary by the incapacities of fallen men to live without it, the power to institute it was given by God to all men precisely in virtue of their common condition. It was not reserved to the church but anteceded it and continued independently of it. The benefits reserved for Christians were of a different, non-temporal, order.

For Ockham the dependence of temporal authority upon God made him the sole cause of it even while not directly instituting it. Ockham sought to explain how by distinguishing the three different modes in which God can be an immediate cause of jurisdiction.[72] By the first mode it is immediately from him without any mediation, whether of decree or election or human ministry in the way that Moses directly received his jurisdiction from God, or Peter his from Christ; by the second it is by means of an intermediary, as when grace is given in baptism or the host consecrated by a priest, or a spiritual office—including the papacy—conferred through appointment or election, although the power is solely from God; by the third mode, however, he only gives what has already been granted or gained by others, so that once given its retention depends solely upon God. It is in that way that all temporal authority is ordinarily (*regulariter*) held from God as sole cause, and applies *inter alia* to that of the emperor. Only exceptionally (*casualiter*) can he or any other temporal ruler be corrected by men.[73] The distinction between jurisdiction exercised *regulariter* and *casualiter* is thus precisely that between jurisdiction conserved by God, having been instituted by men, and jurisdiction which reverts to men when a ruler violates that jurisdiction, by infringing positive or natural—or in the case of the church—evangelical law; by implication God ceases to conserve what he has hitherto directly upheld.

Ockham's justification for adopting this third mode is on the same theological grounds which led him to distinguish the power to have temporalities and rulers from the actual possessions and jurisdiction to which they led: namely that, save in exceptional circumstances as in the example of Moses, there is no evidence that God instituted rulers or temporalities by either of the first two modes, since they can be known only through revelation, and for that there is nothing in the Bible.[74] Even when God directly endowed rulers he did so only as we have seen after men had, through Cain, already instituted temporal rule; even so, there is nothing to say that those kingdoms granted by him originated differently from the Empire

---

[70] *Breviloquium*, ch. 12, 132, l. 16–133, l. 28.
[71] As Lagarde, *La Naissance*, IV, 202, has said.
[72] *Breviloquium*, bk. IV, ch. 5, 149–50,
[73] *Ibid.*, 150, l. 14–26; ch. 6, 151.
[74] *Ibid.*, ch. 7, 151–3.

and other kingdoms.[75] The words of Christ confirm that. When Christ said
'Render unto Caesar' he was not conferring a new jurisdiction; he was simply
commanding that the emperor be given his due, thereby approving the power he
already had.[76] Accordingly if God himself only exceptionally instituted rulers,[77]
he directly upholds all of them. That for Ockham means that he not only permits
them but directly confers their authority upon them.

It is not a particularly convincing attempt to reconcile the human origin of
secular jurisdiction with its divine sanction; for it does not explain how something
not directly caused by God is caused by him other than as conserver—the role in
which throughout Ockham's speculative writings God permitted rather than
actively willed. Ockham does not use the term 'conserver' here, because he was
concerned to show that God did more than permit temporal rulers. But the
grounds for the distinction remain unexplained. Even if we concede, as we can,
that there is a difference between a ruler holding his authority directly from God
and merely being permitted by him to hold it—as he permits but does not
himself will, sin—it does not answer the question of how and whether a wrongful
ruler's jurisdiction is to be distinguished from that of a legitimate ruler—or whether
God differentiates between them—until the moment when the people or their
representatives no longer accept his authority.

Ockham affirms that all sovereignty is from the people, who have the power to
make laws and institute rulers;[78] also that this power is a natural right granted by
God which they can freely exercise and which should, like the other rights of
individuals, not be overridden.[79] But he accepts equally, first that the authority
thus instituted is coercive authority, and as, naturally, husbands have the power of
compelling their wives and children, so politically judges and rulers have the same
power over those who have submitted to them;[80] second, that this jurisdiction is
normally from human law through the power transferred to a ruler by the people
and only exceptionally from God;[81] third, that once conferred voluntarily it cannot,
as we have said before, be withdrawn from a ruler against his will unless guilty
of a crime.[82] As long therefore as jurisdiction remains useful and advantageous
to the common good it cannot be dissolved by those from whom it came originally.

The effect of these provisions is, as we have said before, tantamount to acceptance
of the *status quo*, so long as it conforms to the laws and customs which prevail; and
Ockham frequently stresses the validity of good customs.[83] Consequently his

[75] *Ibid.*, 152, 1. 32–153, l. 14; also bk. III, chs. 10 and 11, 130–2.

[76] *Ibid.*, bk. IV, ch. 7, 152, l. 9–19.

[77] *Ibid.*, bk. III, ch. 11, 132, l. 1–5.

[78] Ad cuius evidentiam est primo sciendiem quod potestas condendi leges et iura humana
primo et principiliter fuit apud populum (*ibid.*, bk. III, ch. 14, 136, l. 19–21).

[79] *Ibid.*, bk. IV, ch. 10, 161, l. 21–23.

[80] *Ibid.*, bk. III, ch. 11, l. 13–20.

[81] *Ibid.*, ch. 14, 136, 1. 20–137, l. 4.

[82] Nam postquam aliqui se subdiderint alicuius sponte dominio ab eius dominio ipso invito
non possunt recedere, quia dominus sine culpa sua non debet privari iure suo (*ibid.*, bk. IV, ch. 13,
165, 1. 29–166, l. 1).

[83] E.g. *ibid.*, bk. III, ch. 14, 136, 1. 30–137, l. 4.

account makes no prescription for the form authority should take or how it should be regulated—other than in an emergency through the withdrawal of power when it does not conform to law or custom; and since positive law may not conform to moral law, the appeal to natural equity against a ruler is circumscribed, if indeed not effectively nullified. The common good, then, which is a temporal ruler's *raison d'être*, does not of its nature include the defence of evangelical liberty—and the oppressions of secular authority are not those which Ockham combats,[84] because it is instituted and regulated by men who are not bound to honour God or the moral law even if they cannot abrogate it.

It is here that the lacuna in Ockham's doctrine of political authority appears—at the very point where we pass from the power God has granted men to their diverse applications of it. It is also the point at which we pass from prescription to contingency. Human authority does not for Ockham conform to an ideal, because it is the work of human will able not to conform. Hence unlike a natural *species specialissima*, whose attributes, it will be recalled, can be inferred from knowledge of one member, the possible forms of human authority can only be enumerated. Ockham regularises their diversity rather than prescribes a non-existent norm: for society no less than for being, reality consists in what actually exists, not in any essences. The only constant is the power to institute; its outcome is diverse.

That is exemplified in his account of the origins of the Roman Empire in the *Breviloquium*. Its legitimacy is proved, as we have already said, from the recognition it received from Christ, John the Baptist and St Paul, among others, so that even though Pilate wrongfully condemned Christ to death he acted nevertheless from a licit authority.[85] Other than that however it cannot be said either when and how the Empire became legitimate or whether it began tyrannically from a usurped authority. If Christ and the apostles did not say, how, asks Ockham, should he presume to do so?[86] This disavowal expresses men's dependence upon authority for what cannot be inferred or known from experience or self-evidently. Here the only certainties are the general theological truth that God has endowed every free man naturally with the power of choosing his own rulers,[87] and the particular truth, equally theological, of the Empire's legitimacy. But its actual origin is not given, and need not have been simultaneous throughout all the regions of the Empire so that some could have been ruled by the Romans illicitly by a usurped authority until the people concerned submitted; it could also have been by just war; or it could have been by divine revelation.[88] These Ockham regards as the principal modes of constituting true kingdoms,[89] although their legitimacy can be transmitted in various other ways, including the donation by which the Roman Empire passed from the Greeks to the Franks under Charlemagne in 800. In the case of the original Empire, however, while all three modes could occur together, Ockham

---

[84] As Lagarde observes, *La Naissance*, IV, 88.
[85] *Breviloquium*, bk. IV, ch. 10, 160; also *Octo Quaestiones*, qq. V and VI.
[86] *Breviloquium*, ibid., 161, l. 6–15.
[87] *Ibid.*, l. 21–4.   [88] *Ibid.*, 161–2.   [89] *Ibid.*, 162, l. 16.

excludes the third since he finds no mention of a special revelation in the Bible such as that given to Moses over the Israelites.[90] Subsequently the same imperial authority was received by Charlemagne in the *translatio* and then by his successors, the German emperors,[91] to establish whose legitimacy was the object of Ockham's argumentation.

That is as far as we need to take it in identifying his theory of political authority. Its focus was the justification of temporal rulers in the need to chastise wrongdoers rather than with its operations. It suffices that it arose from a pact with the faithful for the common good and extended to all, including the pope, who was not exempt from the emperor's power.[92] There was little or nothing in Ockham of the political theorist of societies and institutions that there was in Marsilius of Padua. Ockham was concerned with their legitimacy and autonomy; his arguments were essentially theological, founded upon man's natural need for rulers and his power to institute them. How they do so, and with what results, are secondary, of interest only to illustrate the voluntaristic and hence contingent nature of human jurisdiction. Ockham did not attempt to do more than illustrate it. The forms of political authority were subordinate to the independent right to exercise it, and its exercise was regulated only by the negative limits of not violating right reason or the good customs and laws formed in accordance with it. It is an untidy doctrine which in political terms is almost totally wanting. But those are not Ockham's terms. They belong to his defence of Empire against the claims of the *plenitudo potestatis*. What he says about temporal authority can only be measured in relation to his concept of spiritual power exercised by the church, to which we must briefly turn in conclusion.

To do so is to adopt another standard. The legitimacy of temporal rulers is as the upholders of human law which does not conflict with but can remain in-different to divine law. The church is the upholder of divine law expressed in God's precepts; everything else which does not directly come under them is indifferent and lies outside ecclesiastical authority. It is therefore bound by the very pre-scriptions from which secular rulers are free, and enjoys none of their latitude. With the church there is not the no-man's-land between divine and positive law which enables a temporal ruler *de facto*, if not *de jure*, to act without direct reference to God and independently of the people. Spiritual authority is immediately answer-able to both because it is only a true authority if its exercise conforms with Bible and receives assent from all the faithful.

Here we come to the central difference between Ockham's ecclesiology and his doctrine of temporal authority. Where the latter's universality, which comes from the assent of the people is nominal, effectively qualified out of existence save in emergencies, the only true spiritual authority is that which accords with the faith of the universal church. All the constraints which temporal jurisdiction can effectively avoid through the contingencies of its human institution bind the

---

[90] *Ibid.*, I, 17–29.
[91] E.g. *Octo Quaestiones*, II, 90; IV, 124, 140–3, 197.
[92] *Ibid.*, III, 110–13; *Dialogus*, III, II, bk. II, chs. 11, 12 and 28.

pope to fulfil what is of divine institution. Whether he does so is measured by two main criteria: faithfulness to Christ and accord with the universal church. Ockham's discussion of spiritual authority was principally designed to exhibit the incompatibility of both with the doctrine of the *plenitudo potestatis*. It was accordingly framed in directly opposite terms to his discussion of temporal authority: instead of seeking to reconcile it with God's dispensation, he sought to expose papal deviations from an inviolable norm. In doing so, above all in considering the church's temporal form and institutions, Ockham introduced certain far-reaching conceptions which followed directly from his philosophical and theological principles.

Taking the relation to Christ first, Ockham sought to cut the pope down to human size by comparing him with Christ both temporally and spiritually. We are already familiar with the first aspect. Christ as a passable and mortal man had had neither temporal possessions nor jurisdiction; if therefore Christ had renounced all such powers how then could the pope as his vicar claim them? Christ's law was the law of liberty; far from having had temporal dominion over all men he had held it over nothing. To claim such power in Christ's name was therefore heretical.[93]

These were the pure Franciscan terms in which Ockham had first denounced John XXII over evangelical poverty, and continued to denounce him together with Benedict XII over the *plenitudo potestatis*. He came to complement them with the second comparison between their spiritual qualities. It was in many ways more damaging because it was subversive of the very nature of papal or indeed any ecclesiastical authority exercised by mortal men. There were two aspects. The first and most directly derogatory was that the pope unlike Christ was only a man, *purus viator*; he was therefore as liable to sin and to err and to fall into heresy as any other fallible man; the only difference was that in view of his office his lapse was worse and 'he sins more gravely, perniciously, and dangerously than any other Christian'.[94] For Ockham that possibility was a reality in the case of both popes John XXII and Benedict XII, the first for his heresies over evangelical poverty and the beatific vision, the second for not anathematising his predecessor. In his ceaseless attacks upon each, as well as his extended discussion of a pope's heresy in the *Dialogus* and subsequently,[95] Ockham helped to give a new currency and an immediate application to the accepted canonist doctrine that a pope could fall into heresy and so ceased to be pope by excluding himself from the church. Moreover his office does not sanctify him any more than any ecclesiastical office sanctifies its holder. That is the other aspect. While Ockham unlike Marsilius of Padua, and later Wyclif, did not deny the canonical nature of the papacy, he did deny that it

[93] *An Princeps*, 233, 238, 243; *Octo Quaestiones*, I, 31; *Dialogus*, I, bk. VI, ch. 3; III, I, bk. I, chs. 5, 79; *Breviloquium*, bk. II, ch. 9, 69–70.

[94] *Contra Ioannem* 81–2; also 71–2, 108; *Octo Quaestiones*, II, 61; *Dialogus*, I, bk. V, chs. 3 and 5.

[95] *Dialogus* I, bks. V and VI especially chs 66, 72, 75, 78, where he also discusses how the faithful or sections of the church, like the cardinals or bishops, could err. Also *Contra Benedictum*, 321; *Octo Quaestiones*, I, 17; VIII, 210–18.

prevented the pope from falling into sin; the pope still remains a peccable man as the enormous papal wrongs have shown.[96]

That can be regarded as the complement to Ockham's denial of the need for grace as the requisite of temporal jurisdiction, and of making either authority the preserve of the just. To begin with, office neither necessarily confers grace nor confirms or increases it; and any *viator* not confirmed in grace can deny the truth of whatever is not known self-evidently, or by experience or demonstration, as many of the truths of faith are not known. In the second place someone can only be said not to be able to err if his inerrability can be proved from the Bible or the faith of the church or inferred from it; by none of these modes can that be said of a pope.[97] Consequently the pope, whether as an individual or in virtue of his office, has no claim to greater sanctity than any other believer—and many may have more than he[98]—or to immunity from sin and error.

In neither respect, as man or bishop of Rome, is the pope comparable with Christ. As a man Christ was free from error or sin; the pope is not. Christ could institute new sacraments and dispense with previous ones; the pope cannot. Even if Christ had as a man had a plenitude of temporal power—which he expressly renounced—it would still have not been expedient, either for the pope or for the faithful, to have given the same powers to his vicar, lacking his wisdom and goodness, lest exalted by pride or suffering other human weakness or evil he should corrupt Christ's power to the detriment of the faithful.[99] Accordingly Christ did not give the same power which he possessed to his vicar; they remain unequal; and what Christ can do in performing miracles, or even in expelling the money-lenders from the temple, belongs either to his divine as opposed to his human power or to his spiritual office.[100] So far as the latter is concerned Ockham takes the words of his commission to Peter as incontrovertible proof that it was exclusively for spiritual ministration. When Christ committed his flock to Peter it was not for Peter's own private honour or comfort, or to rule them, that he did so, but for the benefit of the faithful; nor did he tell him to do whatever pleased Peter but what was for the service and need of the common good. Had Peter done otherwise Christ would not have given such a commission to him or his successors. Papal primacy was instituted no less for the benefit of the faithful than just and proper temporal authority is for the benefit of its subjects.[101]

The power of binding and loosing therefore conferred on Peter and his successors, although a general one, is not unqualified; if it were, Peter would have been promised a power equal to that of Christ's divinity, which is absurd and heretical. Not only does it not enable him to do what Christ and God can do; the legitimate rights of rulers and of subjects, faithful and infidel alike, which do not conflict

---

[96] *Dialogus, ibid.,* bk. v, chs. 3 and 5.
[97] *Ibid.,* ch. 3.
[98] *Ibid.*
[99] *Breviloquium,* bk. II, ch. 22, 103–4, bk. v, ch. 8, 183–6; *Dialogus* I, bk. v, ch. 19.
[100] *Breviloquium,* bk. v, ch. 8.
[101] *Ibid.,* bk. II, ch. 5, 59–60, l. 13; *OND,* ch. 93; *Octo Quaestiones,* I, 37 ff, 57; *An Princeps,* 243–50; *De Imp.,* ch. 6.

with good customs or honouring God or his law, are exempt from its ordinary application. They have their own validity, originating as we have seen, before God's law was explicitly given, and binding upon both believers and infidels. There can be no question then of the pope as Peter's successor interfering in their affairs; he is both forbidden to do so under apostolic precept, and the faithful are held by the necessity of salvation to submit to the powers and principalities even if they are of infidels.[102] Peter and his successors for their part are bound by the evangelical law, which is that of liberty; hence they cannot, as we have also mentioned before, impose any new burdensome decrees upon men except from crimes or urgent necessity or manifest utility. That was true of the ceremonies and sacraments of the old law: how much more is it true of the new law? If a pope were able to go beyond its obligations stated in the New Testament he could compel the faithful on the grounds of the greatest utility to perform acts which concerned perfection and were supererogatory such as fasting and abstinence; he could then by the same token make someone enter a religious order, none of which he can ordinarily do.[103]

The power of binding and loosing conferred by Christ on Peter confined him to following Christ's spiritual mission; apart from excluding infidels it expressly excluded the emperor who at that time was an infidel. The only dominion that Peter had over infidels was of baptism for those received into the church in order to make them in some way worthy of entry; over the faithful it consisted in instructing them in good works and the Catholic faith. That was the sense in which Ockham interpreted pope Nicholas I's statement that Christ in founding the church upon the rock of faith and committing to Peter the key of eternal life also committed to him jurisdiction of both the heavenly and the earthly empire. That right was not one of possession and lordship but the right and power of teaching and preaching the Christian faith in the land of the emperor, whether an infidel or believer.[104]

It was in similar terms that Ockham in the *Dialogus* explained the relation of Christ to Peter as head of the church. Christ was its principal founder; without him there could have been no church. He alone was without sin or error, unlike Peter when he denied Christ three times.[105] Peter however was also the rock upon which Christ built his church; as such he could also be called its foundation. But a secondary foundation. The apostles were also. Just as a real building often has many foundation stones, of these secondary foundations Peter could be called the principal. Although none of them was necessary to the church as Christ was, it had nevertheless *de facto* come into existence through Christ's promise to Peter; he was thus principal apostle, whom Christ, in addition to the power of binding and loosing given to all the apostles, had put first in dignity.[106]

In the context of the time, with Marsilius of Padua's outright denial of the

---

[102] *Breviloquium*, bk. II, chs. 14–16, 81–90.

[103] *Ibid.*, ch. 17, 90–93; also ch. 18, 93–5.

[104] *Ibid.*, bk. VI, ch. 1, 194–7; also *Dialogus*, I, bk. V, ch. 16; III, I, bk. IV, ch. 18, III, II, bk. III, ch. 7, *OND*, ch. 93, 686, l. 668–88, l. 723; *Octo Quaestiones*, II, 75–80; *An Princeps*, 243–4, 248.

[105] *Dialogus*, III, I, bk. IV, chs. 18 and 19.

[106] *Ibid.*, ch. 19.

Petrine basis of the church, nothing is more striking than Ockham's insistence upon it. Marsilius had identified Christ with the rock of the church as its only head and founder, citing in support St Augustine's change from Peter to Christ in the *Retractationes*.[107] Ockham, however, took the same change by St Augustine to illustrate that there was more than one foundation, with Christ the principal head and Peter the secondary head.[108] Nor did he make any play on the absence of the pope's name from the Bible. That for him could be explained by the very freedom of action which Christ bequeathed to Peter's successors.[109] Christ did not lay down a set mode for the election of his future vicars any more than God had decreed a set order of political authority. As we shall see again presently it is the very absence of a fixed *ordo* necessary *ex natura rei* that makes Ockham's attitude to the pope and Roman church so damaging to their authority. But, unlike Marsilius, it is not through denying the validity of the pope's office or the authority of its holders; Ockham unconditionally accepts the first as the outcome of Christ's commission to Peter and the second if it conforms to the first. Peter's primacy and the need to have a single head of the church are for Ockham proved by both faith and good custom. All the authorities testify to that; nor is it conceivable that Christ would have left his church achephalous or chosen any but the best form of headship, which is monarchy.[110] But that meant neither that the pope was a monarch in the manner of an Old Testament king,[111] nor that there could never be more than one head of the church.[112] The pope's own position was that of a minister or steward (*dispensator*) who was guardian of the faithful; his was not a despotic power any more than that of temporal kings should be; and his authority did not extend beyond God's precepts to what was supererogatory, because to have the power of making laws in all things which were not against natural and divine law would mean oppressing many of the faithful who were too infirm to follow the way of perfection.[113]

As to the possibility of more than one head of the church, that brings us to the other aspect of Ockham's concept of spiritual power; the antinomy between a divine office, and an ecclesiastical order, exercised by mortal fallible men ever liable to sin and err, and an institution which was infallible and indefectible. The contrast was the focus of Ockham's ecclesiology. It was founded upon his definition of the universal church as the communion of all believers from the time of the apostles to the present bound inerrably in the same faith.[114] It therefore included

[107] *Defensor Pacis*, II, ch. 28; *Retractationes*, I, 21, 1.

[108] *Dialogus*, III, I, ch. 19.

[109] *Ibid.*, III, II, chs. 6 and 7; also bk. I, ch. 5 and tract I, bk. IV, ch. 4.

[110] *Ibid.*, I, bk. IV, chs. 22, 23, 24.

[111] *Breviloquium*, bk. v, ch. 7, 180–3; *Octo Quaestiones*, I, 50–51.

[112] *Dialogus*, I, bk. v, chs. 15 and 30. Ockham was unusual among his contemporaries in not making monarchy the ideal form of government, though he regards it as the best, giving his reasons in its favour in the *Octo Quaestiones*, III, 104–10.

[113] *Breviloquium*, bk. II, chs. 5 and 6, 59–65; *An Princeps*, 251; *Dialogus*, I, bk. v, ch. 15; *OND*, ch. 93.

[114] Sed auctoritas ecclesiae universalis, quae etiam fideles non solum in hac vita simul degentes, sed sibimet succedentes praelatos et populos catholicos comprehendit, valet ad fidem et certitudinem fidei catholicae veritatis (*Contra Ioannem* 65, l. 33–36). And: Haec enim ecclesia

not only the dead as well as the living but excluded those believers among the living who had erred against Christian truth as John XXII had done. The universal church was therefore at once beyond the individual churches—of Rome, Constantinople, Antioch, Lyon, Pisa and the others—which formed it in space, and it could be less, either through the defection of an entire congregation or through the error of individuals.[115] It existed only fully in time through the confirmation of its all members in faith. That was the import of Ockham's definition. As he expressed it in the *Dialogus* in the language of his earlier life, 'Although Christian faith and the faith of the universal church are the same when the church does not err, yet . . . "universal church" consignifies or signifies directly (*in recto*) those Christians whom "Christian faith" does not'.[116] Hence they are not synonymous because Christian believers can err. When they do so they are not part of the universal church.

As interpreted by Ockham this distinction had two overriding consequences. The first was his rejection of any substitute for the one requisite of universality which gave the universal church its sanctity and inviolability. The second was that faith was the sole test of conformity with the universal church and so of legitimate ecclesiastical authority; faith was the regulator both of the claim to be acting on behalf of the universal church and of the measures needed to correct its abuses. The first consequence introduced a division between the visible church and the universal church, whether its hierarchy or among the faithful, which was to become one of the features of later medieval ecclesiology among men such as Dietrich of Niem, Wyclif, and Hus, though each gave it a very different meaning from that which it had for Ockham; the second consequence effectively destroyed the exclusive sacramental prerogatives over faith of the hierarchy, as an *ordo*, for the universal prerogative of baptism which enabled any believer—ecclesiastical or lay—to intervene in matters of faith.

In neither case was Ockham invoking a spiritual or invisible church, in the manner of Dietrich of Niem or Wyclif, to discount the visible church. The whole force of his attitude was that the church in its present existential form *de inesse* is not necessarily the same as the universal church because, even if does not, it could err. It therefore shares the same radical contingency of all temporal existence.[117] In this case by man's freedom to sin and his liability to do so if God does not conserve him in faith. But because Christ has promised that his faith will endure to the end it can be maintained by other means than those constituted *regulariter* to uphold it. That is

---

quae Apostolos, Evangelistas, omnes Romanos pontifices ceterosque episcopos ac prelatos, martyresque et doctores, omnesque catholicos populos usque ad hec tempora comprehendit, maioris auctoritatis esse videtur quam quodcumque concilium generale vel ecclesia, quae nunc in hac peregrinatione consistit (*ibid.*, ch. 66, l. 10–14). Also *Dialogus*, I, bk. I, ch. 4; bk. v, ch. 8; Pt. III, I, bk. IV, ch. 8, ch. 22, *Contra Benedictum*, 261, l. 23–33.

[115] *Dialogus* I, bk. v, ch. 24.
[116] *Ibid.*, I, bk. IV, ch. 9.
[117] E.g. Ad quartum rationem dicitur quod hec est falsa. illa ecclesia errare non potest contra fidem a qua quicumque dissentit . . . Sed illa de inesse est vera: illa ecclesia non errat contra fidem a qua quicumque dissentit ab ea (*ibid.*, bk. v, ch. 24).

the kernel of Ockham's ecclesiology. In an illuminating passage in the *Dialogus* he declares that Christ's mystical body cannot be compared with the human material body, because the human body cannot survive without a head, but Christ's mystical body can be without a head on earth, since it continues to exist in heaven. It could also remain in being without many individual churches, including the Roman church.[118] All the main features of Ockham's ecclesiology flow from this standpoint.

To begin with, in relation to the government of the church, nothing less than the universal church—whether a pope, an independent church such as that of Rome or Paris, a college such as that of the cardinals, or indeed all the faithful— has the attributes of inerrability and indefectability which belong to the universal church alone; for everything else is related to it as part to whole. Nothing is therefore its equal or can perfectly represent it, since it is its universality which the universal church alone by definition possesses and which saves it from the failings to which all other congregations are prone.[119] Not only can a pope fall into error and heresy but so can any part of the church: the whole college of cardinals, the hierarchy, bishops and inquisitors,[120] and indeed every believer, save one solitary individual,[121] or only those like baptised infants and fools not having the use of reason,[122] left to preserve Christ's faith to the end. For the same reason a general council has no claim to universality and infallibility; it is both less than the universal church and of human contrivance, summoned and dissolved by human decree. Although it could correct a pope and elect another in case of utility or necessity, it too could fall into heresy wholly or in part as many past councils have done; and what it can do to restore the situation can also be done by other means, lay and ecclesiastical,[123] as we shall mention shortly.

No body or person can thus claim the attributes of the universal church on earth, for nothing else can properly represent it. In both the *Opus Nonaginta Dierum*[124] and later the *Tractatus Contra Benedictum*[125] Ockham completely rejected John XXII's claim that the church was a fictitious person, for the very reason that Christ's mystical body consists of real persons. It is their totality as individuals which alone makes the universal church universal. Nothing exists beyond them. Ockham's epistemology of individual existence was accordingly the rock upon

---

[118] Ad septimum dicitur quod licet quantum ad multa sit similitudo inter corpus misticum quod est ecclesia et corpus materiale hominis, non tamen est quantum ad omnia simul. Corpus ergo hominis nec ad tempus manet vivum sine capite. Corpus autem Christi misticum sine capite ad tempus vivum manere potest. Sepe caret capite in terris quamvis tunc habeat caput in celis, scilicet Christum . . . Corpus ergo Christi misticum potest esse sine multis membris. Quelibet enim ecclesia particularis est membrum ecclesie . . . et tamen sine illis posset esse corpus Christi misticum . . . Et ideo quamvis romana ecclesia post papam fuit membrum principale ecclesie, sine ista tamen posset ecclesia esse (*ibid.*).

[119] E.g. *ibid.*, bk. V, passim.
[120] *Ibid.*, chs. 1, 2, 6, 7, 8, 9, 22, 23.
[121] *Contra Ioannem* 68; *Epistola ad Fratres Minores*, 15, l. 23–7.
[122] *Dialogus*, I, bk. V, ch. 25.
[123] *Ibid.*, chs. 25, 26; also bk. VI, ch. 70, III, I, bk. III. ch. 11.
[124] Ch. 6, 371–2; ch. 62, 564, l. 206–24.
[125] Ch. 8, 189–91.

which the claims of Peter's successors, whether of the pope himself or the hierarchy or a general council, all foundered. It has its converse in the role of laymen; in virtue of being believers and so individual members of the same church, they could intervene in its affairs on the same grounds of contingency, namely, when, because of necessity or utility, what normally held *regulariter* could be set aside *casualiter*. Just as there need be no pope or there could be several, if the interests of the church in conformity with Christ's precepts dictated it,[126] so the emperor could be involved in the election of a pope; he held that right both as a Christian and as one of the Romans in whom the power of electing a pope had been ultimately vested through Christ, who had not wished to prejudice it by ordaining a specific mode of electing St Peter's successor.[127] That opened a maze of alternatives. The emperor could receive the right of election from the Romans alone, or from the pope, if the Romans transferred their power to the pope, or if the Romans acted to the detriment of the church. On the other hand the power could revert to the Romans if the pope and the electors were killed or heretics, and if the emperor tried to impede an election, they could act without him.[128] The permutations are almost endless. What they show is the absence of a fixed order as part of Christ's own dispensation in not having decreed the precise mode for the fulfilment of his decrees. They also show the absence of any firm and irrevocable divisions between spiritual and temporal office. The office of neither pope nor emperor is necessary *ex natura rei*; both could be in the hands of the same person;[129] and *casualiter* each can intervene in the affairs of the other.[130] The difference is that where the pope is bound by Christ's evangelical law of liberty by which he can only act to enforce God's precepts, the emperor and all laymen are themselves part of the body of the church; they therefore have a defined place within it, not only to defend it but of sharing the common right of all believers to act for the common good;[131] which they can do in accordance with the three modes of natural law mentioned earlier.[132] Hence the very universality of the church makes it open to lay participation and in case of necessity or utility subject to lay coercion or direction, as in the case of electing or summoning a general council.

All ecclesiastical authority, then, unlike temporal jurisdiction depends upon confirmation in faith; no human device such as a general council can claim the infallibility which comes alone from God's power to preserve a believer in his truth. Hence it does not reside in an office given by him.[133]

That brings us to the final aspect of Ockham's ecclesiology; the definition of faith. If universality is the source of the church's infallibility, unanimity is the only measure among *viatores* of Christian truth, when it is not expressly contained in

[126] *Dialogus*, III, I, bk. II, chs. 22, 23, 24, 28; bk. IV, ch. 24.
[127] *Ibid.*, II, bk. III, ch. 7.
[128] *Ibid.*, chs. 4, 7–12; also I, bk. VI, chs. 8–14, 26, 85, 94, 97, 99, 100.
[129] *Octo Quaestiones*, I, 26–7.
[130] *Ibid.*, II, 90, IV, 142; *Dialogus*, note 126.
[131] *Dialogus*, III, II, bk. III, ch. 4.
[132] *Ibid.*, ch. 6.
[133] *Ibid.*, I, bk. V. ch. 25.

the Bible or in the canonical doctrine of the universal church, derived from its conformity with the Bible, or the writings of the evangelists and saints and the acts of martyrs. That is the conclusion to which Ockham came in the course of his running struggle with John XXII over poverty and the beatific vision, and enunciated first sketchily in the *Dialogus*[134] and then more systematically in the *Tractatus Contra Johannem*.[135] In effect it invoked a judgement of reason upon conclusions drawn from the Bible and the doctrines of the church; their unanimity was a sign of the universality which any true inference must share. The difference was that the premises were from faith and so could not provide evident knowledge; hence the stress upon the absence of dissent, which Ockham interpreted as a miracle and so equivalent to a divine revelation. It did not exclude any special revelation say to a pope or a general council, but it must be made manifest and not simply taken on trust as an assertion.[136] Conversely whenever even one believer dissented, that was a sign of its nullity; and just as Christ would always conserve one believer in his faith, so there would always be at least one believer to denounce its infraction.[137] It is an ingenious doctrine, a proto-Christian version of Popper's theory of falsifiability except that there is no evident means of ascertaining the truth of the falsifier; it must be taken as sign to be believed. Its significance however is that it removed the power of pronouncement upon doctrine from the pope and magistracy of the church and made it accessible to all believers having the use of reason on the basis of infallible doctrine. As Ockham distinguished it in the *Dialogus*[138] there were three sources: the Bible; apostolic doctrine not recorded in the Bible but derived from the subsequent relation or writings of the faithful and worthy of belief: for example the primacy of the Roman church which is not mentioned in the Bible but is accepted because it was handed down by the apostles and taught to the faithful; and finally revelation or divine inspiration the credentials for which must be exhibited. The first two were accessible to any believers having the use of reason and some degree of theological understanding, and it was to these

[134] *Ibid.*, I, bk. II, chs. 1, 2, 5, 25.

[135] *Contra Ioannem*, chs. 14 and 15, 62–72.

[136] *Dialogus, ibid*, ch. 25.

[137] Sed forte quaeret aliguis quo modo potest universalis ecclesia quamcumque veritatem catholicam explicite approbare, cum non possit insimul convenire, nec aliquid sententialiter aut iudicialiter definire. Huic respondetur quod, quemadmodum sicut in decretis habitur, d. IV, *Leges*: [*Leges*] moribus utentium approbantur, et tamen non est necesse quod utentes ad approbandum leges simul conveniant neque pro tribunali sendentes leges esse definiant tenendas: ita veritates catholicae ab universali ecclesia approbantur, quando praelati communiter et populi comprehendentes viros et mulieres catholicas easdem veritates sub verbis apertis expressas tamquam catholicas expresse vel tacite confitentur licet nequaquam simul conveniant . . . Hoc autem contingit quandocumque aliquae veritates catholicae per omnes regiones catholicovum publice asseruntur et predicantur, et apud omnes populos catholicos tamquam catholicae divulgantur, et nullus invenitur catholicus, qui tali assertioni resistat. Sicut enim, iuxta promissum Salvatoris, fides catholica est usque ad finem saeculi permansura, ita semper erit aliquis in ecclesia, clericus vel laicus, praelatus vel subditus, qui cuicumque errori qui umquam omnibus fidelibus populis per quoscumque vel quemcumque inculcabitur ut credendus, cum instantia forti resistet (*Contra Ioannem*, 67); also 68–9, 71–2, and *Dialogus*, I, bk. VI, ch. 21, III, I, bk. III, chs. 8, 18, 23, 25.

[138] *Ibid.*, I, bk. II, ch. 25; in ch. 5 (*ibid.*) he also includes accounts from chronicles and histories confirming what is held by the first two sources and what may be deduced from them.

that Ockham addressed himself, insisting that ordinarily the Bible and approved doctrine of the church constituted the sole *regula fidei* by which all that was not explicitly believed was to be judged. Nothing was immune, including the pronouncements of a pope—like John XXII's on the beatific vision, Ockham's main target in the *Contra Johannem*—or of a general council. The authority of the Bible and the church was thus the final arbiter to which all must submit. Even the separate writings of the evangelists come under it, since individually they are outweighed by the combined authority of all the canonical writings and doctrines which constitute the authority of the universal church.[139] Accordingly whatever is only implicit can only be made explicit by reference to the Bible and the faith of the universal church, to be accepted or rejected.[140]

The change in attitude compared with Ockham's repeated declarations of submission to the Roman church in his *Sacrament of the Altar* has been noticed often enough and does not need stressing. It is the measure at once of the distance Ockham had travelled in a few short years, with the *Opus Nonaginta Dierum* once again the transition: this time in his separation of the key of knowledge—of the immutable truths contained in divine law and the doctrine of the universal church—from the key of power—for the exercise of spiritual authority—the first of which John XXII claimed in virtue of holding the second.[141] The effect of Ockham's doctrine of unanimity based exclusively upon valid deductions from the Bible and the church denied the pope or indeed a general council any special right to legislate on matters of faith. Together with the other restrictions upon their freedom to do more than enforce God's precepts, Ockham had in the name of Christ's evangelical law woven a mesh of restrictions around the hierarchy that made it the servants not the rulers of the faithful.

These conceptions left virtually none of the traditional landmarks intact. While not denying the hierarchy any of its accepted attributes, Ockham effectively undermined their indispensability. By reposing all canonical authority in the universal church, mediated by scripture and reason, Ockham, though in a very different way from Wyclif, went far towards the exclusion of the hierarchy from any special role. Fidelity to faith was for him the only regulator; ecclesiastical office was contingent upon its observance. It could therefore be wielded by any or all of the faithful in default of its proper exercise by those who are ordinarily entrusted with it. As Lagarde has observed,[142] Ockham's meaning of the church was wider than a strictly ecclesiological one; it not only included the whole of Christian society, past and present, but allowed for the active intervention of all its members in cases of necessity and utility. It therefore embraced lay society as well; and it was precisely in enumerating the possible forms that lay participation could take, when a pope or the cardinals or the whole hierarchy and clergy failed, that Ockham's influence upon subsequent Conciliar thinking was so suggestive.

---

[139] *Contra Ioannem*, 66; *Dialogus*, I, bk. I, ch. 4; III, I, bk. III, ch. 8.
[140] *Contra Ioannem*, 71-2.
[141] *OND*, ch. 123.
[142] *La Naissance*, v, 50

For him the church was wherever the faithful were;[143] it did not therefore need an official presence or a special jurisdiction.[144] Others could do whatever a pope or general council or any body of the church could normally do. At the same time, unlike Marsilius of Padua and later Wyclif, there was nothing of the Biblical fundamentalist about Ockham. Tradition, expressed in the canons of the universal church, and reason in their interpretation, were the indispensable guides to a proper understanding of faith and the claims made in its name, as right reason was the guide to its enforcement. Ockham thus brought a much more subtle and flexible approach to scripture: he could not only accept the need to interpret what was contained in it, but also to interpolate what was not contained in it, as in the case of electing Peter's successors. That capacity belonged to any number of the universal church who had the power of reason, not office, to enable him to do so. The key of knowledge ultimately came to outweigh the key of power, or rather to contain the power which office alone could not give. As conceived by Ockham, that knowledge meant freedom for the individual believer from the impositions of the pope, as it meant submission to the jurisdiction of temporal rulers. The novelty of Ockham's position was that he used God's law as the justification for both.

That completes our discussion. The degree of rapport between Ockham's philosophy, theology and political ideas must remain to some extent a matter of individual interpretation. What can be said is that many of the same presuppositions —of God's omnipotence, of the contingency of the created order, of the irreducibly individual nature of existence, of the inability of a part to take on the attributes of a whole, of the universal validity of a judgement of reason, of the moral freedom of the will—are brought to bear upon establishing the independence of temporal authority and the limitations of spiritual authority. The difference between them springs from a common emphasis upon individual freedom: of the layman— infidel or believer—to choose his own rulers and enjoy temporal possessions; of the individual believer to enjoy immunity from papal or other ecclesiastical oppression. And each in the name of God's law. The whole of Ockham's intent was to vindicate the *status quo* in temporal affairs so far as the emperor was concerned and to under-mine it in the church so far as the pope was concerned. He was therefore forced to qualify the liberty of the individual subject out of existence while allowing himself every device of necessity and utility to assert that of the individual believer. The absence of a natural law binding upon a ruler's actions contrasts with the omni-presence of divine law circumscribing papal actions and the means it provided of enforcing it. The opposition between them was the focus of Ockham's political philosophy, expressed not in a minutely articulated system, but in the play between the necessary principles given in God's precepts and their contingent application. To the end the dialectic between what holds *de inesse* and what could be *de possibili* remained the joker in the Venerable Inceptor's pack.

---

[143] See note 137.

[144] Lagarde has remarked, *La Naissance*, v, 183, that Ockham talks only of a spiritual *po-testas*, not jurisdiction. See also *Dialogus*, iii, ii, bk. iii, ch. 4.

BIBLIOGRAPHY

Note. This bibliography is restricted to those works which have had a direct bearing upon this book. For a comprehensive list to 1967 see V. Heynck, 'Ockham-Literatur 1919–49', *FS* 32 (1950), 164–83; J. P. Reilly, 'Ockham bibliography, 1950–67', *FcS* 28 (1968), 197–214.

N. Abbagnano, *Guglielmo di Ockham* (Lanciano, 1931)

M. A. Adams, 'Intuitive cognition, certainty and skepticism in William of Ockham', *Traditio* 26 (1970), 389–98

Aristotle, *The Works of Aristotle Translated into English* ed. W. D. Ross, 12 vols (Oxford)

J. Auer, *Die Entwicklung der Gnadenlehre in der Hochscholastik mit bes. Berucks des Kard. Matteo d'Aquasparta*, Vol. I (Freiburg im Breisgau, 1942), vol. II (1951)

L. Baudry, *Le 'Tractatus de principiis theologiae' attribué à Guillaume d'Occam'*, ed. L. Baudry, (Paris, 1936)

—*Guillaume d'Occam: sa vie, ses oeuvres, ses idées sociales et politiques* (Paris, 1950)

—*Lexique philosophique de Guillaume d'Occam: Étude des notions fondamentales* (Paris, 1957)

—'Les Rapports de Guillaume d'Occam et de Walter Burleigh', *Archives* 9 (1934), 155–73

—'A propos de la théorie occamiste de la relation', *Archives* 9 (1934), 199–203

—'Sur trois manuscrits occamistes', *Archives* 10 (1935–6), 129–62

—'Le philosophe et le politique dans Guillaume d'Ockham', *Archives* 14 (1939), 203–30

—'A propos de Guillaume d'Ockham et de Wiclef', *Archives* 14 (1939), 231–51

—'Gauthier de Chatton et son Commentaire des Sentences', *Archives* 18 (1943), 337–69

—'Remarques sur trois manuscrits occamistes', *Archives* 15 (1946), 169–74

—'Guillaume d'Ockham, critique des preuves scotistes sur l'unicité de Dieu', *Archives* 20 (1953), 99–122

—'Les Rapports de la raison et de la foi selon Guillaume d'Ockham', *Archives* 29 (1962), 33–92

H. Becher, 'Gottesbegriff und Gottesbeweis bei Wilhelm von Ockham', *Scholastik* 3 (1928), 369–93

G. Bergmann, 'Some remarks on the ontology of Ockham', *Philosophical Review* 63 (New York, 1954), 560–71

P. Boehner, *Collected Articles on Ockham*, ed. E. M. Buytaert (New York and Louvain, 1958)

—'Scotus teaching according to Ockham': I: 'On the univocity of Being', *FcS* 6 (1946), 100–7; II: 'On the Natura Communis', *ibid.*, 362–75

—'The Notitia Intuitiva of non-existents according to William Ockham. With a critical study of the text of Ockham's *Reportatio* and a revised edition of the *Reportatio* II, q. 14–15', *Traditio* I (1943), 223–75

—'Notitia Intuitiva of non-existents according to Peter Aureoli OFM (1322)', *FcS* 8 (1948), 388–416

C. Bérubé, 'La Conaissance intellectuelle du singulier materiel' *FcS* 11 (1951) 157–201

—'La Conaissance intellectuelle du singulier materiel chez Duns Scotus' *FcS* 13 (1953) 29–49, 27–58

—*La Conaissance de l'individuel au moyen âge*, (Paris and Montreal, 1964)

J. F. Boler, 'Ockham on intuitive cognition', *Journal of the History of Philosophy* 11 (1973), 95–106

C. K. Brampton, 'A note on Aureol, Ockham and MS. Borghese 329', *Gregorianum* 41 (1960), 713–16

—'Guillaume d'Ockham et la "Prima Redactio" de son Commentaire sur les Sentences', *RHE* 56 (1961), 470–6

—'Guillaume d'Ockham, fut-il maître en théologie?', *Études Franciscaines* 13 (1963), 53–9

—'The probable order of Ockham's non-polemical works', *Traditio* 19 (1963), 469–83

—'Guillaume d'Ockham et la date probable de ses opuscules sur l'Eucharistie', *Études Franciscaines* 14 (1964), 77–88

—' A note on the manuscript tradition of Ockham's Tractatus *De Quantitate*', *AFH* 57 (1964), 383–91

—'Chronological gleanings from Martival episcopal register', *AFH* 58 (1965), 369–93

—'Scotus, Ockham and the theory of intuitive cognition', *Antonianum* 40 (1965), 449–66

—'Personalities at the process against Ockham at Avignon', *FcS* 26 (1966), 4–25

—'Ockham and his authorship of the *Summulae Physicorum*', *Isis* 55 (1964), 418–26

S. F. Brown, 'Sources for Ockham's Prologue to the Sentences', *FcS* 26 (1966), 36–65; 27 (1967), 39–107

—'Walter Burleigh's *Treatise de Suppositionibus* and its influence on William of Ockham', *FcS* 32 (1972), 15–64

G. Buescher, *The eucharistic teaching of William Ockham* (St Bonaventure, New York, and Louvain, 1950), Franciscan Institute Publications

E. M. Buytaert, 'The Immaculate Conception in the writings of Ockham', *FcS* 10 (1950), 149–63

D. W. Clark, 'Voluntarism and rationalism in the ethics of William of Ockham', *FcS* 31 (1971), 72–87

—'William of Ockham on right reason', *Speculum* (1973), 13–36

F. Corvini, 'Le *Quaestiones in libros physicorum* nella formazione del pensiero di Guglielmo d'Occam', *Rivista critica di storia della filosofia* 12 (1957), 387–411

A. C. Crombie, *Robert Grosseteste and the Origins of Experimental Science* (reprinted Oxford, 1971)

—*Medieval and Early Modern Science*, 2. vols (revised edition, New York, 1959)

S. J. Day, *Intuitive cognition. A key to the significance of the later scholastics* (St Bonaventure, New York, and Louvain, 1947), Franciscan Institute Publications

W. Dettloff, *Die Lehre von der Acceptatio Divina bei Johannes Duns Scotus* (Werl, 1954)

—*Die Entwicklung der Akzeptations- und Verdienstlehre* (Münster, 1963)

P. Doncoeur, 'Le nominalisme de Guillaume d'Ockham: La théorie de la relation', *Revue Néoscolastique de philosophie* 22 (1921), 5–25

N. A. Fitzpatrick, 'Walter Chatton on the univocity of Being: a reaction to Peter Aureoli and William Ockham', *FcS* 31 (1971) 88–177

O. Fuchs, *The Psychology of Habit According to William Ockham* (St Bonaventure, New York and Louvain 1952), Franciscan Institute Publications

G. Gál, 'Gualteri de Chatton et Guillelmi de Ockham controversia de natura conceptus universalis', *FcS* 27 (1967), 191–212

—'Henricus de Harclay: Quaestio de Significato Conceptus Universalis (Fons doctrinae Guillelmi de Ockham)', *FcS* 31 (1971), 178–234

A. Garvens, 'Die Grundlagen der Ethik Wilhelms von Ockham', *FS* 21 (1934), 243–73, 360–408

A. Ghisalberti, *Guglielmo di Ockham: vita e pensiero* (Milan, 1972)

C. Giacon, *Guglielmo di Occam: Saggio storico-critico sulla formazione et sulla decadenza della scolastica*, 2 vols (Milan, 1941)

H. Grieve, 'Zur Relationslehre Wilhelms von Ockham', *FS* 49 (1966), 248–58

R. Guelluy, *Philosophie et Théologie chez Guillamme d'Ockham* (Louvain, and Paris, 1947)

A. Hamman, *La Doctrine de l'Église et de l'État chez Occam: Étude sur le Breviloquium* (Paris, 1942)

—'La Doctrine de l'Église et de l'état d'après le Breviloquium d'Occam', *FS* 32 (1950), 135–41

B. Heiser, 'The *Primum Cognitum* according to Duns Scotus', *FcS* 2 (1942), 193–216

E. Hochstetter, *Studien zur Metaphysik und Erkenntnislehre Wilhelms von Ockham* (Berlin and Leipzig, 1927)

—'Nominalismus?', *FcS* 9 (1949), 370–403 (Review of Guelluy)

—'Viator Mundi: Einige Bermerkungen zur Situation des Menschen bei Wilhelm von Ockham', *FS* 32 (1950), 1–20

D. P. Henry, 'The early history of the Suppositio', *FcS* 23 (1963), 205–12

—'Ockham and the formal distinction', *FcS* 25 (1965), 285–92

F. Hoffmann, *Die erste Kritik des Ockhamismus durch den Oxforder Kanzler Johannes Lutterell* (Breslau, 1941)

—*Die Schriften des Oxforder Kanzlers Johannes Lutterell: Texte zur Theologie des vierzehnten Jahrhunderts* (Leipzig, 1959)

E. Iserloh, 'Um die Echtheit des *Centiloquium*: Ein Beitrag zur Wertung Ockhams und zur Chronologie seiner Werke', *Gregorianum* 30 (1949), 78–103, 309–46

—*Gnade und Eucharistie in der philosophischen Theologie des Wilhelm von Ockham: Ihre Bedeutung für die Ursachen der Reformation* (Wiesbaden, 1956)

E. F. Jacob, *Essays in the Conciliar Epoch* (3rd edition, Manchester, 1963)

H. Junghans, *Ockham im Lichte der neueren Forschung* (Berlin and Hamburg, 1968)

W. and M. Kneale, *The Development of Logic* (Oxford, 1962; reprinted 1965)

J. Koch, 'Neue Aktenstücke zu dem gegen Wilhelm Ockham in Avignon gefürhten Prozess', *Recherches* 7 (1935), 353–80; 8 (1936), 79–93, 168–97

W. Kölmel, 'Das Naturrecht bei Wilhelm von Ockham', *FS* 35 (1953), 39–85

—*Wilhelm Ockham und seine Kirchenpolitischen Schriften* (Essen, 1962)

—'Wilhelm Ockham—der Mensch zwischen Ordnung und Freiheit', *Miscellanea Medievalia* 3, ed. P. Wilpert (Berlin, 1964), 204–29

G. de Lagarde, *La naissance de l'esprit laïque au declin du moyen-âge*, vols IV–VI (Paris, 1942–6); new edition: IV: *Guillaume d'Ockham, Défense de l'Empire* (Louvain and Paris, 1962); V: *Guillaume d'Ockham, critique des structures ecclésiales* (Louvain and Paris, 1963)

A. van Leeuwen, L'église, règle de foi, dans les écrits de Guillaume d'Occam', *Ephemerides theologicae Lovanienses* II (1934), 247–88

G. Leff, *Gregory of Rimini: Tradition and Innovation in Fourteenth Century Thought* (Manchester, 1961)

—*Heresy in the Later Middle Ages*, 2 vols (Manchester, 1967)

R. McKeon, *Selections from Medieval Philosophers*, edited by R. McKeon (New York, 1958)

E. McMullin, *The Concept of Matter in Greek and Medieval Philosophy*, edited by E. McMullin (University of Notre Dame, 1961)

A. Maier, *Die Vorläufer Galileis* (Rome, 1949)

—*Zwei Grundprobleme der scholastischen Naturphilosophie* (Rome, 1951)

—*An der Grenze von Scholastik und Naturwissenschaft* (Rome, 1952)

A. Maier, *Metaphysische Hintergründe der spätscholastischen Naturphilosophie* (Rome, 1955)

—*Zwischen Philosophie und Mechanik* (Rome, 1956)

—*Ausgehendes Mittelalter*, 2 vols (Rome, 1964 and 1967)

—'Zu einigen Problemen der Ockhamforschung', *AFH* 46 (1953), 161–94 (reprinted in *Ausgehendes Mittelalter*, I, 192–5)

—'Das Problem der Evidenz in der Philosophie des 14 Jahrhunderts', *Scholastik* 38 (1963), 183–225

G. Martin, *Wilhelm von Ockham. Untersuchungen zur Ontologie der Ordnungen* (Berlin, 1949)

—'Ist Ockhams Relationstheorie Nominalismus?', *FS* 32 (1950), 31–49

A. Maurer, 'Ockham's conception of the unity of science' *Mediaeval Studies* 20 (1958) 98–112

M. C. Menges, *The Concept of Univocity Regarding the Predication of God and Creature According to William Ockham* (St Bonaventure, New York, and Louvain, 1952), Franciscan Institute Publications

R. Messner, 'Über die Gegenwartsbedentung der Erkenntnishaltung Bonaventuras und Ockhams', *Antonianum* 28 (1953), 131–47

J. Miethke, 'Ockhams *Summulae in libros physicorum*—eine nicht-authentische Schrift?', *AFH* 60 (1967), 55–78. A convincing refutation of Brampton's rejection of the work as unauthentic (*Isis* 55)

—*Ockhams Weg zur Sozialphilosophie* (Berlin, 1969)

G. E. Mohan, 'The *Questio de Relatione* attributed to William Ockham', *FcS* 11 (1951), 273–303

—'The Prologue to Ockham's Exposition of the *Physics* of Aristotle', *FcS* 5 (1945), 235–46.

E. A. Moody, *The Logic of William of Ockham* (London, 1935; reprinted New York, 1965)

—'Ockham, Buridan and Nicholas of Autrecourt: The Parisian statutes of 1339 and 1340', *FcS* 7 (1947), 113–46

—'Ockham and Aegidius of Rome', *FcS* 9 (1949), 417–42

—*Truth and Consequence in Mediaeval Logic* (Amsterdam, 1963)

J. B. Morrall, 'Some notes on a recent interpretation of William of Ockham's political philosophy', *FcS* 9 (1949), 335–69

—'Ockham and ecclesiology', *Medieval Studies Presented to Aubrey Gwynn S.J.*, ed. J. A. Watt, J. B. Morrall, F. Martin (Dublin, 1961) 481–91

S. Moser, *Grundbegriffe der Naturphilosophie bei Wilhelm von Ockham: Kritischer vergleich der 'Summulae in libros Physicorum' mit der philosophie des Aristoteles* (Innsbruck, 1932)

A. Pelzer, 'Les 51 articles de Guillaume d'Occam censurés en Avignon, en 1326', *RHE* 18 (1922) 240–70. Also in *August Pelzer: Études d'histoire littéraire sur la scholastique médiévale*, ed. E. Pattin and E. van de Vyver (Louvain and Paris, 1964), 508–19 (without the edition of the text)

M. A. Pernoud, 'Innovation in William of Ockham's references to the *Potentia Dei*.', *Antonianum* 45 (1970), 65–97

—'The theory of the *Potentia Dei* according to Aquinas, Scotus and Ockham', *Antonianum* 47 (1972), 69–75

L. Prentice, 'Primary efficiency and its relation to creation, infinite power and omnipotence in the metaphysics of John Duns Scotus', *Antonianum* 40 (1965), 395–441

L. Price, 'William of Ockham and *Suppositio Personalis*', *FcS* 30 (1970), 131–40

A. N. Prior, *Formal Logic* (second edition, Oxford, 1962)

V. Richter, 'Zu Ockhams Handschrift, Vat. Borghese 68', *Gregorianum* 46 (1965), 766–816

R. C. Richards, 'Ockham and scepticism', *New Scholasticism* 42 (1968), 345–63

J. Salamucha, 'Die Aussagenlogik bei Wilhelm Ockham', *FS* 32 (1950), 97–134

R. Scholz, *Wilhelm von Ockham als politischer Denker und sein Breviloquium de principatu tyrannico* (Leipzig, 1944; reprinted Stuttgart, 1952)

T. K. Scott, 'Ockham on evidence, necessity and intuition', *Journal of the History of Philosophy* 7 (1969), 27–49

H. Shapiro, *Motion, Time and Place According to William Ockham* (St Bonaventure, New York, and Louvain, 1957), Franciscan Institute Publications

O. Suk, 'The connection of the virtues according to Ockham', *FcS* 10 (1950), 9–32, 91–113

J. Swiniarski, 'A new presentation of Ockham's theory of supposition with an evaluation of some contemporary criticisms', *FcS* 30 (1970), 181–217

B. Tierney, 'Ockham, the conciliar theory and the canonists', *Journal of the History of Ideas* 15 (1954), 40–70

M. Tweedale, 'Scotus and Ockham on the infinity of the Most Eminent Being', *FcS* 23 (1963), 257–67

C. Vasoli, *Guglielmo d'Occam* (Florence, 1953)

P. Vignaux, *Justification et Prédestination au XIVᵉ siecle. Duns Scot, Pierre d'Aureole, Guillaume d'Occam, Grégoire de Rimini* (Paris, 1934)

—'Nominalisme', *Dictionnaire de Théologie Catholique*, XI, 717–84

—'Occam', *Ibid.*, 876–89

—*Nominalisme au 14ᵉ siècle* (Montreal and Paris, 1948)

—'Note sur l'*esse beatificabile*', *FcS* 9 (1949), 404–16

D. Webering, *Theory of Demonstration According to William Ockham* (St Bonaventure, New York, and Louvain, 1953), Franciscan Institute Publications

—*Wilhelm Ockham: Aufsätze zu seiner Philosophie und Theologie* (Münster, 1950) *FS* 32

J. A. Weisheipl, 'Ockham and some Mertonians', *Mediaeval Studies* 30 (1968), 163–213

A. B. Wolter, 'Ockham and the textbooks: On the origin of possibility', in *Wilhelm Ockham*, *FS* 32 (1950), 70–96

—*The Transcendentals and their Function in the Metaphysics of Duns Scotus* (Washington, 1946)

Index

I NAMES AND WRITINGS

II SUBJECTS

Leff, Gordon.
　　William of Ockham : the metamorphosis of scholastic dis-
course / Gordon Leff. -- Manchester : Manchester University
Press ; Totowa, N.J. : Rowman and Littlefield, [1975]

　　xxiv, 666 p. ; 24 cm.

　　Bibliography: p. 645-649.
　　Includes indexes.
　　ISBN 0-87471-679-9 (Rowman and Littlefield)

1. Ockham, William, d. ca. 1349.　I.Title.